Less managing. More teaching. Greater learning.

INSTRUCTORS...

Would you like your **students** to show up for class more **prepared**? *(Let's face it, class is much more fun if everyone is engaged and prepared...)*

Want ready-made application-level **interactive assignments,** student progress reporting, and auto-assignment grading? *(Less time grading means more time teaching...)*

Want an **instant view of student or class performance** relative to learning objectives? *(No more wondering if students understand...)*

Need to **collect data and generate reports** required for administration or accreditation? *(Say goodbye to manually tracking student learning outcomes...)*

Want to **record and post your lectures** for students to view online?

With McGraw-Hill's *Connect Plus Business Communication,*

INSTRUCTORS GET:

- Interactive Applications – **book-specific interactive assignments** that require students to APPLY what they've learned.
- Simple **assignment management**, allowing you to spend more time teaching.
- **Auto-graded** assignments, quizzes, and tests.
- **Detailed Visual Reporting** where student and section results can be viewed and analyzed.
- Sophisticated **online testing** capability.
- A **filtering and reporting** function that allows you to easily assign and report on materials that are correlated to accreditation standards, learning outcomes, and Bloom's taxonomy.
- An easy-to-use **lecture capture** tool.

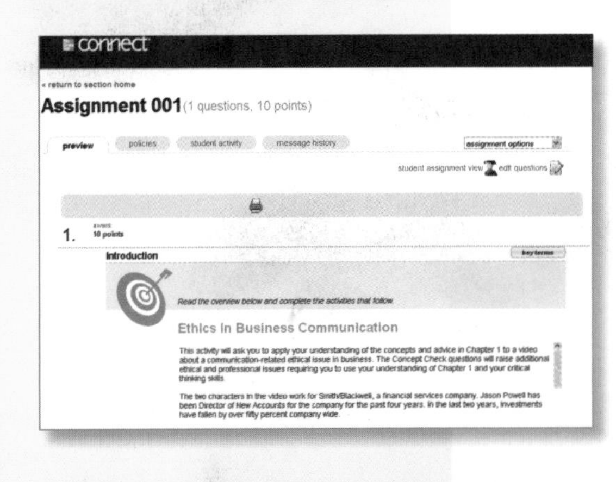

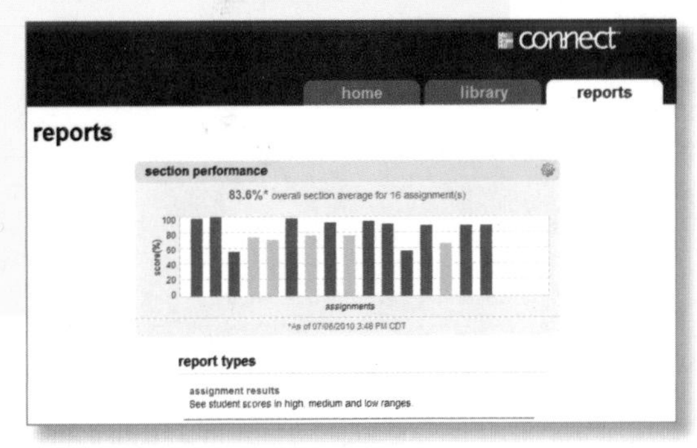

Want an online, **searchable version** of your textbook?

Wish your textbook could be **available online** while you're doing your assignments?

Connect Plus Business Communication eBook

If you choose to use *Connect Plus Business Communication*, you have an affordable and searchable online version of your book integrated with your other online tools.

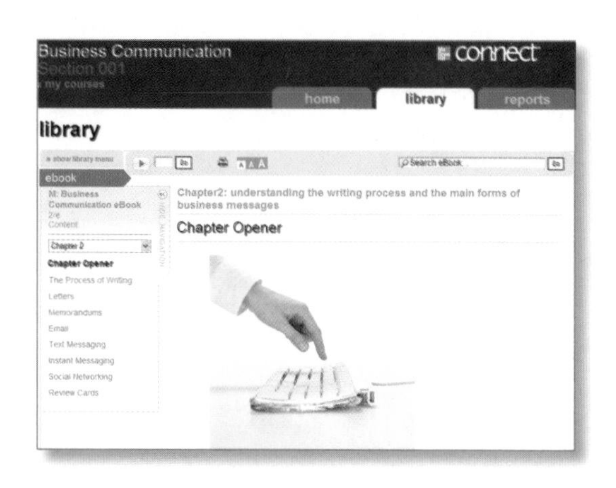

Connect Plus Business Communication eBook offers features like:

- Topic search
- Direct links from assignments
- Adjustable text size
- Jump to page number
- Print by section

Want to get more **value** from your textbook purchase?

Think learning management should [illegible] **interesting**?

Check out the STUDENT RESOURCES section under the *Connect* Library tab.

Here you'll find a wealth of resources designed to help you achieve your goals in the course. You'll find things like **quizzes, PowerPoints, and Internet activities** to help you study. Every student has different needs, so explore the STUDENT RESOURCES to find the materials best suited to you.

Business and Administrative Communication

TENTH EDTION

Business and Administrative Communication

KITTY O. LOCKER
The Ohio State University

DONNA S. KIENZLER
Iowa State University

The McGraw-Hill Companies

BUSINESS AND ADMINISTRATIVE COMMUNICATION

Published by McGraw-Hill/Irwin, a business unit of The McGraw-Hill Companies, Inc., 1221 Avenue of the Americas, New York, NY, 10020.

This book is printed on acid-free paper.

2 3 4 5 6 7 8 9 0 DOW/DOW 1 0 9 8 7 6 5 4 3 2

ISBN 978-0-07-340318-2
MHID 0-07-340318-0

Vice president and editor-in-chief: *Brent Gordon*
Editorial director: *Paul Ducham*
Executive editor: *John Weimeister*
Executive director of development: *Ann Torbert*
Development editor: *Jane Beck*
Vice president and director of marketing: *Robin J. Zwettler*
Marketing director: *Amee Mosley*
Marketing manager: *Donielle Xu*
Vice president of editing, design, and production: *Sesha Bolisetty*
Senior project manager: *Dana M. Pauley*
Senior buyer: *Michael R. McCormick*
Senior designer: *Matt Diamond*
Senior photo research coordinator: *Keri Johnson*
Photo researcher: *Sarah Evertson*
Senior media project manager: *Susan Lombardi*
Media project manager: *Joyce J. Chappetto*
Cover design: *Jesi Lazar*
Typeface: *10.5/12 Palatino*
Compositor: *Laserwords Private Limited*
Printer: *R. R. Donnelley*

Library of Congress Cataloging-in-Publication Data

Locker, Kitty O.
Business and administrative communication / Kitty O. Locker, Donna S. Kienzler.—10th ed.
p. cm.
Includes index.
ISBN-13: 978-0-07-340318-2 (alk. paper)
ISBN-10: 0-07-340318-0 (alk. paper)
1. Business communication. 2. Communication in management. I. Kienzler, Donna S. II. Title.
HF5718.L63 2013
651.7—dc23

2011045377

www.mhhe.com

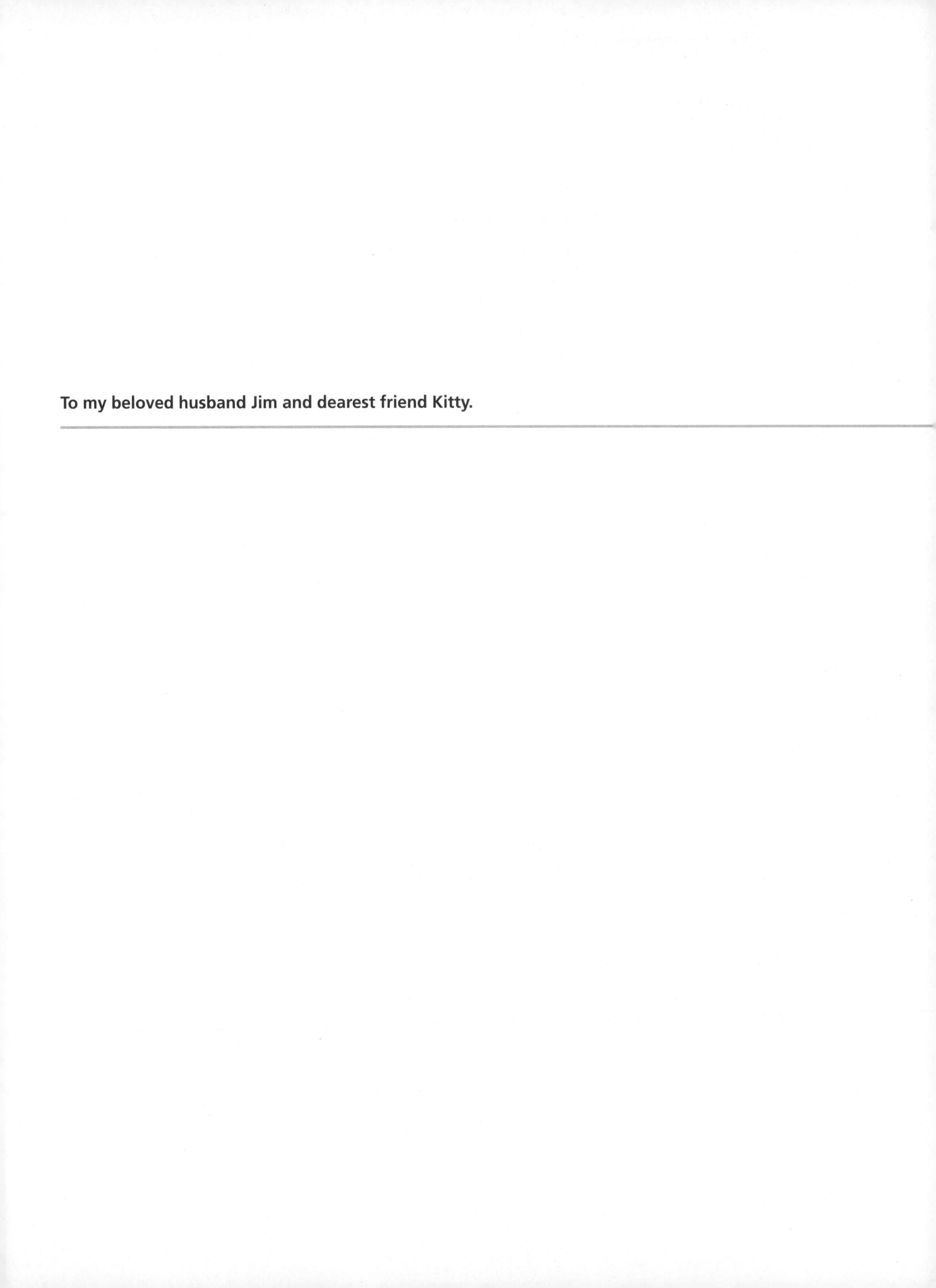

To my beloved husband Jim and dearest friend Kitty.

Kitty O. Locker was an Associate Professor of English at The Ohio State University in Columbus, Ohio, where she coordinated the Writing Center and taught courses in business and technical discourse and in research methods. She also taught as Assistant Professor at Texas A&M University and the University of Illinois.

She wrote *The Irwin Business Communication Handbook: Writing and Speaking in Business Classes* (1993), coauthored *Business Writing Cases and Problems* (1980, 1984, 1987), and coedited *Conducting Research in Business Communication* (1988). She twice received the Alpha Kappa Psi award for Distinguished Publication in Business Communication for her article "'Sir, This Will Never Do': Model Dunning Letters 1592–1873" and for her article " 'As per Your Request': A History of Business Jargon." In 1992, she received the Association for Business Communication's Outstanding Researcher Award.

Her research included work on collaborative writing in the classroom and the workplace, and the emergence of bureaucratic writing in the correspondence of the British East India Company from 1600 to 1800.

Her consulting work included conducting tutorials and short courses in business, technical, and administrative writing for employees of URS Greiner, Ross Products Division of Abbott Laboratories, Franklin County, the Ohio Civil Service Employees Association, AT&T, the American Medical Association, Western Electric, the Illinois Department of Central Management Services, the Illinois Department of Transportation, the A. E. Staley Company, Flo-Con, the Police Executive Leadership College, and the Firemen's Institute. She developed a complete writing improvement program for Joseph T. Ryerson, the nation's largest steel materials service center.

She served as the Interim Editor of *The Bulletin of the Association for Business Communication* and, in 1994–1995, as President of the Association for Business Communication (ABC). She edited ABC's *Journal of Business Communication* from 1998 to 2000.

In 1998, she received ABC's Meada Gibbs Outstanding Teacher Award.

Kitty O. Locker passed away in 2005.

Donna S. Kienzler is a Professor Emeritus of English at Iowa State University in Ames, Iowa, where she taught in the Rhetoric and Professional Communication program. She was the Director of Advanced Communication and oversaw more that 120 sections of business and technical communication annually. She was also an Assistant Director of the university's Center for Excellence in Learning and Teaching, where she taught classes, seminars, and workshops on pedagogy; directed graduate student programming; and directed the Preparing Future Faculty program, a career-training program for graduate students and postdoctoral follows.

Her research focused on pedagogy and ethics. Her article with Helen Ewald, "Speech Act Theory and Business Communication Conventions," won an Association for Business Communication (ABC) Alpha Kappa Psi Foundation Award for distinguished publication in business communication. Her article with Carol David, "Towards an Emancipatory Pedagogy in Service Courses and User Departments," was part of a collection that won a National Council of Teachers of English (NCTE) Award for Excellence in Technical and Scientific Communication: Best Collection of Essays in Technical or Scientific Communication.

She has done consulting work for the Air Force, Tracor Consulting, Green Engineering, Northwestern Bell, Iowa Merit Employment, the Iowa Department of Transportation, the University of Missouri, and her local school district.

She is active in the Association for Business Communication (ABC), where she currently serves on the board of directors as well as on the Business Practices and the Teaching Practices Committees. She also served on ABC's Ad Hoc Committee on Professional Ethics, which developed a Professional Ethics Statement for the national organization.

In 2002, she received ABC's Meada Gibbs Outstanding Teacher Award.

Donna and Kitty became close friends in graduate school at the University of Illinois, Urbana–Champaign, where they shared the same major professor. They remained close friends, and indeed considered each other family, until Kitty's death. During those wonderful years, their favorite topic of conversation was *Business and Administrative Communication;* they discussed content for the original book proposal, content for the first edition, changes for subsequent editions, and future plans for the book. Everything from new sidebars and footnotes to major organizational changes made its way into those long, frequent conversations. These conversations helped Donna carry on Kitty's tradition of excellence.

Welcome to *Business and Administrative Communication* (BAC). This textbook can make learning about business communication easier and more enjoyable.

You'll find that this edition of BAC is as flexible, specific, interesting, comprehensive, and up-to-date as its predecessors. The features that users particularly like have been retained: the anecdotes and examples, the easy-to-follow lists, the integrated coverage of ethics and international business communication, the analyses of sample problems, the wealth of exercises and assignments. But a good book has become even better. This edition of BAC includes major changes.

MAJOR CHANGES TO THE TENTH EDITION

Major changes make the tenth edition even better:

- Entire chapter on using technology in business communications. Also, additions on new technology throughout.
- New material and increased emphasis on electronic communication throughout:
  - Instant messaging and text messaging.
  - Wikis.
  - Social media.
    - Facebook.
    - Twitter.
    - LinkedIn.
    - Blogs.
- New material in the job chapters:
  - New sections:
    - Personal branding.
    - Networking.
    - Using an internship as a job hunting tool.
  - New material:
    - Guidelines for using LinkedIn, Facebook, Twitter, and blogs in the job hunt.
    - Guidelines for older job seekers.
    - Tips for job hunting in a down economy.
- Expanded ethics section, as well as more ethics coverage throughout.
- Expanded material on networking in multiple chapters.
- Expanded coverage of web page design.
- New appendix on APA and MLA documentation.

CONTENT UPDATES

In addition to the major changes, the tenth edition has new material throughout to keep it up-to-date for instructors and interesting for students:

- New chapter openers, Newsworthy Communication, provide examples of chapter content occurring in the news.
  - Toyota's communication strategy to recover from its accelerator problems.
  - Apple's moving response to the earthquake and tsunami in Japan.
  - BP's communication failures regarding its Gulf oil spill.
  - Air New Zealand's "naked" safety message.

- New, up-to-date, interesting examples in text and sidebars:
    - Persuasion techniques to get men to go to their doctors.
    - College ads during football games.
    - A takeoff of NBC's hit sitcom *The Office* used for an effective ethics training program.
    - Costco's adaptations for Taiwan.
- Examples from popular companies such as Zappos, Best Buy, Google, and Microsoft.
- New additions from the ranks of business bestseller books:
    - Nicholas Boothman, *Convince Them in 90 Seconds or Less*
    - Richard. J. Connors, ed., *Warren Buffett on Business: Principles from the Sage of Omaha*
    - Atul Gawande, *The Checklist Manifesto: How to Get Things Right*
    - Chip Heath and Dan Heath, *Switch: How To Change Things When Change Is Hard*
    - Jay Heinrichs, *Thank You for Arguing: What Aristotle, Lincoln, and Homer Simpson Can Teach Us about the Art of Persuasion*
    - Tony Hsieh, *Delivering Happiness: A Path to Profits, Passion, and Purpose*
    - Rosabeth Moss Kanter, *Supercorp: How Vanguard Companies Create Innovation, Profits, Growth, and Social Good*
    - John Kotter and Lorne Whitehead, *Buy In: Saving Your Good Idea from Getting Shot Down*
    - Patrick Lencioni, *The Five Dysfunctions of a Team*
    - Daniel Pink, *Drive: The Surprising Truth about What Motivates Us*
- New exercises, including more ethics exercises.

QUALITIES RETAINED

BAC retains the qualities that have made it a top textbook in business communication:

- **BAC is flexible.** Choose the chapters and exercises that best fit your needs. Choose from in-class exercises, messages to revise, problems with hints, and cases presented as they'd arise in the workplace. Many problems offer several options: small group discussions, individual writing, group writing, or oral presentations.
- **BAC is specific.** BAC provides specific strategies, specific guidelines, and specific examples. BAC takes the mystery out of creating effective messages.
- **BAC is interesting.** Anecdotes from a variety of fields show business communication at work. The lively side columns from *The Wall Street Journal* and a host of other sources provide insights into the workplace.
- **BAC is comprehensive.** BAC includes international communication, communicating across cultures in this country, ethics, collaborative writing, organizational cultures, graphs, and technology as well as traditional concerns such as style and organization. Assignments offer practice dealing with international audiences or coping with ethical dilemmas.
- **BAC is up-to-date.** The tenth edition of BAC incorporates the latest research and practice so that you stay on the cutting edge.

SUPPLEMENTS

The stimulating, user-friendly supplements package has been one of the major reasons that BAC is so popular. All of the supplements are available on the book's website at www.mhhe.com/locker10e.

1. The **Instructor's Resource Manual** contains
   - **Answers to all exercises,** an overview and difficulty rating for each problem, and, for several of the problems in the book, a detailed analysis, discussion questions, and a good solution.
   - **Additional exercises and cases for** diagnostic and readiness tests, grammar and style, and for letters, memos, and reports.
   - **Lesson plans and class activities for each chapter.** You'll find discussion guides, activities to reinforce chapter materials and prepare students for assignments, and handouts for group work, peer editing, and other activities.
   - **Sample syllabi** for courses with different emphases and approaches.
2. The **Test Bank** contains approximately 2,000 test items with answers. Each is tagged with learning objective, level of difficulty (corresponding to Bloom's taxonomy of educational objectives), AACSB standards, and page number.
3. A **Computerized Test Bank** is available to qualified adopters in both Macintosh and Windows formats, and allows professors to generate and edit their own test questions.
4. The **BAC website** at www.mhhe.com/locker10e identifies sites for business, research, ethics, and job hunting. The Instructor's Manual, Test Bank, and PowerPoints are available to instructors. Additional exercises, and quizzes are available to help students improve their writing and communication skills.

CONTINUING THE CONVERSATION

This edition incorporates the feedback I've received from instructors who used earlier editions. Tell me about your own success stories teaching *Business and Administrative Communication.* I look forward to hearing from you!

Donna S. Kienzler

All writing is in some sense collaborative. This book in particular builds upon the ideas and advice of teachers, students, and researchers. The people who share their ideas in conferences and publications enrich not only this book but also business communication as a field.

Many people reviewed the 9th edition, suggesting what to change and what to keep. We thank all of these reviewers for their attention to detail and their promptness!

William Brunkan, *Augustana College*

Marilyn Chalupa, *Ball State University*

Robert Cohn, *Long Island University*

Smiljka Cubelic, *Indiana University–South Bend*

Aparajita De, *University of Maryland–College Park*

Lynda Fuller, *Wilmington University*

Wade Graves, *Grayson County College*

Kathy Hilly, *Sam Houston State University*

Patti Koluda, *Yakima Valley Community College*

Barbara Limbach, *Chadron State College*

Barbara Looney, *Black Hills State University*

Danielle Mitchell, *Pennsylvania State University–Fayette*

Karl Mitchell, *Queens College–CUNY*

Mialisa Moline, *University of Wisconsin–River Falls*

Rodger Glenn Morrison, *Troy University*

Cassie Rockwell, *Santa Monica College*

Valarie Spiser-Albert, *University of Texas–San Antonio*

Mary Young Bowers, *Northern Arizona University*

In addition, the book continues to benefit from people who advised me on earlier editions:

Mark Alexander, *Indiana Wesleyan University*

Bill Allen, *University of LaVerne*

Vanessa Arnold, *University of Mississippi*

Lynn Ashford, *Alabama State University*

Jean Baird, *Brigham Young University–Idaho*

Lenette Baker, *Valencia Community College*

Dennis Barbour, *Purdue University–Calumet*

Laura Barelman, *Wayne State College*

Fiona Barnes, *University of Florida*

Jan Barton-Zimerman, *University of Nebraska–Kearney*

Jaye Bausser, *Indiana University–Purdue University at Fort Wayne*

Sallye Benoit, *Nicholls State University*

Michael Benton, *Bluegrass Community and Technology College*

Raymond W. Beswick, *formerly of Synerude, Ltd.*

Carole Bhakar, *The University of Manitoba*

Cathie Bishop, *Parkland College*

Randi Meryl Blank, *Indiana University*

Yvonne Block, *College of Lake County*

Bennis Blue, *Virginia State University*

John Boehm, *Iowa State University*

Maureen S. Bogdanowicz, *Kapi'olani Community College*

Kendra S. Boggess, *Concord College*

Melanie Bookout, *Greenville Technical College*

Christy Ann Borack, *California State University–Fullerton; Orange Coast College–Costa Mesa*

Charles P. Bretan, *Northwood University*

Paula Brown, *Northern Illinois University*

Vincent Brown, *Battelle Memorial Institute*

John Bryan, *University of Cincinnati*

Phyllis Bunn, *Delta State University*

Trudy Burge, *University of Nebraska–Lincoln*

Janice Burke, *South Suburban College of Cook County*

Nicole Buzzetto-More, *University of Maryland–East Shore*

Robert Callahan, *The University of Texas–San Antonio*

Andrew Cantrell, *University of Illinois*

Danny Cantrell, *West Virginia State College*

Peter Cardon, *University of South Carolina*

Susan Carlson

John Carr, *The Ohio State University*

Kathy Casto

Kelly Chaney, *Southern Illinois University–Carbondale*

Jay Christiansen, *California State University–Northridge*

Lynda Clark, *Maple Woods Community College*

Brendan G. Coleman, *Mankato State University*

Andrea Compton, *St. Charles Community College*

John Cooper, *University of Kentucky*

Donna Cox, *Monroe Community College*

Christine Leigh Cranford, *East Carolina University*

Tena Crews, *State University of West Georgia*

Carla Dando, *Idaho State University*

Susan H. Delagrange, *The Ohio State University*

Mark DelMaramo, *Thiel College*

Moira E. W. Dempsey, *Oregon State University*

Gladys DeVane, *Indiana University*

Linda Di Desidero, *University of Maryland–University College*

Veronica Dufresne, *Finger Lakes Community College*

Jose A. Duran, *Riverside Community College*

Dorothy J. Dykman, *Point Loma Nazarene College*

Marilyn Easter, *San Jose State University*

Anna Easton, *Indiana University*

Donna Everett, *Morehead State University*

Joyce Ezrow, *Ann Arundel Community College*

Susan Fiechtner, *Texas A&M University*

Susan Finnerty, *John Carroll University*

Bartlett Finney, *Park University–Parkville*

Mary Ann Firmin, *Oregon State University*

Melissa Fish, *American River College*

W. Clark Ford, *Middle Tennessee State University*

Louisa Fordyce, *Westmoreland County Community College*

Paula J. Foster, *Foster Communication*

Mildred Franceschi, *Valencia Community College–West Camp*

Linda Fraser, *California State University–Fullerton*

Silvia Fuduric, *Wayne State University*

Lynda Fuller, *Wilmington University*

Robert D. Gieselman, *University of Illinois*
Cheryl Glenn, *Pennsylvania State University*
Mary Greene, *Prince George's Community College*
Jane Greer
Daryl Grider, *West Virginia State College*
Peter Hadorn, *Virginia Commonwealth University*
Ed Hagar, *Belhaven College*
Elaine Hage, *Forsythe Technical Community College*
Barbara Hagler, *Southern Illinois University*
Robert Haight, *Kalamazoo Valley Community College*
Mark Hama, *Angelo State University*
Les Hanson, *Red River Community College–Canada*
Kathy Harris, *Northwestern State University*
Mark Harstein, *University of Illinois*
Maxine Hart, *Baylor University*
Vincent Hartigan, *New Mexico State University*
David Hawes, *Owens Community College*
Charles Hebert, *The University of South Carolina*
Tanya Henderson, *Howard University*
Ruth Ann Hendrickson
Paulette Henry, *Howard University*
Deborah Herz, *Salve Regina University*
Robert Hill, *University of LaVerne*
Kenneth Hoffman, *Emporia State University*
Elizabeth Hoger, *Western Michigan University*
Carole A. Holden, *County College of Morris*
Carlton Holte, *California State University–Sacramento*
Glenda Hudson, *California State University–Bakersfield*
Elizabeth Huettman, *Cornell University*
Melissa Ianetta, *University of Southern Indiana*
Susan Isaacs, *Community College of Philadelphia*
Daphne A. Jameson, *Cornell University*
Elizabeth Jenkins, *Pennsylvania State University*
Carolyn Jewell, *Fayetteville State University*
Lee Jones, *Shorter College*
Paula R. Kaiser, *University of North Carolina–Greensboro*
Jeremy Kemp, *San Jose State University*
Robert W. Key, *University of Phoenix*
Joy Kidwell, *Oregon State University*
Susan E. Kiner, *Cornell University*
Lisa Klein, *The Ohio State University*
Gary Kohut, *University of North Carolina–Charlotte*
Sarah McClure Kolk, *Hope College*
Keith Kroll, *Kalamazoo Valley Community College*
Milton Kukon, *Southern Vermont College*
Linda M. LaDuc, *University of Massachusetts–Amherst*
Suzanne Lambert, *Broward Community College*
Jamie Strauss Larsen, *North Carolina State University*
Newton Lassiter, *Florida Atlantic University*
Barry Lawler, *Oregon State University*
Sally Lawrence, *East Carolina University*
Cheryl Ann Laws, *City University*
Gordon Lee, *University of Tennessee*

Paul Lewellan, *Augustana College*

Kathy Lewis-Adler, *University of North Alabama*

Luchen Li, *Iowa State University*

Bobbi Looney, *Black Hills State University*

Dana Loewy, *California State University–Fullerton*

Andrea A. Lunsford, *Stanford University*

Catherine Macdermott, *Saint Edwards University*

Elizabeth Macdonald, *Thunderbird Graduate School of International Management*

John T. Maguire, *University of Illinois*

Michael D. Mahler, *Montana State University*

Margaret Mahoney, *Iowa State University*

Gianna Marsella

Pamela L. Martin, *The Ohio State University*

Iris Washburn Mauney, *High Point College*

Patricia McClure, *West Virginia State College*

Kelly McCormick–Sullivan, *Saint John Fisher College*

Nancie McCoy-Burns, *University of Idaho*

Brian R. McGee, *Texas Tech University*

Virginia Melvin, *Southwest Tennessee Community College*

Yvonne Merrill, *University of Arizona*

Julia R. Meyers, *North Carolina State University*

Julianne Michalenko, *Robert Morris University*

Paul Miller, *Davidson College*

Scott Miller

Jayne Moneysmith, *Kent State University–Stark*

Josef Moorehead, *California State University–Sacramento*

Gregory Morin, *University of Nebraska–Omaha*

Evelyn Morris, *Mesa Community College*

Frederick K. Moss, *University of Wisconsin–Waukesha*

Andrea Muldoon, *University of Wisconsin–Stout*

Anne Nail, *Amarillo College*

Frank P. Nemecek, *Jr., Wayne State University*

Cheryl Noll, *Eastern Illinois University*

Nancy Nygaard, *University of Wisconsin–Milwaukee*

Robert Von der Osten, *Ferris State University*

Carole Clark Papper

Greg Pauley, *Moberly Area Community College*

Jean E. Perry, *University of Southern California*

Linda N. Peters, *University of West Florida*

Florence M. Petrofes, *University of Texas–El Paso*

Melinda Phillabaum, *IUPUI–Indianapolis*

Evelyn M. Pierce, *Carnegie Mellon University*

Cathy Pleska, *West Virginia State College*

Susan Plutsky, *California State University–Northridge*

Virginia Polanski, *Stonehill College*

Janet Kay Porter, *Leeward Community College*

Susan Prenzlow, *Minnesota State University–Mankato*

Brenda Price, *Bucks County Community College*

Brenner Pugh, *Virginia Commonwealth University*

David Ramsey, *Southeastern Louisiana University*

Greg Rapp, *Portland Community College*

Kathryn C. Rentz, *University of Cincinnati*

Janetta Ritter, *Garland County Community College*
Naomi Ritter, *Indiana University*
Jeanette Ritzenthaler, *New Hampshire College*
Betty Jane Robbins, *University of Oklahoma*
Ralph Roberts, *University of West Florida*
Carol Roever, *Missouri Western State College*
Alisha Rohde
Deborah Roper, *California State University–Dominguez Hills*
Mary Jane Ryals, *Florida State University*
Mary Saga, *University of Alaska–Fairbanks*
Betty Schroeder, *Northern Illinois University*
Nancy Schullery, *Western Michigan University*
Kelly Searsmith, *University of Illinois*
Sherry Sherrill, *Forsythe Technical Community College*
Frank Smith, *Harper College*
Pamela Smith, *Florida Atlantic University*
Don Soucy
Helen W. Spain, *Wake Technical Community College*
Janet Starnes, *University of Texas–Austin*
Natalie Stillman-Webb, *University of Utah–Salt Lake City*
Ron Stone, *DeVry University*
Bruce Todd Strom, *University of Indianapolis*
Judith A. Swartley, *Lehigh University*
Christine Tachick, *University of Wisconsin–Milwaukee*
Mel Tarnowski, *Macomb Community College*
Bette Tetreault, *Dalhousie University*
Barbara Z. Thaden, *St. Augustine's College*
Lori Townsend, *Niagara County Community College–Sanborn*
Linda Travis, *Ferris State University*
Lisa Tyler, *Sinclair Community College*
Donna Vasa, *University of Nebraska–Lincoln*
David A. Victor, *Eastern Michigan University*
Catherine Waitinas, *University of Illinois–Champaign-Urbana*
Vicky Waldroupe, *Tusculum College*
Randall Waller, *Baylor University*
George Walters, *Emporia State University*
Jie Wang, *University of Illinois–Chicago*
Craig Warren, *Pennsylvania State–Erie Behrend College*
Linda Weavil, *Elon College*
Judy West, *University of Tennessee–Chattanooga*
Paula Weston
Gail S. Widner, *University of South Carolina*
Rebecca Wiggenhorn, *Clark State Community College*
Andrea Williams
Paula Williams, *Arkansas Northeastern College*
Marsha Daigle Williamson, *Spring Arbor University*
Bennie Wilson, *University of Texas–San Antonio*
Rosemary Wilson, *Washtenaw Community College*
Janet Winter, *Central Missouri State University*
Annette Wyandotte, *Indiana University Southeast*
Bonnie Thames Yarbrough, *University of North Carolina–Greensboro*
Sherilyn K. Zeigler, *Hawaii Pacific University*

I'm pleased to know that the book has worked so well for so many people and appreciative of suggestions for ways to make it even more useful in this edition. I especially want to thank the students who have allowed me to use their letters and memos, whether or not they allowed me to use their real names in the text.

I am grateful to all the business people who have contributed. The companies where I have done research and consulting work have given me insights into the problems and procedures of business and administrative communication. Special acknowledgment is due Joseph T. Ryerson & Son, Inc., where Kitty created the Writing Skills program that ultimately became the first draft of this book. And I thank the organizations that permitted McGraw-Hill/Irwin to reproduce their documents in this book and in the ancillaries.

Special thanks go to three assistants. Karen Bovenmyer, an Iowa State University graduate student, performed research wonders and checked all citations. Jacob Rawlins, another Iowa State University graduate student, wrote the Newsworthy Communications, and many of the sidebars. He also provided extensive help on editing PDF files and sorted reams of material into useful bundles.

Christopher Toth, assistant professor at Grand Valley State University, updated and edited Chapters 6, 10, 16, 17, and Appendix C, as well as large portions of Chapters 15 and 18 and part of Chapter 9. He provided the résumé and job letter examples as well as the student report and its proposal. He also did the ancillaries, as well as a large part of our half of the picture selection. Even more important to me, he served as my main sounding board. For all those hours of listening and suggesting, in addition to all his other labors for BAC, I thank him heartily.

The publisher, McGraw-Hill/Irwin, provided strong editorial and staff support. I wish to thank Dana Pauley, Michelle Gardner, Matt Diamond, and Sue Lombardi for the appearance of the book and website. Further thanks go to Sarah Evertson for finding such wonderful photos; Gretlyn Cline for her superlative editing; and Michelle Gardner for her good humor, enormous patience, gentle nudges, and outstanding problem-solving abilities.

And, finally, I thank my husband Jim, who provided support, research, editorial assistance, and major PDF work.

A Guided Tour

Business and Administrative Communication, by Kitty O. Locker and Donna S. Kienzler, is a true leader in the business communications field. The 10th edition is designed to teach students how to think critically, communicate effectively, and improve written, oral, and electronic business communication skills. These skills will successfully prepare students to meet a variety of challenges they may face in their future careers.

Beyond covering the broad scope of topics in business communication, this text uses a student-friendly writing style and strong design elements to hold student attention. In addition, real-world examples and real business applications underscore key material within the text.

We invite you to learn about this new edition and its features by paging through this visual guide.

CHAPTER PEDAGOGY

CHAPTER OUTLINE AND LEARNING OBJECTIVES

Each chapter begins with a chapter outline and learning objectives to guide students as they study. The first exercise for each chapter, Reviewing the Chapter, poses questions specifically linked to the chapter's learning objectives.

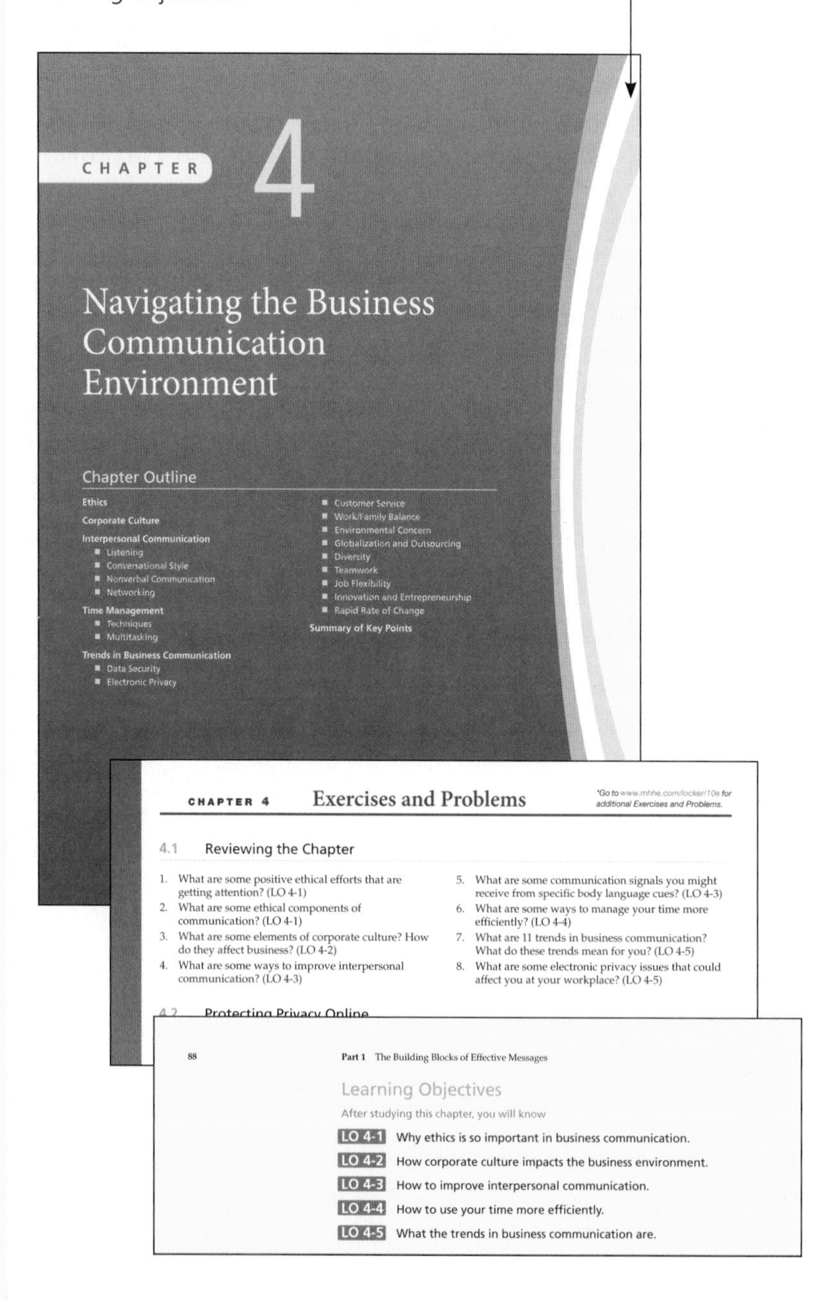

CHAPTER 4

Navigating the Business Communication Environment

Chapter Outline

Ethics
Corporate Culture
Interpersonal Communication
- Listening
- Conversational Style
- Nonverbal Communication
- Networking

Time Management
- Techniques
- Multitasking

Trends in Business Communication
- Data Security
- Electronic Privacy
- Customer Service
- Work/Family Balance
- Environmental Concern
- Globalization and Outsourcing
- Diversity
- Teamwork
- Job Flexibility
- Innovation and Entrepreneurship
- Rapid Rate of Change

Summary of Key Points

CHAPTER 4 Exercises and Problems

Go to www.mhhe.com/locker/10e for additional Exercises and Problems.

4.1 Reviewing the Chapter

1. What are some positive ethical efforts that are getting attention? (LO 4-1)
2. What are some ethical components of communication? (LO 4-1)
3. What are some elements of corporate culture? How do they affect business? (LO 4-2)
4. What are some ways to improve interpersonal communication? (LO 4-3)
5. What are some communication signals you might receive from specific body language cues? (LO 4-3)
6. What are some ways to manage your time more efficiently? (LO 4-4)
7. What are 11 trends in business communication? What do these trends mean for you? (LO 4-5)
8. What are some electronic privacy issues that could affect you at your workplace? (LO 4-5)

4.2 Protecting Privacy Online

88 Part 1 The Building Blocks of Effective Messages

Learning Objectives

After studying this chapter, you will know

LO 4-1 Why ethics is so important in business communication.
LO 4-2 How corporate culture impacts the business environment.
LO 4-3 How to improve interpersonal communication.
LO 4-4 How to use your time more efficiently.
LO 4-5 What the trends in business communication are.

AN INSIDE PERSPECTIVE

Each chapter is introduced with current news articles relevant to the chapter's concepts. These opening articles set the stage for the chapter's content and allow students a glimpse at how the material applies in the business world.

NEWSWORTHY COMMUNICATION

Unconventional Job Tactics

With high U.S. unemployment rates, even the best-qualified candidates may struggle to make an impression in a sea of other job seekers. Some may turn to unconventional methods to get noticed by hiring directors and recruiters.

Nathan Schwagler, for example, chose an innovative way to get past the traditional hiring process at Ingram Micro. He dressed up as a deliveryman, complete with a clipboard, a bouquet of flowers, and a Candygram. He got through security and to the office of Jessica, the company's recruiter. When he finally met her, Schwagler stripped off his coveralls to reveal his business suit underneath and presented Jessica with his résumé, in addition to the flowers and candy.

These kinds of innovative methods to get noticed are on the rise in the United States. One survey of hiring managers conducted by CareerBuilder.com showed that unconventional methods are rising, with 22% of the managers seeing unusual tactics.

But do these unusual tactics work? In some cases. Only 9% of the hiring managers surveyed reported having hired someone who used an unconventional tactic to get noticed. However, most of the unusual tactics they list benefit the hiring company in some way: one candidate submitted a business plan for one of the company's products; another presented a solution to one of the company's problems. As you ponder your tactics, keep in mind that the other 91% of the people hired used standard techniques, including a strong application letter and a well-designed résumé.

"Remember that most innovative methods backfire."

Remember that most innovative methods backfire. Take Nathan Schwagler. After delivering his résumé, he followed up a week later, only to find himself talking with the head of security: Schwagler had been barred from entering the premises or calling again. As one of his professors told him later, "The world is not ready for that type of creativity."

Sources: Rachel Zupek, "Unusual Job Search Tactics," CareerBuilder, accessed April 9, 2011, http://www.careerbuilder.com/article/cb-1076-job-search-unusual-job-search-tactics/; and "More Employers Seeing Unusual Tactics from Job Seekers in 2010, Finds New CareerBuilder Survey," CareerBuilder, June 9, 2010, http://www.careerbuilder.com/share/aboutus/pressreleasesdetail.aspx?id=pr574&sd=6/9/2010&ed=12/31/2010&siteid=cbpr&sc_cmp1=cb_pr574_.

NEWSWORTHY COMMUNICATION

Audiences Change with Time

Every year in late January, the president of the United States gives the State of the Union address to one of the largest and most diverse audiences of any communication. Congress, the news media, foreign leaders and diplomats, students, and members of the American public from all walks of life watch, listen, or read the president's comments each year.

Traditionally, the president uses the State of the Union to recount his successes and to spell out his political goals for the coming year. In 2010, President Barack Obama outlined ambitious plans for health care reform, economic recovery, and an increased focus on education and green energy initiatives. He focused much of his speech on the challenges faced by the people of America and the steps he and his Democratic party were taking to help.

"His tone and presentation reflected the changed audience he faced—one more divided than the one he addressed in 2010."

In 2011, however, the president faced a different audience. Even though many of the *people* listening were the same, the *situation* and the *attitudes* had changed. In spite of President Obama's success with his goals during 2010, many Americans were dissatisfied. Riding a wave of discontent with the government, conservative Republicans had gained control of the House of Representatives in

tions and gained several seats in t

out the election, the tenor of pol

become increasingly pointed and

President Obama responded t

a different kind of State of th

still outlined ambitious plans,

on bipartisan efforts to achieve

more conciliatory and more f

the parties in Congress under

his core n

the same:

care, rebui

strengthen

expanding

tiatives. Hi

tation refl

audience he faced—one more di

he addressed in 2010.

The ability to adjust your me

ence is one key to effective com

President Obama addressed a

of millions, most communicatio

specific audiences—real people

and real concerns. Learning to a

ence will provide you with an excellent foundation for any kind of communication.

Sources: Barak Obama, "Remarks by the President in State of the Union Address," January 28, 2010, transcript, The White House, Office of the Press Secretary, http://www.whitehouse.gov/the-press-office/remarks-president-state-union-address; Barak Obama, "Remarks by the President in State of the Union Address," January 25, 2011, transcript, The White House, Office of the Press Secretary, http://www.whitehouse.gov/the-press-office/2011/01/25/remarks-president-state-union-address.

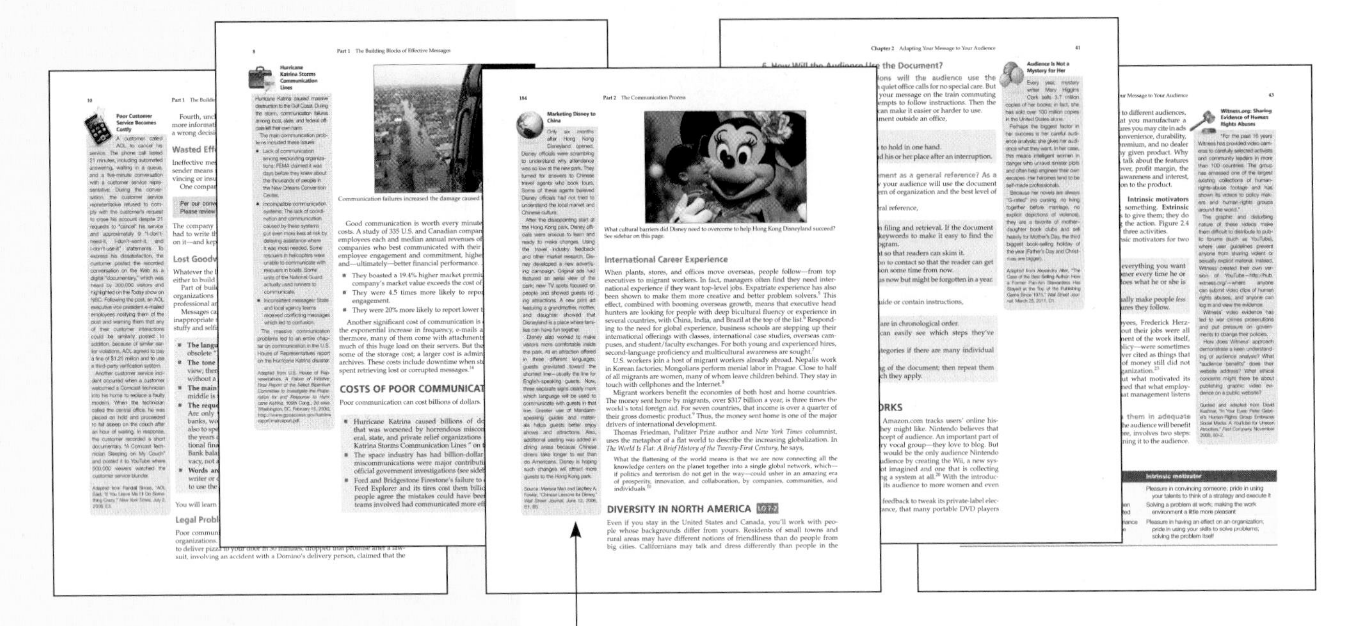

SIDEBARS

These novel and interesting examples effectively enhance student understanding of key concepts. Featured in the margins of every chapter, these sidebars cover topic areas that include International, Legal/Ethical, Just for Fun, Technology, and On the Job. In addition, gold stars identify "classic" sidebars.

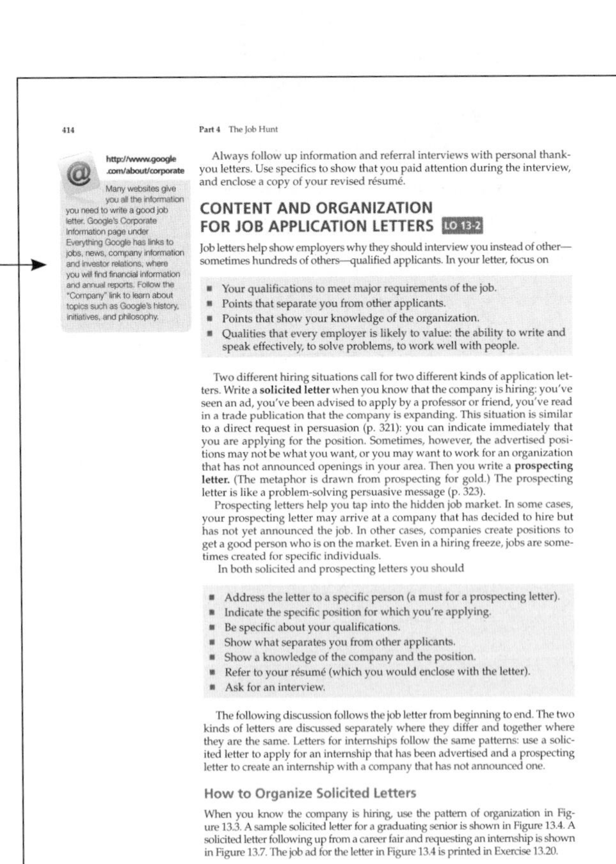

414 Part 4 The Job Hunt

http://www.google.com/about/corporate

Many websites give you all the information you need to write a good job letter. Google's Corporate Information page under Everything Google has links to jobs, news, company information and investor relations, where you will find financial information and annual reports. Follow the "Company" link to learn about topics such as Google's history, initiatives, and philosophy.

Always follow up information and referral interviews with personal thank-you letters. Use specifics to show that you paid attention during the interview, and enclose a copy of your revised résumé.

CONTENT AND ORGANIZATION FOR JOB APPLICATION LETTERS LO 13-2

Job letters help show employers why they should interview you instead of other—sometimes hundreds of others—qualified applicants. In your letter, focus on

- Your qualifications to meet major requirements of the job.
- Points that separate you from other applicants.
- Points that show your knowledge of the organization.
- Qualities that every employer is likely to value: the ability to write and speak effectively, to solve problems, to work well with people.

Two different hiring situations call for two different kinds of application letters. Write a **solicited letter** when you know that the company is hiring: you've seen an ad, you've been advised to apply by a professor or friend, you've read in a trade publication that the company is expanding. This situation is similar to a direct request in persuasion (p. 321): you can indicate immediately that you are applying for the position. Sometimes, however, the advertised positions may not be what you want, or you may want to work for an organization that has not announced openings in your area. Then you write a **prospecting letter.** (The metaphor is drawn from prospecting for gold.) The prospecting letter is like a problem-solving persuasive message (p. 323).

Prospecting letters help you tap into the hidden job market. In some cases, your prospecting letter may arrive at a company that has decided to hire but has not yet announced the job. In other cases, companies create positions to get a good person who is on the market. Even in a hiring freeze, jobs are sometimes created for specific individuals.

In both solicited and prospecting letters you should

- Address the letter to a specific person (a must for a prospecting letter).
- Indicate the specific position for which you're applying.
- Be specific about your qualifications.
- Show what separates you from other applicants.
- Show a knowledge of the company and the position.
- Refer to your résumé (which you would enclose with the letter).
- Ask for an interview.

The following discussion follows the job letter from beginning to end. The two kinds of letters are discussed separately where they differ and together where they are the same. Letters for internships follow the same patterns: use a solicited letter to apply for an internship that has been advertised and a prospecting letter to create an internship with a company that has not announced one.

How to Organize Solicited Letters

When you know the company is hiring, use the pattern of organization in Figure 13.3. A sample solicited letter for a graduating senior is shown in Figure 13.4. A solicited letter following up from a career fair and requesting an internship is shown in Figure 13.7. The job ad for the letter in Figure 13.4 is printed in Exercise 13.20.

INSITE LINKS

These helpful URLs point to websites that include organizations and resources of effective business communication. These examples underscore the role of the web in business communication and serve to motivate and enrich the student learning experience. These websites cover a wide range of reference sources, including corporate, small business, nonprofit, and government websites.

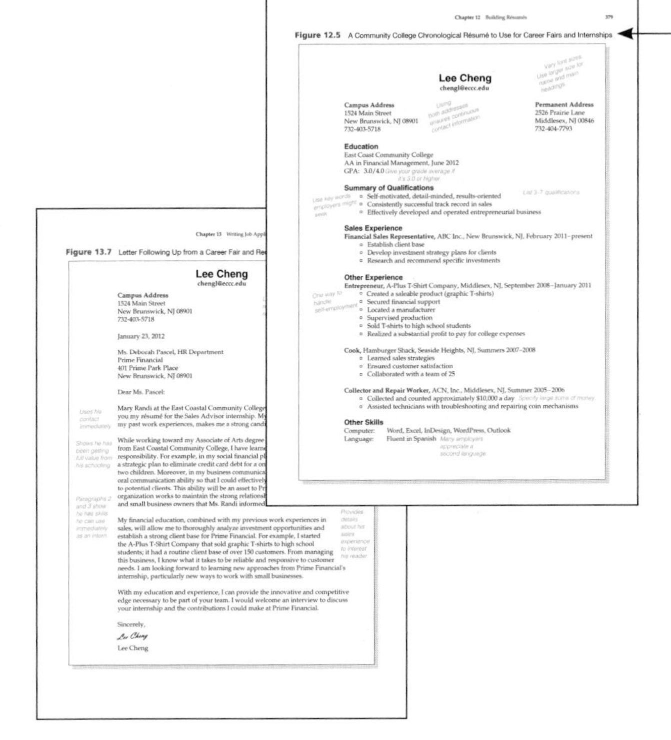

Chapter 12 Building Résumés 379

Figure 12.5 A Community College Chronological Résumé to Use for Career Fairs and Internships

Lee Cheng
chengl@eccc.edu

Vary font sizes. Use larger size for name and main headings

Campus Address
1524 Main Street
New Brunswick, NJ 08901
732-403-5718

Using both addresses ensures continuous contact information

Permanent Address
2526 Prairie Lane
Middlesex, NJ 00846
732-404-7793

Education
East Coast Community College
AA in Financial Management, June 2012
GPA: 3.0/4.0 *Give your grade average if it's 3.0 or higher*

Summary of Qualifications *List 3–7 qualifications*
Use key words employers might seek
- Self-motivated, detail-minded, results-oriented
- Consistently successful track record in sales
- Effectively developed and operated entrepreneurial business

Sales Experience
Financial Sales Representative, ABC Inc., New Brunswick, NJ, February 2011–present
- Establish client base
- Develop investment strategy plans for clients
- Research and recommend specific investments

Other Experience
Entrepreneur, A-Plus T-Shirt Company, Middlesex, NJ, September 2008–January 2011
One way to handle self-employment
- Created a saleable product (graphic T-shirts)
- Secured financial support
- Located a manufacturer
- Supervised production
- Sold T-shirts to high school students
- Realized a substantial profit to pay for college expenses

Cook, Hamburger Shack, Seaside Heights, NJ, Summers 2007–2008
- Learned sales strategies
- Ensured customer satisfaction
- Collaborated with a team of 25

Collector and Repair Worker, ACN, Inc., Middlesex, NJ, Summer 2005–2006
- Collected and counted approximately $10,000 a day *Specify large sums of money*
- Assisted technicians with troubleshooting and repairing coin mechanisms

Other Skills
Computer: Word, Excel, InDesign, WordPress, Outlook
Language: Fluent in Spanish *Many employers appreciate a second language*

Chapter 13 Writing Job Appl

Figure 13.7 Letter Following Up from a Career Fair and Re

Lee Cheng
chengl@eccc.edu

Campus Address
1524 Main Street
New Brunswick, NJ 08901
732-403-5718

January 23, 2012

Ms. Deborah Pascel, HR Department
Prime Financial
401 Prime Park Place
New Brunswick, NJ 08901

Dear Ms. Pascel:

Uses his contact immediately

Mary Randi at the East Coastal Community College
you my résumé for the Sales Advisor internship. My
my past work experiences, makes me a strong candi

Shows he has been getting full value from his schooling

While working toward my Associate of Arts degree
from East Coastal Community College, I have learne
responsibility. For example, in my social financial pl
a strategic plan to eliminate credit card debt for a on
two children. Moreover, in my business communica
oral communication ability so that I could effectively
to potential clients. This ability will be an asset to Pr
organization works to maintain the strong relationsh
and small business owners that Ms. Randi informed

Paragraphs 2 and 3 show he has skills he can use immediately as an intern

My financial education, combined with my previous work experiences in sales, will allow me to thoroughly analyze investment opportunities and establish a strong client base for Prime Financial. For example, I started the A-Plus T-Shirt Company that sold graphic T-shirts to high school students; it had a routine client base of over 150 customers. From managing this business, I know what it takes to be reliable and responsive to customer needs. I am looking forward to learning new approaches from Prime Financial's internship, particularly new ways to work with small businesses.

Provides details about his sales experience to interest his reader

With my education and experience, I can provide the innovative and competitive edge necessary to be part of your team. I would welcome an interview to discuss your internship and the contributions I could make at Prime Financial.

Sincerely,

Lee Cheng

Lee Cheng

FULL-PAGE EXAMPLES

A variety of visual examples featuring full-sized letters, memos, e-mails, reports, and résumés are presented in the text. These examples include the authors' "handwritten" annotations, explaining communication miscues while offering suggestions for improvement.

GOOD AND BAD EXAMPLES

Paired effective and ineffective communication examples are presented so students can pinpoint problematic ways to phrase messages to help improve their communication skills. Commentaries in red and blue inks indicate poor or good methods of message communication and allow for easy comparison.

60 Part 1 The Building Blocks of Effective Messages

Exercising Empathy for Employees and Customers

Although the concept of happy employees leading to happy customers is not new, it is experiencing a resurgence in many different industries. For example, call centers are allowing seasoned employees to work at home while a grocery chain is giving employees a profit-sharing plan that rewards them for excellent customer service.

Companies are finding creative ways to help employees identify with customers. USAA, an insurance agency for the military, provides new employees with MREs (meals ready to eat) during orientation so they will better understand the lifestyle of the members they serve.

Cabela's, an outdoor outfitter, encourages employees to use products they sell by loaning items free of charge in exchange for writing reviews on a company system. The loans are good perks for employees, and they help staff understand the issues customers may have with the products.

At Four Seasons Hotels, employees receive free overnight stays and meals at the hotel for themselves and a guest. They gain a customer's perspective on the hotel, but they also grade the hotel on various services.

The companies exercising empathy for employees and customers believe their customer service helps set them apart from other organizations.

Adapted from Jena McGregor, "Customer Service Champs," *BusinessWeek*, March 5, 2007, 52.

Don't talk about your audience's feelings, either. It's distancing to have others tell us how we feel—especially if they are wrong.

Lacks you-attitude: You'll be happy to hear that Open Grip Walkway Channels meet OSHA requirements.
You-attitude: Open Grip Walkway Channels meet OSHA requirements.

Maybe the audience expects that anything you sell would meet government regulations (OSHA—the Occupational Safety and Health Administration—is a federal agency). The audience may even be disappointed if they expected higher standards. Simply explain the situation or describe a product's features; don't predict the audience's response.

When you have good news, simply give the good news.

Lacks you-attitude: You'll be happy to hear that your scholarship has been renewed.
You-attitude: Congratulations! Your scholarship has been renewed.

4. In positive situations, use *you* more often than *I*. Use *we* when it includes the audience. Talk about the audience, not you or your company.

Lacks you-attitude: We provide health insurance to all employees.
You-attitude: You receive health insurance as a full-time Procter & Gamble employee.

Most readers are tolerant of the word *I* in e-mail messages, which seem like conversation. But edit paper documents to use *I* rarely if at all. *I* suggests that you're concerned about personal issues, not about the organization's problems, needs, and opportunities. *We* works well when it includes the reader. Avoid *we* if it excludes the reader (as it would in a letter to a customer or supplier or as it might in a memo about what *we* in management want *you* to do).

5. In negative situations, avoid the word *you*. Protect your audience's ego. Use passive verbs and impersonal expressions to avoid assigning blame. When you report bad news or limitations, use a noun for a group of which your audience is a part instead of *you* so people don't feel that they're singled out for bad news.

Lacks you-attitude: You must get approval from the director before you publish any articles or memoirs based on your work in the agency.
You-attitude: Agency personnel must get approval from the director to publish any articles or memoirs based on their work at the agency.

Use passive verbs and impersonal expressions to avoid blaming people. **Passive verbs** describe the action performed on something, without necessarily saying who did it. (See Chapter 5 for a full discussion of passive verbs.) In most cases, active verbs are better. But when your audience is at fault, passive verbs may be useful to avoid assigning blame.

Impersonal expressions omit people and talk only about things. Normally, communication is most lively when it's about people—and most interesting to audiences when it's about them. When you have to report a mistake or bad news, however, you can protect your audience's ego by using an impersonal expression, one in which things, not people, do the acting.

Lacks you-attitude: You made no allowance for inflation in your estimate.
You-attitude (passive): No allowance for inflation has been made in this estimate.
You-attitude (impersonal): This estimate makes no allowance for inflation.

CHECKLISTS

Checklists for important messages appear throughout the book. These helpful lists serve as a handy reference guide of items to keep in mind when composing and editing messages.

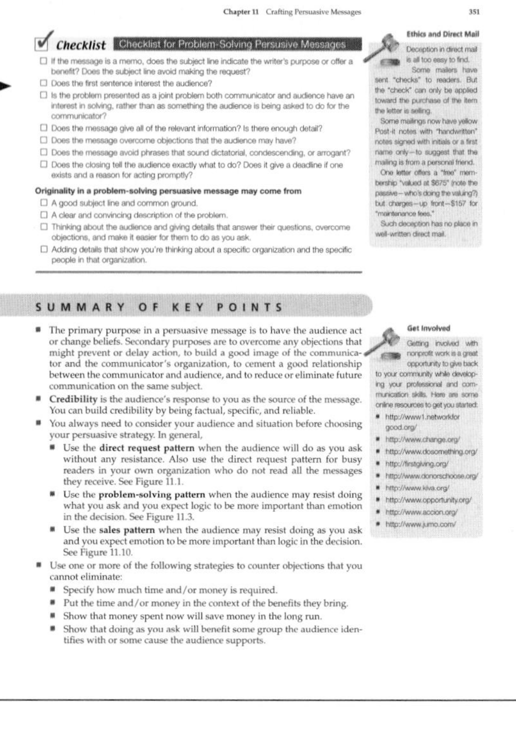

Chapter 11 Crafting Persuasive Messages 351

Checklist Checklist for Problem-Solving Persuasive Messages

- ☐ If the message is a memo, does the subject line indicate the writer's purpose or offer a benefit? Does the subject line avoid making the request?
- ☐ Does the first sentence interest the audience?
- ☐ Is the problem presented as a joint problem both communicator and audience have an interest in solving, rather than as something the audience is being asked to do for the communicator?
- ☐ Does the message give all of the relevant information? Is there enough detail?
- ☐ Does the message overcome objections that the audience may have?
- ☐ Does the message avoid phrases that sound dictatorial, condescending, or arrogant?
- ☐ Does the closing tell the audience exactly what to do? Does it give a deadline if one exists and a reason for acting promptly?

Originality in a problem-solving persuasive message may come from

- ☐ A good subject line and common ground.
- ☐ A clear and convincing description of the problem.
- ☐ Thinking about the audience and giving details that answer their questions, overcome objections, and make it easier for them to do as you ask.
- ☐ Adding details that show you're thinking about a specific organization and the specific people in that organization.

Ethics and Direct Mail

Deception in direct mail is all too easy to find.

Some mailers have sent "checks" to readers. But the "check" can only be applied toward the purchase of the item the letter is selling.

Some mailings now have yellow Post-it notes with "handwritten" notes signed with initials or a first name only—to suggest that the mailing is from a personal friend.

One letter offers a "free" membership "valued at $675" (note the passive—who's doing the valuing?) but charges—up front—$157 for "maintenance fees."

Such deception has no place in well-written direct mail.

SUMMARY OF KEY POINTS

- The primary purpose in a persuasive message is to have the audience act or change beliefs. Secondary purposes are to overcome any objections that might prevent or delay action, to build a good image of the communicator and the communicator's organization, to cement a good relationship between the communicator and audience, and to reduce or eliminate future communication on the same subject.
- **Credibility** is the audience's response to you as the source of the message. You can build credibility by being factual, specific, and reliable.
- You always need to consider your audience and situation before choosing your persuasive strategy. In general,
  - Use the **direct request pattern** when the audience will do as you ask without any resistance. Also use the direct request pattern for busy readers in your own organization who do not read all the messages they receive. See Figure 11.1.
  - Use the **problem-solving pattern** when the audience may resist doing what you ask and you expect logic to be more important than emotion in the decision. See Figure 11.3.
  - Use the **sales pattern** when the audience may resist doing as you ask and you expect emotion to be more important than logic in the decision. See Figure 11.10.
- Use one or more of the following strategies to counter objections that you cannot eliminate:
  - Specify how much time and/or money is required.
  - Put the time and/or money in the context of the benefits they bring.
  - Show that money spent now will save money in the long run.
  - Show that doing as you ask will benefit some group the audience identifies with or some cause the audience supports.

Get Involved

Getting involved with nonprofit work is a great opportunity to give back to your community while developing your professional and communication skills. Here are some online resources to get you started:

- http://www1.networkforgood.org/
- http://www.change.org/
- http://www.dosomething.org/
- http://firstgiving.org/
- http://www.donorschoose.org/
- http://www.kiva.org/
- http://www.opportunity.org/
- http://www.accion.org/
- http://www.jumo.com/

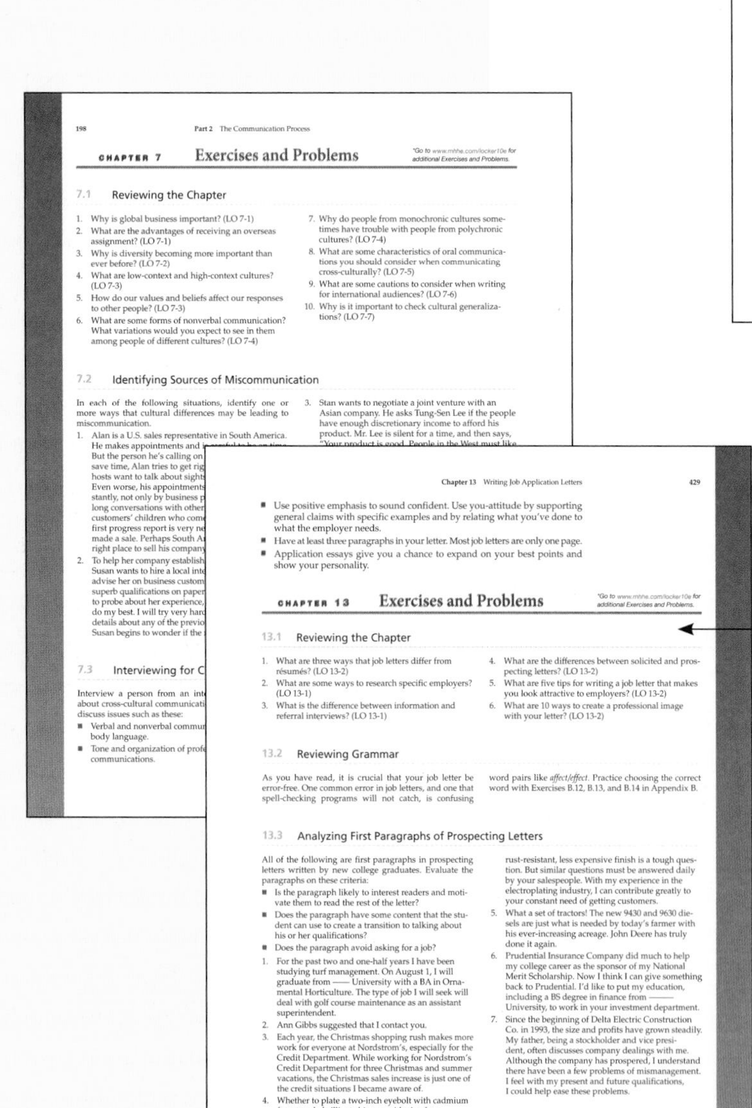

198 Part 2 The Communication Process

CHAPTER 7 Exercises and Problems

*Go to www.mhhe.com/locker10e for additional Exercises and Problems.

7.1 Reviewing the Chapter

1. Why is global business important? (LO 7-1)
2. What are the advantages of receiving an overseas assignment? (LO 7-1)
3. Why is diversity becoming more important than ever before? (LO 7-2)
4. What are low-context and high-context cultures? (LO 7-3)
5. How do our values and beliefs affect our responses to other people? (LO 7-3)
6. What are some forms of nonverbal communication? What variations would you expect to see in them among people of different cultures? (LO 7-4)
7. Why do people from monochronic cultures sometimes have trouble with people from polychronic cultures? (LO 7-4)
8. What are some characteristics of oral communications you should consider when communicating cross-culturally? (LO 7-5)
9. What are some cautions to consider when writing for international audiences? (LO 7-6)
10. Why is it important to check cultural generalizations? (LO 7-7)

7.2 Identifying Sources of Miscommunication

In each of the following situations, identify one or more ways that cultural differences may be leading to miscommunication.

1. Alan is a U.S. sales representative in South America. He makes appointments and i
But the person he's calling on
save time, Alan tries to get rig
hosts want to talk about sight
Even worse, his appointments
stantly, not only by business p
long conversations with other
customers' children who com
first progress report is very ne
made a sale. Perhaps South A
right place to sell his company
2. To help her company establish
Susan wants to hire a local int
advise her on business custom
superb qualifications on paper
to probe about her experience,
do my best. I will try very hard
details about any of the previo
Susan begins to wonder if the
3. Stan wants to negotiate a joint venture with an Asian company. He asks Tung-Sen Lee if the people have enough discretionary income to afford his product. Mr. Lee is silent for a time, and then says,

7.3 Interviewing for C

Interview a person from an int
about cross-cultural communicati
discuss issues such as these:

- Verbal and nonverbal commu
body language.
- Tone and organization of prof
communications.

Chapter 13 Writing Job Application Letters 429

- Use positive emphasis to sound confident. Use you-attitude by supporting general claims with specific examples and by relating what you've done to what the employer needs.
- Have at least three paragraphs in your letter. Most job letters are only one page.
- Application essays give you a chance to expand on your best points and show your personality.

CHAPTER 13 Exercises and Problems

*Go to www.mhhe.com/locker10e for additional Exercises and Problems.

13.1 Reviewing the Chapter

1. What are three ways that job letters differ from résumés? (LO 13-2)
2. What are some ways to research specific employers? (LO 13-1)
3. What is the difference between information and referral interviews? (LO 13-1)
4. What are the differences between solicited and prospecting letters? (LO 13-2)
5. What are five tips for writing a job letter that makes you look attractive to employers? (LO 13-2)
6. What are 10 ways to create a professional image with your letter? (LO 13-2)

13.2 Reviewing Grammar

As you have read, it is crucial that your job letter be error-free. One common error in job letters, and one that spell-checking programs will not catch, is confusing word pairs like *affect/effect*. Practice choosing the correct word with Exercises B.12, B.13, and B.14 in Appendix B.

13.3 Analyzing First Paragraphs of Prospecting Letters

All of the following are first paragraphs in prospecting letters written by new college graduates. Evaluate the paragraphs on these criteria:

- Is the paragraph likely to interest readers and motivate them to read the rest of the letter?
- Does the paragraph have some content that the student can use to create a transition to talking about his or her qualifications?
- Does the paragraph avoid asking for a job?

1. For the past two and one-half years I have been studying turf management. On August 1, I will graduate from —— University with a BA in Ornamental Horticulture. The type of job I will seek will deal with golf course maintenance as an assistant superintendent.
2. Ann Gibbs suggested that I contact you.
3. Each year, the Christmas shopping rush makes more work for everyone at Nordstrom's, especially for the Credit Department. While working for Nordstrom's Credit Department for three Christmas and summer vacations, the Christmas sales increase is just one of the credit situations I became aware of.
4. Whether to plate a two-inch eyebolt with cadmium for a tough, brilliant shine or with zinc for a rust-resistant, less expensive finish is a tough question. But similar questions must be answered daily by your salespeople. With my experience in the electroplating industry, I can contribute greatly to your constant need of getting customers.
5. What a set of tractors! The new 9430 and 9630 diesels are just what is needed by today's farmer with his ever-increasing acreage. John Deere has truly done it again.
6. Prudential Insurance Company did much to help my college career as the sponsor of my National Merit Scholarship. Now I think I can give something back to Prudential. I'd like to put my education, including a BS degree in finance from —— University, to work in your investment department.
7. Since the beginning of Delta Electric Construction Co. in 1993, the size and profits have grown steadily. My father, being a stockholder and vice president, often discusses company dealings with me. Although the company has prospered, I understand there have been a few problems of mismanagement. I feel with my present and future qualifications, I could help ease these problems.

EXERCISES AND PROBLEMS

These hands-on exercises are flexible and can be used as in-class discussions or as individual and group assignments. These workplace exercises allow students to assume a role or perform a task in a variety of realistic business scenarios. Helpful "hints" provide structure and guidance to students for them to complete the exercises.

The first exercise is always a collection of chapter review questions connected to the learning objectives.

A WEALTH OF SUPPLEMENTS IN THE NEW ONLINE LEARNING CENTER

NEW ONLINE LEARNING CENTER

Numerous resources available for both instructors and students are online at www.mhhe.com/locker10e. Instructor resources include downloadable versions of the

- Instructor's Manual.
- Test Bank.
- PowerPoint.

Student resources include

- Practice exercises.
- Quizzes.
- Memo, letter, and résumé templates.
- Links to business communication resources.

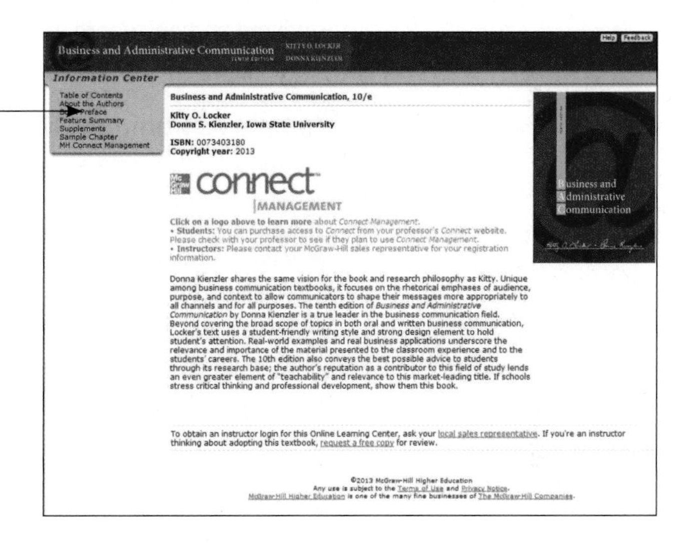

McGraw-Hill *Connect Business Communication*

Less Managing. More Teaching. Greater Learning. McGraw-Hill *Connect Business Communication* is an online assignment and assessment solution that connects students with the tools and resources they'll need to achieve success.

McGraw-Hill *Connect Business Communication* helps prepare students for their future by enabling faster learning, more efficient studying, and higher retention of knowledge.

McGraw-Hill *Connect Business Communication* Features. *Connect Business Communication* offers a number of powerful tools and features to make managing assignments easier, so faculty can spend more time teaching. With *Connect Business Communication,* students can engage with their course work anytime and anywhere, making the learning process more accessible and efficient. *Connect Business Communication* offers you the features described below.

Simple Assignment Management. With *Connect Business Communication,* creating assignments is easier than ever, so you can spend more time teaching and less time managing. The assignment management function enables you to

- Create and deliver assignments easily with selectable end-of-chapter questions and test bank items.
- Streamline lesson planning, student progress reporting, and assignment grading to make classroom management more efficient than ever.
- Go paperless with the eBook and online submission and grading of student assignments.

Smart Grading. When it comes to studying, time is precious. *Connect Business Communication* helps students learn more efficiently by providing feedback and practice material when they need it, where they need it. When it comes to teaching, your time also is precious. The grading function enables you to

- Have assignments scored automatically, giving students immediate feedback on their work and side-by-side comparisons with correct answers.
- Access and review each response; manually change grades or leave comments for students to review.
- Reinforce classroom concepts with practice tests and instant quizzes.

Instructor Library. The *Connect Business Communication* Instructor Library is your repository for additional resources to improve student engagement in and out of class. You can select and use any asset that enhances your lecture. The *Connect Business Communication* Instructor Library includes

- Instructor's Manual.
- PowerPoint Slides.
- Test Bank.
- eBook.

Student Study Center. The *Connect Business Communication* Student Study Center is the place for students to access additional resources. The Student Study Center

- Offers students quick access to lectures, practice materials, eBooks, and more.
- Provides instant practice material and study questions, easily accessible on the go.
- Gives students access to the Personalized Learning Plan described below.

Student Progress Tracking. *Connect Business Communication* keeps instructors informed about how each student, section, and class is performing, allowing for more productive use of lecture and office hours. The progress-tracking function enables you to

- View scored work immediately and track individual or group performance with assignment and grade reports.
- Access an instant view of student or class performance relative to learning objectives.
- Collect data and generate reports required by many accreditation organizations, such as AACSB.

Lecture Capture. Increase the attention paid to lecture discussion by decreasing the attention paid to note taking. For an additional charge Lecture Capture offers new ways for students to focus on the in-class discussion, knowing they can revisit important topics later. Lecture Capture enables you to

- Record and distribute your lecture with the click of a button.
- Record and index PowerPoint presentations and anything shown on your computer so it is easily searchable, frame by frame.
- Offer access to lectures anytime and anywhere by computer, iPod, or mobile device.
- Increase intent listening and class participation by easing students' concerns about note-taking. Lecture Capture will make it more likely you will see students' faces, not the tops of their heads.

McGraw-Hill *Connect Plus Business Communication*

McGraw-Hill reinvents the Textbook learning experience for the modern student with *Connect Plus Business Communication.* A seamless integration of an eBook and *Connect Business Communication, Connect Plus Business Communication* provides all of the *Connect Business Communication* features plus the following:

- An integrated eBook, allowing for anytime, anywhere access to the textbook.
- Dynamic links between the problems or questions you assign to your students and the location in the eBook where that problem or question is covered.
- A powerful search function to pinpoint and connect key concepts in a snap.

In short, *Connect Business Communication* offers you and your students powerful tools and features that optimize your time and energies, enabling you to focus on course content, teaching, and student learning. *Connect Business Communication* also offers a wealth of content resources for both instructors and students. This state-of-the-art, thoroughly tested system supports you in preparing students for the world that awaits.

For more information about Connect, go to www.mcgrawhillconnect.com, or contact your local McGraw-Hill sales representative.

TEGRITY CAMPUS: LECTURES 24/7

Mc Graw Hill tegrity campus

Tegrity Campus is a service that makes class time available 24/7 by automatically capturing every lecture in a searchable format for students to review when they study and complete assignments. With a simple one-click start-and-stop process, you capture all computer screens and corresponding audio. Students can replay any part of any class with easy-to-use browser-based viewing on a PC or Mac.

Educators know that the more students can see, hear, and experience class resources, the better they learn. In fact, studies prove it. With Tegrity Campus, students quickly recall key moments by using Tegrity Campus's unique search feature. This search helps students efficiently find what they need, when they need it, across an entire semester of class recordings. Help turn all your students' study time into learning moments immediately supported by your lecture.

To learn more about Tegrity watch a two-minute Flash demo at http://tegritycampus.mhhe.com.

ASSURANCE OF LEARNING READY

Many educational institutions today are focused on the notion of *assurance of learning,* an important element of some accreditation standards. *Business and Administrative Communication,* 10e, is designed specifically to support your assurance of learning initiatives with a simple, yet powerful solution.

Each Test Bank question for *Business and Administrative Communication,* 10e, maps to a specific chapter learning outcome/objective listed in the text. You can use our Test Bank software, EZ Test and EZ Test Online, or *Connect Business Communication* to easily query for learning outcomes/objectives that directly relate to the learning objectives for your course. You can then use the reporting features of EZ Test to aggregate student results in similar fashion, making the collection and presentation of assurance of learning data simple and easy.

AACSB STATEMENT

The McGraw-Hill Companies is a proud corporate member of AACSB International. Understanding the importance and value of AACSB accreditation, *Business and Administrative Communication,* 10e recognizes the curricula guidelines detailed in the AACSB standards for business accreditation by connecting selected questions in the text and/or the Test Bank to the six general knowledge and skill guidelines in the AACSB standards.

The statements contained in *Business and Administrative Communication,* 10e, are provided only as a guide for the users of this textbook. The AACSB leaves content coverage and assessment within the purview of individual schools, the mission of the school, and the faculty. While *Business and Administrative Communication,* 10e, and the teaching package make no claim of any specific AACSB qualification or evaluation, we have within *Business and Administrative Communication,* 10e, labeled selected questions according to the six general knowledge and skills areas.

MCGRAW-HILL CUSTOMER EXPERIENCE CONTACT INFORMATION

At McGraw-Hill, we understand that getting the most from new technology can be challenging. That's why our services don't stop after you purchase our products. You can e-mail our Product Specialists 24 hours a day to get product-training online. Or you can search our knowledge bank of Frequently Asked Questions on our support website. For Customer Support, call **800-331-5094,** e-mail **hmsupport@mcgraw-hill.com,** or visit **www.mhhe.com/support.** One of our Technical Support Analysts will be able to assist you in a timely fashion.

MHHE AND BLACKBOARD TEAM UP

McGraw-Hill Higher Education and Blackboard have teamed up. What does this mean for you?

1. **Your life, simplified.** Now you and your students can access McGraw-Hill's Connect® and Create™ right from within your Blackboard course—all with one single sign-on. Say goodbye to the days of logging in to multiple applications.
2. **Deep integration of content and tools.** Not only do you get single sign-on with Connect® and Create™, you also get deep integration of McGraw-Hill content and content engines right in Blackboard. Whether you're choosing a book for your course or building Connect® assignments, all the tools you need are right where you want them—inside Blackboard.
3. **Seamless gradebooks.** Are you tired of keeping multiple gradebooks and manually synchronizing grades into Blackboard? We thought so. When a student completes an integrated Connect® assignment, the grade for that assignment automatically (and instantly) feeds your Blackboard grade center.

4. **A solution for everyone.** Whether your institution is already using Blackboard or you just want to try Blackboard on your own, we have a solution for you. McGraw-Hill and Blackboard can now offer you easy access to industry-leading technology and content, whether your campus hosts it, or we do. Be sure to ask your local McGraw-Hill representative for details.

Craft your teaching resources to match the way you teach! With McGraw-Hill Create, www.mcgrawhillcreate.com, you can easily rearrange chapters, combine material from other content sources, and quickly upload content you have written, like your course syllabus or teaching notes. Find the content you need in Create by searching through thousands of leading McGraw-Hill textbooks. Arrange your book to fit your teaching style. Create even allows you to personalize your book's appearance by selecting the cover and adding your name, school, and course information. Order a Create book and you'll receive a complimentary print review copy in three to five business days or a complimentary electronic review copy (eComp) via e-mail in about one hour. Go to www.mcgrawhillcreate.com today and register. Experience how McGraw-Hill Create empowers you to teach *your* students *your* way.

CONTENTS

Preface ix

PART ONE **The Building Blocks of Effective Messages**

1 Succeeding in Business Communication 2

Newsworthy Communication 3
Communication Ability = Promotability 4
"I'll Never Have to Write Because . . ." 5
Communicating on the Job 6
The Cost of Communication 6
Costs of Poor Communication 8
Benefits of Improving Communication 12
Criteria for Effective Messages 12
Using Technology for Communication 12
Following Conventions 13
Understanding and Analyzing Business Communication Situations 14
How to Solve Business Communication Problems 14
How to Use This Book 18
Summary of Key Points 18
Exercises and Problems for Chapter 1 19

2 Adapting Your Message to Your Audience 26

Newsworthy Communication 27
Identifying Your Audiences 28
Ways to Analyze Your Audience 29
Choosing Channels to Reach Your Audience 33
Using Audience Analysis to Adapt Your Message 36
Audience Analysis Works 41
Audience Benefits 42
Audience Benefits Work 46
Writing or Speaking to Multiple Audiences with Different Needs 47
Summary of Key Points 48
Exercises and Problems for Chapter 2 49

3 Building Goodwill 56

Newsworthy Communication 57
You-Attitude 58
Positive Emphasis 63
Tone, Power, and Politeness 68
Reducing Bias in Business Communication 70
Summary of Key Points 76
Exercises and Problems for Chapter 3 76

4 Navigating the Business Communication Environment 86

Newsworthy Communication 87
Ethics 88
Corporate Culture 91
Interpersonal Communication 93
Time Management 99
Trends in Business Communication 101
Summary of Key Points 109
Exercises and Problems for Chapter 4 110

PART TWO The Communication Process

5 Planning, Composing, and Revising 116

Newsworthy Communication 117
The Ways Good Writers Write 118
Activities in the Composing Process 118
Using Your Time Effectively 120
Brainstorming, Planning, and Organizing Business Documents 120
Writing Good Business and Administrative Documents 121
Half-Truths about Business Writing 124
Ten Ways to Make Your Writing Easier to Read 125
Organizational Preferences for Style 138
Revising, Editing, and Proofreading 138
Getting and Using Feedback 142
Using Boilerplate 144
Readability Formulas 144
Summary of Key Points 145
Exercises and Problems for Chapter 5 146

6 Designing Documents 156

Newsworthy Communication 157
The Importance of Effective Design 158
Design as Part of Your Writing Process(es) 158
Design and Conventions 159
Levels of Design 159
Guidelines for Document Design 161
Designing Brochures 167
Designing Web Pages 169
Testing the Design for Usability 172
Summary of Key Points 172
Exercises and Problems for Chapter 6 173

7 Communicating across Cultures 180

Newsworthy Communication 181
Global Business 183
Diversity in North America 184
Ways to Look at Culture 185
Values, Beliefs, and Practices 187
Nonverbal Communication 188
Oral Communication 194
Writing to International Audiences 195
Learning More about International Business Communication 197
Summary of Key Points 197
Exercises and Problems for Chapter 7 198

8 Working and Writing in Teams 204

Newsworthy Communication 205
Team Interactions 206
Working on Diverse Teams 213
Conflict Resolution 214
Effective Meetings 218
Collaborative Writing 220
Summary of Key Points 224
Exercises and Problems for Chapter 8 224

PART THREE

Basic Business Messages

9 Sharing Informative and Positive Messages with Appropriate Technology 232

Newsworthy Communication 233
Communication Hardware 234
Information Overload 236
Using Common Media 237
Organizing Informative and Positive Messages 244
Subject Lines for Informative and Positive Messages 245
Managing the Information in Your Messages 249
Using Benefits in Informative and Positive Messages 250
Ending Informative and Positive Messages 251
Humor in Informative Messages 252
Varieties of Informative and Positive Messages 253
Solving a Sample Problem 257
Summary of Key Points 261
Exercises and Problems for Chapter 9 261

10 Delivering Negative Messages 276

Newsworthy Communication 277
Organizing Negative Messages 279
The Parts of a Negative Message 283
Apologies 287
Tone in Negative Messages 291
Alternative Strategies for Negative Situations 291
Varieties of Negative Messages 293
Solving a Sample Problem 296
Summary of Key Points 300
Exercises and Problems for Chapter 10 300

11 Crafting Persuasive Messages 312

Newsworthy Communication 313
Analyzing Persuasive Situations 315
Choosing a Persuasive Strategy 320
Why Threats Are Less Effective than Persuasion 320
Making Persuasive Direct Requests 321
Writing Persuasive Problem-Solving Messages 323
Tone in Persuasive Messages 332
Varieties of Persuasive Messages 333
Sales and Fund-Raising Messages 336
Solving a Sample Problem 347
Summary of Key Points 351
Exercises and Problems for Chapter 11 352

PART FOUR The Job Hunt

12 Building Résumés 366

Newsworthy Communication 367
A Time Line for Job Hunting 368
Evaluating Your Strengths and Interests 369
Using the Internet in Your Job Search 370
Personal Branding 371
Networking 372
A Caution about Blogs, Social Networking Sites, and Internet Tracking 372
Using an Internship as a Job Hunting Tool 373
How Employers Use Résumés 374
Guidelines for Résumés 375
Kinds of Résumés 378
What to Include in a Résumé 380
References 390
What Not to Include in a Résumé 391
Dealing with Difficulties 392
Electronic Résumés 394
Honesty 397
Summary of Key Points 398
Exercises and Problems for Chapter 12 398

13 Writing Job Application Letters 408

Newsworthy Communication 409
How Content Differs in Job Letters and Résumés 410
How to Find Out about Employers and Jobs 411
Tapping into the Hidden Job Market 412
Content and Organization for Job Application Letters 414
E-Mail Application Letters 422
Creating a Professional Image 423
Application Essays 427
Summary of Key Points 428
Exercises and Problems for Chapter 13 429

14 Interviewing, Writing Follow-Up Messages, and Succeeding in the Job 438

Newsworthy Communication 439
21st Century Interviews 440
Interview Strategy 441
Interview Preparation 441
Interview Channels 444
Interview Practice 445
Interview Customs 445
Traditional Interview Questions and Answers 448
Kinds of Interviews 454
Final Steps for a Successful Job Search 458
Dealing with Rejection 462
Your First Full-Time Job 462
Summary of Key Points 463
Exercises and Problems for Chapter 14 464

PART FIVE Proposals and Reports

15 Planning and Researching Proposals and Reports 468

Newsworthy Communication 469
Varieties of Reports 470
The Report Production Process 471
Report Problems 472
Research Strategies for Reports 474
Source Citation and Documentation 489
Summary of Key Points 491
Exercises and Problems for Chapter 15 492

16 Creating Visuals and Data Displays 498

Newsworthy Communication 499
When to Use Visuals and Data Displays 500
Guidelines for Creating Effective Visuals and Data Displays 501
Integrating Visuals and Data Displays in Your Text 508
Designing Visuals and Data Displays 509
Summary of Key Points 516
Exercises and Problems for Chapter 16 517

17 Writing Proposals and Progress Reports 532

Newsworthy Communication 533
Writing Proposals 534
Writing Progress Reports 545
Summary of Key Points 549
Exercises and Problems for Chapter 17 549

18 Analyzing Information and Writing Reports 552

Newsworthy Communication 553
Using Your Time Efficiently 554
Analyzing Data and Information for Reports 554
Choosing Information for Reports 560
Organizing Information in Reports 561
Presenting Information Effectively in Reports 569
Writing Formal Reports 574
Summary of Key Points 598
Exercises and Problems for Chapter 18 599

19 Making Oral Presentations 606

Newsworthy Communication 607
Identifying Purposes in Oral Presentations 608
Comparing Written and Oral Messages 609
Planning a Strategy for Your Presentation 610
Choosing Information to Include in a Presentation 613
Organizing Your Information 615
Planning PowerPoint Slides 616
Delivering an Effective Presentation 619
Handling Questions 622
Making Group Presentations 624
Summary of Key Points 624
Exercises and Problems for Chapter 19 626

A Formatting Letters, Memos, and E-Mail Messages 631

Formats for Letters 632

Formats for Envelopes 638

Formats for Memos 642

Formats for E-Mail Messages 642

State and Province Abbreviations 649

B Writing Correctly 650

Using Grammar 651

Understanding Punctuation 655

Punctuating Sentences 656

Punctuation within Sentences 658

Special Punctuation Marks 662

Writing Numbers and Dates 663

Words That Are Often Confused 664

Proofreading Symbols 669

Exercises and Problems for Appendix B 671

C Citing and Documenting Sources 676

American Psychological Association (APA) Format 678

Modern Language Association (MLA) Format 678

D Formatting a Scannable Résumé 685

Glossary 687

Notes 697

Photo Credits 710

Name Index 711

Company Index 714

Subject Index 718

Business and Administrative Communication

CHAPTER 1

Succeeding in Business Communication

Chapter Outline

Communication Ability = Promotability

"I'll Never Have to Write Because . . ."

Communicating on the Job

The Cost of Communication

Costs of Poor Communication

- Wasted Time
- Wasted Efforts
- Lost Goodwill
- Legal Problems

Benefits of Improving Communication

Criteria for Effective Messages

Using Technology for Communication

Following Conventions

Understanding and Analyzing Business Communication Situations

How to Solve Business Communication Problems

- Gather Knowledge and Brainstorm Solutions.
- Answer the Five Questions for Analysis.
- Organize Your Information to Fit Your Audiences, Your Purposes, and the Situation.
- Make Your Document Visually Inviting.
- Revise Your Draft to Create a Friendly, Businesslike, Positive Style.
- Edit Your Draft for Standard English; Double-Check Names and Numbers.
- Use the Response You Get to Plan Future Messages.

How to Use This Book

Summary of Key Points

A Communication Recovery from Disaster

In 2009 and 2010 the Toyota Motor Corporation recalled more than 8 million cars and trucks after highly publicized incidents of accelerator pedal failure. In chilling accidents replayed on news reports and the Internet, Toyota accelerator pedals became stuck, causing serious—and sometimes fatal—crashes.

Toyota, the world's largest automaker, had built its business on customer trust and loyalty by providing consistent quality in its cars. But now, in addition to the financial costs of the pedal recalls and the government investigations, the company faced a public relations disaster: customers no longer trusted Toyota to provide safe vehicles.

> *"For Toyota, good communication helped the company recover from the costly and embarrassing recalls."*

The company responded with a carefully designed communication campaign to restore customer trust in the Toyota brand. On February 2, 2010, Jim Lentz, Toyota's president and chief operating officer in the United States, sent a letter to all Toyota customers with a personal apology and a commitment to correct the problems. This letter kicked off a publicity campaign of personal and open letters, newspaper and magazine advertisements, and television commercials that all focused on how Toyota was taking responsibility and improving its operations.

Every company relies on communication with its customers to build trust. When crises hit, as in the case of Toyota's recalls, communication becomes even more important. The quality of written and spoken messages could make the difference between a company's failure and recovery after a crisis. In the late 1990s, Ford Motor Company and the Firestone Tire and Rubber Company were investigated for a series of rollover accidents involving blown-out tires. After first denying the problems and then blaming each other, both companies took years to recover from the crisis—they were still dealing with recalls and complaints in 2006, more than six years after the initial problems.

By contrast, Toyota's straightforward apology and aggressive communication in many forms of media helped restore its image quickly. In fact, by December 2010, Toyota announced that it had "regained the number one spot as the most-considered automobile brand among new-car shoppers." For Toyota, good communication helped the company recover from the costly and embarrassing recalls.

Source: Toyota, "2010 Year-End Progress Report: Major Changes Help Toyota Put Even More Focus on Its Customers," news release, December 20, 2010, http://www.toyota.com/about/news/corporate/2010/12/21-1-Progress.html; and Jim Lentz, "Open Letter to Toyota Customers," Toyota, February 2, 2010, http://www.toyota.com/recall/v2/pdf/ToyotaCustomerLetter.pdf.

Learning Objectives

After studying this chapter, you will know

- **LO 1-1** Why you need to be able to communicate well.
- **LO 1-2** What the costs of communication are.
- **LO 1-3** What the costs of poor communication are.
- **LO 1-4** What role conventions play in business communication.
- **LO 1-5** How to solve business communication problems.

Communication Is Key to Pay

How can you make more money at your job?

The number one way, according to the *Wall Street Journal*, is to "listen to your boss." Specifically, do the work your boss wants done, follow directions, work hard, and let your boss know what you have accomplished. Employees who follow this method collect raises at a rate of 9.9%, while average performers receive 3.6% and poor performers get 1.3%, according to one survey.

Just as important is to make sure you ask your manager to define expectations. Don't assume you know what your manager wants. Make sure you understand what your manager considers an outstanding performance in your position.

Adapted from Perri Capell, "10 Ways to Get the Most Pay out of Your Job," *Wall Street Journal*, September 18, 2006, R1.

The amount of business communication is staggering. The U.S. Postal Service processed 177 billion pieces of mail in 2009, most of which were business communications. Merchants send American consumers 20 billion catalogs annually, through the mail and e-mail. When you consider that most of your business communications are electronic or oral, you can start to imagine the staggering number of business communications that people compose, hear, and read. As one small piece of that, the head of Best Buy says his company handles more than 1.5 billion customer interactions annually. The Radicati Group, a technology market research firm, projects that 294 billion e-mail messages were sent daily in 2010, of which 89.1% were spam.[1]

Business depends on communication. People must communicate to plan products and services; hire, train, and motivate workers; coordinate manufacturing and delivery; persuade customers to buy; and bill them for the sale. Indeed, for many businesses and nonprofit and government organizations, the "product" is information or services rather than something tangible. Information and services are created and delivered by communication. In every organization, communication is the way people get work done.

Communication takes many forms: face-to-face or phone conversations, informal meetings, presentations, e-mail messages, letters, memos, reports, blogs, tweets, text messaging, and websites. All of these methods are forms of **verbal communication,** or communication that uses words. **Nonverbal communication** does not use words. Pictures, computer graphics, and company logos are nonverbal. Interpersonal nonverbal signals include how people sit at meetings, how large offices are, and how long someone keeps a visitor waiting.

COMMUNICATION ABILITY = PROMOTABILITY LO 1-1

Even in your first job, you'll communicate. You'll listen to instructions; you'll ask questions; you may solve problems with other workers in teams. Even "entry-level" jobs require high-level skills in reasoning, mathematics, and communicating. As a result, communication ability consistently ranks first among the qualities that employers look for in college graduates.[2] Warren Buffet told Columbia Business School students that they could increase their value 50% by learning communication skills, and that many of them did not yet have those skills.[3]

As more people compete for fewer jobs, the ones who will build successful careers are those who can communicate well with customers and colleagues. Robert O. Best, Chief Information Officer of UNUMProvident, an insurance corporation, cautions, "You used to be able to get away with being a technical nerd. . . . Those days are over."[4]

The National Commission on Writing surveyed 120 major corporations, employing nearly 8 million workers. Almost 70% of respondents said that at least two-thirds of their employees have specific writing responsibilities included in their position descriptions. These writing responsibilities include:

- E-mail (100% of employees)
- Presentations with visuals, such as PowerPoint slides (100%)
- Memos and correspondence (70%)
- Formal reports (62%)
- Technical reports (59%)

Respondents also noted that communication functions were least likely to be outsourced.[5]

Because communication skills are so important, good communicators earn more. Research has shown that among people with two- or four-year degrees, workers in the top 20% of writing ability earn, on average, more than three times as much as workers whose writing falls into the worst 20%.[6] Jeffrey Gitomer, business consultant and author of best-selling business books, says there are three secrets to getting known in the business world; all of them are communication skills: writing, e-zining (he reaches over 130,000 subscribers each week), and speaking. He states, "Writing leads to wealth."[7]

In spite of the frequency of on-the-job writing and the importance of overall communication skills, employers do not find college students well skilled in writing. A survey of employers conducted on behalf of the Association of American Colleges and Universities found that writing was one of the weakest skills of college graduates.[8] In another large survey, respondents noted that a lack of "effective business communication skills appears to be a major stumbling block among new [job] entrants—even at the college level. Spelling errors, improper use of grammar, and the misuse of words were common in written reports, PowerPoint presentations, and e-mail messages."[9]

Put It in Writing

Raymond Dreyfack credits his writing skills for his successful career at Faberge Perfumes. As he worked in supervisory and management jobs, he kept his eye open for opportunities to solve problems and improve performance. Then, when he had an idea, he wrote a memo to his boss.

Why a memo? The written format forced Dreyfack to organize his initial idea clearly and concisely. Editing memos trained Dreyfack to consider whether his messages reflected the reader's interests and viewpoints. The written format also gave Dreyfack's boss time to consider the idea and reflect on its merits. (If you spring an idea on your boss in the hallway, he or she might find it easier to blurt out a *no* than to give the idea fair consideration.)

Adapted from Raymond Dreyfack, "The Write Way to Jump-Start Your Career," *Supervision* 65, no. 4 (April 2004): 13–15.

"I'LL NEVER HAVE TO WRITE BECAUSE . . ."

Some students think that an administrative assistant will do their writing, that they can use form letters if they do have to write, that only technical skills matter, or that they'll call or text rather than write. Each of these claims is fundamentally flawed.

Claim 1: An administrative assistant will do all my writing.

Reality: Because of automation and restructuring, job responsibilities in offices have changed. Today, many offices do not have typing pools. Most secretaries have become administrative assistants with their own complex tasks such as training, research, and database management for several managers. Managers are likely to take care of their own writing, data entry, and phone calls.

Claim 2: I'll use form letters or templates when I need to write.

Reality: A form letter is designed to cover only routine situations, many of which are computerized or outsourced, Also, the higher you rise, the more frequently you'll face situations that aren't routine, that demand creative solutions.

Claim 3: I'm being hired as an accountant, not a writer.

Reality: Almost every entry-level professional or managerial job requires you to write e-mail messages, speak to small groups, write documents, and present your work for annual reviews. People who do these things well are likely to be promoted beyond the entry level. Employees in jobs as diverse as firefighters, security professionals, and construction project managers are all being told to polish their writing and speaking skills.[10]

Claim 4: I'll just pick up the phone.

Reality: Important phone calls require follow-up letters, memos, or e-mail messages. People in organizations put things in writing to make themselves visible, to create a record, to convey complex data, to make things convenient for the reader, to save money, and to convey their own messages more effectively. "If it isn't in writing, it didn't happen" is a maxim at many companies. Writing is an essential way to record agreements, to make yourself visible, and to let your accomplishments be known.

COMMUNICATING ON THE JOB

Communication—oral, nonverbal, and written—goes to both internal and external audiences. **Internal audiences** are other people in the same organization: subordinates, superiors, peers. **External audiences** are people outside the organization: customers, suppliers, distributors, unions, stockholders, potential employees, trade associations, special interest groups, government agencies, the press, and the general public.

People in organizations produce a large variety of documents. Figures 1.1 and 1.2 list a few of the specific documents produced at Ryerson, a company that fabricates and sells steel, aluminum, other metals, and plastics to a wide variety of industrial clients and has sales offices across the United States, Canada, and China.

All of the documents in Figures 1.1 and 1.2 have one or more of the three basic purposes of organizational writing: to inform, to request or persuade, and to build goodwill. In fact, most messages have multiple purposes. When you answer a question, for instance, you're informing, but you also want to build goodwill by suggesting that you're competent and perceptive and that your answer is correct and complete.

THE COST OF COMMUNICATION LO 1-2

Writing costs money. The annual Social Security statements cost $70 million a year to mail, even with huge economies of scale.[11] The cost does not include employee time in the writing and processing, a major expense.

Business communication involves paper documents, electronic communications, and most of all, interpersonal abilities.

Figure 1.1 Internal Documents Produced in One Organization

Document	Description of document	Purpose(s) of document
Transmittal	Memo accompanying document, telling why it's being forwarded to the receiver	Inform; persuade reader to read document; build image and goodwill
Monthly or quarterly report	Report summarizing profitability, productivity, and problems during period. Used to plan activity for next month or quarter	Inform; build image and goodwill (report is accurate, complete; writer understands company)
Policy and procedure bulletin	Statement of company policies and instructions (e.g., how to enter orders, how to run fire drills)	Inform; build image and goodwill (procedures are reasonable)
Request to deviate from policy and procedure bulletin	Persuasive memo arguing that another approach is better for a specific situation than the standard approach	Persuade; build image and goodwill (request is reasonable; writer seeks good of company)
Performance appraisal	Evaluation of an employee's performance	Inform; persuade employee to improve
Memo of congratulations	Congratulations to employees who have won awards, been promoted	Build goodwill

Document cycling processes also increase costs. In many organizations, all external documents must be approved before they go out. A major document may **cycle** from writer to superior to writer to another superior to writer again 10 or more times before final approval. Longer documents can involve large teams of people and take months to write.

Large organizations handle so much paper that even small changes to their communication practices amount to millions of dollars. Through better use of technology, InterContinental Hotels Group cut communications costs by $2.6 million in two years. Xerox Global Services Europe touts contractual annual savings of up to 1 million Euros for organizations with 4,000 or more employees who switch to its printing services.[12]

Figure 1.2 External Documents Produced in One Organization

Document	Description of document	Purpose(s) of document
Quotation	Letter giving price for a specific product or service	Inform; build goodwill (price is reasonable)
Claims adjustment	Letter granting or denying customer request to be given credit for defective goods	Inform; build goodwill
Job description	Description of qualifications and duties of job. Used for performance appraisals, salaries, and hiring	Inform; persuade good candidates to apply; build goodwill (job duties match level, pay)
10-K report	Report filed with the Securities and Exchange Commission detailing financial information	Inform
Annual report	Report to stockholders summarizing financial information for year	Inform; persuade stockholders to retain stock and others to buy; build goodwill (company is a good corporate citizen)
Thank-you letter	Letter to suppliers, customers, or other people who have helped individuals or the company	Build goodwill

Hurricane Katrina Storms Communication Lines

Hurricane Katrina caused massive destruction to the Gulf Coast. During the storm, communication failures among local, state, and federal officials left their own harm.

The main communication problems included these issues:

- Lack of communication among responding organizations: FEMA claimed it was days before they knew about the thousands of people in the New Orleans Convention Center.
- Incompatible communication systems: The lack of coordination and communication caused by these systems put even more lives at risk by delaying assistance where it was most needed. Some rescuers in helicopters were unable to communicate with rescuers in boats. Some units of the National Guard actually used runners to communicate.
- Inconsistent messages: State and local agency teams received conflicting messages which led to confusion.

The massive communication problems led to an entire chapter on communication in the U.S. House of Representatives report on the Hurricane Katrina disaster.

Adapted from U.S. House of Representatives, *A Failure of Initiative: Final Report of the Select Bipartisan Committee to Investigate the Preparation for and Response to Hurricane Katrina*, 109th Cong., 2d sess. (Washington, DC, February 15, 2006), http://www.gpoaccess.gov/katrinareport/mainreport.pdf.

Communication failures increased the damage caused by Hurricane Katrina.

Good communication is worth every minute it takes and every penny it costs. A study of 335 U.S. and Canadian companies with an average of 13,000 employees each and median annual revenues of $1.8 billion found that those companies who best communicated with their employees enjoyed "greater employee engagement and commitment, higher retention and productivity, and—ultimately—better financial performance. . . .

- They boasted a 19.4% higher market premium (the degree to which the company's market value exceeds the cost of its assets).
- They were 4.5 times more likely to report high levels of employee engagement.
- They were 20% more likely to report lower turnover rates."[13]

Another significant cost of communication is e-mail storage. In addition to the exponential increase in frequency, e-mails are also growing in size. Furthermore, many of them come with attachments. And businesses are storing much of this huge load on their servers. But the cost of the hardware is only some of the storage cost; a larger cost is administering and maintaining the archives. These costs include downtime when storage systems crash and time spent retrieving lost or corrupted messages.[14]

COSTS OF POOR COMMUNICATION LO 1-3

Poor communication can cost billions of dollars. We all can think of examples.

- Hurricane Katrina caused billions of dollars of damage—damage that was worsened by horrendous miscommunications between federal, state, and private relief organizations (see the sidebar "Hurricane Katrina Storms Communication Lines " on this page.).
- The space industry has had billion-dollar mistakes—mistakes where miscommunications were major contributing factors as confirmed by official government investigations (see sidebars on pages 9 and 12).
- Ford and Bridgestone Firestone's failure to coordinate the design of the Ford Explorer and its tires cost them billions of dollars. In hindsight, people agree the mistakes could have been prevented if the different teams involved had communicated more effectively with each other.[15]

- Internal and external communication problems have contributed greatly to delays in Boeing's 787 Dreamliner, delays which have cost Boeing billions in penalties and have caused some customers to switch their orders to Airbus.[16]
- From figures provided by the members of the Business Roundtable, the National Commission on Writing calculated the annual private sector costs of writing training at $3.1 billion.[17] These figures do not include the retail and wholesale trade businesses.
- Even part of the subprime mortgage collapse, which helped spark a global recession, has been connected to poor communication. Documents supposedly explaining some of the riskier investments were so convoluted that even most experts could not understand them. Goldman Sachs paid a $550 million fine to settle allegations that it misled investors in mortgage bonds.[18]

Costs of poor communication are not just financial. People died in the rollovers of Ford Explorers, noted above. In the aftermath of Hurricane Katrina, inaccurate media reports of looting convinced some residents to stay to protect their property instead of evacuating; false reports of shootings at helicopters resulted in some states refusing to send trained emergency workers. According to the presidential commission, inadequate communication among British Petroleum, Halliburton, and Transocean, as well as within their own companies, was a contributing factor in BP's massive oil spill, which caused so much damage, as well as fatalities, in the Gulf of Mexico.[19]

Not all communication costs are so dramatic, however. When communication isn't as good as it could be, you and your organization pay a price in wasted time, wasted effort, lost goodwill, and legal problems.

Wasted Time

Bad writing takes longer to read as we struggle to understand what we're reading. How quickly we can do this is determined by the difficulty of the subject matter and by the document's organization and writing style.

Second, bad writing may need to be rewritten. Poorly written documents frequently cycle to other people for help.

Third, ineffective communication may obscure ideas so that discussions and decisions are needlessly drawn out.

Business Communication Lessons from Mars

The *Mars Climate Orbiter* spacecraft lost contact with NASA mission control just after it arrived at Mars. A subsequent investigation revealed that the main problem was a minor software programming error caused by communication errors.

Like many business projects, the *Mars Climate Orbiter* involved a wide range of people in a range of locations. The programmers who wrote the software that controlled the spacecraft's engines worked in Great Britain, and used metric measurements in their calculations, while the engineers who made the satellite's engines worked in the United States, and used English measurements. Both teams assumed that they were using the same measurement standards, neither team made any attempt to check, and no one else caught the error. With that failure, NASA lost a $125 million satellite and years of effort, while gaining a major public embarrassment.

Adapted from NASA MCO Mission Failure Mishap Investigation Board, *Mars Climate Orbiter Mishap Investigation Board Phase I Report*, November 10, 1999, ftp://ftp.hq.nasa.gov/pub/pao/reports/1999/MCO_report.pdf.

When the *Mars Climate Orbiter* spacecraft crashed as a result of poor communication, the United States lost a $125 million satellite and years of effort.

Poor Customer Service Becomes Costly

A customer called AOL to cancel his service. The phone call lasted 21 minutes, including automated answering, waiting in a queue, and a five-minute conversation with a customer service representative. During the conversation, the customer service representative refused to comply with the customer's request to close his account despite 21 requests to "cancel" his service and approximately 9 "I-don't-need-it, I-don't-want-it, and I-don't-use-it" statements. To express his dissatisfaction, the customer posted the recorded conversation on the Web as a digital "documentary," which was heard by 300,000 visitors and highlighted on the *Today* show on NBC. Following the post, an AOL executive vice president e-mailed employees notifying them of the post and warning them that any of their customer interactions could be similarly posted. In addition, because of similar earlier violations, AOL agreed to pay a fine of $1.25 million and to use a third-party verification system.

Another customer service incident occurred when a customer welcomed a Comcast technician into his home to replace a faulty modem. When the technician called the central office, he was placed on hold and proceeded to fall asleep on the couch after an hour of waiting. In response, the customer recorded a short documentary, "A Comcast Technician Sleeping on My Couch" and posted it to YouTube where 500,000 viewers watched the customer service blunder.

Adapted from Randall Stross, "AOL Said, 'If You Leave Me I'll Do Something Crazy,'" *New York Times*, July 2, 2006, E3.

Fourth, unclear or incomplete messages may require the receiver to gather more information and some receivers may not bother to do so; they may make a wrong decision or refuse to act.

Wasted Efforts

Ineffective messages don't get results. A receiver who has to guess what the sender means may guess wrong. A reader who finds a letter or memo unconvincing or insulting simply won't do what the message asks.

One company sent out past-due bills with the following language:

> Per our conversation, enclosed are two copies of the above-mentioned invoice. Please review and advise. Sincerely, . . .

The company wanted money, not advice, but it didn't say so. The company had to write third and fourth reminders. It waited for its money, lost interest on it—and kept writing letters.

Lost Goodwill

Whatever the literal content of the words, every letter, e-mail, or report serves either to build or to undermine the image the reader has of the writer.

Part of building a good image is taking the time to write correctly. Even organizations that have adopted casual dress still expect writing to appear professional and to be free from typos and grammatical errors.

Messages can also create a poor image because of poor audience analysis and inappropriate style. The form letter printed in Figure 1.3 failed because it was stuffy and selfish. The comments in red show specific problems with the letter.

- **The language is stiff and legalistic.** Note the sexist "Gentlemen:" and obsolete "Please be advised," "herein," and "expedite."
- **The tone is selfish.** The letter is written from the writer's point of view; there are no benefits for the reader. (The writer says there are, but without a shred of evidence, the claim isn't convincing.)
- **The main point is buried** in the middle of the long first paragraph. The middle is the least emphatic part of a paragraph.
- **The request is vague.** How many references does the supplier want? Are only vendor references OK, or would other credit references, like banks, work too? Is the name of the reference enough, or is it necessary also to specify the line of credit, the average balance, the current balance, the years credit has been established, or other information? What "additional financial information" does the supplier want? Annual reports? Bank balance? Tax returns? The request sounds like an invasion of privacy, not a reasonable business practice.
- **Words are misused** (*herein for therein*), suggesting either an ignorant writer or one who doesn't care enough about the subject and the reader to use the right word.

You will learn more about tone in Chapter 3 and language in Chapter 5.

Legal Problems

Poor communication choices can lead to legal problems for individuals and organizations. The news is full of examples. Domino's pizza, which promised to deliver pizza to your door in 30 minutes, dropped that promise after a lawsuit, involving an accident with a Domino's delivery person, claimed that the

Figure 1.3 A Form Letter That Annoyed Customers

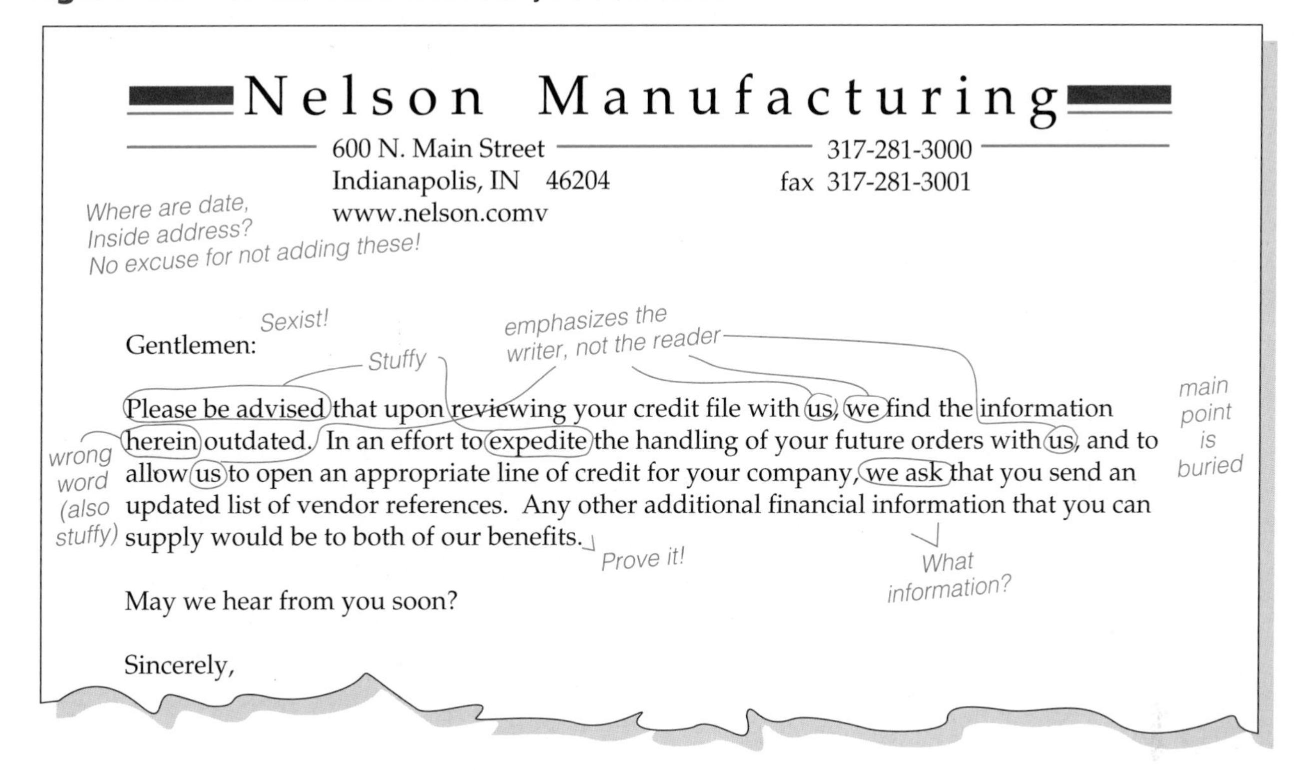
Nelson Manufacturing
600 N. Main Street
Indianapolis, IN 46204
www.nelson.comv
317-281-3000
fax 317-281-3001

Gentlemen:

Please be advised that upon reviewing your credit file with us, we find the information herein outdated. In an effort to expedite the handling of your future orders with us, and to allow us to open an appropriate line of credit for your company, we ask that you send an updated list of vendor references. Any other additional financial information that you can supply would be to both of our benefits.

May we hear from you soon?

Sincerely,

pledge led to accidents. Domino's settled for a sum in the seven-figure range, but dropped the promise because the company feared other lawsuits.[20]

Individual communications can also have legal consequences. Steamy text messages revealed an affair between Detroit mayor Kwame Kilpatrick and one of his aides; both the messages and the affair contradicted testimony the mayor had given under oath. Consequences included loss of office, jail time, and a $1 million fine.

US Representative Mark Foley resigned after his instant messages to House pages were published. E-mails have helped bring about the fall of many executives, including

- Senior Enron executives
- Boeing CEO Harry Stonecipher
- Credit Suisse First Boston banker Frank Quattrone
- Hewlett-Packard Chairperson Patricia Dunn
- Walmart Vice Presidents Julie Roehm and Sean Womack
- South Carolina Governor Mark Sanford

One San Francisco law firm says that 70% of their routine evidence now comes from e-mails.[21]

In particular, letters, memos, e-mails, and instant messages create legal obligations for organizations. When a lawsuit is filed against an organization, the lawyers for the plaintiffs have the right to subpoena documents written by employees of the organization. These documents may then be used as evidence, for instance, that an employer fired an employee without adequate notice or that a company knew about a safety defect but did nothing to correct it.

These documents may also be used as evidence in contexts the writer did not intend. This means that a careless writer can create obligations that the organization does not mean to assume. For instance, a letter from a manager

Columbia Disaster Communication Failures

In 2003, the *Columbia* space shuttle disintegrated on re-entry, resulting in the deaths of all seven crew members. The independent research team investigating the disaster found communication problems to be the root cause of the accident. The researchers concluded that organizational barriers prevented effective communication of critical safety information and restrained communication of professionals.

The report identified the following communication problems:

- Communication flow between managers and subordinates: Managers did not heed the concerns of the engineers regarding debris impacts on the shuttle. Throughout the project, communication did not flow effectively up to or down from program managers.
- Circulation of information among teams: Although engineers were concerned about landing problems and therefore conducted experiments on landing procedures, the concerns were not relayed to managers or to system and technology experts who could have addressed the concerns.
- Communication sources: Managers received a large amount of their information from informal channels, which blocked relevant opinions and conclusions from engineers.

Adapted from Columbia Accident Investigation Board, *Report of Columbia Accident Investigation Board, Volume I*, August 2003, http://www.nasa.gov/columbia/home/CAIB_Vol1.html.

telling a scout troop they may not visit a factory floor because it is too dangerous could be used in a worker's compensation suit.[22]

Careful writers and speakers think about the larger social context in which their words may appear. What might those words mean to other people in the field? What might they mean to a judge and jury?

BENEFITS OF IMPROVING COMMUNICATION

Better communication helps you to

- **Save time.** Eliminate the time now taken to rewrite badly written materials. Reduce reading time, since comprehension is easier. Reduce the time taken asking, "What did you mean?"
- **Make your efforts more effective.** Increase the number of requests that are answered positively and promptly—on the first request. Present your points—to other people in your organization; to clients, customers, and suppliers; to government agencies; to the public—more forcefully.
- **Communicate your points more clearly.** Reduce the misunderstandings that occur when the audience has to supply missing or unclear information. Make the issues clear, so they can be handled.
- **Build goodwill.** Build a positive image of your organization. Build an image of yourself as a knowledgeable, intelligent, capable person.

CRITERIA FOR EFFECTIVE MESSAGES

Good business and administrative communication meets five basic criteria: it's clear, complete, and correct; it saves the audience's time; and it builds goodwill.

- **It's clear.** The meaning the audience gets is the meaning the communicator intended. The audience doesn't have to guess.
- **It's complete.** All of the audience questions are answered. The audience has enough information to evaluate the message and act on it.
- **It's correct.** All of the information in the message is accurate. The message is free from errors in spelling, grammar, word choice, and sentence structure.
- **It saves the audience's time.** The style, organization, and visual or aural impact of the message help the audience read or hear, understand, and act on the information as quickly as possible.
- **It builds goodwill.** The message presents a positive image of the communicator and his or her organization. It treats the receiver as a person, not a number. It cements a good relationship between the communicator and the receiver.

Whether a message meets these five criteria depends on the interactions among the communicator, the audience, the purposes of the message, and the situation. No single set of words will work in all possible situations.

USING TECHNOLOGY FOR COMMUNICATION

In this technological age, different forms of media are encompassing all parts of life. For instance, in 2010, the average American spent 158 hours a month watching television, accounting for approximately half their leisure time.

They also spent 25 hours a month using the Internet, which has become the third most popular news platform, behind only local and national television news. The Internet is now ahead of radio and national and local print newspapers as a news source. However, the greatest use of Internet time is for social networking. Personal e-mail has fallen out of second place to be replaced by gaming.[23]

Technology has even gripped the highest office in the country. President Obama battled with U.S. intelligence agencies to keep his BlackBerry when he took office; he is the first president in the history of our country to use e-mail while in office.

If the highest office in the land demands technology, the business world is no exception. When it comes to technology, business continually embraces all forms that help increase productivity and save money. Almost all office employees are expected to know how to navigate through the web and to use word processing, e-mail, spreadsheet, database, and presentation software. Newer forms of technology, especially social media such as Facebook, Twitter, and texting, are also becoming prominent in business offices. Chapter 9 will discuss communication technologies in more detail.

FOLLOWING CONVENTIONS LO 1-4

Conventions are widely accepted practices you routinely encounter. For example, you wouldn't write an analytical report to your boss who only wanted a "yes" or "no" on whether you could make the scheduled meeting with potential clients. You would send the more appropriate and conventional response—an e-mail.

Similarly, common business communications have conventions. These conventions help people recognize, produce, and interpret different kinds of communications. Each chapter in this textbook presents conventions of traditional business documents. For example, Chapter 13 discusses conventions of job application letters, Chapter 11 highlights conventions of persuasive messages, and Chapter 19 talks about conventions of delivering oral presentations.

Conventions change over time. Consider how the conventions governing movies and television have changed just during your lifetime, allowing more explicit sex and violence. Similarly, conventions change in business. Paper memos have mostly given way to e-mails, and some e-mails are being replaced by text messaging.

The key to using conventions effectively, in spite of their changing nature, is to remember that they always need to fit the rhetorical situation—they always need to be adjusted for the particular audience, context, and purpose. For instance, Chapter 10 provides guidelines on constructing negative messages. However, you will need to adapt these guidelines based on the way your organization presents their negative messages. Some organizations will use a more formal tone than others; some present negative news bluntly, while others ease into it more gently.

Since every organization will be unique in the conventions they follow, the information presented in this text will provide a basic understanding of common elements for particular genres. You will always need to adjust the basics for your particular needs.

The best way to learn conventions in a particular workplace is to see what other workers are doing. How do they communicate with each other? Do their practices change when they communicate with superiors? What kinds of letters and memos do they send? How much do they e-mail? What tone is preferred? Close observation will help your communications fit in with the conventions of your employer.

Wiio's laws

Professor Osmo A. Wiio is a Finnish expert on communication. He has formulated a series of communication laws, expressed humorously but with serious content. These are some of his laws:

1. Communication usually fails, except by accident. (This is the fundamental one among Wiio's laws.)
2. If a message can be interpreted in several ways, it will be interpreted in a manner that maximizes the damage.
3. There is always someone who knows better than you what you meant with your message.
4. The more we communicate, the worse communication succeeds.
5. In mass communication, the important thing is not how things are but how they seem to be.

Can you think of examples supporting Wiio's laws?

Laws are quoted from Osmo A. Wiio, "How All Human Communication Fails, Except by Accident, or a Commentary of Wiio's Laws," last updated July 4, 2010, http://www.cs.tut.fi/~jkorpela/wiio.html.

UNDERSTANDING AND ANALYZING BUSINESS COMMUNICATION SITUATIONS

The best communicators are conscious of the context in which they communicate; they're aware of options.

Ask yourself the following questions:

- **What's at stake—to whom?** Think not only about your own needs but also about the concerns your boss and your audience will have. Your message will be most effective if you think of the entire organizational context—and the larger context of shareholders, customers, and regulators. When the stakes are high, you'll need to take into account people's feelings as well as objective facts.
- **Should you send a message?** Sometimes, especially when you're new on the job, silence is the most tactful response. But be alert for opportunities to learn, to influence, to make your case.
- **What channel should you use?** Paper documents and presentations are formal and give you considerable control over the message. E-mail, texting, tweeting, phone calls, and stopping by someone's office are less formal. Oral channels are better for group decision making, allow misunderstandings to be cleared up more quickly, and seem more personal. Sometimes you may need more than one message, in more than one channel.
- **What should you say?** Content for a message may not be obvious. How detailed should you be? Should you repeat information that the audience already knows? The answers will depend on the kind of message, your purposes, audiences, and the corporate culture. And you'll have to figure these things out for yourself, without detailed instructions.
- **How should you say it?** How you arrange your ideas—what comes first, second, and last—and the words you use shape the audience's response to what you say.

HOW TO SOLVE BUSINESS COMMUNICATION PROBLEMS LO 1-5

When you're faced with a business communication problem, you need to develop a solution that will both solve the organization's problem and meet the psychological needs of the people involved. The strategies in this section will help you solve the problems in this book. Almost all of these strategies can also be applied to problems you encounter on the job. Use this process to create good messages:

- Gather knowledge and brainstorm solutions.
- Answer the five questions for analysis in Figure 1.4.
- Organize your information to fit your audiences, your purposes, and the context.
- Make your document visually inviting.
- Revise your draft to create a friendly, businesslike, positive style.
- Edit your draft for standard spelling, punctuation, and grammar; double-check names and numbers.
- Use the response you get to plan future messages.

Figure 1.4 Questions for Analysis

1. Who is (are) your audience(s)?
2. What are your purposes in communicating?
3. What information must your message include?
4. How can you build support for your position? What reasons or benefits will your audience find convincing?
5. What aspects of the total situation may be relevant?

Just a Deadline; No Directions

School assignments are spelled out, sometimes even in writing. In the workplace, workers are less likely to get details about what a document should include. The transition can be disorienting. One intern reported, "I was less prepared than I thought. . . . I was so used to professors basically telling you what they want from you that I expected to be, if not taught, then told, what exactly it was that they wanted these brochures to accomplish. . . . They have not taken the time to discuss it—they just put things on my desk with only a short note telling me when they needed it done. No directions or comments were included."

Intern's quotation from Chris M. Anson and L. Lee Forsberg, "Moving Beyond the Academic Community," *Written Communication* 7, no. 3 (April 1990): 211.

Gather Knowledge and Brainstorm Solutions.

Problem solving usually starts by gathering knowledge. What are the facts? What can you infer from the information you're given? What additional information might be helpful? Where could you get it? What emotional complexities are involved? This information will usually start to suggest some solutions, and you should brainstorm other solutions. In all but the very simplest problems, there are multiple possible solutions. The first one you think of may not be best. Consciously develop several solutions. Then measure them against your audience and purposes: Which solution is likely to work best?

You will learn more about gathering knowledge in Chapter 15 and more about brainstorming in Chapter 8.

Answer the Five Questions for Analysis.

The five questions in Figure 1.4 help you analyze your audience(s), purpose(s), and the organizational context.

1. **Who is (are) your audience(s)?**

   What audience characteristics are relevant for this particular message? If you are writing or speaking to more than one person, how do the people in your audience differ? How much does your audience know about your topic? How will they respond to your message? What objections might they have?

   Some characteristics of your audience will be irrelevant; focus on ones that matter *for this message.* Whenever you address several people or a group, try to identify the economic, cultural, or situational differences that may affect how various subgroups may respond to what you have to say. For a more complete audience analysis, see the questions in Chapter 2.

2. **What are your purposes in communicating?**

   What must this message do to meet the organization's needs? What must it do to meet your own needs? What do you want your audience to do? To think or feel? List all your purposes, major and minor.

   Even in a simple message, you may have several related purposes: to announce a new policy, to make the audience aware of the policy's provisions and requirements, and to have them feel that the policy is a good one, that the organization cares about its employees, and that you are a competent communicator and manager.

3. **What information must your message include?**

   Make a list of the points that must be included; check your draft to make sure you include them all. To include information without emphasizing it, put it in the middle of a paragraph or document and present it as briefly as possible.

4. **How can you build support for your position? What reasons or benefits will your audience find convincing?**

   Brainstorm to develop reasons for your decision, the logic behind your argument, and possible benefits to the audience if they do as you ask. Reasons and audience benefits do not have to be monetary. Making the

Classroom versus Workplace Contexts

Professors Aviva Freedman and Christine Adam found in a research study that students have to relearn ways to acquire basic knowledge when trying to mesh with their employer's organization once they enter the workforce.

School is structured to help students learn. On the other hand, the workplace is structured to get results, not help the learner/new employee. New college graduate hires frequently don't understand the context of communications. For example, new employees have to figure out which co-workers are trustworthy and can be a guide while not pushing away others.

Moreover, the roles of participants in each situation are different. While school settings have an instructor as the voice of authority, workplace settings are comprised of people with varying degrees of relevant and useful knowledge.

What has been your experience with internships? Have you noticed other ways in which workplace settings differ from classroom expectations?

Adapted from Aviva Freedman and Christine Adam, "Learning to Write Professionally: 'Situated Learning' and the Transition from University to Professional Discourse," *Journal of Business and Technical Communication* 10, no. 4 (October 1996): 395–427.

audience's job easier or more pleasant is a good benefit. In an informative or persuasive message, identify multiple audience benefits. In your message, use those that you can develop most easily and effectively.

Be sure the benefits are adapted to your audience. Many people do not identify closely with their organizations; the fact that the organization benefits from a policy will help the individual only if the saving or profit is passed directly on to the employees. Instead, savings and profits are often eaten up by returns to stockholders, bonuses to executives, and investments in plants and equipment or in research and development.

5. **What aspects of the total situation may be relevant?**

   Should you consider the economy? The time of year? Morale in the organization? Any special circumstances? The organization may be prosperous or going through hard times; it may have just been reorganized or may be stable. All these different situations will affect what you say and how you say it.

   Think about the news, the economy, the weather. Think about the general business and regulatory climate, especially as it affects the organization specified in the problem. Use the real world as much as possible. Think about interest rates, business conditions, and the economy. Is the industry in which the problem is set doing well? Is the government agency in which the problem is set enjoying general support? Think about the time of year. If it's fall when you write, is your business in a seasonal slowdown after a busy summer? Gearing up for the Christmas shopping rush? Or going along at a steady pace unaffected by seasons?

   To answer these questions, draw on your experience, your courses, and your common sense. Read the *Wall Street Journal* or look at a company's website. Sometimes you may even want to phone a local business person to get information.

Organize Your Information to Fit Your Audiences, Your Purposes, and the Situation.

You'll learn different psychological patterns of organization in Chapters 9 through 11. For now, remember these three basic principles:

- Put good news first.
- In general, put the main point or question first. In the subject line or first paragraph, make it clear that you're writing about something that is important to the reader.
- Disregard the above point and approach the subject indirectly when you must persuade a reluctant audience.

Make Your Document Visually Inviting.

A well-designed document is easier to read and builds goodwill. To make a document visually attractive

- Use subject lines to orient the reader quickly.
- Use headings to group related ideas.
- Use lists and indented sections to emphasize subpoints and examples.
- Number points that must be followed in sequence.
- Use short paragraphs—usually eight typed lines or fewer.

If you plan these design elements before you begin composing, you'll save time and the final document will probably be better.

The best medium for a document depends on how it will be used. For example, a document that will be updated frequently may need to be on a website so the reader can easily obtain the most current information. Chapters 6 and 16 will provide more information on the design of documents and visuals.

Succeeding against the Odds

I developed my communication skills as a technique of survival. I was born in poverty and spent two years on the welfare rolls, and I learned early that I had to communicate or die. And so I talked my way out of poverty—I communicated my way to the top. . . .

I read and re-read books on self-improvement, success and communication. The most important lesson I learned from these books is what I call "other focusing." This means, among other things, that if we want to communicate with employees, managers, and even competitors we must ask ourselves not what we want but what they want.

This rule made me a millionaire. For the only way I got to where I am today was by persuading thousands of blacks and whites, some of whom were very prejudiced, that the only way they could get what they wanted was by helping me get what I wanted. All the law and prophecy of communication theory can be found in that formula.

John H. Johnson, owner and publisher of *Ebony* magazine, quoted in Gloria Gordon, "EXCEL Award Winner John H. Johnson Communicates Success," *IABC Communication World* 6, no. 6 (May 1989): 18–19.

Revise Your Draft to Create a Friendly, Businesslike, Positive Style.

In addition to being an organizational member or a consumer, your reader has feelings just as you do. Writing that keeps the reader in mind uses **you-attitude** (see Chapter 3). Read your message as if you were in your reader's shoes. How would you feel if *you* received it?

Good business and administrative writing is both friendly and businesslike. If you're too stiff, you put extra distance between your reader and yourself. If you try to be too chummy, you'll sound unprofessional. When you write to strangers, use simple, everyday words and make your message as personal and friendly as possible. When you write to friends, remember that your message may be read by people you've never even heard of: avoid slang, clichés, and "in" jokes.

Sometimes you must mention limitations, drawbacks, or other negative elements, but don't dwell on them. People will respond better to you and your organization if you seem confident. Expect success, not failure. If you don't believe that what you're writing about is a good idea, why should they?

You emphasize the positive when you

- Put positive information first, give it more space, or set it off visually in an indented list.
- Eliminate negative words whenever possible.
- Focus on what is possible, not what is impossible.

Edit Your Draft for Standard English; Double-Check Names and Numbers.

Business people care about correctness in spelling, grammar, and punctuation. If your grasp of mechanics is fuzzy, if standard English is not your native dialect, or if English is not your native language, you'll need to memorize rules and perhaps find a good book or a tutor to help you. Even software spelling and grammar checkers require the writer to make decisions. If you know how to write correctly but rarely take the time to do so, now is the time to begin to edit and proofread to eliminate careless errors. Correctness in usage, punctuation, and grammar is covered in Appendix B.

Always proofread your document before you send it out. Double-check the reader's name, any numbers, and the first and last paragraphs. Chapter 5 will provide more tips on revising and editing communication.

Use the Response You Get to Plan Future Messages.

Evaluate the **feedback,** or response, you get. The real test of any message is "Did you get what you wanted, when you wanted it?" If the answer is *no,* then the message has failed—even if the grammar is perfect, the words elegant, the approach creative, the document stunningly attractive. If the message fails, you need to find out why.

Analyze your successes, too. You want to know *why* your message worked. There has to be a reason, and if you can find what it is, you'll be more successful more often.

HOW TO USE THIS BOOK

This book has many aids to help you learn the material.

- Chapter outlines, learning objectives, and headings all provide previews of the contents. They can give you hooks on which to hang the information you are reading.
- Examples of written documents provide illustrations of effective and ineffective communications. Comments in red ink highlight problems; those in blue ink note effective practices.
- Terminology is defined in the glossary at the end of the book.
- Sidebars provide workplace examples of ideas discussed in the text. They are categorized for you by the icons that appear beside them. A gold star with any icon signifies a classic example.
  - On-the-job examples have briefcase icons.
  - Ethics and legal examples have gavel icons.
  - Websites have an @ sign.
  - Technology examples have smartphone icons.
  - International examples have globe icons.
  - Fun examples have balloon icons.
- Chapter summaries at the end of each chapter, and review questions at the beginning of each set of chapter exercises, help you review the chapters for retention.

SUMMARY OF KEY POINTS

- Communication helps organizations and the people in them achieve their goals. The ability to write and speak well becomes increasingly important as you rise in an organization.
- People put things in writing to create a record, to convey complex data, to make things convenient for the reader, to save money, and to convey their own messages more effectively.
- Internal documents go to people inside the organization. External documents go to audiences outside: clients, customers, suppliers, stockholders, the government, the media, and the general public.
- The three basic purposes of business and administrative communication are to inform, to request or persuade, and to build goodwill. Most messages have more than one purpose.
- Poor writing wastes time, wastes effort, and jeopardizes goodwill.
- Good business and administrative writing meets five basic criteria: it's clear, complete, and correct; it saves the reader's time; and it builds goodwill.
- To evaluate a specific document, we must know the interactions among the writer, the reader(s), the purposes of the message, and the context. No single set of words will work for all readers in all situations.
- Common business communications have conventions, as do organizations. Business communicators need to know how to adjust conventions to fit a particular audience, context, and purpose.

- To understand business communication situations, ask the following questions:
  - What's at stake—to whom?
  - Should you send a message?
  - What channel should you use?
  - What should you say?
  - How should you say it?
- The following process helps create effective messages:
  - Gather knowledge and brainstorm solutions.
  - Answer the analysis questions in Figure 1.4.
  - Organize your information to fit your audiences, your purposes, and the context.
  - Make your document visually inviting.
  - Revise your draft to create a friendly, businesslike, positive style.
  - Edit your draft for standard English; double-check names and numbers.
  - Use the response you get to plan future messages.

CHAPTER 1 Exercises and Problems

**Go to www.mhhe.com/locker10e for additional Exercises and Problems.*

1.1 Reviewing the Chapter

1. Why do you need to be able to communicate well? (LO 1-1)
2. What are some myths about workplace communication? What is the reality for each myth? (LO 1-1)
3. What are the costs of communication? (LO 1-2)
4. What are the costs of poor communication? (LO 1-3)
5. What role do conventions play in business communication? (LO 1-4)
6. What are the components of a good problem-solving method for business communication opportunities? (LO 1-5)

1.2 Assessing Your Punctuation and Grammar Skills

To help you see where you need to improve in grammar and punctuation, take the Diagnostic Test, B.1, Appendix B.

1.3 Letters for Discussion—Landscape Plants

Your nursery sells plants not only in your store but also by mail order. Today you've received a letter from Pat Sykes, complaining that the plants (in a $572 order) did not arrive in a satisfactory condition. "All of them were dry and wilted. One came out by the roots when I took it out of the box. Please send me a replacement shipment immediately."

The following letters are possible approaches to answering this complaint. How well does each message meet the needs of the reader, the writer, and the organization? Is the message clear, complete, and correct? Does it save the reader's time? Does it build goodwill?

1.

> Dear Sir:
>
> I checked to see what could have caused the defective shipment you received. After ruling out problems in transit, I discovered that your order was packed by a new worker who didn't understand the need to water plants thoroughly before they are

shipped. We have fired the worker, so you can be assured that this will not happen again.

Although it will cost our company several hundred dollars, we will send you a replacement shipment.

Let me know if the new shipment arrives safely. We trust that you will not complain again.

2. Dear Pat:

Sorry we screwed up that order. Sending plants across country is a risky business. Some of them just can't take the strain. (Some days I can't take the strain myself!) We'll send you some more plants sometime next week and we'll credit your account for $372.

3. Dear Mr. Smith:

I'm sorry you aren't happy with your plants, but it isn't our fault. The box clearly says, "Open and water immediately." If you had done that, the plants would have been fine. And anybody who is going to buy plants should know that a little care is needed. If you pull by the leaves, you will pull the roots out. Since you don't know how to handle plants, I'm sending you a copy of our brochure, "How to Care for Your Plants." Please read it carefully so that you will know how to avoid disappointment in the future.

We look forward to your future orders.

4. Dear Ms. Sykes:

Your letter of the 5th has come to the attention of the undersigned.

According to your letter, your invoice #47420 arrived in an unsatisfactory condition. Please be advised that it is our policy to make adjustments as per the Terms and Conditions listed on the reverse side of our Acknowledgment of Order. If you will read that document, you will find the following:

> ". . . if you intend to assert any claim against us on this account, you shall make an exception on your receipt to the carrier and shall, within 30 days after the receipt of any such goods, furnish us detailed written information as to any damage."

Your letter of the 5th does not describe the alleged damage in sufficient detail. Furthermore, the delivery receipt contains no indication of any exception. If you expect to receive an adjustment, you must comply with our terms and see that the necessary documents reach the undersigned by the close of the business day on the 20th of the month.

5. Dear Pat Sykes:

You'll get a replacement shipment of the perennials you ordered next week.

Your plants are watered carefully before shipment and packed in specially designed cardboard containers. But if the weather is unusually warm, or if the truck is delayed, small root balls may dry out. Perhaps this happened with your plants. Plants with small root balls are easier to transplant, so they do better in your yard.

The violas, digitalis, aquilegias, and hostas you ordered are long-blooming perennials that will get even prettier each year. Enjoy your garden!

1.4 Online Messages for Discussion—Responding to Rumors

The Acme Corporation has been planning to acquire Best Products, and Acme employees are worried about how the acquisition will affect them. Ed Zeplin, Acme's human resource manager, has been visiting the Acme chat sites and sees a dramatic rise in the number of messages spreading rumors about layoffs. Most of the rumors are false.

The following messages are possible responses that Ed can post to the chat sides. How well does each message meet the needs of the reader, the writer, and the organization? Is the message clear, complete, and correct? Does it save the reader's time? Does it build goodwill?

1.

It Will Be Great!
Author: L. Ed Zeplin, HR
Date: Tuesday, May 23

I am happy to tell you that the HR news is good. Two months ago, the CEO told me about the merger, and I have been preparing a human resource plan ever since.

I want you to know about this because morale has been bad, and it shouldn't be. You really should wait for the official announcements, and you'll see that the staffing needs will remain strong. My department has been under a lot of pressure, but if you'll be patient, we'll explain everything—the staffing, the compensation.

Our plan should be ready by Monday, and then if you have any questions, just contact your HR rep.

2.

HR Staffing
Author: HR Boss
Date: Tuesday, May 23

The rumors are false. Just ask anyone in HR. There will be no layoffs.

3.

Don't Believe the Rumors
Author: lezeplin@acme.com
Date: Tuesday, May 23

Acme has 475 employees, and Best Products has 132 employees. Our human resource plan for next year calls for 625 employees. If you do the math, you can see that there will be no layoffs. Rather, we will be hiring 18 employees. Of course, as we consolidate operations with Best, there will be some redeployments. However, our plan indicates that we will be able to retain our current staff. All employees are valued at Acme, as our current benefits package testifies.

Our HR plan is based on the best analytic techniques and a business forecast by a top consulting firm. If you're an employee, you should review our business plan, at the Our Goals page on Acme's intranet. Everyone should read Acme's mission statement on our home page, www.acme.com/homepage.html.

4.

Layoff Rumors Do Acme a Disservice
Author: Zeplin in HR
Date: Tuesday, 23 May

If you come here to get your company information, you aren't getting the straight story. The people posting to this discussion board are spreading false rumors, not the truth. If you want to know the truth about Acme, ask the people who have access to the information.

As HR manager, I can assure you we won't be laying off employees after the merger with Best Products. I'm the one who approves the staffing plan, so I should know. If people would ask me, instead of reading the negative, whining lies at this site, they would know the facts, too.

If people really cared about job security, they would be working and exceeding their goals, rather than wasting their time in rumor-mongering on message boards. Hard work: that's the key to success!

5.

The True Story about Lay-Offs
Author: lezeplin@acme.com
Date: Tuesday, 23 May

Whenever there is a merger or acquisition, rumors fly. It's human nature to turn to rumors when a situation seems uncertain. The case of Acme acquiring Best Products is no exception, so I'm not surprised to see rumors about layoffs posted on this message board.

Have no fear! I am working closely with our CEO and with the CEO and human resource manager at Best Products, and we all agree that our current staff is a valuable asset to Acme, to Best, and to our combined companies in the future. We have no plans to lay off any of our valued people. I will continue monitoring this message board and will post messages as I am able to disclose more details about our staffing plans. In the meantime, employees should watch for official information in the company newsletter and on our intranet.

We care about our people! If employees ever have questions about our plans and policies, they should contact me directly.

L. Ed Zeplin, HR Manager

1.5 Discussing Communication Barriers

With a small group, discuss some of the communication barriers you have witnessed in the workplace or classroom. What confuses audiences? What upsets them? What creates ill will? What causes loss of interest? Try to pinpoint exactly how the communication broke down. How closely do the problems you've identified coincide with the content from Chapter 1?

1.6 Identifying Poor Communicators

Almost everyone has come in contact with someone who is a poor communicator. With a small group, discuss some of your experiences with poor communicators either in the workplace or in the classroom. Why was the communicator ineffective? What would have made communication clearer? After your discussion, develop a list of poor communication traits and what can be done to overcome them.

1.7 Discussing Wiio's Laws

Reread the list of Wiio's laws in the sidebar on page 14. With a small group, discuss examples of those laws you have witnessed in

a. The workplace
b. The classroom
c. The news media
d. Social networking sites

1.8 Identifying Changing Conventions

This chapter talks about the need to be aware of conventions and how they shift with time. What are some changing classroom communication conventions you have observed in your classes? What are some changing communication conventions you have observed at your workplace, or those of your family and friends? With a small group, discuss your examples.

1.9 Understanding the Role of Communication in Your Organization

Interview your work supervisor to learn about the kinds and purposes of communication in your organization. Your questions could include the following:

- What kinds of communication (e.g., memos, e-mail, presentations) are most important in this organization?
- What communications do you create? Are they designed to inform, to persuade, to build goodwill—or to do a combination?
- What communications do you receive? Are they designed to inform, to persuade, to build goodwill—or to do a combination?
- Who are your most important audiences within the organization?
- Who are your most important external audiences?
- What are the challenges of communicating in this organization?
- What kinds of documents and presentations does the organization prefer?

As your instructor directs,

a. Share your results with a small group of students.
b. Present your results in a memo to your instructor.
c. Join with a group of students to make a group presentation to the class.
d. Post your results online to the class.

1.10 Introducing Yourself to Your Instructor

Write a memo (at least 1½ pages long) introducing yourself to your instructor. Include the following topics:

Background: Where did you grow up? What have you done in terms of school, extracurricular activities, jobs, and family life?

Interests: What are you interested in? What do you like to do? What do you like to think about and talk about?

Academics: What courses have you liked the best in school? Why? What life skills have you gained? How do you hope to use them? What do you hope to gain from this course?

Achievements: What achievements have given you the greatest personal satisfaction? List at least five. Include things that gave *you* a real sense of accomplishment and pride, whether or not they're the sort of thing you'd list on a résumé.

Goals: What do you hope to accomplish this term? Where would you like to be professionally and personally five years from now?

Use complete memo format with appropriate headings. (See Appendix A for examples of memo format.) Use a conversational writing style; check your draft to polish the style and edit for mechanical and grammatical correctness. A good memo will enable your instructor to see you as an individual. Use specific details to make your memo vivid and interesting. Remember that one of your purposes is to interest your reader!

1.11 Introducing Yourself to Your Collaborative Writing Group

Write a memo (at least 1½ pages long) introducing yourself to the other students in your collaborative writing group. Include the following topics:

Background: What is your major? What special areas of knowledge do you have? What have you done in terms of school, extracurricular activities, jobs, and family life?

Previous experience in groups: What groups have you worked in before? Are you usually a leader, a follower, or a bit of both? Are you interested in a quality product? In maintaining harmony in the group? In working efficiently? What do you like most about working in groups? What do you like least?

Work and composing style: Do you like to talk out ideas while they're in a rough stage or work them out on paper before you discuss them? Would you rather have a complete outline before you start writing or just a general idea? Do you want to have a detailed schedule of everything that has to be done and who will do it, or would you rather "go with the flow"? Do you work best under pressure, or do you want to have assignments ready well before the due date?

Areas of expertise: What can you contribute to the group in terms of knowledge and skills? Are you good at brainstorming ideas? Researching? Designing charts? Writing? Editing? Word processing? Managing the flow of work? Maintaining group cohesion?

Goals for collaborative assignments: What do you hope to accomplish this term? Where does this course fit into your priorities?

Use complete memo format with appropriate headings. (See Appendix A for examples of memo format.) Use a conversational writing style; edit your final draft for mechanical and grammatical correctness. A good memo will enable others in your group to see you as an individual. Use details to make your memo vivid and interesting. Remember that one of your purposes is to make your readers look forward to working with you!

1.12 Describing Your Experiences in and Goals for Writing

Write a memo (at least 1½ pages long) to your instructor describing the experiences you've had writing and what you'd like to learn about writing during this course.

Answer several of the following questions:

- What memories do you have of writing? What made writing fun or frightening in the past?
- What have you been taught about writing? List the topics, rules, and advice you remember.
- What kinds of writing have you done in school? How long have the papers been?
- How has your school writing been evaluated? Did the instructor mark or comment on mechanics and grammar? Style? Organization? Logic? Content? Audience analysis and adaptation? Have you gotten extended comments on your papers? Have instructors in different classes had the same standards, or have you changed aspects of your writing for different classes?
- What voluntary writing have you done—journals, poems, stories, essays? Has this writing been just for you, or has some of it been shared or published?
- Have you ever written on a job or in a student or volunteer organization? Have you ever edited other people's writing? What have these experiences led you to think about real-world writing?
- What do you see as your current strengths and weaknesses in writing skills? What skills do you think you'll need in the future? What kinds of writing do you expect to do after you graduate?

Use complete memo format with appropriate headings. (See Appendix A for examples of memo format.) Use a conversational writing style; edit your final draft for mechanical and grammatical correctness.

CHAPTER 2

Adapting Your Message to Your Audience

Chapter Outline

Identifying Your Audiences

Ways to Analyze Your Audience

- Analyzing Individuals
- Analyzing Members of Groups
- Analyzing the Organizational Culture and the Discourse Community

Choosing Channels to Reach Your Audience

Using Audience Analysis to Adapt Your Message

1. How Will the Audience Initially React to the Message?
2. How Much Information Does the Audience Need?
3. What Obstacles Must You Overcome?
4. What Positive Aspects Can You Emphasize?
5. What Are the Audience's Expectations about the Appropriate Language, Content, and Organization of Messages?
6. How Will the Audience Use the Document?

Audience Analysis Works

Audience Benefits

- Characteristics of Good Audience Benefits
- Ways to Identify and Develop Audience Benefits

Audience Benefits Work

Writing or Speaking to Multiple Audiences with Different Needs

Summary of Key Points

Audiences Change with Time

Every year in late January, the president of the United States gives the State of the Union address to one of the largest and most diverse audiences of any communication. Congress, the news media, foreign leaders and diplomats, students, and members of the American public from all walks of life watch, listen, or read the president's comments each year.

Traditionally, the president uses the State of the Union to recount his successes and to spell out his political goals for the coming year. In 2010, President Barack Obama outlined ambitious plans for health care reform, economic recovery, and an increased focus on education and green energy initiatives. He focused much of his speech on the challenges faced by the people of America and the steps he and his Democratic party were taking to help.

In 2011, however, the president faced a different audience. Even though many of the *people* listening were the same, the *situation* and the *attitudes* had changed. In spite of President Obama's success with his goals during 2010, many Americans were dissatisfied. Riding a wave of discontent with the government, conservative Republicans had gained control of the House of Representatives in the November elections and gained several seats in the Senate. Throughout the election, the tenor of political discourse had become increasingly pointed and divisive.

President Obama responded to his audience with a different kind of State of the Union—one that still outlined ambitious plans, but focused more on bipartisan efforts to achieve them. His tone was more conciliatory and more focused on uniting the parties in Congress under his leadership, but his core messages remained the same: improving health care, rebuilding the economy, strengthening education, and expanding green energy initiatives. His tone and presentation reflected the changed audience he faced—one more divided than the one he addressed in 2010.

"His tone and presentation reflected the changed audience he faced—one more divided than the one he addressed in 2010."

The ability to adjust your message to your audience is one key to effective communication. While President Obama addressed a complex audience of millions, most communications have very small, specific audiences—real people with real situations and real concerns. Learning to adjust to your audience will provide you with an excellent foundation for any kind of communication.

Sources: Barak Obama, "Remarks by the President in State of the Union Address," January 28, 2010, transcript, The White House, Office of the Press Secretary, http://www.whitehouse.gov/the-press-office/remarks-president-state-union-address; Barak Obama, "Remarks by the President in State of the Union Address," January 25, 2011, transcript, The White House, Office of the Press Secretary, http://www.whitehouse.gov/the-press-office/2011/01/25/remarks-president-state-union-address.

Learning Objectives

After studying this chapter, you will know

LO 2-1 Ways to analyze different kinds of audiences.

a. Individuals

b. Groups

c. Organizations

LO 2-2 How to choose channels to reach your audience.

LO 2-3 How to analyze your audience and adapt your message to it.

LO 2-4 How to identify and develop audience benefits.

Knowing who you're talking to is fundamental to the success of any message. You need to identify your audiences, understand their motivations, and know how to reach them.

IDENTIFYING YOUR AUDIENCES

The first step in analyzing your audience is to decide who your audience is. Organizational messages have multiple audiences:

1. A **gatekeeper** has the power to stop your message instead of sending it on to other audiences. The gatekeeper therefore controls whether your message even gets to the primary audience. Sometimes the supervisor who assigns the message is the gatekeeper; sometimes the gatekeeper is higher in the organization. In some cases, gatekeepers may exist outside the organization.
2. The **primary audience** decides whether to accept your recommendations or acts on the basis of your message. You must reach the primary audience to fulfill your purposes in any message.
3. The **secondary audience** may be asked to comment on your message or to implement your ideas after they've been approved. Secondary audiences also include lawyers who may use your message—perhaps years later—as evidence of your organization's culture and practices.
4. An **auxiliary audience** may encounter your message but will not have to interact with it. This audience includes the "read-only" people.
5. A **watchdog audience,** though it does not have the power to stop the message and will not act directly on it, has political, social, or economic power. The watchdog pays close attention to the transaction between you and the primary audience and may base future actions on its evaluation of your message.

As the following examples show, one person can be part of two audiences. Frequently, a supervisor is both the primary audience and the gatekeeper.

Dawn is an assistant account executive in an ad agency. Her boss asks her to write a proposal for a marketing plan for a new product the agency's client is introducing. Her **primary audience** is the executive committee of the client company, who will decide whether to adopt the plan. The **secondary audience** includes the marketing staff of the client company, who will be asked for comments on the plan, as well as the artists, writers, and media buyers who will carry out details of the plan if it is adopted. Her boss, who must approve the plan before it is submitted to the client, is the **gatekeeper.** Her office colleagues who read her plan are her **auxiliary audience.**

Joe works in the information technology department of a large financial institution. He must write a memo explaining a major software change. His boss is the **gatekeeper;** the software users in various departments are the **primary audience.** The **secondary audience** includes the tech people who will be helping the primary audience install and adjust to the new software. The **auxiliary audience** includes department program assistants who forward the memo to appropriate people in each department. A **watchdog audience** is the board of directors.

WAYS TO ANALYZE YOUR AUDIENCE LO 2-1

The most important tools in audience analysis are common sense and empathy. **Empathy** is the ability to put yourself in someone else's shoes, to feel with that person. Use what you know about people and about organizations to predict likely responses.

Analyzing Individuals

When you write or speak to people in your own organization and in other organizations you work closely with, you may be able to analyze your audience as individuals. You may already know them, or can probably get additional information easily. You may learn that one manager may dislike phone calls, so you will know to write your request in an e-mail. Another manager may have a reputation for denying requests made on a Friday, so you will know to get yours in earlier.

A useful schema for analyzing people is the **Myers-Briggs Type Indicator.®** This instrument uses four pairs of dichotomies to identify ways that people differ.[1] One of these dichotomies is well known: Extroversion-Introversion, measuring how individuals prefer to focus their attention and get energy. Extroverted types are energized by interacting with other people. Introverted types get their energy from within.

The other three dichotomies in Myers-Briggs® typology are Sensing-Intuition, Thinking-Feeling, and Judging-Perceiving. The Sensing-Intuition dichotomy measures the way an individual prefers to take in information. Sensing types gather information through their senses, preferring what is real and tangible. Intuitive types prefer to gather information by looking at the big picture, focusing on the relationships and connections between facts.

The Thinking-Feeling dichotomy measures the way an individual makes decisions. Thinking types prefer to use thinking in decision making to consider the logical consequences of a choice or action. Feeling types make decisions based on the impact to people, considering what is important to them and to others involved.

The Judging-Perceiving dichotomy measures how individuals orient themselves to the external world. Judging types like to live in a planned, orderly way, seeking closure. Perceiving types prefer to live in a flexible, spontaneous way, enjoying possibilities.

The descriptors on each of the scales' dichotomies represent a preference, just as we have a preference for using either our right or our left hand to write. If necessary, we can use the opposite style, but we have less practice in it and use it less easily.

You can find your own personality type by taking the Myers-Briggs Type Indicator® instrument at your college's counseling center or student services office. Some businesses administer the Myers-Briggs Type Indicator® instrument to all employees to assist with team building and/or personal growth and development.

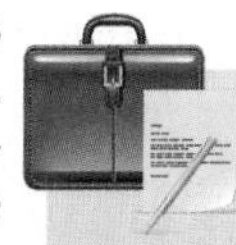

Reading Levels

One of the most relevant demographic measures for writers is the literacy level of your audience. Unfortunately, even in advanced economies you have to ask how well your audience can read and put information to use. In the United States, the answer may be "not very well."

The National Assessment of Adult Literacy (NAAL), conducted by the US Department of Education, found that 14% of adults had difficulty reading well enough to follow simple instructions (such as when to take medication), 12% struggled to use simple forms (deciding where to sign their name on a form), and 22% had trouble working with numbers (simple addition tasks). NAAL also found that 5% of adults were nonliterate—their language skills weren't strong enough to participate in the assessment.

Overall, that translates into 30 million adults in the United States with "below basic" reading and comprehension levels, and another 63 million with only "basic" literacy levels. For business writers, this poses a challenge. When composing a message for a broad audience of employees or customers, you may have to use short sentences, simple words, and clarifying graphics. What other techniques might you use to ensure that audiences with lower literacy levels can understand and use your message?

Adapted from Mark Kutner, Elizabeth Greenberg, and Justin Baer, "National Assessment of Adult Literacy (NAAL): A First Look at the Literacy of America's Adults in the 21st Century," American Institutes for Research, National Center for Education Statistics, U.S. Department of Education, 2006, http://nces.ed.gov/NAAL/PDF/2006470.PDF.

Figure 2.1 Using Personalities in Communication

If your audience is	Use this strategy	Because
Extraverting	Try out ideas orally.	Extraverts like to develop ideas by talking; they are energized by people.
Introverting	Communicate in writing so the audience can think about your message before responding.	Introverts like to think before they communicate. Written messages give them their thinking time.
Sensing	Present all of the needed facts, and get them right. Present your reasoning step by step. Stress practicalities.	Sensing people are good at facts, and expect others to be, also. They trust their own experience more than someone else's account.
Intuiting	Focus on the big picture and underlying patterns first. Save details for later. Use metaphors and analogies in explanations. Stress innovation.	Intuitive people like new possibilities and innovation; they enjoy problem solving and creative endeavors. They can be impatient with details, routine, and repetition.
Thinking	Use logic and principles of consistency and fairness rather than emotion or personal circumstances.	Thinking people make decisions based on logic and abstract principles. They are often uncomfortable with emotion or personal revelations.
Feeling	Stress positives. Show how your ideas value the people needs of the organization. Use tactful language.	Feeling people care about other people and their feelings. They are empathetic and desire harmony.
Judging	Make your communications very organized. Provide all needed information. Follow company procedures. Schedule work in advance; provide time frames for various tasks.	Judging people are eager to make decisions, so they may not seek out additional information. They prefer a structured, orderly work life.
Perceiving	Provide alternatives. Ask for action or a decision by a specific date.	Perceiving people like to gather lots of information before making decisions, and they like to keep all options open as long as possible.

Source: People Types and Tiger Stripes, 4e 2009 Gordon Lawrence. Used with permission. CAPT, Inc.

As Figure 2.1 suggests, you'll be most persuasive if you play to your audience's strengths. Indeed, many of the general principles of business communication appeal to the types most common among managers. Putting the main point up front satisfies the needs of judging types, and some 75% of US managers are judging. Giving logical reasons satisfies the needs of the nearly 80% of U.S. managers who are thinking types.[2]

Analyzing Members of Groups

In many organizational situations, you'll analyze your audience not as individuals but as members of a group: "taxpayers who must be notified that they owe more income tax," "customers who use our accounting services," or "employees with small children." Focus on what group members have in common. Although generalizations won't be true for all members of the group, generalization is necessary when you must appeal to a large group of people with one message. In some cases, no research is necessary: It's easy to guess the attitudes of people who must be told they owe more taxes. In other cases, databases may yield useful information. In still other cases, you may want to do original research.

Databases enable you to map demographic and psychographic profiles of customers or employees. **Demographic characteristics** are measurable features that can be counted objectively: age, sex, race, religion, education level, income, and so on.

Sometimes demographic information is irrelevant; sometimes it's important. Does education matter? Well, the fact that the reader has a degree from

Group membership sometimes gives clues about your audience.

One Huge Audience

Baby boomers number 76 million and account for about half of total U.S. consumer spending. They are expected to spend an additional $50 billion over the next decade. So businesses are subtly beginning to accommodate the needs of this major audience.

Subtle is a key word: boomers do not like to be reminded that they are aging. For instance, many boomers dislike having people talk slowly to them, so ADT Security Services trains new operators to talk quickly and get to the point. CVS stores have installed carpeting to reduce slipping. Arm & Hammer sharpened the color contrast on its cat litter packaging and increased font size 20%.

Euphemisms abound. ADT's medical-alert systems are now "companion services"; bathroom-fixture manufacturer Kohler has "belay" bars instead of grab bars for showers; and Kimberly-Clark's Depends are sometimes labeled as underwear. Small packages of Depends look like underwear and hang on hooks rather than being stacked on shelves like diapers.

Adapted from Ellen Byron, "How to Market to an Aging Boomer: Flattery, Suberfuge, and Euphemism," *Wall Street Journal*, February 5, 2011, A1.

Eastern State rather than from Harvard may not matter, but how much the reader knows about accounting may. Does family structure matter? Sometimes. Some hotels and resorts offer family packages that include baby-sitting, multiple bedrooms, and children's activities.

Age certainly matters. Mutual funds are aiming for young investors by lowering the minimum investment to less than the cost of an iPod, and simplifying choices.[3]

One aspect of age that gets much press is the differences between generations in the office. Many older people believe younger workers have a sense of entitlement, that they expect great opportunities and perks without working for them. On the other hand, many younger workers see their older colleagues as rigid and hostile. Figure 2.2 shows some of the frequently mentioned age differences. While awareness of generational differences may help in some communication situations, such lists are also a good place to attach mental warnings against stereotypes. Plenty of baby boomers also like frequent positive feedback, and almost everyone likes a chance to make a difference.

For most companies, income is a major demographic characteristic. In 2011, Walmart quietly returned to its "everyday low prices" after experimenting with low-priced sale products balanced by slightly higher prices elsewhere. The new pricing had not appealed to Walmart's financially strapped customers. The chain also returned shotguns and rifles to the shelves of many of its stores in an attempt to attract more male customers.[4]

Location is yet another major demographic characteristic. You can probably think of many differences between regional audiences, or urban/rural audiences, in the United States. See Chapter 7 for more information on cross-cultural audiences.

Psychographic characteristics are qualitative rather than quantitative: values, beliefs, goals, and lifestyles. Knowing what your audience finds important allows you to choose information and benefits that the audience will find persuasive. The Choice and Gaylord hotel groups use semantic analysis software on their customer satisfaction surveys. Results can be connected to specific hotels, departments, shifts, employees, and rooms, allowing managers to track trends and respond to problems. Digital marketing companies are combining consumers' web surfing records with personal off-line data from sources such as the Census Bureau, consumer research firms such as Nielsen,

Chinese Internet Companies

Chinese Internet companies are besting their American counterparts for Chinese users, and part of the reason is that they analyze their audience and give them what they want.

- Baidu's Internet search dominates Google's. One reason is that early on, Baidu's search bar was longer and wider than Google's, an important difference because Chinese characters are more complex than English letters, and the larger bar makes them clearer.
- Tencent Holdings popularized instant messaging in China by pairing it with blogging and online gaming, both highly popular in China. Now it has a bigger market value than Yahoo.
- Alibaba e-commerce site Taobao added instant messaging to allow buyers and sellers to haggle over prices, just as business is done off-line in China. eBay couldn't compete and closed its website in China.

Adapted from Loretta Chao, "Something Borrowed . . . ," *Wall Street Journal*, November 16, 2009, R4.

Figure 2.2 Some Generational Differences in the Office

	Baby Boomers	Generation X and Millenials
Birth Dates	Between 1946 and 1964	1964 and on
Work ethic	Long hours in office	Productivity counts, not hours at office
Values	Hard work; consistency; hierarchy; clearly defined roles; serious about work	Work–life balance; flexibility; autonomy, informality; variety of challenges; the workplace can be fun
Preferred channels	Face-to-face, e-mail	Texting, social networks
Motivators	Duty to company	Why a task is important; what's in it for them
Communication style	Through channels and hierarchy; accept annual evaluation	Freely offer opinions, both laterally and upward; want great amounts of attention and praise; want faster feedback
Decorum	Follow basic business decorum	May need to be reminded about basic business decorum

Sources: Ron Alsop, "The 'Trophy Kids' Go to Work," *Wall Street Journal*, October 21, 2008, D1, D4; and Piper Fogg, "When Generations Collide," *Chronicle of Higher Education*, July 18, 2008, B18.

credit card and shopping histories, and real estate and motor vehicle records. The combined data allow marketers to reach narrowly defined audiences, especially convenient for cable TV ads.[5]

Analyzing the Organizational Culture and the Discourse Community

Be sensitive to the culture in which your audiences work and the discourse community of which they are a part. **Organizational culture** is a set of values, attitudes, and philosophies. An organization's culture is revealed verbally in the organization's myths, stories, and heroes, as well as in documents such as employee manuals. It is revealed nonverbally through means such as dress codes, behavior standards, or the allocation of space, money, and power. A **discourse community** is a group of people who share assumptions about what channels, formats, and styles to use for communication, what topics to discuss and how to discuss them, and what constitutes evidence.

In an organization that values equality and individualism, you can write directly to the CEO and address him or her as a colleague. In other companies, you'd be expected to follow a chain of command. Some organizations prize short messages; some expect long, thorough documents. Messages that are consistent with the organization's culture have a greater chance of succeeding.

You can begin to analyze an organization's culture by asking the following questions:

- Is the organization tall or flat? Are there lots of levels between the CEO and the lowest worker, or only a few?
- How do people get ahead? Are the organization's rewards based on seniority, education, being well-liked, saving money, or serving customers? Are rewards available only to a few top people, or is everyone expected to succeed?

Some companies are beginning to accept visible body art and long hair in traditional workplace cultures.

- Does the organization value diversity or homogeneity? Does it value independence and creativity or being a team player and following orders?
- What stories do people tell? Who are the organization's heroes and villains?
- How important are friendship and sociability? To what extent do workers agree on goals, and how intently do they pursue them?
- How formal are behavior, language, and dress?
- What does the work space look like? Do employees work in offices, cubicles, or large rooms?
- What are the organization's goals? Making money? Serving customers and clients? Advancing knowledge? Contributing to the community?

To analyze an organization's discourse community, ask the following questions:

- What media, formats, and styles are preferred for communication?
- What do people talk about? What topics are not discussed?
- What kind of and how much evidence is needed to be convincing?

Write Your Way into Your New Job

You can learn a bit about your organization's discourse community by listening to people and reading the documents that other people write. But the best way to learn is to write. The feedback you get from your supervisor will show you how to adapt your writing for the particular organization. To make the feedback most useful, categorize the comments and generalize. Are you being asked to provide specific supporting details? To write so that people can understand what you say without having to reread? To use a more or less formal style? To include lots of charts or none at all?

Learning to adapt your content, structure, and style to the organization will make you a more effective writer and a more effective worker. And that means that more often you'll be able to get what you want in the organization.

CHOOSING CHANNELS TO REACH YOUR AUDIENCE LO 2-2

A communication **channel** is the means by which you convey your message. Communication channels vary in speed, accuracy of transmission, cost, number of messages carried, number of people reached, efficiency, and ability to

A Channel Pro

Virgin Atlantic Airlines (VAA) uses multiple channels to support its branding as a fun, innovative, honest, caring, and value-offering airline.

- The most-read portion of its Facebook page contains travel tips from crew members, communication that comes across as honest and caring.
- Its website contains a "rapid response" link to Twitter and Facebook for up-to-date communications during crises.
- Its Vtravelled site allows customers to exchange travel information and advice.
- Its Facebook Flight Status app was a first for any airline, as was its iPhone app, Flight Tracker, which includes real-time aircraft positions.
- In response to suggestions from its online community, it launched an airport taxi-sharing service.

VAA's head of e-business says, "Twitter is no more than a sound bite. Facebook can be an article. The website is for in-depth detail. They all need to signpost each other."

Adapted from Patrick Barwise and Sean Meehan, "The One Thing You Must Get Right When Building a Brand," *Harvard Business Review* 88, no. 12 (December 2010): 83–84.

promote goodwill. Depending on the audience, your purposes, and the situation, one channel may be better than another.

A written message makes it easier to

- Present extensive or complex data.
- Present many specific details.
- Minimize undesirable emotions.
- Track details and agreements.

Oral messages make it easier to

- Use emotion to help persuade the audience.
- Focus the audience's attention on specific points.
- Resolve conflicts and build consensus.
- Modify plans.
- Get immediate action or response.

Choosing the right channel can be tricky sometimes. Even in the office, you will have to decide if your message will be more effective as an e-mail, text message, phone call, visit, or sticky note posted on a colleague's computer. In nonstandard situations, choosing a channel can be challenging. If you are the head of a small, nonprofit literacy agency which helps adults learn to read, how do you reach your clients? You cannot afford TV ads, and they cannot read print channels such as flyers. If you are a safety officer for a manufacturer, how do you send out product recall notifications? How many people file the

M&M candies offer a sweet communication channel to organizations.

contact-information cards when they purchase an item? If you are the benefits manager in a large manufacturing plant, how will you get information about your new benefits plan out to the thousand people on the floor? They don't use computers at work and may not have computer access at home.

Businesses are becoming ever more savvy about using the array of channels. Ad money has been moving out of print and TV channels and into online advertising, which totaled $25 billion in 2010. Of those billions, $2 billion were spent on social media sites, Facebook in particular.[6]

Businesses use Twitter, YouTube, and Flickr to highlight new products and services. Many companies have interactive websites and forums where customers can get product information and chat about products; Amazon is the prime example. Diaper companies are giving perks to "mommy" bloggers to talk about their products; car companies are using strong social media influencers to post their opinions online.[7] Nonprofits advertise events, connect with volunteers, and schedule volunteer service on their Facebook pages. And all that social network chatter can now be mined by software which performs semantic analyses providing feedback to advertisers about both products and audiences.

Even traditional paper channels are moving online. Publishers are making their travel books into e-books and cell phone apps. Newspapers are expanding from print to blogs, podcasts, and chatrooms. In fact, Warren Buffet himself warned the *Washington Post*, on whose board he served, that the paper-only model would no longer work.[8] In 2010, 41% of Americans got their national and international news from the Internet, surpassing newspapers (40%) for the first time, and online advertising surpassed print newspaper advertising for the first time.[9]

The big three TV network newscasts are facing similar problems. According to the Pew Research Center, network evening news audiences have been on a downward trend for three decades. Staffers have been cut, as have bureaus and offices. Audience median age is now over 50.[10] In response to declining viewership, networks are posting news in online stories and videos, as well as blogs.

Trolling for Plaintiffs

Law firms are spending millions to develop their online presence—and to get new clients. And this online spending is replacing more traditional spending for yellow pages, TV, and radio ads.

Many of these online sites look like community forums or news boards. They are publicized on forums such as Facebook and Twitter. Many firms, knowing that people generally trust material they find in electronic searches far more than they trust ads, are also adding content so that their sites appear early in a Google search.

The marketing officer for one such law firm told the *Wall Street Journal* that people reaching the firm through social media were twice as likely to become clients as those who made contact through television or print.

Adapted from Nathan Koppel, "Using Social Networking as Legal Tool: Law Firms Say They Are Turning to the Web to Develop Evidence for Suits and Market Themselves to Potential Clients," *Wall Street Journal*, June 15, 2010, B4.

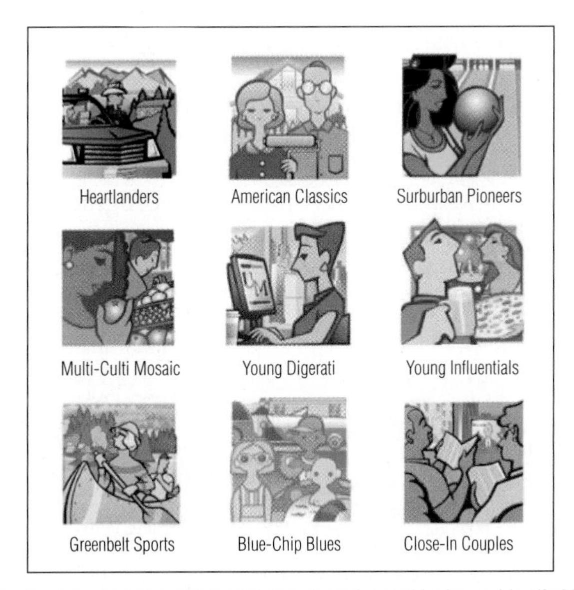

Market research firm Claritas, Inc., combines demographic and psychographic data to identify 66 lifestyle segments, including "Young Digerati" (tech-savvy young adults), "Close-In Couples" (older, African-American couples), and "Blue-Chip Blues" (young families with well-paying blue-collar jobs). PRIZM is a trademark or registered trademark of The Nielsen Company (US), LLC.

Is It the Black Abyss for the White Pages?

White pages may become a relic as more and more telecommunication companies cease to print paper copies.

As land lines steadily decrease, more and more people rely solely on their cell phones, whose numbers usually are not in the white pages. Furthermore, those cell phones store frequently used numbers. For numbers not in their cell phones, most consumers now check the Internet.

Telecommunication companies tout the change as an environmentally friendly one. Verizon notes a savings of 17,000 tons of paper annually by switching to Internet listings in its 12-state area of operation.

Adapted from Michael Felberbaum, "It's Looking Dark for White Pages of Phone Books," *Des Moines Register*, November 12, 2010, 1A.

Creative uses of channels are appearing everywhere (for more on electronic channels, see Chapters 4 and 9):

- Intel is using electronic billboards in New York's Penn Station to promote its Smart TV technology. People with the appropriate mobile app will be personally greeted by the signs.[11]
- Popular bands such as Phish have developed their own apps, with features such as remixing tools and games, for their fans.[12]
- Toy maker Mattel is using Facebook, Twitter, and a series of eight webisodes to celebrate the 50th birthday of Barbie's boyfriend Ken. The webisodes allow Mattel to extend the audience to teenagers and adults who have an emotional tie with the toy and may be collectors.[13]
- Dunkin' Donuts quickie contest for people to submit pictures of themselves drinking iced coffee in the winter generated 140 submissions and 3.9 million product plugs through posts and status updates.[14]
- Digital book store Wowio is selling ads on e-books readers download from its site.[15]
- Bill Cosby recorded a hip-hop album to help carry his message of education and self-respect to new audiences. To sell its cleaning products, Clorox put out an album, "The Blue Sky Project: A Clorox Charity Collection." Companies such as Procter & Gamble and Allstate also offer full-length versions of tunes used in their ads. In regions such as the United Kingdom and Asia, original songs featured in ads often become quite popular.[16]
- Vienna, Austria, raised money for the main public library with a phone sex hotline. Pay by the minute and you got to hear a famous Austrian actress reading passages from the library's collection of erotic fiction from the 18th through 20th centuries.[17]

Creative channels abound. Ads are appearing on hotel shower curtains, the bellies of pregnant women, airport luggage conveyor belts, grocery checkout conveyors, sidewalks, and toilet stall doors. Ads inside subway tunnels appear to be in motion as trains ride by. One company prints ads on cardboard shirt hangers which are distributed free to cleaners. The hangers are touted as a good way to reach male consumers.[18]

As consumers become ever more savvy about ways to ignore advertising, one channel that has received publicity is the vivistitial: ads that take advantage of more receptive times in consumers' lives. One much talked about example is the elevator ad. Captivate offers video programming, such as news headlines and weather, in elevators. The programming is not intrusive: screens are not huge and the video does not have sound. Recall of Captivate ads is two to four times higher than that of TV ads.[19]

USING AUDIENCE ANALYSIS TO ADAPT YOUR MESSAGE LO 2-3

Zeroing in on the right audience with the right message is frequently a formula for success. If you know your audience well and if you use words well, much of your audience analysis and adaptation will be unconscious. If you don't know your audience or if the message is very important, take the time to analyze your audience formally and to revise your message with your analysis in mind. The questions in Figure 2.3 will help guide a careful analysis.

Figure 2.3 Analyzing Your Audience

These questions will help you analyze your audience:

1. How will the audience initially react to the message?
2. How much information does the audience need?
3. What obstacles must you overcome?
4. What positive aspects can you emphasize?
5. What are the audience's expectations about the appropriate language, content, and organization of messages?
6. How will the audience use the document?

A Zappos Channel

[According to Tony Hsieh, founder and CEO of Zappos, the popular Internet footwear business], "There's a lot of buzz these days about 'social media' and 'integration marketing.' As unsexy and low-tech as it may sound, our belief is that the telephone is one of the best branding devices out there. You have the customer's undivided attention for five to ten minutes, and if you get the interaction right, what we've found is that the customer remembers the experience for a very long time and tells his or her friends about it.

. . .

"At Zappos, we don't measure call times (our longest phone call was almost six hours long!). . . . We don't have scripts because we trust our employees to use their best judgment when dealing with each and every customer. . . . We're trying to build a lifelong relationship with each customer one phone call at a time."

Quoted from Tony Hsieh, *Delivering Happiness: A Path to Profits, Passion, and Purpose* (New York: Business Plus, 2010), 143–45. With permission from Central Grand Publishing.

As you answer these questions for a specific audience, think about the organizational culture in which the person works. At every point, your audience's reaction is affected not only by his or her personal feelings and preferences but also by the political environment of the organization, the economy, and current events.

1. How Will the Audience Initially React to the Message?

a. Will the audience see this message as important? Audiences will read and act on messages they see as important to their own careers; they may ignore messages that seem unimportant to them.

When the audience may see your message as unimportant, you need to

- Use a subject line or first paragraph that shows your reader this message is important and relevant.
- Make the action as easy as possible.
- Suggest a realistic deadline for action.
- Keep the message as short as possible.

Customer Analysis

According to Harvey Mackay, author of the business bestseller *Swim with the Sharks without Being Eaten Alive,* the Golden Rule of sales is Know Your Customer. Your customers are not companies, but rather the individuals at companies who decide whether or not to buy your goods or services. To analyze these buyers, he has developed a 66-question customer profile, the Mackay 66.

The profile includes questions about such topics as the individual's education, spouse, children, politics, religion, activities, hobbies, vacations, cars, personality, personal goals, and business goals. In addition to typical questions you might expect, such as employment record, the profile also asks about

- Status symbols in office.
- Sensitive items to be avoided.
- Subjects arousing strong feelings.
- Favorite conversation topics.

Mackay uses the information in these profiles to meet the needs of his customers. (He says he also guards it with his life, because he knows how sensitive it is.)

Adapted from Harvey Mackay, "Knowing Your Customer Is Key," *Des Moines Register,* November 29, 2010, 6E.

b. How will the fact that the message is from you affect the audience's reaction? The audience's experience with you and your organization shapes the way they respond to this new message. Someone who thinks well of you and your organization will be prepared to receive your message favorably; someone who thinks poorly of you and the organization will be quick to find fault with what you say and the way you say it.

When your audience has negative feelings about your organization, your position, or you personally, you need to

- Make a special effort to avoid phrases that could seem condescending, arrogant, rude, hostile, or uncaring.
- Use positive emphasis (Chapter 3) to counteract the natural tendency to sound defensive.
- Develop logic and benefits fully.

2. How Much Information Does the Audience Need?

a. How much does the audience already know about this subject? It's easy to overestimate the knowledge an audience has. People outside your own immediate unit may not really know what it is you do. Even people who once worked in your unit may have forgotten specific details now that their daily work is in management. People outside your organization won't know how *your* organization does things.

When some of your information is new to the audience, you need to

- Make a special effort to be clear. Define terms, explain concepts, use examples, avoid acronyms.
- Link new information to old information that the audience already knows.
- Use paragraphs and headings to break up new information into related chunks so that the information is easier to digest.
- Test a draft of your document with your reader or a subset of your intended audience to see whether the audience can understand and use what you've written.

b. Does the audience's knowledge need to be updated or corrected? Our personal experience guides our expectations and actions, but sometimes needs to be corrected. If you're trying to change someone's understanding of something, you need to

- Acknowledge the audience's initial understanding early in the message.
- Use examples, statistics, or other evidence to show the need for the change, or to show that the audience's experience is not universal.
- Allow the audience to save face by suggesting that changed circumstances call for new attitudes or action.

c. What aspects of the subject does the audience need to be aware of to appreciate your points? When the audience must think of background or old information to appreciate your points, you can

- Preface information with "As you know" or "As you may remember" to avoid suggesting that you think the audience does not know what you're saying.
- Put old or obvious information in a subordinate clause.

3. What Obstacles Must You Overcome?

a. Is your audience opposed to what you have to say? People who have already made up their minds are highly resistant to change. When the audience will oppose what you have to say, you need to

- Start your message with any areas of agreement or common ground that you share with your audience.
- Make a special effort to be clear and unambiguous. Points that might be clear to a neutral audience can be misinterpreted by someone opposed to the message.
- Make a special effort to avoid statements that will anger the audience.
- Limit your statement or request to the smallest possible area. If parts of your message could be delivered later, postpone them.
- Show that your solution is the best solution currently available, even though it isn't perfect.

b. Will it be easy for the audience to do as you ask? Everyone has a set of ideas and habits and a mental self-image. If we're asked to do something that violates any of those, we first have to be persuaded to change our attitudes or habits or self-image—a change we're reluctant to make.

When your request is time-consuming, complicated, or physically or psychologically difficult, you need to

- Make the action as easy as possible.
- Break down complex actions into a list, so the audience can check off each step as it is completed. This list will also help ensure complete responses.
- Show that what you ask is consistent with some aspect of what the audience believes.
- Show how the audience (not just you or your organization) will benefit when the action is completed.

4. What Positive Aspects Can You Emphasize?

a. From the audience's point of view, what are the benefits of your message? Benefits help persuade the audience that your ideas are good ones. Make the most of the good points inherent in the message you want to convey.

- Put good news first.
- Use audience benefits that go beyond the basic good news.

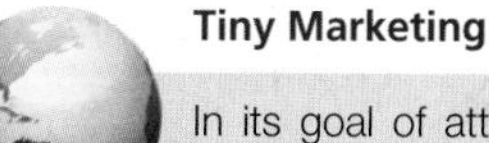

Tiny Marketing

In its goal of attracting 1 billion additional consumers, Procter & Gamble is adding new marketing techniques to its arsenal. Since most of these potential customers are poor women in developing countries who buy single-use packets of products such as shampoo, soap, and detergent, P&G is packaging its products in small portions. The small packages also please the tiny mom-and-pop stores, many just kiosks or closet-sized stores, which serve these customers. These stores aggregated are P&G's largest customer, larger even than Wal-Mart. To attract owners, P&G employs local agents who tidy and price P&G in-store products, distribute promotional items, and stock shelves—sparing owners trips to distributors.

P&G is also developing special products just for these markets. One example is feminine hygiene products. Because many customers lack the money and privacy to change pads frequently, P&G developed a low-priced, extra-absorbent pad, which is now the leading product in Mexico.

What unique marketing practices have you noticed in other countries?

Adapted from Ellen Byron, "P&G's Global Target: Shelves of Tiny Stores: It Woos Poor Women Buying Single Portions; Mexico's 'Hot Zones,'" *Wall Street Journal*, July 16, 2007, A1.

Customer Service Channels

"If you think the privacy of your medical information has been compromised, you can file a complaint with the Office for Civil Rights. A brochure distributed by this office tells people they can call and 'ask for a civil-rights or privacy-complaint form.'

"But you can't really ask for anything, because when you call the number, you can't get a person on the line.

"An automated voice thanks you for calling and then breaks the news:

"'We're sorry, a staff person is not able to receive your call. This number is not able to receive messages.'

"Callers are directed to a website to file a complaint. Twice. And if you don't have a computer, . . . [t]he voice tells you . . . 'most local libraries have computers available that residents can use to access the Internet at no extra cost.'"*

Is this an ethical way to distribute information? What groups of people does this channel discriminate against? Do you know of other organizations that communicate only through the web?

*Quoted from "Not Exactly a Model for Customer Service," *Des Moines Register,* August 23, 2008, 14A.

b. What experiences, interests, goals, and values do you share with the audience? A sense of solidarity with someone can be an even more powerful reason to agree than the content of the message itself. When everyone in your audience shares the same experiences, interests, goals, and values, you can

- Consider using a vivid anecdote to remind the audience of what you share. The details of the anecdote should be interesting or new; otherwise, you may seem to be lecturing the audience.
- Use a salutation and close that remind the audience of their membership in this formal or informal group.

5. What Are the Audience's Expectations about the Appropriate Language, Content, and Organization of Messages?

a. What style of writing does the audience prefer? Good writers adapt their style to suit the reader's preferences. A reader who sees contractions as too informal needs a different style from one who sees traditional business writing as too stuffy. As you write,

- Use what you know about your reader to choose a more or less formal, more or less friendly style.
- Use the reader's first name in the salutation only if both of you are comfortable with a first-name basis.

b. Are there hot buttons or "red flag" words that may create an immediate negative response? You don't have time to convince the audience that a term is broader or more neutral than his or her understanding. When you need agreement or approval, you should

- Avoid terms that carry emotional charges for many people: for example, *criminal, un-American, feminist, fundamentalist, liberal.*
- Use your previous experience with individuals to replace any terms that have particular negative meanings for them.

c. How much detail does the audience want? A message that does not give the audience the amount of or kind of detail they want may fail. Sometimes you can ask your audience how much detail they want. When you write to people you do not know well, you can

- Provide all the detail they need to understand and act on your message.
- Group chunks of information under headings so that readers can go directly to the parts of the message they find most interesting and relevant.
- Be sure that a shorter-than-usual document covers the essential points; be sure that a longer-than-usual document is free from wordiness and repetition.

d. Does the audience prefer a direct or indirect organization? Individual personality or cultural background may lead someone to prefer a particular kind of structure. You'll be more effective if you use the structure and organization your audience prefers.

6. How Will the Audience Use the Document?

a. Under what physical conditions will the audience use the document? Reading a document in a quiet office calls for no special care. But suppose the audience will be reading your message on the train commuting home, or on a ladder as he or she attempts to follow instructions. Then the physical preparation of the document can make it easier or harder to use.

When the reader will use your document outside an office,

- Use lots of white space.
- Make the document small enough to hold in one hand.
- Number items so the reader can find his or her place after an interruption.

b. Will the audience use the document as a general reference? As a specific guide? Understanding how your audience will use the document will enable you to choose the best pattern of organization and the best level of detail.

If the document will serve as a general reference,

- Use a specific subject line to aid in filing and retrieval. If the document is online, consider using several keywords to make it easy to find the document in a database search program.
- Use headings within the document so that readers can skim it.
- Give the office as well as the person to contact so that the reader can get in touch with the appropriate person some time from now.
- Spell out details that may be obvious now but might be forgotten in a year.

If the document will be a detailed guide or contain instructions,

- Check to be sure that all the steps are in chronological order.
- Number steps so that readers can easily see which steps they've completed.
- Group steps into five to seven categories if there are many individual steps.
- Put any warnings at the beginning of the document; then repeat them just before the specific step to which they apply.

Audience Is Not a Mystery for Her

Every year, mystery writer Mary Higgins Clark sells 3.7 million copies of her books; in fact, she has sold over 100 million copies in the United States alone.

Perhaps the biggest factor in her success is her careful audience analysis; she gives her audience what they want. In her case, this means intelligent women in danger who unravel sinister plots and often help engineer their own escapes. Her heroines tend to be self-made professionals.

Because her novels are always "G-rated" (no cursing, no living together before marriage, no explicit depictions of violence), they are a favorite of mother–daughter book clubs and sell heavily for Mother's Day, the third biggest book-selling holiday of the year (Father's Day and Christmas are bigger).

Adapted from Alexandra Alter, "The Case of the Best-Selling Author: How a Former Pan-Am Stewardess Has Stayed at the Top of the Publishing Game Since 1975," *Wall Street Journal*, March 25, 2011, D1.

AUDIENCE ANALYSIS WORKS

Audience analysis is a powerful tool. Amazon.com tracks users' online histories to make suggestions on items they might like. Nintendo believes that much of its success is extending its concept of audience. An important part of its audience is hard-core gamers, a very vocal group—they love to blog. But if Nintendo listened just to them, they would be the only audience Nintendo had. Instead, Nintendo extended its audience by creating the Wii, a new system that the hard-core gamers had not imagined and one that is collecting new users who never imagined owning a system at all.[20] With the introduction of Wii Fit, Nintendo is expanding its audience to more women and even senior citizens.

Best Buy uses its extensive customer feedback to tweak its private-label electronics. The company noticed, for instance, that many portable DVD players

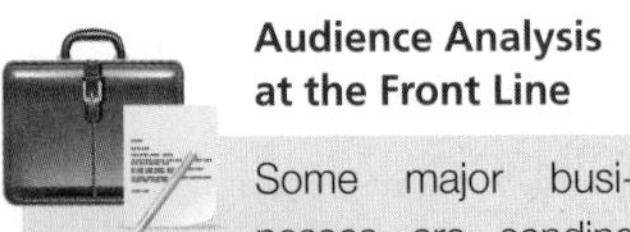

Audience Analysis at the Front Line

Some major businesses are sending their executives out to the front lines for a day or more to increase awareness of both clients' and employees' needs. Such stints are bringing changes to the front lines. A Loews executive who served as a bellhop, pool attendant, and housekeeper at a Florida hotel sweated so much in his polyester uniform that he had both the style and material of the uniforms altered. Executives at DaVita, a firm that runs kidney dialysis centers, learn that patient needs must come first, even before company paperwork.

Other companies which send executives out to be low-level workers include Walt Disney, Continental Airlines, Sysco, and Amazon.com.

What do you think executives learn on the front lines at these companies? Can you think of other companies that would benefit from similar programs for their executives?

Adapted from Joann S. Lublin, "Top Brass Try Life in the Trenches: To Promote Understanding, Firms Require Executives to Perform Entry-Level Jobs," *Wall Street Journal*, June 25, 2007, B1, B3.

The U.S. Census Bureau prepared over 100 posters, similar to this one, to reach various segments of its audience.

Source: "Posters," U.S. Census Bureau: United States Census 2010, http://2010.census.gov/partners/materials/posters-materials.php.

were purchased for young children. So they developed a spill-resistant model with rubberized edges that became a top seller.[21]

Tesco PLC, Britain's largest retailer, signs up customers for its Clubcard. The card gives customers discounts, and it gives Tesco audience data. When Tesco added Asian herbs and ethnic foods in Indian and Pakistani neighborhoods, the data showed the products were also popular with affluent white customers, so Tesco expanded its roll-out. When customers buy diapers the first time, they get coupons for usual baby products such as wipes and toys. They also get coupons for beer, because the data show that new fathers buy more beer.[22]

AUDIENCE BENEFITS LO 2-4

Use your analysis of your audience to create effective **audience benefits,** advantages that the audience gets by using your services, buying your products, following your policies, or adopting your ideas. In informative messages, benefits give reasons to comply with the information you announce and suggest that the information is good. In persuasive messages, benefits give reasons to act and help overcome audience resistance. Negative messages do not use benefits.

Characteristics of Good Audience Benefits

Good benefits meet four criteria. Each of these criteria suggests a technique for writing good benefits.

1. Adapt benefits to the audience. When you write to different audiences, you may need to stress different benefits. Suppose that you manufacture a product and want to persuade dealers to carry it. The features you may cite in ads directed toward customers—stylish colors, sleek lines, convenience, durability, good price—won't convince dealers. Shelf space is at a premium, and no dealer carries all the models of all the brands available for any given product. Why should the dealer stock your product? To be persuasive, talk about the features that are benefits from the dealer's point of view: turnover, profit margin, the national advertising campaign that will build customer awareness and interest, the special store displays you offer that will draw attention to the product.

2. Stress intrinsic as well as extrinsic motivators. **Intrinsic motivators** come automatically from using a product or doing something. **Extrinsic motivators** are "added on." Someone in power decides to give them; they do not necessarily come from using the product or doing the action. Figure 2.4 gives examples of extrinsic and intrinsic motivators for three activities.

Intrinsic motivators or benefits are better than extrinsic motivators for two reasons:

- There just aren't enough extrinsic motivators for everything you want people to do. You can't give a prize to every customer every time he or she places an order or to every subordinate who does what he or she is supposed to do.
- Research shows that extrinsic motivators may actually make people *less* satisfied with the products they buy or the procedures they follow.

In a groundbreaking study of professional employees, Frederick Herzberg found that the things people said they liked about their jobs were all intrinsic motivators—pride in achievement, an enjoyment of the work itself, responsibility. Extrinsic motivators—pay, company policy—were sometimes mentioned as things people disliked, but they were never cited as things that motivated or satisfied them. People who made a lot of money still did not mention salary as a good point about the job or the organization.[23]

Steak 'n Shake restaurant chain wanted to find out what motivated its employees to do their best at work. The company learned that what employees want more than money is respect and the feeling that management listens to them and values their input.[24]

3. Prove benefits with clear logic and explain them in adequate detail. An audience benefit is a claim or assertion that the audience will benefit if they do something. Convincing the audience, therefore, involves two steps: making sure that the benefit really will occur, and explaining it to the audience.

Witness.org: Sharing Evidence of Human Rights Abuses

"For the past 16 years Witness has provided video cameras to carefully selected activists and community leaders in more than 100 countries. The group has amassed one of the largest existing collections of human-rights-abuse footage and has shown its videos to policy makers and human-rights groups around the world."

The graphic and disturbing nature of these videos make them difficult to distribute to public forums (such as YouTube), where user guidelines prevent anyone from sharing violent or sexually explicit material. Instead, Witness created their own version of YouTube—http://hub.witness.org/—where anyone can submit video clips of human rights abuses, and anyone can log in and view the evidence.

Witness' video evidence has led to war crimes prosecutions and put pressure on governments to change their policies.

How does Witness' approach demonstrate a keen understanding of audience analysis? What "audience benefits" does their website address? What ethical concerns might there be about publishing graphic video evidence on a public website?

Quoted and adapted from David Kushner, "In Your Eyes: Peter Gabriel's Human-Rights Group Embraces Social Media. A YouTube for Unseen Atrocities," *Fast Company*, November 2008, 80–2.

Figure 2.4 Extrinsic and Intrinsic Motivators

Activity	Extrinsic motivator	Intrinsic motivator
Making a sale	Getting a commission	Pleasure in convincing someone; pride in using your talents to think of a strategy and execute it
Turning in a suggestion to a company suggestion system	Getting a monetary reward when the suggestion is implemented	Solving a problem at work; making the work environment a little more pleasant
Writing a report that solves an organizational problem	Getting praise, a good performance appraisal, and maybe a raise	Pleasure in having an effect on an organization; pride in using your skills to solve problems; solving the problem itself

If the logic behind a claimed benefit is faulty or inaccurate, there's no way to make that particular benefit convincing. Revise the benefit to make it logical.

Faulty logic:	Moving your account information into Excel will save you time.
Analysis:	If you have not used Excel before, in the short run it will probably take you longer to work with your account information using Excel. You may have been pretty good with your old system!
Revised benefit:	Moving your account information into Excel will allow you to prepare your monthly budget pages with a few clicks of a button.

If the logic is sound, making that logic evident to the audience is a matter of providing enough evidence and showing how the evidence proves the claim that there will be a benefit. Always provide enough detail to be vivid and concrete. You'll need more detail in the following situations:

- The audience may not have thought of the benefit before.
- The benefit depends on the difference between the long run and the short run.
- The audience will be hard to persuade, and you need detail to make the benefit vivid and emotionally convincing.

The apparel industry, which is actively seeking a middle-aged and baby boomer audience, is using details to attract them. Slacks may offer slimming panels, and jeans may offer stretch waists and room for padded hips and thighs. Tops may cover upper arms. The potential market is huge. Women over 35 bought over half the annual $100 billion spent on women's apparel purchases.[25]

Until recently, Islamic women who wanted to go swimming had a problem. To meet their customers' needs, the Australian company Ahiida now makes hooded full-bodied bathing suits, called Burqinis, for Muslim women who wish to go swimming while still maintaining the Islamic customs of full body coverage.

Source: Lisa Miller, "Belief Watch: Surf's Up!" *Newsweek*, January 29, 2007, 15.

4. Phrase benefits in you-attitude. If benefits aren't worded with you-attitude (Chapter 3), they'll sound selfish and won't be as effective as they could be. It doesn't matter how you phrase benefits while you're brainstorming and developing them, but in your final draft, check to be sure that you've used you-attitude.

Lacks you-attitude:	We have the lowest prices in town.
You-attitude:	At Havlichek Cars, you get the best deal in town.

No Substitute for Face Time

In the face of globalization and remote video feeds that simultaneously connect workers and clients all around the world, face-to-face meetings are still critical in global business. Culturally, the world is still incredibly diverse, and to make global coalitions, such as launching a Coca-Cola bottling plant in Albania a few years ago, meeting the right people in person was crucial for Coke's CEO.

Another example is MTV in the center of Islamic nations. Would it be possible to enter MTV into the Arabian market without offending the religious institutions of this region? Not without many carefully planned, face-to-face meetings. The chief of MTV Networks International managed to accomplish the establishment of MTV Arabia by convincing the mayor of Mecca that the new station would provide educational opportunities and would not show skin.

Collaborative technologies such as videoconferencing may be convenient and less expensive than frequent flying, but technology simply cannot take the place of physically sitting down with a colleague or client to solve problems and form alliances.

Adapted from Tom Lowry et al., "It's All About the Face-to-Face," *BusinessWeek*, January 28, 2008, 48–51.

Ways to Identify and Develop Audience Benefits

Brainstorm lots of benefits—perhaps twice as many as you'll need. Then you can choose the ones that are most effective for your audience, or that you can develop most easily. The first benefit you think of may not be the best.

Sometimes benefits will be easy to think of and to explain. When they are harder to identify or to develop, use the following steps to identify and then develop good benefits.

1. Identify the needs, wants, and feelings that may motivate your audience. All of us have basic needs, and most of us supplement those needs with possessions or intangibles we want. We need enough food to satisfy nutritional needs, but we may want our diet to make us look sexy. We need basic shelter, but we may want our homes to be cozy, luxurious, or green. And our needs and wants are strongly influenced by our feelings. We may feel safer in a more expensive car, even though research does not show that car as being safer than cheaper models.

2. Identify the objective features of your product or policy that could meet the needs you've identified. Sometimes just listing the audience's needs makes it obvious which feature meets a given need. Sometimes several features together meet the need. Try to think of all of them.

Suppose that you want to persuade people to come to the restaurant you manage. It's true that everybody needs to eat, but telling people they can satisfy their hunger needs won't persuade them to come to your restaurant rather than going somewhere else or eating at home. Depending on what features your restaurant offered, you could appeal to one or more of the following subgroups:

Subgroup	Features to meet the subgroup's needs
People who work outside the home	A quick lunch; a relaxing place to take clients or colleagues
Parents with small children	High chairs, children's menus, and toys to keep the kids entertained while they wait for their order
People who eat out a lot	Variety both in food and in decor
People on tight budgets	Economical food; a place where they don't need to tip (cafeteria or fast food)
People on special diets	Low-sodium and low-carb dishes; vegetarian food; kosher food
People to whom eating out is part of an evening's entertainment	Music or a floor show; elegant surroundings; reservations so they can get to a show or event after dinner; late hours so they can come to dinner after a show or game

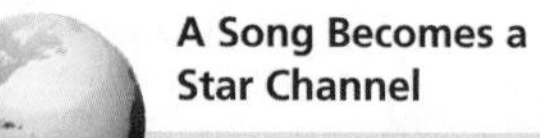

A Song Becomes a Star Channel

Wavin' Flag, a song by Somali-Canadian hip-hop artist K'naan, became a World Cup anthem and top iTunes hit in 17 countries. It also was the centerpiece of Coca-Cola's largest marketing campaign, which reached 160 countries.

Coke liked K'naan's multinational upbringing and the song's melody and chorus. K'naan recorded versions of the song with various multinational pop stars to increase its appeal.

Coke put the profits from the sale of *Wavin' Flag* downloads into its Replenish Africa Initiative, a $30 million effort to provide clean water and better sanitation on that continent.

Adapted from Duane D. Stanford, "Coke's World Cup Song Hits the High Notes," *Bloomberg Businessweek,* July 19, 2010, 24–25.

Whenever you're communicating with customers or clients about features that are not unique to your organization, it's wise to present both benefits of the features themselves and benefits of dealing with your company. If you talk about the benefits of the new healthy choices in children's menus but don't mention your own revised menu, people may go somewhere else!

3. Show how the audience can meet their needs with the features of the policy or product. Features alone rarely motivate people. Instead, link the feature to the audience's needs—and provide details to make the benefit vivid.

Weak: You get quick service.

Better: If you only have an hour for lunch, try our Business Buffet. Within minutes, you can choose from a variety of main dishes, vegetables, and a make-your-own-sandwich-and-salad bar. You'll have a lunch that's as light or filling as you want, with time to enjoy it—and still be back to the office on time.

AUDIENCE BENEFITS WORK

Appropriate audience benefits work so well that organizations spend much time and money identifying them and then developing them.

- Procter & Gamble increased the market share of Gain detergent, and saw annual sales of over a billion dollars, by focusing on a benefit their audience considered important: the scent.[26]
- Hotels study which benefits are worth the money, and which are not. Holiday Inn keeps restaurants and bars in all their hotels, even though they are not money makers, but does not have bellhops. Staybridge Suites cleans less often but has "Sundowner receptions" which give guests a free meal and a chance to socialize.[27]
- *The Daily Sun,* a South African tabloid, is gaining market share, when other newspapers are losing it, by focusing on stories—soccer, sex, soap operas, local witches, supernatural events like evil flying tortoises—its audience wants to read. This audience, primarily newly enfranchised black Africans, has given the paper an audited paid circulation of over a half million.[28]
- Many companies offer their employees health benefits, an arrangement that benefits both the company and employee. Meredith Corporation, publisher of magazines such as *Better Homes and Gardens, Family Circle,* and *Parents,* pays for employee health screenings. Employees who accept the offer get $300 off their health insurance cost; Meredith gets a decrease in corporate health care costs.[29]
- Companies branching out into servicing their products find that they are more successful if they offer benefits in addition to cost saving. One truck company offers its customers fleet-management services, including monitoring fuel consumption and showing drivers how to increase their gas mileage. This service in turn helps its customers appeal to environmentally concerned clients such as government agencies.[30]

Remember that audience benefits must be appropriate for the audience before they work. Tylenol tried a new ad campaign that said, "We put our love into Tylenol." Upset customers who remembered the Tylenol cyanide poisonings wrote in saying they didn't want anyone putting anything into their Tylenol.[31]

THE McPLAYBOOK

Now That's Fast Food

To pump up business 24/7, McDonald's has sped up its new-product introductions. Here's its secret recipe:

Make it easy to eat

McDonald's does more than half its business at drive-through windows. That means it needs snacks and meals that can be held in one hand while the other is on the steering wheel.

Make it easy to prepare

McDonald's restaurant crews turn over entirely within a year, on average. To maintain consistency amid this churn, tasks must be simple to learn and repeat.

Make it quick

It's called fast food for a reason. McDonald's tests all new products for cooking times so customers don't have to wait even a second longer than absolutely necessary.

Make what the customers want

McDonald's prowls the market for new products and then spends months in carefully monitored field tests to ensure that people will buy its new concoctions.

McDonald's plans menu items to meet the needs and expectations of customers, employees, and franchise owners.

Source: From Michael Arndt, "Special Report: McDonald's," Reprinted from the February 5, 2007 issue of *BusinessWeek*. Used with permission of Bloomberg L. P. Copyright © 2011. All rights reserved.

Localizing Incentive Programs

Incentive programs are employee benefits aimed to reward good work performances. Globalization has complicated such programs, because what works in one country may not work in another.

In the United States, top performers might be rewarded with an expensive luxury item such as a watch. In China or India, a moped might be more appropriate.

Travel awards may also differ. US employees generally prefer unstructured, leisurely vacations, such as those offered by beach resorts. Europeans tend to prefer more adventurous trips, perhaps including a strenuous mountain hike or rafting trip. Many Chinese prefer highly structured tours with carefully planned itineraries.

Religion can also be a factor. Many U.S. employees would appreciate a trip to Las Vegas, with a complimentary bottle of champagne in their room. But many religious people in the Middle East or Asia would not want the gambling or the alcohol.

What are some employee incentives you can name that would be appropriate in one country but not another? What are some ways large firms can work with these differences?

Adapted from Irwin Speizer, "Good Intentions, Lost in Translation," *Workforce Management,* November 21, 2005, http://www.workforce.com/archive/feature/benefits-compensations/good-intentions-lost-translation/index.php.

Sometimes it is hard to know what your audience wants. A classic example is "feature creep" in electronic goods. Unfortunately, consumers seem to want lots of features in their electronics when they buy them, but then become frustrated trying to use them and return the devices. In the United States, product returns cost $100 billion.[32] Research has shown that over half the wares are in complete working order; consumers just cannot operate them.[33]

WRITING OR SPEAKING TO MULTIPLE AUDIENCES WITH DIFFERENT NEEDS

Many business and administrative messages go not to a single person but to a larger audience. When the members of your audience share the same interests and the same level of knowledge, you can use the principles outlined above for individual readers or for members of homogeneous groups. But often different members of the audience have different needs.

Researcher Rachel Spilka has shown that talking to readers both inside and outside the organization helped corporate engineers adapt their documents successfully. Talking to readers and reviewers helped writers involve readers in the planning process, understand the social and political relationships among readers, and negotiate conflicts orally rather than depending solely on the document. These writers were then able to think about content as well as about organization and style, appeal to common grounds (such as reducing waste or increasing productivity) that multiple readers shared, and reduce the number of revisions needed before documents were approved.[34]

When it is not possible to meet everyone's needs, meet the needs of gatekeepers and decision makers first.

As you write for multiple audiences, consider these strategies:

Content and number of details

- Provide an overview or executive summary for readers who want just the main points.
- In the body of the document, provide enough detail for decision makers and for anyone else who could veto your proposal.
- If the decision makers don't need details that other audiences will want, provide those details in appendices—statistical tabulations, earlier reports, and so forth.

Organization

- Use headings and a table of contents so readers can turn to the portions that interest them.
- Organize your message based on the decision makers' attitudes toward it.

Level of formality

- Avoid personal pronouns. *You* ceases to have a specific meaning when several different audiences use a document.
- If both internal and external audiences will use a document, use a slightly more formal style than you would in an internal document.
- Use a more formal style when you write to international audiences.

Technical level

- In the body of the document, assume the degree of knowledge that decision makers will have.
- Put background and explanatory information under separate headings. Then readers can use the headings and the table of contents to read or skip these sections, as their knowledge dictates.
- If decision makers will have more knowledge than other audiences, provide a glossary of terms. Early in the document, let readers know that the glossary exists.

SUMMARY OF KEY POINTS

- The **primary audience** will make a decision or act on the basis of your message. The **secondary audience** may be asked by the primary audience to comment on your message or to implement your ideas after they've been approved. The **auxiliary audience** encounters the message but does not have to interact with it. A **gatekeeper** controls whether the message gets to the primary audience. A **watchdog audience** has political, social, or economic power and may base future actions on its evaluation of your message.
- A communication channel is the means by which you convey your message to your audience.
- The following questions provide a framework for audience analysis:
  1. What will the audience's initial reaction be to the message?
  2. How much information does the audience need?

3. What obstacles must you overcome?
4. What positive aspects can you emphasize?
5. What expectations does the audience have about the appropriate language, contents, and organization of messages?
6. How will the audience use the document?

- **Audience benefits** are advantages that the audience gets by using your services, buying your products, following your policies, or adopting your ideas. Benefits can exist for policies and ideas as well as for goods and services.
- Good benefits are adapted to the audience, based on **intrinsic** rather than **extrinsic motivators,** supported by clear logic, explained in adequate detail, and phrased in you-attitude. Extrinsic benefits simply aren't available to reward every desired behavior; further, they reduce the satisfaction in doing something for its own sake.
- To create audience benefits,
  1. Identify the feelings, fears, and needs that may motivate your audience.
  2. Identify the features of your product or policy that could meet the needs you've identified.
  3. Show how the audience can meet their needs with the features of the policy or product.
- When you write to multiple audiences, use the primary audience to determine level of detail, organization, level of formality, and use of technical terms and theory.

CHAPTER 2 Exercises and Problems

**Go to www.mhhe.com/locker10e for additional Exercises and Problems.*

2.1 Reviewing the Chapter

1. Who are the five different audiences your message may need to address? (LO 2-1)
2. What are some characteristics to consider when analyzing individuals? (LO 2-1)
3. What are some characteristics to consider when analyzing groups? (LO 2-1)
4. What are some questions to consider when analyzing organizational culture? (LO 2-1)
5. What is a discourse community? Why will discourse communities be important in your career? (LO 2-1)
6. What are standard business communication channels? (LO 2-2)
7. What kinds of electronic channels seem most useful to you? Why? (LO 2-2)
8. What are considerations to keep in mind when selecting channels? (LO 2-2)
9. What are 12 questions to ask when analyzing your audience? (LO 2-3)
10. What are four characteristics of good audience benefits? (LO 2-4)
11. What are three ways to identify and develop audience benefits? (LO 2-4)
12. What are considerations to keep in mind when addressing multiple audiences? (LO 2-3)

2.2 Reviewing Grammar

Good audience analysis requires careful use of pronouns. Review your skills with pronoun usage by doing grammar exercise B.5, Appendix B.

2.3 Identifying Audiences

In each of the following situations, label the audiences as gatekeeper, primary, secondary, auxiliary, or watchdog audiences (all audiences may not be in each scenario):

1. Kent, Carol, and Jose are planning to start a website design business. However, before they can get started, they need money. They have developed a business plan and are getting ready to seek funds from financial institutions for starting their small business.
2. Barbara's boss asked her to write a direct mail letter to potential customers about the advantages of becoming a preferred member of their agency's travel club. The letter will go to all customers of the agency who are over 65 years old.
3. Paul works for the mayor's office in a big city. As part of a citywide cost-cutting measure, a blue-ribbon panel has recommended requiring employees who work more than 40 hours in a week to take compensatory time off rather than being paid overtime. The only exceptions will be the police and fire departments. The mayor asks Paul to prepare a proposal for the city council, which will vote on whether to implement the change. Before they vote, council members will hear from (1) citizens, who will have an opportunity to read the proposal and communicate their opinions to the city council; (2) mayors' offices in other cities, who may be asked about their experiences; (3) union representatives, who may be concerned about the reduction in income that will occur if the proposal is implemented; (4) department heads, whose ability to schedule work might be limited if the proposal passes; and (5) the blue-ribbon panel and good-government lobbying groups. Council members come up for reelection in six months.
4. Sharon, Steven's boss at Bigster Corporation, has asked him to write an e-mail for everyone in her division, informing them of HR's new mandatory training sessions on new government regulations affecting Bigster's services.

2.4 Analyzing Multiple Audiences

Like most major corporations, the U.S. Census Bureau has multiple, conflicting audiences, among them the president, Congress, press, state governments, citizens (both as providers and users of data), statisticians, and researchers.

- For the bureau, who might serve as gatekeeper, primary, secondary, auxiliary, and watchdog audiences?
- What kinds of conflicting goals might these audiences have?
- What would be appropriate benefits for each type of audience?
- What kinds of categories might the bureau create for its largest audience (citizens)?
- How do some of the posters at the website below differ for different audiences?: "Posters," U.S. Census Bureau: United States Census 2010, http://2010.census.gov/partners/materials/posters-materials.php.

2.5 Choosing a Channel to Reach a Specific Audience

Suppose your organization wants to target a product, service, or program for each of the following audiences. What would be the best channel(s) to reach that group in your city? To what extent would that channel reach all group members?

a. Stay-at-home mothers
b. Vegetarians
c. Full-time students at a university
d. Part-time students at a community college
e. Non-English speakers
f. People who use hearing aids
g. Parents whose children play softball or baseball
h. Attorneys
i. Female owners of small businesses
j. Pet owners

2.6 Identifying and Developing Audience Benefits

Listed here are several things an organization might like its employees to do:

1. Use less paper.
2. Attend a brown-bag lunch to discuss ways to improve products or services.
3. Become more physically fit.
4. Volunteer for community organizations.
5. Write fewer e-mails.
6. Attend mandatory training about new government regulations affecting the business.

As your instructor directs,

a. Identify the motives or needs that might be met by each of the activities.

b. Take each need or motive and develop it as an audience benefit in a full paragraph. Use additional paragraphs for the other needs met by the activity. Remember to use you-attitude!

2.7 Identifying Objections and Audience Benefits

Think of an organization you know something about, and answer the following questions for it:

a. Your organization is thinking about developing a knowledge management system that requires workers to input their knowledge and experience in their job functions into the organizational database. What benefits could the knowledge management system offer your organization? What drawbacks are there? Who would be the easiest to convince? Who would be the hardest?

b. New telephone software would efficiently replace your organization's long-standing human phone operator who has been a perennial welcoming voice to incoming callers. What objections might people in your organization have to replacing the operator? What benefits might your organization receive? Who would be easiest to convince? Who would be the hardest?

c. Your organization is thinking of outsourcing one of its primary products to a manufacturer in another country where the product can be made more cost-efficiently. What fears or objections might people have? What benefits might your organization receive? Who would be easiest to convince? Who would be hardest?

As your instructor directs,

a. Share your answers orally with a small group of students.

b. Present your answers in an oral presentation to the class.

c. Write a paragraph developing the best audience benefit you identified. Remember to use you-attitude.

2.8 Analyzing Benefits for Multiple Audiences

The U.S. Census Bureau lists these benefits from cooperating with the census:

> "Census information affects the numbers of seats your state occupies in the U.S. House of Representatives. And people from many walks of life use census data to advocate for causes, rescue disaster victims, prevent diseases, research markets, locate pools of skilled workers and more.
>
> "When you do the math, it's easy to see what an accurate count of residents can do for your community. Better infrastructure. More services. A brighter tomorrow for everyone. In fact, the information the census collects helps to determine how more than $400 billion dollars of federal funding each year is spent on infrastructure and services like:
>
> - Hospitals
> - Job training centers
> - Schools
> - Senior centers
> - Bridges, tunnels and other public works projects
> - Emergency services"

How well do these benefits meet the four characteristics of good audience benefits discussed in this chapter?

Quoted from "Why It's Important," U.S. Census Bureau: United States Census 2010, accessed May 8, 2010, http://2010.census.gov/2010census/about/why-important.php.

2.9 Addressing Your Audience's Need for Information

"Tell me about yourself."

This may be the most popular opening question of job interviews, but it's also a question that you'll encounter in nearly any social situation when you meet someone new. Although the question may be the same, the answer you give will change based upon the rhetorical situation: the audience, purpose, and context of the question.

For each of the following situations in a–g, ask yourself these questions to help create a good response:

- How will the audience react to your answer? Will the audience see the message as important? What information will you need to include in your answer to keep their attention?
- How will the audience use your answer? Why is the audience asking the question? What information is relevant to the audience and what information can you leave out?
- How much information does the audience need? What information do they already know about you? What level of detail do they need?
- What are the audience's expectations about your answer? What are the appropriate word choices and tone for your answer? What topics should you avoid (at least for now)?
- What are the physical conditions that will affect your answer? Where are you (e.g., Are you outside, in a noisy room, on the phone)? How much time do you have to give your response?

Write your response to the statement "Tell me about yourself." Assume that the question is being asked by

a. A recruiter at a career fair in your university's auditorium.
b. A recruiter in a job interview in a small interview or conference room.
c. An attractive male or female at a popular weekend nightspot.
d. Your instructor on the first day of class.
e. Your new roommate on your first day in the dormitory.
f. A new co-worker on your first day at a new job.
g. A new co-worker on your first day volunteering at your local food pantry.

2.10 Analyzing Individuals

Read about the Myers-Briggs Type Indicator on page 29. On the web, take one of the free tests similar to the Myers-Briggs. Read about your personality type and consider how accurate the description may be. Print your results.

As your instructor directs,

- Share your results orally with a small group of students and discuss how accurately the Type Indicator describes you. Identify some of the differences among your personality types and consider how the differences would affect efforts to collaborate on projects.
- Identify other students in the classroom with the same combination of personality traits. Create a brief oral presentation to the class that describes your Type Indicator and explains how the pros and cons of your personality will affect group dynamics in collaborative work.
- Write a brief memo to your instructor describing your results, assessing how well the results reflect your personality, and suggesting how your personality traits might affect your work in class and in the workplace.

2.11 Getting Customer Feedback

Smart businesses want to know what their customers and clients are saying about their products and services. Many websites can help them do so.

Check some of the common sites for customer comments. Here is a list to get you started:

http://www.amazon.com
http://www.angieslist.com
http://getsatisfaction.com
http://www.my3cents.com
http://www.ratepoint.com
http://www.suggestionbox.com
http://www.thesqueakywheel.com
http://www.yelp.com

What does each site do?
What are good features of each site?
What are drawbacks?

As your instructor directs,

a. Discuss your findings in a memo to your instructor.
b. Share your findings in small groups.
c. As a group, make a presentation to your classmates.

2.12 Identifying International Audience Benefits

Reread the sidebar on page 39 explaining how Procter & Gamble is marketing its products in developing countries. In small groups, discuss different marketing practices you have become aware of in other countries. How do these practices benefit consumers? How do they benefit store owners?

As your instructor directs,

a. Post your findings electronically to share with the class.
b. Present your findings in a memo to your instructor.
c. Present your findings in an oral presentation to the class.

2.13 Evaluating a New Channel

To combat software piracy, Microsoft tried an unusual communication channel. A new software update turned screens black on computers using pirated software; the update also posted a message to switch to legitimate software copies. The update did not prevent people from using their machines, and they could manually change their wallpaper back to its previous design. But the black screen returned every 60 minutes. Microsoft said there was little protest except in China, where ironically the software piracy problem is greatest.

In small groups, discuss this practice.

- What do you think of this channel?
- Is it ethical?
- Will it help or hurt Microsoft profits in China?
- How do you think receivers of the black screen react?

As your instructor directs,

a. Post your findings electronically to share with the class.
b. Present your findings in a memo to your instructor.
c. Present your findings in an oral presentation to the class.

Source: Loretta Chao and Juliet Ye, "Microsoft Tactic Raises Hackles in China: In Antipiracy Move, Software Update Turns Screens Black and Urges Users to Buy Legal Windows Copies," *Wall Street Journal*, October 23, 2008, B4.

2.14 Discussing Ethics

a. What do you think about the practice among some companies of giving perks such as free samples to bloggers to discuss their products? Does your opinion change according to the expense of the perk (free tissues vs. tablet computers, for instance)? How can you tell if bloggers have been influenced by the companies whose products they discuss?
b. What do you think about the practice of law firms using social media to find plaintiffs (see sidebar on page 35)? Is it any worse to use social media than print or TV ads? Why? Look at some of the sites provided by law firms. Try http://www.oil-rig-explosions.com/, http://www.consumerwarningnetwork.com/; http://www.sokolovelaw.com/legal-help/dangerous-drugs/birth-control; http://westwoodscammed.me/.
   How persuasive is the content?
c. What do you think about the practice of tracking consumers' Internet surfing and selling the information to marketers? Does the tracking seem more intrusive when it is combined with off-line records such as shopping and credit card records?
d. What do you think about the practice of companies asking their employees to take health screenings and then giving them hundreds of dollars off their health insurance if they do so? What benefits do you see for employees? Drawbacks? Is this just a way to penalize employees who refuse by making them pay more for health insurance?

2.15 Banking on Multiple Audiences

Bruce Murphy, an executive at KeyBank, is working on a new problem: how to extend banking services to a new audience—people who use banks intermittently or not at all. It is a large group, estimated at 73 million people. Together, they spend an estimated $11 billion in fees at places such as check-cashing outlets, money-wire companies, and paycheck lenders (companies offering cash advances on future paychecks).

However, they are a tough audience. Many of them have a deep distrust of banks or believe banks will not serve them. Murphy also faced another tough audience: bank managers who feared attracting forgeries and other bad checks and thus losing money. One manager actually said, "Are you crazy? These are the very people we're trying to keep out of the bank!"

To attract the new customers, KeyBank cashes payroll and government checks for a 1.5% fee, well below the 2.44% which is average for check-cashing outlets. The bank also started offering free financial education classes. In fact, the bank even has a program to help people with a history of bounced checks to clear their records by paying restitution and taking the financial education class.

The program is growing, both among check-cashing clients and branches offering the services, to the satisfaction of both audiences.

- What are some other businesses that could expand services to underserved populations?
- What services would they offer?
- What problems would they encounter?
- What audience appeals could they use to attract clients or customers?

Source: Adapted from Ann Carrns, "Banks Court a New Client: The Low-Income Earner: KeyCorp Experiments with Check Cashing," *Wall Street Journal,* March 16, 2007, A1, A14.

2.16 Announcing a New Employee Benefit

Your company has decided to pay employees for doing charity work. Employees can spend one hour working with a charitable or nonprofit group for every 40 hours they work. As Vice President of Human Resources, you need to announce this new program.

Pick a specific organization you know something about, and answer the following questions about it:

1. What proportion of the employees are already involved in volunteer work?
2. Is community service or "giving back" consistent with the organization's corporate mission?
3. Some employees won't be able or won't want to participate. What is the benefit for them in working for a company that has such a program?
4. Will promoting community participation help the organization attract and retain workers?

As your instructor directs,

a. Present your answers in an oral presentation to the class.
b. Present your answers in a memo to your instructor.
c. Share your answers with a small group of students and write a joint memo reporting the similarities and differences you found.

2.17 Announcing a Tuition Reimbursement Program

Assume that your organization is considering reimbursing workers for tuition and fees for job-related courses. As Director of Education and Training, you will present to company executives a review of pros and cons for the program. To prepare, you have composed a list of questions you know they may have. Pick a specific organization that you know something about, and answer the following questions about it.

1. What do people do on the job? What courses or degrees could help them do their current jobs even better?
2. How much education do people already have? How do they feel about formal schooling?
3. How busy are employees? Will most have time to take classes and study in addition to working 40 hours a week (or more)?
4. Is it realistic to think that people who get more education would get higher salaries? Or is money for increases limited? Is it reasonable to think that most people could be promoted? Or does the organization have many more low-level than high-level jobs?
5. How much loyalty do employees have to this particular organization? Is it "just a job," or do they care about the welfare of the organization?
6. How competitive is the job market? How easy is it for the organization to find and retain qualified employees?
7. Is knowledge needed to do the job changing, or is knowledge learned 5 or 10 years ago still up-to-date?
8. How competitive is the economic market? Is this company doing well financially? Can its customers or clients easily go somewhere else? Is it a government agency dependent on tax dollars for funding? What about the current situation makes this an especially good time to hone the skills of the employees you have?
9. Do you support the program? Why or why not?

2.18 Crafting a Memo for a Particular Audience

Your supervisor at a fitness center wants to increase the organization's membership and has asked you to write a letter to the three primary population segments in your town: retirees, college students, and working professionals with families. Using the following fitness benefits your supervisor gave you to help you get started, write a version of a letter targeted at each of the three audiences.

- Become a member with no sign-up fees.
- Attend free nutrition classes to help with weight control and optimal fitness.

- Attend any of our many fitness classes, scheduled for your convenience.
- Enjoy the new indoor/outdoor pool with lap lanes and zero-gravity entrance.
- Use the large selection of free-weights and exercise machines.
- Lose weight and feel your healthiest with a personal trainer, who will guide you toward your fitness goals.

Remember these benefits were just to get you started; you are expected to come up with more on your own.

2.19 Analyzing Your Co-Workers

What do your co-workers do? What hassles and challenges do they face? To what extent do their lives outside work affect their responses to work situations? What do your co-workers value? What are their pet peeves? How committed are they to organizational goals? How satisfying do they find their jobs? Are the people you work with quite similar to each other, or do they differ from each other? How?

As your instructor directs,

a. Share your answers orally with a small group of students.

b. Present your answers in an oral presentation to the class.

c. Present your answers in a memo to your instructor.

d. Share your answers with a small group of students and write a joint memo reporting the similarities and differences you found.

2.20 Analyzing the Audiences of Noncommercial Web Pages

Analyze the implied audiences of two web pages of two noncommercial organizations with the same purpose (combating hunger, improving health, influencing the political process, etc.). You could pick the home pages of the national organization and a local affiliate, or the home pages of two separate organizations working toward the same general goal.

Answer the following questions:

- Do the pages work equally well for surfers and for people who have reached the page deliberately?
- Possible audiences include current and potential volunteers, donors, clients, and employees. Do the pages provide material for each audience? Is the material useful? Complete? Up-to-date? Does new material encourage people to return?
- What assumptions about audiences do content and visuals suggest?
- Can you think of ways that the pages could better serve their audiences?

As your instructor directs,

a. Share your results orally with a small group of students.

b. Present your results orally to the class.

c. Present your results in a memo to your instructor. Attach copies of the home pages.

d. Share your results with a small group of students, and write a joint memo reporting the similarities and differences you found.

e. Post your results in an e-mail message to the class. Provide links to the two web pages.

2.21 Analyzing a Discourse Community

Analyze the way a group you are part of uses language. Possible groups include

- Work teams.
- Sports teams.
- Sororities, fraternities, and other social groups.
- Churches, mosques, synagogues, and temples.
- Geographic or ethnic groups.
- Groups of friends.

Questions to ask include the following:

- What specialized terms might not be known to outsiders?
- What topics do members talk or write about? What topics are considered unimportant or improper?
- What channels do members use to convey messages?
- What forms of language do members use to build goodwill? to demonstrate competence or superiority?
- What strategies or kinds of proof are convincing to members?
- What formats, conventions, or rules do members expect messages to follow?
- What are some nonverbal ways members communicate?

As your instructor directs,

a. Share your results orally with a small group of students.

b. Present your results in an oral presentation to the class.

c. Present your results in a memo to your instructor.

d. Share your results with a small group of students, and write a joint memo reporting the similarities and differences you found.

CHAPTER 3

Building Goodwill

Chapter Outline

You-Attitude

- How to Create You-Attitude
- You-Attitude beyond the Sentence Level

Positive Emphasis

- How to Create Positive Emphasis
- How to Check Positive Emphasis

Tone, Power, and Politeness

- Use Courtesy Titles for People You Don't Know Well
- Be Aware of the Power Implications of the Words You Use

Reducing Bias in Business Communication

- Making Language Nonsexist
- Making Language Nonracist and Nonageist
- Talking about People with Disabilities and Diseases
- Choosing Bias-Free Photos and Illustrations

Summary of Key Points

Restoring Goodwill at Delta

Traveling by air can be a frustrating experience. High prices, extra fees, delays, and cancellations can leave a customer feeling frazzled and angry. After a year in which it had the highest number of customer complaints, Delta Air Lines is trying to change its image by sending all 11,000 flight agents back to training.

In day-long seminars, agents learn how to respond to customer complaints and worries with a positive attitude and a focus on improving the customer's experience. The seminars include these key points:

> *"Agents learn how to respond to customer complaints and worries with a positive attitude and a focus on improving the customer's experience."*

- *Be positive.* The agents are taught to smile and express appreciation for the customers' business, especially when the customers are unhappy or when there are problems.
- *Be honest.* If a passenger is late and going to miss her flight, the agents learn to tell her immediately and offer to help rebook, rather than encouraging her to rush through the airport.
- *Recognize the customer's feelings.* Empathizing with a frustrated customer can make the difference between a bad experience and a good experience. Agents may not be able to solve all customers' complaints, but by acknowledging frustration they show that they care and are attempting to help.
- *Don't apologize for the rules.* Baggage fees and other expenses have become part of the flying experience. Agents should stick to the facts, rather than saying they agree with angry customers. Michael Hazelton, a facilitator for the training classes, said, "You may think you are bonding with the customer by agreeing the fees are horrible, but the customer thinks, 'This person just threw his company under the bus.'"
- *Don't place blame.* Customers know when they've made poor decisions, such as arriving late or not allowing enough time to get through airport security. Agents should work to help the customers and solve problems as much as possible.

Of course, better customer service can't solve every problem with flying. But at Delta Air Lines, they believe that an increased focus on the customer will improve peoples' impressions of the flying experience.

Source: Scott McCartney, "Delta Sends Its 11,000 Agents to Charm School," *Wall Street Journal*, February 3, 2011, D3.

Learning Objectives

After studying this chapter, you will know how to

LO 3-1 Create you-attitude.

LO 3-2 Create positive emphasis.

LO 3-3 Improve tone in business communications.

LO 3-4 Reduce bias in business communications.

Goodwill smooths the challenges of business and administration. Companies have long been aware that treating customers well pays off in more sales and higher profits.

- Amazon's corporate mission says "We seek to be Earth's most customer centric company for three primary customer sets: consumer customers, seller customers and developer customers." Jeff Bezos, Amazon's founder and CEO, has a video on YouTube entitled "Everything I Know." It has three points: obsess over customers, invent on behalf of customers, and think long term, because doing so allows you to serve customers better.[1]
- Tony Hsieh built Zappos around customer service, including a service attitude for their vendors.
- Linda Thaler and Robin Koval built the Kaplan Thaler Group into an advertising agency with nearly $1 billion in billings using goodwill, you-attitude, and positive tone.[2]
- A study by Vanderbilt University found that a portfolio of companies whose ACSI (American Consumer Satisfaction Index) scores were above the national average far outperformed the market. Over a 10-year period, the portfolio gained 212%; the Standard & Poor 500-stock index rose 105% over the same period.[3]

Goodwill is important internally as well as externally. More and more organizations are realizing that treating employees well is financially wise as well as ethically sound. Happy employees create less staff turnover, thus reducing hiring and training costs. A University of Pennsylvania study of 3,000 companies found that investing 10% of revenue on capital improvement boosted company productivity 3.9%, but spending the money on employees increased productivity 8.5%, or more than twice as much.[4]

You-attitude, positive emphasis, and bias-free language are three ways to help build goodwill. Messages that show **you-attitude** use the audience's point of view, not the writer's or speaker's. **Positive emphasis** means focusing on the positive rather than the negative aspects of a situation. **Bias-free language** does not discriminate against people on the basis of sex, physical condition, race, ethnicity, age, or any other category. All three help you achieve your purposes and make your messages friendlier, more persuasive, more professional, and more humane. They suggest that you care not just about money but also about the needs and interests of your customers, employees, and fellow citizens.

YOU-ATTITUDE LO 3-1

Putting what you want to say in you-attitude is a crucial step both in thinking about your audience's needs and in communicating your concern to your audience.

How to Create You-Attitude

You-attitude is a style of communication that looks at things from the audience's point of view, emphasizing what the audience wants to know, respecting the audience's intelligence, and protecting the audience's ego.

To apply you-attitude on a sentence level, use the following techniques:

1. **Talk about the audience, not about yourself.**
2. **Refer to the customer's request or order specifically.**
3. **Don't talk about feelings, except to congratulate or offer sympathy.**
4. **In positive situations, use *you* more often than *I*. Use *we* when it includes the audience.**
5. **In negative situations, avoid the word *you*. Protect the audience's ego. Use passive verbs and impersonal expressions to avoid assigning blame.**

Revisions for you-attitude do not change the basic meaning of the sentence. However, revising for you-attitude often makes sentences longer because the revision is more specific and has more information. Long sentences need not be wordy. **Wordiness** means having more words than the meaning requires. We can add information and still keep the writing concise.

Customer Service Becoming Popular with Businesses

More companies are improving customer service to increase both sales and market share.

Walgreens is training pharmacists to work more closely with patients with chronic illnesses such as diabetes. Pharmacists are replacing their normal 3- to 5-minute meetings with regular 20- to 45-minute patient meetings to help them manage their disease.

American Express is training call-center agents to focus on building customer loyalty rather than processing the call quickly.

Even Comcast, which has had well-publicized problems with customer service, is giving its 24,000 call-center agents additional training.

Adapted from Dana Mattioli, "Customer Service as a Growth Engine," *Wall Street Journal*, June 7, 2010, B6.

1. Talk about the audience, not about yourself.

Your audience wants to know how they benefit or are affected. When you provide this information, you make your message more complete and more interesting.

Lacks you-attitude: We have negotiated an agreement with Apex Rent-a-Car that gives you a discount on rental cars.

You-attitude: As a Sunstrand employee, you can now get a 20% discount when you rent a car from Apex.

2. Refer to the customer's request or order specifically.

Refer to the customer's request, order, or policy specifically, not as a generic *your order* or *your policy*. If your customer is an individual or a small business, it's friendly to specify the content of the order. If you're dealing with a company with which you do a great deal of business, give the invoice or purchase order number.

Lacks you-attitude: Your order . . .

You-attitude (to individual): The desk chair you ordered . . .

You-attitude (to a large store): Your invoice #783329 . . .

3. Don't talk about feelings, except to congratulate or offer sympathy.

In most business situations, your feelings are irrelevant and should be omitted.

Lacks you-attitude: We are happy to extend you a credit line of $10,000.

You-attitude: You can now charge up to $10,000 on your American Express card.

It *is* appropriate to talk about your own emotions in a message of congratulations or condolence.

You-attitude: Congratulations on your promotion to district manager! I was really pleased to read about it.

Exercising Empathy for Employees and Customers

Although the concept of happy employees leading to happy customers is not new, it is experiencing a resurgence in many different industries. For example, call centers are allowing seasoned employees to work at home while a grocery chain is giving employees a profit-sharing plan that rewards them for excellent customer service.

Companies are finding creative ways to help employees identify with customers. USAA, an insurance agency for the military, provides new employees with MREs (meals ready to eat) during orientation so they will better understand the lifestyle of the members they serve.

Cabela's, an outdoor outfitter, encourages employees to use products they sell by loaning items free of charge in exchange for writing reviews on a company system. The loans are good perks for employees, and they help staff understand the issues customers may have with the products.

At Four Seasons Hotels, employees receive free overnight stays and meals at the hotel for themselves and a guest. They gain a customer's perspective on the hotel, but they also grade the hotel on various services.

The companies exercising empathy for employees and customers believe their customer service helps set them apart from other organizations.

Adapted from Jena McGregor, "Customer Service Champs," *BusinessWeek*, March 5, 2007, 52.

Don't talk about your audience's feelings, either. It's distancing to have others tell us how we feel—especially if they are wrong.

Lacks you-attitude: You'll be happy to hear that Open Grip Walkway Channels meet OSHA requirements.

You-attitude: Open Grip Walkway Channels meet OSHA requirements.

Maybe the audience expects that anything you sell would meet government regulations (OSHA—the Occupational Safety and Health Administration—is a federal agency). The audience may even be disappointed if they expected higher standards. Simply explain the situation or describe a product's features; don't predict the audience's response.

When you have good news, simply give the good news.

Lacks you-attitude: You'll be happy to hear that your scholarship has been renewed.

You-attitude: Congratulations! Your scholarship has been renewed.

4. In positive situations, use *you* more often than *I*. Use *we* when it includes the audience. Talk about the audience, not you or your company.

Lacks you-attitude: We provide health insurance to all employees.

You-attitude: You receive health insurance as a full-time Procter & Gamble employee.

Most readers are tolerant of the word *I* in e-mail messages, which seem like conversation. But edit paper documents to use *I* rarely if at all. *I* suggests that you're concerned about personal issues, not about the organization's problems, needs, and opportunities. *We* works well when it includes the reader. Avoid *we* if it excludes the reader (as it would in a letter to a customer or supplier or as it might in a memo about what *we* in management want *you* to do).

5. In negative situations, avoid the word *you*. Protect your audience's ego. Use passive verbs and impersonal expressions to avoid assigning blame. When you report bad news or limitations, use a noun for a group of which your audience is a part instead of *you* so people don't feel that they're singled out for bad news.

Lacks you-attitude: You must get approval from the director before you publish any articles or memoirs based on your work in the agency.

You-attitude: Agency personnel must get approval from the director to publish any articles or memoirs based on their work at the agency.

Use passive verbs and impersonal expressions to avoid blaming people. **Passive verbs** describe the action performed on something, without necessarily saying who did it. (See Chapter 5 for a full discussion of passive verbs.) In most cases, active verbs are better. But when your audience is at fault, passive verbs may be useful to avoid assigning blame.

Impersonal expressions omit people and talk only about things. Normally, communication is most lively when it's about people—and most interesting to audiences when it's about them. When you have to report a mistake or bad news, however, you can protect your audience's ego by using an impersonal expression, one in which things, not people, do the acting.

Lacks you-attitude: You made no allowance for inflation in your estimate.

You-attitude (passive): No allowance for inflation has been made in this estimate.

You-attitude (impersonal): This estimate makes no allowance for inflation.

Hallmark is producing a new line of cards for common situations such as depression or chemotherapy. For example, "Get Well Soon," is not appropriate for someone who is battling cancer. Hallmark has changed the tone of their Journey's Collection to reflect the needs of their dual audiences—buyers and receivers of cards.

Source: David Twiddy, "Hallmark Tackles Real-Life Situations," *Chicago Tribune,* February 19, 2007, sec. Business.

A purist might say that impersonal expressions are illogical: An estimate, for example, is inanimate and can't "make" anything. In the pragmatic world of business writing, however, impersonal expressions help you convey criticism tactfully.

You-Attitude beyond the Sentence Level

Good messages apply you-attitude beyond the sentence level by using content and organization as well as style to build goodwill.

To create goodwill with content,

- Be complete. When you have lots of information to give, consider putting some details in an appendix, which may be read later.
- Anticipate and answer questions your audience is likely to have.
- Show why information your audience didn't ask for is important.
- Show your audience how the subject of your message affects them.

You-Attitude with International Audiences

When you communicate with international audiences, look at the world from their point of view.

The United States is in the middle of most of the maps sold in the United States. It isn't in the middle of maps sold elsewhere in the world.

The United States clings to a measurement system that has been abandoned by most of the world. When you write for international audiences, use the metric system.

Even pronouns and direction words need attention. *We* may not feel inclusive to readers with different assumptions and backgrounds. *Here* won't mean the same thing to a reader in Bonn as it does to one in Boulder.

Figure 3.1 A Letter Lacking You-Attitude

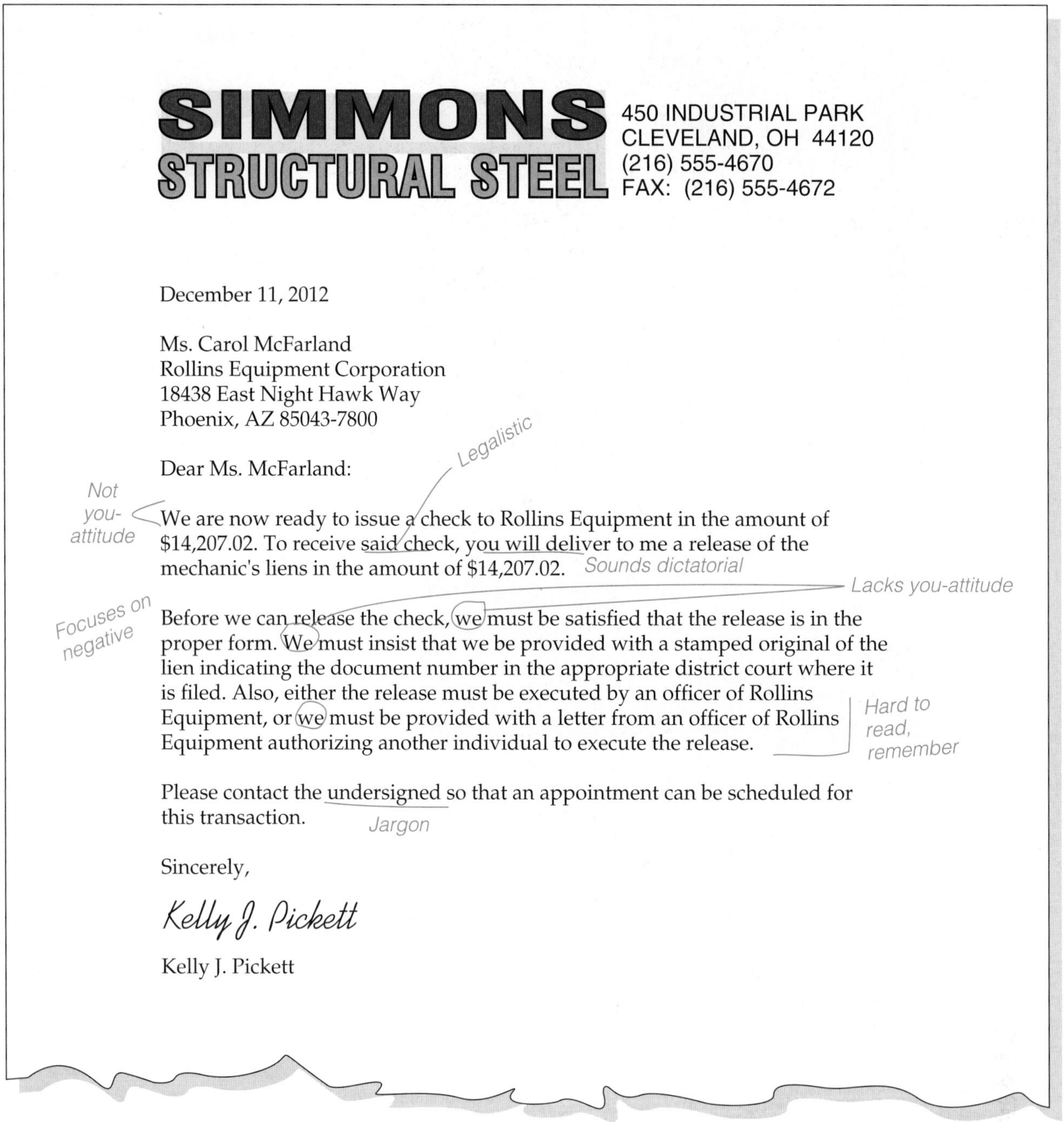

SIMMONS STRUCTURAL STEEL
450 INDUSTRIAL PARK
CLEVELAND, OH 44120
(216) 555-4670
FAX: (216) 555-4672

December 11, 2012

Ms. Carol McFarland
Rollins Equipment Corporation
18438 East Night Hawk Way
Phoenix, AZ 85043-7800

Dear Ms. McFarland:

We are now ready to issue a check to Rollins Equipment in the amount of $14,207.02. To receive said check, you will deliver to me a release of the mechanic's liens in the amount of $14,207.02.

Before we can release the check, we must be satisfied that the release is in the proper form. We must insist that we be provided with a stamped original of the lien indicating the document number in the appropriate district court where it is filed. Also, either the release must be executed by an officer of Rollins Equipment, or we must be provided with a letter from an officer of Rollins Equipment authorizing another individual to execute the release.

Please contact the undersigned so that an appointment can be scheduled for this transaction.

Sincerely,

Kelly J. Pickett

Kelly J. Pickett

To organize information to build goodwill,

- Put information your audience is most interested in first.
- Arrange information to meet your audience's needs, not yours.
- Use headings and lists so readers can find key points quickly.

Consider the letter in Figure 3.1. As the red marginal notes indicate, many individual sentences in this letter lack you-attitude. Fixing individual sentences could improve the letter. However, it really needs to be totally rewritten.

Figure 3.2 shows a possible revision of this letter. The revision is clearer, easier to read, and friendlier.

POSITIVE EMPHASIS LO 3-2

Some negatives are necessary. When you have bad news to give—announcements of layoffs, product defects and recalls, price increases—straightforward negatives build credibility. (See Chapter 10 on how to present bad news.) Sometimes negatives are needed to make people take a problem

Figure 3.2 A Letter Revised to Improve You-Attitude

SIMMONS STRUCTURAL STEEL

450 INDUSTRIAL PARK
CLEVELAND, OH 44120
(216) 555-4670
FAX: (216) 555-4672

December 11, 2012

Ms. Carol McFarland
Rollins Equipment Corporation
18438 East Night Hawk Way
Phoenix, AZ 85043-7800

Dear Ms. McFarland:

Let's clear up the lien in the Allen contract.

Starts with main point from the reader's point of view

Focuses on what reader gets

Rollins will receive a check for $14,207.02 when you give us a release for the mechanic's lien of $14,207.02. To assure us that the release is in the proper form,

1. Give us a stamped original of the lien indicating the document's district court number, and

2. Either
   a. Have an officer of Rollins Equipment sign the release
      or
   b. Give us a letter from a Rollins officer authorizing someone else to sign the release.

List makes it easy to see that reader needs to do two things—and that the second can be done in two ways.

Please call me to tell me which way is best for you.

Emphasizes reader's choice

Sincerely,

Kelly J. Pickett

Kelly J. Pickett
Extension 5318

Extension number makes it easy for reader to phone.

Defining Allowable Negatives

The Des Moines *Register* issued the following standards for contributors to its electronic forum:

"[The Des Moines *Register's*] new updated standards make the distinction between offensive opinion and offensive approach.

We will remove comments including these types of specific information or language:

- Libel. In general terms, that means a comment that includes a false statement of fact that actually harms a person's reputation (as opposed to insulting or offending them).
- Sexually explicit or crude sexual comments about someone.
- Threatening statements or statements that suggest violent acts against someone.
- Crude comments about a child.
- Swearing or obscenity.
- Derogatory phrases to define a group of people.
- Nasty name-calling (language such as "moron" and "white trash").

But we will allow opinions some will find offensive.

We will allow conversation that is simply strident in tone.

We will allow criticism of public officials.

We will allow criticism of people who are subjects of stories.

We will allow opinions that some may find offensive about tough social issues around race and sexual orientation, as long as they don't include the kind of specific language I just described."

Quoted from Carolyn Washburn, "Inviting Robust Conversation, but Spelling Out a Few Rules," *Des Moines Sunday Register,* April 15, 2007.

seriously. In some messages, such as disciplinary notices and negative performance appraisals, one of your purposes is to make the problem clear. Even here, avoid insults or attacks on your audience's integrity or sanity.

Sometimes negatives create a "reverse psychology" that makes people look favorably at your product. German power tool manufacturer Stihl advertises that its chain saws and other tools are *not* sold by chains like Lowe's or Home Depot. Instead, the company emphasizes that its products are sold through independent retailers. While the campaign risks offending potential customers by implying that shopping at big box stores means that they don't appreciate quality, Stihl insists that its high-end products are worth the prices that are charged by specialty stores.[5]

But in most situations, it's better to be positive. Researchers have found that businesspeople responded more positively to positive than to negative language and were more likely to say they would act on a positively worded request.[6] In ground-breaking research for Met Life, Martin Seligman found that optimistic salespeople sold 37% more insurance than pessimistic colleagues. As a result, Met Life began hiring optimists even when they failed to meet the company's other criteria. These "unqualified" optimists outsold pessimists 21% in their first year and 57% in the next.[7]

Positive emphasis is a way of looking at things. Is the bottle half empty or half full? You can create positive emphasis with the words, information, organization, and layout you choose. "Part-time" may be a negative phrase for someone seeking full-time employment, but it may also be a positive phrase for college students seeking limited work hours while they pursue their education. It may become even more positive if connected with flexible hours.

How to Create Positive Emphasis

Create positive emphasis by using the following techniques:

1. Avoid negative words and words with negative connotations.
2. Beware of hidden negatives.
3. Focus on what the audience can do rather than on limitations.
4. Justify negative information by giving a reason or linking it to an audience benefit.
5. Put the negative information in the middle and present it compactly.

Choose the technique that produces the clearest, most accurate communication.

1. Avoid negative words and words with negative connotations. Figure 3.3 lists some common negative words. If you find one of these words in a draft, try to substitute a more positive word. When you must use a negative, use the *least negative* term that will convey your meaning.

The following examples show how to replace negative words with positive words.

Negative:	We have failed to finish taking inventory.
Better:	We haven't finished taking inventory.
Still better:	We will be finished taking inventory Friday.
Negative:	If you can't understand this explanation, feel free to call me.
Better:	If you have further questions, just call me.
Still better:	Omit the sentence.

Figure 3.3 Negative Words to Avoid

afraid	impossible	**Some dis- words:**	**Many un- words:**
anxious	lacking	disapprove	unclear
avoid	loss	dishonest	unfair
bad	neglect	dissatisfied	unfortunate
careless	never		unfortunately
damage	no		unpleasant
delay	not	**Many in- words:**	unreasonable
delinquent	objection	inadequate	unreliable
deny	problem	incomplete	unsure
difficulty	reject	inconvenient	
eliminate	sorry	insincere	
error	terrible	injury	
except	trivial		
fail	trouble		
fault	wait	**Some mis- words:**	
fear	weakness	misfortune	
hesitate	worry	missing	
ignorant	wrong	mistake	
ignore			

Truly Friendly Skies

United pilot Denny Flanagan goes out of his way to create goodwill with his passengers and customers. He takes pictures of pets in cargo compartments and shows their owners that the pets are safely onboard. He phones the parents of unaccompanied minors to keep them up-to-date on delays. He hands out his business cards to all passengers, and the lucky ones with his signature on the back get free books, wine, or discount coupons. When his flights are delayed or diverted, he tries to find snacks like McDonald's hamburgers for his passengers. Before some of his delayed flights he is in the passenger lounge using his cellphone to help passengers with their connections. . . .

Captain Flanagan says, "I just treat everyone like it's the first flight they've ever flown. . . . The customer deserves a good travel experience."

One of those customers noted, "If other folks in the airline industry had the same attitude, it would go a long way to mitigating some of the negative stuff that has come about in the last four or five years."

Quoted from Scott McCartney, "To a United Pilot, The Friendly Skies Are a Point of Pride," *Wall Street Journal*, August 28, 2007, A1, A11. Copyright © 2007 by Dow Jones & Company, Inc. Reproduced with permission of Dow Jones & Company, Inc. via Copyright Clearance Center.

Omit double negatives.

Negative: Never fail to back up your documents.

Better: Always back up your documents.

When you must use a negative term, use the least negative word that is accurate.

Negative: Your balance of $835 is delinquent.

Better: Your balance of $835 is past due.

Getting rid of negatives has the added benefit of making what you write easier to understand. Sentences with three or more negatives are very hard to understand.[8]

2. Beware of hidden negatives. Some words are not negative in themselves but become negative in context. *But* and *however* indicate a shift, so, after a positive statement, they are negative. *I hope* and *I trust that* suggest that you aren't sure. *Patience* may sound like a virtue, but it is a necessary virtue only when things are slow. Even positives about a service or product may backfire if they suggest that in the past the service or product was bad.

Negative: I hope this is the information you wanted. [Implication: I'm not sure.]

Better: Enclosed is a brochure about road repairs scheduled for 2012.

Still better: The brochure contains a list of all roads and bridges scheduled for repair during 2012, specific dates when work will start, and alternate routes.

Negative: Please be patient as we switch to the automated system. [Implication: You can expect problems.]

Better: If you have questions during our transition to the automated system, call Melissa Morgan.

Still better: You'll be able to get information instantly about any house on the market when the automated system is in place. If you have questions during the transition, call Melissa Morgan.

Negative: Now Crispy Crunch tastes better. [Implication: it used to taste terrible.]

Better: Now Crispy Crunch tastes even better.

Removing negatives does not mean being arrogant or pushy.

Negative: I hope that you are satisfied enough to place future orders.

Arrogant: I look forward to receiving all of your future business.

Better: Whenever you need computer chips, a call to Mercury is all it takes for fast service.

When you eliminate negative words, be sure to maintain accuracy. Words that are exact opposites will usually not be accurate. Instead, use specifics to be both positive and accurate.

Negative: The exercycle is not guaranteed for life.

Not true: The exercycle is guaranteed for life.

True: The exercycle is guaranteed for 10 years.

Legal phrases also have negative connotations for most readers and should be avoided whenever possible.

3. Focus on what the audience can do rather than on limitations. When there are limits, or some options are closed, focus on the alternatives that remain.

Negative: We will not allow you to charge more than $5,000 on your VISA account.

Better: You can charge $5,000 on your new VISA card.

or: Your new VISA card gives you $5,000 in credit that you can use at thousands of stores nationwide.

As you focus on what will happen, check for **you-attitude.** In the last example, "We will allow you to charge $5,000" would be positive, but it lacks you-attitude.

When you have a benefit and a requirement the audience must meet to get the benefit, the sentence is usually more positive if you put the benefit first.

Negative: You will not qualify for the student membership rate of $55 a year unless you are a full-time student.

Better: You get all the benefits of membership for only $55 a year if you're a full-time student.

4. Justify negative information by giving a reason or linking it to an audience benefit. A reason can help your audience see that the information is necessary; a benefit can suggest that the negative aspect is outweighed by positive factors. Be careful, however, to make the logic behind your reason clear and to leave no loopholes.

Negative: We cannot sell individual pastel sets.

Loophole: To keep down packaging costs and to help you save on shipping and handling costs, we sell pastel sets in packages of 12.

Suppose the customer says, "I'll pay the extra shipping and handling. Send me six." If you truly sell only in packages of 12, you need to say so:

Better: To keep down packaging costs and to help customers save on shipping and handling costs, we sell pastel sets only in packages of 12.

If you link the negative element to a benefit, be sure it is a benefit your audience will acknowledge. Avoid telling people that you're doing things "for their own good." They may have a different notion of what their own good is. You may think you're doing customers a favor by limiting their credit so they don't get in over their heads and go bankrupt. They may think they'd

Truth Can Be Spoken in Different Ways

"One Iranian told a fable of an ancient king who had an ominous dream. In the dream the king saw himself aged and afflicted, with decaying and falling teeth. Calling together his court astrologers for an interpretation, the shaken king heard the first say, "Your Majesty, I regret to tell you that the interpretation must be bad. The dream means that you will die within a year." In a rage the king threw the brash astrologer out of his court and turned to the second man.

The second astrologer said, "Your Majesty, it is good news, the very best. It means that all your programs and projects will live on after you, and all your sons and daughters will survive you." The king, who was old and knew he might die soon, nevertheless was pleased with this interpretation and richly rewarded the astrologer."

Quoted from John P. Fieg and John G. Blair, *There Is a Difference: 12 Intercultural Perspectives* (Washington, DC: Meridian House International, 1975), 83.

Some stores might say, "Put books you don't want here." But bookseller Joseph-Beth in Lexington, KY, uses positive emphasis.

Four Ways to Say "Yes" Instead of "No"

"'Yes, I want to help.'
Even if you have to say no personally, there is usually an alternative yes. By helping to solve someone's problem—say, by referring them to someone who might be able to help them—you keep the positive energy in motion.

'Yes, you can do better.'
Rather than say, "This is terrible," it's a lot more motivating to say, "You do such terrific work. I'm not sure this is up to your caliber."

'Yes, I see you.'
It only takes a minute to send a thank-you note or respond to an unsolicited résumé.

'Yes, your talents lie elsewhere.'
Warren Buffet says that he's never fired anyone. He has just helped them to find the right job."

Quoted from Linda Kaplan Thaler and Robin Koval, *The Power of Nice: How to Conquer the Business World with Kindness* (New York: Currency, 2006), 84–87.

be better off with more credit so they could expand in hopes of making more sales and more profits.

5. Put the negative information in the middle and present it compactly. Put negatives at the beginning or end only if you want to emphasize the negative. To deemphasize a written negative, put it in the middle of a paragraph rather than in the first or last sentence and in the middle of the message rather than in the first or last paragraphs.

When a letter or memo runs several pages, remember that the bottom of the first page is also a position of emphasis, even if it is in the middle of a paragraph, because of the extra white space of the bottom margin. (The first page gets more attention because it is on top and the reader's eye may catch lines of the message even when he or she isn't consciously reading it; the tops and bottoms of subsequent pages don't get this extra attention.) If possible, avoid placing negative information at the bottom of the first page.

Giving a topic lots of space emphasizes it. Therefore, you can de-emphasize negative information by giving it as little space as possible. Give negative information only once in your message. Don't list negatives with bulleted or numbered lists. These lists take space and emphasize material.

How to Check Positive Emphasis

All five of the strategies listed above help create positive emphasis. However, you should always check to see that the positive emphasis is appropriate, sincere, and realistic.

So's Yer Old Man

It may not come as a surprise to you, but a Harvard professor's computerized study of congressional communications reveals that 27% of the time members of Congress are taunting each other.

The three categories the study expected to find were well-known to political scientists: claiming credit, taking a position, and "advertising" someone or something to get one's name out there. That members of Congress also spend a quarter of their time taunting each other came as a surprise. Taunting was most common among members with a relatively safe position.

Adapted from David A. Fahrenthold, "27% of Communication by Members of Congress Is Taunting, Professor Concludes," *Washington Post*, April 6, 2011, http://www.washingtonpost.com/politics/27percent-of-communication-by-members-of-congress-is-taunting-professor-concludes/2011/04/06/AF1no2qC_story.html.

As you read at the beginning of this section, positive emphasis is not always **appropriate.** Some bad news is so serious that presenting it with positive tone is insensitive, if not unethical. Layoffs, salary cuts, and product defects are all topics in this category.

Some positive emphasis is so overdone that it no longer seems **sincere.** The used-car sales rep selling a rusting auto is one stereotype of insincerity. A more common example for most business people is the employee who gushes praise through gritted teeth over your promotion. Most of us have experienced something similar, and we know how easy it is to see through the insincerity.

Positive emphasis can also be so overdone that it clouds the reality of the situation. If your company has two finalists for a sales award, and only one award, the loser does not have second place, which implies a second award. On the other hand, if all sales reps win the same award, top performers will feel unappreciated. Too much praise can also make mediocre employees think they are doing great. Keep your communications **realistic.**

Restraint can help make positive emphasis more effective. Conductor Otto Klemperer was known for not praising his orchestra. One day, pleased with a particularly good rehearsal, he spoke a brusque "good." His stunned musicians broke into spontaneous applause. Klemperer rapped his baton on his music stand to silence them and said, "Not *that* good."[9]

TONE, POWER, AND POLITENESS LO 3-3

Tone is the implied attitude of the communicator toward the audience. If the words of a document seem condescending or rude, tone is a problem. Norms for politeness are cultural and generational; they also vary from office to office.

Tone is tricky because it interacts with context and power. Language that is acceptable within one group may be unacceptable if used by someone outside the group. Words that might seem friendly from a superior to a subordinate may seem uppity if used by the subordinate to the superior. Similarly, words that may be neutral among peers may be seen as negative if sent by a superior to subordinate.

Paul Goward, the former police chief of Winter Haven, Florida, discovered this lesson about the connection between power and tone. Goward sent an e-mail to about 80 employees asking "Are You a Jelly Belly?" In the e-mail, he provided 10 reasons why his employees should be in better shape; the reasons ranged from health risks to department image. The e-mail added, "If you are unfit, do yourself and everyone else a favor. . . . See a professional about a proper diet. . . . Stop making excuses. . . . We didn't hire you unfit and we don't want you working unfit." The e-mail so offended employees that Goward was forced to resign.[10]

Using the proper tone with employees can have huge economic impact for a business. A Litigation Trends Survey, based on reports from 310 in-house counsel, found employee lawsuits to be the top litigation concern of corporate lawyers. Disgruntled employees are suing more than ever before, and disputes over wages or hours frequently can be brought as class actions, making them even more expensive.[11]

The desirable tone for business writing is businesslike but not stiff, friendly but not phony, confident but not arrogant, polite but not groveling. Several guidelines will help you achieve the tone you want.

Use Courtesy Titles for People You Don't Know Well

Most U.S. organizations use first names for everyone, whatever their age or rank. But many people don't like being called by their first names by people they don't know or by someone much younger. When you talk or write to people outside your organization, use first names only if you've established a personal relationship. If you don't know someone well, use a courtesy title (see *pages 71–72* for more on courtesy titles):

Dear Mr. Reynolds:

Dear Ms. Lee:

Be Aware of the Power Implications of the Words You Use

"Thank you for your cooperation" is generous coming from a superior to a subordinate; it's not appropriate in a message to your superior. Different ways of asking for action carry different levels of politeness.[12]

Order: (lowest politeness)	Turn in your time card by Monday.
Polite order: (midlevel politeness)	Please turn in your time card by Monday.
Indirect request: (higher politeness)	Time cards should be turned in by Monday.
Question: (highest politeness)	Would you be able to turn in your time card by Monday?

Higher levels of politeness may be unclear. In some cases, a question may seem like a request for information to which it's acceptable to answer, "No, I can't." In other cases, it will be an order, simply phrased in polite terms.

You need more politeness if you're asking for something that will inconvenience the audience and help you more than the person who does the action. Generally, you need less politeness when you're asking for something small, routine, or to the audience's benefit. Some discourse communities, however, prefer that even small requests be made politely.

Lower politeness:	To start the scheduling process, please describe your availability for meetings during the second week of the month.
Higher politeness:	Could you let me know what times you'd be free for a meeting the second week of the month?

Solving an Ethical Dilemma Using Goodwill

Most ethical dilemmas boil down to people, balancing the needs or desires of one constituency against those of another: Management versus staff, stockholders versus customers.

Toro, maker of lawnmowers, faced such a dilemma. One of its popular riding mowers is very hard to overturn, but when it does, it can seriously injure the driver. Toro decided to install roll bars behind the driver's seat on new machines but not raise the price because the bars were added for safety.

Then an even harder issue arose. Shouldn't the same ethical treatment be offered on machines already owned? Those owners would be protected but the cost would adversely affect shareholders.

What would you do? Toro installed the bars for all mowers, new and used, a decision they believed would best serve users and shareholders in the long term.

Adapted from Kevin Cashman, "What Exactly Is Ethics?" *Forbes*, March 3, 2007, http://www.forbes.com/2007/03/03/leadership-cashman-ethics-leadership-citizen-cx_kc_0305ethics.html.

Attempts To Create a Unisex Pronoun

For more than 150 years, people have attempted to coin a unisex pronoun. None of the attempts has been successful.

Date	he or she	his or her	him or her
1850	ne	nis	nim
1884	le	lis	lim
1938	se	sim	sis
1970	ve	vis	ver
1977	e	e's	em
1988	ala	alis	alum

Adapted from Dennis E. Baron, "The Epicene Pronoun: Word That Failed," *American Speech* 56 (1981): 83–97; and Ellen Graham, "Business Bulletin," *Wall Street Journal*, December 29, 1988, A1.

REDUCING BIAS IN BUSINESS COMMUNICATION LO 3-4

According to the U.S. Census Bureau, the United States now has more women than men, and more women than men are attending college and attaining postsecondary degrees. The Hispanic population is the fastest growing in the country; it numbered 50.5 million in the 2010 census. Four states (California, Hawaii, New Mexico, and Texas) plus the District of Columbia have a "majority–minority" population, where more than 50% are part of a minority group. The number of people 65 and older is also growing; that population now numbers over 40 million, and 6.5 million of them are still in the workforce.[13] These figures highlight the growing diversity of the workplace and the need to communicate with appropriate language.

Bias-free language is language that does not discriminate against people on the basis of sex, physical condition, race, ethnicity, age, religion or any other category. It includes all audience members, helps to sustain goodwill, is fair and friendly, and complies with the law.

Check to be sure that your language is bias-free. Doing so is ethical; it can also avoid major problems and lawsuits.

- Josef Ackermann, chief executive of Deutsche Bank, was mocked in the international news when he said at a news conference that including women on the bank's all-male executive board would make it "more colorful and prettier too." The publicity added to mistrust of the bank at an awkward time when it was lobbying to dissuade German policy makers from imposing restrictions.[14]
- Conservative advice expert Dr. Laura Schlessinger resigned abruptly from her syndicated radio show after a controversy arising from her multiple use of a racial epithet while talking to an African American caller.
- Famous radio personality Don Imus was fired by CBS after making racist comments about the Rutgers University women's basketball team.

Making Language Nonsexist

Nonsexist language treats both sexes neutrally. Check to be sure that your messages are free from sexism in four areas: job titles, courtesy titles and names, pronouns, and other words and phrases.

Job titles Use neutral titles which do not imply that a job is held only by men or only by women. Many job titles are already neutral: *accountant, banker, doctor, engineer, inspector, manager, nurse, pilot, secretary, technician,* to name a few. Other titles reflect gender stereotypes and need to be changed.

Instead of	Use
Businessman	A specific title: executive, accountant, department head, owner of a small business, men and women in business, businessperson
Chairman	Chair, chairperson, moderator
Fireman	Firefighter
Foreman	Supervisor
Mailman	Mail Carrier
Salesman	Salesperson, sales representative
Waitress	Server
Woman lawyer	Lawyer
Workman	Worker, employee. Or use a specific title: crane operator, bricklayer, etc.

Courtesy titles and names E-mails to people you know normally do not use courtesy titles. However, letters, memos, and e-mails to people with whom you have a more formal relationship require courtesy titles in the salutation *unless* you're on a first-name basis with your reader. (See Appendix A for examples of memo and letter formats.)

When you know your reader's name and gender, use courtesy titles that do not indicate marital status: *Mr.* for men and *Ms.* for women. *Ms.* is particularly useful when you do not know what a woman's marital status is. However, even when you happen to know that a woman is married or single, **you still use *Ms.*** unless you know that she prefers another title. There are, however, two exceptions:

1. If the woman has a professional title, use that title if you would use it for a man.

   Dr. Kristen Sorenson is our new company physician.

   The Rev. Elizabeth Townsley gave the invocation.

2. If the woman prefers to be addressed as *Mrs.* or *Miss,* use the title she prefers rather than Ms. (You-attitude takes precedence over nonsexist language: address the reader as she—or he—prefers to be addressed.) To find out if a woman prefers a traditional title,

- Check the signature block in previous correspondence. If a woman types her name as *(Miss) Elaine Anderson* or *(Mrs.) Kay Royster,* use the title she designates.
- Notice the title a woman uses in introducing herself on the phone. If she says, "This is Robin Stine," use Ms. when you write to her. If she says, "I'm Mrs. Stine," use the title she specifies.
- When you're writing job letters or crucial correspondence, call the company and ask the receptionist which title your reader prefers.

In addition to using parallel courtesy titles, use parallel forms for names.

Not Parallel	Parallel
Members of the committee will be Mr. Jones, Mr. Yacone, and Lisa.	Members of the committee will be Mr. Jones, Mr. Yacone, and Ms. Melton. or Members of the committee will be Irving, Ted, and Lisa.

When you know your reader's name but not the gender, either

- Call the company and ask the receptionist, or
- Use the reader's full name in the salutation:

  Dear Chris Crowell:

  Dear J. C. Meath:

Booming Business

As the 78 million U.S. baby boomers age, more and more companies are making products with adaptations for physical infirmities:

- Appliance control panels with adjustable typefaces and color combinations.
- Ovens, dishwashers, and washer/dryer sets mounted higher so people have to bend over less.
- Sink fixtures with levers instead of knobs, for hands with limited mobility.
- Cellphones with large keys and large numbers on the screen.

Nissan and Ford Motor Companies fit their design engineers with special body suits that mimic aging bodies. The suits have an expanded waist, limited mobility in key joints, and goggles that mimic the effect of cataracts.

Marketing these new features requires a delicate touch, because no one likes to be reminded that their body is failing.

When you know neither the reader's name nor gender, you have three options:

- Omit the salutation and use a subject line in its place. (See Figure A.4, Simplified Format.)
  SUBJECT: RECOMMENDATION FOR BEN WANDELL
- Use the reader's position or job title:
  Dear Loan Officer:
  Dear Registrar:
- Use a general group to which your reader belongs:
  Dear Investor:
  Dear Admissions Committee:

Pronouns When you refer to a specific person, use the appropriate gender pronouns:

In his speech, John Jones said that . . .

In her speech, Judy Jones said that . . .

When you are referring not to a specific person but to anyone who may be in a given job or position, traditional gender pronouns are sexist.

Sexist: a. Each supervisor must certify that the time sheet for his department is correct.

Sexist: b. When the nurse fills out the accident report form, she should send one copy to the Central Division Office.

Business communication uses four ways to eliminate sexist generic pronouns: use plurals, use second-person *you,* revise the sentence to omit the pronoun, or use pronoun pairs. Whenever you have a choice of two or more ways to make a phrase or sentence nonsexist, choose the alternative that is the smoothest and least conspicuous.

The following examples use these methods to revise sentences *a* and *b* above.

1. Use plural nouns and pronouns.

   Nonsexist: a. Supervisors must certify that the time sheets for their departments are correct.

   Note: When you use plural nouns and pronouns, other words in the sentence may need to be made plural too. In the example above, plural supervisors have plural time sheets and departments.

   Avoid mixing singular nouns and plural pronouns.

   Nonsexist but lacks agreement: b. When the nurse fills out the accident report, they should send one copy to the Central Division Office.

   Since *nurse* is singular, it is incorrect to use the plural *they* to refer to it. The resulting lack of agreement is acceptable orally but is not yet acceptable in writing. Instead, use one of the other ways to make the sentence nonsexist.

2. Use *you.*

   Nonsexist: a. You must certify that the time sheet for your department is correct.

   Nonsexist: b. When you fill out an accident report form, send one copy to the Central Division Office.

   You is particularly good for instructions and statements of the responsibilities of someone in a given position.

3. Substitute an article (*a, an,* or *the*) for the pronoun, or revise the sentence so that the pronoun is unnecessary.

Nonsexist: a. The supervisor must certify that the time sheet for the department is correct.

Nonsexist: b. The nurse will
1. Fill out the accident report form.
2. Send one copy of the form to the Central Division Office.

4. When you must focus on the action of an individual, use pronoun pairs.

Nonsexist: a. The supervisor must certify that the time sheet for his or her department is correct.

Nonsexist: b. When the nurse fills out the accident report form, he or she should send one copy to the Central Division Office.

Other words and phrases If you find any terms similar to those in the first column in Figure 3.4 in your messages or your company's documents, replace them with terms similar to those in the second column.

Not every word containing *man* is sexist. For example, *manager* is not sexist. The word comes from the Latin *manus* meaning *hand;* it has nothing to do with maleness.

Avoid terms that assume that everyone is married or is heterosexual.

Biased: You and your husband or wife are cordially invited to the reception.

Better: You and your guest are cordially invited to the reception.

Making Language Nonracist and Nonageist

Language is **nonracist** and **nonageist** when it treats all races and ages fairly, avoiding negative stereotypes of any group. Use the following guidelines to check for bias in documents you write or edit.

Give someone's race or age only if it is relevant to your story. When you do mention these characteristics, give them for everyone in your story—not just the non-Caucasian, non-young-to-middle-aged adults you mention.

Figure 3.4 Getting Rid of Sexist Terms and Phrases

Instead of	Use	Because
The girl at the front desk	The woman's name or job title: "Ms. Browning," "Rosa," "the receptionist"	Call female employees *women* just as you call male employees *men.* When you talk about a specific woman, use her name, just as you use a man's name to talk about a specific man.
The ladies on our staff	The women on our staff	Use parallel terms for males and females. Therefore, use *ladies* only if you refer to the males on your staff as *gentlemen.* Few businesses do, since social distinctions are rarely at issue.
Manpower Manhours Manning	Personnel Hours or worker hours Staffing	The power in business today comes from both women and men.
Managers and their wives	Managers and their guests	Managers may be female; not everyone is married.

New Technology Access for People with Visual and Hearing Impairments

In October 2010, President Obama signed into law a bill aimed at making technologies that are staples of life more accessible. The law mandates

- Easier Internet connections on smart phones.
- Audible descriptions of action on TV.
- Captions for dialogue on TV.
- TV remotes with buttons or switches for easier access to closed captioning.
- Equipment compatible with hearing aids for Internet phone calls.

Adapted from "Bill Will Improve Technology Access for Blind, Deaf," *Des Moines Register*, October 9, 2010, 3A.

Organizations are making their business sites more accommodating to people with disabilities.

Refer to a group by the term it prefers. As preferences change, change your usage. Fifty years ago, *Negro* was preferred as a more dignified term than *colored* for African Americans. As times changed, *Black* and *African American* replaced it. Gallup polls show that the majority of black Americans (about 60%) have no preference between the two terms. However, among those who do care, polls show a slight trend toward African American.[15]

Oriental has now been replaced by *Asian*.

The term *Latino* is the most acceptable group term to refer to Mexican Americans, Cuban Americans, Puerto Ricans, Dominicans, Brazilianos, and other people with Central and Latin American backgrounds. (*Latina* is the term for an individual woman.) Better still is to refer to the precise group. The differences among various Latino groups are at least as great as the differences among Italian Americans, Irish Americans, Armenian Americans, and others descended from various European groups.

Baby boomers, older people, and *mature customers* are more generally accepted terms than *Senior Citizens* or *Golden Agers.*

Avoid terms that suggest that competent people are unusual. The statement "She is an intelligent purple woman" suggests that the writer expects most purple women to be stupid. "He is an asset to his race" suggests that excellence in the race is rare. "He is a spry 70-year-old" suggests that the writer is amazed that anyone that old can still move.

Talking about People with Disabilities and Diseases

A disability is a physical, mental, sensory, or emotional impairment that interferes with the major tasks of daily living. According to the U.S. Census Bureau, 19% of Americans currently have a disability; of those, about 48% who were 21–64 and had a "nonsevere disability" were employed full-time.[16] The number of people with disabilities will rise as the population ages.

To keep trained workers, more and more companies are making accommodations for disabilties. Companies such as Sylvania, American Express, and

General Motors are offering accommodations such as telecommuting, flexible hours, workshift changes, and assignment changes.[17]

When talking about people with disabilities, use **people-first language** to focus on the person, not the condition. People-first language names the person first, then adds the condition. Use it instead of the traditional noun phrases that imply the condition defines the person. In 2010, President Obama signed Rosa's Law, which replaces "mentally retarded" with "an individual with an intellectual disability," in most federal statutes.[18]

Instead of	Use	Because
The mentally retarded	People with an intellectual disability	The condition does not define the person or his or her potential.
Cancer patients	People being treated for cancer	

Avoid negative terms, unless the audience prefers them. You-attitude takes precedence over positive emphasis: use the term a group prefers. People who lost their hearing as infants, children, or young adults often prefer to be called *deaf*, or *Deaf* in recognition of Deafness as a culture. But people who lose their hearing as older adults often prefer to be called *hard of hearing*, even when their hearing loss is just as great as that of someone who identifies him- or herself as part of the Deaf culture.

Using the right term requires keeping up with changing preferences. If your target audience is smaller than the whole group, use the term preferred by that audience, even if the group as a whole prefers another term.

Some negative terms, however, are never appropriate. Negative terms such as *afflicted, suffering from,* and *struck down* also suggest an outdated view of any illness as a sign of divine punishment.

Instead of	Use	Because
Confined to a wheelchair	Uses a wheelchair	Wheelchairs enable people to escape confinement.
AIDS victim	Person with AIDS	Someone can have a disease without being victimized by it.
Abnormal	Atypical	People with disabilities are atypical but not necessarily abnormal.

Choosing Bias-Free Photos and Illustrations

When you produce a document with photographs or illustrations, check the visuals for possible bias. Do they show people of both sexes and all races? Is there a sprinkling of various kinds of people (younger and older, people using wheelchairs, etc.)? It's OK to have individual pictures that have just one sex or one race; the photos as a whole do not need to show exactly 50% men and 50% women. But the general impression should suggest that diversity is welcome and normal.

Check relationships and authority figures as well as numbers. If all the men appear in business suits and the women in maids' uniforms, the pictures are sexist even if an equal number of men and women are pictured. If the only nonwhites pictured are factory workers, the photos support racism even when an equal number of people from each race are shown.

R-E-S-P-E-C-T

"Most major airlines and hotel chains provide disability training to employees. . . . I recognize when someone has been trained—to offer me a Braille menu, use my name when addressing me, or take a moment to orient me to a new environment. What I appreciate even more, though, is . . . simple, common courtesy.

"I don't care how many pages in an employee manual somewhere are devoted to . . . the dos and don'ts of interacting with someone who is deaf, blind, or mentally retarded. Among hundreds of experiences in airports and hotels, the one distinction that separates the (mostly) pleasing from the (occasionally) painful in my encounters has been the honest friendliness and respect with which I have or have not been treated.

"Ask me where I'd like to sit, whether I need help getting there, and what other kinds of help I need.

"Please, assume that I know more about my disability than anyone else ever could.

"Respect me as you do any other customer who is paying for the same service, and have the grace to apologize if something does go wrong.

"Too many companies, it seems to me, are busy shaking in their boots over the imagined high cost of accommodating people with disabilities when, in many instances, a good old-fashioned refresher course in manners would cover most bases."

Quoted from Deborah Kendrick, "Disabled Resent Being Patronized," *Columbus Dispatch*, July 21, 1996, 3B. Reprinted with permission.

SUMMARY OF KEY POINTS

- **You-attitude** is a style of communication that looks at things from the audience's point of view, emphasizing what the audience wants to know, respecting the audience's intelligence, and protecting the audience's ego.
  1. Talk about the audience, not about yourself.
  2. Refer to the audience's request or order specifically.
  3. Don't talk about feelings except to congratulate or offer sympathy.
  4. In positive situations, use *you* more often than *I*. Use *we* when it includes the audience.
  5. In negative situations, avoid the word *you*. Protect the audience's ego. Use passive verbs and impersonal expressions to avoid assigning blame.
- Apply you-attitude beyond the sentence level by using organization and content as well as style to build goodwill.
- **Positive emphasis** means focusing on the positive rather than the negative aspects of a situation. To create positive emphasis
  1. Avoid negative words and words with negative connotations.
  2. Beware of hidden negatives.
  3. Focus on what the audience can do rather than on limitations.
  4. Justify negative information by giving a reason or linking it to an audience benefit.
  5. Put the negative information in the middle and present it compactly.
- Check to see that your positive emphasis is appropriate, sincere, and clear.
- The desirable tone for business communication is businesslike but not stiff, friendly but not phony, confident but not arrogant, polite but not groveling.
- Bias-free language is fair and friendly; it complies with the law. It includes all members of your audience; it helps sustain goodwill.
- Check to be sure that your language is nonsexist, nonracist, and nonageist.
- Communication should be free from sexism in four areas: job titles, courtesy titles and names, pronouns, and other words and phrases.
- *Ms.* is the nonsexist courtesy title for women. Whether or not you know a woman's marital status, use *Ms. unless* the woman has a professional title or unless you know that she prefers a traditional title.
- Four ways to make pronouns nonsexist are to use plurals, to use *you*, to revise the sentence to omit the pronoun, and to use pronoun pairs.
- When you talk about people with disabilities or diseases, use the term they prefer.
- When you produce newsletters or other documents with photos and illustrations, picture a sampling of the whole population, not just part of it.

CHAPTER 3 Exercises and Problems

**Go to www.mhhe.com/locker10e for additional Exercises and Problems.*

3.1 Reviewing the Chapter

1. What are five ways to create you-attitude? (LO 3-1)
2. What are five ways to create positive emphasis? (LO 3-2)
3. How can you improve the tone of business messages? (LO 3-3)
4. What are different categories to keep in mind when you are trying to reduce bias in business messages? (LO 3-4)
5. What techniques can you use when you are trying to reduce bias in business messages? (LO 3-4)

3.2 Evaluating the Ethics of Positive Emphasis

The first term in each pair is negative; the second is a positive term that is sometimes substituted for it. Which of the positive terms seem ethical? Which seem unethical? Briefly explain your choices.

cost	investment
second mortgage	home equity loan
tax	user fee
nervousness	adrenaline
problem	challenge
price increase	price change
for-profit hospital	tax-paying hospital
used car	pre-owned car
credit card fees	usage charges

3.3 Eliminating Negative Words and Words with Negative Connotations

Revise each of the following sentences to replace negative words with positive ones. Be sure to keep the meaning of the original sentence.

1. You will lose customer goodwill if you are slow in handling returns and issuing refunds.
2. Do not put any paper in this box that is not recyclable.
3. When you write a report, do not make claims that you cannot support with evidence.
4. Don't drop in without an appointment. Your counselor or case worker may be unavailable.
5. I am anxious to discuss my qualifications in an interview.

3.4 Focusing on the Positive

Revise each of the following sentences to focus on the options that remain, not those that are closed off.

1. Scholarship applications that arrive December 1 or later cannot be processed.
2. You cannot use flextime unless you have the consent of your supervisor.
3. As a first-year employee, you are not eligible for dental insurance.
4. I will be out of the country October 25 to November 10 and will not be able to meet with you then.
5. You will not get your first magazine for at least four weeks.

3.5 Identifying Hidden Negatives

Identify the hidden negatives in the following sentences and revise to eliminate them. In some cases, you may need to add information to revise the sentence effectively.

1. The seminar will help you become a better manager.
2. Thank you for the confidence you have shown in us by ordering one of our products. It will be shipped to you soon.
3. This publication is designed to explain how your company can start a recycling program.
4. I hope you find the information in this brochure beneficial to you and a valuable reference as you plan your move.
5. In thinking about your role in our group, I remember two occasions where you contributed something.
6. [In job letter] This job in customer service is so good for me; I am so ready to take on responsibility.

3.6 Improving You-Attitude and Positive Emphasis

Revise these sentences to improve you-attitude and positive emphasis. Eliminate any awkward phrasing. In some cases, you may need to add information to revise the sentence effectively.

1. You'll be happy to learn that the cost of tuition will not rise next year.
2. Although I was only an intern and didn't actually make presentations to major clients, I was required to prepare PowerPoint slides for the meetings and to answer some of the clients' questions.
3. At DiYanni Homes we have more than 30 plans that we will personalize just for you.

4. Please notify HR of your bank change as soon as possible to prevent a disruption of your direct deposit.
5. I'm sorry you were worried. You did not miss the deadline for signing up for a flexible medical spending account.
6. We are in the process of upgrading our website. Please bear with us.
7. You will be happy to hear that our cellphone plan does not charge you for incoming calls.
8. The employee discount may only be used for purchases for your own use or for gifts; you may not buy items for resale. To prevent any abuse of the discount privilege, you may be asked to justify your purchase.
9. I apologize for my delay in answering your inquiry. The problem was that I had to check with our suppliers to see whether we could provide the item in the quantity you say you want. We can.
10. If you mailed a check with your order, as you claim, we failed to receive it.
11. This job sounds perfect for me.

3.7 Eliminating Biased Language

Explain the source of bias in each of the following, and revise to remove the bias.

1. We recommend hiring Jim Ryan and Elizabeth Shuman. Both were very successful summer interns. Jim drafted the report on using rap music in ads, and Elizabeth really improved the looks of the office.
2. All sales associates and their wives are invited to the picnic.
3. Although he is blind, Mr. Morin is an excellent group leader.
4. Unlike many blacks, Yvonne has extensive experience designing web pages.
5. Chris Renker
   Pacific Perspectives
   6300 West Corondad Blvd.
   Los Angles, CA
   Gentlemen:
6. Enrique Torres has very good people skills for a man.
7. *Parenting 2012* shows you how to persuade your husband to do his share of child care chores.
8. Mr. Paez, Mr. O'Connor, and Tonya will represent our office at the convention.
9. Sue Corcoran celebrates her 50th birthday today. Stop by her cubicle at noon to get a piece of cake and to help us sing "The Old Grey Mare Just Ain't What She Used to Be."
10. Because older customers tend to be really picky, we will need to give a lot of details in our ads.

3.8 Analyzing You-Attitude

Your book gives some examples of occasions when you-attitude is inappropriate. What are some other examples? Why are they inappropriate? How would you fix them?

3.9 Analyzing Positive Tone

LaQuinta ran a series of ads using cartoons, like the one on this page, featuring people making the best of disasters. You can see the whole series at this website: http://www.lq.com/lq/brightside/index.jsp.

What do you think of these ads? Does the use of negatives help or hinder them? What overall impression of LaQuinta do the ads leave with you?

wake up on the bright side
SALES 2006
"WELL ... LOOKS LIKE MY LAPTOP'S FRIED. BUT WHAT A FANTASTIC OPPORTUNITY FOR A LITTLE VENTRILOQUISM."
For reservations, visit LQ.com

Reprinted with permission.

3.10 Analyzing Goodwill

A recent study by a law professor shows that credit card companies make offers to people fresh out of bankruptcy. In the study of 341 families, almost 100% received credit card offers within a year after completing bankruptcy proceedings, and 87% of those offers mentioned the bankruptcy proceedings. In fact, 20% of the offers came from companies the family had owed before the bankruptcy.

In small groups, discuss whether you think this practice is ethical. Why or why not? What reasons exist for not offering new credit to people who have just gone through bankruptcy? Why might such people need new credit cards?

Adapted from Marie Beaudette, "Study: Credit Card Offers Flood Once-Bankrupt Consumers," *Des Moines Register*, August 10, 2007, 6D.

3.11 Analyzing Ethics

[Female lawyers and their female corporate clients recently had a "shoe event" at a Manhattan boutique to network.]

"Such women-only networking events are proliferating at law firms and an array of other companies, including [accounting, investing, and industrial companies]. There are spa retreats, conferences at resorts, evenings at art galleries and cooking demonstrations, all organized by women who want to network and socialize with clients in their own way—at least some of the time.

"The top brass at such companies support the events for several reasons, most notably, they help to boost the bottom line. . . .

"Still, holding women-only networking events raises some complicated issues. Are these single-sex events just as exclusionary as the traditional spectator sports events and steak-and-cigar dinners have been for men? What about women who have male clients and vice versa?"

How do you feel about women-only events? Are they ethical?

Quoted from Carol Hymowitz, "High Power and High Heels: Companies Move beyond Sports, Steak and Scotch to Cultivate New Clients," *Wall Street Journal*, March 26, 2007, B1.

3.12 Analyzing a Form Letter

Analyze the following form letter.

Is it a goodwill message?

Where does it show you-attitude? Where does it need more you-attitude?

Evaluate the use of positive tone.

What is your overall impression of the letter?

Debbie Harrington
1436 Gooden Road
Lincoln, NE 54367

THE FOLLOWING INFORMATION IS TIME SENSITIVE; PLEASE REVIEW CAREFULLY

James Honda of Lincoln has partnered with Automobile Resellers, Inc., to replenish drastically reduced vehicle inventories. James Honda of Lincoln is in need of a number of high-demand pre-owned vehicles and records indicate that you may own one of these vehicles. Your 2007 Honda Civic has been classified as a high-demand vehicle. The purpose of this letter is to request the opportunity to BUY BACK your vehicle for perhaps more than you thought possible.

Bring this letter for admittance to this event. Simply present it to a dealership representative who will assist you in this BUY BACK process. Also, you may have won up to $20,000. To see if your claim number is a guaranteed cash prize winner, simply visit James Honda of Lincoln on the event date and claim your prize.

During this exciting event, James Honda of Lincoln has agreed to aggressively price its entire inventory of new and pre-owned cars, trucks, vans, and sport utilities. With rates as low as 0% and rebates up to $5,000, we are confident that you can upgrade your 2007 Honda Civic and in many cases reduce your current monthly payment with little out-of-pocket expense.

Due to the nature of this event it will not be advertised to the general public. Your status as a customer as well as your possession of a high-demand vehicle entitles you to attend this exciting event.

Appointments are recommended due to the anticipated response of this event. To schedule an appointment or if you are unable to attend on the below event date, please contact James Honda of Lincoln toll-free at 800.123.4567.

EVENT DATE:
Saturday, Nov 21st—9:00 a.m. to 6:00 p.m.

EVENT SITE:
JAMES HONDA OF LINCOLN
220 Kitty Hawk
Lincoln, NE 54367

As your instructor directs,

- Share your findings orally with a small group of students.
- Share your findings orally with the class.
- Post your findings in an e-mail to the class.
- Summarize your findings in a memo to your instructor.

3.13 Revising a Form Letter

Revise this form letter to improve positive tone and you-attitude (and to catch spelling and punctuation errors):

Dear customer,

We wish you a Happy New Year from Happy Catalog. Its been awhile since we heard from you. We have a special offer to welcome you back.

Our customers are the focus of what we do. All of our efforts center on exceeding our customer expectations.

Happy Catalog stands behind everything we sell, as we have since 1986. We will provide you with even better service, tailored to meet you needs and guaranteed to offer more of the helpful, unique and hard to find merchandise we're known for. Whether you choose to shop by phone, mail, or e-mail us, we promise to continually improve our process to better serve you. If you have been disappointed in any way, please accept our sincerest apology.

We have a special offer, exclusively for you, to welcome you back. When you use the enclosed coupon, you'll save 20% on any order, regardless of order size. Hurry, this offer will expire the beginning of February.

Welcome back! Thank you for your business.

Sincerly,
I. M. President
Happy Catalog.

3.14 Advising a Hasty Subordinate

Three days ago, one of your subordinates forwarded to everyone in the office a bit of e-mail humor he'd received from a friend. Titled "You know you're Southern when . . . ," the message poked fun at Southern speech, attitudes, and lifestyles. Today you get this message from your subordinate:

> Subject: Should I Apologize?
>
> I'm getting flamed left and right because of the Southern message. I thought it was funny, but some people just can't take a joke. So far I've tried not to respond to the flames, figuring that would just make things worse. But now I'm wondering if I should apologize. What do you think?

Answer the message.

3.15 Responding to a Complaint

You're Director of Corporate Communications; the employee newsletter is produced by your office. Today you get this e-mail message from Caroline Huber:

> Subject: Complaint about Sexist Language
>
> The article about the "Help Desk" says that Martina Luna and I "are the key customer service representatives 'manning' the desk." I don't MAN anything! I WORK.

Respond to Caroline. And send a message to your staff, reminding them to edit newsletter stories as well as external documents to replace biased language.

3.16 Exploring the Positive Effects of Negative Messages

In 2004, Gap Inc. (Gap, Old Navy, and Banana Republic) released a social responsibility report that acknowledged wage, health, and safety violations in many of its overseas factories. Rather than hiding this information, Gap chose to go public and address the problem. In 2006, Ford Motor Company released a series of online documentaries about the company's turnaround efforts which included a film about the company stock receiving a "sell" rating from industry analysts.

Find an example of a company that has shared its problems and its plans to solve those problems with the public. What went wrong? How did the company respond? How did the company report the problem? Can you find the current status of the company and its recovery?

As your instructor directs,

a. Share your findings orally with a small group of students.
b. Post your findings in an e-mail to the class.
c. Summarize your findings in a memo to your instructor.
d. Join with a group of students to create a written report summarizing negative corporate news.

Adapted from Cheryl Dahl, "Gap's New Look: The See-Through," *Fast Company*, September 2004, 69–70.

3.17 Evaluating Bias in Visuals

Evaluate the portrayals of people in one of the following:

- Ads in one issue of a business magazine
- A company's annual report
- A company's web page

Do the visuals show people of both sexes and all races? Is there a sprinkling of people of various ages and physical conditions? What do the visuals suggest about who has power?

As your instructor directs,

a. Share your findings orally with a small group of students.
b. Post your findings in an e-mail to the class.
c. Summarize your findings in a memo to your instructor.
d. Present your findings in an oral presentation to the class.
e. Join with a small group of students to create a written report.

3.18 Revising a Memo for Positive Tone

Revise the following memo to improve positive tone.

TO: All Staff

SUBJECT: Decorating Your Work Area

With the arrival of the holiday season, employees who wish to decorate their work areas should do so only with great caution. Don't do something stupid that might burn down the entire office. If you wish to decorate, don't forget the following guidelines:

1. If using decorative lights, don't place them in obstructive places.
2. Do not overload your workstation with decorations that will interfere with your daily duties.
3. Don't forget to turn off and/or unplug all lights at the end of your workday.
4. Do not use hot lights; they can burn your countertop so it is imperative that everyone take care in selecting your lights.
5. Do not use decorations which will offend people of other religions.
6. Absolutely no candles are allowed.

Don't forget these guidelines, and we'll have a great holiday season. Thank you for your cooperation.

3.19 Dealing with Negative Clients

An executive at one of your largest client companies is known for his negative attitude. He is feared for his sharp tongue and scathing attacks, and he bullies everyone. Everyone you know, including yourself, is afraid of him. Unfortunately, he is also the one who decides whether or not you get your annual contract. Your contract is up for renewal, and you have some new services you think his company would like.

In small groups, discuss at least four ways to handle Mr. Bully. Write up your two best to share with the whole class. Also write up the reasons you think these two approaches will work. Share your two approaches with the whole class, as a short oral presentation or online.

As a class, select the two best approaches from those offered by the small groups. Discuss your criteria for selection and rejection.

3.20 Writing Business Thank-You Notes

Some businesses make a practice of sending goodwill messages to some of their customers.

Pick a business you patronize that might logically send some thank-you notes. Write a suitable note and design a tasteful visual for it. In a separate document, write a memo to your instructor explaining your design and content decisions.

Questions you might want to consider:

- Who is your audience? Will you write to everyone? Will you target big spenders? Trend setters? People who might become long-term customers? How will you identify your categories?
- What tone did you select? What words and phrases help produce that tone? What words and phrases did you avoid? What diction choices did you make to convey sincerity?
- What content did you choose? Why? What content choices did you discard?
- What design features did you choose? Why? What design features did you discard?

3.21 Evaluating You-Attitude and Positive Emphasis in University Websites

As they plan their college visits, many students begin by visiting university websites. Imagine you are a high school senior and a prospective student. Go to the "Prospective Students" part of your school's website and read about housing, course offerings, and student life. Evaluate the information you find for you-attitude and positive emphasis. Compare the text for prospective students with the text on several sites targeted for current students. Does the tone change? In what ways? What information increases or decreases you-attitude?

Now visit the website of another university. Review the same type of information for prospective students and compare it to that of your own school. Which school does a better job? Why?

As your instructor directs,

- Share your findings orally with a small group of students.
- Share your findings orally with the class.
- Post your findings in an e-mail to the class.
- Summarize your findings in a memo to your instructor.

3.22 Evaluating You-Attitude and Positive Emphasis at IRS

The IRS has a page called "Where's My Refund?" In 2007, the page read like this:

> "Where's My Refund?"
>
> "You filed your tax return and you're expecting a refund. You have just one question and you want the answer now—*Where's My Refund?*"
>
> "Whether you split your refund among several accounts, opted for direct deposit to one account or asked IRS to mail you a check, you can track your refund through this secure Web site. You can get refund information even if you filed just to request the telephone excise tax refund."
>
> "To get to your personal refund information, be ready to enter your:"
>
> - Social Security Number (or IRS Individual Taxpayer Identification Number)
> - Filing status (Single, Married Filing Joint Return, Married Filing Separate Return, Head of Household, or Qualifying Widow(er))
> - Exact refund amount shown on your return
>
> "If you don't receive your refund within 28 days from the original IRS mailing date shown on *Where's My Refund?,* you can start a refund trace online."
>
> If *Where's My Refund?* shows that IRS was unable to deliver your refund, you can change your address online.
>
> "*Where's My Refund?* will prompt you when these features are available for your situation. "
>
> "Okay now, *Where's My Re-fund?*"

Now read their current "Where's My Refund" page on their website. What changes have they made? Which version has more you-attitude and positive emphasis? Which version do you like better? Why? Write your answers in a memo to your instructor or classmates.

Quoted from "Where's My Refund?" U.S. Department of the Treasury, updated April 6, 2011, http://www.irs.gov/individuals/article/0,,id=96596,00.html.

3.23 Designing for People with Disabilities

Reread the sidebar on page 75. In small groups discuss these questions:

- What are some other products you can think of that could be redesigned for easier use by people with disabilities?
- What themes would you use to advertise these products? Remember that no one likes to be reminded that they are losing physical capacities.
- What are some changes companies should make to their advertising and product information for easier access by people with disabilities?

As your instructor directs, in small groups

- Summarize your discussion in a memo for your instructor.
- Summarize your discussion in a memo for your class list serve.
- Prepare a short presentation for your classmates.

3.24 Revising a "Goodwill Disaster"

Li, an intern at All-Weather, a window manufacturer, has been asked to write a letter to a recent young customer asking him if some new engineers can tour his gallery to see the products in use. Here is his draft:

Dear Mr. Mason,
Executive Director,
Iconic Art Gallery, St. Paul, MN

You must be glad that you chose All-Weather's energy efficient bow windows, horizontal sliders, and fiberglass doors for your art gallery. As everyone who is anyone knows, we offer the finest quality wood, vinyl, aluminum, steel, and fiberglass composite windows and doors you can find in the US of A. As you also know, our customer service representatives are ready to assist you 24/7 (and more!) with any installation or maintenance needs you may have (even if it's your responsibility or fault, I might add). After doing so much for an important customer such as you, we have a small favor to ask of you, which we're sure you will not deny us. We just hired some new engineers who will join our manufacturing division to continue to make the fine products that we make. Unfortunately, they have never seen how our finished products look outside or inside actual homes or offices. (On a personal note, I confess I don't know what they can learn from one visit to a home or an office.) Our VP (Manufacturing), an asset to All-Weather, says that we should send these engineers out on a field visit. And he should know, shouldn't he, being the VP and all? That is why I'm writing to you (the pleasure is mine, though).

These fresh minds need exposure to actual conditions in actual markets. We think that if they visit your art gallery, they will see how our products are helping you get results your art gallery could never dream of before. If you don't believe me, take a peek inside your exhibits room, whose space seems to have expanded thanks to our bow window that you have installed. I myself remember what a cramped-looking room it was before. No, I'm not asking you to share your admission fees with us, though free exhibition tickets wouldn't hurt (I'm kidding, sir). Also, you should perhaps buy more windows and doors from us (and attract more visitors as a result!). Also, don't forget to mention us favorably to your patrons.

Oh, and by the way, will you please let us know the day and time suitable to you when we might send those engineers to your art gallery? Our orientation program begins in three weeks time. Looking forward to your prompt acceptance of our request (with or without free exhibition tickets).

Sincerely,
Li

Li was trying for a breezy tone which he thought appropriate for a young art gallery owner but obviously went overboard.

Based on your reading of Chapter 3, complete the following tasks:

- List problems in Li's draft.
- Prepare another list of changes that would improve the draft. Be specific in your suggestions. For instance, it's insufficient to say "more you-attitude" or "more politeness." Point to places in the draft where these strategies might be useful. Also, rephrase relevant sentences or paragraphs for more you-attitude or more politeness, whichever is the case.
- What is the primary purpose of the letter? The secondary purpose?
- Revise the draft.

CHAPTER 4

Navigating the Business Communication Environment

Chapter Outline

Ethics

Corporate Culture

Interpersonal Communication

- Listening
- Conversational Style
- Nonverbal Communication
- Networking

Time Management

- Techniques
- Multitasking

Trends in Business Communication

- Data Security
- Electronic Privacy
- Customer Service
- Work/Family Balance
- Environmental Concern
- Globalization and Outsourcing
- Diversity
- Teamwork
- Job Flexibility
- Innovation and Entrepreneurship
- Rapid Rate of Change

Summary of Key Points

NEWSWORTHY COMMUNICATION

A Refreshingly Ethical Project

One of the best-known corporate social responsibility efforts is Pepsi's Refresh Project, launched in February 2010.

In its first year, the Refresh Project promised $20 million in donations to organizations and individuals who submitted "refreshing ideas that change the world." Competition for grants, especially in the $250,000 category, was high, with community, health, and religious organizations forming alliances and dominating voting by encouraging supporters to vote up to the maximum allowed under contest rules. Such competition shut out many smaller, grassroots organizations that couldn't muster the same kind of support among voters.

Despite initial complaints of unfair competition, Pepsi Refresh Project reported 12,642 idea submissions and over 76 million votes. The project awarded $6.4 million in grants to arts and health organizations, and provided funds that helped improve 26 playgrounds and start 47 organizations.

To even the field for the second year of Project Refresh, Pepsi revised voting procedures. Additionally, Pepsi eliminated the $250,000 grant category, but offered twice as many grants of $50,000 or less, which are sought by smaller groups. Jill Beraud, chief marketing officer for PepsiCo Beverages America, explained that the changes were meant to make the competition for Project Refresh grants more democratic.

While some analysts worry that Pepsi is spending too much on promoting an image of social responsibility and not enough on marketing its major brands, PepsiCo remains committed to Project Refresh and plans to expand the initiative to China and Latin America. According to PepsiCo Chairman and Chief Executive Indra K. Nooyi, companies must find ways to make their brands stand apart from other brands in their same market, and social responsibility is one way to do that. As she explained at an industry conference in December 2010, "It's a matter of, 'What does this brand stand for in terms of doing something positive in the world?'"

"What does this brand stand for in terms of doing something positive in the world?"

Source: Valerie Bauerlein, "Pepsi Hits 'Refresh' on Donor Project," *Wall Street Journal*, January 31, 2011, B4.

Learning Objectives

After studying this chapter, you will know

- **LO 4-1** Why ethics is so important in business communication.
- **LO 4-2** How corporate culture impacts the business environment.
- **LO 4-3** How to improve interpersonal communication.
- **LO 4-4** How to use your time more efficiently.
- **LO 4-5** What the trends in business communication are.

In addition to adapting to audiences and building goodwill, business communications are heavily influenced by the environments in which they are created and interpreted. Part of this environment is shaped by national culture, such as the growing concern about business ethics, and part is shaped by corporate culture. Part is shaped by individual behaviors, such as those involved in interpersonal communication. A final part is shaped by widespread trends—trends such as globalization or the green movement. Technology and information overload, which are perhaps the largest of these trends, are discussed extensively in Chapter 9, along with effective ways to deal with them.

Dilbert May Get You Fired

Catfish Bend Casinos in Burlington, Iowa, fired a seven-year employee for placing a Dilbert cartoon on a company bulletin board. The employee posted the cartoon after the company announced the casino was closing and 170 workers would probably be laid off.

The Dilbert cartoon called decision makers "drunken lemurs" and said they had time but no talent.

The employee, who was identified from security tapes, thought the comic was humorous and might cheer up some of his colleagues. Managers found it insulting misconduct. They then tried to block his unemployment benefits, but the judge sided with the employee, calling the posting "a good-faith error in judgment."

Adapted from Clark Kauffman, "Bosses Check Video, Fire Man Who Put up Comic," *Des Moines Register*, December 19, 2007, 1A, 10A.

ETHICS LO 4-1

With the official recognition of a serious worldwide recession in the fall of 2008, along with the subprime mortgage debacle, ethics concerns have become a major part of the business environment. Financial giants such as AIG, Bear Sterns, Lehman Brothers, Merrill Lynch, Wachovia, and Washington Mutual had to be bailed out or went bankrupt. Banks, corporate officials, and rating agencies all were accused of unethical behavior. The SEC charged Goldman Sachs with fraud on securities linked to subprime mortgages; the firm settled out of court for over half a billion dollars.

Even drug companies were not immune. Glaxo pleaded guilty to charges that it knowingly sold adulterated drugs, including the antidepressant Paxil, and paid fines of $750 million. Pfizer paid $2.3 billion for promoting drugs for unauthorized uses.[1]

Billionaires fell as well. Bernie Madoff was sentenced to prison in what may have been the biggest Ponzi scheme in history, one that defrauded thousands of investors of billions of dollars. Hedge-fund manager Raj Rajaratnam was convicted of securities fraud and conspiracy in the biggest insider-trading case to that time.[2]

The Ethics Resource Center, America's oldest nonprofit organization devoted to ethical practice, reported in its 2009 *National Business Ethics Survey®*, that 49% of employees surveyed personally witnessed unethical or illegal behavior; 37% of those witnesses did not report it. The most frequent misconducts were company resource abuse, abusive behavior, lying to employees, e-mail or Internet abuse, conflicts of interest, discrimination, lying to stakeholders, employee benefit violations, health or safety violations, employee privacy breach, improper hiring practices, and falsifying time or expenses.[3]

Some common reasons for not reporting ethical misconduct are

- It's standard practice here.
- It's not a big deal.
- It's not my responsibility (a particularly common reason for junior employees).
- I want to be loyal to my colleagues/manager/company (stated negatively, this reason is "fear of consequences").[4]

On the other side of the coin, positive ethical efforts are also getting attention. The United Nations Global Compact, the world's largest corporate effort for global citizenship, focuses on human rights, labor, environment, and anticorruption measures. More than 5,300 businesses in 130 countries participate.[5] The Clinton Global Initiative has brought together 150 heads of state, 18 Nobel laureates, and hundreds of CEOs, who collectively have committed $63 billion. This money has already impacted the lives of 300 million people in 180 countries.[6]

The United States has its own efforts:

- Bill and Melinda Gates' foundation received double attention when Warren Buffett announced his transfer of billions of dollars to it. The three philanthropists have attracted still more attention with their efforts to convince other billionaires to pledge the majority of their wealth to philanthropy. The list of those who have made the pledge is posted at givingpledge.org; it included 69 pledgers in Spring 2011.
- Google, the "Don't Be Evil" company, has invested over $100 million in Google.org to use "Google's strengths in information and technology to build products and advocate for policies that address global challenges."[7]
- Robin Hood, a venture philanthropy, "robs" the rich (its board members cover all costs, so 100% of money donated goes to fund programs) to help the poor in New York City.[8]

Social entrepreneurs, backed by social investors like Bill Gates, are extending the reach of philanthropy. Grameen Bank founder Muhammad Yunus won the 2006 Nobel Peace Prize for his work with microfinance. The bank says it has brought 68% of its 8.3 million clients out of extreme poverty. Social Finance is launching Social Impact Bonds (SiB). SiBs help social enterprises acquire the sustainable revenues they need to succeed. Financial returns for investors are based on improved social outcomes.[9]

Business ethics includes far more than corporate greed, international pacts, and philanthropy, of course. Much of business ethics involves routine practices, and many of these practices involve communication. How can we make our contracts with our clients and suppliers easier to understand? How can we best communicate with our employees? How much should our hospital disclose about infection rates?

Many basic, daily communication decisions involve an ethics component. Am I including all the information my audience needs? Am I expressing it in ways they will understand? Am I putting it in a format that helps my audience grasp it quickly? Am I including information for all segments of my audience? Am I taking information from other sources accurately? Am I acknowledging my sources? Figure 4.1 lists some of the web resources that deal with business ethics.

Figure 4.2 elaborates on ethical components of communication. As it suggests, language, graphics, and document design—basic parts of any

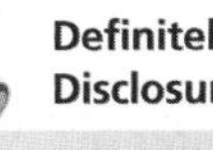

Definitely Not Full Disclosure

"A prominent spine surgeon and researcher at the University of Wisconsin received $19 million in payment over five years from Medtronic Inc., one of the country's largest makers of spinal devices. . . ."

"The surgeon . . . received the payments while helping Medtronic develop and promote a number of spinal products. Medtronic's $19 million in payments . . . went 'greatly' beyond what was evident in disclosures he made to the university. . . .

'[During those five years, the surgeon] told the university that he received $20,000 or more from Medtronic. . . .' The disclosures conform to school policies, which currently don't require researchers to specify amounts received above $20,000. . . .

"Charles Rosen, a University of California, Irvine, spinal surgeon who is also president of the Association for Medical Ethics, said the Wisconsin disclosure policy is similar to that of many universities and medical societies. He said those policies are insufficient. . . ."

"'When you are advocating devices or procedures, it can't be said this is a private matter and that no one should know how much this company is paying me,' he said. 'It should be very public. People should know.'"

Quoted from David Armstrong and Thomas M. Burton, "Medtronic Paid This Researcher More Than $20,000—Much More," *Wall Street Journal*, January 16, 2009.

No Illegal Downloads in France

France became one of the first countries to enforce an antipiracy law against Internet scofflaws. It is going after all illegal downloaders of copyrighted film and music, regardless of where the material was made.

The law was passed after heavy lobbying from involved industries, who claim that illegal downloads cost the French music industry €700 million ($978 million) annually.

Offenders receive two warnings, first by e-mail and then by registered letter. A third offense can lead to legal proceedings plus a one-year Internet blackout for the offender.

Adapted from Max Colchester, "All Eyes on France as Officials Enforce New Antipiracy Law," *Wall Street Journal,* November 27, 2010, B1.

Figure 4.1 Business Ethics Resources on the Web

- **Business Ethics Resources on the Internet**
  http://www.ethicsweb.ca/resources/business
- **Defense Industry Initiative on Business Ethics and Conduct**
  http://dii.org
- **DePaul University's Institute for Business and Professional Ethics**
  http://commerce.depaul.edu/ethics
- **Ethics Resource Center**
  http://www.ethics.org
- **E-Business Ethics**
  http://www.e-businessethics.com
- **Various Codes of Conduct**
  http://www.ethicsweb.ca/resources/business/codes.html

business document—can be ethical or manipulative. Persuading and gaining compliance—activities at the heart of business and organizational life—can be done with respect or contempt for customers, co-workers, and subordinates.

In these days of instant communication, you, like the organization in which you work, must always act in an ethical manner. Consequences for not doing so are becoming more common as disgruntled colleagues/employees now have ample means for whistleblowing. Of course, there are also positive reasons for ethical behavior. In addition to moral reasons, there are business ones. As the Ethics Resource Center notes, customers and employees are attracted

Figure 4.2 Ethical Issues in Business Communications

Manner of conveying the message	Qualities of the message	Larger organizational context of the message
• Is the language audience-friendly? Does it respect the audience? • Do the words balance the organization's right to present its best case with its responsibility to present its message honestly? • Do graphics help the audience understand? Or are graphics used to distract or confuse? • Does the design of the document make reading easy? Does document design attempt to make readers skip key points?	• Is the message an ethical one that is honest and sensitive to all stakeholders? • Have interested parties been able to provide input? • Does the audience get all the information it needs to make a good decision or is information withheld? • Is information communicated so the audience can grasp it or are data "dumped" without any context? • Are the arguments logical? Are they supported with adequate evidence? • Are the emotional appeals used fairly? Do they supplement logic rather than substitute for it? • Does the organizational pattern lead the audience without undue manipulation?	• How does the organization treat its employees? How do employees treat each other? • How sensitive is the organization to stakeholders such as the people who live near its factories, stores, or offices and to the general public? • Does the organization support employees' efforts to be honest, fair, and ethical? • Do the organization's actions in making products, buying supplies, and marketing goods and services stand up to ethical scrutiny? • Is the organization a good corporate citizen, helpful rather than harmful to the community in which it exists? • Are the organization's products or services a good use of scarce resources?

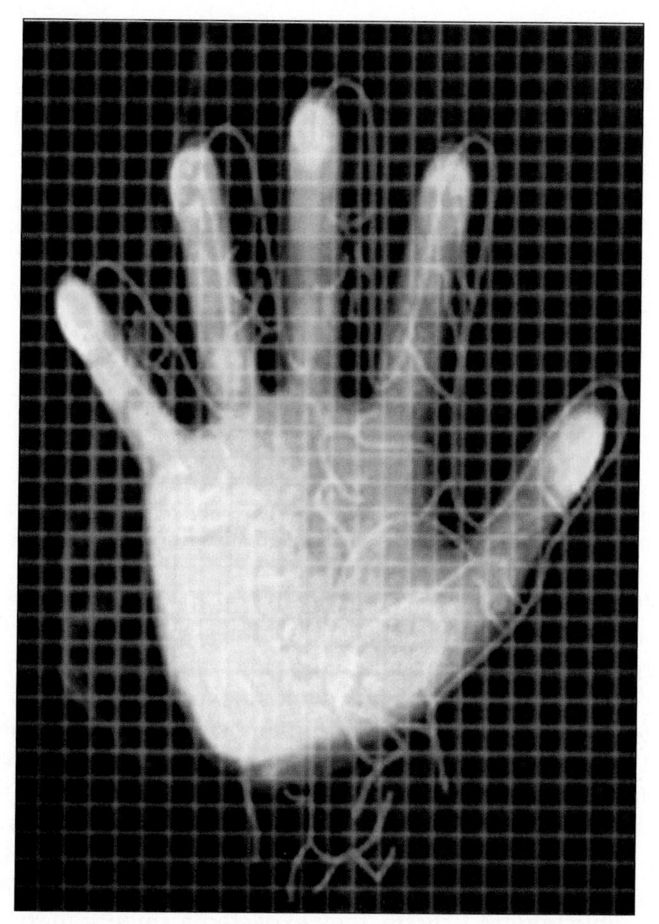

GMAT is now using palm vein scans to eliminate hired test takers. See sidebar on this page.

Business School Ethics

GMAT test scores were canceled for applicants who allegedly supplied or accessed exam questions posted on a website. Business schools were notified that these students had prepared improperly for the exam, and the Graduate Management Admission Council, which oversees the exam, obtained a court order to shut down the site, believed to be maintained in China.

The council also announced that it will be requiring GMAT test takers to take a palm vein scan, an infrared picture of the blood vessels in their hands. This new security measure is a new attempt to wipe out proxies—hired brains that take the test for an applicant.

The efforts to cheat continue in business school. Donald McCabe, a Rutgers University professor of management who has studied academic dishonesty for two decades, says that students in business schools cheat more than other students. His findings are backed up by a Duke University study which found that 56% of master's students in business administration cheat, again the highest rate among graduate students.

Adapted from John Hechinger, "Schools Cancel GMAT Scores," *Wall Street Journal*, September 11, 2008, D6; and "The Ethical Mind: A Conversation with Psychologist Howard Gardner," *Harvard Business Review*, March 2007, 51–56.

to ethical businesses. Rosabeth Moss Kanter, a professor at Harvard Business School, argues in her book, *Supercorp: How Vanguard Companies Create Innovation, Profits, Growth, and Social Good,* that companies desiring to do good have a competitive advantage. In fact, a benevolent viewpoint provides a wider view of society and thus awareness of new opportunities for growth and innovation by solving the problems of unmet needs.

Tony Hsieh, the founder and CEO of Zappos, offers this useful ethics guideline:

> As a guiding principle in life for anything I do, I try to ask myself, *What would happen if everyone in the world acted in the same way? What would the world look like? What would the net effect be on the overall happiness in the world?* [Hsieh's italics]
>
> This thought experiment has been useful to me when thinking about whether to share how we do things at Zappos, or whether to get upset at the waitress who accidentally got my order wrong, or whether to hold the door open for a stranger who's a slightly inconvenient distance away.
>
> The same questions are just as important for deciding what not to do, even if not doing anything is the default choice.[10]

CORPORATE CULTURE LO 4-2

Another strong influence on the business environment is corporate culture (see Chapter 2 for ways to analyze corporate culture). Corporate cultures vary widely. They range from formal—with individual offices, jackets, and hierarchical lines of command—to informal, with open office space, casual attire, and flat organizational structures. Characteristics of popular corporate

Rule 34: Don't Plagiarize

"Do not plagiarize" should have been included in *Unwritten Rules of Management*, the book by William Swanson, CEO of Raytheon. In 2004, Raytheon gave employees free copies of the book, which contained 33 rules. The book quickly became widely read by professionals and executives because of its humorous approach. However, an engineer at Hewlett-Packard discovered that 13 of the rules had been previously published by W. J. King in his 1944 bestseller, *The Unwritten Laws of Engineering*. Further findings uncovered that the additional rules were obtained from Defense Secretary Rumsfeld and humor editorial writer Dave Barry.

Swanson apologized for the mistake, which, he states, began when he asked employees to create a presentation from a file. The presentation was a great hit, which led to the creation of the 33 rules—one for each year he worked for Raytheon. Unfortunately, the rules were not original and the sources were not properly cited.

How can you avoid plagiarism?

Adapted from Lisa Takeuchi Cullen, "Rule No. 1: Don't Copy," *Time*, May 15, 2006, 41.

Thoughtful Perks

Some companies have unique perks:

- On-site laundry pickup and delivery
- Café lunch delivery at desks
- Professional home cleaning
- Two weeks fully paid leave to work for green nonprofits
- Up to $5,000 and an extra week off for vacations abroad
- Charge card to use in a nearby restaurant

Adapted from "10 Perks We Love," *Inc.*, June 2010, 94.

Some employees use exercise balls as desk chairs. The balls require employees to use core muscles to maintain posture. Employees say they are also fun because they can bounce.

cultures include flexible work arrangements, profit sharing, information sharing, good training, health insurance, and wellness programs.

Both large and small companies get cited for their corporate cultures. Google is known for company gyms, well-stocked snack rooms, restaurants, and casual work attire. Dealer.com offers subsidized meals at its café, with organic and locally grown food, wellness seminars on exercise and stress management, chair massages, bike rentals, tennis and basketball courts, fitness center, and half-price ski passes. The company supports its sports teams, including softball, volleyball, soccer, bowling, and dragon-boat racing.[11]

Two companies in the same field may have very different cultures. When Procter & Gamble bought Gillette, they expected a smooth marriage between the world's number one toothbrush, Oral-B, and the world's number two toothpaste, Crest. But cultural differences caused problems. Gillette employees found P&G's culture rigid, its decision making slow. Gillette employees also had to learn P&G's famous acronyms, such as CIB (consumer is boss) and FMOT (first moment of truth, when consumers notice the product). P&G people sent memos, Gillette people called meetings.[12]

Wise companies also use effective corporate cultures to retain hourly workers. Hotels lose two-thirds of their hourly workers annually, according to hotel survey firm Market Metrix. Each departure costs midrange hotels about $5,000 in lost productivity, recruiting, and training. But Joie de Vivre Hospitality has a turnover rate that is half the industry average. The CEO attributes the low rate to a corporate culture that listens to employees, enacts some of their suggestions, and tries to make work fun. In addition to awards, the company sponsors parties, annual retreats, and regularly scheduled dinners. It also offers free classes on subjects such as Microsoft Excel and English as a second language.[13]

Corporate culture is at the heart of the customer service focus at Zappos, the Internet footwear retailer. The company nurtures a touch of weirdness to make work more fun. That same touch of weirdness also encourages innovation. To increase serendipitous interactions, all employees enter and exit through the reception area. Logging in to the company computer requires completing the short multiple-choice test to name the randomly selected employee whose picture is displayed.[14] Tours of corporate offices are always unique, because teams are always changing their décor:

> You might find a popcorn machine or a coffee machine dressed up as a robot in our lobby. As you passed through different departments, you might find an aisle of cowbells . . . , a makeshift bowling alley . . . , employees dressed up as pirates,

employees karaokeing, a nap room, a petting zoo, or a hot dog social. You might see a parade pass by because one of our departments decided that it was the perfect day to celebrate Oktoberfest.[15]

Warren Buffett on Ethics

In a 2008 letter to Berkshire directors, Warren Buffett says this about ethics:

"We *must* continue to measure every act against not only what is legal but also what we would be happy to have written about on the front page of a national newspaper in an article written by an unfriendly but intelligent reporter."

"Sometimes your associates will say 'Everybody else is doing it.' This rationale is almost always a bad one if it is the main justification for a business action. It is totally unacceptable when evaluating a moral decision. Whenever somebody offers that phrase as a rationale, in effect they are saying that they can't come up with a *good* reason. If anyone offers this explanation, tell them to try using it with a reporter or a judge and see how far it gets them."

". . . It's very likely that if a given course of action evokes hesitation *per se*, it's too close to the line and should be abandoned. There's plenty of money to be made in the center of the court. If it's questionable whether some action is close to the line, just assume it is outside and forget it."

INTERPERSONAL COMMUNICATION LO 4-3

Within the corporate environment, some people are more likely to be successful than others, and one major reason for the variation is interpersonal communication skill. Much important communication takes place in hallways, at the coffee machine, and in break rooms. Successful professionals communicate well with different categories of people—co-workers, bosses, clients—in a variety of settings. To do so, they cultivate skills in diverse areas such as listening, conversation, nonverbal communication, and networking. They also practice skills in conflict resolution and teamwork (see Chapter 8 for a discussion of these latter two skills).

These skills are part of what Daniel Goleman has widely popularized as Emotional Intelligence in his books on the subject. He presents much evidence to show that while intelligence and expertise are necessary to climb to the top in organizations, once at the top emotional intelligence, not IQ, predicts the star leaders.[16]

Listening

Listening is crucial to building trust. However, listening on the job may be more difficult than listening in classes. Many classroom lectures are well organized, with signposts and repetition of key points to help hearers follow. But conversations usually wander. A key point about when a report is due may be sandwiched in among statements about other due dates for other projects. Finally, in a classroom you're listening primarily for information. In interchanges with friends and co-workers, you need to listen for feelings, too. Feelings such as being rejected or overworked need to be dealt with as they arise. But you can't deal with a feeling unless you are aware of it.

Listening errors also can result from being distracted by your own emotional response, especially when the topic is controversial. Listeners have to be aware of their emotional responses so that they can clarify the speaker's intent and also allow time for cooling off, if necessary. A "you" attitude is as helpful for listening as it is for writing. Listening is more effective if the listener focuses more on understanding than on formulating a reply. Thinking about your own response too often causes you to miss important information.

Some listening errors also happen because the hearer wasn't paying enough attention to a key point. Be aware of points you need to know and listen for them.

Inattention and emotions can cause listeners to misinterpret a speaker. To reduce listening errors caused by misinterpretation,

- Paraphrase what the speaker has said, giving him or her a chance to correct your understanding.
- At the end of the conversation, check your understanding with the other person. Especially check who does what next.
- After the conversation, write down key points that affect deadlines or how work will be evaluated. Sometimes these key points need to be confirmed in an e-mail.
- Don't ignore instructions you think are unnecessary. Before you do something else, check with the order giver to see if there is a reason for the instruction.

Small Companies, Large Hearts

Some small companies are building philanthropy into their business models. Hook & Ladder Brewing Company donates a portion of all sales to local burned firefighters and other burn survivors. ColorMe Company, which produces arts and crafts materials for children, gives 10% of earnings to children's charities. Toms shoes gives a pair of new shoes to a child in need for every pair of shoes purchased from them.

Charitable contributions like these help attract and keep customers and employees and set such companies apart from their competitors.

What do you think of such philanthropic business models? What potential problems do such models have? Do you think the benefits will outweigh the pitfalls?

Adapted from "H&L History," Hook & Ladder Brewing Company, accessed May 26, 2011, http://www.hookandladderbeer.com/Public/Content.aspx; "Homepage," ColorMe Company, accessed May 26, 2011, http://www.colormecompany.com/; "Official Store," TOMS Company, accessed May 26, 2011, http://www.toms.com/.

- Consider the other person's background and experiences. Why is this point important to the speaker? What might he or she mean by it?

Listening to people is an indication that you're taking them seriously. **Acknowledgment responses**—nods, *uh huhs,* smiles, frowns—help carry the message that you're listening. However, remember that listening responses vary in different cultures.

In **active listening,** receivers actively demonstrate that they've understood a speaker by feeding back the literal meaning, the emotional content, or both. These strategies create active responses:

- Paraphrase the content. Feed back the meaning in your own words.
- Identify the feelings you think you hear.
- Ask for information or clarification.
- Offer to help. ("What can I do to help?")

When dealing with problems, instead of acknowledging what the other person says, many of us immediately respond in a way that analyzes or attempts to solve or dismiss the problem. People with problems need first of all to know that we hear that they're having a rough time. Figure 4.3 lists some of the responses that block communication. Ordering and threatening both tell the other person that the speaker doesn't want to hear what he or she has to say. Preaching attacks the other person. Minimizing the problem suggests the other person's concern is misplaced. It can even attack the other person's competency by suggesting that other people are coping just fine with bigger problems. Even advising shuts off discussion. Giving a quick answer minimizes the pain the person feels and puts him or her down for not seeing (what is to us) the obvious answer. Even if it is a good answer from an objective point of view, the other person may not be ready to hear it. And too often, the off-the-top-of-the-head solution doesn't address the real problem.

Active listening takes time and energy. Even people who are skilled active listeners can't do it all the time. Active listening can reduce the conflict that

Figure 4.3 Blocking Responses versus Active Listening

Blocking response	Possible active response
Ordering, threatening "I don't care how you do it. Just get that report on my desk by Friday."	**Paraphrasing content** "You're saying that you don't have time to finish the report by Friday."
Preaching, criticizing "You should know better than to air the department's problems in a general meeting."	**Mirroring feelings** "It sounds like the department's problems really bother you."
Minimizing the problem "You think *that's* bad. You should see what *I* have to do this week."	**Asking for information or clarification** "What parts of the problem seem most difficult to solve?"
Advising "Well, why don't you try listing everything you have to do and seeing which items are most important?"	**Offering to help solve the problem together** "Is there anything I could do that would help?"

Source: These responses that block communication are based on a list in Thomas Gordon and Judith Gordon Sands, *P.E.T. in Action* (New York: Wyden, 1976), 117–18.

results from miscommunication, but it alone cannot reduce the conflict that comes when two people want apparently inconsistent things or when one person wants to change someone else.

Conversational Style

Deborah Tannen, a linguist who specializes in gender discourse, uses the term **conversational style** to denote our conversational patterns and the meaning we give to them: the way we show interest, politeness, appropriateness.[17] Your answers to the following questions reveal your own conversational style:

- How long a pause tells you that it's your turn to speak?
- Do you see interruption as rude? or do you say things while other people are still talking to show that you're interested and to encourage them to say more?
- Do you show interest by asking lots of questions? or do you see questions as intrusive and wait for people to volunteer whatever they have to say?

Tannen concludes that the following features characterize her own conversational style:

Fast rate of speech.
Fast rate of turn-taking.
Persistence—if a turn is not acknowledged, try again.
Preference for personal stories.
Tolerance of, preference for simultaneous speech.
Abrupt topic shifting.

Different conversational styles are not necessarily good or bad, but people with different conversational styles may feel uncomfortable without knowing why. A subordinate who talks quickly may be frustrated by a boss who speaks slowly. People who talk more slowly may feel shut out of a conversation with people who talk more quickly. Someone who has learned to make requests directly ("Please pass the salt") may be annoyed by someone who uses indirect requests ("This casserole needs some salt").

In the workplace, conflicts may arise because of differences in conversational style. If people see direct questions as criticizing or accusing, they may see an ordinary question ("Will that report be ready Friday?") as a criticism of their progress. One supervisor might mean the question simply as a request for information. Another supervisor might use the question to mean "I want that report Friday."

Researchers Daniel N. Maltz and Ruth A. Borker believe that differences in conversational style (Figure 4.4) may be responsible for the miscommunication that often occurs in **male–female conversations.** Certainly conversational style is not the same for all men and for all women, but research has found several common patterns in the U.S. cultures studied so far.[18] For example, researchers have found that women are much more likely to nod and to say *yes* or *mm hmm* than men are.[19] Maltz and Borker hypothesize that to women, these symbols mean simply "I'm listening; go on." Men, on the other hand, may decode these symbols as "I agree" or at least "I follow what you're saying so far." A man who receives nods and *mms* from a woman may feel that she is inconsistent and unpredictable if she then disagrees with him. A woman may feel that a man who doesn't provide any feedback isn't listening to her.

Encyclopedia of Ethical Failure

"[Stephen] Epstein, the director of the Pentagon's Standards of Conduct Office, is mounting an ethical cleansing offensive from inside the corridors of power. His weapon of choice is the 'Encyclopedia of Ethical Failure,' a hit parade he publishes on the Internet to regale bureaucrats with tales of shenanigans and shockingly bad judgment that have shot down the careers of fellow public servants across government.

"Take the case of the Customs . . . officer who landed a government helicopter on his daughter's grade-school playground: Despite having a supervisor's ill-considered clearance to fly there, . . . the officer was fired for misusing government property. . . .

"Mr. Epstein combs through the press, legal records and internal government investigation reports for material. . . . He often finds humor in the missteps. Two Veterans Affairs bureaucrats were charged with overbilling the government and receiving kickbacks from a supplier. 'The product? . . . Red tape.'"

Figure 4.4 Different Conversational Styles

	Debating	Relating
Interpretation of questions	See questions as requests for information.	See questions as way to keep a conversation flowing.
Relation of new comment to what last speaker said	Do not require new comment to relate explicitly to last speaker's comment. Ignoring previous comment is one strategy for taking control.	Expect new comments to acknowledge the last speaker's comment and relate directly to it.
View of aggressiveness	See aggressiveness as one way to organize the flow of conversation.	See aggressiveness as directed at audience personally, as negative, and as disruptive to a conversation.
How topics are defined and changed	Tend to define topics narrowly and shift topics abruptly. Interpret statements about side issues as effort to change the topic.	Tend to define topics gradually, progressively. Interpret statements about side issues as effort to shape, expand, or limit the topic.
Response to someone who shares a problem	Offer advice, solutions.	Offer solidarity, reassurance. Share troubles to establish sense of community.

Sources: Based on Daniel N. Maltz and Ruth A. Borker, "A Cultural Approach to Male-Female Miscommunication," *Language and Social Identity,* ed. John J. Gumperz (Cambridge: Cambridge University Press, 1982), 213; and Deborah Tannen, *Talking from 9 to 5: Women and Men in the Workplace: Language, Sex and Power* (New York: William Morrow, 1995).

Interpersonal Skills for Doctors

The risk of being sued for medical malpractice lies not so much with training, credentials, or even the number of mistakes made. Rather, it depends on doctors' interpersonal skills. Again and again, patients in malpractice suits say they were rushed, ignored, or treated like objects. A study of surgeons showed that those who had never been sued

- Made orienting comments at visits, so patients knew what was going to happen and when it was best to ask questions.
- Practiced active listening ("Tell me more about that").
- Laughed and were funny during visits.

The difference was all in how they talked to their patients; there was no difference in amount or quality of information.

Adapted from Malcolm Gladwell, *Blink: The Power of Thinking without Thinking* (New York: Back Bay Books, 2007), 40–43.

Research has also shown that in our culture men tend to interrupt more than women; women tend to wait for a pause in the discussion before speaking. When former Secretary of State Madeleine Albright was asked to give advice to professional women hoping to rise in the ranks, she replied, "Learn to interrupt."[20]

Nonverbal Communication

Nonverbal communication—communication that doesn't use words—takes place all the time. Smiles, frowns, who sits where at a meeting, the size of an office, how long someone keeps a visitor waiting—all these communicate pleasure or anger, friendliness or distance, power and status.

Researchers have begun to study a category of nonverbal communication called **social signals**—tone of voice, gestures, proximity to others, facial expressions—as keys to business success. Researchers can study these signals in individuals and then predict accurately who will win raises or business plan contests. The more successful people are more energetic and positive. They do talk more, but they also listen more, drawing other people out.[21]

Most of the time we are no more conscious of interpreting nonverbal signals than we are conscious of breathing. Yet nonverbal signals can be misinterpreted just as easily as can verbal symbols (words). And the misunderstandings can be harder to clear up because people may not be aware of the nonverbal cues that led them to assume that they aren't liked, respected, or approved.

Learning about nonverbal language can help us project the image we want to present and make us more aware of the signals we are interpreting. However, even within a single culture, a nonverbal symbol may have more than one meaning.

In the business world, two sets of nonverbal signals are particularly important: spatial cues and body language.

Spatial Cues In the United States, the size, placement, and privacy of one's office connotes status. Large corner offices have the highest status. An individual office with a door that closes connotes more status than a desk in a common area. Windows also may matter. An office with a window may connote more status than one without.

People who don't know each other well may feel more comfortable with each other if a piece of furniture separates them. For example, a group may work better sitting around a table than just sitting in a circle. Desks can be used as barricades to protect oneself from other people.

Body Language Our body language communicates to other people much about our feelings. Our facial expressions, eye contact, gestures, posture, and body positions all telegraph information about us. In the United States, **open body positions** include leaning forward with uncrossed arms and legs, with the arms away from the body. **Closed** or **defensive body positions** include leaning back, sometimes with both hands behind the head, arms and legs crossed or close together, or hands in pockets. As the labels imply, open positions suggest that people are accepting and open to new ideas. Closed positions suggest that people are physically or psychologically uncomfortable, that they are defending themselves and shutting other people out.

People who cross their arms or legs often claim that they do so only because the position is more comfortable. But notice your own body the next time you're in a perfectly comfortable discussion with a good friend. You'll probably find that you naturally assume open body positions. The fact that so many people in organizational settings adopt closed positions may indicate that many people feel at least slightly uncomfortable in school and on the job.

Some nonverbal communications appear to be made and interpreted unconsciously by many people. Researchers at MIT are showing that when we get excited about something, we have more nervous energy. Another such signal is fluency, or consistency. Consistency in motions (such as in surgery) or

Liar Detection

Although not infallible, these are signs of lying:

Body language: Physical cues such as sweating and fidgeting may be telling.

Details: False stories often lack details. Pushing for details increases chances the liar may slip up.

Unpleasantness: Liars are less cooperative, pleasant, and friendly than truth tellers. They also make more negative statements and complaints.

Eye contact: Failure to make eye contact is often a sign of lying.

Stress signs: Dilated pupils and a rise in voice pitch may be present.

Pauses: Most liars will have pauses in their stories as they make them up.

Inconsistencies: Ask suspected liars to repeat their stories; listen for inconsistencies.

Adapted from Elisabeth Eaves, "Ten Ways to Tell if Someone Is Lying to You," *Forbes*, July 22, 2010, http://www.forbes.com/2006/11/02/tech-cx_ee_technology_liar_slide.html.

(a)

(b)

(a) (left) "THE REAL THING: A real smile involves the whole face, not just the mouth. While muscles pull the corners of the mouth up (1), an involuntary nerve causes the upper eyefold (2) to relax."

(b) (right) "THE SOCIAL SMILE: When faking, the lips are pulled straight across (3). Though this creates cheek folds (4) similar to those of a real smile, the lack of eye crinkles (5) is a dead giveaway."

Quoted from Andy Raskin, "A Face Any Business Can Trust," Business 2.0 4, no. 11 (December 2003): 60.

Are Interruptions Impolite?

In the dominant U.S. culture, interrupting can seem impolite, especially if a lower-status person interrupts a superior.

Simulated negotiations have measured the interruptions by businesspeople in 10 countries. The following list is ordered by decreasing numbers of interruptions:

Korea
Germany
France
China
Brazil
Russia
Taiwan
Japan
United Kingdom
United States

This list does not mean that U.S. businesspeople are more polite, but rather that how people show politeness differs from culture to culture. Chinese and Italians (who also interrupt frequently) use interruptions to offer help, jointly construct a conversation, and show eagerness to do business—all of which are polite.

Based on Jan M. Ulijn and Xiangling Li, "Is Interrupting Impolite? Some Temporal Aspects of Turn-Taking in Chinese-Western and Other Intercultural Encounters," *Text* 15, no. 4 (1995): 600, 621.

Body language can give big clues about our attitude to office visitors.

tone (speech) tells us who is expert, or at least well practiced. Such signals are hard to fake, which may explain their influence.[22]

Body language is complicated by the fact that nonverbal signs may have more than one meaning. A frown may signal displeasure or concentration. A stiff posture that usually means your co-worker is upset may today just be a sign of sore back muscles.

Misunderstandings are even more common when people communicate with people from other cultures or other countries. Knowing something about other cultures may help you realize that a subordinate who doesn't meet your eye may be showing respect rather than dishonesty. But it's impossible to memorize every meaning that every nonverbal sign has in every culture. And in a multicultural workforce, you may not know whether someone retains the meanings of his or her ancestors or has adopted the dominant U.S. meanings. The best solution is to ask for clarification.

Networking

A much underappreciated skill in the business environment is **networking,** the ability to connect with many different kinds of people. Most of us can relate to the people in our immediate work group, although even there differences in ability to connect impact performance. But true networking is creating connections with still more people. It involves creating connections before they are needed, creating diverse connections in widely spread areas, knowing which people to turn to when you need additional expertise, knowing people outside the company.

Good networkers know who will help them cut through red tape, who can find an emergency supplier, who will take on extra work in a crisis. Informal conversations, about yesterday's game and Li's photography exhibit as well as what's happening at work, connect them with the **grapevine,** an informal source of company information. Participation in civic, school, religious, and professional organizations connects them to a larger environment. They attend conferences, trade shows, fundraisers, and community events. They use social networking sites such as LinkedIn (see Chapter 9 for more on electronic networks).

Networking becomes even more important as you climb the corporate ladder. Good managers interact with their employees continually, not just when they need something. They listen to lunchroom conversations; they chat with employees over coffee.

Much research shows that networking is crucial to job success. In *Emotional Intelligence,* Daniel Goleman tells of research in a division at Bell Labs to determine what made the star performers in the division. Everyone in the division had a high academic IQ, which meant that IQ was not a good predictor of job productivity (although academic knowledge and IQ are good predictors of success on earlier career ladder rungs). But networking skill was a good predictor. The stars put effort into developing their network, and they cultivated relationships in that network *before* they were needed.[23]

Goleman identifies three different kinds of workplace networks: conversational (who talks to whom), expertise (who can be turned to for advice), and trust (who can be trusted with sensitive information like gripes). Unsurprisingly, the stars of an organization are often heavily networked in all three varieties.[24]

Good networkers share certain interpersonal communication behaviors. They adapt their behavior and attitude to the people around them. They subtly mirror the postures, behaviors, and emotional states of people near them. They share some personal and emotional information about themselves, a sharing that helps build trust. They capitalize on the benefits of physical proximity—trading some phone calls for actual office visits, attending both informal and formal gatherings. One study showed that people with these skills penetrated the center of their workplace network in just 18 months; people lacking in these skills took 13 years.[25]

Authoritative Body Language

Carol Kinsey Goman, author of *The Silent Language of Leaders: How Body Language Can Help—or Hurt—How You Lead,* offers these tips to increase your image of authority:

- Keep your head straight up. Head tilts show concern or interest for individuals, but may be processed as submission signals in power situations.
- Expand your space. Stand tall, spread your elbows a little, widen your stance, and spread your materials on the table at the next meeting. Authority is demonstrated through height and space.
- Use the tonal arc, in which your voice rises in pitch through a sentence but drops back down at the end. Ending on a higher pitch often indicates uncertainty or a need for approval.
- Look serious when the subject is serious. Smiles are frequently inappropriate in power situations.
- Do not nod to express listening or engagement; nodding undercuts authority.
- Minimize movements, especially gestures.
- Have a firm handshake.

Adapted from Carol Kinsey Goman, "10 Common Body Language Traps for Women in the Workplace," *On Leadership* (blog), *Washington Post,* May 2, 2011, http://www.washingtonpost.com/blogs/on-leadership/post/10-common-body-language-traps-for-women-in-the-workplace/2011/03/03/AFIOGFbF_blog.html.

TIME MANAGEMENT LO 4-4

As your work environment becomes more complex, with multiple networks, responsibilities, and projects, good time management becomes crucial. Although much time management advice sounds like common sense, it is amazing the number of people who do not follow it.

Techniques

Probably the most important time management technique is to prioritize the demands on your time, and make sure you spend the majority of your time on the most important demands. If your career success depends on producing reports, news articles, and press releases about company business, then that is what you need to spend the majority of your time doing.

Randy Pausch, in his highly popular video and book *The Last Lecture,* makes this point about prioritizing most eloquently. His lecture is a moving reminder to make time for friends and family. His colleagues noted that he would regularly tell his students they could always make more money later, but they could never make more time.[26]

In *The 7 Habits of Highly Effective People,* Stephen Covey presents a useful time management matrix which sorts activities by urgency and importance; see Figure 4.5. Obviously we should focus our time on important, urgent activities, but Covey also advises putting significant time into quadrant II, important but nonurgent activities, which he calls the heart of effective management. Quadrant II activities include networking, planning, and preparing.[27]

Gossip Networking

Although it has a tarnished reputation, gossip can benefit both individuals and organizations, research shows. Gossiping is a form of networking. According to Joe Labianca, a professor at the University of Kentucky's Center for Research on Social Networks in Business, the more workers gossip, the better their understanding of the work environment and the higher their peers rate their influence. Gossip disseminates valuable information about workers, such as who doesn't do their share or who is impossible to work with.

And guess what? Managers gossip, too. In fact, they may have more "gossip partners" than nonmanagers.

Adapted from Giuseppe Labianca, "It's Not 'Unprofessional' to Gossip at Work," *Harvard Business Review*, (September 2010): 29.

Figure 4.5 Stephen Covey's Time Management Matrix. Covey advises putting significant time into quadrant II.

	Urgent	Not Urgent
Important	I ACTIVITIES: Crises Pressing problems Deadline-driven projects	II ACTIVITIES: Prevention, PC activities Relationship building Recognizing new opportunities Planning, recreation
Not Important	III ACTIVITIES: Interruptions, some calls Some mail, some reports Some meetings Proximate, pressing matters Popular activities	IV ACTIVITIES: Trivia, busy work Some mail Some phone calls Time wasters Pleasant activities

Source: Stephen R. Covey, *The 7 Habits of Highly Effective People: Restoring the Character* (New York: Free Press, 2004), 150–54. Reprinted with permission of the author.

These are some other common tips for time management:

- Keep lists—both daily and long term. Prioritize items on your list.
- Ask yourself where you want to be in three or five years and work accordingly.
- Do large, important tasks first, and then fill in around them with smaller tasks.
- Break large tasks into small ones. Remember that you do not always have to work sequentially. If you have been putting off a report because you cannot decide how to write its introduction, start with the conclusions or some other part that is easy for you to write.
- Find blocks of time: put your phone on answering machine, ignore e-mail, avoid the break room, move discretionary meetings. Put these blocks at your most productive time; save e-mail and meetings for less productive times.
- Avoid time sinks: some people, long phone conversations, constant e-mail checks.
- Decide at the end of today's work session what you will do in tomorrow's session, and set yourself up to do it. Find the necessary file; look up the specifications for that proposal.
- At end of week, evaluate what you didn't get done. Should you have done it for promotion, goodwill, ethics?

Multitasking

Many workers believe they can manage some of their time crunch problems by multitasking. Unfortunately, decades of research on the subject show that this is a false belief. It is particularly false when long-term learning or communication tasks are involved.[28] Just think of all the e-mails that get sent to unintended audiences while the writer is multitasking, or all the phone calls for which the caller, busy multitasking, forgets who is being called or why in the short time between dialing and pickup.

Research shows that when we think we are multitasking, we are really switching back and forth between tasks. And there is always a start-up delay involved in returning to a previous task, no matter how brief the delay. These delays may make it faster to do the tasks sequentially, in which case we will probably do them better, too. In fact, some research shows it can take up to 50% longer to multitask.[29] Other research shows that multitasking hurts overall attention and memory, even when not multitasking.[30]

When we return to a task following an interruption—either from someone else, like a phone call, or from ourselves, like a visit to FaceBook—it may take us close to half an hour to get back into the original task.[31] Sometimes, we do not get back to the task correctly. Pilots who are interrupted in their preflight checklist may miss an item when they return to it. One crash, in which 153 people died, has been blamed on an error resulting from such an interruption.[32]

As the Old Song Says, "I Got Rhythm"

One of the newest electronic security methods is keystroke authentication. It turns out that your typing pattern, the pressure of your fingers on the keys and your typing speed, is unique. It allows you to prove electronically that you are who you say you are.

Keystroke patterning has a long history. The military began using it over a hundred years ago to identify individual senders of Morse code by their tapping rhythms. As the location of those senders shifted, military trackers got data on enemy movements.

Currently, the biggest users of keystroke patterning are banks and credit unions, who are employing it in addition to standard password authentication. Since identity theft has become such a major problem, banks and credit unions are under a federal mandate to use stronger authentication measures to protect online customers.

Adapted from Kathleen Kingsbury, "Telltale Fingertips: With Biometrics, How You Type Can Allow Websites to Know Who You Are—Or Aren't," *Time Bonus Section*, January 2007, A10.

TRENDS IN BUSINESS COMMUNICATION LO 4-5

Both business and business communication are constantly changing. One of the biggest changes for most people is the shift to electronic communications. This all-encompassing trend is the subject of Chapter 9. Related to this shift are trends in data security and electronic privacy. Other trends are customer service, work/family balance, environmental concern, globalization and outsourcing, diversity, teamwork, job flexibility, innovation and entrepreneurship. As this list of trends suggests, rapid change itself is another major trend in the business environment.

Data Security

As business communication becomes increasingly electronic, concerns about data theft mushroom. Just as individuals take steps—like not providing important identification numbers by e-mail—to prevent identity theft, organizations take steps to protect their data. The need for them to do so becomes always more urgent as hackers continue to produce more sophisticated software. In 2011, Sony reported the theft of names, birthdates, and possibly credit card numbers for 77 million people.[33]

Not all the lost data comes from hackers. Lost or stolen laptops and smart phones containing sensitive data also add to the problem. Flash drives, because of their small size, are an even bigger problem. Corporate security measures include bans on personal electronic devices. Some companies are even disabling extra USB connections to ensure employees cannot attach these devices. Others are performing random checks of laptops to look for unauthorized or unsecured files and using scans of fingerprints, eyes, or faces to limit and track access to specific computers.[34]

Data security problems affect individuals, too. When hackers get names and e-mail addresses, they can send **phishing messages,** e-mails that try to lure receivers to send sensitive information. When hackers can connect the names and addresses to actual firms the readers use, such as banks and stores, the phishing e-mails look so official that even executives and professionals are convinced to respond.

Electronic Privacy

As organizations respond to growing security concerns, their efforts often encroach on workers' privacy. Organizations are monitoring many different kinds

Identity theft is such a growing concern that some companies make it the main focus of their business.

of electronic interactions. According to a survey by the American Management Association of 304 companies,

- 73% store and review e-mail.
- 66% monitor Internet usage.
- 65% block inappropriate websites.
- 48% use video surveillance.
- 45% record time spent on phone and numbers dialed.
- 43% store and review computer files.[35]

The same study also showed that 45% track keystrokes (and time spent at the computer). Because of findings from such monitoring, some companies are blocking access to particular websites, especially Facebook, YouTube, sports and online shopping sites. Many organizations claim that heavy usage of these sites slows down company communications such as file transfers and e-mail. In 2009, Senator Chuck Grassley called for a halt of funds to the National Science Foundation after a report was released that found that some employees spent up to 20% of their workday looking at porn instead of reviewing grant proposals.[36]

Other surveillance techniques use GPS (global positioning system) chips to monitor locations of company vehicles, as well as arrival and departure times at job sites. EZ-Pass, the electronic toll collection system, records are being used in courts as proof of infidelity. Workers may tell their spouses they are in a meeting, but EZ-Pass has a record of where and when their vehicle entered or exited that day.[37] Cellphones and computers give approximate location signals that are accurate enough to help law enforcement officials locate suspects.

The division between corporate data security and personal privacy has become increasingly complex and blurry. Corporate surveillance does not necessarily stop when employees leave their offices or cars. It can continue to the company parking areas and even employees' homes. Companies such as Google, Delta Air Lines, and even Burger King have fired workers for content on their personal blogs. Although many workers believe their blogs are protected by the first amendment, the truth is that in most states, companies can fire employees for almost any reason except discrimination.[38]

A survey by the American Management Association found that over a quarter of companies fired employees for e-mail misuse.[39] New technologies make it increasingly easy for companies—and lawyers—to track employees. "E-discovery" software can aid searchers in sorting millions of documents and e-mails in just days to find relevant ones for court cases. They go far beyond finding specific words and terms. In some of the best, if you search for "dog," you will also find documents with "man's best friends" and even the notion of "walk." Other programs can find concepts rather than just key words. Still others look at activities—who did what when, who talked to whom—to extract patterns. They find anomalies, such as switching media from e-mail to phone or a face-to-face communication, or when a document is edited an unusual number of times by unusual people.[40]

Other media are also connected with privacy issues. Some Twitter users have found the hard way that their messages are not private. Paul Chambers lost his job and was convicted of threatening to blow up an airport after sending a joking tweet to his friends.[41] Detroit mayor Kwame Kilpatrick was charged with perjury and forced to resign after text messages he sent were used against him by prosecutors. Embarrassing photos of hapless individuals pepper the web. Employees have also been fired for posting on their personal Facebook site disparaging comments about their employers. And even "old" technology can threaten privacy. Illinois Governor Blagojevich was impeached on the bases of taped phone conversations.

Although more individuals are starting to sue over their firings, and a few are winning, the legal scale is still weighted in favor of employers. In 2010 the Supreme Court ruled that searches on work equipment are reasonable and not a violation of Fourth Amendment rights.

Someone's Watching

The anonymous life exists no more, if it ever did. Now private incidents are constantly being publicized on the Internet. New sites are constantly springing up that allow ordinary citizens to post blogs, comments, pictures, or videos about faux pas ranging from bad driving to leaving doggie droppings. Anyone, from your next door neighbor to the guy sitting next to you on the bus while you are loudly talking on your cellphone, can report a complaint about your social infraction on these websites.

For example, a North Carolina driver found himself accused of reckless driving. Unfortunately, the posting doesn't stop there; readers added the driver's full name and cellphone number. Other "violators" have had home address, occupation, and employer's name posted.

Check out some of these sites:

Platewire.com

Mybikelane.com

Litterbutt.com

Rudepeople.com

How would you feel if one of your actions were deemed obnoxious enough to show up on one of these websites? Do you think the self-policing of these types of websites can really make a difference?

Adapted from Jennifer Saranow, "The Snoop Next Door: Bad Parking, Loud Talking—No Transgression Is Too Trivial to Document Online," *Wall Street Journal,* January 12, 2007, W1.

Some companies are seeking to help individuals protect their privacy by offering services that delete messages and documents from multiple phones at a set time. Users can set an expiration time for their messages, which will be used to delete the messages from their own phones, the recipients' phones, and the messaging service's computer servers.[42] Other companies, for example, allow users to choose what kinds of ads they will see or to opt out altogether. Companies like Microsoft and Mozilla are beginning to include do-not-track features in their popular Internet browsers, to keep advertisers and others from monitoring online habits.[43]

In 2009, the Federal Trade Commission endorsed industry self-regulation to protect consumer privacy. Websites and companies that collect consumer data such as searches performed and websites visited are to (1) clearly notify consumers that they do so, (2) provide an easy way to opt out, (3) protect the data, and (4) limit its retention, but breaches of these guidelines continue to occur.[44]

A highly publicized study by the *Wall Street Journal* of the 50 most popular websites in the United States found that those sites installed 3,180 tracking files on the test computer. Twelve sites, including Dictionary.com, Comcast.net, and MSN.com, installed over 100 tracking tools each. Some tracking files could track sensitive health and financial data; other files could transmit keystrokes; still other files could reattach trackers that a person deleted. Apps on smart phones are performing similar trackings.[45]

Customer Service

One effect of the recession was to push more businesses into focusing on their customer service. Amazon, for instance, is well-known for its mission to be "Earth's most customer centric company." But it is far from alone. Customer satisfaction is increasingly important for all businesses; in fact, it is a leading indicator of financial success.[46] Companies with higher scores on the American Customer Satisfaction Index (ACSI) tend to see better sales and stock performance than do companies with lower scores.[47] In an age where unhappy customers can share their experiences with thousands of web users, focusing on customer satisfaction is vital.

Improving customer service doesn't always mean spending extra money. Companies are learning to cross-train employees, so they can fill in where needed. Other companies are giving extra attention to their best customers to keep them loyal. Walgreens is training its pharmacists to work more closely with patients with chronic illnesses such as diabetes.[48] A tried and true way of improving customer service is increasing the oral communication skills of sales reps and customer service agents.

Work/Family Balance

In addition to improving customer satisfaction, businesses are also focusing on their own employees. To reduce turnover, and increase employee satisfaction, companies are trying to be more family friendly by proving flextime, telecommuting, time off for family needs, and extended career breaks for caregiving. The balance of work and family is becoming such a popular topic that the *Wall Street Journal* now runs a regular column called "Work and Family."

At Cisco, 95% of employees take advantage of flextime, and 90% do some of their work off-site (the average is two days a week). Mothers of young

Many organizations promote virtual offices, which allow employees to work from home.

Santa Letters

Even letters to Santa Claus reflect the wider business environment.

During good times, children tend to ask for everything they see. But tougher economic times are reflected in children's letters. The letters talk of grim topics such as lost jobs and homes. They plead for basic necessities—rent money for mom, diapers for the baby, socks and warm clothing for everyone.

The Chicago main post office alone receives over 12,000 letters to Santa. Employees and volunteers sort them by gender and family size, then put them in the lobby where customers can select a child to help. Hundreds do so.

Adapted from Stacy St. Clair, "Letters to Santa Reflect Reality of Grim Economy: Kids' Requests for Toys Are Replaced with Wishes for Pajamas—or Rent Money for Their Parents," *Des Moines Register*, December 11, 2008, 3A.

children can take extended leave of up to two years, including one with full benefits. Cisco also offers job sharing and some positions that work full-time from home. Microsoft offers in-home sick care for sick children, as well as local centers for mildly ill children.[49]

At times, employees find ways other than physical presence to demonstrate their commitment and enthusiasm for organizational goals. Thanks to technology advances, employees can use laptops, e-mail, or cellphones to do work at any time, including weekends and evenings. The downside of this trend is that sometimes work and family life are not so much balanced as blurred. For instance, many employers are giving portable media players to workers for training courses, language lessons, and general organizational announcements to hear on their own time. Some employees are also expected to conduct business 24-hours a day because of different time zones of workplaces. The flexibility of employees is necessary in an age of downsizing and globalization, but it means that families are being impacted.

Dilbert's company, the one of cartoon fame, no longer uses the phrase work/family balance; instead, it uses "'work-life integration' so it's easier to make you work when you would prefer being with loved ones."[50]

Environmental Concern

As global warming becomes an issue of increasing concern, more and more companies are trying to soften their environmental impact. They do so for a variety of reasons in addition to environmental concerns. Sometimes such awareness saves money; sometimes executives hope it will create favorable publicity for the company. However, many marketing experts say that green advertising is now just standard operating procedure.[51] Environmental activist groups such as Greenpeace and Friends of the Earth go even further. These groups have sharply and publicly criticized some large companies for exaggerating their commitment to the environment. One study claims that 95% of the "green" products it examined made claims that were lies, unsupported by proof, or couched in meaningless language ("all-natural").[52]

Fortune's 2007 list of the 20 most admired companies was organized around environmental awareness. The top companies on it owed a significant part of their growth to strategies and products aimed at helping the environment.

Walmart is boosting its purchase of local, small-farmer grown produce, both domestically and internationally. GE has spent more than $5 billion in research and development for its ecomagination initiative; it has committed itself to an additional $10 billion by 2015. Revenues from its energy-efficient and environmentally sound products and services crossed $18 billion in 2009, almost two times the company average.[53]

Globalization and Outsourcing

In the global economy, importing and exporting are just a start. More and more companies have offices and factories around the world:

- McDonald's serves food in over 119 countries on six continents.[54]
- 3M operates in over 65 countries; 65% of its sales are international.[55]
- UPS serves over 220 countries and territories.[56]
- Coca-Cola sells its beverages in over 200 countries.[57]
- Walmart has 4,600 stores outside the continental United States, including ones in Central America, South America, China, India, and Japan.[58]

Alternate energy has become a leading environmental issue, bringing both business and good publicity to some companies.

McDonald's now serves food in China.

The site of the store, factory, or office may not be the site of all the jobs. A data center in Washington can support many workers in India as businesses are outsourcing domestically and globally. **Outsourcing** means going outside the company for products and services that once were produced by the company's employees. Companies can outsource technology services, customer service, tax services, legal services, accounting services, benefit communications, manufacturing, and marketing. Outsourcing is often a win–win solution: the company saves money or gets better service, and the outsourcers make a profit. In *The World Is Flat,* Thomas Friedman says "the accountant who wants to stay in business in America will be the one who focuses on designing creative, complex strategies. . . . It means having quality-time discussions with clients."[59] He sees the work of the future as customization, innovation, service, and problem solving.[60]

All the challenges of communicating in one culture and country increase exponentially when people communicate across cultures and countries. Succeeding in a global market requires **intercultural competence,** the ability to communicate sensitively with people from other cultures and countries, based on an understanding of cultural differences. To learn more about international communication, see Chapter 7.

Diversity

Women, people of color, and immigrants have always been part of the U.S. workforce. But for most of this country's history, they were relegated to clerical, domestic, or menial jobs. Now, U.S. businesses realize that barriers to promotion hurt the bottom line as well as individuals. Success depends on using the brains and commitment as well as the hands and muscles of every worker.

In the last decade, we have also become aware of other sources of diversity beyond those of gender, race, and country of origin: age, religion, class,

Japanese Companies Woo Former Female Employees

Faced with a looming worker shortage as baby boomers retire, Japanese companies have begun courting their former women employees. Some are accepting former employees' requests to work part-time and offering coaches until the women get back up to speed. Other companies are offering perks to female employees to retain them. Some companies are offering day care centers and coupons for babysitting and house-cleaning services; other companies allow women to work shorter hours or reject overtime work until their youngest child finishes high school.

"'It's not difficult to set up a [female-friendly] system,' says [the] manager of a division promoting women at Mizuho's [one of Japan's major banks] corporate banking unit. 'The hardest part is changing people's mentality. It takes a long time.'"

Adapted and quoted from Miho Inada, "Japanese Companies Woo Women Back to Work," *Wall Street Journal,* July 23, 2007, B1.

Team Communication Saves Lives

Communication breakdowns during patient transfers between units or personnel shifts are the largest source of medical error. The hospital accreditation board is now requiring hospitals to establish standards for transfer communications. To help hospitals, the Institute for Healthcare Improvement is working with hospitals on a communication rubric known as SBAR:

- Situation: describe briefly, get attention.
- Background: offer enough to provide context for the problem.
- Assessment: your assessment of overall condition.
- Recommendation: your specific recommendations.

Kaiser Permanente, the large health care organization, pioneered using the model, which helps doctors and nurses convey the most critical information in just 60 seconds. The model increases communication between doctors who don't want nurses' opinions and nurses who are reluctant to provide their opinions.

One Kaiser physician administrator says, "In almost all serious avoidable episodes of patient harm, communication failure plays a central role. . . . By teaching caregivers new models of 'structured communication,'. . . we can make sure that we are all in the same movie."

Adapted from Laura Landro, "Hospitals Combat Errors at the 'Hand-Off': New Procedures Aim to Reduce Miscues as Nurses and Doctors Transfer Patients to Next Shift," *Wall Street Journal*, June 28, 2006, D1, D2.

regional differences, sexual orientation, and physical disabilities are now areas of diversity. Helping each worker reach his or her potential requires more flexibility from managers as well as more knowledge about intercultural communication. And it's crucial to help workers from different backgrounds understand each other—especially in today's global economy. To learn more about diversity and the workforce, read Chapter 7.

Teamwork

More and more companies are getting work done through teams. Teamwork brings together people's varying strengths and talents to solve problems and make decisions. Often, teams are cross-functional (drawing from different jobs or functions) or cross-cultural (including people from different nations or cultural groups served by the company).

Teams, including cross-functional teams, helped Sarasota Memorial Hospital resolve major problems with customer and employee satisfaction. For example, team members from the emergency room recorded every step in the process from pulling into the parking lot through decisions about patient care, and then they eliminated unnecessary steps. The ER team worked with the laboratory staff to improve the process of getting test results. At Michelin, the French tire maker, teams bring together people from the United States and Europe. According to the company's chemical purchasing manager for Europe, the exchange between the two continents helps employees on both sides of the Atlantic understand each other's perspectives and needs.[61]

Increasing emphasis on teamwork is a major reason given by organizations such as AT&T, Intel, Hewlett-Packard, and the U.S. Interior Department for calling telecommuting workers back to the office.[62] To learn more about working in teams, see Chapter 8.

Job Flexibility

In traditional jobs, people did what they were told to do. But today, jobs that are routine can readily be done in other countries at lower cost. Many U.S. jobs have already been subject to such "offshoring," and more are sure to follow. The work that remains in the United States is more likely to be complex work requiring innovation, flexibility, and adaptation to new learning.

Today's workers do whatever needs to be done, based on the needs of customers, colleagues, and anyone else who depends on their work. They help team members finish individual work; they assist office mates with pressing deadlines. They are resourceful: they know how to find information and solution ideas. They work extra hours when the task demands it. They are ready to change positions and even locations when asked to do so. They need new skill sets even when they don't change jobs.

At Sarasota Memorial Hospital, food service workers do more than bring food to patients; they open containers, resolve problems with meals, help patients read their menus, and adjust orders to meet patients' preferences. This attentiveness not only serves the patients; it is part of a team-spirited approach to patient care that in this case frees nurses to do other work.[63] The experience at Sarasota Memorial is backed up by research suggesting that the most effective workers don't see work as assigned tasks. Instead, they define their own goals based on the needs of customers and clients.[64]

Your parents may have worked for the same company all their lives. You may do that, too, but you have to be prepared to job-hunt throughout your career. That means continuing to learn—keeping up with new technologies, new economic and political realities, new ways of interacting with people.

Innovation and Entrepreneurship

As global competition increases, and industrial milieus change ever more quickly, innovation becomes more and more important. *Fortune*'s 2008 list of most admired companies was organized around innovation. Apple, at the top of the list, also got the top marks for innovation.

Many companies rely on all employees for suggestions. A classic article in the *Harvard Business Review* made famous the examples of 3M (where researchers can spend 15% of their time on ideas that don't need management approval), Thermo Electron (where managers can "spin out" promising new businesses), and Xerox (where employees write business proposals competing for corporate funds to develop new technologies).[65] 3M also sends 9,000 employees, in 35 countries, into customers' workplaces to work beside people there and to note problems the company can solve. American Express established a $50 million innovation fund to finance employees' ideas.[66] Google is famous for its 20% rule: technical employees can spend about 20% of their time on projects outside their main job, and even their managers cannot remove that free margin.[67]

The spirit of innovation is inspiring some workers to start their own businesses. The U.S. Census Bureau counted 21.4 million nonemployer businesses (self-employed workers without employees) in 2008.[68] In fact, these businesses are the majority of all U.S. businesses. These entrepreneurs have to handle all the communication in the business: hiring, training, motivating, and evaluating employees; responding to customer complaints; drafting surveys; writing business plans; making presentations to venture capitalists; and marketing the product or service.

World-Class Innovation

Ideo, the world-famous design consulting firm, has over 1,000 patents and 346 design awards. Their message to the world is that creativity is not a burst of inspiration but rather a teachable process—understand, observe, brainstorm, prototype—that can be incorporated into businesses of all sizes.

One of their clients, the giant health care provider Kaiser Permanente, now has its own innovation center that follows the Ideo way. That center tackled the all-too-common problem of medication errors, errors that harm more than 1.5 million people in the United States alone. A team shadowed doctors, nurses, and pharmacists as they prescribed, administered, and filled medications. They made videos; they kept journals. And they discovered that interruptions were the cause of most errors. So the team brainstormed solutions, including "Leave Me Alone!" aprons and red "Do Not Cross!" lines in front of medication stations. The program has reduced interruptions by 50%.

Adapted from Linda Tischler, "A Designer Takes On His Biggest Challenge Ever," *Fast Company*, February 2009, 78–83, 101.

Rapid Rate of Change

As any employee who has watched his or her job shift can testify, change—even change for the better—is stressful. Even when change promises improvements, people have to work to learn new skills, new habits, and new attitudes.

Rapid change means that no college course or executive MBA program can teach you everything you need to know for the rest of your working life. You'll need to stay abreast of professional changes by reading trade journals as well as professional websites and blogs, participating in professional Listservs, and attending professional events. Take advantage of your company's training courses and materials; volunteer for jobs that will help you gain new skills and knowledge. Pay particular attention to your communication skills; they become even more important as you advance up your career ladder. A survey of 1,400 financial executives found that 75% considered oral, written, and interpersonal skills even more important for finance professionals now than they were just a few years ago.[69]

The skills you polish along the way can stand you in good stead for the rest of your life: critical thinking, computer savvy, problem solving, and the ability to write, speak, and work well with other people are vital in most jobs. It's almost a cliché, but it is still true: the most important knowledge you gain in college is how to learn.

SUMMARY OF KEY POINTS

- The economic news continues to create concern over lapses in business ethics. On the other hand, positive ethical efforts are also increasing.
- Corporate cultures range from informal to formal and impact such widely diverse areas as worker performance and sales.

- Interpersonal communication includes such areas as listening, conversational style, body language, and networking. Its importance in career success is receiving new recognition.
- Time management skills are also crucial to job success. Probably the most important time management technique is to prioritize the demands on your time, and make sure you spend the majority of your time on the most important demands.
- Decades of research on multitasking show that it does not increase job performance and may actually hinder it.
- Eleven trends in business, government, and nonprofit organizations affect business and administrative communication: data security, electronic privacy, customer service, work/family balance, environmental concern, globalization and outsourcing, diversity, teamwork, job flexibility, innovation and entrepreneurship, and rapid change.

CHAPTER 4 Exercises and Problems

*Go to www.mhhe.com/locker/10e for additional Exercises and Problems.

4.1 Reviewing the Chapter

1. What are some positive ethical efforts that are getting attention? (LO 4-1)
2. What are some ethical components of communication? (LO 4-1)
3. What are some elements of corporate culture? How do they affect business? (LO 4-2)
4. What are some ways to improve interpersonal communication? (LO 4-3)
5. What are some communication signals you might receive from specific body language cues? (LO 4-3)
6. What are some ways to manage your time more efficiently? (LO 4-4)
7. What are 11 trends in business communication? What do these trends mean for you? (LO 4-5)
8. What are some electronic privacy issues that could affect you at your workplace? (LO 4-5)

4.2 Protecting Privacy Online

As companies demand ever-more accurate audiences to whom they can pitch their products and services, the debate over online tracking vs. privacy continues.

Working in small groups, discuss some of the challenges you see to protecting your privacy on the Internet.

- Should companies be allowed to track your online activity? Is it OK if they notify you they are tracking you? Do you like targeted placement ads, similar to Google's recommendations for you? Where do you find a balance between allowing Internet sites to use your information to provide better service and protecting your privacy?
- Are employers justified in monitoring employees' e-mail, Twitter, and Internet usage on company machines?
- Are employers justified in monitoring employees' Facebook accounts? Do you think it is fair when employees get fired for comments they post on their Facebook site?
- What do you think of companies like Google tracking searches to produce sites like Google Flu Trends, which shows where people are getting sick during flu season?

4.3 Following Trends in Business Communication

Pick three of the trends discussed in this chapter and explain how they have impacted business communications in an organization where you—or a friend or family member—have worked.

As your instructor directs,

a. Share your information in small groups.
b. Present your group findings to your classmates.
c. Post your information online for your classmates.

4.4 Applying Ethics Guidelines

Reread the ethics guidelines by Warren Buffett (sidebar on page 93) and Tony Hsieh (end of Ethics section). In small groups, apply them to some business ethics situations currently in the news.

- How would the situations be handled by Buffett? Hsieh?
- Do you approve of those solutions?
- Do you find one statement more helpful than the other? Why?

4.5 Making Ethical Choices

Indicate whether you consider each of the following actions ethical, unethical, or a gray area. Which of the actions would you do? Which would you feel uncomfortable doing? Which would you refuse to do?

Discuss your answers with a small group of classmates. In what ways did knowing you would share with a group change your answers?

1. Taking home office supplies (e.g., pens, markers, calculators, etc.) for personal use.
2. Inflating your evaluation of a subordinate because you know that only people ranked *excellent* will get pay raises.
3. Making personal long-distance calls on the company phone.
4. Updating your Facebook page and visiting the pages of friends during business hours.
5. Writing a feasibility report about a new product and de-emphasizing test results that show it could cause cancer.
6. Coming in to the office in the evening to use the company's computer for personal projects.
7. Designing an ad campaign for a cigarette brand.
8. Working as an accountant for a company that makes or advertises cigarettes.
9. Working as a manager in a company that exploits its nonunionized hourly workers.
10. Writing copy for a company's annual report hiding or minimizing the fact that the company pollutes the environment.
11. "Padding" your expense account by putting on it charges you did not pay for.
12. Telling a job candidate that the company "usually" grants cost-of-living raises every six months, even though you know that the company is losing money and plans to cancel cost-of-living raises for the next year.
13. Laughing at the racist or sexist jokes a client makes, even though you find them offensive.
14. Reading the *Wall Street Journal* on company time.

4.6 Analyzing Business Ethics

New Oriental Education & Technology Group offers Chinese students intensive courses to prepare for SAT, GRE, and TOEFL exams. The object of the courses is to enable their students to achieve scores that will get them into American colleges and universities. The courses provide traditional prep help, such as cramming vocabulary words, but they also offer more controversial techniques.

- They avail themselves of websites where students download the test questions they remember immediately after the exam. Since the tests do recycle some questions to ensure score consistency over time, they can prep students for actual exam questions.
- They provide tricks (e.g., females in the test passages are always smarter than males) that help students choose correct answers just by looking at the choices, without understanding the passages.
- Since many of their students are good at math, they recommend that five minutes into the math section, their students should flip back to the reading and finish it. Flipping is prohibited, but this timing helps students escape the attention of the proctors, who look for it at the beginning and end of each test section.
- They help students prepare essays and speeches on topics—such as biographies of famous Americans, that can be memorized and adapted to many situations, thus avoiding extemporaneous performances.

The upside of their efforts is that many of their students do fulfill dreams of getting into American schools. The downside is that many of these same students have such poor English skills that they cannot understand the lectures or participate in class discussions. Nor can they write class papers without help. Unfortunately, they score so well that they even sometimes test out of the transitional programs many schools have to help students with shaky English skills.

Is New Oriental an ethical business?

What would Warren Buffett say (see pg. 93)?

What would Tony Hsieh say (see end of Ethics section)?

What are New Oriental's effects on its students?

Why do American schools accept these students?

What could be done to make the situation more ethical?

Source: Daniel Golden, "U.S. College Test Prep in China Is: [sic]" *Bloomberg Businessweek,* May 9, 2011, 58–63.

4.7 Analyzing Philanthropic Websites

Working in small groups, go to the websites of some of the large philanthropic organizations such as the Gates Foundation, Google.org, or the Clinton Global Initiative. What commonalities do you see? Which aspects do you like best? If you were a rich multibillionaire who was going to leave a billion dollars to a philanthropy, which one would you choose? Why? Write your findings and answers to these questions in a memo to share with your class.

4.8 Analyzing Pro Bono Work

Pro bono legal work, free legal work for those in need, has long been a law tradition. But now some elite firms are so eager for pro bono work—to boost their image or ranking, to get high-profile cases, and to attract top law students—that they are paying for it.

- What do you think of organizations that charge law firms to do pro bono work?
- What do you think of law firms that do pro bono work just to boost their image or ranking? Does their motivation matter?
- When law firms pay to work on high-profile cases, what happens to welfare cases, landlord–tenant disputes, or divorce cases among poorer couples?

Discuss your answers in small groups.

4.9 Analyzing a Letter

Dr. Joseph Biederman, Professor of Psychiatry at Harvard Medical School and Chief of Clinical and Research Programs in Pediatric Psychopharmacology and Adult ADHD, wrote a letter to the editor of the *Wall Street Journal* that appeared December 19, 2008, on page A16. The letter reputes the claim that he had a significant relationship with pharmaceutical manufacturers. Find the letter in your library's electronic copy of the *Wall Street Journal.* (In ProQuest, the letter is listed under the title "I was Doing the Right Thing." Authors of letters to the editor are listed as Anonymous in ProQuest.)

For a memo to your instructor, analyze the letter.

- What was your first impression?
- Is the letter convincing to you?
- What part makes you most sympathetic to the doctor?
- Is there any part that works against the doctor?
- Who are the audiences?
- What is the purpose of the letter?

After you analyze the letter as it is, look up some articles about Dr. Biederman. Three that appeared in the *Wall Street Journal,* including the one referenced in the letter, are

- David Armstrong, "Harvard Researchers Fail To Report Drug Payments," *Wall Street Journal,* June 9, 2008, A2.
- David Armstrong and Alicia Mundy, "J&J Emails Raise Issues of Risperdal Promotion," *Wall Street Journal,* November 25, 2008, B1.
- Jennifer Levitz, "Drug Researcher Agrees to Curb Role," *Wall Street Journal,* December 31, 2008, B3.

Do these articles change your opinion of the letter? Why?

Include both parts of your analysis, of the letter itself and the impact of the articles, in a memo to your instructor.

4.10 Analyzing Corporate Culture

Some businesses are deciding not to hire people with visible body art. Do you think such policies are allowable expressions of corporate culture, or are they a form of discrimination? Discuss your answers in small groups.

4.11 Analyzing Corporate Culture

Go to *Fortune*'s 100 Best Companies to Work For website: http://money.cnn.com/magazines/fortune/bestcompanies/2011/full_list/.

Look up six companies you find interesting. What are unique features of their corporate culture? What features seem to be common with many companies? Which features did you find particularly appealing? Write up your findings in a memo for your instructor.

4.12 Analyzing Customer Service

Go to a business on campus or in your community where you can observe customer service for a half hour. Make sure you observe at least three different kinds of service.

- Where did you go? Why?
- What categories of service did you observe?
- What examples of good service did you see?
- What examples of service that could be improved did you see? How would you improve it?
- If you were the manager of the business, what changes would you make to impact customer service?

Write up your findings in a memo to your instructor.

4.13 Analyzing Nonverbal Communication

Choose one of your courses and make notes on nonverbal communications you see in the classroom.

- What are some dominant traits you see among the students?
- What are some interesting behaviors you see in individual students?
- Does the nonverbal communication differ from the beginning and end of the class?
- What are nonverbal communications from the instructor?
- Overall, what does the nonverbal communication in the classroom tell you about student learning in that class?

Write up your findings in a memo to your instructor.

4.14 Analyzing Body Language

Go to a location such as your campus or city library where you can watch people at work and rest. Spend a half hour observing examples of body language around you. Make sure your half hour includes examples of at least one group at work, individuals at work, and individuals relaxing.

- What were some interesting examples of body language you noted?
- What were some common features of body language?
- Did you see any unique body language?
- Could you make assumptions about group relations based on the body language you saw exhibited by members of the group?
- How did the body language of individuals who were relaxing differ from that of the group members?

Write up your findings in a memo for your instructor.

4.15 Analyzing Your Time Management

For two days, write down exactly how you spend your time. Be specific. Don't just say "two hours studying." Instead, note how long you spent on each item of study (e.g., 15 min. reviewing underlinings in sociology chapter, 20 min. reviewing class notes, an hour and 20 min. reading accounting chapter). Include time spent on items such as grooming, eating, talking with friends (both in person and on phone), texting, watching television, and sleeping.

Now analyze your time record. Does anything surprise you? How much time did you spend studying? Is it enough? Did you spend more time studying your most important subjects? Your hardest subjects? Did you spend time on projects that are due later in the term? Did you spend time on health-related items? Do you see items on which you spent too much time? Too little time? Did you spend any time on items that would fit in Covey's quadrant II (see page 100)?

As your instructor directs,

a. Share your findings in small groups.
b. Write up your findings in a memo for your instructor.

4.16 Analyzing the Business Environment Where You Work

In a memo to your instructor, describe and analyze the business environment at an organization where you have worked. Use this chapter as a guide for content. What aspects of the environment did you like? Dislike? What aspects helped your job performance? What aspects hindered your job performance?

4.17 Participating in a Networking Event

In this exercise, you are going to participate in a networking event, an abbreviated "talk and walk."

To prepare for the event,

- Prepare business cards for yourself, using a computer application of your choice.
- Prepare a list of people in your class that you would like to meet (give a visual description if you do not know their names).
- Prepare a list of questions you would like to have answered.
- Collect materials to use for taking notes during the event.

During the event, you will have six three-minute sessions to talk with a fellow student. Your instructor will time the sessions and tell you when to change people.

After the event, analyze what you have learned. Here are some questions to get you started:

- Who was the most interesting? Why?
- Who did you like the most? Why?
- Who would you most like to have on a team in this class? Why?
- Did you meet anyone who might become a professional contact? Explain.
- What lessons did you learn about networking?

As your instructor directs,

- Share your analyses in small groups; then prepare an informal oral report for the class.
- Write up your analysis in a memo to your teacher.
- Write up your analysis in a memo to post on your class website.

CHAPTER 5

Planning, Composing, and Revising

Chapter Outline

The Ways Good Writers Write

Activities in the Composing Process

Using Your Time Effectively

Brainstorming, Planning, and Organizing Business Documents

Writing Good Business and Administrative Documents

Half-Truths about Business Writing

- Half-Truth 1: "Write as You Talk."
- Half-Truth 2: "Never Use *I*."
- Half-Truth 3: "Never Use *You*."
- Half-Truth 4: "Never Begin a Sentence with *And* or *But*."
- Half-Truth 5: "Never End a Sentence with a Preposition."
- Half-Truth 6: "Big Words Impress People."
- Half-Truth 7: "Never Have a Sentence with More than 20 Words, or a Paragraph with More than 8 Lines."

Ten Ways to Make Your Writing Easier to Read

- As You Choose Words
- As You Write and Revise Sentences
- As You Write and Revise Paragraphs

Organizational Preferences for Style

Revising, Editing, and Proofreading

- What to Look for When You Revise
- What to Look for When You Edit
- How to Catch Typos

Getting and Using Feedback

Using Boilerplate

Readability Formulas

Summary of Key Points

NEWSWORTHY COMMUNICATION

Writing Practice for John Grisham

Best-selling author John Grisham knows the secret to writing success. His legal thrillers have sold more than 250 million copies worldwide, and nine of his novels have been adapted into successful films. But before his first book was published in 1988, Grisham was a working lawyer in Southaven, Mississippi. Like fellow lawyers-turned-writers Scott Turow and Erle Stanley Gardner (who created the character Perry Mason), Grisham honed his writing skills drafting and redrafting legal briefs.

Lawyers learn early to take special care in writing their briefs, which are the written arguments submitted to judges and opposing lawyers, two intimidating audiences. Judges study the materials' fairness, and opposing lawyers naturally search for flaws. Each brief must present the lawyer's arguments clearly, concisely, and persuasively.

> *"What lawyers understand better than most writers is that the really hard work takes place before setting pen to paper."*

How do lawyers do it? Freedman writes, "What lawyers understand better than most writers is that the really hard work takes place before setting pen to paper." In other words, to *write* effectively, lawyers must first *plan* effectively. Using the main facts and evidence in the case, lawyers create strategies, plan organizations, and focus arguments all before they start to write. And once they do begin writing, they draft, revise, rework, edit, and redraft, each step taking them closer to a strong, well-written legal brief.

According to Freedman, a good brief needs a strong central theme, plain language, focused arguments, and relentless revision and editing. The same tips hold true for any business document. While most memos, letters, and reports will not receive the same level of antagonistic scrutiny as legal briefs, using careful planning, drafting, and revision techniques will focus and improve any document.

Sources: Adam Freedman, "Why Trial Lawyers Say It Better," *Wall Street Journal*, January 29, 2011, http://online.wsj.com/article/SB10001424052748703555804576102384190154812.html; and "John Grisham Bio," JohnGrisham.com, accessed May 24, 2011, http://www.jgrisham.com/bio/.

Learning Objectives

After studying this chapter, you will know

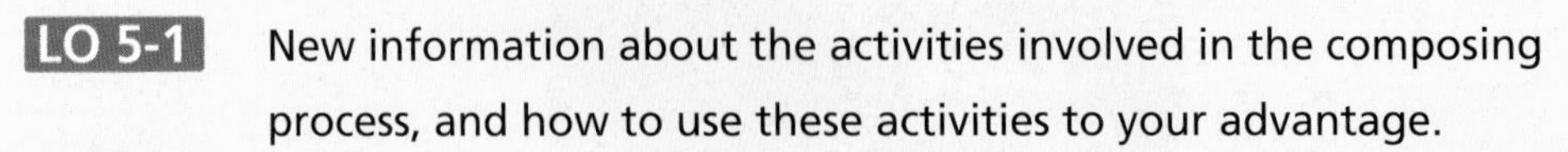

LO 5-1 New information about the activities involved in the composing process, and how to use these activities to your advantage.

LO 5-2 New guidelines for effective word choice, sentence construction, and paragraph organization.

LO 5-3 New techniques to revise, edit, and proofread your communications.

Ethics and the Writing Process

As you plan a message,

- Be sure you have identified the real audiences and purposes of the message.
- In difficult situations, seek allies in your organization and discuss your options with them.

As you compose,

- Provide accurate and complete information.
- Use reliable sources of material. Document when necessary.
- Warn your readers of limits or dangers in your information.
- Promise only what you can deliver.

As you revise,

- Check to see that your language does not use words that show bias.
- Use feedback to revise text and visuals that your audience may misunderstand.
- Check your sources.
- Assume that no document is confidential. E-mail documents and IMs (instant messages) can be forwarded and printed without your knowledge; both electronic and paper documents, including drafts, can be subpoenaed for court cases.

Skilled performances look easy and effortless. In reality, as every dancer, musician, and athlete knows, they're the products of hard work, hours of practice, attention to detail, and intense concentration. Like skilled performances in other arts, writing rests on a base of work.

THE WAYS GOOD WRITERS WRITE

No single writing process works for all writers all of the time. However, good writers and poor writers seem to use different processes.[1] Good writers are more likely to

- Realize that the first draft can be revised.
- Write regularly.
- Break big jobs into small chunks.
- Have clear goals focusing on purpose and audience.
- Have several different strategies to choose from.
- Use rules flexibly.
- Wait to edit until after the draft is complete.

The research also shows that good writers differ from poor writers in identifying and analyzing the initial problem more effectively, understanding the task more broadly and deeply, drawing from a wider repertoire of strategies, and seeing patterns more clearly. Good writers also are better at evaluating their own work.

Thinking about the writing process and consciously adopting the processes of good writers will help you become a better writer.

ACTIVITIES IN THE COMPOSING PROCESS LO 5-1

Composing can include many activities: planning, brainstorming, gathering, organizing, writing, evaluating, getting feedback, revising, editing, and proofreading. The activities do not have to come in this order. Not every task demands all activities.

Planning

- Analyzing the problem, defining your purposes, and analyzing the audience.

- Brainstorming information to include in the document.
- Gathering the information you need—from the message you're answering, a person, printed sources, or the web.
- Selecting the points you want to make, and the examples, data, and arguments to support them.
- Choosing a pattern of organization, making an outline, creating a list.

MBAs Can't Write

The writing and presentation skills of MBAs have long been a complaint of employers. Too many words, employers say, and too many big words. Graduates are particularly inept at preparing short persuasive communications or writing for multiple audiences.

Now MBA programs are acting on the complaints. The Wharton School of Business now requires 12 communication classes, twice what it required before. Other business schools are adding writing coaches, and having the writing coaches assign writing grades to papers for other courses.

Adapted from Diana Middleton, "Students Struggle for Words," *Wall Street Journal*, March 3, 2011, B8.

Writing

- Putting words on paper or a screen. Writing can be lists, possible headings, fragmentary notes, stream-of-consciousness writing, incomplete drafts, and ultimately a formal draft.

Revising

- Evaluating your work and measuring it against your goals and the requirements of the situation and audience. The best evaluation results from *re-seeing* your draft as if someone else had written it. Will your audience understand it? Is it complete? Convincing? Friendly?
- Getting feedback from someone else. Is all the necessary information there? Is there too much information? Is your pattern of organization appropriate? Does a revision solve an earlier problem? Are there obvious mistakes?
- Adding, deleting, substituting, or rearranging. Revision can be changes in single words or in large sections of a document.

Editing

- Checking the draft to see that it satisfies the requirements of standard English. Here you'd correct spelling and mechanical errors and check word choice and format. Unlike revision, which can produce major changes in meaning, editing focuses on the surface of writing.
- Proofreading the final copy to see that it's free from typographical errors.

Note the following points about these activities:

- **The activities do not have to come in this order.** Some people may gather data *after* writing a draft when they see that they need more specifics to achieve their purposes.
- **You do not have to finish one activity to start another.** Some writers plan a short section and write it, plan the next short section and write it, and so on through the document. Evaluating what is already written may cause a writer to do more planning or to change the original plan.
- **Most writers do not use all activities for all the documents they write.** You'll use more activities when you write more complex or difficult documents about new subjects or to audiences that are new to you.

For many workplace writers, pre-writing is not a warm-up activity to get ready to write the "real" document. It's really a series of activities designed to gather and organize information, take notes, brainstorm with colleagues, and plan a document before writing a complete draft. And for many people, these activities do not include outlining. Traditional outlining may lull writers into a false sense of confidence about their material and organization, making it difficult for them to revise their content and structure if they deviate from the outline developed early in the process.

Overcoming Writer's Block

According to psychologist Robert Boice, who has made a career study of writer's block, these actions help overcome writer's block:

1. **Prepare for writing.** Collect and arrange material. Talk to people; interact with some of your audiences. The more you learn about the company, its culture, and its context, the easier it will be to write—and the better your writing will be.
2. **Practice writing regularly and in moderation.** Try to write almost daily. Keep sessions to a moderate length; Boice suggests an hour to an hour and a half.
3. **Talk positively to yourself:** "I can do this." "If I keep working, ideas will come." "It doesn't have to be perfect; I can make it better later."
4. **Talk to other people about writing.** Value the feedback you get from them. Talking to other people expands your repertoire of strategies and helps you understand your writing community.

Adapted from Robert Boice, *Advice for New Faculty Members: Nihil Nimus* (Boston: Allyn & Bacon, 2000), 111–12.

Not all writing has to be completed in office settings. Some people work better outside, in coffee shops, or from home.

USING YOUR TIME EFFECTIVELY

To get the best results from the time you have, spend only one-third of your time actually "writing." Spend at least another one-third of your time analyzing the situation and your audience, gathering information, and organizing what you have to say. Spend the final third evaluating what you've said, revising the draft(s) to meet your purposes and the needs of the audience and the organization, editing a late draft to remove any errors in grammar and mechanics, and proofreading the final copy.

Do realize, however, that different writers, documents, and situations may need different time divisions to produce quality communications, especially if documents are produced by teams. Geographic distance will add even more time to the process.

BRAINSTORMING, PLANNING, AND ORGANIZING BUSINESS DOCUMENTS

Spend significant time planning and organizing before you begin to write. The better your ideas are when you start, the fewer drafts you'll need to produce a good document. Start by using the analysis questions from Chapter 1 to identify purpose and audience. Use the strategies described in Chapter 2 to analyze audience and identify benefits. Gather information you can use for your document. Select the points you want to make—and the examples and data to support them.

Sometimes your content will be determined by the situation. Sometimes, even when it's up to you to think of information to include in a report, you'll find it easy to think of ideas. If ideas won't come, try the following techniques:

- **Brainstorming.** Think of all the ideas you can, without judging them. Consciously try to get at least a dozen different ideas before you stop. Good brainstorming depends on generating many ideas.
- **Freewriting.**[2] Make yourself write, without stopping, for 10 minutes or so, even if you must write "I will think of something soon." At the end of 10 minutes, read what you've written, identify the best point in the draft, then set it aside, and write for another 10 uninterrupted minutes. Read this draft, marking anything that's good and should be kept, and

then write again for another 10 minutes. By the third session, you will probably produce several sections that are worth keeping—maybe even a complete draft that's ready to be revised.

- **Clustering.**[3] Write your topic in the middle of the page and circle it. Write down the ideas the topic suggests, circling them, too. (The circles are designed to tap into the nonlinear half of your brain.) When you've filled the page, look for patterns or repeated ideas. Use different colored pens to group related ideas. Then use these ideas to develop your content.
- **Talk to your audiences.** As research shows, talking to internal and external audiences helps writers to involve readers in the planning process and to understand the social and political relationships among readers. This preliminary work helps reduce the number of revisions needed before documents are approved.[4]

Thinking about the content, layout, or structure of your document can also give you ideas. For long documents, write out the headings you'll use. For short documents, jot down key points—information to include, objections to answer, benefits to develop. For an oral presentation, a meeting, or a document with lots of visuals, try creating a **storyboard,** with a rectangle representing each page or unit. Draw a box with a visual for each main point. Below the box, write a short caption or label.

WRITING GOOD BUSINESS AND ADMINISTRATIVE DOCUMENTS

Good business and administrative writing is closer to conversation and less formal than the style of writing that has traditionally earned high marks in college essays and term papers. (See Figure 5.1.)

Most people have several styles of talking, which they vary instinctively depending on the audience. Good writers have several styles, too. An e-mail to

Figure 5.1 Different Levels of Style

Feature	Conversational style	Good business style	Traditional term paper style
Formality	Highly informal	Conversational; sounds like a real person talking	More formal than conversation would be, but retains a human voice
Use of contractions	Many contractions	OK to use occasional contractions	Few contractions, if any
Pronouns	Uses first- and second-person pronouns	Uses first- and second-person pronouns	First- and second-person pronouns kept to a minimum
Level of friendliness	Friendly	Friendly	No effort to make style friendly
How personal	Personal; refers to specific circumstances of conversation	Personal; may refer to reader by name; refers to specific circumstances of audiences	Impersonal; may generally refer to readers but does not name them or refer to their circumstances
Word choice	Short, simple words; slang	Short, simple words but avoids slang	Many abstract words; scholarly, technical terms
Sentence and paragraph length	Incomplete sentences; no paragraphs	Short sentences and paragraphs	Longer sentences and paragraphs
Grammar	Can be ungrammatical	Uses standard English	Uses more formal standard English
Visual impact	Not applicable	Attention to visual impact of document	No particular attention to visual impact

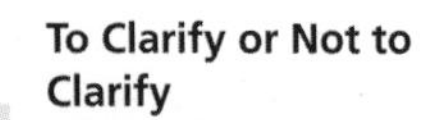

To Clarify or Not to Clarify

Former Federal Board Chair Alan Greenspan was known for his lack of clarity. After one speech, a headline in the *Washington Post* read "Greenspan Hints Fed May Cut Interest Rates," while the corresponding headline in the *New York Times* read "Doubt Voiced by Greenspan on a Rate Cut." Even his wife joked that he had to propose twice before she understood what he was saying.

His replacement, Ben Bernanke, has a different style. As he aims for more transparent communications, he is trying to make the Fed clearer about goals for economic growth.

Adapted from Greg Ip, "'Transparent' Vision: New Fed Chairman Hopes to Downplay Impact of His Words," *Wall Street Journal*, September 6, 2006, A1; and Daniel Kadlec, "5 Ways the New Fed Chairman Will Be Different," *Time*, November 7, 2005, 49–50.

your boss about the delays from a supplier will be informal, perhaps even chatty; a letter to the supplier demanding better service will be more formal.

Reports tend to be more formal than letters and memos, since they may be read many years in the future by audiences the writer can barely imagine. Reports tend to avoid contractions, personal pronouns, and second person (since so many people read reports, *you* doesn't have much meaning). See Chapter 18 for more about report style.

Keep the following points in mind as you choose a level of formality for a specific document:

- Use a friendly, informal style to someone you've talked with.
- Avoid contractions, slang, and even minor grammatical lapses in paper documents to people you don't know. Abbreviations are OK in e-mail messages if they're part of the group's culture.
- Pay particular attention to your style when you write to people you fear or when you must give bad news. Research shows our style changes in stressful contexts. We tend to rely on nouns rather than on verbs and deaden our style when we are under stress or feel insecure.[5] Confident people are more direct. Edit your writing so that you sound confident, whether you feel that way or not.

More and more organizations are trying to simplify their communications. Alan Greenspan, former chair of the Federal Reserve, was infamously known for his lack of clarity in communications, but his successor is striving to bring about new clarity in the board's communications (see sidebar on this page).

In the financial world, the US Securities and Exchange Commission's *A Plain English Handbook: How to Create Clear SEC Disclosure Documents* asks for short sentences, everyday words, active voice, bullet lists, and descriptive headings. It cautions against legal and highly technical terms. Warren Buffett wrote the preface, saying that the handbook was good news for him, because too often he had been unable to decipher the documents filed by public companies. He offers his own writing tip: write to a specific person. He says he pretends he is writing to his sisters when he writes his Berkshire Hathaway annual reports. The SEC has more recently applied the handbook standards to the brochures investment advisers give to clients and has urged them on hedge funds.[6]

In 2010, the Plain Writing Act became law. It requires all federal agencies to use clear prose that the public can readily understand. PlainLanguage.gov explains the law, provides a 112-page manual to help agencies use plain language, and offers examples of good federal communication.

Of course, the news is full of examples where these efforts have failed. The same negative examples, however, also show the great need for clear, simple style. A major factor in the subprime mortgage disaster was documents written in prose so complex that even experts couldn't understand it. Many homeowners who signed adjustable rate mortgages and subsequently lost their homes claim they did not understand all the consequences of what they were signing. Experts outside the mortgage business agree with the homeowners that the language was too complex for most people to understand.[7]

Communication consultants like Gerard Braud urge clients to simplify their prose. He warns, "All communication affects [the] bottom line. . . . When a reader, listener, viewer or member of a live audience has to take even a nanosecond to decipher what you are saying because you are making it more complicated than it needs to be, you may lose that person."[8]

Good business style allows for individual variation. Figure 5.2 shows the opening paragraphs from Warren Buffett's letter to shareholders in Berkshire Hathaway's 2010 annual report. Buffett's direct style suggests integrity and

Figure 5.2 Opening Paragraphs of Warren Buffett's 2010 Letter to Shareholders

BERKSHIRE HATHAWAY INC.

To the Shareholders of Berkshire Hathaway Inc.:

Buffett's letter start with a short financial summary of the past year.

The per-share book value of both our Class A and Class B stock increased by 13% in 2010. Over the last 46 years (that is, since present management took over), book value has grown from $19 to $95,453, a rate of 20.2% compounded annually.*

The highlight of 2010 was our acquisition of Burlington Northern Santa Fe, a purchase that's working out even better than I expected. It now appears that owning this railroad will increase Berkshire's "normal" earning power by nearly 40% pre-tax and by well over 30% after-tax. Making this purchase increased our share count by 6% and used $22 billion of cash. Since we've quickly replenished the cash, the economics of this transaction have turned out very well.

He explains his assumptions.

A "normal year," of course, is not something that either Charlie Munger, Vice Chairman of Berkshire and my partner, or I can define with anything like precision. But for the purpose of estimating our current earning power, we are envisioning a year free of a mega-catastrophe in insurance and possessing a general business climate somewhat better than that of 2010 but weaker than that of 2005 or 2006. Using these assumptions, and several others that I will explain in the "Investment" section, I can estimate that the normal earning power of the assets we currently own is about $17 billion pre-tax and $12 billion after-tax, excluding any capital gains or losses. Every day Charlie and I think about how we can build on this base.

Social benefits

Both of us are enthusiastic about BNSF's future because railroads have major cost and environmental advantages over trucking, their main competitor. Last year BNSF moved each ton of freight it carried a record 500 miles on a single gallon of diesel fuel. That's *three* times more fuel-efficient than trucking is, which means our railroad owns an important advantage in operating costs. Concurrently, our country gains because of reduced greenhouse emissions and a much smaller need for imported oil. When traffic travels by rail, society benefits.

. . .

Historic examples

Money will always flow toward opportunity, and there is an abundance of that in America. Commentators today often talk of "great uncertainty." But think back, for example, to December 6, 1941, October 18, 1987, and September 10, 2001. No matter how serene today may be, tomorrow is *always* uncertain.

Don't let that reality spook you. Throughout my lifetime, politicians and pundits have constantly moaned about terrifying problems facing America. Yet our citizens now live an astonishing six times better than when I was born. The prophets of doom have overlooked the all-important factor that *is* certain: Human potential is far from exhausted, and the American system for unleashing that potential—a system that has worked wonders for over two centuries despite frequent interruptions for recessions and even a Civil War—remains alive and effective.

Why do you think he used these dates?

We are not natively smarter than we were when our country was founded nor do we work harder. But look around you and see a world beyond the dreams of any colonial citizen. Now, as in 1776, 1861, 1932 and 1941, America's best days lie ahead.

Performance

Colorful metaphor

Charlie and I believe that those entrusted with handling the funds of others should establish performance goals at the onset of their stewardship. Lacking such standards, managements are tempted to shoot the arrow of performance and then paint the bull's-eye around wherever it lands.

* All per-share figures used in this report apply to Berkshire's A shares. Figures for the B shares are 1/1500th of those shown for A.

Source: Copyrighted material. Reprinted with permission of the author.

Evaluating "Rules" about Writing

Some "rules" are grammatical conventions. For example, standard edited English requires that each sentence have a subject and verb, and that the subject and verb agree. Business writing normally demands standard grammar, but exceptions exist. Promotional materials such as brochures, advertisements, and sales letters may use sentence fragments to mimic the effect of speech.

Other "rules" may be conventions adopted by an organization so that its documents will be consistent. For example, a company might decide to capitalize job titles (e.g., *Production Manager*) even though grammar doesn't require the capitals.

Still other "rules" are attempts to codify "what sounds good." "Never use *I*" and "use big words" are examples of this kind of "rule." To evaluate these "rules," you must consider your audience, purposes, and situation. If you want the effect produced by an impersonal style and polysyllabic words, use them. But use them only when you want the distancing they produce.

clarity. Later in the letter, Buffett adds some of the colorful prose for which he is famous:

- We're prepared. Our elephant gun has been reloaded, and my trigger finger is itchy.
- [Deriding those who dismiss important facts as anomalies] I always love explanations of that kind: The Flat Earth Society probably views a ship's circling of the globe as an annoying, but inconsequential, anomaly.
- The fundamental principle of auto racing is that to finish first, you must first finish.
- Credit is like oxygen. When either is abundant, its presence goes unnoticed. When either is missing, that's *all* that is noticed.[9]

HALF-TRUTHS ABOUT BUSINESS WRITING

Many generalizations about business writing are half-truths and must be applied selectively, if at all.

Half-Truth 1: "Write as You Talk."

Most of us use a colloquial, conversational style in speech that is too informal for writing. We use slang, incomplete sentences, and even grammatical errors.

Unless our speech is exceptionally fluent, "writing as we talk" can create awkward, repetitive, and badly organized prose. It's OK to write as you talk to produce your first draft, but edit to create a good written style.

Half-Truth 2: "Never Use *I*."

Using *I* too often can make your writing sound self-centered; using it unnecessarily will make your ideas seem tentative. However, when you write about things you've done or said or seen, using *I* is both appropriate and smoother than resorting to awkward passives or phrases like *this writer.*

Half-Truth 3: "Never Use *You.*"

Certainly writers should not use *you* in formal reports, as well as other situations where the audience is not known or *you* may sound too informal. But *you* is widely used in situations such as writing to familiar audiences like our office mates, describing audience benefits, and writing sales text.

Half-Truth 4: "Never Begin a Sentence with *And* or *But.*"

Beginning a sentence with *and* or *also* makes the idea that follows seem like an afterthought. That's OK when you want the effect of spontaneous speech in a written document, as you may in a sales letter. If you want to sound as though you have thought about what you are saying, put the *also* in the middle of the sentence or use another transition: *moreover, furthermore.*

But tells the reader that you are shifting gears and that the point which follows not only contrasts with but also is more important than the preceding ideas. Presenting such verbal signposts to your reader is important. Beginning a sentence with *but* is fine if doing so makes your paragraph read smoothly.

Half-Truth 5: "Never End a Sentence with a Preposition."

Prepositions are those useful little words that indicate relationships: *with, in, under, to, at.* In job application letters, reports, and important presentations, avoid ending sentences with prepositions. Most other messages are less formal; it's OK to end an occasional sentence with a preposition. Noting exceptions to the rule, Sir Winston Churchill famously scolded an editor who had presumptuously corrected a sentence ending with a preposition, "This is the kind of impertinence up with which I will not put."[10] Analyze your audience and the situation, and use the language that you think will get the best results.

Building a Better Style

To improve your style,

- Try telling someone what you really mean. Then write the words.
- Try reading your draft out loud to someone sitting about three feet away—about as far away as you'd sit in casual conversation. If the words sound awkward, they'll seem awkward to a reader, too.
- Ask someone else to read your draft out loud. Readers stumble because the words on the page aren't what they expect to see. The places where that person stumbles are places where your writing can be better.
- Read widely and write a *lot.*
- Use the 10 techniques starting on this page to polish your style.

Half-Truth 6: "Big Words Impress People."

Learning an academic discipline requires that you master its vocabulary. After you get out of school, however, no one will ask you to write just to prove that you understand something. Instead, you'll be asked to write or speak to people who need the information you have.

Sometimes you may want the sense of formality or technical expertise that big words create. But much of the time, big words just distance you from your audience and increase the risk of miscommunication. If you feel you need to use big words, make sure you use them correctly. When people misuse big words, they look foolish.

Half-Truth 7: "Never Have a Sentence with More than 20 Words, or a Paragraph with More than 8 Lines."

While it is true that long sentences and paragraphs may sometimes be hard to read, such is not always the case. Long sentences with parallel clauses (see pages 134–135) may be quite clear, and a longer paragraph with a bulleted list may be quite readable. Your audience, purpose, and context should guide length decisions. Instructions for complicated new software may need shorter sentences and paragraphs, but an instruction paragraph on the six criteria for legitimate travel expenses may be longer than eight lines and still quite clear.

If your audience, however, believes in rigid guidelines, then you should follow them also.

TEN WAYS TO MAKE YOUR WRITING EASIER TO READ LO 5-2

Direct, simple writing is easier to read. One study tested two versions of a memo report. The "high-impact" version had the "bottom line" (the purpose of the report) in the first paragraph, simple sentences in normal word order, active verbs, concrete language, short paragraphs, headings and lists, and first- and second-person pronouns. The high-impact version took 22% less time to read. Readers said they understood the report better, and tests showed that they really did understand it better.[11] Another study showed that high-impact instructions were more likely to be followed.[12]

As You Choose Words

The best word depends on context: the situation, your purposes, your audience, the words you have already used.

1. Use words that are accurate, appropriate, and familiar. Accurate words mean what you want to say. Appropriate words convey the attitudes you want and fit well with the other words in your document. Familiar words are easy to read and understand.

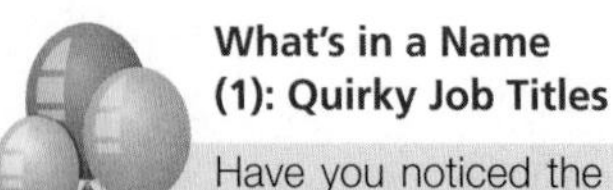

What's in a Name (1): Quirky Job Titles

Have you noticed the fun job titles at some companies lately? A mortgage company with a Wealth Creation Specialist, a chamber of commerce with a Director of First Impressions (receptionist)?

McLellan Marketing Group—headed by Top Dog, of course—has a Duchess of Details (project manager) and a Warden (accountant). The Top Dog says the titles give customers an immediate impression of the company so they can judge compatibility.

Even national companies have joined in the retitling craze. Best Buy's computer-help Geek Squad employs Special Agents, Field Marshals, and Mission Controllers. Build-a-Bear (stores where you choose, stuff, and dress your own teddy bear) has its Chief Executive Bear and Database Adminbearstrator.

Experts say the new titles work when they fit the corporate culture and company clients.

Adapted from Patt Johnson, "Quirky Names Try to Better Match What People Do," *Des Moines Register*, March 10, 2008, 1D.

Sometimes choosing the accurate word is hard. Most of us have word pairs that confuse us. Grammarian Richard Lederer tells Toastmasters that these 10 pairs are the ones you are most likely to see or hear confused.[13]

Affect/Effect	Disinterested/Uninterested
Among/Between	Farther/Further
Amount/Number	Fewer/Less
Compose/Comprise	Imply/Infer
Different from/Different than	Lay/Lie

For help using the pairs correctly, see Appendix B.

Some meanings are negotiated as we interact one-on-one with another person, attempting to communicate. Individuals are likely to have different ideas about value-laden words like *fair* or *empowerment*. The *Wall Street Journal* notes that the Securities and Exchange Commission has upped the ante on the definition of *rich* as it regulates the net worth requirement for those eligible to invest in hedge funds. That definition is important because it often becomes the government's definition of *rich*:

> The SEC. . . . says investors need to have investible assets of at least $2.5 million, excluding equity in any homes or businesses, to be eligible to sign on a hedge fund's dotted line. That's a huge jump from the current requirement, which says individuals have to have a net worth of at least $1 million, including the value of primary residences, or an annual income of $200,000 for the previous two years for individuals or $300,000 for couples."[14]

Some word choices have legal implications.

- Confusion about the definition of *wetlands* has reduced these natural resources by more than half.[15]
- Some employees, such as assistant managers in small franchises, are working to be reclassified as nonprofessionals. The word choice affects the workers' paychecks, because under labor laws employers are exempt from paying extra when professionals and administrators work overtime.[16]
- Medicare dropped its opposition to defining obesity as an illness, thus allowing Medicare to cover the payment for some treatments.[17]

As the last example indicates, some word choices have major health repercussions. Smokers have sued tobacco companies for duping them into believing that "light" cigarettes were less harmful. *Recall*, when used in warnings about defective pacemakers and defibrillators, causes patients to ask for replacements, even though the replacement surgery is riskier than the defective device. For this reason, some physician groups prefer *safety advisory* or *safety alert*.[18]

Accurate denotations To be accurate, a word's denotation must match the meaning the writer wishes to convey. Denotation is a word's literal or dictionary meaning. Most common words in English have more than one denotation. The word *pound*, for example, means, or denotes, a unit of weight, a place where stray animals are kept, a unit of money in the old British system, and the verb *to hit*. Coca-Cola spends millions each year to protect its brand names so that *Coke* will denote only that brand and not just any cola drink.

When two people use the same word or phrase to mean, or denote, different things, **bypassing** occurs. For example, a large mail-order drug company notifies clients by e-mail when their prescription renewals get stopped because the doctor has not verified the prescription. Patients are advised to call their doctors and remind them to verify. However, the company's website posts a sentence telling clients that the prescription is *being processed.* The drug company means the renewal is in the system, waiting for the doctor's verification. The patients believe the doctor has checked in and the renewal is moving forward. The confusion results in extra phone calls to the company's customer service number, delayed prescriptions, and general customer dissatisfaction.

Problems also arise when writers misuse words.

> The western part of Pennsylvania was transferred from Columbus to Philadelphia.

(Pennsylvania did not move. Instead, a company moved responsibility for sales in western Pennsylvania.)

> Three major divisions of Stiners Corporation are poised to strike out in opposite directions.

(Three different directions can't be opposite each other.)

> Stiners has grown dramatically over the past five years, largely by purchasing many smaller, desperate companies.

This latter statement probably did not intend to be so frank. More likely, the writer relied on a computer's spell checker, which accepted *desperate* for *disparate,* meaning "fundamentally different from one another."

Appropriate connotations Words are appropriate when their **connotations,** that is, their emotional associations or colorings, convey the attitude you want. A great many words carry connotations of approval or disapproval, disgust or delight. Words in the first column below suggest approval; words in the second column suggest criticism.

Positive word	Negative word
assume	guess
curious	nosy
cautious	fearful
firm	obstinate
flexible	wishy-washy

A supervisor can "tell the truth" about a subordinate's performance and yet write either a positive or a negative performance appraisal, based on the connotations of the words in the appraisal. Consider an employee who pays close attention to details. A positive appraisal might read, "Terry is a meticulous team member who takes care of details that others sometimes ignore." But the same behavior might be described negatively: "Terry is hung up on trivial details."

Advertisers carefully choose words with positive connotations.

- In this youth-conscious society, hearing aids become personal communication assistants.[19]
- Expensive cars are never *used;* instead, they're *pre-owned, experienced,* or even *previously adored.*[20]
- Insurers emphasize what you want to *protect* (your home, your car, your life), rather than the losses you are insuring against (fire damage, auto accident, death).
- Credit card companies tell about what you can do with the card (charge a vacation), not the debt, payments, and fees involved.

What's in a Name (2): How Local Is "Local"?

Some consumers prefer to purchase food produced locally on the assumption that the food will be fresher and contain fewer chemicals. But what does *local* mean? One woman in Washington, D.C., found "local" strawberries whose packaging indicated they were actually grown in California.

Some states and retailers have established definitions for what qualifies as locally grown: Vermont says within state or 30 miles of sales place; Walmart says *local* means produce came from the state where it is being sold. However, definitions vary widely, and, given the diversity of crops and their growing regions, a nationwide standard is unlikely.

So, despite the economic boon to retailers of labeling a product as locally produced, the advantage to consumers is not always clear.

Adapted from "Locally Grown Produce? It All Depends on How You Define It," *Des Moines Register*, April 2, 2011, 8A.

Words may also connote categories. Some show status. Both *salesperson* and *sales representative* are nonsexist job titles. But the first sounds like a clerk in a store; the second suggests someone selling important items to corporate customers. Some words connote age: *adorable* generally connotes young children, not adults. Other words, such as *handsome* or *pretty*, connote gender.

Connotations change over time. The word *charity* had acquired such negative connotations by the 19th century that people began to use the term *welfare* instead. Now, *welfare* has acquired negative associations. Most states have *public assistance programs* instead.

Ethical implications of word choice How positively can we present something and still be ethical? *Pressure-treated lumber* sounds acceptable. But naming the material injected under pressure—*arsenic-treated lumber*—may lead the customer to make a different decision. We have the right to package our ideas attractively, but we have the responsibility to give the public or our superiors all the information they need to make decisions.

Word choices have ethical implications in other contexts as well. When scientists refer to 100-year floods, they mean a flood so big that it has a 1% chance of happening in any given year. However, a "1% annual chance flood" is awkward and has not become standard usage. On the other hand, many nonscientists believe a 100-year flood will happen only once every hundred years. After a 100-year flood swamped the Midwest in 1993, many people moved back into flood-prone homes; some even dropped their flood insurance. Unfortunately, both actions left them devastated by a second 100-year flood in 2008.[21]

Perhaps one of the best-known examples of ethical implications deals with the interrogation technique of waterboarding. President Bush's attorney general said waterboarding was not torture; President Obama's attorney general said it was.[22]

Familiar words Use familiar words, words that are in almost everyone's vocabulary. Use the word that most exactly conveys your meaning, but whenever you can choose between two words that mean the same thing, use the shorter, more common one. Try to use specific, concrete words. They're easier to understand and remember.[23]

A series of long, learned, abstract terms makes writing less interesting, less forceful, and less memorable. When you have something simple to say, use simple words.

The following list gives a few examples of short, simple alternatives:

Formal and stuffy	Short and simple
ameliorate	improve
commence	begin
enumerate	list
finalize	finish, complete
prioritize	rank
utilize	use
viable option	choice

There are some exceptions to the general rule that "shorter is better":

- Use a long word if it is the only word that expresses your meaning exactly.
- Use a long word—or phrase—if it is more familiar than a short word: *a word in another language for a geographic place or area* is better than *exonym*.

- Use a long word if its connotations are more appropriate. *Exfoliate* is better than *scrape off dead skin cells.*
- Use a long word if your audience prefers it.

2. Use technical jargon sparingly; eliminate business jargon. There are two kinds of **jargon.** The first is the specialized terminology of a technical field. Many public figures enjoy mocking jargon. Even the *Wall Street Journal* does its share, mocking quotes like this one from a computer industry press release announcing a new "market offering":

> [The] offerings are leading-edge service configuration assurance capabilities that will help us to rapidly deploy high-demand IP services, such as level 3 virtual private networks, multi-cast and quality of service over our IP/MPLS network.[24]

A job application letter is one of the few occasions when it's desirable to use technical jargon: using the technical terminology of the reader's field helps suggest that you're a peer who also is competent in that field. In other kinds of messages, use technical jargon only when the term is essential and known to the reader. If a technical term has a "plain English" equivalent, use the simpler term.

The second kind of jargon is the **businessese** that some writers still use: *as per your request, enclosed please find, please do not hesitate.* None of the words in this second category of jargon are necessary. Indeed, some writers call these terms *deadwood,* since they are no longer living words. If any of the terms in the first column of Figure 5.3 show up in your writing, replace them with more modern language.

As You Write and Revise Sentences

At the sentence level, you can do many things to make your writing easy to read.

3. Use active voice most of the time. "Who does what" sentences with active voice make your writing more forceful.

A verb is in **active voice** if the grammatical subject of the sentence does the action the verb describes. A verb is in **passive voice** if the subject is acted upon. Passive voice is usually made up of a form of the verb *to be* plus a past participle. *Passive* has nothing to do with *past.* Passive voice can be past, present, or future:

were received	(in the past)
is recommended	(in the present)
will be implemented	(in the future)

To spot a passive voice, find the verb. If the verb describes something that the grammatical subject is doing, the verb is in active voice. If the verb describes something that is being done to the grammatical subject, the verb is in passive voice.

Active Voice	Passive Voice
The customer received 500 widgets.	Five hundred widgets were received by the customer.
I recommend this method.	This method is recommended by me.
The state agencies will implement the program.	The program will be implemented by the state agencies.

DUTA [Don't Use That Acronym]

Used properly, acronyms can be both convenient and powerful. Marketers in Washington, D.C., for example, use mostly unknown acronyms in their subway and billboard advertising to target government employees at specific agencies. It doesn't matter that most people have no idea what the ads are about; the signs are targeted for government procurement agents and program managers.

But acronyms can fail when the intended audience doesn't understand what an acronym stands for or when a single acronym has multiple meanings, sometimes even within the same organization. In Washington D.C., even some of the bureaucrats in the intended audience don't understand the ads.

To look up the definition of an acronym, try using www.AcronymFinder.com, an acronym dictionary used by businesses, lawyers, students, and savvy writers seeking acronym definitions. The site has over 1 million visitors and 4 million page views a month. In May 2011, the site listed more than 750,000 acronyms, including 90 SAFEs, 147 FASTs, and 202 CATs. No wonder acronyms can be confusing.

Adapted from Thomas Catan, "To Understand Washington Ads, You've Got to Be a Code Breaker," *Wall Street Journal,* March 7, 2011, A1.

Figure 5.3 Getting Rid of Business Jargon

Instead of	Use	Because
At your earliest convenience	The date you need a response	If you need it by a deadline, say so. It may never be convenient to respond.
As per your request; 65 miles per hour	As you requested; 65 miles an hour	*Per* is a Latin word for *by* or *for* each. Use *per* only when the meaning is correct; avoid mixing English and Latin.
Enclosed please find	Enclosed is; Here is	An enclosure isn't a treasure hunt. If you put something in the envelope, the reader will find it.
Hereto, herewith	Omit	Omit legal jargon.
Please be advised; Please be informed	Omit—simply start your response	You don't need a preface. Go ahead and start.
Please do not hesitate	Omit	Omit negative words.
Pursuant to	According to; or omit	*Pursuant* does not mean *after.* Omit legal jargon in any case.
This will acknowledge receipt of your letter.	Omit—start your response	If you answer a letter, the reader knows you got it.
Trusting this is satisfactory, we remain	Omit	Eliminate-*ing* endings. When you are through, stop.

Menu Word Choice

Some restaurants use humorous names for their dishes so patrons will talk about them to their friends.

- Sticky Fingers RibHouses, a South Carolina–based chain, calls its onion appetizer Git-R-D'onions.
- David Burke at Bloomingdales, New York, offers Angry Roasted Hen-in-Law: a roasted chicken which comes with a knife in its back.
- Spy City Café, next to Washington's Spy Museum, serves Disguise Dogs, hotdogs which come with a selection of 15 toppings ("disguises").

Adapted from Judy Mandell, "Name That Dish: Menu Writing Gets Creative," *USA Weekend,* March 18, 2007, 19.

To change from passive voice to active voice, you must make the agent the new subject. If no agent is specified in the sentence, you must supply one to make the sentence active.

Passive Voice	Active Voice
The request was approved by the plant manager.	The plant manager approved the request.
A decision will be made next month. No agent in sentence.	The committee will decide next month..
A letter will be sent informing the customer of the change. No agent in sentence.	[You] Send the customer a letter informing her about the change.

Passive voice has at least three disadvantages:

- If all the information in the original sentence is retained, passive voice makes the sentence longer. Passive voice takes more time to understand.[25]
- If the agent is omitted, it's not clear who is responsible for doing the action.
- Using much passive voice, especially in material that has a lot of big words, can make the writing boring and pompous.

Passive voice is desirable in these situations:

a. Use passive voice to emphasize the object receiving the action, not the agent.

> Your order was shipped November 15.

The customer's order, not the shipping clerk, is important.

b. Use passive voice to provide coherence within a paragraph. A sentence is easier to read if "old" information comes at the beginning of a sentence. When you have been discussing a topic, use the word again as your subject even if that requires passive voice.

The bank made several risky loans in the late 1990s. These loans were written off as "uncollectible" in 2001.

Using *loans* as the subject of the second sentence provides a link between the two sentences, making the paragraph as a whole easier to read.

c. Use passive voice to avoid assigning blame.

The order was damaged during shipment.

Active voice would require the writer to specify *who* damaged the order. The passive voice is more tactful here.

According to PlainLanguage.gov, changing writing to active voice is the most powerful change that can be made to government documents.[26] But even the self-proclaimed prescriptivist style editor Bill Walsh, a copy chief at the *Washington Post,* admits that sometimes passive voice is necessary—although not as often as many writers think.[27]

What's in a Name (3): Medicine Names

"Prozac. Viagra. Lipitor.

"The names of these incredibly popular medicines don't have defined meanings. But millions of dollars are spent creating just the right sound and image.

"Research shows letters with a hard edge like P, T or K convey effectiveness. X seems scientific. L, R or S provides a calming or relaxing feel. Z means speed. . . .

"Most companies prefer a name that says something about the drug, like Allegra, which alludes to the allergy relief it provides. . . .

"The name cannot make a claim about a drug. The hair-loss treatment Rogaine, for instance, was originally called Regain until the FDA rejected it. . . .

"The FDA rejects 35 percent to 40 percent of the brands it reviews. In Europe, the rejection rate approaches 50 percent."

Quoted from Tom Murphy, "Starts with P, T, K? Payoff Big for Right Drug Name: Companies Spend Millions of Dollars on Processing a Winning Medicine Brand," *Des Moines Register,* January 18, 2008, 6D.

4. Use verbs—not nouns—to carry the weight of your sentence. Put the weight of your sentence in the verb to make your sentences more forceful and up to 25% easier to read.[28] When the verb is a form of the verb *to be,* revise the sentence to use a more forceful verb.

Weak: The financial advantage of owning this equipment instead of leasing it is 10% after taxes.

Better: Owning this equipment rather than leasing it will save us 10% after taxes.

Nouns ending in *-ment, -ion,* and *-al* often hide verbs.

Weak	Better
make an adjustment	adjust
make a payment	pay
make a decision	decide
reach a conclusion	conclude
take into consideration	consider
make a referral	refer
provide assistance	assist

Use verbs to present the information more forcefully.

Weak: We will perform an investigation of the problem.

Better: We will investigate the problem.

Weak: Selection of a program should be based on the client's needs.

Better: Select the program that best fits the client's needs.

5. Eliminate wordiness. Writing is **wordy** if the same idea can be expressed in fewer words. Unnecessary words increase writing time, bore your reader, and make your meaning more difficult to follow, since the reader must hold all the extra words in mind while trying to understand your meaning. Don Bush, the "friendly editor" columnist for *intercom,* calls wordiness the most obvious fault of technical writing.[29]

Good writing is concise, but it may still be lengthy. Concise writing may be long because it is packed with ideas. In Chapter 3, we saw that revisions to create you-attitude and positive emphasis and to develop benefits were frequently *longer* than the originals because the revision added information not given in the original.

Meaningless Sentences

[Editor Bill Walsh of the *Washington Post* gives these examples of meaningless sentences]

- *A donation of your car, truck or boat is tax-deductible to the maximum extent of the law.*

In other words, you're allowed to deduct it as much as you're allowed to deduct it. Good news: Your toenail clippings are also deductible to the maximum extent of the law.

- *You can use this scholarship at any participating school in the world.*

I have no doubt that this is true. But it raises one major question. . . .

- *Area schools will be back in session Monday, disappointing thousands of children who would rather stay home and watch John Wayne movies.*

No, they wouldn't. (How old are you, anyway?)

Quoted from Bill Walsh, *The Elephants of Style: A Trunkload of Tips on the Big Issues and Gray Areas of Contemporary American English* (New York: McGraw-Hill, 2004), 140, 149.

Sometimes you may be able to look at a draft and see immediately how to condense it. When the solution isn't obvious, try the following strategies to condense your writing:

a. Eliminate words that add nothing.
b. Combine sentences to eliminate unnecessary words.
c. Put the meaning of your sentence into the subject and verb to cut the number of words.

You eliminate unnecessary words to save the reader's time, not simply to see how few words you can use. You aren't writing a telegram, so keep the little words that make sentences complete. (Incomplete sentences are fine in lists where all the items are incomplete.)

The following examples show how to use these methods.

a. Eliminate words that add nothing. Cut words if the idea is already clear from other words in the sentence. Substitute single words for wordy phrases.

Wordy: Keep this information on file for future reference.
Better: Keep this information for reference.
or: File this information.
Wordy: Ideally, it would be best to put the billing ticket just below the monitor and above the keyboard.
Better: If possible, put the billing ticket between the monitor and the keyboard.

Phrases beginning with *of, which,* and *that* can often be shortened.

Wordy: the question of most importance
Better: the most important question
Wordy: the estimate which is enclosed
Better: the enclosed estimate
Wordy: We need to act on the suggestions that our customers offer us.
Better: We need to act on customer suggestions.

Sentences beginning with *There are* or *It is* can often be tighter.

Wordy: There are three reasons for the success of the project.
Tighter: Three reasons explain the project's success.
Wordy: It is the case that college graduates advance more quickly in the company.
Tighter: College graduates advance more quickly in the company.

Check your draft. If you find these phrases, or any of the unnecessary words shown in Figure 5.4, eliminate them.

b. Combine sentences to eliminate unnecessary words. In addition to saving words, combining sentences focuses the reader's attention on key points, makes your writing sound more sophisticated, and sharpens the relationship between ideas, thus making your writing more coherent.

Wordy: I conducted this survey by telephone on Sunday, April 21. I questioned two groups of upperclass students—male and female—who, according to the Student Directory, were still living in the dorms. The purpose of this survey was to find out why some upperclassstudents continue to live in the dorms even though they are no longer required by the University to do so. I also wanted to find out if there were any differences between male and female upperclass students in their reasons for choosing to remain in the dorms.

Figure 5.4 Words to Cut

Cut the following words	Cut redundant words	Substitute a single word for a wordy phrase	
quite	~~a period of~~ three months	~~at the present time~~	now
really	during ~~the course of~~ the negotiations	~~due to the fact that~~	because
very	during ~~the year of~~ 2004	~~in order to~~	to
	maximum ~~possible~~	~~in the event that~~	if
	~~past~~ experience	~~in the near future~~	soon (or give the date)
	plan ~~in advance~~	~~on a regular basis~~	regularly
	refer ~~back~~	~~prior to the start of~~	before
	~~the color~~ blue	~~until such time as~~	until
	~~the state of~~ Texas		
	~~true~~ facts		

Tighter: On Sunday, April 21, I phoned upperclass men and women living in the dorms to find out (1) why they continue to live in the dorms even though they are no longer required to do so, and (2) whether men and women gave the same reasons.

c. Put the meaning of your sentence into the subject and verb to cut the number of words. Put the core of your meaning into the subject and verb of your main clause.

Wordy: The reason we are recommending the computerization of this process is because it will reduce the time required to obtain data and will give us more accurate data.

Better: Computerizing the process will give us more accurate data more quickly.

Wordy: The purpose of this letter is to indicate that if we are unable to mutually benefit from our seller/buyer relationship, with satisfactory material and satisfactory payment, then we have no alternative other than to sever the relationship. In other words, unless the account is handled in 45 days, we will have to change our terms to a permanent COD basis.

Better: A good buyer/seller relationship depends upon satisfactory material and payment. You can continue to charge your purchases from us only if you clear your present balance in 45 days.

6. Vary sentence length and sentence structure. Readable prose mixes sentence lengths and varies sentence structure. A really short sentence (under 10 words) can add punch to your prose. Really long sentences (over 30 or 40 words) are danger signs. The first-place Golden Gobbledygook Award, in the Legalese Hall of Shame, goes to a four-page, 1,000-word sentence in an indictment filed in Oklahoma.[30]

You can vary sentence patterns in several ways. First, you can mix simple, compound, and complex sentences. (See Appendix B for more information on sentence structure.) **Simple sentences** have one main clause:

We will open a new store this month.

Compound sentences have two main clauses joined with *and, but, or,* or another conjunction. Compound sentences work best when the ideas in the two clauses are closely related.

What's in a Name (4): Names Influence Eating Behaviors

Can renaming a food make it more appealing? Can the name make you eat more? Well, yes, especially if you're dieting.

Researchers called Jelly Belly candies "fruit chews" or "candy chews." Dieters rated "candy chews" as being less tasty than "fruit chews." In addition, dieters consumed 70% more jelly beans when the candies were called "fruit chews" than they did when the candies were called "candy chews."

Adapted from Christopher Shea, "Salad Is a Magic Word," *Wall Street Journal,* April 23–24, 2011, C4.

We have hired staff, and they will complete their training next week.

We wanted to have a local radio station broadcast from the store during its grand opening, but the DJs were already booked.

Complex sentences have one main and one subordinate clause; they are good for showing logical relationships.

When the stores open, we will have specials in every department.

Because we already have a strong customer base in the northwest, we expect the new store to be just as successful as the store in the City Center Mall.

You can also vary sentences by changing the order of elements. Normally the subject comes first.

We will survey customers later in the year to see whether demand warrants a third store on campus.

To create variety, occasionally begin the sentence with some other part of the sentence.

Later in the year, we will survey customers to see whether demand warrants a third store on campus.

Use these guidelines for sentence length and structure:

- Always edit sentences for conciseness. Even a short sentence can be wordy.
- When your subject matter is complicated or full of numbers, make a special effort to keep sentences short.
- Use longer sentences to show how ideas are linked to each other, to avoid a series of short, choppy sentences, and to reduce repetition.
- Group the words in long and medium-length sentences into chunks that the reader can process quickly.
- When you use a long sentence, keep the subject and verb close together.

Let's see how to apply the last three principles.

Use long sentences to show how ideas are linked to each other, to avoid a series of short, choppy sentences, and to reduce repetition. The following sentence is hard to read not simply because it is long but because it is shapeless. Just cutting it into a series of short, choppy sentences doesn't help. The best revision uses medium-length sentences to show the relationship between ideas.

Too long: It should also be noted in the historical patterns presented in the summary, that though there were delays in January and February which we realized were occurring, we are now back where we were about a year ago, and that we are not off line in our collect receivables as compared to last year at this time, but we do show a considerable over-budget figure because of an ultraconservative goal on the receivable investment.

Choppy: There were delays in January and February. We knew about them at the time. We are now back where we were about a year ago. The summary shows this. Our present collect receivables are in line with last year's. However, they exceed the budget. The reason they exceed the budget is that our goal for receivable investment was very conservative.

Better: As the summary shows, although there were delays in January and February (of which we were aware), we have now regained our position of a year ago. Our present collect receivables are in line with last year's, but they exceed the budget because our goal for receivable investment was very conservative.

Group the words in long and medium-length sentences into chunks. The "better" revision above has seven chunks. At 27 and 24 words, respectively, these sentences aren't short, but they're readable because no chunk is longer than 10 words. Any sentence pattern will get boring if it is repeated sentence after sentence. Use different sentence patterns—different kinds and lengths of chunks—to keep your prose interesting.

Keep the subject and verb close together. Often you can move the subject and verb closer together if you put the modifying material in a list at the end of the sentence. For maximum readability, present the list vertically.

Hard to read: Movements resulting from termination, layoffs and leaves, recalls and reinstates, transfers in, transfers out, promotions in, promotions out, and promotions within are presently documented through the Payroll Authorization Form.

Better: The Payroll Authorization Form documents the following movements:

- Termination
- Layoffs and leaves
- Recalls and reinstates
- Transfers in and out
- Promotions in, out, and within

7. Use parallel structure.

Parallel structure puts words, phrases, or clauses in the same grammatical and logical form. In the following faulty example, *by reviewing* is a gerund, while *note* is an imperative verb. Make the sentence parallel by using both gerunds or both imperatives.

Faulty: Errors can be checked by reviewing the daily exception report or note the number of errors you uncover when you match the lading copy with the file copy of the invoice.

Parallel: Errors can be checked by reviewing the daily exception report or by noting the number of errors you uncover when you match the lading copy with the file copy of the invoice.

Also parallel: To check errors, note

1. The number of items on the daily exception report.
2. The number of errors discovered when the lading copy and the file copy are matched.

Note that a list in parallel structure must fit grammatically into the umbrella sentence that introduces the list.

Faulty: The following suggestions can help employers avoid bias in job interviews:

1. Base questions on the job description.
2. Questioning techniques.
3. Selection and training of interviewers.

Parallel: The following suggestions can help employers avoid bias in job interviews:

1. Base questions on the job description.
2. Ask the same questions of all applicants.
3. Select and train interviewers carefully.

Also parallel: Employers can avoid bias in job interviews by

1. Basing questions on the job description.
2. Asking the same questions of all applicants.
3. Selecting and training interviewers carefully.

Limerick Law

Federal Judge Ronald Leighton thought a 465-page lawsuit (the title alone was eight pages) was too long. In a limerick, he demanded a "short and plain" statement of allegations:

Plaintiff has a great deal to say,
But it seems he skipped
Rule 8(a).
His Complaint is too long,
Which renders it wrong,
Please rewrite and refile today.

Adapted from "Nobles & Knaves," *Washington Times*, July 13, 2008, B02.

Words must also be logically parallel. In the following faulty example, *juniors, seniors,* and *athletes* are not three separate groups. The revision groups words into nonoverlapping categories.

Faulty: I interviewed juniors and seniors and athletes.

Parallel: I interviewed juniors and seniors. In each rank, I interviewed athletes and nonathletes.

Parallel structure is a powerful device for making your writing tighter, smoother, and more forceful. As Figure 5.5 shows, parallelism often enables you to tighten your writing. To make your writing as tight as possible, eliminate repetition in parallel lists; see Figure 5.6.

8. Put your readers in your sentences. Use second-person pronouns *(you)* rather than third-person *(he, she, one)* to give your writing more impact. *You* is both singular and plural; it can refer to a single person or to every member of your organization.

Third-person: Funds in a participating employee's account at the end of each six months will automatically be used to buy more stock unless a "Notice of Election Not to Exercise Purchase Rights" form is received from the employee.

Second-person: Once you begin to participate, funds in your account at the end of each six months will automatically be used to buy more stock unless you turn in a "Notice of Election Not to Exercise Purchase Rights" form.

Be careful to use *you* only when it refers to your reader.

Incorrect: My visit with the outside sales rep showed me that your schedule can change quickly.

Correct: My visit with the outside sales rep showed me that schedules can change quickly.

Figure 5.5 Use Parallelism to Tighten Your Writing.

These are the benefits the customer gets.
- Use tracking information.
- Our products let them scale the software to their needs.
- The customer can always rely on us.

Faulty

Customer Benefits
- Tracking information
- Scalability
- Reliability

Parallel

Figure 5.6 Eliminate Repeated Words in Parallel Lists.

PowerPoint Reports
- They work best when the audience is well-defined.
- They work best when visuals can carry the message.
- They work best when oral comments can explain and connect ideas.

Wordy

PowerPoint reports work best when
- The audience is well-defined.
- Visuals can carry the message.
- Oral comments can explain and connect ideas.

Concise

As You Write and Revise Paragraphs

Paragraphs are visual and logical units. Use them to chunk your sentences.

9. Begin most paragraphs with topic sentences. A good paragraph has **unity;** that is, it discusses only one idea, or topic. The **topic sentence** states the main idea and provides a scaffold to structure your document. Your writing will be easier to read if you make the topic sentence explicit and put it at the beginning of the paragraph.[31]

Hard to read (no topic sentence):	In fiscal 2012, the company filed claims for refund of federal income taxes of $3,199,000 and interest of $969,000 paid as a result of an examination of the company's federal income tax returns by the Internal Revenue Service (IRS) for the years 2008 through 2010. It is uncertain what amount, if any, may ultimately be recovered.
Better (paragraph starts with topic sentence):	The company and the IRS disagree about whether the company is responsible for back taxes. In fiscal 2012, the company filed claims for a refund of federal income taxes of $3,199,000 and interest of $969,000 paid as a result of an examination of the company's federal income tax returns by the Internal Revenue Service (IRS) for the years 2008 through 2010. It is uncertain what amount, if any, may ultimately be recovered.

A good topic sentence forecasts the structure and content of the paragraph.

Plan B also has economic advantages.

(Prepares the reader for a discussion of B's economic advantages.)

We had several personnel changes in June.

(Prepares the reader for a list of the month's terminations and hires.)

Employees have complained about one part of our new policy on parental leaves.

(Prepares the reader for a discussion of the problem.)

When the first sentence of a paragraph is not the topic sentence, readers who skim may miss the main point. If the paragraph does not have a topic sentence, you will need to write one. If you can't think of a single sentence that serves as an "umbrella" to cover every sentence, the paragraph probably lacks unity. To solve the problem, either split the paragraph into two or eliminate the sentence that digresses from the main point.

10. Use transitions to link ideas. Transition words and sentences signal the connections between ideas to the reader. Transitions tell whether the next sentence continues the previous thought or starts a new idea; they can tell whether the idea that comes next is more or less important than the previous thought. Figure 5.7 lists some of the most common transition words and phrases.

These sentences use transition words and phrases:

Kelly wants us to switch the contract to Ames Cleaning, and I agree with her. (continuing the same idea)

Kelly wants us to switch the contract to Ames Cleaning, but I prefer Ross Commercial. (contrasting opinions)

As a result of our differing views, we will be visiting both firms. (showing cause and effect)

Figure 5.7 Transition Words and Phrases

To show addition or continuation of the same idea
and
also
first, second, third
in addition
likewise
similarly

To introduce another important item
furthermore
moreover

To introduce an example
for example (e.g.)
for instance
indeed
to illustrate
namely
specifically

To contrast
in contrast
on the other hand
or

To show that the contrast is more important than the previous idea
but
however
nevertheless
on the contrary

To show cause and effect
as a result
because
consequently
for this reason
therefore

To show time
after
as
before
in the future
next
then
until
when
while

To summarize or end
finally
in conclusion

Writing for International Audiences

When you're writing for readers in another country, be careful to adjust your writing style to the new culture. Even the English language changes when you leave the United States. American spelling in documents for audiences who have learned British English can be annoying to readers. Remember that spelling is cultural, so adjust your writing to suit your readers, even if that means writing *grey, analyse, colour, centre,* and *familiarise.* Adjusting your style and your spelling for international audiences demonstrates respect for their cultures.

If you're adapting your text for an international audience, go beyond a dictionary. Localize your document by asking a native speaker from your target country (or countries) to read the document and note any problematic words, phrases, images, or examples.

Adapted from James Calvert Scott, "American and British Business-Related Spelling Differences," *Business Communication Quarterly* 67, no. 3 (2004): 153–67.

These are transitional sentences:

Now that we have examined the advantages of using Ames Cleaning, let's look at potential disadvantages. (shows movement between two sections of evaluation)

These pros and cons show us three reasons we should switch to Ross Commercial. (shows movement away from evaluation sections; forecasts the three reasons)

ORGANIZATIONAL PREFERENCES FOR STYLE

Different organizations and bosses may legitimately have different ideas about what constitutes good writing. If the style doesn't seem reasonable, ask. Often the documents that end up in files aren't especially good; later, other workers may find these and copy them, thinking they represent a corporate standard. Bosses may in fact prefer better writing.

Recognize that a style may serve other purposes than communication. An abstract, hard-to-read style may help a group forge its own identity. Researchers James Suchan and Ronald Dulek have shown that Navy officers preferred a passive, impersonal style because they saw themselves as followers. An aircraft company's engineers saw wordiness as the verbal equivalent of backup systems. A backup is redundant but essential to safety, because parts and systems do fail.[32]

Building a good style takes energy and effort, but it's well worth the work. Good style can make every document more effective; good style can help make you the good writer so valuable to every organization.

REVISING, EDITING, AND PROOFREADING LO 5-3

Once you have your document written, you need to polish it.

A popular myth is that Abraham Lincoln wrote the Gettysburg address, perhaps the most famous American presidential speech, on the back of an envelope on the train as he traveled to the battlefield's dedication. The reality is that Lincoln wrote at least a partial draft of the speech before leaving for the trip and continued to revise it up to the morning of its delivery. Furthermore, the speech was on a topic he passionately believed in, one he had been pondering for years.[33]

Like Lincoln, good writers work on their drafts; they make their documents better by judicious revising, editing, and proofreading.

- **Revising** means making changes in content, organization, and tone that will better satisfy your purposes and your audience.
- **Editing** means making surface-level changes that make the document grammatically correct.
- **Proofreading** means checking to be sure the document is free from typographical errors.

When Words Hurt

In the summer of 2006, a large, midwestern state university was gearing up to host the first national Special Olympics, a competition featuring people with intellectual disabilities. Visitors would be arriving from all over the country, and the small university town wanted to put on its best face for the crowds. The student newspaper created a 14-page, full-color visitors' guide to the town and inserted it into the campus paper. Unfortunately, they named it "[Name of Town] for Dummies" after the popular book series.

The editor-in-chief quickly apologized for the insensitive word choice, while the newspaper removed the inserts and replaced them with reprinted publications featuring a new headline.

Adapted from Lisa Rossi, "Olympics Section Goof Sends Paper Running," *Des Moines Register,* July 1, 2006, 1A, 4A.

What to Look for When You Revise

When you're writing to a new audience or have to solve a particularly difficult problem, plan to revise the draft at least three times. The first time, look for content and clarity: Have I said enough and have I said it clearly? The second time, check the organization and layout: Have I presented my content so it can be easily absorbed? Finally, check style and tone: Have I used you-attitude? The Thorough Revision Checklist summarizes the questions you should ask.

Often you'll get the best revision by setting aside your draft, getting a blank page or screen, and redrafting. This strategy takes advantage of the thinking you did on your first draft without locking you into the sentences in it.

As you revise, be sure to read the document through from start to finish. This is particularly important if you've composed in several sittings or if you've used text from other documents. Such documents tend to be choppy, repetitious, or inconsistent. You may need to add transitions, cut repetitive parts, or change words to create a uniform level of formality throughout the document.

If you're really in a time bind, do a light revision, as outlined in the Light Revision Checklist. The quality of the final document may not be as high as with a thorough revision, but even a light revision is better than skipping revision altogether.

Sometimes revising and proofreading is more pleasant if done in an informal setting.

Revisioning a Novel

Michael Chabon is a Pulitzer Prize author. And his novel, *The Yiddish Policemen's Union*, had a blurb in his publisher's sales catalog plus an on-sale date when his editor made him revise it.

He spent eight months reworking the entire book, adding a flashback structure and paring down the language.

Altogether, he spent five years and four drafts working on the novel. In the process, he moved to a different plot and changed from a first-person to a third-person narrator. His editor sent him detailed notes in the margins of the drafts. On the final draft, she went over the manuscript page by page with him.

The novel won both Hugo and Nebula awards, science fiction's highest awards.

Adapted from Sam Schechner, "Chabon's Amazing Rewrite Adventures," *Wall Street Journal*, April 27, 2007, W3.

Checklist Thorough Revision Checklist

Content and clarity

- ☐ Does your document meet the needs of the organization and of the reader—and make you look good?
- ☐ Have you given readers all the information they need to understand and act on your message?
- ☐ Is all the information accurate and clear?
- ☐ Is the message easy to read?
- ☐ Is each sentence clear? Is the message free from apparently contradictory statements?
- ☐ Is the logic clear and convincing? Are generalizations and benefits backed up with adequate supporting detail?

Organization and layout

- ☐ Is the pattern of organization clear? Is it appropriate for your purposes, audience, and context?
- ☐ Are transitions between ideas smooth? Do ideas within paragraphs flow smoothly?
- ☐ Does the design of the document make it easy for readers to find the information they need? Is the document visually inviting?
- ☐ Are the points emphasized by layout ones that deserve emphasis?
- ☐ Are the first and last paragraphs effective?

Style and tone

- ☐ Does the message use you-attitude and positive emphasis?
- ☐ Is the message friendly and free from sexist language?
- ☐ Does the message build goodwill?

Checklist Light Revision Checklist

- ☐ Have you given readers all the information they need to understand and act on your message?
- ☐ Is the pattern of organization clear and helpful?
- ☐ Is the logic clear and convincing? Are generalizations and benefits backed up with adequate supporting detail?
- ☐ Does the design of the document make it easy for readers to find the information they need?
- ☐ Are the first and last paragraphs effective?

What to Look for When You Edit

Even good writers need to edit, since no one can pay attention to surface correctness while thinking of ideas. Editing should always *follow* revision. There's no point in taking time to fix a grammatical error in a sentence that may be cut when you clarify your meaning or tighten your style. Some writers edit more accurately when they print out a copy of a document and edit the hard copy.

Check your material to make sure you have acknowledged all information and opinions you have borrowed from outside the organization (see Chapter 18 for help on documentation). Using material from outside the organization without acknowledging the source is plagiarism. Even when you use company information, you may need to acknowledge the source if your audience is skeptical or generally not aware of the existence of the information.

Check your communication to make sure your sentences say what you intend.

Not: Take a moment not to sign your policy.

But: Take a moment now to sign your policy.

Not: I wish to apply for the job as assistant manger.

But: I wish to apply for the job as assistant manager.

An extra "not" caused Arkansas to accidentally pass a law allowing its citizens of any age, even children, to marry if their parents agreed. The unintended law said this:

> In order for a person who is younger than eighteen (18) years of age and who is not pregnant to obtain a marriage license, the person must provide the county clerk with evidence of parental consent to the marriage.[34]

Walden O'Dell, former CEO of Diebold, an Ohio manufacturer of ATMs and other machines, wrote in a fund-raising letter for President Bush that he was "committed to helping Ohio deliver its electoral votes to the president." That wording raised ethics questions because Diebold makes voting machines.[35]

When you edit, you also need to check that the following are accurate:

- Sentence structure.
- Subject–verb and noun–pronoun agreement.
- Punctuation.
- Word usage.
- Spelling—including spelling of names.
- Numbers.

You also need to know the rules of grammar and punctuation to edit. Errors such as sentence fragments and run-on sentences disturb most educated readers and make them wonder what other mistakes you might be making. Errors in punctuation can change the meaning of a sentence. Lynne Truss, author of the *New York Times* bestseller on punctuation *Eats, Shoots & Leaves,* offers "a popular 'Dear Jack' letter" to show the need for care:[36]

> Dear Jack,
> I want a man who knows what love is all about. You are generous, kind, thoughtful. People who are not like you admit to being useless and inferior. You have ruined me for other men. I yearn for you. I have no feelings whatsoever when we're apart. I can be forever happy—will you let me be yours?
>
> Jill

Résumé Proofreading Errors

- "Position Desired: Profreader." It doesn't look good. . .
- "Skills: Familiar with all faucets of accounting." Accountant by day, plumber by night.
- "Resume Section Title: Educatio" You're "n" trouble.
- "Experience: Detailed-oriented saleman." We have our doubts.
- "Experience: Demonstrated ability in multi-tasting." You'll love our vending machine.
- "Carrier Objective: To become a manager." A man on the move.
- "Languages: Speak English and Spinach." Must be what they teach at the culinary academy.
- "Awards/Accomplishments: Dum major with my high school band." Don't be so hard on yourself.
- "Experience: Child care provider: Organized activities; prepared lunches and snakes." Probably best to stick with graham crackers and milk.

Quoted from "Cover Letter Statements," Robert Half International, accessed March 20, 2011, http://www.resumania.com/ResumaniaArchive.

The Cost of a Typo

Most small proofreading errors are embarrassing to a company. Some errors, though still small, can be very costly and even dangerous. In February 2011, Johnson & Johnson recalled more than 667,000 packages of Sudafed because of an error on the directions. Instead of the standard warning, each of the packages instructed users "do not *not* divide, crush, chew, or dissolve the tablet."

Although no accidents or problems were reported from the incorrect instructions, the one repeated word cost the company time, money, and some of its reputation for quality. Not every typo requires a recall, but any one can be costly.

Adapted from Melly Alazraki, "Johnson & Johnson Recalls Sudafed Because of a Typo," February 25, 2011, http://www.dailyfinance.com/2011/02/25/johnson-and-johnson-recalls-sudafed-because-of-a-typo/.

Dear Jack,
I want a man who knows what love is. All about you are generous, kind, thoughtful people, who are not like you. Admit to being useless and inferior. You have ruined me. For other men I yearn! For you I have no feelings whatsoever. When we're apart I can be forever happy. Will you let me be? Yours,

Jill

Writers with a good command of grammar and mechanics can do a better job than the computer grammar checkers currently available. But even good writers sometimes use a good grammar handbook for reference. On the other hand, even good editors—such as Bill Walsh, Copy Desk Chief for the Business Desk of the *Washington Post*—warn writers that handbooks should be used with a clear goal of clarifying text, not blindly following rules.[37]

Appendix B reviews grammar and punctuation, numbers, and words that are often confused.

Most writers make a small number of errors over and over. If you know that you have trouble with dangling modifiers or subject–verb agreement, for example, specifically look for them in your draft. Also look for any errors that especially bother your boss and correct them.

How to Catch Typos

To catch typos use a spell-checker. But you still need to proofread by eye. Spell checkers work by matching words; they will signal any group of letters not listed in their dictionaries. However, they cannot tell you when you've used the wrong word but spelled it correctly.

Don't underestimate the harm that spelling errors can create. A large, midwestern university lost its yearbook after an uncaught typo referred to the Greek community as the "geeks on campus." Greeks boycotted the yearbook, which went deeply into debt and out of business. The impact of typos on job documents is well-known (see sidebar on this page for example). Proofread every document both with a spell checker and by eye, to catch the errors a spell checker can't find.

Proofreading is hard because writers tend to see what they know should be there rather than what really is there. Since it's always easier to proof something you haven't written, you may want to swap papers with a proofing buddy. (Be sure the person looks for typos, not content.)

To proofread,

- Read once quickly for meaning, to see that nothing has been left out.
- Read a second time, slowly. When you find an error, correct it and then *re-read that line*. Readers tend to become less attentive after they find one error and may miss other errors close to the one they've spotted.
- To proofread a document you know well, read the lines backward or the pages out of order.

Always triple-check numbers, headings, the first and last paragraphs, and the reader's name.

GETTING AND USING FEEDBACK

Getting feedback almost always improves a document. In many organizations, it's required. All external documents must be read and approved before they go out. The process of drafting, getting feedback, revising, and getting

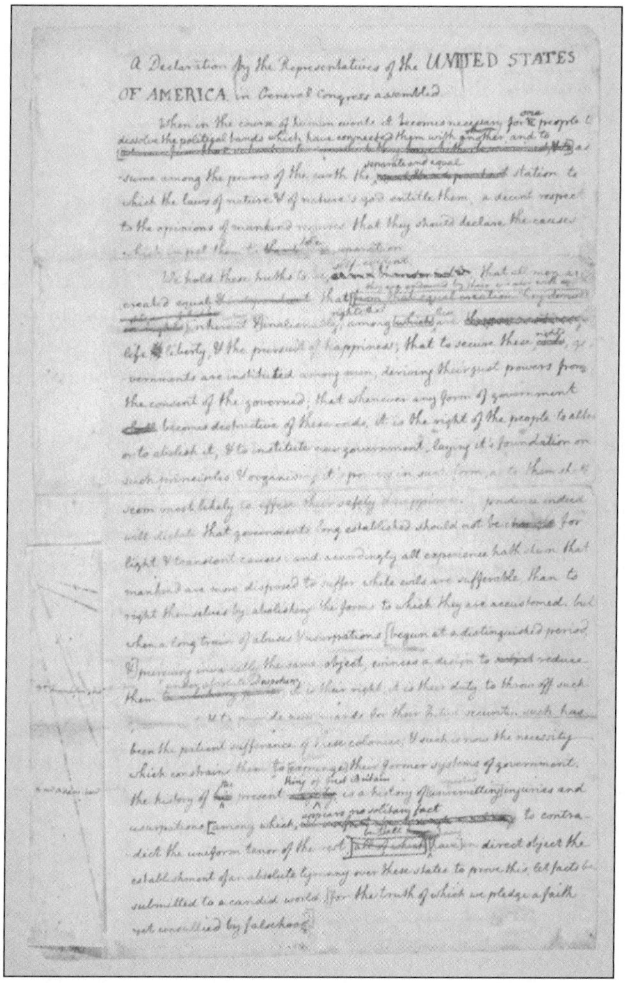

Even history-shaping documents, like the Declaration of Independence, become better with editing.

more feedback is called **cycling.** One researcher reported that documents in her clients' firms cycled an average of 4.2 times before reaching the intended audience.[38] Another researcher studied a major 10-page document whose 20 drafts made a total of 31 stops on the desks of nine reviewers on four different levels.[39] Being asked to revise a document is a fact of life in business.

You can improve the quality of the feedback you get by telling people which aspects you'd especially like comments about. For example, when you give a reader the outline or planning draft, you probably want to know whether the general approach and content are appropriate, and if you have included all major points. After your second draft, you might want to know whether the reasoning is convincing. When you reach the polishing draft, you'll be ready for feedback on style and grammar. The Checklist on the next page lists questions to ask.

It's easy to feel defensive when someone criticizes your work. If the feedback stings, put it aside until you can read it without feeling defensive. Even if you think that the reader hasn't understood what you were trying to say, the fact that the reader complained usually means the section could be improved. If the reader says "This isn't true" and you know the statement is true, several kinds of revision might make the truth clear to the reader: rephrasing the statement, giving more information or examples, or documenting the source.

Too Much Feeback?

When college admissions officers review applications, part of the information they consider is the personal essay. Now students are getting help on those essays.

A thriving industry has grown up around the college essay. Numerous books, websites, and training seminars have been developed to help students write college essays that will win them admission into their college of choice. None of the sources actually write the essay, but all offer advice, suggestions, and examples to help students craft their own papers.

People in the new industry claim they are doing nothing wrong. After all, parents have always been able to help their children write and revise their applications. The new industry also blames the universities for creating the demand for writing assistance. Yet admissions officers worry that the college essay industry is doing more harm than good. They note that the prep services lead to formulaic essays that look prepped and may not match the information on the application form. Outstanding essays may not be matched by writing and verbal skills scores. Plagiarism site Turnitin.com says 11% of the admissions essays it checked contained at least one-quarter unoriginal material. Other critics claim that the costly services put students who cannot afford the extra help at a disadvantage.

What do you think? Are the essay prep services ethical?

Adapted from June Kronholz, "Perfect College Essay Takes Lots of Practice—and Extra Help," *Wall Street Journal,* July 11, 2005, A1, A8; and "The Admissions Police," *Wall Street Journal,* April 6, 2007, W1, W10.

Your Edits May Be Showing

"When SCO Group, a litigious Lindon (Utah) software company, filed a breach of contract suit in Michigan against Daimler Chrysler[, . . . a] CNET News reporter, poking through the Microsoft Word filing, discovered that the case had originally been drawn up as a suit against Bank of America in a California court. . . .

"[H]idden in a Word, Excel, or PowerPoint file may [be] the names of the author and anyone who edited the document, reviewers' comments, . . . and deleted text. . . .

"A *Wired News* analysis of a Word document circulated by California Attorney General Bill Lockyer urging other attorneys to crack down on file-sharing showed that the text had been edited or reviewed by an official of the Motion Picture Association of America. . . .

"Nearly every business exchanges electronic documents with partners, competitors, and customers. . . . [To remove sensitive information,] select "Track Changes" from the tools menu and view the document as "Final Showing Markup." Make sure that all your changes have been either accepted or rejected by the program—a step that removes the tracking information. And make sure all versions but the last have been deleted."

Quoted from Stephen H. Wildstrom, "Don't Let Word Give Away Your Secrets," *BusinessWeek,* April 19, 2004, 26.

Reading feedback carefully is a good way to understand the culture of your organization. Are you told to give more details or to shorten messages? Does your boss add headings and bullet points? Look for patterns in the comments, and apply what you learn in your next document.

USING BOILERPLATE

Boilerplate is language—sentences, paragraphs, even pages—from a previous document that a writer legitimately includes in a new document. In academic papers, material written by others must be quoted and documented—to neglect to do so would be plagiarism. However, because businesses own the documents their employees write, old text may be included without attribution.

Many legal documents, including apartment leases and sales contracts, are almost completely boilerplated. Writers may also use boilerplate they wrote for earlier documents. For example, a section from a proposal describing the background of the problem could also be used in the final report. A section from a progress report describing what the writer had done could be used with only a few changes in the methods section of the final report.

Writers use boilerplate both to save time and energy and to use language that has already been approved by the organization's legal staff. However, research has shown that using boilerplate creates two problems.[40] First, using unrevised boilerplate can create a document with incompatible styles and tones. Second, boilerplate can allow writers to ignore subtle differences in situations and audiences.

READABILITY FORMULAS

Readability formulas attempt to measure objectively how easy something is to read. However, since they don't take many factors into account, the formulas are at best a very limited guide to good style.

Computer packages that analyze style may give you a readability score. Some states' "plain English" laws require consumer contracts to meet a certain readability score. Some companies require that warranties and other consumer documents meet certain scores.

Readability formulas depend heavily on word length and sentence length. See the BAC website to calculate readability using the two best-known readability formulas: the Gunning Fog Index and the Flesch Reading Ease Scale. Research has shown,[41] however, that using shorter words and sentences will not necessarily make a passage easy to read. Short words are not always easy to understand, especially if they have technical meanings (e.g., *waive, bear market, liquid*). Short, choppy sentences and sentence fragments are actually harder to understand than well-written medium-length sentences.

No reading formula yet devised takes into account three factors that influence how easy a text is to read: the complexity of the ideas, the organization of the ideas, and the layout and design of the document.

Instead of using readability formulas, test your draft with the people for whom it is designed. How long does it take them to find the information they need? Do they make mistakes when they try to use the document? Do they think the writing is easy to understand? Answers to these questions can give much more accurate information than any readability score.

✓Checklist Questions to Ask Readers

Outline or planning draft

- ☐ Does the plan seem on the right track?
- ☐ What topics should be added? Should any be cut?
- ☐ Do you have any other general suggestions?

Revising draft

- ☐ Does the message satisfy all its purposes?
- ☐ Is the message adapted to the audience(s)?
- ☐ Is the organization effective?
- ☐ What parts aren't clear?
- ☐ What ideas need further development and support?
- ☐ Do you have any other suggestions?

Polishing draft

- ☐ Are there any problems with word choice or sentence structure?
- ☐ Did you find any inconsistencies?
- ☐ Did you find any typos?
- ☐ Is the document's design effective?

SUMMARY OF KEY POINTS

- Processes that help writers write well include not expecting the first draft to be perfect, writing regularly, modifying the initial task if it's too hard or too easy, having clear goals, knowing many different strategies, using rules as guidelines rather than as absolutes, and waiting to edit until after the draft is complete.
- Writing processes can include many activities: planning, gathering, brainstorming, organizing, writing, evaluating, getting feedback, revising, editing, and proofreading. **Revising** means changing the document to make it better satisfy the writer's purposes and the audience. **Editing** means making surface-level changes that make the document grammatically correct. **Proofreading** means checking to be sure the document is free from typographical errors. The activities do not have to come in any set order. It is not necessary to finish one activity to start another. Most writers use all activities only when they write a document whose genre, subject matter, or audience is new to them.
- To think of ideas, try **brainstorming, freewriting** (writing without stopping for 10 minutes or so), and **clustering** (brainstorming with circled words on a page).
- Good style in business and administrative writing is less formal, more friendly, and more personal than the style usually used for term papers.
- Use the following techniques to make your writing easier to read.

  As you choose words,

  1. Use words that are accurate, appropriate, and familiar. Denotation is a word's literal meaning; connotation is the emotional coloring that a word conveys.
  2. Use technical jargon sparingly; eliminate business jargon.

As you write and revise sentences,

3. Use active voice most of the time. Active voice is better because it is shorter, clearer, and more interesting.
4. Use verbs—not nouns—to carry the weight of your sentence.
5. Eliminate wordiness. Writing is wordy if the same idea can be expressed in fewer words.
   a. Eliminate words that add nothing.
   b. Combine sentences to eliminate unnecessary words.
   c. Put the meaning of your sentence into the subject and verb to cut the number of words.
6. Vary sentence length and sentence structure.
7. Use parallel structure. Use the same grammatical form for ideas that have the same logical function.
8. Put your readers in your sentences.

As you write and revise paragraphs,

9. Begin most paragraphs with topic sentences so that readers know what to expect in the paragraph.
10. Use transitions to link ideas.

- If the writing situation is new or difficult, plan to revise the draft at least three times. The first time, look for content and completeness. The second time, check the organization, layout, and reasoning. Finally, check style and tone.

CHAPTER 5 Exercises and Problems

*Go to www.mhhe.com/locker10e for additional Exercises and Problems.

5.1 Reviewing the Chapter

1. What are some techniques of good writers? Which ones do you use regularly? (LO 5-1–3)
2. What are ways to get ideas for a specific communication? (LO 5-1)
3. What activities are part of the composing process? Which one should you be doing more often or more carefully in your writing? (LO 5-1)
4. What are some half-truths about style? (LO 5-2)
5. What are some ways you can make your sentences more effective? (LO 5-2)
6. What are some ways you can make your paragraphs more effective? (LO 5-2)
7. How can you adapt good style to organization preferences? (LO 5-2)
8. How do revising, editing, and proofreading differ? Which one do you personally need to do more carefully? (LO 5-3)
9. How can you get better feedback on your writing? (LO 5-3)

5.2 Interviewing Writers about Their Composing Processes

Interview someone about the composing process(es) he or she uses for on-the-job writing. Questions you could ask include the following:

- What kind of planning do you do before you write? Do you make lists? formal or informal outlines?
- When you need more information, where do you get it?
- How do you compose your drafts? Do you dictate? Draft with pen and paper? Compose on screen? How do you find uninterrupted time to compose?
- When you want advice about style, grammar, and spelling, what source(s) do you consult?
- Does your superior ever read your drafts and make suggestions?
- Do you ever work with other writers to produce a single document? Describe the process you use.
- Describe the process of creating a document where you felt the final document reflected your best work. Describe the process of creating a document you found difficult or frustrating. What sorts of things make writing easier or harder for you?

As your instructor directs,

a. Share your results orally with a small group of students.
b. Present your results in an oral presentation to the class.
c. Present your results in a memo to your instructor.
d. Share your results with a small group of students and write a joint memo reporting the similarities and differences you found.

5.3 Analyzing Your Own Writing Processes

Save your notes and drafts from several assignments so that you can answer the following questions:

- Which practices of good writers do you follow?
- Which of the activities discussed in Chapter 5 do you use?
- How much time do you spend on each of the activities?
- What kinds of revisions do you make most often?
- Do you use different processes for different documents, or do you have one process that you use most of the time?
- What parts of your process seem most successful? Are there any places in the process that could be improved? How?
- What relation do you see between the process(es) you use and the quality of the final document?

As your instructor directs,

a. Discuss your process with a small group of other students.
b. Write a memo to your instructor analyzing in detail your process for composing one of the papers for this class.
c. Write a memo to your instructor analyzing your process during the term. What parts of your process(es) have stayed the same throughout the term? What parts have changed?

5.4 Identifying Words with Multiple Denotations

a. Each of the following words has several denotations. How many can you list without going to a dictionary? How many additional meanings does a good dictionary list?

browser	log	see
court	table	check

b. List five other words that have multiple denotations.

5.5 Evaluating the Ethical Implication of Connotations

In each of the following pairs, identify the more favorable term. When is its use justifiable?

1. wasted/sacrificed
2. illegal alien/immigrant
3. friendly fire/enemy attack
4. terminate/fire
5. inaccuracy/lying
6. budget/spending plan
7. feedback/criticism

5.6 Correcting Errors in Denotation and Connotation

Identify and correct the errors in denotation or connotation in the following sentences:

1. In our group, we weeded out the best idea each person had thought of.
2. She is a prudent speculator.
3. The three proposals are diametrically opposed to each other.
4. While he researched companies, he was literally glued to the web.
5. Our backpacks are hand sewn by one of roughly 16 individuals.
6. Raj flaunted the law against insider trading.

5.7 Using Connotations to Shape Response

Write two sentences to describe each of the following situations. In one sentence, use words with positive connotations; in the other, use negative words.

1. Chris doesn't spend time on small talk.
2. Chris often starts work on a new project without being told to do so.
3. As a supervisor, Chris gives very specific instructions to subordinates.

5.8 Choosing Levels of Formality

Identify the more formal word in each pair. Which term is better for most business documents? Why?

1. adapted to	geared to
2. befuddled	confused
3. assistant	helper
4. pilot project	testing the waters
5. cogitate	think

5.9 Eliminating Jargon and Simplifying Language

Revise these sentences to eliminate jargon and to use short, familiar words.

1. When the automobile company announced its strategic downsizing initiative, it offered employees a career alternative enhancement program.
2. Any alterations must be approved during the 30-day period commencing 60 days prior to the expiration date of the agreement.
3. As per your request, the undersigned has obtained estimates of upgrading our computer system. A copy of the estimated cost is attached hereto.
4. Please be advised that this writer is in considerable need of a new computer.
5. Enclosed please find the proposed draft for the employee negative retention plan. In the event that you have alterations which you would like to suggest, forward same to my office at your earliest convenience.

5.10 Changing Verbs from Passive to Active Voice

Identify passive voice in the following sentences and convert it to active voice. In some cases, you may need to add information to do so. You may use different words as long as you retain the basic meaning of the sentence. Remember that imperative verbs are active voice, too.

1. For a customer to apply for benefits, an application must be completed.
2. The cost of delivering financial services is being slashed by computers, the Internet, and toll-free phone lines.
3. When the vacation schedule is finalized it is recommended that it be routed to all supervisors for final approval.
4. As stated in my résumé, I have designed web pages for three student organizations.
5. Material must not be left on trucks outside the warehouse. Either the trucks must be parked inside the warehouse or the material must be unloaded at the time of receiving the truck.

5.11 Using Strong Verbs

Revise each of the following sentences to replace hidden verbs with action verbs.

1. An understanding of stocks and bonds is important if one wants to invest wisely.
2. We must undertake a calculation of expected revenues and expenses for the next two years.
3. The production of clear and concise documents is the mark of a successful communicator.
4. We hope to make use of the company's website to promote the new product line.
5. If you wish to be eligible for the Miller scholarship, you must complete an application by January 31.
6. When you make an evaluation of media buys, take into consideration the demographics of the group seeing the ad.
7. We provide assistance to clients in the process of reaching a decision about the purchase of hardware and software.

5.12 Reducing Wordiness

1. Eliminate words that say nothing. You may use different words.
   a. There are many businesses that are active in community and service work.
   b. The purchase of a new computer will allow us to produce form letters quickly. In addition, return on investment could be calculated for proposed repairs. Another use is that the computer could check databases to make sure that claims are paid only once.
   c. Our decision to enter the South American market has precedence in the past activities of the company.
2. Combine sentences to show how ideas are related and to eliminate unnecessary words.
   a. Some customers are profitable for companies. Other customers actually cost the company money.
   b. If you are unable to come to the session on HMOs, please call the human resources office. You will be able to schedule another time to ask questions you may have about the various options.
   c. Major Japanese firms often have employees who know English well. U.S. companies negotiating with Japanese companies should bring their own interpreters.

5.13 Improving Parallel Structure

Revise each of the following sentences to create parallelism.

1. The orientation session will cover the following information:
   - Company culture will be discussed.
   - How to use the equipment.
   - You will get an overview of key customers' needs.
2. Five criteria for a good web page are content that serves the various audiences, attention to details, and originality. It is also important to have effective organization and navigation devices. Finally, provide attention to details such as revision date and the webmaster's address.
3. When you leave a voicemail message,
   - Summarize your main point in a sentence or two.
   - The name and phone number should be given slowly and distinctly.
   - The speaker should give enough information so that the recipient can act on the message.
   - Tell when you'll be available to receive the recipient's return call.

5.14 Putting Readers in Your Sentences

Revise each of the following sentences to put readers in them. As you revise, use active voice and simple words.

1. Mutual funds can be purchased from banks, brokers, financial planners, or from the fund itself.
2. I would like to take this opportunity to invite you back to Global Wireless. As a previous customer we have outstanding new rate plans to offer you and your family. We invite you to review the rate plans on the attached page and choose the one that best fits your needs. All our customers are important to us.
3. Another aspect of the university is campus life, with an assortment of activities and student groups to participate in and lectures and sports events to attend.

5.15 Editing Sentences to Improve Style

Revise these sentences to make them smoother, less wordy, and easier to read. Eliminate jargon and repetition. Keep the information; you may reword or reorganize it. If the original is not clear, you may need to add information to write a clear revision.

1. There are many different topics that you will read about on a monthly basis once you subscribe to *Inc.*
2. With the new organic fertilizer, you'll see an increase in the quality of your tomatoes and the number grown.
3. New procedure for customer service employees: Please be aware effective immediately, if a customer is requesting a refund of funds applied to their account a front and back copy of the check must be submitted if the transaction is over $500.00. For example, if the customer is requesting $250.00 back, and the total amount of the transaction is $750.00, a front and back copy of the check will be needed to obtain the refund.

4. The county will benefit from implementing flextime.
   - Offices will stay open longer for more business.
   - Staff turnover will be lower.
   - Easier business communication with states in other time zones.
   - Increased employee productivity.
5. There is a seasonality factor in the workload, with the heaviest being immediately prior to quarterly due dates for estimated tax payments.

5.16 Practicing Plain Language

Working with a partner, create three sentences that feature problematic elements that mask meaning.

- Sentence 1: wordiness and/or euphemisms
- Sentence 2: jargon from your field of study
- Sentence 3: words with multiple denotations or connotations

Then exchange your sentences with another team and rewrite their sentences into plain language.

5.17 Using Topic Sentences

Make each of the following paragraphs more readable by opening each paragraph with a topic sentence. You may be able to find a topic sentence in the paragraph and move it to the beginning. In other cases, you'll need to write a new sentence.

1. At Disney World, a lunch put on an expense account is "on the mouse." McDonald's employees "have ketchup in their veins." Business slang flourishes at companies with rich corporate cultures. Memos at Procter & Gamble are called "reco's" because the model P&G memo begins with a recommendation.
2. The first item on the agenda is the hiring for the coming year. George has also asked that we review the agency goals for the next fiscal year. We should cover this early in the meeting since it may affect our hiring preferences. Finally, we need to announce the deadlines for grant proposals, decide which grants to apply for, and set up a committee to draft each proposal.
3. Separate materials that can be recycled from your regular trash. Pass along old clothing, toys, or appliances to someone else who can use them. When you purchase products, choose those with minimal packaging. If you have a yard, put your yard waste and kitchen scraps (excluding meat and fat) in a compost pile. You can reduce the amount of solid waste your household produces in four ways.

5.18 Revising Paragraphs

Revise each paragraph to make it easier to read. Change, rearrange, or delete words and sentences; add any material necessary.

a. Once a new employee is hired, each one has to be trained for a week by one of our supervisors at a cost of $1,000 each which includes the supervisor's time. This amount also includes half of the new employee's salary, since new hires produce only half the normal production per worker for the week. This summer $24,000 was spent in training 24 new employees. Absenteeism increased in the department on the hottest summer days. For every day each worker is absent we lose $200 in lost production. This past summer there was a total of 56 absentee days taken for a total loss of $11,200 in lost production. Turnover and absenteeism were the causes of an unnecessary expenditure of over $35,000 this summer.

b. One service is investments. General financial news and alerts about companies in the customer's portfolio are available. Quicken also provides assistance in finding the best mortgage rate and in providing assistance in making the decision whether to refinance a mortgage. Another service from Quicken is advice for the start and management of a small business. Banking services, such as paying bills and applying for loans, have long been available to Quicken subscribers. The taxpayer can be walked through the tax preparation process by Quicken. Someone considering retirement can use Quicken to ascertain whether the amount being set aside for this purpose is sufficient. Quicken's website provides seven services.

5.19 Revising, Editing, and Proofreading a Letter

Dana Shomacher, an enthusiastic new hire of six months at Bear Foods, wants Stan Smith, regional head of HR at the grocery chain, to allow her to organize and publicize a food drive for Coastal Food Pantry. Revise, edit, and proof her memo.

> Hey Stan,
>
> I have this great idea for great publicity for Bear Foods that won't cost anything and will get us some really great publicity. Its something great we can do for our community. I wont Bear to conduct a food drive for Coastal Food Pantry. Their was an article in the Tribune about how they were having trouble keeping up with food requests and I thought what a great fit it would be for Bear.
>
> All our employees should donate food and we should also get our customer to donate also. We could set out some shopping carts for the donations. I could write an announcement for the Tribune and get some postures made for our front windows.
>
> I am willing to take care of all details so you won't have to do anything except say yes to this memo.
>
> Dana

After you have fixed Dana's memo, answer these questions in a memo to your instructor.

- What revisions did you make? Why?
- Many grocery stores already contribute to local food pantries. In addition to some staples, they provide items such as bakery goods that are past their sale date but still quite tasty, sacks for bagging groceries at the pantry, and even shopping carts to transport groceries to the cars of pantry clients. If Bear already contributes to Coastal, how should that fact change the content of Dana's memo?
- What edits did you make? Why?
- What impression do you think this letter made on the head of human resources? Explain. Do you think he granted Dana's request? Why or why not?

Submit both your version of Dana's memo and your analysis memo.

5.20 Writing Paragraphs

As your instructor directs, write a paragraph on one or more of the following topics.

a. Discuss your ideal job.
b. Summarize a recent article from a business magazine or newspaper.
c. Explain how technology is affecting the field you plan to enter.
d. Explain why you have or have not decided to work while you attend college.
e. Write a profile of someone who is successful in the field you hope to enter.

As your instructor directs,

a. Label topic sentences, active voice, and parallel structure.
b. Edit a classmate's paragraphs to make the writing even tighter and smoother.

5.21 Identifying Buzzwords and Jargon

This is an actual press release published in the *Des Moines Register* with an article on buzzwords.

> Wal-Mart Stores, Inc., the largest private employer with more than 1.8 million employees and the largest corporate mover of people, selected Capital Relocation Services as the sole source provider for the implementation of its Tier III and Tier IV relocation programs. These two programs account for the vast majority of the company's

relocations. Capital was awarded the business following an intensive RFP and due diligence process.

"We're very excited about the synergy that Wal-Mart's selection of Capital brings to both companies," commented Mickey Williams, Capital's CEO. "We are also pleased to welcome to Capital the existing Wal-Mart PMP Relocation team that has been on-site at Wal-Mart's Bentonville headquarters for 14 years. They will continue to serve Wal-Mart and Sam's Club's Associates and will have an active role in the implementation of the new policy."

"What really enabled us to stand out was our focus on the strategic results Wal-Mart was looking for, and connecting that to their relocation program," added Williams. "Additionally, we demonstrated what would need to be done to achieve those results."

Mr. Williams continued, "Several years ago, we realized that traditional relocation solutions weren't enough. The challenge was that relocation management had become a logistics focused straightjacket. The emphasis was on efficiency and not on effectiveness. In a time of unprecedented change, relocation management programs were becoming increasingly inflexible."

"We realized that our continued success required us to stop thinking of ourselves solely as a relocation management company—we had to start thinking and acting as a talent management support company; after all that is the underlying purpose of relocation management in the first place. Wal-Mart's selection of Capital is a big confirmation that our approach is the right one."

Now answer these questions:

1. What is this press release about? What is it saying?
2. Why did Capital Relocation Services get the new contract?
3. Underline the buzzwords and jargon in the press release. What do these words do in the press release?
4. What is the purpose of this press release? Does it meet its purpose? Why or why not?

Write a memo to your instructor evaluating the press release as an effective document.

Source: Larry Ballard, "Decipher a Honcho's Buzzwords, Such as 'Unsiloing,'" *Des Moines Register,* January 21, 2008, 1D

5.22 Checking Spelling and Grammar Checkers

Each of the following paragraphs contains errors in grammar, spelling, and punctuation. Which errors does your spelling or grammar checker catch? Which errors does it miss? Does it flag as errors any words that are correct?

a. Answer to an Inquiry

   Enclosed are the tow copies you requested of our pamphlet, "Using the Internet to market Your products. The pamphelt walks you through the steps of planning the Home Page (The first page of the web cite, shows examples of other web pages we have designed, and provide a questionaire that you can use to analyze audience the audience and purposes."

b. Performance Appraisal

   Most staff accountants complete three audits a month. Ellen has completed 21 audits in this past six months she is our most productive staff accountant. Her technical skills our very good however some clients feel that she could be more tactful in suggesting ways that the clients accounting practices courld be improved.

c. Brochure

   Are you finding that being your own boss crates it's own problems? Take the hassle out of working at home with a VoiceMail Answering System. Its almost as good as having your own secratery.

d. Presentation Slide

   How to Create a Web Résumé

   - Omit home adress and phone number
   - Use other links only if they help an employer evaluate you.
     - Be Professional.
     - Carefully craft and proof read the phrase on the index apage.

5.23 Revising Documents using "Track Changes"

"Track Changes" is a feature in some word processors that records alterations made to a document. It is particularly useful when you are collaborating with a colleague to create, edit, or revise documents. Track Changes will highlight any text that has been added or deleted to your document but it also allows you to decide, for each change, whether to accept the suggestion or reject it and return to your original text. In addition to Track Changes, many word processors include a comment feature that allows you to ask questions or make suggestions without altering the text itself.

For this exercise, you will electronically exchange a document with one of your classmates. With the Track Changes feature turned on, you will review each other's documents, make comments or ask questions, insert additions, and make deletions to improve the writing, and then revise your work based upon the changes and comments.

As your instructor directs, select the electronic file of the document you created for exercise 5.20 "Writing Paragraphs" or another document that you have created for this class. Exchange this file with your peer review partner. Open your partner's file and select Track Changes. Review the document and make suggestions that will help your peer improve the writing. For instance, you can

- Look for accurate, appropriate, and ethical wording as well as instances of unnecessary jargon.
- Look for active voice and concise prose.
- Look for structural issues like topic sentences, tightly written paragraphs, varied sentence structure and length, and focus upon the thesis statement. Suggest where sentences can be combined or where sentences need parallel structure.
- Look for you-attitude.
- Ask questions (using comments) when the text isn't clear or make suggestions to tighten the writing or improve word choices.

Return the document to its author and open yours to review the changes and comments your partner added to your document. For each change, decide whether to Accept or Reject the suggestion.

Continue to revise the document. Then submit a copy of your original version and the revised version to your instructor.

5.24 Using the SEC's *A Plain English Handbook*

Go the Securities and Exchange Commission's *A Plain English Handbook,* at http://www.sec.gov/pdf/handbook.pdf. Scroll down to Appendix B and look at the four before and after examples. What kinds of changes have been made? What are examples of each kind? Can you understand the revised version? Did you understand the original version?

5.25 Investigating the Plain Language Act in Federal Agencies

Look at some of the plain language guidelines for some of the agencies listed on the PlainLanguage.gov site, at http://www.plainlanguage.gov/plLaw/fedGovt/index.cfm.

- Work in small groups, with each group checking the adaptations of a different agency. Report back to the class. As a class, discuss how different agencies adapt the act to their focus.
- In your groups, also look at some of the before and after examples. Share a particularly good one with the class, explaining the changes in the improved message.
- You might want to look at the humorous but true nine easy steps to making a sentence unreadable, found at http://www.plainlanguage.gov/testExamples/indexExample.cfm?record=6&search=humor.

5.26 Valuing drafts

Suppose your state has an open records law, a law that gives citizens broad access to records of communications made by public officials, including records reflecting the development of various decisions and laws. Now suppose your state legislature is considering legislation that would enable government officials to keep drafts secret. Are you for or against the new legislation?

Hints:

1. Why do you think the new legislation is being proposed?
2. What is a draft? Do you want to see brainstorming notes of Senator Doe? Suppose in your state a law is a draft until it has been signed by the governor. Would that fact modify your opinion?

3. Can you think of criteria that would exclude some but not all drafts?
4. Where in the process do you think most of the significant changes are made in policy? Early? Late? Somewhere in-between?
5. When does it become hard to change a policy?
6. Suppose the policy could also be applied to drafts of corporate officials who set company policies with public impact. Now are you for or against the new legislation?

As your instructor directs,

a. Discuss your opinions in small groups.
b. As a group present your opinions to the class.
c. Post your opinions online for your classmates to read.

CHAPTER 6

Designing Documents

Chapter Outline

The Importance of Effective Design

Design as Part of Your Writing Process(es)

Design and Conventions

Levels of Design

Guidelines for Document Design

1. Use White Space.
2. Use Headings.
3. Limit the Use of Words Set in All Capital Letters.
4. Use No More than Two Fonts in a Single Document.
5. Decide Whether to Justify Margins.
6. Put Important Elements in the Top Left and Lower Right Quadrants.
7. Use a Grid to Unify Graphic Elements.
8. Use Highlighting, Decorative Devices, and Color in Moderation.

Designing Brochures

- Analyzing Your Rhetorical Situation
- Drafting the Text
- Selecting Appropriate Visuals
- Creating the Design
- Printing the Brochure

Designing Web Pages

- Attracting and Maintaining Attention
- Creating a Usable Home Page
- Providing Easy Navigation
- Following Conventions
- Increasing Accessibility

Testing the Design for Usability

Summary of Key Points

Newsworthy Communication

A Sign of the System

Designing directional signs for streets and subway systems should be easy, right? According to *Helvetica and the New York City Subway System,* by Paul Shaw, creating a unified, effective sign system takes extensive planning and careful design.

When the three independent subway systems in New York City merged in 1940, the signs were a confusing hodge-podge of detailed antique mosaics and hand-painted placards. By the 1960s, the subway systems were a mess, what one task force called "the most squalid public environment of the United States," and the signs were one symptom of the problem.

> *"Now the Transit Authority's distinctive signs are a recognized symbol of New York City."*

In 1966, New York's Transit Authority contracted with design firm Unimark International to redesign the signs and coordinate their placement in the subway system. The designers carefully analyzed the needs of the people who used the subway to find the best places to put each sign. They also proposed a standard look for each sign, using the newly designed typeface Helvetica.

The Transit Authority accepted Unimark's proposal, but did not allow the designers to implement the plan. Rather, the Transit Authority relied on their own plans: they used a different typeface and ignored the recommendations on sign placement. Additionally, the Transit Authority did not remove the old signs when the new signs were placed.

The result was chaos. Soon, New York contacted Unimark again. This time, the designers carried their vision throughout the subway system, using Helvetica and color-coded disks that still help commuters navigate the subways today. Now the Transit Authority's distinctive signs are a recognized symbol of New York City.

Although most designers rarely get to work on something as large as redesigning a city's transit system, the process of designing for the audience that Unimark used in New York should apply to any document.

Source: Michael Bierut, "When in Helvetica," *Wall Street Journal,* March 26, 2011, C8.

Learning Objectives

After studying this chapter, you will know

- LO 6-1 Why document design is important in business communication.
- LO 6-2 The four levels of document design, and how they can help you critique documents.
- LO 6-3 Guidelines for document design.
- LO 6-4 How to design brochures.
- LO 6-5 How to design web pages.
- LO 6-6 How to do basic usability testing on your documents.

Good Document Design Saves Money

Document design changes are not just cosmetic. Infomap, a communications consulting company, reports these savings among its customers:

- A major brokerage firm found 5,000 document inconsistencies by using Information Mapping services. After creating a new document system, the firm experienced a 30% reduction in costly errors.
- A leading credit card company reduced the average length of phone calls to its customer service center by 60 seconds each after improving the design of its reference materials. This time reduction reduced costs by 20%.
- A leading health care provider redesigned its customer claims manual and saw the number of calls to the help desk decrease by 50%.
- A major government agency struggling with information overload used Information Mapping to create "uniform information architecture" agency wide. Newly trained "mappers" changed over 60,000 pages, and the agency reported over $17 million dollars of cost savings.

Adapted from "Expertise—Success Stories," Information Mapping, accessed May 23, 2011, http://infomap.com/index.cfm/expertise/success_stories.

Good document design saves time and money, reduces legal problems, and builds goodwill. Effective design groups ideas visually, making the structure of the document more inviting and obvious so the document is easier to read. Easy-to-read documents enhance your credibility and build an image of you as a professional, competent person. Many workplaces expect you to be able to create designs that go beyond the basic templates you'll find in common business software programs. Good design is important not only for reports, web pages, brochures, and newsletters but also for announcements and one-page letters and memos.

THE IMPORTANCE OF EFFECTIVE DESIGN LO 6-1

When document design is poor, both organizations and society suffer. The *Challenger* space shuttle blew up because its O-rings failed in the excessive cold. Poor communication—including charts that hid, rather than emphasized, the data about O-ring performance—contributed to the decision to launch. More recently, after the *Columbia* space shuttle disintegrated during reentry, poor communication was again implicated in NASA's failure to ensure the spacecraft was safe. Mission leaders insisted that engineers had not briefed them on the seriousness of the damage to the shuttle when a piece of foam struck it on takeoff. But after studying transcripts of meetings, Edward R. Tufte, who specializes in visual presentations of evidence, concluded that engineers did offer their concerns and supporting statistics. However, they did so using visuals that obscured the seriousness.[1] In 2000, the badly designed Florida ballot confused enough voters to cloud the outcome of the U.S. presidential election.

DESIGN AS PART OF YOUR WRITING PROCESS(ES)

Design isn't something to "tack on" when you've finished writing. Indeed, the best documents, slides, and screens are created when you think about design at each stage of your writing process(es).

- As you plan, think about your audience. Are they skilled readers? Are they busy? Will they read the document straight through or skip around?
- As you write, incorporate lists and headings. Use visuals to convey numerical data clearly and forcefully.

- Get feedback from people who will be using your document. Do they find the document hard to understand? Do they need additional visuals?
- As you revise, check your draft against the guidelines in this chapter.

Redesigning the Newspaper

The publishers of the *Wall Street Journal* spent two years researching, creating, and testing designs for the *Journal*'s new look before they unveiled it. After getting advice from their customers in the form of surveys, focus groups, and test marketing, the *Journal*'s publishers chose to redesign their newspaper in specific ways:

- They expanded their use of headings and white space to make it easier to read and follow articles from page to page.
- They created a hierarchy, through headline size and story placement, to indicate relative importance of news.
- They changed to a narrower paper size that would make the *Journal* more convenient to hold.
- They added more color to help highlight important topics and help readers find information more easily.
- They created a new font, called Exchange, which is easy to read even when printed in a small size in tight columns.

Adapted from L. Gordon Crovitz, "What Is Changing—What Isn't—in the *Wall Street Journal*," *Wall Street Journal*, December 4, 2006, A17; L. Gordon Crovitz, "What to Expect in Your *Journal*, Starting Jan. 2," *Wall Street Journal*, December 30–31, 2006, A11; and Mario R. Garcia, "The Relevance of Good Design," *Wall Street Journal*, January 2, 2007, G8.

DESIGN AND CONVENTIONS

Like all aspects of communication, effective design relies heavily on conventions. These conventions provide a design language. For instance, most graphical interfaces are organized around the desktop metaphor, where we use files, folders, tabs, and trashcans. Commercial websites use the metaphor of the shopping cart. We have a mental image of the way brochures, business letters, or business cards are supposed to look.

Conventions may vary by audience, geographic area, industry, company, or even department, but they do exist. Some conventions work well with some audiences but not with others, so careful audience analysis is necessary. The British and Americans prefer serif typefaces; the French and Dutch prefer sans serif. Instruction pictures for office equipment generally show feminine hands using the equipment. Some female readers will relate more readily to the instructions; others will be offended at the implied assumption that only women perform such low-level office jobs.[2]

Conventions also change over time. Résumés used to be typed documents; now most companies ask for electronic ones. Today we rarely use Courier font; we italicize titles rather than underlining them, and we space once rather than twice after periods at ends of sentences.

Conventions also change with new software. When Microsoft Word 2007 and Word 2008 were launched, they broke long-standing Word conventions. They used the font Cambria for headings and Calibri for body text, instead of the traditional Times New Roman. The default spacing changed from single to 1.5. Time will tell if these settings become new conventions.

Many Word users were also frustrated at first with the overall interface of the program, because it broke too many conventions at once. Instead of the classic drop-down menus that have been present since early versions of Word, the menus now use a more visual interface, with a small icon representing each task a user wants to perform. For example, if you want to insert a picture, a little picture icon indicates that option. Similarly if you want to do a word count, a little icon with "ABC 123" indicates this option.

Violating conventions is risky: violations may not be interpreted correctly, or they may signal that the author or designer is unreliable or unknowledgeable. Brochures with text that does not fit properly into the folded panels, freehand drawings in a set of installation instructions, or bar charts with garish color designs can destroy the reader's trust.[3]

LEVELS OF DESIGN LO 6-2

Visual communications expert Charles Kostelnick distinguishes four levels of design (see Figure 6.1). These levels provide an organized way to think about the design choices you can make in your own documents, presentations, and visuals. They're also useful when you analyze the documents you encounter in a professional setting: one of the best ways to get ideas for your own document designs is to analyze the design elements in successful documents.

When you look at communication design, look for Kostelnick's four levels:[4]

- Intra—Design choices for individual letters and words. Intra-level design choices include the font and its size you choose; whether you use bold, italics, or color changes to emphasize key words; and the way you use capital letters. The serif font used for body text on this page is an intra-level choice, as is the sans serif font used for headings.

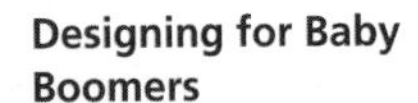

Designing for Baby Boomers

As baby boomers turn 60, many start to lose the ability to see as clearly as they once did. Tiny buttons on cellphones, small typeface on bottles of pills, and even the low lighting in some restaurants all make reading a difficult task. But this baby boomer generation is not bashful when it comes to denouncing issues with poor document design.

As a result, some corporations are trying to help this large population see and function better in our society. For example, Romano's Macaroni Grill supplies reading glasses and large-print menus on request. Target is modifying its labeling on prescription bottles by putting the most important information—patient name, medication, dosage—in large boldface capital letters. Some remote controls and cellphones now have large text and buttons specifically designed for this older audience. Some laundry labels on garments use larger print. Even Microsoft has given users the option to enlarge the size of text on computer screens.

Overall, those companies that are willing to adapt their products to the unique needs of the 77 million baby boomers are more likely to be successful in the future.

Adapted from Katie Hafner, "Their Parents' Eyes," *New York Times*, August 4, 2007, B1.

Figure 6.1 Four Levels for Examining Visual Language

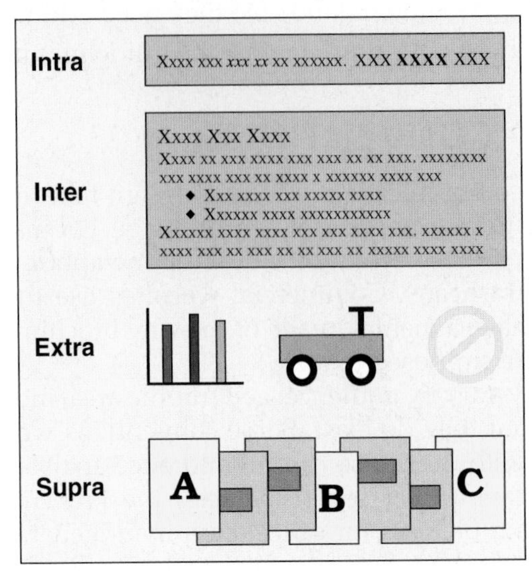

Source: Kostelnick, Charles; Roberts, David D.; Dragga, Sam, *Designing Visual Language*: Strategies for Professional Communicators 1st Edition, © 1998. Reprinted by permission of Pearson Education, Inc., Upper Saddle River, NJ.

- Inter—Design choices for blocks of text. Inter-level design choices include the ways you use headings, white space, indents, lists, and even text boxes. The headings and bulleted lists that organize information on this page are inter-level choices.
- Extra—Design choices for graphics that go with the text. Extra-level design choices include the way you use pictures, photographs, data displays, charts, and graphs, and the ways in which you emphasize information on those graphics. The figures in this chapter are extra-level design choices.
- Supra—Design choices for entire documents. Supra-level design choices include paper size, headers and footers, and the index and table of contents, as well as color schemes and layout grids that define the look of all sections of a document. The placement of the page numbers in this book, the two-column layout grid on all of the pages in this chapter, and the navigation text in the header on this page are supra-level choices.

The U.S. Census 2010 poster in Figure 6.2 illustrates all levels of design. At the intra-level, this poster uses a sans serif font throughout the whole document. Other intra-level elements include words in all capital letters and the boldface sentence. Inter-level elements involve the centered text throughout the notice and chunking text above and below the image. The main text below the image uses a pyramid shape, while the text above the image uses a reverse pyramid. This choice helps the viewer focus attention on the image. The main image containing faces that form the shape of the United States is part of the extra-level. This image is used to highlight the textual element that encourages viewers to help paint the newest portrait of America. The supra-level includes the size of the poster, which measures 16″ × 20″ so that all the information can be clearly seen when posted. Another unifying piece of information on a supra-level that can be found in all census promotional material is the "United States Census 2010: It's in our hands" tag and slogan in the bottom right corner. Visually, this information is treated like a page footer and can be found somewhere on every promotional census material.

Figure 6.2 This United States 2010 Census poster uses all four levels of design.

Source: "Posters," U.S. Census Bureau: United States Census 2010, http://2010.census.gov/partners/pdf/ActionPoster.pdf

GUIDELINES FOR DOCUMENT DESIGN LO 6-3

Use the guidelines in Figure 6.3 to create visually attractive documents.

1. Use White Space.

White space—the empty space on the page—makes material easier to read by emphasizing the material that it separates from the rest of the text. To create white space,

Figure 6.3 Guidelines for Page Design

1. Use white space to separate and emphasize points.
2. Use headings to group points and lead the reader through the document.
3. Limit the use of words set in all capital letters.
4. Use no more than two fonts in a single document.
5. Decide whether to justify margins based on the situation and the audience.
6. Put important elements in the top left and lower right quadrants of the page.
7. Use a grid of imaginary columns to unify graphic elements.
8. Use highlighting, decorative devices, and color in moderation.

- Use headings.
- Use a mix of paragraph lengths (most no longer than seven typed lines). It's OK for a paragraph or two to be just one sentence. First and last paragraphs, in particular, should be short.
- Use lists.
  - Use tabs or indents—not spacing—to align items vertically.
  - Use numbered lists when the number or sequence of items is exact.
  - Use **bullets** (large dots or squares like those in this list) when the number and sequence don't matter.

When you use a list, make sure that all of the items in it are parallel (see "Parallel Structure" in Chapter 5, p. 135) and fit into the structure of the sentence that introduces the list.

Increasing white space can easily improve the look of your message. Figure 6.4 shows an original typed document. Notice how this document is visually uninviting. In Figure 6.5, the same document has improved white space by using lists, headings, and shorter paragraphs. Audiences scan documents for information, so anything you can do visually to help ease their reading will reflect positively on you as the communicator. Keep in mind that

Figure 6.4 A Document with Poor Visual Impact

Full capital letters make title hard to read

MONEY DEDUCTED FROM YOUR WAGES TO PAY CREDITORS

Long paragraph is visually uninviting

When you buy goods on credit, the store will sometimes ask you to sign a Wage Assignment form allowing it to deduct money from your wages if you do not pay your bill. When you buy on credit, you sign a contract agreeing to pay a certain amount each week or month until you have paid all you owe. The Wage Assignment Form is separate. It must contain the name of your present employer, your social security number, the amount of money loaned, the rate of interest, the date when payments are due, and your signature. The words "Wage Assignment" must be printed at the top of the form and also near the line for your signature. Even if you have signed a Wage Assignment agreement, Roysner will not withhold part of your wages unless all of the following conditions are met: 1. You have to be more than forty days late in payment of what you owe; 2. Roysner has to receive a correct statement of the amount you are in default and a copy of the Wage Assignment form; and 3. You and Roysner must receive a notice from the creditor at least twenty days in advance stating that the creditor plans to make a demand on your wages. This twenty-day notice gives you a chance to correct the problems yourself. If these conditions are all met, Roysner must withhold 15% of each paycheck until your bill is paid and give this money to your creditor.

If you think you are not late or that you do not owe the amount stated, you can argue against it by filing a legal document called a "defense." Once you file a defense, Roysner will not withhold any money from you. However, be sure you are right before you file a defense. If you are wrong, you have to pay not only what you owe but also all legal costs for both yourself and the creditor. If you are right, the creditor has to pay all these costs.

Important information is hard to find

Figure 6.5 A Document Revised to Improve Visual Impact

Money Deducted from Your Wages to Pay Creditors

First letter of each main word capitalized—Title split onto two lines

When you buy goods on credit, the store will sometimes ask you to sign a Wage Assignment form allowing it to deduct money from your wages if you do not pay your bill.

Have You Signed a Wage Assignment Form?

Headings divide document into chunks

When you buy on credit, you sign a contract agreeing to pay a certain amount each week or month until you have paid all you owe. The Wage Assignment Form is separate. It must contain

- The name of your present employer,
- Your social security number,
- The amount of money loaned,
- The rate of interest,
- The date when payments are due, and
- Your signature.

List with bullets where order of items doesn't matter

Single-space list when items are short.

The words "Wage Assignment" must be printed at the top of the form and also near the line for your signature.

Headings must be parallel. Here all are questions

When Would Money Be Deducted from Your Wages to Pay a Creditor?

Even if you have signed a Wage Assignment agreement, Roysner will not withhold part of your wages unless all of the following conditions are met:

White space between items emphasizes them

1. You have to be more than 40 days late in payment of what you owe;

2. Roysner has to receive a correct statement of the amount you are in default and a copy of the Wage Assignment form; and

3. You and Roysner must receive a notice from the creditor at least 20 days in advance stating that the creditor plans to make a demand on your wage. This 20-day notice gives you a chance to correct the problem yourself.

Double-space between items in list when most items are two lines or longer.

Numbered list where number or order of items matter

If these conditions are all met, Roysner must withhold fifteen percent (15%) of each pay-check until your bill is paid and give this money to your creditor.

What Should You Do If You Think the Wage Assignment Is Incorrect?

If you think you are not late or that you do not owe the amount stated, you can argue against it by filing a legal document called a "defense." Once you file a defense, Roysner will not withhold any money from you. However, be sure you are right before you file a defense. If you are wrong, you have to pay not only what you owe but also all legal costs for both yourself and the creditor. If you are right, the creditor has to pay all these costs.

Design and Driver Safety

The New York City Department of Transportation decided to revise 250,000 street signs throughout the city. Current signs use all capital letters. The new signs will use a font called Clearview and feature both capital and lowercase letters.

The newly designed street signs are expected to improve safety, according to the Federal Highway Administration. Drivers will be able to decipher words more easily because of their shapes and, in turn, pay more attention to the road.

The price to replace all of the signs is anticipated to be $27.5 million. The project will be completed by 2018.

Adapted from "New York to Replace 250,000 Street Signs," United Press International, article published October 1, 2010, http://www.upi.com/Odd_News/2010/10/01/New-York-to-replace-250000-street-signs/UPI-10711285863676/.

these devices take space. When saving space is essential, it's better to cut the text and incorporate white space and headings.

2. Use Headings.

Psychological research has shown that our short-term memories can hold only seven plus or minus two bits of information.[5] Only after those bits are processed and put into long-term memory can we assimilate new information. Large amounts of information will be easier to process if they are grouped into three to seven chunks rather than presented as individual items.

Headings are words, short phrases, or short sentences that group points and divide your document into sections. Headings enable your reader to see at a glance how the document is organized, to turn quickly to sections of special interest, and to compare and contrast points more easily. Headings also break up the page, making it look less formidable and more interesting. To use headings effectively,

- Make headings specific.
- Make each heading cover all the material until the next heading.
- Keep headings at any one level parallel.

In a letter or memo, type main headings even with the left margin in bold or in a larger or different font. Capitalize the first letters of the first word and of other major words; use lowercase for all other letters. (See Figure 6.5 for an example.) In single-spaced text, triple-space between the previous text and the heading; double-space between the heading and the text that follows.

If you need subdivisions under a main heading, again type the heading even with the left margin, but this time make the subheading visually distinct from the major heading by varying font size or using italics. Use subheadings only when you have at least two subdivisions under a given main heading.

In a report, you may need more than two levels of headings. Figure 18.3 in Chapter 18 shows levels of headings for reports.

Research continues to show that headings help readers. In a study that examined forensic child abuse reports from Canadian children's hospitals, researchers discovered that headings play an important role. Headings and subheadings helped improve the accessibility of information about the severity of the child's injuries between the physicians who authored the reports and the social workers, lawyers, and police officers who later used them.[6]

3. Limit the Use of Words Set in All Capital Letters.

We recognize words by their shapes.[7] (See Figure 6.6.) In capitals, all words are rectangular; letters lose the descenders and ascenders that make reading faster and more accurate.[8] In addition, many people interpret text in full capitals as "shouting," especially when that text appears in online documents. In those cases, full capitals might elicit a negative response from your audience. Use full capitals sparingly, if at all.

Figure 6.6 Full Capitals Hide the Shape of a Word

Full capitals hide the shape of a word and slow reading 19%.

FULL CAPITALS HIDE THE SHAPE OF A WORD AND SLOW READING 19%.

4. Use No More than Two Fonts in a Single Document.

Fonts are unified styles of type. Popular fonts are Times Roman, Calibri, Palatino, Helvetica, or Arial, and each comes in various sizes and usually in bold and italic. In **fixed** fonts every letter takes the same space; an *i* takes the same space as a *w*. Courier and Prestige Elite are fixed fonts. Most fonts are **proportional** and allow wider letters to take more space than narrower letters. Times Roman, Palatino, Helvetica, and Arial are proportional fonts. Most business documents use no more than two fonts.

Serif fonts have little extensions, called serifs, from the main strokes. (In Figure 6.7, look at the feet on the *r*'s in New Courier and the flick on the top of the *d* in Lucinda.) New Courier, Elite, Times Roman, Palatino, and Lucinda Calligraphy are serif fonts. Helvetica, Arial, Geneva, and Technical are **sans serif** fonts since they lack serifs (*sans* is French for *without*). Sans serif fonts are good for titles and tables.

You should choose the fonts you use carefully, because they shape reader response just as font size does. Research suggests that people respond positively to fonts that fit the genre and purpose of the document.[9] For example, a font like Broadway (see Figure 6.7) is appropriate for a headline in a newsletter, but not for the body text of a memo.

Twelve-point type is ideal for letters, memos, and reports. Smaller type is harder to read, especially for older readers. You can create emphasis and levels of headings by using bold, italics, and different sizes. Bold is easier to read than italics, so use bolding if you need only one method to emphasize text. In a complex document, use bigger type for main headings and slightly smaller type for subheadings and text.

If your material will not fit in the available pages, cut it. Putting some sections in tiny type saves space but creates a negative response—a negative response that may extend to the organization that produced the document.

5. Decide Whether to Justify Margins.

Word-processing programs allow you to use **full justification** so that type lines up evenly on both the right and left margins. This paragraph you are reading justifies both margins. Margins justified only on the left, sometimes called **ragged right margins,** have lines ending in different places. In this chapter, sidebar columns with bullets use ragged right margins.

Figure 6.7 Examples of Different Fonts

This sentence is set in 12-point Times Roman.

This sentence is set in 12-point Arial.

This sentence is set in 12-point New Courier.

This sentence is set in 12-point Lucinda Calligraphy.

This sentence is set in 12-point Broadway.

This sentence is set in 12-point Technical.

Cultural Differences in Document Design

Cultural differences in document design are based on reading practices and experiences with other documents. Language is one source of these differences. For example, English and other European languages are written in horizontal lines moving from left to right down the page. Hebrew and Arabic languages are read from right to left. This affects where readers of these languages look first when they see a page of text.

People in the United States focus first on the left side of a website. Middle Eastern people focus first on the right side, so websites in Arabic and Hebrew orient text, links, and graphics from right to left.

Translations also affect the layout of a document. To convey the same message, Spanish and French take up more room than English does. Writing concise text for brochures, packages, and web pages is more challenging in the wordier languages. The problem is even more complex in designing bilingual or multilingual documents. For example, a company selling in Canada must use both English and French on its packages, and the French type must be printed at least as large as the English. On some products, such as a bottle of medicine or perfume, this requirement leaves little room for fancy graphics.

Adapted from "The Effects of Cross Cultural Interface Design Orientation on World Wide Web User Performance," by Albert N. Badre, accessed May 23, 2011, ftp://ftp.cc.gatech.edu/pub/gvu/tr/2001/01-03.html; and "Multilingual Labeling Broadens Product Appeal," by Pan Demetrakakes, BNet, accessed May 23, 2011, http://findarticles.com/p/articles/mi_m0UQX/is_7_67/ai_106423172/.

http://infomap.com/index.cfm/themethod/demos

Information Mapping uses grids and tables to present complex information in an easy-to-find format. Review some of the online demos on the Information Mapping website, and notice how the 'after' documents make strong use of tables, lists, and white space to draw your attention to important points.

Try the fun interactive demo at http://infomap.com/movies/demo.htm to see how they convert time savings to money savings.

http://www.degraeve.com/color-palette and http://www.colorhunter.com/

Do you have a hard time generating aesthetically pleasing color schemes? Have you ever wanted to create a color scheme that matches a prominent photo in your document?

Color Hunter and Color Palette Generator websites allow you to upload a photo from any URL address. After you complete this step, the websites create a color palette that matches the primary colors found within the image.

Use full justification when you

- Can use proportional fonts.
- Want a more formal look.
- Want to use as few pages as possible.

Use ragged right margins when you

- Cannot use a proportional font.
- Want an informal look.
- Want to be able to revise an individual page without reprinting the whole document.
- Use very short line lengths.

6. Put Important Elements in the Top Left and Lower Right Quadrants.

Readers of English are accustomed to reading pages of text from left to right, developing this habit over a lifetime. Effective document designers tap into our habit. They know that we start in the upper left-hand corner of the page, read to the right, move down, and then to the right again. Actually, the eye moves in a Z pattern.[10] (See Figure 6.8.) Therefore, the four quadrants of the page carry different visual weights. The top left quadrant, where the eye starts, is the most important; the bottom right quadrant, where the eye ends, is next most important.

7. Use a Grid to Unify Graphic Elements.

Many document designers use a **grid system** to design pages. In its simplest form, a grid imposes two or three imaginary columns on the page. In more complex grids, these columns can be further subdivided. Then all the graphic elements—text indentations, headings, visuals, and so on—are lined up within the columns. The resulting symmetry creates a more pleasing page and unifies long documents.

Figure 6.9 uses grids to organize a page with visuals and a newsletter page.

Figure 6.8 Put Important Elements in the Top Left and Bottom Right Quadrants

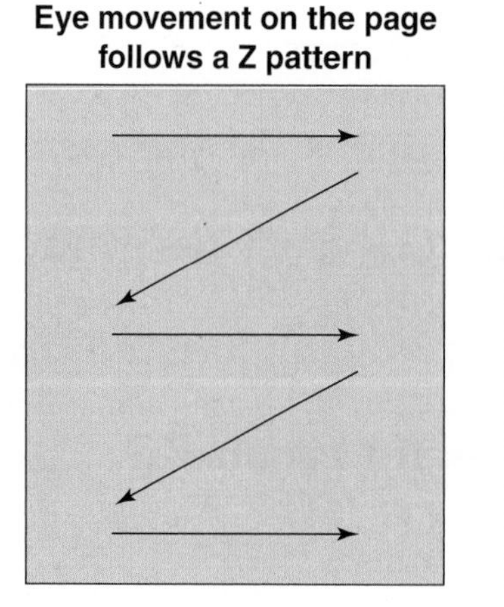

Eye movement on the page follows a Z pattern

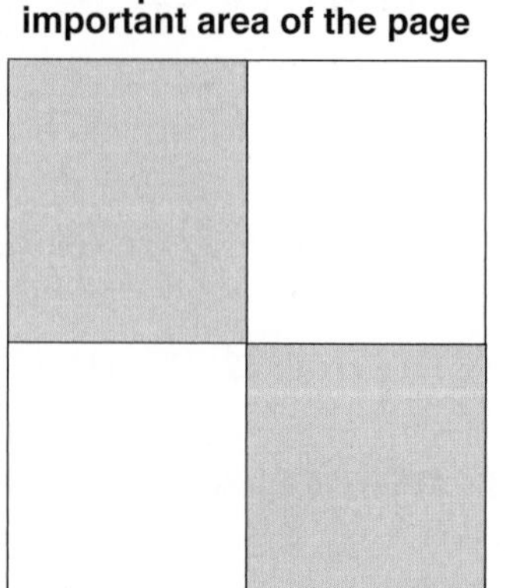

Figure 6.9 Examples of Grids to Design Pages

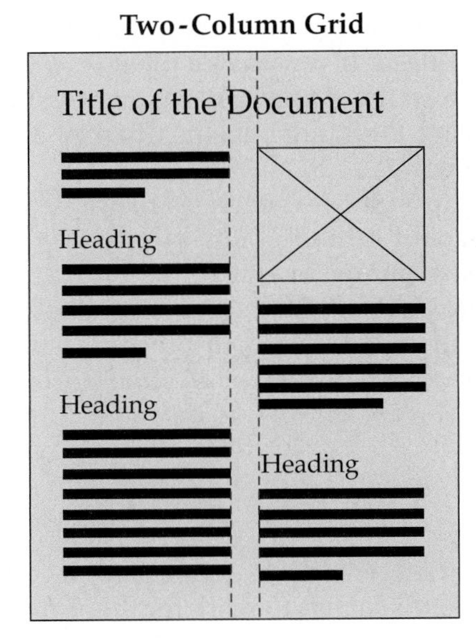

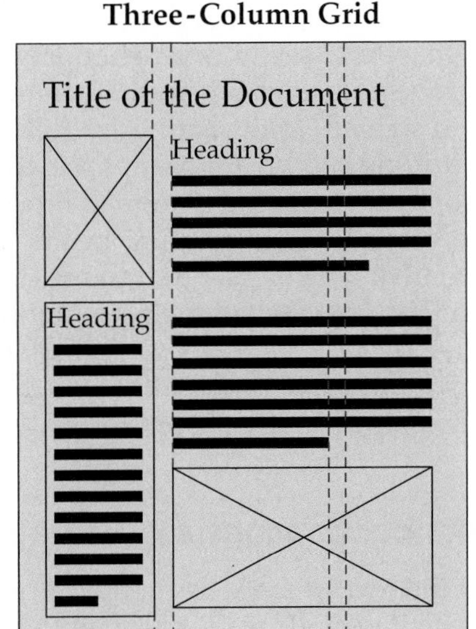

Forecasting Color

The Pantone Color Institute is one of the premier organizations for deciding what colors are trendy. There are over 1,900 Pantone hues and picking the up-and-coming colors is a full-time job.

The Color Institute has an entire team who jets around the globe, attends trade shows, and studies psychological research to determine upcoming trends. The team compiles its findings into a report that sells to businesses for $750. Each issue gives advice on how businesses can market their products using the latest color trends.

Consumer psychology plays a big part in forecasting. At one time, the color brown was associated with mud or wood, but it has undergone a transformation to being associated with quality food or good taste. A once unpopular color—orange—has become trendy in recent years; you can see the color on video cameras, blenders, and cars.

The economy can also have a big impact on color trends. In leaner times, people tend to favor neutrals.

Adapted from Alyssa Abkowitz, "The Color Committee Gets to Work," *Fortune*, October 26, 2009, 34–37.

8. Use Highlighting, Decorative Devices, and Color in Moderation.

Many word-processing programs have arrows, pointing fingers, and a host of other **dingbats** that you can insert. Clip art packages and presentation software allow you to insert more and larger images into your text. Used in moderation, highlighting and decorative devices make pages more interesting. However, don't overdo them. A page or screen that uses every possible highlighting device just looks busy and hard to read.

Color works well to highlight points. Use color for overviews and main headings, not for small points. Red is appropriate for warnings in North America. Since the connotations of colors vary among cultures, check with experts before you use color with international or multicultural audiences. (For more information on color, see the discussion in Chapter 16.)

DESIGNING BROCHURES LO 6-4

Designing a good brochure incorporates all elements of document design. To create an effective brochure, you must analyze your rhetorical situation, draft the text, select appropriate visuals, create the design, and print.

Analyzing Your Rhetorical Situation

In all forms of business communication, you should begin by considering your audience and purpose. A brochure designed to promote awareness of your company will have a different look than a brochure telling people how to do something and persuading them to do it. Try to identify a **central selling point,** an overarching benefit the audience will get. Identify any objections the audience may have and brainstorm ways to deal with these in your brochure. Finally, consider how the audience will get the brochure and where they will use it.

http://colorschemedesigner.com

Have you ever wondered how color documents might look to a person with color deficiencies? Well, now you can see! This website provides the ability to create a color scheme you might incorporate into your professional documents. It also has a drop-down menu that allows you to see how your color creations will be perceived by people with color deficiencies. Since nearly 14.5% of the population has some sort of color deficiency, you should consider how the colors you choose in your designs may affect your audience.

Drafting the Text

Once you have developed a clear understanding of your rhetorical situation, draft the text to see how much room you need. If you have a lot of text, you'll need to use a bigger brochure layout or a series of brochures. However, make sure to tighten your writing by following the guidelines in Chapter 5. Use you-attitude and positive emphasis throughout.

People are more likely to read brochures if the text engages their attention. So be sure to use interesting headlines and selling points by making them informative as well as attention-grabbing, funny, or out of the ordinary. Or you might use sidebars with testimonial quotes, examples, or vignettes. You could add elements to get your readers involved with your brochure, such as a coupon for a free or discount offer, a quiz, or a puzzle. Interesting stories can also hold your readers' attention.

Selecting Appropriate Visuals

After the text is drafted, choose appropriate visuals to accompany it. Use a visual that tells a story. Remember that the visual has to work for the audience. A photo of a campus landmark may not mean much to an audience thinking about attending a summer program on campus. For additional information about incorporating visuals, including ethics, see Chapter 16.

Creating the Design

Before inserting textual and visual elements into your brochure, you might use thumbnail sketches to test layouts. You will need to choose the image you want to project for yourself or your organization. (Clean and clear? Postmodern and hip?) Make every choice—color, font, layout, paper—a conscious one. The three-fold brochure shown in Figure 6.10 is the most common layout, but many other arrangements are possible.

Put your central selling point on the cover. Then, use a grid to align the elements within the panels. Make sure that the Z pattern emphasizes important points for each spread the reader encounters. In a three-fold brochure, the Z pattern needs to work for the cover alone, for inside pages 1 and 2 (as the reader begins to unfold the brochure),and for inside pages 1, 3, and 4 (when the brochure is fully opened).

Figure 6.10 Three-Fold Brochure on 8.5″ × 11″ Paper

Side 1
Inside p. 2 | Back cover | **Cover**

Side 2
Inside p. 1 | Inside p. 3 | Inside p. 4

Folded
Cover
Inside p. 3
Inside p. 2

When creating a three-fold brochure, mimic this scheme so your final document prints correctly.

Follow these additional design principles when creating your brochure:

- Use proportional fonts.
- Use two fonts—one for headings and one for body text—to create visual variety.
- Avoid italic type and underlining, which can make text hard to read.
- Use color effectively (by using the color scheme designer mentioned in the sidebar on page 168).
- Repeat design elements (headings, small photos) across panels to create a unified look.
- Create contrast (between text and visuals, between a larger font for headings and a smaller one for text).
- Include enough white space—use lists and headings or short paragraphs with extra space between them. Ragged right margins generally work better with short line lengths.

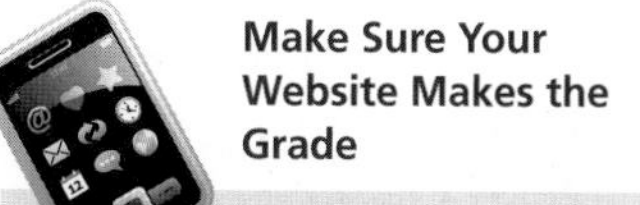

Make Sure Your Website Makes the Grade

"Ninety-seven percent of the 1,000-plus corporate Web sites that Forrester Research Inc. has evaluated received failing grades. Companies with bad Web sites are turning off customers and leaving money on the table. And usually it's due to common mistakes that can be broken down into four categories:

1. Value. The first mistake that companies make is copying features from competitors.
2. Navigation. Companies often opt for cute menus instead of clear menus.
3. Presentation. Web sites need to be easy to read and understand.
4. Trust. People are concerned about online privacy and security. Calling attention to privacy policy can actually help sales."

Quoted from Ben Worthen, "Why Most Web Sites Receive Failing Grades," *Wall Street Journal*, August 21, 2007.

Printing the Brochure

Printing can be accomplished on your personal inkjet printer. For better laser-quality results, however, you might go to Kinkos or Copyworks. If your organization demands an even higher professional look or you have thousands of copies to print, take your brochure to a commercial printer.

If you opt for four-color printing, use glossy paper to add a professional tone to your design. Four-color printing will look best; however, it will also cost you or your organization the most money. To get the effect of color with the least expense, use black print on colored paper.

DESIGNING WEB PAGES LO 6-5

Like effective brochures, web pages also incorporate principles of rhetorical analysis and document design. To create effective web pages, you must attract and maintain the audience's attention, create a usable home page, provide easy navigation, follow conventions, and increase accessibility.

Attracting and Maintaining Attention

The amount of time you have to attract and keep an audience's attention on your website is minimal. Researchers tracked how long users took to read or scan web pages; 52% of the visits were shorter than 10 seconds. In fact, 25% were less than four seconds. Only 10% were longer than two minutes. Therefore, any mishaps in design could cause audiences to completely skip your website.[11]

Jakob Nielsen, a web guru and usability consultant, provides research showing that web audiences use an F-shaped pattern when viewing web pages. First, they quickly read across the top of the page. Then they move down the page some and read across again, but for a shorter distance. Finally, they scan down the left side. All this happens quickly. The F-shaped pattern means that your most important information must be at the top of the page. In addition, make sure that headings, paragraphs, and items in lists start with words important to your reader.[12]

http://www.oswd.org

Open Source Web Design has thousands of clean, professional design templates for web pages available for download. Most of these templates are free to use: the authors ask only that you keep their contact information on the pages you create using the template.

http://www.usableweb.com/

Usable Web offers a collection of links about information architecture, human factors, user interface issues, and usable design specific to the World Wide Web. Log on to find tips on how to improve the overall design and look of your website and its features.

Creating a Usable Home Page

Your home page is crucial. Not only must it open quickly, but visitors must be able to find what they want quickly. Studies show that users grow impatient after waiting 10 seconds for a page to load, and most will leave the site immediately.[13] In addition, first-time visitors tend not to scroll down beyond the first screen of text.

To keep visitors around long enough to find (or buy) what they want, make using the first screen extremely easy.

- Provide an introductory statement or graphic orienting the surfing reader to the organization sponsoring the page.
- Make completing a task as easy as possible.
- Offer an overview of the content of your page, with links to take readers to the parts that interest them.
- Provide navigation bars vertically on the left of the screen or horizontally on the top and bottom. A site index and an internal search engine are valuable tools.
- Make it clear what readers will get if they click on a link.

Ineffective phrasing:	Employment. Openings and skill levels are determined by each office.
Better phrasing:	Employment. Openings listed by skill level and by location.

Providing Easy Navigation

While websites have increased the value they have to offer, the biggest problem now is navigation, especially as sites grow and become more complex. A web page's navigation should be intuitive to the audience and make accessing information easy. If the audience has to work too hard to figure out how to use your web page, chances are they will leave the site. After eBay fell behind Amazon for site visitors, they launched an overhaul of the website before the holiday shopping season in 2010 to organize thousands of listings and upgrade their outdated technology. Some of the new elements on the home page include recommendations to users based on previous searches, mentions of the hottest items, and consolidated lists with the best deals.[14]

Following Conventions

Jakob Nielsen urges his readers to follow conventions of web pages and get back to design basics. He reminds designers that users want quality basics. Here are some of the top web design mistakes he lists:

- Bad search engines
- Links that don't change color when visited
- Large text blocks
- Fixed font size
- Content that doesn't answer users' questions

He also cautions against violating design conventions. Users will expect your website to act like the other sites they visit. If it doesn't, the site will be harder to use and visitors will leave. Nielsen warns that some conventions, such as banner ads, have outlived their usefulness. Banner blindness is so prevalent that anything that looks like a banner will be ignored, as one nonprofit health site discovered. The site had a box at the top of their home page telling users what to do if they thought they were having a heart attack, but research showed that users were ignoring the box because they thought it was an ad.[15]

As you design web pages, use the following guidelines:

- Use a white or light background for easy scanning.
- Keep graphics small. Specify the width and height so that the text can load while the graphics are still coming in.
- Provide visual variety in your text. Use indentations, bulleted or numbered lists, and headings. Start lists with impact words—remember the F pattern.
- Unify multiple pages with a small banner, graphic, or label so surfers know who sponsors each page.
- Use alternative text ("ALT tag") for visually impaired viewers.
- On each page, provide a link to the home page.
- Keep animation to a minimum, and allow viewers to control its use. If you have an animated site introduction page, include an easy-to-spot Skip Intro button.
- If your web pages include music or sound effects, put an Off button where the user can see it immediately. Computer users may be at work, in a library or at another location where your brand's theme song would be disruptive—or embarrassing.

Appropriately enough, the web has many additional resources on web page design, as well as technical pages on HTML, XML, and Java.

Increasing Accessibility

As you design a website, you also should try to make it accessible to people with disabilities. The law is beginning to consider a website a public space and therefore subject to the 1990 Americans with Disabilities Act. Target settled a class action suit with the National Federation of the Blind by agreeing to pay $6 million in damages and to make their site more accessible. More legal proceedings got Apple to agree to make iTunes more accessible. One of the most sought features in these legal actions is text attached to links and graphics that can be accessed by screen-reading software.[16] For more ways to make your web page accessible, see the sidebar on this page.

One additional concern in terms of accessibility is the location where people view your web pages. With the proliferation of smartphones and other tablet computers, you need to optimize your website for these alternative viewing platforms. The retail world is trying to catch up, but has been slow. Halfway through 2010, only 12% of the top 500 U.S. online retailers had compatible sites for smartphones. Yet, 85% of customers surveyed expect the ability to shop easily on their phones, according to research by Tealeaf, a software company that monitors online consumer patterns. Some of the survey participants suggested that mobile shopping was sometimes more frustrating that sitting in traffic.[17]

Making Your Web Page Accessible

Users with hearing impairments need captions for audio material on the web.

Blind users need words, not images. Words can be voiced by a screen reader or translated into Braille text. To make your web page accessible for people with vision impairments,

- Put a link to a text-only version of the site in the upper-left-hand corner.
- Put navigation links, a site map, and search box at the top of the screen, preferably in the upper left-hand corner.
- Arrange navigation links alphabetically so that blind users can use a screen reader to jump to the links they want.
- Provide alternative text (an "Alt tag") for all images, applets, and submit buttons.
- Provide a static alternative to flash or animation.
- In hypertext links, use text that makes sense when read alone. A person listening to the audio will not understand "Click here." "Click to order a copy" or "Click for details" offers a better clue.

The Web Accessibility Initiative (www.w3.org) points out that accessible websites are easier for a variety of people to use—not just those with obvious impairments.

TESTING THE DESIGN FOR USABILITY LO 6-6

Usability testing is an important step in document design. A document that looks pretty may or may not work for the audience. To know whether your design is functional, test it with your audience.

According to Jakob Nielsen, testing a draft with five users will reveal 85% of the problems with the document.[18] If time and money permit additional testing, revise the document and test the new version with another five users. Test the document with the people who are most likely to have trouble with it: very old or young readers, people with little education, people who read English as a second language.

Three kinds of tests yield particularly useful information:

- Watch someone as he or she uses the document to do a task. Where does the user pause, re-read, or seem confused? How long does it take? Does the document enable the user to complete the task accurately?
- Ask the user to "think aloud" while completing the task, interrupt the user at key points to ask what he or she is thinking, or ask the user to describe the thought process after completing the document and the task. Learning the user's thought processes is important, since a user may get the right answer for the wrong reasons. In such a case, the design still needs work.
- Ask users to put a plus sign (+) in the margins by any part of the document they like or agree with, and a minus sign (−) by any part of the document that seems confusing or wrong. Then use interviews or focus groups to find out the reasons for the plus and minus judgments.

Jakob Nielsen also urges usability testing for web design. In fact, he recommends testing at various stages of the design process—good advice for complex paper documents as well. He also warns that the best usability testing involves *watching* people use the communication. Listening to what they think they do can be misleading.[19] (Would you have told a researcher that you look at a web page using an F pattern?)

SUMMARY OF KEY POINTS

- Good document design can save time and money, and can prevent legal problems.
- Effective design groups ideas visually, making the structure of the document more inviting and obvious so the document is easier to read.
- The best documents are created when you think about design at each stage of the writing process.
  - As you plan, think about the needs of your audience.
  - As you write, incorporate lists, headings, and visuals.

  - Get feedback from people who will be using your document.
  - As you revise, check your draft against the guidelines in this chapter.
- Effective design relies heavily on conventions, which vary by audience.
- The four levels of design—intra, inter, extra, and supra—help you organize and analyze design choices.
- These guidelines help writers create visually attractive documents:
  1. Use white space.
  2. Use headings.
  3. Limit the use of words set in all capital letters.
  4. Use no more than two fonts in a single document.
  5. Decide whether to justify margins.
  6. Put important elements in the top left and lower right quadrants.
  7. Use a grid to unify visuals and other graphic elements.
  8. Use highlighting, decorative devices, and color in moderation.
- To create an effective brochure, you must analyze your rhetorical situation, draft the text, select appropriate visuals, create the design, and print.
- To create effective web pages, you must attract and maintain the audience's attention, create a usable home page, provide easy navigation, follow conventions, and increase accessibility.
- To conduct a usability test, observe people reading the document or using it to complete a task.

CHAPTER 6 Exercises and Problems

**Go to www.mhhe.com/locker10e for additional Exercises and Problems.*

6.1 Reviewing the Chapter

1. Why is document design important in business communication? (LO 6-1)
2. What are the four levels of document design? (LO 6-2)
3. What are some guidelines for document design? (LO 6-3)
4. What are some basic guidelines for designing brochures? Web pages? (LO 6-4)
5. What are some basic guidelines for designing web pages? (LO 6-5)
6. How can you perform basic usability testing on your documents? (LO 6-5)

6.2 Evaluating Page Designs

Use the guidelines in Chapter 6 to evaluate each of the following page designs. What are their strong points? What could be improved?

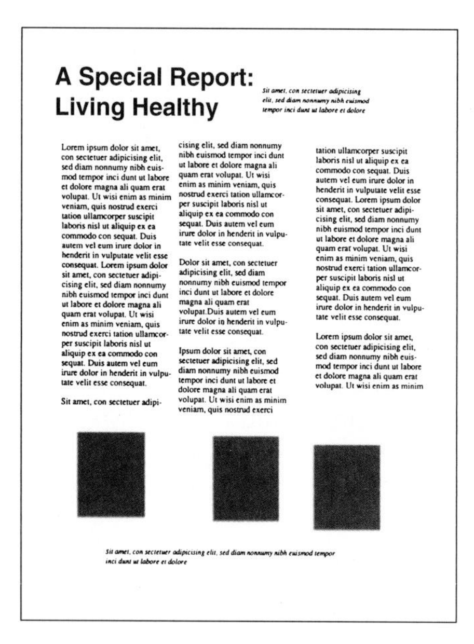

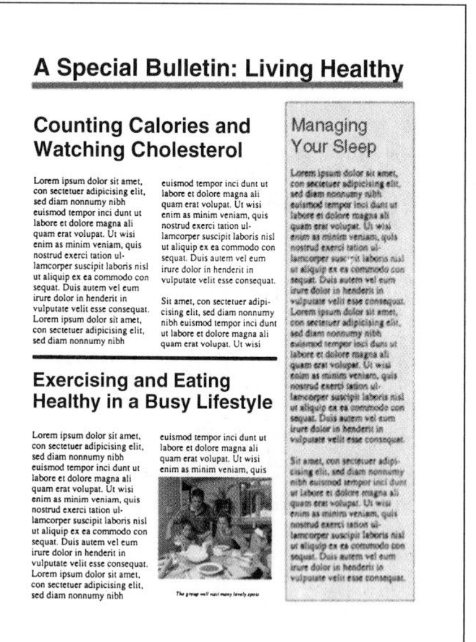

As your instructor directs,

a. Discuss the design elements you see on these sample pages with a small group of classmates.

b. Write a memo to your instructor evaluating the design elements on each of the sample pages. Be sure to address the four levels of design, as well as the guidelines for page and visual design discussed in this chapter.

c. In an oral presentation to the class, explain the process you'd use to redesign one of the sample pages. What design elements would make the page stronger or weaker? What design elements would you change, and how? Given the title of the document, what audience characteristics might your design take into account?

6.3 Recognizing Typefaces

Some companies commission a unique typeface, or wordmark, for their logos. Other companies use a standard font. When a logo is used consistently and frequently, it becomes associated with the organization. Can you name the brands that go with each letter of the alphabet below?

As your instructor directs,

a. Discuss the visual design of these brand visuals with a small group of classmates. What features distinguish them from other, similar brands? What makes them so recognizable?

b. Select one of the brand visuals represented and research it to determine its history. How has the visual changed over time? Write a memo to your instructor evaluating those changes, and identifying some of the design strategies (and business strategies) involved in each change.

Source: "Alphabet Soup," © *Issue: The Journal of Business and Design*, Vol. 2, No. 2, Fall 1997, pp. 24–25.

ISSUE: ISSUE:

Alphabet Soup You don't always need to see the whole word to recognize the name of the brand. One letter will do. Used effectively, a distinctive logotype becomes the corporate signature. That is why many companies commission the design of a unique typeface, or wordmark, that incorporates clues to their line of business or operating philosophy. Other companies have adopted an off-the-shelf typeface that they have made their own through the use of designated corporate colors, upper or lower case styling, condensed or expanded leading and other techniques. As with any branding tool, a logotype must be used consistently and frequently to work. Test your familiarity with some of the best-known logotypes by naming the brand that goes with each letter in this alphabet.

24 25

Source: "Alphabet Soup." Reprinted with permission from © *Issue: The Journal of Business and Design*, Vol. 2, No. 2, Fall 1997, pp. 24–25. Published by Corporate Design Foundation and sponsored by Potlatch Corporation.

6.4 Evaluating the Ethics of Design Choices

Indicate whether you consider each of the following actions ethical, unethical, or a gray area. Which of the actions would you do? Which would you feel uncomfortable doing? Which would you refuse to do?

1. Putting the advantages of a proposal in a bulleted list, while discussing the disadvantages in a paragraph.
2. Using a bigger type size so that a résumé visually fills a whole page.
3. Using tiny print and very little white space on a credit card contract to make it less likely that people will read it.
4. Putting important information on the back of what looks like a one-page document.
5. Putting the services that are not covered by your health plan in full caps to make it less likely that people will read the page.

6.5 Using Headings

Reorganize the items in each of the following lists, using appropriate headings. Use bulleted or numbered lists as appropriate.

a. Rules and Procedures for a Tuition Reimbursement Plan

1. You are eligible to be reimbursed if you have been a full-time employee for at least three months.
2. You must apply before the first class meeting.
3. You must earn a "C" or better in the course.
4. You must submit a copy of the approved application, an official grade report, and a receipt for tuition paid to be reimbursed.
5. You can be reimbursed for courses related to your current position or another position in the company, or for courses which are part of a degree related to a current or possible job.
6. Your supervisor must sign the application form.
7. Courses may be at any appropriate level (high school, college, or graduate school).

b. Activities in Starting a New Business

- Getting a loan or venture capital.
- Getting any necessary city or state licenses.
- Determining what you will make, do, or sell.
- Identifying the market for your products or services.
- Pricing your products or services.
- Choosing a location.
- Checking zoning laws that may affect the location.
- Identifying government and university programs for small business development.
- Figuring cash flow.
- Ordering equipment and supplies.
- Selling.
- Advertising and marketing.

6.6 Evaluating Page Designs

1. Collect several documents that you receive as a consumer, a student, or an employee: forms, letters, memos, newsletters, e-mail, announcements, ads, flyers, and reports. Use the guidelines in this chapter to evaluate each of them.
2. Compare these documents in a specific category to the documents produced by competing organizations. Which documents are more effective? Why?

As your instructor directs,

a. Discuss the documents with a small group of classmates.
b. Write a memo to your instructor evaluating three or more of the documents, and comparing them to similar documents produced by competitors. Include originals or photocopies of the documents you discuss in an appendix to your memo.
c. Write a letter to one of the originating organizations, recommending ways it can improve the design of the documents.
d. In an oral presentation to the class, explain what makes one document strong and another one weak.

6.7 Evaluating Websites

Compare three web pages in the same category (for example, shelters for the homeless, organizations, car companies, university departments, food banks). Which page(s) are most effective? Why? What weaknesses do the pages have?

As your instructor directs,

a. Discuss the pages with a small group of classmates.
b. Write a memo to your instructor evaluating the pages. Include URLs of the pages in your memo.
c. In an oral presentation to the class, explain what makes one page good and another one weak.
d. Post your evaluation in an e-mail message to the class. Include the URLs so classmates can click to the pages you discuss.

6.8 Comparing Websites

Alexa.com is a website that tracks the performance and popularity of other websites. In addition to ranking websites, the site allows users to input several websites and compare their rank and number of page views on a colored graph. The comparisons can range between seven days and a year. Visit the site to see which websites currently have the honor of being the top-rated. Where does your organization's or school's website rank? How can a tool like this be useful for businesses? What limitations does this tool have?

As your instructor directs,

a. Share your findings with a small group of classmates.

b. Put your findings in a memo to your instructor.

6.9 Creating a Brochure

Create a brochure for a campus, nonprofit, government or business organization. As you work,

- Analyze your intended audience. What are their needs? What factors are most likely to persuade them to read your brochure?
- Choose a story: What's the important information? What idea do you want your audience to take away?
- Make page design choices that create a usable document and generate a positive response from your audience.
- Make visual design choices that enhance and expand on your text without being simply decorative.

As your instructor directs,

a. Write a memo to your instructor explaining your choices for content and design.

b. In an oral presentation to the class, display your brochure and explain your content and design choices.

6.10 Creating a Web Page

Create a web page for a campus, nonprofit, government or business organization that does not yet have one. As you work,

- Analyze your intended audience. What are their needs? What factors are most likely to persuade them to use this site?
- Choose a story: What's the important information? What action do you want them to take while they're browsing this site?
- Make page design choices that create a usable site and generate a positive response from your audience.
- Make visual design choices that enhance and expand on your text without being distracting.

As your instructor directs,

a. Write a memo to your instructor explaining your choices for content and design.

b. In an oral presentation to the class, display your site and explain your page and visual design choices. Provide the URL, or display images of the site as presentation visuals, so that classmates can evaluate your design as you present it.

6.11 Testing a Document

Ask someone to follow a set of instructions or to fill out a form. (Consider consumer instructions, forms for financial aid, and so forth.)

- Time the person. How long does it take? Is the person able to complete the task?
- Observe the person. Where does he or she pause, reread, seem confused?
- Interview the person. What parts of the document were confusing?

As your instructor directs,

a. Discuss the changes needed with a small group of classmates.

b. Write a memo to your instructor evaluating the document and explaining the changes that are needed. Include the document as an appendix to your memo.

c. Write to the organization that produced the document recommending necessary improvements.

d. In an oral presentation to the class, evaluate the document and explain what changes are needed.

6.12 Improving a Financial Aid Form

You've just joined the financial aid office at your school. The director gives you the following form and asks you to redesign it. The director says:

> We need this form to see whether parents have other students in college besides the one requesting aid. Parents are supposed to list all family members that the parents support—themselves, the person here, any other kids in college, and any younger dependent kids.
>
> Half of these forms are filled out incorrectly. Most people just list the student going here; they leave out everyone else.

If something is missing, the computer sends out a letter and a second copy of this form. The whole process starts over. Sometimes we send this form back two or three times before it's right. In the meantime, students' financial aid is delayed—maybe for months. Sometimes things are so late that they can't register for classes, or they have to pay tuition themselves and get reimbursed later.

If so many people are filling out the form wrong, the form itself must be the problem. See what you can do with it. But keep it to a page.

As your instructor directs,

a. Analyze the current form and identify its problems.
b. Revise the form. Add necessary information; reorder information; change the chart to make it easier to fill out.
c. Write a memo to the director of financial aid pointing out the changes you made and why you made them.

Hints:

- Where are people supposed to send the form? What is the phone number of the financial aid office? Should they need to call the office if the form is clear?
- Does the definition of *half-time* apply to all students or just those taking courses beyond high school?
- Should capital or lowercase letters be used?
- Are the lines big enough to write in?
- What headings or subdivisions within the form would remind people to list all family members whom they support?
- How can you encourage people to return the form promptly?

Please complete the chart below by listing all family members for whom you (the parents) will provide more than half support during the academic year (July 1 through June 30). Include yourselves (the parents), the student, and your dependent children, even if they are not attending college.

EDUCATIONAL INFORMATION, 201_ – 201_						
FULL NAME OF FAMILY MEMBER	AGE	RELATIONSHIP OF FAMILY MEMBER TO STUDENT	NAME OF SCHOOL OR COLLEGE THIS SCHOOL YEAR	FULL-TIME	HALF-TIME* OR MORE	LESS THAN HALF-TIME
STUDENT APPLICANT						

*Half-time is defined as 6 credit hours or 12 clock hours a term.

When the information requested is received by our office, processing of your financial aid application will resume.

Please sign and mail this form to the above address as soon as possible. Your signature certifies that this information, and the information on the FAF, is true and complete to the best of your knowledge. If you have any questions, please contact a member of the need analysis staff.

Signature of Parent(s) ____________________ Date ____________

CHAPTER 7

Communicating across Cultures

Chapter Outline

Global Business
- Local Culture Adaptations
- International Career Experience

Diversity in North America

Ways to Look at Culture

Values, Beliefs, and Practices

Nonverbal Communication
- Body Language
- Touch
- Space
- Time
- Other Nonverbal Symbols

Oral Communication
- Understatement and Exaggeration
- Compliments

Writing to International Audiences

Learning More about International Business Communication

Summary of Key Points

Newsworthy Communication

Communicating Compassion

When disaster strikes, like the March 2011 earthquake and tsunami in Japan, a company's ability to communicate well and efficiently becomes doubly important. This is especially true for international corporations, which need to navigate not only the natural disasters, but also the complications of cross-cultural communication.

Apple, Inc., relies on suppliers in Japan for many components of its computers and other consumer products. When the earthquake struck, Apple was preparing to release its latest version of the popular iPad in Japan. It was a critical time for the company's continued success. Hours after the earthquake, however, Apple suspended the iPad's launch, and all its employees in Japan received the following message from CEO Steve Jobs:

"To Our Team in Japan,

"We have all been following the unfolding disaster in Japan. Our hearts go out to you and your families, as well as all of your countrymen who have been touched by this tragedy.

"If you need time or resources to visit or care for your families, please see HR and we will help you. If you are aware of any supplies that are needed, please also tell HR and we will do what we can to arrange delivery.

"Again, our hearts go out to you during this unimaginable crisis.

"Please stay safe."

The message itself was important—a statement of encouragement and support from the head of the company. But the way Apple continued to respond made the difference for thousands of employees and even more nonemployees. In cities with no power or Internet, Apple's self-contained stores stayed open, providing free wireless access, free use of computers and phones, charging stations, food, and places to sleep for stranded employees. Hundreds crowded into the stores to contact family and friends.

> *"The actions of the local employees and the executive teams that helped thousands of people were admirable and appropriate gestures from a truly international company."*

Apple's International HR chief was in Japan at the time and he, with other executives, went to the retail store to spend the night with the employees. The executive team authorized thousands of dollars in taxi charges and hotel rooms to help their employees get to their families.

In high-context cultures like Japan, which place great importance on personal relationships, oral agreements, and nonverbal actions, Apple's response to the disaster was perfectly suited. The written message from Steve Jobs was good; the actions of the local employees and the executive teams that helped thousands of people were admirable and appropriate gestures from a truly international company.

Sources: Ricardo Bilton, "Steve Jobs Responds to Japan Quake," *International Business Times*, March 17, 2011, http://www.ibtimes.com/art/services/print.php?articleid5123928; and Kevin Rose, "Apple's Role in Japan during the Tohoku Earthquake," *Kevinrose.com* (blog), March 16, 2011, http://kevinrose.com/blogg/2011/3/14/apples-role-in-japan-during-the-tohoku-earthquake.html.

Learning Objectives

After studying this chapter, you will know

LO7-1 Why global business is important.

LO7-2 Why diversity is becoming more important.

LO7-3 How our values and beliefs affect our responses to other people.

LO7-4 How nonverbal communication impacts cross-cultural communications.

LO7-5 How to adapt oral communication for cross-cultural communications.

LO7-6 How to adapt written communications for international audiences.

LO7-7 Why it is important to check cultural generalizations.

HBR on Chinese versus Russian Entrepreneurs

As business opportunities continue to expand in China and Russia, the *Harvard Business Review* offers this summary of the differences between entrepreneurs in the two countries:

- Chinese tend to think concretely and appreciate harmonious and balanced ideas. Russians tend to think abstractly and tolerate contradictory positions.
- Chinese networks tend to be small and close knit: family, friends, and colleagues. Russia's institutional chaos has hastened the formation of new, loosely knit networks.
- Members of Chinese networks exhibit higher levels of trust, Russians lower levels.

Because of these characteristics, Chinese networks are harder to enter than the more fluid Russian networks. However, once you are in, you will be more trusted in a Chinese network than in a Russian one.

However, HBR notes that Americans will always be expected to be different and that trying too hard to fit in will undermine trust.

Our values, priorities, and practices are shaped by the culture in which we grow up. Understanding other cultures is crucial if you want to work in an organization with a diverse group of employees, benefit from a global supply chain, sell your products to other cultures in our country, sell to other countries, manage an international plant or office, or work in this country for a multinational company headquartered in another country.

The successful intercultural communicator is

- Aware of the values, beliefs, and practices in other cultures.
- Sensitive to differences among individuals within a culture.
- Aware that his or her preferred values and behaviors are influenced by culture and are not necessarily "right."
- Sensitive to verbal and nonverbal behavior.
- Willing to ask questions about preferences and behaviors.
- Flexible and open to change.

The first step in understanding another culture is to realize that it may do things very differently, and that the difference is not bad or inferior. The second step is understanding that people within a single culture differ.

When pushed too far, the kinds of differences summarized in this chapter can turn into stereotypes, which can be just as damaging as ignorance. Psychologists have shown that stereotypes have serious consequences and that they come into play even when we don't want them to. Asking African American students to identify their race before answering questions taken from the Graduate Record Examination, the standardized test used for admission to graduate schools, cut in half the number of items they got right. Similarly, asking students to identify their sex at the beginning of Advanced Placement (AP) calculus tests, used to give high school students college credits, lowered the scores of women. If the sex question were moved to the end of the test, about 5% more women would receive AP credit.[1]

Don't try to memorize the material in this chapter as a rigid set of rules. Instead, use the examples to get a sense for the kinds of things that differ from one culture to another. Test these generalizations against your experience. When in doubt, ask.

GLOBAL BUSINESS LO 7-1

As we saw in Chapter 4, exports are essential both to the success of individual businesses and to a country's economy as a whole. Even many small businesses have global supply chains. Most major businesses operate globally, and an increasing share of profits comes from outside the headquarters country:

- McDonald's has restaurants in over 115 countries and has 66% of its income internationally.
- 3M operates in over 65 countries and has 65% of its sales internationally.
- Procter & Gamble brands are sold in 180 countries.
- Unilever sells products in over 180 countries; more than 50% of its business is in emerging markets.
- Walmart's international sales earn "only" 29% of the company's sales, but that percentage is a huge $109 billion.[2]

Other businesses are following suit. Movie studios, for instance, are turning down scripts that would play well in the United States because they would not play well abroad. Such decisions are seen as sound, since foreign ticket sales are now two-thirds of the global film market. Studios are hiring more foreign actors for blockbusters, rewriting scripts for international audiences, and cutting back on comedies (American humor is frequently not funny abroad).[3] Other companies depend on international vendors or operations for services such as call centers, data centers, and accounting centers.

Local Culture Adaptations

As they expand globally, U.S. retailers are catering to local tastes and customs. When expanding to China, Walmart enraged consumers when they sold dead fish and meat packaged in Styrofoam, which shoppers saw as old merchandise. Walmart quickly learned to compensate by leaving meat uncovered and installing fish tanks to sell live fish. They also sell live tortoises and snakes; Johnson's Baby Oil is stocked next to moisturizers containing sheep placenta, a native wrinkle "cure." Walmart lures customers on foot or bikes with free shuttle buses and home deliveries for large items. Perhaps the biggest change is Walmart's acceptance of organized labor in China; in July 2006 it accepted its first union ever into its stores.

The costs for failing to adapt to local cultures can be high. AlertDriving, a Toronto company that provides training for companies' drivers, opened its services in more than 20 countries before it became aware of problems. The driving lessons had been poorly translated, and the instructions did not fit with local laws and customs. To make matters worse, the company did not learn about some of the problems for years because some clients considered criticism disrespectful. Eventually AlertDriving had to spend a million dollars to retranslate and rework all of its materials for local cultures, a costly lesson in cultural awareness.[4]

Beyond Stereotypes

Learning about different cultures is important for understanding the different kinds of people we work with. However, leadership coaches Keith Caver and Ancella Livers caution that people are individuals, not just representatives of a cultural group. Based on their work with African American executives and middle managers, Caver and Livers have found that coworkers sometimes treat these individuals first as representatives of black culture, and only second as talented and experienced managers.

As an example, Caver and Livers cite the all-too-common situation of a newly hired black manager who participates in a management development activity. The new manager is prepared to answer questions about her area of business expertise, but the only questions directed toward her are about "diversity." African American clients of Caver and Livers have complained that they are often called upon to interpret the behavior of famous black Americans such as Clarence Thomas or Jesse Jackson, and they wonder whether their white colleagues would feel their race qualifies them to interpret the deeds of famous white Americans.

In this example, stereotypes make well-intentioned efforts at communication offensive. To avoid such offense, consider not only culture, but also people's individual qualities and their roles and experiences. A person who communicates one way in the role of son or daughter may communicate very differently as engineer or client.

Adapted from Keith A. Caver and Ancella B. Livers, "Dear White Boss," *Harvard Business Review* 80, no. 11 (November 2002), 76–81.

Marketing Disney to China

Only six months after Hong Kong Disneyland opened, Disney officials were scrambling to understand why attendance was so low at the new park. They turned for answers to Chinese travel agents who book tours. Some of these agents believed Disney officials had not tried to understand the local market and Chinese culture.

After the disappointing start at the Hong Kong park, Disney officials were anxious to learn and ready to make changes. Using the travel industry feedback and other market research, Disney developed a new advertising campaign. Original ads had featured an aerial view of the park; new TV spots focused on people and showed guests riding attractions. A new print ad featuring a grandmother, mother, and daughter showed that Disneyland is a place where families can have fun together.

Disney also worked to make visitors more comfortable inside the park. At an attraction offered in three different languages, guests gravitated toward the shortest line—usually the line for English-speaking guests. Now, three separate signs clearly mark which language will be used to communicate with guests in that line. Greater use of Mandarin-speaking guides and materials helps guests better enjoy shows and attractions. Also, additional seating was added in dining areas because Chinese diners take longer to eat than do Americans. Disney is hoping such changes will attract more guests to the Hong Kong park.

Source: Merissa Marr and Geoffrey A. Fowler, "Chinese Lessons for Disney," *Wall Street Journal,* June 12, 2006, B1, B5.

What cultural barriers did Disney need to overcome to help Hong Kong Disneyland succeed? See sidebar on this page.

International Career Experience

When plants, stores, and offices move overseas, people follow—from top executives to migrant workers. In fact, managers often find they need international experience if they want top-level jobs. Expatriate experience has also been shown to make them more creative and better problem solvers.[5] This effect, combined with booming overseas growth, means that executive head hunters are looking for people with deep bicultural fluency or experience in several countries, with China, India, and Brazil at the top of the list.[6] Responding to the need for global experience, business schools are stepping up their international offerings with classes, international case studies, overseas campuses, and student/faculty exchanges. For both young and experienced hires, second-language proficiency and multicultural awareness are sought.[7]

U.S. workers join a host of migrant workers already abroad. Nepalis work in Korean factories; Mongolians perform menial labor in Prague. Close to half of all migrants are women, many of whom leave children behind. They stay in touch with cellphones and the Internet.[8]

Migrant workers benefit the economies of both host and home countries. The money sent home by migrants, over $317 billion a year, is three times the world's total foreign aid. For seven countries, that income is over a quarter of their gross domestic product.[9] Thus, the money sent home is one of the major drivers of international development.

Thomas Friedman, Pulitzer Prize author and *New York Times* columnist, uses the metaphor of a flat world to describe the increasing globalization. In *The World Is Flat: A Brief History of the Twenty-First Century,* he says,

> What the flattening of the world means is that we are now connecting all the knowledge centers on the planet together into a single global network, which—if politics and terrorism do not get in the way—could usher in an amazing era of prosperity, innovation, and collaboration, by companies, communities, and individuals.[10]

DIVERSITY IN NORTH AMERICA LO 7-2

Even if you stay in the United States and Canada, you'll work with people whose backgrounds differ from yours. Residents of small towns and rural areas may have different notions of friendliness than do people from big cities. Californians may talk and dress differently than people in the

Midwest. The cultural icons that resonate for baby boomers may mean little to Millennials. For many workers, local diversity has become as important as international diversity.

The last two decades have seen a growing emphasis on diversity. This diversity comes from many sources:

- Gender
- Race and ethnicity
- Regional and national origin
- Social class
- Religion
- Age
- Sexual orientation
- Physical ability

Many young Americans are already multicultural. According to 2009 U.S. census figures, 37% of Americans aged 15 to 24 are African American, Latino, Asian, or Native American.[11] Some of them are immigrants or descendants of immigrants. In 2009, the largest numbers of immigrants to the United States have come from Mexico, India, China, the Philippines, Dominican Republic, Cuba, Vietnam, and Korea.[12] In 2002 Latinos became the largest minority group in the United States. The U.S. Census Bureau predicts that by 2042, the non-Hispanic white population will be less than 50% of the country's total population.[13] Already California, the District of Columbia, Hawaii, New Mexico, and Texas have a population that is more than 50% minorities; the Census Bureau labels these states as having a "majority–minority" population.[14]

Bilingual Canada has long compared the diversity of its people to a mosaic. But now immigrants from Italy, China, and the Middle East add their voices to the medley of French, English, and Inuit. Radio station CHIN in Toronto offers information in 30 languages.[15]

According to 2010 U.S. census figures, about 9 million people identified themselves as belonging to two or more races.[16] U.S. census figures also show that 19.7% of the population nationally and 42.3% in California speak a language other than English at home.[17] In cities such as Los Angeles and San Jose, over half the population speaks a language other than English at home (60.3% and 53.7%, respectively).[18]

Faced with these figures, organizations are making special efforts to diversify their workforces. Microsoft, for instance, has 40 different Employee Networks; in addition to various ethnic groups (Chinese Employees is the largest), they cover various family roles (Working Parents), disabilities (Visually Impaired Persons), age groups (Boomers), and backgrounds (U.S. Military Veterans). Various groups focus on a variety of functions, including member support, diversity advocacy, cultural awareness, and educational outreach. They also provide resources for recruiting and training.[19]

These companies are smart; new evidence shows that diversity can improve business. Research analyzing the relationship between diversity levels and business performance of 250 U.S. businesses found a correlation between diversity and business success; companies with high levels of racial and ethic minorities have the highest profits, the highest market shares, and highest number of customers. On the other hand, organizations with low levels of diversity have the lowest profits, the lowest market shares, and the lowest number of customers.[20]

Adapting Costco to Taiwan

By offering an American experience with a local twist, Costco has found success in Asian markets. In Costco's Taiwan location, such twists include selling its store-brand steak thinly sliced to accommodate local preferences, offering local favorites such as sea cucumbers and mahjong sets, and including local variations on traditional American favorites in its frozen foods section, like Peking duck pizza alongside pepperoni pizza.

Besides product management, Costco Taiwan has had to find ways to convince customers that an annual membership, a relatively new idea in Taiwan, is worth their investment. One way Costco Taiwan has done this is by following the chain's U.S. policy of trying to guarantee the lowest market prices for products.

Another, more surprising tactic, is a return policy. Costco's Taiwan chief Richard Chang explains that returning merchandise is an unfamiliar practice in Asian markets, but Costco Taiwan is trying to change that by making returns, even of half a watermelon, "so pleasurable that you are going to tell your family and friends. That's something money can't buy. We consider that part of our advertising."

These practices have made the store the second most profitable in the 567-store chain.

Adapted from Andria Cheng, "Costco Cracks Taiwan Market," *Wall Street Journal*, April 2, 2010, B5.

WAYS TO LOOK AT CULTURE

Each of us grows up in a culture that provides patterns of acceptable behavior and belief. We may not be aware of the most basic features of our own culture until we come into contact with people who do things differently. In India, children might be expected to touch the bare feet of elders to show respect, but in the United States such touching would be inappropriate.[21]

Anthropologist Edward Hall first categorized cultures as high-context or low-context, categories which are popular in the business milieu, although no longer in vogue in anthropology. In **high-context cultures,** most of the information is inferred from the social relationships of the people and the context of a message; little is explicitly conveyed. Chinese, Japanese, Arabic, and Latin American cultures are high-context. In **low-context cultures,** context is less important; most information is explicitly spelled out. German, Scandinavian, and North American cultures are low-context.

High- and low-context cultures value different kinds of communication and have different attitudes toward oral and written communication. As Figure 7.1 shows, low-context cultures like those of the United States favor direct approaches and may see indirectness as dishonest or manipulative. The written word is seen as more important than oral statements, so contracts are binding but promises may be broken. Details matter. Business communication practices in the United States reflect these low-context preferences.

Another way of looking at cultures is by using Geert Hofstede's cultural dimensions. Based on data collected by IBM, Hofstede's five dimensions are power/inequality, individualism/collectivism, masculinity/femininity, uncertainty avoidance, and long-term/short-term orientation. They are now applied to 74 countries and regions. To illustrate, Hofstede analyzes the United States as extremely high in individualism, but also high in masculinity, with men dominating a significant portion of the power structure. It has a lower power-distance index, indicating more equality at all social levels. It also has a lower uncertainty avoidance index, meaning that it has fewer rules and greater tolerance for a variety of ideas and beliefs than do many countries.[22]

The discussion that follows focuses on national and regional cultures. But business communication is also influenced by the organizational culture and by personal culture, such as gender, race and ethnicity, social class, and so forth. As Figure 7.2 suggests, all of these intersect to determine what kind of

Figure 7.1 Views of Communication in High- and Low-Context Cultures

	High-context (Examples: Japan, Saudi Arabia)	**Low-context (Examples: Germany, North America)**
Preferred communication strategy	Indirectness, politeness, ambiguity	Directness, confrontation, clarity
Reliance on words to communicate	Low	High
Reliance on nonverbal signs to communicate	High	Low
Importance of relationships	High	Low
Importance of written word	Low	High
Agreements made in writing	Not binding	Binding
Agreements made orally	Binding	Not binding
Attention to detail	Low	High

Source: Robert T. Moran, Philip R. Harris, and Sarah V. Moran, *Managing Cultural Differences: Global Leadership Strategies for the 21st Century,* 7th ed. (Boston: Elsevier, 2007), 49–52.

Figure 7.2 National Culture, Organizational Culture, and Personal Culture Overlap

communication is needed in a given situation. Sometimes one kind of culture may be more important than another. For example, in a study of aerospace engineers in Europe, Asia, and the United States, researchers found that the similarities of the professional discourse community outweighed differences in national cultures.[23]

VALUES, BELIEFS, AND PRACTICES LO 7-3

Values and beliefs, often unconscious, affect our response to people and situations. Most North Americans, for example, value "fairness." "You're not playing fair" is a sharp criticism calling for changed behavior. In some countries, however, people expect certain groups to receive preferential treatment. Many people in the United States value individualism. Other countries may value the group. Japan's traditional culture emphasized the group, but there is evidence that this cultural value is changing.

Religion also affects business communication and business life. Practicing Muslims, Jews, and Christians observe days of rest and prayer on Friday, Saturday, and Sunday, respectively. During the holy month of Ramadan, Muslims fast from sunup to sundown; scheduling a business luncheon with a Muslim colleague during Ramadan would be inappropriate. A sampling of international holidays, including Ramadan, appears in Figure 7.3.

Even everyday practices differ from culture to culture. North Americans and Europeans put the family name last; Asians put it first. North American and European printing moves from left to right; Arabic reads from right to left. In the United States, a meeting on the fourth floor is actually on the fourth floor; in England, it is actually on the fifth floor of the building, because the British distinguish between ground and first floors. In Korea, the building may not have a fourth floor, or it may just be "F" floor, because the word for *four* sounds like the word for *death*.[24]

Common business practices also differ among cultures. In Middle Eastern—or predominantly Muslim—countries, business cards are exchanged only with the right hand, never with the "unclean" left hand. In China, business cards are exchanged with both hands; they are commented upon and put in a card case. In Russia, where hierarchy is important, cards should show your status with items like your title and the founding date of your company. In India, where education is specially valued, your card might show your graduate degrees.[25]

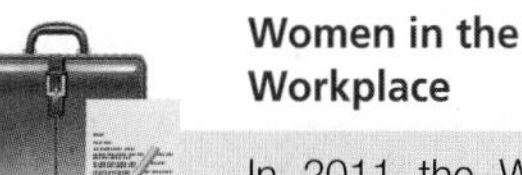

Women in the Workplace

In 2011 the White House released a comprehensive report on the status of U.S. women; it was the first update in nearly 50 years. Drawn from federal statistics, the report highlights women's changing roles, showing a shift toward education and employment. Women caught up with men in college attendance; in fact, younger women are more likely than younger men to obtain a college degree. And more women go on to graduate school than do men. Women are also flocking to the workplace; the number of women age 20 or older working outside the home doubled over the period covered by the report.

These gains, however, have not carried over into wage equity: in 2009 women still earned only about 75 percent of what their male counterparts earned. Women also continue to fill a major share of administrative jobs, but lag behind men in pursuing higher-paying science- and math-oriented careers. The report also points out that U.S. single-parent families are still headed predominantly by women, resulting in more women than men living below the poverty line.

Adapted from "White House Releases First Comprehensive Federal Report on the Status of American Women in Almost 50 Years," press release, White House, March 01, 2011, http://www.whitehouse.gov/the-press-office/2011/03/01/white-house-releases-first-comprehensive-federal-report-status-american-.

Figure 7.3 A Sampling of International Holidays

Holiday	Date	Celebrated in	Commemorates
Chinese New Year (Spring Festival)	January or February (date varies)	Countries with Chinese residents	Beginning of lunar new year
Independence Day	March 6	Ghana	1957 independence from Great Britain
St. Patrick's Day	March 17	Ireland	Ireland's patron saint
Mardi Gras	Day before Lent	Countries with Christian residents, most famously Brazil	Day of feasting before Lent
Cinco de Mayo	May 5	Mexico	1867 victory over the French
St. Jean-Baptiste Day	June 24	Québec province of Canada	Québec's national holiday
Canada Day	July 1	Canada	1867 proclamation of Canada's status as dominion
Bastille Day	July 14	France	1789 fall of the Bastille prison during the French Revolution
Ramadan	Ninth month of lunar year	Countries with Muslim residents	Atonement; fasting from sunup to sundown
Respect for the Aged Day	September 15	Japan	Respect for elderly relatives and friends
Chun Ben	Last week of September	Cambodia, other Buddhist countries	The dead and actions for one's salvation
Yom Kippur	September or October (dates vary)	Countries with Jewish residents	Day of atonement
Diwali	October or November	Countries with Hindu residents	Festival of lights celebrating renewal of life
Christmas	December 25	Countries with Christian residents	Birth of Jesus
Boxing Day	December 26	British Commonwealth	Tradition of presenting small boxed gifts to service workers

In today's electronically connected world, cultural practices can change swiftly. For instance, in China, where age has traditionally been revered, few political or business leaders now turn gray, even those who are in their fifties or sixties. Workers are also becoming less group oriented and more individualistic.[26] In such fluid contexts, communication becomes even more important. If you don't know, ask.

NONVERBAL COMMUNICATION LO 7-4

Chapter 4 discussed the significance of nonverbal communication in interpersonal communication. **Nonverbal communication** is also important in intercultural settings. Be aware of usage differences in such areas as body language, touch, space, and time.

Living and working in another country require being sensitive to cultural beliefs and practices. The Japanese holiday Shichi-go-san (seven-five-three) is celebrated on November 15th when boys (ages 3 and 5) and girls (ages 3 and 7) are taken by their parents to a Shinto shrine to give thanks for their health and growth, and to pray for their future. Shichi-go-san dates back to ancient times when the families of samurai and noblemen would mark milestones in their children's growth.

Cross-Cultural Collaboration Gone Wrong

When Daimler-Benz and Chrysler proposed a $36 billion merger in 1998, both parties thought it was a good plan.

The merger was supposed to strengthen each other's place in the automotive market. But in 2007, a third party Cerberus Capital Management bought Daimler-Chrysler for just $7.4 billion. What went wrong?

The cultural differences reflected in the practices of the two companies were a significant factor. For example, the German workers of Daimler-Benz were used to daily, company-sanctioned beer breaks while the American workers worried that alcohol consumption during work would lead to accidents and legal suits.

In addition, the German professionals were used to a formal, hierarchical structure in the organization and formal business attire.

Differences in the corporate lifestyle later led to questions as to who got the better end of the deal. U.S. assembly line workers earned more wages per hour than their German counterparts. However, the German workers, who received a six-week annual vacation, fully paid health care and education, and a triennial soul-soothing spa break, undoubtedly had a better benefits package. In addition, while the Daimler plant produced 850,000 vehicles a year with 120,000 employees, Chrysler manufactured 3 million with approximately the same number of employees. These cultural differences eventually overshadowed the positives of this merger.

Adapted from Associated Press, "A Chronology in the Takeover Saga of Global Automaker DaimlerChrysler AG," *Associated Press Archive*, May 14, 2007; Roberto A. Weber and Colin F. Camerer, "Cultural Conflict and Merger Failure: An Experimental Approach," *Management Science* 49, no. 4 (2003); and Carol Williams, "Steering around Culture Clashes," *Los Angeles Times*, January 17, 1999, C1.

Body Language

Just as verbal languages differ, so body languages differ from culture to culture. The Japanese value the ability to sit quietly. They may see the U.S. tendency to fidget and shift as an indication of lack of mental or spiritual balance. Even in North America, interviewers and audiences usually respond negatively to nervous gestures such as fidgeting with a tie or hair or jewelry, tapping a pencil, or swinging a foot.

People use body language to signal such traits as interest, respect, emotional involvement, confidence, and agreement. For example, Americans working in the Middle East are cautioned to avoid pointing their finger at people or showing the soles of their feet when seated. They also need to avoid misreading handholding among Arab men, for whom it is an expression of affection and solidarity.[27]

Eye contact North American whites see eye contact as a sign of attention; in fact, lack of eye contact is slightly suspect. But in many cultures, dropped eyes are a sign of appropriate deference to a superior. Japanese show respect by lowering their eyes when speaking to superiors. In some Latin American and African cultures, such as Nigeria, it is disrespectful for lower-status people to prolong eye contact with their superiors. Similarly, in the United States, staring is considered rude. For the English, however, polite people pay strict attention to speakers and blink their eyes to show understanding. In China, a widening of the eyes shows anger, in the United States—surprise. Among Arab men, eye contact is important; it is considered impolite not to face someone directly.[28] In Muslim countries, women and men are not supposed to have eye contact.

These differences can lead to miscommunication in the multicultural workplace. Superiors may feel that subordinates are being disrespectful when the subordinates are being fully respectful—according to the norms of their culture.

Facial Expression The frequency of smiling and the way people interpret smiles may depend on the purpose smiles serve in a particular culture. In the United States, smiling varies from region to region. In Germany, Sweden, and the "less-smiley" U.S. cultures, smiling is more likely to be reserved for close relationships and genuine joy. Frequent smiles in other situations would

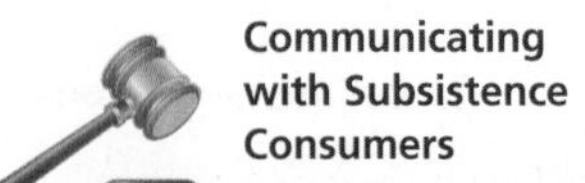

Communicating with Subsistence Consumers

Subsistence consumers may earn little money, but they still need to buy necessities. Corporations are learning how best to communicate with them.

Many of them lack basic reading skills, so visual cues are important. Cues such as store layout, package design, and brand logos need to remain consistent for them. Many buy products that look attractive because of packaging colors or pictures. They also tend to buy only brands they recognize by appearance, so changes in colors or visual design have negative impacts.

To better serve these customers, stores need to

- Price products in whole or half numbers, and display these prices graphically—such as a picture of the money needed to buy the product.
- Display pictures of product categories, so shoppers can find the goods they need.
- Train store personnel to form relationships with consumers and offer friendly, individualized assistance.

Adapted from Jose Antonio Rosa, Madhubalan Viswanathan, and Julie A. Ruth, "Emerging Lessons: For Multinational Companies, Understanding the Needs of Poorer Consumers Can Be Profitable and Socially Responsible," *Wall Street Journal*, October 20, 2008, R12.

Fast food chains are adapting to international cultures.

therefore seem insincere. For other people, including those in Thailand, smiling can be a way to create harmony and make situations pleasant.

Research has shown that when they are interpreting emotions, Americans focus on the mouth, so smiles are important. Japanese often focus on the eyes. This distinction is apparent even in their emoticons. American use :) for a happy face and :(for a sad one; Japanese use ^-^for a happy face and ;_; for a sad one.[29]

Gestures U.S. citizens sometimes assume that they can depend on gestures to communicate if language fails. But the meanings of gestures vary widely in different cultures. Kissing is usually an affection gesture in the United States but is a greeting gesture in other countries. In Greece, people may nod their heads to signify *no* and shake their heads to signify *yes.*[30]

Gestures that mean approval in the United States may have very different meanings in other countries. The "thumbs up" sign, which means "good work" or "go ahead" in the United States and most of western Europe, is a vulgar insult in Iraq, Iran, and Bangladesh. The circle formed with the thumb and first finger that means *OK* in the United States is obscene in Brazil and Germany. In India, the raised middle finger means you need to urinate.[31]

The V-sign is another gesture with multiple meanings. Made with the palm facing out, it was famously used by Churchill during WWII and by the hippies in the 60s and 70s. Made with the palm facing in, it is the equivalent of giving someone the finger in countries such as the United Kingdom, Ireland, and Australia. An American president made interesting headlines when he inadvertently used the V-sign on a visit to Australia.

Touch

Repeated studies have shown that babies need to be touched to grow and thrive and that older people are healthier both mentally and physically if they are touched. But some people are more comfortable with touch than others.

HARRY BAUMERT/THE REGISTER
A MULTIPLE-EXPOSURE PHOTOGRAPH IN ONE FRAME

What in the United States could mean "wait" or "hold on" in Nigeria indicates putting on a curse. In India it means "stop" or "enough."

What in the United States illustrates "a small amount," in Japan illustrates the degree of something, as in, "I know little English."

This means "peace" in the United States; it is the same as showing the middle finger in Australia and New Zealand. It can mean the number 2 in many places.

In the United States, this gesture means "well done" or "thumps up," but in Iraq, Iran and Bangladesh it means "up yours."

This refers to the Texas longhorns, but in Norway it salutes the devil; in Argentina it means your wife is cheating on you.

In the United States, this could mean small or contained. In Lebanon it means "wait"; and in Italy, "what the #$%! do you want?"

In India, an open hand wave could be interpreted as a "no."

In some cultures, hands folded as if in prayer means "I'm in deep thought; don't bother me."

An "O" with the thumb and index means "OK" in the U.S., but is an obscenity in Brazil and Germany.

The meanings of gestures vary with cultures.

Source: Mike Kilen, "Watch Your Language: Rude or Polite? Gestures Vary with Cultures," *Des Moines Register,* May 30, 2006, E1–2.

Each kind of person may misinterpret the other. A person who dislikes touch may seem unfriendly to someone who's used to touching. A toucher may seem overly familiar to someone who dislikes touch.

Most parts of North America allow opposite-sex couples to hold hands or walk arm-in-arm in public but frown on the same behavior in same-sex couples. People in some other countries have the opposite expectation: male friends or female friends can hold hands or walk arm-in-arm, but an opposite-sex couple should not touch in public.

In U.S. business settings, people generally shake hands when they meet, but little other touching is considered appropriate. In Mexico, greetings may involve greater physical contact. Men may embrace one another, and women may kiss one another. In many European settings, business colleagues may shake hands when they encounter one another throughout the day. In countries along the Mediterranean, hugs and shoulder pats are common as well. In some European countries, greetings include light kisses. The typical pattern is to kiss the person's right cheek and then the left (or to kiss the air near the cheek). In Italy this pattern stops with two kisses; Belgians continue for three, and the French for four.[32]

Mac and PC's Overseas Adventures

"When Apple Inc. wanted to bring its series of 'Mac vs. PC' ads to international markets, it faced a difficult issue: What's funny in one culture can seem ill-mannered in another.

"In the American ads . . . a nerdy PC guy keeps getting trumped by his hip Mac counterpart, who uses pointed banter that demonstrates how Macs are better. In one . . . spot, PC is proudly having a camera taped to his head so he can do video chatting—only to discover that Mac already has a built-in camera. . . .

"But in Japanese culture, where direct-comparison ads have long been frowned upon, it's rude to brag about one's strengths. So for Japanese versions of the ads, two local comedians from a troupe called the Rahmens made subtle changes to emphasize that Macs and PCs are not that different. Instead of clothes that cast PC clearly as a nerd and Mac as a hipster, PC wears plain office attire and Mac weekend fashion, highlighting the work/home divide between the devices more than personality differences. . . .

"PC's body language is a big source of the humor in Japan: Mac looks embarrassed when the PC touches his shoulder, or hides behind Mac's legs to avoid viruses. . . .

"The international campaigns reflect a growing move by U.S. companies to refine their ad campaigns for overseas markets."

Quoted from Geoffrey A. Fowler, Brian Steinberg, and Aaron O. Patrick, "Mac and PC's Overseas Adventures: Globalizing Apple's Ads Meant Tweaking Characters, Clothing, Body Language," *Wall Street Journal,* March 1, 2007, B1.

That's Not What We Meant!

Translating a product's advertising slogan is especially tricky, because the product's benefits have to be packed into just a few words. A poor translation can be embarrassing, as in the following examples:

Kentucky Fried Chicken's slogan in English: *Finger lickin' good.*

Meaning in Chinese translation: *Eat your fingers off.*

Otis Engineering Corporation's slogan: *Completion equipment.*

Meaning in Russian translation: *Equipment for orgasms.*

Parker Pen Company's slogan: *Avoid embarrassment.*

Meaning in Spanish translation: *Avoid pregnancy.*

Perdue Farms' slogan: *It takes a tough man to make a tender chicken.*

Meaning in Spanish translation: *It takes a sexually excited man to make a chicken affectionate.*

Examples quoted from Anton Piëch, "Speaking in Tongues," *Inc.*, June 2003, 50.

https://www.cia.gov/library/publications/the-world-factbook/.

World Factbook published by the Central Intelligence Agency is a good starting point for learning about the people of another country. Extensive country-by-country information includes history, government, and economics.

Space

Personal space is the distance people want between themselves and other people in ordinary, nonintimate interchanges. Some research shows that many North Americans, North Europeans, and Asians want a bigger personal space than do many Latin Americans, French, Italians, and Arabs. Even people who prefer lots of personal space are often forced to accept close contact on a crowded elevator or subway, or in a small conference room.

Even within a culture, some people like more personal space than do others. In many cultures, people who are of the same age and sex take less personal space than do mixed-age or mixed-sex groups.

Time

Differences in time zones complicate international phone calls and video conferences. But even more important are different views of time and attitudes toward time. Offices in the United States keep time by the calendar and the clock. Being "on time" is seen as a sign of dependability. Other cultures may keep time by the seasons, the moon, the sun, internal "body clocks," or a personal feeling that "the time is right."

North Americans who believe that "time is money" are often frustrated in negotiations with people who take a much more leisurely approach. Part of the problem is that people in many other cultures want to establish a personal relationship before they decide whether to do business with each other.

The problem is made worse because various cultures mentally measure time differently. Many North Americans measure time in five-minute blocks. Someone who's five minutes late to an appointment or a job interview feels compelled to apologize. If the executive or interviewer is running half an hour late, the caller expects to be told about the likely delay upon arriving. Some people won't be able to wait that long and will need to reschedule their appointments. But in other cultures, half an hour may be the smallest block of time. To someone who mentally measures time in 30-minute blocks, being 45 minutes late is no worse than being 10 minutes late is to someone who is conscious of smaller units.

Different cultures have different lead times for scheduling events. In some countries, you need to schedule important meetings at least two weeks in advance. In other countries, not only are people not booked up so far in advance, but a date two weeks into the future may be forgotten.

Anthropologist Edward Hall distinguishes between **monochronic cultures,** which focus on clock time, and **polychronic cultures,** which focus on relationships. People in monochronic cultures tend to schedule their time and do one task at a time; people in polychronic cultures tend to want their time unstructured and do multiple tasks at the same time. When U.S. managers feel offended because a Latin American manager also sees other people during "their" appointments, the two kinds of time are in conflict.[33]

Other Nonverbal Symbols

Many other symbols can carry nonverbal meanings: clothing, colors, age, and height, to name a few.

Clothing In North America, certain styles and colors of clothing are considered more "professional" and more "credible." Some clothing denotes not only status but also occupational group. Cowboy boots, firefighter hats, and judicial robes all may, or may not, signal specific occupations. Tool belts, coveralls, hard hats, and stethoscopes may signal broader occupational groupings.

Eating pizza with chopsticks illustrates how new cultural values interact with native culture to constantly create hybrid cultures.

Colors Colors can also carry meanings in a culture. Chinese tradition associates red with good fortune. Korean Buddhists use red to announce death. Black is the color of joy in Japan, the color of death in the United States.[34] White is the color of funerals in eastern countries; in the United States it is the color of brides. UPS found its company color working against it when it entered the Spanish market. The brown trucks that distinguish the delivery company's brand in the United States are not a good image in Spain, where hearses are traditionally brown. When UPS realized its mistake, it altered its uniforms and truck colors in Spain, emphasizing the company logo rather than the color brown.[35]

Age In the United States, youth is valued. People color their hair and even have face-lifts to look as youthful as possible. In Japan, younger people generally defer to older people. Americans attempting to negotiate in Japan are usually taken more seriously if at least one member of the team is noticeably gray-haired.

Height Height connotes status in many parts of the world. Executive offices are usually on the top floors; the underlings work below. Even being tall can help a person succeed. A recent study found that white, non-Hispanic males of below-average height earned 10% less than males of above-average height. Each additional inch of height was linked to 2.5% greater income. Perhaps surprisingly, the measurement that produced this effect was the man's height when he was a teenager. Those who grew later in life did not enjoy the income benefits of greater height. For white women in the study, actual adult height was associated with greater income. The researchers lacked sufficient data on other ethnic groups except to say that there seems to be a height–income effect for black males that resembles the effect for white males.[36]

More Than Words

Does the language you speak affect the way you perceive the world? Linguistic research suggests that the answer is yes—language not only reflects our thoughts, but, in many ways, shapes our thoughts. Here are just a few examples:

- Russian speakers, who have a larger vocabulary for blues, are better able to distinguish among shades of blue.
- Some indigenous tribes use combinations of *north, south, east,* and *west* instead of *left* and *right* for direction ("you have a bug on your northeast foot"); they have superior spatial orientation, even in unfamiliar landscapes.
- The Piraha, an Amazonian tribe, uses words like *few* and *many* instead of number words; its people are unable to keep track of exact quantities.
- Studies conducted at Stanford found that Spanish and Japanese speakers could not remember who caused accidental events as well as English speakers could. The reason? Spanish and Japanese do not normally mention the agents of accidents: "The glass broke itself," rather than "Dana broke the glass."

Adapted from Lera Boroditsky, "Lost in Translation," *Wall Street Journal,* July 24, 2010, W3.

http://www.cyborlink.com/
http://www.kwintessential.co.uk/

Cyborlink.com and Kwintessential.co.uk provide information on business communication in various countries. On both sites, choose a country to explore and you will get general information on topics such as negotiations, gift giving, personal space, and much more.

Walmart is one of many companies that have expanded internationally.

ORAL COMMUNICATION LO 7-5

Effective oral communication requires cultural understanding. As Figure 7.4 suggests, even an act as specific as a business introduction may differ across cultures. These are general patterns, not absolutes, but they help communicators stay alert for audience preferences.

During business meetings, even words as distinct as *yes* and *no* may cause confusion. In some cultures where saying *no* is considered rude, a *yes* may mean merely "I heard you."

Learning at least a little of the language of the country where you hope to do business will help you in several ways. First, learning the language will give you at least a glimpse into the culture. In English, for example, we say that a clock "runs." The French say "*Il marche*"—literally, "It is walking." Second, learning some of the language will help you manage the daily necessities of finding food and getting where you need to go while you're there. Finally, in business negotiations, knowing a little of the language gives you more time to think. You'll catch part of the meaning when you hear your counterpart speak; you can begin thinking even before the translation begins.

Frequently you will need good translators when you travel abroad on business. Brief them with the technical terms you'll be using; explain as much of the context of your negotiations as possible. A good translator can also help you interpret nonverbal behavior and negotiating strategies. Some translators can help their clients establish trust and credibility with international businesses.

Understatement and Exaggeration

To understand someone from another culture, you must understand the speaker's conversational style. The British have a reputation for understatement. Someone good enough to play at Wimbledon may say he or she "plays a little tennis." In many contexts, Americans accept exaggeration as a way to express positive thinking. Particularly in advertising, Americans expect some hype. Germans, in contrast, generally see exaggeration as a barrier to clear

Figure 7.4 Cultural Contrasts in Business Introductions

	United States	Japan	Arab countries
Purpose of introduction	Establish status and job identity; network	Establish position in group, build harmony	Establish personal rapport
Image of individual	Independent	Member of group	Part of rich culture
Information	Related to business	Related to company	Personal
Use of language	Informal, friendly; use first name	Little talking	Formal; expression of admiration
Values	Openness, directness, action	Harmony, respect, listening	Religious harmony, hospitality, emotional support

Source: Adapted from Farid Elashmawi and Philip R. Harris, *Multicultural Management 2000: Essential Cultural Insights for Global Business Success* (Houston: Gulf, 1998), 113.

communication. German customers are likely to be intolerant of claims that seem logically unsupportable. An American writing for a German audience should ensure that any claims are literally true.[37]

Compliments

The kinds of statements that people interpret as compliments and the socially correct ways to respond to compliments also vary among cultures. Statements that seem complimentary in one context may be inappropriate in another. For example, women in business may be uncomfortable if male colleagues or superiors compliment them on their appearance: the comments may suggest that the women are being treated as visual decoration rather than as contributing workers.

WRITING TO INTERNATIONAL AUDIENCES LO 7-6

Most cultures are more formal than that of the United States. When you write to international audiences, you may need to use titles, not first names. Avoid contractions, slang, and sports metaphors.

Not: Let's knock these sales figures out of the ballpark.

But: Our goal is to increase sales 7%.

Do write in English unless you're extremely fluent in your reader's language. Be clear, but be adult. Don't write in second-grade English.

Not: We will meet Tuesday. Our meeting room will be Hanscher North. We will start at 9:30 AM.

But: We will meet Tuesday at 9:30 AM in Hanscher North.

The patterns of organization that work for United States audiences may need to be modified in international correspondence. For instance, most North Americans develop an argument linearly; points in a contract such as price, quantity, and delivery date are presented in order, one at a time. However, business people from other cultures may think holistically rather than sequentially, and the business relationship may be far more important than the actual contract, which may not even be considered binding.

In other documents, negative messages may need more buffering and requests may need to be indirect. A U.S. manager asking a direct question in an e-mail ("Were the contract numbers checked against Accounting's figures?") could cause hurt feelings among some international recipients, who might take the question as an accusation.

Safety Problem: Multiple Languages

All mining is dangerous, but platinum mining is particular so. The mineral is frequently a mile below the surface and in very hard rock. Safety at Anglo's platinum mines was further complicated by a lack of a common language. Workers, who come from various countries and tribes, speak a dozen languages, and are frequently not able to warn each other of dangers.

For over a hundred years, Anglo has taught its miners Fanagolo, a 200-word pidgin language created for mining tasks. But today's workers find the language racially offensive.

Now Anglo is offering English and Afrikaans classes, and encouraging all its miners to learn one of the two languages.

Adapted from Robert Guy Matthews, "A Mile Down, Saving Miners' Lives," *Wall Street Journal*, July 19, 2010, B1.

Figure 7.5 Cultural Contrasts in Oral Communication

	United States	Europe	Asia
Opening a conversation	Take the initiative	England: take the initiative	Japan: wait for an invitation to speak
Interrupting	Wait until speaker finishes	Italy: interruptions common; more than one person may speak at once	Japan: do not interrupt; silence periods common
Vocal characteristics	Modulated pace and volume	Spaniards may speak louder than the French	Indians speak English much faster than Americans
Disagreements	Stated calmly and directly	Spain: often accompanied by emotional outbursts	Japan: often communicated by silence
Praise	Key motivational factor	Russia: saved for extraordinary behavior, otherwise seen as false	Indonesia: may be offensive (suggests supervisor surprised by good job)

Source: Adapted from Richard M. Steers, Carlos J. Sanchez-Runde, and Luciara Nardon, *Management across Cultures: Challenges and Strategies* (New York: Cambridge University Press, 2010), 222–23.

As Figures 7.5 and 7.6 suggest, the style, structure, and strategies that would motivate a U.S. audience may need to be changed for international readers. Relationships become more important, as do politeness strategies. The information in the figures suggests general patterns, not definitive delineations, but such suggestions help communicators look for ways to be more effective. Most writers will benefit from researching a culture before composing messages for people in it.

Response time expectations may also need to be modified. U.S. employees tend to expect fast answers to e-mails. However, other cultures with hierarchical organization structures may need extra response time to allow for approval by superiors. Pressing for a quick response may alienate the people whose help is needed and may result in false promises.[38]

In international business correspondence, list the day before the month:

Not: April 8, 2008

But: 8 April 2008

Spell out the month to avoid confusion.

Figure 7.6 Cultural Contrasts in Written Persuasive Documents

	United States	Japan	Arab countries
Opening	Request action or get reader's attention	Offer thanks; apologize	Offer personal greetings
Way to persuade	Immediate gain or loss of opportunity	Waiting	Personal connections; future opportunity
Style	Short sentences	Modesty; minimize own standing	Elaborate expressions; many signatures
Closing	Specific request	Desire to maintain harmony	Future relationship, personal greeting
Values	Efficiency; directness; action	Politeness; indirectness; relationship	Status; continuation

Source: Adapted from Farid Elashmawi and Philip R. Harris, *Multicultural Management 2000: Essential Cultural Insights for Global Business Success* (Houston: Gulf, 1998), 139.

Business people from Europe and Japan who correspond frequently with North America are beginning to adopt U.S. directness and patterns of organization. Still, it may be safer to modify your message somewhat; it certainly is more courteous.

LEARNING MORE ABOUT INTERNATIONAL BUSINESS COMMUNICATION LO 7-7

Learning to communicate with people from different backgrounds shouldn't be a matter of learning rules. Instead, use the examples in this chapter to get a sense for the kinds of factors that differ from one culture to another. Test these generalizations against your experience. Remember that people everywhere have their own personal characteristics. And when in doubt, ask.

You can also learn by seeking out people from other backgrounds and talking with them. Many campuses have centers for international students. Some communities have groups of international business people who meet regularly to discuss their countries. By asking all these people what aspects of the dominant U.S. culture seem strange to them, you'll learn much about what is "right" in their cultures.

Multicultural Diabetes Education

New York City's 11 public hospitals are tailoring diabetes education for different cultures.

The programs start with communications in the patients' native tongues. Handouts come in 11 languages, from Albanian to Urdu. Phone-based translation services allow medical staff to communicate in still more languages. If patients miss their appointments, phone calls and letters in their native language remind them.

Correct portion sizes are illustrated with photos of plates of lamb *korma*, fried plantains, and General Tso's chicken. Cooking classes for Caribbean emigrants demonstrate flavoring rice with fresh herbs and spices rather than tripe or pig snouts. An online guide for Indian foods lists nutritional information for classic dishes such as *roti* (flat bread) and *dal* (bean or pea dishes).

The goal of the program is to make good health care more accessible.

Adapted from Theo Francis, "Treating Diabetes and Understanding Cultures: With Minorities at Risk, Doctors Work to Make Diet Advice Hit Home," *Wall Street Journal*, October 23, 2007, D2.

SUMMARY OF KEY POINTS

- Culture provides patterns of acceptable behavior and beliefs.
- The successful intercultural communicator is
  - Aware of the values, beliefs, and practices in other cultures.
  - Sensitive to differences among individuals within a culture.
  - Aware that his or her preferred values and behaviors are influenced by culture and are not necessarily "right."
  - Sensitive to verbal and nonverbal behavior.
  - Willing to ask about preferences and behaviors.
  - Flexible and open to change.
- In high-context cultures, most of the information is inferred from the context of a message; little is explicitly conveyed. In low-context cultures, context is less important; most information is explicitly spelled out.
- Nonverbal communication is communication that doesn't use words. Nonverbal communication can include body language, space, time, and other miscellaneous matters such as clothing, colors, age, and height.
- Nonverbal signals can be misinterpreted just as easily as can verbal symbols (words).
- No gesture has a universal meaning across all cultures. Gestures that signify approval in North America may be insults in other countries, and vice versa.
- Personal space is the distance someone wants between him- or herself and other people in ordinary, nonintimate interchanges.
- North Americans who believe that "time is money" are often frustrated in negotiations with people who want to establish a personal relationship before they decide whether to do business with each other.
- The patterns of organization that work for North American audiences may need to be modified in international correspondence.

CHAPTER 7 Exercises and Problems

*Go to www.mhhe.com/locker10e for additional Exercises and Problems.

7.1 Reviewing the Chapter

1. Why is global business important? (LO 7-1)
2. What are the advantages of receiving an overseas assignment? (LO 7-1)
3. Why is diversity becoming more important than ever before? (LO 7-2)
4. What are low-context and high-context cultures? (LO 7-3)
5. How do our values and beliefs affect our responses to other people? (LO 7-3)
6. What are some forms of nonverbal communication? What variations would you expect to see in them among people of different cultures? (LO 7-4)
7. Why do people from monochronic cultures sometimes have trouble with people from polychronic cultures? (LO 7-4)
8. What are some characteristics of oral communications you should consider when communicating cross-culturally? (LO 7-5)
9. What are some cautions to consider when writing for international audiences? (LO 7-6)
10. Why is it important to check cultural generalizations? (LO 7-7)

7.2 Identifying Sources of Miscommunication

In each of the following situations, identify one or more ways that cultural differences may be leading to miscommunication.

1. Alan is a U.S. sales representative in South America. He makes appointments and is careful to be on time. But the person he's calling on is frequently late. To save time, Alan tries to get right to business. But his hosts want to talk about sightseeing and his family. Even worse, his appointments are interrupted constantly, not only by business phone calls but also by long conversations with other people and even the customers' children who come into the office. Alan's first progress report is very negative. He hasn't yet made a sale. Perhaps South America just isn't the right place to sell his company's products.
2. To help her company establish a presence in Asia, Susan wants to hire a local interpreter who can advise her on business customs. Kana Tomari has superb qualifications on paper. But when Susan tries to probe about her experience, Kana just says, "I will do my best. I will try very hard." She never gives details about any of the previous positions she's held. Susan begins to wonder if the résumé is inflated.
3. Stan wants to negotiate a joint venture with an Asian company. He asks Tung-Sen Lee if the people have enough discretionary income to afford his product. Mr. Lee is silent for a time, and then says, "Your product is good. People in the West must like it." Stan smiles, pleased that Mr. Lee recognizes the quality of his product, and he gives Mr. Lee a contract to sign. Weeks later, Stan still hasn't heard anything. If Asians are going to be so nonresponsive, he wonders if he really should try to do business with them.
4. Elspeth is very proud of her participatory management style. On assignment in India, she is careful not to give orders but to ask for suggestions. But people rarely suggest anything. Even a formal suggestion system doesn't work. And to make matters worse, she doesn't sense the respect and camaraderie of the plant she managed in the United States. Perhaps, she decides gloomily, people in India just aren't ready for a woman boss.

7.3 Interviewing for Cultural Information

Interview a person from an international community about cross-cultural communication. You might want to discuss issues such as these:

- Verbal and nonverbal communication, including body language.
- Tone and organization of professional communications.
- Attitude toward materialism.
- Time awareness differences.
- Concepts of personal space.

Compare the person's responses with your own values and write a memo to your instructor reflecting on the similarities and differences.

7.4 Analyzing Ads

Search for international ads on YouTube using keywords such as "Cell phone ads China" "Domino pizza in India." Compare them to a similar ad created in the Unites States.

- What are some differences you see in the advertisement?
- How do they inform about the cultural values of the commodities shown in the advertisement?

Discuss your findings in small groups. As a group, prepare a short presentation for your classmates.

7.5 Comparing Company Web Pages for Various Countries

Many multinationals have separate web pages for their operations in various countries. For example, Coca-Cola's pages include pages for Belgium, France, and Japan. Analyze three of the country pages of a company of your choice.

- Is a single template used for pages in different countries, or do the basic designs differ?
- Are different images used in different countries? What do the images suggest?
- If you can read the language, analyze the links. What information is emphasized?
- To what extent are the pages similar? To what extent do they reveal national and cultural differences?

As your instructor directs,

a. Write a memo analyzing the similarities and differences you find. Attach printouts of the pages to your memo.
b. Make an oral presentation to the class. Paste the web pages into PowerPoint slides.
c. Join with a small group of students to create a group report comparing several companies' web pages in three specific countries. Attach printouts of the pages.
d. Make a group oral presentation to the class.

7.6 Researching Other Countries

Choose two countries in two different continents other than North America. Look them up in both cyborlink .com and kwintessential.co.uk. Note information a new manager in those countries would need to know. Working in small groups (make sure your group covers multiple continents and does not duplicate countries), share your information.

a. Which country would be the easiest one for a young U.S. manager to gain international experience? Why?
b. Which country would be the hardest? Why?
c. Which country would you like to be sent to by a company? Why?

7.7 Creating a Web Page

Create a web page of international information for managers who are planning assignments in another country or who work in this country for a multinational company headquartered in another country.

Assume that this page can be accessed from another of the organization's pages. Offer at least seven links. (More is better.) You may offer information as well as links to other pages with information. At the top of the page, offer an overview of what the page covers. At the bottom of the page, put the creation/update date and your name and e-mail address.

As your instructor directs,

a. Turn in a copy of your page(s). On another page, give the URLs for each link.
b. Write a memo to your instructor (1) identifying the audience for which the page is designed and explaining (2) the search strategies you used to find material on this topic, (3) why you chose the pages and information you've included, and (4) why you chose the layout and graphics you've used.
c. Present your page orally to the class.

Hints:

- Limit your page to just one country or one part of the world.
- You can include some general information about working abroad and culture, but most of your links should be specific to the country or part of the world you focus on.

- Consider some of these topics: history, politics, geography, culture, money, living accommodations, transportation, weather, business practices, and so forth.
- Chunk your links into small groups under headings.

7.8 Comparing International Information

In small groups, find at least four websites providing information about a specific international community. Also, if possible, meet with a member of that community and discuss your findings. Do you find any clashing sources of evidence? What do the contradictions tell you about your sources? What do they tell you about that international community in general?

Discuss your findings in small groups. As a group, prepare a short presentation for your classmates.

7.9 Planning an International Trip

Assume that you're going to the capital city of another country on business two months from now. (You pick the country.) Use a search engine to find out

- What holidays will be celebrated in that month.
- What the climate will be.
- What current events are in the news there.
- What key features of business etiquette you might consider.
- What kinds of gifts you should bring to your hosts.
- What sight-seeing you might include.

As your instructor directs,

a. Write a memo to your instructor reporting the information you found.

b. Post a message to the class analyzing the pages. Include the URLs as hotlinks.

c. Make an oral presentation to the class.

d. Join with a small group of students to create a group report on several countries in a region.

e. Make a group oral presentation to the class.

7.10 Recommending a Candidate for an Overseas Position

Your company sells customized computer systems to businesses large and small around the world. The Executive Committee needs to recommend someone to begin a three-year term as Manager of Eastern European Marketing.

As your instructor directs,

a. Write a memo to each of the candidates, specifying the questions you would like each to answer in a final interview.

b. Assume that it is not possible to interview the candidates. Use the information here to write a memo to the CEO recommending a candidate.

c. Write a memo to the CEO recommending the best way to prepare the person chosen for his or her assignment.

d. Write a memo to the CEO recommending a better way to choose candidates for international assignments.

e. Write a memo to your instructor explaining the assumptions you made about the company and the candidates that influenced your recommendation(s).

Information about the candidates:

All the candidates have applied for the position and say they are highly interested in it.

1. **Deborah Gere,** 39, white, single. Employed by the company for eight years in the Indianapolis and New York offices. Currently in the New York office as Assistant Marketing Manager, Eastern United States; successful. University of Indiana MBA. Speaks Russian fluently; has translated for business negotiations that led to the setting up of the Moscow office. Good technical knowledge, acceptable managerial skills, excellent communication skills, good interpersonal skills. Excellent health; excellent emotional stability. Swims. One child, age 12. Lived in the then–Soviet Union for one year as an exchange student in college; business and personal travel in Europe.
2. **Claude Chabot,** 36, French, single. Employed by the company for 11 years in the Paris and London offices. Currently in the Paris office as Assistant Sales Manager for the European Economic Community; successful. No MBA, but degrees from MIT in the

United States and l'Ecole Supérieure de Commerce de Paris. Speaks native French; speaks English and Italian fluently; speaks some German. Good technical knowledge, excellent managerial skills, acceptable communication skills, excellent interpersonal skills. Excellent health, good emotional stability. Plays tennis. No children. French citizen; lived in the United States for two years, in London for five years (one year in college, four years in the London office). Extensive business and personal travel in Europe.

3. **Linda Moss,** 35, African American, married. Employed by the company for 10 years in the Atlanta and Toronto offices. Currently Assistant Manager of Canadian Marketing; very successful. Howard University MBA. Speaks some French. Good technical knowledge, excellent managerial skills, excellent communication skills, excellent interpersonal skills. Excellent health; excellent emotional stability. Does Jazzercize classes. Husband is an executive at a U.S. company in Detroit; he plans to stay in the States with their children, ages 11 and 9. The couple plans to commute every two to six weeks. Has lived in Toronto for five years; business travel in North America; personal travel in Europe and Latin America.
4. **Steven Hsu,** 42, of Asian American descent, married. Employed by the company for 18 years in the Los Angeles office. Currently Marketing Manager, Western United States; very successful. UCLA MBA. Speaks some Korean. Excellent technical knowledge, excellent managerial skills, good communication skills, excellent interpersonal skills. Good health, excellent emotional stability. Plays golf. Wife is an engineer who plans to do consulting work in eastern Europe. Children ages 8, 5, and 2. Has not lived outside the United States; personal travel in Europe and Asia.

Your committee has received this memo from the CEO.

To: Executive Committee

From: Ed Conzachi *EC*

Subject: Choosing a Manager for the New Eastern European Office

Please write me a memo recommending the best candidate for Manager of East European Marketing. In your memo, tell me whom you're choosing and why; also explain why you have rejected the unsuccessful candidates.

This person will be assuming a three-year appointment, with the possibility of reappointment. The company will pay moving and relocation expenses for the manager and his or her family.

The Eastern European division currently is the smallest of the company's international divisions. However, this area is poised for growth. The new manager will supervise the Moscow office and establish branch offices as needed.

The committee has invited comments from everyone in the company. You've received these memos.

To: Executive Committee

From: Robert Osborne, U.S. Marketing Manager *RO*

Subject: Recommendation for Steve Hsu

Steve Hsu would be a great choice to head up the new Moscow office. In the past seven years, Steve has increased sales in the Western Region by 15%—in spite of recessions, earthquakes, and fires. He has a low-key, participative style that brings out the best in subordinates. Moreover, Steve is a brilliant computer programmer. He probably understands our products better than any other marketing or salesperson in the company.

Steve is clearly destined for success in headquarters. This assignment will give him the international experience he needs to move up to the next level of executive success.

To: Executive Committee

From: Becky Exter, Affirmative Action Officer *BE*

Subject: Hiring the New Manager for East European Marketing

Please be sensitive to affirmative action concerns. The company has a very good record of appointing women and minorities to key positions in the United States and Canada; so far our record in our overseas divisions has been less effective.

In part, perhaps, that may stem from a perception that women and minorities will not be accepted in countries less open than our own. But the experience of several multinational firms has been that even exclusionary countries will accept people who have the full backing of their companies. Another concern may be that it will be harder for women to establish a social support system abroad. However, different individuals have different ways of establishing support. To assume that the best candidate for an international assignment is a male with a stay-at-home wife is discriminatory and may deprive our company of the skills of some of its best people.

We have several qualified women and minority candidates. I urge you to consider their credentials carefully.

To: Executive Committee

From: William E. Dortch, Marketing Manager, European Economic Community *WED*

Subject: Recommendation for Debbie Gere

Debbie Gere would be my choice to head the new Moscow office. As you know, I recommended that Europe be divided and that we establish an Eastern European division. Of all the people from the States who have worked on the creation of the new division, Debbie is the best. The negotiations were often complex. Debbie's knowledge of the language and culture was invaluable. She's done a good job in the New York office and is ready for wider responsibilities. Eastern Europe is a challenging place, but Debbie can handle the pressure and help us gain the foothold we need.

To: Ed Conzachi, President

From: Pierre Garamond, Sales Representative, European Economic Community *PG*

Subject: Recommendation for Claude Chabot

Claude Chabot would be the best choice for Manager of Eastern European Marketing. He is a superb supervisor, motivating us to the highest level of achievement. He understands the complex legal and cultural nuances of selling our products in Europe as only a native can. He also has the budgeting and managerial skills to oversee the entire marketing effort.

You are aware that the company's record of sending U.S. citizens to head international divisions is not particularly good. European Marketing is an exception, but our records in the Middle East and Japan have been poor. The company would gain stability by appointing Europeans to head European offices, Asians to head Asian offices, and so forth. Such people would do a better job of managing and motivating staffs which will be comprised primarily of nationals in the country where the office is located. Ending the practice of reserving the top jobs for U.S. citizens would also send a message to international employees that we are valued and that we have a future with this company.

To: Executive Committee

From: Elaine Crispell, Manager, Canadian Marketing *EC*

Subject: Recommendation for Linda Moss

Linda Moss has done well as Assistant Manager for the last two and a half years. She is a creative, flexible problem solver. Her productivity is the highest in the office. Though she could be called a "workaholic," she is a warm, caring human being.

As you know, the Canadian division includes French-Speaking Montreal and a large Native Canadian population; furthermore, Toronto is an international and intercultural city. Linda has gained intercultural competence both on a personal and professional level.

Linda has the potential to be our first woman CEO 15 years down the road. She needs more international experience to be competitive at that level. This would be a good opportunity for her, and she would do well for the company.

7.11 Researching Diversity at Your School

Research your university's policies and practices regarding diversity. Conduct the following research:

- Locate your university's position statement on diversity for both employment and educational opportunities.
- Find diversity data for your university's student body.
- Gather pictures of the student body you can find from the Internet, brochures, and posters throughout your university.
- Analyze your findings. Do the pictures you find resemble the statistics you find?

As your instructor directs,

a. Write an e-mail to your instructor explaining your findings, opinions, and conclusions.
b. Share your results with a small group of students.
c. Write an e-mail message to the president of the university outlining your opinion on how your university is achieving diversity and what, if anything, needs to be done to improve its efforts.
d. Make a short oral presentation to the class discussing your findings and conclusions.

7.12 Researching Diversity Programs of Companies

Find three businesses that are successfully globalizing or outsourcing.

- Specify their successes. What actions, behaviors, and policies do they follow to be successful at globalizing and/or outsourcing their organization?
- Note what other organizations can learn from these examples.

Find three businesses that are having problems globalizing or outsourcing.

- Specify their problems. What actions, behaviors, and policies do they follow that are causing the problems?
- Note what other organizations can learn from these examples.

As your instructor directs,

a. Write an e-mail to your instructor explaining your findings, opinions, and conclusions.
b. Share your results with a small group of students.
c. Make a short oral presentation to the class discussing your findings and conclusions.

CHAPTER 8

Working and Writing in Teams

Chapter Outline

Team Interactions
- Roles in Teams
- Leadership in Teams
- Decision-Making Strategies
- Feedback Strategies
- Characteristics of Successful Student Teams
- Peer Pressure and Groupthink

Working on Diverse Teams

Conflict Resolution
- Steps in Conflict Resolution
- Criticism Responses
- You-Attitude in Conflict Resolution

Effective Meetings

Collaborative Writing
- Planning the Work and the Document
- Composing the Drafts
- Revising the Document
- Editing and Proofreading the Document
- Making the Team Process Work

Summary of Key Points

Newsworthy Communication

A Team Disaster

Complex operations like deepwater oil drilling involve hundreds of people and, sometimes, multiple corporations working in close cooperation. The Deepwater Horizon disaster in April 2010 exposed the failures of the corporate and individual teams who were involved with the operation.

In a report released in early 2011, the presidential commission on the Deepwater Horizon disaster placed responsibility for the massive oil spill on well owner BP and two of its contractors, Transocean and Halliburton. But the problems that led to the disaster are not confined to the companies involved in the Gulf spill. Commission cochairman William K. Reilly stated that what the commission observed was "a system-wide problem" exemplified by communication failures at every level.

"Successful teams, whether composed of individuals or corporations, must be built on excellent cooperation and communication."

At the most basic level, the workers on the rig did not understand who had authority during an emergency. Written safety guidelines on the rig required multiple people to make decisions about responding to emergencies, but crew members wasted critical minutes when the rig caught fire attempting to decide whether they could shut off the well. As the captain of the rig and 10 other managers and crew members discussed the situation, Andrea Fleytas, a 23-year-old rig worker, took charge and radioed a distress signal to the Coast Guard. She was promptly reprimanded for doing so without the captain's permission.

As the disaster unfolded, larger issues emerged surrounding the cooperation of the companies that should have been working together on the Horizon. The commission report found that all three companies had failed to communicate with each other or with their employees about dangers, procedures, and similar situations.

Successful teams, whether composed of individuals or corporations, must be built on excellent cooperation and communication. People on the teams must be aware of correct procedures and their own roles and responsibilities. In the case of the Deepwater Horizon disaster, failures in teamwork at all levels ended up in a human and environmental tragedy.

Sources: Stephen Power and Ben Casselman, "White House Probe Blames BP, Industry in Gulf Blast," *Wall Street Journal*, January 6, 2011, A2; and Douglas A. Blackmon, Vanessa O'Connell, Alexandra Berzon, and Ana Campoy, "There Was 'Nobody in Charge,'" *Wall Street Journal*, May 28, 2010, A6–A7.

Learning Objectives

After studying this chapter, you will know

LO 8-1 Different kinds of productive and nonproductive roles in teams.

LO 8-2 Group decision-making strategies.

LO 8-3 Characteristics of successful teams.

LO 8-4 Techniques for resolving conflict.

LO 8-5 Techniques for making meetings effective.

LO 8-6 Techniques for collaborative writing.

http://www.teamtechnology.co.uk/

Log on to this website to find a wide range of articles and resources about interacting effectively in team settings. More specifically, click on "Team Roles" to find some interactive links to aid in assessing yourself as a team member as well as determining roles of your fellow group members.

Teamwork is crucial to success in an organization. Some teams produce products, provide services, or recommend solutions to problems. Other teams—perhaps in addition to providing a service or recommending a solution—also produce documents. Today teamwork is facilitated by technology tools such as wikis, Google Docs, chats, Skype, and teleconferencing.

Teamwork comes into play when a job is too big or the time is too short for one person to do the work, and again when no one person has the needed knowledge and skills. High stakes also call for teamwork, both because the efforts of multiple talented people are needed and because no one person wants the sole responsibility for a possible failure.

Interpersonal communication, communication between people, is crucial for good teamwork. It relies heavily on interpersonal skills such as listening and networking. Chapter 4 discusses interpersonal skills vital for good teamwork. Skills in conflict resolution, meeting organization, and collaborative writing also help teamwork. These skills will make you more successful in your job, social groups, community service, and volunteer work. On writing teams, giving careful attention to both teamwork and writing process (see Chapter 5) improves both the final product and members' satisfaction with the team.

TEAM INTERACTIONS LO 8-1

http://www.effectivemeetings.com/

Log onto EffectiveMeetings.com for articles offering advice about making meetings effective. What advice offered in these articles do you think would be helpful for conducting meetings with your fellow group members?

Teams can focus on different dimensions. **Informational dimensions** focus on content: the problem, data, and possible solutions. **Procedural dimensions** focus on method and process. How will the team make decisions? Who will do what? When will assignments be due? **Interpersonal dimensions** focus on people, promoting friendliness, cooperation, and team loyalty.

Different kinds of communication dominate during these stages of the life of a task team: formation, coordination, and formalization.

During **formation,** when members meet and begin to define their task, teams need to develop some sort of social cohesiveness and to develop procedures for meeting and acting. Interpersonal and procedural comments reduce the tension that always exists in a new team. Insistence on information in this first stage can hurt the team's long-term productivity.

Teams are often most effective when they explicitly adopt ground rules. Figure 8.1 lists some of the most common ground rules used by workplace teams.

During formation, conflicts frequently arise when the team defines tasks and procedures. Successful teams clarify what each member is supposed to do. They also set procedures: When and how often will they meet? Will decisions

Figure 8.1 Possible Team Ground Rules

- Start team meetings on time; end on time.
- Attend regularly.
- Come to the meeting prepared.
- Leave the meeting with a clear understanding of what each member is to do next.
- Focus comments on the issues.
- Avoid personal attacks.
- Listen to and respect members' opinions.
- Everyone speaks on key issues and procedures.
- Address problems as you become aware of them. If you have a problem with another person, tell that person, not everyone else.
- Do your share of the work.
- Communicate immediately if you think you may not be able to fulfill an agreement.
- Produce your work by the agreed-upon time.

be made by a leader, as is the case with many advisory groups? By consensus or vote? Will the team evaluate individual performances? Will someone keep minutes? Interpersonal communication is needed to resolve the conflict that surfaces during this phase. Successful teams analyze their tasks thoroughly before they begin to search for solutions.

Coordination is the longest phase and the phase during which most of the team's work is done. While procedural and interpersonal comments help maintain direction and friendliness, most of the comments need to deal with information. Good information is essential to good decisions. Successful teams deliberately seek numerous possible solutions. Conflict may occur as the team debates these solutions. Successful teams carefully consider as many solutions as possible before choosing one. They particularly avoid the temptation of going with the first solution that arises.

In **formalization,** the group finalizes its work. The success of this phase determines how well the group's decision will be implemented. In this stage, the group seeks to forget earlier conflicts.

Developing Team Cohesiveness

In *The Five Dysfunctions of a Team,* Patrick Lencioni suggests a simple method for helping to establish social cohesiveness in a new team. His low-risk exercise involves having everyone on the team answer a short list of questions about themselves.

The questions, while personal, are not particularly probing, and the group could create the list of questions together. He suggests questions about hometown, number of siblings, a few facts about one's childhood, hobbies, first job, and worst job.

Simply by answering even innocuous questions about themselves, team members begin to relate to each other and see each other as interesting people. This in turn encourages greater empathy and understanding.

Have you tried Lencioni's technique in a team you belonged to? Did it help in team formation? What questions do you think would work best?

Adapted from Patrick Lencioni, *The Five Dysfunctions of a Team: A Leadership Fable* (San Francisco: Jossey-Bass, 2002), 198.

Roles in Teams

Individual members can play multiple roles within teams, and these roles can change during the team's work. Roles can be positive or negative.

Positive roles and actions that help the team achieve its task goals include the following.

- **Seeking information and opinions**—asking questions, identifying gaps in the team's knowledge.
- **Giving information and opinions**—answering questions, providing relevant information.
- **Summarizing**—restating major points, summarizing decisions.
- **Synthesizing**—pulling ideas together, connecting different elements of the team's efforts.
- **Evaluating**—comparing team processes and products to standards and goals.
- **Coordinating**—planning work, giving directions, and fitting together contributions of team members.

Teamwork Myths

Myth: Harmony is good.
Reality: Well-managed conflict can generate more creative solutions and help a group's performance.
Myth: Add new members for fresh ideas and energy.
Reality: The longer group membership stays stable, the better groups perform.
Myth: With today's technology, in-the-room team meetings are no longer necessary.
Reality: Long-distance teams have a considerable disadvantage. So much so that many businesses pay the money to bring them together at key times.
Myth: Larger teams are better, particularly when they include representatives of all constituencies.
Reality: Large size is one of the worst impediments to team effectiveness. It allows individuals to shirk their share of the workload and requires more effort poured into coordinating activities.

Adapted from J. Richard Hackman, "Six Common Misperceptions about Teamwork," *Harvard Business Review* (blog), June 7, 2011, http://blogs.hbr.org/cs/2011/06/six_common_misperceptions_abou.html.

Positive roles and actions that help the team build loyalty, resolve conflicts, and function smoothly include the following behaviors (also see the list in Figure 8.2):

- **Encouraging participation**—demonstrating openness and acceptance, recognizing the contributions of members, calling on quieter team members.
- **Relieving tensions**—joking and suggesting breaks and fun activities.
- **Checking feelings**—asking members how they feel about team activities and sharing one's own feelings with others.
- **Solving interpersonal problems**—opening discussion of interpersonal problems in the team and suggesting ways to solve them.
- **Listening actively**—showing team members that they have been heard and that their ideas are being taken seriously.

Negative roles and actions that hurt the team's product and process include the following:

- **Blocking**—disagreeing with everything that is proposed.
- **Dominating**—trying to run the team by ordering, shutting out others, and insisting on one's own way.
- **Clowning**—making unproductive jokes and diverting the team from the task.
- **Overspeaking**—taking every opportunity to be the first to speak; insisting on personally responding to everyone else's comments.
- **Withdrawing**—being silent in meetings, not contributing, not helping with the work, not attending meetings.

Some actions can be positive or negative depending on how they are used. Active participation by members helps teams move forward, but too much talking from one member blocks contributions from others. Criticizing ideas is necessary if the team is to produce the best solution, but criticizing every idea raised without ever suggesting possible solutions blocks a team. Jokes in moderation can defuse tension and make the team work more fun. Too many jokes or inappropriate jokes can make the team's work more difficult.

Leadership in Teams

You may have noted that "leader" was not one of the roles listed above. Being a leader does *not* mean doing all the work yourself. Indeed, someone who

Figure 8.2 The Five Characteristics of an Effective Team

1. They trust one another.
2. They engage in unfiltered conflict around ideas.
3. They commit to decisions and plans of action.
4. They hold one another accountable for delivering against those plans.
5. They focus on the achievement of collective results.

Quoted from Patrick Lencioni, *The Five Dysfunctions of a Team: A Leadership Fable* (San Francisco: Jossey-Bass, 2002), 189–90.

implies that he or she has the best ideas and can do the best work is likely playing the negative roles of blocking and dominating.

Effective teams balance three kinds of leadership, which parallel the three team dimensions:

- Informational leaders generate and evaluate ideas and text.
- Interpersonal leaders monitor the team's process, check people's feelings, and resolve conflicts.
- Procedural leaders set the agenda, make sure that everyone knows what's due for the next meeting, communicate with absent team members, and check to be sure that assignments are carried out.

While it's possible for one person to assume all these responsibilities, in many teams, the three kinds of leadership are taken on by three (or more) different people. Some teams formally or informally rotate or share these responsibilities, so that everyone—and no one—is a leader.

Studies have shown that people who talk a lot, listen effectively, and respond nonverbally to other members of the team are considered to be leaders.[1]

Decision-Making Strategies LO 8-2

Probably the least effective decision-making strategy is to let the person who talks first, last, loudest, or most determine the decision. Most teams instead aim to air different points of view with the objective of identifying the best choice, or at least a choice that seems good enough for the team's purposes. The team discussion considers the pros and cons of each idea. In many teams, someone willingly plays **devil's advocate** to look for possible flaws in an idea. To give ideas a fair hearing, someone should also develop an idea's positive aspects.

After the team has considered alternatives, it needs a method for picking one to implement. Typical selection methods include voting and consensus. **Voting** is quick but may leave people in the minority unhappy with and uncommitted to the majority's plan. Coming to **consensus** takes time but usually results in speedier implementation of ideas. Airing preferences early in the process, through polls before meetings and straw votes during meetings, can sometimes help teams establish consensus more quickly. Even in situations where consensus is not possible, good teams ensure everyone's ideas are considered. Most people will agree to support the team's decision, even if it was not their choice, as long as they feel they have been heard.

Business people in different nations have varying preferences about these two methods. An international survey of 15,000 managers and employees found that four-fifths of the Japanese respondents preferred consensus, but a little more than one-third of the Americans did. Other nations in which consensus was preferred included Germany, the Netherlands, Belgium, and France.[2]

Two strategies that are often useful in organizational teams are the standard problem-solving process and dot planning.

The standard problem-solving process has multiple steps:

1. Identify the task or problem. What is the team trying to do?
2. Understand what the team has to deliver, in what form, by what due date. Identify available resources.
3. Gather information, share it with all team members, and examine it critically.

Make the Most of Your Brainstorming

Matt Bowen, president of the Aloft Group Inc. marketing and PR agency, has advice on running successful brainstorming meetings:

- Identify a clear, concrete goal before you start. That allows you to establish some boundaries for ideas—about practicality or cost, for example—and helps you keep your brainstorming session focused.
- Let everyone involved in the meeting know what the goal is ahead of time. That gives everyone a chance to have ideas ready when they come to the meeting: if people "prebrainstorm," you can focus your meeting on refining ideas.
- Set limits on meeting size and duration. Bowen recommends limiting a brainstorming meeting to one hour, with no more than five to seven participants. An hour is enough time for a focused discussion, and it's easier for everyone to participate and be heard in a small team.
- Let the ideas flow freely. Bowen recommends practicing active listening skills that encourage people both to share their ideas and to build on each other's ideas.
- Remember that there are no bad ideas: any idea, however impractical, might inspire the best solution, and spending time weeding out weak ideas can stifle creativity.
- Brainstorm with a diverse team. The best ideas come out of teams made up of people with very different perspectives.

Adapted from Kelly K. Spors, "Productive Brainstorms Take the Right Mix of Elements," *Wall Street Journal*, July 24, 2008, B5.

4. Establish criteria. What would the ideal solution include? Which elements of that solution would be part of a less-than-ideal but still acceptable solution? What legal, financial, moral, or other limitations might keep a solution from being implemented?
5. Generate alternate solutions. Brainstorm and record ideas for the next step.
6. Measure the alternatives against the criteria.
7. Choose the best solution.

Dot planning offers a way for large teams to choose priorities quickly. First, the team brainstorms ideas, recording each on pages that are put on the wall. Then each individual gets two strips of three to five adhesive dots in different colors. One color represents high priority, the other lower priority. People then walk up to the pages and stick dots by the points they care most about. Some teams allow only one dot from one person on any one item; others allow someone who is really passionate about an idea to put all of his or her dots on it. The dots make it easy to see which items the team believes are most and least important.

What happens if your team can't agree, or can't reach consensus? Team-building expert Bob Frisch suggests some strategies for working through a team-decision deadlock. In addition to using standard group techniques (setting clear goals, brainstorming solutions, and weighing the pros and cons of each solution), you should

- Use the current sticking point as the start for a new round of brainstorming. If there are two solutions that your team can't choose between, break the deadlock by brainstorming new solutions that combine the old ones. That will get the team making progress again and get new ideas on the table.
- Instead of rushing to a decision, allow time for team members to consider the options. Sometimes people refuse to compromise in order to avoid making a bad snap decision. Giving your team time to consider the options will take the pressure off. For especially complex decisions, schedule multiple meetings with time in between to do some research and to digest the pros and cons of each solution.
- Allow team members to make their decisions confidentially. People might refuse to state an opinion—or change an opinion—if they feel their opinions and reasoning will be judged negatively by the group. A secret ballot or other confidential form of "discussion" can help break a deadlock by giving team members an opportunity to voice their opinions without being judged or embarrassed.[3]

Feedback Strategies

As soon as the team begins to put its decisions into play, it needs to begin generating and heeding feedback. Sometimes this feedback will be external; it will come from supervisors, suppliers, clients, and customers. It should also, however, come from within the team. Teams frequently evaluate individual team members' performances, team performance, task progress, and team procedures.

Feedback should be frequent and regular. Many teams have weekly feedback as well as feedback connected to specific stages of their task. Regular feedback is a good way to keep team members contributing their share of the work in a timely fashion. While feedback needs to be honest and incorporate criticism, such critiques can be phrased as positively as possible ("please get your figures in for the Wednesday update" rather than "do you think you can make the Wednesday deadline this time?"). And don't forget to praise.

Research shows that teams with a higher ratio of positive-to-negative interactions do better work.[4]

One form of feedback that has been gaining popularity with organizations is **360-degree feedback.** This is a form of employee-development assessment in which a team member receives feedback from peers, managers, subordinates, customers, suppliers—from anyone touched by that person's work. Organizations or teams that use this model successfully typically apply it to everyone on the team, including team leaders. Research has shown this method is particularly effective when workers believe they can improve from the feedback. The method is also more effective when the feedback is positive and constructive.[5]

Who Does What

Working successfully on a team depends on being open about preferences, constraints, and skills and then using creative problem-solving techniques.

A person who prefers to outline the whole project in advance may be on a team with someone who expects to do the project at the last minute. Someone who likes to talk out ideas before writing may be on a team with someone who wants to work on a draft in silence and revise it before showing it to anyone. By being honest about your preferences, you make it possible for the team to find a creative solution that builds on what each person can offer.

In one team, Rob wanted to wait to start the project because he was busy with other class work. David and Susan, however, wanted to go ahead now because their schedules would get busier later in the term. A creative solution would be for David and Susan to do most of the work on parts of the project that had to be completed first (such as collecting data and writing the proposal) and for Rob to do work that had to be done later (such as creating tables, revising, editing, proofreading, and making bound copies).

What are your work preferences? What are the preferences of other people on your team? How can you work together to accommodate everyone's schedules and preferences?

Characteristics of Successful Student Teams LO 8-3

Studies of student teams completing class projects have found that students in successful teams were not necessarily more skilled or more experienced than students in less successful teams. Instead, successful and less successful teams communicated differently.

- Successful teams assign specific tasks, set clear deadlines, and schedule frequent meetings. They also regularly communicate as a team about each member's progress. In less successful teams, members are not sure what they are supposed to be doing or when it is needed. Less successful teams meet less often.
- Successful teams recognize that they have to build trust with each other through goodwill, active listening, and consistent participation. Teams who trust each other tend to work together to solve problems that impact the whole team. Less successful teams expect members to complete their own parts, and fail to bring those parts together into a coherent whole, behaviors which also appear in unsuccessful workplace teams.[6]
- Successful teams recognize the contribution of every team member to the team's success, and take time to acknowledge each member during team meetings. When team members know that their efforts are noticed and appreciated by their peers, they're much more willing to contribute to the team. Less successful teams take individual contributions for granted.
- Successful teams listen carefully to each other and respond to emotions as well as words. Less successful teams pay less attention to what is said and how it is said.
- In successful teams members work more evenly and actively on the project.[7] Successful teams even find ways to use members who don't like working in teams. For example, a student who doesn't want to be a "team player" can be a freelancer for her team, completing assignments by herself and e-mailing them to the team. Less successful teams have a smaller percentage of active members and frequently have some members who do very little on the final project.
- Successful teams make important decisions together. In less successful teams, a subgroup or an individual makes decisions.
- Successful teams listen to criticism and try to improve their performance on the basis of it. In less successful teams, criticism is rationalized.
- Successful teams deal directly with conflicts that emerge; unsuccessful teams try to ignore conflicts.

Research has shown that student teams produce better documents when they disagree over substantive issues of content and document design. The

Checklists for Teams

As knowledge continues to grow, more and more tasks have to be accomplished by teams. One person no longer has the knowledge or skills to do them. Indeed, one person may not know enough to even supervise them. Teams perform organ transplants, run marketing campaigns, and create proposals for billion dollar projects.

Construction is a good example. In the past, construction on grand edifices, such as palaces and cathedrals, was overseen by a master builder. Now skyscrapers are constructed by 16 different trades. To coordinate their work, the structural engineering firm in charge uses enormous checklists for work to be done and dates. The checklists are created by a team, with at least one person from each of the 16 trades. As work is completed, or problems arise, new checklists are created.

McNamara/Salvia, a large construction firm in Boston, also uses a communication checklist. After each major step in construction, for instance elevator installation, all trades involved meet to discuss progress. When questions or problems arise, more items are added to the checklist. Problems are discussed and resolved by representatives of the relevant trades, who then sign off on proposed solutions.

Adapted from Atul Gawande, *The Checklist Manifesto: How to Get Things Right* (New York: Henry Holt, 2009), chap. 3.

disagreement does not need to be angry: someone can simply say, "Yes, and here's another way we could do it." Deciding among two (or more) alternatives forces the proposer to explain the rationale for an idea. Even when the team adopts the original idea, considering alternatives rather than quickly accepting the first idea produces better writing.[8]

As you no doubt realize, these characteristics of good teams actually apply to most teams, not just student teams. A survey of engineering project teams found that 95% of the team members thought that good communication was the reason for team success, and poor communication the reason for team failures.[9]

Peer Pressure and Groupthink

Teams that never express conflict may be experiencing groupthink. Groupthink is the tendency for teams to put such a high premium on agreement that they directly or indirectly punish dissent.

Many people feel so much reluctance to express open disagreement that they will say they agree even when objective circumstances would suggest the first speaker cannot be right. In a series of classic experiments in the 1950s, Solomon Asch showed the influence of peer pressure. People sitting around a table were shown a large card with a line and asked to match it to the line of the same length on another card. It's a simple test: people normally match the lines correctly almost 100% of the time. However, in the experiment, all but one of the people in the group had been instructed to give false answers for several of the trials. When the group gave an incorrect answer, the focal person accepted the group's judgment 36.8% of the time. When someone else also gave a different answer—even if it was another wrong answer—the focal person accepted the group's judgment only 9% of the time.[10]

The experimenters varied the differences in line lengths, hoping to create a situation in which even the most conforming subjects would trust their own senses. But some people continued to accept the group's judgment, even when one line was seven inches longer than the other.

A classic example of groupthink, and one illustrating the sometimes constraining influence of a powerful team leader, occurred during President Kennedy's administration. The deliberations of Kennedy and his advisers illustrated classic characteristics of groupthink such as premature agreement and suppression of doubts. Kennedy guided the discussions in a way that minimized disagreements. The result was the disastrous decision to launch the Bay of Pigs invasion, whose failure led to the Cuban Missile Crisis. However, Kennedy subsequently analyzed what had gone wrong with the decision process, and he had his advisers do likewise. He used these analyses to change the process for the Cuban Missile Crisis. Although the team again included Kennedy and many of the same advisers, it avoided groupthink. Kennedy ordered the team to question, allowed free-ranging discussions, used separate subteam meetings, and sometimes left the room himself to avoid undue influence of the discussions.[11]

Teams that "go along with the crowd" and suppress conflict ignore the full range of alternatives, seek only information that supports the positions they already favor, and fail to prepare contingency plans to cope with foreseeable setbacks. A business suffering from groupthink may launch a new product that senior executives support but for which there is no demand. Student teams suffering from groupthink turn in inferior documents.

The best correctives to groupthink are to consciously search for additional alternatives, to test one's assumptions against those of a range of other people, and to protect the right of people on a team to disagree. When power roles are a factor, input may need to be anonymous.

WORKING ON DIVERSE TEAMS

In any organization, you will work with people whose backgrounds and working styles differ from yours. Residents of small towns and rural areas have different notions of friendliness than do people from big cities. Marketing people tend to have different values and attitudes than researchers or engineers. In addition, differences arise from gender, class, race and ethnicity, religion, age, sexual orientation, and physical ability. Even people who share some of these characteristics are likely to differ in personality type.

These differences affect how people behave on teams and what they expect from teams. For example, in a business negotiation, people from Asia are more likely to see the goal of negotiation as development of a relationship between the parties. In contrast, American negotiators (especially the lawyers on the team) are more likely to see the purpose of a negotiation as producing a signed contract.[12] Such differences are likely to affect what people talk about and how they talk. Some western cultures use direct approaches; other cultures, especially eastern cultures, consider such approaches rude and respond by withholding information.

Other pitfalls of team differences exist. Sometimes people who sense a difference may attribute problems in the team to prejudice, when other factors may be responsible. Also, a significant body of research shows that accurate interpretation of emotions in diverse teams is influenced by factors such as gender, nationality, race, and status.[13] On the other hand, another body of

Diverse teams can extend the range of group efforts and ideas.

Here a Team, There a Team

At ICU Medical, any worker can form a team to tackle any problem he or she wishes. What's more, the CEO has never vetoed a team decision.

Teams elect their own leaders, assign tasks, set meetings and deadlines. Most teams have 5 to 7 people, and 12 to 15 teams generally finish a project each quarter. Teams have changed the company's production process and set up a 401(k) plan.

Serving on a team is voluntary, although some employees with special expertise get invited to join teams frequently. But team participation does not give employees a break from their regular job duties, which still must be performed satisfactorily.

To help teams function smoothly, ICU has a team handbook, created—you guessed it—by yet another team. The 25-page handbook addresses issues like what to do at the first meeting and other frequently asked questions. Teams also must post notes about their meetings on the company intranet, where all employees can offer feedback.

As a final team incentive, ICU rewards successful teams, with the size of the reward reflecting the importance of the project.

Would you like to work at ICU?

Adapted from Erin White, "How a Company Made Everyone a Team Player," *Wall Street Journal,* August 13, 2007, B1.

Team Stats

Most white-collar workers have to collaborate, but they are not always happy about doing so. Here are some team statistics.

- The majority of workers (54%) prefer working in groups of three.
- 10% of workers prefer to work alone.
- 82% of workers collaborate, and 42% do so constantly.
- Women (51%) like working collaboratively to learn more than men (40%) do.
- Men (36%) like working collaboratively to perform a task more than women (25%) do, but obviously neither group is close to a majority.
- Younger workers (18–24) like working collaboratively to learn (60%).

Do you see any of these statistics reflected in your teams?

Adapted from Matt Vella, "Indata: White-Collar Workers Shoulder Together—Like It or Not," *BusinessWeek,* April 28, 2008, 58.

research shows that ethnically diverse teams produce more and higher-quality ideas.[14] Research has also found that over time, as team members focus on their task, mission, or profession, cultural differences become less significant than the role of being a team member.[15]

Sometimes the culture to which the team belongs is a distinct asset, uniting strangers in positive ways and giving them strengths to use in high-stakes situations. With their team skills enhanced by the organizational culture, airline crews and emergency teams may perform heroically in a crisis.

Savvy team members play to each other's strengths and devise strategies for dealing with differences. These efforts can benefit the whole team. A study of multicultural teams published in the *Harvard Business Review* found acknowledging cultural gaps openly and cooperatively working through them an ideal strategy for surmounting cultural differences. For example, a U.S. and U.K. team used their differing approaches to decision making to create a higher-quality decision. The U.K. members used their slower approach to analyze possible pitfalls, and the U.S. members used their "forge ahead" approach to move the project along. Both sides appreciated the contributions of the other members.[16]

CONFLICT RESOLUTION LO 8-4

Conflicts are going to arise in any group of intelligent people who care about their task. Yet many of us feel so uncomfortable with conflict that we pretend it doesn't exist. However, unacknowledged conflicts rarely go away: they fester, making the next interchange more difficult.

To reduce the number of conflicts in a team,

- Make responsibilities and ground rules clear at the beginning.
- Discuss problems as they arise, rather than letting them fester till people explode.
- Realize that team members are not responsible for each others' happiness.

In spite of these efforts, some conflict is a part of any team's life and that conflict needs to be resolved. When a conflict is emotionally charged, people will need a chance to calm themselves before they can arrive at a well-reasoned solution. Meeting expert John Tropman recommends the "two-meeting rule" for emotional matters: Controversial items should be handled at two different meetings. The first meeting is a chance for everyone to air a point of view about the issue. The second meeting is the one at which the team reaches a decision. The time between the two meetings becomes a cooling-off period.[17]

Figure 8.3 suggests several possible solutions to conflicts that student teams experience. Often the symptom arises from a feeling of not being respected or appreciated by the team. Therefore, many problems can be averted if people advocate for their ideas in a positive way. One way to do this is to devote as much effort to positive observations as possible. Another technique is to state analysis rather than mere opinions. Instead of "I wouldn't read an eight-page brochure," the member of a team could say, "Tests we did a couple of years ago found a better response for two-page brochures. Could we move some of that information to our website?" As in this example, an opinion can vary from person to person; stating an opinion does not provide a basis for the team to make a decision. In contrast, analysis provides objective information for the team to consider.

Figure 8.3 Troubleshooting Team Problems

Symptom	Possible solutions
We can't find a time to meet that works for all of us.	*a.* Find out why people can't meet at certain times. Some reasons suggest their own solutions. For example, if someone has to stay home with small children, perhaps the team could meet at that person's home. *b.* Assign out-of-class work to "committees" to work on parts of the project. *c.* Use technology (e.g., Skype, wikis, e-mail) to share, discuss, and revise drafts.
One person isn't doing his or her fair share.	*a.* Find out what is going on. Is the person overcommitted? Does he or she feel unappreciated? Is he or she unprepared? Those are different problems you'd solve in different ways. *b.* Early on, do things to build team loyalty. Get to know each other as writers and as people. Sometimes do something fun together. *c.* Encourage the person to contribute. "Mary, what do you think?" "Jim, which part of this would you like to draft?" Then find something to praise in the work. "Thanks for getting us started." *d.* If someone misses a meeting, assign someone else to bring the person up to speed. People who miss meetings for legitimate reasons (job interviews, illness) but don't find out what happened may become less committed to the team. *e.* Consider whether strict equality is the most important criterion. On a given project, some people may have more knowledge or time than others. Sometimes the best team product results from letting people do different amounts of work. *f.* Even if you divide up the work, make all decisions as a team: what to write about, which evidence to include, what graphs to use, what revisions to make. People excluded from decisions become less committed to the team.
I seem to be the only one on the team who cares about quality.	*a.* Find out why other members "don't care." If they received low grades on early assignments, stress that good ideas and attention to detail can raise grades. Perhaps the team should meet with the instructor to discuss what kinds of work will pay the highest dividends. *b.* Volunteer to do extra work. Sometimes people settle for something that's just OK because they don't have the time or resources to do excellent work. They might be happy for the work to be done—if they don't have to do it. *c.* Be sure that you're respecting what each person can contribute. Team members sometimes withdraw when one person dominates and suggests that he or she is "better" than other members. *d.* Fit specific tasks to individual abilities. People generally do better work in areas they see as their strengths. A visual learner who doesn't care about the written report may do an excellent job on the accompanying visuals.
People in the team don't seem willing to disagree. We end up going with the first idea suggested.	*a.* Brainstorm so you have multiple possibilities to consider. *b.* After an idea is suggested, have each person on the team suggest a way it could be improved. *c.* Appoint someone to be a devil's advocate. *d.* Have each person on the team write a draft. It's likely the drafts will be different, and you'll have several options to mix and match. *e.* Talk about good ways to offer criticism. Sometimes people don't disagree because they're afraid that other team members won't tolerate disagreement.
One person just criticizes everything.	*a.* Ask the person to follow up the criticism with a suggestion for improvement. *b.* Talk about ways to express criticism tactfully. "I think we need to think about *x*" is more tactful than "You're wrong." *c.* If the criticism is about ideas and writing (not about people), value it. Ideas and documents need criticism if we are to improve them.

A Team of Rivals

A major focus of Doris Kearns Goodwin's book *Team of Rivals* is Abraham Lincoln's leadership style, particularly the way he built his leadership team. President Obama said if he could take only one book, apart from the Bible, with him to the White House it would be this book. The following are some of Goodwin's key points:

- Lincoln chose his cabinet from his most able rivals, men who were guaranteed to hold different views. His ability to weave these men into an effective team showed great emotional intelligence.
- These men were confident enough that they were not afraid to question Lincoln or argue with him. The resulting exchange of ideas strengthened Lincoln's decision making.
- These men also had temperaments different from Lincoln's, helping Lincoln find a balanced approach to leading the war.
- Lincoln shared both credit for successes and responsibility for failures, including failures of others. Goodwin calls this tactic creating "a reservoir of good feeling." Through this approach Lincoln earned the intense loyalty of his team.

Adapted from Doris Kearns Goodwin, "Leadership Lessons from Abraham Lincoln," *Harvard Business Review* 87, no.4 (2009): 43–47.

Steps in Conflict Resolution

Dealing successfully with conflict requires attention both to the issues and to people's feelings. The following techniques will help you resolve conflicts constructively.

1. Make sure the people involved really disagree. Sometimes different conversational styles, differing interpretations of data, or faulty inferences create apparent conflicts when no real disagreement exists.

Someone who asks "Are those data accurate?" may just be asking for source information, not questioning the conclusions the team drew from the data.

Sometimes someone who's under a lot of pressure may explode. But the speaker may just be venting anger and frustration; he or she may not in fact be angry at the person who receives the explosion. One way to find out if a person is just venting is to ask, "Is there something you'd like me to do?"

2. Check to see that everyone's information is correct. Sometimes people are operating on outdated or incomplete information. People may also act on personal biases or opinions rather than data.

3. Discover the needs each person is trying to meet. Sometimes determining the real needs makes it possible to see a new solution. The **presenting problem** that surfaces as the subject of dissension may or may not be the real problem. For example, a worker who complains about the hours he's putting in may in fact be complaining not about the hours themselves but about not feeling appreciated. A supervisor who complains that the other supervisors don't invite her to meetings may really feel that the other managers don't accept her as a peer. Sometimes people have trouble seeing beyond the presenting problem because they've been taught to suppress their anger, especially toward powerful people. One way to tell whether the presenting problem is the real problem is to ask, "If this were solved, would I be satisfied?" If the answer is *no,* then the problem that presents itself is not the real problem. Solving the presenting problem won't solve the conflict. Keep probing until you get to the real conflict.

4. Search for alternatives. Sometimes people are locked into conflict because they see too few alternatives. People tend to handle complexity by looking for ways to simplify. In a team, someone makes a suggestion, so the team members discuss it as if it is the only alternative. The team generates more alternatives only if the first one is unacceptable. As a result, the team's choice depends on the order in which team members think of ideas. When a decision is significant, the team needs a formal process to identify alternatives before moving on to a decision. Many teams use brainstorming when they search for alternatives.

5. Repair negative feelings. Conflict can emerge without anger and without escalating the disagreement, as the next section shows. But if people's feelings have been hurt, the team needs to deal with those feelings to resolve the conflict constructively. Only when people feel respected and taken seriously can they take the next step of trusting others on the team.

Criticism Responses

Conflict is particularly difficult to resolve when someone else criticizes or attacks us directly. When we are criticized, our natural reaction is to defend ourselves—perhaps by counterattacking. The counterattack prompts the critic to defend him- or herself. The conflict escalates; feelings are hurt; issues become muddied and more difficult to resolve.

Just as resolving conflict depends on identifying the needs each person is trying to meet, so dealing with criticism depends on understanding the real concern of the critic. Constructive ways to respond to criticism and get closer to the real concern include paraphrasing, checking for feelings, checking inferences, and buying time with limited agreement.

Paraphrasing To **paraphrase,** repeat in your own words the verbal content of the critic's message. The purposes of paraphrasing are (1) to be sure that you have heard the critic accurately, (2) to let the critic know what his or her statement means to you, and (3) to communicate that you are taking the critic and his or her feelings seriously.

Criticism:	You guys are stonewalling my requests for information.
Paraphrase:	You think that we don't give you the information you need.

Checking for feelings When you check the critic's feelings, you identify the emotions that the critic seems to be expressing verbally or nonverbally. The purposes of checking feelings are to try to understand (1) the critic's emotions, (2) the importance of the criticism for the critic, and (3) the unspoken ideas and feelings that may actually be more important than the voiced criticism.

Criticism:	You guys are stonewalling my requests for information.
Feelings check:	You sound pretty angry, yes?

Always *ask* the other person if you are right in your perception. Even the best reader of nonverbal cues is sometimes wrong.

Checking for inferences When you check the inferences you draw from criticism, you identify the implied meaning of the verbal and nonverbal content of the criticism, taking the statement a step further than the words of the critic to try to understand *why* the critic is bothered by the action or attitude under discussion. The purposes of checking inferences are (1) to identify the real (as opposed to the presenting) problem and (2) to communicate the feeling that you care about resolving the conflict.

Criticism:	You guys are stonewalling my requests for information.
Inference:	Are you saying that you need more information from our team?

Inferences can be faulty. In the above interchange, the critic might respond, "I don't need more information. I just think you should give it to me without my having to file three forms in triplicate every time I want some data."

Buying time with limited agreement Buying time is a useful strategy for dealing with criticisms that really sting. When you buy time with limited agreement, you avoid escalating the conflict (as an angry statement might do) but also avoid yielding to the critic's point of view. To buy time, restate the part of the criticism you agree to be true. (This is often a fact, rather than the interpretation or evaluation the critic has made of that fact.) *Then let the critic respond, before you say anything else.* The purposes of buying time are (1) to allow you time to think when a criticism really hits home and threatens you, so that you can respond to the criticism rather than simply reacting defensively, and (2) to suggest to the critic that you are trying to hear what he or she is saying.

Criticism:	You guys are stonewalling my requests for information.
Limited agreement:	It's true that the cost projections you asked for last week still aren't ready.

Scientific Teams

For centuries Western innovation has been led by individuals, like Da Vinci, Darwin, and Einstein. But in recent years, teamwork has become the model that drives innovation, especially in the sciences.

Benjamin Jones, a professor at Northwestern University's Kellogg School of Management, analyzed 19.9 million papers and 2.1 million patents, and found that 99% of scientific subfields have seen not only increased levels of teamwork but also increases in the sizes of teams.

According to Jones, the best research now comes from teams. Among the most cited studies, papers authored by teams are cited more than twice as often as papers by individual authors. Papers cited more than one thousand times—"home run papers"—are more than six times as likely to be the result of team research.

What is behind this shift toward teamwork? In part, Jones claims, researchers develop narrow expertise during years of graduate study, requiring them to rely on colleagues in other fields to provide connections between areas of study. Additionally, the complex nature of twenty first-century problems demands collaborative efforts in order to truly transform our understanding of those problems.

Adapted from Jonah Lehrer, "Sunset of the Solo Scientist," *Wall Street Journal,* February 5, 2011, C12.

International Teams

IBM programmer Rob Nicholson has 50 colleagues from three countries—England, India, and Canada—on his software team.

Global teams such as his have to work to overcome language and cultural barriers. Workers worried about having their jobs outsourced have to learn to share information. Workers from more polite or reserved cultures have to conquer their reluctance to interrupt people and instead contact colleagues immediately with questions.

The team collaborates through sophisticated electronic communications. Team wikis allow members to post reports on their own progress and comment on the work of other team members. Team members get automatic alerts when major components of their project change. Completed program segments are put into a shared database. Phones display photos and personal details of team members so new programmers can learn about their teammates and where to go for help. Instant messaging keeps team members in touch.

A vital task for this team is dividing the work into small pieces. Most projects are divided into two-week chunks; those chunks are further divided into pieces that one programmer can complete in one or two days. The task list is kept on the team wiki. As programmers complete their tasks, they take the top task from the wiki list.

When the software fails a test, the entire team stops programming and focuses on finding the problem. In fact, the British office has rigged a red emergency light on its testing machine.

Clear and frequent communications among team members are a vital key for the success of the project.

Adapted from Phred Dvorak, "How Teams Can Work Well Together from Far Apart," *Wall Street Journal*, September 17, 2007, B4.

DO NOT go on to justify or explain. A "Yes, but . . ." statement is not a time-buyer.

You-Attitude in Conflict Resolution

You-attitude means looking at things from the audience's point of view, respecting the audience, and protecting the audience's ego. The *you* statements that many people use when they're angry attack the audience; they do not illustrate you-attitude. Instead, substitute statements about your own feelings. In conflict, *I* statements show good you-attitude!

Lacks you-attitude:	You never do your share of the work.
You-attitude:	I feel that I'm doing more than my share of the work on this project.
Lacks you-attitude:	Even you should be able to run the report through a spelling checker.
You-attitude:	I'm not willing to have my name on a report with so many spelling errors. I did lots of the writing, and I don't think I should have to do the proofreading and spell checking, too.

EFFECTIVE MEETINGS LO 8-5

Meetings have always taken a large part of the average manager's week. Although technology has eliminated some meetings, the increased number of teams means that meetings are even more frequent. In spite of their advantages for communication, meetings are not always good. Many productive workers see them as all too often a waste of time, interrupting valuable work, while less productive workers see them as a pleasant break. However, meetings can easily be made more effective.

Meetings can have multiple purposes:

- To share information.
- To brainstorm ideas.
- To evaluate ideas.
- To develop plans.
- To make decisions.
- To create a document.
- To motivate members.

When meetings combine two or more purposes, it's useful to make the purposes explicit. For example, in the meeting of a company's board of directors, some items are presented for information. Discussion is possible, but the group will not be asked to make a decision. Other items are presented for action; the group will be asked to vote. A business meeting might specify that the first half hour will be time for brainstorming, with the second half hour devoted to evaluation.

Formal meetings are run under strict rules, like the rules of parliamentary procedure summarized in *Robert's Rules of Order.* Motions must be made formally before a topic can be debated. Each point is settled by a vote. **Minutes** record each motion and the vote on it. Formal rules help the meeting run smoothly if the group is very large or if the agenda is very long. **Informal meetings,** which are much more common in the workplace, are run more loosely. Votes may not be taken if most people seem to agree. Minutes may not be kept. Informal meetings are better for team-building and problem solving.

Planning the **agenda** is the foundation of a good meeting. A good agenda indicates

- A list of items for consideration.
- Whether each item is presented for information, for discussion, or for a decision.
- Who is sponsoring or introducing each item.
- How much time is allotted for each item.

Although a time schedule on an agenda is frequently not followed exactly, it does inform participants about the relative importance of the agenda items. In general, the information on an agenda should be specific enough that participants can come to the meeting prepared with ideas, background information, and any other resources they need for completing each agenda item.

Many groups start their agendas with routine items on which agreement will be easy. Doing so gets the meeting off to a positive start. However, it may also waste the time when people are most attentive. Another approach is to put routine items at the end. If there's a long list of routine items, sometimes you can dispense with them in an omnibus motion. An **omnibus motion** allows a group to approve many items together rather than voting on each separately. A single omnibus motion might cover multiple changes to operational guidelines, or a whole slate of candidates for various offices, or various budget recommendations. It's important to schedule controversial items early in the meeting, when energy levels are high, and to allow enough time for full discussion. Giving a controversial item only half an hour at the end of the day or evening makes people suspect that the leaders are trying to manipulate them.

Pay attention to people and process as well as to the task at hand. At informal meetings, a good leader observes nonverbal feedback and invites everyone to participate. If conflict seems to be getting out of hand, a leader may want to focus attention on the group process and ways that it could deal with conflict, before getting back to the substantive issues. Highly sensitive topics may require two or more meetings, the first to air the subject and people's feelings and the second to vote. The time between the two gives participants time to cool off and informally discuss the issues involved.

If the group doesn't formally vote, the leader should summarize the group's consensus after each point. At the end of the meeting, the leader should summarize all decisions and remind the group who is responsible for implementing or following up on each item. If no other notes are taken, someone should record the decisions and assignments. Long minutes will be most helpful if assignments are set off visually from the narrative.

If you're planning a long meeting, for example, a training session or a conference, recognize that networking is part of the value of the meeting. Allow short breaks at least every two hours and generous breaks twice a day so participants can talk informally to each other. If participants will be strangers, include some social functions so they can get to know each other. If they will have different interests or different levels of knowledge, plan concurrent sessions on different topics or for people with different levels of expertise.

Fun at Berkshire Hathaway's Annual Meeting

[In his 2011 letter to the shareholders of Berkshire Hathaway, Warren Buffett gives a three-page preview of what to anticipate at the annual meeting. Here are some colorful excerpts.]

- If you decide to leave during the day's question periods, please do so while *Charlie* is talking. (Act fast; he can be terse.)
- On Sunday, around 1 p.m., I will be at Borsheims with a smile and a shoeshine, selling jewelry. . . . I've told Susan Jacques, Borsheims' CEO, that I'm still a hot shot salesman. But I see doubt in her eyes. So cut loose and buy something from me for your wife or sweetheart (presumably the same person). Make me look good.
- Gorat's and Piccolo's will again be open exclusively for Berkshire shareholders on Sunday. . . . These restaurants are my favorites and—still being a growing boy—I will eat at both of them on Sunday evening.

Quoted from Warren Buffett, "Letters 2010," Berkshire Hathaway Inc., accessed May 24, 2011, http://www.berkshirehathaway.com/letters/2010ltr.pdf.

COLLABORATIVE WRITING LO 8-6

Whatever your career, it is likely that some of the documents you produce will be written with a team. Collaborative writing is often prompted by one of the following situations:

- The task is too big or the time is too short for one person to do all the writing.
- No one person has all the knowledge required to do the writing.
- The stakes for the task are so high that the organization wants the best efforts of as many people as possible; no one person wants the sole responsibility for the success or failure of the document.

Collaborative writing can be done by two people or by a much larger group. The team can be democratic or run by a leader who makes decisions alone. The team may share or divide responsibility for each stage in the writing process. There are several ways teams commonly divide the work. One person might do the main writing, with others providing feedback. Another approach is to divide the whole project into smaller tasks and to assign each task to a different team member. This approach shares the workload more evenly but is harder to coordinate, although technology, such as wikis or Google docs, helps. Sometimes team members write together simultaneously, discussing and responding to each other's ideas. This approach helps consensus but is time-consuming.

Research in collaborative writing suggests strategies that produce the best writing. As noted earlier, research has found that student teams that voiced disagreements as they analyzed, planned, and wrote a document produced significantly better documents than those that suppressed disagreement, going

Many important historical documents resulted from collaborative efforts. Thomas Jefferson may have written the foundation for the Declaration of Independence, but he received many suggestions and changes from other key players, including John Adams and Benjamin Franklin. The document underwent 47 alterations before it was finalized and presented to Congress.

Write Meeting Minutes Minutes Later (not Months)

During congressional hearings on the cholesterol drug Vytorin, representatives from Merck and Schering-Plough (the drug's manufacturers) were grilled by lawmakers over a set of meeting minutes.

The minutes were from a meeting held between the drug manufacturers and the outside contractors who had researched the drug's effectiveness. According to the minutes, those consultants had recommended changing the way they evaluated the results of their research to "fudge" the data and make it seem that Vytorin was more effective than it really is. But when they testified before Congress, the researchers claimed that Vytorin's manufacturers had suggested that change in their research process—and that those minutes had been written by Merck employees almost a year after the meeting. In fact, those minutes hadn't been written until after the congressional investigation began—a delay which made it look like Vytorin's manufacturers were "fudging" more than test data.

Meeting minutes serve two main purposes: they preserve a record of what happened and what was decided, and they capture the facts so that if there's a dispute later, it's easier to untangle the truth. In either case, the best practice is to write the minutes right after the meeting, so that everything is still remembered correctly.

Adapted from Alica Mundy and Ron Winslow, "Accuracy of Vytorin Minutes Raises Doubt," *Wall Street Journal*, April 12, 2008, A3.

along with whatever was first proposed.[18] A case study of two collaborative writing teams in a state agency found that the successful team distributed power in an egalitarian way, worked to soothe hurt feelings, and was careful to involve all team members. In terms of writing process, the successful team understood the task as a response to a rhetorical situation (with a specific audience, purpose, and situation), planned revisions as a team, saw supervisors' comments as legitimate, and had a positive attitude toward revision.[19] Ede and Lunsford's detailed case studies of collaborative teams in business, government, and science create a description of effective collaborative writers: "They are flexible; respectful of others; attentive and analytical listeners; able to speak and write clearly and articulately; dependable and able to meet deadlines; able to designate and share responsibility, to lead and to follow; open to criticism but confident in their own abilities; ready to engage in creative conflict."[20]

Being Taken Seriously

It's frustrating to speak in a meeting and have people ignore what you say. Here are some tips for being taken seriously:

- Link your comment to the comment of a powerful person, even if logic suffers a bit. For example, say, "John is saying that we should focus on excellence, AND I think we can become stronger by encouraging diversity."
- Show that you've done your homework. Laura Sloate, who is blind, establishes authority by making sure her first question is highly technical: "In footnote three of the 10K, you indicate. . . ."
- Find an ally in the organization and agree ahead of time to acknowledge each other's contributions to the meeting, whether you agree or disagree with the point being made. Explicit disagreement signals that the comment is worth taking seriously: "Duane has pointed out. . . , but I think that. . . ."
- Use the style of language that powerful people in your organization use.
- Repeat your ideas. Put important ideas in a memo before the meeting.

Adapted from Joan E. Rigdon, "Managing Your Career," *Wall Street Journal,* December 1. 1993, B1; Cynthia Crossen, "Spotting Value Takes Smarts, Not Sight, Laura Sloate Shows," *Wall Street Journal,* December 10, 1987. A1, A14; and Anne Fisher, "Ask Annie: Putting Your Money Where Your Mouth Is," *Fortune,* September 3, 2001, 238.

Planning the Work and the Document

Collaborative writing is most successful when the team articulates its understanding of the document's purposes, audiences, and contexts, and explicitly discusses the best way to achieve rhetorical goals. Businesses schedule formal planning sessions for large projects to set up a time line specifying intermediate and final due dates, meeting dates, who will attend each meeting, and who will do what. Putting the plan in writing reduces misunderstandings during the project.

When you plan a collaborative writing project,

- Make your analysis of the problem, audience, context, and purposes explicit so you know where you agree and where you disagree. It usually helps to put these in writing.
- Plan the organization, format, and style of the document before anyone begins to write to make it easier to blend sections written by different authors. Decide who is going to do what and when each piece of the project will be due.
- Consider your work styles and other commitments when making a timeline. A writer working alone can stay up all night to finish a single-authored document. But members of a team need to work together to accommodate each other's styles and to enable members to meet other commitments.
- Decide how you will give constructive feedback on each person's work.
- Build some leeway into your deadlines. It's harder for a team to finish a document when one person's part is missing than it is for a single writer to finish the last section of a document on which he or she has done all the work.

All team members need to give input on important planning issues, especially to analysis and organization.

Composing the Drafts

When you draft a collaborative writing project,

- Decide who will write what. Will one person write an entire draft? Will each team member be assigned a portion of the draft? Will the whole team write the draft together? Most writers find that composing alone is faster than composing in a group. However, composing together may

Corporate Annual Meetings

Corporate annual meetings have become more interesting as activists become more vocal. PETA representatives press restaurant operators on the ethical treatment of the animals slaughtered for them. Environmentalists pressure manufacturers about their water treatments. Shareholders confront executive compensation plans they believe to be out of line.

All the action is moving corporate officials to stage-manage their annual meetings. Companies have been assigning "escorts" to activists, requiring questions to be submitted ahead of time in writing, setting speaker time limits of one to three minutes, and using stationary microphones, rather than roving ones, to ensure orderly proceedings. Many companies are googling the sponsors of shareholder resolutions. Some firms are moving meeting locations to out-of-the-way locations: U-Haul's parent company held one annual meeting in a tiny Nevada town. Home Depot hired several dozen beefy "greeters" to enforce speaker time limits. Some activists find they are greeted by an official who sits by them at the meeting and escorts them to the door afterward.

Some companies are going too far. Walmart had to apologize after a report that they had investigated some resolution sponsors. And some companies still believe in showing courtesy to shareholders as a way to generate goodwill.

Adapted from Erin White, "Stage-Managing the Annual Meeting: Companies Keep Tight Rein on Activists, Limit Speeches; Beefy 'Greeters' at the Depot," *Wall Street Journal*, April 16, 2007, B1, B3.

reduce revision time later, since the group examines every choice as it is made. Even so, it is still generally faster to have individuals compose drafts.

- Decide how you will share drafts. Will you use wikis or Google docs so everyone can work on a draft? International teams particularly need to use electronic media to compose drafts.
- Carefully label and date drafts so everyone is working on the most current version. Make sure everyone knows the date of the latest draft.
- If the quality of writing is crucial, have the best writer(s) draft the document after everyone has gathered the necessary information.

Revising the Document

Revising a collaborative document requires attention to content, organization, and style. The following guidelines can make the revision process more effective:

- Evaluate the content and discuss possible revisions as a team. Brainstorm ways to improve each section so the person doing the revisions has some guidance.
- Evaluate the organization and discuss possible revisions as a team. Would a different organization make the message clearer?
- Recognize that different people favor different writing styles. If the style satisfies the demands of standard English and the conventions of business writing, accept it even if you wouldn't say it that way.
- When the team is satisfied with the content of the document, one person—probably the best writer—should make any changes necessary to make the writing style consistent throughout.

Editing and Proofreading the Document

Since writers' mastery of standard English varies, a team report needs careful editing and proofreading.

- Have at least one person check the whole document for correctness in grammar, mechanics, and spelling and for consistency in the way that format elements (particularly headings), names, and numbers are handled.
- Run the document through a spell checker.
- Even if you use a computerized spell checker, at least one human being should proofread the document too.

Like any member of the writing team, those handling the editing tasks need to consider how they express their ideas. In many situations, the editor plays the role of diplomat, careful to suggest changes in ways that do not seem to call the writer's abilities into question. Describing the reason for a change is typically more helpful than stating an opinion. Writers are more likely to allow editing of their prose if they know a sentence has a dangling modifier, or a paragraph needs work on parallel structure. Using words like *could* and *should* to modify a direction can add a tone of politeness.

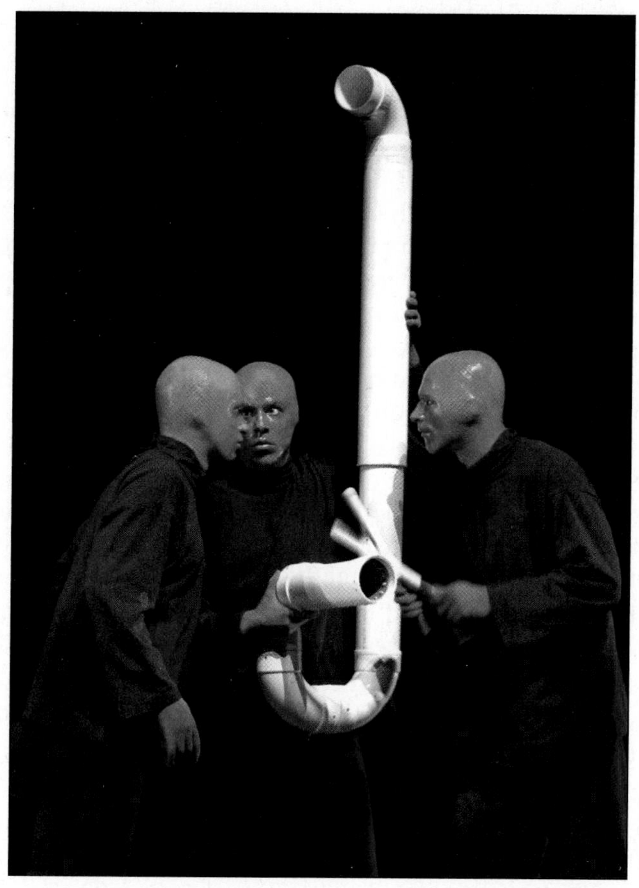

The Blue Man Group uses consensus to create their shows and run their business.

Making the Team Process Work

The information in this chapter can help your team interact effectively, run meetings efficiently, and deal with conflict constructively. The following suggestions apply specifically to writing teams:

- Give yourselves plenty of time to discuss problems and find solutions. Writing a team report may require hours of discussion time in addition to the time individuals spend doing research and writing drafts.
- Take the time to get to know team members and to build team loyalty. Team members will work harder and the final document will be better if the team is important to members.
- Be a responsible team member. Produce your drafts on time.
- Be aware that people have different ways of expressing themselves in writing.
- Because talking is "looser" than writing, people on a team can think they agree when they don't. Don't assume that because the discussion went smoothly, a draft written by one person will necessarily be acceptable.
- Allow more time at all stages of the writing process than you would if you were writing the document by yourself.

Blue Man Group Work

The Blue Man Group started in 1988 as a trio of performance artists doing street theater in New York City. Today, Blue Man Group is an entertainment franchise with about 70 Blue Men employed in nine theater shows plus touring concerts. They fill stadiums, they've founded their own creativity-based early childhood program, and they've been nominated for a Grammy. How did they do it? Teamwork.

As Matt Goldman, one of the founding Blue Men, notes, "Three is the smallest unit where you can have an outsider." The Blue Man Group uses consensus to create their music, original instruments, and shows—and to run their business. They discuss decisions until they reach a point where all three members can agree. That lets each member bring his/her own unique contributions to the process, while ensuring that the whole team is satisfied with the result. "It takes longer, but we find if you keep talking things through, you reach a better choice."

Working as part of a team is one of the most challenging communication tasks you can face in a professional setting. As a team member, you'll use your audience analysis skills to build goodwill with people inside *and* outside of your team, and your organizational skills to keep both your communication and your work moving smoothly.

Sources: Liz Welch, "How We Did It: The Blue Man Group, from Downtown Performance Art to Global Entertainment Empire," *Inc.*, August 2008, 110–12; and "What Is Blue Man Group?" Blue Man Productions, Inc., accessed May 31, 2011, http://www.blueman.com/about/whatis.

SUMMARY OF KEY POINTS

- Effective teams balance information leadership, interpersonal leadership, and procedural team management.
- Successful teams set clear deadlines, schedule frequent meetings, deal directly with conflict, have an inclusive decision-making style, and have a higher proportion of members who worked actively on the project.
- Groupthink is the tendency for groups to put such a high premium on agreement that they directly or indirectly punish dissent. The best correctives to groupthink are to consciously search for additional alternatives, to test one's assumptions against those of a range of other people, and to protect the right of each person in the group to disagree.
- To resolve conflicts, first make sure that the people involved really disagree. Next, check to see that everyone's information is correct. Discover the needs each person is trying to meet. The presenting problem that surfaces as the subject of dissension may or may not be the real problem. Search for alternatives. Repair negative feelings.
- Constructive ways to respond to criticism include paraphrasing, checking for feelings, checking inferences, and buying time with limited agreement.
- Use statements about your own feelings to own the problem and avoid attacking the audience. In conflict, *I* statements are good you-attitude!
- To make meetings more effective,
  - State the purpose of the meeting at the beginning.
  - Distribute an agenda that indicates whether each item is for information, discussion, or action, and how long each is expected to take.
  - Allow enough time to discuss controversial issues.
  - Pay attention to people and process as well as to the task at hand.
  - If you don't take formal votes, summarize the group's consensus after each point. At the end of the meeting, summarize all decisions and remind the group who is responsible for implementing or following up on each item.
- Collaborative writing means working with other writers to produce a single document. Writers producing a joint document need to pay attention not only to the basic steps in the writing process but also to the processes of team formation and conflict resolution. They also need to allow more time than they would for single-authored documents.

CHAPTER 8 Exercises and Problems

**Go to www.mhhe.com/locker10e for additional Exercises and Problems.*

8.1 Reviewing the Chapter

1. What are 10 kinds of productive roles in teams? Which roles do you prefer to play? (LO 8-1)
2. What are five kinds of nonproductive roles in teams? (LO 8-1)
3. What are some team decision-making strategies? (LO 8-2)
4. Name five characteristics of successful teams. (LO 8-3)
5. What is groupthink? Have you ever experienced it? (LO 8-2)
6. What are some techniques for resolving conflict? (LO 8-4)
7. What are some techniques for responding to criticism? (LO 8-4)
8. What are some techniques for making meetings effective? (LO 8-5)

9. What are some techniques for collaborative writing? (LO 8-6)
10. Have you ever been part of a team that wrote a document as a whole group rather than assigning out pieces? If so, how did the process work for your team? (LO 8-6)

8.2 Brainstorming Ways to Resolve Conflicts

Suggest one or more ways that each of the following teams could deal with the conflict(s) it faces.

1. Mike and Takashi both find writing hard. Elise has been getting better grades than either of them, so they offer to do all the research if she'll organize the document and write, revise, edit, and proofread it. Elise thinks that this method would leave her doing a disproportionate share of the work. Moreover, scheduling the work would be difficult, since she wouldn't know how good their research was until the last minute.
2. Because of their class and work schedules, Lars and Andrea want to hold team meetings from 8 to 10 pm, working later if need be. But Juan's wife works the evening shift, and he needs to be home with his children, two of whom have to be in bed before 8. He wants to meet from 8 to 10 am, but the others don't want to meet that early.
3. Lynn wants to divide up the work exactly equally, with firm due dates. Marcia is trying to get into medical school. She says she'd rather do the lion's share of the work so that she knows it's good.
4. Jessie's father is terminally ill. This team isn't very important in terms of what's going on in her life, and she knows she may have to miss some team meetings.
5. Sherry is aware that she is the person on her team who always points out the logical flaws in arguments: she's the one who reminds the team that they haven't done all the parts of the assignment. She doesn't want her team to turn in a flawed product, but she wonders whether the other team members see her as too critical.
6. Jim's team missed several questions on their team quiz. Talking to Tae-Suk after class, Jim learns that Tae-Suk knew all the answers. "Why didn't you say anything?" Jim asks angrily. Tae-Suk responds quietly, "Todd said that he knew the answers. I did not want to argue with him. We have to work together, and I do not want anyone to lose face."

8.3 Comparing Meeting Minutes

Have two or more people take minutes of each class or team meeting for a week. Compare the accounts of the same meeting.

- To what extent do they agree on what happened?
- Does one contain information missing in other accounts?
- Do any accounts disagree on a specific fact?
- How do you account for the differences you find?

As your instructor directs,

a. Discuss your findings with your team.
b. Share your team findings orally with the class.
c. Describe and analyze your findings in a memo to your instructor.

8.4 Learning about Annual Meetings

The sidebar on page 219 previewed the annual meeting of Berkshire Hathaway. Read Buffett's complete three-page preview at http://www.berkshirehathaway.com/letters/2010ltr.pdf. Prepare to discuss the preview in small groups by answering these questions:

- What is the tone of the preview?
- What useful hints does Buffett give to his shareholders?
- What activities will occur at the meeting?

Now look up the announcement for the annual conference of a professional society to which you belong.

- What is the tone of the conference preview?
- Does it give useful hints?
- What activities will occur at the meeting?

Which meeting would you rather attend, Buffett's or that of your professional society? Why? Discuss the answers to these questions in small groups.

8.5 Recommending a Policy on Student Entrepreneurs

Assume that your small team comprises the officers in student government on your campus. You receive this e-mail from the Dean of Students:

> As you know, campus policy says that no student may use campus resources to conduct business-related activities. Students can't conduct business out of dorm rooms or use university e-mail addresses for business. They can't post business web pages on the university server.
>
> On the other hand, a survey conducted by the Kauffman Center for Entrepreneurial Leadership showed that 7 out of 10 teens want to become entrepreneurs.
>
> Should campus policy be changed to allow students to use dorm rooms and university e-mail addresses for business? (And then what happens when roommates complain and our network can't carry the increased e-mail traffic?) Please recommend what support (if any) should be given to student entrepreneurs.

Your team will be writing a report recommending what (if anything) your campus should do for student entrepreneurs and supporting your recommendation.

Hints:

- Does your campus offer other support for entrepreneurs (courses, a business plan competition, a start-up incubator)? What should be added or expanded?
- Is it realistic to ask alumni for money to fund student start-ups?
- Are campus dorms, e-mail, phone, and delivery services funded by tax dollars? If your school is a public institution, do state or local laws limit business use?

You need to

- Send e-mail messages to team members describing your initial point of view on the issue and discussing the various options.
- Help your team write the report.
- Write a memo to your instructor telling how satisfied you are with
  - The decision your team reached.
  - The process you used to reach it.
  - The document your team produced.

8.6 Recommending a Fair Way to Assign Work around the Holidays

Assume that your team comprises a hospital's Labor-Management Committee. This e-mail arrives from the hospital administrator:

> Subject: Allocating Holiday Hours
>
> It's that time of year again, and we're starting to get requests for time off from every department. We have shifts where every physician and half the nurses want time off. Don't these people realize that we can't close down over a holiday? And what's worse is that some of the shift leads are giving preferential treatment to their friends. The head of the nurses' union has already started complaining to me.
>
> We need a comprehensive, hospital-wide procedure for assigning holiday vacation time that doesn't make us shut down wards. It needs to be flexible, because people like to take a week off around Christmas. But we have to set limits: no more than one-quarter of the staff can take time off at any one time. And those nurses like to swap shifts with each other to arrange their days off into larger blocks, so we need to cover that too.

> Write up a policy to keep these people in line. Be sure to throw in the safety concerns and regulatory stuff.

Your team will be performing these tasks:

a. Write a team response recommending a new policy and supporting your recommendations. Include two transmittal e-mails: one to the hospital administrator, and one to the hospital's medical and nursing staff. Take care to address the two audiences' different needs and expectations with good you-attitude and positive emphasis.
b. Create a one-page notice describing your new policy. This notice should be suitable for posting at the duty desk for each ward: that is, in full view of both your employees and your customers (the patients). Create an effective visual design that emphasizes and organizes the text.

You personally need to

- Send e-mail messages to team members describing your initial point of view on the issue and discussing the various options.
- Help your team write the documents.
- Write a memo to your instructor telling how satisfied you are with
  - The decisions your team reached.
  - The process you used to reach them.
  - The documents your team produced.

8.7 Recommending a Dress Policy

Assume that your small team comprises your organization's Labor-Management Committee

This e-mail arrives from the CEO:

> In the last 10 years, we became increasingly casual. But changed circumstances seem to call for more formality. Is it time to reinstate a dress policy? If so, what should it be?

Your team will be writing a response recommending the appropriate dress for employees and supporting your recommendation.

Hint:

Agree on an office, factory, store, or other workplace to use for this problem.

You need to

- Send e-mail messages to team members describing your initial point of view on the issue and discussing the various options.
- Help your team write the response.
- Write a memo to your instructor telling how satisfied you are with
  - The decision your team reached.
  - The process you used to reach it.
  - The document your team produced.

8.8 Responding to an Employee Grievance

Assume that your small team comprises the Labor-Management committee at the headquarters of a chain of grocery stores. This e-mail arrives from the vice president for human resources:

> As you know, company policy requires that employees smile at customers and make eye contact with them. In the past 9 months, 12 employees have filed grievances over this rule. They say they are being harassed by customers who think they are flirting with them. A produce clerk claims customers have propositioned her and followed her to her car. Another says "Let *me* decide who I am going to say hello to

> with a big smile." The union wants us to change the policy to let workers *not* make eye contact with customers, and to allow workers to refuse to carry groceries to a customer's car at night. My own feeling is that we want to maintain our image as a friendly store that cares about customers, but that we also don't want to require behavior that leads to harassment. Let's find a creative solution.

Your team will be writing a group response recommending whether to change the policy and supporting your recommendation.

You need to

- Send e-mail messages to team members describing your initial point of view on the issue and discussing the various options.
- Help your team write the response.
- Write a memo to your instructor telling how satisfied you are with
    - The decision your team reached.
    - The process you used to reach it.
    - The document your team produced.

8.9 Answering an Ethics Question

Assume that your team comprises your organization's Ethics Committee. You receive the following anonymous note:

> People are routinely using the company letterhead to write letters to members of Congress, senators, and even the president stating their positions on various issues. Making their opinions known is of course their right, but doing so on letterhead stationery implies that they are speaking for the company, which they are not.
>
> I think that the use of letterhead for anything other than official company business should be prohibited.

Your team will be determining the best solution to the problem and then communicating it in a message to all employees.

You need to

- Send e-mail messages to team members describing your initial point of view on the issue and discussing the various options.
- Help your team write the message.
- Write a memo to your instructor telling how satisfied you are with
    - The decision your team reached.
    - The process you used to reach it.
    - The document your team produced.

8.10 Interviewing Workers about Collaborating

Interview someone who works in an organization about his or her on-the-job collaboration activities. Possible questions to ask include the following:

- How often do you work on collaborative projects?
- Do your collaborative projects always include people who are in your immediate office? How often do you collaborate with people via technology?
- How do you begin collaborative projects? What are the first steps you take when working with others?
- How do you handle disagreements?
- What do you do when someone isn't doing his/her share of the work on a collaborative project?
- What do you do to see every person meets team deadlines?
- How do you handle unexpected problems? Illness? Injury? Broken equipment?
- What advice can you give about effectively collaborating on projects?

As your instructor directs,

a. Share your information with a small team of students in your class.
b. Present your findings orally to the class.
c. Present your findings in a memo to your instructor.
d. Join with other students to present your findings in a team report.

8.11 Networking for Team Formation

In this exercise, you are going to participate in a networking event, an abbreviated "talk and walk."

To prepare for the event,

- Prepare business cards for yourself, using a computer application of your choice.
- Prepare a list of people in your class whom you would like to meet (give visual descriptions if you do not know their names).
- Prepare a list of questions you would like to have answered.
- Collect materials to use for taking notes during the event.

During the event, you will have six three-minute sessions to talk with a fellow student. Your instructor will time the sessions and tell you when to change people.

After the event, analyze what you have learned. Here are some questions to get you started:

- Who was the most interesting? Why?
- Who did you like the most? Why?
- Who would you most like to have on a team in this class? Why?
- Did you meet anyone you didn't want to work with? Explain.
- What lessons did you learn about networking?

Write up your analysis in a memo to your teacher.

8.12 Writing a Team Action Plan

Before you begin working on a team project, develop a team action plan to establish a framework that will hold your team members accountable for their work.

After reading the project assignment sheet and meeting your team, decide upon answers for the following questions:

- Will you have a team leader? If so, who? Why is that person qualified to be the team leader? What are that person's responsibilities? How will you proceed if the team leader is unable to meet those responsibilities?
- What will be each team member's role? What is each team member's qualification for that role?
- How are you dividing your work? Why did you choose to divide the work the way you did?
- What are the tasks your team needs to accomplish? For each task in the assignment, identify a concrete deliverable (What do you need to hand in?), a concrete measure for success (How will your team decide if you completed that task well?), and a work schedule (When does each task need to be done?)
- How will you resolve disagreements that may arise while working on the project? How will your team make decisions: By majority? By consensus?
- When and where will you hold meetings? Decide whether you can hold meetings if all team members are not present. How will you inform team members of what occurred at meetings if they were not present?
- Define what "absence" means for your team. Are all absences equal? How should a team member who's going to be absent let the team know? How far in advance does your team need to know about an absence? How many absences from one team member will be too many? What are the consequences of too many absences?
- Create a policy dealing with people who don't attend class during your preparation days or during your presentation; people who don't attend meetings outside class; people who miss deadlines, don't do their work at all or in a timely manner, or who consistently turn in incomplete or poor-quality work. What penalties will you apply? (Some ideas: you might consider loss of points, grade reductions, failure, a team firing, or a team intervention.)
- Will you report problem members to your instructor? If so, at what point? What role do you want your instructor to have in dealing with problem members?

After your team determines and agrees on an action plan, the team's secretary should send your answers in a memo to your instructor, who will keep the document on file in case a problem arises.

8.13 Writing Team Meeting Minutes

As you work in a collaborative team setting, designate a different member to take minutes for each meeting.

As your instructor directs, your minutes should include:

- Name of the team holding the meeting.
- Members who were present.
- Members who were absent.
- Place, time, and date of meeting.
- Work accomplished, and who did it, during the meeting.

- Actions that need to be completed, the person responsible, and the due date.
- Decisions made during the meeting.
- New issues raised at the meeting but not resolved should be recorded for future meetings.
- Signature of acting secretary.

Remember to keep your minutes brief and to the point. When the minutes are complete, e-mail them to your fellow team members and cc: them to your instructor.

8.14 Keeping a Journal about a Team

As you work on a team, keep a journal after each team meeting.

- Who did what?
- What roles did you play in the meeting?
- What decisions were made? How were they made?
- What conflicts arose? How were they handled?
- What strategies could you use to make the next meeting go smoothly?
- Record one observation about each team member.

At the end of the project, analyze your journals. In a memo to your instructor, discuss

- Patterns you see.
- Roles of each team member, including yourself.
- Decision making in your team.
- Conflict resolution in your team.
- Strengths of your team.
- Areas where your team could improve.
- Strengths of the deliverables.
- Areas where the deliverables could be improved.
- Changes you would make in the team and deliverables if you had the project to do over.

8.15 Analyzing the Dynamics of a Team

Analyze the dynamics of a task team of which you were a member. Answer the following questions:

1. Who was the team's leader? How did the leader emerge? Were there any changes in or challenges to the original leader?
2. Describe the contribution each member made to the team and the roles each person played.
3. Did any members of the team officially or unofficially drop out? Did anyone join after the team had begun working? How did you deal with the loss or addition of a team member, both in terms of getting the work done and in terms of helping people work together?
4. What planning did your team do at the start of the project? Did you stick to the plan or revise it? How did the team decide that revision was necessary?
5. How did your team make decisions? Did you vote? reach decisions by consensus?
6. What problems or conflicts arose? Did the team deal with them openly? To what extent did they interfere with the team's task?
7. Evaluate your team both in terms of its task and in terms of the satisfaction members felt. How did this team compare with other task teams you've been part of? What made it better or worse?
8. What were the strengths of the team? Weaknesses?
9. How did the team's strengths and weaknesses impact the quality of the work produced?
10. If you had the project to do over again, what would you do differently?

As you answer the questions,

- Be honest. You won't lose points for reporting that your team had problems or did something "wrong."
- Show your knowledge of good team dynamics. That is, if your team did something wrong, show that you know what *should* have been done. Similarly, if your team worked well, show that you know *why* it worked well.
- Be specific. Give examples or anecdotes to support your claims.

As your instructor directs,

a. Discuss your answers with the other team members.
b. Present your findings in an individual memo to your instructor.
c. Join with the other team members to write a collaborative memo to your instructor.

8.16 Dealing with a "Saboteur"

It's often said that "there's no *I* in *team*" because on the best teams, everyone works together for the good of the group. What happens when you encounter a team member who believes that "there's a *me* in *team*" and ignores or undermines the team's success in order to achieve personal goals?

Consider this scenario. You're on a team of four students, and you've all been working for the past month to complete a major class project. When you were planning out your project, one team member—let's say Lee—argued with your team's decisions, but agreed to go along with the majority. Lee contributed the bare minimum to your team's work, sat silently during meetings, and when you asked for help overcoming a problem with the project, Lee responded with a shrug, "I told you at the start that I thought this was a bad idea. I guess we're all going to get a failing grade."

Now you're at your last team meeting before the assignment is due. Lee reveals a decision to quit the team and turn in a separate project. Lee doesn't want a grade that "will suffer from all your 'second-rate' efforts," and tells you that s/he already complained to your instructor about the rest of you.

As your instructor directs,

a. Write a memo to your instructor in which you explain your individual response to this scenario. What would you do? How should your team proceed?

b. Work as a group to establish a working policy that might address this scenario before it happens.

- What policies would you need to protect the group from individual members who are out for themselves?
- What policies would you need to protect team members from having the team take advantage of them?
- What is your instructor's role in your team's policy?
- How would your team evaluate each member's contributions fairly?

CHAPTER 9

Sharing Informative and Positive Messages with Appropriate Technology

Chapter Outline

Communication Hardware
- Smartphones
- Portable media players
- Videoconferences

Information Overload

Using Common Media
- Face-to-Face Contacts
- Phone Calls
- Instant Messaging and Text Messaging
- Wikis
- Social Media
- E-mails, Letters, and Paper Memos

Organizing Informative and Positive Messages

Subject Lines for Informative and Positive Messages
- Making Subject Lines Specific
- Making Subject Lines Concise
- Making Subject Lines Appropriate for the Pattern of Organization
- Pointers for E-Mail Subject Lines

Managing the Information in Your Messages

Using Benefits in Informative and Positive Messages

Ending Informative and Positive Messages

Humor in Informative Messages

Varieties of Informative and Positive Messages
- Transmittals
- Summaries
- Thank-You and Positive Feedback Notes
- Positive Responses to Complaints

Solving a Sample Problem
- Problem
- Analysis of the Problem
- Discussion of the Sample Solutions

Summary of Key Points

A Positive Message that Backfired

Sharing good news is often considered the easiest part of a writer's job. However, just as with any message, writers must craft positive messages carefully and pay attention to their audience and the situation.

In March 2011, Transocean issued its annual report to its shareholders and the United States Securities and Exchange Commission. As the largest offshore oil drilling contractor in the world, Transocean had enjoyed a profitable year with, according to standard industry measures, an exemplary safety record. In the filing, the company stated, "We recorded the best year in safety performance in our Company's history."

Unfortunately, Transocean is the owner of Deepwater Horizon, the oil rig that exploded in the Gulf of Mexico, April 2010. The accident killed 11 workers, injured another 17, and triggered the largest—and most publicized—oil spill in the history of the United States. Millions of barrels of oil gushed into the ocean over three months, causing an environmental disaster.

But in its report, Transocean attempted to minimize the Deepwater Horizon accident to place greater emphasis on its good news: "Notwithstanding the tragic loss of life in the Gulf of Mexico, we achieved an exemplary statistical safety record as measured by our total recordable incident rate and total potential severity rate."

The strategy backfired. News articles about the report focused on the phrase "the best year in safety performance" and the six-figure bonuses and salary increases for the executives, all only months after the disaster in the Gulf of Mexico. Days after the annual report's filing, Transocean apologized for the wording.

> *"Writers must craft positive messages carefully and pay attention to their audience and the situation."*

By failing to craft its positive annual report with sensitivity to the situation and public opinion, Transocean saw a positive message turned into another negative strike against the company.

Sources: Transocean website, accessed June 7, 2011, http://www.deepwater.com; CNN Wire Staff, "Despite Gulf Oil Spill, Rig Owner Executives Get Big Bonuses," Cable News Network, April 4, 2011, http://edition.cnn.com/2011/BUSINESS/04/03/gulf.spill.bonuses/index.html; and CNN Wire Staff, "Gulf Oil Rig Owner Apologizes for Calling 2010 'Best Year' Ever," Cable News Network, April 4, 2011, http://www.cnn.com/2011/US/04/04/gulf.spill.bonuses/index.html?hpt=T2.

Learning Objectives

After studying this chapter, you will know

LO 9-1 How technology is changing business communication.

LO 9-2 When and how to use common business media effectively.

LO 9-3 How to organize informative and positive messages.

LO 9-4 How to compose some of the common varieties of informative and positive messages.

A Vision of the Future

Have you ever dreamed about moving objects without using a muscle? Do you wish you could control objects using only your brain?

Thought-conversion technology is the main focus of a company called Emotiv. Right now, the company has advanced the technology to a point where users can move objects with their thoughts in a video game environment. Users wear a wireless headset that contains 16 electrodes that press against the scalp. The device has the capability to measure brain waves and turn thoughts into electronic actions.

Expanded from the science behind EEGs, thought-conversion technology could be the wave of the future. Emotiv doesn't want consumers just to be able to play video games. Eventually, they hope to develop the system so that users can control everything they do on their computer and around the house by mental power.

What implications would a device like this have for the business world? How could it increase productivity? What, if any, drawbacks would there be to a device like this?

Adapted from David H. Freedman, "Reality Bites," *Inc.*, December 2008, 92–99.

Business messages must meet the needs of the sender (and the sender's organization), be sensitive to the audience, and accurately reflect the topic being discussed. Informative and positive messages are the bread-and-butter messages in organizations.

When we need to convey information to which the receiver's basic reaction will be neutral, the message is **informative.** If we convey information to which the receiver's reaction will be positive, the message is a **positive or good news message.** Neither message immediately asks the receiver to do anything. You usually do want to build positive attitudes toward the information you are presenting, so in that sense, even an informative message has a persuasive element. Chapter 10 will discuss messages where the receiver will respond negatively; Chapter 11 will discuss messages where you want the receiver to change beliefs or behavior.

Informative and positive messages include acceptances; positive answers to requests; information about meetings, procedures, products, services, or options; announcements of policy changes that are neutral or positive; and changes that are to the receiver's advantage.

Even a simple informative or good news message usually has several purposes:

Primary purposes:

To give information or good news to the receiver or to reassure the receiver.
To have the receiver view the information positively.

Secondary purposes:

To build a good image of the sender.
To build a good image of the sender's organization.
To cement a good relationship between the sender and the receiver.
To deemphasize any negative elements.
To reduce or eliminate future messages on the same subject.

Informative and positive messages are not necessarily short. Instead, the length of a message depends on your purposes, the audience's needs, and the complexity of the situation.

In addition to these concerns, you also have to ensure you are communicating with appropriate tools and media.

COMMUNICATION HARDWARE LO 9-1

Businesses are quick to adopt new forms of technology that can enhance the experience of workers and improve the bottom line. New software programs and devices continually enter the market to help businesses. However,

Technology plays a large role in the changing face of business communication. Conference rooms are frequently equipped with laptops, projectors and videoconferencing equipment, making it possible for people to have meetings across continents and time zones.

acquiring new technology and helping workers master it entail an enormous capital investment. Learning to use new-generation software and improved hardware takes time and may be especially frustrating for people who were perfectly happy with old technology.

Some of the most popular workplace tools that improve productivity are smartphones, portable media players, and videoconferences.

Smartphones

Smartphones, such as Apple's iPhone or any in the Android lineup, allow users to send and receive e-mail, access websites, conduct word processing, learn their next tasks, update a job's status, complete a time sheet, and make telephone calls. Many of these devices have touch screens or full QWERTY keyboards. These devices can also broadcast streaming video and audio. Every day more applications become available for these smartphones, which can enhance productivity. With the full functionality of these devices, employees can be connected to their work 24/7. However, this does not mean they should be. Be considerate and try to limit business calls to business hours.

Portable Media Players

Portable media players (like iPods and MP3 players) feature the ability to broadcast streaming video and audio. Some organizations give employees these devices pre-loaded with recordings of meetings, new product information, or general announcements. These devices help keep employees connected, even when they're not in the office.

Videoconferences

With rising travel costs, many businesses are seeking alternatives to traditional face-to-face meetings. One solution is videoconferences, which allow two or more parties to communicate and hold meetings with full audio and visual capabilities. They can occur across different time zones or between different nations instantaneously. As an added benefit, meetings never have to be delayed or postponed because of late flights or weather problems.

Cellphone Blindness

"How blind to their surroundings can people be when they are talking on their cellphones?

Enough to miss seeing a clown riding a unicycle as they walked across the Western Washington University campus, according to a study conducted by a professor and his students. Seventy-five percent of the people who were walking and talking on their phones did not see the clown—until he was pointed out to them.

While the idea of cellphone users being so oblivious they fail to see a unicycling clown is humorous, Ira Hyman, a psychology professor who conducted the study, said the implications are serious and show that people should not be talking on cellphones while driving.

Numerous studies already have shown that people fail to notice things while they're talking on their cellphones. But many of those studies were conducted in a laboratory setting, typically in driving simulators."

What do you think? Should talking on cellphones while driving be banned?

Quoted from "Cell Phone Talkers Miss the Obvious, School's Study Finds," *Des Moines Register*, November 5, 2009, 4A.

Cellular phone technology is spreading worldwide.

One type of videoconferencing is telepresence, which uses high-end 50-inch plasma screens and broadcast-quality cameras to create virtual meetings that are almost lifelike. Pepsi, Bank of American, and Proctor & Gamble are just some of the companies that have adopted this technology. These state-of-the-art telepresence rooms can be pricey, costing up to $300,000. Some of the cost is associated with the equipment necessary to create a room, but most of the cost comes from the large amounts of bandwidth required for the conferencing. Projected revenue for telepresence services will reach $2.3 billion by 2015.[1]

Lower-cost alternatives for videoconferencing exist as well. Services like Skype, Apple's FaceTime, or GoToMeeting allow employees to connect and collaborate remotely with web cameras that are standard on many newer laptops or tablets. Cisco and Logitech have also introduced systems that require HDTVs and a broadband connection for videoconferencing in the comfort of your home.

INFORMATION OVERLOAD

One of the realities of communication today is information overload. Technology enables other people to bombard us with junk mail, sales calls, advertisements, and spam. Spam clutters mailboxes—or leads to filters that stop some needed e-mail. Spam also means that many people do not open e-mail if they do not recognize the sender or the topic.

Basex, a knowledge economy research and advisory company, surveyed knowledge workers and found that over 50% of them felt that the amount of information coming to them daily was detrimental to accomplishing their work. In fact, 94% of them reported that at some point they were overwhelmed by information to the point of incapacity.[2] A similar survey by Xerox of government and education workers found that 58% spent almost half their work time sorting, filing, or deleting information, and that this effort amounts to over $31 billion spent annually on managing information.[3]

On another level, even more routine communications are becoming overwhelming. With fast and cheap e-mails, plus the genuine belief in more transparent business procedures, businesses send more announcements of events, procedures, policies, services, and employee news. Departments send newsletters. Employees send announcements of and best wishes for births, birthdays, weddings, and promotions. Customers send comments about products, service, policies, and advertisements.

Yet another factor in overload is inappropriate e-mails. This group includes jokes, personal information, and non-job-related e-mails, as well as e-mails that are unnecessarily long, trivial, and irrelevant. Too many people forward too many messages to uncaring receivers, and the "Reply to All" button is getting a notorious reputation.

According to the Radicati Group, a technology market research firm, the average corporate e-mail user sends and receives 167 e-mails per day.[4] Radicati calculates that 294 billion e-mail messages were sent *daily* in 2010, of which 89.1% were spam.[5] An internal survey at Intel found that employees were spending an average of 20 hours a week on e-mails, 30% of which were unnecessary.[6]

With this flood of information, you need to protect your communication reputation.

WARNING: You do not want to be the person whose e-mails or voice-mail messages are opened last because they take so long to get to the point, or even worse, the person whose messages are rarely opened at all because you send so many that aren't important or necessary.

One research study on e-mail overload found that length was not the problem: most e-mails in the study were short, four lines or less. Rather, the study found three factors that contributed to the perception of e-mail overload. The first, unstable requests, included requests that got refined in the process of e-mail correspondence and frequently morphed into requests for more work. The second, pressure to respond, included requests for information within hours. People in the study noted that they were never away from their e-mail, and that these requests could come any time. The third factor, delegation of tasks and shifting interactants, included tasks that were indirectly delegated (Could anyone get me the figures on X for the noon meeting?) or that recipients of the group e-mail then gave to their own subordinates.[7]

Some organizations and software applications are taking a stand to help employees deal with information overload. For instance, software add-ons for e-mail systems can now prioritize messages after analyzing which senders have the most importance. Companies such as Intel are declaring e-mail-free days, where employees are encouraged to meet face-to-face.

USING COMMON MEDIA LO 9-2

In the office, most informative and positive communications are made through six channels: face-to-face contacts, phone calls, instant messages and text messaging, e-mails, letters, and paper memos. Many people have personal preferences that need to be recognized. They may keep up with their e-mail but avoid listening to voice-mail messages; they may enjoy drop-in visitors but think instant messages are silly. Similarly, some channels seem better fitted for some situations than others.

Face-to-Face Contacts

Some businesses are encouraging their employees to write fewer e-mails and visit each other's desks more often. They believe such visits contribute to a friendlier, more collaborative work environment. Visits are a good choice when

- You know a colleague welcomes your visits.
- You are building a business relationship with a person.
- A real-time connection saves messages (e.g., setting a meeting agenda).
- Your business requires dialogue or negotiation.
- You need something immediately (like a signature).
- Discretion is vital and you do not want to leave a paper trail.
- The situation is complex enough that you want as many visual and aural cues as possible.

Phone Answering Machine Pet Peeves

- Callback numbers that are mumbled or given too quickly.
- Messages longer than 30 seconds.
- Messages that require serious note taking (when an e-mail would have been better).
- Too much or too little information.
- Demands to contact people without saying why.
- Messages expecting an immediate response.
- Angry messages.

Use these tips for effective face-to-face contact:

- Ensure the timing is convenient for the recipient.
- If you are discussing something complex, have appropriate documents in hand.
- Don't usurp their space. Don't put your papers on top of their desk or table without their permission.
- Look for "time to go" signs. Some people have a limited tolerance for small talk, especially when they are hard at work on a task.

Phone Calls

Phone calls provide fewer contextual cues than face-to-face visits, but more cues than electronic or paper messages. Phone calls are a good choice when

- Tone of voice is important.
- A real-time connection saves multiple phone calls or e-mails (e.g., setting a meeting time).
- You need something immediately (like an OK).
- You do not want to leave a paper trail (but remember that phone records are easily obtained).

Use these tips for effective phone calls (also see sidebar on this page):

- Ensure the timing is convenient for the recipient; try to limit cellphone calls to business hours:
- Promptly return calls to your answering machine.
- Speak clearly, especially when giving your name and phone number (even more important when leaving your name and phone number on an answering machine). Do not assume they have a phone that records your number.
- Use an information hook: I am calling about. . . .
- Keep the call short and cordial. If you need to leave a message, keep it brief: 1–2 sentences. Most people resent long messages on their answering machines.
- Repeat your phone number at the end of the call. Too often, people don't write the number down at the beginning of the call.
- Focus on the call; do not do other work. Most people can tell if you are reading e-mail or web pages while talking to them, and they get the message that their concern is not important to you.

Remember that unplanned phone calls are an interruption in a busy worker's day. If that person works in an open office, as many do, the call will also interrupt other employees to some extent.

Instant Messaging and Text Messaging

Formerly limited primarily to students, instant and text messaging are beginning to gain acceptance in the business world, especially among people who work closely together. Instant messaging services, like AOL Instant Messenger, Google chat, and Yahoo Messenger, have quickly found their way into office settings. Because they are less intrusive than phone calls or visits, these messages are good for short messages on noncritical topics, such as running commentary or questions on tasks you and your colleagues are working on simultaneously. And because they are generally answered immediately, they can decrease the time needed to solve an issue. Some organizations also believe that IMing fosters better collaborations among employees, particularly those who work from home.

You will probably find more enthusiasm for these media among your younger colleagues. But not always! Many parents have been initiated to these messages by their children. Even among users, audience distinctions will be important, especially with abbreviations. Although even the *Oxford English Dictionary* lists LOL, BFF, IMHO, and OMG, some people will not recognize other abbreviations. And abbreviations like OMG disturb some readers.

Remember that, like e-mails, these messages can be saved, forwarded, and printed. They too leave a paper trail, and many businesses monitor them. Do not use them to send sensitive information, such as files or passwords, and always keep them professional in both mechanics and content. Florida Congressman Mark Foley lost his position for holding sexual and otherwise inappropriate IM conversations with underage pages.

Wikis

With the popularity of websites like Wikipedia, the business world has been quick to follow suit. Many organizations are using wikis, an online form of content knowledge management, in which users can post information or collaborate on projects. The access to these wikis is limited to employees of the particular organization using them, much like intranets. Employees can use wikis to:

- Bookmark and summarize web pages.
- Upload drafts of working documents.
- Create new entries about workplace practices.

Other employees can then quickly search for information using keywords or modify existing uploaded documents.

Wikis are a great way for corporations to create knowledge databases of workplace practices for their particular organization. In addition, wikis reduce the e-mailing of drafts between employees who are collaborating on a project. As an added bonus, every change made to documents on a wiki can be tracked. Moreover, when employees leave an organization, their job knowledge is still stored on the wiki and can be a valuable resource for new employees.

Social Media

Many organizations are adapting social media tools at an ever increasing rate. And they have good reason to do so. In addition to reaching thousands of clients in a single message, social media offer a relatively inexpensive way to connect. Employees can post profiles, updates, blogs, or useful links, all for free.

For businesses, the challenge of social media is figuring out how to harness the positives to increase productivity, particularly when dealing with customers. Dell Inc. has created a social media university for employees who are interested in learning the basics of social media by taking four courses. Over 9,000 employees started the program to better integrate social media into their positions.[8]

Facebook and Divorce

While sharing too much information on Facebook is known to be a danger at workplaces, here is a new situation demanding great caution: divorce.

Mounting evidence exists online for lawyers to sort and use in divorce cases. In fact, 81% of the American Academy of Matrimonial Lawyers have used or encountered evidence from social media sites over the last five years. Facebook is the largest source of virtual evidence, accounting for 66%.

Divorce lawyers recounted cases where the husband went on vacation with a new mistress and posted pictures to his Facebook profile. Unfortunately, the husband forgot that he was still friends with his wife. In another situation, a father who wanted custody of the children showed evidence of the mother logged onto Facebook's Farmville when she should have been attending the children's sporting events.

These are just more reminders to be conscious of what you're sharing online.

Adapted from Leanne Italie, "Divorce Lawyers Revel in Online Evidence," *Des Moines Register*, July 4, 2010, 1E, 2E.

Like Dell, many organizations use social networking sites to establish an identity and harness a relationship with clients. The United States Army has a social media division in charge of recruiting. Even the Pope has encouraged priests to tap into digital media options.

Some businesses seem to adapt easily to social media. Blendtec, a manufacturer of blenders, became a media star with a series of YouTube videos, *Will It Blend?* which put various objects (computer games, iPod, iPad) in its blenders. The video with the iPhone has been viewed over 9 million times, and Blendtec sales have increased sevenfold. Other businesses have to be more cautious. Mutual funds were slow to embrace social media, partly because of industry regulations.[9]

Four of the most common ways to connect with customers are Facebook, Twitter, LinkedIn, and blogs.

Facebook Facebook is a social networking tool where users create a profile and then can chat and share interests with other users. The site has over 600 million users worldwide and has become the most popular site in the United States, surpassing Google in 2010 by having 8.9% of all Internet visits.[10]

Beyond buying advertising space, organizations use Facebook as a communication channel with customers by providing updates about business activities, introducing new products, informing about upcoming events, encouraging participation in philanthropic causes, or offering discounts or incentives.

Organizations can also create focus groups where they can receive or share feedback from clients about products and services. Dr Pepper measures the social conversation about their brand from their 8.5 million fan base and adjusts marketing messages accordingly. As a result, Dr Pepper gets free marketing when users pass their messages on to other Facebook friends.[11]

As an added bonus to businesses, Facebook connections can increase awareness about their brand by boosting their presence in search engines. Best of all, Facebook easily integrates with other social media platforms, such as Twitter, which offer organizations a complete media link to consumers.

Employees within the same organization can build stronger relationships by friending each other. In some organizations, teams have even established Facebook groups to promote camaraderie and create a place to discuss project documents and other concerns.

Facebook users, however, need to be aware of the public nature of Facebook. In fact, poor judgment has cost some workers their jobs as a result of posting controversial updates about their employers or uploading inappropriate photos. For example, an Atlanta police officer was terminated after posting sensitive job information; Virgin Atlantic fired 13 crew members after they posted mean comments about passengers and spiteful opinions about the airline's safety standards.[12]

Twitter Twitter is a microblog that allows users to let their followers know what they're doing by posting tweets, short messages of 140 characters or less.

Twitter offers another way for organizations to create a following, share information, brand themselves, and even eavesdrop on what people say about their competitors. Organizations can follow what other people tweet about them and use the service to provide an additional form of customer service. For example, when a patron in a Fort Worth branch of Chipotle tweeted about the restaurant lacking corn tortillas, the corporate office called the manager before the customer even left the store.[13]

Similar to many restaurants and other organizations, Chipotle has service representatives dedicated to social media relations. With over 55 million tweets sent per day worldwide, it can be overwhelming for organizations to manage their image and plan appropriate 140-word responses.

As is true for all social media, Twitter users must be careful what they say. Tweets can be searched on Google and can be recalled in defamation lawsuits. Comedian Gilbert Gottfriend, the voice of the Aflac duck, got fired over insensitive tweets about the Japanese earthquake and tsunami. New York Congressman Anthony Weiner had to step down after sexual tweets were reported in the media. As a final note to make us all even more cautious, in 2010, the Library of Congress announced that it would archive all tweets.

LinkedIn LinkedIn allows professionals to connect with colleagues and other industry members. Over 100 million people use the site. Unlike Facebook or Twitter, which can easily blur the professional and personal line, LinkedIn profiles tend to remain strictly work oriented.

Professionals can use the site to network and earn recommendations from past and current clients. These referrals, in turn, could create more business opportunities. Employees can also join industry associations or alumni groups to expand their network of connections. LinkedIn Answers provides a forum for industry professionals to ask questions and share their expertise, which may also spark new clients. For job searches, LinkedIn allows users to search for new job opportunities, post a résumé, or recruit new employees.

Blogs Blogs allow businesses to connect with customers and clients in a more social way than they can on traditional websites. Internal corporate blogs allow managers and employees to share ideas and information.

Many public corporate blogs offer information relevant to their business; a catering service may offer food safety tips and recipes; a travel agency may offer travel tips and descriptions of exotic destinations. Other popular content includes employee stories, glimpses inside the business, insider business tips, and question-and-answer features.

Good blogs present their content in ways that inspire conversations and encourage readers to comment and then to share the information. The best blogs offer a unique perspective that enables them to stand out from the millions of other blogs on the Internet. While all blogs should be visually attractive, bloggers need to remember that many of their readers will have opted to turn off the visuals. Too many visuals will create an empty-looking blog.

Other Social Media Other new social media sites are on the rise. Here are a few that professionals have been quick to adapt to their business needs:

- Xing—Similar features as LinkedIn, but more popular in Europe and India.
- Google+—Google's version of Facebook containing many similar options.
- Ning—A site for users to create their own social networking site adapted to their business.
- NetParty—A site for professionals to connect online to meet up for happy hour and other after-work activities.
- Yammer—A Facebook–Twitter mashup tool exclusively for internal corporate communications.
- Sermo—Site dedicated exclusively to the medical profession; helps doctors solicit opinions, share information, and improve patient care.

Information about Your Medicine

Informing people about their medicines is not so simple. Hospitals annually treat 1.9 million people for medication problems; emergency rooms treat an addition 838,000. These figures for 2008, the latest available, are up 52% from 2004.

Part of the problem results from the growing complexity of medication regimes, particularly for the elderly and those with multiple, chronic conditions. These regimes are becoming so complex that even well-educated patients make mistakes.

Another group with special problems consists of patients with low literacy. In one study, only 34% of such patients could accurately demonstrate the precise number of pills they were to take, even after correctly repeating "take two twice a day."

These patients are not alone. Another study showed that more than half of adults misunderstood at least one of the common prescription warnings.

Experts are recommending language changes on medicine labels: "use only on your skin" to replace "for external use only," or "limit your time in the sun" to replace "avoid prolonged or excessive exposure to direct sunlight." They are also recommending new drug information sheets.

Adapted from Laura Landro, "'Use Only as Directed' Isn't Easy," *Wall Street Journal*, April 26, 2011, D1.

The realm of social media is expanding exponentially. Some systems are designed specifically for businesses, such as IBM's BluePages, where 26,000 employees have blogs on which they post opinions about their work and technology in general. More than 100,000 employees work on 20,000 wikis.[14] On the site PatientsLikeMe, consenting participants provide detailed medical histories and discuss side effects of prescribed drugs they're taking. The company then packages this information and sells it to drug and insurance companies, a knowledge transfer which participants believe will help find cures faster. The site can also be used by pharmaceutical companies to invite clinical trial subjects, helping speed up research.[15]

Another way that businesses are trying to reach customers is through **widgets,** tiny software programs that can be dragged, dropped, and embedded into social media sites. Widgets are changing the way people use the Internet. In the past, people surfed from page to page, but now widgets can bring the power of all those pages into a central location, like a social networking site.

Of course, like all technological tools, social media sites have some drawbacks. If workers spend much of their day immersed in social media, how much of their regular work routine is not being completed? A survey of 1,400 large U.S. companies reported that more than half prohibit social media use.[16] However, how do organizations differentiate between social media use for professional and personal purposes, especially when some employees have a single account? A final thought about social media: once workers post information about themselves, electronic copies of that information are stored indefinitely.

E-Mails, Letters, and Paper Memos

When people think of business communications, many think of e-mails, letters, and paper memos. Letters go to someone outside your organization; paper memos go to someone in your organization; e-mails can go anywhere. Today most memos are sent as e-mails rather than paper documents.

E-mails, letters, and memos use different formats. The most common formats are illustrated in Appendix A. The simplified letter format is very similar to memo format: it uses a subject line and omits the salutation and the complimentary close. Thus, it is a good choice when you don't know the reader's name.

E-mails, instant and text messages, telephone calls, social media entries, and web searches can all be tracked by your employer and used in lawsuits. You should always observe professional practices while in the workplace.

The differences in audience and format are the only differences among these documents. All of these messages can be long or short, depending on how much you have to say and how complicated the situation is. All of these messages can be informal when you write to someone you know well, or more formal when you write to someone you don't know, to several audiences, or for the record. All of these messages can be simple responses that you can dash off in minutes; they can also take hours of analysis and revision when you're facing a new situation or when the stakes are high.

E-mails are commonly used for these purposes:

- To accomplish routine, noncontroversial business activities (setting up meetings/appointments, reminders, notices, quick updates, information sharing).
- To save time: many people can look through 60–100 e-mails an hour.
- To save money: one e-mail can go to many people, including global teams.
- To allow readers to deal with messages at their convenience, when timing is not crucial.
- To communicate accurately.
- To provide readers with details for reference (meetings).
- To create a paper trail.

E-mails do not work well for some purposes. Negative critiques and bad news generally have better outcomes when delivered in person. Sarcasm and irony are too frequently misinterpreted to be safely used. Similarly, avoid passing on gossip in your e-mails. The chances of having your gossip forwarded with your name attached are just too great.

Salutations for e-mails are in a state of transition. *Dear* is saved mostly for formal e-mails; *Hey* is generally considered too informal for business use. Many writers are now starting their e-mails with *Hi* or *Hello* (e.g., "Hi Udi,"). And when e-mailing people with whom they are in constant contact, many writers use no salutation at all.

Many people read their e-mails quickly. They may read for only a few seconds or lines to decide if the e-mail is pertinent. Value your readers' time by designing your e-mail to help them:

- Put the most important information in the first sentence.
- If your e-mail is more than one screen long, use an overview, headings, and enumeration to help draw readers to successive screens.
- Limit your e-mail to one topic. Delete off-topic material.

Another factor in e-mail miscommunication is the lack of nonverbal cues. Many of the billions of e-mails sent daily contain intentional and unintentional emotions that can cause misinterpretation of information. One study showing this misinterpretation found that study participants believed they could accurately convey emotions in e-mail but doubted the abilities of their co-workers to do so.[17]

Remember that e-mails are public documents and may be widely forwarded. Save lowercase and instant message abbreviations for friends, if you use them at all. Even a quick confirmation to your boss should look professional.

E-Mail Pet Peeves

- Missing or vague subject lines.
- Copying everyone rather than just the people that might find the information useful/interesting.
- Too much information/too little information.
- Too many instant messaging acronyms.
- Lack of capitalization and punctuation.
- Long messages without headings or bullets.
- Delayed response e-mails that don't include the original message. Sometimes readers have no idea what the e-mails are responding about.
- Writers who send a general request to multiple people, creating confusion about who is responsible for handling the request.
- People who expect an immediate answer.
- People who never respond to queries.
- People who don't read their e-mail carefully enough to absorb a simple message.
- People who send too many unimportant e-mails.
- Superfluous images and attachments.
- Flaming.

Not this:

> that time should work. bring the donuts and coffee!!! i'm hungry!
> CU L8r

But this:

> 3 works for me, too. I'll bring copies of the Wolford schedule. See you there.

Never put anything in an e-mail that would embarrass you or harm your career if your employer, colleague, parent, or child saw it. Examples abound of public and corporate officials forced to resign because of misbehaviors documented in e-mails they sent to others. But the senders don't have to be officials to cause the organization trouble.

- An employee e-mail arranging for a group to leave work early and go drinking at a topless bar was used as evidence of poor oversight in a product-contamination lawsuit against the company.[18]
- An American employee responded to a request for floor mats from an American GI in Iraq by saying "We would NEVER ship to Iraq. If you were sensible, you and your troops would pull out of Iraq." The e-mail quickly circulated on the Internet, getting the employee fired and the business boycotted.[19]
- Leaked e-mails from the Climate Research Unit at East Anglia University, UK, showing bias and exclusion not only created a furor for that research group, but also called into question all research on global warming.

A survey by the American Management Association found that over a quarter of companies have fired employees for e-mail misuse.[20] And of course WikiLeaks has reminded everyone of the dangers hiding in even supposedly secure e-mails.

ORGANIZING INFORMATIVE AND POSITIVE MESSAGES LO 9-3

The patterns of organization in this chapter and others follow standard conventions of business. The patterns will work for many of the writing situations most people in business, nonprofits, and government face. Using the appropriate pattern can help you compose more quickly, create a better final product, and demonstrate you know the conventions.

WARNING: The patterns should never be used blindly. You must always consider whether your audience, purpose, and context would be better served with a different organization.

If you decide to use a pattern:

- Be sure you understand the rationale behind each pattern so that you can modify the pattern when necessary.
- Realize not every message that uses the basic pattern will have all the elements listed.
- Realize sometimes you can present several elements in one paragraph; sometimes you'll need several paragraphs for just one element.

Figure 9.1 shows how to organize informative and positive messages. Figures 9.2 and 9.3 illustrate two ways that the basic pattern can be applied.

Figure 9.1 How to Organize Informative and Positive Messages

1. **Start with good news or the most important information.** Summarize the main points. If the audience has already raised the issue, make it clear that you're responding.
2. **Give details, clarification, background.** Answer all the questions your audience is likely to have; provide all the information necessary to achieve your purposes. If you are asking or answering multiple questions, number them. Enumeration increases your chances of giving or receiving all the necessary information. Present details in the order of importance to the reader or in some other logical order.
3. **Present any negative elements—as positively as possible.** A policy may have limits; information may be incomplete; the audience may have to satisfy requirements to get a discount or benefit. Make these negatives clear, but present them as positively as possible.
4. **Explain any benefits.** Most informative messages need benefits. Show that the policy or procedure helps your audience, not just the company. Give enough detail to make the benefits clear and convincing. In letters, you may want to give benefits of dealing with your company as well as benefits of the product or policy.
   In a good news message, it's often possible to combine a short benefit with a goodwill ending.
5. **Use a goodwill ending: positive, personal, and forward-looking.** Shifting your emphasis away from the message to the specific audience suggests that serving the audience is your real concern.

Use To/CC/BCC Lines to Your Advantage

To

Send your e-mail only to people who will really want or need it. If you are sending to multiple people, decide in which order to place the names. Is organizational rank important? Should you alphabetize the list? Don't hit "reply to all" unless all will appreciate your doing so.

CC

CC stands for "carbon copy," from the days of typewriters when carbon paper was used to make multiple copies. CC people who are not directly involved in the business of the e-mail but are interested in it. Marketing may not be helping you produce your new software, but they may want to stay abreast of the changes so they can start generating marketing ideas. A committee might CC a secretary who does not attend committee meetings but does maintain the committee's paper records.

Sometimes the CC line is used politically. For example, an administrative assistant doing routine business may CC the boss to give added weight to the e-mail.

BCC

BCC stands for "blind carbon copy," a copy that the listed receivers do not know is being sent. Blind copies can create ill will when they become known, so be careful in their use.

The letter in Figure 9.2 announces a change in a magazine's ownership. Rather than telling subscribers that their magazine has been acquired, which sounds negative, the first two paragraphs describe the change as a merger that will give subscribers greater benefits from the combined magazine. Paragraph 3 provides details about how the arrangement will work, along with a way to opt out. A possible negative is that readers who already have subscriptions to both magazines will now receive only one. The company addresses this situation positively by extending the subscription to the jointly published magazine. The goodwill ending has all the desired characteristics: it is positive ("we're confident"), personal ("your continued loyalty"), and forward-looking ("you will enjoy").

The memo in Figure 9.3 announces a new employee benefit. The first paragraph summarizes the new benefits. Paragraphs 2–3 give details. Negative elements are stated as positively as possible. The last section of the memo gives benefits and a goodwill ending.

SUBJECT LINES FOR INFORMATIVE AND POSITIVE MESSAGES

A **subject line** is the title of a document. It aids in filing and retrieving the document, tells readers why they need to read the document, and provides a framework in which to set what you're about to say. Subject lines are standard in memos and e-mails. Letters are not required to have subject lines (see Appendix A, Formats for Letters, Memos, and E-Mail Messages).

A good subject line meets three criteria: it is specific, concise, and appropriate to the kind of message (positive, negative, persuasive).

Making Subject Lines Specific

The subject line needs to be specific enough to differentiate its message from others on the same subject, but broad enough to cover everything in the message.

Too general: Training Sessions

Better: Dates for 2012 Training Sessions

Figure 9.2 A Positive Letter

eBusCompanyToday

P.O. Box 12345
Tampa, FL 33660
813-555-5555

June 17, 2012

Dear Ms. Locker:

Main point presented as good news

We're excited to share some great news! *eBusCompanyToday* has merged with another business magazine, *High-Tech Business News*. This merged publication will be called *High-Tech Business News* and will continue to be edited and published by the *eBusCompanyToday* staff.

Details focus on benefits to the reader

The "new" *High-Tech Business News* is a great tool for navigating today's relentlessly changing marketplace, particularly as it's driven by the Internet and other technologies. It reports on the most innovative business practices and the people behind them; delivers surprising, useful insights; and explains how to put them to work. Please be assured that you will continue to receive the same great editorial coverage that you've come to expect from *eBusCompanyToday*.

You will receive the "new" *High-Tech Business News* in about 4 weeks, starting with the combined August/September issue. If you already subscribe to *High-Tech Business News*, your subscription will be extended accordingly. And if you'd rather not receive this publication, please call 1-800-555-5555 within the next 3 weeks.

Option to cancel is offered but not emphasized

Positive, personal, forward-looking ending

Thank you for your continued loyalty to *eBusCompanyToday*; we're confident that you will enjoy reading *High-Tech Business News* every month.

Sincerely,

Alan Schmidt

Alan Schmidt, Editor and President

High-Tech Business News is published monthly except for two issues combined periodically into one and occasional extra, expanded or premium issues.

Figure 9.3 A Positive Memo, Sent to Chamber of Commerce Employees and Members

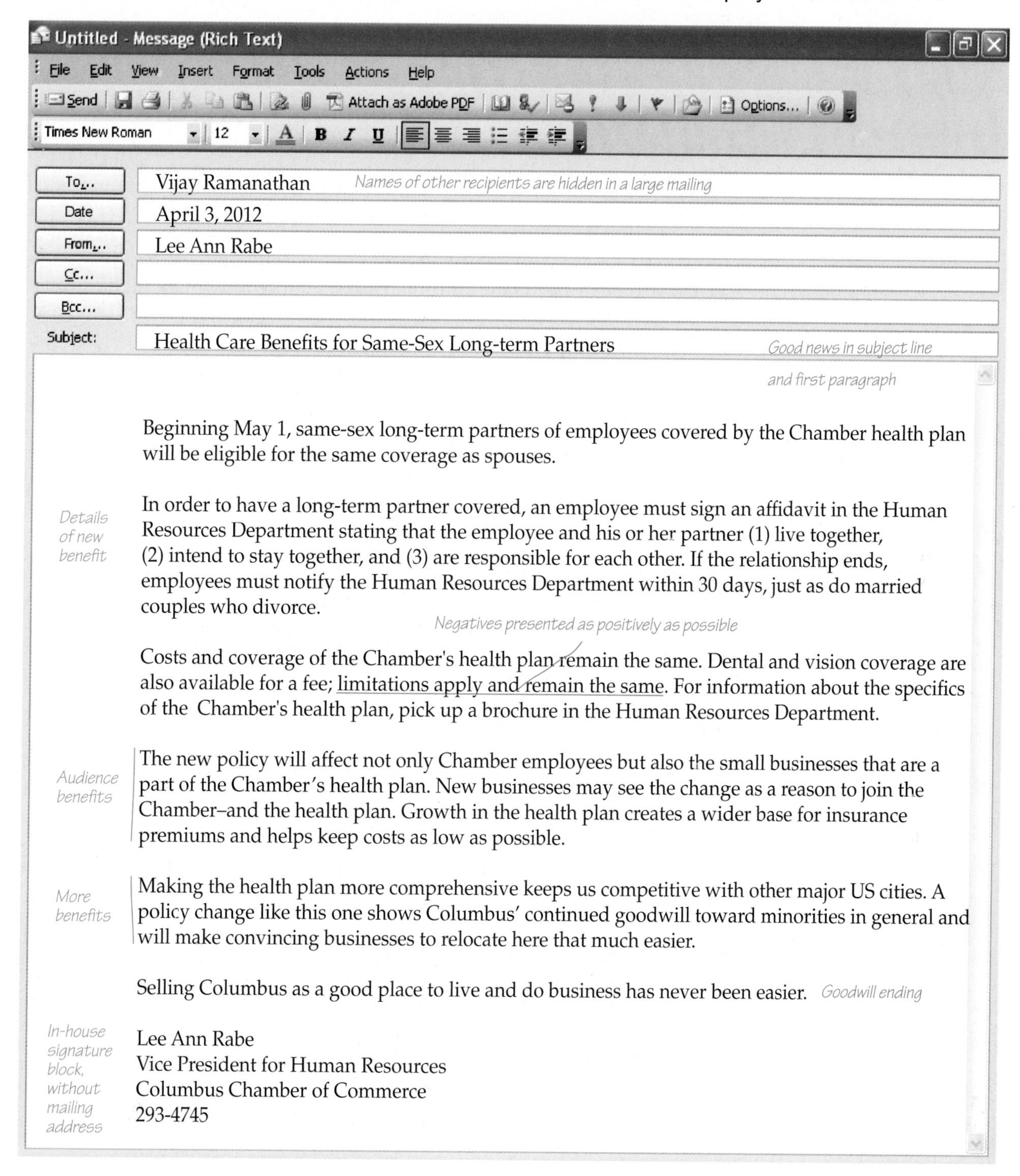

Making Subject Lines Concise

Most subject lines are relatively short. MailerMailer, a web-based e-mail management service, found that e-mails whose subject lines were 35 characters or fewer were significantly more likely to be opened by readers than subject lines with more than 35 characters.[21]

Wordy: Student Preferences in Regards to Various Pizza Factors

Better: Students' Pizza Preferences

If you can't make the subject both specific and short, be specific.

Making Subject Lines Appropriate for the Pattern of Organization

Since your subject line introduces your reader to your message, it must satisfy the psychological demands of the situation; it must be appropriate to your purposes and to the immediate response you expect from your reader. In general, do the same thing in your subject line that you would do in the first paragraph.

When you have good news for the reader, build goodwill by highlighting it in the subject line. When your information is neutral, summarize it concisely for the subject line.

Subject: Discount on Rental Cars Effective January 2

Starting January 2, as an employee of Amalgamated Industries you can get a 15% discount on cars you rent for business or personal use from Roadway Rent-a-Car.

Subject: Update on Arrangements for Videoconference with France

In the last month, we have chosen the participants and developed a tentative agenda for the videoconference with France scheduled for March 21.

Pointers for E-Mail Subject Lines

Many people skim through large lists of e-mails daily, so subject lines in e-mails are even more important than those in letters and memos. Subject lines must be specific, concise, and catchy. In these days of spam, some e-mail users get so many messages that they don't bother reading messages if they don't recognize the sender or if the subject doesn't catch their interest. Create a subject line that will help your e-mail get read:

- Use important information in the subject line. Many people delete blanks and generic tags such as "hello," "your message," "thank you," and "next meeting," if they don't recognize the sender, especially now that so much spam has common business tags.
- Put good news in the subject line.
- Name drop to make a connection: Lee Pizer gave me your name.
- Make e-mail sound easy to deal with: Two Short Travel Questions.

The following subject lines would be acceptable for informative and good news e-mail messages:

Travel Plans for Sales Meeting
Your Proposal Accepted
Reduced Prices during February
Your Funding Request Approved

Do not use indefinite dates such as Today, Tomorrow, Next Week, or even Wednesday, as subject lines. They are no longer clear if read at a later time.

When you reply to a message, check to see that the automatic subject line "Re: [subject line of message to which you are responding]" is still appropriate. If it isn't, you may want to create a new subject line. And if a series of messages arises, you probably need a new subject line. "Re: Re: Re: Re: Question" is not an effective subject line.

MANAGING THE INFORMATION IN YOUR MESSAGES

Information control is important. You want to give your audience the information they need, but you don't want to overwhelm them with information. Sometimes you will have good reasons for not providing all the information they want.

When you are the person in the know, it is easy to overestimate how much your audience knows. As a patient seeking medical treatment, you understand how much you would appreciate being told how long the wait is. When you leave a medical facility, you know how difficult it is to remember accurately those complicated instructions given to you orally by a doctor or nurse. Unfortunately, most of the huge medical industry seems to be just discovering these facts now. Medical offices are beginning to communicate waiting times and send patients home with written instructions for self-care and follow-up visits.

But, of course, information management is not always that simple. Pharmaceutical companies struggle with how much information to provide about their drugs. In 2004, the FDA publicized an analysis showing that young people on antidepressants had a 2% risk of suicidal thoughts. There were no actual suicides reported in the studies, just suicidal thoughts. Nevertheless, the FDA put a Black Box warning—the strongest possible warning—on antidepressants. Parents and physicians began backing away from the medications. Use of SSRI (selective serotonin reuptake inhibitors) medications in young people declined 14%, and suicides increased 18% among young people the first year of the warnings.[22]

Sometimes pharmaceutical companies, and other organizations, get in trouble because their information management withholds information that others—shareholders, regulators, customers, etc.—believe should be revealed. Glaxo-SmithKline was sued by shareholders and patients for not fully disclosing the risks of its diabetes drug Avandia. Merck faced similar lawsuits for its painkiller Vioxx. Both drugs were linked to an increased risk of heart attacks.[23] In a different venue, responding to donor desires for more transparency about how charities spend their money, the IRS revised the charities' annual tax form to require more information. This form must be made available on request.[24]

Other concerns about managing information are more prosaic.

- If you send out regularly scheduled messages on the same topic, such as monthly updates of training seminars, try to develop a system that lets people know immediately what is new. Use color for new or changed entries. Put new material at the top.

Goldman Sachs' Communication Policies

These are some statements from Goldman Sachs' communication policies:

- "It is the policy of the firm to make no comment on rumors whatsoever, even to deny rumors you believe to be untrue."
- "Prior to recommending that a customer purchase, sell or exchange any security, salespeople must have reasonable grounds for believing that the recommendation is suitable."
- "Firm employees frequently provide so-called 'trade ideas' to multiple recipients. Such trade ideas are designed to help clients take advantage of market conditions and intelligence, but are not intended to be specific buy/sell recommendations."
- "All sales correspondence from or to employees working from home offices must be routed through regional offices for purposes of review, approval, distribution and retention."
- "Casual correspondence, thank you notes, confirmations or schedules for meetings, invitations, and other correspondence that does not relate to business does not require approval."
- "Each individual's correspondence must be sampled no less often than annually."
- "'To All' memos . . . must be approved as described . . . in the Employee Handbook."

Quoted from Max Abelson and Caroline Winter, "The Goldman Rules," *Bloomberg Businessweek*, April 25, 2011, 90–91.

- If you are answering multiple questions, use numbers.
- If your e-mail is long (more than one screen), use overviews, headings, and bullets so readers can find the information they need.
- If you are asking people to complete processes involving multiple steps or complicated knowledge, use checklists. Once maligned as too elementary, checklists are being recognized as a major tool to prevent errors. Atul Gawande has popularized the trend with his book, *The Checklist Manifesto: How to Get Things Right*, showing how checklists are used in fields as diverse as aviation, construction, and medicine to eliminate mistakes.
- If you send messages with an attachment, put the most vital information in the e-mail too. Don't make readers open an attachment merely to find out the time or location of a meeting.

Check your message for accuracy and completeness. Remember all the e-mails you receive about meetings that forget to include the time, place, or date, and don't let your e-mails fall in that incomplete category. Make a special effort to ensure that promised attachments really are attached. Be particularly careful with the last messages you send for the day or the week, when haste can cause errors.

USING BENEFITS IN INFORMATIVE AND POSITIVE MESSAGES

Not all informative and positive messages need benefits. You don't need benefits when

- Presenting factual information only.
- The audience's attitude toward the information doesn't matter.
- Stressing benefits may make the audience sound selfish.
- The benefits are so obvious that to restate them insults the audience's intelligence.

You do need benefits when

- Presenting policies.
- Shaping your audience's attitudes toward the information or toward your organization.
- Stressing benefits presents the audience's motives positively.
- Some of the benefits may not be obvious.

Benefits are hardest to develop when you are announcing policies. The organization probably decided to adopt the policy because it appeared to help the organization; the people who made the decision may not have thought at all about whether it would help or hurt employees. Yet benefits are most essential in this kind of message so employees see the reason for the change and support it.

When you present benefits, be sure to present advantages *to the audience.* Most new policies help the organization in some way, but few workers will see their own interests as identical with those of the organization. Employees' benefits need to be spelled out, as do those of customers. To save money, an organization may change health care providers, but the notice to employees should spell out new benefits for employees and their families. Airlines announced their new check-in kiosks to customers as a way to avoid lines and save travelers' time.

To develop benefits for informative and positive messages, use the steps suggested in Chapter 2. Be sure to think about benefits that come from the activity or policy itself, in addition to any financial benefits. Does a policy improve customers' experience or the hours employees spend at work?

Wacky Warning Contest Winners

M-LAW (Michigan Lawsuit Abuse Watch) posts these winners:

- "Do not iron while wearing shirt" (on iron-on T-shirt transfer).
- "Caution: Safety goggles recommended" (on letter opener).
- "Do not put any person in this washer" (on clothes washer).
- "Never use a lit match or open flame to check fuel level" (instructions for a personal water craft).
- "Harmful if swallowed" (on a fishing lure with a three-pronged hook).
- "If you do not understand, or cannot read, all directions, cautions and warnings, do not use this product" (on bottle of drain cleaner).
- "This product not intended for use as a dental drill" (on electric drill for carpenters).
- "Remove child before folding" (on baby stroller).

Adapted from "M-LAW's Wacky Warning Labels: 11th Annual Wacky Warning Label Contest Winners," Michigan Lawsuit Abuse Watch, accessed June 7, 2011, http://www.mlaw.org/wwl/photos.html.

ENDING INFORMATIVE AND POSITIVE MESSAGES

Ending a letter or memo gracefully can be a problem in short informative and positive messages. In a one-page memo where you have omitted details and proof, you can tell readers where to get more information. In long messages, you can summarize your basic point. In a short message containing all the information readers need, either write a goodwill paragraph that refers directly to the reader or the reader's organization, or just stop. In many short e-mails, just stopping is the best choice.

Goodwill endings should focus on the business relationship you share with your reader rather than on the reader's hobbies, family, or personal life. Use a paragraph that shows you see your reader as an individual. Possibilities include complimenting the reader for a job well done, describing a benefit, or looking forward to something positive that relates to the subject of the message.

> Thank you so much for sending those two extra sales tables. They were just what I needed for Section IV of the report.

When you write to one person, a good last paragraph fits that person so specifically that it would not work if you sent the same basic message to someone else or even to a person with the same title in another organization. When you write to someone who represents an organization, the last paragraph can refer to your company's relationship to the reader's organization. When you write to a group (for example, to "All Employees"), your ending should apply to the whole group.

> Remember that the deadline for enrolling in this new benefit plan is January 31.

Some writers end every message with a standard invitation:

> If you have questions, please do not hesitate to ask.

That sentence implies both that your message did not answer all questions, and that readers will hesitate to contact you. Both implications are negative. But revising the line to say "feel free to call" is rarely a good idea. People in business aren't shrinking violets; they will call if they need help. Don't make more work for yourself by inviting calls to clarify simple messages. Simply omit this sentence.

HUMOR IN INFORMATIVE MESSAGES

Some writers use humor to ensure their messages are read. Humor is a risky tool because of its tendency to rile some people. However, if you know your audience well, humor may help ensure that they read and remember your messages.

If you decide to use humor, these precautions will help keep it useful.

- Do not direct it against other people, even if you are sure they will never see your message. The Internet abounds with proof that such certainties are false. In particular, never aim humor against a specific group of people.
- Political, religious, and sexual humor should always be avoided; it is against discrimination policies in many businesses.
- Use restraint with your humor; a little levity goes a long way.

Used with care, however, humor in carefully chosen situations can help your communications. An information technology person sent the following e-mail in his small, nonprofit organization:[25]

> My set of screw driver tips is missing. I may well have loaned them to someone, perhaps weeks ago. If you have them, please return them to me. I use them when someone reports that they have a screw loose.

He got his tips back promptly. Because he has a reputation for clever e-mails, people regularly read his messages.

Information for Healthy Eating

To help consumers make better choices in the grocery store and fight the alarming rates of obesity in the country, some supermarket chains are creating informational signage displayed near healthy foods. These signs help consumers quickly understand that the products have met federal guidelines. They also help simplify choices between similar products.

Stop & Shop and Giant Food have introduced the "Healthy Ideas" system, which provides labels on over 3,000 nutritious foods sold in their stores. Similarly, Price Chopper and HyVee supermarkets started the "NuVal" system, which rates the nutritional value of foods on a scale of 1 to 100. Another system, the "Guiding Stars," has been used in Hannaford Bros. supermarkets since 2006. This system gives stars to foods in three categories: good, better, and best.

Adapted from: Timothy W. Martin, "Grocers Launch Labels to Identify Healthy Foods," *Wall Street Journal*, January 2, 2009, A4.

Signs with information about nutritional content of food help consumers make healthier choices.

VARIETIES OF INFORMATIVE AND POSITIVE MESSAGES LO 9-4

Many messages can be informative, negative, or persuasive depending on what you have to say. A transmittal, for example, can be positive when you're sending glowing sales figures or persuasive when you want the reader to act on the information. A performance appraisal is positive when you evaluate someone who's doing superbly, negative when you want to compile a record to justify firing someone, and persuasive when you want to motivate a satisfactory worker to continue to improve. Each of these messages is discussed in the chapter of the pattern it uses most frequently. However, in some cases you will need to use a pattern from a different chapter.

Transmittals

When you send someone something, you frequently need to attach a memo or letter of transmittal explaining what you're sending. A transmittal can be as simple as a small yellow Post-it™ note with "FYI" ("for your information") written on it, or it can be a separate typed document.

Organize a memo or letter of transmittal in this order:

1. Tell the reader what you're sending.
2. Summarize the main point(s) of the document.
3. Indicate any special circumstances or information that would help the reader understand the document. Is it a draft? Is it a partial document that will be completed later?
4. Tell the reader what will happen next. Will you do something? Do you want a response? If you do want the reader to act, specify exactly what you want the reader to do and give a deadline.

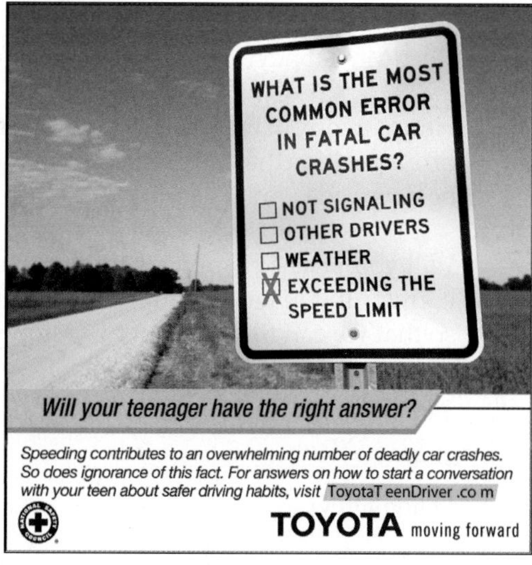

Toyota conducted an ad campaign to encourage safe driving among teenagers, who hold the highest rate for being in an accident. In the ads, Toyota attempted to inform the public about safety issues of driving recklessly, while also appealing to the viewers' emotions.

Source: Toyota Advertisements, *Wall Street Journal,* October 4, 2006, A1, and September 27, 2006, A1.

Frequently transmittals have important secondary purposes. Consider the writer's purpose in Figure 9.4, a transmittal from a lawyer to her client. The primary purpose of this transmittal is to give the client a chance to affirm that his story and the lawyer's understanding of it are correct. If there's anything wrong, the lawyer wants to know *before* she files the brief. But an important secondary purpose is to build goodwill: "I'm working on your case; I'm earning my fee." The greatest number of complaints officially lodged against lawyers are for the lawyer's neglect—or what the client perceives as neglect—of the client's case.

Summaries

You may be asked to summarize a conversation, a document, or an outside meeting for colleagues or superiors. (Minutes of an internal meeting are usually more detailed. See Chapter 8 for advice on writing minutes of meetings.)

Figure 9.4 A Transmittal

DREW & Associates

100 Barkley Plaza • Denver, CO 80210 • 303.555.4783 • Fax 303.555.4784

October 8, 2012

Mr. Charles Gibney
Personnel Manager
Roydon Interiors
146 East State Street
Denver, CO 80202

Dear Mr. Gibney:

Paragraph one tells reader what is enclosed and summarizes main points.

Here is a copy of the brief we intend to file with the Tenth Circuit Court in support of our position that the sex discrimination charge against Roydon Interiors should be dropped.

Will you please examine it carefully to make sure that the facts it contains are correct? If you have changes to suggest, please call my office by October 22nd, so that we can file the brief by October 24th.

Last paragraph asks for action by a specific date.

Sincerely,

Diana Drew

Diana Drew

In a summary of a conversation for internal use, identify the people who were present, the topic of discussion, decisions made, and who does what next.

To summarize a document, start with the main point. Then go on to give supporting evidence or details. In some cases, your audience may also want you to evaluate the document. Should others in the company read this report? Should someone in the company write a letter to the editor responding to this newspaper article?

When you visit a client or go to a conference, you may be asked to share your findings and impressions with other people in your organization. Chronological accounts are the easiest to write but the least useful for the reader. Your company doesn't need a blow-by-blow account of what you did; it needs to know what *it* should do as a result of the meeting.

Summarize a visit with a client or customer in this way:

1. Put the main point from your organization's point of view—the action to be taken, the perceptions to be changed—in the first paragraph.
2. Provide an **umbrella paragraph** to cover and foreshadow the points you will make in the report.
3. Provide necessary detail to support your conclusions and cover each point. Use lists and headings to make the structure of the document clear.

In the following example, the revised first paragraph summarizes the sales representative's conclusions after a call on a prospective client:

Weak original:

> On October 10th, Rick Patel and I made a joint call on Consolidated Tool Works. The discussion was held in a conference room, with the following people present:
>
> 1. Kyle McCloskey (Vice President and General Manager)
> 2. Bill Petrakis (Manufacturing Engineer)
> 3. Garett Lee (Process Engineering Supervisor)
> 4. Courtney Mansor-Green (Project Engineer)

Improved revision:

> Consolidated Tool Works is an excellent prospect for purchasing a Matrix-Churchill grinding machine. To get the order, we should
>
> 1. Set up a visit for CTW personnel to see the Matrix-Churchill machine in Kansas City;
> 2. Guarantee 60-day delivery if the order is placed by the end of the quarter; and
> 3. Extend credit terms to CTW.

Compliment Carefully

Compliments can be valuable for building goodwill in informative messages. But too often they offer backhanded compliments. Consider these examples:

- "That dress looks better on you every year."
- "You short people sure are intelligent."
- "You must have been really pretty when you were young."

If you decide to use a compliment in your message, proceed carefully. Make sure you are being sincere and specific and that your compliment can't be misunderstood. You should also limit your compliments to those that will be most significant to your reader. Using compliments correctly can help you build goodwill and good relationships with others.

Adapted from Elizabeth Bernstein, "Why Do Compliments Cause So Much Grief?" *Wall Street Journal*, May 4, 2010, D1.

Thank-You and Positive Feedback Notes

We all like to feel appreciated. Praising or congratulating people can cement good feelings between you and them and enhance your own visibility.

> Congratulations, Sam, on winning the Miller sales award. I bet winning that huge Lawson contract didn't hurt any!

Make your praise sound sincere by offering specifics and avoiding language that might seem condescending or patronizing. For example, think how silly it would sound to praise an employee for completing basic job requirements

Dear Professor Carlton,

Thank you for all your help this semester. My writing skills have improved greatly as have my organizational skills. The extra time you gave me really paid off. I've already had three job interviews due to the job packet I prepared for your course. I will miss your funny dog stories!!! Thanks again for everything!

Pat Robbins

Thank-you notes can be written on standard business stationery, using standard formats. But one student noticed that his professor really liked dogs and told funny dog stories in class. So the student found a dog card for a thank-you note.

or to gush that one's mentor has superior knowledge. In contrast, thanks for a kind deed and congratulations or praise on completing a difficult task are rewarding in almost any situation.

Sending a **thank-you note** will make people more willing to help you again in the future. Thank-you letters can be short but must be prompt. They need to be specific to sound sincere.

> Chris, thank you for the extra-short turnaround time. You were a major reason we made the deadline.

Most thank-you notes are e-mails now, so handwritten ones stand out.

If you make it a habit to watch for opportunities to offer thanks and congratulations, you may be pleasantly surprised at the number of people who are extending themselves. During his six-year term, Douglas Conant, Chief Executive of Campbell, sent over 16,000 handwritten thank-you notes to employees ranging from top executives to hourly workers. Linden Labs has a "Love Machine" that allows employees to send other employees a note of thanks. These notes are tracked in a database, which is accessed during performance reviews.[26] As Kenneth Blanchard and Spencer Johnson, authors of the business best seller *The One Minute Manager*, note, "People who feel good about themselves produce good results."[27]

Hey Manager! Are You Getting the Employee Input You Need?

Probably not, according to research reported in the *Harvard Business Review.* Even employees who do speak up sometimes frequently have issues on which they keep silent.

The most common reason for holding back is a sense of futility, not fear of retribution. This is especially true for routine problems and opportunities.

And even that fear deterrent may not be just what you think. You may think it applies only to serious problems: allegations about illegal or unethical activities. But it too, like the sense of futility, applies to routine problems and opportunities. Silence on these day-to-day issues prevents action to avoid larger problems in the future.

When you become a manager, what steps will you take to promote effective communication to and from your employees?

Adapted from James R. Deter, Ethan R Burris, and David A Harrison, "Debunking Four Myths about Employee Silence," *Harvard Business Review* 88, no.6 (June 2010): 26.

Positive Responses to Complaints

Complaining customers expect organizations to show that they are listening and want to resolve the problem. When you grant a customer's request for an adjusted price, discount, replacement, or other benefit to resolve a complaint, do so in the very first sentence.

> Your Visa bill for a night's lodging has been adjusted to $163. Next month a credit of $37 will appear on your bill to reimburse you for the extra amount you were originally asked to pay.

Don't talk about your own process in making the decision. Don't say anything that sounds grudging. Give the reason for the original mistake only if it reflects credit on the company. (In most cases, it doesn't, so the reason should be omitted.)

SOLVING A SAMPLE PROBLEM

Workplace problems are richer and less well defined than textbook problems and cases. But even textbook problems require analysis before you begin to write. Before you tackle the assignments for this chapter, examine the following problem. See how the analysis questions from Chapter 1 probe the basic points required for a solution. Study the two sample solutions to see what makes one unacceptable and the other one good. Note the recommendations for revision that could make the good solution excellent. The checklist at the end of the chapter can help you evaluate a draft.

Problem

At Interstate Fidelity Insurance (IFI) there is often a time lag between receiving a payment from a customer and recording it on the computer. Sometimes, while the payment is in line to be processed, the computer sends out additional notices: past-due notices or collection letters. Customers are frightened or angry and write or call asking for an explanation. In most cases, if they just waited a little while, the situation would be straightened out. But policyholders are afraid that they'll be without insurance because the company thinks the bill has not been paid.

IFI doesn't have the time to check each individual situation to see if the check did arrive and has been processed. It wants you to write a letter that will persuade customers to wait. If something is wrong and the payment never reached IFI, IFI would send a legal notice to that effect saying the policy would be canceled by a certain date (which the notice would specify) at least 30 days after the date on the original premium bill. Continuing customers always get this legal notice as a third chance (after the original bill and the past-due notice).

Prepare a form letter that can go out to every policyholder who claims to have paid a premium for automobile insurance and resents getting a past-due notice. The letter should reassure readers and build goodwill for IFI.

I Agreed to What?

Every piece of software or app installed on a computer or smartphone comes with an End User License Agreement (EULA) that acts as a contract between the user and the company. But these long statements, written in heavy legalese, sometimes ask users to agree to odd conditions.

One agreement placed online in April 2010 by the British online store Gamestation says, "By placing an order via this Web site, you agree to grant us a non-transferable option to claim, for now and forever more, your immortal soul." Proving that most do not read these agreements, more than 7,500 people agreed to the terms in only one day.

Adapted from Eric Felten, "Video Game Tort: You Made Me Play You," *Wall Street Journal,* September 3, 2010, W17.

Analysis of the Problem

1. Who is (are) your audience(s)?

   Automobile insurance customers who say they've paid but have still received a past-due notice. They're afraid they're no longer insured. Since it's a form letter, different readers will have different situations: in some cases payments did arrive late, in some cases the company made a mistake, in some the reader never paid (check was lost in mail, unsigned, bounced, etc.).

2. What are your purposes in writing?

   To reassure readers that they're covered for 30 days. To inform them that they can assume everything is OK *unless* they receive a second notice. To avoid further correspondence on this subject. To build goodwill for IFI: (a) we don't want to suggest IFI is error-prone or too cheap to hire enough people to do the necessary work; (b) we don't want readers to switch companies; (c) we do want readers to buy from IFI when they're ready for more insurance.

3. What information must your message include?

   Readers are still insured. We cannot say whether their checks have now been processed (company doesn't want to check individual accounts). Their insurance will be canceled if they do not pay after receiving the second past-due notice (the legal notice).

4. How can you build support for your position? What reasons or benefits will your audience find convincing?

   We provide personal service to policyholders. We offer policies to meet all their needs. Both of these points would need specifics to be interesting and convincing.

5. What aspects of the total situation may affect audience response? The economy? The time of year? Morale in the organization? The relationship between the communicator and audience? Any special circumstances?

   The insurance business is highly competitive—other companies offer similar rates and policies. The customer could get a similar policy for about the same money from someone else. The economy is making money tight, so customers will want to keep insurance costs low. Yet the fact that prices are steady or rising means that the value of what they own is higher—they need insurance more than ever.

   Many insurance companies are refusing to renew policies (car, liability, home). These refusals to renew have gotten lots of publicity, and many people have heard horror stories about companies and individuals whose insurance has been canceled or not renewed after a small number of claims. Readers don't feel very kindly toward insurance companies.

   People need car insurance. If they have an accident and aren't covered, they not only have to bear the costs of that accident alone but also (depending on state law) may need to place as much as $50,000 in a state escrow account to cover future accidents. They have a legitimate worry.

   We are slow in processing payments. We don't know if the checks have been processed. We will cancel policies if their checks don't arrive.

Discussion of the Sample Solutions

The solution in Figure 9.5 is unacceptable. The red marginal comments show problem spots. Since this is a form letter, we cannot tell customers we have their checks; in some cases, we may not. The letter is far too negative. The explanation in paragraph 2 makes IFI look irresponsible and uncaring. Paragraph 3 is far too negative. Paragraph 4 is too vague; there are no benefits; the ending sounds selfish. A major weakness with the solution is that it lifts phrases straight out of the problem; the writer does not seem to have thought about the problem or about the words he or she is using. Measuring the draft against the answers to the questions for analysis suggests that this writer should start over.

Figure 9.5 An Unacceptable Solution to the Sample Problem

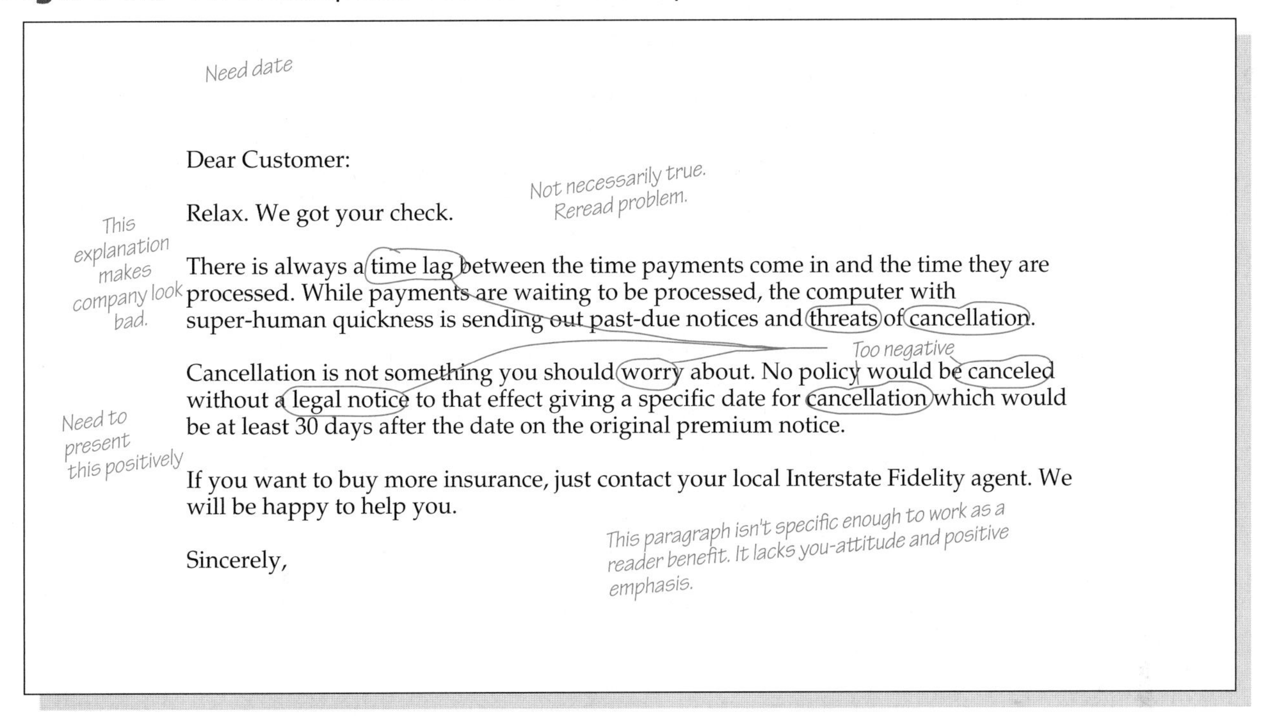

Dear Customer:

Relax. We got your check.

There is always a time lag between the time payments come in and the time they are processed. While payments are waiting to be processed, the computer with super-human quickness is sending out past-due notices and threats of cancellation.

Cancellation is not something you should worry about. No policy would be canceled without a legal notice to that effect giving a specific date for cancellation which would be at least 30 days after the date on the original premium notice.

If you want to buy more insurance, just contact your local Interstate Fidelity agent. We will be happy to help you.

Sincerely,

The solution in Figure 9.6 is much better. The blue marginal comments show the letter's good points. The message opens strongly with the good news that is true for all audiences. Paragraph 2 explains IFI's policy in more positive terms. The negative information is buried in paragraph 3 and is presented positively: the notice is information, not a threat; the 30-day extension is a "grace period." Telling the reader now what to do if a second notice arrives eliminates the need for a second exchange of letters. Paragraph 4 offers benefits for being insured by IFI. Paragraph 5 promotes other policies the company sells and prepares for the last paragraph.

As the red comments indicate, this good solution could be improved by personalizing the salutation and by including the name and number of the local agent. Computers could make both of those insertions easily. This good letter could be made excellent by revising paragraph 4 so that it doesn't end on a negative note and by using more benefits. For instance, can agents advise clients of the best policies for them? Does IFI offer good service—quick, friendly, nonpressured—that could be stressed? Are agents well trained? All of these might yield ideas for additional benefits.

You—A Most Important Subject

On the job, one of the most important subjects you can communicate about is your own performance. Make sure your boss knows what you are doing. You don't have to brag; simply noting your accomplishments is usually enough, because many employees do not take the time to do so.

Remember that raises are based not on the hard work you actually do, but the hard work your boss knows about. Furthermore, bosses count the work they want done, which is not always the work employees emphasize.

Provide your boss with paper copies of your work; CC him/her on major e-mails, if appropriate. Have 30-second blurbs ready for times when you and your boss are alone in the elevator or break room: "We got the McCluskey contract ready a day early" or "the new G7 database is going to IT tomorrow."

Checklist — Checklist for Informative and Positive Messages

- ☐ In positive messages, does the subject line give the good news? In either message, is the subject line specific enough to differentiate this message from others on the same subject?
- ☐ Does the first paragraph summarize the information or good news? If the information is too complex to fit into a single paragraph, does the paragraph list the basic parts of the policy or information in the order in which the memo discusses them?
- ☐ Is all the information given in the message? What information is needed will vary depending on the message, but information about dates, places, times, and anything related to money usually needs to be included. When in doubt, ask!
- ☐ In messages announcing policies, is there at least one benefit for each segment of the audience? Are all benefits ones that seem likely to occur in this organization?

- ☐ Is each benefit developed, showing that the benefit will come from the policy and why the benefit matters to this audience? Do the benefits build on the specific circumstances of the audience?
- ☐ Does the message end with a positive paragraph—preferably one that is specific to the readers, not a general one that could fit any organization or policy?

And, for all messages, not just informative and positive ones,

- ☐ Does the message use you-attitude and positive emphasis?
- ☐ Is the tone friendly?
- ☐ Is the style easy to read?
- ☐ Is the visual design of the message inviting?
- ☐ Is the format correct?
- ☐ Does the message use standard grammar? Is it free from typos?

Originality in a positive or informative message may come from

- ☐ Creating good headings, lists, and visual impact.
- ☐ Developing benefits.
- ☐ Thinking about audiences; giving details that answer their questions and make it easier for them to understand and follow the policy.

Figure 9.6 A Good Solution to the Sample Problem

Need date

Dear Customer: *Better: use computer to personalize. Put in name and address of a specific reader*

Your auto insurance is still in effect. *Good ¶ 1. True for all readers*

Past-due notices are mailed out if the payment has not been processed within three days after the due date. This may happen if a check is delayed in the mail or arrives without a signature or account number. When your check arrives with all the necessary information, it is promptly credited to your account. *Good you-attitude*

Good to treat notice as information, tell reader what to do if it arrives

Even if a check is lost in the mail and never reaches us, you still have a 30-day grace period. If you do get a second notice, you'll know that we still have not received your check. To keep your insurance in force, just stop payment on the first check and send a second one.

Benefits of using IFI

IFI is always checking to ensure that you get any discounts you're eligible for: multicar, accident-free record, good student. If you have a claim, your agent finds quality repair shops quickly, whatever car you drive. You get a check quickly—usually within 3 working days—without having to visit dealer after dealer for time-consuming estimates. *Too negative*

Better to put in agent's name, phone number

Need to add benefits of insuring with IFI

Today, your home and possessions are worth more than ever. You can protect them with Interstate Fidelity's homeowners' and renters' policies. Let your local agent show you how easy it is to give yourself full protection. If you need a special rider to insure a personal computer, jewelry, a coin or gun collection, or a fine antique, you can get that from IFI, too. *Good specifics*

Whatever your insurance needs—auto, home, life, or health—one call to IFI can do it all.

Sincerely, *Acceptable ending*

SUMMARY OF KEY POINTS

- Good communicators need to thoughtfully select one of the common modes of communications: face-to-face contact, phone calls, instant messages and text messaging, social media, letters, e-mails, and paper memos.
- Informative and positive messages normally use the following pattern of organization:
  1. Start with good news or the most important information; summarize the main points.
  2. Give details, clarification, background.
  3. Present any negative elements—as positively as possible.
  4. Explain any benefits.
  5. Use a goodwill ending: positive, personal, and forward-looking.
- A **subject line** is the title of a document. A good subject line meets three criteria: it's specific; it's reasonably short; and it's adapted to the kind of message (positive, negative, persuasive). If you can't make the subject both specific and short, be specific.
- The subject line for an informative or positive message should highlight any good news and summarize the information concisely.
- Good messages provide the necessary information without overwhelming their audience.
- Use benefits in informative and positive messages when you want to shape your audience's attitudes toward the information or toward your organization.
- **Goodwill endings** should focus on the business relationship you share with your audience or the audience's organization. The last paragraph of a message to a group should apply to the whole group.
- Humor is a risky tool. Use it carefully in written messages, and only when you and your audience know each other well.
- Use the analysis questions listed in Chapter 1 to probe the basic points needed for successful informative and positive messages.

CHAPTER 9 Exercises and Problems

Go to www.mhhe.com/locker10e for additional Exercises and Problems.

9.1 Reviewing the Chapter

1. What technological changes are occuring in business communication? (LO 9-1)
2. What are the multiple purposes of informative and good news messages? (LO 9-2)
3. How does information overload impact your communications? (LO 9-2)
4. When do you use face-to-face contacts? Phone calls? Instant messages? Text messaging? Social media? Letters? Memos and e-mails? (LO 9-2)
5. What are some tips for effectively using face-to-face contacts? Phone calls? Instant messages? Text messaging? Social media? Letters? Memos and e-mails? (LO 9-2)
6. How do you organize informative and positive messages? (LO 9-3)
7. What are some concerns to consider when choosing and ordering the information in your message? (LO 9-3)
8. What are tips for composing some of the common varieties of informative and positive messages? (LO 9-4)

9.2 Reviewing Grammar

Good letters and e-mails need correct grammar. Practice yours by doing the exercises from Appendix B on correcting sentence errors (B.8) and editing for grammar and usage (B.9).

9.3 Describing the Role of Technology Where You Work

Analyze the role of technology in an organization where you—or a friend or family member—have worked.

- What kinds of communication technology do you use most?
- What are some of the newest communication technologies introduced there?
- What kinds of technology upgrades do you wish would be made?
- Are certain kinds of technology used for certain situations? (for instance, are layoffs announced face-to-face or by e-mail?)
- What kinds of data security measures are in force?
- Has anyone there gotten in trouble for misuse of technology?

As your instructor directs,

a. Share your information in small groups.
b. Present your group findings to your classmates.
c. Post your information online for your classmates.

9.4 Saying Yes to a Subordinate—E-Mails for Discussion

Today, you get this request from a subordinate.

> Subject: Request for Leave
>
> You know that I've been feeling burned out. I've decided that I want to take a three-month leave of absence this summer to travel abroad. I've got five weeks of vacation time saved up; I would take the rest as unpaid leave. Just guarantee that my job will be waiting when I come back!

You decide to grant the request. The following messages are possible responses. How well does each message meet the criteria in the checklist for informative and positive messages?

1.
> Subject: Re: Request for Leave
>
> I highly recommend Italy. Spend a full week in Florence, if you can. Be sure to visit the Brancacci Chapel—it's been restored, and the frescoes are breathtaking. And I can give you the names of some great restaurants. You may never want to come back!

2.
> Subject: Your Request for Leave
>
> As you know, we are in a very competitive position right now. Your job is important, and there is no one who can easily replace you. However, because you are a valued employee, I will permit you to take the leave you request, as long as you train a replacement before you leave.

3.
> Subject: Your Request for Leave Granted
>
> Yes, you may take a three-month leave of absence next summer using your five weeks of accumulated vacation time and taking the rest as unpaid leave. And yes, your job will be waiting for you when you return!
>
> I'm appointing Garrick to take over your duties while you're gone. Talk with him to determine how much training time he'll need, and let me know when the training is scheduled.
>
> Have a great summer! Let us know every now and then how you're doing!

9.5 Introducing a Suggestion System—Memos for Discussion

Your organization has decided to institute a suggestion system. Employees on hourly pay scales will be asked to submit suggestions. (Managers and other employees on salary are not eligible for this program; they are supposed to be continually suggesting ways to improve things as part of their regular jobs.) If the evaluating committee thinks that the suggestion will save money, the employee will receive 10% of the first year's estimated annual savings. If the suggestion won't save money but will improve work conditions, service, or morale, the employee will get a check for $100.

The following memos are possible approaches. How well does each message meet the criteria in the checklist for informative and positive messages?

1.

Subject: Suggestion System (SS)

I want to introduce you to the Suggestion System (SS). This program enables the production worker to offer ideas about improving his job description, working conditions, and general company procedures. The plan can operate as a finely tuned machine, with great ideas as its product.

Operation will begin October 1. Once a week, a designate of SS will collect the ideas and turn them over to the SS Committee. This committee will evaluate and judge the proposed changes.

Only employees listed as factory workers are eligible. This excludes foremen and the rest of supervisory personnel. Awards are as follows:

1. $100 awards will be given to those ideas judged operational. These are awarded monthly.
2. There will be grand prizes given for the best suggestions over the six-month span.

Ideas are judged on feasibility, originality, operational simplicity, and degree of benefit to the worker and company. Evaluation made by the SS Committee is final. Your questions should be channeled to my office.

2.

Subject: Establishment of Suggestion System

We announce the establishment of a Suggestion System. This new program is designed to provide a means for hourly employees to submit suggestions to company management concerning operations and safety. The program will also provide an award system to compensate nonmanagement employees for implemented suggestions.

Here is how the program will work: beginning October 1, suggestions can be submitted by hourly workers to the company on Form 292, which will be furnished to all plants and their departments by October 1st. On the form, the submitting employee should include the suggestion, his or her name, and the department number. The form can be deposited in a suggestion drop box, which will be located near the personnel office in each plant.

Any suggestion dealing with the improvement of operations, safety, working conditions, or morale is eligible for consideration. The award structure for the program will be as follows:

1. For an implemented suggestion which improves safety or efficiency with no associated monetary benefits or cost reduction: $100.00.
2. For an implemented suggestion which makes or saves the company money: 10% of the first year's estimated annual savings or additional revenue.

It is hoped that we will have a good initial and continuous response from all hourly employees. This year, we are out to try to cut production costs, and this program may be the vehicle through which we will realize new savings and increased revenues. New ideas which can truly increase operational efficiency or cut safety problems will make the company a nicer place for all employees. A safer work environment is a better work environment. If department operations can be made more efficient, this will eventually make everyone's job just a little easier, and give that department and its employees a sense of pride.

3.

Subject: New Employee Suggestion System

Beginning October 1, all of you who are hourly employees of Tyfor Manufacturing will be able to get cash awards when your suggestions for improving the company are implemented.

Ideas about any aspect of Tyfor Manufacturing are eligible: streamlining behind-the-counter operations, handling schedule problems, increasing the life of line machines.

- If your idea cuts costs or increases income (e.g., increasing production, decreasing line accidents), you'll receive 10% of the first year's estimated annual savings.
- If the idea doesn't save money but does improve service, work conditions, or morale, you'll receive a check for $100.

To submit a suggestion, just pick up a form from your manager. On the form, explain your suggestion, describe briefly how it could be implemented, and show how it will affect Tyfor Manufacturing. Return the completed form in the new suggestion box behind the back counter. Suggestions will be evaluated at the end of each month. Turn in as many ideas as you like!

Think about ways to solve the problems you face every day. Can we speed up the materials check-in process? Cut paperwork? Give customers faster service? Decrease the percentage of line flaws?

Your ideas will keep Tyfor Manufacturing competitive. Ten years ago, Tyfor Manufacturing was the only supplier in the Midwest. Now we have three regional competitors, in addition to numerous international ones. Efficiency, creativity, and quality can keep Tyfor Manufacturing ahead.

Employees whose ideas are implemented will be recognized in the regional Tyfor Manufacturing newsletter. The award will also be a nice accomplishment to add to any college application or résumé. By suggesting ways to improve Tyfor Manufacturing, you'll demonstrate your creativity and problem-solving abilities. And you'll be able to share the credit for keeping Tyfor Manufacturing a profitable manufacturing concern.

9.6 Critiquing a Letter—Economic Stimulus Payment Notice

The following letter was sent to more than 130 million households after the U.S. Congress passed a stimulus package in early 2008. Critique it in small groups. Here are some questions to get you started:

1. What are the purposes of this letter?
2. How well does this letter inform the audience of its purpose?

3. Does the letter violate any of the guidelines for constructing informational messages you read about in this chapter? If so, which ones?
4. What kind of impression is given to readers by the document design choices?

As your instructor directs,

a. Write a memo to your instructor summarizing your group discussion.
b. As a group, record your answers to the questions, plus other observations you made. Trade summaries with another group. Where did they agree with you? Disagree? What observations did they make that your group did not? Write a memo to your instructor summarizing the differences between the two critiques. Submit the memo and the two critiques to your instructor.

Department of the Treasury
Internal Revenue Service

Notice 1377 (February 2008)
Catalog Number 51255B

www.irs.gov

Economic Stimulus Payment Notice

Dear Taxpayer:

We are pleased to inform you that the United States Congress passed and President George W. Bush signed into law the Economic Stimulus Act of 2008, which provides for economic stimulus payments to be made to over 130 million American households. Under this new law, you may be entitled to a payment of up to $600 ($1,200 if filing a joint return), plus additional amount for each qualifying child.

We are sending this notice to let you know that based on this new law the IRS will begin sending the one-time payments starting in May. To receive a payment in 2008, individuals who qualify will not have to do anything more than file a 2007 tax return. The IRS will determine eligibility, figure the amount, and send the payment. This payment should not be confused with any 2007 income tax refund that is owed to you by the federal government. Income tax refunds for 2007 will be made separately from this one-time payment.

For individuals who normally do not have to file a tax return, the new law provides for payments to individuals who have a total of $3,000 or more in earned income, Social Security benefits, and/or certain veterans' payments. Those individuals should file a tax return for 2007 to receive a payment in 2008.

Individuals who qualify may receive as much as $600 ($1,200 if married filing jointly). Even if you pay no income tax but have a total of $3,000 or more in earned income, Social Security benefits, and/or certain veterans' payments, you may receive a payment of $300 ($600 if married filing jointly).

In addition, individuals eligible for payments may also receive an additional amount of $300 for each child qualifying for the child tax credit.

For taxpayers with adjusted gross income (AGI) of more than $75,000 (or more than $150,000 if married filing jointly), the payment will be reduced or phased out completely.

To qualify for the payment, an individual, spouse, and any qualifying child must have a valid Social Security number. In addition, individuals cannot receive a payment if they can be claimed as a dependent of another taxpayer or they filled a 2007 Form 1040NR, 1040NR-EZ, 1040-PR, or 1040-SS.

All individuals receiving payments will receive a notice and additional information shortly before the payment is made. In the meantime, for additional information, please visit the IRS website at *www.irs.gov*.

Source: Internal Revenue Service, "Economic Stimulus Payment Notice," February 2008, http://www.irs.gov/pub/irs-utl/economic_stimulus_payment_notice.pdf.

9.7 Critiquing a Letter—Introducing Kindle

The following letter was sent to Amazon shareholders after Kindle went on the market. Critique the letter in small groups. Here are some questions to get you started:

1. What are the purposes of this letter?
2. How well are these purposes accomplished?
3. What information does Bezos provide about Kindle? Why do you think he chose this information?
4. How is the information organized?
5. Where do you see you-attitude and positive tone? Do they contribute to the letter's effectiveness? Why or why not?

As your instructor directs,

a. Write a memo to your instructor summarizing your group discussion.

b. As a group, record your answers to the questions, plus other observations you made. Trade summaries with another group. Where did they agree with you? Disagree? What observations did they make that your group did not? Write a memo to your instructor summarizing the differences between the two critiques. Submit the memo and the two critiques to your instructor.

Jeffrey Bezos (Amazon Founder and Chief Executive Officer) letter to shareholders

To our shareowners:

November 19, 2007, was a special day. After three years of work, we introduced Amazon Kindle to our customers.

Many of you may already know something of Kindle—we're fortunate (and grateful) that it has been broadly written and talked about. Briefly, Kindle is a purpose-built reading device with wireless access to more than 110,000 books, blogs, magazines, and newspapers. The wireless connectivity isn't WiFi—instead it uses the same wireless network as advanced cellphones, which means it works when you're at home in bed or out and moving around. You can buy a book directly from the device, and the whole book will be downloaded wirelessly, ready for reading, in less than 60 seconds. There is no "wireless plan," no year-long contract you must commit to, and no monthly service fee. It has a paper-like electronic-ink display that's easy to read even in bright daylight. Folks who see the display for the first time do a double-take. It's thinner and lighter than a paperback, and can hold 200 books. Take a look at the Kindle detail page on Amazon.com to see what customers think—Kindle has already been reviewed more than 2,000 times.

As you might expect after three years of work, we had sincere hopes that Kindle would be well received, but we did not expect the level of demand that actually materialized. We sold out in the first 5 1/2 hours, and our supply chain and manufacturing teams have had to scramble to increase production capacity.

We started by setting ourselves the admittedly audacious goal of improving upon the physical book. We did not choose that goal lightly. Anything that has persisted in roughly the same form and resisted change for 500 years is unlikely to be improved easily. At the beginning of our design process, we identified what we believe is the book's most important feature. It disappears. When you read a book, you don't notice the paper and the ink and the glue and the stitching. All of that dissolves, and what remains is the author's world.

We knew Kindle would have to *get out of the way,* just like a physical book, so readers could become engrossed in the words and forget they're reading on a device. We also knew we shouldn't try to copy every last feature of a book—we could never out-book the book. We'd have to add new capabilities—ones that could never be possible with a traditional book.

The early days of Amazon.com provide an analog. It was tempting back then to believe that an online bookstore should have all the features of a physical bookstore. I was asked about a particular feature dozens of times: "How are you going to do electronic book signings?" Thirteen years later, we still haven't figured that one out!

Instead of trying to duplicate physical bookstores, we've been inspired by them and worked to find things we could do in the new medium that could never be done in the old one. We don't have electronic book signings, and similarly we can't provide a comfortable spot to sip coffee and relax. However, we can offer literally millions of titles, help with purchase decisions through customer reviews, and provide discovery features like "customers who bought this item also bought." The list of useful things that can be done only in the new medium is a long one.

I'll highlight a few of the useful features we built into Kindle that go beyond what you could ever do with a physical book. If you come across a word you don't recognize, you can look it up easily. You can search your books. Your margin notes and underlinings are stored on the server-side in the "cloud," where they can't be lost. Kindle keeps your place in each of the books you're reading, automatically. If your eyes are tired, you can change the font size. Most important is the seamless, simple ability to find a book and have it in 60 seconds. When I've watched people do this for the first time, it's clear the capability has a profound effect on them. Our vision for Kindle is every book ever printed in any language, all available in less than 60 seconds.

Publishers—including all the major publishers—have embraced Kindle, and we're thankful for that. From a publisher's point of view, there are a lot of advantages to Kindle. Books never go out of print, and they never go out of stock. Nor is there ever waste from over-printing. Most important, Kindle makes it more convenient for readers to buy more books. Anytime you make something simpler and lower friction, you get more of it.

We humans co-evolve with our tools. We change our tools, and then our tools change us. Writing, invented thousands of years ago, is a grand whopper of a tool, and I have no doubt that it changed us dramatically. Five hundred years ago, Gutenberg's invention led to a significant step-change in the cost of books. Physical books ushered in a new way of collaborating and learning. Lately, networked tools such as desktop computers, laptops, cellphones and PDAs have changed us too. They've shifted us more toward information snacking, and I would argue toward shorter attention spans. I value my BlackBerry—I'm convinced it makes me more productive—but I don't want to read a three-hundred-page document on it. Nor do I want to read something hundreds of pages long on my desktop computer or my laptop. As I've already mentioned in this letter, people do more of what's convenient and friction-free. If our tools make information snacking easier, we'll shift more toward information snacking and away from long-form reading. Kindle is purpose-built for long-form reading. We hope Kindle and its successors may gradually and incrementally move us over years into a world with longer spans of attention, providing a counterbalance to the recent proliferation of info-snacking tools. I realize my tone here tends toward the missionary, and I can assure you it's heartfelt. It's also not unique to me but is shared by a large group of folks here. I'm glad about that because missionaries build better products. I'll also point out that, while I'm convinced books are on the verge of being improved upon, Amazon has no sinecure as that agent. It will happen, but if we don't execute well, it will be done by others.

Your team of missionaries here is fervent about driving free cash flow per share and returns on capital. We know we can do that by putting customers first. I guarantee you there is more innovation ahead of us than behind us, and we do not expect the road to be an easy one. We're hopeful, and I'd even say optimistic, that Kindle, true to its name, will "start a fire" and improve the world of reading.

As always, I attach our 1997 letter to shareholders. You'll see that Kindle exemplifies our philosophy and long-term investment approach as discussed in that letter. Happy reading and many thanks!

Jeffrey P.Bezos
Founder and Chief Executive Officer
Amazon.com, Inc.

9.8 Critiquing a Letter—Airline Merger

The following letter was sent by Northwest Airlines before their merger with Delta. Critique the letter in small groups. Here are some questions to get you started:

1. What are the purposes of this letter?
2. How well are these purposes accomplished?
3. What information does the letter provide that an ordinary traveler would find useful?
4. How is the information organized?
5. Where do you see you-attitude and positive tone? Do they contribute to the letter's effectiveness? Why or why not?

As your instructor directs,

a. Write a memo to your instructor summarizing your group discussion.

b. As a group, record your answers to the questions, plus other observations you made. Trade summaries with another group. Where did they agree with you? Disagree? What observations did they make that your group did not? Write a memo to your instructor summarizing the differences between the two critiques. Submit the memo and the two critiques to your instructor.

Dear Steven Schmidt,

As a valued Northwest Airlines customer and WorldPerks® member, I wanted you to be among the first to hear that we have announced a merger with Delta Air Lines. Subject to regulatory review, our two airlines are joining forces to create America's premier global airline which, upon closing of the merger, will be called Delta Air Lines.

By combining Northwest and Delta, we are building a stronger, more resilient airline that will be a leader in providing customer service and value. Our combined airline will offer unprecedented access to the world, enabling you to fly to more destinations, have more flight choices and more ways than ever to earn and redeem your WorldPerks miles.

You can be assured that your WorldPerks miles and Elite program status will be unaffected by this merger. In addition, you can continue to earn miles through use of partners like WorldPerks Visa®. And once the new Delta Air Lines emerges you can look forward to being a part of the world's largest frequent flyer program with expanded benefits.

The combined Delta Air Lines will serve more U.S. communities and connect to more worldwide destinations than any global airline. Our hubs—both Delta's and Northwest's—will be retained and enhanced. We will be the only U.S. airline to offer direct service from the United States to all of the world's major business centers in Asia, Latin America, Europe, Africa and around North America.

Both airlines bring tremendous strengths to this new partnership. Our complementary service networks form an end-to-end system that is truly greater than the sum of its parts. This is a merger by addition, not subtraction, which means all of our hubs—both Northwest's and Delta's—will be retained. In addition, building on both airlines' proud decades-long history of serving small communities, we plan to enhance global connections to small towns and cities across the U.S.

All of these positive benefits of our combination mean that we can:

- Offer a true global network where our customers will be able to fly to more destinations, have more schedule options and more opportunities to earn and redeem frequent flyer miles in what will become the world's best and most comprehensive frequent flyer program.
- Continue to serve our current roster of destinations and to maintain our hubs in Atlanta, Cincinnati, Detroit, Memphis, Minneapolis/St. Paul, New York, Salt Lake City, Amsterdam, and Tokyo.
- Improve our customers' travel experience, through new products and services including enhanced self-service tools, better bag-tracking technology, more onboard services, including more meal options, new seats and refurbished cabins.

While we work to secure approval of our merger, which may take up to 6 to 8 months, it will be business-as-usual at both airlines. We will continue to operate as independent airlines and the people of Northwest will remain focused on providing you with the very best in safe, reliable and convenient air travel. At the same time, both airlines will be planning for a seamless integration of our two airlines, one that delivers to you the enhanced benefits that will earn—and retain—your preference.

As we work through this process, we will keep you informed at every step along the way. Thank you for your business and we look forward to serving you on your next Northwest flight.

Sincerely,
Bob Soukup
Managing Director, WorldPerks

9.9 Discussing an Ethics Situation : Fired for an E-mail

"[In November 2006] Justen [sic] Deal, a 22-year-old Kaiser Permanente employee, blasted an email throughout the giant health maintenance organization. His message charged that HealthConnect—the company's ambitious $4 billion project to convert paper files into electronic medical records—was a mess.

"In a blistering 2,000-word treatise, Mr. Deal wrote: 'We're spending recklessly, to the tune of over $1.5 billion in waste every year, primarily on HealthConnect. . . .

"'For me, this isn't just an issue of saving money,' he wrote. 'It could very well become an issue of making sure our physicians and nurses have the tools they need to save lives.'"

Mr. Deal, who had believed he would be protected by Kaiser's policy encouraging people to report ethical problems, was fired. The CIO resigned, although the HMO said the timing was a coincidence. The appropriate California watchdog agency is now monitoring the system, and the Los Angeles *Times* ran a story with some of the same criticisms Mr. Deal had made.

Would you risk your job for an ethics issue this large? A smaller ethics issue? How could Mr. Deal have handled differently the problem he saw?

Quoted from Rhonda L. Rundle, "Critical Case: How an Email Rant Jolted a Big HMO: A 22-Year-Old's Tirade Made Trouble for Kaiser. Mr. Deal Got Fired, Famous," *Wall Street Journal,* April 24, 2007.

9.10 Analyzing Goldman Sachs' Communication Policies

Reread the Goldman Sachs sidebars quoting some statements from Goldman Sachs' communication policies, *United States Policies for the Preparation, Supervision, Distribution and Retention of Written and Electronic Communications.* Answer the following questions:

- What are the implications of this guideline?

  "Prior to recommending that a customer purchase, sell or exchange any security, salespeople must have reasonable grounds for believing that the recommendation is suitable."
- Does this guideline contradict the above guideline?

  "Firm employees frequently provide so-called "trade ideas" to multiple recipients. Such trade ideas are designed to help clients take advantage of market conditions and intelligence, but are not intended to be specific buy/sell recommendations."
- What are the implications of the multiple statements that the firm surveys employee communications?
- Do you think that following these guidelines could have helped Goldman Sachs avoid its half-billion dollar fine?

9.11 Managing Overdraft Information

Banks make billions of dollars from overdraft fees. They maintain that the overdraft service allows customers to make vital purchases even when their account is empty.

On the other side, many customers are furious at how the current system allows them to rack up hundreds of dollars in overdraft fees without knowing they are doing so. Many of them claim they did not know they had overdraft service until they saw the fees. They want to be alerted when a purchase will result in an overdraft. They also object to the bank practice of processing a large purchase before several small ones that occurred at almost the same time, so that each small purchase gets an overdraft fee that it would not have gotten if the large purchase had been processed last.

In small groups, discuss how much overdraft information should be shared. Here are some questions to get you started:

- For what groups are overdraft services a benefit?
- Which groups do such services hurt most?
- Should people be automatically enrolled in such services, as is now the case for most customers?
- Should banks notify customers that they are about to incur an overdraft fee? How would third-party processors affect such notifications?

Write a memo to your instructor summarizing your group's discussion.

Source: Kelly Evans, "Consumers Vent on Overdraft Fees," *Wall Street Journal,* March 26, 2009, D2.

9.12 Offering Restaurant Nutrition Information

The Food and Drug Administration wants restaurants to provide more nutritional information, including calorie counts of offerings, so that customers can make more nutritious choices. You own a restaurant and are considering whether or not you should change your menu to comply. On the one hand, you know obesity is a national problem, and you might be able to attract health-conscious customers if you change your menu. On the other hand, the large majority of your customers do not seem to be counting calories. Their favorites on your menu are the comfort food selections such as fried chicken, mashed potatoes, pies, and cakes. Furthermore, it would cost you over $50,000 for a lab to test your menu items and provide nutritional content and calorie counts. In small groups, discuss whether or not your restaurant will comply. What are some compromises you can think of? Write a memo to your instructor summarizing your group's conclusions.

9.13 Revising a Letter

You work for a credit card company and asked your assistant to draft a letter to new customers who have recently opened an account. The purpose of the letter is to inform clients of the services available to them, persuade them to use the services, and build goodwill.

Subject: Credit Card

Dear Sir or Madame,

This letter will let you know about our organization and what we can do for you. We believe that you will like using our services, as we offer many convenient ones.

Before we tell you about the great services we have to offer, we want to let you know how glad we our to have you as a new customer. We got out of our way to make sure you get the best benefits. 2% back on grocery purchases, no annual fee, and reward dollars—who could ask for anything more?! Shop, Shop, Shop and the rewards will pile up. Go online to sign up for rewards so you don't lose out. While your there, don't forget to enroll in e-mail alerts to remind you of upcoming due dates.

We have been helping clients for almost a quarter of a century and are happy your apart of the family. Like a family member who just drops in, you get to chose your payment due date. Now how's that for convenience!

Thank you for joining our service. We look forward to continuing our business relationship with you.

Sincerely,

This draft definitely needs some work. It lacks you-attitude and needs attention to the organization. Moreover, the new services are not clearly explained, and there are many mechanical errors.

As your instructor directs,

a. Write a memo to your subordinate, explaining what revisions are necessary.
b. Revise the letter.

9.14 Accommodating a Hearing-Impaired Employee

You're manager of Human Resources at your company. Two weeks ago, you got this e-mail message:

> Subject: Accommodations for Employee
>
> Our work team includes a hearing-impaired employee. She is our most productive team member on the floor, but at team meetings, she can't effectively contribute. I e-mailed her about my concerns, and she says the conversations are too hard to follow. What can we do so she can contribute her ideas?

One of your staffers has researched the issue for you and brought you several recommendations. Based on the staffer's research, you have determined that you will contract with a sign language interpreter to be present at the regular staff meetings. You will also have your staffer meet with the work team to share some basic guidelines for communicating, such as looking directly at the deaf team member when speaking, speaking slowly, using facial expressions when possible, and avoiding any statements not intended for the interpreter to translate (the interpreter will translate anything spoken during the meeting). These plans are part of your existing policy of complying with the Americans with Disabilities Act (ADA).

Write an e-mail message to the affected employees, telling them about the new practices for your employee.

9.15 Giving Employees Their Birthday Off

Your company holds a birthday celebration for everyone in your unit. After the last three celebrations, co-workers noticed a discrepancy. Some co-workers believe that Jane had much more effort, time, and money spent on her party than did Kurt and Barbara, both of whom do the same quantity and quality of work as Jane.

After some complaints about the unfairness of office birthday parties when one co-worker gets a much more lavish celebration, the management has decided to institute a new policy regarding employee birthdays. From now on, all employees will be given the day off to celebrate their birthday however they like.

Write a memo to all employees announcing the change in policy.

Hints:

- Choose an organization you know something about.
- Be sure to provide benefits for employees like Jane, who had a much better party than other co-workers.

9.16 Creating a Human Resources Web Page

As firms attempt to help employees balance work and family life (and as employers become aware that personal and family stresses affect performance at work), Human Resource departments sponsor an array of programs and provide information on myriad subjects. However, some people might be uncomfortable asking for help, either because the problem is embarrassing (who wants to admit needing help to deal with drug abuse, domestic violence, or addiction to gambling?) or because focusing on nonwork issues (e.g., child care) might lead others to think they aren't serious about their jobs. The web allows organizations to post information that employees can access privately—even from home.

Create a web page that could be posted by Human Resources to help employees with one of the challenges they face. Possible topics include

- Appreciating an ethnic heritage.
- Buying a house.
- Caring for dependents: child care, helping a child learn to read, living with teenagers, elder care, and so forth.
- Staying healthy: exercise, yoga, massage, healthy diet, and so forth.
- Dealing with a health problem: alcoholism, cancer, diabetes, heart disease, obesity, and so forth.
- Dressing for success or dressing for casual days.
- Managing finances: basic budgeting, deciding how much to save, choosing investments, and so forth.
- Nourishing the spirit: meditation, religion.
- Getting out of debt.
- Planning for retirement.
- Planning vacations.
- Reducing stress.
- Resolving conflicts on the job or in families.

Assume that this page can be accessed from another of the organization's pages. Offer at least seven links. (More is better.) You may offer information as well as links to other pages with information. At the top of the page, offer an overview of what the page covers. At the bottom of the page, put the creation/update date and your name and e-mail address.

As your instructor directs,

a. Turn in one printed copy of your web page(s). On another page, give the URLs for each link.
b. Electronically submit your web page files.
c. Write a memo to your instructor identifying the audience for which the page is designed and explaining (1) the search strategies you used to find material on this topic, (2) why you chose the pages and information you've included, and (3) why you chose the layout and graphics you've used.
d. Present your page orally to the class.

Hints:

- Pick a topic you know something about.
- Realize that audience members will have different needs. You could explain the basics of choosing day care or stocks, but don't recommend a specific day care center or a specific stock.
- If you have more than nine links, chunk them in small groups under headings.
- Create a good image of the organization.

9.17 Praising Work Done Well

Write an e-mail to a co-worker (with a copy to the person's supervisor) thanking him or her for helping you or complimenting him or her on a job well done. Use details to give your note sincerity.

9.18 Giving Good News

Write to a customer or client, to a vendor or supplier, or to your boss announcing good news. Possibilities include a product improvement, a price cut or special, an addition to your management team, a new contract, and so forth.

9.19 Investigating E-mail

Interview a professional you know about his/her use of e-mail. You might consider questions such as these:

- How many e-mails do you receive on an average day? Send?
- How much time do you spend handling e-mails on an average day?
- What are the most common kinds of e-mails you receive? Send?
- What are the most difficult kinds of e-mails for you to write? Why?
- What are your pet peeves about e-mails?

Write up your findings in an informational memo to your instructor.

9.20 Reminding Guests about the Time Change

Annually in the United States, cities switch to daylight saving time and then back again. The time change can be disruptive for hotel guests, who may lose track of the date, forget to change the clocks in their rooms, and miss appointments as a result.

Prepare a form letter to leave in each hotel room reminding guests of the impending time change. What should guests do?

Write the letter.

Hints:

- Use an attention-getting page layout so readers don't ignore the message.
- Pick a specific hotel or motel chain you know something about.
- Use the letter to build goodwill for your hotel or motel chain. Use specific references to services or features the hotel offers, focusing not on what the hotel does for the reader, but on what the reader can do at the hotel.

9.21 Announcing a New Employee Benefit

Your company has decided to pay employees for doing charity work. Employees can spend 1 hour working with a charitable on nonprofit group for every 40 they work. Employees will be paid for this hour, so their salaries will not fall. People who choose not to participate will work and be paid for the same number of hours as before. Supervisors are responsible for ensuring that essential business services are covered during business hours. Any employee who will be away during regular business hours (either to volunteer or to take off an hour in compensation for volunteering off-shift or on a weekend) will need to clear the planned absence with his or her supervisor. Your office is collecting a list of organizations that would welcome volunteers. People can work with an organized group or do something informal (such as tutoring at a local school or coaching kids at a local playground). People can volunteer 1 hour every week, 2 hours every other week, or a half-day each month. Volunteer hours cannot be banked from one month to the next; they must be used each month. The program starts January 1 (or June 1). The various groups that people work with will be featured in company publications.

As Vice President of Human Resources, write a memo to all employees announcing this new program.

Hints:

- Pick a business, government, or nonprofit organization that you know something about.
- What proportion of your employees are already involved in volunteer work?
- Is community service or "giving back" consistent with your corporate mission?
- Some employees won't be able or won't want to participate. What is the benefit for them in working for a company that has such a program?
- Will promoting community participation help your organization attract and retain workers?

9.22 Announcing an Employee Fitness Center

Your company is ready to open an employee fitness center with on-site aerobics and yoga classes, exercycles, tread mills, and weight machines. The center will be open 6 am to 10 pm daily; at least one qualified instructor will be on duty at all times. Employees get first preference; if there is extra room, clients, spouses, and children 14 and older may also use the facilities. Locker rooms and showers will also be available.

Your company hopes that the fitness center will help out-of-shape employees get the exercise they need to be more productive. Other companies have saved between $2.30 and $10.10 for every $1.00 spent on wellness programs. The savings come from lower claims on medical insurance, less absenteeism, and greater productivity.

Write the memo announcing the center.

Hints:

- Who pays the medical insurance for employees? If the employer pays, then savings from healthier employees will pay for the center. If another payment plan is in effect, you'll need a different explanation for the company's decision to open the fitness center.
- Stress benefits apart from the company's saving money. How can easier access to exercise help employees? What do they do? How can exercise reduce stress, improve strength, help employees manage chronic illnesses such as diabetes and high blood pressure, and increase productivity at work?
- What kind of record does the company have of helping employees be healthy? Is the fitness center a departure for the company, or does the company have a history of company sports teams, stop-smoking clinics, and the like?
- What is the company's competitive position? If the company is struggling, you'll need to convince readers that the fitness center is a good use of scarce funds. If the company is doing well, show how having fit employees can make people even more productive.
- Stress fun as a benefit. How can access to the center make employees' lives more enjoyable?

9.23 Announcing New Smoking Policy

During a recent board meeting, your organization's officers decided to respond to complaints from workers and clients about smokers who gather outside the main entrance to your office building. Complaints ranged from the effects of secondhand smoke to the message the smokers shed on the organization's image to outside clients who need to enter the building. The board decided that smoking will be allowed only in a designated area at the far end of the parking lot. Smokers can no longer congregate near the building's main entrance.

As vice president, write a memo to all employees announcing the immediate change in the smoking policy.

In addition, write a memo to your instructor that analyzes your rhetorical situation (context, audiences, and purposes) and the ethical decisions you had to make to construct this memo.

Hints:

- Pick a business, government, or nonprofit organization that you know something about.
- What benefits can you stress to employees about the new policy?
- Some employees, particularly those who smoke, may be disgruntled with the new policy. What benefits can you stress for them and how will you overcome their negative feelings?

9.24 Providing Information to Job Applicants

Your company is in a prime vacation spot, and as personnel manager you get many letters from students asking about summer jobs. Company policy is to send everyone an application for employment, a list of the jobs you expect to have open that summer with the rate of pay for each, a description of benefits for seasonal employees, and an interview schedule. Candidates must come for an interview at their own expense and should call to schedule a time in advance. Competition is keen: Only a small percentage of those interviewed will be hired.

Write a form letter to students who've written to you asking about summer jobs. Give them the basic information about the hiring procedure and tell them what to do next. Be realistic about their chances, but maintain their interest in working for you.

9.25 Announcing a Premium Holiday

Rather than paying fees to an insurer, your company is self-insured. That is, you set aside corporate funds to pay for medical bills. If claims are light, the company saves money.

Employees pay a monthly fee for part of the amount of their health insurance. However, with one month to go in the fiscal year, you have more than enough set aside to cover possible costs. You're going to pass along some of the savings to employees (who, by staying healthy, have kept medical costs down). Next month will be a "premium holiday." You will not deduct the monthly premium from employees' checks. As a result, they will have a slightly higher take-home pay next month. The holiday is just for one month; after it, the premium for health insurance will again be deducted each month.

Write a memo to all employees.

9.26 Announcing a Tuition Reimbursement Program

Your organization has decided to encourage employees to take courses by reimbursing each eligible employee a maximum of $3,500 in tuition and fees during any one calendar year. Anyone who wants to participate in the program must apply before the first class meeting; the application must be signed by the employee's immediate supervisor. The Office of Human Resources will evaluate applications. That office has application forms; it also has catalogs from nearby schools and colleges.

The only courses employees may choose are those either related to the employee's current position (or to a position in the company that the employee might hold someday) or part of a job-related degree program. Again, the degree must be one that would help the employee's current position or that would qualify him or her for a promotion or transfer in the organization.

Only tuition and fees are covered, not books or supplies. People whose applications are approved will be reimbursed when they have completed the course with a grade of C or better. An employee cannot be reimbursed until he or she submits a copy of the approved application, an official grade report, and a statement of the tuition paid. If someone is eligible for other financial aid (scholarship, veterans benefits), the company will pay tuition costs not covered by that aid as long as the employee does not receive more than $3,500 and as long as the total tuition reimbursement does not exceed the actual cost of tuition and fees.

Part-time employees are not eligible; full-time employees must work at the company a year before they can apply to participate in the program. Courses may be at any appropriate level (high school, college, or graduate). However, the Internal Revenue Service currently requires workers to pay tax on any reimbursement for graduate programs. Undergraduate and basic education reimbursements of $3,500 or less a year are not taxed.

As Director of Human Resources, write a memo to all employees explaining this new benefit.

Hints:

- Pick an organization you know something about. What do its employees do? What courses or degrees might help them do their jobs better?
- How much education do employees already have? How do they feel about formal schooling?
- The information in the problem is presented in a confusing order. Put related items together.
- The problem stresses the limits of the policy. Without changing the provisions, present them positively.
- How will having a better educated workforce help the organization? Think about the challenges the organization faces, its competitive environment, and so forth.

9.27 Summarizing Information

Summarize one or more of the following:

1. An article from a recent edition of *Bloomberg Businessweek* or *Harvard Business Review.*
2. A tip from Jakob Nielsen's Alertboxes, http://www.alertbox.com.
3. An article about college, career development, or job searching from Quintessential Careers, http://www.quintcareers.com/articles.html.
4. Online information about options for recycling or donating used, outdated computers.
5. Options for consolidating student loans and other finances.
6. Online information about protecting your credit card or debit card.
7. An article or web page assigned by your instructor.

As your instructor directs,

a. Write a summary of no more than 100 words.
b. Write a 250- to 300-word summary.
c. Write a one-page summary.
d. In a small group compare your summaries. How did the content of the summaries vary? How do you account for any differences?

9.28 Writing a Thank-You Letter

Write a thank-you letter to someone who has helped you achieve your goals.

As your instructor directs,

a. Turn in a copy of the letter.
b. Mail the letter to the person who helped you.
c. Write a memo to your instructor explaining the situation and choices you made in writing the thank-you letter.

CHAPTER 10

Delivering Negative Messages

Chapter Outline

Organizing Negative Messages
- Giving Bad News to Clients and Customers
- Giving Bad News to Superiors
- Giving Bad News to Peers and Subordinates

The Parts of a Negative Message
- Subject Lines
- Buffers
- Reasons
- Refusals
- Alternatives
- Endings

Apologies

Tone in Negative Messages

Alternative Strategies for Negative Situations
- Recasting the Situation as a Positive Message
- Recasting the Situation as a Persuasive Message

Varieties of Negative Messages
- Claims and Complaints
- Rejections and Refusals
- Disciplinary Notices and Negative Performance Appraisals
- Layoffs and Firings

Solving a Sample Problem
- Problem
- Analysis of the Problem
- Discussion of the Sample Solutions

Summary of Key Points

Newsworthy Communication

Metaphors in Negative News

Sharing negative messages is never easy, but announcing to all of your employees that your company is failing could be the most difficult message a CEO has to share. But in February 2011, only days before announcing a major deal with Microsoft, Nokia CEO Stephen Elop did just that.

Nokia, in spite of being the world's largest maker of mobile phones, has been struggling to maintain its market lead in the face of increased competition from Apple's iPhone and Google's range of Android handsets. With shrinking demand for feature phones and no hit smartphone under its belt, Nokia is in real danger.

> *"By the time Elop finishes the memo, he has delivered the message . . . as an opportunity to innovate and shape the future of mobile communication."*

Elop shared the harsh realities of the situation with all Nokia employees in an internal memo, framing the entire message as an opportunity to improve. He began with a dramatic story: an oil platform worker forced to choose between a fire behind him and the icy North Atlantic waters in front of him. Elop then challenged his workers: "We too, are standing on a 'burning platform,' and we must decide how we are going to change our behaviour."

Using that story as a frame, Elop then outlined the advances of Nokia's competitors and Nokia's own missteps. "While competitors poured flames on our market share, what happened at Nokia? We fell behind, we missed big trends, and we lost time. . . . We poured gasoline on our own burning platform. I believe we have lacked accountability and leadership to align and direct the company through these disruptive times. We had a series of misses. We haven't been delivering innovation fast enough. We're not collaborating internally. Nokia, our platform is burning."

The 1,300-word memo details market losses, failed devices, corporate failures, and bad decisions. And yet, by the time Elop finishes the memo, he has delivered the message not as the death-knell of the company, but as an opportunity to innovate and shape the future of mobile communication. He concludes his memo by returning to the burning platform once again: "The burning platform, upon which the man found himself, caused the man to shift his behaviour, and take a bold and brave step into an uncertain future. He was able to tell his story. Now, we have a great opportunity to do the same."

By delivering his negative message in a carefully constructed memo, Stephen Elop avoided creating further problems for an already struggling company. Rather, he took the bold step of being direct and honest and asked for all of his employees to help Nokia regain its lead in the market.

Sources: Chris Ziegler, "Nokia CEO Stephen Elop Rallies Troops in Brutally Honest 'Burning Platform' Memo," Engadget.com, February 8, 2011, http://www.engadget.com/2011/02/08/nokia-ceo-stephen-elop-rallies-troops-in-brutally-honest-burnin/.

Learning Objectives

After studying this chapter, you will know

LO 10-1 Different ways to organize negative messages.

LO 10-2 Ways to construct the different parts of negative messages.

LO 10-3 How to improve the tone of negative messages.

LO 10-4 Ways to construct different kinds of negative messages.

In a negative message, the basic information we have to convey is negative; we expect the audience to be disappointed or angry. Some jobs entail conveying more negative messages than others. Customer service representatives, employee relations personnel, and insurance agents all have to say no on a regular basis.

Negative communications such as refusals, rejections, recalls, and apologies are hard to compose. Yet they are so important. Good ones restore corporate reputations as well as customer and employee goodwill. Bad ones can lead to lawsuits. Corporate officers can be promoted or fired on the basis of a negative communication. Employees reporting negative situations (whistle-blowing) are frequently penalized; one study found the percentage being penalized to be 82%. In spite of the penalties, the study found that 19% of corporate fraud was uncovered by employees.[1]

Negative messages are a vital part of business and administrative communication. One Silicon Valley company calculated the costs of negative communications from a sales person known for negative interpersonal skills and e-mails. Their costs included managerial time, HR time, anger management training and counseling, among others, and came to $160,000 for just one year. The company also deducted 60% of that cost from the employee's bonus. A British study estimated the costs of bullying in firms with 1,000 employees to be about $2 million a year per firm.[2]

The other side of the coin, and a classic illustration of how to handle negatives, is the 1982 Tylenol recall. When Johnson and Johnson learned that seven people in the Chicago area had died from cyanide-laced Tylenol capsules, they immediately communicated their knowledge. They ordered the entire supply withdrawn from store shelves, and they offered to replace Tylenol capsules in people's homes with tablets. This decision cost the company tens of millions of dollars. But it was the right decision. When Tylenol was released again several months later in new, tamper-resistant containers, it recovered its market share. The company's forthright communications of the situation confirmed its integrity.[3] This chapter will follow the 1982 Tylenol path and look at some of the preferred ways to convey negative messages.

Negative messages include rejections and refusals, announcements of policy changes that do not benefit the audience, requests the audience will see as insulting or intrusive, negative performance appraisals, disciplinary notices, and product recalls or notices of defects.

A negative message always has several purposes:

Primary purposes:

- To give the audience the bad news.
- To have the audience read, understand, and accept the message.
- To maintain as much goodwill as possible.

Sometimes corporations earn more bad publicity by keeping quiet about negative events than they would by explaining them. Rolls-Royce received much negative publicity when it delayed responding to the failure of one of its engines on an Airbus A380 superjumbo jet.

Secondary purposes:

- To maintain, as much as possible, a good image of the communicator and the communicator's organization.
- To reduce or eliminate future communication on the same subject so the message doesn't create more work for the sender.

In many negative situations, the communicator and audience will continue to deal with each other. Even when further interaction is unlikely (for example, when a company rejects a job applicant or refuses to renew a customer's insurance), the firm wants anything the audience may say about the company to be positive or neutral rather than negative.

Some messages that at first appear to be negative can be structured to create a positive feeling: a decision that may be negative in the short term may be shown to be a positive one in the long term; or the communication of a problem can be directly connected to an effective solution.

Even when it is not possible to make the audience happy with the news we must convey, we still want the audience to feel that

- They have been taken seriously.
- Our decision is fair and reasonable.
- If they were in our shoes, they would make the same decision.

ORGANIZING NEGATIVE MESSAGES LO 10-1

The best way to organize a negative message depends on your audience and on the severity of the negative information. This chapter presents several possible patterns and connects them with their most likely contexts. Be sure to always consider your particular situation when choosing an organizing pattern.

Giving Bad News to Clients and Customers

When you must give bad news to clients and customers, you need to be clear, but you also need to maintain goodwill. People are increasingly skeptical and have a hard time trusting organizations. One study found that in order to

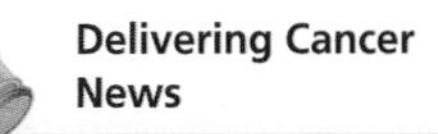

Delivering Cancer News

Oncologists, doctors who specialize in treating cancer, have one of the toughest jobs when it comes to delivering negative news. These doctors often inform patients that they have a difficult battle to face or that there is almost no hope and death may be imminent.

Some medical schools now insist that students learn how to deliver bad news to patients, particularly those suffering from cancer. These medical programs have added classes where students learn to give the negative news through verbal and nonverbal forms of communication. Some of these schools also use role-playing with patient actors. The medical students have to inform the actors of an unwanted diagnosis and appropriately deal with the actor's response. Some studies suggest that the manner in which bad news is presented to a patient has significant effects on their overall health.

As an additional resource for doctors to be upfront with their patients, the American Society of Clinical Oncology has developed a booklet. It helps patients understand their options when they learn they have cancer. The goal is to help improve their quality of life, maximize their remaining time, and plan for end-of-life care. The society believes that currently less than 40% of patients have conversations with their doctors about their options.

Adapted from Dawn Sagario, "Doctors Learn to Convey Facts in Appropriate, Thoughtful Way," *Des Moines Register*, October 17, 2006, E1, E2; "Oncology Group Promotes Candor on End-of-Life-Care," *Des Moines Register*, February 8, 2011, 6A.

Figure 10.1 How to Organize Negative Messages

Negative messages to clients and customers	Negative messages to superiors	Negative messages to peers and subordinates
1. **When you have a reason that the audience will understand and accept, give the reason before the refusal.** A good reason prepares the audience to expect the refusal. 2. **Give the negative information or refusal just once, clearly.** Inconspicuous refusals can be missed altogether, making it necessary to say *no* a second time. 3. **Present an alternative or compromise, if one is available.** An alternative not only gives the audience another way to get what they want but also suggests that you care about them and helping them meet their needs. 4. **End with a positive, forward-looking statement.**	1. **Describe the problem.** Tell what's wrong, clearly and unemotionally. 2. **Tell how it happened.** Provide the background. What underlying factors led to this specific problem? 3. **Describe the options for fixing it.** If one option is clearly best, you may need to discuss only one. But if your superiors will think of other options, or if different people will judge the options differently, describe all the options, giving their advantages and disadvantages. 4. **Recommend a solution and ask for action.** Ask for approval so that you can make the necessary changes to fix the problem.	1. **Describe the problem.** Tell what's wrong, clearly and unemotionally. 2. **Present an alternative or compromise, if one is available.** An alternative not only gives the audience another way to get what they want but also suggests that you care about them and helping them meet their needs. 3. **If possible, ask for input or action.** People in the audience may be able to suggest solutions. And workers who help make a decision are far more likely to accept the consequences.

accept a message as true, more than 70% of people need exposure to it more than three times.[4] Compromises or alternatives can help you achieve clarity and goodwill. See the first column in Figure 10.1 for a way to organize these messages.

Figure 10.2 illustrates another basic pattern for negative messages. This letter omits the reason for the policy change, probably because the change benefits the company, not the customer. Putting the bad news first (though pairing it immediately with an alternative) makes it more likely that the recipient will read the letter. If this letter seemed to be just a routine renewal, or if it opened with the good news that the premium was lower, few recipients would read the letter carefully, and many would not read it at all. Then, if they had accidents and found that their coverage was reduced, they'd blame the company for not communicating clearly. Emphasizing the negative here is both good ethics and good business.

Giving Bad News to Superiors

Your superior expects you to solve minor problems by yourself. But sometimes, solving a problem requires more authority or resources than you have. When you give bad news to a superior, also recommend a way to deal with the problem. Turn the negative message into a persuasive one. See the middle column in Figure 10.1.

Giving Bad News to Peers and Subordinates

When passing along serious bad news to peers and subordinates, many people use the organization suggested in the last column in Figure 10.1.

Figure 10.2 A Negative Letter

Vickers

Insurance Company

3373 Forbes Avenue
Rosemont, PA 19010
(215) 572-0100

Liability Coverage
Is Being Discontinued—
Here's How to Replace It!

Negative information highlighted so reader won't ignore message
Negative
Alternative

Dear Policyholder:

Negative

When your auto insurance is renewed, it will no longer include liability coverage unless you select the new Assurance Plan. Here's why.

Liability coverage is being discontinued. It, and the part of the premium which paid for it, will be dropped from all policies when they are renewed.

Positive information underlined for emphasis

This change could leave a gap in your protection. But you can replace the old Liability Coverage with Vickers' new Assurance Plan.

Alternative
No reason is given. The change probably benefits the company rather than the reader, so it is omitted.

With the new Assurance Plan, you receive benefits for litigation or awards arising from an accident—regardless of who's at fault. The cost for the Assurance Plan at any level is based on the ages of drivers, where you live, your driving record, and other factors. If these change before your policy is renewed, the cost of your Assurance Plan may also change. The actual cost will be listed in your renewal statement.

To sign up for the Assurance Plan, just check the level of coverage you want on the enclosed form and return it in the postage-paid envelope within 14 days. You'll be assured of the coverage you select.

Forward-looking ending emphasizes reader's choice

Sincerely,

C. J. Morgan

C. J. Morgan
President

Alternative

P.S. The Assurance Plan protects you against possible legal costs arising from an accident. Sign up for the plan today and receive full coverage from Vickers.

No serious negative (such as being downsized or laid off) should come as a complete surprise, nor should it be delivered by e-mail. Researchers Timmerman and Harrison note that managers may be inclined to use electronic forms of communication to deliver bad news, but they should resist the temptation in most situations. Their study outlines four factors that should be considered when choosing a medium for delivering bad news: the

When Chrysler cut 25% of its dealers, it sent the bad news the same day it went public with the list of cut dealerships. Thus, many dealers first heard about their cuts on the news, not from Chrysler's letter, and created even more bad press for Chrysler.

severity of the message, the complexity of the explanation, the type of explanation, and the relationship between the superior and subordinates. Timmerman and Harrison suggest managers must always juggle the efficiency of delivering the message with its impact on receivers. Typically, managers who deliver bad news in face-to-face settings are more appreciated and accepted by employees.[5]

Managers can prepare for possible negatives by giving full information as it becomes available. It is also possible to let the people who will be affected by a decision participate in setting the criteria. Someone who has bought into the criteria for retaining workers is more likely to accept decisions using such criteria. And in some cases, the synergism of groups may make possible ideas that management didn't think of or rejected as "unacceptable."

Some workplaces incorporate employee suggestion systems to help reduce excess costs and improve organizational effectiveness. Nokia, for example, runs a BlogHub and Sphere. Both are social media sites that employees can use to critique products, rant about the company, and ask questions. Mangers hope that these sites, which allow employees to give anonymous honest opinions, will spawn new ideas and innovations.[6]

When the bad news is less serious, as in Figure 10.3, try using the pattern in the first column of Figure 10.1 unless your knowledge of the audience suggests that another pattern will be more effective. The audience's reaction is influenced by the following factors:

- Do you and the audience have a good relationship?
- Does the organization treat people well?
- Has the audience been warned of possible negatives?
- Has the audience bought into the criteria for the decision?
- Do communications after the negative decision build goodwill?

Figure 10.3 A Negative Memo to Subordinates

Memo

Date: January 10, 2012
To: All Employees
From: Floyd E. Mattson FEM

Subject: Group Dental Insurance

First Bank is always seeking to provide employees with a competitive benefits package that meets their needs.

In response to many requests, the Human Resource Department solicited bids for expanded dental coverage. At this time none of the responses from insurers serving our area are affordable for us. We continue to negotiate, but with costs rising at 20% per year, success seems unlikely. Other banks in the area are in a similar situation, so our current benefits package matches or exceeds what they offer.

First Bank continues to offer enrollment in an employee-funded group plan with ABC Dental. The coverage includes 37 dentists in our county and pays 50 percent of allowable fees. Many of our employees have found this coverage helpful. Employees also may use their medical savings account for dental care. Consider one of these options for the present, and First Bank will continue to investigate new opportunities for expanded coverage.

Reason given before negative | Positive | Alternatives | Positive close

THE PARTS OF A NEGATIVE MESSAGE LO 10-2

This section provides more information about wording each part of a negative message.

Subject Lines

Many negative messages put the topic, but not the specific negative, in the subject line.

Subject: Status of Conversion Table Program

Other negative message subject lines focus on solving the problem.

Subject: Improving Our Subscription Letter

How to Tell a Partner about an STD

"Dating etiquette demands it—and so does public health. If you have a sexually transmitted disease, you need to tell your partner.

But finding the right moment for that awkward conversation isn't easy. Whether out of fear, shame, or anger, people diagnosed with STDs often fail to tell.

So how about sending an e-card? That's an approach developed in part by the San Francisco Department of Public Health. Called the inSPOT program, it lets you send specialized STD alert e-cards to break the news. Since its launch a few years ago, more than 30,000 people have sent more than 49,500 cards. Considering the 19 million new STD cases diagnosed each year in the U.S., that's a drop in the bucket, but it's certainly a step in the right direction.

E-cards come in various designs, and the sender can choose a specific STD from a pull-down menu. One message reads: 'It's not what you brought to the party, it's what you left with. I left with an STD. You might have, too. Get checked out soon.' It then directs recipients to testing centers in their area. The e-cards can be sent anonymously, and according to inSPOT, it doesn't collect data about site users or card recipients."

Use a negative subject line in messages when you think readers may ignore what they believe is a routine message. Also use a negative subject line when the reader needs the information to make a decision or to act.

> Subject: Elevator to Be Out Friday, June 17

Many people do not read all their messages, and a neutral subject line may lead them to ignore the message.

Buffers

Traditionally, textbooks recommended that negative messages open with buffers. A buffer is a neutral or positive statement that allows you to delay the negative. Some research suggests that buffers do not make readers respond more positively,[7] and good buffers are hard to write. However, in special situations, you may want to use a buffer. The first sentence in the First Bank letter (Figure 10.3) is a buffer.

To be effective, a buffer must put the reader in a good frame of mind, not give the bad news but not imply a positive answer either, and provide a natural transition to the body of the letter. The kinds of statements most often used as buffers are good news, facts and chronologies of events, references to enclosures, thanks, and statements of principle.

1. **Start with any good news or positive elements the letter contains.**

> Starting Thursday, June 26, you'll have easier access to your money 24 hours a day at First National Bank.

Letter announcing that the drive-up windows will be closed for two days while new automatic teller machines are installed

2. **State a fact or provide a chronology of events.**

> As a result of the new graduated dues schedule—determined by vote of the Delegate Assembly last December and subsequently endorsed by the Executive Council—members are now asked to establish their own dues rate and to calculate the total amount of their remittance.

Announcement of a new dues structure that will raise most members' dues

3. **Refer to enclosures in the letter.**

> A new sticker for your car is enclosed. You may pick up additional ones in the office if needed.

Letter announcing increase in parking rental rates

4. **Thank the reader for something he or she has done.**

> Thank you for scheduling appointments for me with so many senior people at First National Bank. My visit there March 14 was very informative.

Letter refusing a job offer

5. **State a general principle.**

> Good drivers should pay substantially less for their auto insurance. The Good Driver Plan was created to reward good drivers (those with five-year accident-free records) with our lowest available rates. A change in the plan, effective January 1, will help keep those rates low.

Letter announcing that the company will now count traffic tickets, not just accidents, in calculating insurance rates—a change that will raise many people's premiums

Some audiences will feel betrayed by messages whose positive openers delay the central negative point. Therefore, use a buffer only when the audience (individually or culturally) values harmony or when the buffer serves another purpose. For example, when you must thank the reader somewhere in the letter, putting the "thank you" in the first paragraph allows you to start on a positive note.

Buffers are hard to write. Even if you think the reader would prefer to be let down easily, use a buffer only when you can write a good one.

Reasons

Research shows that audiences who described themselves as "totally surprised" by negative news had many more negative feelings and described their feelings as being stronger than did those who expected the negative.[8] A clear and convincing reason prepares the audience for the negative, resulting in people who more easily accept it.

The following reason is inadequate.

Weak reason: The goal of the Knoxville CHARGE-ALL Center is to provide our customers faster, more personalized service. Since you now live outside the Knoxville CHARGE-ALL service area, we can no longer offer you the advantages of a local CHARGE-ALL Center.

If the reader says, "I don't care if my bills are slow and impersonal," will the company let the reader keep the card? No. The real reason for the negative is that the bank's franchise allows it to have cardholders only in a given geographic region.

Real reason: Each local CHARGE-ALL center is permitted to offer accounts to customers in a several-state area. The Knoxville CHARGE-ALL center serves customers east of the Mississippi. You can continue to use your current card until it expires. When that happens, you'll need to open an account with a CHARGE-ALL center that serves Texas.

Don't hide behind "company policy": your audience will assume the policy is designed to benefit you at their expense. If possible, show how your audience benefits from the policy. If they do not benefit, don't mention policy at all.

Weak reason: I cannot write an insurance policy for you because company policy does not allow me to do so.

Better reason: Gorham insures cars only when they are normally garaged at night. Standard insurance policies cover a wider variety of risks and charge higher fees. Limiting the policies we write gives Gorham customers the lowest possible rates for auto insurance.

Avoid saying that you *cannot* do something. Most negative messages exist because the communicator or company has chosen certain policies or cutoff points. In the example above, the company could choose to insure a wider variety of customers if it wanted to do so.

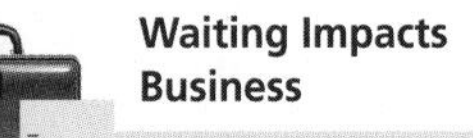

Waiting Impacts Business

The longer customers wait, the more annoyed they can become. A team of marketing professors examined the waiting experiences of 844 customers at banks, hair salons, restaurants, and oil change shops. The researchers identified five pieces of advice that affect how customers respond to waiting.

1. Give customers a focus other than the wait: If customers are doing something, they are less focused on how long the wait lasts.
2. Try to reduce anxiety of waiting: Providing wait estimates or music can help reduce customer anxiety.
3. Show fairness in waiting: If customers are waiting, they don't want to see (or perceive) other people getting special treatment.
4. Create a relaxed environment: Make sure seating, temperatures, and noise levels are all appropriate when customers wait.
5. Support regular customers.

Adapted from David Elbert, "Waiting Warps Customers' Sense of Time, Raises Dander," *Des Moines Register*, November 29, 2009, 1D, 2D.

As a middle manager, you will often enforce policies that you did not design and announce decisions that you did not make. Don't pass the buck by saying, "This was a terrible decision." Carelessly criticizing your superiors is never a good idea.

If you have several reasons for saying *no*, use only those that are strong and watertight. If you give five reasons and the audience dismisses two of the them, the audience may feel that they've won and should get the request.

Weak reason:	You cannot store large bulky items in the dormitory over the summer because moving them into and out of storage would tie up the stairs and the elevators just at the busiest times when people are moving in and out.

If students say they will move large items before or after the two days when most people are moving in or out, you are still not going to grant the request, because you do not have the storage room. If you do not have a good reason, omit the reason rather than use a weak one. Even if you have a strong reason, omit it if it makes the company look bad.

Reason that hurts company:	Our company is not hiring at the present time because profits are down. In fact, the downturn has prompted top management to reduce the salaried staff by 5% just this month, with perhaps more reductions to come.
Better:	Our company does not have any openings now.

Refusals

Deemphasize the refusal by putting it in the same paragraph as the reason, rather than in a paragraph by itself.

Sometimes you may be able to imply the refusal rather than stating it directly.

Direct refusal:	You cannot get insurance for just one month.
Implied refusal:	The shortest term for an insurance policy is six months.

Be sure the implication is crystal clear. Any message can be misunderstood, but an optimistic or desperate audience is particularly unlikely to understand a negative message. One of your purposes in a negative message is to close the door on the subject. You do not want to have to send a second message saying that the real answer is *no.*

Alternatives

Giving your audience an alternative or a compromise, if one is available, is a good idea for several reasons:

- It offers the audience another way to get what they want.
- It suggests that you really care about your audience and about helping to meet their needs.
- It enables your audience to reestablish the psychological freedom you limited when you said *no.*
- It allows you to end on a positive note and to present yourself and your organization as positive, friendly, and helpful.

When you give an alternative, give your audience all the information they need to act on it, but don't take the necessary steps. Let your audience decide whether to try the alternative.

Negative messages limit your audience's freedom. People may respond to a limitation of freedom by asserting their freedom in some other arena. Sharon and Jack Brehm calls this phenomenon **psychological reactance.**[9] Psychological reactance is at work when a customer who has been denied credit no longer buys even on a cash basis, a subordinate who has been passed over for a promotion gets back at the company by deliberately doing a poor job, or someone who has been laid off sabotages the company's computers.

An alternative allows your audience to react in a way that doesn't hurt you. By letting your audience decide for themselves whether they want the alternative, you allow them to reestablish their sense of psychological freedom.

The specific alternative will vary depending on the circumstances. In Figure 10.4, the company suggests using a different part. In different circumstances, the writer might offer different alternatives.

Disgruntled Customer with a Hammer

Providing good customer service should be a goal of any business. When it's not, customers get angry and can exert their frustrations in negative ways.

In Bristow, Virginia, Mona Shaw, a 75-year-old woman who wanted phone, Internet, and cable service installed, vented her frustrations with Comcast by going to their office and smashing a keyboard, monitor, and telephone . . . with a hammer.

She claims her frustration was the result of poor customer service. She waited for an installation technician who showed up two days late. Once there, he never finished the job. To top things off, two days later Comcast cut all her services. The tipping point came when she waited two hours to talk to a Comcast manager before being informed he had left for the day.

For her brash response, Shaw received a fine and three-month suspended sentence. She is also forbidden to go near the Comcast office. She eventually got her phone, Internet, and cable working, but with different providers.

Adapted from "Woman, 75, Fined for Smashing Comcast Office with Hammer in Customer Service Dispute," *Associated Press Archive,* October 19, 2007.

Endings

If you have a good alternative, refer to it in your ending: "If you can use A515 grade 70, please let me know."

The best endings look positively to the future.

> Wherever you have your account, you'll continue to get all the service you've learned to expect from CHARGE-ALL, and the convenience of charging items at over a million stores, restaurants, and hotels in the United States and abroad–and in Knoxville, too, whenever you come back to visit!

Letter refusing to continue charge account for a customer who has moved

Avoid endings that seem insincere.

> We are happy to have been of service, and should we be able to assist you in the future, please contact us.

This ending lacks you-attitude and would not be good even in a positive message. In a situation where the company has just refused to help, it's likely to sound sarcastic.

APOLOGIES

Apologizing is never an easy task, but it's something most of us do. New research suggests that people, on average, say they're sorry four times a week. And most people have an easier time saying they're sorry to friends and strangers than they do family members or partners.[10]

Organizations have to routinely offer apologies, too. The news frequently has stories of corporations providing apologies. Southwest Airlines CEO offered an apology to customers and safety regulators for poor maintenance measures in an effort to restore a tarnished reputation.[11] Descriptions of other apologies from JetBlue and the *Los Angeles Times* can be found in sidebars in this chapter.

Timing is crucial for apologies. After Toyota vehicles had an issue with sticking gas pedals that forced a recall of about 6 million cars, they issued full page pledges in most major newspapers to their customers on how they're fixing the situation. The president of Toyota, Akio Toyoda, also issued a formal apology. However, some critics were upset that Toyota Motors sent an American sales executive, Jim Lentz, to initially handle questions rather than Toyado himself as the face of the company. Others believe that Toyota mishandled the situation by offering a slow response, minimizing the problem, and delaying the recall.[12]

Figure 10.4 A Refusal with an Alternative

"Serving the needs of America since 1890"
1800 Olney Avenue • Philadelphia, PA 19140 • 215•555•7800 • Fax: 215•555•9803

April 27, 2012

Mr. H. J. Moody
Canton Corporation
2407 North Avenue
Kearney, NE 68847

Subject: Bid Number 5853, Part Number D-40040

Dear Mr. Moody:

Buffer Thank you for requesting our quotation on your Part No. D-40040.

Reason Your blueprints call for flame-cut rings 1/2" thick A516 grade 70. To use that grade, we'd have to grind down from 1" thick material. However, if you can use A515 grade 70, which we stock in 1/2" thick, you can cut the price by more than half.

Quantity	Description	Gross Weight	Price/Each
75	Rings Drawing D-40040, A516 Grade 70 1" thick x 6" O.D. x 2.8" I.D. ground to .5" thick.	12 lbs.	$15.08
75	Rings Drawing D-40040, A515 Grade 70 1/2" thick x 6" O.D. x 2.8" I.D.	6 lbs.	$6.91

Alternative (Depending on circumstances, different alternatives may exist.)

If you can use A515 grade 70, please let me know.

Leaves decision up to reader to re-establish psychological freedom

Sincerely,

Valerie Prynne

Valerie Prynne

VP:wc

Not all negative messages, however, need to include apologies. In business documents, apologize only when you are at fault. If you need to apologize, do it early, briefly, and sincerely. Do so only once, early in the message. Do not dwell on the bad things that have happened. The reader already knows this negative information. Instead, focus on what you have done to correct the situation.

Schwinn needed a new product line to attract sophisticated cyclists. This apology for its old, boring line moves quickly to a discussion of its new technology. By evoking an experience every cyclist has had, the headline also suggests that falling is a minor event.

No explicit apology is necessary if the error is small and if you are correcting the mistake.

Negative: We're sorry we got the nutrition facts wrong in the recipe.

Better: You're right. We're glad you made us aware of this. The correct amounts are 2 grams of fat and 4 grams of protein.

Do not apologize when you are not at fault. The phrase "I'm sorry" is generally interpreted to mean the sorry person is accepting blame or responsibility. When you have done everything you can and when a delay or problem is due to circumstances beyond your control, you aren't at fault and don't need to apologize. It may, however, be appropriate to include an explanation so the reader knows you weren't negligent. In the previous example acknowledging an error, the writer might indicate the source of the error (such as a reference book or a government website). If the news is bad, put the explanation first. If you have good news for the reader, put it before your explanation.

Negative: I'm sorry that I could not answer your question sooner. I had to wait until the sales figures for the second quarter were in.

Better (neutral or bad news): We needed the sales figures for the second quarter to answer your question. Now that they're in, I can tell you that. . . .

Better (good news): The new advertising campaign is a success. The sales figures for the second quarter are finally in, and they show that. . . .

If the delay or problem is long or large, it is good you-attitude to ask the audience whether they want to confirm the original plan or make different arrangements.

Negative: I'm sorry that the chairs will not be ready by August 25 as promised.

Better: Because of a strike against the manufacturer, the desk chairs you ordered will not be ready until November. Do you want to keep that order, or would you like to look at the models available from other suppliers?

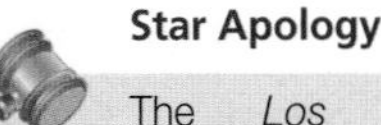

Star Apology

The *Los Angeles Times* ran an article that implied associates of rapper Sean Combs (a.k.a. "Diddy") carried out the 1994 robbery and shooting of rapper Tupac Shakur, and that Combs knew about it ahead of time. The *Times* initially reported that FBI records, interviews with people at the crime scene, and statements to the FBI by an informant were the source of the article. However, none were actually named in the article.

Combs and his lawyers were outraged about the attacks on his character and stated that he had no involvement in the murder.

After The Smoking Gun website posted doubt about the validity of the FBI documents, the *Times* ran its own investigation. The Smoking Gun noted the documents appeared to be written on a typewriter, not a computer, and contained unusual blacked-out sections. These investigations of the sources of the article led the *Times* to eventually retract its story and offer a public apology.

Public apologies are never easy but sometimes are necessary.

Adapted from "*LA Times* Apologizes, Says Documents Used for Tupac Shakur Story Likely Fabricated," *Associated Press Archive,* March 27, 2008.

JetBlue's Nightmare

On February 14, 2007, JetBlue attempted to continue operations during an ice storm. They boarded passengers and rolled planes to runways for de-icing, betting that planes would be able to take off as the storm subsided.

Other planes were subsequently parked at terminal gates, preventing JetBlue planes from returning to the gates to unload passengers. Hundreds of passengers were held aboard planes, some for as long as 11 hours. Thousands more passengers and mounds of baggage were stranded at the terminal.

JetBlue's problems were exacerbated by the company's poor communication:

- Posting delays for flights instead of cancellations kept passengers waiting for hours.
- Passengers stranded on planes reported they were not given information about their status because the flight crews were not being informed.
- The JetBlue phone number was overloaded. Callers experienced lengthy holds, and many could not get through at all.
- The airline's computer system and crew-scheduling software were inadequate for the task of scheduling crews after the storm, slowing the return to full service.

JetBlue publicly apologized and offered refunds, free flight vouchers, and penalty-free rebooking. Besides the damage to the company's reputation, estimated costs to JetBlue included $14 million in customer refunds, $16 million in vouchers, and $4 million in staff overtime.

Sources: Allan Sloan, with Temma Ehrenfeld, "Skies Were Cloudy before Jet Blew It," *Newsweek,* March 5, 2007, 26; and Jesus Sanchez and Alana Semuels, "JetBlue Struggles to Get Past Last Week's Fiasco," *Chicago Tribune,* February 19, 2007.

This cereal box mocks the accelerating trend for apologies in the workplace.

Source: The Denver Post and The Flip Side Staff, "Eating Crow," *Columbus Dispatch,* September 8, 2004, F8.

Sometimes you will be in a fortunate position where you can pair your apology with an appropriate benefit.

- When the Hallmark Flowers web site stopped taking orders the week before Mother's Day, Hallmark sent an e-mail asking customers to try again and offering free shipping for a day.[13]
- When Apple sharply cut the price on the iPhone a few months after it came on the market, Steve Jobs offered an apology to earlier buyers and provided them with a $100 Apple store credit.
- Many airlines now have computer programs that generate apology letters for customers on flights with lengthy delays or other major problems; the letters frequently offer additional frequent-flyer miles or discount vouchers for future trips.[14]

Sincere apologies go hand in hand with efforts to rectify the problem. Some hospitals have found that disclosing medical errors, apologizing, and quickly offering a financial settlement to the victims actually reduces litigation and prevents future mistakes. After a program was established at the University of Illinois Medical Center in Chicago to help communicate with wronged patients, the number of lawsuits declined 40% in four years, even though the number of procedures increased by 23%. When mistakes happen, the hospital also tries to establish new protocols to avoid similar problems in the future.[15]

It's easy to get angry in negative situations; avoid that temptation.

TONE IN NEGATIVE MESSAGES LO 10-3

Tone—the implied attitude of the author toward the reader and the subject—is particularly important when you want readers to feel that you have taken their requests seriously. Check your draft carefully for positive emphasis and you-attitude (see Chapter 3), both at the level of individual words and at the level of ideas. In many situations, empathizing with your audience will help you create a more humane message.

Figure 10.5 lists some of the words and phrases to avoid in negative messages. Figure 3.3 in Chapter 3 suggests more negative words to avoid.

Even the physical appearance and timing of a message can convey tone. An obvious form rejection letter suggests that the writer has not given much consideration to the reader's application. An immediate negative suggests that the rejection didn't need any thought. A negative delivered just before a major holiday seems especially unfeeling.

ALTERNATIVE STRATEGIES FOR NEGATIVE SITUATIONS

Whenever you face a negative situation, consider recasting it as a positive or persuasive message. Southwest Airlines, the low-cost airline, is famous for saying no to its customers. It says no to such common perks as reserve seats,

Workplace Violence

An increasing number of people respond violently to bad news.

In August 2010, a man killed nine people at a distributor in Hartford, Connecticut, after he signed a resignation letter as the result of disciplinary action. He brought two handguns, which he used to shoot his victims, to work in a red metal lunchbox.

In another incident in July 2010, a former employee of Emcore, a fiber optics company in Albuquerque, New Mexico, killed two co-workers and himself and injured four more.

These workplace incidents are only a few of many that routinely occur in businesses. In fact, the Bureau of Labor Statistics reports that in 2008, the year with the most recent statistics, 421 workers nationwide were homicide victims. Typically, workplace violence ensues when a person feels mistreated or betrayed by an organization. Many businesses now have formal workplace procedures to cope with these incidents.

Adapted from Ross Arrowsmith, "Gunman Came Prepared to Connecticut Shooting," *Workplace Violence News,* August 4, 2010, http://workplaceviolencenews.com/2010/08/04/gunman-came-prepared-to-connecticut-shooting/; Ben Casselman, "Albuquerque Shooting Leaves 3 Dead," *Wall Street Journal,* July 13, 2010, http://online.wsj.com/article/SB10001424052748704288204575363133284257738.html; and U.S. Bureau of Labor Statistics, "Workplace Shootings," July 2010, http://www.bls.gov/iif/oshwc/cfoi/osar0014.htm.

Figure 10.5 Avoid These Phrases in Negative Messages

Phrase	Because
I am afraid that we cannot	You aren't fearful. Don't hide behind empty phrases.
I am sorry that we are unable	You probably are able to grant the request; you simply choose not to. If you are so sorry about saying no, why don't you change your policy and say *yes*?
I am sure you will agree that	Don't assume that you can read the reader's mind.
Unfortunately	*Unfortunately* is negative in itself. It also signals that a refusal is coming.

International Firing

"When doing business in another country, it is often easy to assume that things there are the same as in your country. . . . It is wise to know the proper way to dismiss an employee when working with other cultures. This is a difficult task to perform in a familiar territory but it is especially tricky when one is in a foreign country and does not always fully understand the local culture. An American manager stationed in Indonesia reportedly discovered this when he tried to fire an oil-rig employee. Rather than notifying the employee privately of this dismissal, the manager publicly told the timekeeper to send the man 'packing.' In Indonesia, this public dismissal was considered unacceptable 'loss of face' which offended both the dismissed man and his friends. So, rather than leave quietly, the man grabbed fire axes and ran after the American manager. Reportedly, the American was barely rescued in time. Obviously, it is dangerous to ignore local management practices and customs!"

Quoted from David A. Ricks, *Blunders in International Business,* 4th ed. (Malden, MA: Blackwell Publishing, 2006), 105.

meals, and interairline baggage transfers. But it recasts all those negatives into its two biggest positives, low-cost fares and conveniently scheduled frequent flights.[16]

Recasting the Situation as a Positive Message

If the negative information will directly lead to a benefit that you know readers want, use the pattern of organization for informative and positive messages:

Situation:	Your airline has been mailing out quarterly statements of frequent-flier miles earned. To save money, you are going to stop mailing statements and ask customers to look up that information at your website.
Negative:	Important Notice: This is your last Preferred Passenger paper statement.
Positive emphasis:	New, convenient online statements will replace this quarterly mailing. Now you can get up-to-the-minute statements of your miles earned. Choose e-mail updates or round-the-clock access to your statement at our website, www.aaaair.com. It's faster, easier, and more convenient.

After Taco Bell had a law firm voluntarily withdraw a suit that questioned the amount of meat in their ground beef, the company turned the negative situation into a positive. Taco Bell bought full pages in the *Wall Street Journal* and *New York Times* and ran advertisements with a headline, "Thank you for suing us." They used the rest of the space to discuss the ingredients in their ground beef and to avoid a public relations scandal.[17]

Recasting the Situation as a Persuasive Message

Often a negative situation can be recast as a persuasive message. If your organization has a problem, ask the audience to help solve it. A solution that workers have created will be much easier to implement.

When the Association for Business Communication raised dues, the Executive Director wrote a persuasive letter urging members to send in renewals early so they could beat the increase. The letter shared some of the qualities of

After an alligator escaped from his cage at the Los Angeles Zoo, a spokesperson recast the negative situation as a positive by telling reporters that the escape proved the alligator was smart and healthy.

Source: Justin Scheck and Ben Worthen, "When Animals Go AWOL, Zoos Try to Tame Bad PR," *Wall Street Journal,* January 1, 2008, A1, A10.

any persuasive letter: using an attention-getting opener, offsetting the negative by setting it against the benefits of membership, telling the reader what to do, and ending with a picture of the benefit the reader received by acting. More recent increases, however, have been announced directly.

If you are criticizing someone, your real purpose may be to persuade the reader to act differently. Chapter 11 offers patterns for problem-solving persuasive messages.

VARIETIES OF NEGATIVE MESSAGES LO 10-4

Some of the most common negative messages are claims and complaints. Three of the most difficult kinds of negative messages to write are rejections and refusals, disciplinary notices and negative performance appraisals, and layoffs and firings.

Claims and Complaints

Claims and complaint messages are needed when something has gone wrong: you didn't get the files you needed in time for the report; the supplier didn't send enough parts; the copy machine breaks down daily. Many claims and complaints are handled well with a quick phone call or office visit, but sometimes you will need a paper trail.

Technology has certainly influenced the way complaints are processed. United Airlines stopped their customer relations phone service. Complaint responses are now handled by United representatives through e-mail and letters. The company believes customers will get a better quality of feedback.[18] Delta Air Lines has a team of customer service agents who monitor social media applications like Twitter for real-time complaints. When travelers complain about the company, the agents try to solve problems before they go viral by offering updated gate information or rebooking details. Sometimes they even bend the rules to null complaints in the Twittersphere. In one instance, a passenger got frequent flier miles that she wasn't entitled to receive because she posted complaining tweets about Delta.[19]

A lot of consumers are angry these days, and organizations should be responsive to their complaints. According to the Edelman Trust Barometer, people believe negative news about an organization with a low trust level after one or two encounters, while people believe positive news only after four or five.[20]

Organizations, like Delta, need fast response times in handling complaints before a situation tarnishes their brand. The speed of complaints is growing faster with websites exclusively dedicated to the issue. Sites such as Angie's List, Consumer Affairs, Planet Feedback, Ripoff Report, Tello, and Yelp offer forums for disgruntled customers. Many of these sites also have smartphone applications that allow consumers to report incidents almost instantaneously. To stay on top of the reviews, new electronic tools are emerging that help organizations scan for key words and monitor reviews related to their brand.

When writing a claim or complaint, you generally will use a direct organization: put a clear statement of the problem in the first sentence. An indirect approach, such as starting with a buffer, may be interpreted as a weak claim.

Give supporting facts—what went wrong, the extent of the damage. Give identifiers such as invoice numbers, warranty codes, and order dates. If this is a claim, specify what is necessary to set things right (be realistic!). Avoid anger and sarcasm; they will only lessen your chances of a favorable settlement. In particular, avoid saying you will never use the company, service, machine again. Such a statement may eliminate your audience's will to rectify the problem. See Figure 10.6 for the *Wall Street Journal*'s suggestions for e-mail claims to airlines.

Turning Tables on Complaints

While consumers have many avenues for complaining, the organizations that are complained about may feel a bit powerless. However, the Alamo Drafthouse, a movie theater in Austin, Texas, found a way to turn the tables on one complainer.

The movie theater has one simple rule: don't text or use a phone during the movie. One woman broke this simple rule and was kicked out of the theater. She then called the theater to complain about the situation; she believed they were ripping her off.

The theater now uses this woman's ridiculous message as a public service announcement that shows before all movies begin to remind movie goers of the one simple rule. In other words, instead of allowing the customer, who was clearly in the wrong, to create negative publicity, the theater owners created a positive situation for their business. You can watch the video at the web address in the source below.

In another instance, a pizza shop in New York turned the tables by printing T-shirts for employees with the negative reviews they received online at Yelp. The strategy helped increase business and create more loyal customers.

What do you think? Are the actions of these businesses justified? How else can organizations gain more power in this electronic age when it is so easy for anonymous consumers to complain?

Adapted from Lani Rosales, "Austin Business Proves That Social Media Cuts Both Ways," AGBeat, June 6, 2011, http://agentgenius.com/real-estate-technology-new-media/austin-business-proves-that-social-media-cuts-both-ways/.

Figure 10.6 Airline Complaint Tips

These tips can improve your chances of a favorable response from an airline:

- Ask for the compensation you want.
- Be realistic. You will not get compensation for a routine delay.
- Be direct and short. Do provide flight, reservation, and frequent-flyer numbers.
- Don't threaten. Particularly don't say you will never fly with them again.
- Write to Customer Service. Your complaint will eventually end up there no matter where you send it.

Source: Scott McCartney, "What Airlines Do When You Complain," Wall Street Journal, March 20, 2007, D1.

Rejections and Refusals

When you refuse requests from people outside your organization, try to give an alternative if one is available. For example, you may not be able to replace for free an automotive water pump that no longer is on warranty. But you may be able to offer your customer a rebuilt one that is much less expensive than a new pump.

Politeness and length help. In two different studies, job applicants preferred rejection letters that said something specific about their good qualities, that

Hallmark has expanded their line of cards to address the health concerns many people are experiencing. The inside of this card says, "They'll have no follow-up questions."

phrased the refusal indirectly, that offered a clear explanation of the procedures for making a hiring decision, that offered an alternative (such as another position the applicant might be qualified for), and that were longer.[21] Furthermore, businesses that follow this pattern of organization for rejection letters will retain applicants who still view the organization favorably, who will recommend the organization to others interested in applying there, and who will not file lawsuits.[22]

Double-check the words in a refusal to be sure the reason can't backfire if it is applied to other contexts. The statement that a plant is too dangerous for a group tour could be used as evidence against the company in a worker's compensation claim. Similarly, writing resignation letters for a variety of reasons—leaving a job, opting out of a fellowship—can be a delicate practice and can have serious future implications. Many audiences will see the letter as a statement that their organization is not good enough. The best letters try to neutralize these feelings. A negative and poorly worded resignation letter can impact your chances for receiving a positive recommendation or reference in the future.

When you refuse requests within your organization, use your knowledge of the organization's culture and of the specific individual to craft your message. Some organizations share more negative information than others. Some individuals prefer a direct no; others may find a direct negative insulting. The sample problem at the end of this chapter is a refusal to someone within the company.

Disciplinary Notices and Negative Performance Appraisals

Performance appraisals, discussed in detail in Chapter 11, will be positive when they are designed to help a basically good employee improve. But when an employee violates company policy or fails to improve after repeated negative appraisals, the company may discipline the employee or build a dossier to support firing him or her.

Present disciplinary notices and negative performance appraisals directly, with no buffer. A buffer might encourage the recipient to minimize the message's importance—and might even become evidence in a court case that the employee had not been told to shape up "or else." Cite quantifiable observations of the employee's behavior, rather than generalizations or inferences based on it.

Weak: Lee is apathetic about work.

Better: Lee was absent 15 days and late by one hour 6 days in the quarter beginning January 1.

Weak: Vasu is careless with her written documents.

Better: Vasu had multiple spelling errors in her last three client letters; a fourth letter omitted the date of the mandatory federal training seminar.

Not all disciplinary notices are as formal as performance appraisals. Blanchard and Johnson, of *One Minute Manager* fame, present what they call the One Minute Reprimand. Much of the effectiveness of these reprimands comes from the fact that supervisors tell their employees from the beginning, before any reprimands are needed, that there will be explicit communication about both positive and negative performances. The reprimand itself is to come immediately after negative behavior and specify exactly what is wrong. It distinguishes between positive feelings for the employee and negative feelings for his or her performance in the specific situation.[23]

Dumpster Diving Anyone?

Northwest Airlines, which filed for bankruptcy and underwent reorganization before merging with Delta, sent out a handbook for employees who might lose their jobs. The handbook, titled "Ground Operations Restructuring Q&A and Employee Support," offered employees some useful information about retirement benefits and résumé assistance. However, the handbook also offered some unconventional assistance, such as a listing of "101 Ways to Save Money."

Here are a few of the tips: (quoted list)

- Buy spare parts for your car at the junkyard
- Get hand-me-down clothes and toys for your kids from family and friends
- Buy old furniture at yard sales and refinish it yourself
- Hang clothes out to dry
- Borrow a dress for a big night out or go to a consignment shop
- Don't be shy about pulling something you like out of a dumpster

Northwest employees were appalled by this list of outrageous suggestions. The vice president for ground operations quickly apologized, and the chief executive officer sent a letter of apology to the affected employees who received the handbook.

Adapted and quoted from Michelle Singletary, "Dumpster-Diving Advice Doesn't Fly," *Washington Post*, August 24, 2006, D2.

Effective Negative Letters

Researcher Catherine Schryer asked writers at an insurance company to evaluate the firm's letters denying claims. She found four differences between the letters judged effective and the letters judged ineffective:

- Good letters were easier to read. Poor letters contained more jargon; longer words and sentences; and stiff, awkward phrasing.
- Good letters gave fuller reasons for the rejection. Poor letters often used boilerplate and did not explain terms.
- Good letters were less likely to talk about the reader's emotions ("angry," "disappointed").
- Good letters were more likely to portray the writer and reader as active agents.

Adapted from Catherine Schryer, "Walking a Fine Line: Writing Negative Letters in an Insurance Company," *Journal of Business and Technical Communication* 14 (October 2000): 445–97.

Layoffs and Firings

If a company is in financial trouble, management needs to communicate the problem clearly. Sharing information and enlisting everyone's help in finding solutions may make it possible to save jobs. Sharing information also means that layoff notices, if they become necessary, will be a formality; they should not be new information to employees.

Give the employee an honest reason for the layoff or firing. Based on guidance from your organization's human resource experts, state the reasons in a way that is clear but does not expose the organization to legal liabilities.

Show empathy for affected employees; think about how you would feel if you were losing your job. Show how the company will help them with severance pay and other aid, such as job search advice. Remember that many studies show that layoffs may temporarily help the bottom line, but they rarely provide long-term savings. They also hurt the productivity of remaining employees.[24]

Firings for unsatisfactory performance have always been a part of business. Now, however, as technology blurs the line between work and home, firings are also happening for personal reasons, even if the behavior is not tied to work and occurs off-site. The CEO of HBO was asked to resign after he was accused of assaulting his girlfriend in a parking lot. Kaiser Aluminum's CFO had to resign because of a personal relationship with another employee, as did Boeing's former president and CEO Harry Stonecipher.[25]

Information about layoffs and firings is normally delivered orally but accompanied by a written statement explaining severance pay or unemployment benefits that may be available. RadioShack made negative headlines when it fired 400 employees with a two-sentence e-mail.

SOLVING A SAMPLE PROBLEM

Solving negative problems requires careful analysis. The checklist at the end of the chapter can help you evaluate your draft.

Problem

You're Director of Employee Benefits for a Fortune 500 company. Today, you received the following memo:

From: Michelle Jagtiani
Subject: Getting My Retirement Benefits

Next Friday will be my last day here. I am leaving [name of company] to take a position at another firm.

Please process a check for my retirement benefits, including both the deductions from my salary and the company's contributions for the last six and a half years. I would like to receive the check by next Friday if possible.

You have bad news for Michelle. Although the company does contribute an amount to the retirement fund equal to the amount deducted for retirement from the employee's paycheck, employees who leave with less than seven years of employment get only their own contributions. Michelle will get back only the money that has been deducted from her own pay, plus 4½% interest compounded quarterly. Her payments and interest come to just over $17,200; the amount could be higher depending on the amount of her last paycheck, which will include compensation for any unused vacation days and sick leave. Furthermore, since the amounts deducted were not considered taxable income, she will have to pay income tax on the money she will receive.

You cannot process the check until after her resignation is effective, so you will mail it to her. You have her home address on file; if she's moving, she needs to let you know where to send the check. Processing the check may take two to three weeks.

Write a memo to Michelle.

www.useit.com/alertbox/20000123.html

General guidelines for saying no can be applied to specific situations. Web guru Jakob Neilsen explains how to tell users that your website can't do what they want. Neilsen suggests telling users "no" upfront when your website cannot do something. Otherwise, users will spend too much time looking for the desired feature, and in the process will develop negative feelings for the site.

He also suggests if your site cannot meet a user's needs, that you direct them to another site that will. This referral builds goodwill and will make your site the starting point for the customer's next search. If an item will be available reasonably soon, you can allow customers to preorder or provide their e-mail for notification when the product or service becomes available.

Log onto Neilsen's site and read the rest of his advice for telling users no. Can you think of other ways to tell website users "no" that Neilsen hasn't suggested?

Analysis of the Problem

Use the analysis questions in the first chapter to help you solve the problem.

1. Who is (are) your audience(s)?

   Michelle Jagtiani. Unless she's a personal friend, I probably wouldn't know why she's leaving and where she's going.

   There's a lot I don't know. She may or may not know much about taxes; she may or may not be able to take advantage of tax-reduction strategies. I can't assume the answers because I wouldn't have them in real life.

2. What are your purposes in communicating?

   To tell her that she will get only her own contributions, plus 4½% interest compounded quarterly; that the check will be mailed to her home address two to three weeks after her last day on the job; and that the money will be taxable as income.

   To build goodwill so that she feels that she has been treated fairly and consistently. To minimize negative feelings she may have.

   To close the door on this subject.

3. What information must your message include?

   When the check will come. The facts that her check will be based on her contributions, not the employer's, and that the money will be taxable income. How lump-sum retirement benefits are calculated. The fact that we have her current address on file but need a new address if she's moving.

4. How can you build support for your position? What reasons or benefits will your audience find convincing?

   Giving the amount currently in her account may make her feel that she is getting a significant sum of money. Suggesting someone who can give free tax advice (if the company offers this as a fringe benefit) reminds her of the benefits of working with the company. Wishing her luck with her new job is a nice touch.

5. What aspects of the total situation may be relevant?

   Since this is right after taxes are due, she may be particularly interested in the tax advice. With the weak economy, she may have been counting on the extra money. On the other hand, most people take another job to get more money, so maybe she is too. I don't know for sure. Since she and I don't know each other, I don't know about her special circumstances.

Discussion of the Sample Solutions

The solution in Figure 10.7 is not acceptable. The subject line gives a bald negative with no reason or alternative. The first sentence has a condescending tone that is particularly offensive in negative messages; it also focuses on what is being taken away rather than what remains. Paragraph 2 lacks you-attitude and is vague. The memo ends with a negative. There is nothing anywhere in the memo to build goodwill.

The solution in Figure 10.8, in contrast, is effective. The policy serves as a buffer and explanation. The negative is stated clearly but is buried in the paragraph to avoid overemphasizing it. Paragraph 2 emphasizes the positive by specifying the amount in the account and the fact that the sum might be even higher.

Paragraph 3 contains the additional negative information that the amount will be taxable but offers the alternative that it may be possible to reduce taxes. The writer builds goodwill by suggesting a specific person the reader could contact.

Paragraph 4 tells the reader what address is in the company files (Michelle may not know whether the files are up-to-date), asks that she update it if necessary, and ends with the reader's concern: getting her check promptly.

The final paragraph ends on a positive note. This generalized goodwill is appropriate when the writer does not know the reader well.

Figure 10.7 An Unacceptable Solution to the Sample Problem

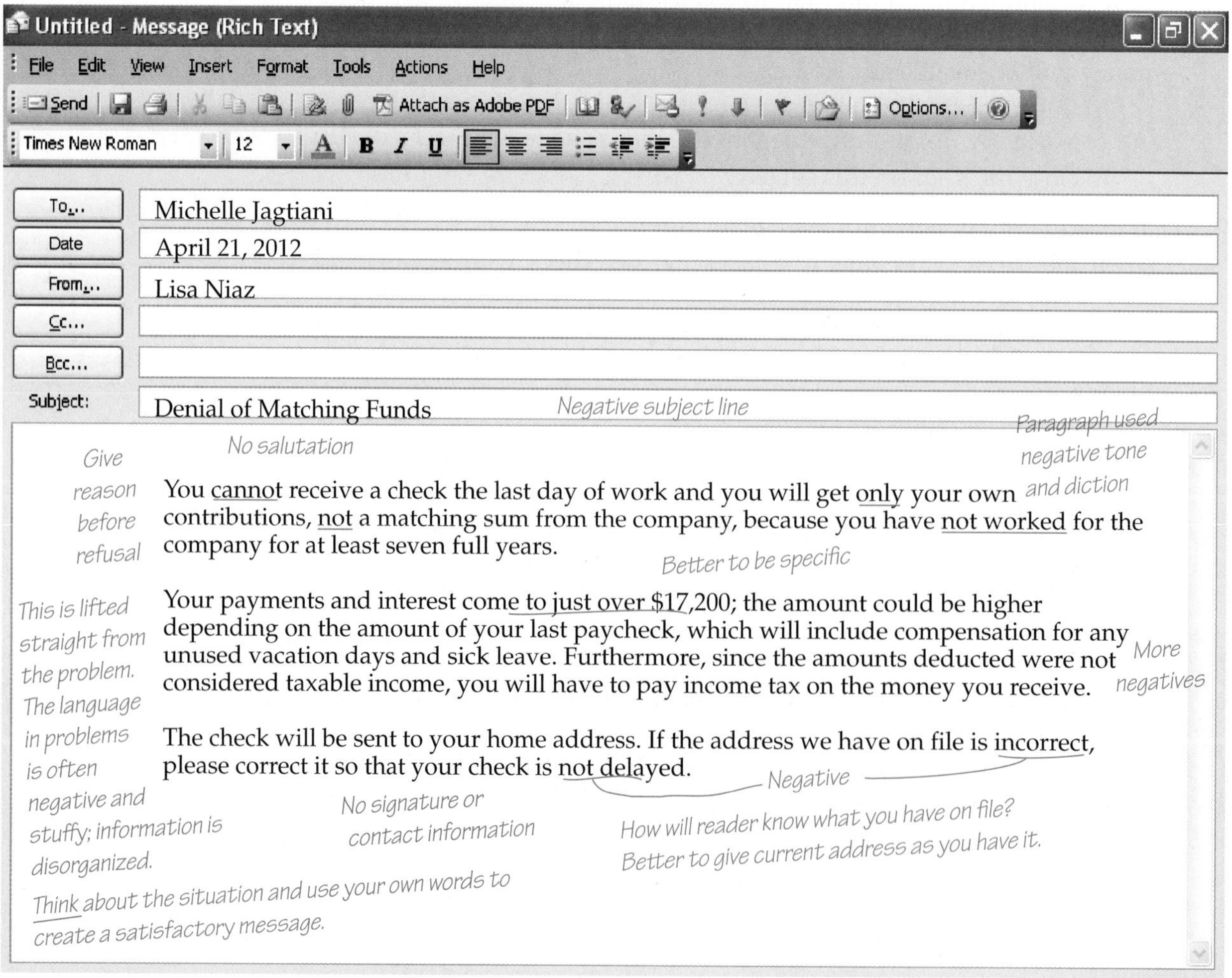

Untitled - Message (Rich Text)

File Edit View Insert Format Tools Actions Help

Send Attach as Adobe PDF Options...

Times New Roman 12

To...: Michelle Jagtiani

Date: April 21, 2012

From...: Lisa Niaz

Cc...:

Bcc...:

Subject: Denial of Matching Funds — *Negative subject line*

No salutation

Give reason before refusal

Paragraph used negative tone and diction

You cannot receive a check the last day of work and you will get only your own contributions, not a matching sum from the company, because you have not worked for the company for at least seven full years.

Better to be specific

Your payments and interest come to just over $17,200; the amount could be higher depending on the amount of your last paycheck, which will include compensation for any unused vacation days and sick leave. Furthermore, since the amounts deducted were not considered taxable income, you will have to pay income tax on the money you receive.

More negatives

The check will be sent to your home address. If the address we have on file is incorrect, please correct it so that your check is not delayed.

Negative

This is lifted straight from the problem. The language in problems is often negative and stuffy; information is disorganized.

No signature or contact information

How will reader know what you have on file? Better to give current address as you have it.

Think about the situation and use your own words to create a satisfactory message.

Figure 10.8 An Effective Solution to the Sample Problem

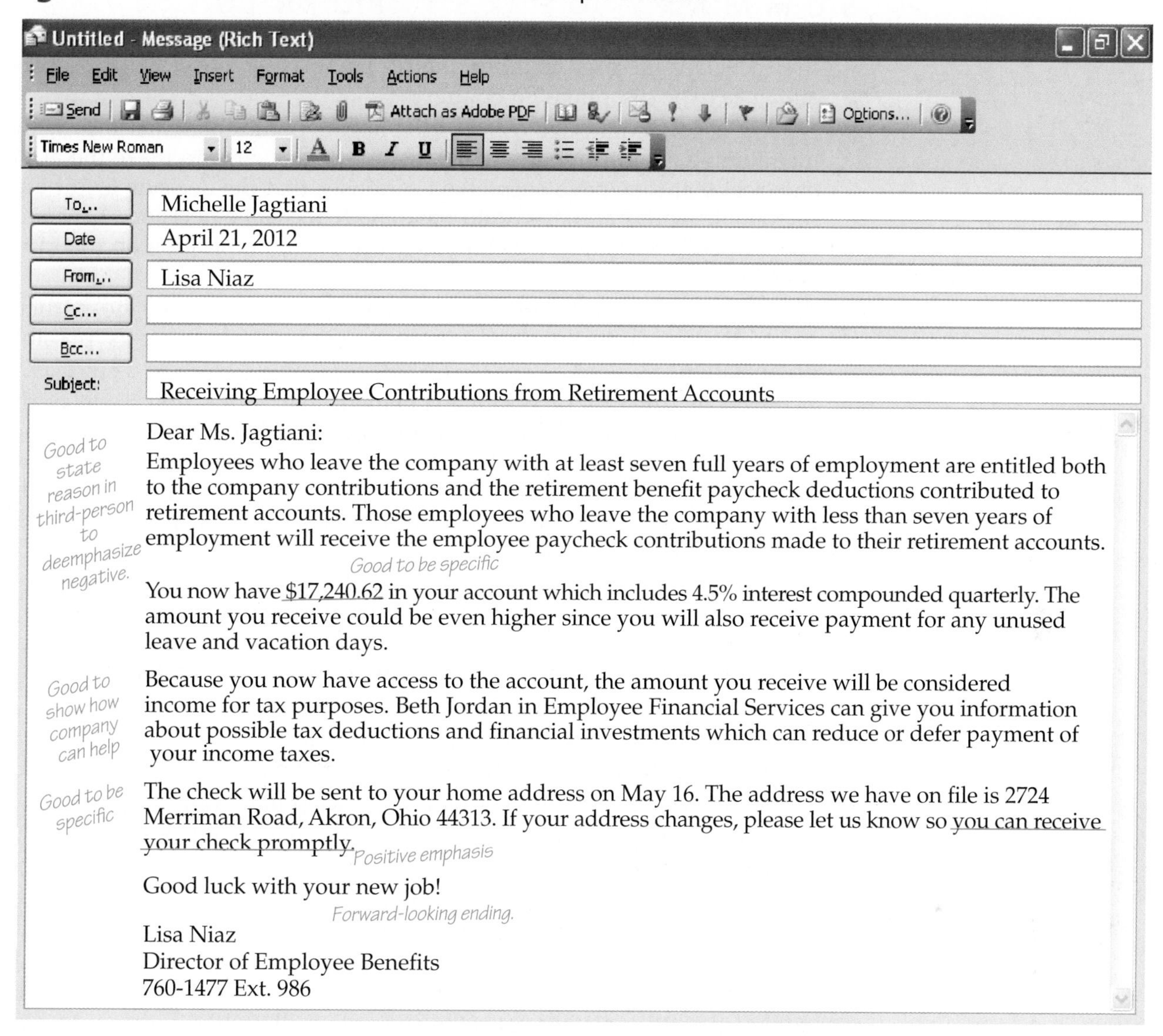
Untitled - Message (Rich Text)

To... Michelle Jagtiani
Date April 21, 2012
From... Lisa Niaz
Cc...
Bcc...
Subject: Receiving Employee Contributions from Retirement Accounts

Dear Ms. Jagtiani:

Employees who leave the company with at least seven full years of employment are entitled both to the company contributions and the retirement benefit paycheck deductions contributed to retirement accounts. Those employees who leave the company with less than seven years of employment will receive the employee paycheck contributions made to their retirement accounts.

You now have $17,240.62 in your account which includes 4.5% interest compounded quarterly. The amount you receive could be even higher since you will also receive payment for any unused leave and vacation days.

Because you now have access to the account, the amount you receive will be considered income for tax purposes. Beth Jordan in Employee Financial Services can give you information about possible tax deductions and financial investments which can reduce or defer payment of your income taxes.

The check will be sent to your home address on May 16. The address we have on file is 2724 Merriman Road, Akron, Ohio 44313. If your address changes, please let us know so you can receive your check promptly.

Good luck with your new job!

Lisa Niaz
Director of Employee Benefits
760-1477 Ext. 986

Checklist Negative Messages

- ☐ Is the subject line appropriate?
- ☐ Is the organization and content appropriate for the audience?
- ☐ If a buffer is used, does it avoid suggesting either a positive or a negative response?
- ☐ Is the reason, if it is given, presented before the refusal? Is the reason watertight, with no loopholes?
- ☐ Is the negative information clear?
- ☐ Is an alternative given if a good one is available? Does the message provide all the information needed to act on the alternative but leave the choice up to the audience?
- ☐ Does the last paragraph avoid repeating the negative information?
- ☐ Is tone acceptable—not defensive, but not cold, preachy, or arrogant either?

Originality in a negative message may come from

- ☐ An effective buffer, if one is appropriate.
- ☐ A clear, complete statement of the reason for the refusal.
- ☐ A good alternative, clearly presented, which shows that you're thinking about what the audience really needs.
- ☐ Adding details that show you're thinking about a specific organization and the specific people in that organization.

SUMMARY OF KEY POINTS

- In a negative message, the basic information is negative; we expect the audience to be disappointed or angry.
- A good negative message conveys the negative information clearly while maintaining as much goodwill as possible. The goal is to make the audience feel that they have been taken seriously, that the decision is fair and reasonable, and that they would have made the same decision. A secondary purpose is to reduce or eliminate future communication on the same subject.
- The best way to organize negative messages depends on the particular audiences and situations involved. Figure 10.1 suggests possible organizations.
- A **buffer** is a neutral or positive statement that allows you to delay the negative message. Buffers must put the audience in a good frame of mind, not give the bad news but not imply a positive answer either, and provide a natural transition to the body of the message. Use a buffer only when the audience values harmony or when the buffer serves a purpose in addition to simply delaying the negative.
- A good reason prepares the audience for the negative and must be watertight. Give several reasons only if all are watertight and are of comparable importance. Omit the reason for the refusal entirely if it is weak or if it makes your organization look bad. Do not hide behind company policy.
- Make the refusal crystal clear.
- Giving the audience an alternative or a compromise
  - Offers the audience another way to get what they want.
  - Suggests that you really care about the audience and about helping to meet their needs.
  - Allows you to end on a positive note and to present yourself and your organization as positive, friendly, and helpful.
- When you give an alternative, give the audience all the information they need to act on it, but don't take the necessary steps for them. Letting the audience decide whether to try the alternative allows the audience to reestablish a sense of psychological freedom.
- Many negative situations can be redefined as informative, positive, or persuasive messages.

CHAPTER 10 Exercises and Problems

Go to www.mhhe.com/locker10e for additional Exercises and Problems.

10.1 Reviewing the Chapter

1. What are the reasons behind the patterns of organization for negative messages in different situations (Figure 10.1)? (LO 10-1)
2. What are the parts of negative messages? How may those parts be changed for different contexts? (LO 10-2)
3. When should you not use a buffer? (LO 10-2)
4. When should you not apologize? (LO 10-2)
5. What are some ways you can maintain a caring tone in negative messages? (LO 10-3)
6. What are some different varieties of negative messages? What are some examples from the chapter text and sidebars? (LO 10-4)

10.2 Reviewing Grammar

Negative news is frequently placed in dependent clauses to help de-emphasize it. Unfortunately, some dependent clauses and phrases are dangling or misplaced modifiers. Do the exercise from Appendix B on improving modifiers (B.6) to help you learn to recognize this error.

10.3 Letters for Discussion—Credit Refusal

As director of customer service at C'est Bon, an upscale furniture store, you manage the store's credit. Today you are going to reject an application from Frank Steele. Although his income is fairly high, his last two payments on his college loans were late, and he has three bank credit cards, all charged to the upper limit, on which he's made just the minimum payment for the last three months.

The following letters are possible approaches to giving him the news. How well does each message meet the criteria in the checklist for negative messages?

1.

> Dear Mr. Steele:
>
> Your request to have a C'est Bon charge account shows that you are a discriminating shopper. C'est Bon sells the finest merchandise available.
>
> Although your income is acceptable, records indicate that you carry the maximum allowable balances on three bank credit cards. Moreover, two recent payments on your student loans have not been made in a timely fashion. If you were given a C'est Bon charge account, and if you charged a large amount on it, you might have difficulty paying the bill, particularly if you had other unforeseen expenses (car repair, moving, medical emergency) or if your income dropped suddenly. If you were unable to repay, with your other debt you would be in serious difficulty. We would not want you to be in such a situation, nor would you yourself desire it.
>
> Please reapply in six months.
>
> Sincerely,

2.

> Dear Frank:
>
> No, you can't have a C'est Bon credit card—at least not right now. Get your financial house in order and try again.
>
> Fortunately for you, there's an alternative. Put what you want on layaway. The furniture you want will be held for you, and paying a bit each week or month will be good self-discipline.
>
> Enjoy your C'est Bon furniture!
>
> Sincerely,

3.

> Dear Mr. Steele:
>
> Over the years, we've found that the best credit risks are people who pay their bills promptly. Since two of your student loan payments have been late, we won't extend store credit to you right now. Come back with a record of six months of on-time payments of all bills, and you'll get a different answer.

You might like to put the furniture you want on layaway. A $50 deposit holds any item you want. You have six months to pay, and you save interest charges.

You might also want to take advantage of one of our Saturday Seminars. On the first Saturday of each month at 11 AM, our associates explain one topic related to furniture and interior decorating. Upcoming topics are

How to Wallpaper a Room	February 5
Drapery Options	March 6
Persian Carpets	April 1

Sincerely,

10.4 E-Mails for Discussion—Saying *No* to a Colleague

A colleague in another state agency has e-mailed you asking if you would like to use the payroll software her agency developed. You wouldn't. Switching to a new program would take a lot of time, and what you have works well for you.

The following messages are possible approaches to giving her the news. How well does each message meet the criteria in the checklist for negative messages?

1.

Subject: Re: Use Our Software?

No.

2.

Subject: Re: Use Our Software?

Thanks for telling me about the payroll software your team developed. What we have works well for us. Like every other agency, we're operating on a bare-bones budget, and no one here wants to put time (that we really don't have) into learning a new program. So we'll say, no, thanks!

3.

Subject: Re: Use Our Software?

The payroll software your team developed sounds very good.

I might like to use it, but the people here are computer phobic. They HATE learning new programs. So, being a good little computer support person, I soldier on with the current stuff. (And people wonder why state government is SO INEFFICIENT! Boy, the stories I could tell!)

Anyway, thanks for the offer. Keep me posted on the next development—maybe it will be something so obviously superior that even the Neanderthals here can see its advantages!

10.5 Analyzing a Bad News Message

Today you received the following message in your mailbox:

> Dear (Your Name),
>
> Thank you for your membership with Fit4Life. We hope you are enjoying our fitness club and that you're reaching your health and wellness goals along the way. As always, we're excited to help you in any way.
>
> We're writing to let you know about an upcoming change in your Fit4Life monthly dues. Effective June 15, the dues for your membership will increase $10 per month—plus any associated taxes.
>
> We strive to keep dues increases as infrequent and minimal as possible. If you have questions about the increase or if there is anything else we can do to improve your experience with Fit4Life, please contact me on your next visit to the club.
>
> Thank you again for your membership with Fit4Life. We enjoy serving you and look forward to seeing you soon!
>
> Sincerely,
>
> Lawrence Josel
>
> Fit4Life General Manager

As your instructor directs,

a. Write an e-mail in which you analyze this message using the guidelines for negative messages that you learned in this chapter.

b. Rewrite this message so that it does a better job of delivering the negative news. Then, write a memo to your instructor explaining why you chose to make these revisions.

10.6 Revising a Negative Message

Rewrite the following negative message:

> Dear Madam:
>
> Unfortunately, because you have not paid your account for the last three months, we have absolutely NO CHOICE but to turn off your heat soon. We know that winter is upon us and it's a horrible time to be without heat, but you really brought this on yourself.
>
> Next time, we recommend PAYING your bills ON TIME.
>
> If you get us your outstanding payments soon, you can keep your heat.
>
> As always, we appreciate your business and value you as our customer.
>
> Sincerely,
>
> WarmHomes Customer Service Team

10.7 Notifying Baby Boomers about Housing Rules

Erin and TJ Bouda are baby boomers who live in a 55-plus Clearwater, Florida, housing development run by WaterBlue Homeowners Association. They have lived in their current house for five years and plan to live the rest of their lives in this home.

A few months ago, the Boudas started raising their three-year-old grandson, Riley, because his mother has a substance abuse problem and his father is deceased. Unfortunately, WaterBlue Homeowners Association has a policy that prohibits children under 18 years of age as permanent residents. Two neighbors of the Boudas have already complained about Riley.

Take on the role of the homeowners association and write to the Boudas telling them that their grandson has to leave (which is not an option) or that they have to give up their home. As you write, be sure to consider the audience and the effect your letter will have on them.

Hints:

- What reasons besides "policy" can you offer the Boudas to help them understand the situation?
- What help can you offer them?
- Are there any alternatives that you can offer?

10.8 Notifying College Seniors That They May Not Graduate

State University asks students to file an application to graduate one term before they actually plan to graduate. The application lists the courses the student has already had and those he or she will take in the last term. Your office reviews the lists to see that the student will meet the requirements for total number of hours, hours in the major, and general education requirements. Some students have forgotten a requirement or not taken enough courses and cannot graduate unless they take more courses than those they have listed.

As your instructor directs,

Write form e-mail messages to the following audiences. Leave blanks for the proposed date of graduation and specific information that must be merged into the message:

a. Students who have not taken enough total hours.
b. Students who have not fulfilled all the requirements for their majors.
c. Students who are missing one or more general education courses.
d. Advisers of students who do not meet the requirements for graduation.

10.9 Correcting a Mistake

Today, as you reviewed some cost figures, you realized they didn't fit with the last monthly report you filed. You had pulled the numbers together from several sources, and you're not sure what happened. Maybe you miscopied, or didn't save the final version after you'd checked all the numbers. But whatever the cause, you've found errors in three categories. You gave your boss the following totals:

Personnel	$2,843,490
Office supplies	$43,500
Telephone	$186,240

E-mail your boss to correct the information.

As your instructor directs,

Write e-mail messages for the following situations:

a. The correct numbers are

Personnel	$2,845,490
Office supplies	$34,500
Telephone	$186,420

b. The correct numbers are

Personnel	$2,845,490
Office supplies	$84,500
Telephone	$468,240

Variations for each situation:

1. Your boss has been out of the office; you know she hasn't seen the data yet.
2. Your boss gave a report to the executive committee this morning using your data.

Hints:

- How serious is the mistake in each situation?
- In which situations, if any, should you apologize?
- Should you give the reason for the mistake? Why or why not?
- How do your options vary depending on whether your job title gives you responsibility for numbers and accounting?

10.10 Refusing to Pay an Out-of-Network Bill

Your employees' health insurance allows them to choose from one of three health maintenance organizations (HMOs). Once employees have selected an HMO, they must get all medical care (except for out-of-state emergency care) from the HMO. Employees receive a listing of the doctors and hospitals affiliated with each HMO when they join the company and pick an HMO and again each October when they have a one-month "open enrollment period" to change to another of the three HMOs if they choose.

As Director of Employee Benefits, you've received an angry e-mail from Alvin Reineke. Alvin had just received a statement from his HMO stating that it would not pay for the costs of his hernia operation two months ago at St. Catherine's Hospital in your city. Alvin is furious: one of the reasons he accepted a job with your company six months ago was its excellent health care coverage. He feels the company lied to him and should pay for his (rather large) hospital bill since the HMO refuses to do so.

The HMO which Alvin had selected uses two hospitals, but not St. Catherine's. When Alvin joined the company six months ago, he (like all new employees) received a thick booklet explaining the HMO options. Perhaps he did not take the time to read it carefully. But that's not your fault. Alvin can change plans during the next open enrollment, but even if he switched to an HMO that included St. Catherine's, that HMO wouldn't pay for surgery performed before he joined that HMO.

Write an e-mail message to Alvin giving him the bad news.

Hints:

- What tone should you use? Should you be sympathetic? Should you remind him that this is his own fault?
- Is there any help you can give Alvin (e.g., information about credit-union short-term loans or even information about negotiating payment terms with the hospital)?
- What can you do to make Alvin feel that the company has not lied to him?

10.11 Announcing a Reduction in Benefits

In years past, your company has had a generous health insurance policy, fully funded by the employer. Employees pay only a $10 copayment for doctor visits and a $6 copayment for prescriptions. However, the cost of health insurance has risen much faster than the company's other expenses and much faster than the prices your company can charge its customers. Most other companies now expect their employees to contribute part of the cost of their health insurance through payroll deductions, and management has determined that your company must begin doing the same. For a group insurance policy similar to the one employees have received in the past, they will now have to pay $50 per month, and the copayment for doctor visits will rise to $15 per visit. The coverage for prescriptions will vary, with the $6 copayment applying only to generic drugs. For brand-name drugs, employees will have to pay more.

As your instructor directs,

Write an e-mail message to the employees of

a. A large advertising agency in a big city. The agency's billings have fallen 30% in the last six months, and 10% of the staff have already been laid off.

b. A manufacturing company. The company is still making a profit, but just barely. Unless the company saves money, layoffs may be necessary.

c. A successful service business. The business is doing well, but most of the employees earn only the minimum wage. They do not own stock in the company.

10.12 Recommending a Policy on Uncivil Behavior

Assume that your small team comprises your organization's Labor-Management Committee. This e-mail arrives from the CEO:

> I read that PepsiCo created a policy to deal with unfriendly behavior on the job, and that sounds like a good idea. When someone's rude, inconsiderate, or shows bad manners, that can ruin your day and ruin your productivity. I know that we have harassment policies, but what about a rudeness policy? Put one together, and send it to me.

As a team, write a response recommending an appropriate policy for dealing with uncivil behavior in the workplace.

Hint:

Be sure to define what your organization considers unacceptable behavior, describe the roles of employees and managers in reporting such behaviors, and outline clear guidelines for dealing with violations.

Source: Adapted from Diane Bandow and Debra Hunt, "Developing Policies about Uncivil Workplace Behavior," *Business Communication Quarterly* 71, no. 1 (2008), 103–6.

10.13 Complaining about the Dead

You are traveling on a first-class flight from New Delhi to London. When you wake, you find the corpse of a woman, who died in the economy section of the airplane, sitting next to you. After flagging down the flight attendant, you're told the crew moved the woman who died so her family could have some privacy to grieve. They could not put the body in the aisle or the attendant station for safety reasons. Needless to say, you're appalled by the situation.

As your instructor directs,

- Write a complaint letter to the airline.
- Write an apology letter from the perspective of the airline who has just received your complaint.

Source: Jennifer Quinn, "Passenger Dies on International Flight, Body Moved to First-Class Cabin," *Associated Press Archive,* March 19, 2007.

10.14 E-Mailing Bad News about Lab Hours

You're the administrator of your university's computer labs. Many students have asked for longer lab hours, and you presented the request to your superiors. However, you've just been informed that, beginning next term, the hours for the computer labs are being reduced. The labs will open one hour later each morning as a cost-saving measure.

Write an e-mail message, including subject line, to all students, informing them of this change.

10.15 Telling Employees to Remove Personal Websites

You're Director of Management and Information Systems (MIS) in your organization. At your monthly briefing for management, a vice president complained that some employees have posted personal web pages on the company's web server.

"It looks really unprofessional to have stuff about cats and children and musical instruments. How can people do this?"

You took the question literally. "Well, some people have authorization to post material—price changes, job listings, marketing information. Someone who has authorization could put up anything."

Another manager said, "I don't think it's so terrible—after all, there aren't any links from our official pages to these personal pages."

A third person said, "But we're paying for what's posted—so we pay for server space and connect time. Maybe it's not much right now, but as more and more people become web-literate, the number of people putting up unauthorized pages could spread. We should put a stop to this now."

The vice president agreed. "The website is carefully designed to present an image of our organization. Personal pages are dangerous. Can you imagine the flak we'd get if someone posted links to pornography?"

You said, "I don't think that's very likely. If it did happen, as system administrator, I could remove the page."

The third speaker said, "I think we should remove all the pages. Having any at all suggests that our people have so much extra time that they're playing on the web. That suggests that our prices are too high and may make some people worry about quality. In fact, I think that we need a new policy prohibiting personal pages on the company's web server. And any pages that are already up should be removed."

A majority of the managers agreed and told you to write a message to all employees. Create an e-mail message to tell employees that you will remove the personal pages already posted and that no more will be allowed.

Hint:

- Suggest other ways that people can post personal web pages.
- Give only reasons that are watertight and make the company look good.

10.16 Refusing to Waive a Fee

As the Licensing Program Coordinator for your school, you evaluate proposals from vendors who want to make or sell merchandise with the school's name, logo, or mascot. If you find the product acceptable, the vendor pays a $250 licensing fee and then 6.5% of the wholesale cost of the merchandise manufactured (whether or not it is sold). The licensing fee helps to support the cost of your office; the 6.5% royalty goes into a student scholarship fund. At well-known universities or those with loyal students and alumni, the funds from such a program can add up to hundreds of thousands of dollars a year.

On your desk today is a proposal from a current student, Meg Winston.

I want to silk-screen and sell T-shirts printed with the name of the school, the mascot, and the words "We're Number One!" (A copy of the design I propose is enclosed.) I ask that you waive the $250 licensing fee you normally require and limit the 6.5% royalty only to those T-shirts actually sold, not to all those made.

I am putting myself through school by using student loans and working 30 hours a week. I just don't have $250. In my marketing class, we've done feasibility analyses, and I've determined that the shirts can be sold if the price is low enough. I hope to market these shirts in an independent study project with Professor Doulin, building on my marketing project earlier this term. However, my calculations show that I cannot price the shirts competitively if just one shirt must bear the 6.5% royalty for all the shirts produced in a batch. I will of course pay the 6.5% royalty on all shirts sold and not returned. I will produce the shirts in small batches (50–100 at a time). I am willing to donate any manufactured but unsold shirts to the athletic program so that you will know I'm not holding out on you.

By waiving this fee, you will show that this school really wants to help students get practical experience in business, as the catalog states. I will work hard to promote these shirts by getting the school president, the coaches, and campus leaders to endorse them, pointing out that the money goes to the scholarship fund. The shirts themselves will promote school loyalty, both now and later when we're alumni who can contribute to our alma mater.

I look forward to receiving the "go-ahead" to market these shirts.

The design and product are acceptable under your guidelines. However, you've always enforced the fee structure across the board, and you see no reason to make an exception now. Whether the person trying to sell merchandise is a student or not doesn't matter; your policy is designed to see that the school benefits whenever it is used to sell something. Students aren't the only ones whose cash flow is limited; many businesses would find it easier to get into the potentially lucrative business of selling clothing, school supplies, and other items with the school name or logo if they got the same deal Meg is asking for. (The policy also lets the school control the kinds of items on which its name appears.) Just last week, your office confiscated about 400 T-shirts and shorts made by a company that had used the school name on them without permission; the company has paid the school $7,500 in damages.

Write a letter to Meg rejecting her special requests. She can get a license to produce the T-shirts, but only if she pays the $250 licensing fee and the royalty on all shirts made.

10.17 Correcting Misinformation

You're the director of the city's Division of Water. Your mail today contains this letter:

When we bought our pool, the salesman told us that you would give us a discount on the water bill when we fill the pool. Please start the discount immediately. I tried to call you three times and got nothing but busy signals.

Sincerely,

Larry Shadburn-Butler

Larry Shadburn-Butler

The salesperson was wrong. You don't provide discounts for pools (or anything else). At current rates, filling a pool with a garden hose costs from $8.83 (for a 1,800-gallon pool) to $124.67 (for 26,000 gallons) in the city. Filling a pool from any other water source would cost more. Rates are 30% higher in the suburbs and 50% higher in unincorporated rural areas. And you don't have enough people to answer phones. You tried a voicemail system but eliminated it when you found people didn't have time to process all the messages that were left. But the city budget doesn't allow you to hire more people.

As your instructor directs,

a. Write a letter to Mr. Shadburn-Butler.

b. Write a letter to all the stores that sell swimming pools, urging them to stop giving customers misinformation.

c. Write a notice for the one-page newsletter that you include with quarterly water bills. Assume that you can have half a page for your information.

10.18 Analyzing Job Rejection Letters

1. Here are three rejections letters to an applicant who applied for an accounting position.

Letter 1

We realize that the application process for the accounting position at AlphaBank required a substantial amount of thought, time, and effort on your part. Therefore, we would like to express our sincere appreciation for your willingness to participate in the search process.

The task of selecting a final candidate was difficult and challenging due to the quality of the applicant pool. We regret to inform you that we selected another candidate who we believe will best meet the needs of AlphaBank.

We thank your for your interest in employment at AlphaBank and extend our best wishes as you pursue your professional goals.

Letter 2

Thank you for your interest in the accounting position at AlphaBank. I'm sorry to inform you that you were not one of the finalists. The position has now been filled.

The search committee and I wish you the best in your future employment searches.

Letter 3

Thank you for your interest in the accounting position at AlphaBank.

I'm sorry to inform you that the search committee has decided to offer the position to another candidate. This was an extremely difficult decision for us to make. We were all impressed with your résumé and credentials.

Again, thank you for your interest in AlphaBank.

1. Analyze these three job rejection letters by answering the following questions:

- Do these letters use buffers? If so, how effective are they?
- What reasons do the letters give, if any?
- Does the letter attempt to build goodwill with the audience? If yes, how so?
- Do any of the letters offer an alternative?

- How do you think recipients will react to each of the letters? Which (if any) are more preferable?

As your instructor directs,

a. Discuss your findings in a small group.
b. Present your findings orally to the class.
c. Present your findings in a memo to your instructor.

2. Collect job rejection letters mailed to seniors on your campus. Analyze the letters, answering the following questions:

- Do these letters use buffers? If so, how effective are they?
- What reasons do the letters give, if any?
- Do the letters attempt to build goodwill with the audience? If yes, how so?
- Do any of the letters offer an alternative?
- How do you think recipients will react to each of the letters? Which (if any) are more preferable?

As your instructor directs,

a. Discuss your finding in a small group.
b. Present your findings orally to the class.
c. Present your findings in a memo to your instructor.
d. Join with other students to write a report based on your findings.

10.19 Creating Equal Work Distribution

You noticed recently that Clare, the woman who works next to you at a call center, takes extended lunches and makes a lot of personal phone calls. As the result of her phone calls and breaks, you and your co-workers complete more work throughout the day. After discussing the situation with a close friend, you decide you are going to tell the boss about her behavior.

As your instructor directs,

- Write a memo or e-mail to your boss in which you discuss Clare's behavior and ask for a resolution.
- Partner up with a classmate and role-play the situation of telling the boss. One of you is the employee and one of you is the boss.
- Partner up with a classmate and role-play the situation of confronting Clare. One of you is the employee and one of you is Clare.

Hints:

- How can you deliver the negative news without sounding like a tattletale?
- How can you make the situation seem severe enough so that your boss takes action?

10.20 Dumping Your Trash

With the economic downturn, organizations are looking for any possible cost-cutting measures. Today, your supervisors tell you about a new program they are starting next week to reduce costs. From now on, employees will be responsible for dumping their own trash into a common bin. Employees who work for the state of Texas, the University of Washington, and Dartmouth College already participate in this project and have saved their organizations thousands of dollars. Your supervisors believe the same savings will happen at your company.

All employees in your organization will have two cans at their desks: a large one for recyclables and smaller one for trash. In addition to the estimated money that the organization will save from custodial needs, they also hope to gain more revenue from the recycling bins.

As your instructor directs,

a. Write to everyone in your company and explain the new trash policy.
b. Write a complaint memo to your supervisors as an employee concerned about the new trash policy.
c. After the two messages are drafted, write a memo to your instructor that discusses which message was easier to create and why. You should also discuss which message you believe makes a stronger argument.

Hints:

- Pick a business, government, or nonprofit organization you know something about.
- What benefits can you stress to employees about the new policy?
- How can you complain to your supervisor so that he/she takes you seriously?
- What are the disadvantages of reducing work for the lowest-paid employees?

Based on Sudeep Reddy, "Memo to All Staff: Dump Your Trash," *Wall Street Journal*, November 1, 2010, A3.

10.21 Turning Down a Faithful Client

You are Midas Investment Services' specialist in estate planning. You give talks to various groups during the year about estate planning. You ask nonprofit groups (churches, etc.) just to reimburse your expenses; you charge for-profit groups a fee plus expenses. These fees augment your income nicely, and the talks also are marvelous exposure for you and your company.

Every February for the last five years, Gardner Manufacturing Company has hired you to conduct an eight-hour workshop (two hours every Monday night for four weeks) on retirement and estate planning for its employees who are over 60 or who are thinking of taking early retirement. These workshops are popular and have generated clients for your company. The session last February went smoothly, as you have come to expect.

Today, out of the blue, you got a letter from Hope Goldberger, Director of Employee Benefits at Gardner, asking you to conduct the workshops every Tuesday evening *next* month at your usual fee. She didn't say whether this is an extra series or whether this will replace next February's series.

You can't do it. Your spouse, a geneticist is giving an invited paper at an international conference in Paris next month and the two of you are taking your children, ages 13 and 9, on a three-week trip to Europe. (You've made arrangements with school authorities to have the kids miss three weeks of classes.) You've been looking forward to and planning the trip for the last eight months.

Unfortunately, Midas Investment Services is a small group, and the only other person who knows anything about estate planning is a terrible speaker. You could suggest a friend at another financial management company, but you don't want Gardner to turn to someone else permanently; you enjoy doing the workshops and find them a good way to get leads.

Write the letter to Ms. Goldberger.

10.22 Getting Information from a Co-worker

Your boss has been pressuring you because you are weeks late turning in a termination report. However, you cannot begin your section of the report until your colleague, Matt Churetta, finishes his section. Right now, he is the problem. Here is a series of e-mail exchanges between you and Matt:

7/25/2012

Matt,

The boss wants the termination report now. Send over your section as soon as you finish.

Thanks,

Matt's reply:

7/31/2012

My apologies about the report.

On another note, I'm waiting to see my oncology surgeon to see what the course of treatment will be for the esophageal cancer. I will keep you posted on the process.

Please let me know if there is anything else coming up.

Thanks,

8/15/2012

Matt,

I had no idea that you are dealing with esophageal cancer. Definitely keep me posted on your condition. Best wishes as you work through your treatment.

I need your section of the termination report as soon as you finish it. The boss has been waiting patiently for the finished version.

Thanks,

Matt's reply:

8/26/2012

Report is coming along. The last two weeks have been difficult dealing with all the tests, doctors' appointments, etc. I will beat this deal!!!

Take Care,

It is now September, and over a month has passed from the termination report's original due date. While you are sympathetic to Matt's situation, the boss is demanding the finished report.

As your instructor directs,

a. Write an e-mail to Matt telling him you have to have his portion of the report as soon as possible. You are concerned for your job security, as well as his, if this report is not finalized soon.

b. Write a memo to your boss explaining the situation.

c. Write a memo to your instructor that focuses on the ethical choices you had to make while constructing the two messages.

10.23 Sending Negative Messages to Real Audiences

As your instructor directs, write a negative letter that responds to one of the following scenarios:

- Write a letter to the owner of a restaurant where you received poor service.
- Write a letter to a company whose product unsatisfactorily met your expectations or needs.
- Identify a current political topic on which you disagree with your congressional representative. Write a letter that outlines your views for him/her and calls for change.
- Identify a television advertisement with which you disagree. Write a letter to the company explaining your position and request that the advertisement be altered or taken off the air.

Hints:

- For all of these scenarios, your main goal should be to promote change.
- Express your complaint as positively as possible.
- Remember to consider your audience's needs; how can you build support for your position?

CHAPTER 11

Crafting Persuasive Messages

Chapter Outline

Analyzing Persuasive Situations

1. What Do You Want People to Do?
2. What Objections, If Any, Will the Audience Have?
3. How Strong Is Your Case?
4. What Kind of Persuasion Is Best for the Situation?
5. What Kind of Persuasion Is Best for the Organization and the Culture?

Choosing a Persuasive Strategy

Why Threats Are Less Effective than Persuasion

Making Persuasive Direct Requests

Writing Persuasive Problem-Solving Messages

- Subject Lines for Problem-Solving Messages
- Developing a Common Ground
- Dealing with Objections
- Offering a Reason for the Audience to Act Promptly
- Building Emotional Appeal
- Putting It All Together

Tone in Persuasive Messages

Varieties of Persuasive Messages

- Performance Appraisals
- Letters of Recommendation

Sales and Fund-Raising Messages

- Organizing a Sales or Fund-Raising Message
- Strategy in Sales Messages and Fund-Raising Appeals
- Writing Style

Solving a Sample Problem

- Problem
- Analysis of the Problem
- Discussion of the Sample Solutions

Summary of Key Points

Newsworthy Communication

Bet You Watch This Safety Video

Most airline passengers ignore the preflight safety presentation, where the flight crew details important procedures in case of emergency. Even though the information is vital, the presentation is standard and routine.

New Zealand's national airline is uniquely persuading its passengers to watch the safety presentation: the company filmed its safety video with the crew members wearing nothing but skin-painted uniforms. The saucy video uses safety equipment to protect the actors' privacy. The safety video is complemented by television commercials for the airline that feature a new slogan: "At Air New Zealand, our fares have nothing to hide."

"New Zealand's national airline is uniquely persuading its passengers to watch the safety presentation."

New Zealand's approach got plenty of attention. In the first four days after its release, it had more than 1 million views on YouTube.

Source: Adapted from "New Zealand Safety Video Bares Painted Plane Crew," *Des Moines Register*, July 4, 2009, 4A.

Learning Objectives

After studying this chapter, you will know how to

LO 11-1 Analyze a persuasive situation.

LO 11-2 Identify basic persuasive strategies.

LO 11-3 Write persuasive direct requests.

LO 11-4 Write persuasive problem-solving messages.

LO 11-5 Write sales and fund-raising messages.

LO 11-6 Use rational and emotional appeals to support persuasive messages.

Persuasion is almost universal in good business communications. If you are giving people information, you are persuading them to consider it good information, or to remember it, or even to use it. If you are giving people negative news, you are trying to persuade them to accept it. If you work for a company, you are a "sales representative" for it. Your job depends on its success.

Some messages, however, seem more obviously persuasive to us than others. Employees try to persuade their supervisors to institute flex hours or casual Fridays; supervisors try to persuade workers to keep more accurate records, thus reducing time spent correcting errors; or to follow healthier lifestyles, thus reducing health benefit costs. You may find yourself persuading your colleagues to accept your ideas, your staff to work overtime on a rush project, and your boss to give you a raise.

Whether you're selling safety equipment or ideas, effective persuasion is based on accurate logic, effective emotional appeal, and credibility or trust. Reasons have to be ones the audience finds important; emotional appeal is based on values the audience cares about; credibility depends on your character and reputation.

Persuasive messages include requests, proposals and recommendations, sales and fund-raising messages, job application letters, and efforts to change people's behavior, such as collection letters, criticisms or performance appraisals where you want the subordinate to improve behavior, and public-service ads designed to reduce drunk driving, drug use, and so on. Reports are persuasive messages if they recommend action.

This chapter gives general guidelines for persuasive messages. Chapter 17 discusses proposals; reports are the subject of Chapter 18. Chapter 13 covers job application letters.

All persuasive messages have several purposes:

Primary purpose:

- To have the audience act or change beliefs.

Secondary purposes:

- To build a good image of the communicator.
- To build a good image of the communicator's organization.
- To cement a good relationship between the communicator and audience.
- To overcome any objections that might prevent or delay action.
- To reduce or eliminate future communication on the same subject so the message doesn't create more work for the communicator.

ANALYZING PERSUASIVE SITUATIONS LO 11-1

Choose a persuasive strategy based on your answers to five questions. Use these questions to analyze persuasive situations:

1. What do you want people to do?
2. What objections, if any, will the audience have?
3. How strong is your case?
4. What kind of persuasion is best for the situation?
5. What kind of persuasion is best for the organization and the culture?

1. What Do You Want People to Do?

Identify the specific action you want and the person who has the power to do it. If your goal requires several steps, specify what you want your audience to do *now*. For instance, your immediate goal may be to have people come to a meeting or let you make a presentation, even though your long-term goal is a major sale or a change in policy.

2. What Objections, If Any, Will the Audience Have?

If you're asking for something that requires little time, money, or physical effort and for an action that's part of the person's regular duties, the audience is likely to have few objections.

Often, however, that is not the case, and you'll encounter some resistance. People may be busy and have what they feel are more important things to do. They may have other uses for their time and money. To be persuasive, you need to show your audience that your proposal meets their needs; you need to overcome any objections.

The easiest way to learn about objections your audience may have is to ask. Particularly when you want to persuade people in your own organization or

Giving Water

Without access to clean water, many people in Africa and Asia struggle with disease and unsanitary conditions. Scott Harrison has made it his mission to provide clean water to as many people as possible. Through his organization, called charity: water, he has given access to clean water to nearly 1 million people, with the help of thousands of individual donors. The organization's success depends on its successful marketing, which is built on three principles:

1. *All money from new donors goes directly into providing water.* Harrison asks only his top supporters to cover administrative costs.
2. *Donors can track their donation's impact.* The organization lets donors name wells and see their location on Google Earth.
3. *Use social media and new media.* Harrison's organization has raised over a million dollars through Twitter and other Internet media. Entertaining web videos and creative social media campaigns garner extensive support.

So far, charity: water has raised over 10 million dollars; it is continuing to gain support from around the world.

Adapted from Nicholas D. Kristof, "Clean, Sexy Water," *New York Times*, July 11, 2009, http://www.nytimes.com/2009/07/12/opinion/12kristof.html.

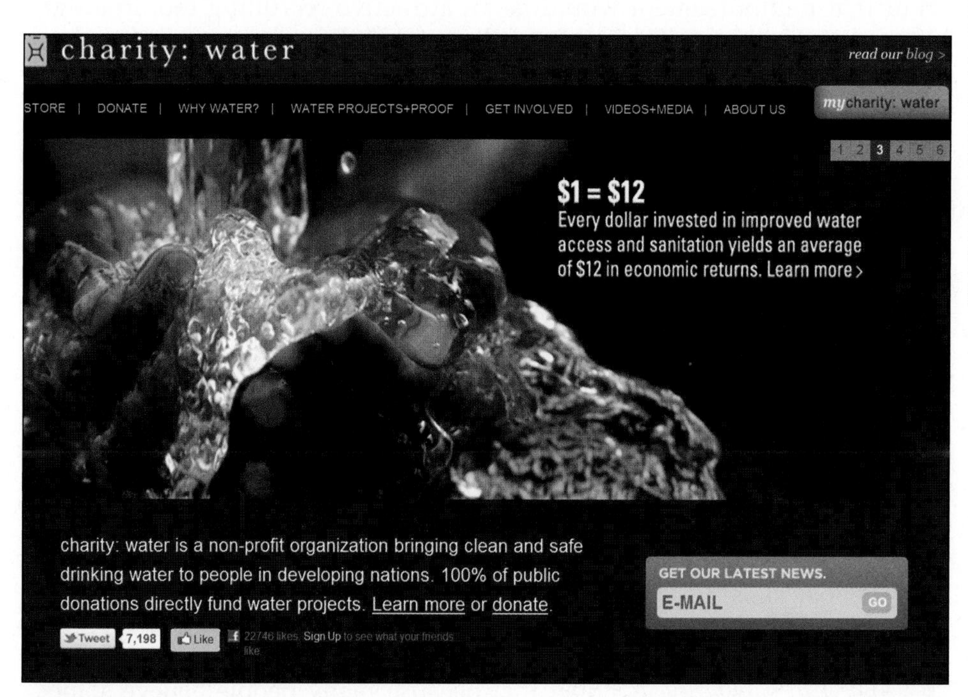

Charity: water's website presents a persuasive argument that clean water can be made available for millions of people.

Men's Health

Real men don't ask for directions and they certainly don't go to the doctor. These old stereotypes may have some truth in them. One study found that only 57% of men have visited the doctor in the past year, while 74% of women have. The federal government's Agency for Healthcare Research and Quality is trying to persuade more men to get health care with a series of humorous newspaper and television ads.

The ads, which can be viewed online at www.ahrq.gov/healthymen/, use dark humor to show how timely medical care can prevent serious diseases and early death. In one ad, a real estate broker tells a family they will have many happy years in their new home, but then turns to the father and tells him that he will die in three years from a preventable disease. She adds that it could have been detected early with a simple test, but he didn't get the test.

Other ads in the series feature men participating in weddings, graduations, and other family activities wearing hospital gowns. The messages, entitled "Real Men Wear Gowns," encourage men to get regular checkups and testing to benefit them and their families.

Adapted from Laura Landro, "New Ads Try to Shock Men into Going to See the Doctor," *Wall Street Journal*, June 15, 2010, D3.

your own town, talk to knowledgeable people. Phrase your questions nondefensively, in a way that doesn't lock people into taking a stand on an issue: "What concerns would you have about a proposal to do *x*?" "Who makes a decision about *y*?" "What do you like best about [the supplier or practice you want to change]?" Ask follow-up questions to be sure you understand: "Would you be likely to stay with your current supplier if you could get a lower price from someone else? Why?"

People are likely to be most aware of and willing to share objective concerns such as time and money. They will be less willing to tell you that their real objection is emotional. People have a **vested interest** in something if they benefit directly from keeping things as they are. People who are in power have a vested interest in retaining the system that gives them their power. Someone who designed a system has a vested interest in protecting that system from criticism. To admit that the system has faults is to admit that the designer made mistakes. In such cases, you'll need to probe to find out what the real reasons are.

Whether your audience is inside or outside your organization, they will find it easier to say *yes* when you ask for something that is consistent with the person's self-image.

3. How Strong Is Your Case?

The strength of your case is based on three aspects of persuasion: argument, credibility, and emotional appeal.

Argument refers to the reasons or logic you offer. Sometimes you may be able to prove conclusively that your solution is best. Sometimes your reasons may not be as strong, the benefits may not be as certain, and obstacles may be difficult or impossible to overcome. For example, suppose that you wanted to persuade your organization to offer a tuition reimbursement plan for employees. You'd have a strong argument if you could show that tuition reimbursement would improve the performance of marginal workers or that reimbursement would be an attractive recruiting tool in a tight job market. However, if dozens of fully qualified workers apply for every opening you have, your argument would be weaker. The program might be nice for workers, but you'd have a hard job proving that it would help the company.

Some arguments are weakened by common errors known as logical **fallacies.** These are some common types of logical fallacies:[1]

- *Hasty generalization.* Making general assumptions based on limited evidence. "Most of my friends agree that the new law is a bad idea. Americans do not support this law."
- *False cause.* Assuming that because one event follows another, the first event caused the second. "In the 1990s farmers increased their production of corn for ethanol. Soon after, more Americans began using ethanol fuel in their cars."
- *Weak analogy.* Making comparisons that don't work. "Outlawing guns because they kill people is like outlawing cars because they kill people."
- *Appeal to authority.* Quoting from a famous person who is not really an expert. "Hollywood actor Joe Gardner says this hand mixer is the best on the market today."
- *Appeal to popularity.* Arguing that because many people believe something, it is true. "Thousands of Americans doubt the reality of climate change, so climate change must not be happening."

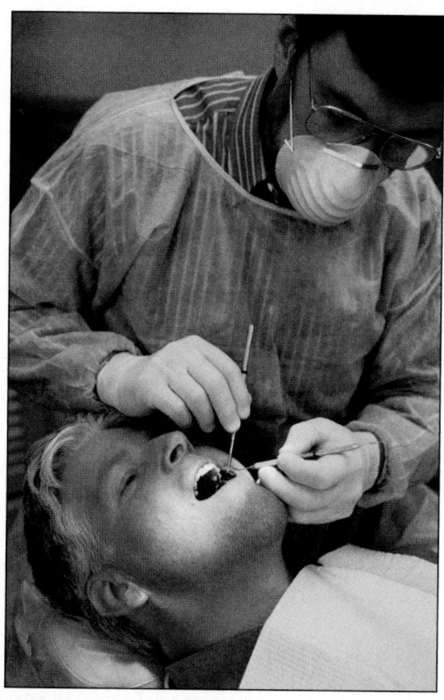

As the recession affected professionals, even dentists increased their sales messages—using e-mails, phone calls, and tweets in addition to their postcard reminders—to persuade their patients to keep coming for dental appointments.

Source: Maureen Scarpelli, "Dentists Step Up Marketing as Patients Skip Their Visits," *Wall Street Journal,* August 11, 2009, B5.

- *Appeal to ignorance.* Using lack of evidence to support the conclusion. "There's nothing wrong in the plant; all the monitors are in the safety zone."
- *False dichotomy.* Setting up the situation to look like there are only two choices. "If you are not with us, you are against us."

Credibility is the audience's response to you as the source of the message. Credibility in the workplace has three sources: expertise, image, and relationships.[2] Citing experts can make your argument more credible. In some organizations, workers build credibility by getting assigned to high-profile teams. You build credibility by your track record. The more reliable you've been in the past, the more likely people are to trust you now.

We are also more likely to trust people we know. That's one reason that new CEOs make a point of visiting as many branch offices as they can. Building a relationship with someone—even if the relationship is based on an outside interest, like sports or children—makes it easier for that person to see you as an individual and to trust you.

When you don't yet have the credibility that comes from being an expert or being powerful, build credibility by the language and strategy you use:

- **Be factual.** Don't exaggerate. If you can test your idea ahead of time, do so, and report the results. Facts about your test are more convincing than opinions about your idea.
- **Be specific.** If you say "X is better," show in detail *how* it is better. Show the audience exactly where the savings or other benefits come from so that it's clear that the proposal really is as good as you say it is.
- **Be reliable.** If you suspect that a project will take longer to complete, cost more money, or be less effective than you originally thought, tell your audience *immediately.* Negotiate a new schedule that you can meet.

Emotional appeal means making the audience *want* to do what you ask. People don't make decisions—even business decisions—based on logic alone. As John Kotter and Holger Rathgeber, authors of the popular business book *Our Iceberg Is Melting*, found, "feelings often trump thinking."[3] Jonah Lehrer, author of *How We Decide*, goes a step further. He offers research that shows people make better decisions—ones that satisfy them better—about large purchases such as a couch when they followed their emotions: "The process of thinking requires feeling, for feelings are what let us understand all the information that we can't directly comprehend. Reason without emotion is impotent."[4]

De Tijd, a Belgian business newspaper, won a European Marketing Council award for its emotional appeal to get human resource managers to use its pension brochure. Every manager who published a job ad in the newspaper received a handwritten letter from Cyriel, age 84, applying for the position. The message on the last page of Cyriel's application read, "Save your employees from having to do like Cyriel: to look for a job when they retire. Offer your employees our brochure." Sales of the brochure increased 24%.[5]

4. What Kind of Persuasion Is Best for the Situation?

Different kinds of people require different kinds of persuasion. What works for your boss may not work for your colleague. But even the same person may require different kinds of persuasion in different situations. Many people who make rational decisions at work do not do so at home, where they may decide to smoke and overeat even though they know smoking and obesity contribute to many deaths.

For years, companies have based their persuasion techniques on the idea that money is most people's primary motivator. And sometimes it is, of course. How many people buy an extra item to reach the $25 amount for free shipping at Amazon? But research in the last decade has shown that people are also motivated by other factors, including competition and community perceptions. Utility companies, for example, have found that people are more likely to conserve energy if they see how their use compares to their neighbors' use. And patients are more likely to take their medications regularly if there is a system to notify doctors or family members when they do. These factors, derived from behavioral economics, open up new ways to persuade people to act.[6]

Even when money is the motivator, companies are beginning to use it differently, especially when trying to persuade their employees to lead healthier lives. Many of these new techniques stem from **behavioral economics,** a branch of economics that uses insights from sociology and psychology. It finds that people often behave irrationally, although still predictably, and not in their own best interests. Techniques include lotteries and short-term financial incentives. Employees who enroll in weight-loss or smoking-cessation programs and stick with them might be eligible for a daily lottery (people tend to give greater weight to the small probability of a lottery than to the much larger probability of long-term health improvements from a healthier lifestyle) or a regular series of payments (people tend to value short-term benefits over long-term health improvements). Capitalizing on the well-known aversion to loss, companies are also asking employees in such programs to put a dollar or two each day into the program. Employees who meet their goals get their money back plus matching funds.[7]

In *Drive: The Surprising Truth about What Motivates Us*, Daniel Pink summarizes decades of research that shows many businesses are using the wrong kinds of persuasion on their employees who do knowledge work,

work that demands sophisticated understanding, flexible problem solving, and creativity. According to this research, once basic levels of financial fairness are reached, "carrot" motivators, such as financial ones, do not work for employees who are expected to be innovative. In fact, carrot motivators will actually decrease innovation; they turn creative work into drudgery.

"Stick" motivators, in the form of ill-chosen goals, are also harmful and can lead to unethical and illegal behavior. Managers hit short-term goals to get performance bonuses, even when they know the short-term goals will cause long-term problems. Sears set sales quotas on its auto repair personnel, who then made national news by overcharging and performing unnecessary repairs. Mortgage issuers offered financial incentives for new mortgages, which got offered to people who could not afford them, leading to a worldwide recession.

So what does motivate knowledge workers? Pink says it is three drives: "our deep-seated desire to direct our own lives, to expend and expand our abilities, and to live a life of purpose."[8]

5. What Kind of Persuasion Is Best for the Organization and the Culture?

A strategy that works in one organization may not work somewhere else. One **corporate culture** may value no-holds-barred aggressiveness. In another organization with different cultural values, an employee who used a hard-sell strategy for a request would antagonize people.

Organizational culture (see Chapter 2) isn't written down; it's learned by imitation and observation. What style do high-level people in your organization use to persuade? When you show a draft to your boss, are you told to tone down your statements or to make them stronger? Role models and advice are two ways organizations communicate their culture to newcomers.

Different kinds of persuasion also work for different **social cultures.** In North Carolina, police are using a new combination to persuade drug dealers to shut down. The combination includes iron-clad cases against the dealers, but also pressure from loved ones—mothers, grandmothers, mentors—along with a second chance. Texas used a famous antilitter campaign based on the slogan "Don't Mess with Texas." Research showed the typical Texas litterer was 18–35, male, a pickup driver, and a lover of sports and country music. He did not respond to authority (Don't litter) or cute owls (Give a hoot; don't pollute). Instead, the campaign aimed to convince this target audience that people like him did not pollute. Ads featured Texan athletes and musicians making the point that Texans don't litter. The campaign was enormously successful: during its first five years, Texas roadside litter decreased 72% and roadside cans 81%.[9] The campaign is still going 25 years later.[10]

What counts for "evidence" also varies by culture. In general, people count a scientist as an expert only when that scientist agrees with a position held by most of those who share their cultural values. This remains true even if the scientist got a degree from a major university, is on the faculty at another major university, and is a member of the National Academy of Sciences.[11]

Different **native cultures** also have different preferences for gaining compliance. In one study, students who were native speakers of American English judged direct statements ("Do this"; "I want you to do this") clearer and more effective than questions ("Could you do this?") or hints ("This is needed"). Students who were native speakers of Korean, in contrast, judged direct statements to be *least* effective. In the Korean culture, the clearer a request is, the

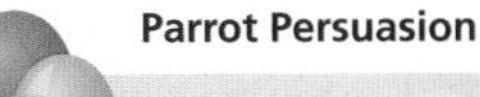

Parrot Persuasion

The tiny island of St. Lucia in the Caribbean is the only home of the St. Lucia Parrot, a beautiful blue, green, and red bird which was on the brink of extinction; only 100 of the parrots remained in the wild.

St. Lucia's forestry department hired Paul Butler, a new college grad, to head an effort to preserve the parrot. Butler faced an enormous task. The St. Lucia Parrot had few legal protections, and the citizens of the island didn't seem to care.

Armed with a tiny budget and a passion for the project, Butler embarked on a public relations campaign to convince St. Lucians that their parrot was special and should be protected. He arranged for puppet shows, T-shirts, and bumper stickers. He had volunteers in parrot costumes visit local schools. He even convinced a phone company to make calling cards with the lovely parrot next to the not-so-lovely bald eagle.

St. Lucia's forestry department was happy with his campaign: the St. Lucia Parrot population has improved to between 600 and 700 birds.

Adapted from Chip Heath and Dan Heath, *Switch: How to Change Things When Change Is Hard* (New York: Broadway Books, 2010), 149–51.

Selling Education

At the end of every year, college football teams in the United States participate in highly anticipated title contests and bowl games. As part of each televised event, the two universities whose teams are playing in the games are given 30-second advertising spots during halftime.

What do the universities do with their time? A *Wall Street Journal* study of 112 university commercials found that most are an odd mixture of messages: academics, the arts, athletics, and scientific achievements, all trying to appeal to high school students, their parents, alumni, and taxpayers. The study found that with so many audiences and confused messages, most of the ads were unsuccessful. A few, however, stood out.

- Some ads used famous alumni, like Jon Hamm (Missouri) or Tom Brokaw (Iowa), to talk about their schools.
- Rice University used historical footage of John F. Kennedy delivering his famous speech at the Rice campus about putting a man on the moon.
- Minnesota delivered an ad focused on the research of professor Massoud Amin, who is developing a better power grid.

The most successful ads showed an understanding of their audience and focused on a single, clear message.

Adapted from Darren Everson, "Those Halftime College Ads: A Review," *Wall Street Journal*, November 19, 2010, D12.

ruder and therefore less effective it is.[12] Another study notes that communicators from countries such as China, Japan, and Korea prefer to establish personal relationships before they address business issues. They also show modesty and humility, debasing their egos in favor of collective relationships and disdaining personal profit.[13]

Researchers are studying the sale of counterfeit drugs, which is a huge business, both in the United States and abroad. They have found that the quality of the fakes matters only in the United States; people in other countries are willing to accept a price–quality trade-off. United States citizens harbor ill will toward big drug companies; people in other countries do not. United States citizens consider the consumption of counterfeit drugs unethical; people in China and Russia do not.

So what should drug companies do? In countries placing a low priority on drug quality, companies can highlight the dangers of such drugs, including the contaminants that are common in them. In cultures lacking ethical concerns, drug companies can stress social concerns. Diluted malaria drugs, for instance, can help the parasite causing the disease to develop drug resistance.[14]

CHOOSING A PERSUASIVE STRATEGY LO 11-2

If your organization prefers a specific approach, use it. If your organization has no preference, or if you do not know your audience's preference, use the following guidelines to help you choose a strategy. These guidelines work in many cases but not all.

- Use the **direct request pattern** when
  - The audience will do as you ask without any resistance.
  - You need responses only from people who will find it easy to do as you ask.
  - The audience may not read all of the message.
- Use the **problem-solving pattern** when the audience may resist doing as you ask and you expect logic to be more important than emotion in the decision.
- Use the **sales pattern** when the audience may resist doing as you ask and you expect emotion to be more important than logic in the decision.

WARNING: You always need to consider your audience and situation before choosing your persuasive strategy.

WHY THREATS ARE LESS EFFECTIVE THAN PERSUASION

Sometimes people think they will be able to mandate change by ordering or threatening subordinates. Real managers disagree. Research shows that managers use threats only for obligatory duties such as coming to work on time. For more creative duties—like being part of a team or thinking of ways to save the company money—good managers persuade. Persuasion not only keeps the lines of communication open, it fosters better working relationships and makes future discussions go more smoothly.[15]

Threats are even less effective in trying to persuade people whose salaries you don't pay.

A **threat** is a statement—explicit or implied—that someone will be punished if he or she does (or doesn't do) something. Various reasons explain why threats don't work:

1. **Threats don't produce permanent change.** Many people obey the speed limit only when a marked police car is in sight.
2. **Threats won't necessarily produce the action you want.** If you punish whistleblowers, you may stop hearing about problems you could be solving—hardly the response you'd want!
3. **Threats may make people abandon an action—even in situations where it would be appropriate.** Criticizing workers for chatting with each other may reduce their overall collaboration.
4. **Threats produce tension.** People who feel threatened put their energies into ego defense rather than into productive work.
5. **People dislike and avoid anyone who threatens them.** A supervisor who is disliked will find it harder to enlist cooperation and support on the next issue that arises.
6. **Threats can provoke counteraggression.** Getting back at a boss can run the gamut from complaints to work slowdowns to sabotage.

In *The Tipping Point,* Malcolm Gladwell describes classic fear experiments conducted at Yale University. The point of the experiments was to get students to go to the health center for tetanus shots. Students were given high-fear or low-fear versions of booklets explaining why they should get the shots. The high-fear booklet included gruesome pictures and text; the low-fear booklet did not. As you might predict, more of the students reading the high-fear booklet said they would get the shots than those reading the low-fear version. But only 3% of students in either group actually did so. However, one small change upped the percentage to 28% (evenly spread across both groups). That change was including a campus map with the health center circled and the times shots were available listed. The map shifted the persuasion from abstract material about the dangers of tetanus to practical, personal advice.[16]

Making Ethics Training Fun

BearingPoint, a management and technology consulting firm, has taken a different approach to its ethics training.

Russ Berland, BearingPoint's chief compliance officer, faced the problem of reworking the company's ethics and compliance program from a rarely used legal manual into a regularly consulted solution to ethics problems. After interviewing associates from around the country, he found that many of them had experienced ethical dilemmas, and their stories were interesting and compelling.

Berland and his associates then came up with a brilliant idea: instead of simply reworking the manual, they decided to put the drama of real-life situations on television. They hired a director and filmed 10 episodes in a weekend, with the plan to release one episode each Monday. Using the format of NBC's hit sitcom *The Office,* the episodes talked about sticky ethics subjects with comic exaggeration.

The series was an instant hit. Employees not only watched the videos, they responded to them, talked about them, and searched for the next episodes before they were released. With humor and heart, BearingPoint helped persuade employees to "take" their ethics training.

Adapted from Dan Heath and Chip Heath, "The Power of Razzle-Dazzle," *Fast Company,* December 2009/January 2010, 69–70; BearingPoint's ethics videos are online at http://fastcompany.com/aggrieva.

MAKING PERSUASIVE DIRECT REQUESTS LO 11-3

When you expect quick agreement, you can generally save your audience's time by presenting the request directly (see Figure 11.1). Also use the direct request pattern for busy people who do not read all the messages they receive and in organizations whose cultures favor putting the request first.

This pattern is also frequently used to persuade in dire situations. In 2008, at the height of the United States' financial crisis, Ben Bernanke and Henry Paulson, then treasury secretary, bluntly asked Congress for $700 billion to rescue the banks and prevent a deep, prolonged recession.[17]

Figure 11.1 How to Organize a Persuasive Direct Request

1. **Consider asking immediately for the information or service you want.** Delay the request if it seems too abrupt or if you have several purposes in the message.
2. **Give your audience all the information they will need to act on your request.** Number your questions or set them off with bullets so readers can check to see that all have been answered.
3. **Ask for the action you want.** Do you want a check? A replacement? A catalog? Answers to your questions? If you need an answer by a certain time, say so. If possible, show why the time limit is necessary.

In written direct requests, put the request, the topic of the request, or a question in the subject line.

> Subject: Request for Updated Software
>
> My copy of HomeNet does not accept the nicknames for Gmail accounts.

> Subject: Status of Account #3548-003
>
> Please get me the following information about account #3548-003.

> Subject: Do We Need an Additional Training Session in October?
>
> The two training sessions scheduled for October will each accommodate 20 people. Last month, you said that 57 new staff accountants had been hired. Should we schedule an additional training session in October? Or can the new hires wait until the next regularly scheduled session in February?

Figure 11.2 illustrates a direct request. Note that a direct request does not contain benefits and does not need to overcome objections: it simply asks for what is needed.

Figure 11.2 A Direct Request

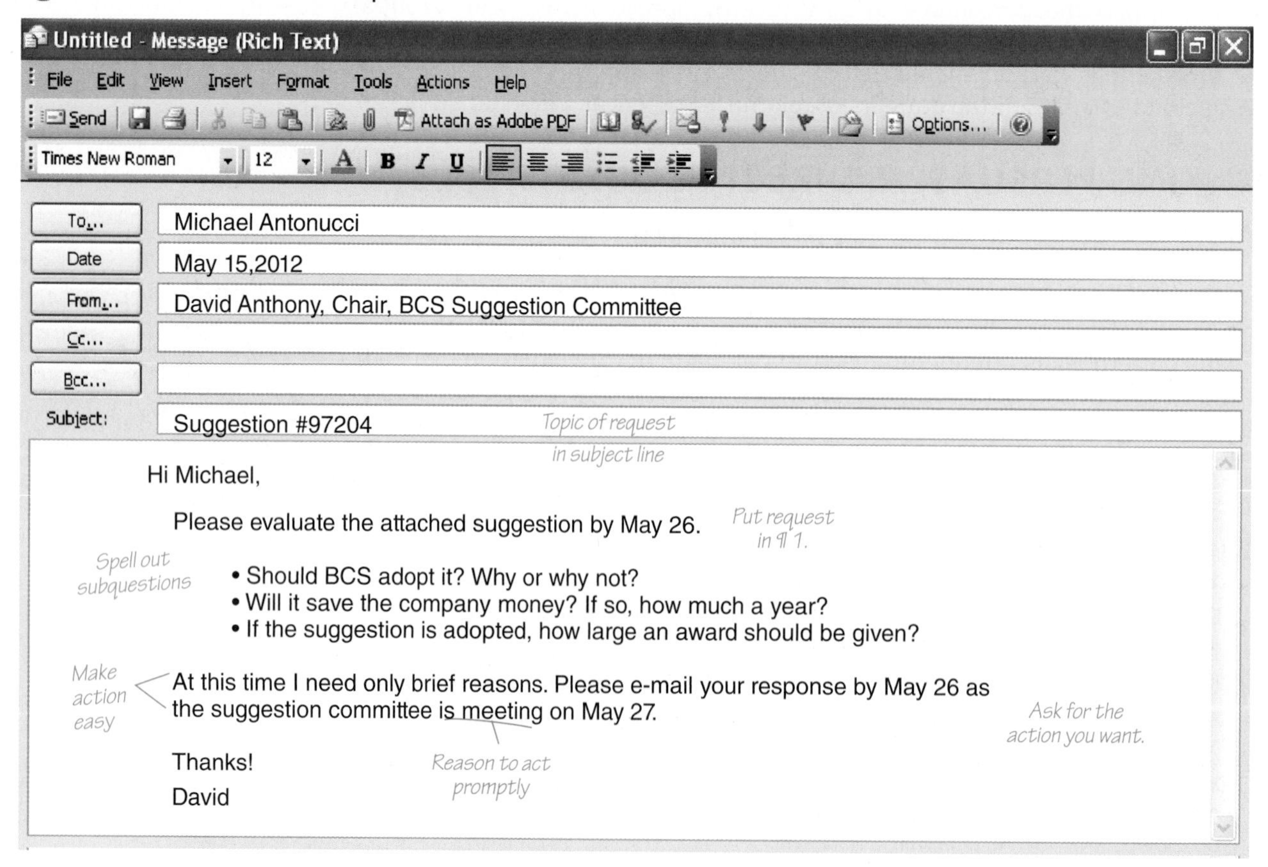

Direct requests should be clear. Don't make people guess what you want.

Indirect request: Is there a newer version of the 2003 *Chicago Manual of Style?*

Direct request: If there is a newer version of the 2003 *Chicago Manual of Style,* please send it to me.

In a claim, a message asking for correction or compensation for goods or services, explain the circumstances so that the reader knows what happened. Be sure to include all the relevant details: date of purchase, model or invoice number, and so on.

In more complicated direct requests, anticipate possible responses. Suppose you're asking for information about equipment meeting certain specifications. Explain which criteria are most important so that the reader can recommend an alternative if no single product meets all your needs. You may also want to tell the reader what your price constraints are and ask whether the item is in stock or must be special-ordered.

During the recession, the Campaign for a Commercial-Free Childhood urged parents to write to toy manufacturers asking them to suspend advertising toys to children during the holiday season. The CCFC offered parents a sample letter, one which put the request in the first sentence. Anticipating strong reactions from toy manufacturers, the CCFC pointed out that it is wrong to make children expect toys that their parents cannot afford. The letter offered the alternative of advertising the toys to parents, who of course buy the toys, rather than to children. (See Exercise 11.26 for more details and the text of the sample letter.)[18]

WRITING PERSUASIVE PROBLEM-SOLVING MESSAGES LO 11-4

Generally, you will use an indirect approach and the problem-solving pattern of organization (see Figure 11.3) when you expect resistance from your audience but can show that doing what you want will solve a problem you and your audience share. This pattern allows you to disarm opposition by showing all the reasons in favor of your position before you give your audience a chance to say *no.* As always, you need to analyze your audience and situation before you choose this approach to ensure it is a good one for the occasion.

Figure 11.3 How to Organize a Persuasive Problem-Solving Message

1. **Catch the audience's interest by mentioning a common ground.** Show that your message will be interesting or beneficial. You may want to catch attention with a negative (which you will go on to show can be solved).
2. **Define the problem you both share (which your request will solve).** Present the problem objectively: don't assign blame or mention personalities. Be specific about the cost in money, time, lost goodwill, and so on. You have to convince people that *something* has to be done before you can convince them that your solution is the best one.
3. **Explain the solution to the problem.** If you know that the audience will favor another solution, start with that solution and show why it won't work before you present your solution.

   Present your solution without using the words *I* or *my*. Don't let personalities enter the picture; don't let the audience think they should say *no* just because you've had other requests accepted recently.
4. **Show that any negative elements (cost, time, etc.) are outweighed by the advantages.**
5. **Summarize any additional benefits of the solution.** The main benefit—solving the problem—can be presented briefly since you described the problem in detail. However, if there are any additional benefits, mention them.
6. **Ask for the action you want.** Often your audience will authorize or approve something; other people will implement the action. Give your audience a reason to act promptly, perhaps offering a new benefit. ("By buying now, we can avoid the next quarter's price hikes.")

Figure 11.4 A Problem-Solving Persuasive Message

Untitled - Message (Rich Text)

To...: All Staff Members
Date: February 16, 2012
From...: Melissa J. Gutridge
Cc...:
Bcc...:
Subject: Client Locations

As we all know, successfully mainstreaming our clients into the community is very important and involves daily interaction with the public. Our clients enjoy the times they get to go to the mall or out to lunch instead of remaining here all day. Recently, however, clients have been taken out on activities without other staff members knowing the client's location or escort.

We need to know where all clients are at all times because social workers,psychologists, and relatives constantly stop by unannounced. Last week Janet's father stopped by to pick her up for a doctor's appointment and she was not here. No one knew where she was or who had escorted her. Naturally her father was very upset and wanted to know what kind of program we were running. Such situations damage the good reputation of our staff and program.

Starting Monday, February 20, a sign-out board will be located by Betty's desk. Please write down where you and the client are going and when you expect to be back. When signing out, help clients sign themselves out. We can turn this into a learning experience for our clients. Then when a social worker stops by to see someone who isn't here, we can simply look at the sign-out board to tell where the client is and when he or she will return.

Please help keep up the superb reputation you have helped Weststar earn as a quality center for adults with handicaps. Sign out yourself and clients at all times.

Thank you,
Melissa

The message in Figure 11.4 uses the problem-solving pattern of organization. Benefits can be brief in this kind of message since the biggest benefit comes from solving the problem.

Subject Lines for Problem-Solving Messages

When you have a reluctant audience, putting the request in the subject line just gets a quick *no* before you've had a chance to give all your arguments. One option is to use a neutral subject line. In the following example, the first is the most neutral. The remaining two increasingly reveal the writer's preference.

Subject: A Proposal to Change the Formula for Calculating Retirees' Benefits

Subject: Arguments for Expanding the Marysville Plant

Subject: Why Cassano's Should Close Its West Side Store

Another option is to use common ground or a benefit—something that shows the audience that this message will help them.

> Subject: Reducing Energy Costs in the Louisville Office
>
> Energy costs in our Louisville office have risen 12% in the last three years, even though the cost of gas has remained constant and the cost of electricity has risen only 5%.

Although your first paragraph may be negative in a problem-solving message, your subject line should be neutral or positive.

Developing a Common Ground

A common ground avoids the me-against-you of some persuasive situations and suggests that both you and your audience have a mutual interest in solving the problems you face. To find a common ground, we analyze the audience; understand their biases, objections, and needs; and identify with them to find common goals. This analysis could be carried out in a cold, manipulative way. It should, however, be based on a respect for and sensitivity to the audience's position.

Audiences are highly sensitive to manipulation. No matter how much you disagree with your audience, respect their intelligence. Try to understand why they believe or do something and why they may object to your position. If you can understand your audiences' initial positions, you'll be more effective—and you won't alienate your audience by talking down to them.

The best common grounds are specific. Often a negative—a problem the audience will want to solve—makes a good common ground.

Vague common ground:	We all want this plant to be profitable.
Improved specific common ground:	We forfeited a possible $1,860,000 in profits last month due to a 17% drop in productivity.

In your common ground, emphasize the parts of your proposal that fit with what your audience already does or believes. Some HMOs are trying to improve patients' health (and cut the costs of providing care for them) by reaching out to individual patients and persuading them to take medications, get needed tests, and manage chronic conditions. Often, they first have to overcome patients' belief that HMOs want to limit their access to care. They do so by emphasizing the patients' needs and health.

Use audience analysis to evaluate possible common grounds. Suppose you want to install a system to play background music in a factory. To persuade management to pay for the system, a possible common ground would be increasing productivity. However, to persuade the union to pay for the system, you'd need a different common ground. Workers would see productivity as a way to get them to do more work for the same pay. A better common ground would be that the music would make the factory environment more pleasant.

Dealing with Objections

If you know that your audience will hear other points of view, or if your audience's initial position is negative, you have to deal with their objections to persuade them. The stronger the objection is, the earlier in your message you should deal with it.

That Personal Touch

Selling a home in a crowded market can be difficult. Real estate brokers and homeowners often need to turn to unconventional methods to help their homes stand out. One Atlanta broker, Rhonda Duffy, asks her clients to include a personal touch in selling their homes: Each homeowner writes a personal letter to potential buyers.

While the letters do review the important facts about the home, they accomplish much more. Through the letters, homeowners can paint a picture of the best features and intangible benefits of the home. The letters show that real people have lived in the home and have been happy there. These personal letters can make a big impact on buyers, most of whom are not just investing in property, but are looking for a lifestyle. The letters also make the homes memorable. Duffy explains, "It's 'the letter house' instead of 'the green carpet house.'"

Adapted from Amy Hoak, "Desperate Times, Desperate Measures," *Wall Street Journal*, December 13, 2010, R10.

It Came from Where?

New companies face an uphill battle to persuade people to trust them and their products. The problem is even worse if the new companies are located in a country not usually associated with the product they are selling. Take chocolate, for example. Although the cocoa beans used to produce the world's best chocolate come from South America and Africa, consumers associate fine chocolate with European companies.

Companies from emerging markets employ several different strategies to deal with consumer perceptions. Some try actively to change perceptions, by playing up their countries on product labeling. Others hide their countries of origin or use companies in the United States or Europe as their primary labels.

The most successful, however, work for years to establish their brand by producing quality products and offering excellent service. Carmakers like Toyota, Nissan, and Honda established themselves through years of investment and quality to become some of the most trusted brands in the auto business.

Adapted from Rohit Deshpandé, "Why You Aren't Buying Venezuelan Chocolate," *Harvard Business Review* 88, no. 12 (December 2010): 25–27.

The best way to deal with an objection is to eliminate it. When hail damaged mail-order apples just before harvest, the orchard owner inserted a note in each crate being shipped:

> Note the hail marks which have caused minor skin blemishes in some of these apples. They are proof of their growth at a high mountain altitude where the sudden chills from hailstorms help firm the flesh, develop the natural sugars, and give these apples their incomparable flavor.

No one asked for a refund; in fact, some customers requested the hail-marked apples the next year.[19]

If an objection is false and is based on misinformation, give the response to the objection without naming the objection. (Repeating the objection gives it extra emphasis.) In a brochure, you can present responses with a "question/answer" format.

When objections have already been voiced, you may want to name the objection so that your audience realizes that you are responding to that specific objection. However, to avoid solidifying the opposition, don't attribute the objection to your audience. Instead, use a less personal attribution: "Some people wonder . . ."; "Some citizens are afraid that. . . ."

If real objections remain, try one or more of the following strategies to counter objections:

1. Specify how much time and/or money is required—it may not be as much as the audience fears.

> Distributing flyers to each house or apartment in your neighborhood will probably take two afternoons.

2. Put the time and/or money in the context of the benefits they bring.

> The additional $252,500 will (1) allow the Essex Shelter to remain open 24 rather than 16 hours a day, (2) pay for three social workers to help men find work and homes, and (3) keep the Neighborhood Bank open, so that men don't have to cash Social Security checks in bars and so that they can save for the $800 deposit they need to rent an apartment.

3. Show that money spent now will save money in the long run.

> By buying a $1,000 safety product, we can avoid $5,000 in OSHA fines.

4. Show that doing as you ask will benefit some group or cause the audience supports, even though the action may not help the audience directly. This is the strategy used in fund-raising letters.

> By being a Big Brother or a Big Sister, you'll give a child the adult attention he or she needs to become a well-adjusted, productive adult.

5. Show the audience that the sacrifice is necessary to achieve a larger, more important goal to which they are committed.

> These changes will mean more work for all of us. But we've got to cut our costs 25% to keep the plant open and to keep our jobs.

The Central Asia Institute uses positive images and language to show how financial contributions help promote world peace by building schools in Asian countries. See https://www.ikat.org/

6. Show that the advantages as a group outnumber or outweigh the disadvantages as a group.

> None of the locations is perfect. But the Backbay location gives us the most advantages and the fewest disadvantages.

Use the following steps when you face major objections:

1. **Find out why your audience members resist what you want them to do.** Sit down one-on-one with people and listen. Don't try to persuade them; just try to understand.
2. **Try to find a win–win solution.** People will be much more readily persuaded if they see benefits for themselves. Sometimes your original proposal may have benefits that the audience had not thought of, and explaining the benefits will help. Sometimes you'll need to modify your original proposal to find a solution that solves the real problem and meets everyone's needs.
3. **Let your audience save face.** Don't ask people to admit that they have been wrong all along. If possible, admit that the behavior may have been appropriate in the past. Whether you can do that or not, always show how changed circumstances or new data call for new action.
4. **Ask for something small.** When you face great resistance, you won't get everything at once. Ask for a month's trial. Ask for one step that will move toward your larger goal. For example, if your ultimate goal is to eliminate prejudice in your organization, a step toward that goal might be to convince managers to make a special effort for one month to recognize the contributions of women or members of minorities in group meetings.
5. **Present your arguments from your audience's point of view.** Offer benefits that help the audience, not just you. Take special care to avoid words that attack or belittle your audience. Present yourself as someone helping your audience achieve their goals, not someone criticizing or giving orders from above.

Hard Tests for Persuasion

How do you get your employees to agree to be tested for AIDS? This was a huge concern for SABMiller, a South African brewer who faced losing about 15% of its workforce within three years. Their first step was to hire an outside testing firm to allay fears that a positive HIV test would become company gossip or hurt careers. Participants also joined raffles for free radios and TVs. The company paid for antiretroviral treatment for infected employees.

How do you get employees to leave their jobs? France Telecom's need for a major workforce reduction inspired them to be creative. In addition to traditional means such as early retirement plans and retirement bonuses, they developed a program to shift people to public sector jobs at other institutions. They also helped employees start their own businesses, offering assistance with writing business plans, applying for loans, and purchasing equipment. They paid for consultations with business people and new educational courses.

What other hard tests for businesses can you identify? What persuasive solutions can you imagine?

Adapted from William Echikson and Adam Coher, "SABMiller's AIDS Test Program Gets Results: Effort Benefits Business, Saves Employee Lives; Building Confidence Is Key," *Wall Street Journal*, August 18, 2006, A7; and Leila Abboud, "At France Telecom, Battle to Cut Jobs Breeds Odd Tactics: Company Offers Money, Advice on Starting New Business if Employees Will Leave," *Wall Street Journal*, August 14, 2006, A1.

From Full Time to Part Time

Many employees dream about working fewer hours or even cutting back to part-time work. But managers agree that most employees ask their boss the wrong way. Too often employees focus on why *they* want part-time work; managers want to hear about advantages and disadvantages for the company.

You might use these persuasive arguments to convince your employer to let you work fewer hours:

- Demonstrate that you understand and appreciate corporate policies on part-time work.
- Stress that your dedication to your work won't fade when you start working fewer hours.
- Agree to be reached outside the office if your colleagues need you.
- Present a plan detailing how the rest of your work will get done.
- Suggest a trial period to show your plan will work.
- Above all, treat the situation as a persuasive message: develop a common ground with your employer, anticipate objections, and suggest solutions.

Adapted from Erin White, "Build a Case before Asking to Work Less," *Wall Street Journal,* October 24, 2006, B7.

Organizational changes work best when the audience buys into the solution. And that happens most easily when they themselves find it. Management can encourage employees to identify problems and possible solutions. If that is not possible because of time, sensitive information, or organizational cultural constraints, a good second alternative is to fully explain to employees how the decision for organizational change was made, the reasons behind the change, what alternatives were considered, and why they were rejected. A study of over 100 employers found that workers who received such explanations were more than twice as likely to support the decision as those workers who did not.[20]

Offering a Reason for the Audience to Act Promptly

The longer people delay, the less likely they are to carry through with the action they had decided to take. In addition, you want a fast response so you can go ahead with your own plans.

Request action by a specific date. Try to give people at least a week or two: they have other things to do besides respond to your requests. Set deadlines in the middle of the month, if possible. If you say, "Please return this by March 1," people will think, "I don't need to do this till March." Ask for the response by February 28 instead. Similarly, a deadline of Friday, 5 pm, will frequently be seen as Monday morning. If such a shift causes you problems, if you were going to work over the weekend, set a Thursday deadline. If you can use a response even after the deadline, say so. Otherwise, people who can't make the deadline may not respond at all.

Your audience may ignore deadlines that seem arbitrary. Show why you need a quick response:

- **Show that the time limit is real.** Perhaps you need information quickly to use it in a report that has a due date. Perhaps a decision must be made by a certain date to catch the start of the school year, the Christmas selling season, or an election campaign. Perhaps you need to be ready for a visit from out-of-town or international colleagues.
- **Show that acting now will save time or money.** If business is slow and your industry isn't doing well, then your company needs to act now (to economize, to better serve customers) in order to be competitive. If business is booming and everyone is making a profit, then your company needs to act now to get its fair share of the available profits.
- **Show the cost of delaying action.** Will labor or material costs be higher in the future? Will delay mean more money spent on repairing something that will still need to be replaced?

Building Emotional Appeal

Emotional appeal helps make people care. Stories and psychological description are effective ways of building emotional appeal.

Even when you need to provide statistics or numbers to convince the careful reader that your anecdote is a representative example, **telling a story** first makes your message more persuasive. In *Made to Stick,* Chip and Dan Heath report on research done at Carnegie Mellon supporting the value of stories. After a survey (completing the survey for money ensured all participants had cash for the real experiment), participants received an envelope with a letter requesting they donate to Save the Children. Researchers tested two letters: one was full of grim statistics about starving Africans. The other letter told the story of seven-year-old Rokia. Participants receiving the Rokia letter gave more

Emotional appeals can be intense. The Save Darfur campaign used this ad to raise awareness of horrifying brutality and genocide. Do you think this graphic of a half-buried hand works to solicit support for this cause? Or is the emotional appeal too intense?

Persuasion at Davos

The Davos economic forum had something new in 2009: a simulation of a refugee camp. Crossroads Foundation staged the simulations, which were cosponsored by the United Nations High Commissioner on Refugees and the Global Risk Forum.

The one-hour simulations were held 4–5 times a day for 15–30 participants. Everyone was given a specific role to play. The idea was to give Davos attendees a taste of what life is like for the 32.9 million refugees in the world.

The "refugee camp" came complete with muddy tent floors, barbed wire, and sadistic guards. Sound effects included exploding bombs, screaming women, and wailing children. One of the actresses involved even stepped on a pretend land mine and was carried away with artificial blood streaming.

What do you think this simulation was trying to persuade executives to do? How effective do you think it was?

Adapted from Alessandra Galloni and Bob Davis, "Sign of the Times: CEOs Play 'Refugees' at Forum," *Wall Street Journal*, January 30, 2009, A6.

than twice as much money as those receiving the statistics letter. A third group received a letter with both sets of information: the story and the statistics. This group gave a little more than the statistics group, but far less than the group that had the story alone. The researchers theorized that the statistics put people in an analytical frame of mind which canceled the emotional effect of the story.[21]

As with other appeals, the **emotional appeal** should focus on the audience. To customers who had fallen behind with their payments, a credit card company sent not the expected stern collection notice but a hand-addressed, hand-signed greeting card. The front of the card pictured a stream running through a forest. The text inside noted that sometimes life takes unexpected turns and asked people to call the company to find a collaborative solution. When people called the 800 number, they got credit counseling and help in creating a payment plan. Instead of having to write off bad debts, the company received payments—and created goodwill.[22]

In his marketing book *Buyology,* marketing guru Martin Lindstrom points out that advertisers deliberately create somatic markers, icons that associate the advertised goods with some value you admire. Car tires pretty much look the same, but if you head for Michelin instead of Goodyear, you may be responding to carefully crafted somatic markers. The cute baby once used in their ads translates into safety for your child. The plump Michelin man suggests the protective padding of good tires and thus sturdy durability. The high-end Michelin travel and food guides bring an association of top-of-the line quality.[23]

Short but Persuasive

A horse breeder had a problem with city folk feeding his horses. People would try to feed the horses, who are vegetarians, items like hot dogs and hamburgers. The horses would drop the food in the field, and the breeder had to continually police the fields to keep the spoiling food from attracting flies and vermin.

So the breeder put up a sign: "Do Not Feed the Horses." The problem got worse, because the sign put the idea into the minds of new people.

The breeder put up another sign: "Please Do Not Feed the Horses." The problem got still worse. (This guy is so polite, he won't mind.)

Finally, the breeder put up this sign: "We Eat Only Apples and Carrots." His problem was solved.

Adapted from Nicholas Boothman, *Convince Them in 90 Seconds *or Less* (New York: Workman Publishing, 2010), 267.

Emotional appeal is often used in public service announcements. Here the AdCouncil uses the emotional appeal of the young child to underscore Tyler's need for help.

Sometimes emotional appeals go too far and alienate audiences. Germany's Federal Constitutional Court ruled that a PETA ad campaign was an offense against human dignity and not protected by freedom of speech laws. The campaign compared factory farms and animal slaughterhouses to Jewish concentration camps and the Holocaust.[24]

Sense impressions—what the reader sees, hears, smells, tastes, feels—evoke a strong emotional response. **Psychological description** means creating a scenario rich with sense impressions so readers can picture themselves using your product or service and enjoying its benefits. The flyer for a university's food services in Figure 11.5 gets your gastric juices flowing.

You can also use psychological description to describe the problem your product, service, or solution will ease. Psychological description works best early in the message to catch readers' attention.

> Because our smokers take their breaks on the front patio, clients visiting our office frequently pass through a haze of acrid smoke—as well as through a group of employees who are obviously not working.

Putting It All Together

The Campaign for a Commercial-Free Childhood sent a letter to toy manufacturers direct from the CCFC, in addition to the letters from parents discussed in the Making Persuasive Direct Requests section earlier in this chapter. The

Figure 11.5 Using Psychological Description to Develop Benefits

The Colonial Room

When you dine in the Illini Union Colonial Room, it's easy to imagine yourself a guest in a fine Virginian mansion. Light from the gleaming chandeliers reflects from a hand-carved mirror hanging over the dark, polished buffet. Here you can dine in quiet elegance amid furnishings adapted from 18th century Williamsburg and the Georgian homes of the James River Valley in Virginia.

Perhaps you'd like a dinner of stuffed rainbow trout. Or the pork fricassee. The menu features a variety of complete meals which are changed daily, as well as the regular a la carte service. Whatever your choice, you'll enjoy an evening of fine dining at very reasonable prices.

The Illini Union Colonial Room is located on the northeast corner of the first floor. Dinners are served Monday through Friday from 5:30 to 7:30 p.m. Please call 333-0690 for reservations, and enjoy the flavor of the Colonies tonight.

The Cafeteria

In the Illini Union Cafeteria, you start out with an empty tray and silverware. Then comes the food, several yards of it, all yours for the choosing. By the time you've finished, your empty tray has become a delicious meal.

In the morning, the warm aroma of breakfast fills the air. Feast your eyes and then your appetite on the array of eggs, bacon, pancakes, toast, sausage, rolls, juices, and coffee . . . They're all waiting to wake you up with good taste. Have a hearty breakfast or make it quick and tasty. The warm, freshly baked sweet rolls and coffeecakes practically beg to be smothered in butter and savored with a cup of hot coffee.

By 11 a.m. the breakfast menu has made way for lunch. Here come the plump Reuben sandwiches and the toasty grilled cheese. Soups and salads make their appearance. A variety of vegetables are dressed up to entice you and several main dishes lead the luncheon parade. Any number of complete meals can take shape as you move along.

What? Back for dinner? Well, no wonder! The Cafeteria sets out a wide selection of entrees and side dishes. Veal parmigiana steams for your attention but the roast beef right next to it is rough competition. Tomorrow the fried chicken might be up for selection. Choose the dinner combination that best fits your appetite and your pocket.

The newly remodeled Cafeteria is on the ground floor and is open for breakfast from 7 to 11 a.m. Monday through Saturday and 8 to 11 a.m. on Sunday. Lunch is served from 11 a.m. to 1:15 p.m. Monday through Saturday and 11 a.m. to 2 p.m. on Sunday. Dinner is served from 4:45 to 7 p.m. Monday through Friday.

A meal in a restaurant is expensive. A meal at home is a chore. But a meal at the Cafeteria combines good food and reasonable prices to make dining a pleasure.

organization's letter, which was two pages, used most of the elements discussed in this section of the chapter in its quest to stop holiday toy advertising to children.

Although major secondary purposes of the CCFC's letter were avoiding either disappointing children at the holidays or forcing parents to buy toys they could ill afford, the CCFC could not use these purposes as common grounds with toy manufacturers, who might see their own sales as a much greater goal. Therefore they highlighted a different way to sell toys:

> We understand the need to create awareness of your products. We urge you to do that by advertising directly to parents.

Undercutting Persuasion to Be Ethical

Companies and executives spend time and money to persuade employees to be ethical in their actions. But even the best managers may not see unethical behavior. The *Harvard Business Review* listed five reasons why:

1. Ill-Conceived Goals: If goals are expressed in the wrong way (like a goal for a number of billable hours), they may encourage employees to lie or cheat in order to achieve them.
2. Motivated Blindness: Managers may overlook their employees' unethical choices if those choices benefit the managers' interests.
3. Indirect Blindness: Managers may not hold their employees accountable for unethical behavior by contractors or other third parties.
4. The Slippery Slope: Managers may miss unethical behavior when it develops slowly over time.
5. Overvaluing Outcomes: If the employees are meeting the right outcomes, managers may ignore the unethical behavior.

To ensure ethical practice, companies and executives must find ways around these barriers.

Adapted from Max H. Bazerman and Ann E. Tenbrusel, "Ethical Breakdowns," *Harvard Business Review* 89, no.4 (April 2011): 58–65.

The letter anticipated many objections from toy manufacturers. To counter claims that parents did not need to cut back on toy buying, the CCFC cited information gathered by the Associated Press. To counter claims that advertising directly to children does not lead to toy requests and hence family stress, the CCFC referred to a review of research in the academic journal *Applied Developmental Psychology*. To counter claims that the toy industry was cutting back on ads to children, they referred to media figures.

The letter also used emotional appeals:

> As you know, children are more vulnerable to advertising than adults. Seductive advertising designed explicitly to exploit their vulnerabilities will create unrealistic expectations in kids too young to understand the economic crises and will make parenting in these uncertain times even more difficult.

The fast approach of the holiday sales push provided the reason for prompt action. For more details about this campaign, including the full text of CCFC's letter and some responses from toy manufacturers, see Exercise 11.26.[25]

TONE IN PERSUASIVE MESSAGES

The best phrasing for tone depends on your relationship to the your audience. When you ask for action from people who report directly to you, polite orders ("Please get me the Ervin file") and questions ("Do we have the third-quarter numbers yet?") will work. When you need action from co-workers, superiors, or people outside the organization, you need to be more polite.

How you ask for action affects whether you build or destroy positive relationships with other employees, customers, and suppliers. Avoiding messages that sound parental or preachy is often a matter of tone. Adding "Please" is a nice touch. Tone will also be better when you give reasons for your request or reasons to act promptly.

Parental: Everyone is expected to comply with these regulations. I'm sure you can see that they are commonsense rules needed for our business.

Better: Even on casual days, visitors expect us to be professional. So please leave the gym clothes at home!

Writing to superiors is trickier. You may want to tone down your request by using subjunctive verbs and explicit disclaimers that show you aren't taking a *yes* for granted.

Arrogant: Based on this evidence, I expect you to give me a new computer.

Better: If department funds permit, I would like a new computer.

Passive verbs and jargon sound stuffy. Use active imperatives—perhaps with "Please" to create a friendlier tone.

Stuffy: It is requested that you approve the above-mentioned action.

Better: Please authorize us to create a new subscription letter.

It can be particularly tricky to control tone in e-mail messages, which tend to sound less friendly than paper documents or conversations. For important requests, compose your message offline and revise it carefully before you send it.

Major requests that require great effort or changes in values, culture, or lifestyles should not be made in e-mail messages.

VARIETIES OF PERSUASIVE MESSAGES

Performance appraisals and letters of recommendation are two important kinds of persuasive messages.

Performance Appraisals

Good supervisors give their employees regular feedback on their performances. The feedback may range from a brief "Good job!" to a hefty bonus. Blanchard and Johnson's *One Minute Manager* is a popular business guide for brief but effective performance feedback.

Performance appraisals have a tarnished reputation. Employees may not want to be honest with their supervisor about their need for improvement or training. A supervisor who praises an employee may need to reward that person. On the other hand, a supervisor who criticizes a poor performance may then need to explain why this person wasn't managed more effectively. Supervisors of Army Major Nidal Hasan, who killed 13 at Fort Hood, praised him in performance appraisals, even though they knew he was often late for work, disappeared when on call, saw few patients, and pushed his religious views on those around him.[26]

Critics also complain about vague criteria and feedback, or stock phrases. They note that "not a team player" is being used to eliminate the need to give high achievers well-deserved promotions. Even widely touted techniques such as 360-degree feedback (anonymous input from supervisors, peers, and subordinates) have their critics. Some companies are suspending this form of appraisal because of conflicting input with vague support.[27]

Companies are recognizing the need to lavish more praise on their workers, especially younger ones. Land's End and Bank of America hired consultants to teach their supervisors how to compliment workers. The Scooter Store Inc. hired a "celebrations assistant," whose duties included handing out 100–500 celebration balloons and tossing 25 pounds of confetti—per week. (The celebrations assistant became averse to confetti, so her praise came in the form of text messaging.) Such companies see the praise as a way to maintain work quality and keep good workers.[28]

Performance appraisal documents are more formal ways by which supervisors evaluate, or appraise, the performance of their subordinates. In most organizations, employees have access to their appraisals; sometimes they must sign the document to show that they've read it. The superior normally meets with the subordinate to discuss the appraisal.

As a subordinate, you should prepare for the appraisal interview by listing your achievements and goals. What have you accomplished during the appraisal period? What supporting details will you need? Where do you want to be in a year or five years? What training and experience do you need to reach your goals? If you need training, advice, or support from the organization to improve, the appraisal interview is a good time to ask for this help. As you prepare, choose the persuasive strategy that will best present your work.

Appraisals need to both protect the organization and motivate the employee. Sometimes these two purposes conflict. Most of us will see a candid appraisal as negative; we need praise and reassurance to believe that we're valued and can do better. But the praise that motivates someone to improve can come back to haunt the company if the person does not eventually do acceptable work. An organization is in trouble if it tries to fire someone whose evaluations never mention mistakes.

Put Positive Emphasis in Performance Appraisals

Positive emotional appeal is a great tool for performance reviews and other "management moments" where you need to give motivating feedback to a co-worker, teammate, or employee.

Julia Stewart, the chair and CEO of the restaurant company DineEquity, describes how she uses positive emotional appeals when she gives feedback to employees. "I'd go behind the counter, get on the food prep line, and catch an employee doing something right. I'd say, 'Great job—that's the perfect way to portion that taco' and then turn to the next person down the line and ask, 'Did you see how well this was done?' Or I'd stand in the middle of the kitchen and half-shout, 'Who did the walk-in here today?' There would be silence, and then someone would confess, 'I did.' And I'd compliment him on the job and ask the people in the kitchen to gather around so they could see what had gone right and what could be done even better the next time."

This type of positive emphasis is a great persuasive tool: your audience associates your feedback with the positive emotional feeling of being praised, which makes them more likely to view your recommendations as positive and act on them.

Adapted from Daisy Wademan Dowling, "DineEquity Chairman and CEO Julia A. Stewart on Leaders as Teachers," *Harvard Business Review* 87, no. 3 (March 2009): 29.

When you are writing performance appraisals that need to document areas for improvement, avoid labels (*wrong, bad*) and inferences. Instead, cite specific observations that describe behavior.

Inference:	Sam is an alcoholic.
Vague observation:	Sam calls in sick a lot. Subordinates complain about his behavior.
Specific observation:	Sam called in sick a total of 12 days in the last two months. After a business lunch with a customer last week, Sam was walking unsteadily. Two of his subordinates have said that they would prefer not to make sales trips with him because they find his behavior embarrassing.

Sam might be an alcoholic. He might also be having a reaction to a physician-prescribed drug; he might have a mental illness; he might be showing symptoms of a physical illness other than alcoholism. A supervisor who jumps to conclusions creates ill will, closes the door to solving the problem, and may provide grounds for legal action against the organization.

Be specific in an appraisal.

Too vague:	Sue does not manage her time as well as she could.
Specific:	Sue's first three weekly sales reports have been three, two, and four days late, respectively; the last weekly sales report for the month is not yet in.

Without specifics, Sue won't know that her boss objects to late reports. She may think that she is being criticized for spending too much time on sales calls or for not working 80 hours a week. Without specifics, she might change the wrong things in a futile effort to please her boss.

It is also important that specifics be included in performance appraisals for good employees to help them continue to shine and also to receive their well-deserved raises and promotions.

Appraisals are more useful to subordinates if they make clear which areas are most important and contain specific recommendations for improvement. No one can improve 17 weaknesses at once. Which two should the employee work on this month? Is getting in reports on time more important than increasing sales?

Phrase goals in specific, concrete terms. The subordinate may think that "considerable progress toward completing" a report may mean that the project should be 15% finished. The boss may think that "considerable progress" means 50% or 85% of the total work.

Sometimes a performance appraisal reflects mostly the month or week right before the appraisal, even though it is supposed to cover six months or a year. Many managers record specific observations of subordinates' behavior two or three times a month. These notes jog the memory so that the appraisal doesn't focus unduly on recent behavior.

A recent trend in performance appraisals is attempting to make them objective. Instead of being subjectively evaluated on intangible qualities like "works well with others," employees are monitored on how well they meet quantifiable goals. Nurses might be ranked on items such as low infection rates and high patient-satisfaction scores. Technical support personnel might be ranked on number of projects completed on time and customer-satisfaction scores.[29] If you will be evaluated by the numbers, try to have a say in setting your goals so you are not judged on items to which you only indirectly contribute. Make sure your goals stay updated so you are not judged on goals which are no longer a priority for your position or your efforts on new goals are not being measured.

Figure 11.6 shows a performance appraisal for a member of a collaborative business communication student group.

Figure 11.6 A Performance Appraisal

February 13, 2012

To: Barbara Buchanan

From: Brittany Papper BAP

Subject: Your Performance Thus Far in Our Collaborative Group

Subject line indicates that memo is a performance appraisal

Overall evaluation

You have been a big asset to our group. Overall, our communications group has been one of the best groups I have ever worked with, and I think that only minor improvements are needed to make our group even better.

These headings would need to be changed in a negative performance appraisal.

Strengths

Specific observations provide dates, details of performance

You demonstrated flexibility and compatibility at our last meeting before we turned in our proposal on February 9 by offering to type the proposal since I had to study for an exam in one of my other classes. I really appreciated this because I definitely did not have the time to do it. I will definitely remember this if you are ever too busy with your other classes and cannot type the final report.

Another positive critical incident occurred February 2. We had discussed researching the topic of sexual discrimination in hiring and promotion at Midstate Insurance. As we read more about what we had to do, we became uneasy about reporting the information from our source who works at Midstate. I called you later that evening to talk about changing our topic to a less personal one. You were very understanding and said that you agreed that the original topic was a touchy one. You offered suggestions for other topics and had a positive attitude about the adjustment. Your suggestions ended my worries and made me realize that you are a positive and supportive person.

Other strengths

Your ideas are a strength that you definitely contribute to our group. You're good at brainstorming ideas, yet you're willing to go with whatever the group decides. That's a nice combination of creativity and flexibility.

Areas for Improvement

Two minor improvements could make you an even better member.

The first improvement is to be more punctual to meetings. On February 2 and February 5 you were about 10 minutes late. This makes the meetings last longer. Your ideas are valuable to the group, and the sooner you arrive the sooner we can share in your suggestions.

Specific recommendations for improvement

Positive cast to suggestion

Specific behavior to be changed

The second suggestion is one we all need to work on. We need to keep our meetings positive and productive. I think that our negative attitudes were worst at our first group meeting February 3. We spent about half an hour complaining about all the work we had to do and about our busy schedules in other classes. In the future if this happens, maybe you could offer some positive things about the assignment to get the group motivated again.

Overall Compatibility

Positive, forward-looking ending

I feel that this group has gotten along very well together. You have been very flexible in finding times to meet and have always been willing to do your share of the work. I have never had this kind of luck with a group in the past and you have been a welcome breath of fresh air. I don't hate doing group projects any more!

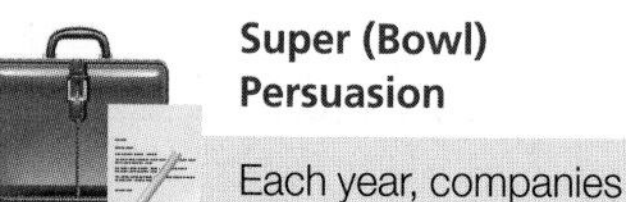

Super (Bowl) Persuasion

Each year, companies pay millions of dollars to feature 30-second ads in the biggest television event of the year: the Super Bowl. Many companies use the game spots to launch promotions or to set the tone for their annual advertising campaigns. For some, the Super Bowl is a jackpot. For many others, however, the expensive ads fail to connect with consumers. So what makes the difference?

The Super Bowl ads have become almost as much an event as the game itself. Consumers are looking for something new, clever, and most often, funny. In 2011, Volkswagen received the most positive reviews with its ad featuring a boy dressed as Darth Vader discovering that the Force can control his father's new car. Other ads, however, particularly ones that did not offer any surprises or anything new, failed to impress consumers.

High-profile advertising in events like the Super Bowl is a risky venture. Companies must use careful persuasion techniques to succeed.

Adapted from Emily Steel, "At Super Bowl, Many Ads Fail to Score," *Wall Street Journal*, February 7, 2011, B1.

Letters of Recommendation

You may write letters of recommendation when you want to recommend someone for an award or for a job. Letters of recommendation must be specific. General positives that are not backed up with specific examples and evidence are seen as weak recommendations. Letters of recommendation that focus on minor points also suggest that the person is weak.

Either in the first or the last paragraph, summarize your overall evaluation of the person. Early in the letter, perhaps in the first paragraph, show how well and how long you've known the person. In the middle of the letter, offer specific details about the person's performance. At the end of the letter, indicate whether you would be willing to rehire the person and repeat your overall evaluation. Figure A.3 in Appendix A shows a sample letter of recommendation.

Although experts are divided on whether you should include negatives, the trend is moving away from doing so. Negatives can create legal liabilities, and many readers feel that any negative weakens the letter. Other people feel that presenting but not emphasizing honest negatives makes the letter more convincing. In either case, you must ensure that your recommendation is honest and accurate.

In many discourse communities, the words "Call me if you need more information" in a letter of recommendation mean "I have negative information that I am unwilling to put on paper. Call me and I'll tell you what I really think."

In an effort to protect themselves against lawsuits, some companies state only how long they employed someone and the position that person held. Such bare-bones letters have themselves been the target of lawsuits when employers did not reveal relevant negatives.

SALES AND FUND-RAISING MESSAGES LO 11-5

Sales and fund-raising messages are a special category of persuasive messages. They are known as **direct marketing** because they ask for an order, inquiry, or contribution directly from the audience. Direct marketing which includes printed (direct mail), verbal (telemarketing), and electronic (e-mails, social media, websites, infomercials) channels, is a $300 billion industry.[30]

This section focuses on two common channels of direct marketing: sales and fund-raising letters. Large organizations hire professionals to write their direct marketing materials. If you own your own business, you can save money by doing your firm's own direct marketing. If you are active in a local group that needs to raise money, writing the fund-raising letter yourself is likely to be the only way your group can afford to use direct mail. If you can write an equally effective e-mail message, you can significantly cut the costs of a marketing campaign or supplement the success of your direct mail with direct e-mail.

The principles in this chapter will help you write solid, serviceable letters and e-mails that will build your business and help fund your group.

Sales, fund-raising, and promotional messages have multiple purposes:

Primary purpose:

To have the reader act (order the product, send a donation).

Secondary purpose:

To build a good image of the writer's organization (to strengthen the commitment of readers who act, and make readers who do not act more likely to respond positively next time).

Organizing a Sales or Fund-Raising Message

Use the sales persuasion pattern to organize your message (see Figure 11.7).

Opener The opener of your message gives you a chance to motivate your audience to read the rest of the message.

A good opener will make readers want to read the message and provide a reasonable transition to the body of the message. A very successful subscription letter for *Psychology Today* started out,

> Do you still close the bathroom door when there's no one in the house?

The question was both intriguing in itself and a good transition into the content of *Psychology Today:* practical psychology applied to the quirks and questions we come across in everyday life.

It's essential that the opener not only get attention but also be something that can be linked logically to the body of the message. A sales letter started,

> Can You Use $50 This Week?

Certainly that gets attention. But the letter only offered the reader the chance to save $50 on a product. Readers may feel disappointed or even cheated when they learn that instead of getting $50, they have to spend money to save $50.

To brainstorm possible openers, use the four basic modes: questions, narration, startling statements, and quotations.

1. Questions

> Dear Subscriber,
>
> **ARE YOU NUTS?** Your subscription to PC Gamer is about to expire!
> **No reviews. No strategies. No tips.**
> *No PC Gamer. Are you willing to suffer the consequences?*

This letter urging the reader to renew *PC Gamer* is written under a large banner question: Do you want to get eaten alive? The letter goes on to remind its audience, mostly young males, of the magazine's gaming reviews, early previews, exclusive demo discs, and "awesome array of new cheats for the latest games"—all hot buttons for computer gaming fans.

Good questions are interesting enough that the audience want the answers, so they read the letter.

Poor question: Do you want to make extra money?
Better question: How *much* extra money do you want to make next year?

A series of questions can be an effective opener. Answer the questions in the body of the letter.

Figure 11.7 How to Organize a Sales or Fund-Raising Message

1. Open by catching the audience's attention.
2. In the body, provide reasons and details.
3. End by telling the audience what to do and providing a reason to act promptly.

Persuading to Save

In the past several decades, the percentage of income Americans save has decreased dramatically. Until the early 1980s, Americans saved nearly 10% of their income. In 2009, however, we saved a paltry 0.9%. Some banks are trying to encourage their customers to save regularly by some unusual methods.

Eight credit unions in Michigan started a program called "Save to Win." This strange cross between a savings program and a lottery taps into many Americans' love of gambling. Customers who put at least $25 into a one-year CD receive an entry into a monthly drawing for $400 and an annual jackpot for $100,000. The CDs are insured, but pay slightly less than the conventional rate. The program is working, and some of the winners are putting their winnings directly into savings accounts.

Adapted from Jason Zweig, "Using the Lottery Effect to Make People Save," *Wall Street Journal,* July 18, 2009, B1.

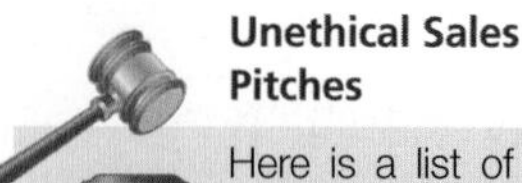

Unethical Sales Pitches

Here is a list of questionable tactics that some salespeople use to tailor their persuasive messages to you:

- Ask you to tell them about yourself, and pretend to be interested in the same things you are.
- Look for your weak spots: emotional appeals that you're less likely to resist.
- Tell you that they're offering a one-of-a-kind deal.
- Tell you that if you don't take their offer, someone else will.
- Give you a "free" gift for listening to their pitch, hoping that you'll feel obligated to buy their product.

What about these tactics makes them unethical? How can you craft persuasive messages using similar techniques—good psychological descriptions, for example—without being unethical?

Adapted from Jonathan Clements, "Don't Get Hit by the Pitch: How Advisers Manipulate You," *Wall Street Journal*, January 3, 2007, D1.

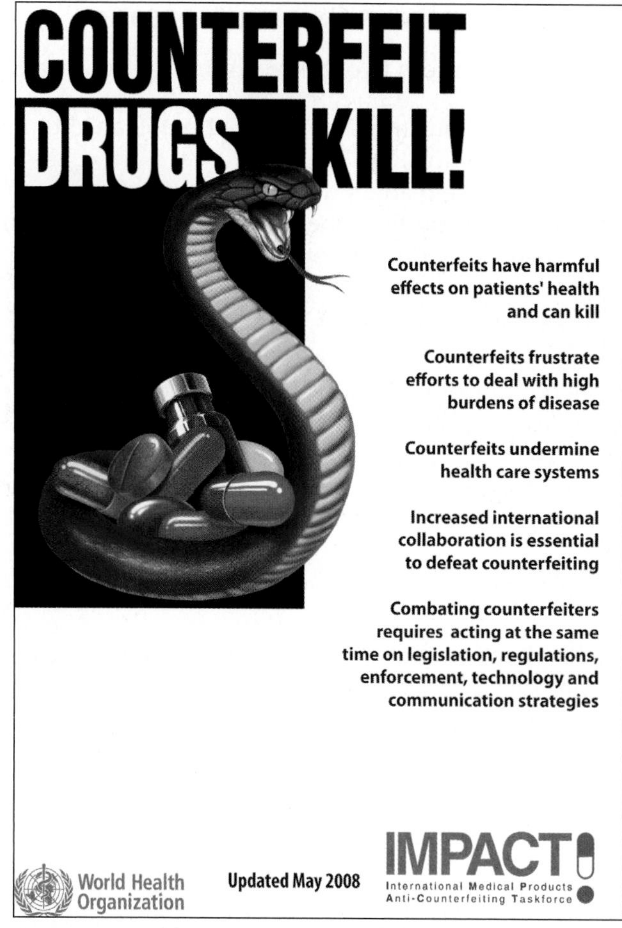

This World Health Organization poster juxtaposes lifesaving medicines with a deadly cobra in a visual "startling statement."

2. Narration, stories, anecdotes

Dear Reader:

She hoisted herself up noiselessly so as not to disturb the rattlesnakes snoozing there in the sun.

To her left, the high desert of New Mexico. Indian country. To her right, the rock carvings she had photographed the day before. Stick people. Primitive animals.

Up ahead, three sandstone slabs stood stacked against the face of the cliff. In their shadow, another carving. A spiral consisting of rings. Curious, the young woman drew closer. Instinctively, she glanced at her watch. It was almost noon. Then just at that moment, a most unusual thing happened.

Suddenly, as if out of nowhere, an eerie dagger of light appeared to stab at the topmost ring of the spiral. It next began to plunge downward—shimmering, laser-like.

It pierced the eighth ring. The seventh. The sixth. It punctured the innermost and last. Then just as suddenly as it had appeared, the dagger of light was gone. The young woman glanced at her watch again. Exactly twelve minutes had elapsed.

Coincidence? Accident? Fluke? No. What she may have stumbled across that midsummer morning three years ago is an ancient solar calendar. . . .

This subscription letter for *Science84* argues that it reports interesting and significant discoveries in all fields of science—all in far more detail than do other media. The opener both builds suspense so that the reader reads the subscription letter and suggests that the magazine will be as interesting as the letter and as easy to read.

3. Startling statements

> Dear Membership Candidate:
>
> I'm writing to offer you a job.
>
> It's not a permanent job, understand. You'll be working for only as much time as you find it rewarding and fun.
>
> It's not even a paying job. On the contrary, it will cost *you* money.

This fund-raising letter from Earthwatch invites readers to participate in its expeditions, subscribe to its journal, and donate to its programs. Earthwatch's volunteers help scientists and scholars dig for ruins, count bighorns, and monitor changes in water; they can work as long as they like; they pay their own (tax-deductible) expenses.

Variations of this mode include special opportunities, twists, and challenges.

4. Quotations

> "I never tell my partner that my ankle is sore or my back hurts. You can't give in to pain and still perform."
>
> —Jill Murphy
> Soloist

The series of which this letter is a part sells season tickets to the Atlanta Ballet by focusing on the people who work to create the season. Each letter quotes a different member of the company. The opening quote is used on the envelope over a picture of the ballerina and as an opener for the letter. The letters encourage readers to see the artists as individuals, to appreciate their hard work, and to share their excitement about each performance.

Body The body of the message provides the logical and emotional links that move the audience from their first flicker of interest to the action that is wanted. A good body answers the audience's questions, overcomes their objections, and involves them emotionally.

All this takes space. One of the industry truisms is "The more you tell, the more you sell." Tests show that longer letters bring in more new customers or new donors than do shorter letters. A four-page letter is considered ideal for mailings to new customers or donors.

Can short letters work? Yes, when you're writing to old customers or when the mailing is supported by other media. E-mail direct mail is also short—generally just one screen. The Direct Marketing Association says a postcard is the mailing most likely to be read.[31] The shortest message on record may be the two-word postcard that a fishing lake resort sent its customers: "They're biting!"

Fraud Victims

Financial scams and fraud cost Americans billions of dollars each year. According to studies of scammers, the victims of fraud aren't the uneducated or naïve. Most victims are well-educated, middle-aged men who have an excellent understanding of finances. So why are they falling prey to scammers? The studies offer these reasons:

- **Overconfidence.** Because of their education and experience in investing, most victims trust their own judgment without consulting experts for advice.
- **Pure motives.** Many victims are taken in because they want to provide an inheritance for their children or grandchildren. The motivation to help may encourage the victims to make unwise decisions.
- **Emotional reactions.** In one experiment during the Christmas season, the Better Business Bureau and a local television station in Idaho set up a fake bell ringer with a plastic Halloween bucket. Even though he had no identifying signs, shoppers automatically gave him money while he rang his bell.
- **Pro/con lists.** Research has shown that when people attempt to make lists of positives and negatives about a decision, whichever side they focus on first has the greatest impact on their choice.

Adapted from Karen Blumenthal, "Fraud Doesn't Always Happen to Someone Else," *Wall Street Journal*, August 12, 2009, D1.

The Master Salesman

Dale Carnegie was an unsuccessful businessman, a failed actor, and an undistinguished author of western novels when he began teaching public speaking at a Harlem YMCA in 1912. His course in public speaking eventually turned into a self-help business empire, built on his still-popular book, *How to Win Friends and Influence People,* published in 1936.

Carnegie's *How to Win Friends* remains one of the most influential business books of all time. Warren Buffett has based his career on the principles in the book, and Lee Iacocca says it changed his life.

What is it about the book that makes it so powerful? In 30 simple principles, Carnegie lays out a course of self-improvement, based on self-confidence and powerful public speaking, that ties directly into business success. His ideas weren't new when he wrote the book, and they are certainly not new now. Carnegie once said, however, "I present, reiterate, and glorify the obvious—because the obvious is what people need to be told."

Adapted from Dan Winters, "The Best Salesman in Business," *Fortune,* May 3, 2010, 202–4.

Content for the body of the message can include

- Information the audience will find useful even if they do not buy or give.
- Stories about how the product was developed or what the organization has done.
- Stories about people who have used the product or who need the organization's help.
- Word pictures of people enjoying the benefits offered.

Because consumers are more likely to choose or favor the familiar, linking your sales message to the things people do or use every day is a good way to increase your message's perceived importance. Of course, that requires that you do a good job of audience analysis up front. Stanford University researchers showed that children given chicken nuggets and French fries preferred the taste of the food in McDonald's packaging, even though all the food came from the same source. The familiarity effect works on adults, too. In another study, adults tasting the same peanut butter from three different jars preferred the spread from the jar with a name brand label.[32]

Costs are generally mentioned near the end of the body and are connected to specific benefits. Sometimes costs are broken down to monthly, weekly, or daily amounts: "For less than the cost of a cup of coffee a day, you can help see that Eren is no longer hungry."

Action Close The action close in the message must do four things:

1. **Tell the audience what to do:** Specify the action you want. Avoid *if* ("If you'd like to try . . .") and *why not* ("Why not send in a check?"). They lack positive emphasis and encourage your audience to say *no.*
2. **Make the action sound easy:** "Fill in the information on the reply card and mail it today." If you provide an envelope and pay postage, say so.
3. **Offer a reason for acting promptly.** People who think they are convinced but wait to act are less likely to buy or contribute. Reasons for acting promptly are easy to identify when a product is seasonal or there is a genuine limit on the offer—time limit, price rise scheduled, limited supply, and so on. Sometimes you can offer a premium or a discount if your audience acts quickly. When these conditions do not exist, remind readers that the sooner they get the product, the sooner they can benefit from it; the sooner they contribute funds, the sooner their dollars can go to work to solve the problem.
4. **End with a positive picture** of the audience enjoying the product (in a sales message) or of the audience's money working to solve the problem (in a fund-raising message). The last sentence should never be a selfish request for money.

The action close can also remind people of central selling points, and mention when the customer will get the product.

Using a P.S. In a direct mail letter or e-mail, the postscript, or P.S., occupies a position of emphasis by being the final part of the message. Direct mail often uses a deliberate P.S. after the signature block. It may restate the central selling point or some other point the letter makes, preferably in different words so that it won't sound repetitive when the reader reads the letter through from start to finish.

Here are four of the many kinds of effective P.S.'s.
Reason to act promptly:

> P.S. Once I finish the limited harvest, that's it! I do not store any SpringSweet Onions for late orders. I will ship all orders on a first-come, first-served basis and when they are gone they are gone. Drop your order in the mail today . . . or give me a call toll free at 800-531-7470! (In Texas: 800-292-5437)

Sales letter for Frank Lewis Alamo Fruit

Description of a premium the reader receives for giving:

> P.S. And . . . we'll be pleased to send you—as a new member—the exquisite, full-color Sierra Club Wilderness Calendar. It's our gift . . . absolutely FREE to you . . . to show our thanks for your membership at this critical time.

Fund-raising letter for Sierra Club

Reference to another part of the package:

> P.S. Photographs may be better than words, but they still don't do justice to this model. Please keep in mind as you review the enclosed brochure that your SSJ will look even better when you can see it firsthand in your own home.

Sales letter for the Danbury Mint's model of the Duesenberg SSJ

Restatement of central selling point:

> P.S. It is not easy to be a hungry child in the Third World. If your parents' crops fail or if your parents cannot find work, there are no food stamps . . . no free government-provided cafeteria lunches.
>
> Millions of hungry schoolchildren will be depending on CARE this fall. Your gift today will ensure that we will be there—that CARE won't let them down.

Fund-raising letter for CARE

Tempest in a Water Glass

Everyone needs water, so how much persuasion does it take to sell it? As the *Wall Street Journal* reported, there's a lot of persuasion involved in the water business—and some controversy as well.

Bottled water is big business in France: French citizens consume 145 liters per person per year, compared to 85 liters a year for Americans. When the public water companies that serve Paris ran advertisements promoting tap water over bottled with the slogan "Which brand delivers excellent water to your house all year round?" the major bottled water companies responded in kind. Their ad featured a toilet bowl and the catchphrase "I don't drink the water I use to flush."

Think about the persuasive techniques involved in the two ad campaigns. What psychological descriptions of their target audience do the ads employ? How do you think the Parisian Water Works ought to respond to the bottled water ads?

Adapted from David Gauthier-Villars, "Water Fight in France Takes a Dirty Turn," *Wall Street Journal*, February 1, 2007, B7.

Strategy in Sales Messages and Fund-Raising Appeals

In both sales messages and fund-raising appeals, the basic strategy is to help your audience see themselves using your products/services or participating in the goals of your charity. Too often, communicators stress the new features of their gadgets, rather than picturing the audience using it, or the statistics about their cause, rather than stories about people helping that cause.

Sales Messages The basic strategy in sales messages is satisfying a need. Your message must remind people of the need your product meets, prove that the product will satisfy that need, show why your product is better than similar products, and make people *want* to have the product. Use psychological description (p. 330) to show people how the product will help them. Details about how the product is made can carry the message of quality. Testimonials from other buyers can help persuade people that the product works. In fact, sales trainer and best-seller business author Jeffrey Gitomer cites customer testimonials as one of the best ways to overcome price resistance.[33]

Generally, the price is not mentioned until the last fourth of the message, after the content makes the audience *want* the product.

Combining Charity with Marketing

When Crate & Barrel, the upscale furniture retailer, set out to support education with donations, they didn't just give money to needy schools. Instead, they sent out coupons in their mailers, inviting their customers to use the DonorsChoose website to decide how and where Crate & Barrel would donate its money.

The response? Customers loved the program. Not only did the coupons inspire a higher rate of customer involvement—11% of the coupons were redeemed, compared to 2% in a normal mass mailing—but the coupons also improved customers' perceptions of the company: 75% of the customers who used the DonorsChoose coupons said they now considered Crate & Barrel a company with a positive attitude toward the community, while 82% said they'd be more likely to buy the company's products in the future.

Think about the nonprofit organizations that you support: how might they convince local businesses to try the same approach?

Adapted from Emily Steel, "Novel Program Blends Charity and Marketing," *Wall Street Journal*, December 20, 2006, B1, B5.

You can make the price more palatable with the following techniques:

- **Link the price to the benefit the product provides.** "Your piece of history is just $39.95."
- **Link the price to benefits your company offers.** "You can reach our customer service agents 24/7."
- **Show how much the product costs each day, each week, or each month.** "You can have all this for less than the cost of a cup of coffee a day." Make sure that the amount seems small and that you've convinced people that they'll use this product sufficiently.
- **Allow customers to charge sales or pay in installments.** Your bookkeeping costs will rise, and some sales may be uncollectible, but the total number of sales will increase.

Fund-Raising Appeals In a fund-raising appeal, the basic emotional strategy is **vicarious participation**. By donating money, people participate vicariously in work they are not able to do personally. This strategy affects the pronouns you use. Throughout the appeal, use *we* to talk about your group. However, at the end, talk about what *you* the audience will be doing. End positively, with a picture of the audience's dollars helping to solve the problem.

Fund-raising appeals require some extra strategy. To achieve both your primary and secondary purposes, you must give a great deal of information. This information (1) helps to persuade people; (2) gives supporters evidence to use in conversations with others; and (3) gives people who are not yet supporters evidence that may make them see the group as worthwhile, even if they do not give money now.

In your close, in addition to asking for money, suggest other ways people can help: doing volunteer work, scheduling a meeting on the subject, writing letters to Congress or the leaders of other countries, and so on. By suggesting other ways to participate, you not only involve your audience but also avoid one of the traps of fund-raising appeals: sounding as though you are interested in your audience only for the money they can give.

Deciding How Much to Ask For Most messages to new donors suggest a range of amounts, from $50 or $100 (for employed people) up to perhaps double what you *really* expect to get from a single donor. A second strategy is to ask for a small, set amount that nearly everyone can afford ($15 or $25).

One of the several reasons people give for not contributing is that a gift of $25 or $100 seems too small to matter. It's not. Small gifts are important both in themselves and to establish a habit of giving. The American Heart Association recently determined that first-time donors responding to direct mail give an average of $21.84 and give $40.62 over a lifetime. But multiplied by the 7.6 million donors who respond to the AHA's mailings, the total giving is large. Also, over $20 million of the money that the AHA receives from estate settlements after a person's death comes from people who have a relationship as direct-mail donors.[34]

You can increase the size of gifts by using the following techniques:

- **Link the gift to what it will buy.** Tell how much money it costs to buy a brick, a hymnal, or a stained glass window for a church; a book or journal subscription for a college library; a meal for a hungry child. Linking amounts to specific gifts helps the audience feel involved and often motivates them to give more: instead of saying, "I'll write a check for $25," the person may say, "I'd like to give a ———" and write a check to cover it.

- **Offer a premium for giving.** Public TV and radio stations have used this ploy with great success, offering books, CDs, DVDs, umbrellas, and carryall bags for gifts at a certain level. The best premiums are things that people both want and will use or display, so that the organization will get further publicity when other people see the premium.
- **Ask for a monthly pledge.** People on modest budgets could give $15 or $25 a month; more prosperous people could give $100 a month or more. These repeat gifts not only bring in more money than the donors could give in a single check but also become part of the base of loyal supporters, which is essential to the continued success of any organization that raises funds.

Annual appeals to past donors often use the amount of the last donation as the lowest suggested gift, with other gifts 25%, 50%, or even 100% higher.

Always send a thank-you message to people who respond to your appeal, whatever the size of their gifts. By telling about the group's recent work, a thank-you message can help reinforce donors' commitment to your cause.

Logical Proof in Fund-Raising Messages The body of a fund-raising message must prove that (1) the problem deserves attention, (2) the problem can be solved or at least alleviated, (3) your organization is helping to solve or alleviate it, (4) private funds are needed, and (5) your organization will use the funds wisely.

1. The problem deserves attention. No one can support every cause. Show why your audience should care about solving this problem.

If your problem is life-threatening, give some statistics: Tell how many people are killed in the United States every year by drunk drivers, or how many children in the world go to bed hungry every night. Also tell about one individual who is affected.

If your problem is not life-threatening, show that the problem threatens some goal or principle your audience find important. For example, a fund-raising letter to boosters of a high school swim team showed that team members' chances of setting records were reduced because timers relied on stopwatches. The letter showed that automatic timing equipment was accurate and produced faster times, since the timer's reaction time was no longer included in the time recorded.

2. The problem can be solved or alleviated. People will not give money if they see the problem as hopeless—why throw money away? Sometimes you can reason by analogy. Cures have been found for other deadly diseases, so it's reasonable to hope that research can find a cure for cancer and AIDS. Sometimes you can show that short-term or partial solutions exist. For example, UNICEF shows how simple changes—oral rehydration, immunization, and breast feeding—could save the lives of millions of children. These solutions don't affect the underlying causes of poverty, but they do keep children alive while we work on long-term solutions.

3. Your organization is helping to solve or alleviate the problem. Prove that your organization is effective. Be specific. Talk about your successes in the past. Your past success helps readers believe that you can accomplish your goals.

Donating to Operating Expenses?

Wouldn't you want to make sure that your charitable donations went to support worthwhile causes, rather than overhead expenses within a nonprofit organization? Many people do, and so look for nonprofits that either limit their spending on overhead or can guarantee that gifts will go toward specific programs, not overhead.

However, even nonprofit organizations have bills to pay. As the *Wall Street Journal* reports, some nonprofits are challenged with the tasks of soliciting donations while convincing donors that money spent on overhead is still money well spent. One solution? Some nonprofits ask for donations specifically to cover their operating expenses by asking for money to support their teams or their business plans.

Philanthropy advisers suggest that donors also consider how effectively the charity uses its money. Some organizations that spend 70% of their funds on their core mission do a better job than those who spend 80%.

The very best way to judge a charity? Be one of their volunteers.

How would asking for a donation to pay for a nonprofit's overhead be different than asking for donations to support a worthy cause? What persuasive strategies could you use to make that request?

Adapted from Rachel Emma Silverman and Sally Beatty, "Save the Children (but Pay the Bills, Too)," *Wall Street Journal*, December 26, 2006, D1, D2.

www.habitat.org

Habitat for Humanity's website provides information for potential and current donors, volunteers, and clients.

These are some of the specifics that the charity:water website gives about its efforts:

> Our Progress So Far: 3,962 projects funded. 1,794,983 people will get clean water. 19 countries, 25 local partners.[35]

4. Private funds are needed to accomplish your group's goals. We all have the tendency to think that taxes, or foundations, or church collections yield enough to pay for medical research or basic human aid. If your group does get some tax or foundation money, show why more money is needed. If the organization helps people who might be expected to pay for the service, show why they cannot pay, or why they cannot pay enough to cover the full cost. If some of the funds have been raised by the people who will benefit, make that clear.

5. Your organization will use the funds wisely. Prove that the money goes to the cause, not just to the cost of fund-raising. This point is becoming increasingly important as stories become more common of "charities" that give little money to their mission. One study of 80 professional fund-raisers serving over 500 charities found the median percentage of proceeds going to the charity was 24%; only five charities received more than 75%. In fact, one fund-raising company charged charities more money than the company raised.[36]

Enclosures In Fund-Raising Letters

Fund-raising letters sometimes use inexpensive enclosures to add interest and help carry the message.

Brochures are inexpensive, particularly if you photocopy them. Mailings to alumni have included "Why I Teach at Earlham" (featuring three professors) and letters from students who have received scholarships.

Seeds don't cost much. Mailings from both Care and the New Forests Fund include four or five seeds of the leucaena, a subtropical tree that can grow 20 feet in a year. Its leaves feed cattle; its wood provides firewood or building materials; its roots reduce soil erosion. (Indeed, the enclosure easily becomes the theme for the letter.)

Reprints of newspaper or magazine articles about the organization or the problem it is working to solve add interest and credibility. Pictures of people the organization is helping build emotional appeal.

Major campaigns may budget for enclosures: pictures of buildings, CDs of oral history interviews, and maps of areas served.

Emotional Appeal in Fund-Raising Messages Emotional appeal is needed to make people pull out their checkbooks. How strong should emotional appeal be? A mild appeal is unlikely to sway anyone who is not already committed, but your audience will feel manipulated by appeals they find too strong and reject them. Audience analysis may help you decide how much emotional appeal to use. If you don't know your audience well, use the strongest emotional appeal *you* feel comfortable with.

Emotional appeal is created by specifics. It is hard to care about, or even to imagine, a million people; it is easier to care about one specific person. Details and quotes help us see that person as real. Sensory details also help people connect to a cause. Covenant House, an organization that takes in homeless youth, does both. They provide vivid pictures both of children arriving at their door and of individuals who have turned their lives around. They also use relevant sensory details: a child crawling into bed on a cold night, feeling warm and safe under soft blankets, versus a girl crawling into a cardboard box on the street to try to stay warm on a cold night.[37]

Sample Fund-Raising Letter The letter from UNICEF (Figure 11.8) seeks aid for people in Darfur. It stresses the enormity of the problem—"4.7 million people," "millions of families," "millions of children"—and what UNICEF has already done to help them. It moves on to the specific need for "additional emergency supplies of therapeutic nutritional supplements," and shows them to be life-saving aids. It applies specifics to donations: $25 will buy 49 packets. The close continues the sense of urgency, while the P.S. reemphasizes the good that has already been done with the nutritional packets.

Writing Style

Direct mail is the one kind of business writing where elegance and beauty of language matter; in every other kind, elegance is welcome but efficiency is all that finally counts. Direct mail imitates the word choice and rhythm of conversation. The best sales, fund-raising, and promotional writing is closer to the language of poetry than to that of academia: it shimmers with images, it echoes with sound, it vibrates with energy.

Figure 11.8 A Fund-Raising Letter

CHILDREN ARE STARVING IN DARFUR

Emotional appeal in headline

Will you help rush 49 packets of ready-to-eat therapeutic nutritional supplement to save malnourished children in Darfur?

Dear Dr. Kienzler,

In spite of intense world pressure and the sustained work of UNICEF, the humanitarian crisis in Darfur continues to worsen. Continued violence has affected 4.7 million people - half of them children - with refugee camps filled to capacity.

Letter opens with startling statement about enormity of problem

Hundreds of thousand of lives have been lost, and the exodus of millions of families has torn this country apart. UNICEF has been coordinating relief for the world's largest refugee relocation effort, establishing and maintaining emergency shipments of food, clean water, and medical supplies.

Pragraph shows what UNICEF has been doing

The recent suspension of humanitarian aid organizations by the government of Sudan has left UNICEF as the only remaining major source of emergency support for millions of children struggling to survive in Darfur. Today, UNICEF supports 260 primary health facilities and mobile clinics . . . has trained and deployed nearly 1,000 community healthy workers . . . and has been the primary source of vaccines, cold chain equipment, and operational staff for polio and measles immunization campaigns.

Fund raising letters may use format features such as underlining and ellipses

UNICEF also directly maintains over 100 therapeutic and supplementary feeding centers. But with millions of children and no readily available source of food, and tens of thousands of children already suffering from severe malnutrition, UNICEF needs to provide additional emergency supplies of therapeutic nutritional supplements.

Sentence shows situation is not hopeless

The specially formulated high-protein, high-energy paste revives children with remarkable results and can reverse the most severe effects of malnutrition. Your gift today of $25 can supply 49 packets - and just three of these packets daily can help a malnourished child recover with minimal adverse health effects.

Shows impact of reasonable individual gift

Every minute counts. Please act now.

Need for immediate action

Sincerely,

Caryl M. Stren

Caryl M. Stren
President & CEO

P. S. By providing nutritional supplies and other assistance, UNICEF successfully treated over 53,000 malnourished children in Darfur last year, saving them from almost-certain death. Please send a generous gift today to continue these vital efforts.

Reiteration of successful effort

Source: Reprinted with permission from the U.S. Fund for UNICEF.

The Changing Role of Catalogs

If sales from mass-mailer catalogs have been declining in recent years, replaced by e-commerce sales through websites, isn't it time to retire paper catalogs? Not necessarily: catalogs are still one way for companies to build customer interest and persuade customers to make purchases—even if those purchases are online.

Catalogs can be an integral part of a company's marketing plan:

- Instead of showing a company's entire stock, a good catalog will save space (and costs!) by listing a representative sampling. The idea is to attract the widest possible range of customers, with the widest possible interests.
- Good catalogs increase customer involvement with the products, either by providing them with a shopping experience "in hand" or by directing them to an interactive website.

Think about the catalogs that you receive in the mail. How do you use them? What would you need to see in a catalog to convince you to visit its website or a physical store?

Adapted from Louise Lee, "Catalogs, Catalogs, Everywhere," *BusinessWeek*, December 4, 2006, 32–34.

Catalogs are still an excellent way for companies to build customer interest and persuade customers to buy—even if the sales are made at the company's website.

Many of the things that make writing vivid and entertaining *add* words because they add specifics or evoke an emotional response. Individual sentences should flow smoothly. The passage as a whole may be fun to read precisely because of the details and images that "could have been left out."

Make Your Writing Interesting If the style is long-winded and boring, the reader will stop reading. Eliminating wordiness is crucial. You've already seen ways to tighten your writing in Chapter 5. Direct mail goes further, breaking some of the rules of grammar. In the following examples, note how sentence fragments and ellipses (spaced dots) are used in parallel structure to move the reader along:

> Dear Member-elect:
>
> If you still believe that there are nine planets in our solar system . . . that wine doesn't breathe . . . and that you'd recognize a Neanderthal man on sight if one sat next to you on the bus . . . check your score. There aren't. It does. You wouldn't.

Subscription letter for *Natural History*

Use Psychological Description Psychological description (p. 330) means describing your product or service with vivid sensory details. In a sales letter, you can use psychological description to create a scenario so readers can picture themselves using your product or service and enjoying its benefits. You can also use psychological description to describe the problem your product or service will solve.

A *Bon Appétit* subscription letter used psychological description in its opener and in the P.S., creating a frame for the sales letter:

> Dear Reader:
>
> First, fill a pitcher with ice.
>
> Now pour in a bottle of ordinary red wine, a quarter cup of brandy, and a small bottle of Club soda.
>
> Sweeten to taste with a quarter to half cup of sugar, garnish with slices of apple, lemon, and orange. . . .

> . . . then *move your chair to a warm, sunny spot.* You've just made yourself Sangria—one of the great glories of Spain, and the perfect thing to sit back with and sip while you consider this invitation. . . .
>
> . . .
>
> P.S. One more thing before you finish your Sangria. . . .

It's hard to imagine any reader really stopping to follow the recipe before finishing the letter, but the scenario is so vivid that one can imagine the sunshine even on a cold, gray day.

Make Your Letter Sound Like a Letter, Not an Ad Maintain the image of one person writing to one other person that is the foundation of all letters. Use an informal style with short words and sentences, and even slang.

You can also create a **persona**—the character who allegedly writes the letter—to make the letter interesting and keep us reading. Use the rhythms of speech, vivid images, and conversational words to create the effect that the author is a "character."

The following opening creates a persona who fits the product:

> Dear Friend:
>
> There's no use trying. I've tried and tried to tell people about my fish. But I wasn't rigged out to be a letter writer, and I can't do it. I can close-haul a sail with the best of them. I know how to pick out the best fish of the catch, I know just which fish will make the tastiest mouthfuls, but I'll never learn the knack of writing a letter that will tell people why my kind of fish—fresh-caught prime-grades, right off the fishing boats with the deep-sea tang still in it—is lots better than the ordinary store kind.

Sales letter, Frank Davis Fish Company

This letter, with its "Aw, shucks, I can't sell" persona, with language designed to make you see an unassuming fisherman ("rigged out," "close-haul"), was written by a professional advertiser.[38]

Humiliation for Debt Collection

Humiliation is becoming a major persuader in Spain, a country with an overwhelmed legal system. Since the courts can't help, many companies believe the only way to collect debt is to shame debtors in front of their neighbors. It is particularly persuasive in this country where one's honor and public image are so important.

Debt collection companies are becoming ingenious in creating humiliation. Collectors arrive at homes dressed as bull fighters, Zorro, Franciscan friars, or even the Pink Panther. The Scottish Collector threatens to send a Scottish bagpipe player to debtors' homes. Sometimes they phone the neighbors.

One collection agency acquired the guest list for a lavish but unpaid wedding reception. They began calling guests and charging them for the food they ate. Needless to say, the debtors paid their bill.

What do you think about this collection method? Do you agree with U.S. law which prohibits it?

Adapted from Thomas Catan, "Spain's Showy Debt Collectors Wear a Tux, Collect the Bucks: Their Goal: Publicly Humiliate Non-Payers; Seeing the Pink Panther at the Door," *Wall Street Journal,* October 11, 2008, A1.

SOLVING A SAMPLE PROBLEM

Little things add up to big issues, especially where workplace quality of life is at stake.

Problem

FirstWest Insurance's regional office has 300 employees, all working the same 8-to-5 shift. Many of them schedule their lunch break during the noon hour, and that's where the problem started: there was only one microwave in the canteen. People had to wait up to 30 minutes to heat their lunches. As Director of Human Resources, you implemented lunch shifts to break the gridlock. That program failed: people were used to their schedules and resisted the change. In your second attempt, you convinced FirstWest's Operations Vice President to approve a purchase order for a second microwave oven.

Now there's a new problem: fish. FirstWest recently recruited five new employees. They're from the Philippines, and fish is a prominent part of their diet. Each afternoon, they take lunch together and reheat their meals—often containing fish—and each afternoon, the air conditioning system in your closed-air building sends the aroma of spiced fish wafting through the whole office.

Face-to-face Persuasion

When you present your persuasive messages in a spoken, face-to-face format, remember that your interpersonal interactions are an important part of your message. A recent study of successful retail salespeople identified some strong techniques you can use when you're speaking persuasively:

- Use their name. People respond well when you show that you care enough about them to use their name.
- Show your interest. Build goodwill and rapport by asking about, noticing, and remembering details about your audience's history and preferences.
- Identify mutual interests. Turn your persuasive pitch into a conversation by inviting stories from your audience and sharing your own in return.
- Be polite and honest. Many people react to persuasive messages by being on guard against potential dishonesty. Demonstrate your respect for your audience by backing up your claims with evidence: show them, don't tell them, and invite them to judge for themselves.
- Give—and seek—information. Take the pressure off your persuasive message by changing it into an informative message instead of sales. Build rapport by inviting your audience to share their knowledge with you.

Adapted from Dwayne D. Gremler and Kevin P. Gwinner, "Rapport-Building Behaviors Used by Retail Employees," *Journal of Retailing* 84, no. 3 (2008): 308–24.

Other employees have complained bitterly about the "foul odor." You've spoken to the new employees, and while they're embarrassed by the complaints, they see no reason to change. After all, they're just as disgusted by the smell of cooking beef: why haven't you asked the American employees not to reheat hamburger? And having just purchased a second oven, you know that management won't pay $1,000 for a new microwave with a filter system that will eliminate the odors. It's time to set a microwave-use policy.

Analysis of the Problem

Use the problem analysis questions in the first chapter to think through the problem.

1. Who is (are) your audience(s)?

   You'll be addressing all of the employees at this location. That's a broad audience, but they have certain characteristics in common, at least regarding this topic. They're all on a similar lunch schedule, and many of them use the canteen and the microwaves. They've also responded poorly to a previous attempt to change their lunch habits.

   Many members of your audience won't see this as their problem: only the new employees are doing something objectionable. The new employees will react poorly to being singled out.

2. What are your purposes in writing?

   To help eliminate cooking odors. To solve a minor issue before it begins to impact morale.

3. What information must your message include?

   The effects of the present situation. The available options and their costs (in money, and also in time, effort, and responsibility).

4. How can you build support for your position? What reasons or benefits will your audience find convincing?

   Improving the workplace environment—and eliminating a minor but persistent irritation—should improve morale. While expensive solutions exist, this is a matter that can, and should, be solved with cooperative behaviors.

5. What aspects of the total situation may be relevant?

   This issue is a minor one, and it may be difficult to get people to take it seriously. The easy solution—mandating what the new employees are allowed to bring for lunch—is discriminatory. For budgetary reasons, company management will not invest in a third (and much more expensive) microwave for the canteen.

Discussion of the Sample Solutions

The solution shown in Figure 11.9 is unacceptable. By formatting the communication as a notice designed to be posted in the canteen, the author invites the audience to publicly embarrass their co-workers: a form of threat. The subject line displays the author's biases in a way that discourages further discussion on the topic and eliminates the possibility of a broader consensus for any solution to the problem. The author uses emotional appeals to place blame on a small segment of the audience, but the lack of logical observations or arguments (and the presence of clip art and emoticons) undermines the author's seriousness. The demand to stop cooking food with strong smells is vague: does this include pizza? popcorn? The author concludes with a threat, again eliminating the possibility of consensus-based actions.

Figure 11.9 An Unacceptable Solution to the Sample Problem

ATTENTION!!!!

DON'T BRING DISGUSTING LUNCHES!!

Negative, biased subject line and clip art

Some of you (you KNOW!!! who you are) have been bringing in foul-smelling food and cooking it in the microwave at lunch. We've all smelled the result. It's not fair that everyone has to put up with your stink. *Negative diction*

I'm writing to tell everyone that this is the END. As of today, no one is allowed to cook any food with a strong smell in the canteen microwave ovens. *Vague diction*

The microwaves are a privilege and not a right. If you people continue to abuse company property, the microwaves will be removed from the canteen for good. ☹ *Don't use emoticons in serious communications* *Threatens*

Thank you in advance for your cooperation in this matter.

Close does not sound sincere after threat

Clip art not appropriate for this serious communication

✓ Checklist — Checklist for Direct Requests

- ☐ If the message is a memo, does the subject line indicate the request? Is the subject line specific enough to differentiate this message from others on the same subject?
- ☐ Does the first paragraph summarize the request or the specific topic of the message?
- ☐ Does the message give all of the relevant information? Is there enough detail?
- ☐ Does the message answer questions or overcome objections that readers may have without introducing unnecessary negatives?
- ☐ Does the closing tell the reader exactly what to do? Does it give a deadline if one exists and a reason for acting promptly?

Originality in a direct request may come from

- ☐ Good lists and visual impact.
- ☐ Thinking about readers and giving details that answer their questions, overcome any objections, and make it easier for them to do as you ask.
- ☐ Adding details that show you're thinking about a specific organization and the specific people in that organization.

The second solution, shown in Figure 11.10, is a more effective persuasive message. The author recognizes that this persuasive situation centers on goodwill, and begins with a neutral subject line (as a more directed subject could

The "Default" Choice Is Yes

Have you ever been presented with an online form that had response boxes prechecked for you? One way to sidestep your customers' objections is to provide them with default responses: choices they can make that encourage an easy, objection-free response. Here are some common types of defaults:

- **Benign** default choices give customers a range of responses that you've chosen for them: you present a sample of the best or most likely responses ("Press one for English, para Espanol oprima numero dos").
- **Persistent** default choices use the customer's last response to the same situation as their current response (such as a billing form which assumes that your billing address is the same as your mailing address).
- **Smart** default choices use what you know about past customer behavior to suggest current choices that they're likely to agree with (such as retailer websites that offer a list of other products you may be interested in based on what you've selected already).
- **Forced** defaults are selections your customers must make in order to access a product or service (such as the licensing agreement for most software packages).

These defaults offer quick, convenient ways to encourage customers to respond in predictable ways. They can also allow you to constrain your customers' choices. What ethical concerns do you need to consider before you use defaults in your persuasive messages?

Adapted from Daniel G. Goldstein et al., "Nudge Your Customers toward Better Choices," *Harvard Business Review* 86, no. 12 (December 2008): 99–105.

Figure 11.10 A Good Solution to the Sample Problem

Date: November 15, 2012

To: FirstWest Grand Harbor Co-Workers

From: Arnold M. Morgan, Human Resources Director AMM

Subject: Canteen Microwave Policies *Neutral subject line*

Creates common ground

We all notice when someone uses the microwaves in the first-floor canteen to reheat strong-smelling food. These odors are distracting—whether they're the scent of burned popcorn, a fish lunch, or fresh-baked brownies—and none of us need any extra distractions in our busy days! Let's work together to "clear the air."

Cause of problem

How is it that we all smell food cooking in the first-floor canteen? Our building has a closed-air ventilation system: it's good for the environment and it saves on heating and cooling costs by recirculating air throughout the building. It also circulates any odors in the air. That's why we can smell food from the first-floor canteen down in the basement archives and up in the third-floor conference rooms: we're all sharing the same air.

We're all sharing the same microwaves, too. Due to popular demand, we recently purchased a second microwave to relieve crowding at lunchtime. We've looked into purchasing a third microwave—an odor-eliminating, air-filtration microwave—but that would cost $1,000, plus $20/month for filters. That seems expensive, especially since there are simple things each of us can do to reduce problems with odors.

Easy solutions to problem

- **Use containers with lids** when you heat up your food. Not only will this help contain any odors, it will reduce the mess in the microwaves.
- **Clean up any mess you make** when you cook. If you cook something with a strong odor—or something that spatters!—take a minute when you're done and wipe the oven down with a damp paper towel.
- **Stay with your food** while it's cooking. When food overcooks or burns, it smells more strongly, so watching your food and removing it from the oven before it overcooks is the easiest way to avoid creating a distracting smell.

We work together as a team every day to serve our customers and succeed as an organization. Please take a little time to use the microwaves responsibly, and help us make sure that the only smell in our workplace is success!

ends on positive note

detract from goodwill). The opening paragraph creates common ground by describing the problem in terms of group experience, rather than by assigning blame. It includes fish odors in with pleasant odors (brownies) and suggests that the memo's purpose is to propose a consensus-based solution.

The problem is spelled out in detail, balancing the emotional, goodwill-centered problem with rational arguments based on process and cost. The solution is presented as small, easily accommodated, changes. The memo ends by linking cooperation with the audience benefit of group participation and identity.

✓ Checklist — Checklist for Problem-Solving Persuasive Messages

- ☐ If the message is a memo, does the subject line indicate the writer's purpose or offer a benefit? Does the subject line avoid making the request?
- ☐ Does the first sentence interest the audience?
- ☐ Is the problem presented as a joint problem both communicator and audience have an interest in solving, rather than as something the audience is being asked to do for the communicator?
- ☐ Does the message give all of the relevant information? Is there enough detail?
- ☐ Does the message overcome objections that the audience may have?
- ☐ Does the message avoid phrases that sound dictatorial, condescending, or arrogant?
- ☐ Does the closing tell the audience exactly what to do? Does it give a deadline if one exists and a reason for acting promptly?

Originality in a problem-solving persuasive message may come from

- ☐ A good subject line and common ground.
- ☐ A clear and convincing description of the problem.
- ☐ Thinking about the audience and giving details that answer their questions, overcome objections, and make it easier for them to do as you ask.
- ☐ Adding details that show you're thinking about a specific organization and the specific people in that organization.

Ethics and Direct Mail

Deception in direct mail is all too easy to find.

Some mailers have sent "checks" to readers. But the "check" can only be applied toward the purchase of the item the letter is selling.

Some mailings now have yellow Post-it notes with "handwritten" notes signed with initials or a first name only—to suggest that the mailing is from a personal friend.

One letter offers a "free" membership "valued at $675" (note the passive—who's doing the valuing?) but charges—up front—$157 for "maintenance fees."

Such deception has no place in well-written direct mail.

SUMMARY OF KEY POINTS

- The primary purpose in a persuasive message is to have the audience act or change beliefs. Secondary purposes are to overcome any objections that might prevent or delay action, to build a good image of the communicator and the communicator's organization, to cement a good relationship between the communicator and audience, and to reduce or eliminate future communication on the same subject.
- **Credibility** is the audience's response to you as the source of the message. You can build credibility by being factual, specific, and reliable.
- You always need to consider your audience and situation before choosing your persuasive strategy. In general,
  - Use the **direct request pattern** when the audience will do as you ask without any resistance. Also use the direct request pattern for busy readers in your own organization who do not read all the messages they receive. See Figure 11.1.
  - Use the **problem-solving pattern** when the audience may resist doing what you ask and you expect logic to be more important than emotion in the decision. See Figure 11.3.
  - Use the **sales pattern** when the audience may resist doing as you ask and you expect emotion to be more important than logic in the decision. See Figure 11.10.
- Use one or more of the following strategies to counter objections that you cannot eliminate:
  - Specify how much time and/or money is required.
  - Put the time and/or money in the context of the benefits they bring.
  - Show that money spent now will save money in the long run.
  - Show that doing as you ask will benefit some group the audience identifies with or some cause the audience supports.

Get Involved

Getting involved with nonprofit work is a great opportunity to give back to your community while developing your professional and communication skills. Here are some online resources to get you started:

- http://www1.networkforgood.org/
- http://www.change.org/
- http://www.dosomething.org/
- http://firstgiving.org/
- http://www.donorschoose.org/
- http://www.kiva.org/
- http://www.opportunity.org/
- http://www.accion.org/
- http://www.jumo.com/

  - Show the audience that the sacrifice is necessary to achieve a larger, more important goal to which they are committed.
  - Show that the advantages as a group outnumber or outweigh the disadvantages as a group.
  - Turn the disadvantage into an opportunity.
- Threats don't produce permanent change. They won't necessarily produce the action you want, they may make people abandon an action entirely (even in situations where abandoning would not be appropriate), and they produce tension. People dislike and avoid anyone who threatens them. Threats can provoke counteraggression.
- To encourage people to act promptly, set a deadline. Show that the time limit is real, that acting now will save time or money, or that delaying action will cost more.
- Build emotional appeal with stories and psychological description.
- Performance appraisals should cite specific observations, not inferences. They should contain specific suggestions for improvement and identify the two or three areas that the worker should emphasize in the next month or quarter.
- Letters of recommendation must be specific and tell how well and how long you've known the person.
- A good opener makes readers want to read persuasion messages and provides a reasonable transition to the body of the message. Four modes for openers are questions, narration, startling statements, and quotations. A good body answers the audience's questions, overcomes their objections, and involves them emotionally. A good action close tells people what to do, makes the action sound easy, gives them a reason for acting promptly, and ends with a benefit or a picture of their contribution helping to solve the problem.
- In a fund-raising appeal, the basic strategy is vicarious participation. By donating money, people participate vicariously in work they are not able to do personally.
- The primary purpose in a fund-raising appeal is to get money. An important secondary purpose is to build support for the cause so that people who are not persuaded to give will still have favorable attitudes toward the group and will be sympathetic when they hear about it again.

CHAPTER 11 Exercises and Problems

*Go to www.mhhe.com/locker10e for additional Exercises and Problems.

11.1 Reviewing the Chapter

1. What are four questions you should answer when analyzing persuasive situations? Which question do you think is the most important? Why? (LO 11-1)
2. What are three basic persuasive strategies? In what kinds of situations is each preferred? (LO 11-2)
3. Why aren't threats effective persuasion tools? (LO 11-2)
4. How do you start the body of persuasive direct requests? Why? (LO 11-3)
5. How do you organize persuasive problem-solving messages? (LO 11-4)
6. How do you develop a common ground with your audience? (LO 11-4)
7. What are 10 ways to deal with objections? (LO 11-4 and LO 11-6)
8. What are ways to build emotional appeal? (LO 11-4 and LO 11-6)
9. What are four good beginnings for sales and fund-raising messages? (LO 11-5)
10. What are ways to de-emphasize costs or donation requests? (LO 11-5)
11. What kinds of rational evidence should you use to support your persuasion? (LO 11-6)
12. What kinds of emotional appeals should you use to support your persuasion? (LO 11-6)

11.2 Reviewing Grammar

Persuasion uses lots of pronouns. Correct the sentences in Exercise B.4, Appendix B, to practice making pronouns agree with their nouns, as well as practicing subject–verb agreement.

11.3 Writing Psychological Description

For one or more of the following groups, write two or three paragraphs of psychological description that could be used in a brochure, news release, or direct mail message directed to members of that group.

1. Having a personal trainer.

   Audiences: Professional athletes
   Busy managers
   Someone trying to lose weight
   Someone making a major lifestyle change after a heart attack

2. Volunteering time to a local charity event (you pick the charity) as part of a team from your workplace.

   Audiences: Your workplace colleagues
   Your boss
   Finance department
   PR department

3. Using vending machines newly installed in school cafeterias and stocked with healthful snacks, such as yogurt, raisins, carrots with dip, and all-natural juices.

   Audiences: High school students
   Parents
   High school faculty

4. Attending a fantasy sports camp (you pick the sport), playing with and against retired players who provide coaching and advice.
5. Attending a health spa where clients get low-fat and low-carb meals, massages, beauty treatments, and guidance in nutrition and exercise.

Hints:

- For this assignment, you can combine benefits or programs as if a single source offered them all.
- Add specific details about particular sports, activities, and so on, as material for your description.
- Be sure to use vivid details and sense impressions.
- Phrase your benefits with you-attitude.

11.4 Evaluating Subject Lines

Evaluate the following subject lines. Is one subject line in each group clearly best? Or does the "best" line depend on company culture, whether the message is a paper memo or an e-mail message, or on some other factor?

1. Subject: Request
   Subject: Why I Need a New Computer
   Subject: Increasing My Productivity
2. Subject: Who Wants Extra Hours?
   Subject: Holiday Work Schedule
   Subject: Working Extra Hours During the Holiday Season
3. Subject: Student Mentors
   Subject: Can You Be an E-Mail Mentor?
   Subject: Volunteers Needed
4. Subject: More Wine and Cheese
   Subject: Today's Reception for Japanese Visitors
   Subject: Reminder
5. Subject: Reducing Absenteeism
   Subject: Opening a Day Care Center for Sick Children of Employees
   Subject: Why We Need Expanded Day Care Facilities

11.5 Evaluating P.S.'s

Evaluate the following P.S.'s. Will they motivate readers to read the whole messages if readers turn to them first? Do they create a strong ending for those who have already read the message?

1. P.S. It only takes one night's stay in a hotel you read about here, one discounted flight, one budget-priced cruise, or one low-cost car rental to make mailing back your Subscription Certificate well worth it.

   P.P.S. About your free gift! Your risk-free subscription to CONSUMER REPORTS TRAVEL LETTER comes with a remarkable 314-page book as a FREE GIFT.

2. P.S. Help spread the tolerance message by using your personalized address labels on all your correspondence. And remember, you will receive a free *Teaching Tolerance* magazine right after your tax-deductible contribution arrives.

3. P.S. Every day brings more requests like that of Mr. Agyrey-Kwakey—for our "miracle seeds." And it's urgent that we respond to the emergency in Malaysia and Indonesia by replanting those forests destroyed by fire. Please send your gift today and become a partner with us in these innovative projects around the world.
4. P.S. Even as you read this letter, a donated load of food waits for the ticket that will move it to America's hungry. Please give today!

11.6 Choosing a Persuasive Approach

For each of the following situations requiring a persuasive message, choose the persuasive approach that you feel would work best. Explain your reasoning; then give a short list of the types of information you'd use to persuade your audience.

1. Asking for an extension on a project.
2. Requesting a job interview.
3. Requesting a free trial of a service.
4. Inviting customers to a store opening.
5. Reporting a co-worker's poor work performance.
6. Asking your supervisor to reconsider a poor performance review.
7. Requesting a new office computer.
8. Requesting time off during your company's busy season.

As your instructor directs,

a. Write a memo, letter, or e-mail that addresses one of the situations in this exercise, drawing on details from your personal experiences. (You might address a real problem that you've faced.)
b. Write a memo to your instructor listing the choices you've made and justifying your approach.

11.7 Identifying Observations

Susan has taken the following notes about her group's meetings. Which of the following are specific observations that she could use in a performance appraisal of group members? If she had it to do over again, what kinds of details would turn the inferences into observations?

1. Feb. 22: Today was very frustrating. Sam was totally out of it—I wonder if he's on something. Jim was dictatorial. I argued, but nobody backed me up. Masayo might just as well have stayed home. We didn't get anything done. Two hours, totally wasted.
2. February 24: Jim seems to be making a real effort to be less domineering. Today he asked Sam and me for our opinions before proposing his own. And he noticed that Masayo wasn't talking much and brought her into the conversation. She suggested some good ideas.
3. February 28: Today's meeting was OK. I thought Masayo wasn't really focusing on the work at hand. She needs to work on communicating her ideas to others. Sam was doing some active listening, but he needs to work at being on time. Jim was involved in the project. He has strong leadership skills. There were some tense moments, but we got a lot done, and we all contributed. I got to say what I wanted to say, and the group decided to use my idea for the report.
4. March 5: This week most of us had midterms, and Masayo had an out-of-town gymnastics trip. We couldn't find a time to meet. So we did stuff by e-mail. Sam and Jim found some great stuff at the library and on the web. Jim created a tentative schedule that he sent to all of us and then revised. I wrote up a draft of the description of the problem. Then Masayo and I put everything together. I sent my draft to her; she suggested revisions (in full caps so I could find them in the e-mail message). Then I sent the message to everyone. Masayo and Jim both suggested changes, which I made before we handed the draft in.
5. March 15: We were revising the proposal, using Prof. Jones's comments. When we thought we were basically done, Masayo noticed that we had not responded to all of the specific comments about our introductory paragraph. We then went back and thought of some examples to use. This made our proposal better and more complete.

As your instructor directs,

a. Based on Susan's notes, write a performance appraisal memo addressed to Prof. Jones. For each group member, including Susan, note specific areas of good performance and make specific suggestions for improvement.
b. Write a memo to your instructor describing the process you used to make your recommendations. Be sure to identify each of the observations you used to provide specific details, and each of the inferences that needed more information.

11.8 Revising a Form Memo

You've been hired as a staff accountant; one of your major duties will be processing expense reimbursements. Going through the files, you find this form memo:

> Subject: Reimbursements
>
> Enclosed are either receipts that we could not match with the items in your request for reimbursement or a list of items for which we found no receipts or both. Please be advised that the Accounting Department issues reimbursement checks only with full documentation. You cannot be reimbursed until you give us a receipt for each item for which you desire reimbursement. We must ask that you provide this information. This process may be easier if you use the Expense Report Form, which is available online.
>
> Thank you for your attention to this matter. Please do not hesitate to contact us with questions.

You know this memo is horrible. Employees have to use the Expense Report Form; it is not optional. In addition to wordiness, a total lack of positive emphasis and you-attitude, and a vague subject line, the document design and organization of information bury the request.

Create a new memo that could be sent to people who do not provide all the documentation they need in order to be reimbursed.

11.9 Creating Persuasive Videos

As they try to undo the harm from YouTube drinking videos starring their institutions, school officials are making their own YouTube videos. Some, such as deans lecturing on course offerings, are ludicrously bad. Other videos are slick promotional films. Still others, such as videos of classes, are somewhere in between.

Some schools are sponsoring contests to persuade students to create videos showing what they like about the school. One humorous one showed a student in a three-piece suit dancing across campus to "It's Raining Men." The student creator said he wanted a school where people dance around and have a good time.

What would you put in a video to convince students—and parents who foot the bills—to consider your school? Share your ideas in small groups.

Source: Susan Kinzie, "Colleges Putting Their Own Spin on YouTube," *Washington Post,* May 12, 2008, A01.

11.10 Creating Alternative Activities

You are residence director at Expensive Private University. Enrollment at your school has been declining because of repeated publicity about excessive drinking among the students. Last year 23 were treated for alcohol poisoning at the local hospital, and one died.

You have been ordered by the president of EPU to develop alcohol-free activities for the campus and ways to persuade students to participate. She wants your plans by the end of June so EPU can work on implementing them for the next academic year. Write the memo to her detailing your plans. Write a second memo to your instructor explaining your persuasive strategies.

Hints:

- Who are your audiences?
- Do they share any common ground?
- What objections will your audiences have?
- What are some ways you can deal with those objections?
- What pitfalls do you need to avoid?

11.11 Evaluating Persuasion Strategies

In June 2009, the Lorillard Tobacco Company responded to new legislation regulating the tobacco industry with a full-page ad in the *Wall Street Journal*. With a classmate or in a small group, evaluate the ad to pick out its persuasion strategies. Use the following questions in your evaluation:

- What audience is this message intended to reach?
- What strategies does the message use in its introduction and conclusion?
- What persuasion strategies does the message use?
- Which phrases are designed to create emotion in readers?
- How does the corporate author of the message affect how you perceive the persuasive arguments? How would your perceptions change if this same message were written by a government watchdog group? an antitobacco group?

Write a memo to your instructor with your evaluation of the ad.

FDA—Tobacco Regulation: Truth and Consequences

As the Family Smoking Prevention and Tobacco Control Act (H.R.1256/S.982)—which mandates that the Food and Drug Administration (FDA) regulate the tobacco industry—moves through the U.S. Senate, this is a critical time for lawmakers and all Americans to take a closer look at the major flaws in this legislation, and consider the serious consequences that could result.

The FDA Is the Wrong Agency

Putting the FDA in charge of an inherently dangerous product is inconsistent with the agency's mission to ensure the safety and efficacy of our nation's food, drugs, biologics, and medical devices. With the legacy of recent food and drug contaminations still reverberating, the FDA is an agency that is already overwhelmed in its mission to protect Americans. A March 2009 poll by the American Society for Quality (ASQ) reveals that Americans are losing confidence in the FDA's "Gold Standard" ability to protect the nation's food and drug supply. The survey found 61 percent of U.S. adults feel the food recall process in only fair or poor, while 73 percent of adults say they are as equally concerned about food safety as the war on terror.

A Boost to the Black Market

History clearly demonstrates that when consumer choice is thwarted by government policy, whether through exorbitant taxes, regulatory burdens, or outright bans, black markets arise to take advantage of the situation. This legislation will increase the price of tobacco products in order to pay for FDA regulation, which will only make it more lucrative and attractive for those who want to illegally profit (and likely deprive the federal and state governments of billions of dollars in taxes as a result) from this regulatory effort. And with huge profits—and low penalties for arrest and conviction—illicit cigarette trafficking now has begun to rival drug trafficking as a funding choice for terrorist groups. A congressional investigation led by Rep. Peter King (R-NY), ranking member of the House Homeland Security Committee, in April 2008 found that cigarette smugglers with ties to terrorist groups are acquiring millions of dollars from illegal cigarette sales and funneling the cash to organizations such as al Qaeda and Hezbollah.

Prohibition in Disguise

We believe the proponents of these new regulations would like nothing more than to outlaw smoking completely in our society. This bill is but a first big step in that direction, allowing the FDA to mandate changes to cigarettes as we know them and prevent new, potentially safer products from entering the marketplace. Should we let the FDA prohibit smoking or demand that the American people and those they elect to make such important decisions be the final arbiter of this issue?

A Blow to Safer Products

The regulations in this legislation would also require that the FDA approve any new tobacco product that claims to lessen the risk from smoking before it can be marketed. However, the standard that such new product must meet—that it is appropriate for the protection of the public health, determined with respect to the risks and benefits to the population as a whole, including users and non-users of the tobacco product—may well be impossible to meet, thereby assuring that no safer products ever come to market. Indeed, this bill will stifle the innovation that may provide promising hope for safer, less harmful tobacco products.

With respect to these specific issues, we urge the Senate to thoroughly review the current legislation and find an effective and different regulatory solution.

Lorillard Tobacco Company

Source: Lorillard Tobacco Company, "FDA-Tobacco Regulation: Truth and Consequences," advertisement, *Wall Street Journal,* June 3, 2009, A7.

11.12 Asking for More Time and/or Resources

Today, this message from your boss shows up in your e-mail inbox:

Subject: Want Climate Report

This request has come down from the CEO. I'm delegating it to you. See me a couple of days before the board meeting—the 4th of next month—so we can go over your presentation.

I want a report on the climate for underrepresented groups in our organization. A presentation at the last board of directors' meeting showed that while we do a good job of hiring women and minorities, few of them rise to the top. The directors suspect that our climate may not be supportive and want information on it. Please prepare a presentation for the next meeting. You'll have 15 minutes.

Making a presentation to the company's board of directors can really help your career. But preparing a good presentation and report will take time. You can look at exit reports filed by Human Resources when people leave the company, but you'll also need to interview people—lots of people. And you're already working 60 hours a week on three major projects, one of which is behind schedule. Can one of the projects wait? Can someone else take one of the projects? Can you get some help? Should you do just enough to get by? Ask your boss for advice—in a way that makes you look like a committed employee, not a shirker.

11.13 Persuading Employees Not to Share Files

Your computer network has been experiencing slowdowns, and an investigation has uncovered the reason. A number of employees have been using the system to download and share songs and vacation photos. You are concerned because the bulky files clog the network, and downloading files opens the network to computer viruses and worms. In addition, management does not want employees to spend work time and resources on personal matters. Finally, free downloads of songs are often illegal, and management is worried that a recording firm might sue the company for failing to prevent employees from violating its copyrights.

As director of Management Information Systems (MIS), you want to persuade employees to stop sharing files unrelated to work. You are launching a policy of regularly scanning the system for violations, but you prefer that employees voluntarily use the system properly. Violations are hard to detect, and increasing scanning in an effort to achieve system security is likely to cause resentment as an intrusion into employees' privacy.

Write an e-mail message to all employees, urging them to refrain from downloading and sharing personal files.

11.14 Not Doing What the Boss Asked

Today, you get this e-mail message:

> To: All Unit Managers
>
> Subject: Cutting Costs
>
> Please submit five ideas for cutting costs in your unit. I will choose the best ideas and implement them immediately.

You think your boss's strategy is wrong. Cutting costs will be easier if people buy into the decision rather than being handed orders. Instead of gathering ideas by e-mail, the boss should call a meeting so that people can brainstorm, teaching each other why specific strategies will or won't be easy for their units to implement.

Reply to your boss's e-mail request. Instead of suggesting specific ways to cut costs, persuade the boss to have a meeting where everyone can have input and be part of the decision.

11.15 Handling a Sticky Recommendation

As a supervisor in a state agency, you have a dilemma. You received this e-mail message today:

> From: John Inoye, Director of Personnel, Department of Taxation
>
> Subject: Need Recommendation for Peggy Chafez
>
> Peggy Chafez has applied for a position in the Department of Taxation. On the basis of her application and interview, she is the leading candidate. However, before I offer the job to her, I need a letter of recommendation from her current supervisor.
>
> Could you please let me have your evaluation within a week? We want to fill the position as quickly as possible.

Peggy has worked in your office for 10 years. She designed, writes, and edits a monthly statewide newsletter that your office puts out; she designed and maintains the department website. Her designs are creative; she's a very hard worker; she seems to know a lot about computers.

However, Peggy is in many ways an unsatisfactory staff member. Her standards are so high that most people find her intimidating. Some find her abrasive. People have complained to you that she's only interested in her own work; she seems to resent requests to help other people with projects. And yet both the newsletter and the web page are projects that need frequent interaction. She's out of the office a lot. Some of that is required by her job (she takes the newsletters to the post office, for example), but some people don't like the fact that she's out of the office so much. They also complain that she doesn't return voice-mail and e-mail messages.

You think managing your office would be a lot smoother if Peggy weren't there. You can't fire her: state employees' jobs are secure once they get past the initial six-month probationary period. Because of budget constraints, you can hire new employees only if vacancies are created by resignations. You feel that it would be pretty easy to find someone better.

If you recommend that John Inoye hire Peggy, you will be able to hire someone you want. If you recommend that John hire someone else, you may be stuck with Peggy for a long time.

As your instructor directs,

a. Write an e-mail message to John Inoye.

b. Write a memo to your instructor listing the choices you've made and justifying your approach.

Hints:

- Polarization may make this dilemma more difficult than it needs to be. What are your options? Consciously look for more than two.
- Is it possible to select facts or to use connotations so that you are truthful but still encourage John to hire Peggy? Is it ethical? Is it certain that John would find Peggy's work as unsatisfactory as you do? If you write a strong recommendation and Peggy doesn't do well at the new job, will your credibility suffer? Why is your credibility important?

11.16 Persuading Tenants to Follow the Rules

As resident manager of a large apartment complex, you receive free rent in return for collecting rents, doing simple maintenance, and enforcing the complex's rules. You find the following notice in the files:

> Some of you are failing to keep any kind of standard of sanitation code, resulting in the unnecessary cost on our part to hire exterminators to rid the building of roaches.
>
> Our leases state breach of contract in the event that you are not observing your responsibility to keep your apartment clean.
>
> We are in the process of making arrangements for an extermination company to rid those apartments that are experiencing problems. Get in touch with the manager no later than 10 pm Monday to make arrangements for your apartment to be sprayed. It is a fast, odorless operation. You are also required to put your garbage in plastic bags. Do not put loose garbage or garbage in paper bags in the dumpster, as this leads to rodent or roach problems.
>
> Should we in the course of providing extermination service to the building find that your apartment is a source of roaches, then you will be held liable for the cost incurred to rid your apartment of them.

The message is horrible. The notice lacks you-attitude, and it seems to threaten anyone who asks to have his or her apartment sprayed.

The annual spraying scheduled for your complex is coming up. Under the lease, you have the right to enter apartments once a year to spray. However, for spraying to be fully effective, residents must empty the cabinets, remove kitchen drawers, and put all food in the refrigerator. People and pets need to leave the apartment for about 15 minutes while the exterminator sprays.

Tell residents about the spraying. Persuade them to prepare their apartments to get the most benefit from it, and persuade them to dispose of food waste quickly and properly so that the bugs don't come back.

Hints:

- What objections may people have to having their apartments sprayed for bugs?
- Why don't people already take garbage out promptly and wrap it in plastic? How can you persuade them to change their behavior?
- Analyze your audience. Are most tenants students, working people, or retirees? What tone would be most effective for this group?

11.17 Asking an Instructor for a Letter of Recommendation

You're ready for the job market, transfer to a four-year college, or graduate school, and you need letters of recommendation.

As your instructor directs,

a. Assume that you've orally asked an instructor for a recommendation, and he or she has agreed to write one, but asks, "Why don't you write up something to remind me of what you've done in the class? Tell me what else you've done, too. And tell me what they're looking for. Be sure to tell me when the letter needs to be in and to whom it goes." Write the e-mail.

b. Assume that you've been unable to talk with the instructor whose recommendation you want. When you call, no one answers the phone; you stopped by once and no one was in. Write asking for a letter of recommendation.

c. Assume that the instructor is no longer on campus. Write him or her asking for a recommendation.

Hints:

- Be detailed about what the organization is seeking and the points you'd like the instructor to mention.
- How well will this instructor remember you? How much detail about your performance in his or her class do you need to provide?
- Specify the name and address of the person to whom the letter should be written; specify when the letter is due.

11.18 Writing a Performance Appraisal for a Member of a Collaborative Group

During your collaborative writing group meetings, keep a log of events. Record specific observations of both effective and ineffective things that group members do. Then evaluate the performance of the other members of your group. (If there are two or more other people, write a separate appraisal for each of them.)

In your first paragraph, summarize your evaluation. Then in the body of your memo, give the specific details that led to your evaluation by answering the following questions:

- What specifically did the person do in terms of the task? Brainstorm ideas? Analyze the information? Draft the text? Suggest revisions in parts drafted by others? Format the document or create visuals? Revise? Edit? Proofread? (In most cases, several people will have done each of these activities together. Don't overstate what any one person did.) What was the quality of the person's work?
- What did the person contribute to the group process? Did he or she help schedule the work? Raise or resolve conflicts? Make other group members feel valued and included? Promote group cohesion? What roles did the person play in the group?

Support your generalizations with specific observations. The more observations you have and the more detailed they are, the better your appraisal will be.

As your instructor directs,

a. Write a midterm performance appraisal for one or more members of your collaborative group. In each appraisal, identify the two or three things the person should try to improve during the second half of the term.

b. Write a performance appraisal for one or more members of your collaborative group at the end of the term. Identify and justify the grade you think each person should receive for the portion of the grade based on group process.

c. Give a copy of your appraisal to the person about whom it is written.

11.19 Writing a Self-Assessment for a Performance Review

Your company privileges good communication skills. In fact, during their second year, all employees are sent to a four-month communication course. As part of your annual review, you must prepare a self-assessment that includes your assessment of your progress in the communication course. Assume that your business communication course is the company's communication course and prepare the communications part of your self-assessment. The company expects this portion to be a page long.

11.20 Evaluating Sales and Fund-Raising Messages

Collect the sales and fund-raising messages that come to you, your co-workers, landlord, neighbors, or family. Use the following questions to evaluate each message:

- What mode does the opener use? Is it related to the rest of the message? How good is the opener?
- What central selling point or common ground does the message use?
- What kinds of proof does the message use? Is the logic valid? What questions or objections are not answered?
- How does the message create emotional appeal?
- Is the style effective?
- Does the close tell people what to do, make action easy, give a reason for acting promptly, and end with a positive picture?
- Does the message use a P.S.? How good is it?
- Is the message visually attractive? Why or why not?
- What other items besides the letter or e-mail are in the package?

As your instructor directs,

a. Share your analysis of one or more messages with a small group of your classmates.

b. Analyze one message in a presentation to the class. Make a copy of the message to use as a visual aid in your presentation.
c. Analyze one message in a memo to your instructor. Provide a copy of the message along with your memo.
d. With several other students, write a group memo or report analyzing one part of the message (e.g., openers) or one kind of letter (e.g., political messages, organizations fighting hunger, etc.). Use at least 10 messages for your analysis if you look at only one part; use at least 6 messages if you analyze one kind of message. Provide copies as an appendix to your report.

11.21 Writing a Fund-Raising Appeal

Write a 2½- to 4-page letter to raise money from *new donors* for an organization you support. You must use a real organization, but it does not actually have to be conducting a fund-raising drive now. Assume that your letter would have a reply card and postage-paid envelope. You do NOT have to write these, but DO refer to them in your letter.

Options for organizations include

- Tax-deductible charitable organizations—religious organizations; hospitals; groups working to feed, clothe, and house poor people.
- Lobbying groups—Mothers Against Drunk Driving, the National Abortion Rights Action League, the National Rifle Association, groups working against nuclear weapons, etc.
- Groups raising money to fight a disease or fund research.
- Colleges trying to raise money for endowments, buildings, scholarships, faculty salaries.

For this assignment, you may also use groups which do not regularly have fund-raising drives but which may have special needs. Perhaps a school needs new uniforms for its band. Perhaps a sorority or fraternity house needs repairs, remodeling, or expansion.

11.22 Asking to Telecommute

You need to relocate to another city, where the company you work for does not have a branch office. You would prefer to remain working at this company, so telecommuting would be an ideal situation. Write a proposal in memo format to persuade your employer to allow you to work from a remote location.

Hints:

- Establish common ground: you want to stay, and many firms would rather allow an employee to telecommute than risk losing a valued team member.
- Point out potential benefits to your employer: you may save the company money on office resources, extend their usual business hours, or provide customer service to a remote location.
- Provide for oversight: outline a framework for evaluating your performance and participating on team projects, and perhaps offer a trial period.

11.23 Calling in a Favor

Last month, your co-worker Mike asked you for a favor: he needed to take an afternoon off to look after one of his children, but he didn't have any vacation or leave time left. Your supervisor had authorized him to take the time off as long as he could get someone else to cover his client meetings for him. You agreed, and spent the day covering for him.

Now you're in the same position: you need to take a morning off, and your supervisor wants you to convince someone to cover for you. You'll be missing a conference call with a client that cannot be rescheduled, and which will take an hour. Mike is the obvious choice—he knows the client, and he owes you a favor—but you know that he's very busy and might object to taking on more work.

Write a short memo or e-mail to Mike asking him to return the favor and cover for you.

Hints:

- Your informal relationship with Mike allows you to exchange favors. It also means that you can use more informal language and tone in your e-mail. (Not too informal, though: any e-mail can be forwarded.)
- Be sure to build common ground and goodwill as part of your opening.
- Mike may object to taking on more work. What other objections might he raise? Be sure to address those objections in your e-mail.

11.24 Creating a Healthy Snackfood Counter

You work in a friendly environment where people like to bring in treats to share with their co-workers. They do it so often that there's an area in your workplace that people jokingly call "Snackfood Counter," lined with donuts, candy, chips, pretzels, soda, and other not-too-healthy fare.

Write a memo, suitable for distributing to a wide audience at your workplace, to convince your co-workers to make the switch to healthy snacks. Build common ground, offset any negatives with benefits, and provide concrete suggestions for future actions. Be sure to build and maintain goodwill: people contribute to Snackfood Counter to be friendly, and may interpret your request as a complaint.

11.25 Recostuming Happy Halloween

Your team has been put in charge of organizing your company's Halloween event. Employees may come to work dressed in a costume. During the lunch hour, you'll hold a costume contest with prizes for the most original costumes (and a prize for the department or team with the highest rate of participation), followed by a party for your staff members. Last year's party was a big hit: about 30% of your employees dressed up, and you anticipate that the number will be higher this year.

However, last year there were a number of (moderately) racy and (somewhat) tasteless costumes, and some complaints about those costumes. The team who organized last year's Halloween ignored those complaints "because we're all adults here, and we can all take a joke." Well, this year, we *won't* all be adults: your company is also sponsoring a trick-or-treat event for kids from 10 local foster homes. Immediately following the costume contest and lunch, there will be dozens of (supervised) kids, ages 2–8, going office-to-office for candy. Your Human Resources department has provided the candy and treats, but it's up to you to make sure that the costume contest is kid-friendly.

As your instructor directs:

- Write a memo, suitable for distributing to all staff, which establishes guidelines for participating in the costume contest and persuades your co-workers to comply.
- Create a sign, suitable for posting in the common areas of your workplace, that establishes your costume guidelines and invites your co-workers to participate in the event.

Hints:

- Adults are more likely to comply with a policy decision when they understand the rationale behind that decision. Be sure to communicate your decision process as well as your guidelines.
- Choose a persuasive message format, create common ground and goodwill, and use creativity in both your language and your visual design.

11.26 Campaigning against Holiday Toy Ads

Discussions on pages 323 and 330 outlined the campaign of CCFC (Campaign for a Commercial-Free Childhood) against holiday toy ads directed at children.

This is the sample letter to toy manufacturers from parents suggested by CCFC:

> I am writing to urge you to suspend all advertising to children this holiday season. With the global economic crisis intensifying, many families will have to scale back their holiday shopping this year. It's wrong to create unrealistic expectations in children or to foment family stress by encouraging kids to lobby for gifts that their parents may not be able to afford.
>
> I understand the need to create awareness of your products. I urge you to do that by advertising directly to parents instead of enlisting children as lobbyists for their holiday gifts. Since it's parents, not children, who can truly understand their family's financial situation in these difficult times, it is more important than ever that you respect their authority as gatekeepers. Please target parents instead of children with your holiday advertising.

Source: "Tell Toy Companies: Target Parents, Not Kids, with Holiday Ads," Campaign for a Commercial-Free Childhood, Judge Baker Children's Center, accessed June 30, 2011, http://salsa.democracyinaction.org/o/621/t/6914/campaign.jsp?campaign_KEY=26139

This is the letter to toy manufacturers from the CCFC:

Campaign for a Commercial-Free Childhood
c/o Judge Baker Children's Center
53 Parker Hill Avenue, Boston, MA 02120-3225
Phone: 617-278-4172• Fax: 617-232-7343
Email: CCFC@JBCC.Harvard.edu
Website: www.commercialfreechildhood.org

PLEASE NOTE: This letter was sent to 24 companies, not just Mattel. A complete list can be found at: www.commercialfreechildhood.org/actions/holidaymarketers.htm

October 27, 2008

Mr. Robert Eckert
Chief Executive Officer, Mattel
333 Continental Boulevard
El Segundo, CA 90245

Dear Mr. Eckert:

As families struggle to cope with the global economic crisis, we are writing to urge you to suspend all holiday marketing aimed at children. With fears of a recession or even a depression intensifying, Americans routinely list the economy as their number one concern. There is little doubt that many parents will have to scale back their holiday purchases significantly and experts predict that parents will spend less money on toys and gifts for children this holiday season. [1] Under normal circumstances it is unfair to bypass parents and target children directly with marketing, but with an uncertain future and budgets tighter than ever, it is particularly egregious to foment family conflict by advertising toys and games directly to kids that their parents may not be able to afford.

Research demonstrates that children's exposure to advertising is linked to the things they ask their parents to buy and family stress. [2] Using advertising to encourage children to nag for products may be good for sales, but it creates considerable family conflict. Even in normal times, buying holiday gifts causes financial strain for many families. A 2005 poll found that approximately one-third of Americans took more than three months to pay off their holiday credit card debt and 14% carried credit card debt into the next holiday season. [3]

Early reports indicate that spending on advertising to children will not reflect the current economic downturn. To date, spending forecasts for forth quarter television advertising on children's television have not been affected. [4] If parents are cutting their purchases back this holiday season while commercial pressures on children remain at record levels, the burden on families will be tremendous.

As you know, children are more vulnerable to advertising than adults. Seductive advertising designed explicitly to exploit their vulnerabilities will create unrealistic expectations in kids too young to understand the economic crises and will make parenting in these uncertain times even more difficult. **We understand the need to create awareness of your products. We urge you to do that by advertising directly to parents instead of enlisting children as lobbyists for their holiday gifts.** Since it's parents, not children, who can truly understand their family's financial situation in these difficult times, it is more important than ever that you respect their authority as gatekeepers: Target parents instead of children this holiday season.

Please note that we are sending this letter to CEO's of all the leading toy and game manufacturers and will be happy to offer public praise for any company that puts America's families first by suspending their holiday advertising to children. We would also welcome the opportunity to discuss this matter with you further.

Sincerely,

Susan Linn, Ed.D.

[1] Anderson, M. (2008, Oct 8). Holiday spending on toys expected to be less. *The Associated Press.* Accessed October 17, 2008 from http://www.thenewstribune.com/1031/v-lite/story/502479.html.
[2] Buijen, M. & Valkenburg (2003). The effects of television advertising on materialism, parent–child conflict, and unhappiness: A review of research. *Applied Developmental Psychology*, 24, 437–456.
[3] Center for a New American Dream (2005). Hot Holiday Gift for Kids This Year? — A Piggy Bank, Say Fed Up Americans. Accessed October 17, 2008 from http://www.newdream.org/holiday/poll05.php.
[4] Freidman, W. (2008, Oct 13). So Far, Kids' TV Saved from Ad Hits. *MediaPost's Media Daily News.* Accessed October 17, 2008 from http://www.mediapost.com/publications/?fa=Articles.showArticle&art_aid=92573.

Source: Reprinted with permission of Judge Baker Children's Center, Boston, MA.

This is the response from the TIA (Toy Industry Association):

Toy Industry Association's Statement

The Toy Industry Association notes with interest, but begs to disagree with, the Campaign for a Commercial-Free Childhood's suggestion that marketing of toys be focused this year on parents and not on children.

We believe parents should know what their children want and are perfectly capable of deciding, as they have always done, how to fit satisfaction of those desires into the family budget. Children are a vital part of the gift selection process and should not be removed from it.

We offer several thoughts to guide families through the gift buying process:

- Children have their own ideas about what appeals to them and parents are not necessarily going to know, without their children's input, if a new toy is going to excite them. We have faith in parents' ability to hear from their children what they would like and then make a decision as to what, and how much, to give them.
- In fact, most parents and grandparents appreciate knowing which items are on their child's wish lists before they go out to purchase a gift for them, as it makes shopping easier. If children are not aware of what is new and available, how will they be able to tell their families what their preferences are?
- Parents do a pretty good job of budgeting and making purchase decisions. While there is certainly greater economic disturbance going on now, families have always faced different levels of economic well-being and have managed to tailor their spending to their means.

Toy Industry Association, Inc.

Source: Reprinted with permission of Judge Baker Children's Center, Boston, MA.

This is the statement on the website of the TIA:

TIA Statement on Marketing to Children

TIA Position Statement for Holiday Season 2008

The Toy Industry Association and its members are proud of the toys and games we produce and their role in play, which is an important, life-shaping experience in the growth of a child. We believe it is appropriate to market toys and games both to children and to their parents, so long as it is done responsibly.

Ultimately, TIA and its members understand that a parent or primary caregiver knows his or her child best. Our research confirms that parents agree that they should be involved in all aspects of their child's life, including the child's television viewing, computer time, and purchasing decisions.

The toy industry believes firmly in self-regulation and is committed to follow best practices in marketing to our consumers, as reflected in various national codes and industry guidelines. These include the Children's Advertising Review Unit of the Council of Better Business Bureaus (of which TIA is a long-standing member) in the United States and the codes of the International Chamber of Commerce and local self-regulatory codes internationally. We are actively involved with various self-regulatory organizations in continually reviewing and improving those guidelines as needed.

Children are the reason our industry exists. We are parents ourselves and we treat all children with the same care and respect.

Source: Industry Statements, from http://www.toyassociation.org/AM/Template.cfm?Section=Industry_Statements&TEMPLATE=/CM/HTMLDisplay.cfm&CONTENTID=1474 (accessed April 5, 2009).

In small groups, discuss these four documents. Here are some questions to get you started:

1. Do the openers grab your attention? Why or why not?
2. What persuasive strategies do they use?
3. What arguments do they use? How do they build credibility?
4. What common ground do they use?
5. What emotional appeals do they use?
6. How do they deal with objections?
7. What are the differences between the TIA response to CCFC and the TIA's statement on its own website?
8. Do the documents convince you? Why or why not? Which document is the most persuasive?
9. How could these documents be improved?

As your instructor directs,

a. As a group, share your analyses with the class in a five-minute presentation.
b. Prepare three documents for your instructor.
    - Write a detailed analysis of one of the documents.
    - On the basis of that analysis, rewrite the document.
    - Write a memo explaining the changes you made and why you kept some of the original document (if you did).

CHAPTER 12

Building Résumés

Chapter Outline

A Time Line for Job Hunting

Evaluating Your Strengths and Interests

Using the Internet in Your Job Search

Personal Branding

Networking

A Caution about Blogs, Social Networking Sites, and Internet Tracking

Using an Internship as a Job Hunting Tool

How Employers Use Résumés

Guidelines for Résumés

- Length
- Emphasis
- Details
- Writing Style
- Key Words
- Layout and Design

Kinds of Résumés

What to Include in a Résumé

- Name and Contact Information
- Career Objective
- Summary of Qualifications
- Education
- Honors and Awards
- Experience
- Other Skills
- Activities
- Portfolio

References

What Not to Include in a Résumé

Dealing with Difficulties

- "I Don't Have Any Experience."
- "All My Experience Is in My Family's Business."
- "I Want to Change Fields."
- "I've Been Out of the Job Market for a While."
- "I Was Laid Off."
- "I Was Fired."

Electronic Résumés

- Sending Your Résumé Electronically
- Posting Your Résumé on the Web

Honesty

Summary of Key Points

Changing Channels

Channels for job documents are changing so rapidly that newspapers and business magazines are running articles on the subject. In 2010, *Fortune* ran an eight-page story on LinkedIn, "How LinkedIn Will Fire Up Your Career." Calling it Facebook for grownups, *Fortune* says that LinkedIn is the only social site that matters for careers.

"Fortune says that LinkedIn is the only social site that matters for careers."

The numbers for LinkedIn are impressive. The site has over 60 million profiles and more than a half million groups—based on companies, schools, and affinities—you can join to help you make connections. You can attach your résumé, pack your profile with key words that make you easy to find, connect to your blog and Twitter account, and invite colleagues to comment on your work (and approve all comments before they appear on your profile).

Your profile will be in good company. The average member is college-educated and makes $107,000. Every *Fortune* 500 company is represented.

You do have your profile there, right?

Source: Jessi Hempel, "How LinkedIn Will Fire Up Your Career," *Fortune*, April 2010, 74–82.

Learning Objectives

After studying this chapter, you will know how to

LO 12-1 Prepare a detailed time line for your job search.

LO 12-2 Prepare a résumé that makes you look attractive to employers.

LO 12-3 Deal with common difficulties that arise during job searches.

LO 12-4 Handle the online portion of job searches.

LO 12-5 Keep your résumé honest.

You will probably change jobs many times during your career. Although no longitudinal study has ever been completed, the U.S. Bureau of Labor Statistics has started one, the National Longitudinal Survey of Youth. It shows that the average person born in the latter years of the baby boom held an average of 11 jobs from age 18 to age 44. In fact, 25% of them have held 15 jobs or more. Even in middle age, when job changing slows down, 68% of jobs ended in fewer than five years. This means that you should keep your résumé up to date.[1]

A **résumé** is a persuasive summary of your qualifications for a job with a specific employer. If you're on the job market, having a résumé is a basic step in the job hunt. When you're employed, having an up-to-date résumé makes it easier to take advantage of opportunities that may come up for even better jobs. If you're several years away from job hunting, preparing a résumé now will help you become more conscious of what to do in the next two or three years to make yourself an attractive candidate.

This chapter covers paper and electronic résumés. Job application letters (sometimes called cover letters) are discussed in Chapter 13. Chapter 14 discusses interviews and communications after the interview. All three chapters focus on job hunting in the United States. Conventions, expectations, and criteria differ from culture to culture: different norms apply in different countries.

All job communications should be tailored to your unique qualifications and the specifications of the job you want. Adopt the wording or layout of an example if it's relevant to your own situation, but don't be locked into the forms in this book. You've got different strengths; your résumé will be different, too.

A TIME LINE FOR JOB HUNTING LO 12-1

Many employers consider the way you do your job hunt to be evidence of the way you will work for them. Therefore, you should start preparing yourself several years ahead of your formal applications.

Informal preparation for job hunting should start soon after you arrive on campus. Check out the services of your college placement and advising offices. Join extracurricular organizations on campus and in the community to increase your knowledge and provide a network for learning about jobs. Find a job that gives you experience. Note which courses you like—and why you like them. If you like thinking and learning about a subject, you're more likely to enjoy a job in that field. Select course projects and paper topics that will help you prepare for a job—and look good on your résumé.

Once you have selected a major, start reading job ads, particularly those posted on your professional organization's website. What kinds of jobs are available? Do you need to change your course selections to better fit them? What kinds of extras are employers seeking? Do they want communication skills? Extra statistics courses? International experience? Learn this information early while you still have time to add to the knowledge and skill sets you are acquiring. Attend job seminars and job fairs. Join your professional association and its listserv.

Formal preparation for job hunting should begin a full year *before you begin interviewing*. Enroll for the services of your campus placement office. Ask friends who are on the job market about their experiences in interviews; find out what kinds of job offers they get. Check into the possibility of getting an internship or a co-op job that will give you relevant experience before you interview.

The year you interview, register with your Placement Office early. An active job search takes significant chunks of time, so plan accordingly. If you plan to graduate in the spring, prepare your résumé and plan your interview strategy early in the fall. Initial campus interviews occur from October to February for May or June graduation. In January or February, write to any organization you'd like to work for that hasn't interviewed on campus. From February to April, you're likely to visit one or more offices for a second interview.

Try to have a job offer lined up *before* you get the degree. People who don't need jobs immediately are more confident in interviews and usually get better job offers. If you have to job-hunt after graduation, plan to spend at least 30 hours a week on your job search. The time will pay off in a better job that you find more quickly.

What Employers Want, I

You can increase your odds of getting an interview by understanding what hiring managers are thinking while they evaluate your résumé. The following are questions managers ask themselves:

Can this applicant fill the needs of the company? Your résumé should stress all of your most relevant skills and experience which match the position opening. Rather than submitting a generic résumé for every position you apply for, create a customized résumé based on your review of the job opening.

Will this applicant stay with the company long term? Managers seek employees who are most likely to stay with a company long term because the hiring process is long, difficult, and costly. The cost of replacing an employee averages $13,355 according to a study conducted by the Employment Policy Foundation. To avoid costly turnover, managers look at your résumé to see if you have a stable work history.

Will this applicant be professional? Your résumé represents your ability to communicate. Unfortunately, managers will eliminate résumés for the slightest problems since they may receive hundreds of résumés for one position. Make sure your résumé is easy to follow and does not contain typos or grammatical mistakes.

Adapted from Robert Half International, "What Employers Think When They Read Your Résumé," CareerBuilder, September, 23, 2008, http://www.careerbuilder.com/Article/CB-427-Resumes-Cover-Letters-What-Employers-Think-When-They-Read-Your-R%C3%A9sum%C3%A9/.

EVALUATING YOUR STRENGTHS AND INTERESTS

A self-assessment is the first step in producing a good résumé. Each person could do several jobs happily. Richard Bolles, a nationally recognized expert in career advising for over a third of a century and author of the *What Color Is Your Parachute* books, says most people who don't find a job they like fail because they lack information about themselves.[2] Personality and aptitude tests can tell you some of your strengths, but you should still answer for yourself questions like these:

- What skills and strengths do you have?
- What achievements have given you the most satisfaction? *Why* did you enjoy them? What jobs would offer these kinds of satisfactions?
- What work conditions do you like? Would you rather have firm deadlines or a flexible schedule? Do you prefer working independently or with other people? Do you prefer specific instructions and standards for evaluation or freedom and uncertainty? How comfortable are you with pressure? How much challenge do you want?
- What kind of work/life balance do you want? Are you willing to take work home? To work weekends? To travel? How important is money to you? Prestige? Time to spend with family and friends?
- How fast do you want to move up? Are you willing to pay your dues for several years before you are promoted?
- Where do you want to live? What features in terms of weather, geography, cultural and social life do you see as ideal?
- Is it important to you that your work achieve certain purposes or values, or do you see work as just a way to make a living? Are an organization's culture and ethical standards important to you? If so, what values will you look for?

What Employers Want, II

Careerbuilder.com asked hiring managers what the top five attributes are when they hire new graduates.

1. **Relevant experience:** Managers look for a candidate's ability to make his/her job experience relevant to the company—and find this ability lacking. Most managers say they view volunteer activities as relevant experience.
2. **Professionalism during the interview:** Managers want to see candidates who dress professionally, who have researched the company, and who are prepared to answer standard interview questions.
3. **Fit within the company culture:** Managers want candidates whose personalities and work styles fit well.
4. **Education:** Managers consider the school, degree, major, GPA, and relevant courses.
5. **Enthusiasm:** Managers want candidates who are clearly interested in the job and show the energy they would bring to their work.

Adapted from Laura Morsch, "Five Must-Haves for New Grads," Experience, Inc., accessed April 3, 2011, http://tribe.experience.com/alumnus/article?channel_id=career_management&source_page=additional_articles&article_id=article_1156346148348.

Once you know what is most important to you, check to see what businesses are looking for (see Figure 12.4). Then analyze the job market to see where you could find what you want. Each possibility will require somewhat different training and course selection, underscoring the need for you to begin considering your job search process early in your college career.

USING THE INTERNET IN YOUR JOB SEARCH

The Internet is a crucial tool for job seekers as well as employers.

Probably the most common use of the Internet for job candidates is to search for openings (see Figure 12.1). In addition to popular job boards like Monster and CareerBuilder job candidates typically search for jobs posted on organizations' Facebook pages, LinkedIn sites, and Twitter (TwitJobSearch.com). They also check electronic listings in local newspapers and professional societies. However, you do need to be careful when responding to online ads. Some of them turn out to be pitches from career or financial services firms, or even phishing ads—ploys from identity thieves seeking your personal information.

Phishing ads often look like real postings; many have company names and logos nearly identical to those of real employers. People behind phishing ads may even e-mail job candidates to build up trust. Privacy experts caution job candidates to be particularly careful with job postings that lack details about the hiring company or job description, and ads that list a large salary range.[3]

In addition to searching for ads, every job candidate should check the Internet for information about writing résumés and application letters, researching specific companies and jobs, and preparing for interviews. Many comprehensive sites give detailed information that will help you produce more effective documents and be a better-prepared job candidate.

As you search the Web, remember that not all sites are current and accurate. In particular, be careful of .com sites: some are good, others are not. Check your school's career site for help. Check the sites of other schools: Stanford, Berkeley, and Columbia have particularly excellent career sites. And even good sources can have advice that is bad for you. Figure 12.2 lists some of the best sites.

A relatively new use of the Internet for job searchers is online job fairs. At online fairs, you can browse through virtual booths, leave your résumé at promising ones, and sometimes even apply on the spot, all without leaving your home. Other advantages of online job fairs are their wide geographic and 24-hour access.

Figure 12.1 Job Listings on the Web

Job Sites

America's Job Bank
www.jobbankinfo.org

CareerBuilder.com
www.careerbuilder.com

Careers.org
www.careers.org

EmploymentGuide.com
www.employmentguide.com

Federal Jobs Career Central
www.fedjobs.com

Indeed.com
www.indeed.com

Monster.com
www.monster.com

MonsterTrak
http://college.monster.com

Job listings from the *Chicago Tribune, Detroit News, Los Angeles Times, Miami Herald, Philadelphia Inquirer, San Jose Mercury News,* and other city newspaper's websites.

Figure 12.2 Comprehensive Web Job Sites Covering the Entire Job Search Process

About.com (Part of New York Times Company)
 http://jobsearch.about.com
Campus Career Center
 www.campuscareercenter.com
CareerBuilder
 www.careerbuilder.com
Career Rookie
 www.careerrookie.com
College Central
 www.collegecentral.com
College Grad Job Hunter
 www.collegegrad.com
The Five O'Clock Club
 www.fiveoclockclub.com
JobHuntersBible.com (Dick Bolles)
 www.jobhuntersbible.com
Monster.com
 www.monster.com
MonsterCollege
 http://college.monster.com/?wtime_n=monstertrak
OWL (Purdue Online Writing Lab)
 http://owl.english.purdue.edu
Quintessential Careers
 www.quintcareers.com
The Riley Guide
 www.rileyguide.com
Spherion Career Center
 www.spherion.com/corporate/ret-registered.jsp
wetfeet
 www.wetfeet.com/undergrad
Vault
 www.vault.com

As you do all this research for your job hunt, you will probably begin to find conflicting advice. When evaluating suggestions, consider the age of the advice; what was true five years ago may not be true today, because the job search process is changing so. Also consider your industry; general advice that works for most may not work for your industry. Above all, consider what advice helps you present yourself as favorably as possible.

PERSONAL BRANDING

A specialized use of the Internet is for **personal branding**, a popular term for marketing yourself, including job searching. It covers an expectation that you will use various options, from the traditional résumé and cover letter to social media, to market your expertise. According to one recent survey, 83% of employers use social media to find new employees. Of those, 89% use LinkedIn, 28% use Facebook, and 14% use Twitter.[4] As has always been true of job searches, you will use these tools to show your value (what do you offer employers?) and quality (why should they hire you instead of other candidates?). These are some of the most popular tools:

- **LinkedIn:** This site allows you to include useful information beyond your résumé, and, unlike your web page, it has a powerful search engine behind it.
- **Personal web page:** Your web page allows you to connect to examples of your professional work.
- **Blogs:** A blog in particular can contribute to your professional image if it focuses on your professional specialty and current issues in your field. However, keeping a blog up to date is time-consuming work during an already stressful period.

Rebranding Yourself

Whether you are looking to advance in your career or to change careers entirely, you may need to do some personal rebranding. *Rebranding* is the effort you make to change other people's perceptions about who you are and what you do well. But it is not always an easy process. Here are five tips to help you with your rebranding:

1. **Set your goals.** Who do you want to be? What skills will you need to get there?
2. **Define your points of difference.** What makes you special? How can your differences help you be noticed and connected with your new brand?
3. **Develop a narrative.** How do your past experiences and skills strengthen your new career?
4. **Reintroduce yourself.** How will you tell your friends and co-workers about your new brand?
5. **Prove your worth.** How can you show that you will be a contributing member of your new field?

These five steps will help you on your path to a new personal brand.

Adapted from Dorie Clark, "Reinventing Your Personal Brand," *Harvard Business Review*, 89, no. 3 (2011): 78–81.

Digital Dirt

Do you wonder if your employer can find out if you committed a crime, experienced financial difficulties, really attended college, or received a driving ticket? According to a survey of executive recruiters by ExecuNet, an executive job-search and networking organization, 75% of recruiters use search engines to uncover information about job candidates.

Prospective employers can use employment screening services to obtain records from private, state and federal agencies. Employers also check social networking sites such as Facebook, and Google names to find blogs and personal websites.

Remember that nothing on the Web is private. Do not post or write anything on the Internet that you do not want a prospective employer to see—starting today.

How can you clean up your reputation online?

- Google yourself. If you find something you would rather your prospective employer did not see, contact the website and ask for it to be removed.
- Clean up your Facebook or personal website. Remove any pictures that may not present a professional image or may be misunderstood by an outsider, especially pictures showing you drinking or dressed inappropriately.
- Cover negative information by increasing your positive online presence, including creating a professional web page with many links to your accomplishments.

Adapted from Jared Flesher, "How to Clean up Your Digital Dirt before It Trashes Your Job Search," *Wall Street Journal*, January 12, 2006, http://online.wsj.com/article/C60112FLESHER.html.

- **Facebook:** Keep content professional. Avoid inappropriate language and all content involving alcohol, other drugs, and incomplete attire. Remember that Facebook has a history of making personal information public.
- **Twitter:** Share useful information such as thoughtful comments about news in your field as you work to build up your Twitter network. Aim for quality, not numbers. Also, follow companies you would like to work for.
- **Professional forums:** Participate thoughtfully: doing so enables people to recognize your name favorably when your application arrives.
- **Cover letter:** Still an excellent tool for personal branding. It gives you more room to provide supporting details about your value and quality.

WARNING: Select your tools carefully; you probably do not have time to use successfully all the tools on this list. Stay professional in all venues; avoid negative comments about people, your school, and your employers. In addition to content, writing (grammar, coherence, style, logic, spelling) will be judged by potential employers. The list of candidates rejected after a basic web search grows daily.

NETWORKING

Many experts now consider networking to be THE most important factor in finding a job. It is important for entry-level work, and becomes even more crucial as you advance in your career.

Networking starts with people you know—friends, family, friends of your parents, classmates, teammates, gym mates, colleagues—and quickly expands to electronic contacts in the social media noted above. Let people know you are looking for a job, and what your job assets are. Use social media to emphasize your field knowledge and accomplishments. Join your school's alumni association to find alumni in businesses that interest you.

The secret to successful networking is reciprocity. Too many people network just for themselves, and they quickly gain a "one-way" reputation that hurts further networking. Good networkers work for a "two-way" reputation; to earn it, they look for ways to reciprocate. They help their contacts make fruitful connections. They share useful information and tips. Successful networks are not just for finding jobs: they are vital for career success.

A CAUTION ABOUT BLOGS, SOCIAL NETWORKING SITES, AND INTERNET TRACKING

Most employers routinely Google job candidates, and many report they are totally turned off by what they find—especially on personal blogs and web pages and social networking sites such as Facebook. If you have a personal blog, web page, or other electronic presence, check sites carefully before you go on the job market.

- Remove any unprofessional material such as pictures of you at your computer with a beer in your hand or descriptions of your last party.
- Remove negative comments about current or past employers and teachers. People who spread dirt in one context will probably do so in others, and no one wants to hire such people.

- Remove political and social rants. While thoughtful, supported opinions can show both education and logic, emotional or extreme statements will turn off most employers.
- Remove any personal information that will embarrass you on the job. If you blog about romance novels, but don't want to be teased about your choice in literature on your new job, make ruthless cuts on your blog.
- Remove inappropriate material posted by friends, relatives, and colleagues.
- Check your blog for writing aptitude. Many employers will consider your blog an extended writing sample. If yours is full of grammatical and spelling errors, obviously you are not a good writer.

Even if you take your blog off-line while you are job searching, employers may still find it in cached data on search engines. The best advice is to plan ahead and post nothing unprofessional on the web.

WARNING: According to a 2010 report on research commissioned by Microsoft, a quarter or more of recruiters also check photo- and video-sharing sites, gaming sites, virtual world sites, and classifieds and auction sites such as Craigslist, Amazon, and eBay.[5]

USING AN INTERNSHIP AS A JOB HUNTING TOOL

Internships are becoming increasingly important as ways to find out about professions, employers, and jobs. Many companies use their internships to find full-time employees. GE, for example, makes about 80% of its new-graduate hires from students who held summer internships with the company; in 2010 PricewaterhouseCoopers offered a full-time job to 90% of its eligible summer interns. A *Wall Street Journal* survey of college recuriters found 25% reporting that more than 50% of their new-graduate hires came from their intern pools. The National Association of Colleges and Employers found in its 2010 survey of internships that 57% of interns became full-time hires (see Figure 12.3). In fact, some industry experts are predicting that within the next few years intern recruiting will largely replace entry-level recruiting.[6]

Figure 12.3 Percentage of Interns Offered Full-Time Jobs

Industry	Percentage
Entertainment/media	85
Oil and gas extraction	81
Construction	80
Accounting	75
Food and beverage	71
Retail	70
Finance/insurance/real estate	67
Engineering	67
Computer and electronics	64
Chemical/pharmaceutical	61

Source: Joe Walker, "Getting Creative to Land an Internship," *Wall Street Journal,* June 8, 2010, D7.

Even if your internship does not lead to a full-time job, it can still give you valuable insight into the profession, as well as contacts you can use in your job search. An increasingly important side benefit is the work you do in your internship, which can become some of the best items in your professional portfolio.

HOW EMPLOYERS USE RÉSUMÉS LO 12-2

Understanding how employers use résumés will help you create a résumé that works for you.

1. **Employers use résumés to decide whom to interview.** See Figure 12.4. (The major exceptions are on-campus interviews, where the campus placement office has policies that determine who meets with the interviewer.) Since résumés are used to screen out applicants, omit anything that may create a negative impression.
2. **Résumés are scanned or skimmed.** At many companies, résumés are scanned electronically. Only résumés that match key words are skimmed by a human being. A human may give a résumé 10 to 30 seconds before deciding to keep or toss it. You must design your résumé to pass both the "scan test" and the "skim test" by emphasizing crucial qualifications.
3. **Employers assume that your letter and résumé represent your best work.** Neatness, accuracy, and freedom from typographical errors are essential. Spelling errors will probably cost you your chance at a job, so proofread carefully.
4. **After an employer has chosen an applicant, he or she submits the applicant's résumé to people in the organization who must approve the appointment.** These people may have different backgrounds and areas of expertise. Spell out acronyms. Explain awards, Greek-letter honor societies, unusual job titles, or organizations that may be unfamiliar to the reader.

Figure 12.4 Employers Want Colleges to Place More Emphasis on These Skills

Skill	Percent
Effective communication, both oral and written	89
Critical thinking and analytical reasoning	81
Application of knowledge to the work world, through internships and other hands-on experiences	79
Ability to analyze and solve complex problems	75
Teamwork	71
Innovation and creativity	70
Understanding of basic concepts and new developments in science and technology	70
Ability to locate, organize, and evaluate information from multiple sources	68
Understanding of global contexts and developments	67
Ability to work with numbers and understand statistics	63

Source: Hart Research Associates, *Raising the Bar: Employers' Views on College Learning in the Wake of the Economic Downturn: A Survey among Employers Conducted on Behalf of the Association of American Colleges and Universities,* January 20, 2010, http://www.aacu.org/leap/documents/2009_EmployerSurvey.pdf.

GUIDELINES FOR RÉSUMÉS

Writing a résumé is not an exact science. What makes your friend look good does not necessarily help you. If your skills are in great demand, you can violate every guideline here and still get a good job. But when you must compete against many applicants, these guidelines will help you look as good on paper as you are in person.

Length

A one-page résumé is sufficient, but do fill the page. Less than a full page suggests that you do not have very much to say for yourself.

If you have more good material than will fit on one page, use a second page. A common myth is that all résumés must fit on one page. According to surveys conducted by international staffing firm Accountemps of executives at the 1,000 largest companies in this country, approval of the two-page résumé is increasing *if* candidates have sufficient good material that relates to the posted job.[7] An experiment that mailed one- or two-page résumés to recruiters at major accounting firms showed that even readers who said they preferred short résumés were more likely to want to interview the candidate with the longer résumé.[8] The longer résumé gives managers a better picture of how you will fit in.

If you do use more than one page, the second page should have at least 10 to 12 lines. Use a second sheet of paper; do not print on the back of the first page. Leave less important information for the second page. Put your name and "Page 2" on the page. If the pages are separated, you want the reader to know whom the qualifications belong to and that the second page is not your whole résumé.

Increasing Expectations for Employees

A survey conducted for the Association of American Colleges and Universities found that employers really are expecting more of their employees. You are not just imagining the change. Compared to past expectations, 88% to 91% expected employees to

- Take on more responsibilities.
- Use a broader skills set.
- Coordinate more with other departments.
- Acquire more learning and skills.
- Deal with more complex challenges.

How does your résumé reflect these new realities?

Adapted from Hart Research Associates, *Raising the Bar: Employers' Views on College Learning in the Wake of the Economic Downtum: A Survey among Employers Conducted on Behalf of the Association of American Colleges and Universities,* January 20, 2010, http://www.aacu.org/leap/documents/2009_EmployerSurvey.pdf.

Emphasis

Emphasize the things you've done that (a) are most relevant to the position for which you're applying, (b) show your superiority to other applicants, and (c) are recent (in the last three to five years). Whatever your age at the time you write a résumé, you want to suggest that you are now the best you've ever been.

Show that you're qualified by giving relevant details on course projects, activities, and jobs where you've done similar work. Be brief about low-level jobs that simply show dependability. To prove that you're the best candidate for the job, emphasize items that set you apart from other applicants: promotions, honors, achievements, experience with computers or other relevant equipment, foreign languages, and so on.

You can emphasize material by putting it at the top or the bottom of a page, by giving it more space, and by setting it off with white space. The beginning and end—of a document, a page, a list—are positions of emphasis. When you have a choice (e.g., in a list of job duties), put less important material in the middle, not at the end, to avoid the impression of "fading out." You can also emphasize material by presenting it in a vertical list, by using informative headings, and by providing details. Headings that name skills listed in the job ad, or skills important for the job (e.g., Managerial Experience) also provide emphasis and help set you apart from the crowd.

Details

Details provide evidence to support your claims, convince the reader, and separate you from other applicants. Numbers make good details. Tell how many people you trained or supervised, how much money you budgeted or saved. Describe the interesting aspects of the job you did.

Too vague: Sales Manager, *The Daily Collegian,* University Park, PA, 2010–2012. Supervised staff; promoted ad sales.

Good details: Sales Manager, *The Daily Collegian,* University Park, PA, 2010–2012. Supervised 22-member sales staff; helped recruit, interview, and select staff; assigned duties and scheduled work; recommended best performers for promotion. Motivated staff to increase paid ad inches 10% over previous year's sales.

Omit details that add nothing to a title, that are less impressive than the title alone, or that suggest a faulty sense of priorities (e.g., listing hours per week spent filing). Either use strong details or just give the office or job title without any details.

Writing Style

Without sacrificing content, be as concise as possible.

Wordy: Member, Meat Judging Team, 2008–09
Member, Meat Judging Team, 2009–10
Member, Meat Judging Team, 2010–11
Captain, Meat Judging Team, 2011–12

Tight: Meat Judging Team, 2008–12; Captain 2011–12

Wordy: Performed foundation load calculations

Tight: Calculated foundation loads

Résumés normally use phrases and sentence fragments. Complete sentences are acceptable if they are the briefest way to present information. To save space and to avoid sounding arrogant, never use *I* in a résumé. *Me* and *my* are acceptable if they are unavoidable or if using them reduces wordiness.

Verbs or gerunds (the *ing* form of verbs) create a more dynamic image of you than do nouns, so use them on résumés that will be read by people instead of scanning programs. In the following revisions of job responsibilities, nouns, verbs, and gerunds are in bold type:

Nouns: Chair, Income Tax Assistance Committee, Winnipeg, MB, 2011–2012. Responsibilities: **recruitment** of volunteers; flyer **design, writing,** and **distribution** for **promotion** of program; **speeches** to various community groups and nursing homes to advertise the service.

Verbs: Chair, Income Tax Assistance Committee, Winnipeg, MB, 2011–2012. **Recruited** volunteers for the program. **Designed, wrote,** and **distributed** a flyer to promote the program; **spoke** to various community groups and nursing homes to advertise the service.

Gerunds: Chair, Income Tax Assistance Committee, Winnipeg, MB, 2011–2012. Responsibilities included **recruiting** volunteers for the program; **designing, writing,** and **distributing** a flyer to promote the program; and **speaking** to various community groups and nursing homes to advertise the service.

Note that the items in the list must be in parallel structure (p. 135).

WARNING: All spelling and grammar should be perfect. If they are not your strong suits, pay an editor. In these days of massive responses to job postings, don't give recruiters an easy elimination of your résumé through careless errors. Remember that spell checks will not catch all errors, as all those store "mangers" will tell you.

Key Words

Now that electronic résumé scans are common, all résumés, but particularly electronic résumés, need to use **key words**—words and phrases the employer will have the computer seek. Key words are frequently nouns or noun phrases: database management, product upgrades, cost compilation/analysis. However, they can also be adjectives such as *responsible*. Key words are frequently the objects of all those action verbs you are using in your résumé; conducted *publicity campaigns*, wrote weekly division *newsletter*.

Key words may include

- Software program names such as Excel.
- Job titles.
- Types of degrees.
- College or company names.
- Job-specific skills, buzzwords, and jargon.
- Professional organizations (spell out the name and then follow it with its abbreviation in parentheses to increase the number of matches).
- Honor societies (spell out Greek letters).
- Personality traits, such as creativity, dependability, team player.
- Area codes (for geographic narrowing of searches).

To find the key words you need in your job search, look through job ads and employer job sites for common terminology. If many ads mention "communication skills," your résumé should too.

Some key words are widely popular. A survey of over 3,000 hirers conducted for CareerBuilder reported these key words as ones searched for most often:[9]

- Problem-solving and decision-making skills (50%)
- Oral and written communications (44%)
- Customer service or retention (34%)
- Performance and productivity improvement (32%)
- Leadership (30%)
- Technology (27%)
- Team-building (26%)
- Project management (20%)
- Bilingual (14%)

In addition to using popular key words, you should double-check to make certain your résumé uses the language of the particular job ad to which you are responding. If the ad uses "software engineers" instead of "computer programmers," then your résumé should also use "software engineers." If the ad talks about "collaboration," you will use that word instead of "teamwork" when you discuss your group work experience.

Use key words liberally in your Summary of Qualifications section. However, to get an interview, your résumé will usually need to put key words into a context proving you have the skills or knowledge. This means that key words will also have to appear in the rest of your résumé, too. Since you will not know exactly what key words are desired, it makes sense to use some synonyms and similar terms: *manager* and *management*, *Excel* and *spreadsheets*, *creative* and *creativity*.

Layout and Design

The layout and design of your résumé will be vital to catch the eye of the employer who is spending only 10 seconds on each document.

WARNING: Do not use résumé templates that come with word-processing software. Many employers see so many résumés from these templates that they learn to recognize—and discount—them.

Almost certainly, you can create a better résumé by adapting a basic style you like to your own unique qualifications. Experiment with layout, fonts, and spacing to get an attractive résumé. Consider creating a letterhead that you use for both your résumé and your application letter.

Decide what are your best selling points and promote them early. Since most résumés will be put into electronic formats (discussed later in chapter), make sure the first screen of information about you is strong, tempting readers to look further.

One of the major decisions you will make is how to treat your **headings**. Do you want them on the left margin, with text immediately below them, as in Figure 12.5? Do you want them alone in the left column, with text in a column to the right, as in Figure 12.7? Generally, people with more text on their résumés use the first option. Putting headings in their own column on the left takes space and thus helps spread a thinner list of accomplishments over the page. But be careful not to make the heading column too wide, or it will make your résumé look unbalanced and empty.

Work with **fonts**, bullets, and spacing to highlight your information. Do be careful, however, not to make your résumé look "busy" by using too many fonts. Generally three fonts should be the top limit, and you should avoid unusual fonts. Keep fonts readable by using at least 10-point type for large fonts such as Arial and 11-point for smaller fonts such as Times New Roman. Use enough white space to group items and make your résumé easy to read, but not so much that you look as if you're padding.

Use **color** sparingly, if at all. Colored text and shaded boxes can prevent accurate scanning. Similarly, white 8½- by 11-inch paper is standard, but do use a good-quality paper.

All of these guidelines are much more flexible for people in creative fields such as advertising and design.

KINDS OF RÉSUMÉS

Two basic categories of résumés are chronological and skills. A **chronological résumé** summarizes what you did in a time line (starting with the most recent events, and going backward in **reverse chronology**). It emphasizes degrees, job titles, and dates. It is the traditional résumé format. Figures 12.5 and 12.8 show chronological résumés.

Use a chronological résumé when

- Your education and experience are a logical preparation for the position for which you're applying.
- You have impressive job titles, offices, or honors.

A **skills résumé**, also called a functional résumé, emphasizes the skills you've used, rather than the job in which you used them or the date of the experience. Figure 12.7 shows a skills résumés. Use a skills résumé when

Figure 12.5 A Community College Chronological Résumé to Use for Career Fairs and Internships

Vary font sizes. Use larger size for name and main headings.

Lee Cheng

chengl@eccc.edu

Campus Address
1524 Main Street
New Brunswick, NJ 08901
732-403-5718

Using both addresses ensures continuous contact information.

Permanent Address
2526 Prairie Lane
Middlesex, NJ 00846
732-404-7793

Education

East Coast Community College
AA in Financial Management, June 2012
GPA: 3.0/4.0 Give your grade average if it's 3.0 or higher.

Summary of Qualifications

List 3–7 qualifications.

Use key words employers might seek.

- Self-motivated, detail-minded, results-oriented
- Consistently successful track record in sales
- Effectively developed and operated entrepreneurial business

Sales Experience

Financial Sales Representative, ABC Inc., New Brunswick, NJ, February 2011–present

- Establish client base
- Develop investment strategy plans for clients
- Research and recommend specific investments

Other Experience

Entrepreneur, A-Plus T-Shirt Company, Middlesex, NJ, September 2008–January 2011

One way to handle self-employment.

- Created a saleable product (graphic T-shirts)
- Secured financial support
- Located a manufacturer
- Supervised production
- Sold T-shirts to high school students
- Realized a substantial profit to pay for college expenses

Cook, Hamburger Shack, Seaside Heights, NJ, Summers 2007–2008

- Learned sales strategies
- Ensured customer satisfaction
- Collaborated with a team of 25

Collector and Repair Worker, ACN, Inc., Middlesex, NJ, Summer 2005–2006

- Collected and counted approximately $10,000 a day Specify large sums of money.
- Assisted technicians with troubleshooting and repairing coin mechanisms

Other Skills

Computer: Word, Excel, InDesign, WordPress, Outlook
Language: Fluent in Spanish Many employers appreciate a second language.

What Happens to Your Résumé?

Each year, technology giant Siemens Global hires more than 10,000 employees out of over 780,000 applicants. One civil engineering position had 187 applications, but only three made it through to the face-to-face interview. How does Siemens find the right people? CNNMoney found four key steps:

1. Hire internally. Like many corporations, Siemens advertises positions both internally and externally, but hires 40% of open positions from inside the company.
2. Use the web. Siemens posts jobs on Monster and CareerBuilder. Recruiters also use LinkedIn both to eliminate candidates and to recruit people who may not be looking for a job.
3. Use computers to scan applications and find applicants who match job requirements.
4. Conduct initial interviews by phone. Only after applicants pass this step can they be sent on to the hiring manager.

For large corporations, using technology and recruiters to screen applicants is vital to finding the right people for jobs.

Adapted from Tami Luhby, "The Secret Life of a Résumé," CNNMoney, May 18, 2011, http://money.cnn.com/fdcp?unique=1305728467379.

- Your education and experience are not the usual route to the position for which you're applying.
- You're changing fields.
- You want to combine experience from paid jobs, activities, volunteer work, and courses to show the extent of your experience in administration, finance, public speaking, and so on.

The two kinds differ in what information is included and how that information is organized. You may assume that the advice in this chapter applies to both kinds of résumés unless there is an explicit statement that the two kinds of résumés would handle a category differently.

WHAT TO INCLUDE IN A RÉSUMÉ

Although the résumé is a factual document, its purpose is to persuade. In a job application form or an application for graduate or professional school, you answer every question even if the answer is not to your credit. In a résumé, you cannot lie, but you can omit some information that does not work in your favor.

Résumés commonly contain the following information. The categories marked with an asterisk are essential.

- Name and Contact Information*
- Career Objective
- Summary of Qualifications
- Education*
- Honors and Awards
- Experience*
- Other skills
- Activities
- Portfolio

You may choose other titles for these categories and add categories that are relevant for your qualifications, such as computer skills or foreign languages.

Education and Experience always stand as separate categories, even if you have only one item under each head. Combine other headings so that you have at least two long or three short items under each heading. For example, if you're in one honor society and two social clubs, and on one athletic team, combine them all under Activities and Honors.

If you have more than seven items under a heading, consider using subheadings. For example, a student who had a great many activities might divide them into Campus Activities and Community Service.

Put your strongest categories near the top and at the bottom of the first page. If you have impressive work experience, you might want to put that category first and Education second.

Name and Contact Information

Use your full **name,** even if everyone calls you by a nickname. You may use an initial rather than spelling out your first or middle name. Put your name in big type.

If you use only one **address,** consider centering it under your name. If you use two addresses (office and home, campus and permanent, until_____ / after_____) set them up side by side to balance the page visually. Use either

A résumé is your most important document at career fairs.

Résumé Blunders

CareerBuilder.com's survey of hiring managers found these résumé howlers:

- Candidate listed God as a reference. (Alas, the candidate didn't include a phone number.)
- Candidate's e-mail address had "lovesbeer" in it.
- Candidate listed "Master of Time and Universe" under his experience.
- Candidate's condition for accepting the position was being allowed to bring his pet monkey to the workplace.
- Candidate sent a 24-page résumé for a five-year career.
- Candidate put a picture of her cat on top of her résumé.

Bullets quoted from Mary Lorenz, "'The Candidate Tried to Hypnotize Me!' and More: Hiring Managers Share Their Strangest Resume Stories," CareerBuilder: The Hiring Site, September 15, 2010, http://thehiringsite.careerbuilder.com/2010/09/15/hiring-managers-share-strangest-resumes/.

post office (two-letter, full caps, no period) abbreviations for the state or spell out the state name, but do be consistent throughout your résumé.

Urbana, IL 61801

Wheaton, Illinois 60187

Give a complete **phone number,** including the area code. Some job candidates give both home and cellphone numbers. Do provide a phone number where you can be reached during the day. Employers usually call during business hours to schedule interviews and make job offers. Do not give lab or dorm phone numbers unless you are sure someone there will take an accurate message for you at all times. Also, be sure that all answering machines have a professional-sounding message.

If you have a **web page,** and you are sure it looks professional (both content and writing), you may wish to include its URL. Be sure your web page does not reveal personal information—such as marital status, ethnicity, religious beliefs, or political stance—that could work against you. Be particularly careful of photographs.

Provide an **e-mail address.** Some job candidates set up a new e-mail address just for job hunting. Your e-mail address should look professional; avoid sexy, childish, or illicit addresses. List your **LinkedIn** site, if you have one.

Career Objective

Career objective statements should sound like the job descriptions an employer might use in a job listing. Keep your statement brief—two lines at most. Tell what you want to do, what level of responsibility you want to hold. The best career objectives are targeted to a specific job at a specific company.

Ineffective career objective: To offer a company my excellent academic foundation in hospital technology and my outstanding skills in oral and written communication

Objectionable Objectives

[These job objectives did not help their writers:]

- "A job." Any one will do.
- "To obtain a position that will allow me to utilize my strengths and reinforce my weaknesses." Are you sure that's a good idea?
- "To become a billionier." A candidate who's not on the money.
- "I am seeking a permanent position to get out of debt." Will we get anything out of the deal?
- "To obtain a position that will enable me to utilize my professional skills and knowledge in a capacity that demonstrates me intelligence." My, oh, my.
- "To work for XYZ Company." We'll forward your résumé to them.
- "My dream job would be as a professional baseball player, but since I can't do that, I'll settle on being an accountant." Your enthusiasm is overwhelming.
- "To learn new skills and gain training which will help me develop my new business." Your dedication is touching.

From Robert Half International, "Resumania Archive," http://www.resumania.com/arcindex.html. Reprinted with permission of Robert Half International.

Better career objective: Hospital and medical sales for Rand Medical requiring experience with state-of-the-art equipment

Good career objectives are hard to write. If you talk about entry-level work, you won't sound ambitious; if you talk about where you hope to be in 5 or 10 years, you won't sound as though you're willing to do entry-level work. When you're applying for a job that is a natural outgrowth of your education and experience, you may omit this category and specify the job you want in your cover letter.

Often you can avoid writing a career objective statement by putting the job title or field under your name:

Joan Larson Ooyen	Terence Edward Garvey	David R. Lunde
Marketing	Technical Writer	Corporate Fitness Director

Note that you can use the field you're in even if you're a new college graduate. To use a job title, you should have some relevant work experience.

If you use a separate heading for a career objective, put it immediately after your contact information, before the first major heading (see Figure 12.7). The résumé in Figure 12.5 does not use a Career Objective because it is being used for various jobs offered at a career fair. If you were particularly interested in several jobs there, you would make targeted résumés for those companies. More and more experts are advising that objectives be clarified in the cover letter rather than wasting valuable space at the top of the résumé.

Summary of Qualifications

A section summarizing the candidate's qualifications seems to have first appeared with scannable résumés, where its key words helped increase the number of matches a résumé produced. But the section proved useful for human readers as well and now is a standard part of many résumés. The best summaries show your knowledge of the specialized terminology of your field and offer specific, quantifiable achievements.

Weak: Staff accountant

Better: Experience with accounts payable, accounts receivable, audits, and month end closings. Prepared monthly financial reports.

Weak: Presentation skills

Better: Gave 20 individual and 7 team presentations to groups ranging from 5 to 100 people.

Some career advisers believe a summary is too repetitious of other sections on a one-page résumé. They believe the space is better used by listing your achievements that set you apart from other candidates.

Education

Education can be your first major category if you've just earned (or are about to earn) a degree, if you have a degree that is essential or desirable for the position you're seeking, or if you can present the information briefly. Put your Education section later if you need all of page 1 for another category or if you lack a degree that other applicants may have (see Figure 12.7).

Under Education, provide information about your undergraduate and graduate degrees, including the location of institutions and the year you received or expect your degree, if these dates are within the last 10 years.

Use the same format for all schools. List your degrees in reverse chronological order (most recent first).

Master of Accounting Science, May 2012, Arizona State University, Tempe, AZ
Bachelor of Arts in Finance, May 2010, New Mexico State University, Las Cruces, NM

BS in Industrial Engineering, May 2012, Iowa State University, Ames, IA
AS in Business Administration, May 2010, Des Moines Area Community College, Ankeny, IA

When you're getting a four-year degree, include community college only if it will interest employers, such as by showing an area of expertise different from that of your major. You may want to include your minor, emphasis, or concentration and any graduate courses you have taken. Include study abroad, even if you didn't earn college credits. If you got a certificate for international study, give the name and explain the significance of the certificate. Highlight proficiency in foreign or computer languages by using a separate category.

To punctuate your degrees, do not space between letters and periods:

A.S. in Office Administration
B.S. in Accounting
Ed.D. in Business Education

Current usage also permits you to omit the periods (BS, MBA), but be consistent with the usage you choose.

Professional certifications can be listed under Education or in a separate category.

If your GPA is good and you graduated recently, include it. If your GPA is under 3.0 on a 4.0 scale, use words rather than numbers: "B– average." If your GPA isn't impressive, calculate your average in your major and your average for your last 60 hours. If these are higher than your overall GPA, consider using them. The National Association of Colleges and Employers, in its Job Outlook 2010 survey, found that 75% of employers do screen job applicants by GPA.[10] If you leave your GPA off your résumé, most employers will automatically assume that it is below a 3.0. If yours is, you will need to rely on internships, work experience, and skills acquired in activities to make yourself an attractive job candidate.

After giving the basic information (degree, field of study, date, school, city, state) about your degree, you may wish to list courses, using short descriptive titles rather than course numbers. Use a subhead like "Courses Related to Major" or "Courses Related to Financial Management" that will allow you to list all the courses (including psychology, speech, and business communication) that will help you in the job for which you're applying. Don't say "Relevant Courses," as that implies your other courses were irrelevant.

Bachelor of Science in Management, May 2012, Illinois State University, Normal, IL
GPA: 3.8/4.0

Courses Related to Management:

Personnel Administration	Business Decision Making
Finance	International Business
Management I and II	Marketing
Accounting I and II	Legal Environment of Business
Business Report Writing	Business Speaking

Listing courses is an unobtrusive way to fill a page. You may also want to list courses or the number of hours in various subjects if you've taken an unusual combination of courses that uniquely qualify you for the position for which you're applying.

The Value of "Soft Skills"

What are MBA programs teaching? Soft skills—lessons in teamwork, leadership, and communication. Specifically, students are working on listening, teamwork, interpersonal communication, presentations, and sensitivity to others. Why? Businesses are requesting MBA graduates with strong soft skills because they believe these students will be employees who can lead, communicate, and negotiate.

In response, schools such as the Stanford Graduate School of Business are requiring all first-year students to take personality tests, participate in teamwork exercises, and examine their people skills. At Tuck, professors designed a program which places students in teams of five to work together throughout their program.

Recruiters note that job candidates need to present their soft skills in language appropriate for the particular job they are seeking.

Adapted from Phred Dvorak, "M.B.A. Programs Hone 'Soft Skills,'" *Wall Street Journal*, February 12, 2007, B3; and Dana Mattioli, "Hard Sell on 'Soft' Skills Can Primp a Résumé: Experience with Facebook, Class Project, Juggling Activities Can Impress Employers," *Wall Street Journal*, May 15, 2007, B6.

BS in Marketing, May 2012, California State University at Northridge
30 hours in marketing
15 hours in Spanish
9 hours in Chicano studies

If your course list is similar to that of others in your major, you should use the space for material that better shows your uniqueness. In that case, another way to fill the page is to include a Projects section, in which you highlight some course projects relevant to the jobs you are seeking.

As you advance in your career, your education section will shrink until finally it probably will include only your degrees and educational institutions.

Honors and Awards

It's nice to have an Honors and Awards section, but not everyone can do so. If you have fewer than three and therefore cannot justify a separate heading, consider a heading Honors and Activities to get that important word in a position of emphasis.

Include the following kinds of entries in this category:

- Academic honor societies. Specify the nature of Greek-letter honor societies (i.e., journalism honorary) so the reader doesn't think they're just social clubs.
- Fellowships and scholarships, including honorary scholarships for which you received no money and fellowships you could not hold because you received another fellowship at the same time.
- Awards given by professional societies.
- Major awards given by civic groups.
- Varsity letters; selection to all-state or all-America teams; finishes in state, national, or Olympic meets. (These could also go under Activities but may look more impressive under Honors. Put them under one category or the other—not both.)

Identify honor societies ("national journalism honorary," "campus honorary for top 2% of business majors") for readers who are not in your discipline. If your fellowships or scholarships are particularly selective or remunerative, give supporting details:

Clyde Jones Scholarship: four-year award covering tuition, fees, room, and board.

Marilyn Terpstra Scholarship: $25,000 annually for four years.

Heemsly Fellowship: 50 awarded nationally each year to top Information Science juniors.

Be careful of listing Dean's List for only one or two semesters. Such a listing reminds readers that in these days of grade inflation you were off the list many more times than you were on it. Omit honors like "Miss Congeniality" or "Muscle Man Star" that work against the professional image you want your résumé to create.

As a new college graduate, try to put Honors on page 1. In a skills résumé, put Honors on page 1 if they're major (e.g., Phi Beta Kappa, Phi Kappa Phi). Otherwise, save them until page 2—Experience will probably take the whole first page.

Experience

You may use other headings if they work better: Work Experience, Summer and Part-Time Jobs, Military Experience, Marketing Experience. In a skills résumé, headings such as "Marketing Experience" allow you to include accomplishments from activities and course projects. Headings that reflect skills mentioned in the job ad are particularly effective.

What to include Under this section in a chronological résumé, include the following information for each job you list: position or job title, organization, city and state (no zip code), dates of employment for jobs held during the last 10 to 15 years, and other details, such as full- or part-time status, job duties, special responsibilities, or the fact that you started at an entry-level position and were promoted. Use strong verbs such as the ones in Figure 12.6 to brainstorm what you've done. Try to give supporting details for highly valued attributes such as communication skills and leadership experience. Include any internships and co-ops you have had. Also, include unpaid jobs and self-employment if they provided relevant skills (e.g., supervising people, budgeting, planning, persuading). Experience information for skills résumés is discussed on page 387.

Normally, go back as far as the summer after high school. Include earlier jobs if you started working someplace before graduating from high school but continued working there after graduation, or if the job is pertinent to the one you are applying for. If you worked full-time after high school, make that clear.

The details you give about your experience are some of the most vital information on your résumé. As you provide these details, use bulleted lists (easy to read) rather than paragraphs which are harder to read and may be skipped over. Remember that items in lists need to have parallel structure; see page 135 for a refresher. Focus on results rather than duties; employers are far more interested in what you accomplished than in what you had to do. Use numbers to support your results wherever possible:

Supervised crew of 15

Managed $120,000 budget; decreased expenses by 19%.

Wrote monthly electronic newsletter; increased hits by 12%.

Emphasize accomplishments that involve money, customers, teamwork, leadership, computer skills, and communication.

Altruism and Jobs

Weak economies send more graduates to investigate working for social causes. And many of these grads find they like making a difference.

Teach for America, the nonprofit that trains top college grads for teaching in poverty school districts, saw applications jump 42% in 2009. The Peace Corps had 16% more applications.

All of these opportunities provide experience and leadership skills valuable on the job market. They also provide strong networks of successful alumni.

Increased competition for these positions means that applicants should highlight business experience, language skills (especially Spanish and French), and volunteer experience.

Will you make a difference?

Adapted from Kyle Stock, "Jobless Professionals Yearn to Do Good: Nonprofits See a Flood of Applications with Business and Legal Know-How," *Wall Street Journal*, June 9, 2009, D6.

Figure 12.6 Action Verbs for Résumés

analyzed	directed	led	reviewed
budgeted	earned	managed	revised
built	edited	motivated	saved
chaired	established	negotiated	scheduled
coached	evaluated	observed	simplified
collected	examined	organized	sold
conducted	helped	persuaded	solved
coordinated	hired	planned	spoke
counseled	improved	presented	started
created	increased	produced	supervised
demonstrated	interviewed	recruited	trained
designed	introduced	reported	translated
developed	investigated	researched	wrote

I Do Good Work

[Create an "I Do Good Work" folder to] back up your claims of top performance with solid evidence.

Before you leave the office this Friday, write down five things you—not necessarily others—believe you did well this week, even if they represent common tasks. Perhaps you returned all phone calls, leaving no loose ends to tie at the end of the week. Or maybe the details you provide in your sales reports enabled you to find additional product fits for the client. Any letters from happy customers or e-mails thanking you for solving a problem should go right in your folder. . . .

Tuck that list away and continue this weekly exercise for the entire month. At the end of the month, narrow the four or five lists to 10 accomplishments that stand out to you. At the end of the year, review the 120 items and cull them to 25. Formalize the language that describes those 25 achievements and print them out in an organized manner . . . along with your references.

"When someone asks, 'What do you bring to this organization?' you won't merely reply, 'I'm good with people,' you'll hand that sales manager or HR person proof," says professional trainer Carol Price.

Quoted from Julie Sturgeon, "All About You," *Selling Power*, September 2000, 57.

Use past tense verbs for jobs you held in the past, and present tense verbs for jobs you still have. Do not list minor duties such as distributing mail or filing documents. If your duties were completely routine, say, at your summer job at McDonald's, do not list them. If the jobs you held in the past were low-level ones, present them briefly or combine them:

2008–2012 Part-time and full-time jobs to finance education

If as an undergraduate you've earned a substantial portion of your college expenses with jobs and scholarship, say so in a separate statement under either Experience or Education. (Graduate students are expected to support themselves.)

These jobs paid 40% of my college expenses.

Paid for 65% of expenses with jobs, scholarships, and loans.

Paying for school expenses just with loans is generally not considered noteworthy.

Formats for setting up Experience There are two basic ways to set up the Experience section of your résumé. In **indented format**, items that are logically equivalent begin at the same space, with carryover lines indented. Indented format emphasizes job titles. It provides work information in this order:

Job title, name of organization, city, state, dates. Other information.

Experience

Engineering Assistant, Sohio Chemical Company, Lima, Ohio, Summers 2011 and 2012.

- Tested wastewater effluents for compliance with Federal EPA standards
- Helped chemists design a test to analyze groundwater quality and seepage around landfills
- Presented weekly oral and written progress reports to Director of Research and Development

Animal Caretaker, Animalcare, Worthington, Ohio, Summers 2008–2010.

Two-margin or **block format** frequently can be used to emphasize *when* you worked, if you've held only low-level jobs. Don't use two-margin format if your work history has gaps.

EXPERIENCE

Summers, 2010–12	Repair worker, Bryant Heating and Cooling, Providence, RI
2010–11	Library Clerk, Boston University Library, Boston, MA. Part-time during school year
2008–10	Food Service Worker, Boston University, Boston, MA. Part-time during school year
Summer, 2009	Delivery person, Domino's Pizza, Providence, RI

The left column can also emphasize steadily increasing job titles.

Experience at Gene Elton, Miami, Florida

Intern

Computer Programmer

Systems Analyst

The right column would list duties and dates.

Use a hyphen to join inclusive dates:

March-August, 2012 (or write out March to August, 2012)
2009–2012 or 2009–12

If you use numbers for dates, do not space before or after the slash:

10/10–5/11

Job Skills Checklist

Having trouble identifying your skills? OWL, Purdue's Online Writing Lab, has an excellent list to help get you going. Connect the skills you identify to experiences in your life that demonstrate the skills; then put the best material into your résumé and cover letter. See this website: http://owl.english.purdue.edu/owl/resource/626/1/.

Skills résumés Skills résumés stress the skills you have acquired rather than specific jobs you have held. They show employers that you do have the desired skill set even if you lack the traditional employment background. They allow you to include skills acquired from activities and course projects in addition to jobs. On the other hand, they are also a clue to employers that you do lack that traditional background, or that you have gaps in your job history, so you will need to make your skill set convincing.

In a skills résumé, the heading of your main section usually changes from "Experience" to "Skills." Within the section, the subheadings will be replaced with the skills used in the job you are applying for, rather than the title or the dates of the jobs you've held (as in a chronological résumé). For entries under each skill, combine experience from paid jobs, unpaid work, classes, activities, and community service.

Use headings that reflect the jargon of the job for which you're applying: *logistics* rather than *planning* for a technical job; *procurement* rather than *purchasing* for a job with the military. Figure 12.7 shows a skills résumé for someone who is changing fields.

A job description can give you ideas for headings. Possible headings and subheadings for skills résumés include

Administration	**Communication**
Budgeting	Editing
Coordinating	Fund-Raising
Evaluating	Interviewing
Implementing	Negotiating
Negotiating	Persuading
Planning	Presenting
Supervising	Writing

Many jobs require a mix of skills. Try to include the skills that you know will be needed in the job you want. You need at least three subheadings in a skills résumé; six or seven is not uncommon. Give enough detail under each subheading so the reader will know what you did. Put the most important category from the reader's point of view first.

In a skills résumé, list your paid jobs under Work History or Employment Record near the end of the résumé (see Figure 12.7). List only job title, employer, city, state, and dates. Omit details that you have already used under Skills.

Other Skills

You may want a brief section in a chronological résumé where you highlight skills not apparent in your work history. These skills may include items such as foreign languages or programming languages. You might want to list software you have used or training on expensive equipment (electron microscopes, NMR machines). As always on your résumé, be completely honest: "two years of high school German," or "elementary speaking knowledge of Spanish." Any knowledge of a foreign language is a plus. It means that a company desiring a second language in its employees would not have to start from scratch in training you. Figure 12.8 lists skills in its Qualifications section.

Figure 12.7 A Skills Résumé for Someone Changing Fields

Molly Schooner
www.ukansas.edu/~Schooner88/home.htm

If you have a professional web page, include its URL.

266 Van Buren Drive
Lawrence, KS 66044
schoonerm@ukansas.edu
785-897-1534 (home)
785-842-4242 (cell)

Objective To contribute my enthusiasm for writing as a Technical Writer at PDF Productions

Job objective includes the position and name of the company.

Skills

Largest section on skills résumé; allows you to combine experiences from work and class.

Computer
- Designed a web page using Dreamweaver www.lawrenceanimalshelter.com
- Used a variety of Macintosh and PC platform programs and languages:

Aspects(online discussion forum)	Adobe Professional
Dreamweaver CS5	HTML
PageMaker	Java Script
XML	Photoshop CS5

Specify computer programs you know well.

Design and Writing

Use parallel structure for bulleted lists.

- Designed a quarterly newsletter for local animal shelter
- Developed professional brochures
- Wrote a variety of professional documents: letters, memos, and reports
- Edited internal documents and promotional materials
- Proofread seven student research papers as a tutor

Organization and Administration
- Coordinated program schedules
- Developed work schedules for five employees
- Led a 10-member team in planning and implementing sorority philanthropy program
- Created cataloging system for specimens
- Ordered and handled supplies, including live specimens

Employment History

Condensed to make room for skills.

Technical Writer, Lawrence Animal Shelter, Lawrence, KS, 2010–present
Undergraduate Lab Assistant, Department of Biology, University of Kansas, Lawrence, KS, 2010–present
Tutor, University of Kansas, Lawrence, KS, 2009–2010

Uses reverse chronology.

Education

Bachelor of Arts, May 2012
University of Kansas, Lawrence, KS
Major: Animal Ecology
Minor: Chemistry
GPA: 3.4/4.0

Give minor when it can be helpful.

Honors

Phi Kappa Phi Honor Society
Alpha Lambda Delta Honor Society, Ecology Honorary
Dean's List, 2007 – present
Raymond Hamilton Scholarship, 2010–2011
($5,000 to a top ecology student in Kansas)

Explain honors your reader may not know.

End with strong items at the bottom of your page, a position of emphasis.

Figure 12.8 A One-Page Chronological Résumé

Jeff Moeller

831.503.4692
51 Willow Street
San José, CA 95112
jmoeller@csmb.edu

Use job title and company name in Career Objective.

Career Objective

To bring my attention to detail and love for computer/video games to Telltale Games as a Game Designer

Qualifications

- Experienced in JavaScript, Lua, and Python
- Intermediate proficiency with Visual Studio; high proficiency with Source Safe
- Excellent communication, interpersonal, and collaboration skills
- Advanced knowledge of computers
- Love of video games

Highlights qualifications specific to the job.

Education

California State University—Monterey Bay
August 2008–May 2012 (expected)
Bachelor of Science in Computer Science and Information Technology

Keeps Education section simple to emphasize experience.

Experience

Online Marketing Consultant—Self-Employed
October 2009–present

Lists job titles on separate lines.

- Manage multiple-client Google Adwords accounts
- Install web software and implement designs for fast turnarounds
- Interface with clients using Basecamp

Editor-in-Chief—Point Network LLC
June 2007–present

Use present tense verbs when you are doing the job now.

- Write and edit for several LucasArts-related gaming news websites
- Design and code websites using Wordpress
- Manage and administrate the LucasForums.com community

Use past tense for jobs that are over.

Online Marketing Assistant—Hayfield Group
May 2010–August 2010; May 2010–August 2011

- Managed all client Google Adwords accounts
- Assisted in or managed planning and executing PPC and SEO campaigns
- Coded the company website and integrated the Drupal CMS
- Prepared website analytics reports using Google Analytics and other analytics suites

Community Manager—Praise Entertainment, Inc.
April 2009–September 2011

- Managed the community at AdminFusion.com, a website geared toward online forum owners
- Organized and ran a monthly contest for community members

Close with strong section.

Honors and Activities

- Member of the gaming press for E3 2010 and 2011
- Member of second place team in 2011 National STEM Video Game challenge (see demo, "Parrot Villa" at www.STEMChallenge.gov/2011_winners)

Include activities that employer might value.

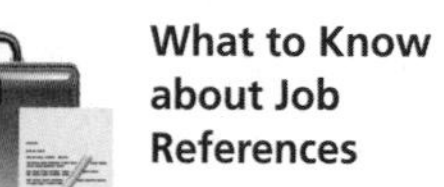

What to Know about Job References

Many job reference myths exist that may undermine your job search:

Myth: I don't have to mention a job that didn't work out, especially if I worked there only a short while.

Fact: Employers check jobs through Social Security, and they will believe the worst of omissions.

Myth: Companies are not legally allowed to give damaging information about applicants.

Fact: Although many companies have formal policies of providing only bare-bones data, many employees within those organizations still engage in providing additional, negative information about applicants. Voice tone, or mentioning that you may not be eligible for rehire, may speak volumes.

Myth: References do not matter once you are hired.

Fact: References may still be checked after you are hired and can be used for grounds for termination.

Myth: References are not needed after you have a job.

Fact: Stay in contact with your references. You never know when you may want to change jobs.

Activities

Employers may be interested in your activities if you're a new college graduate because they can demonstrate leadership roles, management abilities, and social skills as well as the ability to juggle a schedule. If you've worked for several years after college or have an advanced degree (MBA, JD), you can omit Activities and include Professional Activities and Affiliations or Community and Public Service. If you went straight from college to graduate school but have an unusually strong record demonstrating relevant skills, include this category even if all the entries are from your undergraduate days.

Include the following kinds of items under Activities:

- Volunteer work. Include important committees, leadership roles, communication activities, and financial and personnel responsibilities.
- Membership in organized student activities. Include important subcommittees, leadership roles. Include minor offices only if they're directly related to the job for which you're applying or if they show growing responsibility (you held a minor office one year, a bigger office the following year). Include so-called major offices (e.g., vice president) even if you did very little. Provide descriptive details if (but only if) they help the reader realize how much you did and the importance of your work, or if they demonstrate usable job skills.
- Membership in professional associations. Many of them have special low membership fees for students, so you should join one or more.
- Participation in varsity, intramural, or independent athletics. However, don't list so many sports that you appear not to have had adequate time to study.
- Social clubs, if you held a major leadership role or if social skills are important for the job for which you're applying.

As you list activities, add details that will be relevant for your job. Did you handle a six-figure budget for your Greek organization? Plan all the road trips for your soccer club? Coordinate all the publicity for the campus blood drive? Design the posters for homecoming? Major leadership, financial, and creative roles and accomplishments may look more impressive if they're listed under Experience instead of under Activities.

Portfolio

If you have samples of your work available, you may want to end your résumé by stating "Portfolio (or writing samples) available on request." or by giving the URL for your work.

REFERENCES

References are generally no longer included on résumés. Nor do you say "References Available on Request," since no job applicant is going to refuse to supply references. However, you will probably be asked for references at some point in your application process, so it is wise to be prepared.

You will need at least three, usually no more than five, never more than six. As a college student or a new graduate, include at least one professor and at least one employer or adviser—someone who can comment on your work habits and leadership skills. If you're changing jobs, include your current superior. For a skills résumé, choose references who can testify to your abilities in the most important skills areas. Omit personal or character references, who cannot talk about your work. Don't use relatives, friends, or roommates, even if you've worked for them, because everyone will believe they are biased in your favor.

Always ask permission to use the person as a reference. Doing so is not only polite, but ensures the person will remember you when contacted. Instead of the vague "May I list you as a reference?" use, "Can you speak specifically about my work?" Jog the person's memory by taking along copies of work you did for him or her and a copy of your current résumé. Tell the person what qualifications a specific employer is seeking. Keep your list of references up-to-date. If it's been a year or more since you asked someone, ask again—and tell the person about your recent achievements.

On your list of references, provide name, title or position, organization, city, state, phone number, and e-mail for each of your references. If their connection to you is not clear, add an identifying line (former academic adviser; former supervisor at Careltons) so they do not look like personal references. You could also give the full mailing address if you think people are more likely to write than to call. Use courtesy titles *(Dr., Mr., Ms.)* for all or for none. By convention, all faculty with the rank of assistant professor or above may be called *Professor.*

References that the reader knows are by far the most impressive. In fact, employers may ask about you among people they already know: a former classmate may now work for them; a professor in your major department may consult for them. Through these routes, employers can get references about you even in companies whose formal human resources policy provides only dates of employment. Therefore, you should be well thought of by as many people as possible.

Some employers are also checking contacts on social networking sites such as LinkedIn and Facebook to find people who may know you. When you are on the job market, you may want to consider adjusting your privacy settings so that your contacts are visible to only a select few. On sites without such adjustments, you need to be careful with your contact list. Remember that Facebook has a history of making personal information public.

Include the name and address of your placement office if you have written recommendations on file there; that contact information will be all you need.

WHAT NOT TO INCLUDE IN A RÉSUMÉ

Certain items do not belong on résumés used in the United States (standards differ in other countries). These include age, ethnicity, marital status, number of children, and health. Photographs also do not belong on résumés unless you are applying for jobs such as entertainment positions. Although interested parties can frequently find your picture on Facebook, for instance, pictures have long been excluded because of their ability to enable discrimination. For safety reasons, résumés should never include your Social Security number.

Including these kinds of information shows you have not researched the job-hunting process. Since many employers take your performance on the job hunt as an indication of the quality of work you will do for them, résumé lapses indicate that you may not be the best employee.

Since résumés are used to eliminate a large pool of job candidates down to the handful that will be interviewed, do not include controversial activities or associations. This category generally includes work for specific religious or political groups. (If the work is significant, you can include it generically: Wrote campaign publicity for state senator candidate.)

High school facts are generally omitted once you are a junior in college unless you have good reasons for keeping them. These reasons might include showing you have local connections or showing skill in a needed area not covered by college activities (perhaps you are applying for coaching jobs where a

Résumé Checklist

Does the résumé have a good, easy-to-read layout?

Does it include your name, address, city, state, zip code, phone number, and e-mail address at the top of the page?

Does it use bullets or bold to highlight key elements?

Does it list information in order of relevance to the position?

Does it give specifics, not generalities, about your experience?

Did you double check the spelling, grammar and punctuation?

Does it use action verbs to describe your job duties?

Is your résumé truthful?

Is it tailored for a specific employer?

Does a 10-second reading reveal the basics about you?

Does the résumé warrant an interview, if you were an employer?

How does your résumé rate?

Adapted from UC Berkeley Career Center, "Résumé and Letter Writing: Résumé Checklist," in *Job and Internship Guide 2010–2011*, accessed April 3, 2011, http://career.berkeley.edu/Guide/ResumeLetterWriting.pdf.

variety of team sports will help you, and you played basketball in high school and volleyball in college). The fact that you have good high school activities but few if any college activities is not a good reason. In this case, listing high school activities will show you are on a downward trend at a very early age!

Do not pad your résumé with trivial items; they are easily recognized as padding and they devalue the worth of your other items. For instance, except under the most unusual circumstances, graduate students should not list grants for travel to conferences as honors, since such travel grants are ubiquitous. Some community groups, especially religious organizations, list all college graduates in their group-specific "honorary." Since everyone who graduates will belong, these are not considered honors.

As you advance in your career, you will continually cut information from earlier stages of your life, as well as from outside activities, to focus on your recent career achievements.

DEALING WITH DIFFICULTIES LO 12-3

Some job hunters face special problems. This section gives advice for six common problems.

"I Don't Have Any Experience."

If you have a year or more before you job hunt, you can get experience in several ways:

- Take a fast-food job—and keep it. If you do well, you'll be promoted to a supervisor within a year. Use every opportunity to learn about the management and financial aspects of the business.
- Sign on with agencies that handle temporary workers. As an added bonus, some of these jobs become permanent.
- Join a volunteer organization that interests you. If you work hard, you'll quickly get an opportunity to do more: manage a budget, write fund-raising materials, and supervise other volunteers.
- Freelance. Design brochures, create web pages, do tax returns for small businesses. Use your skills—for free, if you have to at first.
- Write. Create a portfolio of ads, instructions, or whatever documents are relevant for the field you want to enter. Ask a professional—an instructor, a local business person, someone from a professional organization—to critique them.

If you're on the job market now, think carefully about what you've really done. Complete sentences using the action verbs in Figure 12.6. Think about what you've done in courses, in volunteer work, in unpaid activities. Especially focus on skills in problem solving, critical thinking, teamwork, and communication. Solving a problem for a hypothetical firm in an accounting class, thinking critically about a report problem in business communication, working with a group in a marketing class, and communicating with people at the senior center where you volunteer are experience, even if no one paid you.

"All My Experience Is in My Family's Business."

In your résumé, simply list the company you worked for. For a reference, instead of a family member, list a supervisor, client, or vendor who can talk about your work. Since the reader may wonder whether "Jim Clarke" is any relation to the owner of

"Clarke Construction Company," be ready to answer interview questions about why you're looking at other companies. Prepare an answer that stresses the broader opportunities you seek but doesn't criticize your family or the family business.

"I Want to Change Fields."

Have a good reason for choosing the field in which you're looking for work. "I want a change" or "I need to get out of a bad situation" does not convince an employer that you know what you're doing.

Think about how your experience relates to the job you want. Sam wants a new career as a pharmaceutical sales representative. He has sold woodstoves, served subpoenas, and worked on an oil rig. A chronological résumé makes his work history look directionless. But a skills résumé could focus on persuasive ability (selling stoves), initiative and persistence (serving subpoenas), and technical knowledge (courses in biology and chemistry).

Learn about the skills needed in the job you want: learn the buzzwords of the industry. Figure 12.7 shows a skills résumé of someone changing fields from animal ecology to technical writing. Her reason for changing could be that she found she enjoyed the writing duties of her jobs more than she enjoyed the ecology field work.

"I've Been Out of the Job Market for a While."

You need to prove to a potential employer that you're up-to-date and motivated:

- Create a portfolio of your work to show what you can do for the employer.
- Do freelance work.
- Be active in professional organizations. Attend meetings.
- Look for volunteer work where you can use and expand relevant work skills.
- Attend local networking events.
- Read the journals and trade publications of your field.
- Learn the software that professionals use in your field.
- Be up-to-date with electronic skills such as IMing, text messaging, and computer searching.
- Take professional training to expand your skill set.

Employment counselors advise that you not leave a gap on your résumé; such a gap makes employers speculate about disasters such as nervous breakdowns or jail time. They suggest you matter-of-factly list an honorable title such as Parent or Caregiver; do not apologize. Better yet is to fill in the gap with substantial volunteer experience. Heading a $75,000 fund-raising drive for a new playground looks good for almost any employer. A side benefit of volunteer work, in addition to new career skills, is networking. Boards of directors and agency executives are frequently well-connected members of the community.

"I Was Laid Off."

In times of large layoffs, this is not an overwhelming obstacle. You do not need to point out the layoff in your application materials; the end date of your last employment will make the point for you. Instead, use your documents to highlight your strengths.

Should I Create a Video Résumé?

What is a video résumé?
Job hunters post short videos as part of their job applications through services such as YouTube, Google video, and video résumé sites.

Who uses video résumés?
Anyone can. Currently, most video résumés are produced by applicants interested in entertainment and media, but job seekers in other industries are starting to use video postings.

What are the benefits to employers?
Employers get an opportunity to screen applicants before asking for an interview. This may save an employer from conducting an interview.

Are there risks?
Yes, discrimination on the basis of sex, age, and ethnicity.

If you decide to create a video posting, you may want to consider these tips for your video résumé:

1. Be brief and concise. Remember that employers generally spend less than 30 seconds per résumé. Don't expect them to spend longer on your video.
2. Be prepared. Avoid reading a script. You should be conversational and natural in your presentation.
3. Tailor the video to the specific employer and position.
4. Be professional. Post a video that is clear, audible, and free from background noise.

Résumé Blasting

Résumé blasting is the process of distributing your résumé to dozens, hundreds, or thousands of résumé sites and databases. Résumé blasting services will do the work for you, for a price. But don't yield to the temptation.

ResumeDoctor.com surveyed over 5,000 recruiters and hiring managers about online job postings. Top complaints were

1. Large numbers of irrelevant responses (92%). Most participants indicated that they receive hundreds of responses per online job posting.
2. Résumés not matching the job description (71%).
3. Job candidates "blasting out" résumés (63%).

Adapted from Universum WetFeet, "Looking Good on Paper," accessed April 2, 2011, http://www.wetfeet.com/Experienced-Hire/Resume—Cover-letter/Articles/Looking-Good-on-Paper.aspx.

Do be prepared to be asked about the layoff in an interview. Why were you laid off when other employees were retained? It helps if you can truthfully give a neutral explanation: the accounting work was outsourced; our entire lab was closed; the company laid off everyone who had worked fewer than five years. Be sure you do not express bitterness or self-pity; neither emotion will help you get your new job. On the other hand, do not be overly grateful for an interview; such excess shows a lack of self-confidence. Be sure to show you are keeping yourself current by doing some of the items in the bulleted list in the previous section.

"I Was Fired."

First, deal with the emotional baggage. You need to reduce negative feelings to a manageable level before you're ready to job-hunt.

Second, take responsibility for your role in the termination.

Third, try to learn from the experience. You'll be a much more attractive job candidate if you can show that you've learned from the experience—whether your lesson is improved work habits or that you need to choose a job where you can do work you can point to with pride.

Fourth, collect evidence showing that earlier in your career you were a good worker. This evidence could include references from earlier employers, good performance evaluations, and a portfolio of good work.

Some common strategies may also give you some help for references. You should check with the Human Resources Department to understand the company's reference policy. Some companies now give no references other than verification of job title and work dates. Others do not give references for employees who worked only a short time.[11] Another option is to ask someone other than your former boss for a reference. Could you ask a supplier or vendor? A different department head?

A different tactic is suggested by Phil Elder, an interviewer for an insurance company. He suggests calling the person who fired you and saying something like this: "Look, I know you weren't pleased with the job I did at _____. I'm applying for a job at _____ now and the personnel director may call you to ask about me. Would you be willing to give me the chance to get this job so that I can try to do things right this time?" All but the hardest of heart, says Elder, will give you one more chance. You won't get a glowing reference, but neither will the statement be so damning that no one is willing to hire you.[12]

Above all, be honest. Do not lie about your termination at an interview or on a job application. The application usually requires you to sign a statement that the information you are providing is true and that false statements can be grounds for dismissal.

ELECTRONIC RÉSUMÉS LO 12-4

In addition to a paper résumé for job fairs, interviews, and potential contacts, you will need electronic versions of your résumé. With a few exceptions noted below, these résumés will have the same content but will be formatted differently so they can be "read" by both software and humans.

Sending Your Résumé Electronically

Many employers are asking to have résumés posted on their organizations' websites. When doing so, be sure you follow their directions exactly. You may also be asked by some employers to send your résumé by e-mail.

Here are some basic guidelines of e-mail job-hunting etiquette:

- Don't use your current employer's e-mail system for your job search. You'll leave potential employers with the impression that you spend company time on writing résumés and other nonwork-related activities.
- Set up a free, Internet-based e-mail account using services such as Hotmail, Gmail, or Yahoo! to manage correspondence related to your job hunt.
- Avoid using silly or cryptic e-mail addresses. Instead of bubbles@aol.com, opt for something business-like: yourname@yahoo.com.
- Write a simple subject line that makes a good first impression: Résumé—Kate Sanchez. A good subject line will improve the chances that your résumé is actually read, since e-mail from unknown senders is often deleted without being opened. If you are responding to an ad, use the job title or job code listed.
- Before sending your résumé into cyberspace, test to see how it will look when it comes out on the other end. E-mail it to yourself and a friend, then critique and fix it.
- Send only one résumé, even if the firm has more than one position for which you qualify. Most recruiters have negative reactions to multiple résumés.
- Experts differ on whether candidates should phone to follow up. Phoning once to be sure your résumé arrived is probably fine.

It's important to heed the specific directions of employers that you are e-mailing. Many do not want attachments because of viruses. While a few may want a Microsoft Word or PDF attachment of your résumé, others may specify that you paste your résumé directly into the body of your e-mail message.

If you are sending your résumé in the text of an e-mail,

- Start all lines at the left margin.
- Do not use bold, underlining, bullets, tabs, or unusual fonts. Instead use keys such as asterisks.
- You can also put some headings in all capital letters, but use this device sparingly.
- To avoid awkward line breaks for your readers, shorten line lengths to 65 characters and spaces.

Beware of Spam Filters

Employers are using filters to keep out spam and damaging computer viruses. Unfortunately, legitimate e-mails, including résumés, are also getting blocked. Applicants who send résumés with an e-mail may be rejected by spam filters for various reasons such as "foul" language (B.S.) or overused phrases (*responsible for* or *duties included).*

What can you do to avoid spam filters?

- Avoid acronyms or titles that may be considered "foul" language.
- Watch overusing words or phrases.
- Avoid words like *free, extend, unbelievable, opportunity, trial, mortgage.*
- Avoid using unusual colors.
- Be careful of using all capitals, exclamation points, or dollar amounts in subject lines.

What preventative steps can you take to avoid being caught by spam filters?

- Set your personal spam filter to high; then send your résumé to your own e-mail account
- Send your résumé to a spam checker.

Adapted from Michael Trust, "How to Stop Your Résumé from Becoming Spam," Careerealism, October 11, 2010, http://www.careerealism.com/stop-resume-spam.

Play Safe

Before posting your job application online, you should verify the site is safe. Here are some criteria:

1. **Have you heard of the site?** If not, be careful. Look for online reviews of the site.
2. **Does it ask you to register before you can search for jobs?** This is a big red flag. Try a different site.
3. **Does it have a comprehensive privacy policy?** Read the policy to see if they sell or rent your information. Putting up your job packet on a nonprivate forum could affect your identity in the future. Do not assume the site is protected if it has a privacy seal.
4. **Can you limit access to your personal contact information?** Identity theft is a growing problem. Good sites allow you to protect personal contact information.
5. **Does it let you delete your résumé after you get a job?** Safe websites should allow you to delete your documents or make them inactive while you are not conducting a job search. You don't want your new boss to think you are still on the job market for an even better position.

Adapted from Susan Joyce, "15 Critical Criteria for Choosing the Best Job Site for You," NETability, Inc., accessed April 3, 2011. http://www.job-hunt.org/choosing.shtml.

Your résumé will look plain to you, but the employers receiving it are used to the look of in-text résumés.

If you are sending your résumé as an attachment, name the document appropriately: Smith Robyn Résumé.docx. Never name it Résumé.docx; you do not want it to get lost in a long directory of documents.

With your résumé include a brief cover letter that will make the receiver want to look at your résumé. In it, mention the types of files you've included. (See Figure 13.8.) Remember, it takes only an instant for readers to delete your e-mail. Do not give them reasons to trash your résumé.

Some people confuse electronic and scannable résumés. The former are résumés you send in or attached to an e-mail. The latter are paper résumés specially formatted for older software. Software programs have greatly improved recently and most can now scan regular résumés posted on websites. However, if you are asked to send a scannable résumé, guidelines for creating one are in Appendix D.

Posting Your Résumé on the Web

You will probably want to post your résumé online. Be selective when you do: stick with well-known sites for safety reasons. Choose one or two of the large popular sites such as Monster or CareerBuilder. Also choose one or two smaller sites, preferably ones specific to your desired occupation or location. A well-chosen niche site can show employers that you know your field. Studies are still showing that about 25% of external hires are made through job boards.[13]

Many responsible career sites recommend that you should not succumb to **résumé blasting**—posting your résumé widely on the web. Many employers consider such blasting to be akin to spam and they respond negatively to job candidates who do it.

If the websites you choose have you place your information into their résumé form, cut and paste from your résumé to avoid typos. Do not use résumé templates unless you are asked to do so; they will rarely present you as well as the layout you have designed for yourself.

For safety reasons, use your e-mail address as contact information instead of your address and phone number. Make sure your e-mail address looks professional; you should not be HotLips@Yahoo.com. To foil identity thieves, some web consultants also recommend that you remove all dates from your résumé, and that you replace employer names with generic descriptions (statewide information technology company). Identity thieves can take information directly from online résumés, or they can call employers and, claiming to be conducting background checks, get additional information.

Since many databases sort résumés by submission date, renew your résumé by making small changes to it at least every two weeks. If you don't get any response to your résumé after a month or two, post it on a different site.

If you post your résumé on your personal website, be sure that all the links go to professional-looking pages, such as documents you have created. Now is not the time to link to pictures of you partying. Also, make sure the first screen includes a current job objective and Summary of Qualifications. One study found that résumés on personal websites were particularly useful for self-employed workers, for whom they attracted clients.[14]

When you have your new job, remove your résumé from all sites. Your new employer will probably take a dim view of finding your résumé on job sites and it is virtually impossible to block your online résumé from people at your current place of employment.

HONESTY LO 12-5

Be absolutely honest on your résumé—and in the rest of your job search. Just ask Marilee Jones, former Dean of Admissions at Massachusetts Institute of Technology (MIT). In 1979, when she applied for an admissions job at MIT, her résumé listed bachelor's and master's degrees from Rensselaer Polytechnic Institute. In reality, she attended there only one year as a part-time student. By 1997, when she was promoted to the deanship, she did not have the courage to correct her résumé. In April 2007, she was forced to resign, even though she was a nationally recognized leader in admissions, after an anonymous tip.[15]

Most businesses now conduct some kind of background check on job applicants. Even graduate schools, particularly business schools, are checking applicants.[16] A survey of over 3,000 hirers conducted for CareerBuilder reported that 49% had caught lies on résumés.

Background checks on job candidates can include a credit check, legal and criminal records, complete employment history, and academic credentials. Such checks turn up some incredible whoppers. Résumés have been found using someone else's photo, listing degrees from nonexistent schools, listing fake Mensa memberships, and even claiming a false connection to the Kennedy clan.[17]

You can omit some material on your résumé, because obviously you cannot include everything about your life to date. For instance, it's still ethical to omit a low GPA, although most employers will assume it is very low indeed to be omitted. But what you do include must be absolutely honest.

Some of the most frequent inaccuracies on résumés are inflated job titles and incorrect dates of employment. While these data are easy to fudge, they are also easy to catch in background checks. It is also possible that some of these particular inaccuracies come from careless records kept by job candidates. Do you remember the exact job title of that first job you held as a sophomore in high school? Keep careful records of your employment history!

If employers do an employment history check, and many do, they will have a complete work history for you. They will be able to spot inaccurate company names and work dates. If you left a company off your résumé, they may wonder why; some may assume your performance at that company was not satisfactory.

Other areas where résumés are commonly inaccurate are

- Degrees: many people conveniently forget they were a few hours short of a degree.
- GPAs: inflating one's grade point seems to be a big temptation.
- Honors: people list memberships in fake honoraries, or fake memberships in real honoraries.
- Fake employers.
- Job duties: many people inflate them.
- Salary increases.
- Fake addresses: people create these to have the "local" advantage.
- Fake contact information for references: this information frequently leads to family members or friends who will give fake referrals.
- Technical abilities.
- Language proficiency.

All dishonesty on a résumé is dangerous, keeping you from being hired if discovered early, and causing you to be fired if discovered later. However, the last two bullets listed above are particular dangerous because your chances are good of being asked at an interview to demonstrate your listed proficiencies.

Résumé Lies Lead to Termination

Listed below are high-level professionals who learned the hard way that eventually employers will discover discrepancies on résumés.

- Dave Edmondson, former chief executive of RadioShack, resigned after lying about having a college degree.
- George O'Leary, former Notre Dame football coach, resigned over inaccuracies in both his academic and athletic backgrounds.
- Jeffrey Papows, former CEO of Lotus Corporation, quit over discrepancies in his military and educational record.
- Kenneth Lonchar, CFO of Veritas software, resigned over inaccuracies in his academic background.

Have you checked your résumé to make sure you have not inflated your credentials?

Adapted from Rachel Zupek, "Infamous Résumé Lies," CareerBuilder, July 7, 2010, http://msn.careerbuilder.com/Article/MSN-1154-Cover-Letters-Resumes-Infamous-R%C3%A9sum%C3%A9-Lies.

SUMMARY OF KEY POINTS

The Cost of a Typo

Typos can cost you a job. Many employers say they will not consider résumés with spelling mistakes or typographical errors.

Why? Employers consider your job documents to be examples of your finest work. If you are careless on them, they assume you will be even more careless in the work you do for them.

Spell check is not enough. Too many "mangers" (managers) with great ability "to to" attend to detail are seeking work in the "pubic area" (public arena). You get the point. Proofread your documents carefully. Get your friends and family to proof them also, but remember, no one cares as much about your documents as you do. If English is not your first language, or your strong suit, consider paying for a professional editor. The success of your career starts with these documents.

- Informal preparation for job hunting should start soon after you arrive on campus. Formal preparation for job hunting should begin a full year before you begin interviewing. The year you interview, register with your placement office early.
- Personal branding and networking, particularly through social media such as LinkedIn, are now an important part of job searching.
- Employers skim résumés to decide whom to interview. Employers assume that the letter and résumé represent your best work.
- Emphasize information that is relevant to the job you want, is recent (last three years), and shows your superiority to other applicants.
- To emphasize key points, put them in headings, list them vertically, and provide details.
- Résumés use sentence fragments punctuated like complete sentences. Items in the résumé must be concise and parallel. Verbs and gerunds create a dynamic image of you.
- A **chronological résumé** summarizes what you did in a time line (starting with the most recent events, and going backward in **reverse chronology**). It emphasizes degrees, job titles, and dates. Use a chronological résumé when
  - Your education and experience are a logical preparation for the position for which you're applying.
  - You have impressive job titles, offices, or honors.
- A **skills résumé** emphasizes the skills you've used, rather than the job in which or the date when you used them. Use a skills résumé when
  - Your education and experience are not the usual route to the position for which you're applying.
  - You're changing fields.
  - You want to combine experience from paid jobs, activities, volunteer work, and courses to show the extent of your experience in administration, finance, speaking, etc.
  - Your recent work history may create the wrong impression (e.g., it has gaps, shows a demotion, shows job-hopping, etc.).
- Résumés contain the applicant's contact information, education, and experience. Career objectives, summary of qualifications, honors and awards, other skills, activities, and a portfolio reference may also be included.
- Many résumés are now sent electronically and are posted on the Internet or the organization's website.
- Remove any unprofessional material from your personal web page, blog, and social networking sites.
- Always be completely honest in your résumé and job search.

CHAPTER 12 Exercises and Problems

*Go to www.mhhe.com/locker10e for additional Exercises and Problems.

12.1 Reviewing the Chapter

1. What should you do soon after starting college to prepare for your job search? (LO 12-1)
2. What should you do a full year before your job search? (LO 12-1)
3. How can you use writing components such as emphasis and details to help set yourself apart from other candidates? (LO 12-2)

4. What are factors you should consider when preparing your contact information? (LO 12-2)
5. Why are career objectives hard to write? (LO 12-2)
6. What are key words? How do you use them in your summary of qualifications? In electronic résumés? (LO 12-2)
7. What kinds of details make your experience look most attractive to potential employers? (LO 12-2)
8. How can activities help make you look attractive to potential employers? (LO 12-2)
9. What can you do to help get the best references possible? (LO 12-2)
10. Pick one of the common problems job hunters may face and explain how you would deal with it if it happened to you during your career. (LO 12-3)
11. What are some basic guidelines of e-mail job-hunting etiquette? (LO 12-4)
12. What safety precautions do you need to take when you post your résumé online? (LO 12-4)
13. What roles are blogs and Facebook pages playing in the job search? (LO 12-4)
14. Why is it more important now than ever before to be completely honest on your résumé? (LO 12-5)

12.2 Reviewing Grammar

Most résumés use lists, and items in lists need to have parallel structure. Polish your knowledge of parallel structure by revising the sentences in Exercise B.7, Appendix B.

12.3 Analyzing Your Accomplishments

List the 10 achievements that give you the most personal satisfaction. These could be things that other people wouldn't notice. They can be accomplishments you've achieved recently or things you did years ago.

Answer the following questions for each accomplishment:

1. What skills or knowledge did you use?
2. What personal traits did you exhibit?
3. What about this accomplishment makes it personally satisfying to you?

As your instructor directs,

a. Share your answers with a small group of other students.
b. Summarize your answers in a memo to your instructor.
c. Present your answers orally to the class.

12.4 Remembering What You've Done

Use the following list to jog your memory about what you've done. For each item, give three or four details as well as a general statement.

Describe a time when you

1. Used facts and figures to gain agreement on an important point.
2. Identified a problem that a group or organization faced and developed a plan for solving the problem.
3. Made a presentation or a speech to a group.
4. Won the goodwill of people whose continued support was necessary for the success of some long-term project or activity.
5. Interested other people in something that was important to you and persuaded them to take the actions you wanted.
6. Helped a group deal constructively with conflict.
7. Demonstrated creativity.
8. Took a project from start to finish.
9. Created an opportunity for yourself in a job or volunteer position.
10. Used good judgment and logic in solving a problem.

As your instructor directs,

a. Identify which job(s) each detail is relevant for.
b. Identify which details would work well on a résumé.
c. Identify which details, further developed, would work well in a job letter.

12.5 Developing Action Statements

Use 10 of the verbs from Figure 12.6 to write action statements describing what you've done in paid or volunteer work, in classes, in extracurricular activities, or in community service.

12.6 Evaluating Career Objective Statements

The following career objective statements are not effective. What is wrong with each statement as it stands? Which statements could be revised to be satisfactory? Which should be dropped?

1. To use my acquired knowledge of accounting to eventually own my own business.
2. A progressively responsible position as a MARKETING MANAGER where education and ability would have valuable application and lead to advancement.
3. To work with people responsibly and creatively, helping them develop personal and professional skills.
4. A position in international marketing which makes use of my specialization in marketing and my knowledge of foreign markets.
5. To bring Faith, Hope, and Charity to the American workplace.
6. To succeed in sales.
7. To design and maintain web pages.

12.7 Deciding How Much Detail to Use

In each of the following situations, how detailed should the applicant be? Why?

1. Ron Oliver has been steadily employed for the last six years while getting his college degree, but the jobs have been low-level ones, whose prime benefit was that they paid well and fit around his class schedule.
2. Adrienne Barcus was an assistant department manager at a clothing boutique. As assistant manager, she was authorized to approve checks in the absence of the manager. Her other duties were ringing up sales, cleaning the area, and helping mark items for sales.
3. Lois Heilman has been a clerk-typist in the Alumni Office. As part of her job, she developed a schedule for mailings to alumni, set up a merge system, and wrote two of the letters that go out to alumni. The merge system she set up has cut in half the time needed to produce letters.
4. As a co-op student, Stanley Greene spends every other term in a paid job. He now has six semesters of job experience in television broadcasting. During his last co-op he was the assistant producer for a daily "morning magazine" show.

12.8 Evaluating Web Résumés

Evaluate five résumés you find on the web. Many schools of business have places where students can post résumés online. You may find other résumés on job boards (see the list in Figure 12.2).

As your instructor directs,

a. Share your results with a small group of students.
b. Write an e-mail message analyzing what works and what doesn't. Provide URLs or links to the pages you discuss.
c. Write a memo analyzing what works and what doesn't. Attach printouts of each page you discuss.
d. Join with a small group of students to analyze the pages.
e. Make a short oral presentation to the class discussing the best (or worst) page you found.

12.9 Writing Job Search Goals

Write a list of goals and tasks you need to accomplish for a successful job search. Which ones are crucial? What steps do you need to start taking now to accomplish these goals and tasks? Make a tentative time line for the steps.

12.10 Writing a Job Description

Write a job description for your "dream position." Include the following:

- Position title
- Position description including tasks, special requirements
- Location
- Work hours
- Working conditions (for example, office space, scheduling, amount of supervision)
- Company culture
- Pay
- Experience and education requirements
- Personal competencies (for example, ability to communicate, work in teams, problem solve, etc.).
- Amount of travel
- Social, political, and ethical issues that may be involved

In small groups, share your descriptions. Did you get some ideas from the dream jobs of other students?

12.11 Performing a Needs Analysis

Identify a specific job posting you are interested in and list its requirements. Analyze the needs of the job and identify your personal strengths and qualifications to obtain it.

As your instructor directs,

a. Work on incorporating your list into a résumé.

b. Compose bullet entries for each qualification using action verbs.

c. Identify areas in which you still need to improve. Brainstorm a list of ways in which you can achieve what you need.

12.12 Researching a Job Ad

For a specific job ad online, list job requirements and key words. Search online for the corporation that has posted the job. Look up the corporation's mission and objectives pages and look for repeating keywords and hot buttons. Find correlations between the job posting and the company's objectives.

As your instructor directs,

a. Share your findings with a group and discuss how the given job posting correlates to the company's overall mission and needs.

b. Identify one such case from your group and present it to the class.

12.13 Editing a Résumé

Below are a job ad and a résumé applying for that job. Using the information you have about Jennifer's two jobs (given below the résumé), critique Jennifer's résumé. Her job letter is Exercise 13.18, if you wish to look at it, too. Redo her résumé to improve it. Then write a memo to your instructor discussing the strengths and weaknesses of the résumé and explaining why you made the changes you did.

Account Manager

Location: Aurora, IL
Job Category: Business/Strategic Management
Career Level: Entry-Level Manager (Manager/Supervisor of Staff)

Quantum National is the market leader in providing research, sales and marketing, health care policy consulting, and health information management services to the health care industry. Quantum has more than 20,000 employees worldwide and offices in 15 countries in Central and South America. Medical Innovation Communications, a division of Quantum National, currently has an opportunity for an Account Manager in our Aurora, IL, office. Medical Innovation Communications provides comprehensive product commercialization at all stages of product development: from phase 2, through national and international product launches to ongoing support.

The Account Manager has global responsibility for managing the client's marketing communications programs, assuring that the client's objectives are met in terms of program quality and on-time delivery.

Responsibilities include:

- Day-to-day client contact to identify and translate marketing objectives into strategic medical communications/education programs.
- Develop proposals, budgets, estimates of job cost, and profitability.
- Lead a team of Project Managers and Marketing Associates through guidance, delegation, and follow-up; and significant interaction with the client.
- Work with New Business Development Teams to develop proposals, budgets, and presenting company capabilities/business pitches to clients.
- Schedule the workflow of a 30-person demonstration and marketing team.

Requirements:

- Bachelors degree.
- Ability to define and respond to client needs, working effectively under tight deadlines.
- Proven client management experience.
- Proven team management experience.
- Superior written and spoken communication skills.

E-mail applications and résumés to pattersj@micquant.com, and direct inquiries to J. Pattersen.

Jennifer Stanton	8523 8th Street	125 A S. 27th Ave
wildechilde@gmail.com	Ames, IA 50011	Omaha, NE 68101
cell: 515-668-9011	515-311-8243	402-772-5106

Objective

To get a job as an account manager.

Education

Iowa State University, Ames, IA—Business
May 2012, maybe December 2012
Minor: Botany
Cumulative GPA: 2.63 / 4.0

Mid-Plains Community College, North Platte, NE—Associate of Arts
May 2008

Bryan High School, Omaha, NE
May 2005

Work Experience

May 2011–August 2011—Summer Internship at FirstWest Insurance, Des Moines, IA

- Worked with a senior account manager to oversee some medical and EAP accounts.
- Made her phone calls to customers.

- Organized meetings with customers.
- I had to write some training "how-to's" for the new billing database.

1998–2010—*Worked in family business*
Worked weekends and summers in my parents' used-book store.

Skills
Microsoft Office
Fluent in Spanish

When you ask, Jennifer tells you about her two jobs:

At her internship this summer, the person she worked with was pretty much an absentee supervisor: Jennifer had to do all the work alone (and she's still a little bitter about that). Her department managed five Employee Assistance Provider accounts with a total of about 36,000 individual policy holders in five midwestern states. She had to set up and maintain work schedules for 12 employees, and manage the expense reports for the entire group. Four of those employees traveled a lot, so there were lots of expense reports to manage; there were so many that Jennifer had to revise the department's budget twice. She spent about four hours of every day returning customer phone calls and linking customers up on conference calls with her department's employees. And those training how-to's? That turned into a 20-page how-to manual, which she wrote up and then had FirstWest's IT department turn into a website for the department to use.

Her parents' family bookstore in Omaha is actually a franchise of a national chain of aftermarket bookstores: Booktopia. The store generates about $450,000 in gross sales per year, and stocks about 100,000 titles (not counting Internet sales and special orders); it employs 5 full-time and 17 part-time employees. In addition to filling in as a floor clerk, stocker, and cashier—all jobs that put her customer-service, cash-handling, and "people skills" to the test—Jennifer has been handling all of the paperwork between the store and the Booktopia corporate office. (Her parents are great salespeople but they're not good at paying attention to details. That's created friction between them and the corporate office.) That paperwork includes all of the store's quarterly and yearly budget, staffing, and marketing reports since 1999.

Note: This exercise was written by Matthew Search.

12.14 Analyzing Job Applicants Based on Their Résumés

Based on your reading of Chapter 12, the following job description and the two résumés below, analyze the two applicants for the position. What are their strengths and weaknesses as highlighted by their résumés? Which of the two candidates would you select? Why?

Job description for Cost Accountant

The position of Cost Accountant is responsible for budgeting, reviewing, analyzing, controlling, and forecasting costs involving different cost centers throughout the production process, including raw material procurement, inventory management, manufacturing, warehousing, and shipping. Other responsibilities include analyzing

G/L reports; ensuring compliance with Generally Accepted Accounting Principles (GAAP) and Cost Accounting Standards (CAS); conducting breakeven (BE), contribution margin, and variance analyses; and preparing periodic reports for upper management. The position requires a bachelor's degree in accounting. A certification in management accounting from the Institute of Management Accountants (IMA) will be a plus. The position also requires a minimum of two years of work experience in cost accounting at a manufacturing company.

STAN GOLDBERG

1010, Buck St., Fairfax, VA
Stanberg@bestwebsite.com

OBJECTIVE

Cost Accountant position in which I can effectively utilize my skills in budgeting, accounting, costing, forecasting, reporting, and teamworking

EXPERIENCE

2005–2006 Abacus Engineering Portland, OR.

Cost Accounting Trainee

- Calculated cost variance for different cost centers.
- Prepared quarterly budget reports
- Coodinated with employees at different levels for data collection

2007–till date Bourke Winodws Fairfax, VA

Costing Manager

- Monitored 12 cost centers
- Implemented policies that reduced costs by 25%
- Supervised a staff of three, including one cost accountant.
- I also produced multiple G/L reports for the production department as well as upper management

EDUCATION

2001–2005 Edward Young University, Perry, OH

- B.A., accounting.
- Currently pursuing CMA of Institute of Management Accounting

INTERESTS

Country music, computers, fishing, golf

Jamal Robinson

1212 S. E. Avenue, Earl, PA
(111) 112-1121-jr8@pearlnews.com

Qualification Summary

Skills in **controling** and reucing costs, experience with GAAP and CAS, skills in cost analyses, project management, CMA (IMA), member of the Financial Management Association International, well-versd with ERP software

Education

- Certification in Management Accounting
  Graduation—2007
  Institute of Management Accountants
- True Blue University, Roald, PA
  Graduation—2006
  Degree—Bachelor of Sciences (BS)
  Major—Accounting, G.P.A. 3.55

Experience

Silverstein Windows and Doors, Earl, PA 2007-Till date

Cost Accountant

- Estimate, review, budget, analyze, and forecast direct / indirect and variable and fixed costs for all stages of production
- Work on the ERP system to genrate reports and data sheets giving cost analyses
- Suggested a procedure in a contract that saved the company $35,000
- Worked with the Marketing Department on the costing / pricing of lower-priced vinyl casement windows

Achievements

- Volunteered more than 100 hours for the Habitat for Humnity Award 2005–2006
- Visted door and widow manufacturing plants in Argentina, Belgium, and Japan
- Received the best employee of the month award at Silverstein Windows and Doors
- Wrote articles for *Financial Control Weekly,* a publication of Costing Professionals Association

References

Available upon request

Note: This exercise was written by Anish Dave.

12.15 Preparing a Résumé

Write a résumé that you could use in your job search.

As your instructor directs,

a. Write a résumé for the field in which you hope to find a job.

b. Write two different résumés for two different job paths you are interested in pursuing. Write a memo to your instructor explaining the differences.

c. Adapt your résumé to a specific company you hope to work for. Write a memo to your instructor explaining the specific adaptations you make and why.

d. Write a résumé for the dream job you developed in Exercise 12.10.

12.16 Critiquing Your Résumé, I

Answer the following overview questions for your résumé:

1. Exactly what position are you applying for? How did you choose the position?
2. What are your concerns with applying for this position?
3. What could the concerns of your audience be with your application? How did you try to address these concerns?

4. How do you think the audience will perceive your résumé? Explain.
5. Does your résumé target your employer and position specifically?

Answer the following questions on your design choices:

1. Does the page look balanced?
2. Does the résumé look original or based on a template?
3. Does the length of your résumé fit your situation and position?
4. Does your résumé include clear headings, bullets, and white space?
5. Do you use fonts appropriate for the career level and industry?
6. Do you use consistent font sizes and spacing throughout the document?
7. Does the design reflect your personality and your career ambitions?

Answer the following questions on the content of your résumé.

1. Are the résumé sections clearly, correctly, and consistently labeled?
2. Does the order of the headings highlight your strongest qualifications?
3. Is the work history listed from most recent to past positions?
4. Do you omit high school information? If not, explain your choice.
5. Do you provide details for your best qualifications?
6. Do you use numbers to support your accomplishments?
7. Is the information provided relevant to the position?
8. Does the information support your claim that you are qualified and the best person for this position?
9. Does the information flow logically and easily?
10. Do your bulleted lists use parallel structure?
11. Do you avoid grammar, punctuation, and spelling errors?

Variation: Review a class member's résumé using the same questions.

12.17 Critiquing Your Résumé, II

Rate your résumé using the résumé checklist in the page 392 sidebar. Write a one-page memo to your instructor stating how you believe your résumé rates. Explain and support your position.

12.18 Creating a Web or Paper Portfolio

Create a web or paper portfolio highlighting your professional and academic accomplishments. Include course projects, workplace samples, and other documents that support your professional accomplishments and goals.

12.19 Evaluating Visual Résumés

Working individually, in pairs, or in small groups, as your instructor directs,

a. Look at five of the example student résumés on VisualCV.com. What features do you like? Why? What features would you change or omit? Why? What are the advantages of VisualCV over your own web page? Disadvantages?
b. Discuss strengths and weaknesses of two résumés in a memo to your teacher, a posting on the class website, or an oral presentation.

12.20 Evaluating LinkedIn Profiles

Working individually, in pairs, or in small groups, as your instructor directs, look at six profiles on LinkedIn. You could use those of your classmates, family members, or local businesspeople.

- Which one has the best résumé? Why?
- How do the profiles and résumés differ?
- Which one has the best recommendations? Why?
- Overall, which one has the best profile? Why?

Discuss your conclusions in a memo to your teacher, a posting on the class website, or an oral presentation.

CHAPTER 13

Writing Job Application Letters

Chapter Outline

How Content Differs in Job Letters and Résumés

How to Find Out about Employers and Jobs

Tapping into the Hidden Job Market

- Information interviews
- Referral interviews

Content and Organization for Job Application Letters

- How to Organize Solicited Letters
- How to Organize Prospecting Letters
- First Paragraphs of Solicited Letters
- First Paragraphs of Prospecting Letters
- Showing a Knowledge of the Position and the Company
- Showing What Separates You from Other Applicants
- The Last Paragraph

E-Mail Application Letters

Creating a Professional Image

- Writing Style
- Positive Emphasis
- You-Attitude
- Paragraph Length and Unity
- Letter Length
- Editing and Proofreading
- Follow-Up

Application Essays

Summary of Key Points

NEWSWORTHY COMMUNICATION

Unconventional Job Tactics

With high U.S. unemployment rates, even the best-qualified candidates may struggle to make an impression in a sea of other job seekers. Some may turn to unconventional methods to get noticed by hiring directors and recruiters.

Nathan Schwagler, for example, chose an innovative way to get past the traditional hiring process at Ingram Micro. He dressed up as a deliveryman, complete with a clipboard, a bouquet of flowers, and a Candygram. He got through security and to the office of Jessica, the company's recruiter. When he finally met her, Schwagler stripped off his coveralls to reveal his business suit underneath and presented Jessica with his résumé, in addition to the flowers and candy.

These kinds of innovative methods to get noticed are on the rise in the United States. One survey of hiring managers conducted by CareerBuilder.com showed that unconventional methods are rising, with 22% of the managers seeing unusual tactics.

But do these unusual tactics work? In some cases. Only 9% of the hiring managers surveyed reported having hired someone who used an unconventional tactic to get noticed. However, most of the unusual tactics they list benefit the hiring company in some way: one candidate submitted a business plan for one of the company's products; another presented a solution to one of the company's problems. As you ponder your tactics, keep in mind that the other 91% of the people hired used standard techniques, including a strong application letter and a well-designed résumé.

> *"Remember that most innovative methods backfire."*

Remember that most innovative methods backfire. Take Nathan Schwagler. After delivering his résumé, he followed up a week later, only to find himself talking with the head of security: Schwagler had been barred from entering the premises or calling again. As one of his professors told him later, "The world is not ready for that type of creativity."

Sources: Rachel Zupek, "Unusual Job Search Tactics," CareerBuilder, accessed April 9, 2011, http://www.careerbuilder.com/article/cb-1076-job-search-unusual-job-search-tactics/; and "More Employers Seeing Unusual Tactics from Job Seekers in 2010, Finds New CareerBuilder Survey," CareerBuilder, June 9, 2010, http://www.careerbuilder.com/share/aboutus/pressreleasesdetail.aspx?id=pr574&sd=6/9/2010&ed=12/31/2010&siteid=cbpr&sc_cmp1=cb_pr574_.

Learning Objectives

After studying this chapter, you will know how to

LO 13-1 Find the information you need to write a good job letter to a specific employer.

LO 13-2 Write a job letter that makes you look attractive to employers.

Multiple Career Changes

You will probably need a cover letter as you change careers during your lifetime. One widely touted figure you may have heard many times is that U.S. workers average seven career changes during their working years.

Unfortunately, that number is a myth. It has been attributed to the U.S. Bureau of Labor Statistics so many times that the bureau now posts a disclaimer on its website.

The bureau does not estimate lifetime career changes for a simple reason: no consensus exists for the definition of a career change. If a worker takes a company promotion to move from being an active engineer to becoming a manager, is that a career change? Just a promotion? The work being done will certainly change. If someone laid off from her financial career takes a landscaping job for six months to pay bills before her next financial job comes along, is that a career change? Will it count as a double career change when she returns to finance?

Adapted from "National Longitudinal Surveys Frequently Asked Questions: Does BLS Have Information on the Number of Times People Change Careers in their Lives?" Bureau of Labor Statistics, last modified September 23, 2010, http://www.bls.gov/nls/nlsfaqs.htm.

The purpose of a job application letter is to get an interview. If you get a job through interviews arranged by your campus placement office or through contacts, you may not need to write a letter. Similarly, if you apply electronically through a company's website, a letter may not be part of the materials you submit. However, if you want to work for an organization that isn't interviewing on campus, or later when you change jobs, you may need a letter. A survey conducted by Robert Half International, the world's largest specialized staffing firm, found 86% of executives said cover letters were still valuable components of job applications in the electronic age.[1]

The co-founder of one software firm says,

> We ignore résumés. . . . Résumés reduce people to bullet points, and most people look pretty good as bullet points.
>
> What we do look at are cover letters. Cover letters say it all. They immediately tell you if someone wants this job or just any job. And cover letters make something else very clear: They tell you who can and who can't write. . . . When in doubt, always hire the better writer.[2]

Job letters can play an important role in your personal branding (p. 371). They can show your personality and, through careful reference to well-chosen details about the organization, interest in a particular job.

Job letters are frequently seen as evidence of your written communication skills, so you want to do your best work in them. Flaws in your letter may well be seen as predicting shoddy job performance in the future.

HOW CONTENT DIFFERS IN JOB LETTERS AND RÉSUMÉS

The job application letter accompanies your résumé and serves as its cover letter. Make the most of your letter; it is your chance to showcase the features that set you apart from the crowd. Here you bring to life the facts presented in your vita; here you can show some personality (don't overdo it). The cover letter is your opportunity to "sell" yourself into an interview.

Although résumés and job letters overlap somewhat, they differ in three important ways:

- The résumé summarizes *all* your qualifications. The letter expands your *best* qualifications to show how you can help the organization meet its needs, how you differ from other applicants, and how much knowledge of the organization you possess.
- The résumé avoids controversial material. The job letter can explain in a positive way situations such as career changes or gaps in employment history.
- The résumé uses short, parallel phrases and sentence fragments. The letter uses complete sentences in well-written paragraphs.

HOW TO FIND OUT ABOUT EMPLOYERS AND JOBS LO 13-1

To adapt your letter to a specific organization, you need information both about the employer and about the job itself. You'll need to know

- **The name and address of the person who should receive the letter.** To get this information, check the ad, call the organization, check its website, or check with your job search contacts. An advantage of calling is that you can find out what courtesy title (p. 69) the individual prefers and get current information.
- **What the organization does, and some facts about it.** Knowing the organization's larger goals enables you to show how your specific work will help the company meet its goals. Useful facts can include market share, new products or promotions, the kind of computer or manufacturing equipment it uses, plans for growth or downsizing, competitive position, challenges the organization faces, and the corporate culture (p. 91).
- **What the job itself involves.** Campus placement offices and web listings often have fuller job descriptions than appear in ads. Talk to friends who have graduated recently to learn what their jobs involve. Conduct information interviews to learn more about opportunities that interest you.

The websites listed in Figure 13.1 provide a wide range of information. For instance, the Forbes and Money sites have good financial news stories; prars.com is a good source for annual reports. As a consumer, you have probably already used the Better Business Bureau (bbb.org) site.

More specific information about companies can be found on their websites. To get specific financial data (and to see how the organization presents itself to the public), get the company's annual report from your library or the web. (Note: Only companies whose stock is publicly traded are required to issue annual reports. In this day of mergers and buyouts, many companies are owned by other companies. The parent company may be the only one to issue an annual report.) Recruiting notebooks at your campus placement office may provide information about training programs and career paths for new hires. To learn about new products, plans for growth, or solutions to industry challenges, read business newspapers such as the *Wall Street Journal*, business magazines such as *Fortune* or *Bloomberg BusinessWeek*, and trade journals.

Figure 13.1 Web Sources for Facts about Companies

Company Facts

http://www.jobbankinfo.org/
http://www.wetfeet.com/
http://www.forbes.com/
http://www.irin.com/tf/IRIN/home?path=/&host=irin.com&
http://www.corporateinformation.com/
http://www.vault.com/
http://www.stockmarketyellowpages.com/
http://www.prars.com/
http://money.cnn.com/
http://www.inc.com/inc5000/
http://www.bbb.org/
http://legacy.www.nypl.org/research/sibl/company/c2index.htm
http://www.lib.berkeley.edu/BUSI/
http://online.wsj.com/public/page/news-career-jobs.html

Salary Calculators

http://salaryexpert.com/
http://www.indeed.com/salary
http://www.payscale.com/
http://www.salary.com/mysalary.asp

Dream Jobs

A survey of over 6,000 employees found that nearly 85% said they were not in their dream jobs. According to survey results, having fun at work was the most important characteristic of a dream job (39%); making a difference in the world was second (17%).

Among the professionals, police and firefighters were the most likely to believe they held dream jobs (35%), followed by teachers (32%), real estate professionals (28%), and engineers (25%). Those least likely to believe they held dream jobs were workers in hotel and food services (9%), manufacturing (9%), and retail (10%).

What is your dream job?

Adapted from CareerBuilder.com, "National 'Dream Jobs' Survey Reveals Four out of Five U.S. Workers Are Still Searching for Their Dream Job," press release, January 25, 2007, http://www.careerbuilder.com/share/aboutus/pressreleasesdetail.aspx?id=pr347&sd=1/25/2007&ed=12/31/2007.

TAPPING INTO THE HIDDEN JOB MARKET

Many jobs are never advertised—and the number rises the higher on the job ladder you go. In fact, some authorities put the percentage of jobs that are not advertised as high as 80%.[3] Many new jobs come not from responding to an ad but from networking with personal contacts. Some of these jobs are created especially for a specific person. These unadvertised jobs are called the **hidden job market.** Information and referral interviews are two organized methods of networking.

Information Interviews

In an **information interview** you talk to someone who works in the area you hope to enter to find out what the day-to-day work involves and how you can best prepare to enter that field. An information interview can let you know whether or not you'd like the job, give you specific information that you can use to present yourself effectively in your résumé and application letter, and create a good image of you in the mind of the interviewer. If you present yourself positively, the interviewer may remember you when openings arise.

In an information interview, you might ask the following questions:

- How did you get started in this field?
- What have you been working on today?
- How do you spend your typical day?
- Have your duties changed a lot since you first started working here?
- What do you like best about your job? What do you like least?
- What do you think the future holds for this kind of work?
- What courses, activities, or jobs would you recommend as preparation for this kind of work?

To set up an information interview, you can phone or write an e-mail like the one in Figure 13.2. If you do e-mail, phone the following week to set up a specific time.

Referral Interviews

Referral interviews are interviews you schedule to learn about current job opportunities in your field. Sometimes an interview that starts out as an information interview turns into a referral interview.

A referral interview should give you information about the opportunities currently available in the area you're interested in, refer you to other people who can tell you about job opportunities, and enable the interviewer to see that you could make a contribution to his or her organization. Therefore, the goal of a referral interview is to put you face-to-face with someone who has the power to hire you: the president of a small company, the division vice president or branch manager of a big company, the director of the local office of a state or federal agency.

Start by scheduling interviews with people you know who may know something about that field—professors, co-workers, neighbors, friends, former classmates. Use your alumni website to get the names and phone numbers of alumni who now work where you would like to work. Talk to them to get advice about improving your résumé and about general job-hunting strategy, but also to get referrals to other people. In fact, go into the interview with the names of people you'd like to talk to. If the interviewer doesn't suggest anyone, say, "Do you think it would be a good idea for me to talk to——?"

Armed with a referral from someone you both know, you can call people with hiring power, and say, "So-and-so suggested I talk with you about

Figure 13.2 E-mail Requesting an Information Interview

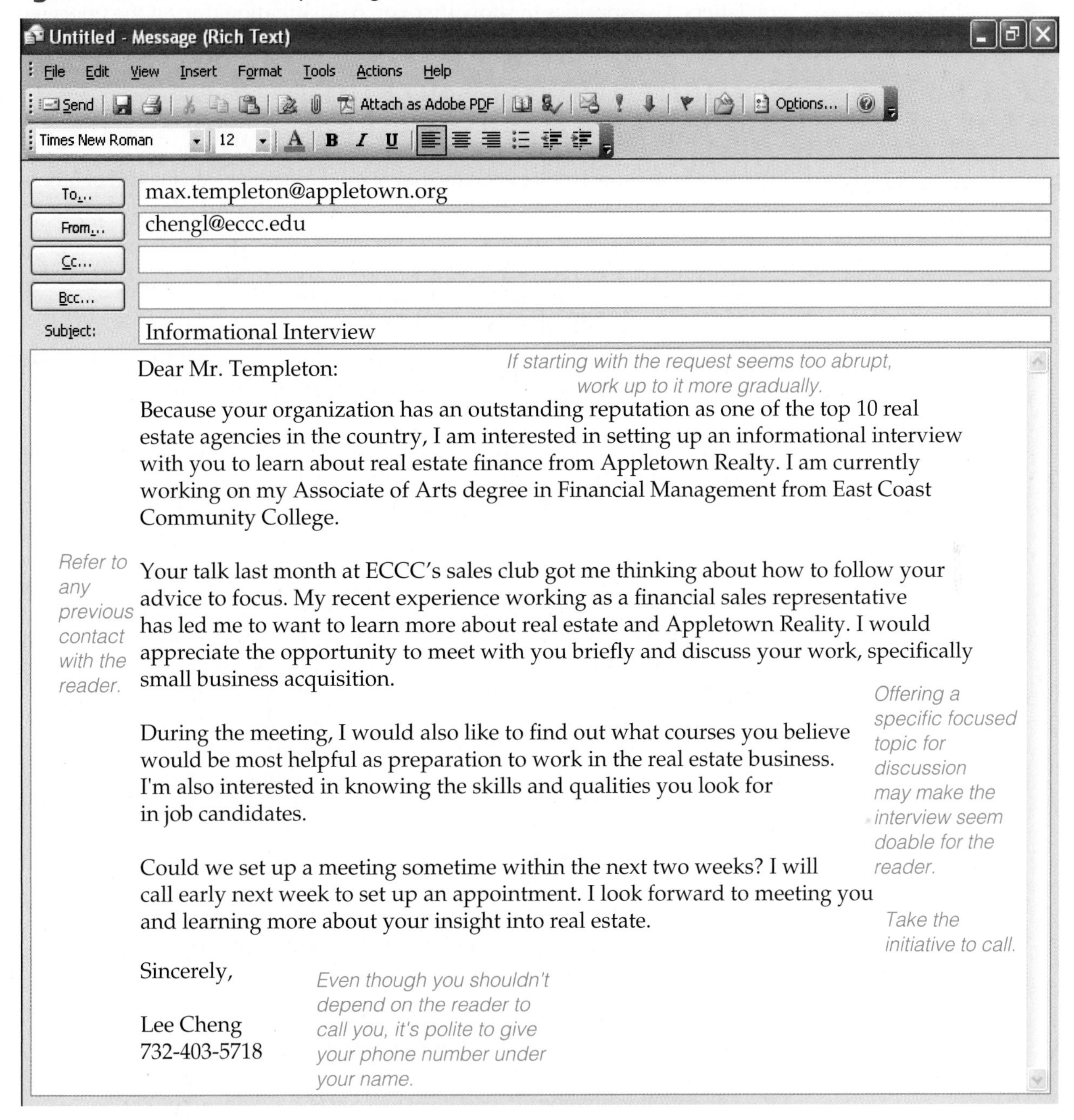
Untitled - Message (Rich Text)

File Edit View Insert Format Tools Actions Help

To... max.templeton@appletown.org
From... chengl@eccc.edu
Cc...
Bcc...
Subject: Informational Interview

Dear Mr. Templeton:

Because your organization has an outstanding reputation as one of the top 10 real estate agencies in the country, I am interested in setting up an informational interview with you to learn about real estate finance from Appletown Realty. I am currently working on my Associate of Arts degree in Financial Management from East Coast Community College.

Your talk last month at ECCC's sales club got me thinking about how to follow your advice to focus. My recent experience working as a financial sales representative has led me to want to learn more about real estate and Appletown Reality. I would appreciate the opportunity to meet with you briefly and discuss your work, specifically small business acquisition.

During the meeting, I would also like to find out what courses you believe would be most helpful as preparation to work in the real estate business. I'm also interested in knowing the skills and qualities you look for in job candidates.

Could we set up a meeting sometime within the next two weeks? I will call early next week to set up an appointment. I look forward to meeting you and learning more about your insight into real estate.

Sincerely,

Lee Cheng
732-403-5718

job-hunting strategy." Even when you talk to the person who could create a job for you, you *do not ask for a job.* But to give you advice about your résumé, the person has to look at it. If there's a match between what you can do and what the organization needs, that person has the power to create a position for you.

WARNING: Many businesspeople are cynical about information and referral interviewing; they know the real purpose of such interviews, and they resent the time needed. Therefore you need to prepare carefully for these interviews. Prepare a list of good questions; know something about the general field or industry; research the specific company.

http://www.google.com/about/corporate

Many websites give you all the information you need to write a good job letter. Google's Corporate Information page under Everything Google has links to jobs, news, company information and investor relations, where you will find financial information and annual reports. Follow the "Company" link to learn about topics such as Google's history, initiatives, and philosophy.

Always follow up information and referral interviews with personal thank-you letters. Use specifics to show that you paid attention during the interview, and enclose a copy of your revised résumé.

CONTENT AND ORGANIZATION FOR JOB APPLICATION LETTERS LO 13-2

Job letters help show employers why they should interview you instead of other—sometimes hundreds of others—qualified applicants. In your letter, focus on

- Your qualifications to meet major requirements of the job.
- Points that separate you from other applicants.
- Points that show your knowledge of the organization.
- Qualities that every employer is likely to value: the ability to write and speak effectively, to solve problems, to work well with people.

Two different hiring situations call for two different kinds of application letters. Write a **solicited letter** when you know that the company is hiring: you've seen an ad, you've been advised to apply by a professor or friend, you've read in a trade publication that the company is expanding. This situation is similar to a direct request in persuasion (p. 321): you can indicate immediately that you are applying for the position. Sometimes, however, the advertised positions may not be what you want, or you may want to work for an organization that has not announced openings in your area. Then you write a **prospecting letter.** (The metaphor is drawn from prospecting for gold.) The prospecting letter is like a problem-solving persuasive message (p. 323).

Prospecting letters help you tap into the hidden job market. In some cases, your prospecting letter may arrive at a company that has decided to hire but has not yet announced the job. In other cases, companies create positions to get a good person who is on the market. Even in a hiring freeze, jobs are sometimes created for specific individuals.

In both solicited and prospecting letters you should

- Address the letter to a specific person (a must for a prospecting letter).
- Indicate the specific position for which you're applying.
- Be specific about your qualifications.
- Show what separates you from other applicants.
- Show a knowledge of the company and the position.
- Refer to your résumé (which you would enclose with the letter).
- Ask for an interview.

The following discussion follows the job letter from beginning to end. The two kinds of letters are discussed separately where they differ and together where they are the same. Letters for internships follow the same patterns: use a solicited letter to apply for an internship that has been advertised and a prospecting letter to create an internship with a company that has not announced one.

How to Organize Solicited Letters

When you know the company is hiring, use the pattern of organization in Figure 13.3. A sample solicited letter for a graduating senior is shown in Figure 13.4. A solicited letter following up from a career fair and requesting an internship is shown in Figure 13.7. The job ad for the letter in Figure 13.4 is printed in Exercise 13.20.

Figure 13.3 How to Organize a Solicited Job Application Letter

1. State that you're applying for the job (phrase the job title as your source phrased it). Tell where you learned about the job (ad, referral, etc.). Include any reference number mentioned in the ad. Briefly show that you have the major qualifications required by the ad: a college degree, professional certification, job experience, etc. Summarize your other qualifications briefly in the same order in which you plan to discuss them in the letter.
2. Develop your major qualifications in detail. Be specific about what you've done; relate your achievements to the work you'd be doing in this new job.
3. Develop your other qualifications, even if the ad doesn't ask for them. Show what separates you from the other applicants who will also answer the ad. Demonstrate your knowledge of the organization.
4. Ask for an interview; tell when you'll be available to be interviewed and to begin work. Thank them for considering your application. End on a positive, forward-looking note.

Passion

[Lucinda B. Watson, career counselor and author of *How They Achieved: Stories of Personal Achievement and Business Success,* transcribes in her book an interview with Ted Bell, the former Vice Chairman and Worldwide Creative Director of Young and Rubicam. An excerpt:]

"My advice to young people is to just be passionate about whatever it is you do. Be the most passionate person in the room. Not the smartest or the cleverest, but the most passionate. Total passion. Say thank you. Say please. Don't take credit, take the blame. Do all that stuff, that's good. But if you are the most passionate person, you'll probably win. Care more about it than anybody and you'll be the one that wins. People love that. People gravitate toward that."

Quoted from Lucinda Watson, *How They Achieved: Stories of Personal Achievement and Business Success* (New York: John Wiley, 2001), 66.

How to Organize Prospecting Letters

When you don't have any evidence that the company is hiring, you cannot use the pattern for solicited letters. Instead, use the pattern of organization in Figure 13.5. A sample prospecting letter for a student desiring to change fields is shown in Figure 13.6.

First Paragraphs of Solicited Letters

When you know that the firm is hiring, announcing that you are applying for a specific position enables the firm to route your letter to the appropriate person, thus speeding consideration of your application. Identify where you learned about the job: "the position of junior accountant announced in Sunday's *Dispatch,*" "William Paquette, our placement director, told me that you are looking for. . . ."

Note how the following paragraph picks up several of the characteristics of the ad:

Ad: Business Education Instructor at Shelby Adult Education. Candidate must possess a Bachelor's degree in Business Education. Will be responsible for providing in-house training to business and government leaders. . . . Candidate should have at least one year teaching experience.

Letter: I am applying for your position in Business Education that is posted on your school website. In December, I will receive a Bachelor of Science degree from North Carolina A & T University in Business Education. My work has given me two years' experience teaching word processing and computer accounting courses to adults plus leadership skills developed in the North Carolina National Guard.

Your **summary sentence** or **paragraph** covers everything you will talk about and serves as an organizing device for your letter.

> Through my education, I have a good background in standard accounting principles and procedures and a working knowledge of some of the special accounting practices of the oil industry. This working knowledge is enhanced by practical experience in the oil fields: I have pumped, tailed rods, and worked as a roustabout.

> My business experience, familiarity with DeVilbiss equipment, and communication skills qualify me to be an effective part of the sales staff at DeVilbiss.

Figure 13.4 A Solicited Letter from a Graduating Senior

Jeff Moeller

831.503.4692
51 Willow Street
San José, CA 95112
jmoeller@csmb.edu

April 4, 2012

Mr. Richard Grove
Telltale Games
P.O. Box 9737
San Rafael, CA 94912

Dear Mr. Grove:

Tell where you learned about the job. If the job has a reference number, provide it.

In paragraph 1, show you have the qualifications the ad lists.

I am applying for your Game Designer position posted on your website. As an avid player of Telltale games, I believe that I have all the qualifications to do a great job. With my degree in Computer Science and Information Technology and my experience creating game content, I will be able to apply many skills to the Game Designer position. My passion for becoming part of the gaming industry, combined with my oral and written communication skills, makes me a great fit for the Telltale team.

This summary sentence forecasts the structure of the rest of the letter.

Shows enthusiasm for the profession and picks up on the programming experience emphasis in the job ad.

Since I was five, I have had a strong interest in computers and video games, and my interest and knowledge have only increased in recent years. Not only do I play video games, I discuss them with others, read news articles about them online, and consider ways to improve or change a specific game. I have also used game editors to create my own content in games. When it comes to computers, I have a keen interest in staying current with the latest technology, and I apply my knowledge hands-on by building systems. These experiences give me an understanding of how modern computers and video game systems function. I also have experience with several programming languages, from both taking courses and learning them on my own. This has increased my eye for detail, a necessary ability for any game designer.

Provides evidence for his achievements in the profession.

My passion for creating video games was recognized this year in President Obama's National STEM video game challenge. With a team of students in Professor Kent Olbernath's game development class at California State University, I produced "Parrot Villa," the first level of an immersive game where players solve mysteries on a unique jungle world. The programming quality and detailed story line helped my team earn second place in the nationwide competition.You can see a demo of "Parrot Villa" at www.STEMChallenge.gov/2011_Winners.

Relates what he has done to what he could do for the company.

Evidence of communication skills is a plus for almost any job.

Along with my enthusiasm for games, I have strong oral and written communication skills. I am a confident public speaker, and I have an ability to relay information in a clear and concise manner. More importantly, though, I have developed the ability in my creative writing courses to create engaging and coherent narratives, which will be a large component of developing new games. In addition to my coursework and experience, I have honed my skills online by writing articles about games. In covering the video game industry for Point Network, I have reviewed Telltale's own *Tales of Monkey Island.*

Shows familiarity with company's products.

Working in the video game industry is my goal, and I would be a great asset to Telltale Games. I would love to come in for an interview to discuss the position and the contributions I can make. I have always enjoyed playing Telltale's games, and I look forward to the possibility of working on them one day soon.

Sincerely,

Jeff Moeller

Jeff Moeller

Figure 13.5 How to Organize a Prospecting Letter

1. Catch the reader's interest.
2. Create a bridge between the attention-getter and your qualifications. Focus on what you know and can do. Since the employer is not planning to hire, he or she won't be impressed with the fact that you're graduating. Summarize your qualifications briefly in the same order in which you plan to discuss them in the letter. This summary sentence or paragraph then covers everything you will talk about and serves as an organizing device for your letter.
3. Develop your strong points in detail. Be specific. Relate what you've done in the past to what you could do for this company. Show that you know something about the company. Identify the specific niche you want to fill.
4. Ask for an interview and tell when you'll be available for interviews. (Don't tell when you can begin work.) Thank them for considering your application. End on a positive, forward-looking note.

Jocks Rock in the Workplace

Some employers are seeking athletes to fill jobs because athletes possess qualities which lead to success in the workplace. For example Gretchen Tonnesen, former flying halfback captain for the Princeton University women's rugby team, now works at JP Morgan Chase & Co. where she examines technology, media, and telecommunications companies for the investment bank. JP Morgan chose her because of her passionate involvement in sports.

Recruiters and employers recognize that college athletes provide leadership, competitiveness, and a sharp focus on goals. Athletes also understand team responsibility, time management, and dedication. In addition, athletes from top schools typically have the drive and stamina that matches the 80-hour high pressure workweeks found in many Wall Street jobs.

By the way, Tonnesen got her job through the Alumni Athlete Network, founded by a Harvard basketball captain. The carefully selected students in the Network's program have average GPAs of 3.6 and average SAT scores of 1320.

How can you capitalize on your extracurricular activities to help your job search?

Adapted from John DeBruicker, "If You're A Jock, You Rock," *BusinessWeek*, September 18, 2006, 67.

First Paragraphs of Prospecting Letters

In a prospecting letter, asking for a job in the first paragraph is dangerous: unless the company plans to hire but has not yet announced openings, the reader is likely to throw the letter away. Instead, catch the reader's interest. Then in the second paragraph you can shift the focus to your skills and experience, showing how they can be useful to the employer and specifying the job you are seeking.

Here are some effective first and second paragraphs that provide a transition to the writer's discussion of his or her qualifications.

First two paragraphs of a letter to the director of publications at an oil company:

> If scarcity of resources makes us use them more carefully, perhaps it would be a good idea to ration words. If people used them more carefully, internal communications specialists like you would have fewer headaches because communications jobs would be done right the first time.
>
> For the last six years I have worked on improving my communications skills, learning to use words more carefully and effectively. I have taught business communication at a major university, worked for two newspapers, completed a Master's degree in English, and would like to contribute my skills to your internal communications staff.

First two paragraphs of a letter applying to be a computer programmer for an insurance company:

> As you know, merging a poorly written letter with a database of customers just sends out bad letters more quickly. But you also know how hard it is to find people who can both program computers and write well.
>
> My education and training have given me this useful combination. I'd like to put my associate's degree in computer technology and my business experience writing to customers to work in State Farm's service approach to insurance.

Notice how the second paragraph provides a transition to a discussion of qualifications.

Questions work well only if the answers aren't obvious. The computer programmer above should *not* ask this question:

> Do you think that training competent and motivated personnel is a serious concern in the insurance industry?

Figure 13.6 A Prospecting Letter from a Career Changer

Molly Schooner
www.ukansas.edu/~Schoonerm88/home.htm

266 Van Buren Drive
Lawrence, KS 66044
schoonerm@ukansas.edu
785-897-1534 (home)
785-842-4242 (cell)

Molly uses a "letterhead" that hamonizes with her résumé. (see Figure 12.7)

March 29, 2012

Mr. Franklin Kohl
PDF Productions
3232 White Castle Road
Minneapolis, MN 85434

In a prospecting letter, open with a sentence which (1) will seem interesting and true to the reader and (2) provides a natural bridge to talking about yourself.

Dear Mr. Kohl:

The Wall Street Journal says that PDF Productions is expanding operations into Kansas, Minnesota, and Nebraska. My experience in technical writing, design, and computers would be an asset to your expanding organization.

Shows knowledge of the organization.

While working at a local animal shelter, I used my technical writing skills to create a website that allows users to easily access information. To improve the website, I conducted usability tests which provided useful feedback that I incorporated to modify the overall design. In addition, I was also responsible for writing and editing the shelter's monthly newsletter, which was distributed to roughly 1,200 "Friends of the Shelter." I have extensive computer and design skills, which I am anxious to put to use for PDF Productions.

Briefly shows a variety of technical writing and computer skills.

Course work has also prepared me well for technical writing. I have written technical material on a variety of levels ranging from publicity flyers for the animal shelter to scientific reports for upper-level science courses. My course work in statistics has shown me how to work with data and present it accurately for various audiences. Because of my scientific background, I also have a strong vocabulary in both life sciences and chemistry. This background will help me get up to speed quickly with clients such as ChemPro and Biostage. My background in science has also taught me just how important specific details can be.

Shows how her course-work is an asset.

Relates what she's done to what she could do for this company.

Names specific clients, showing more knowledge of company.

In May, I will complete my degree from the University of Kansas and will be most interested in making a significant contribution to PDF Productions. I am available every Monday, Wednesday, and Friday for an interview (785-897-1534). Thank you for considering my appliction. I look forward to talking with you about technical writing I can do for PDF Productions.

Sincerely,

Molly Schooner

Molly Schooner

Figure 13.7 Letter Following Up from a Career Fair and Requesting an Internship

Lee Cheng
chengl@eccc.edu

Campus Address
1524 Main Street
New Brunswick, NJ 08901
732-403-5718

Letterhead matches his résumé.

Permanent Address
2526 Prairie Lane
Middlesex, NJ 08846
402-442-7793

January 23, 2012

Ms. Deborah Pascel, HR Department
Prime Financial
401 Prime Park Place
New Brunswick, NJ 08901

Dear Ms. Pascel:

Uses his contact immediately.

Mary Randi at the East Coastal Community College Career Fair suggested I send you my résumé for the Sales Advisor internship. My education, combined with my past work experiences, makes me a strong candidate for Prime Financial.

Shows he has been getting full value from his schooling.

While working toward my Associate of Arts degree in Financial Management from East Coastal Community College, I have learned the value of fiscal responsibility. For example, in my social financial planning course, I developed a strategic plan to eliminate credit card debt for a one-income household with two children. Moreover, in my business communication course, I improved my oral communication ability so that I could effectively communicate my plans to potential clients. This ability will be an asset to Prime Financial as the organization works to maintain the strong relationship with the community and small business owners that Ms. Randi informed me about.

Refers to knowledge gained at career fair.

Paragraphs 2 and 3 show he has skills he can use immediately as an intern.

My financial education, combined with my previous work experiences in sales, will allow me to thoroughly analyze investment opportunities and establish a strong client base for Prime Financial. For example, I started the A-Plus T-Shirt Company that sold graphic T-shirts to high school students; it had a routine client base of over 150 customers. From managing this business, I know what it takes to be reliable and responsive to customer needs. I am looking forward to learning new approaches from Prime Financial's internship, particularly new ways to work with small businesses.

Provides details about his sales experience to interest his reader.

With my education and experience, I can provide the innovative and competitive edge necessary to be part of your team. I would welcome an interview to discuss your internship and the contributions I could make at Prime Financial.

Sincerely,

Lee Cheng

Lee Cheng

Unfortunate Cover Letter Statements

- "Please find my résumé." Did you look under the couch?
- "I have integrity so I will not steal office supplies and take them home." Good to know.
- "Please, please, please hire me for this job. I will be waiting by the phone." Don't wait too long.
- "What interested me about this job is that it's with a prestigious company." Glad to hear it.
- "After perusing my résumé, I am looking forward to hearing from you soon." If you don't mind, we'd appreciate the opportunity to peruse it ourselves before we get back to you.
- "I'm submitting the attached copy of my résumé for your consumption." Yum.
- "I perform my job with effortless efficiency, effectiveness, efficacy, and expertise." And an awful lot of alliteration, apparently.
- "The interview you schedule will undoubtedly reveal my unmatched talent and suitability for the position." Uh, don't count your chickens. . . .
- "But wait . . . there's more. You get all this business knowledge plus a grasp of finance that is second nature." If I act now, will you throw in a set of kitchen knives?

Quoted from "Resumania Archive," Resumania, accessed March 20, 2011, http://www.resumania.com/ResumaniaArchive.

If the reader says *yes,* the question will seem dumb. If the reader says *no,* the student has destroyed his or her common ground. The computer programmer, however, could pose this question:

> How often do you see a programmer with both strong programming skills and good communication skills?

This question would give him or her an easy transition into paragraphs about his/her programming and communication skills.

Showing a Knowledge of the Position and the Company

If you could substitute another inside address and salutation and send out the letter without any further changes, it isn't specific enough. A job application letter is basically a claim that you could do a specific job for a particular company. Use your knowledge of the position and the company to choose relevant evidence from what you've done to support your claims that you could help the company. (See Figures 13.4 and 13.6.)

The following paragraphs show the writer's knowledge of the company.

A letter to PricewaterhouseCoopers's Minneapolis office uses information the student learned in a referral interview with a partner in an accounting firm. Because the reader will know that Herr Wollner is a partner in the Berlin office, the student does not need to identify him.

> While I was studying in Berlin last spring, I had the opportunity to discuss accounting methods for multinational clients of PricewaterhouseCoopers with Herr Fritz Wollner. We also talked about communication among PricewaterhouseCoopers's international offices.
>
> Herr Wollner mentioned that the increasing flow of accounting information between the European offices—especially those located in Germany, Switzerland, and Austria—and the U.S. offices of PricewaterhouseCoopers makes accurate translations essential. My fluency in German enables me to translate accurately; and my study of communication problems in Speech Communication, Business and Professional Speaking, and Business and Technical Writing will help me see where messages might be misunderstood and choose words which are more likely to communicate clearly.

A letter to KMPG uses information the student learned in a summer job.

> As an assistant accountant for Pacific Bell during this past summer, I worked with its computerized billing and record-keeping system, BARK. I had the opportunity to help the controller revise portions of the system, particularly the procedures for handling delinquent accounts. When the KMPG audit team reviewed Pacific Bell's transactions completed for July, I had the opportunity to observe your System 2170. Several courses in computer science allow me to appreciate the simplicity of your system and its objective of reducing audit work, time, and costs.

One or two specific details about the company usually are enough to demonstrate your knowledge. Be sure to use the knowledge, not just repeat it. Never present the information as though it will be news to the reader. After all, the reader works for the company and presumably knows much more about it than you do.

Showing What Separates You from Other Applicants

Your knowledge of the company can separate you from other applicants. You can also use coursework, an understanding of the field, and experience in jobs and extracurricular events to show that you're unique. Stress your accomplishments, not your job responsibilities. Be specific but concise; usually three to five sentences will enable you to give enough specific supporting details.

This student uses both coursework and summer jobs to set herself apart from other applicants. Her research told her Monsanto had recently adopted new accounting methods for fluctuations in foreign currencies. Therefore, she mentions relevant simulations from her coursework.

> My college courses have taught me the essential accounting skills required to contribute to the growth of Monsanto. In two courses in international accounting, I compiled simulated accounting statements of hypothetical multinational firms in countries experiencing different rates of currency devaluation. Through these classes, I acquired the skills needed to work with the daily fluctuations of exchange rates and at the same time formulate an accurate and favorable representation of Monsanto.
>
> Both my summer jobs and my coursework prepare me to do extensive record keeping as well as numerous internal and external communications. As Office Manager for the steamboat *Julia Belle Swain*, I was in charge of most of the bookkeeping and letter writing for the company. I kept accurate records for each workday, and I often entered over 100 transactions in a single day. In business communication I learned how to write persuasive messages and how to present extensive data in reports in a simplified style that is clear and easy to understand.

In your résumé, you may list activities, offices, and courses. In your letter, give more detail about what you did and show how those experiences will help you contribute to the employer's organization more quickly.

When you discuss your strengths, don't exaggerate. No employer will believe that a new graduate has a "comprehensive" knowledge of a field. Indeed, most employers believe that six months to a year of on-the-job training is necessary before most new hires are really earning their pay. Specifics about what you've done will make your claims about what you can do more believable and ground them in reality.

Study Abroad and Overseas Work Programs

Have you considered a studies abroad program or international job?

If so, a variety of resources are available. These websites offer assistance for students interested in study abroad programs:

http://www.ciee.org/

http://studyabroad.com/

http://iiepassport.org/

For information regarding full-time overseas opportunities, visit the following websites:

http://www.monster.com/geo/siteselection/

http://www.jobsabroad.com/search.cfm

http://transitionsabroad.com/

The Last Paragraph

In the last paragraph, indicate when you'd be available for an interview. If you're free anytime, you can say so. But it's likely that you have responsibilities in class and work. If you'd have to go out of town, there may be only certain days of the week or certain weeks that you could leave town for several days. Use a sentence that fits your situation.

> November 5–10 I'll be attending the Oregon Forestry Association's annual meeting and will be available for interviews then.

> Any Monday or Friday I could come to Memphis for an interview.

Email Horror Story

"I sent a digital resume and cover letter via email to apply for a position as a technical writer. Within a few hours, a message from the director in charge of hiring came via email. Full of anticipation, I opened the email to find a terse message: 'your resume is infected with a virus and has been quarantined.' A person cannot recover from an infected resume. I did not pursue the position further."

Quoted from "Horror Stories," ResumeEdge.com, accessed April 5, 2011, http://www.resumeedge.com/contentpartners/interviews13.html.

Should you wait for the employer to call you, or should you call the employer to request an interview? In a solicited letter, it's safe to wait to be contacted: you know the employer wants to hire someone, and if your letter and résumé show that you're one of the top applicants, you'll get an interview. In a prospecting letter, call the employer. Because the employer is not planning to hire, you'll get a higher percentage of interviews if you're assertive.

If you're writing a prospecting letter to a firm that's more than a few hours away by car, say that you'll be in the area the week of such-and-such and could stop by for an interview. Companies pay for follow-up visits, but not for first interviews. A company may be reluctant to ask you to make an expensive trip when it isn't yet sure it wants to hire you.

End the letter on a positive note that suggests you look forward to the interview and that you see yourself as a person who has something to contribute, not as someone who just needs a job.

> I look forward to discussing with you ways in which I could contribute to The Limited's continued growth.

Do not end your letter with a variation of the negative cliché "Please do not hesitate to contact me." Why do you think they would hesitate? Also avoid this other tired cliche: "Thank you for your time." Using an overworked ending dumps you right back in the pool with all the other applicants.

Oh yes, one more thing. Don't forget to sign your letter—with blue or black ink—legibly.

E-MAIL APPLICATION LETTERS

You will probably e-mail most of your applications. If your application is solicited, you can paste your traditional letter into your e-mail. If your application is prospecting, you need a shorter letter that will catch the reader's attention within the first screen (see Figure 13.8). Your first paragraph is crucial; use it to hook the reader.

Some experts are starting to recommend a shorter letter for both situations, but many caution that you need to include enough information to make you, not one of the numerous other applicants, the person for the job. Frequently that is hard to do in one screen.

When you submit an e-mail letter with your résumé,

- Include your name as part of the subject line.
- Put the job number or title for which you're applying in the first paragraph.
- Prepare your letter in a word-processing program. Use a spell checker to make it easier to edit and proof the document; then paste it into the e-mail.
- Use standard business letter features: salutation, standard closing, single-spacing with double-spacing between paragraphs.
- Keep line length to a maximum of 65 characters, including spaces, so receivers won't get a strange mixture of long and short lines.
- Don't put anything in all capital letters.
- Don't use smiley faces or other emotions.
- Put your name at the end of the message.

Figure 13.8 An E-mail with Application Letter and Résumé

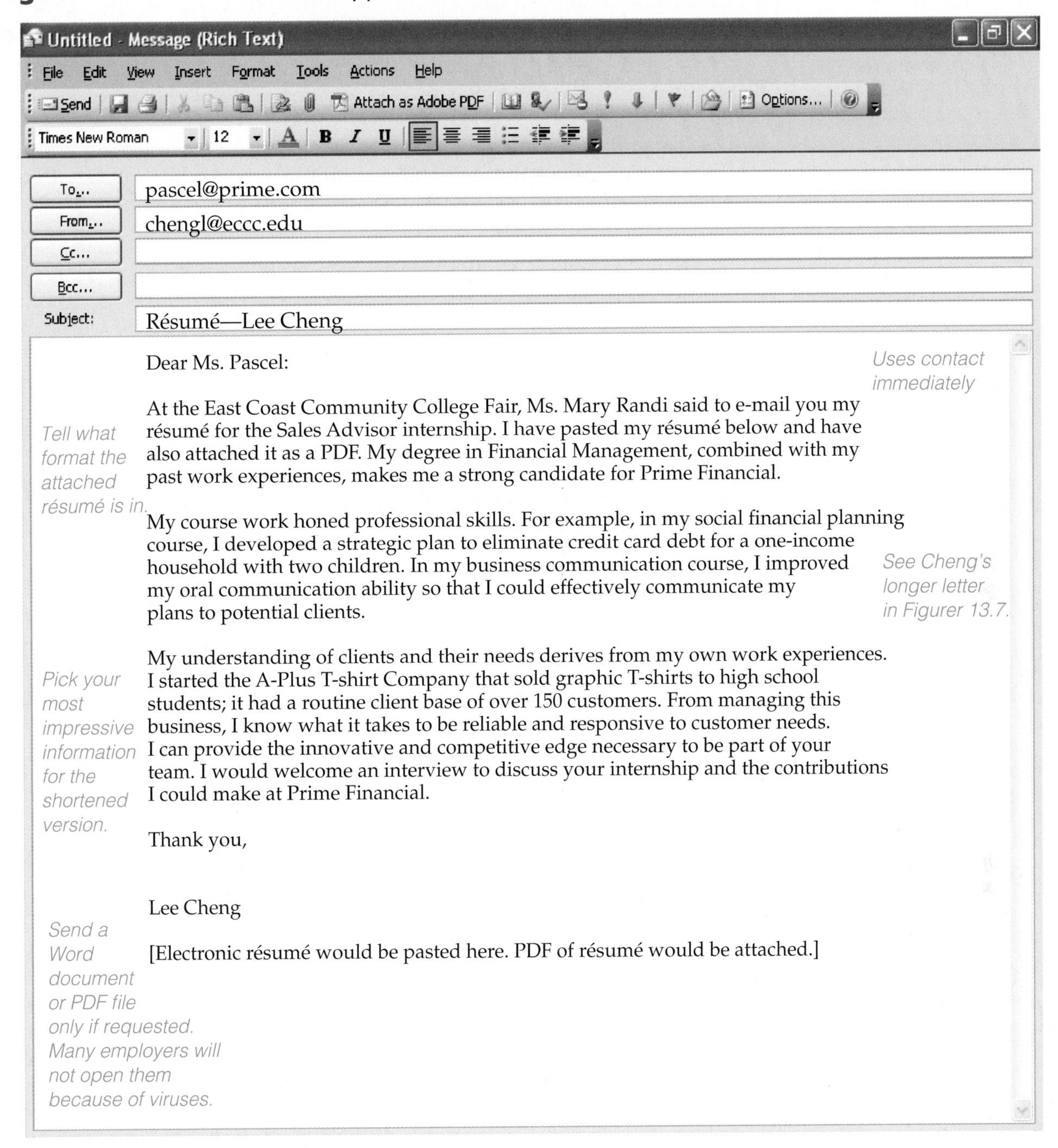
Untitled - Message (Rich Text)

File Edit View Insert Format Tools Actions Help

Send Attach as Adobe PDF Options...

Times New Roman 12

To... pascel@prime.com

From... chengl@eccc.edu

Cc...

Bcc...

Subject: Résumé—Lee Cheng

Dear Ms. Pascel:

At the East Coast Community College Fair, Ms. Mary Randi said to e-mail you my résumé for the Sales Advisor internship. I have pasted my résumé below and have also attached it as a PDF. My degree in Financial Management, combined with my past work experiences, makes me a strong candidate for Prime Financial.

My course work honed professional skills. For example, in my social financial planning course, I developed a strategic plan to eliminate credit card debt for a one-income household with two children. In my business communication course, I improved my oral communication ability so that I could effectively communicate my plans to potential clients.

My understanding of clients and their needs derives from my own work experiences. I started the A-Plus T-shirt Company that sold graphic T-shirts to high school students; it had a routine client base of over 150 customers. From managing this business, I know what it takes to be reliable and responsive to customer needs. I can provide the innovative and competitive edge necessary to be part of your team. I would welcome an interview to discuss your internship and the contributions I could make at Prime Financial.

Thank you,

Lee Cheng

[Electronic résumé would be pasted here. PDF of résumé would be attached.]

Follow all guidelines posted by the company. Do not add attachments unless you know doing so is OK. Test your e-mail by sending it to a friend; have your friend recheck it for appearance and correctness.

CREATING A PROFESSIONAL IMAGE

Every employer wants businesslike employees who understand professionalism. To make your application letter professional,

You(r) Attitude Matters

If you find getting a job difficult, your attitude may be the reason. Here are four common career-blocking attitudes and responses to them:

Attitude:	I deserve a good job because I went to school for four years.
Response:	Employers are looking for who is best for a job, not who "deserves" a job.
Attitude:	I am open to any job. I have no idea what I want to do.
Response:	Employers want workers who are focused.
Attitude:	I don't have experience because no one will give me a chance.
Response:	Employers do not employ people to give them a "chance." Employers are concerned with what an applicant can do for them.
Attitude:	I am so down on myself that it's hard to keep looking for a job.
Response:	Get professional help, because this attitude is poisonous to your life as well as your career.

Adapted from Peter Vogt, "Self-Defeating Attitudes Will Stop Your Job Search Cold," Monster.com, accessed April 8, 2011, http://career-advice.monster.com/job-search/getting-started/self-defeating-attitudes-job-search/article.aspx.

- Create your letter in a word-processing program so you can use features such as spell check. Use a standard font such as Times New Roman, Arial, or Helvetica in 12-point type.
- Address your letter to a specific person. If the reader is a woman, call the office to find out what courtesy title she prefers.
- Don't mention relatives' names. It's OK to use names of other people if the reader knows those people and thinks well of them, if they think well of you and will say good things about you, and if you have permission to use their names.
- Omit personal information not related to the job.
- Unless you're applying for a creative job in advertising, use a conservative style: few contractions; no sentence fragments, clichés, or slang.
- Edit the letter carefully and proof it several times to make sure it's perfect. Errors suggest that you're careless or inept. Double-check the spelling of the receiver's name.
- Print on the same paper (both shade and weight) you used for your résumé. Envelopes should match, too.
- Use a computer to print the envelope address.

Writing Style

Use a smooth, concise writing style (Chapter 5). Use the technical jargon of the field to show your training, but avoid businessese and stuffy words like *utilize, commence,* and *transpire* (for *happen*). Use a lively, energetic style that makes you sound like a real person.

Avoid words that can be interpreted sexually. A model letter distributed by the placement office at a midwestern university included the following sentence:

> I have been active in campus activities and have enjoyed good relations with my classmates and professors.

Sentences like this get shared for laughs; that's not the kind of attention you want to get!

Be sure your letter uses the exact language of the job ad and addresses all items included in the ad. If the ad mentions teamwork, your letter should give examples of teamwork; don't shift the vocabulary to collaboration. Many readers expect their job ad language in applicants' letters. If the language is not there, they may judge the applicant as not fitting the position. And so may their computer, since the vocabulary of the job ad probably contains crucial key words for the computer to find.

Positive Emphasis

Be positive. Don't plead ("Please give me a chance") or apologize ("I cannot promise that I am substantially different from the lot"). Most negatives should be omitted from the letter.

Avoid word choices with negative connotations (see Chapter 3). Note how the following revisions make the writer sound more confident.

Negative: I have learned an excessive amount about writing through courses in journalism and advertising.

Positive:	Courses in journalism and advertising have taught me to recognize and to write good copy. My profile of a professor was published in the campus newspaper; I earned an "A +" on my direct mail campaign for the American Dental Association to persuade young adults to see their dentist more often.

Excessive suggests that you think the courses covered too much—hardly an opinion likely to endear you to an employer.

Negative:	You can check with my references to verify what I've said.
Positive:	Professor Hill can give you more information about my work on his national survey.

Verify suggests that you expect the employer to distrust what you've said.

You-Attitude

Unsupported claims may sound overconfident, selfish, or arrogant. Create you-attitude (Chapter 3) by describing accomplishments and by showing how they relate to what you could do for this employer.

Lacks you-attitude:	An inventive and improvising individual like me is a necessity in your business.
You-attitude:	Building a summer house-painting business gave me the opportunity to find creative solutions to challenges. At the end of the first summer, for example, I had nearly 10 gallons of exterior latex left, but no more jobs. I contacted the home economics teacher at my high school. She agreed to give course credit to students who were willing to give up two Saturdays to paint a house being renovated by Habitat for Humanity. I donated the paint and supervised the students. I got a charitable deduction for the paint and hired the three best students to work for me the following summer. I could put these skills in problem solving and supervising to work as a personnel manager for Burroughs.

Show what you can do for them, not what they can do for you.

Lacks you-attitude:	A company of your standing could offer the challenging and demanding kind of position in which my abilities could flourish.
You-attitude:	Omit.

Remember that the word *you* refers to your reader. Using *you* when you really mean yourself or "all people" can insult your reader by implying that he or she still has a lot to learn about business:

Lacks you-attitude:	Running my own business taught me that you need to learn to manage your time.
You-attitude:	Running my own business taught me to manage my time.

Beware of telling readers information they already know as though they do not know it. This practice can also be considered insulting.

Lacks you-attitude:	Your company has just purchased two large manufacturing plants in France.
You-attitude:	My three college French courses would help me communicate in your newly acquired French manufacturing facilities.

Since you're talking about yourself, you'll use *I* in your letter. Reduce the number of *I*s by revising some sentences to use *me* or *my*.

Under my presidency, the Agronomy Club . . .
Courses in media and advertising management gave me a chance to . . .
My responsibilities as a summer intern included . . .

In particular, avoid beginning every paragraph with *I*. Begin sentences with prepositional phrases or introductory clauses:

As my résumé shows, I . . .
In my coursework in media and advertising management, I . . .
As a summer intern, I . . .
While I was in Italy, . . .

Paragraph Length and Unity

Keep your first and last paragraphs fairly short—preferably no more than four or five typed lines. Vary paragraph length within the letter; it's OK to have one long paragraph, but don't use a series of eight-line paragraphs.

When you have a long paragraph, check to be sure that it covers only one subject. If it covers two or more subjects, divide it into two or more paragraphs.

Use topic sentences at the beginning of your paragraphs to make your letter more readable.

Letter Length

Have at least three paragraphs. A short letter throws away an opportunity to be persuasive; it may also suggest that you have little to say for yourself or that you aren't very interested in the job.

Without eliminating content, tighten each sentence (Chapter 5) to be sure that you're using words as efficiently as possible. If your letter is a bit over a page, use slightly smaller margins or a type size that's one point smaller to get more on the page.

If you have excellent material that will not fit on one page, use it—as long as you have at least 6–12 lines of body text on the second page. The extra space gives you room to be more specific about what you've done and to add details about your experience that will separate you from other applicants. Employers don't *want* longer letters, but they will read them *if* the letter is well written and *if* the applicant establishes early in the letter that he or she has the credentials the company needs. Remember, however, that the trend is toward shorter letters.

Editing and Proofreading

Be sure you edit and proofread your cover letter. Failure to do so can undo all the work you put into it. The web abounds with humorous examples of spelling errors making unintended statements (I'm excellent at spelling and grammer). In fact, some companies post the best bloopers on their web sites. For example, Robert Half International maintains Resumania (resumania.com); Killian Branding, an advertising agency, has "Cover Letters from Hell" on their website (www.killianbranding.com/cover-letters-from-hell/): the "poetic" Night-before-Christmas cover letter is amazing.

Check your content one last time to ensure that everything presents you as a hard-working professional. Make sure you are not revealing any frustration with the job search process in your content or diction. Check your tone to see that it is positive about your previous experiences and yourself. Don't beg or show too much gratitude for commonplaces such as reading your letter.

Follow-Up

Follow up with the employer once if you hear nothing after two or three weeks. It is also OK to ask once after one week if e-mail materials were received. If your job letter was prospecting, it is fine to follow up two or three times. Do not make a pest of yourself, however, by calling or e-mailing too often; doing so could eliminate you from further consideration.

Fatal Spelling Errors

These spelling errors occurred in actual cover letters:

- "I feel my rigorous education and subsequent internship have prepared me for any obstical I might encounter." Except the challenge of finding misspelled words.
- "I prefer a fast-paste work environment." For life's stickiest situations.
- "I am very interested in the newspaper add for the accounting position." And we're divided on your qualifications.
- "I am extremely detailoriented." I'm afraid we're not convinced.
- Name on letterhead: "Sam Mevlin"; Signature: "Sam Melvin" Would the real Sam please come forward?

Robert Half International, "Cover Letter Statements," accessed March 20, 2011, http://www.resumania.com/ResumaniaArchive.

APPLICATION ESSAYS

Some jobs and internships, and many scholarship and graduate school applications, ask for an application essay. In a sense, this essay is an extended cover letter, but one written in an essay format rather than letter format. It will detail your strengths for the job/internship/scholarship/graduate school slot and show why you should be chosen instead of other applicants.

The essay offers you a chance to expand on your best points in more detail than does a cover letter. In so doing, you need to capture your readers' attention and show that you are exceptional. Frequently this means you need to put some of your personality into your essay. Here you can spell out with more interesting details skills you have already acquired from previous experiences and will bring to the new job or internship. Here you can elaborate on your academic achievements so you seem worthy of a scholarship or able to thrive in the rigors of graduate school. You can also expand more on general skills such as communication, critical thinking, and teamwork. Show that you are capable, hard working, and interesting.

The essay also gives you room to include content that you would not put in a cover letter. For instance, you might want to include an anecdote that shows something about you as a developing professional (hint: make it interesting but not melodramatic). Or you might talk some about future goals. How did you arrive at these goals? How would this internship advance your career goals? Why do you want to go to graduate school? What do you want to do after the internship, scholarship, or graduate career is over?

WARNING: Be careful when giving goals for job application essays. You do not want your goals to make the job seem like a quick steppingstone to better opportunities.

Remember to use the good writing techniques you have learned in this course and your other communication classes.

- Follow the directions, especially word and page limits, precisely. If the essay is to respond to a question, make sure it answers the question.
- Have a focal point for your essay, a unifying theme. This will help prevent you from merely listing accomplishments (your résumé did that).
- Start your essay with an interesting paragraph to catch attention. Do not summarize your essay, or your reader may go no further.
- Remember your audience. Show what you can do for this company, or why you want to go to this particular graduate school. But most of all, show what's in it for them if they accept you.

- Use vivid details in the body of the essay. They don't have to be wildly creative for a job essay; showing how you cut production time for the department newsletter by 15% will be interesting to your reader if the job is a good fit for you.
- Use some unique details. If your sentence could be used in many other applications, it is not showing why *you* should get the internship/job/scholarship/graduate school slot.
- Avoid unsupported generalities and clichés.
- Use topic sentences at the beginnings of your paragraphs. Remember these essays are frequently read quickly.
- Let your word choice reveal your personal voice. Since the essay is about you, it's fine to use some first person. Avoid thesaurus diction.
- End with a strong concluding paragraph. Remember, this is their last impression of you. Do not waste it on a boring summary of a one-page essay.

SUMMARY OF KEY POINTS

- Résumés differ from letters of application in the following ways:
  - The résumé summarizes all your qualifications. The letter expands your best qualifications to show how you can help the organization meet its needs, how you differ from other applicants, and that you have some knowledge of the organization.
  - The résumé avoids controversial material. The letter can explain in positive ways situations such as gaps in employment history.
  - The résumé uses short, parallel phrases and sentence fragments. The letter uses complete sentences in well-written paragraphs.
- Information and referral interviews can help you tap into the **hidden job market**—jobs that are not advertised. In an **information interview** you find out what the day-to-day work involves and how you can best prepare to enter that field. **Referral interviews** are interviews you schedule to learn about current job opportunities in your field.
- When you know that a company is hiring, send a **solicited job letter.** When you want a job with a company that has not announced openings, send a **prospecting job letter.** In both letters, you should
  - Address the letter to a specific person.
  - Indicate the specific position for which you're applying.
  - Be specific about your qualifications.
  - Show what separates you from other applicants.
  - Show a knowledge of the company and the position.
  - Refer to your résumé (which you would enclose with the letter).
  - Ask for an interview.
- Use your knowledge of the company, your coursework, your understanding of the field, and your experience in jobs and extracurricular activities to show that you're unique.
- Don't repeat information that the reader already knows; don't seem to be lecturing the reader on his or her business.

- Use positive emphasis to sound confident. Use you-attitude by supporting general claims with specific examples and by relating what you've done to what the employer needs.
- Have at least three paragraphs in your letter. Most job letters are only one page.
- Application essays give you a chance to expand on your best points and show your personality.

CHAPTER 13 Exercises and Problems

*Go to www.mhhe.com/locker10e for additional Exercises and Problems.

13.1 Reviewing the Chapter

1. What are three ways that job letters differ from résumés? (LO 13-2)
2. What are some ways to research specific employers? (LO 13-1)
3. What is the difference between information and referral interviews? (LO 13-1)
4. What are the differences between solicited and prospecting letters? (LO 13-2)
5. What are five tips for writing a job letter that makes you look attractive to employers? (LO 13-2)
6. What are 10 ways to create a professional image with your letter? (LO 13-2)

13.2 Reviewing Grammar

As you have read, it is crucial that your job letter be error-free. One common error in job letters, and one that spell-checking programs will not catch, is confusing word pairs like *affect/effect.* Practice choosing the correct word with Exercises B.12, B.13, and B.14 in Appendix B.

13.3 Analyzing First Paragraphs of Prospecting Letters

All of the following are first paragraphs in prospecting letters written by new college graduates. Evaluate the paragraphs on these criteria:

- Is the paragraph likely to interest readers and motivate them to read the rest of the letter?
- Does the paragraph have some content that the student can use to create a transition to talking about his or her qualifications?
- Does the paragraph avoid asking for a job?

1. For the past two and one-half years I have been studying turf management. On August 1, I will graduate from —— University with a BA in Ornamental Horticulture. The type of job I will seek will deal with golf course maintenance as an assistant superintendent.
2. Ann Gibbs suggested that I contact you.
3. Each year, the Christmas shopping rush makes more work for everyone at Nordstrom's, especially for the Credit Department. While working for Nordstrom's Credit Department for three Christmas and summer vacations, the Christmas sales increase is just one of the credit situations I became aware of.
4. Whether to plate a two-inch eyebolt with cadmium for a tough, brilliant shine or with zinc for a rust-resistant, less expensive finish is a tough question. But similar questions must be answered daily by your salespeople. With my experience in the electroplating industry, I can contribute greatly to your constant need of getting customers.
5. What a set of tractors! The new 9430 and 9630 diesels are just what is needed by today's farmer with his ever-increasing acreage. John Deere has truly done it again.
6. Prudential Insurance Company did much to help my college career as the sponsor of my National Merit Scholarship. Now I think I can give something back to Prudential. I'd like to put my education, including a BS degree in finance from —— University, to work in your investment department.
7. Since the beginning of Delta Electric Construction Co. in 1993, the size and profits have grown steadily. My father, being a stockholder and vice president, often discusses company dealings with me. Although the company has prospered, I understand there have been a few problems of mismanagement. I feel with my present and future qualifications, I could help ease these problems.

13.4 Improving You-Attitude and Positive Emphasis in Job Letters

Revise each of these sentences to improve you-attitude and positive emphasis. You may need to add information.

1. I understand that your company has had problems due to the mistranslation of documents during international ad campaigns.
2. Included in my résumé are the courses in Finance that earned me a fairly attractive grade average.
3. I am looking for a position that gives me a chance to advance quickly.
4. Although short on experience, I am long on effort and enthusiasm.
5. I have been with the company from its beginning to its present unfortunate state of bankruptcy.
6. I wish to apply for a job at Austin Electronics. I will graduate from Florida State in May. I offer you a degree in electrical engineering and part-time work at Best Buy.
7. I was so excited to see your opening. This job is perfect for me.
8. You will find me a dedicated worker, because I really need a job.

13.5 Evaluating Letter Content

Improve the content of these passages from job cover letters. You may need to add content.

1. My internship gave me lots of experience for this job.
2. My job duties at Saxon Sport were to create displays, start an employee newsletter, and on weekends I was part of the sales staff.
3. While at San Fernando State, I participated in lots of activities. I played intramurals in baseball, football, basketball, hockey, and volley ball. I was treasurer and then president of the Marketing Club. I was in the Gaffers' Guild, where I made blown-glass creations. I was also in Campus Democrats.
4. I will be in Boston for a family reunion June 23–25 and will drop by your office then for an interview.
5. I feel any of my bosses would tell you that I try hard and pay attention to to detail.
6. I wish to apply for your job as a computer programmer. I have a computer science minor and two summers of sales experience at Best Buy in their computer department.
7. I am a very hard worker. In fact, I have a reputation for finishing the jobs of other workers.

13.6 Evaluating Rough Drafts

Evaluate the following drafts. What parts should be omitted? What needs to be changed or added? What parts would benefit from specific supporting details?

1.

Dear_____:

There is more to a buyer's job than buying the merchandise. And a clothing buyer in particular has much to consider.

Even though something may be in style, customers may not want to buy it. Buyers should therefore be aware of what customers want and how much they are willing to pay.

In the buying field, request letters, thank-you letters, and persuasive letters are frequently written.

My interest in the retail field inspired me to read The Gap's annual report. I saw that a new store is being built. An interview would give us a chance to discuss how I could contribute to this new store. Please call me to schedule an interview.

Sincerely,

2\.

Dear Sir or Madam:

I am taking the direct approach of a personnel letter. I believe you will under stand my true value in the areas of practical knowledge and promotional capabilities.

I am interested in a staff position with Darden in relation to trying to improve the operations and moral of the Olive Garden Restaurants, which I think that I am capable of doing. Please take a minute not to read my résumé (enclosed) and call to schedule an interview.

Sincerely,

3\.

Dear_____:

I would like to apply for the opening you announced for an Assistant Golf Course Superintendent. I have the qualifications you are asking for.

Every year the Superintendent must go before the greens committee to defend its budget requests. To prepare myself to do this, I took courses in accounting, business and administrative writing, and speech.

I have done the operations necessary to maintain the greens properly.

I look forward to talking with you about this position.

Sincerely,

13.7 Gathering Information about an Industry

Use six recent issues of a trade journal to report on three or four trends, developments, or issues that are important in an industry.

As your instructor directs,

a. Share your findings with a small group of other students.

b. Summarize your findings in a memo to your instructor. Include a discussion of how you could use this information in your job letter and résumé.

c. Present your findings to the class.

d. Join with a small group of other students to write a report summarizing the results of this research.

13.8 Gathering Information about Companies in Your Career Field

Use five different websites, such as those listed in Figure 13.1, to investigate three companies in your career field. Look at salary guides for your level of qualifications, product/service information, news articles about the companies, mission/vision statements, main competitors, annual reports, and financial reports.

As your instructor directs,

a. Share your findings with a small group of other students.

b. Summarize your findings in a memo to your instructor. Include a discussion of how you could use this information in your job letter and résumé.

c. Present your findings to the class.

d. Join with a small group of other students to write a report summarizing the results of this research.

13.9 Gathering Information about a Specific Organization

Gather information about a specific organization, using several of the following methods:

- Check the organization's website.
- Read the company's annual report.

- Pick up relevant information at the Chamber of Commerce.
- Read articles in trade publications and the *Wall Street Journal* or that mention the organization (check the indexes).
- Read recruiting literature provided by the company.

As your instructor directs,

a. Share your findings with a small group of other students.
b. Summarize your findings in a memo to your instructor. Include a discussion of how you could use this information in your job letter and résumé.
c. Present your findings orally to the class.
d. Write a paragraph for a job letter using (directly or indirectly) the information you found.

13.10 Conducting an Information Interview

Interview someone working in a field you're interested in. Use the questions listed on page 412 or the shorter list here:

- How did you get started in this field?
- What do you like about your job?
- What do you dislike about your job?
- What courses and jobs would you recommend as preparation for this field?

As your instructor directs,

a. Share the results of your interview with a small group of other students.
b. Write up your interview in a memo to your instructor. Include a discussion of how you could use this information in your job letter and résumé.
c. Present the results of your interview orally to the class.
d. Write to the interviewee thanking him or her for taking the time to talk to you.

13.11 Conducting a Referral Interview

a. Write to a friend who is already in the workforce, asking about one or more of the following topics:
   - Are any jobs in your field available in your friend's organization? If so, what?
   - If a job is available, can your friend provide information beyond the job listing that will help you write a more detailed, persuasive letter? (Specify the kind of information you'd like to have.)
   - Can your friend suggest people in other organizations who might be useful to you in your job search? (Specify any organizations in which you're especially interested.)
b. List possible networking contacts from your co-workers, classmates, fraternity/sorority members, friends, family friends, former employers and co-workers, neighbors, faculty members, and local business people. Who would be the most valuable source of information for you? Who would you feel most comfortable contacting?

13.12 Writing a Solicited Letter

Write a letter of application in response to an announced opening for a full-time job (not an internship) you would like.

Turn in a copy of the listing. If you use option (a) below, your listing will be a copy. If you choose option (b), you will write the listing.

a. Respond to an ad in a newspaper, in a professional journal, in the placement office, or on the web. Use an ad that specifies the company, not a blind ad. Be sure that you are fully qualified for the job.
b. If you have already worked somewhere, assume that your employer is asking you to apply for full-time work after graduation. Be sure to write a fully persuasive letter.

13.13 Writing a Prospecting Letter

Pick a company you'd like to work for and apply for a specific position that is not being advertised. The position can be one that already exists or one that you would create if you could to match your unique blend of talents.

Address your letter to the person with the power to create a job for you: the president of a small company, or the area vice president or branch manager of a large company.

Create a job description; give your instructor a copy of it with your letter.

13.14 Critiquing a Job Letter

After you have written your job letter for Exercise 13.12 or 13.13, bring it to class and share it with a classmate.

- Read your cover letter aloud to your classmate noting any changes you would like to make and any areas that may not sound appropriate.
- Have your classmate reread your job letter and make suggestions to enhance it.
- Swap letters and go through the exercise again.

Write a memo to your instructor discussing the changes you will make to your job letter on the basis of this exercise.

13.15 Writing a Rhetorical Analysis of Your Job Letter

a. Examine the job letter you wrote for Exercise 13.12 or 13.13 and answer the following questions in a memo to your instructor:
   - Who is your audience? Identify them beyond their name. What will they be looking for?
   - How did you consider this audience when selecting information and the level of detail to use? What information did you exclude? How did you shape the information about you to address your audience's needs?
   - How did you organize your information for this audience?
   - How did you adapt your tone and style for this audience? How did you balance your need to promote yourself without bragging? Where did you use you-attitude, positive tone, and goodwill?
   - How did you show knowledge of the company and the position without telling your audience what they already know?

b. Review a class member's cover letter using the same questions.

13.16 Applying Electronically

Write an e-mail application letter with a résumé in the text of the message.

13.17 Applying at Google

Using the Google sidebar on page 414, research possible jobs at Google. Pick the one most appropriate for you and write an electronic job letter to Google.

13.18 Editing a Cover Letter

In Chapter 12, Exercise 12.13, you critiqued the résumé of Jennifer Stanton. Below is her cover letter. Using the information about Jennifer from Exercise 12.13, redo her letter to improve it. Then write a memo to your instructor discussing the strengths and weaknesses of the letter and explaining why you made the changes you did.

From: wildechilde@gmail.com

To: pattersj@micquant.com

Date: 13 February, 2012

Re: Job!

Dear Ms. Patterson:

My name is Jennifer Stanton and I really want to work with you at Quantum National! Your job looks a whole lot like the one I had at my internship this past summer, so I'm pretty sure I'd be great at it.

I can't start until this Summer, because I'm finishing up my degree at Iowa State. I'm currently working on a degree in Buisness Management, so I'd be a great manager at your business. The one thing I've learned for sure in college is how to balance deadlines to get everything done on time. I've had a few classes where we had to work in teams, and I've been the team leader every time: once I step in, people just want to follow where I lead.

I think my work experience is exactly what you're looking for, too. At my internship last summer, I was basically unsupervised, so I had to learn fast! I managed cliet and department needs, I did the budgets—twice!—and I worked with a sales and marketing team to put together client information packages. I also did the scheduling for the team the whole time, which was my supervisor's job but she delegated it to me, because I am trustworthy. I also worked for years at my family's bookstore, which shows I can hold down a job.

Like I said, I'm really interested in this job. I think that this would be a great place to start my career, and I know I can do the job! Give me a call on my cell when you decide who you're interviewing!

Thanks,

Jennifer Stanton

13.19 Reviewing Cover Letters

All-Weather, Inc., invited applications for the position of Sales Representative (Residential Sales). To be based in Nebraska, this person will be mainly responsible for sales of All-Weather's vinyl windows in local markets, including single- and double-hung windows and casement windows. The job description for the position reads as follows:

The Sales Representative (Residential Sales) will be responsible for successful market penetration of identified market segments. Specifically, the duties include achieving targeted sales, conducting product demonstrations, contacting customers and other stakeholders, gathering market intelligence, preparing market and sales reports, communicating with internal customers, coordinating between customers and the Service and Installation Group, participating in meetings of trade associations and government agencies, attending company training events, and performing other duties assigned by managers. The ideal candidate will be someone with a BS degree, preferably with a technical major. Additionally, the candidate must have at least one year of sales experience, preferably in industrial products. Candidates with experience in brand marketing will also be considered. Among skills for the job, the candidate must possess computer skills, PR and communication skills, teamwork skills, and the ability to perform basic mathematical computations.

Below are two cover letters received from applicants. In a memo to your instructor, discuss the strengths and weaknesses of both. Judging just from their cover letter, which applicant would you prefer to hire? Why?

Figure 1 Antonio Ramirez's Cover Letter

Antonio Ramirez aramirez@bestmail.com 164 Beet St. Houston, TX

October 12, 2012
Ms. Erin Lenhardt
1210 Polaroid Av.
St. Paul, MN

Dear Ms. Lenhardt:
Please consider this letter as my application for the post of Sales Representative (Residential Sales). I learned about your job from the journal *Plastics US* (September issue). I have a bachelor's degree in chemistry from the University of Austin, Texas, and have two years of experience selling PVC resin.
The last two years I have been a Sales Executive in Goodman Petrochemicals in Houston, TX. My responsibilities include selling Goodman's PVC resin to Houston-based PVC processors of rigid and flexible applicatons.
As you suggest in your advertisement, my degree in chemistry will help me explain to customers the important technical attributes of your vinyl windows. My focus during my bachelor's degree was inorganic chemistry, especially hydrocarbons and its practical applications. Apart from my coursework, I also interned at Bright Fenestration Products in Austin, TX.
I look forward to discussing my experience and interst in your organization with you in a face-to-face interview. I'm available for the interview anytime in the next two weeks at a day's notice. I'm confident I will meet—and exceed—all your expetations for this important front line position.

Sincerely,

Antonio Ramirez

Figure 2 Michelle Chang's Cover Letter

Michelle Chang
4334, Sunset Boulevard, Lincoln, NE
mchang@myemail.com

October 14, 2012
Ms. Erin Lenhardt
HR Manager
1210 Polaroid Av.
St. Paul, MN

Dear Ms. Lenhardt:

I wish to apply for the position of Sales Representative (Residential Sales) advertised through Monster.com. After acquiring a bachelor's degree in design, I joined Albatross Advertising in November, 2010, as a trainee in the Accounts Department. Currently, I'm an Account Representative handling three of our most promising brands: *LiteWait* vacuum cleaners, Nebraska Furniture Mart, and Chimney Rock Art Gallery.

My bachelor's degree in design with a major in community and regional planning not only familiarized me with demands of buildings and landscapes in our 21st century living but also acquainted me with concepts of media and design. I joined Albatross because I wanted to see if my education has equipped me to inform, persuade, and help customers with regard to products and brands.

During my nearly two-year tenure at Albatross as Account Representative, I have created and given insightful presentations to clients. As a result of my performance, the agency has entrusted me with three of its most promising accounts, the ones that I mention above.

I would be delighted at an opportunity for a personal interview to further make my case for the job. You can contact me at my e-mail address mentioned above.

Sincerely,

Michelle Chang

13.20 Reviewing a Cover Letter

In the cover letter in Figure 13.4, Jeff Moeller is responding to the following job advertisement from Telltale Games. Using the ad, evaluate Jeff's letter to see how well he shows he is qualified for the job.

Game Designer

Telltale is searching for game designers to work on our growing library of unique episodic games. The game designer will be responsible for generation of detailed concepts covering all aspects of gameplay and story, as well as for prototyping, implementation and polish. Creative writing skills are a plus.

- Responsibilities
  - Work with lead designer to conceive fresh, innovative storytelling games, consistent with company game philosophy and vision

- Design and implement gameplay-related functionality including controls, dialogs, puzzles, and mini-games using Lua
- Implement front end and menu systems, NPC interactions and various other scripted events
- Implement character behaviors in various game scenarios according to story specifications and gameplay needs
- Test and refine gameplay features throughout the development cycle of the project

- Essential Skills and Experience
    - Demonstrated ability to work with artists and other designers
    - Good communication and interpersonal skills
    - Proven experience and proficiency with high level scripting languages (examples: JavaScript, Lua, Python, Perl)
    - Demonstrated ability to write clear, maintainable code
- Preferred Skills and Experience
    - Game industry experience in a design or programming position
    - Experience with Lua
    - Experience with Visual Studio and Source Safe
    - Creative writing skills
    - B.S. in Computer Science, Literature or Creative Writing

Principals only. Sorry, no unsolicited agencies, please!

CHAPTER 14

Interviewing, Writing Follow-Up Messages, and Succeeding in the Job

Chapter Outline

21st Century Interviews

Interview Strategy

Interview Preparation

- Final Research
- Elevator Speech
- Travel Planning
- Attire
- Professional Materials

Interview Channels

- Campus Interviews
- Phone Interviews
- Video Interviews

Interview Practice

Interview Customs

- Behavior
- Note-Taking
- Interview Segments

Traditional Interview Questions and Answers

Kinds of Interviews

- Behavioral Interviews
- Situational Interviews
- Stress Interviews
- Group Interviews

Final Steps for a Successful Job Search

- Following Up with Phone Calls and Written Messages
- Negotiating for Salary and Benefits
- Deciding Which Offer to Accept

Dealing with Rejection

Your First Full-Time Job

Summary of Key Points

Newsworthy Communication

The Four-Day Interview

When President Barack Obama nominated Elena Kagan to fill a place on the United States Supreme Court, he was criticized by leaders and commentators of both parties. In addition to the normal concerns with her political views, many expressed worries about her lack of judicial experience. Kagan, a former dean of the Harvard Law School, had never been a judge and had very little trial experience. It looked like she might have an uphill battle to be confirmed by the Senate Judiciary Committee.

"The confirmation hearings for Elena Kagan were nothing more than an extended job interview for one of the highest profile jobs in the world."

Over four days of intense hearings, the 16 members of the Judiciary Committee grilled Kagan on her experience, her political and social views, her performance and decisions in her jobs, and her published articles and private communications. Throughout the process, Kagan answered the most difficult questions candidly and thoughtfully, with occasional humor. She acknowledged the complexities of the questions and explained her positions without apologizing.

By the end of the hearings, she had won over some of her harshest critics. In fact, Senator Tom Coburn, who had criticized her answers early in the process, said at the end that her hearings had been some of the best in his experience. In the end, she was confirmed by the Judiciary Committee and then by the full Senate.

At the core, the confirmation hearings for Elena Kagan were nothing more than an extended job interview for one of the highest profile jobs in the world. While most job candidates will not face four days of interviews like Kagan, they will be asked to answer in-depth questions about their abilities and experiences, and they will need to explain uncomfortable details of their pasts. In that sense, Kagan's composed and professional conduct during her hearing can be an example to other job seekers.

In the end, Kagan got the job, thanks in large part to her four-day interview.

Sources: Ariane De Vogue and Ann H. Sloan, "The Kagan Hearings: Were They Necessary and Worthwhile?" ABC News, July 2, 2010, http://abcnews.go.com/Politics/Supreme_Court/elena-kagan-hearings-worthwhile/story?id=11068199&page=1; James Gordon Meek, "Elena Kagan Hearings: Supreme Court Justice Nominee Grilled over Military Recruitment Ban at Harvard," *NY Daily News*, June 29, 2010, http://articles.nydailynews.com/2010-06-29/news/27068623_1_elena-kagan-harvard-law-school-gays; and "Kagan Confirmed to Supreme Court," *Washington Post*, accessed April 18, 2011, http://www.washingtonpost.com/wp-srv/package/supremecourt/2010candidates/elena-kagan.html.

Learning Objectives

After studying this chapter, you will know

LO 14-1 What kinds of interviews you may encounter.

LO 14-2 What preparations to make before you start interviewing.

LO 14-3 What to do during an interview.

LO 14-4 How to answer common interview questions.

LO 14-5 What to do after an interview.

LO 14-6 How to succeed at your first full-time job.

Job interviews are scary, even when you've prepared thoroughly. Surveys show that, according to hiring managers, job candidates are more likely to make mistakes during their interviews than at any other point of their job search.[1] But when you are prepared, you can reduce the number of missteps so that you put your best foot forward and get the job you want. The best way to prepare is to know as much as possible about the process and the employer.

"Best" Hires

Fortune magazine offers these tips to increase your chances for a job at one of its "100 Best Companies to Work For."

Know someone at the company; most of these companies rely on employee referrals.

Emphasize your volunteer work; these companies support community outreach.

Be ready for multiple interviews.

Put your inner storyteller to work; you will be asked how you handled various work scenarios.

Do more research about the company than your rivals do.

Be a team player (one manager actually counts the number of times candidates say "I").

Show your willingness to build your career in that company; most are looking for long-term employees.

Show a passion for learning and growing at that company.

Adapted from Anne Fisher, "How to Get Hired by a 'Best' Company," *Fortune*, February 4, 2008, 96.

21ST CENTURY INTERVIEWS LO 14-1

Interviews remain an important part of the hiring process. A survey of 600 managers found that they overwhelmingly preferred evaluating job candidates in person, either by interviews or temporary work performance.[2]

Interviews are changing, however, as employers respond to interviewees who are prepared to answer the standard questions. Today, many employers expect you to

- Follow instructions to the letter.
- Participate in many interviews. You may have one or more interviews by phone, Skype, or video before you have an office interview.
- Take one or more tests, including drug tests, psychological tests, aptitude tests, computer simulations, skills tests, and essay exams where you're asked to explain what you'd do in a specific situation.
- Be approved by the team you'll be joining. In companies with self-managed work teams, the team has a say in who is hired.
- Provide—at the interview or right after it—a sample of the work you're applying to do. You may be asked to write a memo or a proposal, calculate a budget on a spreadsheet, write computer code, or make a presentation.

All the phoning required in 21st-century interviews places a special emphasis on phone skills. Be polite to everyone with whom you speak, including administrative assistants and secretaries. Find out the person's name on your first call and use it on subsequent calls. Be considerate: "Thank you for being so patient. Can you tell me when a better time might be to try to reach Ms. X? I'll try again on [date]." Sometimes, if you call after 5 pm, executives answer their own phones since clerical staff have gone home. However, some of them resent interruptions at that time, so be particularly well prepared and focused.

If you get someone's voice mail, leave a concise message—complete with your name and phone number. Give the phone number slowly so it can be jotted down. Keep your voice pleasant. If you get voice mail repeatedly, call the main company number to speak with a receptionist. Ask whether the person you're trying to reach is in the building. If he or she is on the road, ask when the person is due in.

How to Get a Job at Google

What you have heard is true. Getting hired by Google is difficult, even for highly intelligent people, and even after you make it through the brain-teaser portion of the interview. A former Google recruiter offers these insights:

- Show a willingness to tackle hard problems, including the brain-teasers.
- Have something excellent on your résumé. A 4.0 GPA might work, but a low GPA with your own consulting business, or a major contribution to a nonprofit, may also get you an interview.
- Prepare for behavioral questions, and make sure your answers say positive things about the ways you prefer to work.

Adapted from Phil Stott, "How to Get Hired by Google," Vault.com, accessed April 18, 2011, http://www.vault.com/wps/portal/usa/vcm/detail/Career-Advice/Interviewing/How-to-Get-Hired-by-Google?id=64619.

INTERVIEW STRATEGY

Develop an overall strategy based on your answers to these three questions:

1. **What about yourself do you want the interviewer to know?** Pick two to five points that represent your strengths for that particular job and that show how you will add value to the organization. These facts are frequently character traits (such as enthusiasm), achievements and experiences that qualify you for the job and separate you from other applicants, or unique abilities such as fluency in Spanish. For each strength, think of a specific accomplishment to support it. For instance, be ready to give an example to prove that you're hardworking. Be ready to show how you helped an organization save money or serve customers better.

   Then at the interview, listen to every question to see if you could make one of your key points as part of your answer. If the questions don't allow you to make your points, bring them up at the end of the interview.
2. **What disadvantages or weaknesses do you need to minimize?** Expect that you may be asked to explain weaknesses or apparent weaknesses in your record such as lack of experience, so–so grades, and gaps in your record.

   Plan how to deal with these issues if they arise. Decide if you want to bring them up yourself, particularly disadvantages or weaknesses that are easily discoverable. If you bring them up, you can plan the best context for them during the interview. Many students, for example, have been able to get good jobs after flunking out of school by explaining that the experience was a turning point in their lives and pointing out that when they returned to school they maintained a B or better grade point average. Although it is illegal to ask questions about marital status, married candidates with spouses who are able to move easily sometimes volunteer that information: "My husband is a dentist and is willing to relocate if the company wants to transfer me." See the suggestions later in this chapter under "Answering Traditional Interview Questions" and "Behavioral and Situational Interviews."
3. **What do you need to know about the job and the organization to decide whether or not you want to accept this job if it is offered to you?** Plan *in advance* the criteria on which you will base your decision (you can always change the criteria). Use "Deciding Which Offer to Accept" below to plan questions to elicit the information you'll need to rank each offer.

INTERVIEW PREPARATION LO 14-2

Preparing for your interviews is vital in these days of intense competition for jobs. It can also help you to feel more confident and make a better impression.

Final Research

Research the company interviewing you. Read their web pages, Facebook page, Twitter page, company newsletters, and annual reports. Many companies now have YouTube videos and employee blogs to give you insight into

What Not to Wear at an Interview

CareerBuilder.com surveyed hiring professionals to discover the top fashion mistakes interviewees make:

1. Too-short skirts
2. Overly bright or vividly patterned clothing
3. Wrinkled or stained clothing
4. Poorly fitted clothing
5. Socks that are too short, or don't go with the shoes
6. Patterned hosiery or bare legs
7. Scuffed or inappropriate footwear, including sneakers, stilettos, sandals, and open-toed shoes
8. Extra buttons or tags attached to a new suit
9. Earrings on men; multiple sets of earrings on women
10. Visible tattoos, tongue jewelry, facial piercings
11. Heavy makeup
12. Long or bright fingernails
13. Unnatural hair colors or styles
14. Strong aftershaves, perfumes, or colognes
15. Backpacks, fanny packs, or purses (use a briefcase)
16. Sunglasses on top of your head or headphones around your neck

Adapted from "What Not to Wear to an Interview: Top 20 Wardrobe Malfunctions," CareerBuilder, accessed April 15, 2011, http://www.careerbuilder.com/Article/CB-462-Getting-Hired-What-Not-to-Wear-to-an-Interview/.

the company and its culture. Some of them even offer interview tips. Read about them in trade journals and newspapers. Do a Google search. Ask your professors, classmates, friends, family, and co-workers about them. If possible, find out who will interview you and research them, too.

Also research salaries for the job: What is average? What is the range? Use web tools like indeed.com/salary or salary.com to find salary information by job title and location.

Elevator Speech

After you have finished your research, prepare your elevator speech, a short—two minute max—powerful statement of why you are a good candidate for this particular job. (The name comes from the scenario of being alone with the recruiter for a multifloor elevator ride. What can you say in that short period to convince the recruiter to consider you?) Even though it is short, your elevator speech will need some carefully selected details to be convincing. It will come in handy for questions like "Tell me about yourself" or "Why should I hire you?" It is useful in a variety of situations, including group interviews (p. 458) and receptions where you meet a variety of the company's employees in brief, one-on-one conversations.

Travel Planning

If your interview is not on campus, make sure you can find the building and the closest parking. Plan how much time you will need to get there. Leave time margins for stressors such as traffic jams or broken elevators. If you are fortunate enough to be flown to an interview, don't schedule too tightly. Allow for flight delays and cancellations. Plan how you will get from the airport to the interview site. Take enough cash and credit cards to cover emergencies.

Attire

First impressions are important; employers start judging you from the first second they see you. A major part of that first impression is your appearance.

The outfit you wear to an interview should meet your interviewer's expectations. The most conservative choice is the traditional dark business suit with a light blouse or shirt, plus tie shoes with matching dark socks for men and close-toed pumps with nude, unpatterned hose for women. Although this outfit is probably still the most common choice, you cannot count on it being the right choice. Many companies now expect more casual attire: sport jackets for men, coordinated jackets for women. Skirts should come at least to the knee; low-cut tops should be avoided. Sneakers and sandals are inappropriate.

For campus interviews, you should follow the dress code of your campus career center.

For office interviews, you should show that you understand the organization's culture. Try to find out from your career contacts what is considered appropriate attire. Some interviewers do not mind if you ask them what you should wear to the interview. (Others do mind, so be careful. They believe it means you have not done your homework.)

Paul Capelli, former public relations executive at Amazon.com and now vice president of corporate communications at QVC, suggests that applicants find out what employees wear "and notch it up one step":

> If the dress is jeans and a T-shirt, wear slacks and an open collar shirt . . . If it's slacks and an open collar shirt, throw on a sport coat. If it's a sport coat, throw on a suit. At least match it and go one step up.[3]

You can wear a wide range of apparel to interviews. Find out what is appropriate—and inappropriate—for each interview. Which of these outfits would you wear?

No matter what outfit you choose, make sure it fits well (especially important if it has been a few months since you wore it), is comfortable, and does not show too much cleavage or chest. Avoid casual items such as skin-tight pants, shorts, or sandals.

Choose comfortable shoes. You may do a fair amount of walking during an onsite interview. Check your heels to make sure they aren't run down; make sure your shoes are shined.

Make conservative choices. Have your hair cut or styled conservatively. Jewelry and makeup should be understated; face jewelry, such as eyebrow and nose studs, should be removed. If possible, cover tattoos. Personal hygiene must be impeccable, with close attention paid to fingernails and breath. Make sure your clothes are clean and pressed. Avoid cologne and perfumed after-shave lotions.

Professional Materials

Take extra copies of your résumé. If your campus placement office has already given the interviewer a data sheet, present the résumé at the beginning of the interview: "I thought you might like a little more information about me."

Career Fair Advice

Stanford University's Career Development Center offers the following tips for career fairs:

1. Prepare for the Career Fair. Answer the following questions before you attend:
   - What organizations are attending?
   - How will the employers be organized at the event?
   - What is the starting and ending time?
   - What attire is appropriate?
2. Prepare a résumé to hand out to potential employers. However, if you do not have a résumé, you can still attend the fair to gather information.
3. Set up a plan: Make a prioritized list of organizations you want to visit. However, be open to interesting organizations you run across at the fair.
4. Create a one-minute presentation to give to potential employers outlining your background and qualifications which will meet the organization's needs.
5. Bring questions to ask.
6. Bring a pen and notepad to stay organized during the fair.
7. Collect business cards and write a fact on the back to remember when you write a thank you.
8. Thank employers at the fair for materials you are given.
9. Write a thank-you note to those organizations you wish to pursue.

Adapted from "Preparing for a Career Fair," Stanford University Career Development Center, accessed April 16, 2011, http://studentaffairs.stanford.edu/cdc/services/career-fair-prepare.

Take something to write on and something to write with. It's OK to carry a small notepad with the questions you want to ask on it.

Take copies of your work or a portfolio: an engineering design, a copy of a memo you wrote on a job or in a business writing class, an article you wrote for the campus paper. You don't need to present these unless the interview calls for them, but they can be very effective: "Yes, I have done a media plan. Here's a copy of a plan I put together in my advertising seminar last year. We had a fixed budget and used real figures for cost and rating points, just as I'd do if I joined Foote, Cone & Belding."

Take the names, street addresses, e-mail addresses, and phone numbers of references. Take complete details about your work history and education, including dates and street addresses, in case you're asked to fill out an application form.

If you can afford it, buy a briefcase in which to carry these items. At this point in your life, an inexpensive vinyl briefcase is acceptable. Women should let the briefcase replace a purse.

INTERVIEW CHANNELS LO 14-1

Interviews use other channels in addition to the popular office setting. As a college student, you may well find yourself being interviewed on campus. You may also find you have a phone or video conference, as more and more companies use technology to keep hiring costs in check. Most of the interview advice in this chapter applies to all settings, but some channels do have unique particulars you should consider.

Campus Interviews

Most campus career offices have written protocols and expectations for campus interviews arranged through them. Be sure to follow these expectations so that you look informed.

However, because campus interviewers will see so many students who are all following the same protocols, it is important that you have good details and professional stories about your work to help you stand out from the crowd. Focus on three to four selling points you most want the interviewer to remember about you. If you have a choice, do not schedule your interview late in the day when interviewers are getting tired.

Phone Interviews

Some organizations use phone interviews to narrow the list of candidates they bring in for office visits. Phone interviews give you some advantages. Obviously, you do not have to dress up for them, or find an office. You can use all the materials you want as you speak. You can also take all the notes you want, although copious note-taking will probably impact your speaking quality, and you certainly don't want the sound of keyboard clicking to be heard by your interviewer.

On the other hand, phone interviews obviously deny you the important component of visual feedback. To compensate for this loss, you can ask your interviewer for verbal feedback (e.g., Is this sufficient detail? Would you like more on this topic?).

Although you always want to speak distinctly at an interview, doing so is even more crucial for a phone interview. And speech experts recommend that you smile, lean forward, and even gesture, although no one can see you. Such activities add warmth to your words. Be sure to eliminate all background noise such as music or TV. Finally, just as you did for a campus interview, focus on three to four selling points you most want the interviewer to remember about you.

Video Interviews

Video interviews are becoming more common. You may experience two different kinds. In one, the organization sends you a list of questions and you prepare a video which you send back to them. In the other, the organization conducts live interviews using videoconferencing equipment or programs such as Skype.

If you are preparing a video,

- Practice your answers so you are fluent. You don't want to stumble over your responses, but you also don't want to sound like you have memorized the answers.
- Be thorough. Since the employer can't ask follow-up questions, you want to consider what those questions could be and then be sure to answer them.

If you are participating in a videoconference,

- Do a practice video of yourself ahead of time. Listen to your pronunciation and voice qualities. Watch your video with the sound turned off: check your posture, gestures, facial expressions, and clothing. Do you have nervous mannerisms you need to control?
- During the actual interview, keep your answers under two minutes. Then ask if interviewers want more information. People are generally more reluctant to interrupt a speaker in another location, and body language cues are limited, so ask for feedback ("Would you like to hear about that?").

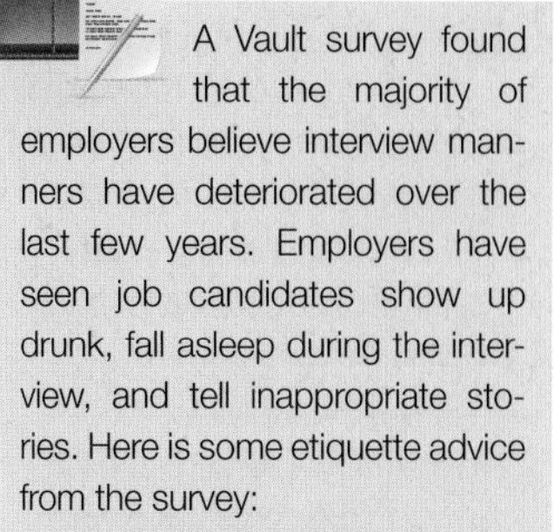

Interview Etiquette: Deteriorating?

A Vault survey found that the majority of employers believe interview manners have deteriorated over the last few years. Employers have seen job candidates show up drunk, fall asleep during the interview, and tell inappropriate stories. Here is some etiquette advice from the survey:

- Be on time. Some employers would eliminate people late for their interview. Other employers do not like people who arrive more than 10–15 minutes early, because they are distracting.
- Turn off your cellphone. Most employers would disqualify someone who answered a call during an interview. They also disapproved of looking at text messages. Such behavior shows a lack of engagement in the interview.
- Show gratitude: Send a thank-you note within 24 hours of the interview.

Adapted from Ingrid Ahlgren, "Job Interview Etiquette 101," Vault.com, accessed April 16, 2011, http://www.vault.com/wps/portal/usa/vcm/detail/Career-Advice/Interviewing/Job-Interview-Etiquette-101?id=1067.

INTERVIEW PRACTICE

Rehearse everything you can: Put on the clothes you'll wear and practice entering a room, shaking hands, sitting down, and answering questions. Ask a friend to interview you. Saying answers out loud is surprisingly harder than saying them in your head. If your department or career center offers practice interviews, take advantage of them.

Some campuses have videotaping facilities so that you can watch your own sample interview. Videotaping is particularly valuable if you can do it at least twice, so you can modify behavior the second time and check the tape to see whether the modification works.

INTERVIEW CUSTOMS LO 14-3

Your interviewing skills will improve with practice. If possible, schedule a few interviews with other companies before your interview with the company that is your first choice. However, even if you're just interviewing for practice, you must still do all the research on that company. If interviewers sense that you aren't interested, they won't take you seriously and you won't learn much from the process. Also, interviewers talk to each other, sharing impressions and stories, sometimes with names attached.

Not all interviews are question and answer sessions. More employers are starting to use other screening devices; they are asking candidates to provide on-the-spot writing samples, or to take personality, critical thinking, or intelligence tests. For example, one securities broker-dealer uses IQ tests, personality tests, and emotional intelligence tests.[4]

Tips for a Successful Interview Meal

David Rand, consultant on professional etiquette, offers these tips to look confident at the interview table.

- Hold premeal drinks in your left hand, so your handshake is not wet and clammy.
- Remember BMW for food placement: bread on the left, meal in the center, and water to your right.
- Unfold your napkin only after your host has done so, or all are seated at the table.
- Use silverware from the outside in. This means your salad fork will be farther from your plate than your dinner fork.
- Always pass the pepper along with salt; don't salt your own food first and then pass.
- When leaving your seat temporarily, place your napkin on your chair; after your meal, place the crumpled napkin back on the table.

Adapted from Rebecca Knight, "MBAs Mind their Manners—An Etiquette and Networking Course Aims to Remove the Angst from the Cocktail Interview," *Financial Times*, February 2, 2009, 11.

Behavior

How you act at the interview is as important as what you say, and first impressions of behavior are as important as they are for appearance.

Employers start judging you from the first second they see you. If you meet multiple people, first impressions will begin anew with each encounter. Always act professionally. Have a pleasant handshake; avoid the limp, dead-fish hand. Be polite to everyone, including people such as security agents, receptionists, and people in the restroom. Their input about you may be sought.

Politeness extends to the interview itself:

- Be punctual, but not too early (no more than 10 minutes early). Many recruiters don't like someone hanging around their reception area.
- Practice active listening (see Chapter 4); it makes speakers feel appreciated and you will likely pick up clues you can use effectively during your interview.
- Do not monopolize the interview time with lengthy monologues. Generally your interviewer will have many questions to cover and will not appreciate an undue amount of time wasted on just one. Check the interviewer's verbal cues and body language for the amount of detail and depth desired. After two to three minutes, ask if the interviewer wants more detail. The best interviews are conversations in which you and your interviewer enjoy your interactions.
- Never say anything bad about current and former employers, a category that includes schools. Candidates who snipe about their employers and instructors will likely continue to do so on their new job and thus appear to be unattractive colleagues.

Be enthusiastic about the job. Enthusiasm helps convince people you have the energy to do the job well. Show how you are a good choice for their job by clearly presenting your carefully chosen accomplishments and strengths. If you are attending an onsite interview, where you could well be asked the same questions by different people, prepare to repeat yourself—with enthusiasm.

Should you be yourself? There's no point in assuming a radically different persona. If you do, you run the risk of getting into a job that you'll hate (though the persona you assumed might have loved it). Furthermore, as interviewers point out, you have to be a pretty good actor to come across convincingly if you try to be someone other than yourself. Yet keep in mind that all of us have several selves: we can be lazy, insensitive, bored, slow-witted, and tongue-tied, but we can also be energetic, perceptive, interested, intelligent, and articulate. Be your best self at the interview.

Interviews can make you feel vulnerable and defensive; to counter this, review your accomplishments—the things you're especially proud of having done. You'll make a better impression if you have a firm sense of your own self-worth.

Every interviewer repeats the advice that you've probably heard: sit up straight, don't mumble, look at people when you talk. It's good advice for interviews. Be aware that many people respond negatively to smoking. Remember to turn off your cellphone.

As much as possible, avoid **nervous mannerisms:** playing with your hair, jingling coins in your pocket, clicking your pen, or repeating verbal spacers such as "like" and "uh." These mannerisms distract your audience and detract from your presentation. It's OK to be a little nervous, however; it shows that you care.

Site visits that involve **meals and semisocial occasions** call for sensible choices. When you order, choose something that's easy to eat without being messy. Watch your table manners. Eat a light lunch, with no alcohol, so that you'll be alert during the afternoon. A survey by the Society for Human Resource Management found that 96% of human resources professionals believe job candidates should not drink at interview meals.[5] At dinner or an evening party, decline alcohol if you don't drink. If you do drink, accept just one drink—you're still being evaluated, and you can't afford to have your guard down. Be aware that some people respond negatively to applicants who drink hard liquor, even if it was offered to them (think of it as another test you have to pass).

Because they may last longer, sometimes site interviews will present you with **minor problems** such as being brought back late from lunch, or being kept overtime with one interviewer so you are late for your appointment with another. Don't let these minor problems throw you. Think of them as a new opportunity to show that you can roll with the punches; move forward calmly.

If you have any **expenses,** be sure you keep all receipts for reimbursement. Many people forget to get taxi or shuttle receipts and thus are not reimbursed for those expenses.

The interview is also a time for you to see if you want to work for this organization. Look for signs of organizational culture (see page 32). How do people treat each other? Are offices or cubbies personalized? How many hours a week do the newest employees work? Is this the place where you want to become another new employee?

Body Language Mistakes

"A new CareerBuilder survey of more than 2,500 hiring managers reveals that failure to make eye contact (67 percent), lack of smile (38 percent) and fidgeting too much (33 percent) would make them less likely to hire someone. . . .

"When asked overall what additional body language mistakes would make them less likely to hire job candidates, hiring managers reported the following:

- Bad posture
- Handshake that is too weak
- Crossing arms over their chest
- Playing with their hair or touching their face
- Using too many hand gestures"

Quoted from CareerBuilder, "New CareerBuilder Survey Reveals Top Body Language Mistakes Candidates Make in Job Interviews," press release, July 28, 2010, http://www.careerbuilder.com/share/aboutus/pressreleasesdetail.aspx?id=pr581&sd=7/29/2010&ed=7/29/2099.

Note-Taking

During or immediately after the interview, write down

- The name of the interviewer (or all the people you talked to, if it's a group interview or an onsite visit).
- Tips the interviewer gave you about landing the job and succeeding in it.
- What the interviewer seemed to like best about you.
- Any negative points or weaknesses that came up that you need to counter in your follow-up messages or phone calls.
- Answers to your questions about the company.
- When you'll hear from the company.

The easiest way to get the interviewer's name is to ask for his or her card. You may be able to make all the notes you need on the back of the card.

Some interviewers say that they respond negatively to applicants who take notes during the interview. However, if you have several interviews back-to-back or if you know your memory is terrible, do take brief notes

Interview Checklist

Here is a checklist of tips for a surefire attitude from Judi James, author of *You're Hired! Interview: Tips And Techniques for a Brilliant Interview.*

Sell yourself to yourself: If you don't believe in yourself, chances are the interviewer won't believe in you either.

Show, don't tell: Prepare short stories of your accomplishments; they are more convincing than simply stating you are a good leader or problem solver. Keep your information relevant to the job.

Avoid JBY syndrome: An interview is not the place to Just Be Yourself (JBY). Interviews are formal events; reflect that formality in your attire and behavior.

Be vivid: Energy, enthusiasm, and charisma help you stand out.

Avoid body language "leakage": Nervous habits such as fidgeting and fiddling can send negative signals.

Make a good entrance: Stand tall, smile, look confident. Practice a firm handshake and making eye contact.

Look the part: Dress appropriately for the company and job.

Adapted from "It's Hire Education—Ten Tips to Succeed in an Interview," *The Sun*, February 5, 2009, 49.

during the interview. That's better than forgetting which company said you'd be on the road every other week and which interviewer asked that *you* get in touch with him or her. Try to maintain eye contact as much as possible while taking notes.

Interview Segments

Every interview has an opening, a body, and a close.

In the **opening** (two to five minutes), good interviewers will try to set you at ease. Some interviewers will open with easy questions about your major or interests. Others open by telling you about the job or the company. If this happens, listen so you can answer questions later to show that you can do the job or contribute to the company that's being described.

The **body** of the interview (10 to 25 minutes) is an all-too-brief time for you to highlight your qualifications and find out what you need to know to decide if you want to accept a site trip. Expect questions that give you an opportunity to showcase your strong points and questions that probe any weaknesses evident from your résumé. (You were neither in school nor working last fall. What were you doing?) Normally the interviewer will also try to sell you on the company and give you an opportunity to raise questions.

You need to be aware of time so that you can make sure to get in your key points and questions: "We haven't covered it yet, but I want you to know that I . . ." "I'm aware that it's almost 10:30. I do have some more questions that I'd like to ask about the company."

In the **close** of the interview (two to five minutes), the interviewer will usually tell you what happens next: "We'll be bringing our top candidates to the office in February. You should hear from us in three weeks." Make sure you know who to contact if the next step is not clearly spelled out or you don't hear by the stated time.

The close of the interview is also the time for you to summarize your key accomplishments and strengths and to express enthusiasm for the job. Depending on the circumstances, you could say: "I've certainly enjoyed learning more about Zappos." "I hope I get a chance to visit your Las Vegas office. I'd really like to see the new computer system you talked about."

TRADITIONAL INTERVIEW QUESTIONS AND ANSWERS LO 14-4

First interviews seek to screen out less qualified candidates rather than to find someone to hire. Negative information will hurt you less if it comes out in the middle of the interview and is preceded and followed by positive information. If you blow a question near the end of the interview, don't leave until you've said something positive—perhaps restating one of the points you want the interviewer to know about you.

As Figure 14.1 shows, successful applicants use different communication behaviors than do unsuccessful applicants. Successful applicants are more likely to use the company name during the interview, show they have researched the company, support their claims with specific details, use appropriate technical language, and ask specific questions about the company and industry. In addition to practicing the content of questions, try to incorporate these tactics.

The ultimate questions in your interviewers' minds are probably these three: What can you do for us? Why should we hire you instead of another

Figure 14.1 The Communication Behaviors of Successful Interviewees

Behavior	Unsuccessful interviewees	Successful interviewees
Statements about the position	Have only vague ideas of what they want to do.	Specific and consistent about the position they want; are able to tell why they want the position.
Use of company name	Rarely use the company name.	Refer to the company by name.
Knowledge about company and position	Make it clear that they are using the interview to learn about the company and what it offers.	Make it clear that they have researched the company; refer to specific website, publications, or people who have given them information.
Level of interest, enthusiasm	Respond neutrally to interviewer's statements: "OK," "I see." Indicate reservations about company or location.	Express approval nonverbally and verbally of information provided by the interviewer; "That's great!" Explicitly indicate desire to work for this particular company.
Nonverbal behavior	Make little eye contact; smile infrequently.	Make eye contact often; smile.
Picking up on interviewer's cues	Give vague or negative answers even when a positive answer is clearly desired ("How are your writing skills?").	Answer positively and confidently; and back up the claim with a specific example.
Use of industry terms and technical jargon	Use almost no technical jargon.	Use appropriate technical jargon.
Use of specifics in answers	Give short answers—10 words or less, sometimes only one word; do not elaborate. Give general responses: "fairly well."	Support claims with specific personal experiences.
Questions asked by interviewee	Ask a small number of general questions.	Ask specific questions based on knowledge of the industry and the company. Personalize questions: "What would my duties be?"

candidate? Will you fit in our company/division/office? However, many interviewers do not ask these questions directly. Instead, they ask other questions to get their answers more indirectly. Some of the more common questions are discussed below. Do some unpressured thinking before the interview so that you'll have answers that are responsive, are honest, and paint a good picture of you. Choose answers that fit your qualifications and the organization's needs.

Check your answers for hidden negatives. If you say you are the kind of person who is always looking for challenges, your interviewer may wonder about hiring you for this entry-level position, which needs someone who does mostly routine work with care. Similarly, if you say you want lots of responsibility, your interviewer may again not see you as a good fit for entry-level positions, which are not known for providing lots of responsibility.

Rehearse your answers mentally, so you feel confident you have good answers. Then get family and friends to interview you. You may be surprised at how much work good mental answers still need when you give them out loud.

Tell Me a Story

One effective way to stand out from the hordes of people being interviewed is to tell a memorable story about yourself.

- Choose a story that shows your personality as well as professional abilities.
- Use a story highly relevant for the particular job.
- Use colorful details, including sensory ones.
- Keep it short—two minutes at the very most.
- Your story is to be an honest anecdote about your professional self, not a fiction.

1. **Tell me about yourself.** Focus on several strengths that show you are a good candidate. Give examples with enough specifics to prove each strength. Don't launch into an autobiography, which will have too many details the interviewer will not care about. Provide professional, not personal, information.
2. **Walk me through your résumé.** Highlight your best features and offer reasons for major decisions. Why did you choose this college? Why did you take that job? Have professional reasons: You went to State U because it has a top-ranked accounting department, not because it is close to home; you took that summer job because it allowed some interaction with the company's accounting department, not because it was the only one you could find.

   Don't try to cover too much; your résumé walk should be no longer than three minutes. But do try to add some interesting detail that is not on your résumé. Above all, do maintain eye contact; do not read your résumé.
3. **What makes you think you're qualified to work for this company? Or, I'm interviewing 120 people for two jobs. Why should I hire you?** This question may feel like an attack. Use it as an opportunity to state your strong points: your qualifications for the job, the things that separate you from other applicants.
4. **What two or three accomplishments have given you the greatest satisfaction?** Pick accomplishments that you're proud of, that create the image you want to project, and that enable you to share one of the things you want the interviewer to know about you. Focus not just on the end result, but on the problem-solving, thinking, and innovation skills that made the achievement possible.
5. **Why do you want to work for us? What is your ideal job?** Even if you're interviewing just for practice, make sure you have a good answer—preferably two or three reasons you'd like to work for that company. If you don't seem to be taking the interview seriously, the interviewer won't take you seriously, and you won't even get good practice.

   If your ideal job is very different from the ones the company has available, the interviewer may simply say there isn't a good match and end the interview. If you're interested in this company, do some research so that what you ask for is in the general ballpark of the kind of work the company offers.
6. **What college subjects did you like best and least? Why?** This question may be an icebreaker; it may be designed to discover the kind of applicant they're looking for. If your favorite class was something outside your major, prepare an answer that shows that you have qualities that can help you in the job you're applying for: "My favorite class was a seminar in the American novel. We got a chance to think on our own, rather than just regurgitate facts; we made presentations to the class every week. I found I really like sharing my ideas with other people and presenting reasons for my conclusions about something."
7. **What is your class rank? Your grade point? Why are your grades so low?** If your grades aren't great, be ready with a nondefensive explanation. If possible, show that the cause of low grades now has been solved or isn't relevant to the job you're applying for: "My father almost died last year, and my schoolwork really suffered." "When I started, I didn't have any firm goals. Once I discovered the field that was right for me, my grades have all been B's or better." "I'm not good at multiple-choice tests. But I am good at working with people."
8. **What have you read recently? What movies have you seen recently?** These questions may be icebreakers; they may be designed to probe your intellectual depth. The term you're interviewing, read at least one book

Cornered
by Mike Baldwin
3-14 © 2011 Mike Baldwin/Dist. by Universal Uclick www.cornered.com
urcornered@gmail.com

"OK, that covers strengths. Do you have any weaknesses?"

or magazine (multiple issues) and see at least one serious movie that you could discuss at an interview. Make thoughtful selections.

9. **Show me some samples of your writing.** Many jobs require the ability to write well. Employers no longer take mastery of basic English for granted, even if the applicant has a degree from a prestigious university.

   The year you're interviewing, go through your old papers and select a few of the best ones, editing them if necessary, so that you'll have samples to present at the interview if you're asked for them.

10. **Describe a major problem you have encountered in your work and how you dealt with it.** Choose a problem that was not your fault: a customer's last-minute change to a large order, a flu outbreak during Christmas rush. In your solution, stress skills you know the company will be seeking.

11. **What are your interests outside work? What campus or community activities have you been involved in?** While it's desirable to be well-rounded, naming 10 interests is a mistake: the interviewer may wonder when you'll have time to work. Select activities that show skills and knowledge you can use on the job: "I have polished my persuasion skills by being a cabin counselor at a camp for troubled preteens."

    If you mention your fiancé, spouse, or children in response to this question ("Well, my fiancé and I like to go sailing"), it is perfectly legal for the interviewer to ask follow-up questions ("What would you do if your spouse got a job offer in another town?"), even though the same question would be illegal if the interviewer brought up the subject first.

12. **What have you done to learn about this company?** An employer may ask this to see what you already know about the company (if you've read the recruiting literature and the website, the interviewer doesn't need to repeat them). This question may also be used to see how active a role you're taking in the job search process and how interested you are in this job.

13. **What adjectives would you use to describe yourself?** Use only positive ones. Be ready to illustrate each with a specific example of something you've done.

14. **What are your greatest strengths?** Employers ask this question to give you a chance to sell yourself and to learn something about your values.

Zappos Interview Questions

Below are some interview questions used at Zappos, where the emphasis is on hiring people compatible with their strong service mission:

- Give me an example from your previous job(s) where you had to think and act outside the box.
- What was the best mistake you made on the job? Why was it the best?
- Tell me about a time you recognized a problem/area to improve that was outside of your job duties and solved [it] without being asked to. What was it, how did you do it?
- Would you say you are more or less creative than the average person? Can you give me an example?
- If it was your first day on the job at Zappos and your task was to make the interview/recruiting process more fun, what would you do for those eight hours?
- What's an example of a risk you took in a previous job? What was the outcome?

Quoted from Tony Hsieh, *Delivering Happiness: A Path to Profit, Passion, and Purpose* (New York: Business Plus, 2010), 172. With permission from Central Grand Publishing.

Pick strengths related to work, school, or activities: "I'm good at working with people." "I really can sell things." "I'm good at solving problems." "I learn quickly." "I'm reliable. When I say I'll do something, I do it." Be ready to illustrate each with a specific example of something you've done. It is important to relate your strengths to the specific position.

15. **What is your greatest weakness?** Use a work-related negative, even if something in your personal life really is your greatest weakness. Interviewers won't let you get away with a "weakness" like being a workaholic or just not having any experience yet. Instead, use one of these strategies:

    a. Discuss a weakness that is not related to the job you're being considered for and will not be needed even when you're promoted. (Even if you won't work with people or give speeches in your first job, you'll need those skills later in your career, so don't use them for this question.) End your answer with a positive that *is* related to the job:

    > [For a creative job in advertising:] I don't like accounting. I know it's important, but I don't like it. I even hire someone to do my taxes. I'm much more interested in being creative and working with people, which is why I find this position interesting.

    > [For a job in administration:] I don't like selling products. I hated selling cookies when I was a Girl Scout. I'd much rather work with ideas—and I really like selling the ideas that I believe in.

    b. Discuss a weakness that you are working to improve:

    > In the past, I wasn't a good writer. But last term I took a course in business writing that taught me how to organize my ideas and how to revise. I may never win a Pulitzer Prize, but now I can write effective reports and memos.

    c. Describe advice you received, and how that advice helped your career.

    > The professor for whom I was an undergraduate assistant pointed out to me that people respond well to liberal praise, and that I was not liberal with mine. As I have worked on providing more positive feedback, I have become a better manager.

16. **What are your career goals? Where do you want to be in five years? Ten years?** This question is frequently a test to see if you fit with this company. Are your goals ones that can be met at this company? Or will the company have the expense of training you only to see you move on promptly to another company?

17. **Why are you looking for another job?** Do not answer this with a negative—"My boss didn't like me," "I didn't like the work"—even if the negative is true. Stress the new opportunities you're looking for in a new job, not why you want to get away from your old one: "I want more opportunity to work with clients."

    Also be careful of hidden negatives: "I couldn't use all my abilities in my last job" sounds like you are complaining. It also suggests that you don't take the initiative to find new challenges. If you are looking for a job with a bigger salary, it is better to use other points when answering this question.

If you were fired, say so. There are various acceptable ways to explain why you were fired:

a. It wasn't a good match. Add what you now know you need in a job, and ask what the employer can offer in this area.
b. You and your supervisor had a personality conflict. Make sure you show that this was an isolated incident, and that you normally get along well with people.
c. You made mistakes, but you've learned from them and are now ready to work well. Be ready to offer a specific anecdote proving that you have indeed changed.

18. **Why do you have a gap in your employment history?** Answer briefly and positively; do not apologize for family decisions.

> I cared for an ill family member. Because of the time it took, it wasn't fair to an employer to start a new job.

> I stayed home with my children while they were young. Now that they are both in school, I can devote myself to top performance in your company.

If you were laid off, be prepared to explain why you were one of the people let go. It helps if you can truthfully say that all new employees with less than three years' experience at the firm were laid off, or that legal services were outsourced, or that the entire training department was disbanded. Be careful you do not display bitter, angry feelings; they will not help you get a new job. It may help you to realize that in tight economies, being laid off is not an issue for many interviewers.

19. **What questions do you have?** This question gives you a chance to cover things the interviewer hasn't brought up; it also gives the interviewer a sense of your priorities and values. Almost all interviewers will ask you for questions, and it is crucial that you have some. A lack of questions will probably be interpreted as a lack of interest in the company and a lack of preparation for the interview. These are some questions you might want to ask:

- What would I be doing on a day-to-day basis?
- What's the top challenge I would face in this job?
- What kind of training program do you have?
- How do you evaluate employees? How often do you review them?
- What will a good employee have done by the time of his or her first evaluation?
- Where would you expect a new trainee (banker, staff accountant) to be three years from now? Five years? Ten years?
- What happened to the last person who had this job?
- How would you describe the company's culture?
- This sounds like a great job. What are the drawbacks?
- How are interest rates (new products from competitors, imports, demographic trends, government regulations, etc.) affecting your company? Questions like these show that you care enough to do your homework and that you are aware of current events.
- What do you like best about working for this company? Ending with a question like this closes your interview on an upbeat note.

Do not ask these questions:

- Questions about information you can easily find (and should have found) on the company's website.
- Questions that indicate dissatisfaction with the job for which you are being interviewed (How soon can I get promoted?).
- Questions about salary and benefits (wait until you have a job offer).

Not all interview questions are proper. Various federal, state, and local laws prohibit questions that would allow employers to discriminate on the basis of protected characteristics such as race, sex, age, disability, and marital status. If you are asked an improper or illegal question during an interview, you have several options:

- You can answer the question, but you may not get hired if you give the "wrong" answer.
- You can refuse to answer the question. Doing so is within your rights, but it may make you look uncooperative or confrontational, so again you may not get hired.
- You can look for the intent behind the question and provide an answer related to the job. For example, if you were asked who would care for your children when you had to work late on an urgent project, you could answer that you can meet the work schedule a good performance requires.

Keep in mind in each situation that legal and illegal questions can be very similar. It is legal to ask if you are over 18, but illegal to ask you how old you are. It is legal to ask you which languages you speak (if that talent is relevant for the job), but it is illegal to ask you what your native language is. Also be careful of variants of illegal questions. Asking when you graduated from high school gives the interviewer a pretty good idea of your age.

You won't be able to anticipate every question you may get. Check with other people at your college or university who have interviewed recently to find out what questions are currently being asked in your field.

KINDS OF INTERVIEWS LO 14-1

Many companies, dissatisfied with hires based on one interview, are turning to multiple interviews. Geoff Smart and Randy Street, in their business best seller *Who: The A Method for Hiring,* present a four-interview system for finding the best employees:

1. Screening interview, which culls the list (done by phone).
2. Topgrading interview, which walks job candidates through their careers so far.
3. Focused interview, which focuses on one desired aspect of the candidate's career.
4. Reference interview, which checks in with candidates' references.[6]

Granted, this system is not for hiring entry-level people, but you won't be entry level very long, if you are even now. Even companies that won't use a

Amy's Ice Cream stores sell entertainment. To find creative, zany employees, Amy Miller gives applicants a white paper bag and a week to do something with it. People who produce something unusual are hired.

four-tiered system to interview you may be supplementing traditional interviews with behavioral, situational, stress, and group interviews.

Behavioral Interviews

Using the theory that past behaviors predict future performance, **behavioral interviews** ask applicants to describe actual past behaviors, rather than future plans. Thus instead of asking "How would you motivate people?" the interviewer might ask, "Tell me what happened the last time you wanted to get other people to do something." Follow-up questions might include, "What exactly did you do to handle the situation? How did you feel about the results? How did the other people feel? How did your superior feel about the results?"

Additional behavioral questions may ask you to describe a situation in which you

- Created an opportunity for yourself in a job or volunteer position.
- Used writing to achieve your goal.
- Went beyond the call of duty to get a job done.
- Communicated successfully with someone you disliked.
- Had to make a decision quickly.
- Took a project from start to finish.
- Used good judgment and logic in solving a problem.
- Worked under a tight deadline.
- Worked with a tough boss.
- Worked with someone who wasn't doing his or her share of the work.

In your answer, describe the situation, tell what you did, and explain what happened. Think about the implications of what you did and be ready to talk about whether you'd do the same thing next time or if the situation were slightly different. For example, if you did the extra work yourself when a team member didn't do his or her share, does that fact suggest that you prefer to work alone? If the organization you're interviewing with values teams, you may want to go on to show why doing the extra work was appropriate in that situation but that you can respond differently in other situations.

A good way to prepare for behavioral interviews is to make a chart. Across the top list jobs, accomplishments, and projects. Down the left side, list qualities employers will want in candidates for the jobs you seek. These qualities should include skills such as communication, teamwork, critical thinking, networking, influencing people, and leadership; traits such as honesty, reliability, and a developed ethical sense; and the ability to meet situations such as those in the list above. Then you fill in the boxes. How does that presentation you made to skeptical administrators demonstrate your communication skills? Your ethics? Your ability to perform under pressure? Make sure each item in your boxes casts you in a favorable light: the ability to work under pressure is generally valued, but if you had to pull three all-nighters to finish your marketing project, employers might see you as a procrastinator.

Mass Interrogation

If you've seen a Senate committee grill a person nominated for a federal job, you've seen a panel interview. This trend is growing even in the private sectors. If you will have a panel interview, here are some tips to help you.

- Take notes. When the panel members introduce themselves, write their names in the same arrangement they are seated.
- Focus on one question at a time rather than getting overwhelmed by the entire experience.
- Address the current questioner, but also make eye contact with other panel members.
- Try to identify the person with the most authority. The body language of the other people usually helps you do so. For instance, everyone may look to them for the answer to a question.
- Ask at least one question of each panel member. Doing so makes you look prepared and invested in the job, and the responses from various panel members help you get a better idea about the company.
- Write a thank-you note to each panel member.

Adapted from Anne Fisher, "1 Job, 11 Interviewers," *Fortune*, November 25, 2008, http://money.cnn.com/2008/11/20/news/economy/interview.fortune/index.

Situational Interviews

Situational interviews put you in situations similar to those you will face on the job. They test your problem-solving skills, as well as your ability to handle problems under time constraints and with minimal preparation. While behavioral interviews asked how you handled something in the past, situational interviews focus on the future. For instance, for jobs with strong service components you could expect to be asked how you would handle an angry client. For jobs with manufacturing companies, you might be asked to imagine a new product.

Frequently situational interviews contain actual tasks candidates are asked to perform. You may be asked to fix some computer coding, sell something to a client, prepare a brochure, or work with an actual spreadsheet. Two favorite tasks are to ask candidates to prepare and give a short presentation with visuals or to work through an online in-box. Both of these tasks test communication and organization skills, as well as the ability to perform under time constraints.

Stress Interviews

Obviously, if the task is complex, performing it at a job interview, particularly with time constraints, is stressful. Thus situational interviews can easily move into stress interviews. The higher you move in your career, the more likely it is that you will have situational or stress interviews. **Stress interviews** deliberately put applicants under stress to see how they handle the pressure. The key is to stay calm; try to maintain your sense of humor.

Sometimes the stress is physical: for example, you're given a chair where the light is in your eyes. Speak up for yourself: ask if the position of the blind can be changed, or move to another chair.

Usually the stress is psychological. Panel interviews, such as those for many political appointments, may be stressful (see sidebar on this page). The group of interviewers may fire rapid questions. However, you can slow the pace down with deliberate answers. In another possibility, a single interviewer may probe every weak spot in your record and ask questions that elicit negatives. If you get questions that put you on the defensive, rephrase

Stress interviews can use physical conditions and people placement to see how candidates respond to uncomfortable situations. You have the option to change some uncomfortable conditions, such as lights shining in your eyes.

STAR: An Interviewing Technique

"One strategy for preparing for behavioral interviews is to use the STAR Technique, as outlined below. (This technique is also referred to as the SAR and PAR techniques.)

Situation or Task

Describe the situation that you were in or the task that you needed to accomplish. You must describe a specific event or situation, not a generalized description of what you have done in the past. Be sure to give enough detail for the interviewer to understand. This situation can be from a previous job, from a volunteer experience, or any relevant event.

Action You Took

Describe the action you took and be sure to keep the focus on you. Even if you are discussing a group project or effort, describe what you did—not the efforts of the team. Don't tell what you might do, tell what you did.

Results You Achieved

What happened? How did the event end? What did you accomplish? What did you learn?"

Quoted from "STAR Interviewing Response Technique for Success in Behavioral Job Interviews," QuintCareers, accessed April 16, 2011, http://www.quintcareers.com/STAR_interviewing.html. Reprinted with permission.

them in less inflammatory terms, if necessary, and then treat them as requests for information.

Q: Why did you major in physical education? That sounds like a pretty Mickey Mouse major.

A: Are you wondering whether I have the academic preparation for this job? I started out in physical education because I've always loved team sports. I learned that I couldn't graduate in four years if I officially switched my major to business administration because the requirements were different in the two programs. But I do have 21 hours in business administration and 9 hours in accounting. And my sports experience gives me practical training in teamwork, motivating people, and management.

Respond assertively. The candidates who survive are those who stand up for themselves and who explain why indeed they *are* worth hiring.

Sometimes the stress comes in the form of unusual questions: Why are manhole covers round? How many tennis balls would fit inside a school bus? If you were a cookie/car/animal, what kind would you be? If you could be any character from a book, who would you be? How you handle the question will be as important as your answer, maybe more important. Can you think creatively under pressure?

Most Common Interview Mistakes

According to a survey of 2,400 hiring managers, these are the most common mistakes job candidates make during their interviews:

- Answering a cellphone or texting during the interview.
- Dressing inappropriately.
- Appearing disinterested.
- Appearing arrogant.
- Speaking negatively about a current or previous employer.
- Chewing gum.
- Not providing specific answers.
- Not asking good questions.

Bullets quoted from CareerBuilder, "Employers Reveal Outrageous and Common Mistakes Candidates Made in Job Interviews, According to New CareerBuilder Survey," news release, January 12, 2011, http://www.careerbuilder.com/share/aboutus/pressreleasesdetail.aspx?id=pr614&sd=1/12/2011&ed=01/12/2011.

Silence can also create stress. One woman walked into her scheduled interview to find a male interviewer with his feet up on the desk. He said, "It's been a long day. I'm tired and I want to go home. You have five minutes to sell yourself." Since she had planned the points she wanted to be sure interviewers knew, she was able to do this. "Your recruiting brochure said that you're looking for someone with a major in accounting and a minor in finance. As you may remember from my résumé, I'm majoring in accounting and have had 12 hours in finance. I've also served as treasurer of a local campaign committee and have worked as a volunteer tax preparer through the Accounting Club." When she finished, the interviewer told her it was a test: "I wanted to see how you'd handle it."

Group Interviews

In group interviews, sometimes called "cattle calls," multiple candidates are interviewed at a time. While many interview tips still apply to these interviews, successful candidates will also practice other techniques. Researching the job and company becomes even more important, because your time to show how you fit the job will be so limited. Have a two-minute summary of your education and experience that shows how you fit this job. Practice it ahead of time so you can share it during the interview.

Arrive early so you have time to meet as many interviewers and interviewees as possible. Get business cards from the interviewers if you can. This pre-interview time may be part of the test, so make the most of it.

During the interview, listen carefully to both interviewers and interviewees. Make eye contact with both groups as well. Participate in the discussion, and look engaged even when you aren't. Watch your body language (see Chapter 4) so you don't give off unintended signals.

Some group interviews are organized around tasks. The group may be asked to solve a problem. Another scenario is that the group will be split into teams, with each team performing a task and then presenting to the whole group. Remember that your participation in these activities is being watched. You will be judged on skills such as communication, persuasion, leadership, organization, planning, analysis, and problem-solving. Do you help move the action forward? Are you too assertive? Too shy? Do you praise the contributions of others? Do you help the group achieve consensus? Are you knowledgeable?

Many group interviews particularly test how you interact with other people. Talking too much may work against you. Making an effort to help quiet people enter the discussion may work in your favor. Connecting your comments to previous comments shows you are a good listener as well as a team player. Be careful not to get caught up in a combative situation.

At the end of the interview, thank each interviewer. Follow up with a written thank you to each interviewer.

FINAL STEPS FOR A SUCCESSFUL JOB SEARCH LO 14-5

What you do after the interview can determine whether you get the job. Many companies expect applicants to follow up on their interviews within a week. If they don't, the company assumes that they wouldn't follow up with clients.

If the employer sends you an e-mail query, answer it promptly. You're being judged not only on what you say but on how quickly you respond. Have your list of references (see page 390) and samples of your work ready to send promptly if requested to do so.

Following Up with Phone Calls and Written Messages

After a first interview, make a follow-up phone call to show enthusiasm for the job, to reinforce positives from the first interview, to overcome any negatives, and to provide information to persuade the interviewer to hire you. Do not stalk the recruiter. Call only once unless you have excellent reasons for multiple calls. If you get voice mail, leave a message. Remember that caller ID will tell the recruiter that you were the person making the multiple hang-ups.

A thank-you note, written within 24 hours of an interview, is essential. Some companies consider the thank-you note to be as important as the cover letter. The note should

- Thank the interviewer for useful information and any helpful action.
- Remind the interviewer of what he or she liked in you.
- Use the jargon of the company and refer to specific things you learned during your interview or saw during your visit.
- Be enthusiastic about the position.
- Refer to the next move, whether you'll wait to hear from the employer or whether you want to call to learn about the status of your application.

If the note is for a site visit, thank your hosts for their hospitality. In the postscript, mention enclosed receipts for your expenses.

Be sure your thank-you is well written and error-free. Double-check the spelling of all names. The note can be an e-mail, but many employers are still impressed by paper thank-you notes. In either case, do not use text messaging abbreviations or emoticons.

Figure 14.2 is an example of a follow-up letter after a site visit.

Negotiating for Salary and Benefits

The best time to negotiate for salary and benefits is after you have the job offer. Try to delay discussing salary early in the interview process, when you're still competing against other applicants.

Prepare for salary negotiations by finding out what the going rate is for the work you hope to do. Ask friends who are in the workforce to find out what they're making. Ask the campus placement office for figures on what last year's graduates got. Check trade journals and the web.

This research is crucial. The White House Report on the status of women shows that women earn about 75% as much as men, at all levels of education. Even when compared to direct male counterparts, the difference is substantial.[7] Knowing what a job is worth will give you the confidence to negotiate more effectively.

The best way to get more money is to convince the employer that you're worth it. During the interview process, show that you can do what the competition can't.

After you have the offer, you can begin negotiating salary and benefits. You're in the strongest position when (1) you've done your homework and know what the usual salary and benefits are and (2) you can walk away from

Interview Bloopers

A recent survey asked executives for the most embarrassing interview moments they had encountered. Here are some examples.

- "The candidate sent his sister to interview in his place."
- "The person was dancing during the interview. He kept saying things like, 'I love life!' and 'Oh yeah!' "
- "The candidate stopped the interview and asked me if I had a cigarette."
- "We had one person who walked out of an interview into a glass door—and the glass shattered."
- "The candidate got his companies confused and repeatedly mentioned the strengths of a competing firm, thinking that's who he was interviewing with."
- "A guy called me by the wrong name during the entire interview."
- "We're a retail company, and when we asked the candidate why she wanted to work for us, she said she didn't want to work in retail anymore."
- "An interviewee put his bubble gum in his hand, forgot about it, and then shook my hand."
- "A candidate fell asleep during the interview."

Bullets quoted from "Dancing, Smoking, Sleeping and Other Bad Interview Moves: Survey Reveals Most Embarrassing Job Interview Blunders," Robert Half International: OfficeTeam, May 28, 2008, http://officeteam.rhi.mediaroom.com/index.php?s=247&item=824.

Figure 14.2 Follow-Up Letter after an Office Visit

405 West College, Apt. 201
Thibodaux, LA 70301
April 2, 2012

Single-space your address and the date when you don't use letterhead.

Mr. Robert Land, Account Manager
Sive Associates
378 Norman Boulevard
Cincinnati, OH 48528

Dear Mr. Land:

After visiting Sive Associates last week, I'm even more sure that writing direct mail is the career for me.

Refers to things she saw and learned during the interview.

I've always been able to brainstorm ideas, but sometimes, when I had to focus on one idea for a class project, I wasn't sure which idea was best. It was fascinating to see how you make direct mail scientific as well as creative by testing each new creative package against the control. I can understand how pleased Linda Hayes was when she learned that her new package for *Smithsonian* beat the control.

Reminds interviewer of her strong points.

Seeing Kelly, Luke, and Gene collaborating on the Sesame Street package gave me some sense of the tight deadlines you're under. As you know, I've learned to meet deadlines, not only for my class assignments but also in working on Nicholls' newspaper. The award I won for my feature on the primary election suggests that my quality holds up even when the deadline is tight!

Thank you for your hospitality while I was in Cincinnati. You and your wife made my stay very pleasant. I especially appreciate the time the two of you took to help me find information about apartments that are accessible to wheelchairs. Cincinnati seems like a very livable city.

Be positive, not pushy. She doesn't assume she has the job.

I'm excited about a career in direct mail and about the possibility of joining Sive Associates. I look forward to hearing from you soon!

Refers to what will happen next.

Sincerely,

Gina Focasio

Gina Focasio
(504) 555-2948

Writer's phone number.

Puts request for reimbursement in P.S. to de-emphasize it; focuses on the job, not the cost of the trip.

P.S. My expenses totaled $454. Enclosed are receipts for my plane fare from New Orleans to Cincinnati ($367), the taxi to the airport in Cincinnati ($30), and the bus from Thibodaux to New Orleans ($57).

Encl.: Receipts for Expenses

this offer if it doesn't meet your needs. Avoid naming a specific salary. Don't say you can't accept less. Instead, say you would find it difficult to accept the job under the terms first offered.

Remember that you're negotiating a package, not just a starting salary. A company that truly can't pay any more money now might be able to review you for promotion sooner than usual, or pay your moving costs, or give you a better job title. Some companies offer fringe benefits that may compensate for lower taxable income: use of a company car, reimbursements for education, child care or elder care subsidies, or help in finding a job for your spouse or partner. And think about your career, not just the initial salary. Sometimes a low-paying job at a company that will provide superb experience will do more for your career (and your long-term earning prospects) than a high salary now with no room to grow.

Work toward a compromise. You want the employer to be happy that you're coming on board and to feel that you've behaved maturely and professionally.

Deciding Which Offer to Accept

The problem with choosing among job offers is that you're comparing apples and oranges. The job with the most interesting work pays peanuts. The job that pays best is in a city where you don't want to live. The secret of professional happiness is taking a job where the positives are things you want and the negatives are things that don't matter as much to you.

To choose among job offers, you need to know what is truly important to *you*. Start by answering questions like the following:

- Are you willing to work after hours? To take work home? To travel? How important is money to you? Prestige? Time to spend with family and friends?
- Would you rather have firm deadlines or a flexible schedule? Do you prefer working alone or with other people? Do you prefer specific instructions and standards for evaluation or freedom and uncertainty? How comfortable are you with pressure? How much variety and challenge do you want?
- What kinds of opportunities for training and advancement are you seeking?
- Where do you want to live? What features in terms of weather, geography, cultural and social life do you see as ideal?
- Is it important to you that your work achieve certain purposes or values, or do you see work as "just a way to make a living"? Are the organization's culture and ethical standards ones you find comfortable? Will you be able to do work you can point to with pride?

No job is perfect but some jobs will fulfill more of your major criteria than will others.

Some employers offer jobs at the end of the office visit. In other cases, you may wait for weeks or even months to hear. Employers may offer jobs orally. You must say something in response immediately, so it's good to plan some strategies in advance.

If your first offer is not from your first choice, express your pleasure at being offered the job, but do not accept it on the phone. "That's great! I assume I have two weeks to let you know?" Then *call* the other companies you're interested in. Explain, "I've just gotten a job offer, but I'd rather work for you. Can you tell me what the status of my application is?" Nobody will put that

Crazy Job-Seeking Stunts

In the struggle to land the perfect job, some job seekers will do almost anything to get noticed and secure a position. A survey conducted by CareerBuilder.com discovered some of the most unconventional methods experienced by hiring managers as candidates attempted to get a job. The following are some of the most bizarre and ones you probably want to avoid:

- Used an official celebrity fan site as a portfolio accomplishment
- Sent a nude photo to the hiring manager
- Performed a stand-up comedy routine
- Waited for the hiring manager at his car
- Dressed as a cat
- Wore a tuxedo
- Brought coffee for the entire office
- Asked the interviewer to dinner
- Provided Yankee tickets for the interviewer
- Provided a baby gift for a pregnant interviewer

Keep in mind, the goal of an interview is to be remembered in a positive way!

Adapted from Rosemary Haefner, "Weirdest Job Seeker Stunts," CareerBuilder, September 24, 2007, http://www.careerbuilder.com/Article/CB-263-Job-Search-Weirdest-Job-Seeker-Stunts.

information in writing, but almost everyone will tell you over the phone. With this information, you're in a better position to decide whether to accept the original offer.

Companies routinely give applicants two weeks to accept or reject offers. Some students have been successful in getting those two weeks extended to several weeks or even months. Certainly if you cannot decide by the deadline, it is worth asking for more time: The worst the company can do is say *no.* If you do try to keep a company hanging for a long time, be prepared for weekly phone calls asking you if you've decided yet.

Make your acceptance contingent upon a written job offer confirming the terms. That letter should spell out not only salary but also fringe benefits and any special provisions you have negotiated. If something is missing, call the interviewer for clarification: "You said that I'd be reviewed for a promotion and higher salary in six months, but that isn't in the letter." Even well-intentioned people can forget oral promises. You have more power to resolve misunderstandings now than you will after six months or a year on the job. Furthermore, the person who made you the promise may no longer be with the company a year later.

When you've accepted one job, notify the other places you visited. Then they can go to their second choices. If you're second on someone else's list, you'll appreciate other candidates' removing themselves so the way is clear for you.

DEALING WITH REJECTION

Because multiple people usually apply for each job opening, most job seekers get far more rejections than job offers. Learn to live with this fact of the job hunt. Form support groups with your friends who are also on the job market. Try to keep an upbeat attitude; it will show in job interviews and make you a more attractive candidate. Remember that candidate selection can be a political process. You may have been competing with the boss's daughter, an inside candidate, or a candidate who was recommended by a respected employee.

YOUR FIRST FULL-TIME JOB LO 14-6

Just like the step from high school to college, the step from college to your first full-time job brings changes that you must negotiate. The new business environment is exhilarating, with many opportunities, but it also contains pitfalls. As you go to being the new kid on the block yet again, remember all the coping strategies you have developed as a newbie in middle school, high school, and college.

- Reread all your materials on the organization, its competition, and the industry.
- Get to know your new colleagues, but also keep networking with people in the field.
- Talk to recent hires in the organization. Ask them what they found to be helpful advice when they were starting.
- Fit into the corporate culture by being observant. Watch what people wear, how they act, how they talk. Watch how they interact during meetings and in the break room. Look at the kinds of e-mails and letters people send. Discover who people go to when they need help.
- Use your breaks effectively. Stop by the coffee station, water cooler, or break room occasionally to plug into the grapevine.

- Find a successful person who is willing to mentor you. Even better, find a support network.
- Ask lots of questions. It may feel embarrassing, but it will feel even worse to still be ignorant several months down the road.
- Seek early opportunities for feedback. What you hear may not always be pleasant, but it will help you become a valued employee more quickly.
- Learn the jargon, but use it sparingly.
- Be pleasant and polite to everyone, including support personnel.
- Be punctual. Arrive for work and meetings on time.
- Be dependable. Do what you say you will do—and by the deadline.
- Be organized. Take a few minutes to plan your daily work. Keep track of papers and e-mails.
- Be resourceful. Few work projects will come to you with the detailed instructions provided by your professors. Think projects through. Ask for suggestions from trusted colleagues. Have a plan before you go to your boss with questions.
- Use technology professionally. Keep your cellphone on vibrate, or turn it off. Resist the temptation to send text messages during meetings. Don't visit inappropriate websites; remember that all computer activity can be tracked. Learn the company's Internet policies.
- Be discreet. Be careful what you say, and where you say it. Above all, be careful what you put in e-mails!
- Proofread all your written messages, including tweets and texts, before you send them. At rushed times, such as the end of the day or week, proofread them twice.
- Go the extra mile. Help out even when you are not asked. Put in extra hours when your help is needed.
- Do your share of grunt work—making coffee or refilling the paper tray.
- Take advantage of voluntary training opportunities.
- Take advantage of company social events, but always act professionally at them. Seriously limit your intake of alcohol.
- Document your work. Collect facts, figures, and documents. You will need this information for your performance reviews.
- Enjoy yourself. Enthusiasm for your new job and colleagues will have you part of the team in short order.

SUMMARY OF KEY POINTS

- Develop an overall strategy based on your answers to these three questions:
  1. What two to five facts about yourself do you want the interviewer to know?
  2. What disadvantages or weaknesses do you need to overcome or minimize?
  3. What do you need to know about the job and the organization to decide whether or not you want to accept this job if it is offered to you?
- Check on dress expectations before the interview.
- Rehearse everything you can. In particular, practice answers to common questions. Ask a friend to interview you. If your campus has practice interviews or videotaping facilities, use them so that you can evaluate and modify your interview behavior.

- Bring an extra copy of your résumé, something to write on and write with, and copies of your work to the interview.
- Record the name of the interviewer, tips the interviewer gave you, what the interviewer liked about you, answers to your questions about the company, and when you'll hear from the company.
- Successful applicants know what they want to do, use the company name in the interview, have researched the company in advance, back up claims with specifics, use appropriate technical jargon, ask specific questions, and talk more of the time.
- **Behavioral interviews** ask the applicant to describe actual behaviors, rather than plans or general principles. To answer a behavioral question, describe the situation, tell what you did, and tell what happened. Think about the implications of what you did and be ready to talk about what you'd do the next time or if the situation were slightly different.
- **Situational interviews** put you in a situation that allows the interviewer to see whether you have the qualities the company is seeking.
- **Stress interviews** deliberately create physical or psychological stress. Change the conditions that create physical stress. Meet psychological stress by rephrasing questions in less inflammatory terms and treating them as requests for information.
- Use follow-up phone calls and written messages to reinforce positives from the first interview, and to provide information to persuade the interviewer to hire you.
- The best time to negotiate for salary and benefits is after you have the job offer.
- If your first offer isn't from your first choice, call the other companies you're interested in to ask the status of your application.

CHAPTER 14 Exercises and Problems

Go to www.mhhe.com/locker10e for additional Exercises and Problems.

14.1 Reviewing the Chapter

1. Name four interview channels. What special considerations do you have to make for them? (LO 14-1)
2. What are three special kinds of interviews you may encounter? What are tips to succeed in them? (LO 14-1)
3. What preparations should you make before an interview? (LO 14-2)
4. What are some behavior tips you should keep in mind during an interview? (LO 14-3)
5. What should you accomplish in the close of an interview? (LO 14-3)
6. What are some common interview questions? What are effective answers for you? (LO 14-4)
7. What do you need to do after an interview? (LO 14-5)
8. When do you negotiate for salary? Why? (LO 14-5)
9. What are some tips to help you succeed at your first full-time job? (LO 14-6)

14.2 Interviewing Job Hunters

Talk to students at your school who are interviewing for jobs this term. Possible questions to ask them include the following:

- What field are you in? How good is the job market in that field this year?
- How long is the first interview with a company, usually?
- What questions have you been asked at job interviews? Were you asked any stress or sexist questions? Any really oddball questions?

- What answers seemed to go over well? What answers bombed?
- At an office visit or plant trip, how many people did you talk to? What were their job titles?
- Were you asked to take any tests (skills, physical, drugs)?
- How long did you have to wait after a first interview to learn whether you were being invited for an office visit? How long after an office visit did it take to learn whether you were being offered a job? How much time did the company give you to decide?
- What advice would you have for someone who will be interviewing next term or next year?

As your instructor directs,

a. Summarize your findings in a memo to your instructor.
b. Report your findings orally to the class.
c. Join with a small group of students to write a group report describing the results of your survey.

14.3 Interviewing an Interviewer

Talk to someone who regularly interviews candidates for entry-level jobs. Possible questions to ask include the following:

- How long have you been interviewing for your organization? Does everyone on the management ladder at your company do some interviewing, or do people specialize in it?
- Do you follow a set structure for interviews? What are some of the standard questions you ask?
- What are you looking for? How important are (1) good grades, (2) leadership roles in extracurricular groups, or (3) relevant work experience? What advice would you give to someone who lacks one or more of these?
- What are the things you see students do that create a poor impression? Think about the worst candidate you've interviewed. What did he or she do (or not do) to create such a negative impression?
- What are the things that make a good impression? Recall the best student you've ever interviewed. Why did he or she impress you so much?
- How does your employer evaluate and reward your success as an interviewer?
- What advice would you have for someone who still has a year or so before the job hunt begins?

As your instructor directs,

a. Summarize your findings in a memo to your instructor.
b. Report your findings orally to the class.
c. Join with a small group of students to write a group report describing the results of your survey.
d. Write to the interviewer thanking him or her for taking the time to talk to you.

14.4 Analyzing a Video Interview

Analyze a video clip of an interview session.

As your instructor directs,

1. In groups of four, search on a video-based website such as Google video or YouTube for terms such as "interview" or "student interview."
2. Watch a video clip of an interview and note the strengths and weaknesses of the interviewee.
3. Discuss your observations with your group and explain why you considered certain responses as strengths and weaknesses.
4. Share your video and analysis with your class.

14.5 Analyzing a Panel Interview

Watch some of the videos of the confirmation hearings (e.g., job interviews) for Elena Kagan. What good interview behaviors do you notice? What interview behaviors do you think could be improved? How does she handle difficult questions?

As your instructor directs,

a. Share your findings with a small group of other students.
b. Describe your findings in a memo to your instructor.
c. Present your findings orally to the class.

14.6 Preparing an Interview Strategy

Prepare your interview strategy.

1. List two to five things about yourself that you want the interviewer to know before you leave the interview.
2. Identify any weaknesses or apparent weaknesses in your record and plan ways to explain them or minimize them.
3. List the points you need to learn about an employer to decide whether to accept an office visit or plant trip.

As your instructor directs,

a. Share your strategy with a small group of other students.
b. Describe your strategy in a memo to your instructor.
c. Present your strategy orally to the class.

14.7 Preparing Questions to Ask Employers

Prepare a list of questions to ask at job interviews.

1. Prepare a list of three to five general questions that apply to most employers in your field.
2. Prepare two to five specific questions for the three companies you are most interested in.

As your instructor directs,

a. Share the questions with a small group of other students.
b. List the questions in a memo to your instructor.
c. Present your questions orally to the class.

14.8 Analyzing Answers to Interview Questions

What might be problematic about these responses to interview questions? How might the answers be improved?

a. Q: Tell me about yourself.
   A: I'm really a fun-loving person. I get along well with everyone.
b. Q: Why are you leaving Software Solutions?
   A: Everyone is leaving. The owner is totally inept. He was even late paying our withholding taxes last year.
c. Q: Tell me about a weakness you have.
   A: I'm a workaholic.
d. Q: What was your least favorite class in college?
   A: Business communication.
e. Q: What was your favorite class in college?
   A: American Indian storytelling.
f. Q: Tell me about a group project that had problems.
   A: Our marketing team had a real deadbeat on it. But I saved our asses by going to the teacher and getting her to take him off.
g. Q: Tell me about a book you have read and enjoyed that wasn't a textbook.
   A: We read *To Kill a Mockingbird* in 10th grade English.
h. Q: What are your interests outside work?
   A: Partying.
i. Q: Where do you see yourself in five years?
   A: In your job.
j. Q: Why do you want this job?
   A: This is a great job for me. It will really increase my skills set.

14.9 Preparing Answers to Tricky Questions

In small groups, find a website that has some trick (sometimes called weird) interview questions such as those at http://finance.yahoo.com/career-work/article/111757/the-25-weirdest-interview-questions-of-2010. Choose four and discuss how you could answer them. Share your best two examples with the class.

14.10 Preparing Answers to Questions You May Be Asked

Prepare answers to each of the interview questions listed in this chapter and to any other questions that you know are likely to be asked of job hunters in your field or on your campus.

As your instructor directs,

a. Write down the answers to your questions and turn them in.

b. Conduct mini-interviews in a small group of students. In the group, let student A be the interviewer and ask five questions from the list. Student B will play the job candidate and answer the questions, using real information about student B's field and qualifications. Student C will evaluate the content of the answer. Student D will observe the nonverbal behavior of the interviewer (A); student E will observe the nonverbal behavior of the interviewee (B).

After the mini-interview, let students C, D, and E share their observations and recommend ways that B could be even more effective. Then switch roles. Let another student be the interviewer and ask five questions of another interviewee, while new observers note content and nonverbal behavior. Continue the process until everyone in the group has had a chance to be "interviewed."

14.11 Writing a Follow-Up Message after an Onsite Visit

Write a follow-up e-mail message or letter after an office visit or plant trip. Thank your hosts for their hospitality; relate your strong points to things you learned about the company during the visit; allay any negatives that may remain; be enthusiastic about the company; and submit receipts for your expenses so you can be reimbursed.

14.12 Clarifying the Terms of a Job Offer

Last week, you got a job offer from your first choice company, and you accepted it over the phone. Today, the written confirmation arrived. The letter specifies the starting salary and fringe benefits you had negotiated. However, during the office visit, you were promised a 5% raise in six months. The job offer says nothing about the raise. You do want the job, but you want it on the terms you thought you had negotiated.

Write to your contact at the company, Damon Winters.

14.13 Researching a Geographic Area

Research a geographic area where you would like to work. Investigate the cost of living, industrial growth in the area, weather and climate, and attractions in the area you could visit. The local Chamber of Commerce is a good place to start your research.

As your instructor directs,

a. Share your findings with a small group of other students.
b. Describe your findings in a memo to your instructor.
c. Present your findings orally to the class.

CHAPTER 15

Planning and Researching Proposals and Reports

Chapter Outline

Varieties of Reports

The Report Production Process

Report Problems

Research Strategies for Reports

- Finding Information Online and in Print
- Evaluating Web Sources
- Analyzing and Designing Surveys
- Conducting Research Interviews
- Using Focus Groups
- Using Online Networks
- Observing Customers and Users

Source Citation and Documentation

Summary of Key Points

Researching the Gulf Disaster

On April 20, 2010, the *Deepwater Horizon*, an oil rig operating in the Gulf of Mexico, exploded, killing 11 crew members and injuring another 17. The explosion tore off the top of the well and oil began spilling into the ocean. For three months, millions of barrels of crude oil poured into the Gulf of Mexico, causing an unprecedented environmental disaster.

Even before the well had been capped, President Barack Obama organized a commission to investigate the cause and results of the accident, and to make recommendations for the future. In January 2011, the National Commission on the BP Deepwater Horizon Oil Spill and Offshore Drilling presented its final report to the president and posted it on their website. The nearly 400-page report details the causes of the accident, the mistakes during the accident, and the errors in corporate and government responses.

A report this size did not happen overnight. The commission members worked for months to gather data, conduct interviews, and make field observations. But all of their research began with a specific plan. When the commission was organized, they were given two tasks: (1) "Examine the performance of the technologies and practices involved in the probable causes of the explosion," and (2) "Identify and recommend available technology, industry best practices, best available standards, and other measures . . . to avoid future occurrence of such events."

"A report this size did not happen overnight. The commission members worked for months to gather data, conduct interviews, and make field observations."

In response to these two tasks, the commission listed the pieces of technology involved in the explosion and the practices of the rig's workers, supervisors, company executives, and contractors. From those lists, the commission determined who to interview and what to research. Over the next several months, as the research progressed, the commission expanded and adjusted their plan.

In January, the commission submitted its report to the president. Careful planning and thorough research helped the commission fulfill its purpose and complete its tasks.

Sources: National Commission on the BP Deepwater Horizon Oil Spill and Offshore Drilling, *Deepwater: The Gulf Oil Disaster and the Future of Offshore Drilling* (Washington, DC: Government Printing Office, 2011); and Committee for the Analysis of Causes of the Deepwater Horizon Explosion, Fire, and Oil Spill to Identify Measures to Prevent Similar Accidents in the Future; National Academy of Engineering; National Research Council, *Interim Report on Causes of the Deepwater Horizon Oil Rig Blowout and Ways to Prevent Such Events* (Washington, DC: National Academies Press, 2010).

Learning Objectives

After studying this chapter, you will know how to

LO 15-1 Define report problems.

LO 15-2 Employ different research strategies.

LO 15-3 Use and document sources.

Proposals and reports depend on research. The research may be as simple as pulling up data with a computer program or as complicated as calling many different people, conducting focus groups and surveys, or even planning and conducting experiments. Care in planning and researching proposals and reports is needed to produce effective documents.

In writing any report, there are five basic steps:

1. Define the problem.
2. Gather the necessary data and information.
3. Analyze the data and information.
4. Organize the information.
5. Write the report.

After reviewing the varieties of reports, this chapter focuses on the first two steps. Chapter 18 discusses the last three steps. You can find tips for creating visuals and data displays in Chapter 16. Chapter 17 covers guidelines for writing proposals.

VARIETIES OF REPORTS

Many kinds of documents are called reports. In some organizations, a report is a long document or one that contains numerical data. In others, one- and two-page memos are called reports. In still others, reports consist of PowerPoint slides delivered orally or printed and bound together. A short report to a client may use letter format. **Formal reports** contain formal elements such as a title page, a transmittal, a table of contents, and a list of illustrations. **Informal reports** may be letters and memos or even computer printouts of production or sales figures. But all reports, whatever their length or degree of formality, provide the information that people in organizations need to make plans and solve problems.

Reports can provide just information, both information and analysis alone, or information and analysis to support a recommendation (see Figure 15.1). Reports can be called **information reports** if they collect data for the reader, **analytical reports** if they interpret data but do not recommend action, and **recommendation reports** if they recommend action or a solution.

The following reports can be information, analytical, or recommendation reports, depending on what they provide:

- **Accident reports** can simply list the nature and causes of accidents in a factory or office. These reports can also analyze the data and recommend ways to make conditions safer.
- **Credit reports** can simply summarize an applicant's income and other credit obligations. These reports can also evaluate the applicant's collateral and creditworthiness and recommend whether or not to provide credit.

Figure 15.1 Variety of Information Reports Can Provide

Information only

Sales reports (sales figures for the week or month).

Quarterly reports (figures showing a plant's productivity and profits for the quarter).

Information plus analysis

Annual reports (financial data and an organization's accomplishments during the past year).

Audit reports (interpretations of the facts revealed during an audit).

Make-good or payback reports (calculations of the point at which a new capital investment will pay for itself).

Information plus analysis plus a recommendation

Recommendation reports evaluate two or more alternatives and recommend which alternative the organization should choose.

Feasibility reports evaluate a proposed action and show whether or not it will work.

Justification reports justify the need for a purchase, an investment, a new personnel line, or a change in procedure.

Problem-solving reports identify the causes of an organizational problem and recommend a solution.

- **Progress and interim reports** can simply record the work done so far and the work remaining on a project. These reports can also analyze the quality of the work and recommend that a project be stopped, continued, or restructured.
- **Trip reports** can simply share what the author learned at a conference or during a visit to a customer or supplier. These reports can also recommend action based on that information.
- **Closure reports** can simply document the causes of a failure or possible products that are not economically or technically feasible under current conditions. They can also recommend action to prevent such failures in the future.

Researching and Reporting at Reuters

Thomson Reuters is the largest business-to-business information services company in the world. Some years ago, it began to reinvent itself by learning more about clients who use its products and services: tax professionals, investment managers, brokers, lawyers, accountants, financial analysts, and researchers.

Thomson Reuters began by identifying eight market segments and exploring each of them in greater detail. It employed both quantitative (surveys) and qualitative (interviews) research methods to collect information. Thomson Reuters even filmed users as they performed their job duties.

The comprehensive approach to research paid off. After thoroughly investigating the eight market segments, Thomson Reuters created a list of product attributes that needed improvement to yield better customer satisfaction. Based on its exhaustive market research, Thomson Reuters redesigned its product portfolio, beginning with what could be done most easily and moving to advanced features. Today, nearly 70% of Thomson Reuter's products have undergone improvements based on its user-oriented market research process, adding both to the company's bottom line and customer satisfaction.

Adapted from Richard J. Harrington and Anthony K. Tjan, "Transforming Strategy One Customer at a Time," *Harvard Business Review* 86, no. 3 (March 2008): 62–72.

THE REPORT PRODUCTION PROCESS

When you write a report, you know the actual writing will take a significant chunk of time. But you should also plan to spend significant time analyzing your data, revising drafts, and preparing visuals and slides.

When you write a report for a class project, plan to complete at least one-fourth of your research before you write the proposal. Begin analyzing your data as you collect it; prepare your list of sources and drafts of visuals as you go along. Start writing your first draft before the research is completed. An early draft can help clarify where you need more research. Save at least one-fourth of your time at the end of the project to think and write after all your data are collected. For a collaborative report, you'll need even more time to write and revise.

Up-front planning helps you use your time efficiently. Start by thinking about the whole report process. Talk to your readers to understand how much detail and formality they want. Look at reports that were produced earlier (sample reports in this text are in Chapter 18). List all the parts of the report you'll need to prepare. Then articulate—to yourself or your team members—the purposes, audiences, and generic constraints for each part. The fuller idea you have of the final product when you start, the fewer drafts you'll need to write and the better your final product will be.

REPORT PROBLEMS LO 15-1

Good reports grow out of real problems: disjunctions between reality and the ideal, choices that must be made. When you write a report as part of your job, the organization may define the problem. To brainstorm problems for class reports, think about issues that face your college or university; housing units on campus; social, religious, and professional groups on campus and in your city; local businesses; and city, county, state, and federal governments and their agencies. Read your campus and local papers and newsmagazines; read the news on the Internet, watch it on TV, or listen to it on National Public Radio.

A good report problem in business or administration meets the following criteria:

1. The problem is
   - Real.
   - Important enough to be worth solving.
   - Narrow but challenging.
2. The audience for the report is
   - Real.
   - Able to implement the recommended action.
3. The data, evidence, and facts are
   - Sufficient to document the severity of the problem.
   - Sufficient to prove that the recommendation will solve the problem.
   - Available to *you.*
   - Comprehensible to *you.*

Often problems need to be narrowed. For example, "improving the college experiences of international students studying in the United States" is far too broad. First, choose one college or university. Second, identify the specific problem. Do you want to increase the social interaction between U.S. and international students? Help international students find housing? Increase the number of ethnic grocery stores and restaurants? Third, identify the specific audience that would have the power to implement your recommendations. Depending on the specific topic, the audience might be the Office of International Studies, the residence hall counselors, a service organization on campus or in town, a store, or a group of investors.

Some problems are more easily researched than others. If you have easy access to the Chinese Student Association, you can survey them about their experiences at the local Chinese grocery. However, if you want to recommend ways to keep the Chinese grocery in business, but you do not have access to their financial records, you will have a much more difficult time solving the problem. Even if you have access, if the records are written in Chinese, you will have problems unless you read the language or have a willing translator.

Research for Developing Countries

Procter & Gamble researchers found that 60% of shoppers at tiny stores in developing countries already know what they want, so they do not spend time browsing. But they do gaze at the cashier's area for 5 seconds as they wait for their purchase or change. So P&G is thinking of ways to persuade store owners to put more P&G products in these areas.

Because running water is in short supply for many low-income Mexican consumers, P&G researchers developed a fabric softener that, when added to the laundry load along with the detergent, can eliminate a rinse cycle in the kinds of washing machines being used.

To keep prices down for these customers, P&G employs "reverse engineering." It starts with the price consumers can afford for the product and then adjusts features and manufacturing accordingly. To hold down the cost of a detergent used for hand washing clothes, P&G used fewer enzymes. The result was a cheaper product, and one that was gentler on the hands than the regular detergent.

Adapted from Ellen Byron, "P&G's Global Target: Shelves of Tiny Stores: It Woos Poor Women Buying Single Portions; Mexico's 'Hot Zones,'" *Wall Street Journal,* July 16, 2007, A1.

Hasbro does extensive research to keep developing games people will play.

Pick a problem you can solve in the time available. Six months of full-time (and overtime) work and a team of colleagues might allow you to look at all the ways to make a store more profitable. If you're doing a report in 6 to 12 weeks for a class that is only one of your responsibilities, limit the topic. Depending on your interests and knowledge, you could choose to examine the prices and brands carried, its inventory procedures, its overhead costs, its layout and decor, or its advertising budget.

Look at the following examples of report problems in the category of technology use:

Too broad:	Texting in class and its effects on college students.
Too time-consuming:	What are the effects of in-class texting on college students?
Better:	What are texting habits of students in XYZ University's Business School?
Better:	How can texting be integrated in XYZ University's business courses?

The first problem is too broad because it covers all college students. The second one is too time-consuming. Scholars are only starting to study the effects, and for you to do a report on this topic, you would need to do your own longitudinal project. The third and fourth problems would both be possibilities. You would select one over the other depending on whether you wanted to focus on students or courses.

How you define the problem shapes the solutions you find. For example, suppose that a manufacturer of frozen foods isn't making money. If the problem is defined as a marketing problem, the researcher may analyze the product's price, image, advertising, and position in the market. But perhaps the problem is really that overhead costs are too high due to poor inventory management, or that an inadequate distribution system doesn't get the product to its target market. Defining the problem accurately is essential to finding an effective solution.

Once you've defined your problem, you're ready to write a purpose statement. The purpose statement goes both in your proposal and in your final report. A good **purpose statement** makes three things clear:

- The organizational problem or conflict.
- The specific technical questions that must be answered to solve the problem.
- The rhetorical purpose (to explain, to recommend, to request, to propose) the report is designed to achieve.

Research and Innovation: Fun and Games at Hasbro

On Fridays, employees at Hasbro spend their lunchtime playing board games and thinking about ways to update games or create new ones. The Friday games are just one of the creative approaches to research and innovation used at the company that manufactures some of America's best-known board games, such as Monopoly, Scrabble, Sorry, and Clue.

In the world of board games, continuous innovation is necessary to fit games to changing consumer lifestyles and preferences. Hasbro invests in extensive market research, such as conducting online surveys, observing children and adults playing games in the company's Game-Works lab, and talking with people about how they want to spend leisure time.

In response to information obtained through these strategies, Hasbro has modified several of its traditional games.

- To accommodate consumers' tight schedules, Hasbro developed "express" versions of Monopoly, Sorry, and Scrabble that can be completed within 20 minutes.
- To address consumers' desire for more balanced lives, The Game of Life now includes life experience, education, and family life as elements of a successful life, rather than basing success only on making the most money.
- Based on 3 million votes cast in an online survey, a revised version of Monopoly replaces Boardwalk with Times Square and Pacific Avenue with Las Vegas Boulevard.
- To attract customers who enjoy using technology to play games, game designers developed electronic versions of games.

Adapted from Carol Hymowitz, "All Companies Need Innovation: Hasbro Finds a New Magic," *Wall Street Journal,* February 26, 2007, B1.

Finding the Facts

Students aren't the only ones who need to sift through mountains of conflicting information on the Internet. Journalists use the Internet to gather data, collect background information, and verify facts. But how do professionals use the Internet wisely? The *Des Moines Register* offers four strategies:

- **Use documents.** Original documents, including public documents, e-mails, and videos tell you what really happened or was said, not what people say they said.
- **Understand context.** Expand your research to include how the information fits into the big picture. What you may see as important data may look different in the larger pattern.
- **Use credible sources.** Make sure the sources you use have good track records of accuracy and fair treatment of both sides of an issue.
- **Present opinions as opinions.** Forecasts of the future are almost always opinions.

Adapted from Carolyn Washburn, "How Register Journalists Work to Bring You the Facts," *Des Moines Register*, October 31, 2010, OP1.

The following purpose statement for a report to the superintendent of Yellowstone National Park has all three elements:

> Current management methods keep the elk population within the carrying capacity of the habitat but require frequent human intervention. Both wildlife conservation specialists and the public would prefer methods that controlled the elk population naturally. This report will compare the current short-term management techniques (hunting, trapping and transporting, and winter feeding) with two long-term management techniques, habitat modification and the reintroduction of predators. The purpose of this report is to recommend which techniques or combination of techniques would best satisfy the needs of conservationists, hunters, and the public.

To write a good purpose statement, you must understand the basic problem and have some idea of the questions that your report will answer. Note, however, that you can (and should) write the purpose statement before researching the specific alternatives the report will discuss.

RESEARCH STRATEGIES FOR REPORTS LO 15-2

Research for a report may be as simple as getting a computer printout of sales for the last month; it may involve finding published material or surveying or interviewing people. **Secondary research** retrieves information that someone else gathered. Library research and online searches are the best known kinds of secondary research. **Primary research** gathers new information. Surveys, interviews, and observations are common methods for gathering new information for business reports.

Finding Information Online and in Print

You can save time and money by checking online and published sources of data before you gather new information. Many college and university libraries

Good research uses multiple media and sources.

PARDON MY PLANET

provide workshops and handouts on research techniques, as well as access to computer databases and research librarians.

Categories of sources that may be useful include

- Specialized encyclopedias for introductions to a topic.
- Indexes to find articles. Most permit searches by key word, by author, and often by company name.
- Abstracts for brief descriptions or summaries of articles. Sometimes the abstract will be all you'll need; almost always, you can tell from the abstract whether an article is useful for your needs.
- Citation indexes to find materials that cite previous research. Citation indexes thus enable you to use an older reference to find newer articles on the topic. The *Social Sciences Citation Index* is the most useful for researching business topics.
- Newspapers for information about recent events.
- U.S. Census reports, for a variety of business and demographic information.

To use a computer database efficiently, identify the concepts you're interested in and choose key words that will help you find relevant sources. **Key words** are the terms that the computer searches for. If you're not sure what terms to use, check the ABI/Inform Thesaurus for synonyms and the hierarchies in which information is arranged in various databases.

Specific commands allow you to narrow your search. For example, to study the effect of the minimum wage on employment in the restaurant industry, you might use a Boolean search (see Figure 15.2):

(minimum wage) *and* (restaurant *or* fast food) *and*
(employment rate *or* unemployment).

This descriptor would give you the titles of articles that treat all three of the topics in parentheses. Without *and,* you'd get articles that discuss the minimum wage in general, articles about every aspect of *restaurants,* and every article that refers to *unemployment,* even though many of these would not be relevant to your topic. The *or* descriptor calls up articles that use the term *fast food* or the term *restaurant.* Many Web search engines, including AltaVista and Google, allow you to specify words that cannot appear in a source.

Figure 15.2 Example of a Boolean Search

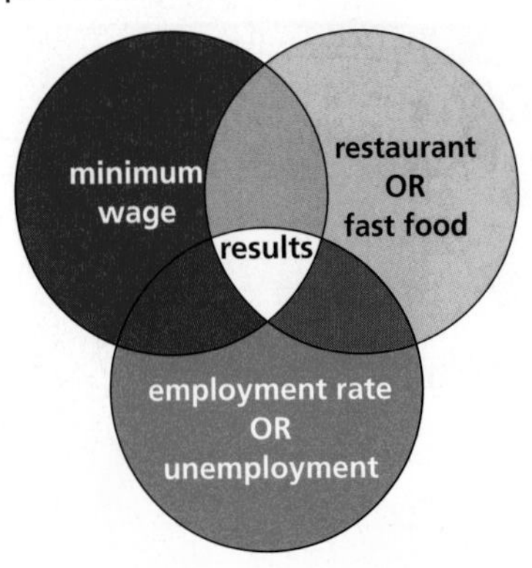

Many words can appear in related forms. To catch all of them, use the database's **wild card** or **truncated code** for shortened terms and root words. To find this feature and others, go to the Advanced Search screen for the search engine you are using. Search engines vary in the symbols they use for searches, so be sure to check for accurate directions.

Web search engines are particularly effective for words, people, or phrases that are unlikely to have separate pages devoted to them. For general topics or famous people, directories like Yahoo! may be more useful. Figure 15.3 lists a few of the specialized sources available.

Figure 15.3 Sources for Web Research

Subject matter directories
SmartPros (accounting and corporate finance) http://smartpros.com/
Rutgers Accounting Web (RAW) http://raw.rutgers.edu/
Education Index http://www.educationindex.com
Resources for Economists on the Internet http://www.aeaweb.org/RFE/
Human Resource Management Resources on the Internet http://www.nbs.ntu.ac.uk/research/depts/hrm/links.php
Global Edge http://www.globaledge.msu.edu/
Management and Entrepreneurship http://www.lib.lsu.edu/bus/managemt.html
KnowThis: Knowledge Source for Marketing http://www.knowthis.com
Internet Marketing Resources http://www.lib.lsu.edu/bus/marketing.html
Statistical Resources on the Web (University of Michigan Documents Center) http://www.lib.umich.edu/government-documents-center/explore/browse/statistics/260/search/

(Continued)

Figure 15.3 Sources for Web Research (Concluded)

News sites

Bloomberg Businessweek
http://www.businessweek.com

CNN/CNNFN
http://www.cnn.com (news)
http://money.cnn.com/ (financial news)

National Public Radio
http://www.npr.org

NewsLink (links to US, Canadian, and international newspapers, magazines, and resources online)
http://newslink.org

New York Times
http://www.nytimes.com

Wall Street Journal
http://online.wsj.com/

Washington Post
http://www.WashingtonPost.com

U.S. government information

FedStats (links from over 100 federal agencies)
http://www.fedstats.gov

U.S. Government Printing Office (free electronic access to government documents)
http://www.gpoaccess.gov/

Bureau of Economic Analysis
http://www.bea.gov/

Bureau of Labor Statistics
http://www.bls.gov/

Census Bureau (including a link to the *Statistical Abstract of the United States*)
http://www.census.gov/

Securities and Exchange Commission Filings and Forms (EDGAR)
http://sec.gov/edgar.shtml

Small Business Administration
http://www.sbaonline.sba.gov/

White House Briefing Room (presidential events and public statements)
http://www.whitehouse.gov/briefing_room/

Reference collections

Hoover's Online (information about businesses)
http://www.hoovers.com/

My Virtual Reference Desk
http://www.refdesk.com/

Tile.Net (reference guide to e-mail newsletters and discussion lists)
http://tile.net/lists/

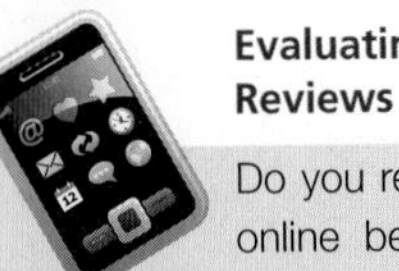

Evaluating Online Reviews

Do you read reviews online before booking a vacation or buying products? If so, read the fine print of the review.

TripAdvisor, a popular travel site, includes a disclaimer that some hotels are writing fake reviews on its website. The disclaimer, posted near questionable reviews, reads: "TripAdvisor has reasonable cause to believe that either this property or individuals associated with the property may have attempted to manipulate our popularity index by interfering with the unbiased nature of our reviews."

The motivation for hotels is an attempt to heighten their own ranking while harming their competitors. This sneaky approach is not unique to travel sites. Other retail stores and businesses routinely confront the same problem when dealing with online reviews. Website administrators are trying to develop ways to combat fake reviewers. The Apple Store, for instance, requires that customers buy an application before they can review it.

Be cautious about the inherent biases you may be reading in reviews before you book your next trip or buy a new product.

Adapted from "Popular Travel Web Site TripAdvisor Warns of Hotels Posting Fake Reviews," *Des Moines Register,* July 16, 2009, 8A.

Evaluating Web Sources

Some of the material on the Web is excellent, but some of it is wholly unreliable. With print sources, the editor or publisher serves as a gatekeeper, so you can trust the material in good journals. To put up a web page, all one needs is access to a server.

Use the following criteria to evaluate websites for your research project:

- **Authors.** What person or organization sponsors the site? What credentials do the authors have?
- **Objectivity.** Does the site give evidence to support its claims? Does it give both sides of controversial issues? Is the tone professional?
- **Information.** How complete is the information? What is it based on?
- **Currency.** How current is the information?
- **Audience.** Who is the intended audience?

Answers to these questions may lead you to discard some of the relevant sites you find. For example, if you find five different web pages about the cell phones and car accidents that all cite the same Toronto study, you have one source, not five. Choose the most complete for your project.

Many students start their research with Wikipedia. If you are one of them, you are not alone. Wikipedia is the largest, most popular encyclopedia ever. It has over 18 million articles in 279 languages and is the seventh visited website in the world.[1] So, while it may be acceptable as a starting place, be aware that many instructors and other professionals do not accept Wikipedia—or any encyclopedia, frequently—as an authoritative source. These are some of their reasons:

- Many remember the beginnings of Wikipedia when it was full of errors.
- Because not all entries are written by experts on the topic, some entries still contain errors.
- Wikipedia makes the news when pranksters maliciously alter entries.
- Thanks to WikiScanner, some editors have been shown to have self-interest. For instance, Diebold deleted paragraphs criticizing its electronic voting machines, and PepsiCo deleted paragraphs on negative health effects in the Pepsi entry. All edits from IP addresses owned by the Church of Scientology have been banned by Wikipedia.[2]
- Because Wikipedia is constantly changing, information you cite may be changed or eliminated if someone goes to check it.
- One final, growing concern is that the volunteers who edit and police Wikipedia are declining at a much faster rate than new contributors are joining.[3]

Analyzing and Designing Surveys

A **survey** questions a group of people. The easiest way to ask many questions is to create a **questionnaire,** a written list of questions that people fill out. An **interview** is a structured conversation with someone who will be able to give you useful information. Organizations use surveys and interviews to research both internal issues such as employee satisfaction and external issues such as customer satisfaction.

A survey that has been the target of much questioning in the press is the one behind the annual college rankings of *U.S. News & World Report.* Critics charge that the rankings are based far too heavily on opinion (peer evaluations from other schools), uncorroborated data supplied by the schools themselves, and irrelevant data (such as rates of alumni giving). Critics also charge schools with gaming the system through practices such as heavy solicitation of students who have almost no chance of being accepted (low acceptance rates help schools' rankings).[4]

Because surveys can be used to show almost anything, people need to be careful when analyzing the results of surveys or designing their own. These are questions commonly asked about surveys:

1. Who did the survey and who paid for it?
2. How many people were surveyed and how were they chosen?
3. How was the survey conducted?
4. What was the response rate?
5. What questions were asked?

1. Who Did the Survey and Who Paid for It? Unfortunately, it is far too easy to introduce bias into surveys. Thus, a good place to start when examining survey results is with the survey producers. Who are they? How were they financed? How comfortable should you be with the results of a survey about a medical device when the survey was financed by the maker of the device? Was a survey about auto model satisfaction financed by the maker of the auto?

2. How Many People Were Surveyed and How Were They Chosen? To keep research costs reasonable, usually only a sample of the total population is polled. How that sample is chosen and the attempts made to get responses from nonrespondents will determine whether you can infer that what is true of your sample is also true of the population as a whole.

A **sample** is a subset of the population. The **sampling units** are those actually sampled. Frequently, the sampling unit is an individual. If a list of individuals is not available then a household can be the sampling unit. The list of all sampling units is the **sampling frame.** For interviews, this could be a list of all addresses, or for companies a list of all Fortune 500 CEOs.[5] The **population** is the group you want to make statements about. Depending on the purpose of your research, your population might be all Fortune 1000 companies, all business students at your college, or all consumers of tea in the mid-Atlantic states.

A **convenience sample** is a group of subjects who are easy to get: students who walk through the union, people at a shopping mall, workers in your own unit. Convenience samples are useful for a rough pretest of a questionnaire and may be acceptable for some class research projects. However, you cannot generalize from a convenience sample to a larger group.

A purposive or **judgment sample** is a group of people whose views seem useful. Someone interested in surveying the kinds of writing done on campus might ask each department for the name of a faculty member who cared about writing, and then send surveys to those people.

In a **random sample,** each person in the population theoretically has an equal chance of being chosen. When people say they did something *randomly* they often mean *without conscious bias.* However, unconscious bias exists. Someone passing out surveys in front of the library will be more likely to approach people who seem friendly and less likely to ask people who seem intimidating, in a hurry, much older or younger, or of a different race, class, or sex. True random samples rely on random digit tables, published in statistics texts and books such as *A Million Random Digits.* An online random number table site can be found at http://ts.nist.gov/WeightsandMeasures/upload/AppendB-HB133-05-Z.pdf.

Social Networking Hoaxes

You should not believe everything you read online. Here are a few recent examples of social networking hoaxes:

- In March 2011, a Twitter spambot sent a hoax message that actor Jackie Chan died from a heart attack. He became a top-five trend within 24-hours on Twitter. Even President Obama offered his condolences. Other death hoaxes have also appeared about Justin Bieber and Miley Cyrus.
- The home furniture store IKEA was part of a hoax on Facebook. An ad suggested that users who fanned their page would receive a $1,000 gift card.
- One of the top continuing hoaxes is targeted at users of freemail accounts (i.e., Gmail, AOL, Yahoo). They receive an e-mail urging them to forward the message so the company can figure out who is still using their accounts. This hoax has been circulating since 1999.

Adapted from A. Hopkinson, "Social Media Death Hoaxes," *Ethics in the News* (blog), April 26, 2011, http://www.ethicsinthenews.com/social-media-death-hoaxes/; Hans Kullin, "IKEA Victim of Facebook Hoax," *Social Media Today,* March 25, 2010, http://socialmediatoday.com/index.php?q=SMC/184215; and "Overload of Malarkey," Snopes, last updated January 27, 2011, http://www.snopes.com/computer/internet/overload.asp.

Speedo conducted extensive research before launching its new LZR Racer Speedo, which enabled many swimmers to break records at the Beijing Olympics.

Source: Christopher Rhodes and Hiroko Tabuchi, "Olympic Swimmers Race to Get Well Suited," *Wall Street Journal,* June 12, 2008, B8.

If you take a true random sample, you can generalize your findings to the whole population from which your sample comes. Consider, for example, a random phone survey that shows 65% of respondents approve of a presidential policy. Measures of variability should always be attached to survey-derived estimates like this one. Typically, a confidence interval provides this measure of variability. Using the confidence interval, we might conclude it is likely that between 58% and 72% of the population approve of the presidential policy when the confidence interval is ± 7%. The accuracy range is based on the size of the sample and the expected variation within the population. Statistics texts tell you how to calculate these measures of variability.

For many kinds of research, a large sample is important for giving significant results. In addition to its electronic data, Nielsen Media Research collects about 2 million television viewing diaries annually to gather viewing data. The large numbers also allow it to provide viewing information for local stations and their advertisers.[6]

Do not, however, confuse **sample size** with randomness. A classic example is the 1936 Literary Digest poll which predicted Republican Alf Landon would beat Democrat incumbent President Franklin Roosevelt. Literary Digest sent out 10 million ballots to its magazine subscribers as well as people who owned cars and telephones, most of whom in 1936 were richer than the average voter—and more Republican.[7]

Many people mistakenly believe any survey provides information about the general population. One survey with a biased sample that got much publicity involved "sexting." "One in five teenagers electronically share nude or semi-nude photos of themselves" declared the news stories. However, the sample for the survey came from a teenage research panel formed by phone and online recruiting, plus recruiting from existing panel members. This sample included many electronically savvy users, users who would be comfortable sending pictures electronically. So the survey showed the figures were true for this panel (and even there, the numbers were raised by responses from 18- and 19-year-old panelists, a group less inhibited than younger teens and more likely to respond), but because the panel was not a representative sample, no conclusions should be drawn about a wider population.[8]

3. How Was the Survey Conducted? **Face-to-face surveys** are convenient when you are surveying a fairly small number of people in a specific location. In a face-to-face survey, the interviewer's sex, race, and nonverbal cues can bias results. Most people prefer not to say things they think their audience will dislike. For that reason, women will be more likely to agree that sexual harassment is a problem if the interviewer is also a woman. Members of a minority group are more likely to admit that they suffer discrimination if the interviewer is a member of the same minority.

Telephone surveys are popular because they can be closely supervised. Interviewers can read the questions from a computer screen and key in answers as the respondent gives them. The results can then be available just a few minutes after the last call is completed.

Phone surveys also have limitations. First, they reach only people who have phones and thus underrepresent some groups such as poor people. Answering machines, caller ID, and cell phones also make phone surveys more difficult. Since a survey based on a phone book would exclude people with unlisted numbers, professional survey-takers use automatic random-digit dialing.

To increase the response rate for a phone survey, call at a time respondents will find convenient. Avoid calling between 5 and 7 PM, a time when many families have dinner.

Mail surveys can reach anyone who has an address. Some people may be more willing to fill out an anonymous questionnaire than to give sensitive information to a stranger over the phone. However, mail surveys are not effective for respondents who don't read and write well. Further, it may be more difficult to get a response from someone who doesn't care about the survey or who sees the mailing as junk mail. Over the phone, the interviewer can try to persuade the subject to participate.

Online surveys deliver questions over the Internet. The researcher can contact respondents with e-mail containing a link to a web page with the survey or can ask people by mail or in person to log on and visit the website with the survey. Another alternative is to post a survey on a website and invite the site's visitors to complete the survey. This approach does not generate a random sample, so the results probably do not reflect the opinions of the entire population.

Mattel, makers of Barbie, conducted an online poll to see what young girls wanted for the doll's next career. Results of the poll surprised Mattel. Although young girls wanted Barbie to be an anchor woman, the career winning the most votes was computer engineer, because various computer organizations for women asked their members to vote.[9] In general, volunteers for online surveys are more educated, more likely to be white, and more likely to be at the ends of the age spectrum than the general population.[10]

Nevertheless, with online surveys costing about one-tenth of phone surveys, they are increasing their acceptance among experts and growing in popularity as response rates for phone surveys continue to drop. The American Customer Satisfaction Index, a phone survey conducted for years by the University of Michigan, began incorporating online polling in 2010. YouGov, which tracks opinions of corporate brands, has a 1 million panel of U.S. adults.

Researching Emotional Purchasing

Most companies use consumer feedback and customer surveys to improve their products and shape their marketing. Traditional interviews and surveys, however, may not tell the whole picture. Campbell Soup found that people did not have logical reasons for their soup-eating habits. Furthermore, even when surveys showed ads were successful and memorable, that reaction didn't translate to additional sales. Words were not capturing people's unconscious soup responses.

To improve the results, Campbell's turned to a new method, "neuromarketing," using advanced biometrics like eye tracking and measurements of changes in pupil diameter, heart rate, skin moisture, and body temperature to learn how customers feel about product packaging. The researchers found that customers who had positive views of Campbell's products at home were overwhelmed by the choices at the store.

Campbell's revised their packaging based on the research, putting greater emphasis on the image of the soup and adding steam to the photograph to make it appear warm and comforting. They also removed or changed elements that did not get an emotional response.

Biometrics may be the marketing research of the future, testing not only what customers say, but also what they truly feel.

Adapted from Ilan Brat, "The Emotional Quotient of Soup Shopping," *Wall Street Journal*, February 17, 2010, B6.

Looking with the Customers' Eyes

IDEO, a design firm based in Palo Alto, California, uses observational research to design work processes that improve the customer's experience. IDEO requires its clients to participate in the research so that they can see how it feels to be one of their own customers. Clients may try using the company's product or go on shopping trips, or they may quietly observe customers. Following an initial observation phase, IDEO works with clients to use the observation data for brainstorming. IDEO then prepares and tests prototypes of the redesigned service, refines the ideas, and puts the revisions into action.

IDEO helped Kaiser Permanente revise its long-term growth plan to be more focused on clients' experiences with the health system. Working in teams with nurses, doctors, and managers from Kaiser, IDEO employees observed patients and occasionally role-played patient experiences. They saw that the check-in process was annoying, and waiting rooms were uncomfortable. Many of the patients arrived with a relative or friend for support, but they were often not allowed to remain together. Sitting alone in examination rooms was unpleasant and unnerving.

Based on these observations, Kaiser realized that it needed to focus more on improving patient experiences than on the original plan of modernizing buildings. The company created more comfortable areas in which patients could wait with family and friends, as well as examination rooms large enough to accommodate two people in addition to the patient. Instructions on where to go were made clearer as well.

Adapted from Bruce Nussbaum, "The Power of Design," *BusinessWeek*, May 17, 2004, 86.

Daily it sends enough surveys to receive back 5,000 completed ones. Although not random, the survey tries to be representative; YouGov ensures respondents reflect the overall population by factors such as age and gender.[11]

4. What Was the Response Rate? A major concern with any kind of survey is the **response rate,** the percentage of people who respond. People who refuse to answer may differ from those who respond, and you need information from both groups to be able to generalize to the whole population. Low response rates pose a major problem, especially for phone surveys. Answering machines and caller ID are commonly used to screen incoming calls resulting in decreased response rates.

Widespread use of cell phones in recent years has also negatively affected the ability of telephone surveyors to contact potential respondents. Including cell phones in a survey adds significantly to both the cost and the complexity (U.S. laws prevent autodialing of cell phones). The National Center for Health Statistics reports that 25% of households have only cell phone service; for adults age 25–29 that number rises to 49%. Many adults having only cell phones are in the lowest household income categories; they also tend to be single and less well educated. Adults 50 and older are significantly overrepresented in landline phone surveys, where they account for 66% of the average sample.[12] These figures show that phone surveys that are landline only, as is true for most, may have significant biases built into their samples.

The problem of nonresponse has increased dramatically in recent years. The response rate for random phone surveys is mostly 10% to 15% and often less than 10%; the rate for cell phone surveys is even less.[13] The mail response rate for the *mandatory* U.S. Census was only 65%, even with the $370.6 million dollars spent promoting response.[14]

To get as high a response rate as possible, good researchers follow up, contacting nonrespondents at least once and preferably twice to try to persuade them to participate in the survey. Sometimes money or other rewards are used to induce people to participate.

5. What Questions Were Asked? Surveys and interviews can be useful only if the questions are well designed. Good questions have these characteristics:

- They ask only one thing.
- They are phrased neutrally.
- They are asked in an order that does not influence answers.
- They avoid making assumptions about the respondent.
- They mean the same thing to different people.

At a telecommunications firm, a survey asked employees to rate their manager's performance at "hiring staff and setting compensation." Although both tasks are part of the discipline of human resource management, they are different activities. A manager might do a better job of hiring than of setting pay levels, or vice versa. The survey gave respondents—and the company using the survey—no way to distinguish performance on each task.[15]

Phrase questions in a way that won't bias the response. In the political sphere, for example, opinions about rights for homosexuals vary according to the way questions are asked. With regard to homosexual relations, the number of people who say such behavior should be "illegal" is greater than the number who say "consenting adults engaged in homosexual activities in private should be prosecuted for a crime."[16]

The order in which questions are asked may matter. Asking about the economy—and its impact on families—before asking about the President will lower opinions of the President during bad economic times; the opposite is true for good economic times.[17]

Avoid questions that make assumptions about your subjects. The question "Does your spouse have a job outside the home?" assumes that your respondent is a married.

Use words that mean the same thing to you and to the respondents. If a question can be interpreted in more than one way, it will be. Words like *often* and *important* mean different things to different people. When a consulting firm called Employee Motivation and Performance Assessment helped Duke Energy assess the leadership skills of its managers, an early draft of the employee survey asked employees to rate how well their manager "understands the business and the marketplace." How would employees know what is in the manager's mind? Each respondent would have to determine what is reasonable evidence of a manager's understanding. The question was rephrased to identify behavior the employees could observe: "resolves complaints from customers quickly and thoroughly." The wording is still subjective ("quickly and thoroughly"), but at least all employees will be measuring the same category of behavior.[18]

As discussed in Chapter 5, **bypassing** occurs when two people use the same words or phrases but interpret them differently. To catch questions that can be misunderstood and to reduce bypassing, avoid terms that are likely to mean different things to different people and pretest your questions with several people who are like those who will fill out the survey. Even a small pretest with 10 people can help you refine your questions.

Survey questions can be categorized in several ways. **Closed questions** have a limited number of possible responses. **Open questions** do not lock the subject into any sort of response. Figure 15.4 gives examples of closed and open questions. The second question in Figure 15.4 is an example of a Likert-type scale.

Closed questions are faster for subjects to answer and easier for researchers to score. However, since all answers must fit into prechosen categories, they cannot probe the complexities of a subject. You can improve the quality of closed questions by conducting a pretest with open questions to find categories that matter to respondents. Analyzing the responses from open questions is usually less straightforward than analyzing responses from closed questions.

Use closed multiple-choice questions for potentially embarrassing topics. Seeing their own situation listed as one response can help respondents feel that it is acceptable. However, very sensitive issues are perhaps better asked in an interview, where the interviewer can build trust and reveal information about himself or herself to encourage the interviewee to answer.

Use an "Other, Please Specify" category when you want the convenience of a closed question but cannot foresee all the possible responses. These responses can be used to improve choices if the survey is to be repeated.

What is the single most important reason that you ride the bus?

_____ I don't have a car.

_____ I don't want to fight rush-hour traffic.

_____ Riding the bus is cheaper than driving my car.

_____ Riding the bus conserves fuel and reduces pollution.

_____ Other (please specify): _____

Watch Your Language

The connotation of a phrase in a survey can unintentionally skew the way people react to a question. A survey used to learn about the leadership skills of managers asked employees whether their manager "takes bold strides" and "has a strong grasp" of complicated issues. Male managers tended to outscore female managers. In a literal sense, males on average take longer strides and have more muscle strength than females. The company changed the wording of the survey. "Has a strong grasp of complex problems" became "discusses complex problems with precision and clarity." After this change, the difference in ratings of female and male managers disappeared. Employees apparently stopped mixing images of size and strength into their ratings of intellectual insight.

Another word-related bias is that respondents tend to agree more than disagree with statements. If a survey about managers asks employees whether their manager is fair, ethical, intelligent, knowledgeable, and so on, they are likely to assign all of these qualities to the manager—and to agree more and more as the survey goes along. To correct for this, some questions should be worded to generate the opposite response. For example, a statement about ethics can be balanced by a statement about corruption, and a statement about fairness can be balanced by a statement about bias or stereotypes.

Adapted from Palmer Morrel-Samuels, "Getting the Truth into Workplace Surveys," *Harvard Business Review* 80, No. 2 (February 2002): 111–18.

http://www.publicagenda.org/pages/20-questions-journalists-should-ask-about-poll-results

Public Agenda provides 20 questions to ask about poll results. Questions include

- Who did the poll and who paid for it?
- How many people were surveyed and how were they chosen?
- How was the survey done?
- What questions were asked?

http://www.gallup.com

Designing survey questions is an important and difficult part of getting valid results. For examples of surveys, including information about their design, visit the Gallup Poll pages of the Gallup Organization's website. The website also includes videos of Gallup's survey work. Some videos discuss the results of particular polls; some also talk about the poll's audience and purpose, important factors in a survey's design. Watch several videos and examine several polls for the ways in which audience and purpose shape the questions in the survey.

Figure 15.4 Closed and Open Questions

Closed questions

Are you satisfied with the city bus service? (yes/no)

How good is the city bus service?

Excellent 5 4 3 2 1 Terrible

Indicate whether you agree (A) or disagree (D) with each of the following statements about city bus service.

A D The schedule is convenient for me.

A D The routes are convenient for me.

A D The drivers are courteous.

A D The buses are clean.

Rate each of the following improvements in the order of their importance to you (1 = most important and 5 = least important).

_____ Buy new buses.

_____ Increase non-rush-hour service on weekdays.

_____ Increase service on weekdays.

_____ Provide earlier and later service on weekdays.

_____ Buy more buses with wheelchair access.

_____ Provide unlimited free transfers.

Open questions

How do you feel about the city bus service?

Tell me about the city bus service.

Why do you ride the bus? (or, Why don't you ride the bus?)

What do you like and dislike about the city bus service?

How could the city bus service be improved?

When you use multiple-choice questions, make the answer categories mutually exclusive and exhaustive. This means you make sure that any one answer fits in only one category and that a category is included for all possible answers. In the following example of overlapping categories, a person who worked for a company with exactly 25 employees could check either *a* or *b*. The resulting data would be hard to interpret.

Overlapping categories: Indicate the number of full-time employees in your company on May 16:

_____ a. 0–25

_____ b. 25–100

_____ c. 100–500

_____ d. over 500

Discrete categories: Indicate the number of full-time employees on your payroll on May 16:

_____ a. 0–25

_____ b. 26–100

_____ c. 101–500

_____ d. more than 500

The number of answer choices for multiple-choice questions can influence the results. During one month of Obama's presidency, polls such as Gallup that asked whether people approved or disapproved of Obama's performance found that more people approved than disapproved. However, the Rasmussen poll for the same month offered people four choices: strongly approve, somewhat approve, somewhat disapprove, and strongly disapprove. With these choices, the disapprovers won.[19]

Branching questions direct different respondents to different parts of the questionnaire based on their answers to earlier questions.

10. Have you talked to an academic adviser this year? (If "no," skip to question 14.)	yes	no

Generally, put early in the questionnaire questions that will be easy to answer. Put questions that are harder to answer or that people may be less willing to answer (e.g., age and income) near the end of the questionnaire. Even if people choose not to answer such questions, you'll still have the rest of the survey filled out.

If subjects will fill out the questionnaire themselves, pay careful attention to the physical design of the document. Use indentations and white space effectively; make it easy to mark and score the answers. Label answer scales frequently so respondents remember which end is positive and which is negative. Include a brief statement of purpose if you (or someone else) will not be available to explain the questionnaire or answer questions. Pretest the questionnaire to make sure the directions are clear. One researcher mailed a two-page questionnaire without pretesting it. One-third of the respondents didn't realize there were questions to answer on the back of the first page.

See Figure 15.5 for an example of a questionnaire for a student report.

Conducting Research Interviews

Schedule interviews in advance; tell the interviewee about how long you expect the interview to take. A survey of technical writers (who get much of their information from interviews) found that the best days to interview subject matter experts are Tuesdays, Wednesdays, and Thursday mornings.[20] People are frequently swamped on Mondays and looking forward to the weekend, or trying to finish their week's work on Fridays.

Interviews can be structured or unstructured. In a **structured interview,** the interviewer uses a detailed list of questions to guide the interview. Indeed, a structured interview may use a questionnaire just as a survey does.

In an **unstructured interview,** the interviewer has three or four main questions. Other questions build on what the interviewee says. To prepare for an unstructured interview, learn as much as possible about the interviewee and the topic. Go into the interview with three or four main topics you want to cover.

Interviewers sometimes use closed questions to start the interview and set the interviewee at ease. The strength of an interview, however, is getting at a person's attitudes, feelings, and experiences. **Situational questions** let you probe what someone does in a specific circumstance. **Hypothetical questions** that ask people to imagine what they would do generally yield less reliable answers than questions about **critical incidents** or key past events.

Situational question:	How do you tell an employee that his or her performance is unsatisfactory.
Hypothetical question:	What would you say if you had to tell an employee that his or her performance was unsatisfactory?
Critical incident question:	You've probably been in a situation where someone who was working with you wasn't carrying his or her share of the work. What did you do the last time that happened?

If People Can Misunderstand the Question, They Will

Q: Give previous experience with dates.
A: Moderately successful in the past, but I am now happily married!

Q: How many autopsies have you performed on dead people?
A: All my autopsies have been on dead people.

Q: James stood back and shot Tommy Lee?
A: Yes.
Q: And then Tommy Lee pulled out his gun and shot James in the fracas?
A: (After hesitation) No sir, just above it.

Q: What is the country's mortality rate?
A: 100%. Everybody dies.

Q: Give numbers of employees broken down by sex.
A: None. Our problem is booze.

Q: Sex?
A: Once a week.

Adapted from James Hartley, *Designing Instructional Text* (London: Kogan Page, 1978), 109; Richard Lederer, *Anguished English* (New York: Wyrick, 1988); and surveys of college students.

Figure 15.5 Questionnaire for a Student Report Using Survey Research

An interesting title can help.

In your introductory ¶,
① tell how to return the survey
② tell how the information will be used

Survey: Why Do Students Attend Athletic Events?

The purpose of this survey is to determine why students attend sports events, and what might increase attendance. All information is to be used solely for a student research paper. Please return completed surveys to Elizabeth or Vicki at the Union help desk. Thank you for your assistance!

Start with easy-to-answer questions

1. Gender (Please circle one) M F

2. What is your class year? (Please circle) 1 2 3 4 Grad Other

The words below each number anchor responses, while still allowing you to average the data.

Seeing a response in a survey can make respondents more willing to admit to feelings they may be embarrassed to volunteer.

3. How do you feel about women's sports? (Please circle)

1	2	3	4	5
I enjoy watching women's sports		I'll watch, but it doesn't really matter		Women's sports are boring/ I'd rather watch men's sports

4. Do you like to attend MSU men's basketball games? (Please circle)
Y N

5. How often do you attend MSU women's basketball games? (Please circle)

1	2	3	4	5
All/most games	Few games a season	Once a season	Less than once a year	Never

6. If you do not attend all of the women's basketball games, why not? (Please check all that apply. If you attend all the games, skip to #7.)

Think about factors that affect the problem you're studying, and write survey questions to get information about them.

__I've never thought to go.
__I don't like basketball.
__I don't like sporting events.
__The team isn't good enough.
__My friends are not interested in going.
__I want to go, I just haven't had the opportunity.
__The tickets cost too much ($5).
__Other (please specify) ____________________

7. To what extent would each of the following make you more likely to attend an MSU women's basketball game? (please rank all)

1	2	3
Much more likely to attend	Possibley more likely	No effect

__Increased awareness on campus (fliers, chalking on the Oval, more articles in the *Gazette*)
__Marketing to students (give-aways, days for residence halls or fraternities/sororities)
__Student loyalty program (awarding points towards free tickets, clothing, food for attending games)
__Education (pocket guide explaining the rules of the game provided at the gate)
__Other (please specify) ____________________

Thank you!
Please return this survey to Elizabeth or Vicki at the Union help desk.

Repeat where to turn in or mail completed surveys.

A **mirror question** paraphrases the content of the last answer: "So you confronted him directly?" "You think that this product costs too much?" Mirror questions are used both to check that the interviewer understands what the interviewee has said and to prompt the interviewee to continue talking. **Probes** follow up an original question to get at specific aspects of a topic:

Question: What do you think about the fees for campus parking?

Probes: Would you be willing to pay more for a reserved space? How much more?
Should the fines for vehicles parked illegally be increased?
Do you think fees should be based on income?

Probes are not used in any definite order. Instead, they are used to keep the interviewee talking, to get at aspects of a subject that the interviewee has not yet mentioned, and to probe more deeply into points that the interviewee brings up.

If you read questions to subjects in a structured interview, use fewer options than you might in a written questionnaire.

I'm going to read a list of factors that someone might look for in choosing a restaurant. After I read each factor, please tell me whether that factor is Very Important to you, Somewhat Important to you, or Not Important to you.

If the interviewee hesitates, reread the scale.

Always tape the interview. Test your equipment ahead of time to make sure it works. If you think your interviewee may be reluctant to speak on tape, take along two tapes and two recorders; offer to give one tape to the interviewee.

Pulitzer Prize winner Nan Robertson offers the following advice to interviewers:

- Do your homework. Learn about the subject and the person before the interview.
- To set a nervous interviewee at ease, start with nuts-and-bolts questions, even if you already know the answers.
- Save controversial questions for the end. You'll have everything else you need, and the trust built up in the interview makes an answer more likely.
- Go into an interview with three or four major questions. Listen to what the interviewee says and let the conversation flow naturally.
- At the end of the interview, ask for office and home telephone numbers in case you need to ask an additional question when you write up the interview.[21]

Well-done interviews can yield surprising results. When the owners of Kiwi shoe polish interviewed people about what they wanted in shoe care products, they learned that shiny shoes were far down on the list. What people cared most about was how fresh and comfortable their shoes were on the inside. So Kiwi developed a new line of products, including "fresh'ins" (thin, lightly scented shoe inserts) and "smiling feet" (cushioning and nonslip pads and strips).[22]

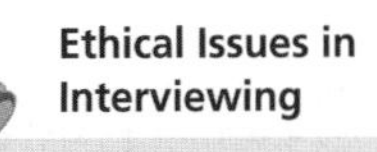

Ethical Issues in Interviewing

If you're trying to get sensitive information, interviewees may give useful information when the interview is "over" and the tape recorder has been turned off. Is it ethical to use that information?

If you're interviewing a hostile or very reluctant interviewee, you may get more information if you agree with everything you can legitimately agree to, and keep silent on the rest. Is it ethical to imply acceptance even when you know you'll criticize the interviewee's ideas in your report?

Most people would say that whatever public figures say is fair game: they're supposed to know enough to defend themselves. Do you agree?

Many people would say that different rules apply when you'll cite someone by name than when you'll use the information as background or use a pseudonym so that the interviewee cannot be identified. Do you agree?

As a practical matter, if someone feels you've misrepresented him or her, that person will be less willing to talk to you in the future. But quite apart from practical considerations, interview strategies raise ethical issues as well.

Using Focus Groups

A focus group, yet another form of qualitative research, is a small group of people convened to provide a more detailed look into some area of interest—a product, service, process, concept, and so on. Because the group setting allows

Interviewee Types

One of the greatest challenges of interviewing people is finding how to help the subjects open up and express real answers to your questions. One former U.S. Army interrogator, Greg Hartley, believes you can help people talk by understanding their personality type and shaping the interview around it. Here are five of his personality types and tips for interacting with them:

- **Teachers.** "Teachers" (consultants, academics, analysts) have extensive knowledge and experience. As an interviewer, take the role of a student and allow the subject to teach, answer questions, and display their expertise.
- **Jargon Dorks.** To cut through the jargon used by some newbies and insecure people, play dumb and ask for definitions and explanations.
- **Complainers.** You may not have trouble getting complainers to talk, but you may need to steer the conversation by using complaints of your own and expressions of empathy.
- **Smartypantses.** These people have to be smarter than everyone else. Making incorrect statements or challenging their opinions will provoke them into talking.
- **Worriers.** Conservative and careful, worriers don't want to say anything that will cause trouble or draw attention. To get them to open up, act as if you already know about their responses.

Adapted from "Make Them Talk," *Inc.*, April 2011, 82.

members to build on each other's comments, carefully chosen focus groups can provide detailed feedback; they can illuminate underlying attitudes and emotions relevant to particular behaviors.

Focus groups also have some problems. The first is the increasing use of professional respondents drawn from databases, a practice usually driven by cost and time limitations. The *Association for Qualitative Research Newsletter* labeled these respondents as a leading industry problem.[23] In order to get findings that are consistent among focus groups, the groups must accurately represent the target population. A second problem with focus groups is that such groups sometimes aim to please rather than offering their own evaluations.

Using Online Networks

An updated version of the focus group is the online network. Del Monte, for instance, has an online community, called "I Love My Dog," of 400 handpicked dog enthusiasts that it can query about dog products. These networks, first cultivated as research tools by technology and video game companies, are being employed by various producers of consumer products and services, including small companies. The networks are often cheaper and more effective than traditional focus groups because they have broader participation and allow for deeper and ongoing probing. Companies can use them for polls, real-time chats with actual consumers, and product trials.[24]

Some of the better online panels include experts as well as users. One small-scale automaker has design engineers and transportation experts on its panel. Although larger than focus groups, these panels carry some of the same drawbacks. They are not necessarily representative, either of current or future customers. Studies have also shown that they tend to discourage innovation.[25] On the other hand, they tend to give responses which members see as positive for the sponsor. Procter & Gamble repeatedly got go-aheads for product development from its online panels, only to see the new products fail field tests.[26]

A still larger online community comes from Twitter and online blogs. These communities are the least controllable of feedback groups, but are becoming more important all the time. Many companies are hiring employees or technology services to monitor comments on social networks and respond quickly. They also use data from Twitter and Facebook to track trends and preferences.

Observing Customers and Users

Answers to surveys and interviews may differ from actual behavior—sometimes greatly. To get more accurate consumer information, many marketers observe users. For example, one problem with asking consumers about their television-watching behavior is that they sometimes underreport the number of hours they watch and the degree to which they watch programs they aren't proud of liking.

Researchers have tried to develop a variety of measurement methods that collect viewing data automatically. Arbitron introduced the Portable People Meter (PPM), which receives an inaudible electronic signal from radio stations and broadcast and cable TV stations. Consumers simply carry the PPM, and it records their media exposure. One of the first results showed that consumers listened to radio more than they had indicated in diaries.[27] Nielsen Media Research has added commercial viewings to its famous TV show numbers; advertisers are naturally anxious to know how many people actually watch commercials instead of leaving to get a snack or fast-forwarding through them on digital video recorders.[28] Nielsen has also started tracking college students' viewing, installing its people meters in commons areas such as dorms. The new data boosted ratings for some shows, such as *Grey's Anatomy* and *America's Next Top Model,* by more than 35%.[29]

Procter and Gamble, maker of products like Swiffer, researches shopping patterns for both in-store and online customers.

The Cost of Plagiarism

Copying from other articles or online sources may seem like a small thing, but it is dishonest and can cost you much more than a poor grade on a school paper. One German politician, Karl-Theodor zu Guttenberg, was forced to resign in 2011 after revelations that he plagiarized large sections of his doctoral thesis.

As Germany's defense minister, zu Guttenberg was one of the country's most powerful and popular politicians. He seemed to be on track to become chancellor someday. But all of that was derailed when a law professor preparing to write a review of zu Guttenberg's thesis ran some passages through Google and found that they matched articles from newspapers and other sources. Later searches by Internet activists found evidence of plagiarism on 75% of the thesis's 400 pages.

Zu Guttenberg's downfall can serve as a warning to business communicators. Plagiarism is not only dishonest, it is costly. And, with Internet research tools, plagiarism is becoming much easier to detect.

Adapted from Marcus Walker and Patrick McGroarty, "German Minister Quits over Scandal," *Wall Street Journal*, March 2, 2011, A13.

Observation can tell marketers more about customers than the customers can put into words themselves. Intuit, a leader in observation studies, sends employees to visit customers and watch how they use Intuit products such as QuickBooks. Watching small businesses struggle with QuickBooks Pro told the company of the need for a new product, QuickBooks Simple Start.[30]

Observation can also be used for gathering in-house information such as how efficiently production systems operate and how well employees serve customers. Some businesses use "mystery shoppers." For instance, McDonald's has used mystery shoppers to check cleanliness, customer service, and food quality. The company posts store-by-store results online, giving store operators an incentive and the information they need to improve quality on measures where they are slipping or lagging behind the region's performance.[31]

Even health care facilities use mystery "shoppers." After they give their reports, the most common changes are improved estimates of waiting times and better explanations of medical procedures. So many organizations use mystery shoppers that there is a Mystery Shopping Providers Association.

Observation is often combined with other techniques to get the most information. **Think-aloud protocols** ask users to voice their thoughts as they use a document or product: "First I'll try. . . ." These protocols are tape-recorded and later analyzed to understand how users approach a document or product. **Interruption interviews** interrupt users to ask them what's happening. For example, a company testing a draft of computer instructions might interrupt a user to ask, "What are you trying to do now? Tell me why you did that." **Discourse-based interviews** ask questions based on documents that the interviewee has written: "You said that the process is too complicated. Tell me what you mean by that."

SOURCE CITATION AND DOCUMENTATION LO 15-3

In effective proposals and reports, sources are cited and documented smoothly and unobtrusively. **Citation** means attributing an idea or fact to its source in the body of the text: "According to the 2010 Census . . . " "Jane Bryant Quinn argues that. . . ." In-text citations provide, in parentheses in the text, the source

A Costly Comment out of Context

Shirley Sherrod was the Agriculture Department's director of rural development in Georgia. Then conservative activist Andrew Breitbart posted video excerpts of her March 2010 speech to an NAACP event. The excerpts seemed to say that she did not give the white farmer who came to her for bankruptcy help the same help she would give to black farmers, in other words, racial discrimination. Fox News and CBS reported on the excerpts the same day they were posted, and Sherrod was asked to resign by government officials, which she did.

In the full video, posted later on other websites, it became clear that the white farmer was an example of a time when she could have discriminated but didn't; he was the person who taught her that white people didn't always have advantages. In fact, the farmer in question told CNN that he and Sherrod were still friends, 20 years later.

Adapted from Marcus K. Garner and Christian Boone, "USDA Reconsiders Firing of Ga. Official over Speech on Race," *Atlanta Journal Constitution,* July 21, 2010, http://www.ajc.com/news/usda-reconsiders-firing-of-574027.html.

where the reference was found. Citing sources demonstrates your honesty and enhances your credibility. **Documentation** means providing the bibliographic information readers would need to go back to the original source. The two usual means of documentation are notes and lists of references.

Failure to cite and document sources is **plagiarism,** the passing off of the words or ideas of others as one's own. Plagiarism can lead to nasty consequences. The news regularly showcases examples of people who have been fired or sued for plagiarism. Now that curious people can type sentences into Google and find the sources, plagiarism is easier than ever to catch. Plagiarism is both unethical and illegal.

Another unethical practice that may occur when using sources is taking material out of context in such a way that the meaning of the material used is counter to the meaning of the material within its full context. An example of this practice discussed in national news occurred when Shirley Sherrod, the Agriculture Department's director of rural development in Georgia, was asked to resign because of a comment that became racist when taken out of context. (See sidebar on this page.)

Note that citation and documentation are used in addition to quotation marks. If you use the source's exact words, you'll use the name of the person you're citing and quotation marks in the body of the proposal or report; you'll indicate the source in parentheses and a list of references or in a footnote or endnote. If you put the source's idea into your own words (paraphrasing), or if you condense or synthesize information, you don't need quotation marks, but you still need to tell whose idea it is and where you found it. See Appendix C for examples of quoting and paraphrasing using both APA and MLA formats.

Long quotations (four typed lines or more) are used sparingly in business proposals or reports. Since many readers skip quotes, always summarize the main point of the quotation in a single sentence before the quotation itself. End the sentence with a colon, not a period, since it introduces the quote. Indent long quotations on the left to set them off from your text. Indented quotations do not need quotation marks; the indentation shows the reader that the passage is a quote.

To make a quotation fit the grammar of your writing, you may need to change one or two words. Sometimes you may want to add a few words to explain something in the longer original. In both cases, use square brackets to indicate words that are your replacements or additions. Omit any words in the original source that are not essential for your purposes. Use ellipses (spaced dots) to indicate your omissions.

Document every fact and idea that you take from a source except facts that are common knowledge. Historical dates and facts are considered common knowledge. Generalizations are considered common knowledge ("More and more women are entering the workforce") even though specific statements about the same topic (such as the percentage of women in the workforce in 1975 and in 2000) would require documentation.

The three most widely used formats for footnotes, endnotes, and bibliographies in reports are those of the American Psychological Association (APA), the Modern Language Association (MLA), and the University of Chicago *Manual of Style* format, which this book uses. Some technical materials use IEEE or CBE formats.

Internal documentation provides in parentheses in the text the source where the reference was found. (See appendix C for a complete explanation and example.)

For a portion of a report in APA and MLA formats, see Appendix C. Appendix C also outlines the APA and MLA formats for the sources most often used in proposals and reports.

If you use a printed source that is not readily available, consider including it as an appendix in your report. For example, you could copy an ad or include an organization's promotional brochure.

SUMMARY OF KEY POINTS

- **Information reports** collect data for the reader; **analytical reports** present and interpret data; **recommendation reports** recommend action or a solution.
- A good purpose statement must make three things clear:
  - The organizational problem or conflict.
  - The specific technical questions that must be answered to solve the problem.
  - The rhetorical purpose (to explain, to recommend, to request, to propose) that the report is designed to achieve.
- Use indexes and directories to find information about a specific company or topic.
- To decide whether to use a website as a source in a research project, evaluate the site's authors, objectivity, information, and revision date.
- A **survey** questions a large group of people, called **respondents** or subjects. A **questionnaire** is a written list of questions that people fill out. An **interview** is a structured conversation with someone who will be able to give you useful information.
- Because surveys can be used to show almost anything, people need to be careful when analyzing the results of surveys or designing their own. These are questions commonly asked about surveys:
  - Who did the survey and who paid for it?
  - How many people were surveyed and how were they chosen?
  - How was the survey conducted?
  - What was the response rate?
  - What questions were asked?
- Qualitative research may also use interviews, focus groups, and online networks.
- Good questions ask just one thing, are phrased neutrally, avoid making assumptions about the respondent, and mean the same thing to different people.
- **Closed questions** have a limited number of possible responses. **Open questions** do not lock the subject into any sort of response. **Branching questions** direct different respondents to different parts of the questionnaire based on their answers to earlier questions. **Hypothetical questions,** which ask what people *might* do, are generally less reliable than **situational questions,** which ask what people *actually* do in specific situations. A **mirror question** paraphrases the content of the last answer. **Probes** follow up an original question to get at specific aspects of a topic.
- A **convenience sample** is a group of subjects who are easy to get. A **judgment sample** is a group of people whose views seem useful. In a **random sample,** each object in the population theoretically has an equal chance of being chosen. A sample is random only if a formal, approved random sampling method is used. Otherwise, unconscious bias can exist.

Internet Pranks

The wealth of good Information available on the Internet is often drowned or diluted by inaccurate, misleading, or blatantly false information. Students who have grown up using the Internet as their primary research tool may have trouble distinguishing between the good and the bad.

One instructor uses the Internet to teach his students to think about sources and information carefully. He begins with an introduction about a dangerous substance called DHMO that is found in many products and causes thousands of deaths each year. He then asks his students to research the substance, directing them specifically to sources like www.dhmo.org, which advocates a government ban on DHMO.

Only after his students start to be convinced does the teacher reveal that DHMO, or dihydrogen monoxide, is simply another term for water, and that the one-sided articles they read were part of an elaborate Internet hoax. This exercise, along with a similar exercise involving a tree octopus, helps the students learn to critique information and its source.

Adapted from Brent Vasicek, "Danger on the Internet: A Lesson in Critical Thinking," Scholastic.com, February 9, 2011, http://blogs.scholastic.com/classroom_solutions/2011/02/danger-on-the-internet-a-lesson-in-critical-thinking.html.

- **Citation** means attributing an idea or fact to its source in the body of the report. **Documentation** means providing the bibliographic information readers would need to go back to the original source.

CHAPTER 15 Exercises and Problems

Go to www.mhhe.com/locker10e for additional Exercises and Problems.

15.1 Reviewing the Chapter

1. What are some criteria for defining report problems? (LO 15-1)
2. What are four criteria for evaluating web sources? (LO 15-2)
3. What questions should you use to analyze a survey? (LO 15-2)
4. What are some criteria for good survey questions? (LO 15-2)
5. What is a random sample? (LO 15-2)
6. What are some disadvantages of focus groups and online networks? (LO 15-2)

15.2 Reviewing Grammar

Reports use lots of numbers. Test your knowledge about writing numbers by doing Exercise B.10 in Appendix B.

15.3 Defining and Evaluating Report Problems

In small teams, turn the following categories into specific report problems you could research for a business communication course. Write three possible report problems for each category.

1. Social media sites
2. Global warming or climate change
3. Globalization
4. Marketing to younger audiences
5. Career planning
6. Technology/cell phone use
7. Credit card debt
8. Campus-based organizations
9. Tuition
10. Housing/parking on campus

Once you have defined three possible problems for each category, evaluate the problems using the following questions:

- Which problem(s) could you address satisfactorily in the time allotted for your course project?
- Which problem(s) are real?
- Which problem(s) are important enough to be worth researching?
- Are the problem(s) narrow enough?
- Who will be able to implement recommended action from your research?
- For which problem(s) could you find adequate resources to create sound solutions?

As your instructor directs,

a. Write a memo to your instructor that shares your evaluation of the problems.
b. Pick two of the categories and present to the class your evaluation of the problems in an oral presentation.
c. Write a preliminary purpose statement for each of the three problems you have identified for a category.

15.4 Identifying the Weaknesses in Problem Statements

Identify the weaknesses in the following problem statements.

- Is the problem narrow enough?
- Can a solution be found in a semester or quarter?
- What organization could implement any recommendations to solve the problem?
- Could the topic be limited or refocused to yield an acceptable problem statement?

1. One possible report topic I would like to investigate would be the differences in women's intercollegiate sports in our athletic conference.
2. How to market products effectively to college students.
3. Should web banners be part of a company's advertising?
4. How can U.S. and Canadian students get jobs in Europe?
5. We want to explore ways our company can help raise funds for the Open Shelter. We will investigate whether collecting and recycling glass, aluminum, and paper products will raise enough money to help.
6. How can XYZ University better serve students from traditionally underrepresented groups?
7. What are the best investments for the next year?

15.5 Writing a Preliminary Purpose Statement

Answer the following questions about a topic on which you could write a formal report.

As your instructor directs,

a. Be prepared to answer the questions orally in a conference.

b. Bring written answers to a conference.

c. Submit written answers in class.

d. Give your instructor a photocopy of your statement after it is approved.

1. What problem will you investigate or solve?
   a. What is the name of the organization facing the problem?
   b. What is the technical problem or difficulty?
   c. Why is it important to the organization that this problem be solved?
   d. What solution or action might you recommend to solve the problem?
   e. Who (name and title) is the person in the organization who would have the power to accept or reject your recommendation?
2. Will this report use information from other classes or from work experiences? If so, give the name and topic of the class and/or briefly describe the job. If you will need additional information (that you have not already gotten from other classes or from a job), how do you expect to find it?
3. List the name, title, and business phone number of a professor who can testify to your ability to handle the expertise needed for this report.
4. List the name, title, and business phone number of someone in the organization who can testify that you have access to enough information about that organization to write this report.

15.6 Choosing Research Strategies

For each of the following reports, indicate the kinds of research that might be useful. If a survey is called for, indicate the most efficient kind of sample to use.

a. How can XYZ store increase sales?

b. What is it like to live and work in [name of country]?

c. Should our organization have a dress code?

d. Is it feasible to start a monthly newsletter for students in your major?

e. How can we best market to mature adults?

f. Can compensation programs increase productivity?

g. What skills are in demand in our area? Of these, which could the local community college offer courses in?

15.7 Evaluating Websites

Choose five websites that are possible resources for a report. Evaluate them on the credibility and trustworthiness of their information. Consider the following questions and compare and contrast your findings.

- What person or organization sponsors the site? What credentials do the authors have?
- Does the site give evidence to support its claims? Does it give both sides of controversial issues?
- Is the tone professional?
- How complete is the information? What is it based on?
- How current is the information?

Based on your findings, which sites are best for your report and why?

As your instructor directs,

a. Write a memo to your instructor summarizing your results.
b. Share your results with a small group of students.
c. Present your results to the class in an oral presentation.

15.8 Choosing Samples for Surveys and Interviews

For the following topics, indicate the types of sample(s) you would use in collecting survey data and in conducting interviews.

a. How can your school save money to limit tuition increases?
b. How can your favorite school organization attract more student members?
c. How can your school improve communication with international students?
d. How should your school deal with hate speech?
e. How can instructors at your school improve their electronic presentations for students?

15.9 Evaluating Survey Questions

Evaluate each of the following questions. Are they acceptable as they stand? If not, how can they be improved?

a. Survey of clerical workers:
   Do you work for the government? ☐
   or the private sector? ☐
b. Questionnaire on grocery purchases:
   1. Do you *usually* shop at the same grocery store?
      a. Yes
      b. No
   2. Do you use credit cards to purchase items at your grocery store?
      a. Yes
      b. No
   3. How much is your average grocery bill?
      a. Under $25
      b. $25–50
      c. $50–100
      d. $100–150
      e. Over $150
c. Survey on technology:
   1. Would you generally welcome any technological advancement that allowed information to be sent and received more quickly and in greater quantities than ever before?
   2. Do you think that all people should have free access to all information, or do you think that information should somehow be regulated and monitored?
d. Survey on job skills:
   How important are the following skills for getting and keeping a professional-level job in U.S. business and industry today?

	Low				High
Ability to communicate	1	2	3	4	5
Leadership ability	1	2	3	4	5
Public presentation skills	1	2	3	4	5
Selling ability	1	2	3	4	5
Teamwork capability	1	2	3	4	5
Writing ability	1	2	3	4	5

15.10 Designing Questions for an Interview or Survey

Submit either a one- to three-page questionnaire or questions for a 20- to 30-minute interview AND the information listed below for the method you choose.

Questionnaire

1. Purpose(s), goal(s).
2. Subjects (who, why, how many).
3. How and where to be distributed.
4. Any changes in type size, paper color, etc., from submitted copy.
5. Rationale for order of questions, kinds of questions, wording of questions.
6. References, if building on questionnaires by other authors.

Interview

1. Purpose(s), goal(s).
2. Subjects (who, and why).
3. Proposed site, length of interview.
4. Rationale for order of questions, kinds of questions, wording of questions, choice of branching or follow-up questions.
5. References, if building on questions devised by others.

As your instructor directs,

a. Create questions for a survey on one of the following topics:
   - Survey students on your campus about their knowledge of and interest in the programs and activities sponsored by a student organization.
   - Survey workers at a company about what they like and dislike about their jobs.
   - Survey people in your community about their willingness to pay more to buy products using recycled materials and to buy products that are packaged with a minimum of waste.
   - Survey two groups on a topic that interests you.

b. Create questions for an interview on one of the following topics:
   - Interview an international student about the forms of greetings and farewells, topics of small talk, forms of politeness, festivals and holidays, meals at home, size of families, and roles of family members in his or her country.
   - Interview a TV producer about what styles and colors work best for people appearing on TV.
   - Interview a worker about an ethical dilemma he or she faced on the job, what the worker did and why, and how the company responded.
   - Interview the owner of a small business about problems the business has, what strategies the owner has already used to increase sales and and profits and how successful these strategies were, and the owner's attitudes toward possible changes in product line, decor, marketing, hiring, advertising, and money management.
   - Interview someone who has information you need for a report you're writing.

15.11 Comparing Online Survey Sites

Visit these online survey websites and analyze their features. What kinds of services do they offer? How useful are they? What are their limitations?

http://www.surveymonkey.com
http://www.polldaddy.com/
http://web-online-surveys.com/
http://www.vizu.com/index.htm
http://freeonlinesurveys.com/

Discuss your findings in small groups.

15.12 Comparing an Online Survey with a Face-to-Face Survey

Surveymonkey.com is an online survey website whose basic features are available free of cost for those who sign up. Design a small survey using the website for a course project or something else. Administer the survey. The website compiles and analyzes the results for you.

Now, distribute the same survey in the form of a questionnaire to the same number of people, but choose new respondents.

Compare the results of the online survey with those of the survey that respondents filled out manually. What similarities and differences do you find in the two results? What might account for these similarities and differences? Do this exercise individually or in a group. Share the results with the class.

15.13 Reviewing Corporate Reports

As companies become increasingly socially and environmentally conscious, they document their social and environmental contributions in reports such as corporate citizenship reports, corporate responsibility reports, corporate sustainability reports, sustainability progress reports, and so on. These reports are available on the companies' websites, often on pages that contain company information.

Go to www.fortune.com, which creates lists of the top 500 and 100 companies as well as the most admired companies. Select a company related to your major and future career field. Visit its website and access one of the reports mentioned above or a report similar to the ones mentioned above. Study the nature and structure of the report; find out whether it informs, analyzes, recommends, or does all three. What kinds of evidence does it use? How well supported are the conclusions? Share your findings in small groups.

15.14 Citing Sources

As your instructor directs,

a. Revise the following list of sources using MLA format.

b. Revise the following list of sources using APA format.

For help, see Appendix C.

1. Shayndi Raice

   Wall Street Journal

   Social Media, Phones Ally

   February 18, 2011

   B7

2. Ben Sisario and Miguel Helft

   The New York Times

   Facebook Is Developing Ways to Share Media

   http://www.nytimes.com/2011/05/27/technology/27facebook.html?ref=technology

   May 26, 2011

   Accessed May 26, 2011

3. Dorie Clark

   Reinventing Your Personal Brand

   Harvard Business Review

   Volume 89, Issue No. 3

   March 2011

   78-81

4. Jakob Nielsen

   Alertbox

   Incompetent Research Skills Curb Users' Problem Solving

   http://www.useit.com/alertbox/search-skills.html

   April 11, 2011

   Accessed March 25, 2011

5. Richard C. Freed, Shervin Freed, Joseph D. Romano

   Writing Winning Business Proposals

   3rd edition

   2010

   McGraw-Hill

   New York

15.15 Writing a Report Based on a Survey

As your instructor directs,

a. Survey 40 to 50 people on some subject of your choice.

b. Team up with your classmates to conduct a survey and write it up as a group. Survey 50 to 80 people if your group has two members, 75 to 120 people if it has three members, 100 to 150 people if it has four members, and 125 to 200 people if it has five members.

c. Keep a journal during your group meetings and submit it to your instructor.

d. Write a memo to your instructor describing and evaluating your group's process for designing, conducting, and writing up the survey.

For this assignment, you do **not** have to take a random sample. Do, however, survey at least two different groups so that you can see if they differ in some way. Possible groups are men and women, business majors and English majors, Greeks and independents, first-year students and seniors, students and townspeople.

As you conduct your survey, make careful notes about what you do so that you can use this information when you write up your survey. If you work with a group, record who does what. Use complete memo format. Your subject line should be clear and reasonably complete. Omit unnecessary words such as "Survey of." Your first paragraph serves as an introduction, but it needs no heading. The rest of the body of your memo will be divided into four sections with the following headings: Purpose, Procedure, Results, and Discussion.

In your first paragraph, briefly summarize (not necessarily in this order) who conducted the experiment or survey, when it was conducted, where it was conducted, who the subjects were, what your purpose was, and what you found out. You will discuss all of these topics in more detail in the body of your memo.

In your **Purpose** section, explain why you conducted the survey. What were you trying to learn? What hypothesis were you testing? Why did this subject seem interesting or important?

In your **Procedure** section, describe in detail *exactly* what you did. "The first 50 people who came through the Union on Wed., Feb. 2" is not the same as "The first 50 people who came through the south entrance of the Union on Wed., Feb. 2, after 8 am, and agreed to answer my questions." Explain any steps you took to overcome possible sources of bias.

In your **Results** section, first tell whether your results supported your hypothesis. Use both visuals and words to explain what your numbers show. (See Chapter 16 on how to design visuals.) Process your raw data in a way that will be useful to your reader.

In your **Discussion** section, evaluate your survey and discuss the implications of your results. Consider these questions:

1. What are the limitations of your survey and your results?
2. Do you think a scientifically valid survey would have produced the same results? Why or why not?
3. Were there any sources of bias either in the way the questions were phrased or in the way the subjects were chosen? If you were running the survey again, what changes would you make to eliminate or reduce these sources of bias?
4. Do you think your subjects answered honestly and completely? What factors may have intruded? Is the fact that you did or didn't know them, were or weren't of the same sex relevant? If your results seem to contradict other evidence, how do you account for the discrepancy? Were your subjects shading the truth? Was your sample's unrepresentativeness the culprit? Or have things changed since earlier data were collected?
5. What causes the phenomenon your results reveal? If several causes together account for the phenomenon, or if it is impossible to be sure of the cause, admit this. Identify possible causes and assess the likelihood of each.
6. What action should be taken?

The discussion section gives you the opportunity to analyze the significance of your survey. Its insight and originality lift the otherwise well-written memo from the ranks of the merely satisfactory to the ranks of the above-average and the excellent.

The whole assignment will be more interesting if you choose a question that interests you. It does not need to be "significant" in terms of major political or philosophic problems; a quirk of human behavior that fascinates you will do nicely.

15.16 Analyzing Annual Reports

Locate two annual reports either in paper or electronic form. Use the following questions to analyze both reports:

- Who is (are) the audience(s)?
- What is (are) the purpose(s) of the report?
- How is the report organized and what does the order of information reflect about the company?
- How does the report validate/support the claims it makes? What type of evidence is used more often—textual or visual? What kinds of claims are used—logical, emotional, or ethical?
- How does the text establish credibility for the report?
- What can you tell about the company's financial situation from the report?
- What role do visuals play in the report? What image do they portray for the company? How do the visuals help establish credibility for the report? What do they imply about power distribution in the company?
- Does the report deal with any ethical issues?

As your instructor directs,

a. Write a memo to your instructor comparing and contrasting the two reports according to your analysis answers. Explain which report you find more effective and why.

b. Share your results orally with a small group of students.

c. Present your results to the class.

CHAPTER 16

Creating Visuals and Data Displays

Chapter Outline

When to Use Visuals and Data Displays

Guidelines for Creating Effective Visuals and Data Displays

1. **Check the Quality of the Data.**
2. **Determine the Story You Want to Tell.**
3. **Choose the Right Visual or Data Display for the Story.**
4. **Follow Conventions.**
5. **Use Color and Decoration with Restraint.**
6. **Be Accurate and Ethical.**

Integrating Visuals and Data Displays in Your Text

Designing Visuals and Data Displays

- Tables
- Pie Charts
- Bar Charts
- Line Graphs
- Gantt Charts
- Photographs
- Drawings
- Maps
- Dynamic Displays

Summary of Key Points

Visualizing in the Army

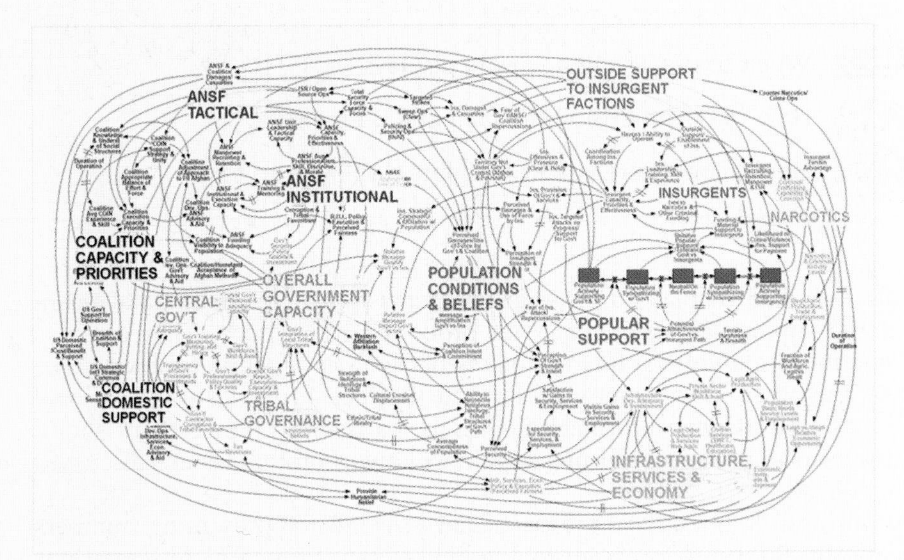

The U. S. Armed Forces thrive on information. With the conflict in Afghanistan, generals, officers, and politicians receive daily briefings on the complex situations in the war zone. These briefings must provide military administration with enough information to make decisions on overall goals and troop movements. And, like similar presentations in the business world, many of these briefings are conducted using Microsoft PowerPoint.

PowerPoint has become an essential business tool since it was first introduced in 1987. It allows presenters to highlight important points and to enhance their information with visuals and data displays. However, some critics claim that PowerPoint is overused and leads to creating bad, uninteresting, or misleading information.

For the U.S. Army, poor use of PowerPoint to present daily briefings has come under increasing criticism. Colonel Lawrence Sellin, a staff officer in army headquarters in Afghanistan, stated, "For headquarters staff, war consists largely of the endless tinkering with PowerPoint slides to conform with the idiosyncrasies of cognitively challenged generals in order to spoon-feed them information." His harsh words about army operations cost him his job.

General McChrystal reportedly responded, "When we understand that slide, we'll have won the war."

Colonel Sellin's criticism was widely reported in the media, along with an image of the now-infamous "spaghetti slide"—a slide used in a daily briefing to show strategy complexity. The slide was aptly named because the strategy looks like a pile of spaghetti with curling lines going in almost every direction (see photo). The leader of the forces in Afghanistan, General McChrystal, reportedly responded, "When we understand that slide, we'll have won the war."

But it is not just the complicated slides that cause misunderstandings. Many of the PowerPoint slides used in the daily briefings are bulleted lists that oversimplify the problems of war.

In spite of these criticisms, communicating visually with PowerPoint can be helpful. When used well, PowerPoint can combine text, images, data, video, and audio into a powerful informative and persuasive message. But like any other form of communication, creating visuals requires careful thought, planning, and attention to the context, the message, and the audience. For the U.S. Army, better visuals could ultimately result in fewer soldier deaths and, perhaps, an earlier end to the war.

Source: Nancy Duarte, "Why We Hate PowerPoints—and How to Fix Them," CNN.com, October 15, 2010, http://www.cnn.com/2010/OPINION/10/15/duarte.powerpoint.fatigue/index.html?hpt=T2; Elisabeth Bumiller, "We Have Met the Enemy and He Is PowerPoint," *New York Times*, April 26, 2010, http://www.nytimes.com/2010/04/27/world/27powerpoint.html?_r=3; and "The PowerPoint Rant That Got a Colonel Fired," *Army Times*, December 6, 2010, http://www.armytimes.com/news/2010/09/army-colonel-fired-for-powerpoint-rant-090210w/.

Learning Objectives

After studying this chapter, you will know

LO 16-1 When to use visuals and data displays.

LO 16-2 How to create effective visuals and data displays.

LO 16-3 How to integrate visuals and data displays into text.

Visuals of Fallen Heroes

After only a few weeks in office, President Obama reversed a controversial policy dealing with visuals. His administration overturned a policy that prohibited the media from photographing caskets of fallen soldiers returning to the United States. Under the new policy, the families of fallen soldiers have the right to choose whether the media can be present at the Dover Air Force Base in Delaware, the place where all deceased soldiers are brought.

Former President George H. W. Bush started the policy in 1991 during the Gulf War. Critics suggest the policy was enacted to prevent the public from seeing the horrors of war and the number of people who had died. On the other hand, critics of the new policy argue that allowing the press to be present creates a spectacle out of a private family matter.

Supporters of the new policy believe the photos are a reminder to all Americans of the sacrifices made by our troops and of the high price of freedom.

How ethical do you believe it is to show the final ceremony of fallen soldiers? If you had a family member who died in war, would you want the press to be present?

Adapted from Julian E. Barnes, "U.S. to Allow Photos of War Dead's Coffins," *The Seattle Times: Politics & Government,* February 27, 2009, http://seattletimes.nwsource.com/html/politics/2008791894_wardead27.html.

Visuals and data displays are design elements that help make data meaningful and support arguments in your proposals and reports. They can also help communicate your points in documents such as brochures, newsletters, reports, and other business messages, where they can add color and emotional appeal, as well as new information. Visuals, particularly PowerPoint slides, are also used to enhance oral presentations; PowerPoint slides are discussed in Chapter 19.

Visuals and data displays are particularly useful for presenting numbers dramatically. Suppose you want to give investors information about various stocks' performances. They would not want to read paragraph after paragraph of statements about which stocks went up and which went down. Organizing the daily numbers into tables would be much more useful.

Tables of stock prices have been the norm until recently. Now, the Internet offers options such as Map of the Market, www.smartmoney.com/map-of-the-market, a graphics tool that helps investors see the top performers. Map of the Market displays visual information for 1,000 U.S. and international stocks, providing details about each company's performance. Each company is shown as a rectangle, and companies are clustered into industry groups. The blocks are color-coded to signify the size of the stock price change or other criteria selected by the user. Size and color provide easy cues for spotting the best and worst performers.

WHEN TO USE VISUALS AND DATA DISPLAYS LO 16-1

The ease of creating visuals and data displays by computer may make people use them uncritically. Use visuals and data displays only to achieve a specific purpose. Never include them in your documents just because you have them; instead, use them to convey information the audience needs or wants.

In your rough draft, use visuals and data displays

- **To see that ideas are presented completely.** A table, for example, can show you whether you've included all the items in a comparison.
- **To find relationships.** Charting sales on a map may show that the sales representatives who made quota all have territories on the East or the West Coast. Is the central United States suffering a recession? Is the product one that appeals to coastal lifestyles? Is advertising reaching the coasts but not the central states? Even if you don't use the visual in your final document, creating the map may lead you to questions you wouldn't otherwise ask.

In the final presentation or document, use visuals and data displays

- **To make points vivid.** Readers skim memos and reports; a visual catches the eye. The brain processes visuals immediately. Understanding words—written or oral—takes more time.
- **To emphasize material** that might be skipped if it were buried in a paragraph. The beginning and end are places of emphasis. However, something has to go in the middle, especially in a long document. Visuals allow you to emphasize important material, wherever it logically falls.
- **To present material more compactly and with less repetition** than words alone would require. Words can call attention to the main points of the visual, without repeating all of the visual's information.

Managing by Data

The best decisions are not necessarily the ones based on analyzing large amounts of data. Sometimes companies that manage with a bent toward numerical data are setting themselves up for failure because some important information isn't quantifiable. Employee morale, changing customer tastes, and new competition are examples.

Data can be called up almost effortlessly using dashboard displays. However, in some cases the recent hype of these data technology tools causes CEOs and other higher ups to rely on them. For example, when executives at Ford and GM were marketing SUVs, whose numbers looked great on the page, they failed to consider the largest factor and ultimately their biggest setback—gas prices.

Even when the numbers are complete, their interpretation can lead to bad calls. For instance, managers relying on data may assume cause/effect relationships that aren't necessarily true. Furthermore, the way data are expressed can also shape interpretations. Notice the difference between saying 10% of employees will leave if management changes versus 90% will stay.

Adapted from David H. Freedman, "Do You Manage by the Numbers? Be Careful If You Do; Your Data May Be Playing Tricks on You," *Inc.*, November 2006, 59–60.

The number of visuals and data displays you will need depends on your purposes, the kind of information, and the audience. You'll use more when you want to show relationships and to persuade, when the information is complex or contains extensive numerical data, and when the audience values visuals and data displays. Some audiences expect oral presentations and reports to use lots of visuals and data displays. Other audiences may see them as frivolous and time spent making them as time wasted. For these audiences, sharply limit the number of visuals and data displays you use—but you should still use them when your own purposes and the information call for them.

GUIDELINES FOR CREATING EFFECTIVE VISUALS AND DATA DISPLAYS LO 16-2

Use these six steps to create effective visuals and data displays:

1. Check the quality of the data.
2. Determine the story you want to tell.
3. Choose the right visual or data display for the story.
4. Follow conventions.
5. Use color and decoration with restraint.
6. Be accurate and ethical.

Let's discuss each of these in more detail.

1. Check the Quality of the Data.

Your data display is only as good as the underlying data. Check to be sure that your data come from a reliable source. See "Evaluating the Source of the Data" in Chapter 18.

Also check that you have data for all factors you should consider. Are some factors missing data from key locations or demographic areas? When Nielsen Media Research, the TV audience measuring organization, switched from paper diaries of TV viewing to "people meters," electronic recording devices, they discovered a marked rise in TV viewing by children and young adults.[1]

If the data may not be reliable, you're better off not using visuals. The visual picture will be more powerful than verbal disclaimers, and the audience will be misled.

2. Determine the Story You Want to Tell.

Every visual should tell a story. Stories can be expressed in complete sentences that describe something that happens or changes. The sentence also serves as the title of the visual.

Environmental Maps

Environmental activists are using the interesting visuals available in Google Earth to show consumers the environmental impact of practices such as clear-cutting and mountain-top removal.

One such group is Appalachian Voices, which fights against the environmental dangers of coal mining. You can visit their website at www.ilovemountains.org/myconnection and enter your zip code to learn whether mountain tops have been removed to provide coal for your electricity providers. The site also provides links to help you protest to your legislators and power company.

Some critics, however, question whether the dramatic visuals will have any impact on consumer buying practices. They suggest that the only people who will be concerned with the images are people already doing environmental work, not the general public.

What do you think? After viewing the website, are you inclined to change any of your buying practices to protect mountain tops or other natural resources?

Adapted from Kevin J. Delaney, "Activists Start Googling: Internet Maps Illustrate Environmental Woes," *Wall Street Journal*, November 15, 2007, B4.

Not a story: U.S. Sales, 2005–2010

Possible stories: Forty Percent of Our Sales Were to New Customers.
Growth Was Highest in the South.
Sales Increased from 2005 to 2010.
Sales Were Highest in the Areas with More Sales Representatives.

Stories that tell us what we already know are rarely interesting. Instead, good stories may

- Support a hunch.
- Surprise you or challenge so-called common knowledge.
- Show trends or changes the audience didn't know existed.
- Have commercial or social significance.
- Provide information needed for action.
- Be personally relevant to the audience.

To find stories,

1. Focus on a topic (where are the most SUVs bought, who likes jazz, etc.).
2. Simplify the data on that topic and convert the numbers to simple, easy-to-understand units.
3. Look for relationships and changes. For example, compare two or more groups: do men and women have the same attitudes? Look for changes over time. Look for items that can be seen as part of the same group. To find stories about entertainers' incomes, for example, you might compare the incomes of writers, actors, and musicians.
4. Process the data to find more stories. Find the average and the median. Calculate the percentage change from one year to the next.

When you think you have a story, test it against all the data to be sure it's accurate.

Some stories are simple straight lines: "Computer Sales Increased." But other stories are more complex, with exceptions or outlying cases. Such stories will need more nuanced titles to do justice to the story. And sometimes the best story arises from the juxtaposition of two or more stories. In Figure 16.1, *BusinessWeek* used four grouped visuals to tell a complex story.

Almost every data set allows you to tell several stories. You must choose the story you want to tell. Dumps of uninterpreted data confuse and frustrate your audience; they undercut the credibility and goodwill you want to create.

Figure 16.1 A Complex Story Told Using Grouped Visuals

A New Era for Agriculture

What happens when farmers plant crops for energy as well as food

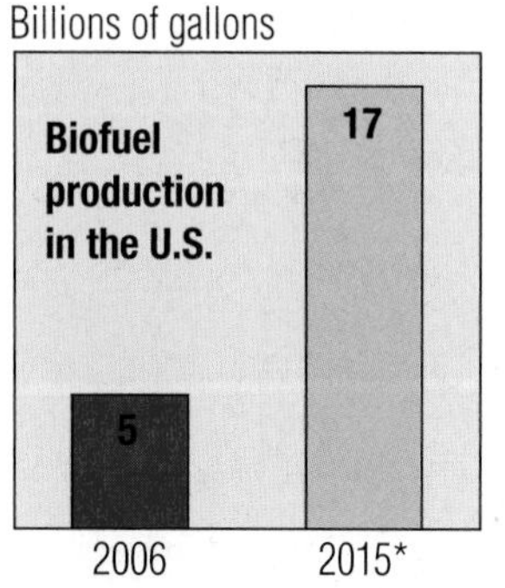

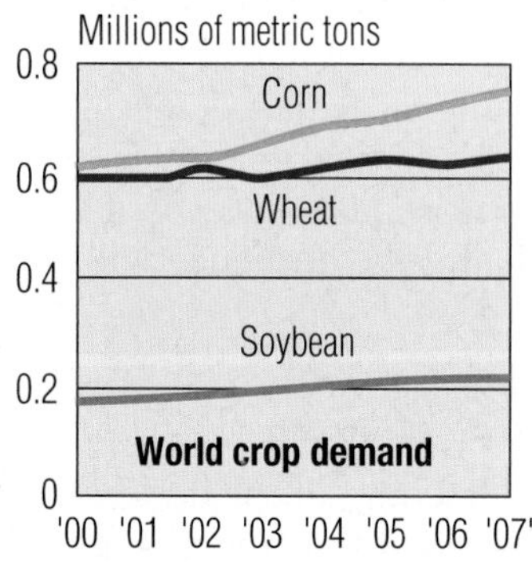

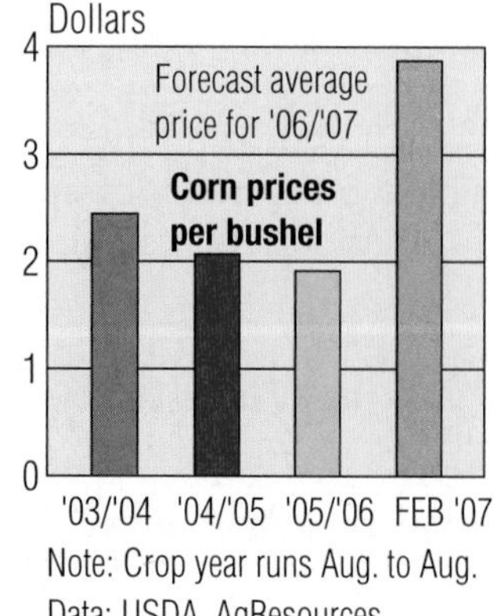

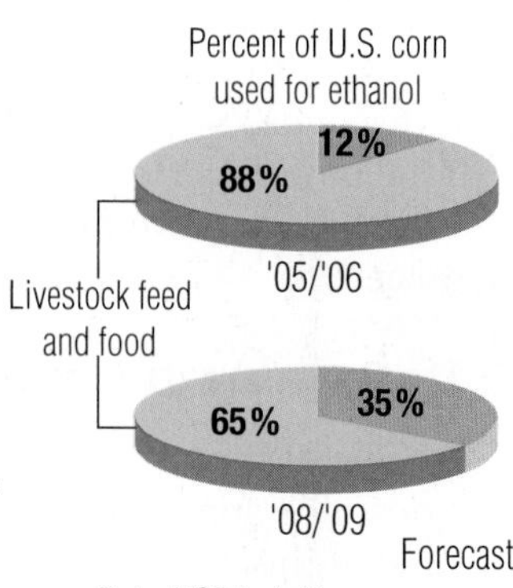

Source: From "A New Era for Agriculture: What Happens When Farmers Plant Crops for Energy as Well as Food." Reprinted from the February 5, 2007 issue of *BusinessWeek*. Used with permission of Bloomberg L.P.

Sometimes several stories will be important. When that's the case, you'll need a separate visual for each.

3. Choose the Right Visual or Data Display for the Story.

Visuals and data displays are not interchangeable. Good writers choose the one that best matches the purpose of the communication. Follow these guidelines to choose the right visuals and data displays:

- Use a **table** when the audience needs to be able to identify exact values. (See Figure 16.2a.)
- Use a chart or graph when you want the audience to focus on relationships.
  - To compare a part to the whole, use a **pie chart.** (See Figure 16.2b.)
  - To compare one item to another item, use a **bar chart.** (See Figure 16.2c.)
  - To compare items over time, use a **bar chart** or a **line graph.** (See Figure 16.2d.)
  - To show frequency or distribution, use a **line graph** or **bar chart.** (See Figure 16.2e.)
  - To show correlations, use a **bar chart,** a **line graph,** or a **dot chart.** (See Figure 16.2f.)
- Use **Gantt charts** to show timelines for proposals or projects.
- Use photographs to create a sense of authenticity or show the item in use. If the item is especially big or small, include something in the photograph that can serve as a reference point: a dime, a person.
- Use drawings to show dimensions, emphasize detail, or eliminate unwanted detail.
- Use maps to emphasize location.

Figure 16.2 Choose the Visual to Fit the Story

US sales reach $44.5 million.

	Millions of dollars		
	2000	2002	2004
Northeast	10.2	10.8	11.3
South	7.6	8.5	10.4
Midwest	8.3	6.8	9.3
West	11.3	12.1	13.5
Totals	37.4	38.2	44.5

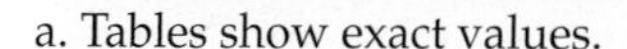

a. Tables show exact values.

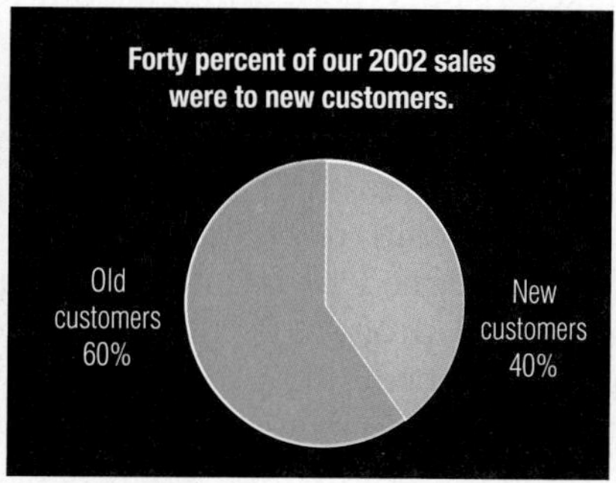

b. Pie charts compare a component to the whole.

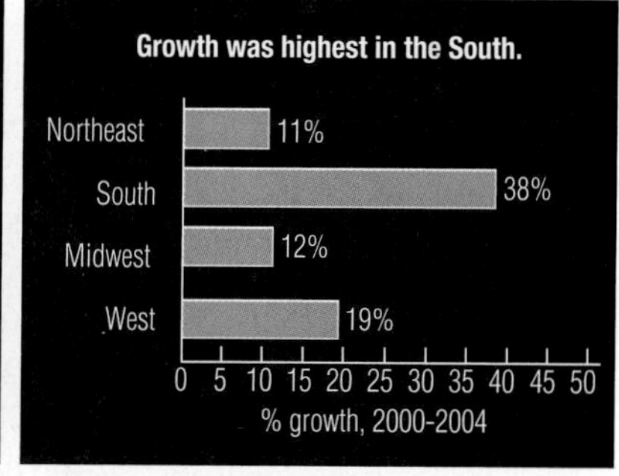

c. Bar charts compare items or show distribution or correlation.

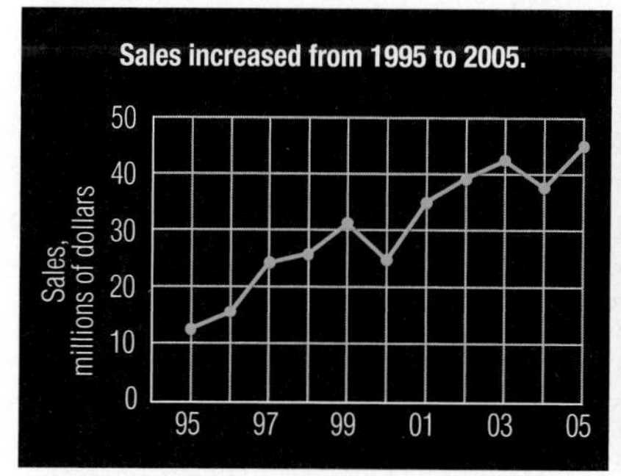

d. Line charts compare items over time or show distribution or correlation.

e. Bar charts can show frequency.

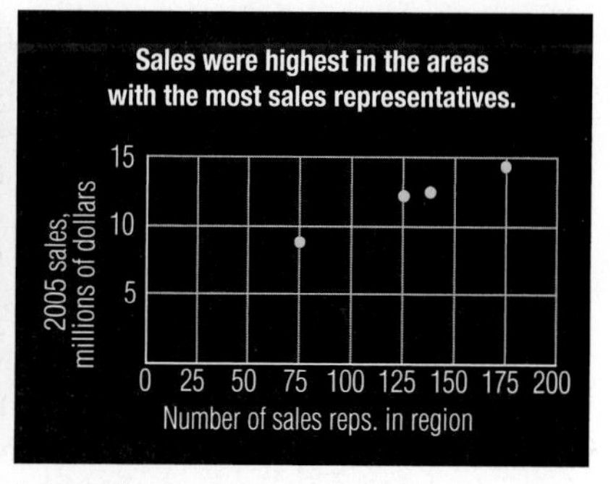

f. Dot charts show correlation.

Fan Cans

How connected are people to college colors? How much can those colors influence behaviors?

Anheuser-Busch found the answers to these questions when it started producing Bud Light cans in school colors. For instance, the fan cans used purple and gold for Louisiana State University; red and gold for Iowa State University. The campaign, known as "Team Pride," didn't use any trademarks or school logos, just the colors. Their intent, beyond increasing sales, was to encourage team spirit on game days.

Many university administrators were upset and demanded the cans be removed from store shelves. Their primary concern was that the fan cans would encourage binge and underage drinking. They also did not want people to think the university endorsed alcohol. The University of Michigan threatened legal action to have the cans removed from the entire state of Michigan. The University of Colorado, Boston College, and Texas A&M all demanded a stop to distribution as well. Anheuser-Busch agreed to drop the color campaigns near any school that made a formal complaint.

What do you think? If fan cans used your school's colors, would they encourage you to drink? Are colors so powerful that they would encourage binge and underage drinking if placed on alcohol?

Adapted from John Hechinger, "Team-Color Bud Cans Leaves Colleges Flat," *Wall Street Journal*, August 21, 2009, A1.

4. Follow Conventions.

Follow conventions when creating visuals and data displays. When you stray from conventions, you may confuse or alienate your audience.

Proposals and reports use formal visuals and data displays, which are typically divided into tables and figures. Tables are numbers or words arrayed in rows and columns. Figures are everything that isn't a table and may include graphs, charts, maps, drawings, and photographs. Formal visuals and data displays use both numbers and titles: "Figure 1. The Falling Cost of Computer Memory, 1992–2012." In an oral presentation, the title is usually used without the number: "The Falling Cost of Computer Memory, 1992—2012." The title should tell the story so the audience knows what to look for in the visual and why it is important.

Other types of documents use informal visuals and data displays, which are inserted directly into the text; they do not have numbers or titles.

Visuals and data displays usually contains these components:

- A title telling the story that the visual or data display shows.
- A clear indication of what the data are. For example, what people *say* they did is not necessarily what they really did. An estimate of what a number will be in the future differs from numbers in the past that have already been measured.
- Clearly labeled units.
- Labels or legends identifying axes, colors, symbols, and so forth.
- The source of the data, if you created the visual from data someone else gathered and compiled.
- The source of the visual or data display, if you reproduce one someone else created.

5. Use Color and Decoration with Restraint.

Color makes visuals more dramatic, but it also creates some problems. Colors may be interpreted positively or negatively depending on their context and the unique experiences of the people viewing them. Figure 16.3 gives some common positive and negative associations found in Western cultures. A good use of color occurs in the weather maps printed daily in many newspapers. Blue seems to fit cold; red seems to fit hot temperatures.

Meanings assigned to colors differ depending on the audience's national background and profession. Blue suggests masculinity in the United States, criminality in France, strength or fertility in Egypt, and villainy in Japan. Red is sometimes used to suggest danger or *stop* in the United States; it means *go* in China and is associated with festivities. Red suggests masculinity or aristocracy in France, death in Korea, blasphemy in some African countries, and luxury in many parts of the world.[2]

These general cultural associations may be replaced by corporate, national, or professional associations. Some people associate blue with IBM or Hewlett-Packard and red with Coca-Cola, communism, or Japan. People in specific professions learn other meanings for colors. Blue suggests *reliability* to financial managers, *water* or *coldness* to engineers, and *death* to health care professionals. Red means *losing money* to financial managers, *danger* to engineers, but *healthy* to health care professionals. Green usually means *safe* to engineers, but *infected* to health care professionals.

Try to avoid graphs that contrast red and green, because the colors will be indistinguishable to people with red–green colorblindness. Almost 10% of men and 2% of women are colorblind. Furthermore, as people get older, their ability to perceive colors also decreases.[3]

Figure 16.3 Colors and Their Common Connotations in Western Culture

Color	Positive	Negative
White	Clean, innocent, pure	Cold, empty, sterile
Red	Strong, brave, passionate	Dangerous, aggressive, domineering
Yellow	Happy, friendly, optimistic	Cowardly, annoying, brash
Brown	Warm, earthy, mature	Dirty, sad, cheap
Green	Natural, tranquil, relaxing	Jealous, inexperienced, greedy
Blue	Strong, trustworthy, authoritative	Cold, depressing, gloomy

Source: Katherine Nolan, "Color It Effective: How Color Influences the User," in *Microsoft Office Online, FrontPage 2003 Help and How-to: Working with Graphics,* accessed June 1, 2011, http://office.microsoft.com/en-us/frontpage-help/color-it-effective-how-color-influences-the-user-HA001042937.aspx.

Remember that color preferences change over time. In the 1970s, avocado green and harvest gold were standard colors for kitchen appliances, but today these colors seem retro to most U.S. audiences.[4]

These various associations suggest that color is safest with a homogenous audience that you know well. In an increasingly multicultural workforce, color may send signals you do not intend.

In any visual, use as little shading and as few lines as are necessary for clarity. Don't clutter up the visual with extra marks. When you design black-and-white graphs, use shades of gray rather than stripes, wavy lines, and checks to indicate different segments or items.

Resist the temptation to make your visual "artistic" or "relevant" by turning it into a picture or adding clip art. **Clip art** consists of predrawn images that you can import into your document or visual. A small drawing of a car in the corner of a line graph showing the number of miles driven is acceptable in an oral presentation but out of place in a written report. Turning a line graph into a highway to show miles driven makes it harder to read: it's hard to separate the data line from lines that are merely decorative. Visuals authority Edward Tufte uses the term **chartjunk** for decorations that at best are irrelevant to the visual and at worst mislead the reader.[5]

6. Be Accurate and Ethical.

To be a trustworthy communicator and to avoid misleading your audience, strive to be ethical in your choice of visuals or data displays and ensure their accuracy. Always double-check them to be sure the information is accurate. In some cases, visuals or data displays have accurate labels but misleading visual shapes. Visuals or data displays communicate quickly; audiences remember the shape, not the labels. If the audience has to study the labels to get the right picture, the visual or data display is unethical even if the labels are accurate.

Figure 16.4 is distorted by **chartjunk** and dimensionality. In an effort to make the visual interesting, the artist used a picture of a young man (presumably an engineer) rather than simple bars. By using a photograph rather than a bar, the chart implies that all engineers are young, nerdy-looking white men. The photograph also makes it difficult to compare the numbers. The number represented by the tallest figure is not quite 5 times as great as the number represented by the shortest figure, yet the tallest figure takes up 12 times as much space and appears even bigger than that. Two-dimensional figures distort data by multiplying the apparent value by the width as well as by the height—four times for every doubling in value. Three dimensional graphs are especially hard for readers to interpret and should be avoided.[6]

Medical Picture Boards

Have you ever wondered what it would be like to explain a medical emergency to nurses or doctors if they did not speak your language? This scenario could happen for an estimated 23 million Americans who have only limited English skills. To resolve the communication barriers, medical professionals are turning to visuals.

Servision Inc. developed picture boards to be used in medical settings. These boards contain common problems such as a cut, fall, burn, itch, etc., and the part of the body that is affected. Other boards illustrate medical conditions such as nausea, pain, and breathing problems. Many of the boards also have English and Spanish words related to the pictures.

Thousands of these picture boards have been adopted by hospitals across the country. As an added bonus, the medical picture boards can also help deaf or mute patients.

Adapted from Linda A. Johnson, "Picture Boards Help Bridge Language Gap in Health Emergencies," *Associated Press Archive,* September 7, 2007.

Train + Antelope = Doctored Photo

China's state-run news organization issued an apology after a photograph, depicting a herd of antelope running beneath a bridge on which China's new high-speed Qinghai-Xizang train zoomed by, was discovered to be fake. The photograph had received honors in 2006 as one of China's top photos of the year. It created a national stir because it eased environmental concerns about the new train connecting China and Tibet.

After the photo was displayed in a Beijing subway terminal, Chinese citizens started to question the authenticity of the photo. The first suspicions were posted on Internet blogs and from there developed momentum. Even scientists who study the antelope argued that the noise from the train would encourage the animals to scatter, instead of running in the tight pack pictured in the photo.

The photographer confessed to forging the photo; he spliced two different pictures together in Photoshop. He has since been stripped of all his awards and has resigned from his position as a photojournalist.

Adapted from Jane Spencer and Juliet Ye, "China Eats Crow over Faked Photo of Rare Antelope: They Didn't Truly Run with a Train to Tibet; Xinhua Agency Recants," *Wall Street Journal,* February 22, 2008, A1.

Cigarette warning labels are more severe in other countries. American audiences have not been receptive to such dire warnings.

Figure 16.4 Chartjunk and Dimensions Distort Data

Source: Adam Lashinsky, "Valley Horror Show: The Incredible Shrinking Engineer," *Fortune,* December 10, 2001, p. 40.

Even simple bar and line graphs may be misleading if part of the scale is missing, or truncated. **Truncated graphs** are most acceptable when the audience knows the basic data set well. For example, graphs of the stock market almost never start at zero; they are routinely truncated. This omission is acceptable for audiences who follow the market closely.

Since part of the scale is missing in truncated graphs, small changes seem like major ones. Figure 16.5 shows three different truncated graphs of US unemployment data. The first graph shows the trend in unemployment from May 2003 to January 2004. The curve falls from the fifth level of the graph to the second, resembling a 60% decline. But a close look at the numbers shows the decline is from a high of 6.3% to a low of 5.6% (a decline of 11%). The period chosen for the horizontal axis also is truncated. The first graph emphasizes the declining trend in unemployment since a tax cut was enacted in 2003. The second graph uses the period November 2002–November 2003 to show unemployment wavering around 6%. The graph accompanies a news article about "cautious" employers and unemployment that "edged lower." The truncated scale on the vertical axis again makes the changes appear larger. The third graph takes a longer view and puts the percentages on a scale starting at zero. On this scale, the changes in the unemployment rate seem less dramatic, and the recent decline looks as if it could be part of a regular pattern that follows recessions (the shaded areas). The graph starting with 1980 shows that the latest ("current") unemployment rate was lower than those after past recessions.[7]

Data can also be distorted when the context is omitted. As Tufte suggests, a drop may be part of a regular cycle, a correction after an atypical increase, or a permanent drop to a new, lower plateau.[8]

To make your data displays more accurate,

- Differentiate between actual and estimated or projected values.
- When you must truncate a scale, do so clearly with a break in the bars or in the background.
- Avoid perspective and three-dimensional graphs.
- Avoid combining graphs with different scales.
- Use images of people carefully in histographs to avoid sexist, racist, or other exclusionary visual statements.

Absolut-ly Not Political

In a Mexican ad campaign, Absolut Vodka used a map of North America showing Mexico and the United States as being about the same size. The map pictured what the border would look like in an "Absolut World": translate that to be a better world from a Mexican perspective. California, Nevada, Texas, and Utah, plus parts of Arizona, Colorado, New Mexico, and Wyoming were all pictured as part of Mexico, as they would have been without the Mexican–American War.

The ad spread quickly through the Internet. While it appealed to its intended Mexican audience, it riled U.S. audiences—so much so that Absolut issued an apology.

Is the map ethical? Would it offend you? Can you think of other examples where maps have been used for political purposes?

Adapted from Frank Jacobs, "264—an Absolut Mexico," *Strange Maps* (blog), April 5, 2008, http://bigthink.com/ideas/21316.

Figure 16.5 Truncated Scales Distort Data

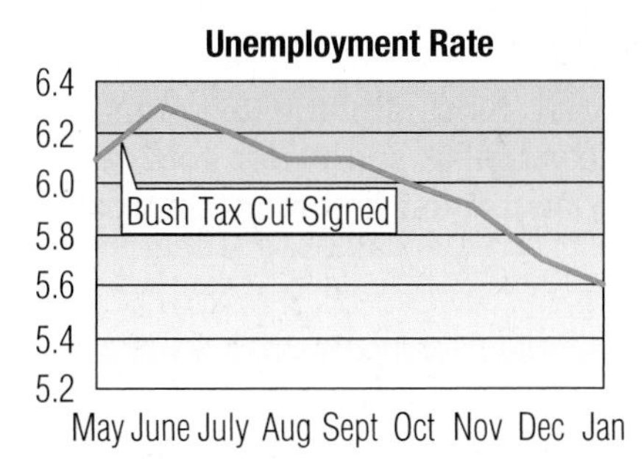

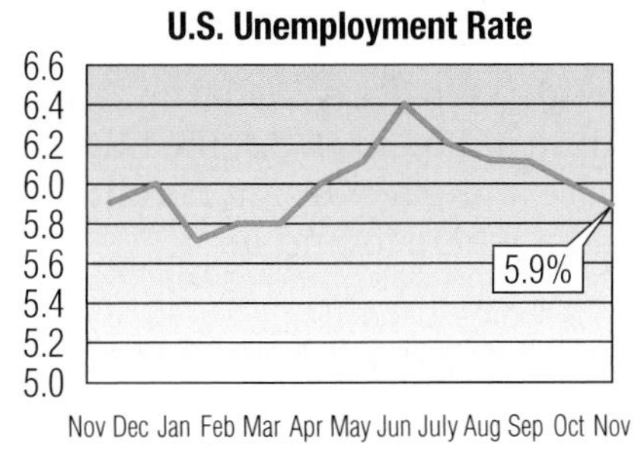

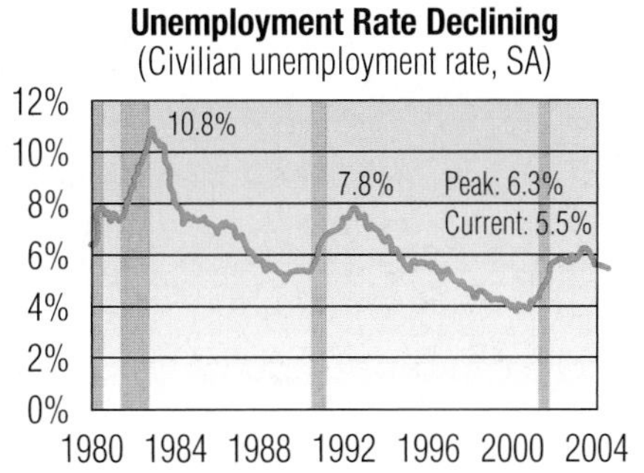

Sources: Jerry Bowyer, "In Defense of the Unemployment Rate," *National Review,* March 5, 2004, http://www.nationalreview.com/articles/209769/defense-unemployment-rate/jerry-bowyer; Mark Gongloff, "Payroll Growth Disappoints," CNN Money, December 5, 2003, http://money.cnn.com/2003/12/05/news/economy/jobs/index.htm; and Joint Economic Committee, "Charts: Economy," August 27, 2004 http://jec.senate.gov.

Finding the Fakes

With the growing trend of altered photos, a researcher set out to find an easy way to spot them. Hany Farid, a computer scientist and forensic imagine specialist at Dartmouth College, developed a system to spot manipulated images and tell what kind of camera snapped the original picture.

Since most photo editing software programs leave a digital signature, his system can tell if manipulation occurred by cross-checking it with a database of more than 10,000 digital camera models. One drawback to the program, however, is that it tells only if a photo has been altered, not what has been edited.

When the program is available for public use, Farid hopes the system will help law enforcement agencies and the newspaper industry.

Adapted from Oliver Staley, "Innovator: Hany Farid," *Bloomberg Businessweek*, January 3, 2011, 37.

Photographs in particular have received close attention for accuracy and ethics concerns. British Airways faced a scandal when their internal staff magazine promoting mobile-boarding passes showed a picture of an iPhone displaying a boarding pass. The first-class passenger's name was "Bin Laden/Osama." No one knows exactly who altered the photo, but British Airways had to deal with a public relations nightmare.[9]

Photographers have always been able to frame their pictures in ways that cut objects they do not want. Pictures of homes for real estate sales can omit the collapsing garage; shots of collapsed homeless people can omit the image of social workers standing by to give aid.

Adobe Photoshop and similar photoediting software have added a new dimension to the problem with their easy photo-altering aids. After recent major worldwide occurrences, such as the Haitian earthquake, the death of Osama bin Laden, the Japanese earthquake and tsunami, handfuls of fabricated pictures have popped up on the Internet. Some were so convincing that even the Associated Press was fooled and sent them across their newswire.[10]

Not long after the oil spill in the Gulf, BP faced another scandal when a photo posted on their website was discovered to be altered. The photo showed BP's Houston Deepwater Horizon command center with control operators closely monitoring live video feeds on large screens. The three fake underwater images were inserted to cover blank screens.[11]

Other controversies have involved the use of digital alterations to increase the beauty of ad models to unnatural degrees. You can watch the short video at www.dove.us/?source=email#/features/videos/default.aspx[cp-documentid=7049579] to see an illustration. First the model's looks are greatly enhanced with makeup and hairstyling. But even that gorgeous result is not good enough. The video shows the made-up model having her brows raised and her neck thinned and elongated with digital alterations for her billboard display.

In another disgrace, *Practical Parenting and Pregnancy* magazine came under fire for airbrushing the baby on the cover. The photographer admitted to eliminating some creases on the baby's chubby arms.[12]

In his discussion of photography ethics, John Long notes that it's easy to think of small changes to photographs as harmless. He argues that any change to the picture is deceptive, because when people see a photo, they assume that it's a true record of a real event. When you change a photo, you use that assumption to deceive.[13] In an attempt to be more ethical, some countries like England and France are trying to push legislation that would require disclaimers on altered photographs.

INTEGRATING VISUALS AND DATA DISPLAYS IN YOUR TEXT LO 16-3

Refer in your text to every visual and data display. Normally the text gives the table or figure number but not the title. Put the visual as soon after your reference as space and page design permit. If the visual must go on another page, tell the reader where to find it:

As Figure 3 shows (page 10), . . .

(See Table 2 on page 14.)

Summarize the main point of a visual or data display *before* you present the visual itself. Then when readers get to it, they'll see it as confirmation of your point.

Weak: Listed below are the results.

Better: As Figure 4 shows, sales doubled in the last decade.

How much discussion a visual or data displays needs depends on the audience, the complexity of the visual, and the importance of the point it makes. Use these guidelines:

- If the material is new to the audience, provide a fuller explanation than if similar material is presented to this audience every week or month.
- If the visual is complex, help the reader find key points.
- If the point is important, discuss its implications in some detail.

In contrast, one sentence about a visual or data display may be enough when the audience is already familiar with the topic and the data, when the visual is simple and well designed, and when the information in the visual is a minor part of your proof.

When you discuss visuals and data displays, spell out numbers that fall at the beginning of a sentence. If spelling out the number or year is cumbersome, revise the sentence so that it does not begin with a number.

Forty-five percent of the cost goes to pay wages and salaries.

In 2002, euronotes and coins became legal tender.

Put numbers in parentheses at the end of the clause or sentence to make the sentence easier to read:

Hard to read: As Table 4 shows, teachers participate (54%) in more community service groups than do members of the other occupations surveyed; dentists (20.8%) participate in more service groups than do members of five of the other occupations.

Better: As Table 4 shows, teachers participate in more community service groups than do members of the other occupations surveyed (54%); dentists participate in more service groups than do five of the other occupations (20.8%).

DESIGNING VISUALS AND DATA DISPLAYS

Once you know your story—what you're saying, how you're saying it, and how you want text and visuals to combine to say it—then you're in a position to choose and create visuals and data displays. Each type of visual can do different things for you. Here are some of the most common types of visuals and data displays, and here's when, where and how they're most effective.

Tables

Use tables only when you want the audience to focus on specific numbers. Graphs convey less specific information but are more memorable. Figure 16.6 illustrates the basic structure of tables, and Figure 16.7 illustrates a completed table. The **boxhead** is the variable whose label is at the top; the **stub** is the variable listed on the side. When constructing tables,

- Use common, understandable units. Round off to simplify the data (e.g., 35% rather than 35.27%; 44.5 million rather than 44,503,276).
- Provide column and row totals or averages when they're relevant.
- Put the items you want audiences to compare in columns rather than in rows to facilitate mental subtraction and division.
- When you have many rows, shade alternate rows (or pairs of rows) or double-space after every five rows to help audiences line up items accurately.

Visuals That Translate Well

When preparing visuals, keep in mind cultural differences:

- Make sure any symbols in the visual will have the correct meaning in the culture of your audience. For example, a red cross symbolizes first aid in North America, but in Muslim countries the symbol with that meaning is typically a green crescent.
- If you use punctuation marks as symbols, be sure they are meaningful to your audience. A question mark in English and certain other languages might signal a help function or answers to questions. But in languages without this symbol, it has no meaning.
- In showing humans, respect the cultural norms of your audience. Europeans tend to accept images of nudity, but some cultures can be offended by images of even a bare leg or other body part.
- Organize the information according to the reading customs of the audience. North American and European audiences will tend to read visual information as they do text: from left to right. Asians view from right to left, and Middle Easterners in a rotation moving counterclockwise.
- Learn your audience's conventions for writing numbers. In the United States, a period indicates the decimal point, and commas separate groups of three digits. In much of Europe, a comma represents the decimal point, and a space goes between each group of three digits. For US and French readers, 3,333 would have different values.

Adapted from Gerald J. Alred, Charles T. Brusaw, and Walter E. Oliu, *The Business Writer's Handbook,* 8th ed. (New York: St. Martin's Press, 2006), 248–50, 558–62; and *The Chicago Manual of Style,* 16th ed. (Chicago: University of Chicago Press, 2010), 471.

Figure 16.6 Table Structure

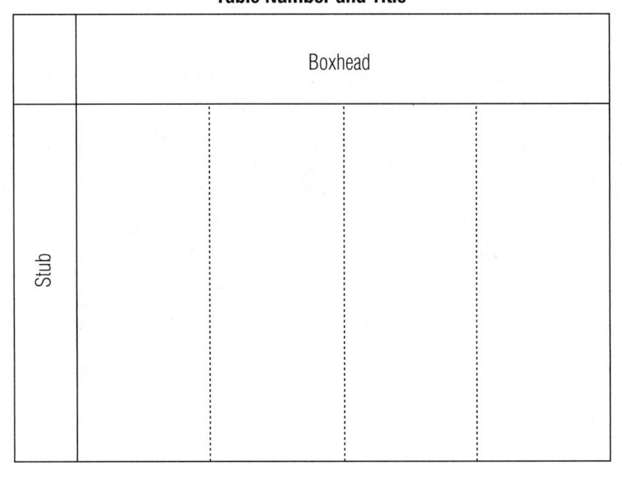

Pie Charts

Pie charts force the audience to measure area. However, people can judge position or length (which a bar chart uses) more accurately than they judge area, thus making information in pie charts more difficult for an audience to understand accurately. The data in any pie chart can be put in a bar chart. Therefore, use a pie chart only when you are comparing one segment to the whole. When you are comparing one segment to another segment, use a bar chart, a line graph, or a map—even though the data may be expressed in percentages. In Figure 16.8, notice how it's nearly impossible to tell the difference in graduation rates between the two pie charts.

Figure 16.7 Tables Show Exact Values for Top U.S. Search Sites for June 2010

Rank	Site	Searches (000)	Share of Searches	MoM % Change
	All Search	9,137,637	100%	
1	Google	5,935,561	65.0%	−0.1%
2	Yahoo! Search	1,250,246	13.7%	−0.1%
3	MSN/WindowsLive/Bing	1,221,873	13.4%	0.4%
4	AOL Search	192,187	2.1%	0.0%
5	Ask.com Search	184,518	2.0%	0.0%
6	My Web Search Search	98,789	1.1%	−0.1%
7	Comcast Search	44,633	0.5%	0.0%
8	NexTag Search	24,377	0.3%	0.0%
9	WhitePages.com Network Search	23,769	0.3%	0.0%
10	Yellow Pages Search	17,588	0.2%	0.0%

Source: The Nielsen Company, "Top U.S. Search Sites for June 2010," July 13, 2010, http://blog.nielsen.com/nielsenwire/online_mobile/top-u-s-search-sites-for-june-2010/.

Figure 16.8 Difficult to Compare Two Pie Charts

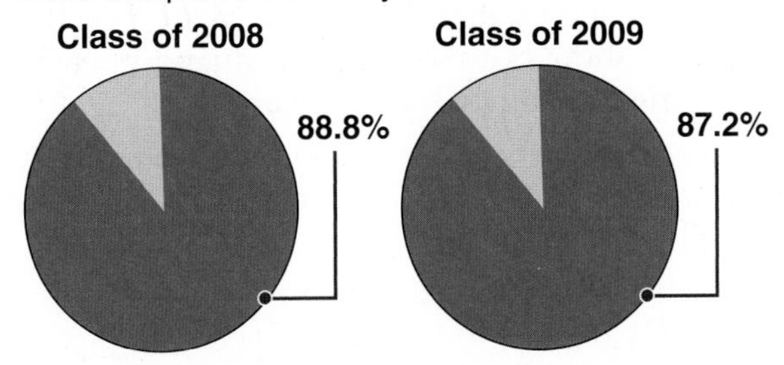
Graduation rate dips
Slightly fewer students graduated in 2009 compared with the year before.
Class of 2008
88.8%
Class of 2009
87.2%

Note: The state changed the way it calculates graduation rates. These are the only two years available under the new method.

Source: Iowa Department of Education

Source: Sheena Dooley, "Academic Progress Flat Despite More Teachers," *Des Moines Register;* November 7, 2010, 1A.

When constructing pie charts,

- Make the chart a perfect circle. Avoid 3D circles; they distort the data.
- Start at 12 o'clock with the largest percentage or the percentage you want to focus on. Go clockwise to each smaller percentage or to each percentage in some other logical order.
- Limit the number of segments to no more than seven. If your data have more divisions, combine the smallest or the least important into a single "miscellaneous" or "other" category.
- Label the segments outside the circle. Internal labels are hard to read.

The Power of the Golden Arches

Company logos have big business implications. In a 2007 taste test with 63 children aged 3 to 5, researchers found that the children preferred food if it came in McDonald's packaging. Even though the children were served the same chicken nuggets from McDonald's in two different bags, 59% of children preferred chicken nuggets in the McDonald's packaging; only 23% suggested there was no difference. The same held true for milk with 61% of children preferring the McDonald's cup, fries with 77% preference, and carrots with 54% preference. The researchers also found that the children who lived in houses with more televisions were more likely to prefer McDonald's branded food.

Assuming these results hold true for a larger random sampling of children, what should McDonald's do with this information? What ethical implications exist in this study's results?

Adapted from Nicholas Bakalar, "If It Says McDonald's, Then It Must Be Good," *New York Times,* August 17, 2007, 7.

Bar Charts

Bar charts are easy to interpret because they ask people to compare distance along a common scale, which most people judge accurately. Bar charts are useful in a variety of situations: to compare one item to another, to compare items over time, and to show correlations. Use horizontal bars when your labels are long; when the labels are short, either horizontal or vertical bars will work. When constructing bar charts,

- Order the bars in a logical or chronological order.
- Put the bars close enough together to make comparison easy.
- Label both horizontal and vertical axes.
- Put all labels inside the bars or outside them. When some labels are inside and some are outside, the labels carry the visual weight of longer bars, distorting the data.
- Make all the bars the same width.
- Use different colors for different bars only when their meanings are different: estimates as opposed to known numbers, negative as opposed to positive numbers.
- Avoid using 3D perspective; it makes the values harder to read and can make comparison difficult.

Personality from Photos

"Your appearance tells a lot more about you than you may think. And all it takes is a snapshot.

A new study finds that people can draw accurate conclusions about your personality—such as how extroverted you are—from a single photograph. And when the picture is spontaneous and unposed, it can reveal a virtual personality profile—how easy going you are, how open you are to new experiences, your political orientation, and how religious you are.

Simine Vazire, a Washington University psychologist, and researchers at other universities assessed college students' personalities through questionnaires they and their friends filled out. Ten personality traits were measured.

The researchers took two full-length pictures of each student, one a standardized pose with hands by their sides and a neutral facial expression, and a second for which students weren't told how to pose.

Judges did best with unposed pictures: They were right most of the time for 9 of 10 character traits."

Quoted from "Study Says Pictures Reveal Personality," *Des Moines Register*, December 27, 2009, 3AA.

Several varieties of bar charts exist. See Figure 16.9 for examples.

- **Grouped bar charts** allow you to compare either several aspects of each item or several items over time. Group together the items you want to compare. Figure 16.9a shows that sales were highest in the West each year. If we wanted to show how sales had changed in each region, the bars should be grouped by region, not by year.
- **Segmented, subdivided, or stacked bars** sum the components of an item. It's hard to identify the values in specific segments; grouped bar charts are almost always easier to use.
- **Deviation bar charts** identify positive and negative values, or winners and losers.
- **Paired bar charts** show the comparison between two items.
- **Histograms or pictograms** use images to create the bars.

Line Graphs

Line graphs are also easy to interpret. Use line graphs to compare items over time, to show frequency or distribution, and to show possible correlations. When constructing line graphs,

- Label both horizontal and vertical axes. When time is a variable, it is usually put on the horizontal axis.
- Avoid using more than three different lines on one graph. Even three lines may be too many if they cross each other.
- Avoid using perspective. Perspective makes the values harder to read and can make comparison difficult.

Gantt Charts

Gantt charts are bar charts used to show schedules. They're most commonly used in proposals to show when elements of a project will be completed. Figure 16.10 is a Gantt chart for a marketing plan. From the chart, it is easy to see which activities must be completed first to finish the total plan on time. When using Gantt charts,

- Color-code bars to indicate work planned and work completed.
- Outline **critical activities,** which must be completed on time if the project is to be completed by the due date.
- Indicate progress reports, major achievements, or other accomplishments.

Photographs

Photographs convey a sense of authenticity. The photo of a prototype helps convince investors that a product can be manufactured; the photo of a devastated area can suggest the need for government grants or private donations. You may need to **crop,** or trim, a photo for best results. However, make sure to be ethical with any cropping you do.

Figure 16.9 Varieties of Bar Charts

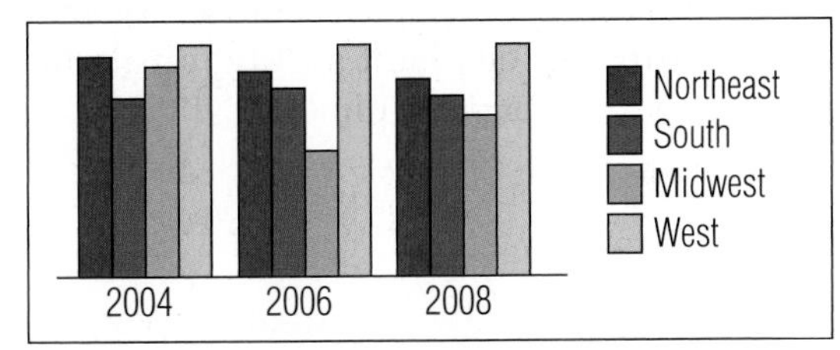

a. Grouped bar charts compare several aspects of each item, or several items over time.

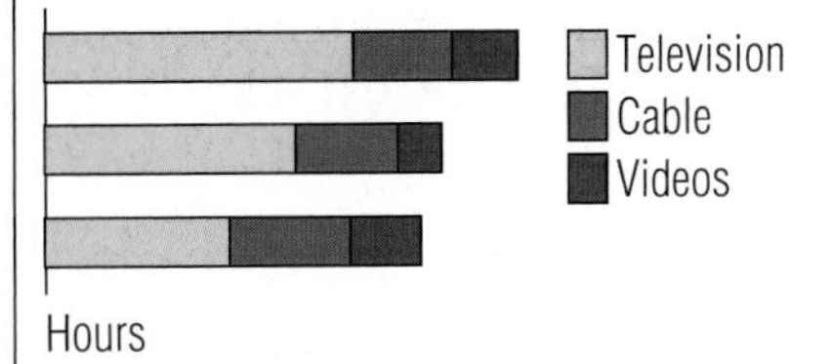

b. Segmented, subdivided, or **stacked bars** sum the components of an item.

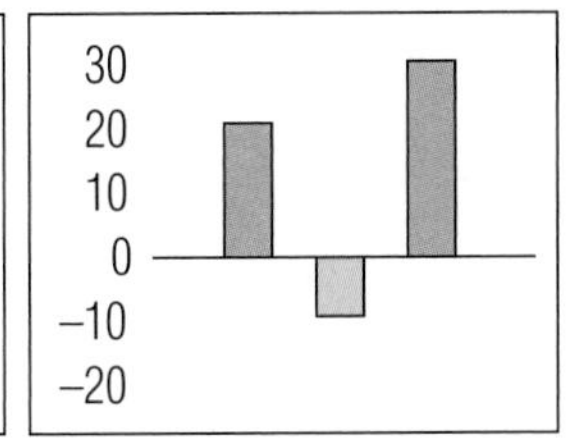

c. Deviation bar charts identify positive and negative values.

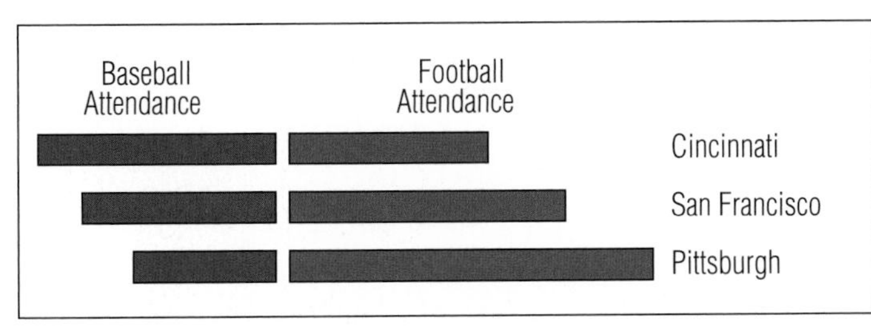

d. Paired bar charts show the comparison between two items.

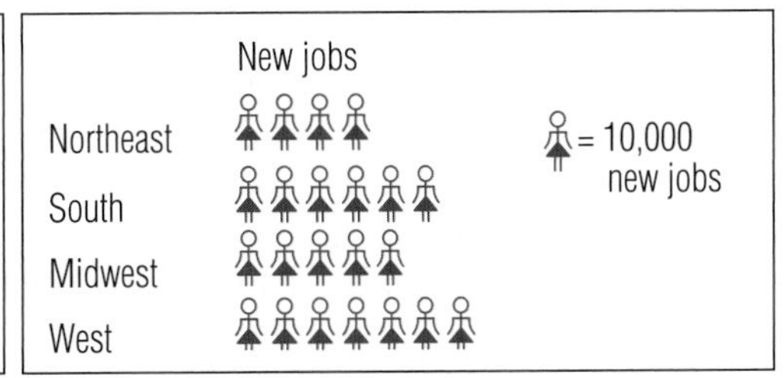

e. Histograms or **pictograms** use images to create the bars.

A growing problem with photos is that they may be edited or staged, purporting to show something as reality even though it never occurred. See the discussion of ethics and accuracy earlier in this chapter.

Figure 16.10 Gantt Charts Show the Schedule for Completing a Project

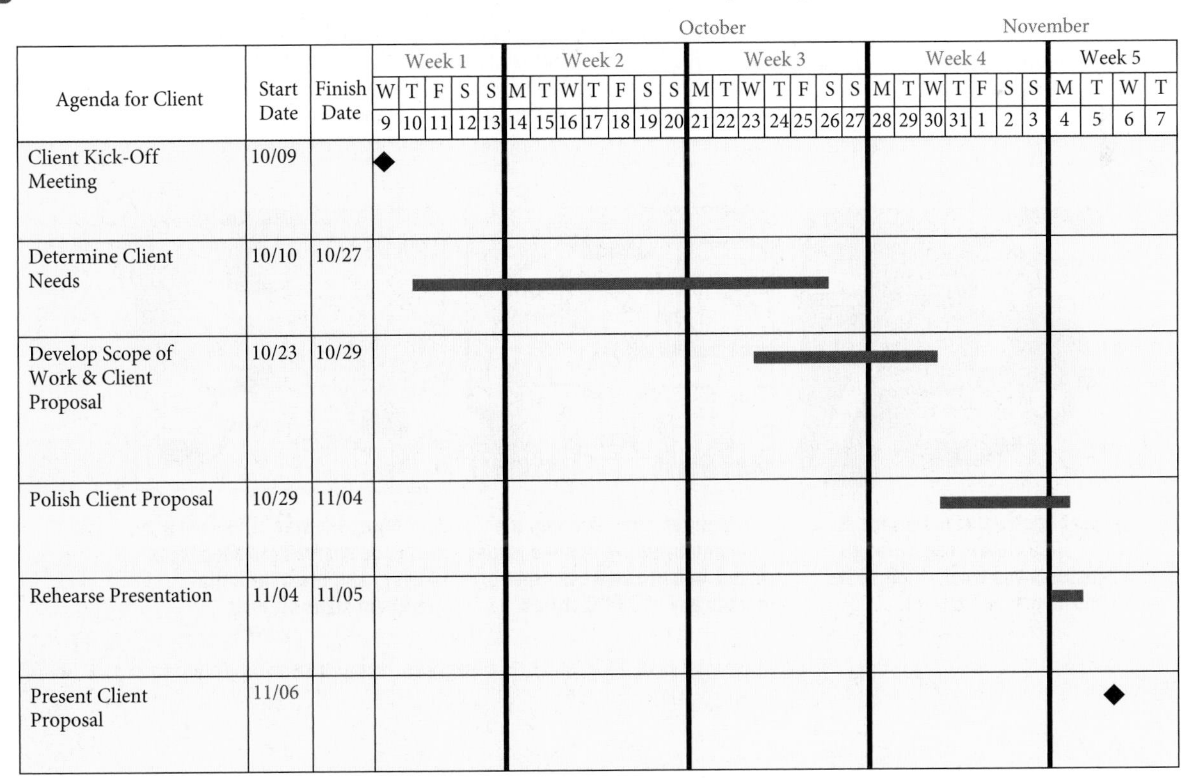

On the other hand, sometimes photos are obviously edited to serve a purpose. The consulting, technology, and outsourcing company Accenture got much publicity from their advertisement showing an elephant surfing on its hind legs. The ad's text said, "Who says you can't be big and nimble?"[14]

Drawings

The richness of detail in photos makes them less effective than drawings for focusing on details. With a drawing, the artist can provide as much or as little detail as is needed to make the point; different parts of the drawing can show different layers or levels of detail. Drawings are also better for showing structures underground, undersea, or in the atmosphere.

In the drawings in Figure 16.11, no attempt is made to show the details of warehousing and transportation facilities. Such details would distract

Figure 16.11 Sketches Can Show Processes

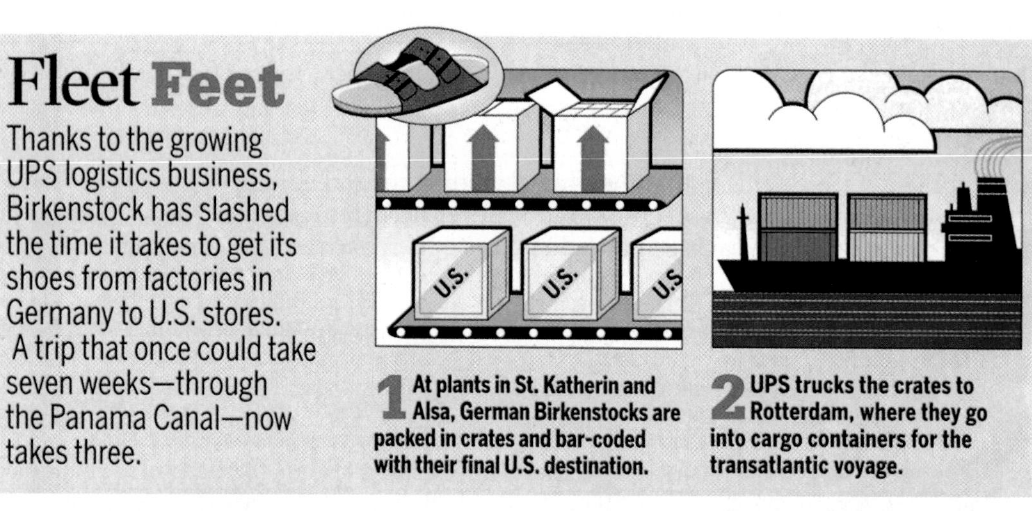

Fleet Feet
Thanks to the growing UPS logistics business, Birkenstock has slashed the time it takes to get its shoes from factories in Germany to U.S. stores. A trip that once could take seven weeks—through the Panama Canal—now takes three.
U.S.
U.S.
U.S.
1 At plants in St. Katherin and Alsa, German Birkenstocks are packed in crates and bar-coded with their final U.S. destination.
2 UPS trucks the crates to Rotterdam, where they go into cargo containers for the transatlantic voyage.

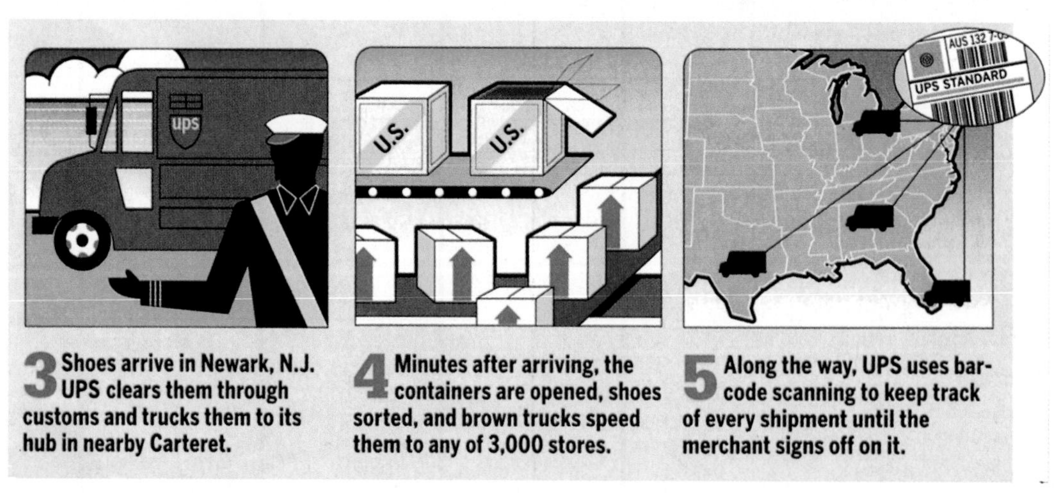

ups
U.S.
U.S.
UPS STANDARD
3 Shoes arrive in Newark, N.J. UPS clears them through customs and trucks them to its hub in nearby Carteret.
4 Minutes after arriving, the containers are opened, shoes sorted, and brown trucks speed them to any of 3,000 stores.
5 Along the way, UPS uses bar-code scanning to keep track of every shipment until the merchant signs off on it.

Source: From Dan Foust, "Big Brown's New Bag." Reprinted from the July 19, 2004 issue of *BusinessWeek*. Used with permission of Bloomberg L.P. Copyright © 2011. All rights reserved.

from the main point. Here, the drawings show how UPS Logistics handles the various activities required to move Birkenstock sandals from the shoe company's German factories to thousands of stores in the United States.

Drawings can also be used to insert creativity into the presentation of information. *Time* magazine used a Seek & Find drawing, like those in magazines asking children to find the hidden items in a picture, to highlight consumer goods whose prices would likely rise as corn is turned into ethanol.[15]

Maps

Use maps to emphasize location or to compare items in different locations. Figure 16.12 shows the prevalence of binge drinking among adults by state.

Figure 16.12 Prevalence of Binge Drinking among Adults

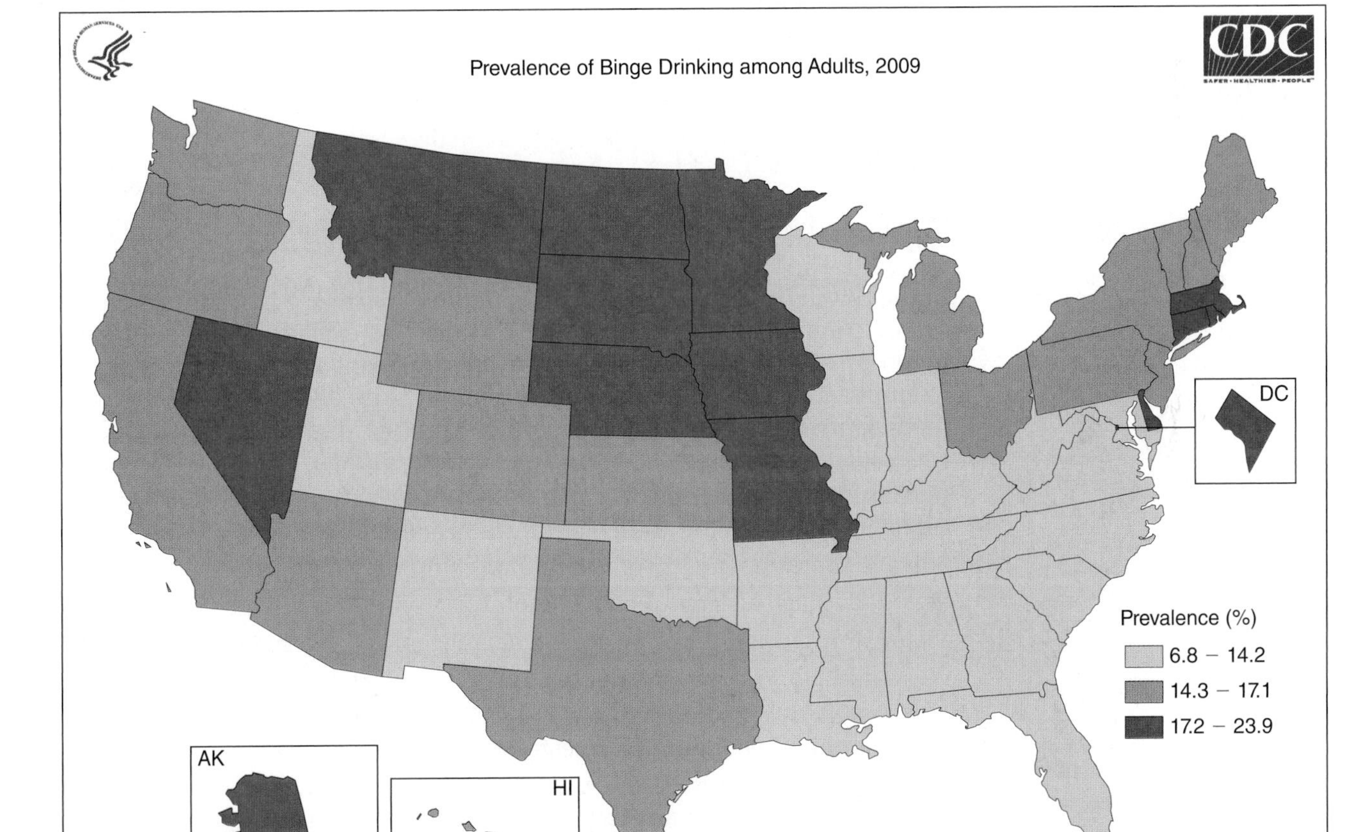

Source: Center for Disease Control, "Prevalence of Binge Drinking among Adults, 2009," accessed June 3, 2011, http://www.cdc.gov/alcohol/index.htm.

A map is appropriate because the emphasis is on the distribution of binge drinking in various regions. Several computer software packages now allow users to generate local, state, national, or global maps, adding color or shadings, and labels. When using maps,

- Label states, provinces, or countries if it's important that people be able to identify levels in areas other than their own.
- Avoid using perspective. Perspective makes the values harder to read and can make comparison difficult.

Dynamic Displays

Online visuals are expanding the possibilities of data displays. Many of these displays are interactive, allowing users to adapt them to personal needs. At BabyNameWizard.com, you can see the popularity of various names over the years, or you can track the popularity of one name. Some displays are animated. At CReSIS, the Center for Remote Sensing of Ice Sheets, you can see the effects of global warming on coastal areas around the world as coasts flood while you watch.

SUMMARY OF KEY POINTS

- Visuals and data displays help make data meaningful for your audience and support your arguments.
- In the rough draft, use visuals and data displays to see that ideas are presented completely and to see what relationships exist. In the final presentation or document, use visuals and data displays to make points vivid, to emphasize material that the reader might skip, and to present material more compactly and with less repetition than words alone would require.
- Use visuals and data displays when you want to show relationships and to persuade, when the information is complex or contains extensive numerical data, and when the audience values visuals.
- Always check the quality of your data.
- Pick data to tell a story, to make a point.
- Visuals and data displays are not interchangeable. The best selection depends on the kind of data and the point you want to make with the data.
- Follow conventions to avoid alienating your audience.
- Use color and decoration with restraint.
- Present data accurately and ethically. **Chartjunk** denotes decorations that at best are irrelevant to the visual and at worst mislead the reader. **Truncated graphs** omit part of the scale and visually mislead readers. Graphs and charts with 3D mislead readers.
- Summarize the main point of a visual or data display before it appears in the text.

CHAPTER 16 Exercises and Problems

Go to www.mhhe.com/locker10e for additional Exercises and Problems.

16.1 Reviewing the Chapter

1. When should you use visuals and data displays? (LO 16-1)
2. What are some specific ways to create effective visuals and data displays? (LO 16-2)
3. What are some concerns that must be addressed to keep your visuals and data displays accurate and ethical? (LO 16-2)
4. What are some guidelines for integrating visuals and data displays into your text? (LO 16-3)
5. What are some guidelines for constructing bar charts? (LO 16-2)

16.2 Evaluating the Ethics of Design Choices

Indicate whether you consider each of the following actions ethical, unethical, or a gray area. Which of the actions would you do? Which would you feel uncomfortable doing? Which would you refuse to do?

1. Using photos of Hawaiian beaches in advertising for Bermuda tourism, without indicating the location of the beaches.
2. Editing a photo by inserting an image of a young black person into a picture of an all-white group, and using that photo in a recruiting brochure designed to attract minority applicants to a university.
3. Altering people in your photographs so that they look skinnier and younger. (Watch the short video mentioned in the ethics discussion of this chapter.)
4. Modifying real estate photos by changing the physical appearance of houses or stores.
5. Including pictures in restaurant menus that are exaggerated in presentation quality, color appearance, and portion size.
6. Creating photos of Osama bin Laden's dead body after the White House withheld releasing the real images.

16.3 Evaluating Visuals

Evaluate each of the following visuals.

- Is visual's message clear?
- Is it the right visual for the story?
- Is the visual designed appropriately? Is color, if any, used appropriately?
- Is the visual free from chartjunk?
- Does the visual distort data or mislead the reader in any way?

1.

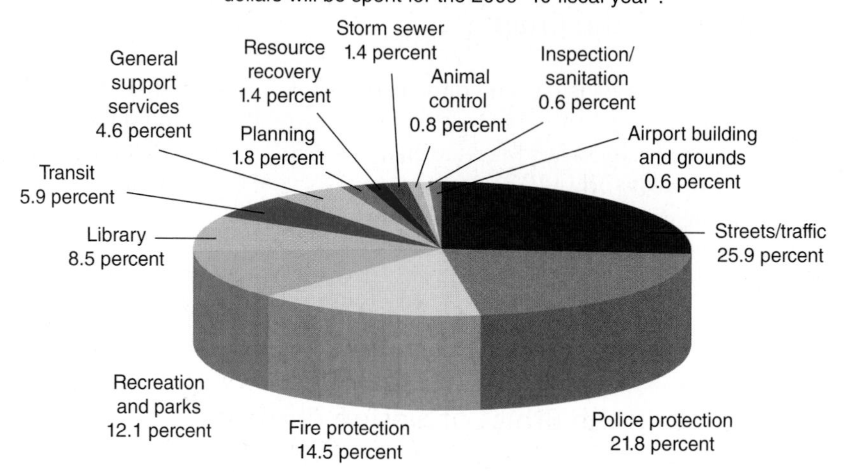

Source: "Where Property Taxes Go," *Ames Tribune,* February, 3, 2009, A2.

2.

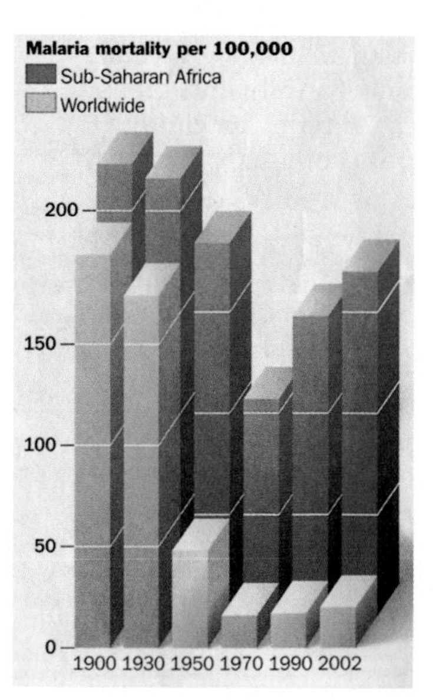

Source: Data provided by World Health Organization.

3.

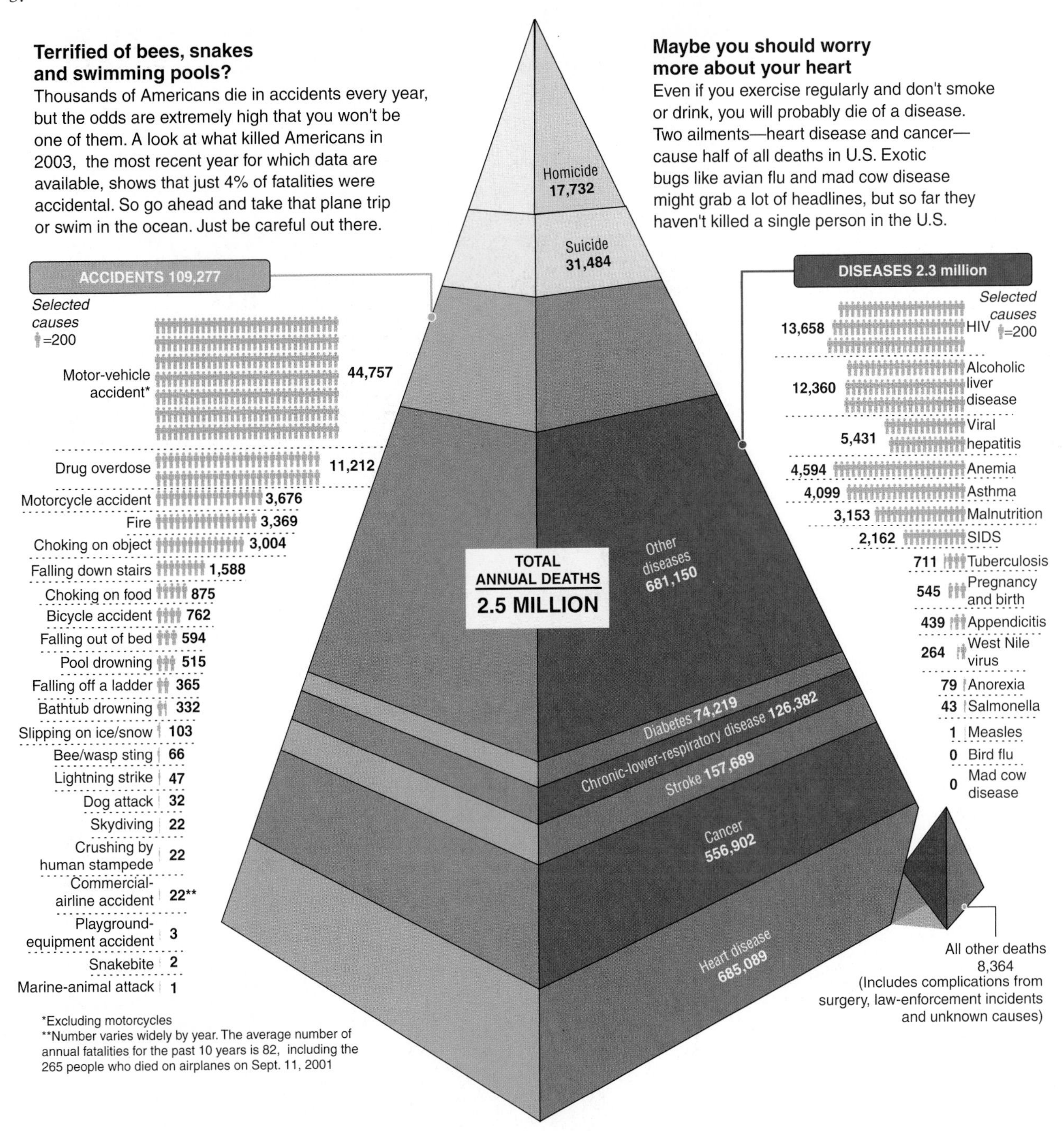

Terrified of bees, snakes and swimming pools?
Thousands of Americans die in accidents every year, but the odds are extremely high that you won't be one of them. A look at what killed Americans in 2003, the most recent year for which data are available, shows that just 4% of fatalities were accidental. So go ahead and take that plane trip or swim in the ocean. Just be careful out there.
Maybe you should worry more about your heart
Even if you exercise regularly and don't smoke or drink, you will probably die of a disease. Two ailments—heart disease and cancer—cause half of all deaths in U.S. Exotic bugs like avian flu and mad cow disease might grab a lot of headlines, but so far they haven't killed a single person in the U.S.
ACCIDENTS 109,277
Selected causes
=200
Motor-vehicle accident* 44,757
Drug overdose 11,212
Motorcycle accident 3,676
Fire 3,369
Choking on object 3,004
Falling down stairs 1,588
Choking on food 875
Bicycle accident 762
Falling out of bed 594
Pool drowning 515
Falling off a ladder 365
Bathtub drowning 332
Slipping on ice/snow 103
Bee/wasp sting 66
Lightning strike 47
Dog attack 32
Skydiving 22
Crushing by human stampede 22
Commercial-airline accident 22**
Playground-equipment accident 3
Snakebite 2
Marine-animal attack 1
*Excluding motorcycles
**Number varies widely by year. The average number of annual fatalities for the past 10 years is 82, including the 265 people who died on airplanes on Sept. 11, 2001
Homicide 17,732
Suicide 31,484
TOTAL ANNUAL DEATHS
2.5 MILLION
Other diseases 681,150
Diabetes 74,219
Chronic-lower-respiratory disease 126,382
Stroke 157,689
Cancer 556,902
Heart disease 685,089
DISEASES 2.3 million
Selected causes
=200
13,658 HIV
12,360 Alcoholic liver disease
5,431 Viral hepatitis
4,594 Anemia
4,099 Asthma
3,153 Malnutrition
2,162 SIDS
711 Tuberculosis
545 Pregnancy and birth
439 Appendicitis
264 West Nile virus
79 Anorexia
43 Salmonella
1 Measles
0 Bird flu
0 Mad cow disease
All other deaths 8,364
(Includes complications from surgery, law-enforcement incidents and unknown causes)

Sources: Centers for Disease Control and Prevention; National Transportation Safety Board.

4.

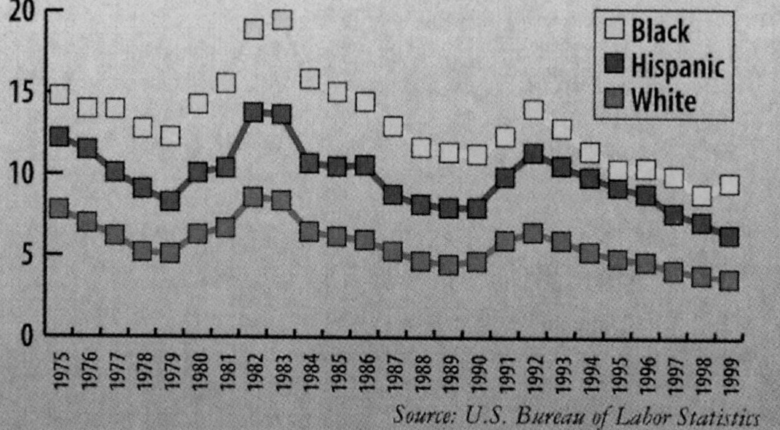

Source: From American Demographics, June 2000. With permission.

5.

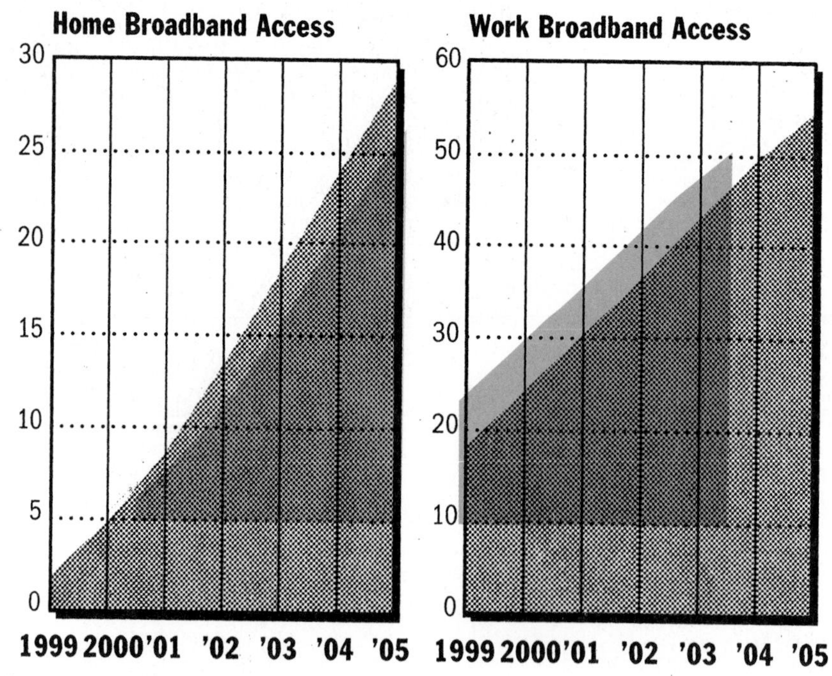

Source: From *The Wall Street Journal,* March 26, 2001, Copyright © 2001 by Dow Jones & Company, Inc. Reproduced with permission of Dow Jones & Company, Inc. via Copyright Clearance Center.

6.

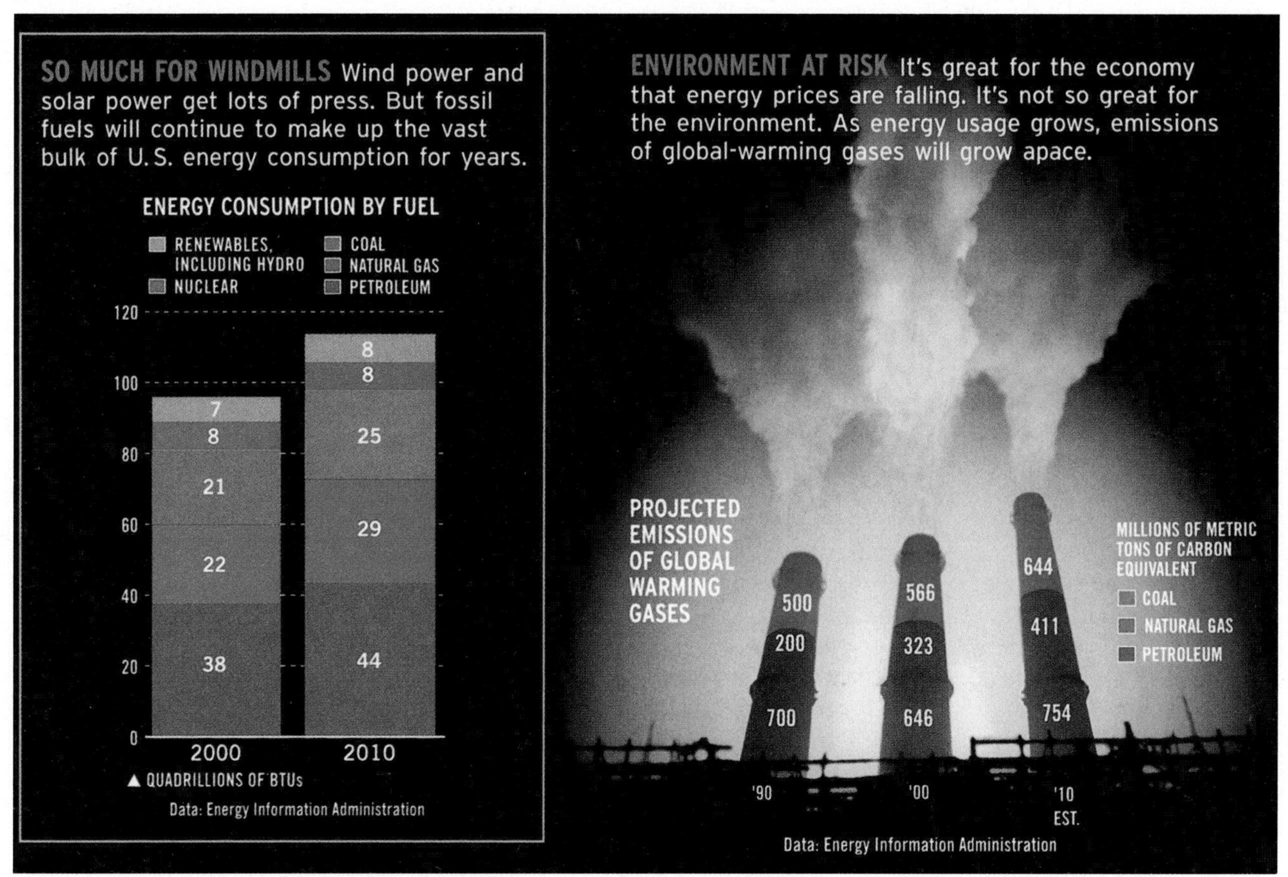

Source: Reprinted from the August 27, 2001 issue of *BusinessWeek* by special permission. Used with permission of Bloomberg L.P. Copyright © 2011. All rights reserved.

7.

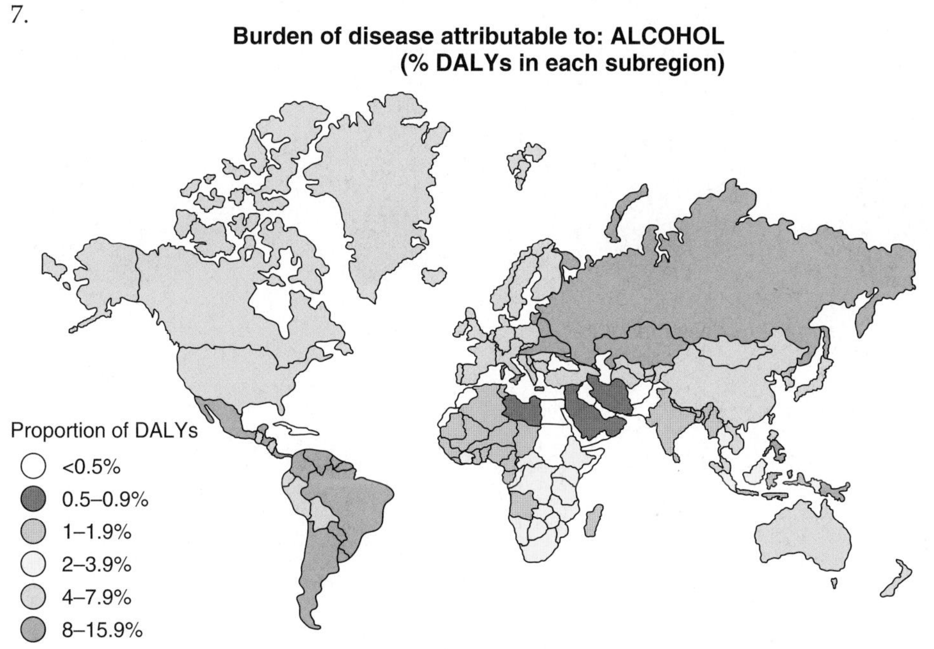

Worldwide alcohol causes 1.8 million deaths (3.2% of total) and 58.3 million (4% of total) of Disability-Adjusted Life Years (DALYs). Unintentional injuries alone account for about one-third of the 1.8 million deaths, while neuro-psychiatric conditions account for close to 40% of the 58.3 million DALYs. The burden is not equally distributed among the countries, as is shown on the map.

Source: World Health Organization, "Alcohol," in *Management of Substance Abuse,* http://www.who.int/substance_abuse/facts/alcohol/en/ (accessed May 5, 2009).

8.

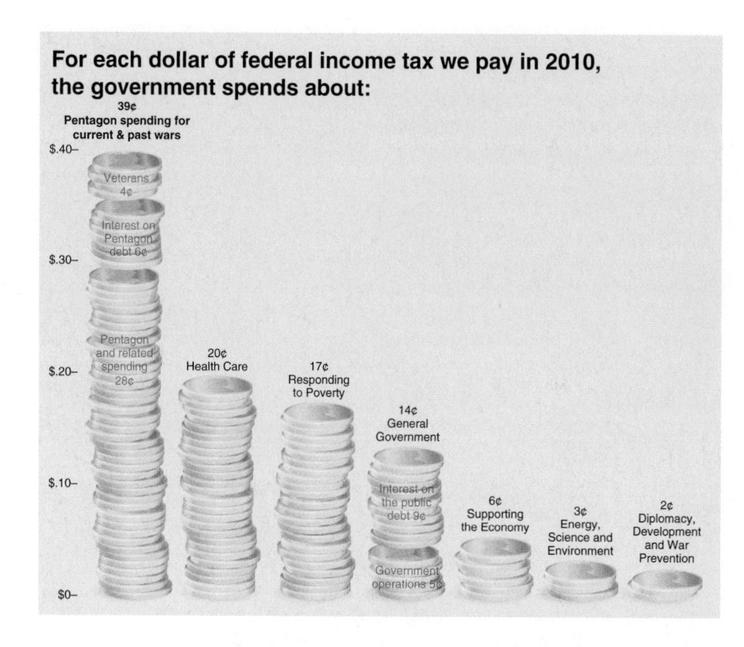

Source: Friends Committee on National Legislation, "Where Do Our Income Tax Dollars Go?" October 2010, http://fcnl.org/assets/issues/budget/Taxes10coin_chart.pdf.

9.

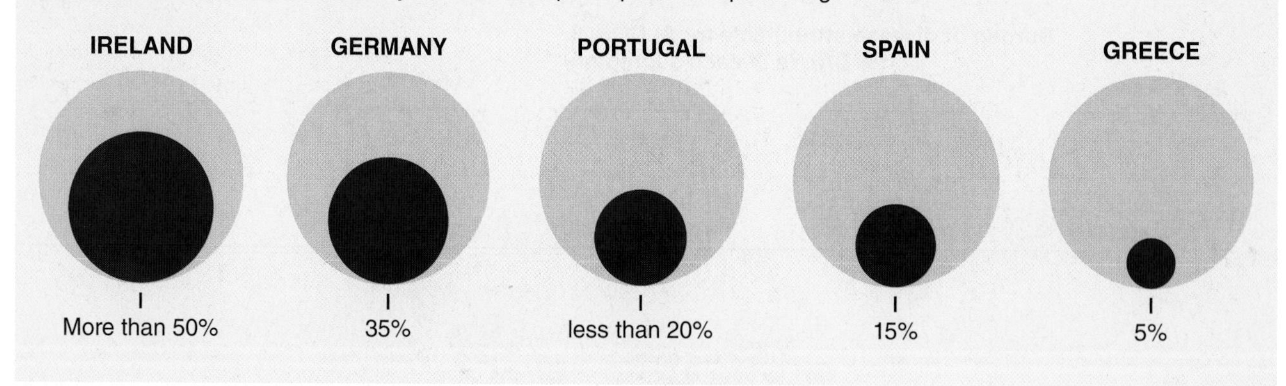

Source: Neil Shah, "Weaker Euro Set to Spur Irish Turnaround," *Wall Street Journal,* June 29, 2010, A14.

16.4 Visualizing Healthy Eating Habits

With soaring obesity rates in the United States, the government continues to produce visuals that encourage healthy eating habits. While the food pyramids have been the norm, their messages have been largely ignored by U.S. citizens. The newest version of the visual to encourage healthy eating uses a plate with various portion sizes for fruits, grains, vegetables, protein, and dairy.

Evaluate each of the visuals.

Which version of the visual is right for the story?

Which healthy eating visual is clearest?

Which is most informative?

Which visual will most likely encourage healthy eating habits?

Which visuals contain chartjunk?

Which did you prefer? Why?

1.

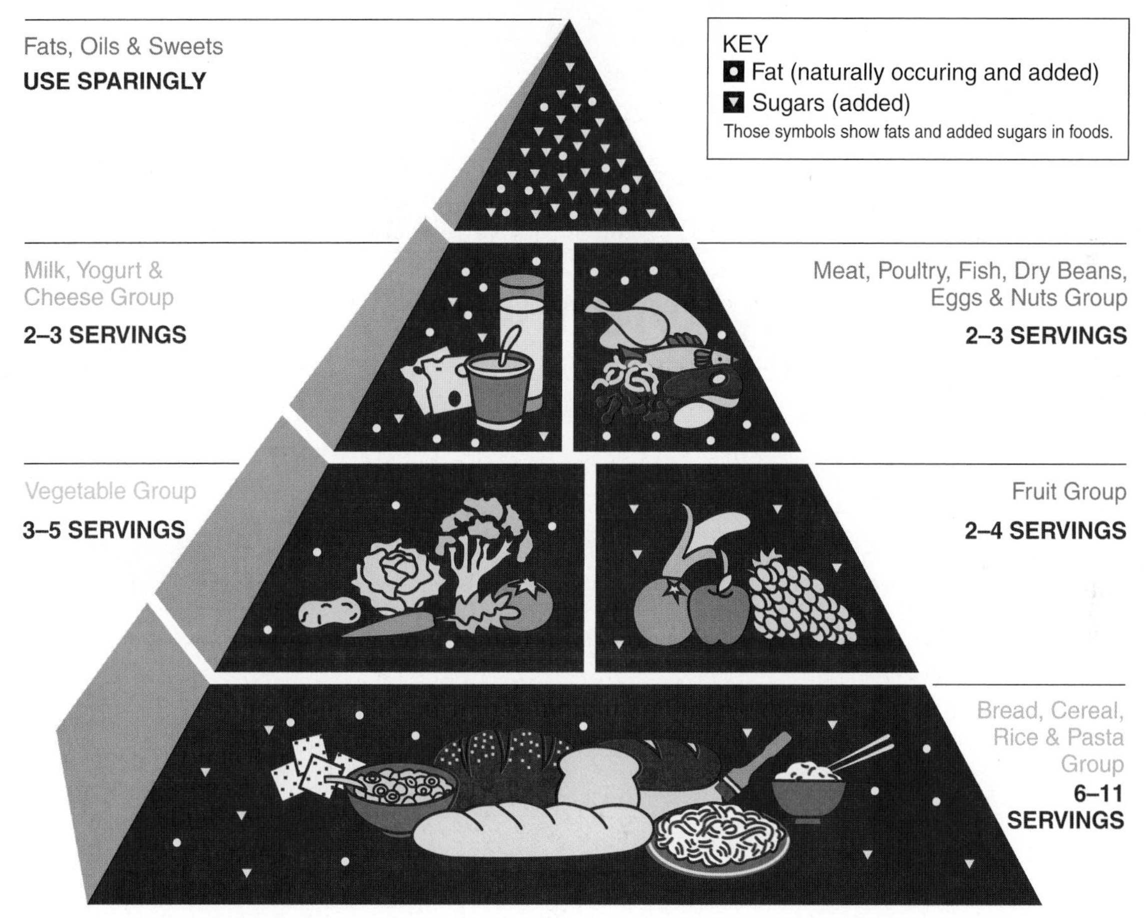

Source: http://www.cnpp.usda.gov/Publications/MyPyramid/OriginalFoodGuidePyramids/FGP/FGPPamphlet.pdf (accessed May 5, 2009).

2.

Anatomy of MyPyramid

One size doesn't fit all

USDA's new MyPyramid symbolizes a personalized approach to healthy eating and physical activity. The symbol has been designed to be simple. It has been developed to remind consumers to make healthy food choices and to be active every day. The different parts of the symbol are described below.

Activity

Activity is represented by the steps and the person climbing them, as a reminder of the importance of daily physical activity.

Moderation

Moderation is represented by the narrowing of each food group from bottom to top. The wider base stands for foods with little or no solid fats or added sugars. These should be selected more often. The narrower top area stands for foods containing more added sugars and solid fats. The more active you are, the more of these foods can fit into your diet.

Personalization

Personalization is shown by the person on the steps, the slogan and the URL. Find the kinds and amounts of food to eat each day at Mypyramid.gov.

Current Food Pyramid

MyPyramid.gov

STEPS TO A HEALTHIER YOU

Proportionality

Proportionality is shown by the different widths of the food group bands. The widths suggest how much food a person should choose from each group. The widths are just a general guide, not exact proportions. Check the Web site for how much is right for you.

Variety

Variety is symbolized by the 6 color bands representing the 5 food groups of the Pyramid and oils. This illustrates that foods from all groups are needed each day for good health.

Gradual Improvement

Gradual improvement is encouraged by the slogan. It suggests that individuals can benefit from taking small steps to improve their diets and lifestyle each day.

USDA U.S. Department of Agriculture
Center for Nutrition Policy
and Promotion
April 2005 CNPP-16

USDA is an equal opportunity provider and employer

GRAINS | VEGETABLES | FRUITS | OILS | MILK | MEAT& BEANS

Source: United States Department of Agriculture, "Steps to a Healthier You," in MyPyramid.gov, http://www.mypyramid.gov (accessed May 5, 2009).

3.

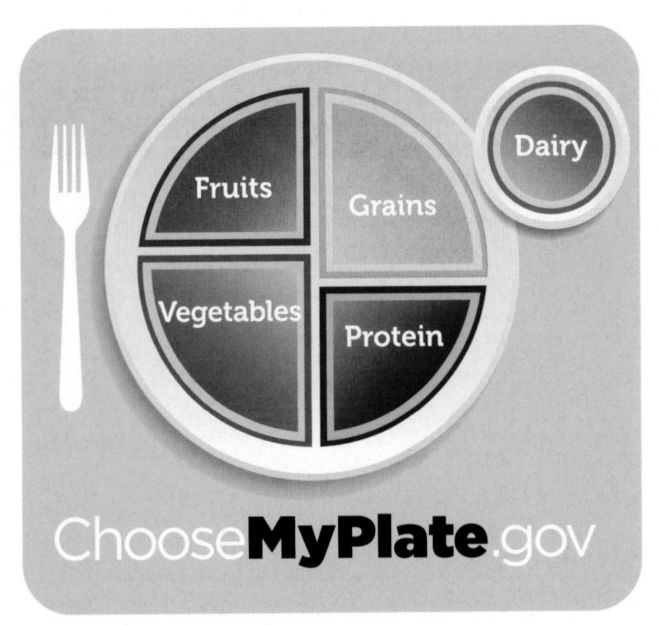

Source: United States Department of Agriculture, "Choose My Plate," in ChooseMyPlate.gov, accessed June 3, 2011, http://www.choosemyplate.gov/images/MyPlateImages/JPG/myplate_green.jpg.

16.5 Creating a Web Guide to Graphs

Create a web page explaining how to create effective visuals and data displays. Offer principles to a specific audience. Your web page should also provide at least seven links to examples of good and poor visuals and data displays. (More is better.) At the top of your web page, offer an overview of what the page contains. At the bottom of the page, put the creation/update date and your name and e-mail address.

As your instructor directs,

a. Turn in one copy of your page(s). On another page, give the URLs for each link.
b. Electronically submit your web page files.
c. Write a memo to your instructor (1) identifying the audience for which the page is designed and explaining (2) the search strategies you used to find material on this topic, (3) why you chose the pages and information you've included, and (4) why you chose the layout and graphics you've used.
d. Present your page orally to the class.

Hints:

- Searching for words *(graphs, maps, Gantt charts, data)* will turn up only pages with those words. Check pages on topics that may use graphs to explain their data: finance, companies' performance, sports, cost of living, exports, and so forth.
- In addition to finding good and bad visuals on the web, you can also scan in examples you find in newspapers, magazines, and textbooks.
- If you have more than nine links, chunk them in small groups under headings.

16.6 Creating Visuals

As your instructor directs,

a. Identify visuals that you might use to help analyze each of the following data sets.
b. Identify and create a visual for one or more of the stories in each set.
c. Identify additional information that would be needed for other stories related to these data sets.

1. Active Internet home users.

Country	Worldwide Active Internet Home Users, June 2009			
	May 2009	June 2009	Growth (%)	Difference
Australia	11,237,351	11,514,606	2.47	277,255
Brazil	25,566,439	25,600,214	0.13	33,775
France	31,099,132	30,971,894	−0.41	−127,238
Germany	36,703,500	37,093,495	1.06	389,995
Italy	17,769,768	18,069,093	1.80	319,325
Japan	49,711,242	50,048,857	0.68%	337,615
Spain	19,826,831	19,726,429	−0.51	−100,402
Switzerland	3,765,629	3,637,642	−3.40	−127,987
U.K.	29,048,332	29,956,108	3.13	907,776
U.S.	156,557,641	172,770,464	10.36	16,212,823

Source: From Enid Burns, "Active Home Internet Users by Country," April 2007, in *Trends and Statistics: The Web's Richest Source.* Reprinted with permission.

2. Daily Change in Traffic to NCAA-Related Sports Websites, during "March Madness" (U.S., Home and Work).

Site	Wed: 3/15 UA (000)	Thurs: 3/16 UA (000)	Fri: 3/17 UA (000)	Wed Fri Growth
CBS Sportsline.com Network	1,958	3,603	3,135	84%
AOL Sports (Web-only)	761	999	1,006	31%
FOX Sports on MSN	1,510	1,953	2,237	29%
Yahoo! Sports	2,121	2,601	2,377	23%
SI.com	724*	819*	773*	13%*
ESPN	3,074	3,312	2,941	8%
Total Unduplicated UA (Unique Audience)	**8,005**	**9,659**	**9,573**	**21%**

*These estimates are calculated on smaller sample sizes and are subject to increased statistical variability as a result.
From Enid Burns, "March Madness Invades Office Life," *Trends & Statistics: The Web's Richest Resource.* Reprinted with permission.

3. Customer Satisfaction with Airlines.

	Base-line	95	96	97	98	99	00	01	02	03	04	05	06	07	08	09	10	Previous Year % Change	First Year % Change
Airlines	**72**	**69**	**69**	**67**	**65**	**63**	**63**	**61**	**66**	**67**	**66**	**66**	**65**	**63**	**62**	**64**	**66**	**3.1**	**−8.3**
Southwest Airlines	78	76	76	76	74	72	70	70	74	75	73	74	74	76	79	81	79	−2.5	1.3
All Others	NM	70	74	70	62	67	63	64	72	74	73	74	74	75	75	77	75	−2.6	7.1
Continental Airlines	67	64	66	64	66	64	62	67	68	68	67	70	67	69	62	68	71	4.4	6.0
American Airlines	70	71	71	62	67	64	63	62	63	67	66	64	62	60	62	60	63	5.0	−10.0
Delta Air Lines (Delta)	77	72	67	69	65	68	66	61	66	67	67	65	64	59	60	64	62	−3.1	−19.5
US Airways	72	67	66	68	65	61	62	60	63	64	62	57	62	61	54	59	62	5.1	−13.9
Northwest Airlines (Delta)	69	71	67	64	63	53	62	56	65	64	64	64	61	61	57	57	61	7.0	−11.6
United Airlines	71	67	70	68	65	62	62	59	64	63	64	61	63	56	56	56	60	7.1	−15.5

Source: "Airlines" in *The American Customer Satisfaction Index: Scores by Industry*, http://www.theacsi.org. Reprinted with permission.

16.7 Interpreting Data

As your instructor directs,

a. Identify at least five stories in one or more of the following data sets.
b. Create visuals for three of the stories.
c. Write a memo to your instructor explaining why you chose these stories and why you chose these visuals to display them.
d. Write a memo to some group that might be interested in your findings, presenting your visuals as part of a short report. Possible groups include career counselors, radio stations, advertising agencies, and Mothers Against Drunk Driving.
e. Brainstorm additional stories you could tell with additional data. Specify the kind of data you would need.

1. Data on tipping.

Tipping Made Easy

The vast majority (74 percent) of Americans tip their waiter or waitress a percentage of the final bill, about 17 percent on average. But 22 percent tip a flat amount instead, $4.67 on average.

	PEOPLE WHO TIP A PERCENTAGE OF THE BILL		PEOPLE WHO TIP A FLAT AMOUNT		PEOPLE WHO DON'T TIP
		AVG. PERCENT		AVG. AMOUNT	
Waiter or waitress	74%	17%	22%	$4.67	2%
Bartender	20%	16%	48%	$1.85*	18%
Barber, hair stylist, or cosmetician	26%	17%	52%	$4.21	18%
Cab or limousine driver	31%	14%	43%	$5.55	16%
Food delivery person	31%	15%	50%	$2.88	12%
Hotel maid	14%	14%	53%	$8.08**	26%
Skycap or bellhop	N/A	N/A	71%	$3.68***	10%
Masseuse	26%	16%	28%	$7.50	25%
Usher at theatre, sporting events, etc.	5%	13%	17%	$5.26	70%

** for one drink; ** for a two-night stay; *** for two bags*
Note: "No Answer/Refused" not shown

Source: Taylor Nelson Sofres Intersearch

Beauty Gets Bucks

While only 11 percent of all Americans say they give a bigger tip to service providers they find attractive, single people are twice as likely to make a habit of it (16 percent) than their married counterparts (8 percent).

PERCENTAGE OF AMERICANS WHO SAY THEY TIP MORE WHEN THEIR SERVICE PROVIDER IS:

	OVERALL	MEN	WOMEN	MARRIED	UNMARRIED	WHITE	BLACK
Older than others who usually do the job	20%	17%	22%	16%	24%	18%	30%
A student	25%	24%	27%	25%	26%	24%	36%
A parent	17%	14%	19%	17%	16%	16%	27%
Attractive	11%	17%	5%	8%	16%	11%	14%
Someone I know	38%	38%	38%	34%	42%	39%	29%
A female	6%	9%	3%	4%	9%	6%	8%
A male	3%	3%	3%	3%	4%	3%	6%
Disabled	33%	34%	32%	33%	34%	32%	47%
A racial minority	3%	3%	3%	2%	4%	2%	9%
Flirtatious	11%	17%	5%	7%	15%	11%	9%

Source: Taylor Nelson Sofres Intersearch

Source: From *American Demographics*, June 2000. With permission.

2. Statistics on high school graduates.

a. Curriculum levels completed, by gender

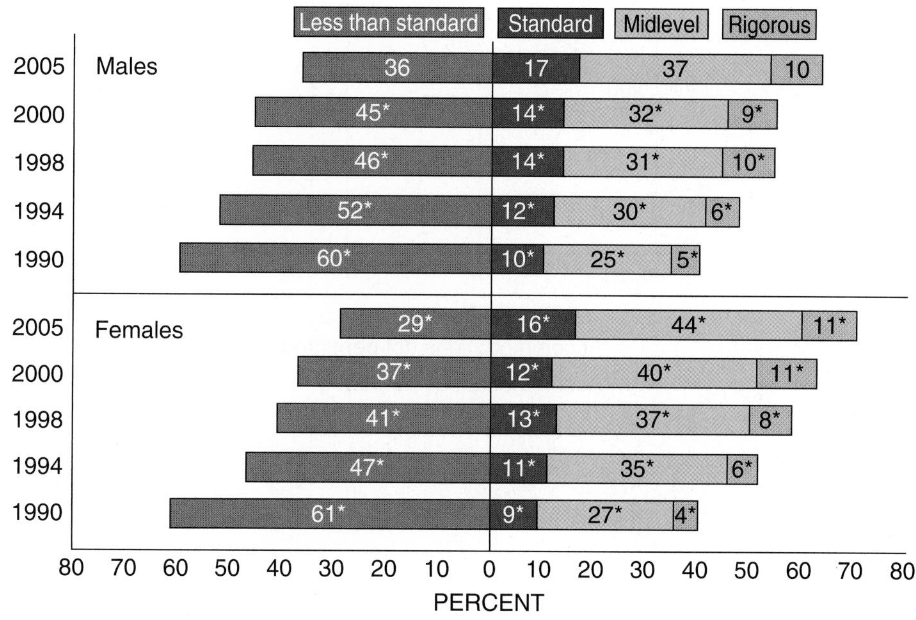

*Significantly different from 2005.

Source: "Curriculum Levels Completed, by Gender," in *U.S. Department of Education, Institute of Education Sciences, National Center for Education Statistics, High School Transcript Study (HSTS), various years, 1990–2005,* http://nationsreportcard.gov/hsts_2005/hs_stu_5b_2.asp (accessed May 5, 2009).

b. Trend in grade point average by gender

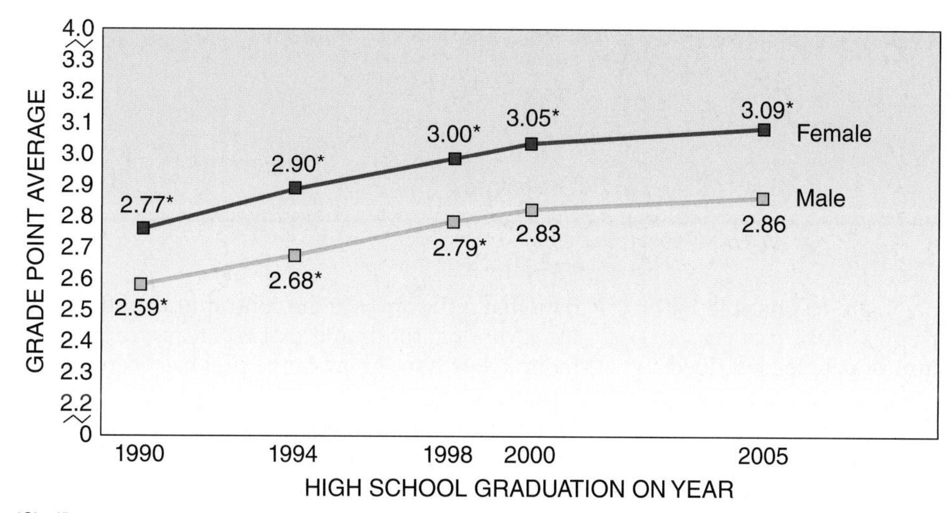

*Significantly different from 2005.

Source: "Trend in Grade Point Average, by Gender," in *U.S. Department of Education, Institute of Education Sciences, National Center for Education Statistics, High School Transcript Study (HSTS), various years, 1990–2005,* http://nationsreportcard.gov/hsts_2005/hs_stu_5b_3.asp (accessed May 5, 2009).

c. Trend in twelfth-grade average NAEP reading scores

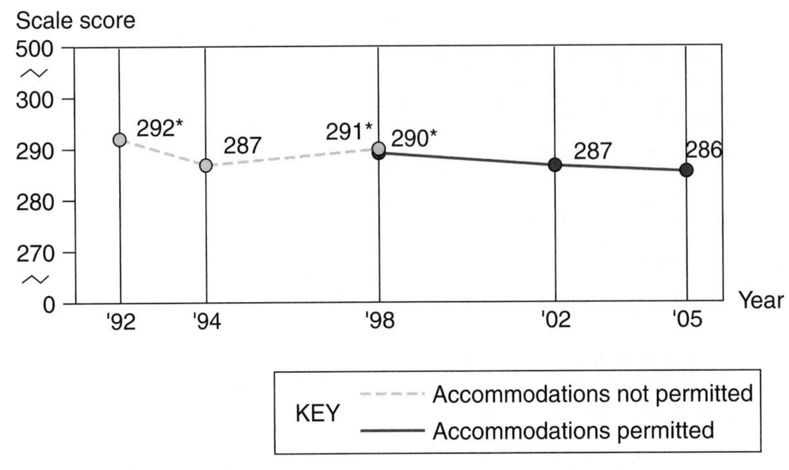

*Significantly different from 2005.

Source: "Trend in Twelfth-Grade Average NAEP Reading Scores," in *U.S. Department of Education, Institute of Education Sciences, National Center for Education Statistics, High School Transcript Study (HSTS), various years, 1990–2005,* http://nationsreportcard.gov/reading_math_grade12_2005/s0202.asp (accessed May 5, 2009).

16.8 Creating Graphs for Two Audiences and Scenarios

"Assume that you work for a local nonprofit organization with the following income expense for 2011 (see Table 1).

Table 1

Income		Expenses	
Description	$ Amount	Description	$ Amount
Government grants	$375,000	Program services	$741,935
Fees for services	$273,467	Administrative costs	$ 88,500
Contributions	$114,763	Miscellaneous	$ 5,230
Special events	$ 58,450		
Sale of products produced by participants in your program	$ 12,468		
Total income	$834,148	Total expenses	$835,665

As directors of the organization, you are responsible for bringing in more money and must present the past year's financial information to two groups of people, described in the following scenarios:

1. Within the community is a core group of consistent contributors who give the same amount each year, although the cost of running your organization continues to go up. You must convince these contributors to give additional funds during your presentation at the annual fund-raising banquet. You need to create graphic representations of financial data that will convince the contributors of the need for additional funds and that will reassure them the money they have given in the past has been spent wisely.
2. Your organization is eligible for a new grant from a federal government agency. You have to write a proposal explaining why your organization needs the money and demonstrating that it is fiscally responsible. There is a strict page limit, so you must present financial information concisely but in enough detail to make a strong case."

With a group of two or three peers, as your instructor directs,

a. Create a graphic representation of the financial data for the presentation and the proposal.
b. Write a memo that justifies the choices you made in creating the graphics for the different audiences and situations.
c. Prepare a brief presentation to the class that justifies your choices in creating the graphics.

Quoted from Susan M. Katz, "Creating Appropriate Graphics for Business Situations," *Business Communication Quarterly,* 71, 1, March 2008, pp: 71–75.

16.9 Graphing Data from the Web

Find data on the web about a topic that interests you. Some sites with data include the following:

Catalyst (women in business)
 http://www.catalyst.org/page/64/browse-research-knowledge
ClickZ (digital marketing)
 http://www.clickz.com/showPage.html?page=stats
FEDSTATS (links to 70 US government agencies)
 http://www.fedstats.gov/
United Nations Environment Program
 http://na.unep.net/
U.S. Congress Joint Economic Committee
 http://jec.senate.gov/public/index.cfm?p=Charts

As your instructor directs,

a. Identify at least five stories in the data.
b. Create visuals for three of the stories.
c. Write a memo to your instructor explaining why you chose these stories and why you chose these visuals to display them.
d. Write a memo to some group which might be interested in your findings, presenting your visuals as part of a short report.
e. Print out the data and include it with a copy of your memo or report.

16.10 Creating a Visual Argument

With a partner, research one of the following topics:

- Having English-only laws in the workplace.
- Introducing new technology into the marketplace.
- Laying off employees during economic downturns.
- Requiring employers to offer insurance plans.
- Banning smoking in the workplace for insurance purposes.
- Hiring/recruiting and diversity in the workplace.
- Current hot business topic.

Then, prepare a four-minute slideshow presentation to share with your peers. The presentation should include only visual elements and contain no words. With the visuals, you should take a stand and present an argument about one of the topics. Recall the guidelines outlined in this chapter about effectively using visuals.

Remember that your presentation needs to be captivating to the audience and effectively convey your purpose. Finally, don't forget to cite all source material.

As your instructor directs,

a. Submit a copy of your slideshow presentation, including both hard and electronic versions.
b. Write a brief memo in which you explain in words the argument you were trying to make.
c. Submit a list of works cited for each of the visuals you used.

CHAPTER 17

Writing Proposals and Progress Reports

Chapter Outline

Writing Proposals

- Proposal Questions
- Proposal Style
- Proposals for Class Research Projects
- Proposals for Action
- Sales Proposals
- Business Plans and Other Proposals for Funding
- Budget and Costs Sections

Writing Progress Reports

- Chronological Progress Reports
- Task Progress Reports
- Recommendation Progress Reports

Summary of Key Points

Newsworthy Communication

Proposals by Corporate Investors

Public companies invite proposals from their shareholders on the company's response to its stakeholders. Corporate investors, led by religious groups and socially responsible investors, have increasingly been bringing forth environmental and social proposals. Often companies work with proponents of these proposals to arrive at mutually agreeable outcomes.

> *"Corporate investors . . . have increasingly been bringing forth environmental and social proposals."*

The growth in these proposals has been tremendous—from around 7% to 32% between 2004 and 2007—counting those that garnered at least 15% votes. Among specific issues that these proposals address are companies' sexual orientation policies, pollution policies, labor policies, efforts on climate change, and political contributions. Some of these proposals find mention in the following year's annual or corporate sustainability report, while some others result in specific agreements with the company. Proposals can be resubmitted, so it's in the companies' interest to take proposals seriously.

Two major examples come from Exxon. The Sisters of St. Dominic were the lead filers on a proposal, which got 31% support, asking for greenhouse gas reduction. A different proposal from an individual investor, which got 27% support, asked for the development of renewable energy sources. Another instance is Domini Social Investments' proposal asking Home Depot to produce a report on its sustainably harvested lumber. Home Depot agreed to publish on its website its wood purchasing policy, including quantitative information.

Adapted from William J. Holstein, "A Bumper Crop of Green Proposals," *BusinessWeek*, June 26, 2008, http://www.businessweek.com/managing/content/jun2008/ca20080626_395541.htm.

Learning Objectives

After studying this chapter, you will know how to

LO 17-1 Write proposals.

LO 17-2 Prepare budget and costs sections.

LO 17-3 Write progress reports.

Proposals and progress reports are two documents that frequently are part of larger, longer projects. **Proposals** argue for the work that needs to be done and who will do it. **Progress reports** let people know how you are coming on the project.

WRITING PROPOSALS LO 17-1

In the workplace, much work is routine or specifically assigned by other people. But sometimes you or your organization will want to consider new opportunities, and you will need to write a proposal for that work. Generally, proposals are created for projects that are longer or more expensive than routine work, that differ significantly from routine work, or that create larger changes than does normal work.

Proposals argue for work that needs to be done; they offer a method to find information, evaluate something new, solve a problem, or implement a change. (See Figure 17.1.) Proposals have two major goals: to get the project accepted and to get you or your organization accepted to do the work. To accomplish these goals, proposals must stress benefits for all affected audiences. A proposal for an organization to adopt flex hours would offer benefits for both employees and management, as well as for key departments such as finance.

Proposals may be competitive or noncompetitive. **Competitive proposals** compete against each other for limited resources. Applications for research funding are often highly competitive. Many companies will bid for corporate or government contracts, but only one will be accepted. In FY 2010, the National Science Foundation spent $6.9 billion supporting research. The National Institute of Health supports almost 50,000 research projects at a cost of $31.2 billion annually.[1] These funds are awarded mainly through competitive proposals.

Noncompetitive proposals have no real competition. For example, a company could accept all of the internal proposals it thought would save money or

Figure 17.1 Relationship among Situation, Proposal, and Final Report

Company's current situation	The proposal offers to	The final report will provide
We don't know whether we should change.	Assess whether change is a good idea.	Insight, recommending whether change is desirable.
We need to/want to change, but we don't know exactly what we need to do.	Develop a plan to achieve desired goal.	A plan for achieving the desired change.
We need to/want to change, and we know what to do, but we need help doing it.	Implement the plan, increase (or decrease) measurable outcomes.	A record of the implementation and evaluation process.

Source: Adapted from Richard C. Freed, Shervin Freed, and Joseph D. Romano, *Writing Winning Business Proposals: Your Guide to Landing the Client, Making the Sale, Persuading the Boss*, 3rd ed (New York: McGraw-Hill, 2010).

improve quality. And often a company that is satisfied with a vendor asks for a noncompetitive proposal to renew the contract. Noncompetitive proposals can still be enormous. In 2009 the Census Bureau submitted to Congress a $1 billion proposal for the 2010 census jobs.[2]

Proposal Questions

To write a good proposal, you need to have a clear view of the opportunity you want to fill or the problem you hope to solve and the kind of research or other action needed to solve it. A proposal must answer the following questions convincingly:

- **What problem are you going to solve or what opportunity do you hope to fill?** Show that you understand the problem or the opportunity and the organization's needs. Define the problem or opportunity as the audience sees it, even if you believe it is part of a larger problem that must first be solved. Sometimes you will need to show that the problem or opportunity exists. For instance, management might not be aware of subtle discrimination against women that your proposal will help eliminate.
- **Why does the problem need to be solved now or the opportunity explored immediately?** Show that money, time, health, or social concerns support solving the problem or exploring the opportunity immediately. Provide the predicted consequences if the problem is not solved now or if the opportunity is not explored immediately.
- **How are you going to solve it?** Prove that your methods are feasible. Show that a solution can be found in the time available. Specify the topics you'll investigate. Explain how you'll gather data. Show your approach is effective and desirable.
- **Can you do the work?** Show that you, or your organization, have the knowledge, means, personnel, and experience to do the work well. For larger projects, you will have to show some evidence such as preliminary data, personnel qualifications, or similar projects in the past.
- **Why should you be the one to do it?** Show why you or your company should do the work. For many proposals, various organizations could do the work. Why should the work be given to you? Discuss the benefits—direct and indirect—you and your organization can provide.
- **When will you complete the work?** Provide a detailed schedule showing when each phase of the work will be completed.
- **How much will you charge?** Provide a detailed budget that includes costs for items such as materials, salaries, and overhead. Give careful thought to unique expenses that may be part of the work. Will you need to travel? Pay fees? Pay benefits in addition to salary for part-time workers?
- **What exactly will you provide for us?** Specify the tangible products you'll produce; develop their benefits.

Since proposals to outside organizations are usually considered legally binding documents, get expert legal and financial advice on the last two bullets. Even if the proposal will not be legally binding (perhaps it is an internal proposal), safeguard your professional reputation. Be sure you can deliver the promised products at the specified time using resources and personnel available to you.

MBA Business Plans

Some students working toward MBA degrees participate in business plan contests. Groups of students write a business plan and present it to real-world bankers and venture capitalists. The stakes are high. Major contests have big cash awards and a shot at really starting the business the students have been planning. Even the losers benefit from the writing practice and the feedback they can use to continue improving their plans.

Among the winners is Sarah Takesh, who took first place in the National Social Ventures Competition, earning $25,000 for a fashion company called Tarsian and Blinkley. In Takesh's business, which she has since launched, Afghan workers apply local handicrafts to produce clothing sold in boutiques in New York and San Francisco. Although the items are beautiful, Takesh's fashion sense was less important to the judges than her insights about international trade.

Another contest winner, KidSmart, is a plan for a company offering a new product: a smoke alarm that alerts children with a recording of a parent's voice, rather than the earsplitting beeps of a traditional smoke alarm. The KidSmart business plan won the $100,000 grand prize in Moot Corp, sponsored by the University of Texas. The four-person KidSmart team supported its presentation with video footage showing that its smoke detector is better at waking children than the traditional beeps.

Adapted from Patrick J. Sauer, "How to Win Big Money and Get Ahead in Business," *Inc.* 25, no. 9 (September 2003): 95–96 +.

Proposal Style

Good proposals are clear and easy to read. Remember that some of your audience may not be experts in the subject matter. Highly statistical survey and data analysis projects may be funded by finance people; medical and scientific studies may be approved by bureaucrats. This means you should use the language your readers understand and expect to see. Anticipate and answer questions your readers may have. Support generalizations and inferences with data and other information. Stress benefits throughout the proposal, and make sure you include benefits for all elements of your audience.

Watch your word choice. Avoid diction that shows doubt.

Weak: "*If* we can obtain X. . . ."
"We *hope* we can obtain X."
"We will *try* to obtain X."

Better: "We plan to obtain X."
"We expect to obtain X."

Avoid bragging diction: "huge potential," "revolutionary process." Also avoid "believing" diction: "we believe that. . . ." Use facts and figures instead. Be particularly careful to avoid bragging diction about yourself.

Use the expected format for your proposal. Shorter proposals (one to four pages) are generally in letter or memo format; longer proposals are frequently formal reports. Government agencies and companies often issue **requests for proposals,** known as **RFPs.** Follow the RFP's specified format to the letter. Use the exact headings, terminology, and structure of the RFP when responding to one. Competitive proposals are often scored by giving points in each category. Evaluators look only under the headings specified in the RFP. If information isn't there, the proposal may get no points in that category.

Beginnings and endings of proposals are important. If you are not following an RFP, your proposal should begin with a clear statement of what you propose doing, why you propose doing it, and what the implications are of the proposed action, or why the action is important. Proposals should end with a brief but strong summary of major benefits of having you do the work. In some circumstances, an urge to action is appropriate:

If I get your approval before the end of the month, we can have the procedures in place in time for the new fiscal year.

Allow a generous amount of time before the due date for polishing and finishing your proposal:

- Edit carefully.
- Make a final check that you have included all sections and pieces of information requested in the RFP. Many RFPs call for appendices with items such as résumés and letters of support. Do you have all of yours?
- Ensure that your proposal's appearance will create a good impression. This step includes careful proofreading.
- Allow enough time for production, reproduction, and administrative approvals before the deadline for receipt of the proposal. If multiple signatures are needed, it may take more than a day to get them all. If you are submitting a government grant, the grants.gov server may be clogged with heavy usage on the final due date, or even the day before, so don't wait until the last minute.

Proposals for Class Research Projects

You may be asked to submit a proposal for a report that you will write for a class. Your instructor wants evidence that your problem is meaningful but not too big to complete in the allotted time, that you understand it, that your method will give you the information you need, that you have the knowledge and resources to collect and analyze the data, and that you can produce the report by the deadline.

A proposal for a student report usually has the following sections:

1. In your first paragraph (no heading), summarize in a sentence or two the topic and purposes of your report.
2. **Problem/Opportunity.** What problem or opportunity exists? Why does it need to be solved or explored? Is there a history or background that is relevant?
3. **Feasibility.** Are you sure that a solution can be found in the time available? How do you know? (This section may not be appropriate for some class projects.)
4. **Audience.** Who in the organization would have the power to implement your recommendation? What secondary audiences might be asked to evaluate your report? What audiences would be affected by your recommendation? Will anyone in the organization serve as a gatekeeper, determining whether your report is sent to decision makers? What watchdog audiences might read the report? Will there be other readers?

   For each of these audiences give the person's name and job title and answer the following questions:

   - What is the audience's major concern or priority? What "hot buttons" must you address with care?
   - What will the audience see as advantages of your proposal? What objections, if any, is the audience likely to have?
   - How interested is the audience in the topic of your report?
   - How much does the audience know about the topic of your report?

   List any terms, concepts, or assumptions that one or more of your audiences may need to have explained. Briefly identify ways in which your audiences may affect the content, organization, or style of the report.
5. **Topics to investigate.** List the questions and subquestions you will answer in your report, the topics or concepts you will explain, the aspects of the problem or opportunity you will discuss. Indicate how deeply you will examine each of the aspects you plan to treat. Explain your rationale for choosing to discuss some aspects of the problem or opportunity and not others.
6. **Methods/procedure.** How will you get answers to your questions? Whom will you interview or survey? What questions will you ask? What published sources will you use? Give the full bibliographic references. Your methods section should clearly indicate how you will get the information needed to answer questions posed in the other sections of the proposal.
7. **Qualifications/facilities/resources.** Do you have the knowledge and skills needed to conduct this study? Do you have adequate access to the organization? Is the necessary information available to you? Are you aware of any supplemental information? Where will you turn for help if you hit an unexpected snag?

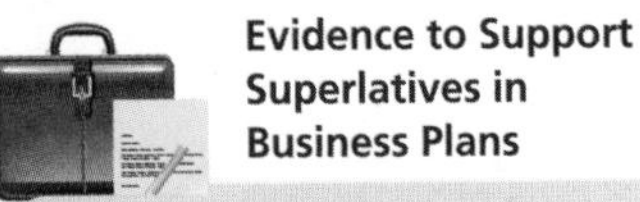

Evidence to Support Superlatives in Business Plans

Dave Lavinsky, a cofounder of Growthink, a professional consulting firm, advises small business owners to draft their business plans carefully because investors will evaluate the potential of the business based on the intelligence shown in the plan.

Specifically, Dave advises his clients to provide evidence for superlatives (*best* customer service, *finest* quality) in the plan.

He advises business owners to cite third-party research or offer other concrete evidence when making superlative claims. For instance, if a firm believes that the market for its products is growing exponentially, it should cite some independent research that validates this claim. Similarly, if a firm claims in the business plan that it has the best people working for it, the plan should include details of qualifications and experiences of the personnel to support the claim.

The practice of always supporting superlative claims in the business plan will increase a firm's fundraising chances by making it appear more credible in the eyes of the investors.

Adapted from Dave Lavinsky, "Business Plan Readers No Longer Believe the Hype," in *BusinessWeek: Small Biz: Tips*, March 20, 2009, http://www.businessweek.com/smallbiz/tips/archives/2009/03/business_plan_r.html.

You'll be more convincing if you have already scheduled an interview, checked out books, or printed online sources.

8. **Work schedule.** For each activity, list both the total time you plan to spend on it and the date when you expect to finish it. Some possible activities you might include could be gathering information, analyzing information, preparing a progress report, writing the report draft, revising the draft, preparing visuals, and editing and proofreading the report. Think of activities needed to complete your specific project.

   These activities frequently overlap. Many writers start analyzing and organizing information as it comes in. They start writing pieces of the final document and preparing visuals early in the process.

   Organize your work schedule in either a chart or calendar. A good schedule provides realistic estimates for each activity, allows time for unexpected snags, and shows that you can complete the work on time.
9. **Call to action.** In your final section, indicate that you'd welcome any suggestions your instructor may have for improving the research plan. Ask your instructor to approve your proposal so that you can begin work on your report.

Figure 17.2 shows a student proposal for a long report.

Proposals for Action

Some proposals call for action or change in your organization. Normally, proposals for action recommend new programs or ways to solve problems. As manager of compensation planning, Catherine Beck had to propose a compensation system when telephone companies Bell Atlantic and Nynex Corporation merged and again a few years later when Bell Atlantic merged with GTE to form Verizon. When two companies merge, each has its own pay scale, bonus policy, and so on; the problem is that the merged companies will need a single, unified system. In these two mergers, Beck had to recommend the system she thought would work best in the new company.[3]

Writing a proposal for action requires considerable research. Beck worked with a team of human resource and other managers plus compensation experts. Together they began by studying the existing policies of the merging organizations. They compared the two systems, looking for their underlying principles. In the first merger, between Bell Atlantic and Nynex, they determined that the two plans were so different that they would have to create a completely new system. In the second merger, of Bell Atlantic and GTE, they concluded that the plans were similar enough to be modified and combined into a single system. After this internal research leading to an initial decision, preparing a proposal and implementing a system for tens of thousands of management employees took months in both mergers.[4]

Often, writing a proposal requires gathering information from outside the organization, too. Basic steps include reading articles in trade and professional journals, looking up data online, and talking to employees or customers.

Remember that all proposals, including in-house ones, need benefits for all levels of audiences. These benefits help ensure buy-in.

Sales Proposals

To sell expensive goods or services, you may be asked to submit a proposal.

To write a good sales proposal, be sure that you understand the buyer's priorities. A phone company lost a $36 million sale to a university because it assumed the university's priority would be cost. Instead, the university wanted a state-of-the-art system. The university accepted a higher bid.

Figure 17.2 Proposal for a Student Team Report

March 24, 2011

To: Professor Christopher Toth

From: JASS LLC (Jordan Koole, Alex Kuczera, Shannon Jones, Sean Sterling)

In the subject line ① indicate that this is a proposal ② specify the kind of report ③ specify the topic.

Subject: Proposal to Research and Make Recommendations on the Feasibility of Expanding RAC Inc. to South Korea

Summarize topic and purpose of report.

RAC Inc. has recently approached our company to determine the possibility of expanding internationally. We believe South Korea could be suitable for this expansion based on our initial investigation of technology in the country. This proposal provides a brief look at South Korea and gives an overview of our research topics and procedures in preparation for the formal research report.

Problem

If the "Problem" section is detailed and well-written, you may be able to use it unchanged in your report.

After establishing a solid consumer base in the U.S., RAC Inc. is looking to expand their business internationally so that they do not fall behind their competitors. They have asked us to research South Korea as a possible alternative site for the manufacturing of their slate tablets.

Country Overview

This section is a "Background" section for this proposal. Not all proposals include background.

After some initial research, we believe that South Korea is a suitable country to research for RAC's international manufacturing of new technology. South Korea has a population of 48.3 million, with 27% of the population located in the capital city Seoul and in Busan. They have a labor force of 24.62 million, ranking as the 25th highest workforce in the world (CIA Factbook, 2011). The official language is Korean, but English, Chinese, and Japanese are taught as second languages (U.S. Department of State, 2010). Proposal uses in-text citations.

In 1950, North Korea invaded South Korea, beginning the Korean War. After three years of fighting and pushing troops across both borders, North and South Korea signed an armistice and agreed to a demilitarized zone (DMZ), which currently serves as the border between the two countries and is protected by both countries' military (U.S. Department of State, 2010). While relations between the two countries are still tense and a few minor skirmishes along the border have occurred, we are not concerned about South Korea's stability.

In fact, since the devastation of the Korean War, the economy of South Korea has recovered and has joined the ranks of the most economically prosperous nations. They have risen to the 13th highest GDP in the world and have the 45th highest GDP per capita at the equivalent of $30,200. They have a very low unemployment rate that has dropped in the last year to 3.3% (CIA Factbook, 2011).

South Korea is now ranked the 7th largest exporter in the world and the 9th largest importer. Their economic policy has emphasized exporting products, explaining why their exports are so high (U.S. Department of State, 2010). Their main exports include computers and component parts, semiconductors, and wireless telecommunication equipment. South Korea is known for making excellent products in these areas. They export mainly to the U.S., China, and Japan, and import primarily from the same countries. As one of the most economically healthy countries in the world, South Korea is situated as a prime country for RAC Inc.'s possible expansion.

Not all class reports will need a "Feasibility" section.

(Continued)

Figure 17.2 Proposal for a Student Team Report (Continued)

Include a header on all additional pages.

RAC Inc. Proposal
March 24, 2011
Page 2

List your major audiences. Identify their knowledge, interests, and concerns.

Audience

Our formal report will have multiple layers of audiences.

- *Gatekeeper*: Professor Toth has the power to accept or reject our proposal for the formal report before it is passed on to Ms. Katie Nichols from RAC Inc.
- *Primary*: Ms. Katie Nichols, CEO of RAC Inc., and the board of directors are our primary audiences, along with other influential members of RAC Inc. They will decide whether to accept the recommendation found in the formal report.
- *Secondary*: Employees of RAC Inc., the legal department of RAC Inc., as well as current RAC Inc. employees who may be transferred to South Korea may all be affected by the primary audience's decision. In addition, the potential employees in South Korea who would work for RAC Inc. also make up this audience.
- *Auxiliary*: Other employees not involved with the expansion effort into South Korea and any Americans or South Koreans who will read about the expansion in the news serve this role.
- *Watchdog*: Stockholders of RAC Inc., the South Korean government, the Securities and Exchange Commission (SEC), the U.S. Department of Commerce, and other companies that may want to expand internationally to South Korea all have economic, social, and political power. Competitors of RAC Inc. already in South Korea (Samsung and LG) may also pay close attention.

Indicate what you'll discuss briefly and what you'll discuss in more detail. This list should match your audiences' concerns.

Topics to Investigate

We plan to answer the following questions in detail:

1. What information does RAC Inc. need to know about South Korean culture, politics, economy, and workforce to be succesful?

All items in list must be grammatically parallel. Here, all are questions.

- Culture—What differences exist between Korean and American cultures that might influence the move?
- Politics—How will relationships between North and South Korea and relationships between the U.S. and South Korea affect business with South Korea?
- Economics—What is the current economic state of the country? How could free trade between the U.S. and South Korea affect business?
- Workforce—What is the availabe workforce? How will the economy of the country affect the overall workforce?

2. How should RAC Inc. adapt their business practices to successfully expand into the South Korean market?

- Competition—Who is the competition in South Korea? How could they affect the business?
- Location—What city could RAC Inc. expand to for production of the slate tablet? Where should they locate the headquarters? Where should they host the initial product launch?
- Slate Tablet—What changes, if any, are needed to market and sell the product in South Korea?

Figure 17.2 Proposal for a Student Team Report (Continued)

RAC Inc. Proposal
March 24, 2011
Page 3

3. What other issues may RAC Inc. have by introducing their product into South Korea?

- Business Culture—How will the differences in business culture influence the expansion to South Korea?
- Technology—To what extent will the advanced state of South Korean technology influence marketing the tablet?
- Marketing—How will competitors' similar products sold in South Korea influence business?
- Integration—How receptive are the people of South Korea to new products from different companies and countries?

If it is well written, "Topics to Investigate" section will become the "Scope" section of the report—with minor revisions.

Methods and Resources

We expect to obtain our information from: (1) various websites, (2) books, and (3) interviews with a native South Korean. The following websites and books appear useful.

If you'll administer a survey or conduct interviews, tell how many subjects you'll have, how you'll choose them, and what you'll ask them. This group does not use a survey.

Central Intelligence Agency. (2011). *The world factbook: South Korea.* Retrieved March 18, 2011, from https:/ /www.cia.gov/library/publications/the-world-factbook/geos/ks.html#.

Fackler, M. (2011, January 6). Lessons learned, South Korea makes quick economic recovery. *The New York Times.* Retrieved from http:// www.nytimes.com/2011/01/07/world/asia/07seoul.html?_r=2.

Jeon, Kyung-Hwan. (2010, September 7). Why your business belongs in South Korea. Retrieved from http:/ /www.openforum.com/articles/why-your-business-belongs-in-south-korea-kyung-hwan-jeon.

Life in Korea. (n.d.). Cultural spotlight. Retrieved March 31, 2011, from http:/ /www.lifeinkorea.com/Culture/spotlight.cfm.

Manyin, M. E. (2004). *South Korea–U.S. economic relations.* Washington, D.C: CRS of Congress.

Manyin, M. E. (2007). *The proposed South Korea–U.S. free trade.* Washington, D.C.: CRS of Congress.

Moon, K. (2004). South Korea–U.S. relations. *The Asian Perspective 28.4.* Retrieved from http:/ /www.asianperspective.org/articles/v28n4-c.pdf.

Ogg, E. (2010, May 28). What makes a tablet a tablet? *CNet News.* Retrieved March 19, 2011, from http:/ /news.cnet.com/8301-31021_3-20006077-260.html?tag=newsLeadStoriesArea.1.

Savada, A.M. & Shaw, W. (1990). South Korea: A country study. *South Korea.* Retrieved March 18, 2011, from http:/ /countrystudies.us/south-korea/.

Settimi, C. (2010, September 1). Asia's 200 best under a billion. *Forbes.* Retrieved from http://www.forbes.com/2010/09/01/ bub-200-intro-asia-under-billion-10-small-companies.html.

Taylor, C. (2006, July 14). The future is in South Korea. *CNN Money.* Retrieved from http:/ /money.cnn.com/2006/06/08/technology/business2_futureboy0608/index.htm.

If you're using library or web research, list sources you hope to use. Use full bibliographic citations.

This list uses APA format.

Your list of sources should convince your instructor that you have made initial progress on the report.

(Continued)

Figure 17.2 Proposal for a Student Team Report (Concluded)

RAC Inc. Proposal
March 24, 2011
Page 4

UK Trade & Investment. (2011). 100 opportunities for UK companies in South Korea. Retrieved March 19, 2011, from http:/ /www.ukti.gov.uk/export/countries/asiapacific/fareast/koreasouth/item/119500.html.

U.S. Deparment of State. (2010, December 10). Background note: South Korea. Retrieved March 18, 2011, from http:/ /www.state.gov/r/pa/ei/bgn/2800.htm.

World Business Culture. (n.d.). Doing business in South Korea. Retrieved March 19, 2011, from http:/ /www.worldbusinessculture.com/Business-in-South-Korea.html.

Qualifications

Cite knowledge and skills from other classes, jobs, and activities that will enable you to conduct the research and interpret your data.

We are all members of JASS LLC who have backgrounds in finance, accounting, computer science, and technology. These diverse backgrounds in the business and technology world give us a good perspective and insight for this project. In addition, we are all enrolled in a business communication course that provides us with knowledge on producing high-quality documents. We are dedicated to producing a thoroughly researched report that will provide solid evidence on the feasibility of an international expansion for RAC Inc. into South Korea.

Work Schedule

The following schedule will enable us to finish this report on time.

Activity	Total Time	Completion Date
Gathering information	12 hours	March 30
Analyzing information	8 hours	April 2
Organizing information	4 hours	April 7
Writing draft/creating visuals	8 hours	April 10
Revising draft	3 hours	April 12
Preparing presentation slides	3–4 hours	April 14
Editing draft	3 hours	April 17
Proofreading report	3 hours	April 18
Rehearsing presentation	2 hours	April 20
Delivering presentaion	1 hour	April 21

Good reports need good revision, editing, and proofreading as well as good research.

Allow plenty of time

Time will depend on the length and topic of your report, your knowledge of the topic, and your writing skills.

Call to Action

We are confident that JASS LLC can complete the above tasks as scheduled. We would appreciate any suggestions for improving our project plan. Please approve our proposal so that we may begin work on the formal report.

It's tactful to indicate you'll accept suggestions. End on a positive, forward-looking note.

Make sure your proposal presents your goods or services as solving the problem your audience perceives. Don't assume that the buyer will understand why your product or system is good. For everything you offer, show the benefits of each feature. Be sure to present the benefits using you-attitude.

Use language appropriate for your audience. Even if the buyers want a state-of-the-art system, they may not want the level of detail that your staff could provide; they may not understand or appreciate technical jargon.

Sales proposals, particularly for complicated systems costing millions of dollars, are often long. Provide a one-page cover letter to present your proposal succinctly. The best organization for this letter is usually a modified version of the sales pattern in Chapter 11:

1. Catch the reader's attention and summarize up to three major benefits you offer.
2. Discuss each of the major benefits in the order in which you mentioned them in the first paragraph.
3. Deal with any objections or concerns the reader may have. In a sales proposal, these objections probably include costs. Connect costs with benefits.
4. Mention other benefits briefly.
5. Ask the reader to approve your proposal and provide a reason for acting promptly.

Business Plans and Other Proposals for Funding

Proposals for funding include both **business plans** (documents written to raise capital for new business ventures) and proposals submitted to foundations, corporations, and government agencies, to seek money for public service projects. In a proposal for funding, stress the needs your project will meet and show how your project helps fulfill the goals of the organization you are asking for funds. Every funding agency has a mission, so be sure to align your idea to fit their needs in obvious ways. Try to weave their mission throughout your proposal's content. Remember effective you-attitude—write for the needs of your audience, not yourself.

Since venture capitalists and other investors are not known for their patience, business plans in particular need to have a concise, compelling beginning describing exactly what you plan to do and what need it will fill. Pay careful attention to the Executive Summary. This overview section is one of the most important places in any proposal. After reading this opening, the reviewer will make initial decisions about you, your writing, your idea, and your logic. Therefore, it must spark enthusiasm for your idea; the reviewer's interest will never increase later on in your proposal. This section should also provide an overview of all of the major topics you will cover in the body.

Your business plan should answer these questions:

- What is your product or service?
- How well developed is it? Is a mock-up or demo available?
- Who is your market? How large is it? Why does this market need your product or service?
- How will you promote your product or service?
- Who are your competitors? How will you be better?
- Who is also providing support for your business?
- Who will be working with you? How many more employees will you need? What will you pay them? What benefits will you give them?

Financial information is important in any proposal, but it is even more crucial in a business plan. You will need to show how much of your own money you are

Writing an Effective Business Plan

How do entrepreneurs raise the capital needed to launch a new business? They write a business plan. When you write one, you need to persuade an investor that your concept for an organization is solid and that you're the best person to carry it out. Venture capitalists and successful entrepreneurs give the following advice about writing a solid business plan:

- Keep it short and simple—a good business plan articulates what the company will do and how it will benefit the customer. Specify the product or service. Begin with an executive summary.
- Introduce the management team—a good business plan explains the people behind the product.
- Anticipate problems and challenges—a good business plan answers the tough questions about your idea. Venture capitalists will already know the problem; they want to be sure you do too.
- Show there is a market—a good business plan identifies a target market and demonstrates that people will use the product or service offered.
- Show a path to profit—a good business plan explains how the business will make money.
- Make it personal—a good business plan is not a template; it shows passion about ideas.

Adapted from Greg Farrell, "Business Plans Should Be Simple, Passionate," *USA Today,* July 31, 2006, 5E.

investing, what investors you already have supporting you, and how you plan to use the money you get. Many investors want to see a five-year financial forecast. Explain with convincing detail how you expect to make money. What is your time frame for financial success? What is your estimated monthly income the first year?

Anticipate problems (investors will already know them; this shows you do, too); show how you plan to solve them. Use details to help convince your audience. Many business plans are too general to convince investors. Details show you have done your homework; they can also show your business acumen.

Proposals are also a major part of nonprofits' fund-raising activity; they write grant proposals to governmental organizations, foundations, and individuals to raise money for their organization. The writing process involves considerable research and planning, and often is preceded by informal conversations and formal presentations to potential funders. The funding process is often seen as a relationship-building process that involves researching, negotiating with, and persuading funders that the proposal not only meets their guidelines, but also is a cause worthy of a grant.

Every funding source has certain priorities; some have detailed lists of the kind of projects they fund. Be sure to do research before applying. Check recent awards to discover foundations that may be interested in your project. See Figure 17.3 for additional resources.

When you write proposals for funding, be sure you follow all format criteria to the letter. Be particularly obedient to specifications about page count, type size, margins, and spacing (single or double spacing). When flooded with applications, many funders use these criteria as preliminary weeding devices. One state Department of Education threw out funding applications from 30 school districts because they were not double-spaced as required.[5]

Finally, be sure to pay close attention to deadlines by reading the fine print. Turn your materials in early. The National Endowment for the Humanities encourages fund seekers to submit drafts six weeks before the deadline to allow time for their staff to review materials.[6]

Keys to Successful Business Plans

Of the thousands of business plans presented to potential investors each year, only a few succeed. John W. Mullens, at the London Business School, offers five reasons why business plans fail.

- **No problem.** Plans must fix a problem or fill a need instead of just being examples of cool technology or good ideas.
- **Unrealistic ambition.** Successful business plans recognize a specific market, instead of aiming at the entire population.
- **Flawed spreadsheets.** Carefully prepared revenue models can work on paper, but successful business plans must work in the real economy.
- **Wrong team.** Investors are not necessarily impressed by education and work experience, unless those contribute to the success of the business.
- **Perfect plan.** Successful plans recognize realistic challenges to the business plan, instead of presenting everything in the best light.

Mullens suggests three keys for success: (1) A clear problem and a logical solution; (2) hard evidence that you have done your research; (3) complete candor about challenges and risks associated with your plan.

Adapted from John W. Mullens, "Why Business Plans Don't Deliver," *Wall Street Journal*, June 22, 2009, R3.

Budget and Costs Sections LO 17-2

For a class research project, you may not be asked to prepare a budget. However, many proposals do require budgets, and a good budget is crucial to making the winning bid. In fact, your budget may well be the most carefully scrutinized part of your proposal.[7]

Ask for everything you need to do a quality job. Asking for too little may backfire, leading the funder to think that you don't understand the scope of the project. Include less obvious costs, such as overhead. Also include costs that will be paid from other sources. Doing so shows that other sources also have confidence in your work. Pay particular attention to costs that may appear to

Figure 17.3 Additional Resources for Writing Business Plans and Funding Proposals

Organization	URL	Description
U.S. Small Business Administration	http://www.sba.gov/category/navigation-structure/starting-managing-business/starting-business	Offers detailed advice for writing a business plan.
Philanthropic Research Inc.	http://www.guidestar.org	Publishes free information about grants and grantmakers.
U.S. Department of Health and Human Services	http://www.grants.gov	Offers information on grant programs of all federal grant-making agencies, as well as downloadable grant applications.
The Foundation Center	http://foundationcenter.org/	Indexes foundations by state and city as well as by field of interest.

benefit you more than the sponsor such as travel and equipment. Make sure they are fully justified in the proposal.

Do some research. Read the RFP to find out what is and isn't fundable. Talk to the program officer (the person who administers the funding process) and read successful past proposals to find answers to the following questions:

- What size projects will the organization fund in theory?
- Does the funder prefer making a few big grants or many smaller grants?
- Does the funder expect you to provide in-kind or cost-sharing funds from other sources?

Think about exactly what you'll do and who will do it. What will it cost to get that person? What supplies or materials will he or she need? Also think about indirect costs for using office space, about retirement and health benefits as well as salaries, about office supplies, administration, and infrastructure.

Make the basis of your estimates specific.

Weak:	75 hours of transcribing interviews	$1,500
Better:	25 hours of interviews; a skilled transcriber can complete 1 hour of interviews in 3 hours; 75 hours @ $20/hour	$1,500

Figure your numbers conservatively. For example, if the going rate for skilled transcribers is $20 an hour, but you think you might be able to train someone and pay only $12 an hour, use the higher figure. Then, even if your grant is cut, you'll still be able to do the project well.

Tapping into the Research Experts

Where else can you go besides Google to find the information you need for your next report? You might try your local library. While you can find a wealth of information on Google, libraries subscribe to commercial databases that can give you access to powerful tools for writing your company's business or marketing plan. An added plus is that librarians are experts at navigating those databases.

Small business owners, in particular, can benefit. Many libraries even hold classes for entrepreneurs and provide networking opportunities with other local agencies and organizations geared to help the small business person. So the next time you are working out a business problem, visit your local library.

Adapted from Tara Siegel Bernhard, "Enterprise: Big Help for Small Businesses at the Library; Commercial Databases, Assistance on Research and Classes Are Offered," *Wall Street Journal*, August 29, 2006, B4.

WRITING PROGRESS REPORTS LO 17-3

When you're assigned to a single project that will take a month or more, you'll probably be asked to file one or more progress reports. A progress report reassures the funding agency or employer that you're making progress and allows you and the agency or employer to resolve problems as they arise. Different readers may have different concerns. An instructor may want to know whether you'll have your report in by the due date. A client may be more interested in what you're learning about the problem. Adapt your progress report to the needs of the audience.

Christine Barabas's study of the progress reports in a large research and development organization found that poor writers tended to focus on what they had done and said very little about the value of their work. Good writers, in contrast, spent less space writing about the details of what they'd done but much more space explaining the value of their work for the organization.[8]

When you write progress reports, use what you know about emphasis, positive tone, and you-attitude. Don't present every detail as equally important. Use emphasis techniques to stress the major ones. Readers will generally not care that Jones was out of the office when you went to visit him and that you had to return a second time to catch him. Trivial details like this should be omitted.

In your report, try to exceed expectations in at least some small way. Perhaps your research is ahead of schedule or needed equipment arrived earlier than expected. However, do not present the good news by speculating on the reader's feelings; many readers find such statements offensive.

Poor:	You will be happy to hear the software came a week early.
Better:	The software came a week early, so Pat can start programming earlier than expected.

Remember that your audience for your report is usually in a position of power over you, so be careful what you say to them. Generally it is not wise to blame them for project problems even if they are at fault.

The Political Uses of Progress Reports

Progress reports can do more than just report progress. You can use progress reports to

- **Enhance your image.** Details about the number of documents you've read, people you've surveyed, or experiments you've conducted create a picture of a hardworking person doing a thorough job.
- **Float trial balloons.** Explain, "I could continue to do X [what you approved]; I could do Y instead [what I'd like to do now]." The detail in the progress report can help back up your claim. Even if the idea is rejected, you don't lose face because you haven't made a separate issue of the alternative.
- **Minimize potential problems.** As you do the work, it may become clear that implementing your recommendations will be difficult. In your regular progress reports, you can alert your boss or the funding agency to the challenges that lie ahead, enabling them to prepare psychologically and physically to act on your recommendations.

Poor: We could not proceed with drafting the plans because you did not send us the specifications for the changes you want.

Better: Chris has prepared the outline for the plan. We are ready to start drafting as soon as we receive the specifications. Meanwhile, we are working on. . . .

Subject lines for progress reports are straightforward. Specify the project on which you are reporting your progress.

Subject: Progress on Developing a Marketing Plan for Fab Fashions

If you are submitting weekly or monthly progress reports on a long project, number your progress reports or include the time period in your subject line. Include information about the work completed since the last report and work to be completed before the next report.

Make your progress report as positive as you *honestly* can. You'll build a better image of yourself if you show that you can take minor problems in stride and that you're confident of your own abilities.

The preliminary data sets were two days late because of a server crash. However, Nidex believes they will be back on schedule by next week. Past performance indicates their estimate is correct, and data analysis will be finished in two weeks, as originally scheduled.

Focus on your solutions to problems rather than the problems themselves:

Negative: Southern data points were corrupted, and that problem set us back three days in our data analysis.

Positive: Although southern data points were corrupted, the northern team was able to loan us Chris and Lee to fix the data set. Both teams are currently back on schedule.

In the above example the problem with the southern data points is still noted, because readers may want to know about it, but the solution to the problem is emphasized.

Do remember to use judicious restraint with your positive tone. Without details for support, glowing judgments of your own work may strike readers as ill-advised bragging, or maybe even dishonesty.

Overdone positive tone, lack of support: Our data analysis is indicating some great new predictions; you will be very happy to see them.

Supported optimism: Our data analysis is beginning to show that coastal erosion may not be as extensive as we had feared; in fact, it may be almost 10% less than originally estimated. We should have firm figures by next week.

Progress reports can be organized in three ways: by chronology, by task, and to support a recommendation. Some progress reports may use a combination: they may organize material chronologically within each task section, for instance.

Chronological Progress Reports

The chronological pattern of organization focuses on what you have done and what work remains.

1. **Summarize your progress in terms of your goals and your original schedule.** Use measurable statements.

Poor: Progress has been slow.

Better: Analysis of data sets is about one-third complete.

2. **Under the heading "Work Completed," describe what you have already done.** Be specific, both to support your claims in the first paragraph and to allow the reader to appreciate your hard work. Acknowledge the people who have helped you. Describe any serious obstacles you've encountered and tell how you've dealt with them.

Poor: I have found many articles about Procter & Gamble on the web. I have had a few problems finding how the company keeps employees safe from chemical fumes.

Better: On the web, I found Procter & Gamble's home page, its annual report, and mission statement. No one whom I interviewed could tell me about safety programs specifically at P&G. I have found seven articles about ways to protect workers against pollution in factories, but none mentions P&G.

3. **Under the heading "Work to Be Completed," describe the work that remains.** If you're more than three days late (for school projects) or two weeks late (for business projects) submit a new schedule, showing how you will be able to meet the original deadline. You may want to discuss "Observations" or "Preliminary Conclusions" if you want feedback before writing the final report or if your reader has asked for substantive interim reports.
4. **Express your confidence in having the report ready by the due date.** If you are behind your original schedule, show why you think you can still finish the project on time.

Even in chronological reports you need to do more than merely list work you have done. Show the value of that work and your prowess in achieving it, particularly your ability at solving problems. The student progress report in Figure 17.4 uses the chronological pattern of organization.

Task Progress Reports

In a task progress report, organize information under the various tasks you have worked on during the period. For example, a task progress report for a team report project might use the following headings:

Finding Background Information on the Web and in Print
Analyzing Our Survey Data
Working on the Introduction of the Report and the Appendices

Under each heading, the team could discuss the tasks it has completed and those that remain.

Task progress reports are appropriate for large projects with distinct topics or projects.

Recommendation Progress Reports

Recommendation progress reports recommend action: increasing the funding or allotted time for a project, changing its direction, canceling a project that isn't working out. When the recommendation will be easy for the reader to accept, use the direct request pattern of organization from Chapter 11. If the recommendation is likely to meet strong resistance, the problem-solving pattern may be more effective.

Figure 17.4 A Student Chronological Progress Report

Date: April 11, 2012

To: Ms. Katie Nichols, CEO of RAC. Inc

From: S. Jones SJ

Subject: Progress on JASS LLC's South Korean Feasibility Study

¶ 1: Summarize results in terms of purpose, schedule.

JASS LLC has collected information on South Korea that will enable us to answer the Topics to Investigate section from our proposal. We are currently analyzing and compiling the information for the formal report that will be submitted on April 21. Although we are slightly behind our original work schedule, we have planned an additional meeting on April 12 and will be back on track.

Work Completed Bold headings

Be very specific about what you've done.

To invesigate the feasibility of RAC Inc. expanding operations into South Korea, JASS LLC submitted a research proposal to Professor Toth that defined our topics to investigate and provided a list of preliminary sources. For this proposal, I wrote part of the problem, country overview, and qualifications sections. I also discovered three sources included in the methods section. These sources will give RAC Inc. important information regarding the competition, the available workforce, and the state of technology in South Korea. Serving as editor for the proposal, I also assisted with improving our writing style and formatting. Since submitting the proposal and getting approval, I have found six additional sources that should prove useful in our formal report.

Show how you've solved minor problems.

Due to scheduling conflicts with our course projects, we were unable to complete the first draft of the report as we had originally planned. However, we scheduled an additional meeting for tomorrow to accomplish this task and to get our group back on schedule. For tomorrow's meeting, I have read and analyzed eight sources and will be ready to compile information into our report draft. Specify steps you will take to correct deviations from schedule.

Work to Be Completed

Specify the work that remains.

During our additional meeting, JASS LLC will write the first full draft of our formal report by organizing information that the four of us have researched. We will also be prepared to conference with Professor Toth about our rough draft by the end of this week. After we receive his feedback, we will move into the revising and editing stages for the formal report. Finally, we still need to assemble our presentation slides and begin rehearsing together.

We will be prepared to submit our formal report and to deliver our presentation for you on April 21.

End on a positive note.

SUMMARY OF KEY POINTS

- Proposals argue for the work that needs to be done and who will do it.
- A proposal must answer the following questions:
  - What problem are you going to solve?
  - Why does the problem need to be solved now?
  - How are you going to solve it?
  - Can you do the work?
  - Why should you be the one to do it?
  - When will you complete the work?
  - How much will you charge?
  - What exactly will you provide for us?
- In a proposal for a class research project, prove that your problem is the right size, that you understand it, that your method will give you the information you need to solve the problem, that you have the knowledge and resources, and that you can produce the report by the deadline.
- In a project budget, ask for everything you will need to do a good job. Research current cost figures so yours are in line.
- Business plans need to pay particular attention to market potential and financial forecasts.
- In a proposal for funding, stress the needs your project will meet. Show how your project will help fulfill the goals of the organization you are asking for funds.
- Progress reports let people know how you are coming on a project.
- Progress reports may be organized by chronology, by task, or to support a recommendation.
- Use positive emphasis in progress reports to create an image of yourself as a capable, confident worker.

CHAPTER 17 Exercises and Problems

*Go to www.mhhe.com/locker10e for additional Exercises and Problems.

17.1 Reviewing the Chapter

1. What are six questions a good proposal should answer? (LO 17-1)
2. What are some guidelines for preparing a budget for a proposal? (LO 17-2)
3. What are the differences between chronological and task progress reports? (LO 17-3)

17.2 Writing a Proposal for a Student Report

Write a proposal to your instructor to do the research for a formal or informal report.

The headings and the questions in the section titled "Proposals for Class Research Projects" are your RFP; be sure to answer every question and to use the headings exactly as stated in the RFP. Exception: where alternate heads are listed, you may choose one, combine the two ("Qualifications and Facilities"), or treat them as separate headings in separate categories.

17.3 Proposing a Change

No organization is perfect, especially when it comes to communication. Propose a change that would improve communication within your organization. The change can be specific to your unit or can apply to the whole organization; it can relate to how important information is distributed, who has access to important information, how information is accessed, or any other change in communication practices that you see as having a benefit. Direct your proposal to the person or committee with the power to authorize the change.

17.4 Proposing to Undertake a Research Project

Pick a project you would like to study whose results could be used by your organization. Write a proposal to your supervisor requesting time away from other duties to do the research. Show how your research (whatever its outcome) will be useful to the organization.

17.5 Writing a Proposal for Funding for a Nonprofit Group

Pick a nonprofit group you care about. Examples include professional organizations, a charitable group, a community organization, or your own college or university.

As your instructor directs,

a. Check the web or a directory of foundations to find one that makes grants to groups like yours. Brainstorm a list of businesses that might be willing to give money for specific projects. Check to see whether state or national levels of your organization make grants to local chapters.
b. Write a proposal to obtain funds for a special project your group could undertake if it had the money. Address your proposal to a specific organization.
c. Write a proposal to obtain operating funds or money to buy something your group would like to have. Address your proposal to a specific organization.

17.6 Writing a Sales Proposal

Pick a project that you could do for a local company or government office. Examples include

- Creating a brochure or web page.
- Revising form letters.
- Conducting a training program.
- Writing a newsletter or an annual report.
- Developing a marketing plan.
- Providing plant care, catering, or janitorial services.

Write a proposal specifying what you could do and providing a detailed budget and work schedule.

As your instructor directs,

a. Phone someone in the organization to talk about its needs and what you could offer.
b. Write an individual proposal.
c. Join with other students in the class to create a team proposal.
d. Present your proposal orally.

17.7 Presenting a Stockholder Proposal

Visit the websites of the following companies and locate their latest proxy statements or reports. These are generally linked from the "about us/company information–investor relations" or "investors" pages. Find shareholder proposals under the heading "proposals requiring your vote," "stockholder proposals," or "shareholder proposals."

- Ford Motor Company
- Citigroup
- AT&T
- J. P. Morgan Chase & Co.
- Southwest Airlines
- Home Depot
- Procter & Gamble
- Boeing
- Google
- Dow Chemical

As a team, select one proposal, and the management response following it, and give an oral presentation answering these questions:

1. What is the problem discussed in the proposal?
2. What is the rationale given for the urgency to solve the problem?
3. How does the proposal seek to solve it?
4. What benefits does the proposal mention that will accrue from the solution?
5. What is the management response to the proposal and what are the reasons given for the response? Does the management response strike you as justified? Why or why not?

Hint: it may help you to do some research on the topic of the proposal.

17.8 Writing a Progress Report to Your Superior

Describe the progress you have made this week or this month on projects you have been assigned. You may describe progress you have made individually, or progress your unit has made as a team.

17.9 Writing a Progress Report

Write a memo to your instructor summarizing your progress on your report.

In the introductory paragraph, summarize your progress in terms of your schedule and your goals. Under a heading titled *Work Completed,* list what you have already done. (This is a chance to toot your own horn: if you have solved problems creatively, say so. You can also describe obstacles you've encountered that you have not yet solved.) Under *Work to Be Completed,* list what you still have to do. If you are more than two days behind the schedule you submitted with your proposal, include a revised schedule, listing the completion dates for the activities that remain.

17.10 Writing a Progress Report for a Team Report

Write a memo to your instructor summarizing your team's progress.

In the introductory paragraph, summarize the team's progress in terms of its goals and its schedule, your own progress on the tasks for which you are responsible, and your feelings about the team's work thus far.

Under a heading titled *Work Completed,* list what has already been done. Be most specific about what you yourself have done. Describe briefly the chronology of team activities: number, time, and length of meetings; topics discussed and decisions made at meetings.

If you have solved problems creatively, say so. You can also describe obstacles you've encountered that you have not yet solved. In this section, you can also comment on problems that the team has faced and whether or not they've been solved. You can comment on things that have gone well and have contributed to the smooth functioning of the team.

Under *Work to Be Completed,* list what you personally and other team members still have to do. Indicate the schedule for completing the work.

CHAPTER 18

Analyzing Information and Writing Reports

Chapter Outline

Using Your Time Efficiently

Analyzing Data and Information for Reports

- Evaluating the Source of the Data
- Analyzing Numbers
- Analyzing Words
- Analyzing Patterns
- Checking Your Logic

Choosing Information for Reports

Organizing Information in Reports

- Basic Patterns for Organizing Information
- Specific Varieties of Reports

Presenting Information Effectively in Reports

1. Use Clear, Engaging Writing.
2. Keep Repetition to a Minimum.
3. Introduce Sources and Visuals.
4. Use Forecasting, Transitions, Topic Sentences, and Headings.

Writing Formal Reports

- Title Page
- Letter or Memo of Transmittal
- Table of Contents
- List of Illustrations
- Executive Summary
- Introduction
- Background or History
- Body
- Conclusions and Recommendations

Summary of Key Points

Reporting on Life

Each year, most publicly held companies produce annual reports. Because the reports can affect stock prices and credit ratings, companies take great care to produce detailed, attractive, and persuasive reports that fit within government guidelines.

Nicholas Felton, a graphic designer in New York City, has taken the idea of an annual report one step farther. Each year since 2005, he has produced a personal annual report, filled with the minute details of his life—encounters with other individuals, places he traveled, restaurants and shops he visited, and so on. With custom-designed charts and graphs, Felton tells his own story of the previous year in "The Feltron Annual Report," which he produces as a printed brochure and sells on his website.

"Like Nicholas Felton, companies then compile the data into charts, graphs, and text that will help their readers understand and interpret the data."

Felton's creative approach to cataloging his life in an annual report has caught the attention of others. A 2010 *New York Times* profile of him reported that other people have begun similar personal data collections. In fact, Felton got so many requests that he started a website to help people track their movements and record their personal data.

Companies gather data for months or even years to produce reports. They analyze the data, looking for patterns that will shape the narratives of their final documents. And, like Nicholas Felton, companies then compile the data into charts, graphs, and text that will help their readers understand and interpret the data.

Sources: "Feltron," Nicholas Felton, accessed June 16, 2011, http://feltron.com/; and "An Annual Report on One Man's Life," *Bits* (blog), *New York Times*, February 9, 2010, http://bits.blogs.nytimes.com/2010/02/09/an-annual-report-on-one-mans-life/.

Learning Objectives

After studying this chapter, you will know

LO 18-1 Ways to analyze data, information, and logic.

LO 18-2 How to choose information for reports.

LO 18-3 Different ways to organize reports.

LO 18-4 How to present information effectively in reports.

LO 18-5 How to prepare the different components of formal reports.

Careful analysis, smooth writing, and effective document design work together to make effective reports, whether you're writing a 2½-page memo report or a 250-page formal report complete with all the report components.

Chapter 15 covered the first two steps in writing a report:

1. Define the problem.
2. Gather the necessary data and information.

This chapter covers the last three steps:

3. Analyze the data and information.
4. Organize the information.
5. Write the report.

USING YOUR TIME EFFICIENTLY

To use your time efficiently, think about the parts of the report before you begin writing. Much of the introduction can come from your proposal (see Chapter 17), with only minor revisions. You can write six sections even before you've finished your research: Purpose, Scope, Assumptions, Methods, Criteria, and Definitions. Mock up tables and figures early using the guidelines in Chapter 16.

The background reading for your proposal can form the first draft of your list of references. Save a copy of your questionnaire or interview questions to use as an appendix. You can print appendixes before the final report is ready if you number their pages separately. Appendix A pages would be A-1, A-2, and so forth; Appendix B pages would be B-1, B-2, and so forth.

You can write the title page and the transmittal as soon as you know what your recommendation will be.

After you've analyzed your data, write the body, the conclusions and recommendations, and the executive summary. Prepare a draft of the table of contents and the list of illustrations.

When you write a long report, list all the sections (headings) that your report will have. Mark those that are most important to your reader and your logic, and spend most of your time on them. Write the important sections early. That way, you won't spend all your time on Background or History of the Problem. Instead, you'll get to the heart of your report.

ANALYZING DATA AND INFORMATION FOR REPORTS LO 18-1

Good reports begin with good data. Analyzing the data you have gathered is essential to produce the tight logic needed for a good report. Analyze your data with healthy skepticism. Check to see that they correspond with expectations or other existing data. If they don't, check for well-supported explanations of the difference.

Be suspicious of all data, even from reputable sources. Ask yourself "How do they know?" or "What could prevent that data from being right?"

- If you read in the paper that 300,000 people attended a demonstration at the National Mall in Washington, D.C., ask yourself how they know. Unless they were able to get a photo from a satellite, they are estimating, and such estimates have been known to vary by 100,000 or more, depending on whether the estimator wants a larger or smaller crowd.
- Want to know how many centenarians live in the United States? Surely the Census Bureau knows? Well, not exactly. An accurate count is obscured by lack of birth records, low literacy levels, cognitive disabilities, and the human desire to hit a milestone number.
- Did you read in a job-hunt article that U.S. workers average seven career changes during their working years? That number is a myth. It has been attributed to the U.S. Bureau of Labor Statistics so many times that the bureau now posts a disclaimer on its website. The bureau does not estimate lifetime career changes for a simple reason: no consensus exists for the definition of a career change. Is a promotion a career change? Is a layoff, a temporary subsistence job, and a return to work 0, 1, or 2 career changes?
- Have you heard that Thanksgiving is the busiest travel day of the year? Actually, no day in November has made the top 35 busiest airline days for years, according to the U.S. Department of Transportation (busiest days occur in the summer, when school is out). Even for those traveling by car, July 4, Labor Day, and Christmas are busier holidays.[1]
- Sometimes the discrepancies are not fun facts. Some states are meeting No Child Left Behind federal mandates for continued funding by lowering grade-level proficiency standards (see sidebar on this page).[2]

Spreadsheets can be particularly troublesome. Cell results derived by formulas can be subtly, or grossly, wrong by incorrectly defining ranges, for example. It is easy to generate results that are impossible, such as sums that exceed known totals. Always have an estimate of the result of a calculation. Using spreadsheets, you can easily be wrong by a factor of 10, 100, or even 1,000. Studies have found up to 80% of spreadsheets have errors, such as misplaced decimal points, transposed digits, and wrong signs. Some of these errors are enormous. Fidelity's Magellan fund's dividend estimate spreadsheet was $2.6 billion off when a sign was wrongly transposed from minus to plus. Fannie Mae, the financer of home mortgages, once discovered a $1.136 billion error in total shareholder equity, again from a spreadsheet mistake.[3]

Try to keep ballpark figures, estimates of what the numbers should be, in mind as you look at numerical data. Question surprises before accepting them.

Analyzing data can be hard even for experts. Numerous studies exist in scholarly journals challenging the data-based conclusions of earlier articles. One example is the fate of unmarried, college-educated women over 30. A famous *Newsweek* cover story, "Too Late for Prince Charming?" reported the Yale and Harvard study that suggested such women had only a 20% chance of finding husbands, and only a 2.6% chance by the time they reached 40. Twenty years later an economist at the University of Washington examined 30 years of census data. Her figures for the decade of the original study showed that women aged 40–44 with advanced degrees were only 25% less likely to be married than comparably aged women with just high school diplomas. By 2000, those women with postcollege education were slightly more likely to be married than those who had finished only high school.[4]

Changing Standards

Under the No Child Left Behind law, every child in the United States must become proficient in reading and math by 2014. Schools that fail to show consistent improvement risk losing funding from both state and federal education programs.

Some states, according to research by the U.S. Department of Education, have been meeting the goals of NCLB in a unique way: by changing what it means to be proficient. The NCLB law requires states to set standards and measure achievement. As the 2014 goal deadline approaches, however, states are changing those standards to make sure their schools meet the requirements of the law.

Between 2005 and 2007, fifteen states lowered the standards for fourth and eighth graders on at least one subject test. Eight other states raised their standards. The result? *Proficient* means something different in every state. According to these different standards, a proficient math student in Massachusetts would be five or six years more advanced than a student in the same grade in Tennessee.

Do you think it is ethical for states to lower their standards for proficiency? Would your opinion change if the states were doing this so they could continue to receive money badly needed for educating children? Is raising standards fair?

Adapted from John Hechinger, "Some States Drop Testing Bar," *Wall Street Journal*, October 30, 2009, A3.

Measuring Innovation

It is commonly accepted wisdom that one measure of a company's innovation is the number of patents it commands. In recent years, however, research has shown that companies increasingly use patents as a defensive strategy rather than a strategy for innovation.

A Boston University study found that software companies with more patents actually reduced their research and development expenditure vis-à-vis sales. Additionally, with companies vying for patents for the smallest addition to product features, patents may be a dubious measure of innovation.

Recent studies on patents also show a growing trend of acquiring patents on design or form of products rather than their technical aspects. Companies such as Samsung Electronics and Nike have earned a name for themselves for innovation by acquiring patents based on product design.

Compared to patents themselves, patent citations, or the references to a company's patent by patents of other companies, may be a better metric of innovation. A high number of patent citations may show that the company's patent truly represents innovation and may be licensed for a fee or royalties. Companies such as Procter & Gamble have adopted this strategy.

Adapted from Jena McGregor, "Are Patents the Measure of Innovation?" *BusinessWeek*, May 4, 2007, http://www.businessweek.com/innovate/content/may2007/id20070504_323562.htm.

Evaluating the Source of the Data

When evaluating the source of your data, question the authors, objectivity, completeness, and currency of the source.

Identify the **authors.** Which people or organization provided the data? What credentials do they have? If you want national figures on wages and unemployment, the U.S. Bureau of Labor Statistics would be a good source. But if you want the figures for your local town, your local Chamber of Commerce might be a more credible source. Use the strategies outlined in Chapter 15 to evaluate web sources.

Assess the **objectivity** of the source. Does the source give evidence to support claims? Is the surrounding prose professional and unbiased? If the subject supports multiple viewpoints, are other opinions referenced or explained? When the source has a vested interest in the results, scrutinize the data with special care. To analyze a company's financial prospects, use independent information as well as the company's annual report and press releases.

Drug and medical device companies, and the researchers funded by them, keep appearing in the news with reports of undue influence. Duke University researchers checked 746 studies of heart stents published in one year in medical journals. They found that 83% of the papers did not disclose whether authors were paid consultants for companies, even though many journals require that information. Even worse, 72% of the papers did not say who funded the research.[5] A study in the prestigious *New England Journal of Medicine* noted that positive studies of antidepressant trials got published and negative ones did not: "According to the published literature, it appeared that 94% of the trials conducted were positive. By contrast, the FDA analysis showed that 51% were positive."[6]

If your report is based upon secondary data from library and online research, look at the sample, the sample size, and the exact wording of questions to see what the data actually measure. (See Chapter 15 for more information on sampling and surveying.) Does the sample have a built-in bias? A survey of city library users may uncover information about users, but it may not find what keeps other people away from the library.

Try to assess the **completeness** of the data. What are they based on? Two reputable sources can give different figures because they take their data from different places. Suppose you wanted to know employment figures. The Labor Department's monthly estimate of nonfarm payroll jobs is the most popular, but some economists like Automatic Data Processing's monthly estimate, which is based on the roughly 20 million paychecks it processes for clients. Both survey approximately 400,000 workplaces, but the Labor Department selects employers to mirror the U.S. economy, while ADP's sample is skewed, with too many construction firms and too few of the largest employers. On the other hand, the government has trouble counting jobs at businesses that are opening and closing, and some employers do not return the survey. (Both organizations do attempt to adjust their numbers to compensate accurately.)[7]

Also check the **currency** of the data. Population figures should be from the 2010 census, not the 2000 one. Technology figures in particular need to be current. Do remember, however, that some large data sets are one to two years behind in being analyzed. Such is the case for some government figures, also. If you are doing a report in 2012 that requires national education data from the Department of Education, for instance, 2011 data may not even be fully collected. And even the 2010 data may not be fully analyzed, so indeed the 2009 data may be the most current available.

Sharp uses what it calls "academic marketing" to sell air purifiers in Japan. Ads in Japanese newspapers and magazines provide data, diagrams, and charts in support of Sharp's plasmacluster technology.

Source: Daisuke Wakabayashi, "Using 'Academic Marketing' to Sell Air Purifiers," *Wall Street Journal,* December 26, 2008, B4.

Analyzing Numbers

Many reports analyze numbers—either numbers from databases and sources or numbers from a survey you have conducted. The numerical information, properly analyzed, can make a clear case in support of a recommendation.

Recognize that even authorities can differ on the numbers they offer, or on the interpretations of the same data sets. Researchers from the United Nations and Johns Hopkins University differed on their estimates of Iraqi deaths in the war by 500% (see sidebar on this page).[8] The cover story of the January 4, 2008, *National Journal* was an explanation of how the two estimates could vary so wildly (research design and execution flaws; sampling error; lack of transparency with the data).[9] You will be best able to judge the quality of data if you know how it was collected.

In their books, *The Tipping Point* and *Freakonomics,* Malcolm Gladwell and Steven D. Levitt and Stephen J. Dubner reach different conclusions about the data on dropping crime rates for New York City. Gladwell attributes the drop to the crackdown by the new police chief on even minor crimes such as graffiti and public drunkenness. Levitt and Dubner first explain why the cause was not a crackdown on crime (the years don't match well; other cities also experienced the drop) and attribute it to the legalization of abortion (at the time of the crime drop the first wave of children born after Roe v. Wade was hitting late teen years and thus prime crime time; that group was short on the category most likely to become criminal: unwanted children). They also provide corroborating evidence from other countries.[10]

When you have multiple numbers for salaries or other items, an early analysis step is to figure the average (or mean), the median, and the range. The **average** or **mean** is calculated by adding up all the figures and dividing by

Getting the Data Right

A 2006 report by Johns Hopkins University claimed that 655,000 Iraqis had died in the war in Iraq, a figure that diverged wildly from other estimates—sometimes more than 1,000%. The Hopkins figure is 500% more than that of the United Nations. Such a difference from other reports calls into question the accuracy of the Hopkins report.

To understand why the figure is so much higher than other research reports, it is important to consider how the data were gathered. The Hopkins researchers used cluster sampling for interviews, a methodology that makes sense given the country's war-zone status. Researchers randomly selected neighborhoods and then conducted door-to-door interviews with "clusters" of individuals from within those neighborhoods. Such a technique saves time and money and is common in research within developing countries.

But the key to this kind of technique is to use enough cluster points. A lack of cluster points can mean that the population sampled isn't representative of the population in Iraq. The Hopkins researchers did not use enough cluster points. In addition, the Hopkins researchers didn't gather demographic data from their participants for comparison to census data. Doing so would have added to the believability of their results.

Getting the data right is important because numbers can have a significant impact on decisions and policies. In terms of casualties, the decisions made based on the numbers reported have an impact on millions of Iraqis and Americans.

Adapted from Stephen E. Moore, "655,000 War Dead?" *Wall Street Journal,* October 18, 2006, A20.

Sun and Statistics

Recent research suggests that patients with low levels of vitamin D, which can be gained from moderate exposure to the sun, have higher risks of cancer, heart disease, and autoimmune disorders.

The Indoor Tanning Association quickly jumped at this new finding. They used their interpretation of the statistics about low vitamin D levels as a way to promote indoor tanning, suggesting that UV rays can prevent cancer.

The medical community was outraged at the ITA's twisted approach to the statistics. Doctor Lichtenfeld of the American Cancer Society suggested that UV ray promotion was "like recommending smoking to reduce stress." The ITA advertisements failed to suggest there were any downsides to tanning, such as the link between prolonged exposure to UV rays and melanoma. They also omitted that the tanner the skin, the longer it takes to absorb vitamin D.

How ethical is the ITA's use of research statistics? Would you be more likely to tan indoors if you saw one of their advertisements?

Adapted from Pat Wingert, "Teens, Tans, and Truth," *Newsweek*, May 19, 2008, 42–43.

the number of samples. The **mode** is the number that occurs most often. The **median** is the number that is exactly in the middle in a ranked list of observations. When you have an even number, the median will be the average of the two numbers in the center of the list. The **range** is the difference between the high and low figures for that variable.

Averages are particularly susceptible to a single extreme figure. In 2007, three different surveys reported the average cost of a wedding at nearly $30,000. Many articles picked up that figure because weddings are big business. However, the median cost in those three surveys was only about $15,000. And even that is probably on the high side, since the samples were convenience samples for a big wedding website, a bride magazine, and a maker of wedding invitations, and thus probably did not include smaller, less elaborate weddings.[11]

Often it's useful to simplify numerical data: rounding it off, combining similar elements. Then you can see that one number is, for instance, about 2½ times another. Graphing it can also help you see patterns in your data. (See Chapter 16 for a full discussion of tables and graphs as a way of analyzing and presenting numerical data.) Look at the raw data as well as at percentages. For example, a 50% increase in shoplifting incidents sounds alarming. An increase from two to three shoplifting incidents sounds less so but could be the same data, just stated differently.

Analyzing Words

Be sure you are clear about definitions on which data are based. For instance, China and the United States are jockeying for first place in number of Internet users. Different sources give different results, and one reason is that they are defining "Internet user" in different ways: Is a user anyone who has access to the Internet at home, school, or work? What about a four-year-old child who has access to the Internet through her family but does not use it? Is anyone who has used the Internet only once in the past six months a user?[12]

State accurately what your data show. For example, suppose that you've asked people who use computers if they could be as productive without them and the overwhelming majority say *no*. This finding shows that people *believe* that computers make them more productive, but it does not prove that they in fact are more productive.

Also try to measure words against numbers. A study of annual reports in the United Kingdom found a large increase (375%) in narrative information and noted that accounting narratives were being used to manage impressions of annual performance.[13] Numbers require interpretation and context for easy comprehension.

Analyzing Patterns

Patterns can help you draw meaning from your data. If you have library sources, on which points do experts agree? Which disagreements can be explained by early theories or numbers that have now changed? Which disagreements are the result of different interpretations of the same data? Which are the result of having different values and criteria? In your interviews and surveys, what patterns do you see?

- Have things changed over time?
- Does geography account for differences?
- Do demographics such as gender, age, or income account for differences?

- What similarities do you see?
- What differences do you see?
- What confirms your hunches?
- What surprises you?

Many descriptions of sales trends are descriptions of patterns derived from data.

Checking Your Logic

Check that your data actually measure what you want them to. A common belief is that satisfied customers will be repeat customers. But a *Harvard Business Review* study found little relationship between the two groups; customers who said on surveys they were satisfied did not necessarily make repeat purchases. Instead, the best predictor of repeat purchases was that the customer would recommend the company to others.[14]

Another common logic error is confusing causation with correlation. *Causation* means that one thing causes or produces another. *Correlation* means that two things happening at the same time are positively or negatively related. One might cause the other, but both might be caused by a third. For instance, consider a study that shows pulling all-nighters hurts grades: students who pull all-nighters get lower grades than those who do not pull all-nighters. But maybe it is not the all-nighter causing the poor grades; maybe students who need all-nighters are weaker students to begin with.

Correlation and causation are easy to confuse, but the difference is important. The Census Bureau publishes figures showing that greater education levels are associated with greater incomes. A widely held assumption is that more education causes greater earnings. But might people from richer backgrounds seek more education? Or might some third factor, such as intelligence, lead to both greater education and higher income?[15]

Some spurious correlations are amusing. The *Wall Street Journal* reported with tongue in cheek the Tiger Woods phenomenon. During the 11 years of 1997–2008, the April bond market performed positively when Woods won the Masters golf tournament, and negatively when he did not.[16]

Consciously search for at least three possible causes for each phenomenon you've observed and at least three possible solutions for each problem. The more possibilities you brainstorm, the more likely you are to find good options. In your report, discuss in detail only the possibilities that will occur to readers and that you think are the real reasons and the best solutions.

When you have identified causes of the problem or the best solutions, check these ideas against reality. Can you find support in references or in numbers? Can you answer claims of people who interpret the data in other ways?

Make the nature of your evidence clear to your reader. Do you have observations that you yourself have made? Or do you have inferences based on observations or data collected by others? Old data may not be good guides to future action.

If you can't prove the claim you originally hoped to make, modify your conclusions to fit your data. Even when your market test is a failure or your experiment disproves your hypothesis, you can still write a useful report.

- Identify changes that might yield a different result. For example, selling the product at a lower price might enable the company to sell enough units.
- Divide the discussion to show what part of the test succeeded.

Charity Data

Many people believe they "know" "facts" and figures that are not so. When you encounter these false beliefs, you need to be sure you provide reliable data to counteract them. One area subject to common misperceptions is charity donations. Below are some common myths paired with realities.

Myth: Most charitable giving goes to help the needy. Reality: Less than one-third of individually donated money to nonprofits goes to the economically disadvantaged. And only 8% provides basic needs like food and shelter.

Myth: The wealthy look after those in need. Reality: Only about a quarter of their donations go to the poor, and only 4% to basic needs.

Myth: Religious donations go to those in need. Reality: Less than one-fifth of money donated goes to the poor.

Myth: Americans give generously to international causes. Reality: Only 8% of US individual donations support any international cause whatsoever.

Adapted from Sheryl Sandberg [board member of Google.org, Google's philanthropic arm], "The Charity Gap," *Wall Street Journal*, April 4, 2007, A15.

Movie Rankings

In late 2009, James Cameron's *Avatar* took the worldwide box office by storm. It set records in the United States and overseas to become the top-grossing movie of all time, with over $2.7 billion in ticket sales. That huge number, however, reflects higher ticket prices and charges for 3-D glasses that distort the movie's place in history.

For many years, movie studios have focused on box office grosses as evidence of success. But the ever-increasing grosses do not take into account inflation, or rising population figures. Some have tried to even the playing field by estimating the number of tickets sold or adjusting ticket prices for inflation. With those revised numbers, *Avatar* is no longer the top all-time grossing movie. In fact, it comes in at number 14. The top-grossing movie of all time remains 1939's best picture, *Gone with the Wind.* But even box office numbers adjusted for inflation don't tell a completely accurate story, because popular older movies like *Gone with the Wind* were released in theaters every few years until the advent of home video.

Like other comparative lists, the all-time worldwide box office rankings depend on how the numbers are counted.

Adapted from Carl Bialik, "What It Takes for a Movie to Be No. 1," *Wall Street Journal,* January 30–31, 2010, A2; and "All Time Box Office Adjusted for Ticket Price Inflation," *Box Office Mojo,* accessed June 16, 2011, http://www.boxofficemojo.com/alltime/adjusted.htm.

As employees become buried in paperwork, it becomes even more important to select carefully and interpret clearly the information to be included in reports.

- Discuss circumstances that may have affected the results.
- Summarize your negative findings in progress reports to let readers down gradually and to give them a chance to modify the research design.
- Remember that negative results aren't always disappointing to the audience. For example, the people who commissioned a feasibility report may be relieved to have an impartial outsider confirm their suspicions that a project isn't feasible.

A common myth associated with numbers is that numbers are more objective than words: "numbers don't lie." But as the above examples show, numbers can be subject to widely varying interpretation.

CHOOSING INFORMATION FOR REPORTS LO 18-2

Don't put information in reports just because you have it or just because it took you a long time to find it. Instead, choose the information that your reader needs to make a decision. NASA received widespread criticism over the way it released results from an $11.3 million federal air safety study. NASA published 16,208 pages of findings with no guide to understanding them. Critics maintain the lapse was deliberate because the data contained hundreds of cases of pilot error.[17]

If you know your readers well, you may already know their priorities. For example, the supervisor of a call center knows that management will be looking for certain kinds of performance data including costs, workload handled, and customer satisfaction. To write regular reports, the supervisor could set up a format in which it is easy to see how well the center is doing in each of these areas. Using the same format month after month simplifies the reader's task.

If you don't know your readers, you may be able to get a sense of what is important by showing them a tentative table of contents (a list of your headings) and asking, "Have I included everything?" When you cannot contact an external audience, show your draft to colleagues and superiors in your organization.

How much information you need to include depends on whether your audience is likely to be supportive, neutral, or skeptical. If your audience is likely to be pleased with your research, you can present your findings directly. If your audience will not be pleased, you will need to explain your thinking in a persuasive way and provide substantial evidence.

You must also decide whether to put information in the body of the report or in appendixes. Put material in the body of the report if it is crucial to your proof, if your most significant readers will want to see it there, or if it is short. (Something less than half a page won't interrupt the reader.) Frequently decision makers want your analysis of the data in the report body rather than the actual data itself. Supporting data that will be examined later by specialists such as accountants, lawyers, and engineers are generally put in an appendix.

Anything that a careful reader will want but that is not crucial to your proof can go in an appendix. Appendixes can include

- A copy of a survey questionnaire or interview questions.
- A tally of responses to each question in a survey.
- A copy of responses to open-ended questions in a survey.
- A transcript of an interview.
- Complex tables and visuals.
- Technical data.
- Previous reports on the same subject.

Tell Them a Story

To persuade people, tell them a story or anecdote that proves your point.

Experiments show that people are more likely to believe a point and more likely to be committed to it when points were made by examples, stories, and case studies. Stories alone were more effective than a combination of stories and statistics; the combination was more effective than statistics alone. In another experiment, attitude changes lasted longer when the audience had read stories than when they had only read numbers. Research suggests that stories are more persuasive because people remember them.

In many cases, you'll need to provide statistics or numbers to convince the careful reader that your anecdote is a representative example. But give the story first. It's more persuasive.

Adapted from Dean C. Kazoleas, "A Comparison of the Persuasive Effectiveness of Qualitative versus Quantitative Evidence," *Communication Quarterly* 41, no. 1 (Winter 1993): 40–50; and Joanne Martin and Melanie E. Powers, "Truth of Corporate Propaganda," in *Organizational Symbolism*, ed. Louis R. Pondy, et al. (Greenwich, CT: JAI Press, 1983), 97–107.

ORGANIZING INFORMATION IN REPORTS LO 18-3

Most sets of data can be organized in several logical ways. Choose the way that makes your information easiest for the audience to understand and use. If you were compiling a directory of all the employees at your plant, for example, alphabetizing by last name would be far more useful than listing people by height, social security number, or length of service with the company, although those organizing principles might make sense in lists for other purposes.

The following three guidelines will help you choose the arrangement that will be the most useful for your audience:

1. **Process your information before you present it to your audience.** The order in which you became aware of information usually is not the best order to present it to your audience.
2. **When you have lots of information, group it into three to seven categories.** The average person's short-term memory can hold only seven chunks, though the chunks can be of any size.[18] By grouping your information into seven categories (or fewer), you make your report easier to comprehend.
3. **Work with the audience's expectations, not against them.** Introduce ideas in the overview in the order in which you will discuss them.

Basic Patterns for Organizing Information

Organize information in a way that will work best for your audience. Here are basic patterns for organizing information that are particularly useful in reports:

- Comparison/contrast.
- Problem-solution.
- Elimination of alternatives.
- SWOT analysis.
- General to particular or particular to general.
- Geographic or spatial.
- Functional.
- Chronological.

A Plan to Fail

In the days following the tragic oil spill in the Gulf of Mexico, BP assured the U.S. government and conservation experts that it was acting in accordance with its 582-page emergency spill response plan. As the details of the plan came to light, however, they revealed deep problems with the company's planning.

For example, the plan, written in 2009, lists Professor Peter Lutz as a wildlife expert. Unfortunately, the professor died in 2005. Additionally, the plan gives detailed instructions on treating sea creatures affected by spills, including walruses, sea otters, sea lions, and seals—none of which live in the Gulf of Mexico.

According to an AP study, the response plan did not address obvious problems and contained serious errors and omissions. Consequently, when the crude oil began to gush into the gulf, BP's employees were left scrambling for solutions without guidance or resources.

Adapted from Justin Pritchard, "Spill Response Plan Was Severely Flawed," *Des Moines Register*, June 10, 2010, 1A.

Any of these patterns can be used for a whole report or for only part of it.

Comparison/contrast Many reports use comparison/contrast sections within a larger report pattern. Comparison/contrast can also be the purpose of the whole report. Recommendation studies usually use this pattern. You can focus either on the alternatives you are evaluating or on the criteria you use. See Figure 18.1 for ways to organize these two patterns in a report.

Focus on the alternatives when

- One alternative is clearly superior.
- The criteria are hard to separate.
- The audience will intuitively grasp the alternative as a whole rather than as the sum of its parts.

Focus on the criteria when

- The superiority of one alternative to another depends on the relative weight assigned to various criteria. Perhaps Alternative A is best if we are most concerned about Criterion 1, cost, but worst if we are most concerned about Criterion 2, proximity to target market.
- The criteria are easy to separate.
- The audience wants to compare and contrast the options independently of your recommendation.

Figure 18.1 Two Ways to Organize a Comparison/Contrast Report

Focus on alternatives	
Alternative A	Opening a New Store on Campus
Criterion 1	Cost of Renting Space
Criterion 2	Proximity to Target Market
Criterion 3	Competition from Similar Stores
Alternative B	Opening a New Store in the Suburban Mall
Criterion 1	Cost of Renting Space
Criterion 2	Proximity to Target Market
Criterion 3	Competition from Similar Stores

Focus on criteria	
Criterion 1	Cost of Renting Space for the New Store
Alternative A	Cost of Campus Locations
Alternative B	Cost of Locations in the Suburban Mall
Criterion 2	Proximity to Target Market
Alternative A	Proximity on Campus
Alternative B	Proximity in the Suburban Mall
Criterion 3	Competition from Similar Stores
Alternative A	Competing Stores on Campus
Alternative B	Competing Stores in the Suburban Mall

A variation of the comparison/contrast pattern is the **pro-and-con pattern.** In this pattern, under each specific heading, give the arguments for and against that alternative. A report recommending new plantings for a university quadrangle uses the pro-and-con pattern:

Advantages of Monocropping
  High Productivity
  Visual Symmetry
Disadvantages of Monocropping
  Danger of Pest Exploitation
  Visual Monotony

This pattern is least effective when you want to de-emphasize the disadvantages of a proposed solution, for it does not permit you to bury the disadvantages between neutral or positive material.

Problem-solution Identify the problem; explain its background or history; discuss its extent and seriousness; identify its causes. Discuss the factors (criteria) that affect the decision. Analyze the advantages and disadvantages of possible solutions. Conclusions and recommendation can go either first or last, depending on the preferences of your audience. This pattern works well when the audience is neutral.

A report recommending ways to eliminate solidification of a granular bleach during production uses the problem–solution pattern:

Recommended Reformulation for Vibe Bleach
Problems in Maintaining Vibe's Granular Structure
  Solidification during Storage and Transportation
  Customer Complaints about "Blocks" of Vibe in Boxes
Why Vibe Bleach "Cakes"
  Vibe's Formula
  The Manufacturing Process
  The Chemical Process of Solidification
Modifications Needed to Keep Vibe Flowing Freely

Elimination of alternatives After discussing the problem and its causes, discuss the *impractical* solutions first, showing why they will not work. End with the most practical solution. This pattern works well when the solutions the audience is likely to favor will not work, while the solution you recommend is likely to be perceived as expensive, intrusive, or radical.

A report on toy commercials, "The Effect of TV Ads on Children," eliminates alternatives:

Alternative Solutions to Problems in TV Toy Ads
  Leave Ads Unchanged
  Mandate School Units on Advertising
  Ask the Industry to Regulate Itself
  Give FCC Authority to Regulate TV Ads Directed at Children

SWOT Analysis A SWOT analysis is frequently used to evaluate a proposed project, expansion, or new venture. The analysis discusses **S**trengths, **W**eaknesses, **O**pportunities, and **T**hreats of the proposed action. Strengths and weaknesses are usually factors within the organization; opportunities and threats are usually factors external to the organization.

Cupid by the Numbers

Online dating sites collect mountains of data about their users—interests, hobbies, demographics, and characteristics—all of which are used to match users with potential partners. One site, however, is using all of that data to do more.

OkCupid, founded by four Harvard-educated mathematicians, maintains a blog called OkTrends, which mines user data to note interesting, amusing, and controversial trends. By running computer calculations and comparisons, the blog has compiled features like "Rape Fantasies and Hygiene by State," and "How Your Race Affects the Messages You Get."

While some of the data presented on OkTrends is useful to OkCupid's users (like how to pose for a profile picture and what greetings to use), much of it is posted simply to show trends and interesting facts (like iPhone users have more sex than other smartphone users). It also serves to drive traffic to the OkCupid site—visits have doubled since the OkTrends blog was introduced.

Adapted from Jason Del Ray, "In Love with Numbers: Getting the Most Out of Your Data," *Inc.*, October 2010, 105–6.

Annual Reports

Report Watch posts annual lists of the best annual reports. They also post tips for creating good annual reports:

- Start with an eye-catching, interest-grabbing cover.
- Live up to the cover's promise in the body of the report.
- Don't overemphasize or underplay important points
- Offer a longer-term, strategic view of the future in addition to information about the past year.
- Use clear headings and bullets to help readers who skim.
- Use a clear, readable style.
- Make all visuals striking, relevant, and creative.

Adapted from Report Watch, "Report Essentials," Report watch, accessed June 16, 2011, http://www.reportwatch.net/reportessentials/.

A report recommending an in-house training department uses a SWOT analysis to support its recommendation:

Advantages of In-House Training
Disadvantages of In-House Training
Competitor Training Businesses
Opportunities for Training Expansion

This report switches the order of threats (Competitor Training Businesses) and opportunities to end with positive information.

General to particular or particular to general General to particular starts with the problem as it affects the organization or as it manifests itself in general and then moves to a discussion of the parts of the problem and solutions to each of these parts. Particular to general starts with the problem as the audience defines it and moves to larger issues of which the problem is a part. Both are good patterns when you need to redefine the audience's perception of the problem to solve it effectively.

The directors of a student volunteer organization, VIP, have defined their problem as "not enough volunteers." After studying the subject, the writer is convinced that problems in training, supervision, and campus awareness are responsible for both a high dropout rate and a low recruitment rate. The general-to-particular pattern helps the audience see the problem in a new way:

Why VIP Needs More Volunteers
Why Some VIP Volunteers Drop Out
  Inadequate Training
  Inadequate Supervision
  Feeling That VIP Requires Too Much Time
  Feeling That the Work Is Too Emotionally Demanding
Why Some Students Do Not Volunteer
  Feeling That VIP Requires Too Much Time
  Feeling That the Work Is Too Emotionally Demanding
  Preference for Volunteering with Another Organization
  Lack of Knowledge about VIP Opportunities
How VIP Volunteers Are Currently Trained and Supervised
Time Demands on VIP Volunteers
Emotional Demands on VIP Volunteers
Ways to Increase Volunteer Commitment and Motivation
  Improving Training and Supervision
  Improving the Flexibility of Volunteers' Hours
  Providing Emotional Support to Volunteers
  Providing More Information about Community Needs and VIP Services

Geographic or spatial In a geographic or spatial pattern, you discuss problems and solutions by units according to their physical arrangement. Move from office to office, building to building, factory to factory, state to state, region to region, etc.

A sales report uses a geographic pattern of organization:

Sales Have Risen in the European Community
Sales Are Flat in Eastern Europe
Sales Have Fallen Sharply in the Middle East

Sales Are Off to a Strong Start in Africa
Sales Have Risen Slightly in Asia
Sales Have Fallen Slightly in South America
Sales Are Steady in North America

Functional In functional patterns, discuss the problems and solutions of each functional unit. For example, a small business might organize a report to its venture capitalists by the categories of research, production, and marketing. A government report might divide data into the different functions an agency performed, taking each in turn:

Major Accomplishments FY 12
  Regulation
  Education
  Research
  International coordination

Chronological A chronological report records events in the order in which they happened or are planned to happen. Many progress reports are organized chronologically:

Work Completed in October
Work Planned for November

If you choose this pattern, be sure you do not let the chronology obscure significant points or trends.

Specific Varieties of Reports

Informative, recommendation, and justification reports will be more successful when you work with the audience's expectations for that kind of report.

Informative and closure reports **Informative** and **closure reports** summarize completed work or research that does not result in action or recommendation.

Informative reports often include the following elements:

- Introductory paragraph summarizing the problems or successes of the project.
- Purpose and scope section(s) giving the purpose of the report and indicating what aspects of the topic it covers.
- Chronological account of how the problem was discovered, what was done, and what the results were.
- Concluding paragraph with suggestions for later action. In a recommendation report, the recommendations would be based on proof. In contrast, the suggestions in a closure or informative report are not proved in detail.

Figure 18.2 presents this kind of informative closure report.

Closure reports also allow a firm to document the alternatives it has considered before choosing a final design.

Figure 18.2 An Informative Memo Report Describing How a Company Solved a Problem

March 14, 2012

To: Donna S. Kienzler

From: Sara A. Ratterman SAR

Informal short reports use letter or memo format.

Subject: Recycling at Bike Nashbar

First paragraph summarizes main points.

Two months ago, Bike Nashbar began recycling its corrugated cardboard boxes. The program was easy to implement and actually saves the company a little money compared to our previous garbage pickup.

Purpose and scope of report.

In this report, I will explain how and why Bike Nashbar's program was initiated, how the program works and what it costs, and why other businesses should consider similar programs.

Bold headings.

The Problem of Too Many Boxes and Not Enough Space in Bike Nashbar

Cause of problem.

Every week, Bike Nashbar receives about 40 large cardboard boxes containing bicycles and other merchandise. As many boxes as possible would be stuffed into the trash bin behind the building, which also had to accommodate all the other solid waste the shop produces. Boxes that didn't fit in the trash bin ended up lying around the shop, blocking doorways, and taking up space needed for customers' bikes. The trash bin was emptied only once a week, and by that time, even more boxes would have arrived.

Triple space before heading.

The Importance of Recycling Cardboard Rather than Throwing It Away

Double space after heading.

Arranging for more trash bins or more frequent pickups would have solved the immediate problem at Bike Nashbar but would have done nothing to solve the problem created by throwing away so much trash in the first place.

Double space between paragraphs within heading.

Further seriousness of problem.

According to David Crogen, sales representative for Waste Management, Inc., 75% of all solid waste in Columbus goes to landfills. The amount of trash the city collects has increased 150% in the last five years. Columbus's landfill is almost full. In an effort to encourage people and businesses to recycle, the cost of dumping trash in the landfill is doubling from $4.90 a cubic yard to $9.90 a cubic yard next week. Next January, the price will increase again, to $12.95 a cubic yard. Crogen believes that the amount of trash can be reduced by cooperation between the landfill and the power plant and by recycling.

How Bike Nashbar Started Recycling Cardboard

Capitalize first letter of major words in heading.

Solution.

Waste Management, Inc., is the country's largest waste processor. After reading an article about how committed Waste Management, Inc., is to waste reduction and recycling, I decided to see whether Waste Management could recycle our boxes. Corrugated cardboard (which is what Bike Nashbar's boxes are made of) is almost 100% recyclable, so we seemed to be a good candidate for recycling.

Figure 18.2 An Informative Memo Report Describing How a Company Solved a Problem *(Continued)*

Donna S. Kienzler
March 14, 2012
Page 2

Reader's name, date, page number.

To get the service started, I met with a friendly sales rep, David Crogen, that same afternoon to discuss the service.

Waste Management, Inc., took care of all the details. Two days later, Bike Nashbar was recycling its cardboard.

How the Service Works and What It Costs

Talking heads tell reader what to expect in each section.

Details of solution.

Waste Management took away our existing 8-cubic-yard garbage bin and replaced it with two 4-yard bins. One of these bins is white and has "cardboard only" printed on the outside; the other is brown and is for all other solid waste. The bins are emptied once a week, with the cardboard going to the recycling plant and the solid waste going to the landfill or power plant.

Since Bike Nashbar was already paying more than $60 a week for garbage pickup, our basic cost stayed the same. (Waste Management can absorb the extra overhead only if the current charge is at least $60 a week.) The cost is divided 80/20 between the two bins: 80% of the cost pays for the bin that goes to the landfill and power plant; 20% covers the cardboard pickup. Bike Nashbar actually receives $5.00 for each ton of cardboard it recycles.

Double space between paragraphs.

Each employee at Bike Nashbar is responsible for putting all the boxes he or she opens in the recycling bin. Employees must follow these rules:

- The cardboard must have the word "corrugated" printed on it, along with the universal recycling symbol.

Indented lists provide visual variety.

- The boxes must be broken down to their flattest form. If they aren't, they won't all fit in the bin and Waste Management would be picking up air when it could pick up solid cardboard. The more boxes that are picked up, the more money that will be made.
- No other waste except corrugated cardboard can be put in the recycling bin. Other materials could break the recycling machinery or contaminate the new cardboard.
- The recycling bin is to be kept locked with a padlock provided by Waste Management so that vagrants don't steal the cardboard and lose money for Waste Management and Bike Nashbar.

(Continued)

Figure 18.2 An Informative Memo Report Describing How a Company Solved a Problem *(Concluded)*

Donna S. Kienzler
March 14, 2012
Page 3

Dis-advantages of solution.

Minor Problems with Running the Recycling Program

The only problems we've encountered have been minor ones of violating the rules. Sometimes employees at the shop forget to flatten boxes, and air instead of cardboard gets picked up. Sometimes people forget to lock the recycling bin. When the bin is left unlocked, people do steal the cardboard, and plastic cups and other solid waste get dumped in the cardboard bin. I've posted signs where the key to the bin hangs, reminding employees to empty and fold boxes and relock the bin after putting cardboard in it. I hope this will turn things around and these problems will be solved.

Advantages of solution.

Advantages of the Recycling Program

The program is a great success. Now when boxes arrive, they are unloaded, broken down, and disposed of quickly. It is a great relief to get the boxes out of our way, and knowing that we are making a contribution to saving our environment builds pride in ourselves and Bike Nashbar.

Our company depends on a clean, safe environment for people to ride their bikes in. Now we have become part of the solution. By choosing to recycle and reduce the amount of solid waste our company generates, we can save money while gaining a reputation as a socially responsible business.

Why Other Companies Should Adopt Similar Programs

Argues that her company's experience is relevant to other companies.

Businesses and institutions in Franklin County currently recycle less than 4% of the solid waste they produce. David Crogen tells me he has over 8,000 clients in Columbus alone, and he acquires new ones every day. Many of these businesses can recycle a large portion of their solid waste at no additional cost. Depending on what they recycle, they may even get a little money back.

The environmental and economic benefits of recycling as part of a comprehensive waste reduction program are numerous. Recycling helps preserve our environment. We can use the same materials over and over again, saving natural resources such as trees, fuel, and metals and decreasing the amount of solid waste in landfills. By conserving natural resources, recycling helps the U.S. become less dependent on imported raw materials. Crogen predicts that Columbus will be on a 100% recycling system by the year 2020. I strongly hope that his prediction will come true.

Recommendation reports Recommendation reports evaluate two or more alternatives and recommend one of them. (Doing nothing or delaying action can be one of the alternatives.)

Recommendation reports normally open by explaining the decision to be made, listing the alternatives, and explaining the criteria. In the body of the report, each alternative will be evaluated according to the criteria using one of the two comparison/contrast patterns. Discussing each alternative separately is better when one alternative is clearly superior, when the criteria interact, or when each alternative is indivisible. If the choice depends on the weight given to each criterion, you may want to discuss each alternative under each criterion.

Whether your recommendation should come at the beginning or the end of the report depends on your audience and the culture of your organization. Most audiences want the "bottom line" up front. However, if the audience will find your recommendation hard to accept, you may want to delay your recommendation until the end of the report when you have given all your evidence.

Justification reports **Justification reports** justify a purchase, investment, hiring, or change in policy. If your organization has a standard format for justification reports, follow that format. If you can choose your headings and organization, use this pattern when your proposal will be easy for your audience to accept:

1. **Indicate what you're asking for and why it's needed.** Since the audience has not asked for the report, you must link your request to the organization's goals.
2. **Briefly give the background of the problem or need.**
3. **Explain each of the possible solutions.** For each, give the cost and the advantages and disadvantages.
4. **Summarize the action needed to implement your recommendation.** If several people will be involved, indicate who will do what and how long each step will take.
5. **Ask for the action you want.**

If the reader will be reluctant to grant your request, use this variation of the problem-solving pattern described in Chapter 11:

1. **Describe the organizational problem (which your request will solve).** Use specific examples to prove the seriousness of the problem.
2. **Show why easier or less expensive solutions will not solve the problem.**
3. **Present your solution impersonally.**
4. **Show that the disadvantages of your solution are outweighed by the advantages.**
5. **Summarize the action needed to implement your recommendation.** If several people will be involved, indicate who will do what and how long each step will take.
6. **Ask for the action you want.**

How much detail you need to give in a justification report depends on the corporate culture and on your audience's knowledge of and attitude toward your recommendation. Many organizations expect justification reports to be short—only one or two pages. Other organizations may expect longer reports with much more detailed budgets and a full discussion of the problem and each possible solution.

The Importance of Annual Reports

A survey, conducted by WithumSmith & Brown and MGT Design Inc., found that the annual report is the most important publication that a company produces. To understand the value of annual reports, the survey asked individual investors, portfolio managers, and securities analysts (the primary audiences for annual reports) about the ways that they read and use the reports to make decisions.

Here are some of their findings:

- 75% said the annual report is the most important publication that a company produces.
- 79% said the annual report is an important tool for investment decisions.
- 66% prefer photos and/or illustrations in annual reports.
- 90% said that important concerns facing the industry, such as environment issues and corporate governance, should be addressed in the report.
- 81% prefer a print version over electronic versions. Respondents said the print documents were easier to read, highlight, annotate, and file.

Taken together, these findings suggest that the annual report is an important communication for organizations and well worth the time spent creating it.

Adapted from Kirk Holderbaum, "Survey Reveals Importance of Corporate Annual Reports," Commerce & Industry Association of New Jersey, accessed May 29, 2011, 66, http://www.withum.com/fileSave/Commerce_Kirk_0207.pdf.

PRESENTING INFORMATION EFFECTIVELY IN REPORTS LO 18-4

The advice about style in Chapter 5 also applies to reports, with three exceptions:

1. **Use a fairly formal style, without contractions or slang.**
2. **Avoid the word *you*.** In a document with multiple audiences, it will not be clear who *you* is. Instead, use the company's name.

Who Did What?

The passive verbs and impersonal constructions in U.S. reports of coal mine disasters ("coal dust was permitted to accumulate" and "an accident occurred") suggest that accidents are inevitable. Who permitted the coal dust to accumulate? What could have been done to prevent the accumulation? Mine disaster reports contain sentences like the following: "The . . . fatality occurred when the victim proceeded into an area . . . before the roof was supported." *Why* did the man who was killed go into the area? Had a supervisor checked to see that the roof was supported? Who ordered what?

British reports of mine disasters, in contrast, focus on people and what they did to limit the damage from the disaster. Perhaps as a result, British mines have a much lower incidence of disasters than do U.S. coal mines.

Adapted from Beverly A. Sauer, "Sense and Sensibility in Technical Documentation: How Feminist Interpretation Strategies Can Save Lives in the Nation's Mines," *Journal of Business and Technical Communication* 7 (January 1993): 63–83.

3. **Include in the report all the definitions and documents needed to understand the recommendations.** The multiple audiences for reports include readers who may consult the document months or years from now; they will not share your special knowledge. Explain acronyms and abbreviations the first time they appear. Explain as much of the history or background of the problem as necessary. Add as appendixes previous documents on which you are building.

The following points apply to any kind of writing, but they are particularly important in reports:

1. Use clear, engaging writing.
2. Keep repetition to a minimum.
3. Introduce sources and visuals.
4. Use forecasting, transitions, topic sentences, and headings to make your organization clear to your reader.

Let's look at each of these principles as they apply to reports.

1. Use Clear, Engaging Writing.

Most people want to be able to read a report quickly while still absorbing its important points. You can help them do this by using accurate diction. Not-quite-right word choices are particularly damaging in reports, which may be skimmed by readers who know little about the subject. Occasionally you can simply substitute a word:

Incorrect: With these recommendations, we can overcome the solutions to our problem.

Correct: With these recommendations, we can overcome our problem.

Also correct: With these recommendations, we can solve our problem.

Sometimes you'll need to completely recast the sentence.

Incorrect: The first problem with the incentive program is that middle managers do not use good interpersonal skills in implementing it. For example, the hotel chef openly ridicules the program. As a result, the kitchen staff fear being mocked if they participate in the program.

Better: The first problem with the incentive program is that some middle managers undercut it. For example, the hotel chef openly ridicules the program. As a result, the kitchen staff fear being mocked if they participate in the program.

A strong writing style is especially important when you are preparing a report that relies on a wealth of statistics. Most people have difficulty absorbing number after number. To help your audiences, use text to highlight the message you want the statistics to convey. Examples and action-oriented details keep the audience engaged.

Warren Buffett says this about clear, engaging writing in annual reports, which can certainly present a wealth of statistics:

> I really have a mental picture of my sisters in mind and it's Dear Doris and Birdie. And I envision them as people who have a very significant part of their net worth in the company, who are bright but who have been away for a year and who are not business specialists.
>
> And once a year I tell them what's going on. . . . I think that should be the mental approach.[19]

2. Keep Repetition to a Minimum.

Some repetition in reports is legitimate. The conclusion restates points made in the body of the report; the recommendations appear in the transmittal, the abstract or executive summary, and in the recommendations sections of the report. However, repetitive references to earlier material ("As we have already seen") may indicate that the document needs to be reorganized. Read the document through at a single sitting to make sure that any repetition serves a useful purpose.

Legal Liability and Report Drafts

During civil litigation (such as a tort case charging that a product has injured a user), rough drafts may be important to establish the state of mind and intent of a document's drafters.

To protect the company, one lawyer recommends labeling all but the final draft "Preliminary Draft: Subject to Change." That way, if there's ever a lawsuit, the company will be able to argue that only the final report, not the drafts, should be used as evidence.

Adapted from Elizabeth McCord, "'But What You Really Meant Was . . . Multiple Drafts and Legal Liability," paper presented at the Association for Business Communication Midwest Regional Conference, Akron, OH, April 3–5, 1991.

3. Introduce Sources and Visuals.

The first time you cite an author's work, use his or her full name as it appears on the work: "Thomas L. Friedman points out. . . . " In subsequent citations, use only the last name: "Friedman shows. . . . " Use active rather than passive verbs.

The verb you use indicates your attitude toward the source. *Says* and *writes* are neutral. *Points out, shows, suggests, discovers,* and *notes* suggest that you agree with the source. Words such as *claims, argues, contends, believes,* and *alleges* distance you from the source. At a minimum, they suggest that you know that not everyone agrees with the source; they are also appropriate to report the views of someone with whom you disagree.

The report text should refer to all visuals:

As Table 1 shows, . . .
See Figure 4.

4. Use Forecasting, Transitions, Topic Sentences, and Headings.

Forecasts are overviews that tell the audience what you will discuss in a section or in the entire report. Make your forecast easy to read by telling the audience how many points there are and using bullets or numbers (either words or figures). In the following example, the first sentence in the revised paragraph tells the reader to look for four points; the numbers separate the four points clearly. This overview paragraph also makes a contract with readers, who now expect to read about tax benefits first and employee benefits last.

Paragraph without numbers:

Employee stock ownership programs (ESOPs) have several advantages. They provide tax benefits for the company. ESOPs also create tax benefits for employees and for lenders. They provide a defense against takeovers. In some organizations, productivity increases because workers now have a financial stake in the company's profits. ESOPs are an attractive employee benefit and help the company hire and retain good employees.

Revised paragraph with numbers:

Employee stock ownership programs (ESOPs) provide four benefits. First, ESOPs provide tax benefits for the company, its employees, and lenders to the plan. Second, ESOPs help create a defense against takeovers. Third, ESOPs may increase productivity by giving workers a financial stake in the company's profits. Fourth, as an attractive employee benefit, ESOPs help the company hire and retain good employees.

Transitions are words, phrases, or sentences that tell audiences whether the discussion is continuing on the same point or shifting points.

There are economic advantages, too.

(Tells audience that we are still discussing advantages but that we have now moved to economic advantages.)

An alternative to this plan is . . .

(Tells audience that a second option follows.)

The second factor . . .

(Tells audience that the discussion of the first factor is finished.)

These advantages, however, are found only in A, not in B or C.

(Prepares audience for a shift from A to B and C.)

A **topic sentence** introduces or summarizes the main idea of a paragraph. Audiences who skim reports can follow your ideas more easily if each paragraph begins with a topic sentence.

Hard to read (no topic sentence):	Another main use of ice is to keep the fish fresh. Each of the seven kinds of fish served at the restaurant requires one gallon twice a day, for a total of 14 gallons. An additional 6 gallons a day are required for the salad bar.
Better (begins with topic sentence):	Twenty gallons of ice a day are needed to keep food fresh. Of this, the biggest portion (14 gallons) is used to keep the fish fresh. Each of the seven kinds of fish served at the restaurant requires one gallon twice a day. An additional 6 gallons a day are required for the salad bar.

Headings (see Chapter 6) are single words, short phrases, or complete sentences that indicate the topic in each section. A heading must cover all of the material under it until the next heading. For example, *Cost of Tuition* cannot include the cost of books or of room and board; *College Costs* could include all costs. You can have just one paragraph under a heading or several pages. If you do have several pages between headings you may want to consider using subheadings. Use subheadings only when you have two or more divisions within a main heading.

Topic headings focus on the structure of the report. As you can see from the following example, topic headings are vague and give little information.

Recommendation
Problem
  Situation 1
  Situation 2
Causes of the Problem
  Background
  Cause 1
  Cause 2
Recommended Solution

Talking heads, in contrast, tell the audience what to expect. Talking heads, like those in the examples in this chapter, provide a specific overview of each section and of the entire report.

Recommended Reformulation for Vibe Bleach
Problems in Maintaining Vibe's Granular Structure
Solidification during Storage and Transportation
Customer Complaints about "Blocks" of Vibe in Boxes
Why Vibe Bleach "Cakes"
Vibe's Formula
The Manufacturing Process
The Chemical Process of Solidification
Modifications Needed to Keep Vibe Flowing Freely

Headings must be parallel (see Chapter 5); that is, they must use the same grammatical structure. Subheads must be parallel to each other but do not necessarily have to be parallel to subheads under other headings.

Not parallel:

Are Students Aware of VIP?
Current Awareness among Undergraduate Students
Graduate Students
Ways to Increase Volunteer Commitment and Motivation
We Must Improve Training and Supervision
Can We Make Volunteers' Hours More Flexible?
Providing Emotional Support to Volunteers
Provide More Information about Community Needs and VIP Services

Parallel:

Campus Awareness of VIP
Current Awareness among Undergraduate Students
Current Awareness among Graduate Students
Ways to Increase Volunteer Commitment and Motivation
Improving Training and Supervision
Improving the Flexibility of Volunteers' Hours
Providing Emotional Support to Volunteers
Providing More Information about Community Needs and VIP Services

In a complicated report, you may need up to three levels of headings. Figure 18.3 illustrates one way to set up headings. Follow these standard conventions for headings:

- Although the figure shows only one example of each level of headings, in an actual report you would use a subheading only when you had at least two subsections under the next higher heading.
- Avoid having a subhead come immediately after a heading. Instead, some text should follow the main heading before the subheading. (If you have nothing else to say, give an overview of the division.)
- Avoid having a heading or subheading all by itself at the bottom of the page. Instead, have at least one line (preferably two) of type. If there isn't room for a line of type under it, put the heading on the next page.
- Don't use a heading as the antecedent for a pronoun. Instead, repeat the noun.

Figure 18.3 Setting Up Headings in a Single-Spaced Document

Center the title; use bold and a bigger font.

Typing Titles and Headings for Reports *14-point type.*

For the title of a report, use a bold font two point sizes bigger than the largest size in the body of the report. You may want to use an even bigger size or a different font to create an attractive title page. Capitalize the first word and all major words of the title.

Heading for main divisions *Two empty spaces (triple space)*

Typing Headings for Reports *12-point type.*

One empty space (double space)

12-point type for body text

Center main headings, capitalize the first and all major words, and use bold. In single-spaced text, leave two empty spaces before main headings and one after. Also leave an extra space between paragraphs. You may also want to use main headings that are one point size bigger than the body text.

This example provides just one example of each level of heading. However, in a real document, use headings only when you have at least two of them in the document. In a report, you'll have several.

Two empty spaces (triple space)

Typing Subheadings *Bold; left margin*

One empty space

Most reports use subheadings under some main headings. Use subheadings only if you have at least two of them under a given heading. It is OK to use subheadings in some sections and not in others. Normally you'll have several paragraphs under a subheading, but it's OK to have just one paragraph under some subheadings.

12-point type

Subheadings in a report use the same format as headings in letters and memos. Bold subheadings and set them at the left margin. Capitalize the first word and major words. Leave two empty spaces before the subheading and one empty space after it, before the first paragraph under the subheading. Use the same size font as the body paragraphs.

One empty space (normal paragraph spacing)

Period after heading

Typing Further Subdivisions. For a very long report, you may need further subdivisions under a subheading. Bold the further subdivision, capitalizing the first word and major words, and end the phrase with a period. Begin the text on the same line. Use normal spacing between paragraphs. Further subdivide a subheading only if you have at least two such subdivisions under a given subheading. It is OK to use divisions under some subheadings and not under others.

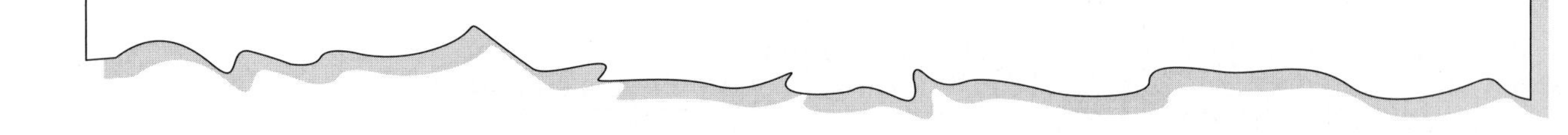

WRITING FORMAL REPORTS LO 18-5

Formal reports are distinguished from informal letter and memo reports by their length and by their components. A full formal report may contain the following components (see Figures 18.4 and 18.5):

- Cover
- Title Page
- Letter or Memo of Transmittal
- Table of Contents
- List of Illustrations
- Executive Summary

Figure 18.4 The Components in a Report Can Vary

More formal ←——	———	——→ Less formal
Cover	Title Page	Introduction
Title Page	Table of Contents	Body
Transmittal	Executive Summary	Conclusions
Table of Contents	Body	Recommendations
List of Illustrations	Introduction	
Executive Summary	Body	
Body	Conclusions	
Introduction	Recommendations	
Body		
Conclusions		
Recommendations		
References/Works Cited		
Appendixes		
Questionnaires		
Interviews		
Computer Printouts		
Related Documents		

http://www.pewinternet.org/

To see examples of the ways in which reports are written and disseminated, visit the Pew Internet & American Life Project at the above website.

The project produces reports on the impact of the Internet on American lives, collecting and analyzing data on real-world developments as they intersect with the virtual world. Following data collection, the results are written into the reports and posted as PDFs to the website.

Visit the Project's web pages to see examples of the ways in which reports are first presented and then rewritten by the press for their audience and purpose.

- Report Body
  - Introduction (Orients the reader to the report. Usually has subheadings for Purpose and Scope; depending on the situation, may also have Limitations, Assumptions, Methods, Criteria, and Definitions.)
  - Background or History of the Problem (Orients the reader to the topic of the report. Serves as a record for later readers of the report.)
  - Body (Presents and interprets data in words and visuals. Analyzes causes of the problem and evaluates possible solutions. Specific headings will depend on the topic of the report.)
  - Conclusions (Summarizes main points of report.)
  - Recommendations (Recommends actions to solve the problem. May be combined with Conclusions; may be put at beginning of body rather than at the end.)
- Notes, References, or Works Cited (Documents sources cited in the report.)
- Appendixes (Provides additional materials that the careful reader may want: transcripts of interviews, copies of questionnaires, tallies of all the questions, complex tables, computer printouts, previous reports.)

As Figure 18.4 shows, not every formal report necessarily has all these components. In addition, some organizations call for additional components or arrange these components in a different order. As you read each section below, you may want to turn to the corresponding pages of the long report in Figure 18.5 to see how the component is set up and how it relates to the total report.

Figure 18.5 A Formal Report

Center all text on the title page.
Use a large font size for the main title.
Use a slightly smaller font size for the subheading.
No punctuation.
Name of audience, job title, organization, city, state, and zip code.
No punctuation.
Name of writer(s), organization, city, state, and zip code.
Date report is released.

Slated for Success

RAC Inc. Expanding to South Korea

Prepared for

Ms. Katie Nichols
CEO of RAC Inc.
Grand Rapids, Michigan, 49503

Prepared by

JASS LLC
Jordan Koole
Alex Kuczera
Shannon Jones
Sean Sterling
Allendale, MI 49401

April 21, 2011

Figure 18.5 A Formal Report *(Continued)*

This student group designed their own letterhead, assuming they were doing this report as consultants.

This letter uses block format.

JASS LLC
1 Campus Drive
Allendale, MI 49401

April 21, 2011

Ms. Katie Nichols, CEO
RAC Inc.
1253 W. Main Street
Grand Rapids, MI 49504

In paragraph 1, release the report. Note when and by whom the report was authorized. Note the report's purpose.

Dear Ms. Nichols:

In this document you will find the report that you requested in March. We have provided key information and made recommendations on a plan of action for the expansion of a RAC Inc. slate tablet manufacturing plant into South Korea.

Give recommendations or thesis of report.

Our analysis of expansion into South Korea covered several important areas that will help you decide whether or not RAC Inc. should expand and build a manufacturing plant in South Korea. To help us make our decision, we looked at the government, economy, culture, and most important the competition. South Korea is a technologically advanced country and its economy is on the rise. Our research has led us to recommend expansion into South Korea. We strongly believe that RAC Inc. can be profitable in the long run and become a successful business in South Korea.

Note sources that were helpful.

JASS LLC used several resources in forming our analysis. The Central Intelligence Agency's *World Factbook*, the U.S. Department of State, World Business Culture, and Kwintessential were all helpful in answering our research questions.

Thank the audience for the opportunity to do the research.

Thank you for choosing JASS to conduct the research into South Korea. If you have any further questions about the research or recommendation please contact us (616-331-1100, info@jass.com) and we will be happy to answer any questions referring to your possible expansion into South Korea at no charge. JASS would be happy to conduct any further research on this issue or any other projects that RAC Inc. is considering. We look forward to building on our relationship with you in the future.

Offer to answer questions about the report.

Sincerely,

Jordan Koole

Jordan Koole
JASS Team Member

Center inital page numbers at the bottom of the page. Use a lowercase roman numeral for initial pages of report.

i

(Continued)

Figure 18.5 A Formal Report *(Continued)*

Main headings are parallel, as are subheadings within a section.

Table of Contents does not list itself.

Table of Contents

Letter of Transmittal i
Executive Summary iii
Introduction 1
  Purpose and Scope 1
  Assumptions 1
  Methods 1
  Limitations 1
  Definitions 1
  Criteria 1
Government 2
  Government Control 2
  Business Regulations 2
  Taxes 3
  Free Trade 3
  Concerns about North Korea 3
  Summary 3
Economy 4
  Economic Growth 4
  GDP and Other Important Economic Measures 5
  Imports and Exports 5
  Dollars and Cents 5
  Summary 5
South Korean Culture 6
  Business Culture 6
  Honor and Respect 6
  Religion 7
  Summary 7
Market Possibilities and Competitors 7
  Technology Use 7
  Competition 8
  Integration 9
  Summary 9
Location, Location, Location 9
Conclusions and Recommendations 10
References 11

Use lowercase roman numerals for initial pages.

Introduction begins on page 1.

Capitalize first letter of each major word in headings.

Indentions show level of heading at a glance.

Line up right margin (justify).

List of Illustrations

Add a "List of Illustrations" at the bottom of the page or on a separate page if the report has many visuals.

Figure 1 South Korea's GDP Growth from 1911 to 2008 4
Figure 2 Comparison of GDP Growth Rates 5
Table 1 Comparison of Specifications for Existing Tablets 8

Figures and tables are numbered independently.

Figure 18.5 A Formal Report *(Continued)*

Report title.

Slated for Success

Many audiences read only the Executive Summary, not the report. Include enough information to give audiences the key points you make.

RAC Inc. Expanding to South Korea

Start with recommendation or thesis.

Executive Summary

To continue growth and remain competitive on a global scale, RAC Inc. should expand its business operations into South Korea. The country is a technologically advanced nation and would provide a strong base for future expansion. Slate tablet competitors of RAC Inc. in South Korea are doing quite well. Since RAC Inc. can compete with them in the United States, we are confident that RAC can remain on par with them in this foreign market.

The research we have done for this project indicates that this expansion will be profitable, primarily because the South Korean economy is flourishing. The workforce in South Korea is large, and finding talented employees to help set up and run the facility will be easy. In addition, the regulations and business structure are similar to those in the United States and will provide an easy transition into this foreign nation. The competition will be fierce; however, we believe that RAC Inc. will be profitable because of its track record with the Notion Tab in the United States.

Provide brief support for recommendations.

To ensure a successful expansion, JASS LLC recommends the following:

1. **RAC Inc. should establish its headquarters and manufacturing plant in Busan.**
   - Purchase a building to have a place to begin manufacturing the Notion Tab.
   - Educate RAC employees about South Korean culture and business practices before they begin working directly with South Koreans to avoid being disrespectful.
   - Explore hiring South Koreans; the available workforce is large.
   - Ensure that the Notion name is appropriate when translated into Korean. If not, change the name to better market the product.
   - Market and sell the product in both Busan and Seoul.
2. **After one year RAC should determine the acceptance and profitability of the expansion.**
   - Conduct a customer satisfaction survey with people who purchased the Notion Tab living in Seoul and Busan to determine the acceptance of the product.
   - Compare and contrast first-year sales with a competitor's similar product.
3. **If the tablet is competitive and profitable, RAC Inc. should expand its product line into all large cities in South Korea.**
   - To gain an edge on the competition, create a marketing plan that will offer the Notion Tab at some discount in the new cities.
   - Explore integrating other RAC Inc. products into South Korea. These products could also be manufactured at the new manufacturing plant in Busan.

Language in the Executive Summary can come from the report. Make sure any repeated language is well-written!

The Abstract or Executive Summary contains the logical skeleton of the report: the recommendation(s) and supporting evidence.

iii

(Continued)

Figure 18.5 A Formal Report *(Continued)*

A running header is optional.

Slated for Success 1

Introduction

Center main headings.

To avoid getting left behind by competition in global expansion, RAC Inc. has contacted JASS LLC to perform an analysis about expanding into South Korea. JASS has researched South Korea to determine if RAC Inc. will be successful in expanding into this foreign market.

"Purpose" and "Scope" can be separate sections if either is long.

Purpose and Scope

RAC Inc. is a successful business in the United States and has had substantial growth over the last five years. With their competitors beginning to venture into foreign markets to gain more global market share, RAC Inc. is looking to expand into the international market as well. The purpose of our research is to decide whether or not RAC Inc. should expand its business into South Korea.

Tell what you discuss and how thoroughly you discuss each topic.

Give topics in the order you'll discuss them.

Topics in "Scope" section should match those in the report.

This report will cover several topics about South Korea including their government, economy, culture, technology market competition, and possible locations. Our research will not include any on-site research in South Korea. We are also not dealing directly with the South Korean people.

List any relevant topics you do not discuss.

Assumptions

Assumptions cannot be proved. But if they are wrong, the report's recommendation may no longer be valid.

The recommendations that we make are based on the assumption that the relationship between North and South Korea will remain the same as of the first part of 2011. We are also assuming that the technological state of South Korea will remain constant and not suffer from a natural disaster or an economic crash. In addition, we assume that the process of expansion into South Korea is the same with RAC Inc. as it has been with other American companies. Another assumption that we are making is that RAC Inc. has a good name brand and is competitive in the United States with Apple, Samsung, LG and other electronic companies.

If you collected original data (surveys, interviews, and observations), tell how you chose your subjects, whatkind of sample you used, and when you collected the information. This report does not use original data; it just provides a brief discussion of significant sources.

Methods

The information in our report comes from online sources and reference books. We found several good sources, but the best information that we obtained came from The Central Intelligence Agency's *World Factbook*, the U.S. Department of State, World Business Culture, and Kwintessential. These resources have given us much useful information on which we have based our recommendation.

These limitations are listed because the students correctly assumed their teacher would want to know them. Limitations such as these would never be listed in a real consulting report, since they would disqualify the firm.

Limitations

If your report has limitations, state them.

The information in the report was limited to what we retrieved from our sources. We were not able to travel to South Korea to conduct on-site research. JASS was also limited by the language barrier that exists between the United States and South Korea. Other limitations exist because we have not been immersed in the Korean culture and have not gotten input from South Koreans on the expansion of companies into their country.

Definitions

Define key terms your audience will need to read your report.

There are a few terms that we use throughout the report that we would like to explain beforehand. The first term is slate tablet, an industry term, which from this point on is referred to as a tablet. Another term we would like to clarify is the city Busan. Some sources referred to it as Pusan. From this point forward, we use only Busan. An abbreviation we use is GDP, which stands for gross domestic product. The South Korean and United States Free Trade Agreement signed in 2007 is abbreviated as KORUS FTA, its official name in the United States government.

Figure 18.5 A Formal Report *(Continued)*

Slated for Success 2

This section outlines the criteria used to make the overall recommendation.

Criteria

JASS LLC has established criteria that need to be favorable before we give a positive recommendation about South Korea. The criteria include the government, economy, culture, and market competition. We have weighted our criteria by percentages:

- Government = 20%
- Economy = 20%
- South Korean culture = 20%
- Market possibilities and competitors = 40%

We will examine each separately and give each criterion a favorable or not favorable recommendation. Market competition is weighted the heaviest and must be favorable or somewhat favorable for us to give a positive recommendation. Market competition can be given a favorable, nonfavorable, or somewhat favorable recommendation based on various external factors in the marketplace. We need a minimum of a 70% total to give a positive recommendation overall.

Triple-space before major headings and double-space after them.

Government

Begin most paragraphs with topic sentences.

South Korea is recognized as a republic government by the rest of the world. A republic government is a democracy where the people have supreme control over the government (South Korea: Political structure, 2009). This foundation makes it similar to the United States' democracy. There is a national government as well as provincial-level governments (similar to state-level governments) with different branches. Larger cities, like Seoul and Busan, have their own city government as well. The government is considered multipartied and has multiple parties vying for positions (South Korea: Political structure, 2009). The Republic of South Korea shares its power among three branches of government, thus providing checks and balances inside the government. The three branches of the government are the presidential, legislative, and judicial (U.S. Department of State, 2010). In this section, we will discuss government control, business regulations, taxes, free trade, and concerns about North Korea.

List subtopics in the order in which they are discussed.

Government Control

It's OK to have subheadings under some headings and not others.

The Grand National Party (GNP) controls the major policy-making branches of the government. President Lee Myung-Bak and Prime Minister Kim Hwang-Sik are both members of the GNP. Winning control of the National Assembly in April 2008 (South Korea: Political structure, 2009), the GNP is considered the conservative party in South Korea and is similar to the Republican Party in the United States. Their policies favor conservatism and are considered pro-business (Grand National Party, 2011). RAC Inc. should not expect much interference from the government with their business venture into South Korea, unless the GNP loses control of the government in the next election.

Use subheadings only when you have two or more sections.

Business Regulations

South Korea ranks 16th on the ease of doing business index (World Bank Group, 2011a). This index measures the regulations that a government imposes on businesses and how easy it is to start and run a business in a given country. Factors this index measures include the ease of starting a business, doing taxes, and enforcing contracts. For comparison, the United States is ranked fifth on this list (World Bank Group, 2011b). While there are more regulations on business in South Korea, they are still near the top of the list. The relatively low rating on regulation can be due in part to the Grand National Party controlling the government. There are a few general regulations that RAC Inc. should know before going into South Korea. For more specific business regulations, RAC Inc. may need to do further research before expanding.

(Continued)

Figure 18.5 A Formal Report *(Continued)*

Slated for Success 3

South Korea has been known for having long workweeks and long working days. South Korea leads the world in hours worked with an average of 2,357 hours per worker per year (Olson, 2008). However, the government has recently passed laws regulating the workweek. In 2003, they shortened their workweek from six days down to the traditional five-day workweek within the public sector. They also shortened the workweek for the public sector down to 40 hours a week (Kirk, 2001). The private sector, however, continues to work long hours because it has not yet been regulated. But the government hinted at regulating the private sector in the future when the public sector law was passed (Kirk, 2001). Nonetheless, no legislation has come through the National Assembly, and South Koreans continue to be the hardest-working people in the world.

Period goes outside of parenthesis.

The South Korean government has also been known to have strong import restrictions placed on companies (Central Intelligence Agency, 2011). As a result, companies have been forced to gather resources from South Korea instead of importing them. This approach helped South Korea grow its GDP and other economic health measures. It has also influenced the South Korean consumers' view of foreign products.

RAC Inc. may need to be concerned about these regulations when expanding to South Korea. In general, however, regulations on business in South Korea are similar to those of the United States because of the closeness in government structures. While the conservative Grand National Party is in control of the major branches of the government, they are likely to shoot down any attempts at business regulations. The result is that future regulations on business in South Korea will remain low.

Taxes

The total tax rate in South Korea is lower than that of the United States. (The total tax rate measures all of the mandatory taxes that a company has to pay on their operations in a given country.) The United States has a 46% tax rate, while South Korea has only a 29% tax rate (World Bank Group, 2011a, 2011b). This lower rate means that a company is able to keep more of their profits in South Korea than in the United States. Lower taxes are a positive factor for RAC Inc. to consider.

Free Trade

In June 2007, South Korea and the United States announced that they had drafted a free trade agreement with each other known as the KORUS FTA (Manyin, 2007). Even though it has been agreed upon since that date, neither nation's legislature has ratified the agreement. Ratification stalled in 2007 because of concerns by a Democratic-controlled congress in the United States and opposition lead by current President Barack Obama. In 2010, President Obama got both sides back together and drafted a new agreement that is pending the approval of both nations' legislatures (AFP, 2010). The highlights of the agreement are an immediate reduction of tariffs and duty-free trade on 95% of all goods exchanged between the countries in three years. In 10 years, all tariffs will be eliminated between the two nations. There would be access between the two countries' service sectors, allowing for faster international deliveries between the two nations (Office of the U.S. Trade Representative, 2011).

The KORUS FTA will be a positive for potential companies expanding into the region by creating a stable political and economic relationship between the United States and South Korea. KORUS FTA will give companies an open door into the region and an ability to conduct business with little to no interference between the governments. However, both nations' legislatures need to ratify the agreement before this trade agreement can make positive impacts for RAC Inc.

Concerns about North Korea

North and South Korea have been separated since 1945. These two countries were at war between 1950 and 1953. Since this conflict, there have been moments of tension, including some moments in 2010. Currently there is no escalation of hostilities (U.S. Department of State, 2010). We are assuming this state of conflict will not change in the near future. Improved relations would be ideal for the region, the world, and RAC Inc.

Figure 18.5 A Formal Report *(Continued)*

Slated for Success 4

Summary

This team provides a "summary" section at the end of each major section to highlight important points.

JASS LLC believes that South Korea's politics favor RAC Inc. expanding into the country. The Grand National Party allows for a favorable government for all businesses. South Korea has low regulations by the government, and they have lower taxes. The restrictions on importing and future workweek regulations are factors that need to be researched more by RAC Inc. if they decide to expand their operations. The KORUS FTA shows the stable relations between the United States and South Korea. The situation with North Korea is as stable as can be at this time. These factors allow JASS to give the government criterion a favorable rating.

Economy

Headings must cover everything under that heading until the next one.

South Korea's economy is considered one of the largest in the world. According to the CIA's *World Factbook*, the country recently became part of the top 20 economies in the world. They are considered a high-tech industrialized country (2011). Major industries in South Korea's economy include electronics, telecommunications, automobile production, chemicals, ship building, and the steel industries. Natural resources from South Korea include coal, tungsten, graphite, molybdenum, lead, and hydropower (U.S. Department of State, 2010). Not only is South Korea one of the largest economies in the world, it is one of the fastest growing. Economic growth, along with the GDP, imports and exports, and currency will be addressed in this section.

Economic Growth

Capitalize all main words of headings and subheadings.

World War II and the Korean War ravished the country and its economic base, and the country has had to rebuild its entire economy. Their GDP was among the poorest in the world in 1960. Since then, South Korea has had record growth in economic measures such as GDP and GDP per capita (South Korea's GDP Growth, 2010). According to the CIA's *World Factbook*, "a system of close government and business ties, including directed credit and import restrictions, made this success possible. The government promoted the import of raw materials and technology at the expense of consumer goods, and encouraged savings and investment over consumption" (2011). Figure 1 shows how the economy of South Korea has grown over time using GDP as a measure.

Refer to figure in text. Tell what point it makes.

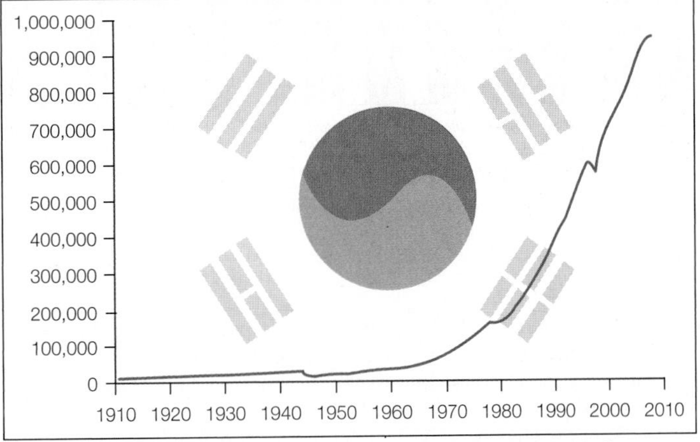

Figure 1: South Korea's GDP (PPP) Growth from 1911 to 2008 (Source: South Korea's GDP Growth, 2010)

Number figures and tables independently.

Cite source of data.

(Continued)

Figure 18.5 A Formal Report *(Continued)*

Since the 1960s, the GDP has had only one dip, a result of the Asian Economic crisis in the late 1990s that affected most Asian countries. In 2004, South Korea became a part of the trillion-dollar economy club, making them one of the world's top economies (Central Intelligence Agency, 2011).

However the economy faces challenges in maintaining steady growth in the future. These challenges include an aging population, inflexible workforce, and an overdependence on exports. Right now, though, South Korea's economy continues to grow. Their industrial production growth rate was 12.1% in 2010, making them the 11th fastest-growing nation in the production industry. In 2010, their GDP grew by 6.8%, the 28th largest growth of GDP in the world (Central Intelligence Agency, 2011). This growth makes South Korea a viable place of expansion.

GDP and Other Important Economic Measures

The official GDP of South Korea was $1.467 trillion in 2010 (Central Intelligence Agency, 2011). This GDP is the 13th highest in the world. GDP measures the total value of goods produced by a country's economy. Figure 2 shows a comparison of GDP growth rates for top countries. GDP per capita in South Korea is $30,200, which is the 44th largest in the world. This measures the output of goods and services per person in the country. It is also an indicator of the average worker's

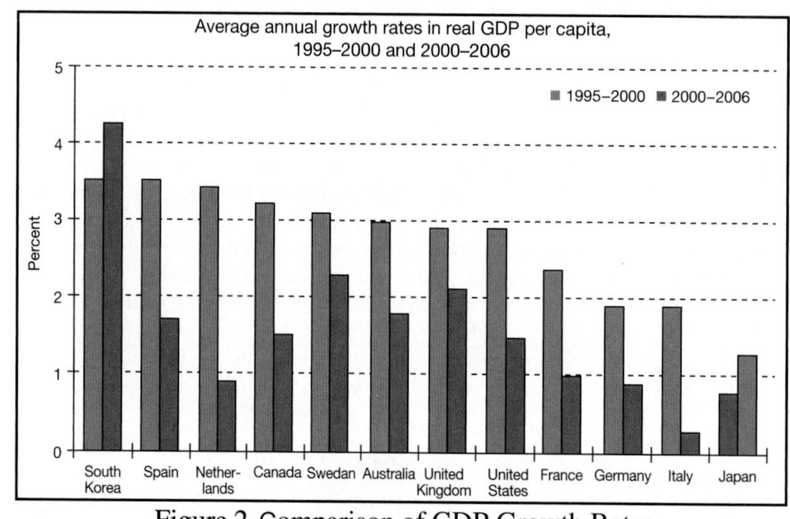

Label both axes of graphs. See chapter 16 for more information on creating data displays.

Figure 2: Comparison of GDP Growth Rates
(Source: U.S. Bureau of Labor Statistics, 2008)

Number figures consecutively throughout the report.

Figure captions need to be descriptive.

salary in the country. South Korea only has 15% of their population living in poverty. They have a labor force of 24.62 million which is the 25th largest labor force in the world, with an unemployment rate of 3.3% (Central Intelligence Agency, 2011). These numbers need to be considered when starting operations in South Korea. South Korea also has a service-driven economy with 57.6% of the country's GDP output in the service industry and 68.4% of the labor force employed in the service industry (Central Intelligence Agency, 2011). All of these numbers and high world rankings of the economic measures show that South Korea has a stable and healthy economy where a business could prosper.

Figure 18.5 A Formal Report *(Continued)*

Imports and Exports

The South Korean economy has grown exponentially because of the government's policy on exporting products instead of importing them. As a result, South Korea has traditionally had more exports than imports. They are the world's seventh largest exporter: $466.3 billion dollars' worth of goods in 2010. The countries they export to are China, the United States, Japan, and Hong Kong (Central Intelligence Agency, 2011). Exporting has helped the South Korean economy grow into what it is today and has made it an important economy in the global marketplace.

With the world becoming more globalized, South Korea now also imports a large amount of goods. South Korea is practically on an island because the only land border is with North Korea, which is not connected to the global marketplace. These factors have made it more important over time for South Korea to import products and relax the government's stance on limiting imports. South Korea is the ninth largest importer in the world. The total dollar amount of imports was $417.9 billion in 2010. Major import partners are China, Japan, the United States, Saudi Arabia, and Australia (Central Intelligence Agency, 2011).

South Korea exports were $48.4 billion greater than its imports while trading with its partners throughout the world (Central Intelligence Agency, 2011). This balance has stayed positive helping the South Korean economy grow. This balance can also be taken as a sign that South Korea's economy is healthy and has useful products and services for their people and consumers worldwide.

Dollars and Cents

South Korea's currency is the won. Asian currencies are traditionally inflated compared to the United States dollar and other currencies around the world. The won is no exception. According to *MSN Money,* the exchange rate as of April 10, 2011, was 1090.513 won to 1 American dollar (KRWUS, 2011).

Summary

With all of these economic factors, JASS LLC believes that the economy is strong enough to support expansion. South Korea has been one of the world's fastest-growing economic markets and has become a major player in today's global economy. All measures and statistics of the economy lead JASS to give a favorable rating to the economy of South Korea.

South Korean Culture

For RAC Inc. to be successful in South Korea, they need to understand its people and culture. Unlike the United States with its numerous cultures, South Korea is primarily made up of South Koreans. Their family heritage and customs are extremely important to them, passing down through generations (Life, n.d.). South Korean society is a class system primarily based on economic status, but also partly based on education. Major status symbols are the size of one's residence, whether it is a house or a condominium, having a chauffeur, and the style and quality of one's clothes (Advameg, Inc., 2011).

Not only is South Korean society based on a class system, but there is also a long tradition of male superiority, in public, though not private, situations. In this section, we will report findings about the business culture, honor and respect, and religion as it relates to RAC's interests.

Outlines subsections for this part of report

(Continued)

Figure 18.5 A Formal Report *(Continued)*

Slated for Success 7

Business Culture

Division of labor by gender is something that RAC Inc. should be extremely aware of, because of its impact on the workforce and social patterns. In public, men are the household head (*boju*) making decisions for their wives and daughters, and women are expected to be submissive. However in private settings, husbands tend to leave the decision making to their wives (Kwintessential, 2010).

Many South Koreans, however, believe that women's work is to take care of the home and house work, even if they work outside the home. Women doing the same job as men are paid only 63.4% of what their male counterparts earn (Advameg, Inc., 2011). RAC Inc. may see this as being sexist, but for many South Koreans, it is an integral part of their culture.

When hiring, many South Koreans rely on social connections for new employees, especially in small companies. Larger companies tend to hire headhunters for finding candidates in upper-level management. South Korean job advancement reflects a strong tradition of seniority, and sometimes will bypass qualified women for a man with higher seniority. New or empty job positions that need to be filled will first be filled by the most senior of employees before someone from the outside is brought in. Only in more recent times is this tradition being challenged (World Business Culture, n.d.).

Use "n.d." for a source with no date.

In the United States, many important meeting and business deals happen in an office, whereas in South Korea these happen in bars and restaurants. Entertainment is as much a part of their culture as it is of their business (Kwintessential, 2010). If RAC employees are invited for dinner, they should accept the invitation. While out, many South Koreans are apt to decide if RAC employees are trustworthy and honorable, thus deciding if they will do business with them or not. Although it may be considered taboo to drink while doing business in America, the Koreans enjoy their alcohol and want to share it with people with whom they wish to do business. They will not look poorly on RAC employees if they don't but joining South Koreans could help build goodwill (World Business Culture, n.d.).

Honor and Respect

Honor and respect work hand-in-hand with Korean culture. Their values stem from their ancestors, elders, and belief in Confucianism (see Religion). These follow them into the workplace where they value collective group harmony and respect for authority, as well as embracing the importance of family, clan, and friendship (World Business Culture, n.d.). When American companies come to South Korea, the traditional values can cause tension between the two styles of management. Being on time, knowing facts (especially technical details), having patience, presenting gifts with both hands, and thanking Koreans with small gifts are things to keep in mind to be both honorable and respectful (Kwintessential, 2010). Something as small as a business card holds a great deal of honor to many Koreans; it is taboo to either write on or fold them (World Business Culture, n.d.).

South Korean managers have a primary goal of encouraging their employees to work together as a unit. They spend most of their day ensuring that the team has a good working relationship. Managers also take a holistic interest in their employees, including their personal lives (World Business Culture, n.d.). This approach contrasts to how American companies may work.

Religion

South Korea has a wide range of religious beliefs, including Shamanism, Confucianism, Buddhism, Christianity, and Islam. Shamanism has evolved from indigenous folk; they believe in the existence of a myriad of gods (such as mountain, house, and fire) and spirits of the dead, all of which influence people's fortunes. Korean Buddhists believe that human suffering is caused mainly by desire; therefore, they try to reach enlightenment by cultivating an attitude of detachment. Others try to seek fulfillment by offering prayers to Kwanum, the Bodhisattva of Compassion. Within Christianity, Catholicism and Protestantism have became the two most popular (Advameg, Inc., 2011).

Figure 18.5 A Formal Report *(Continued)*

Slated for Success 8

Confucianism emphasizes propriety in the five sets of human relationships between sovereign and subject, father and son, husband and wife, senior and junior, and friend and friend. It is also a political and social philosophy that emphasizes the values of *in* (translated as "human-heartedness"). Death and the afterlife are other areas of strong involvement from South Koreans. They believe in ancestral spirits and observe Confucian rituals concerning funerals, mourning practices, and memorial services (Advameg, Inc., 2011).

Summary

Although the culture of South Korean can be vastly different from that of the United Stares, RAC Inc. can overcome these differences. JASS recommends that additional education in Korean culture and business practices be given to any RAC employee that would be directly doing business with them to prevent disrespect. As for religious practices, they are similar to what exists in the United States, though RAC may have to allow special days off work for religious ceremonies. Being honorable and respectful is at the heart of Korean culture and should not be difficult for RAC to adapt. JASS finds the culture favorable for expanding into South Korea.

Market Possibilities and Competitors

Tablets are one of the newest products to emerge in the last few years and are growing in popularity. The tablet is marketed as a computer that is more mobile than a laptop, with the ease of use of a smartphone (Ogg, 2010). With app development supported by several companies, tablets constantly offer new features.

Use author's name in parentheses when it isn't introduced in the sentence.

Currently, the most popular product around the world, with millions of products sold, is Apple's iPad and iPad 2 (iPad 2, 2011). This product, along with products from Samsung, LG, Motorola, and other companies, will create a tough foreign market for RAC to enter. However, since RAC Inc. is competing with these companies and their products in the United States, a successful integration of RAC's Notion Tab is definitely possible. In this section, we will cover information on technology use in South Korea, competition—LG and Samsung—and integration of the Notion Tab.

Technology Use

Tablets are one of the fastest-growing devices in the technology field worldwide; South Koreans have been quick to embrace this technology. In general, the country is on the cutting edge with new technologies such as tablets and NFC (near field communication). Earlier this decade, a greater number of South Korean homes had faster Internet connections than United States homes (Borland & Kanellos, 2004). As of 2009, the year with the latest data, South Korea has the 11th most Internet users worldwide, with 39.4 million (Central Intelligence Agency, 2011).

About 90% of South Koreans own a cellular phone (Koreans love, 2009). Along with the normal calling and texting, they also have Digital Multimedia Broadcasting (DMB), which is used for watching videos, listening to radio, and datacasting (Cho, 2006). The country is set up nicely for technology companies like RAC Inc. to produce and sell their products.

(Continued)

Figure 18.5 A Formal Report *(Continued)*

Competition

Since RAC Inc. has decided what specifications their Notion Tab will have, they should understand what the competition offers with their tablets. Currently, LG and Samsung are the leading competition for RAC Inc. in South Korea. The current specs for LG's G-Slate, Samsung's Galaxy Tab and Apple's iPad 2 are as outlined in Table 1. Refer to figure or table before it appears in text.

Specs	G-Slate	Galaxy Tab	iPad 2	Notion Tab
Processor	1 Ghz NVidia Terga 2 Dual-Core	1 Ghz NVidia Terga 2 Dual-Core	1 Ghz Dual-Core A5	1 Ghz NVidia Terga 2 Dual-Core
Memory	1 GB	1 GB	512 MB	1 GB
Hard Drive	32 GB	16 GB or 32 GB	16 GB, 32 GB, 64 GB	32 GB or 64 GB
Screen Resolution	1280 × 768	1280 × 800	1024 × 768	1024 × 768
Camera	Front and Rear	Front and Rear	Front and Rear	Front and Rear
Display Size	8.9" LCD	8.9" or 10.1" LCD	9.7" LED	9.0" LCD
Operation System	Android 3.0 (Honeycomb)	Android 3.0 (Honeycomb)	iOS 4.3	Android 3.0 (Honeycomb)
Price	$699.99	$469.99–$599.99	$499.99	$499.99

Because tables are numbered separately from other visuals, reports can have both a Figure 1 and a Table 1

Table 1: Comparsion of Specifications for Existing Tablets
(Sources: LG Slate, 2011; Samsung Galaxy Tab, 2011; iPad 2, 2011)

LG

The LG Corporation is the second largest company in South Korea behind Samsung (see below). Their revenues, as of 2009, were $78.89 billion (in U.S. dollars). LG is not as diversified as Samsung, but they do produce products in the fields of electronics, telecommunications, and chemicals (LG Corp, 2011). LG will be one of the main rivals for RAC Inc. in South Korea. LG released their version of a tablet, the G-Slate, as it is called in the United States, in March 2011. The specifications of this tablet are outlined in Table 1 (LG Slate, 2011). LG is relatively new to the field of tablets, so JASS believes RAC Inc. will not have to worry as much about LG as it does about Samsung.

Samsung

Samsung is the largest company in the world, and in South Korea, based upon revenue. As of 2009, their revenue was $172.5 billion (in U.S. dollars). Samsung is part of a larger group of corporations that comprise a diverse set of areas; technology is the biggest (Samsung, 2011). Samsung would be RAC Inc.'s largest competitor in South Korea. Samsung has a tablet, called the Galaxy Tab, launched at the end of 2010. They have a newer version hitting retail stores sometime late 2011. The specifications of this tablet are outlined in Table 1 (Samsung Galaxy, 2011). The Galaxy Tab is actually the second version of their tablet that they have released, with updated technology and software. As a hometown Seoul business, Samsung will present a challenge for RAC Inc. to win the loyalties of the South Korean people and increase market share.

Integration

One way RAC Inc. could improve receptiveness from the South Korean people, and possibly cut costs for their Notion Tab, is to partner with a South Korean company to more readily manufacture their product. Some of these companies are Digitech Systems, Nextchip, and Partron. Digitech Systems has an emphasis on touch screens for phones and other devices, which is a major component of tablets. Nextchip deals with the sensors that are used in touch screens, which is another important element of the device. And finally, Partron deals with basic parts for mobile phones and telecommunication devices (Settimi, 2010).

Figure 18.5 A Formal Report *(Continued)*

Slated for Success 10

If RAC Inc. does expand to South Korea, they will need to have a telecommunications company to carry the service, at least the data service for their Notion Tab. The best option JASS has researched is SK Telecom. SK Telecom, part of the SK group, is South Korea's largest telecommunications group for cellular phone service in the region. They have 50.5% of the market share (SK Telecom, 2011). The other two options are LG Telecom and KT, formally Korea Telecom. LG Telecom would not be a good choice since they are a subsidiary of a competitor, LG (LG Telecom, 2010). KT would also not be the best choice because they are not the largest provider in the country and all of the competitors use SK Telecom as their data service (KT, 2011).

Summary

The people of South Korea are in sync with the latest technology trends such as NFC and DMB. Their affinity with technology has led JASS to choose South Korea as a viable option. However, there are disadvantages as well. The main competitors of RAC Inc. in South Korea, LG and Samsung, are major hurdles. They are the top two companies in South Korea, with Samsung being the largest in the world. Because of these factors, we have determined this criterion is only somewhat favorable for expansion. This criterion could go either way; therefore, JASS cannot give it a full favorable recommendation for expansion into South Korea.

Location, Location, Location

South Korea offers many suitable cities for RAC's expansion. We researched many before picking a city that will generate the most benefits for RAC Inc. Our research covered possible locations for RAC's headquarters, operations, and Notion Tab product launches. We researched the cities of Seoul, Busan, Incheon, Daegu and Cheongju. We picked these cities to research based on size and location. The factors we used in determining the right cities are economic status, population, proximity to North Korea, proximity to shipping ports (coastline), and direct competition to Samsung and LG, whose headquarters are in Seoul. The entire country of South Korea is technologically advanced, so any of these cities could be a possibility for expansion.

JASS has decided that the city with the highest potential to expand business operations is the centrally located Busan. Busan is the second largest city in South Korea with population of 3.4 million. Busan is also the largest port city in South Korea and the fifth largest port city in the world (Park, 2009). Because Busan is a port city, it will allow easy importation of raw materials, as well as easier exportation of finished product to other countries and back to the United States. If manufacturing is cheaper in South Korea, RAC Inc. may decide to create more products in South Korea and ship them back to the United States.

JASS also recommends that the headquarters be in Busan, allowing close proximity to the manufacturing plant, if any issues arise. RAC Inc. should initially launch the Notion Tab in Seoul and Busan. These are the two largest cities in South Korea and have a high-density population. Launching the Notion Tab in these cities will result in the greatest benefit for RAC Inc.

(Continued)

Figure 18.5 A Formal Report *(Continued)*

Slated for Success 11

Conclusions repeat points made in the report. Recommendations are actions the audience should take.

Some companies ask for Conclusions and Recommendations at the beginning of the report.

Conclusions and Recommendations

All of the research that we have done supports the decision to expand into South Korea. The government, economy, and culture criteria all received favorable recommendations for a total of 60%. Market possibilities and competition received half support for an additional 20%. Together, South Korea has earned 80% based on our criteria.

Therefore, we believe that RAC Inc. could profitably expand into South Korea. The Notion Tab is a high-quality product, and it will be easily integrated into this technologically advanced county. In conclusion, we recommend that RAC Inc. should expand into South Korea.

To ensure a successful expansion, JASS LLC recommends the following:

1. **RAC Inc. should establish its headquarters and manufacturing plant in Busan.**
   - Purchase a building to have a place to begin manufacturing the Notion Tab.
   - Educate RAC employees about South Korean culture and business practices before they begin working directly with South Koreans to avoid being disrespectful.
   - Explore hiring South Koreans; the available workforce is large.
   - Ensure that the Notion name is appropriate when translated into Korean. If not, change the name to better market the product.
   - Market and sell the product in both Busan and Seoul.

Numbering points makes it easier for the audience to follow and discuss them.

2. **After one year RAC should determine the acceptance and profitability of the expansion.**
   - Conduct a customer satisfaction survey with people who purchased the Notion Tab living
   - in Seoul and Busan to determine the acceptance of the product.
     Compare and contrast first-year sales with a competitor's similar product.

Make sure all items in a list are parallel.

3. **If the tablet is competitive and profitable, RAC Inc. should expand its product line into all large cities in South Korea.**
   - To gain an edge on the competition, create a marketing plan that will offer the Notion Tab
   - at some discount in the new cities.
     Explore integrating other RAC Inc. products into South Korea. These products could also be manufactured at the new manufacturing plant in Busan.

Because many readers turn to the "Recommendations" first, provide enough information so that the reason is clear all by itself. The ideas in this section must be logical extensions of the points made and supported in the body of the report.

Figure 18.5 A Formal Report *(Continued)*

Slated for Success 12

References

This report uses APA citation style.

Advameg, Inc. (2011). Culture of South Korea. *Countries and Their Cultures.* Retrieved April 2, 2011, from http://www.everyculture.com/Ja-Ma/South-Korea.html.

AFP. (2010, December 5). U.S., South Korea sign sweeping free-trade agreement. *Taipei Times.* Retrieved from http://www.taipeitimes.com/News/front/archives/2010/12/05/200349014.

Borland, J., & Kanellos, M. (2004, July 28). South Korea leads the way. *CNET News.* Retrieved from http://news.cnet.com/South-Korea-leads-the-way/2009-1034_3-5261393.html.

Central Intelligence Agency. (2011). *The world factbook: South Korea.* Retrieved March 18, 2011, from https://www.cia.gov/library/publications/the-world-factbook/geos/ks.html#.

Cho, J. (2006, February 12). Korea: Terrestrial-DMB adds color to Korean lifestyle. *Asia Media Archives.* Retrieved from http://www.asiamedia.ucla.edu/article-eastasia.asp?parentid=38998.

Grand National Party. (2011, April 1). In *Wikipedia.* Retrieved April 6, 2011, from http://en.wikipedia.org/wiki/Grand_National_Party.

iPad 2 specs. (2011). *OS X Daily.* Retrieved from http://osxdaily.com/2011/03/02/ipad-2-specs.

Kirk, D. (2001, July 26). World business briefing: Asia: South Korea: Shorter workweek. *New York Times.* Retrieved from http://www.nytimes.com/2001/07/26/business/world-business-briefing-asia-south-korea-shorter-workweek.html.

Compare this list of sources with those in the proposal. Notice how the authors had to adjust the list as they completed research.

Koreans love their mobile phones. (2009, January 28). *Korean JoongAng Daily.* Retrieved from http://joongangdaily.joins.com/article/view.asp?aid=2900275.

KRWUS. (2011). *MSN Money.* Retrieved April 10, 2011, from http://investing.money.msn.com/investments/currency-exchange-rates/?symbol=%2fKRWUS.

KT. (2011, April 1). In *Wikipedia.* Retrieved April 2, 2011, from http://en.wikipedia.org/wiki/KT_%28telecommunication_company%29.

Kwintessential. (2010). *South Korea: Language, culture, customers and etiquette.* Retrieved from http://www.kwintessential.co.uk/resources/global-etiquette/south-korea-country-profile.html.

LG Corp. (2011, April 1). In *Wikipedia.* Retrieved April 2, 2011, from http://en.wikipedia.org/wiki/LG.

LG Slate full specifications and product details. (2011, February 2). *Gadgetian.* Retrieved April 3, 2011, from http: //gadgetian.com/7069/lg-g-slate-t-mobile-specs-price/.

LG Telecom. (2010, November 29). In *Wikipedia.* Retrieved April 2, 2011, from http://en.wikipedia.org/wiki/LG_Telecom.

Life in Korea. (n.d.). *Cultural spotlight.* Retrieved March 31, 2011, from http://www.lifeinkorea.com/Culture/spotlight.cfm.

List all the printed and online sources cited in your report. Do not list sources you used for background but did not cite.

(Continued)

Figure 18.5 A Formal Report *(Concluded)*

Manyin, M. E. (2007). *The proposed South Korea–U.S. free trade agreement*. Washington, DC: CRS of Congress.

Office of the U.S. Trade Representative. (2011, February 10). Korea–U.S. free trade agreement. *Executive Office of the President: Office of the United States Trade Representative*. Retrieved April 3, 2011, from http://www.ustr.gov/trade-agreements/free-trade-agreements/korus-fta.

Ogg, E. (2010, May 28). What makes a tablet a tablet? *CNet News*. Retrieved March 23, 2011, from http://news.cnet.com/8301-31021_3-20006077-260.html?tag=newsLeadStoriesArea.1.

Olson, P. (2008, May 21). The world's hardest-working countries. *Forbes*. Retrieved from http://www.forbes.com/2008/05/21/labor-market-workforce-lead-citizen-cx_po_0521 countries.html.

Park, K. (2009, March 3). Empty containers clog Busan port as trade slumps. *Bloomberg*. Retrieved from http://www.bloomberg.com/apps/news?pid=newsarchive&sid=ah2Znx0vQ580.

Samsung. (2011, April 5). In *Wikipedia*. Retrieved April 8, 2011, from http://en.wikipedia.org/wiki/Samsung

Samsung Galaxy Tab. (2011, March 22). Retrieved from http://www.phonearena.com/phones/Samsung-GALAXY-Tab-8.9_id5333.

Settimi, C. (2010, September 1). Asia's 200 best under a billion. *Forbes*. Retrieved from http://www.forbes.com/2010/09/01/bub-200-intro-asia-under-billion-10-small-companies.html.

SK Telecom. (2011, April 8). In *Wikipedia*. Retrieved April 10, 2011, from http://en.wikipedia.org/wiki/SK_Telecom.

South Korea: Political structure. (2009, June 11). *The Economist*. Retrieved from http://www.economist.com/node/13805244.

South Korea's GDP Growth. (2010, May 28). In *Wikipedia*. Retrieved April 10, 2011, from http://en.wikipedia.org/wiki/File:South_Korea's_GDP_(PPP)_growth_from_1911_to_2008.png.

U.S. Bureau of Labor of Statistics. (2008, March). "Around the world in eight charts." Retrieved from http://www.bls.gov/spotlight/2008/around_the_world/.

U.S. Department of State. (2010, December 10). *Background note: South Korea*. Retrieved March 21, 2011, from http://www.state.gov/r/pa/ei/bgn/2800.htm.

World Bank Group. (2011a). Ease of doing business in Korea, Rep. *Doing Business: Measuring Business Regulations*. Retrieved from http://www.doingbusiness.org/data/exploreeconomies/korea/.

World Bank Group (2011b). Ease of doing business in United States. *Doing Business: Measuring Business Regulations*.Retrieved from http://www.doingbusiness.org/data/exploreeconomies/united-states/.

World Business Culture. (n.d.). *Doing business in South Korea*. Retrieved March 22, 2011, from http://www.worldbusinessculture.com/Business-in-South-Korea.html.

Title Page

The title page of a report usually contains four items: the title of the report, the person or organization for whom the report is prepared, the person or group who prepared the report, and the release date. Some title pages also contain a brief summary or abstract of the contents of the report; some title pages contain decorative artwork.

The title of the report should be as informative as possible. Like subject lines, report titles are straightforward.

Poor title: New Plant Site

Better title: Eugene, Oregon, Site for the New Kemco Plant

Large organizations that issue many reports may use two-part titles to make it easier to search for reports electronically. For example, U.S. government report titles first give the agency sponsoring the report, then the title of that particular report.

Small Business Administration: Management Practices Have Improved for the Women's Business Center Program

In many cases, the title will state the recommendation in the report: "Why the United Nations Should Establish a Seed Bank." However, the title should omit recommendations when

- The reader will find the recommendations hard to accept.
- Putting all the recommendations in the title would make it too long.
- The report does not offer recommendations.

If the title does not contain the recommendation, it normally indicates what problem the report tries to solve or the topic the report discusses.

Eliminate any unnecessary words:

Wordy: Report of a Study on Ways to Market Life Insurance to Urban Professional People Who Are in Their Mid-40s

Better: Marketing Life Insurance to the Mid-40s Urban Professional

The identification of the receiver of the report normally includes the name of the person who will make a decision based on the report, his or her job title, the organization's name, and its location (city, state, and zip code). Government reports often omit the person's name and simply give the organization that authorized the report.

If the report is prepared primarily by one person, the *Prepared by* section will have that person's name, his or her title, the organization, and its location (city, state, and zip code). In internal reports, the organization and location are usually omitted if the report writer works at the headquarters office.

If several people write the report, government reports normally list all their names, using a separate sheet of paper if the group working on the report is large. Practices in business differ. In some organizations, all the names are listed; in others, the division to which they belong is listed; in still others, the name of the chair of the group appears.

The **release date,** the date the report will be released to the public, is usually the date the report is scheduled for discussion by the decision makers. The report is frequently due four to six weeks before the release date so that the decision makers can review the report before the meeting.

If you have the facilities and the time, try using type variations, color, and artwork to create a visually attractive and impressive title page. However, a plain typed page is acceptable. The format in Figure 18.5 will enable you to create an acceptable typed title page.

Letter or Memo of Transmittal

Use a letter of transmittal if you are not a regular employee of the organization for which you prepare the report; use a memo if you are a regular employee.

The transmittal has several purposes: to transmit the report, to orient the reader to the report, and to build a good image of the report and of the writer. An informal writing style is appropriate for a transmittal even when the style in the report is more formal. A professional transmittal helps you create a good image of yourself and enhances your credibility. Personal statements are appropriate in the transmittal, even though they would not be acceptable in the report itself.

Organize the transmittal in this way:

1. **Transmit the report.** Tell when and by whom it was authorized and the purpose it was to fulfill.
2. **Summarize your conclusions and recommendations.** If the recommendations will be easy for the audience to accept, put them early in the transmittal. If they will be difficult, summarize the findings and conclusions before the recommendations.
3. **Mention any points of special interest in the report. Show how you surmounted minor problems you encountered in your investigation. Thank people who helped you.** These optional items can build goodwill and enhance your credibility.
4. **Point out additional research that is necessary, if any.** Sometimes your recommendation cannot be implemented until further work is done. If you'd be interested in doing that research, or if you'd like to implement the recommendations, say so.
5. **Thank the audience for the opportunity to do the work and offer to answer questions.** Provide contact information. Even if the report has not been fun to do, expressing satisfaction in doing the project is expected. Saying that you'll answer questions about the report is a way of saying that you won't charge the audience your normal hourly fee to answer questions (one more reason to make the report clear!).

The letter of transmittal on page i of Figure 18.5 uses this pattern of organization.

Table of Contents

In the table of contents, list the headings exactly as they appear in the body of the report. If the report is less than 25 pages, you'll probably list all the levels of headings. In a long report, pick a level and put all the headings at that level and above in the table of contents.

Page ii of Figure 18.5 shows the table of contents.

List of Illustrations

A list of illustrations enables audiences to refer to your visuals.

Report visuals comprise both tables and figures. *Tables* are words or numbers arranged in rows and columns. *Figures* are everything else: bar graphs, pie charts, flow charts, maps, drawings, photographs, computer printouts, and so on. Tables and figures may be numbered independently, so you may have both a Table 1 and a Figure 1. In a report with maps and graphs but no other visuals, the visuals are sometimes called Map 1 and Graph 1. Whatever you call the illustrations, list them in the order in which they appear in the report; give the name of each visual as well as its number.

See Chapter 16 for information about how to design and label visuals.

Executive Summary

An **executive summary** or **abstract** tells the audience what the document is about. It summarizes the recommendation of the report and the reasons for the recommendation or describes the topics the report discusses and indicates the depth of the discussion. It should be clear even to people who will read only the abstract.

A good abstract is easy to read, concise, and clear. Edit your abstract carefully to tighten your writing and eliminate any unnecessary words.

Wordy: The report describes two types of business jargon, *businessese* and *reverse gobbledygook.* It gives many examples of each of these and points out how their use can be harmful.

Tight: The report describes and illustrates two harmful types of business jargon, *businessese* and *reverse gobbledygook.*

Abstracts generally use a more formal style than other forms of business writing. Avoid contractions and colloquialisms. Try to avoid using the second-person *you.* Because reports may have many different audiences, *you* may become inaccurate. It's OK to use exactly the same words in the abstract and the report.

Summary abstracts present the logic skeleton of the report: the thesis or recommendation and its proof. Use a summary abstract to give the most useful information in the shortest space.

> To market life insurance to mid-40s urban professionals, Interstate Fidelity Insurance should advertise in upscale publications and use direct mail.
>
> Network TV and radio are not cost-efficient for reaching this market. This group comprises a small percentage of the prime-time network TV audience and a minority of most radio station listeners. They tend to discard newspapers and general-interest magazines quickly, but many of them keep upscale periodicals for months or years. Magazines with high percentages of readers in this group include *Architectural Digest, Bon Appetit, Forbes, Golf Digest, Metropolitan Home, Southern Living,* and *Smithsonian.*
>
> Any advertising campaign needs to overcome this group's feeling that they already have the insurance they need. One way to do this would be to encourage them to check the coverage their employers provide and to calculate the cost of their children's expenses through college graduation. Insurance plans that provide savings and tax benefits as well as death benefits might also be appealing.

One way to start composing an abstract is to write a sentence outline. A **sentence outline** not only uses complete sentences rather than words or phrases but also contains the thesis sentence or recommendation and the evidence that proves that point. Combine the sentences into paragraphs, adding transitions if necessary, and you'll have your abstract.

Descriptive abstracts indicate what topics the report covers and how deeply it goes into each topic, but they do not summarize what the report says about each topic. Phrases that describe the report ("this report covers," "it includes,"

Executive Summary of a Government Plan

On February 18, 2009, the Obama administration announced a "Homeowner Affordability and Stability" plan to counter the home mortgage crisis. The executive summary of the plan—given to the press—included the following:

- First, a statement of background, which included bullet points listing the effects of the crisis (for example, that nearly 6 million households will face foreclosure), and ending with the purpose of the plan (that the plan will help nearly 7 to 9 million families to "restructure" their mortgages to avoid foreclosure).
- Then, the two main components of the plan ("affordability" and "stability") together with their subcomponents (a few subcomponents are given below as examples):
- "Affordability"
  - "Enabling refinancing"
  - "Reducing monthly payments"
- "Stability"
  - "Helping homeowners stay in their homes"
  - "Not aiding speculators"
  - "Protecting neighborhoods"

The summary provided numbers and, where appropriate, examples to inform and explain the plan. A busy reader—or one who wanted to know the broad contours of the plan without going through its nuts and bolts—would likely benefit from reading the summary before deciding whether to read the whole plan.

Adapted from "Homeowner Affordability and Stability Plan Executive Summary," *BusinessWeek,* February 18, 2009, http://www.businessweek.com/bwdaily/dnflash/content/feb2009/db20090218_403370.htm.

Analyzing Numbers, "West Concord, MA, has . . . one of the highest [per capita incomes] in the nation. . . . It also has one of the highest number of single men in Massachusetts. Why? On the outskirts of West Concord is a medium-to-maximum security prison!

So, when one naively juxtaposes these data points, one can be led to assume that there are plenty of single, wealthy men there—when that isn't the case. . . . Think before arriving to conclusions indicated by data crunching."

Quoted from Thomas M. Bodenberg, Letter to the Editor, *American Demographics*, August 2001, 8.

"it summarizes," "it concludes") are marks of a descriptive abstract. An additional mark of a descriptive abstract is that the audience can't tell what the report says about the topics it covers.

> This report recommends ways Interstate Fidelity Insurance could market insurance to mid-40s urban professionals. It examines demographic and psychographic profiles of the target market. Survey results are used to show attitudes toward insurance. The report suggests some appeals that might be successful with this market.

Introduction

The **Introduction** of the report always contains a statement of purpose and scope and may include all the parts in the following list.

- **Purpose.** The purpose statement identifies the problem the report addresses, the technical investigations it summarizes, and the rhetorical purpose (to explain, to recommend).
- **Scope.** The scope statement identifies how broad an area the report surveys. For example, Company XYZ is losing money on its line of computers. Does the report investigate the quality of the computers? The advertising campaign? The cost of manufacturing? The demand for computers? A scope statement allows the reader to evaluate the report on appropriate grounds.
- **Assumptions.** Assumptions in a report are like assumptions in geometry: statements whose truth you assume, and which you use to prove your final point. If they are wrong, the conclusion will be wrong too.

  For example, to plan cars that will be built five years from now, an automobile manufacturer commissions a report on young adults' attitudes toward cars. The recommendations would be based on assumptions both about gas prices and about the economy. If gas prices radically rose or fell, the kinds of cars young adults wanted would change. If there were a major recession, people wouldn't be able to buy new cars.

  Almost all reports require assumptions. A good report spells out its assumptions so that audiences can make decisions more confidently.
- **Methods.** If you conducted surveys, focus groups, or interviews, you need to tell how you chose your subjects, and how, when, and where they were interviewed. If the discussion of your methodology is more than a paragraph or two, you should probably make it a separate section in the body of the report rather than including it in the introduction. Reports based on scientific experiments usually put the methods section in the body of the report, not in the Introduction.

  If your report is based solely on library or online research, provide a brief description of significant sources. See Appendix C on how to cite and document sources.
- **Limitations.** Limitations make your recommendations less valid or valid only under certain conditions. Limitations usually arise because time or money constraints haven't permitted full research. For example, a campus pizza restaurant considering expanding its menu may ask for a report but not have enough money to take a random sample of students and townspeople. Without a random sample, the writer cannot generalize from the sample to the larger population.

  Many recommendations are valid only for a limited time. For instance, a campus store wants to know what kinds of clothing will appeal to college men. The recommendations will remain valid for only a short time: three years from now, styles and tastes may have changed, and the clothes that would sell best now may no longer be in demand.

- **Criteria.** The criteria section outlines the factors or standards that you are considering and the relative importance of each. If a company is choosing a city for a new office, is the cost of office space more or less important than the availability of skilled workers? Check with your audience before you write the draft to make sure that your criteria match those of your audiences.
- **Definitions.** Many reports define key terms in the introduction. For instance, a report on unauthorized Internet use by employees might define what is meant by "unauthorized use." A report on the corporate dress code might define such codes broadly to include general appearance, so it could include items such as tattoos, facial piercings, and general cleanliness. Also, if you know that some members of your primary, or secondary audience will not understand technical terms, define them. If you have only a few definitions, you can put them in the Introduction. If you have many terms to define, put a **glossary** in an appendix. Refer to it in the Introduction so that audiences know that you've provided it.

Background or History

Formal reports usually have a section that gives the background of the situation or the history of the problem. Even though the current audience for the report probably knows the situation, reports are filed and consulted years later. These later audiences will probably not know the background, although it may be crucial for understanding the options that are possible.

In some cases, the history section may cover many years. For example, a report recommending that a U.S. hotel chain open hotels in Romania may give the history of that country for at least several decades. In other cases, the background section is much briefer, covering only a few years or even just the immediate situation.

The purpose of most reports is rarely to provide a history of the problem. Do not let the background section achieve undue length.

Body

The body of the report is usually its longest section. Analyze causes of the problem and offer possible solutions. Present your argument with all its evidence and data. Data that are necessary to follow the argument are included with appropriate visuals and explanatory text. Extended data sets, such as large tables and long questionnaires, are generally placed in appendixes. It is particularly important in the body that you use headings, forecasting statements, and topic sentences to help lead your audience through the text. Audiences will also appreciate clear, concise, and engaging prose. Remember to cite your sources (see Appendix C) and to refer in the text to all visuals and appendixes.

Conclusions and Recommendations

Conclusions summarize points you have made in the body of the report; **Recommendations** are action items that would solve or ameliorate the problem. These sections are often combined if they are short: *Conclusions and Recommendations.* No new information should be included in this section.

Many audiences turn to the recommendations section first; some organizations ask that recommendations be presented early in the report. Number the recommendations to make it easy for people to discuss them. If the recommendations will seem difficult or controversial, give a brief paragraph of rationale after each recommendation. If they'll be easy for the audience to accept, you can simply list them without comments or reasons. The recommendations will also be in the executive summary and perhaps in the title and the transmittal.

SUMMARY OF KEY POINTS

- Good reports begin with good data. Make sure your data come from reliable sources.
- Analyze report numbers and text for accuracy and logic.
- Choose an appropriate organizational pattern for your information and purposes. The most common patterns are comparison/contrast, problem-solving, elimination of alternatives, SWOT analysis, general to particular, particular to general, geographic or spatial, functional, and chronological.
- Reports use the same style as other business documents, with three exceptions:
    1. Reports use a more formal style, without contractions or slang, than do many letters and memos.
    2. Reports rarely use the word *you.*
    3. Reports should include all the definitions and documents needed to understand the recommendations.
- To create good report style,
    1. Use clear, engaging writing.
    2. Keep repetition to a minimum.
    3. Introduce all sources and visuals.
    4. Use forecasting, transitions, topic sentences, and headings.
- **Headings** are single words short phrases, or complete sentences that describe all of the material under them until the next heading. **Talking heads** tell the audience what to expect in each section.
- Headings must use the same grammatical structure. Subheads under a heading must be parallel to each other but do not necessarily have to be parallel to subheads under other headings.
- The title page of a report usually contains four items: the title of the report, whom the report is prepared for, whom it is prepared by, and the date.
- If the report is 25 pages or less, list all the headings in the table of contents. In a long report, pick a level and put all the headings at that level and above in the contents.
- Organize the transmittal in this way:
    1. Release the report.
    2. Summarize your conclusions and recommendations.
    3. Mention any points of special interest in the report. Show how you surmounted minor problems you encountered in your investigation. Thank people who helped you.
    4. Point out additional research that is necessary, if any.
    5. Thank the reader for the opportunity to do the work and offer to answer questions.

- **Summary abstracts** present the logic skeleton of the article: the thesis or recommendation and its proof. **Descriptive abstracts** indicate what topics the article covers and how deeply it goes into each topic, but do not summarize what the article says about each topic.
- A good abstract or executive summary is easy to read, concise, and clear. A good abstract can be understood by itself, without the report or references.
- The **Introduction** of the report always contains a statement of purpose and scope. The **Purpose** statement identifies the organizational problem the report addresses, the technical investigations it summarizes, and the rhetorical purpose (to explain, to recommend). The **Scope** statement identifies how broad an area the report surveys. The introduction may also include **Limitations,** problems or factors that limit the validity of your recommendations; **Assumptions,** statements whose truth you assume, and which you use to prove your final point; **Methods,** an explanation of how you gathered your data; **Criteria** used to weigh the factors in the decision; and **Definitions** of terms audiences may not know.
- A **Background** or **History** section is usually included because reports are filed and may be consulted years later by people who no longer remember the original circumstances.
- The **Body** of the report, usually the longest section, analyzes causes of the problem and offers possible solutions. It presents your argument with all evidence and data.
- **Conclusions** summarize points made in the body of the report; **Recommendations** are action items that would solve or ameliorate the problem. These sections are often combined if they are short.

CHAPTER 18 Exercises and Problems

**Go to www.mhhe.com/locker10e for additional Exercises and Problems.*

18.1 Reviewing the Chapter

1. What are some criteria to check to ensure you have quality data? (LO 18-1)
2. What kinds of patterns should you look for in your data and text? (LO 18-1)
3. What are some guidelines for choosing information for reports? (LO 18-2)
4. Name seven basic patterns for organizing reports. For four of them, explain when they would be particularly effective or ineffective. (LO 18-3)
5. What are three ways that style in reports differs from conventional business communication style? (LO 18-4)
6. Name four good writing principles that are particularly important in reports. (LO 18-4)
7. How do you introduce sources in the text of the report? (LO 18-4)
8. Why should reports try to have a topic sentence at the beginning of each paragraph? (LO 18-4)
9. What are the characteristics of an effective report title? (LO 18-5)
10. What goes in the letter of transmittal? (LO 18-5)
11. What is the difference between summary and descriptive abstracts? (LO 18-5)
12. What goes in the introduction of a report? (LO 18-5)
13. What is the difference between conclusions and recommendations? (LO 18-5)

18.2 Identifying Assumptions and Limitations

Indicate whether each of the following would be an assumption or a limitation in a formal report.

a. Report on Ways to Encourage More Students to Join XYZ Organization
   1. I surveyed a judgment sample rather than a random sample.
   2. These recommendations are based on the attitudes of current students. Presumably, students in the next several years will have the same attitudes and interests.

b. Report on the Feasibility of Building Hilton Hotels in Romania

1. This report is based on the expectation that the country will be politically stable.
2. All of my information is based on library research. The most recent articles were published two months ago; much of the information was published a year ago or more. Therefore some of my information may be out of date.

c. Report on Car-Buying Preferences of Young Adults

1. These recommendations may change if the cost of gasoline increases dramatically or if there is another deep recession.
2. This report is based on a survey of adults ages 20 to 24 in California, Texas, Illinois, Ontario, and Massachusetts.
3. These preferences are based on the cars now available. If a major technical or styling innovation occurs, preferences may change.

18.3 Revising an Executive Summary

The following Executive Summary is poorly organized and too long. Rearrange information to make it more effective. Cut information that does not belong in the summary. You may use different words as you revise.

In this report I will discuss the communication problems which exist at Rolling Meadows Golf Club. The problems discussed will deal with channels of communication. The areas which are causing problems are internal. Radios would solve these internal problems.

Taking a 15-minute drive on a golf cart in order to find the superintendent is a common occurrence. Starters and rangers need to keep in touch with the clubhouse to maintain a smooth flow of players around the course. The rangers have expressed an interest in being able to call the clubhouse for advice and support.

Purchasing two-channel FM radios with private channels would provide three advantages. First, radios would make the golf course safer by providing a means of notifying someone in the event of an emergency. Second, radios would make the staff more efficient by providing a faster channel of communication. Third, radios would enable clubhouse personnel to keep in touch with the superintendent, the rangers, and the starters.

During the week, radios can be carried by the superintendent, the golf pro, and another course worker. On weekends and during tournaments, one radio will be used by the golf professional. The other two will be used by one starter and one ranger. Three radios is the minimum needed to meet basic communication needs. A fourth radio would provide more flexibility for busy weekends and during tournaments.

Tekk T-20 radios can be purchased from Page-Com for $129 each. These radios have the range and options needed for use on the golf course. Radios are durable and easy to service. It is possible that another brand might be even less expensive.

Rolling Meadows Golf Club should purchase four radios. They will cost under $600 and can be paid for from the current equipment budget.

18.4 Comparing Report Formats

Locate five business or organizational reports (or white papers as they're sometimes called) on the Internet. A good online collection of organizational reports is the website of the Council on Library and Information Resources (CLIR) accessible at http://www.clir.org/pubs/reports/. Additionally, you can find reports linked from the websites of the Fortune 500 organizations, or you can search for them on Google using keywords such as "reports," "business reports," "company reports," or "organizational reports."

The reports you find could be about the organizations' environmental sustainability efforts, their products, or any other aspect of their operations.

Compare the organization (the reports' contents or the way they're structured) of the five reports you select. What similarities and differences do you see in the formatting of all these reports? Make a table of your findings. Discuss your findings in small groups.

18.5 Comparing Style in Annual Reports

Locate two annual reports on the Internet. A good source is Report Watch, http://www.reportwatch.net/ Compare the style of the two reports. Here are some questions to get you started:

1. How do they use visuals to keep attention?
2. What differences do you see in the letters from the CEOs?
3. How do they present number-heavy information? Do they rely mainly on tables and graphs? Do they give prose summaries?
4. Is the writing easy to understand?
5. Do you see places where negative information is given a positive spin?
6. Is one report easier to understand than the other? Why?
7. Is one report more interesting than the other? Why?
8. Is one report more convincing than the other? Why?

As your instructor directs,

a. Work in small groups to do your comparison. Share your findings in a five-minute oral presentation to the class.
b. Work in small groups to do your comparison. Share your findings in a memo posted on the class website.
c. Work individually to do your comparison. Share your findings in a memo to your instructor.

18.6 Evaluating a Report from Your Workplace

Consider the following aspects of a report from your workplace:

- Content. How much information is included? How is it presented?
- Emphasis. What points are emphasized? What points are deemphasized? What verbal and visual techniques are used to highlight or minimize information?
- Visuals and layout. Are visuals used effectively? Are they accurate and free from chartjunk? What image do the pictures and visuals create? Are color and white space used effectively? (See Chapter 16 on visuals.)

As your instructor directs,

a. Write a memo to your instructor analyzing the report.
b. Join with a small group of students to compare and contrast several reports. Present your evaluation in an informal group report.
c. Present your evaluation orally to the class.

18.7 Analyzing and Writing Reports

Reread the sidebar about the Pew Internet and American Life Project at http://www.pewinternet.org/ on page 575. Go to the website and browse through the reports. Select a report and answer the following questions:

- Who is the report's audience?
- What is its purpose?
- How were the data collected?
- What did the data collection measure?
- Why was the data collection important?

Given your analysis of the report's audience, purpose, and data collection, consider the strategies used in the report to convey the information. Answer these questions:

- What tone did the writer adopt?
- How was the report organized and designed to meet the needs of the audience?
- What language choices did the writer make?

Finally, examine the press releases that are written about the report (the press releases for each report are included as links) for the ways the information in the report is adapted for a different audience and purpose. How do the content, organization, tone, and language choices differ from those of the original report? Do you see any ethical issues involved in condensing the report into a press release?

As your instructor directs,

- Write a report of your findings to your instructor.
- Present your findings to the class using presentation software.

18.8 Preparing an Information Report

Visit the website of the Global Reporting Initiative (http://www.globalreporting.org/Home), a group of analysts from various industries and professions that is committed to advancing the cause of socially responsible reporting by organizations. Prepare an information report, either as a memo to your instructor or as a PowerPoint presentation for the class, describing the organization, the people behind it, their guidelines, their work, and their impact on the corporate world.

18.9 Recommending Action

Write a report recommending an action that your unit or organization should take. Possibilities include

- Buying more equipment for your department.
- Hiring an additional worker for your department.
- Making your organization more family-friendly.
- Making a change that will make the organization more efficient.
- Making changes to improve accessibility for customers or employees with disabilities.

Address your report to the person who would have the power to approve your recommendation.

As your instructor directs,

a. Create a document or presentation to achieve the goal.

b. Write a memo to your instructor describing the situation at your workplace and explaining your rhetorical choices (medium, strategy, tone, wording, graphics or document design, and so forth).

18.10 Writing a Recommendation Report

Write a report evaluating two or more alternatives. Possible topics include the following:

1. Should students in your major start a monthly newsletter?
2. Should your student organization write an annual report? Would doing so help the next year's officers?
3. Should your student organization create a wiki, blog, or newsletter to facilitate communication with a constituency?
4. Should your workplace create a newsletter to communicate internally?
5. Should a local restaurant open another branch? Where should it be?

In designing your study, identify the alternatives, define your criteria for selecting one option over others, carefully evaluate each alternative, and recommend the best course of action.

18.11 Writing an Informative or Closure Report

Write an informative report on one of the following topics.

1. What should a U.S. manager know about dealing with workers from ______ [you fill in the country or culture]? What factors do and do not motivate people in this group? How do they show respect and deference? Are they used to a strong hierarchy or to an egalitarian setting? Do they normally do one thing at once or many things? How important is clock time and being on time? What factors lead them to respect someone? Age? Experience? Education? Technical knowledge? Wealth? Or what? What conflicts or miscommunications may arise between workers from this culture and other workers due to cultural differences? Are people from this culture similar in these beliefs and behaviors, or is there lots of variation?
2. What benefits do companies offer? To get information, check the web pages of three companies in the same industry. Information about benefits is usually on the page about working for the company.
3. Describe an ethical dilemma encountered by workers in a specific organization. What is the background of the situation? What competing loyalties exist? In the past, how have workers responded? How has the organization responded? Have whistle-blowers been rewarded or punished? What could the organization do to foster ethical behavior?
4. Describe a problem or challenge encountered by an organization where you've worked. Describe the problem, show why it needed to be solved, tell who did what to try to solve it, and tell how successful the efforts were. Possibilities include
   - How the organization is implementing work teams, downsizing, or changing organizational culture.
   - How the organization uses e-mail or voice mail.
   - How the organization uses telecommuting.
   - How managers deal with stress, make ethical choices, or evaluate subordinates.
   - How the organization is responding to changing U.S. demographics, the Americans with Disabilities Act, or international competition and opportunities.

18.12 Writing a Consultant's Report—Restaurant Tipping

Your consulting company has been asked to conduct a report for Diamond Enterprises, which runs three national chains: FishStix, The Bar-B-Q Pit, and Morrie's. All are medium-priced, family-friendly restaurants. The CEO is thinking of replacing optional tips with a 15% service fee automatically added to bills.

You read articles in trade journals, surveyed a random sample of 200 workers in each of the chains, and conducted an e-mail survey of the 136 restaurant managers. Here are your findings:

1. Trade journals point out that the Internal Revenue Service (IRS) audits restaurants if it thinks that servers underreport tips. Dealing with an audit is time-consuming and often results in the restaurant's having to pay penalties and interest.
2. Only one Morrie's restaurant has actually been audited by the IRS. Management was able to convince the IRS that servers were reporting tips accurately. No penalty was assessed. Management spent $1,000 on CPA and legal fees and spent over 80 hours of management time gathering data and participating in the audit.
3. Restaurants in Europe already add a service fee (usually 15%) to the bill. Patrons can add more if they choose. Local custom determines whether tips are expected and how much they should be. In Germany, for example, it is more usual to round up the bill (from 27 € to 30 €, for example) than to figure a percentage.
4. If the restaurant collected a service fee, it could use the income to raise wages for cooks and hosts and pay for other benefits, such as health insurance, rather than giving all the money to servers and bussers.
5. Morrie's servers tend to be under 25 years of age. FishStix employs more servers over 25, who are doing this for a living. The Bar-B-Q Pit servers are students in college towns.
6. In all three chains, servers oppose the idea. Employees other than servers generally support it.

	Retain tips	Change to service fee added to bill	Don't care
FishStix servers (n = 115)	90%	7%	3%
Bar-B-Q servers (n = 73)	95%	0%	5%
Morrie's servers (n = 93)	85%	15%	0%
Morrie's nonservers (n = 65)	25%	70%	5%
FishStix nonservers (n = 46)	32%	32%	37%
Bar-B-Q nonservers (n = 43)	56%	20%	25%

(Numbers do not add up to 100% due to rounding.)

7. Servers said that it was important to go home with money in their pockets (92%), that their expertise increased food sales and should be rewarded (67%), and that if a service fee replaced tips they would be likely to look for another job (45%). Some (17%) thought that if the manager distributed service-fee income, favoritism rather than the quality of work would govern how much tip income they got. Most (72%) thought that customers would not add anything beyond the 15% service fee, and many (66%) thought that total tip income would decrease and their own portion of that income would decrease (90%).
8. Managers generally support the change.

	Retain tips	Change to service fee added to bill	Don't care
FishStix managers (n = 44)	20%	80%	0%
Bar-B-Q managers (n = 13)	33%	67%	0%
Morrie's managers (n = 58)	55%	45%	0%

9. Comments from managers include: "It isn't fair for a cook with eight years of experience to make only $12 an hour while a server can make $25 an hour in just a couple of months," and "I could have my pick of employees if I offered health insurance."
10. Morale at Bar-B-Q seems low. This is seen in part in the low response rate to the survey.
11. In a tight employment market, some restaurants might lose good servers if they made the change. However, hiring cooks and other nonservers would be easier.
12. The current computer systems in place can handle figuring and recording the service fee. Since bills are printed by computer, an additional line could be added. Allocating the service-fee income could take extra managerial time, especially at first.

Write the report.

18.13 Writing a Library Research Report

Write a library research report.

As your instructor directs,

Turn in the following documents:

a. The approved proposal.
b. Two copies of the report, including

    Cover.

    Title Page.

    Letter or Memo of Transmittal.

    Table of Contents.

    List of Illustrations.

    Executive Summary or Abstract.

    Body (Introduction, all information, recommendations). Your instructor may specify a minimum length, a minimum number or kind of sources, and a minimum number of visuals.

    References or Works Cited.
c. Your notes and at least one preliminary draft.

Choose one of the following topics.

1. **Selling to College Students.** Your car dealership is located in a university town, but the manager doubts that selling cars to college students will be profitable. You agree that college incomes are low to nonexistent, but you see some students driving late-model cars. Recommend to the dealership's manager whether to begin marketing to college students, suggesting some tactics that would be effective.
2. **Advertising on the Internet.** You work on a team developing a marketing plan to sell high-end sunglasses. Your boss is reluctant to spend money for online advertising because she has heard that the money is mostly wasted. Also, she associates the ads with spam, which she detests. Recommend whether the company should devote some of its advertising budget to online ads. Include samples of online advertising that supports your recommendation.
3. **Improving Job Interview Questions.** Turnover among the sales force has been high, and your boss believes the problem is that your company has been hiring the wrong people. You are part of a team investigating the problem, and your assignment is to evaluate the questions used in job interviews. Human resource personnel use tried-and-true questions like "What is your greatest strength?" and "What is your greatest weakness?" The sales manager has some creative alternatives, such as asking candidates to solve logic puzzles and seeing how they perform under stress by taking frequent phone calls during the interview. You are to evaluate the current interviewing approaches and propose changes that would improve hiring decisions.
4. **Selling to Walmart.** Your company has a reputation for making high-quality lamps and ceiling fans sold in specialty stores. Although the company has been profitable, it could grow much faster if it sold through Walmart. Your boss is excited about her recent discussions with that retailer, but she has heard from associates that Walmart can be a demanding customer. She asked you to find out if there is a downside to selling through Walmart and, if so, whether manufacturers can afford to say no to a business deal with the retail giant.
5. **Making College Affordable.** The senator you work for is concerned about fast-rising costs of a college education. Students say they cannot afford their tuition bills. Colleges say they are making all the cuts they can without compromising the quality of education. In order to propose a bill that would help make college affordable for those who are qualified to attend, the senator has asked you to research alternatives for easing the problem. Recommend one or two measures the senator could include in a bill for the Senate to vote on.
6. With your instructor's permission, investigate a topic of your choice.

18.14 Writing a Recommendation Report

Write an individual or a team report.

As your instructor directs,

Turn in the following documents:

1. The approved proposal.
2. Two copies of the report, including

   Cover.

   Title Page.

   Letter or Memo of Transmittal.

   Table of Contents.

   List of Illustrations.

   Executive Summary or Abstract.

   Body (Introduction, all information, recommendations). Your instructor may specify a minimum length, a minimum number or kind of sources, and a minimum number of visuals.

   Appendixes if useful or relevant.
3. Your notes and at least one preliminary draft.

Pick one of the following topics.

1. **Improving Customer Service.** Many customers find that service is getting poorer and workers are getting ruder. Evaluate the service in a local store, restaurant, or other organization. Are customers made to feel comfortable? Is workers' communication helpful, friendly, and respectful? Are workers knowledgeable about products and services? Do they sell them effectively? Write a report analyzing the quality of service and recommending what the organization should do to improve.
2. **Recommending Courses for the Local Community College.** Businesses want to be able to send workers to local community colleges to upgrade their skills; community colleges want to prepare students to enter the local workforce. What skills are in demand in your community? What courses at what levels should the local community college offer?
3. **Improving Sales and Profits.** Recommend ways a small business in your community can increase sales and profits. Focus on one or more of the following: the products or services it offers, its advertising, its decor, its location, its accounting methods, its cash management, or any other aspect that may be keeping the company from achieving its potential. Address your report to the owner of the business.
4. **Increasing Student Involvement.** How could an organization on campus persuade more of the

students who are eligible to join or to become active in its programs? Do students know that it exists? Is it offering programs that interest students? Is it retaining current members? What changes should the organization make? Address your report to the officers of the organization.

5. **Evaluating a Potential Employer.** What training is available to new employees? How soon is the average entry-level person promoted? How much travel and weekend work are expected? Is there a "busy season," or is the workload consistent year-round? What fringe benefits are offered? What is the corporate culture? Is the climate nonracist and nonsexist? How strong is the company economically? How is it likely to be affected by current economic, demographic, and political trends? Address your report to the Placement Office on campus; recommend whether it should encourage students to work at this company.
6. With your instructor's permission, choose your own topic.

CHAPTER 19

Making Oral Presentations

Chapter Outline

Identifying Purposes in Oral Presentations

Comparing Written and Oral Messages

Planning a Strategy for Your Presentation

- Choosing the Kind of Presentation
- Adapting Your Ideas to the Audience
- Planning a Strong Opening
- Planning a Strong Conclusion

Choosing Information to Include in a Presentation

- Choosing Data
- Choosing Demonstrations

Organizing Your Information

Planning PowerPoint Slides

- Designing PowerPoint Slides
- Using Figures and Tables
- Using PowerPoint Technology to Involve Your Audience

Delivering an Effective Presentation

- Dealing with Fear
- Using Eye Contact
- Developing a Good Speaking Voice
- Standing and Gesturing
- Using Notes and Visuals

Handling Questions

Making Group Presentations

Summary of Key Points

Steve Jobs, Orator

When most company CEOs give presentations, the news media may provide a brief report in the business or technology sections. However, when Steve Jobs, CEO of Apple Inc., gave a presentation, he almost always got extra attention, and often ended up as a lead story on many news websites. Part of the attention was directed at Apple's innovative products, of course, but the rest was devoted to Jobs himself: as a dynamic CEO, a technology innovator, and a master presenter.

Communications coach Carmine Gallo watched all of Steve Jobs's presentations as he prepared to write his book *The Presentation Secrets of Steve Jobs: How to Be Insanely Great in Front of Any Audience.* Gallo, like many other presentation experts, believes that Jobs is the epitome of the modern CEO presenter. He captivated, enthralled, and sold his products in carefully orchestrated presentations. So what makes the difference?

Gallo believes that Jobs's success as a presenter depended on five key points:

1. A simple headline that carries over from the presentation to all marketing materials ("The World's Thinnest Laptop," for example).
2. A villain, who can motivate the audience to unite behind the hero (Apple).
3. A simple slide, focused on visuals and with no bulleted lists. Gallo found that Jobs once used only 7 words on 10 slides.
4. A demonstration of the product. Jobs never talked about a product when he could show it off instead.
5. A holy smokes moment, where he wowed the audience with something new.

"He captivated, enthralled, and sold his products in carefully orchestrated presentations."

Finally, these five points would not be nearly as powerful without Jobs's careful attention to detail. He rehearsed each presentation multiple times and anticipated glitches and problems. And, most of all, he understood the audience in the room and prepared his presentation for them.

Anyone can incorporate some of the successful strategies used by Steve Jobs, particularly focusing on the audience, simplifying the message and the slides, and preparing and practicing the presentation.

Sources: Carmine Gallo, "Uncovering Steve Jobs' Presentation Secrets," *BusinessWeek,* October 6, 2009, http://www.businessweek.com/print/smallbiz/content/oct2009/sb2009106_706829.htm; and Jon Thomas, "No Presenter Is Perfect, Not Even Steve Jobs," *Presentations Advisors,* March 9, 2010, http://www.presentationadvisors.com/no-presenter-is-perfect-not-even-steve-jobs.

Learning Objectives

After studying this chapter, you will know how to

LO 19-1 Plan effective presentations.

LO 19-2 Select and organize information for effective presentations.

LO 19-3 Deliver effective presentations.

LO 19-4 Handle questions during presentations.

The power to persuade people to care about something you believe in is crucial to business success. Making a good oral presentation is more than just good delivery: it also involves developing a strategy that fits your audience and purpose, having good content, and organizing material effectively. The choices you make in each of these areas are affected by your purposes, audience, and situation.

IDENTIFYING PURPOSES IN ORAL PRESENTATIONS

Oral presentations have the same three basic purposes that written documents have: to inform, to persuade, and to build goodwill. Like written messages, most oral presentations have more than one purpose.

Informative presentations inform or teach the audience. Training sessions in an organization are primarily informative. Secondary purposes may be to persuade new employees to follow organizational procedures, rather than doing something their own way, and to help them appreciate the organizational culture.

Persuasive presentations motivate the audience to act or to believe. Giving information and evidence is an important means of persuasion. Stories and visuals are also effective. In addition, the speaker must build goodwill by appearing to be credible and sympathetic to the audience's needs. The goal in many presentations is a favorable vote or decision. For example, speakers making business presentations may try to persuade the audience to approve their proposals, to adopt their ideas, or to buy their products. Sometimes the goal is to change behavior or attitudes or to reinforce existing attitudes. For example, a speaker at a meeting of factory workers may stress the importance of following safety procedures.

Goodwill presentations entertain and validate the audience. In an after-dinner speech, the audience wants to be entertained. Presentations at sales meetings may be designed to stroke the audience's egos and to validate their commitment to organizational goals.

Make your purpose as specific as possible.

Weak: The purpose of my presentation is to discuss saving for retirement.

Better: The purpose of my presentation is to persuade my audience to put their 401k funds in stocks and bonds, not in money market accounts and CDs.

or: The purpose of my presentation is to explain how to calculate how much money someone needs to save in order to maintain a specific lifestyle after retirement.

Your purpose statement is the principle that guides your choice of strategy and content, so write it down before you start preparing your presentation. Note that the purpose is *not* the introduction of your talk; it may not be explicit in your presentation at all.

COMPARING WRITTEN AND ORAL MESSAGES

Giving a presentation is in many ways very similar to writing a message. All the chapters on using you-attitude and positive emphasis, developing benefits, analyzing your audience, and designing visuals remain relevant as you plan an oral presentation.

Oral messages make it easier to

- Use emotion to help persuade the audience.
- Focus the audience's attention on specific points.
- Answer questions, resolve conflicts, and build consensus.
- Modify a proposal that may not be acceptable in its original form.
- Get immediate action or response.

Written messages make it easier to

- Present extensive or complex data.
- Present many specific details of a law, policy, or procedure.
- Minimize undesirable emotions.

Oral and written messages have many similarities. In both, you should

- Adapt the message to the specific audience.
- Show the audience how they would benefit from the idea, policy, service, or product.
- Overcome any objections the audience may have.
- Use you-attitude and positive emphasis.
- Use visuals to clarify or emphasize material.
- Specify exactly what the audience should do.

Oral presentation skills are a big asset in the business world.

Why It's So Hard

"We may grudgingly admit that, like it or not, verbal blunders have the inevitability of gravity. The next question is why? It's because speaking is one of the most complicated human activities that we do, at any age. The average adult English speaker has a vocabulary of around thirty thousand words. . . . Most of us in modern America, apart from the very solitary and the very garrulous, speak anywhere from 7,500 to 22,500 words a day. Grabbing these words, one every four hundred milliseconds on average, and arranging them in sequences that are edited and reviewed for grammar and appropriateness before they're spoken requires a symphony of neurons working quickly and precisely. Pronouncing words in any language requires that your brain coordinate with your body in order to turn the electricity of nerve impulses into waves of sound. . . .

"Given the speeds involved, why aren't we better equipped to puts units of language in the right order? The problem is that sounds, words, and grammatical items aren't arranged in our brains as though on a library's shelves, with all the items ordered and catalogued by topics and authors. Rather, they're associated with one another in a matrix or a web."

Quoted from Michael Erard, *Um . . . Slips, Stumbles and Verbal Blunders and What They Mean* (New York: Pantheon Books, 2007), 61–62.

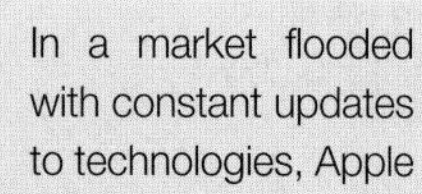

Keeping It Simple

In a market flooded with constant updates to technologies, Apple makes its products stand out from the crowd. One reason is the simple messages provided by former CEO Steve Jobs, which are echoed consistently in online marketing, television ads, and in Apple Stores around the world. When Jobs introduced the iPad in January 2010, for example, he called it "truly magical and revolutionary." His introduction helped catapult the iPad to a commanding share of the new tablet market.

Other technology companies have not been as successful in articulating their messages. RIM, the maker of longtime smartphone leader BlackBerry, introduced its answer to the iPad in late 2010. In his introduction of the Playbook, RIM's CEO Jim Balsillie said, "There's tremendous turbulence in the ecosystem, of course, in mobility. And that's sort of an obvious thing, but also there's tremendous architectural contention at play. And so I'm going to really frame our mobile architectural distinction. We've taken two fundamentally different approaches in their causalness. It's a causal difference, not just nuance. It's not just a causal direction that I'm going to articulate here—and feel free to go as deep as you want—it's really as fundamental as causalness."

Remember, for successful presentations, keep it simple.

Adapted from Diane Brady and Hugo Miller, "Failure to Communicate," *Bloomberg Businessweek,* October 11–17, 2010, 76–80.

PLANNING A STRATEGY FOR YOUR PRESENTATION LO 19-1

How will you reach your specific goals with a specific audience?

In all oral presentations, simplify what you want to say. Identify the one idea you want the audience to take home. Simplify your supporting detail so it's easy to follow. Simplify visuals so they can be taken in at a glance. Simplify your words and sentences so they're easy to understand. Researchers at Bell Labs are practicing these techniques. Where once they spent their days on basic research and academic papers, they now are condensing their scientific work into eight-minute PowerPoint presentations for potential corporate partners and venture capital as the Labs' new director seeks to make it profitable.[1]

An oral presentation needs to be simpler than a written message to the same audience. If readers forget a point, they can turn back to it and reread it. Headings, paragraph indentation, and punctuation provide visual cues to help readers understand the message. Listeners, in contrast, must remember what the speaker says. Whatever they don't remember is lost. Even asking questions requires the audience to remember which points they don't understand.

Analyze your audience for an oral presentation just as you do for a written message. If you'll be speaking to co-workers, talk to them about your topic or proposal to find out what questions or objections they have. For audiences inside the organization, the biggest questions are often practical ones: Will it work? How much will it cost? How long will it take? How will it impact me?

Think about the physical conditions in which you'll be speaking. Will the audience be tired at the end of a long day of listening? Sleepy after a big meal? Will the group be large or small? The more you know about your audience, the better you can adapt your message to them.

Choosing the Kind of Presentation

Choose one of three basic kinds of presentations: monologue, guided discussion, or interactive.

In a **monologue presentation,** the speaker talks without interruption; questions are held until the end of the presentation, at which time the speaker functions as an expert. The speaker plans the presentation in advance and delivers it without deviation. This kind of presentation is the most common in class situations, but it's often boring for the audience. Good delivery skills are crucial, since the audience is comparatively uninvolved.

In a **guided discussion,** the speaker presents the questions or issues that both speaker and audience have agreed on in advance. Rather than functioning as an expert with all the answers, the speaker serves as a facilitator to help the audience tap its own knowledge. This kind of presentation is excellent for presenting the results of consulting projects, when the speaker has specialized knowledge, but the audience must implement the solution if it is to succeed. Guided discussions need more time than monologue presentations, but produce more audience response, more responses involving analysis, and more commitment to the result.

An **interactive presentation** is a conversation, even if the speaker stands up in front of a group and uses charts and overheads. Most sales presentations are interactive presentations. The sales representative uses questions to determine the buyer's needs, probe objections, and gain provisional and then final commitment to the purchase. Even in a memorized sales presentation, the buyer will talk a significant portion of the time. Top salespeople let the buyer do the majority of the talking.

Technology also continues to offer new ways for audience interaction. Audience response devices (see sidebar on this page) allow people to answer multiple-choice, true/false, and yes/no questions; software then quickly tabulates the responses into charts and graphs the audience can see. Some new audience response systems use mobile phones, twitter, and the web; they also display results in charts. The question for you will be how much such a system tempts your audience to send its own tweets instead of listening to you.

Adapting Your Ideas to the Audience

Measure the message you'd like to send against where your audience is now. If your audience is indifferent, skeptical, or hostile, focus on the part of your message the audience will find most interesting and easiest to accept.

Make your ideas relevant to your audience by linking what you have to say to their experiences and interests. Showing your audience that the topic affects them directly is the most effective strategy. When you can't do that, at least link the topic to some everyday experience.

Planning a Strong Opening

The beginning and the end of a presentation, like the beginning and the end of a written document, are positions of emphasis. Use those key positions to interest the audience and emphasize your key point. You'll sound more natural and more effective if you talk from notes but write out your opener and close in advance and memorize them. (They'll be short: just a sentence or two.)

Good presentations adapt their ideas to a particular audience.

Audience Feedback

Just as when you're speaking with someone face-to-face, when you're presenting in front of a group it's important to look for feedback from your audience. Pay attention to body language, and ask your audience questions: the feedback that you get will help you build rapport with your audience so that you can express your message more clearly.

In some settings, such as when you're presenting to a large group, you might use other tools to gather audience feedback. For example, you could build a group discussion into your presentation: give your audience some questions to discuss in small groups, then invite them to share their answers with the room. Give questionnaires to your audience, either before your presentation or during a break. Have a member of your team tabulate audience responses, then build them into the remainder of your talk.

Audience response devices give you another option for getting instant audience feedback. These devices—popular with training departments—allow your audience to respond quickly to multiple-choice or yes/no questions during presentations. Software tabulates the responses as numbers, charts, or graphs for all to see. These devices are particularly good for feedback in situations where people may want anonymity.

Look at the product websites of some popular audience response devices:

- www.meridiaars.com/
- www.optiontechnologies.com
- www.qwizdom.com
- www.turningtechnologies.com

How do these devices compare to each other? How might you use them in your own presentations?

Mastering Toasts

To some, Toastmasters International still reflects its roots: helping nervous groomsmen prepare wedding toasts. But it has grown into an organization with over 250,000 members and is growing at about 10% every year. Its 2011 International Speech Contest drew 38,000 contestants from 113 countries. So what is it all about?

Toastmasters helps its members learn and practice public speaking. But their aim is not at high-stakes motivational speaking. Rather, "We help the new supervisor who just got promoted and doesn't feel comfortable talking to the five people working for him," says Daniel Rex, the executive director. "We teach people skills, but what we really teach is confidence."

Their success in teaching has been noticed. Official branches of the organization can be found in many major corporations, and other companies sponsor Toastmasters classes for their employees. The principles taught—confidence, simplicity, personal branding, and audience engagement—are important for any presenter to learn.

Adapted from Joel Stein, "Making Every Word Count," *Bloomberg Businessweek,* January 24–30, 2011, 112–13.

Consider using one of four common modes for openers: startling statement, narration or anecdote, quotation, or question. The more you can do to personalize your opener for your audience, the better. Recent events are better than things that happened long ago; local events are better than events at a distance; people they know are better than people who are only names.

Startling Statement

> Twelve of our customers have canceled orders in the past month.

This presentation to a company's executive committee went on to show that the company's distribution system was inadequate and to recommend a third warehouse located in the Southwest.

Narration or Anecdote The same presentation could also start with a relevant story.

> Last week Joe Murphy, purchasing agent for Westtrop's, our biggest client, came to see me. I knew something was wrong right away, because Joe was wearing a jacket instead of his usual cowboy shirt and smile. "Ajit," he said, "I have to tell you something. I didn't want to do it, but I had to change suppliers. We've been with you a long time, but it's just not working for us now."

Elements such as dialogue and sensory details will give stories more impact.

Quotation A quotation could also start the presentation. This quotation came from Boyers, a major account for the company:

> "Faster and easier!" That's what Boyers said about their new supplier.

Quotations work best when they are directly connected to the audience, as opposed to quotes from famous people.

Question Asking the audience to raise their hands or reply to questions gets them actively involved in a presentation. Tony Jeary skillfully uses this technique in sessions devoted to training the audience in presentation skills. He begins by asking the audience members to write down their estimate of the number of presentations they give per week:

> "How many of you said one or two?" he asks, raising his hand. A few hands pop up. "Three, four, six, eight?" he asks, walking up the middle of the aisle to the back of the room. Hands start popping up like targets in a shooting gallery. Jeary's Texas drawl accelerates and suddenly the place sounds like a cattle auction. "Do I hear 10? Twelve? Thirteen to the woman in the green shirt! Fifteen to the gentleman in plaid," he fires, and the room busts out laughing.[2]

Most presenters will not want to take a course in auctioneering, as Jeary did to make his questioning routine more authentic. However, Jeary's approach both engages the audience and makes the point that many jobs involve a multitude of occasions requiring formal and informal presentation skills.

Your opener should interest the audience and establish a rapport with them. Some speakers use humor to achieve those goals. However, an inappropriate joke can turn the audience against the speaker. Never use humor that's directed against the audience or an inappropriate group. Humor directed at yourself or your team is safer, but even there, limit it. Don't make your audience squirm with too much self-revelation.

Humor isn't the only way to set an audience at ease. Smile at your audience before you begin; let them see that you're a real person and a nice one.

Planning a Strong Conclusion

The end of your presentation should be as strong as the opener. For your close, you could do one or more of the following:

- Restate your main point.
- Refer to your opener to create a frame for your presentation.
- End with a vivid, positive picture.
- Tell the audience exactly what to do to solve the problem you've discussed.

When Mike Powell described his work in science to an audience of nonscientists, he opened and then closed with words about what being a scientist feels like. He opened humorously, saying, "Being a scientist is like doing a jigsaw puzzle . . . in a snowstorm . . . at night . . . when you don't have all the pieces . . . and you don't have the picture you are trying to create." Powell closed by returning to the opening idea of "being a scientist," but he moved from the challenge to the inspiration with this vivid story:

> The final speaker at a medical conference [I] attended . . . walked to the lectern and said, "I am a thirty-two-year-old wife and mother of two. I have AIDS. Please work fast."[3]

When you write out your opener and close, be sure to use oral rather than written style. As you can see in the example close above, oral style uses shorter sentences and shorter, simpler words than writing does. Oral style can even sound a bit choppy when it is read by eye. Oral style uses more personal pronouns, a less varied vocabulary, and more repetition.

Prezi Presentations

Prezi, a free online tool, provides business communicators with another option when planning presentations. While PowerPoint's presentation philosophy is based on older techniques of clicking through actual physical slides, Prezi uses modern technologies to create a different experience.

Rather than a series of consecutive slides, Prezi creates one large canvas. The presenter can place text and images anywhere on the canvas, and zoom in and out on areas or pan to different areas of the canvas. This approach allows presenters to display hierarchies and spatial relationships between items in ways that PowerPoint's linear progression doesn't allow.

Prezi's zooming and panning approach may be more engaging than PowerPoint, especially to viewers who are not familiar with it. But, just as with PowerPoint's transitions and animations, Prezi's movements can become distracting if used unwisely. Overuse of Prezi's movements can create a dizzying effect on the audience.

CHOOSING INFORMATION TO INCLUDE IN A PRESENTATION LO 19-2

Choose the information that is most interesting to your audience, that answers the questions your audience will have and that is most persuasive for them. Limit your talk to three main points. In a long presentation (20 minutes or more) each main point can have subpoints. Your content will be easier to understand if you clearly show the relationship between each of the main points.

Turning your information into a **story** also helps. For example, a presentation about a plan to reduce scrap rates on the second shift can begin by setting the scene and defining the problem: Production expenses have cut profits in half. The plot unfolds as the speaker describes the facts that helped her trace the problem to scrap rates on the second shift. The resolution to the story is her group's proposal.

In an informative presentation, link the points you make to the knowledge your audience has. Show the audience members that your information answers their questions, solves their problems, or helps them do their jobs. When you explain the effect of a new law or the techniques for using a new machine, use specific examples that apply to the decisions they make and the work they do. If your content is detailed or complicated, give people a written outline or handouts. The written material both helps the audience keep track of your points during the presentation and serves as a reference after the talk is over.

How Not to Give a Presentation

John R. Brant has some excellent advice on how to give an awful presentation:

- Have a dull opening: If you really want to lose your audience in the first few minutes, read a prepared statement to them from a slide or a handout.
- Bury them in slides: Bore your audience with more slides than they'll be able to remember, or speed through your slides so quickly that your PowerPoint turns into a blur.
- Use the wrong humor: Make everyone uncomfortable with self-deprecating humor.
- Show them your back: Demonstrate how disconnected you are with your audience by turning your back to them, and avoid the possibility of rapport-building eye contact by looking at the screen instead of at your audience.

Think about the uninspiring presentations you've seen from other students, or even from your instructors. What could the presenters have done to improve their work and gain your interest?

Adapted from John R. Brandt, "Missing the (Power) Point," *Industry Week*, January 2007, 48.

To be convincing, you must answer the audience's questions and objections. However, don't bring up negatives or inconsistencies unless you're sure that the audience will think of them. If you aren't sure, save your evidence for the question phase. If someone does ask, you'll have the answer.

Choosing Data

As part of choosing what to say, you should determine what data to present, including what to show in visuals. Any data you mention should be necessary for the points you are making. Databases and PowerPoint have given employees direct access to ready-made and easy-to-create slides. The temptation is to overuse them rather than starting with decisions about what the audience needs to know.

Statistics and numbers can be convincing if you present them in ways that are easy to hear. Simplify numbers by reducing them to two significant digits and putting them in a context.

Hard to hear: Our 2010 sales dropped from $12,036,288,000 to $9,124,507,000.

Easy to hear: Our 2010 sales dropped from $12 billion to $9 billion. This is the steepest decline our company has seen in a quarter century.

Double-check your presentation statistics and numbers to ensure they are accurate. Mark Hurd, former chairman and CEO of Hewlett-Packard, gave as the best advice he ever got, "It's hard to look smart with bad numbers."[4]

Choosing Demonstrations

Demonstrations can prove your points dramatically and quickly. Dieticians had long known that coconut oil, used on movie popcorn, was bad for you. But no one seemed to care. Until, that is, the folks at the Center for Science in the Public Interest (CSPI) took up the cause. They called a press conference to announce that a medium movie popcorn (and who eats just a medium?) had more saturated fat than a bacon-and-eggs breakfast, a Big Mac and fries lunch, and a steak dinner with all the trimmings—combined. They provided the full buffet for TV cameras. The story played on all the major networks as well as the front pages of many newspapers. Even better, people remembered the story and popcorn sales plunged.[5]

In their book *Made to Stick: Why Some Ideas Survive and Others Die*, Chip Heath and Dan Heath say that ideas are remembered—and have lasting impact on people's opinions and behavior—when they have six characteristics:

1. **Simplicity:** they are short but filled with meaning: the demonstration above could be comprehended in seconds.
2. **Unexpectedness:** they have some novelty for us: a bag of movie popcorn is worse than a whole day's meals of fatty foods.
3. **Concreteness:** the ideas must be explained with psychological description (see Chapter 11) or in terms of human actions: the display of fatty foods was graphic.
4. **Credibility:** ideas have to carry their own credibility if they do not come from an acknowledged expert. In the demonstration above, people could see the effects for themselves.
5. **Emotions:** the ideas must make people feel some emotion, and it has to be the right emotion. Antismoking campaigns for teenagers have not been successful using fear, but they have had some success using resentment at the duplicity of cigarette companies.
6. **Stories:** the ideas have to tell stories.

The Heaths call the combination of these six factors stickiness. And the concept really works. Amounts of saturated fats are not exciting ideas, but CSPI changed movie popcorn with its demonstration.[6]

An Alternative to PowerPoint

"Barbara Waugh was Worldwide Personnel Manager at Hewlett-Packard Labs. [Several years ago, she was researching how to make HP Labs the best in the business. Waugh's data helped her narrow the problem to three areas needing improvement: programs (clearer priorities and fewer projects), people (elimination of poor performers and more freedom for good performers), and processes (better information sharing). Next, Waugh's challenge was to present these ideas to top managers in a way they could understand and accept.] The last thing she wanted was to preach through PowerPoint. So instead of creating bullet-point slides, she drew on her experience with street theatre and created a "play" about HP Labs. She worked passages from the surveys into dialogue and then recruited executives to act as staff members, and junior people to act as executives. The troupe performed for 30 senior managers. 'At the end of the play, the managers were very quiet,' Waugh remembers. 'Then they started clapping. It was exciting. They really got it. They finally understood.'"

Quoted from Katherine Mieszkowski, "I Grew Up Thinking That Change Was Cataclysmic. The Way We've Done It Here Is to Start Slow and Work Small." *Fast Company,* December 1998, 152.

ORGANIZING YOUR INFORMATION

Most presentations use a direct pattern of organization, even when the goal is to persuade a reluctant audience. In a business setting, the audience is in a hurry and knows that you want to persuade them. Be honest about your goal, and then prove that your goal meets the audience's needs too.

In a persuasive presentation, start with your strongest point, your best reason. If time permits, give other reasons as well and respond to possible objections. Put your weakest point in the middle so that you can end on a strong note.

Often one of five standard patterns of organization will work:

- **Chronological.** Start with the past, move to the present, and end by looking ahead. This pattern works best when the history helps show a problem's complexity or magnitude, or when the chronology moves people to an obvious solution.
- **Problem–causes–solution.** Explain the symptoms of the problem, identify its causes, and suggest a solution. This pattern works best when the audience will find your solution easy to accept.
- **Excluding alternatives.** Explain the symptoms of the problem. Explain the obvious solutions first and show why they won't solve the problem. End by discussing a solution that will work. This pattern may be necessary when the audience will find the solution hard to accept.
- **Pro–con.** Give all the reasons in favor of something, then those against it. This pattern works well when you want the audience to see the weaknesses in its position.
- **1–2–3.** Discuss three aspects of a topic. This pattern works well to organize short informative briefings. "Today I'll review our sales, production, and profits for the last quarter."

Make your organization clear to your audience. Written documents can be reread; they can use headings, paragraphs, lists, and indentations to signal levels of detail. In a presentation, you have to provide explicit clues to the structure of your discourse.

Early in your talk—perhaps immediately after your opener—provide an **overview** of the main points you will make.

> First, I'd like to talk about who the homeless in Columbus are. Second, I'll talk about the services The Open Shelter provides. Finally, I'll talk about what you—either individually or as a group—can do to help.

An overview provides a mental peg that hearers can hang each point on. It also can prevent someone from missing what you are saying because he or she wonders why you aren't covering a major point that you've saved for later.

Offer a clear signpost as you come to each new point. A **signpost** is an explicit statement of the point you have reached. Choose wording that fits your style. The following statements are three different ways that a speaker could use to introduce the last of three points:

> Now we come to the third point: what you can do as a group or as individuals to help homeless people in Columbus.

New to Admissions: PowerPoint

The University of Chicago Business School took a novel approach to their application process in 2007 when they began asking students to submit PowerPoint presentations in addition to other admission requirements. Since knowing how to create effective slides is crucial for people in business, the inclusion of four slides into the application materials seems almost natural. In fact, Microsoft estimates that 30 million presentations are given per day using their software.

Rose Martinelli, an admissions officer, stated that "we wanted to have a freeform space for students to be able to say what they think is important." The school hopes the new medium will help attract students who can think outside the box, an ability which often bodes well in business.

If you were applying to this school, would you be excited about showing off your presentation skills? What type of material would you include on your slides? What slide design techniques would help you stand out from the pack?

Adapted from Justin Pope, "School Adds PowerPoint for Entrance," *Des Moines Register,* August 8, 2007, D5.

@http://www.ted.com/

TED offers "riveting talks by remarkable people, free to the world." You can sort talks by categories such as business or science, or by tags such as persuasive, informative, funny, "most e-mailed this week," or "rated jaw-dropping."

So much for what we're doing. Now let's talk about what you can do to help.

You may be wondering, what can I do to help?

PLANNING POWERPOINT SLIDES

Once you have planned a strategy for your presentation, you need to decide if you will use PowerPoint. Not all presentations benefit from PowerPoint slides. Information design expert Edward Tufte wrote a famous essay blasting the slides. However, the slides have become ubiquitous at presentations, so your audience might expect them. And they definitely offer advantages for talks that benefit from visuals that can be seen at a distance. These visuals can give your presentation a professional image and greater impact.

Well-designed visuals can serve as an outline for your talk (see Figure 19.1), eliminating the need for additional notes. Visuals can help your audience follow along with you, and help you keep your place as you speak. Your visuals should highlight your main points, not give every detail. Elaborate on your visuals as you talk; most people find it mind-numbing to have slide after slide read to them. **If the audience can read the entire presentation for themselves, why are you there?**

Designing PowerPoint Slides

As you design slides for PowerPoint and other presentation programs, keep the following guidelines in mind:

- Use a consistent background
- Use a big font size: 44 or 50 point for titles, 32 point for subheads, and 28 point for examples. You should be able to read the smallest words easily when you print a handout version of your slides.
- Use bullet-point phrases rather than complete sentences.
- Use clear, concise language.
- Make only three to five points on each slide. If you have more, consider using two slides.
- Customize your slides with your organization's logo, and add visuals: charts, pictures, downloaded web pages, photos, and drawings.

Figure 19.1 Poorly Formatted Presentation Slides (Top) and Well-Formatted Slides (Bottom)

Use simplified graphs and charts

Build goodwill

Summmarize main points

Use a consistent background

Use simplified headings

Use clipart or images that match the topic

Use animation to make words and images appear and move during your presentation—but only in ways that help you control information flow and build interest. Avoid using animation or sound effects just to be clever; they will distract your audience.

http://norvig.com/Gettysburg/index.htm

Not every speech needs visuals. As Peter Norvig shows, Lincoln's Gettysburg Address is hurt, not helped, by adding bland PowerPoint slides.

Use **clip art** in your presentations only if the art is really appropriate to your points. Internet sources have made such a wide variety of drawings and photos available that designers really have no excuse for failing to pick images that are both appropriate and visually appealing. Even organizations on tight budgets can find free and low-cost resources, such as the public domain (that is, not copyrighted) collections of the U.S. Fish and Wildlife Service (http://digitalmedia.fws.gov) and the National Oceanic and Atmospheric Administration (http://www.photolib.noaa.gov/).

Choose a consistent **template,** or background design, for your entire presentation. Make sure that the template is appropriate for your subject matter and audience. For example, use a globe only if your topic is international business and palm trees only if you're talking about tropical vacations. One problem with PowerPoint is that the basic templates may seem repetitive to people who see lots of presentations made with the program. For an important presentation, you may want to consider customizing the basic template. You can also find many professionally designed free templates online to help lend your presentation a more unique look. Make sure your template does not detract from your information.

Choose a light **background** if the lights will be off during your presentation and a dark background if the lights will be on. Slides will be easier to read if you use high contrast between the words and backgrounds. See Figure 19.2 for examples of effective and ineffective color combinations.

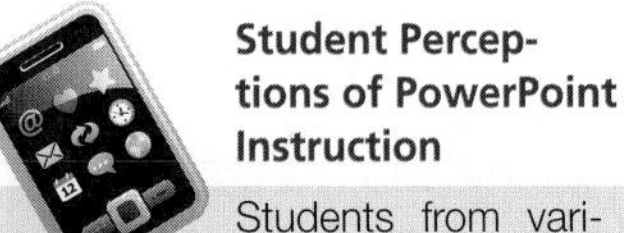

Student Perceptions of PowerPoint Instruction

Students from various business majors took a survey assessing their perceptions of PowerPoint instruction in their courses. The survey revealed that only 27% of students thought that PowerPoint was "interesting and fresh" as an educational tool.

The researchers also discovered that those students who didn't see PowerPoint as interesting viewed traditional lecture as a better way to handle classroom discussion and encourage social interaction. Moreover, students were also likely to suggest that PowerPoint provoked boredom and attention difficulties.

What are your perceptions of PowerPoint? How effectively do you learn from PowerPoint instruction? What could make your classroom learning experience more effective?

Adapted from Lisa A. Burke and Karen. E. James, "PowerPoint Based Lectures in Business Education: An Empirical Investigation of Student-Perceived Novelty and Effectiveness," *Business Communication Quarterly* 71, no. 3 (September 2008): 277–96.

http://www.authorstream.com/

Created a great PowerPoint that you would like to share with the rest of the world? Interested in viewing some intricately crafted PowerPoint presentations? Well, Author Stream is just the place. You can join for free and upload your PowerPoint presentations on just about any topic. Author Stream also allows you to rate and comment on other users' PowerPoint presentations. An additional feature lets you keep track of people who embed your presentation on their website and the number of times it gets viewed.

Figure 19.2 Effective and Ineffective Colors for Presentation Slides

Effective

Use high contrast between words and background.

Repeat colors in words and design elements.

Ineffective

Limit the number of bright colors.

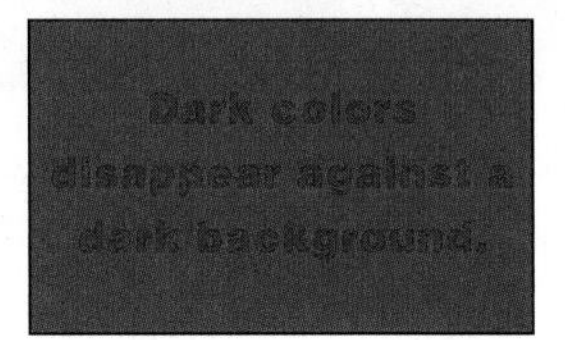

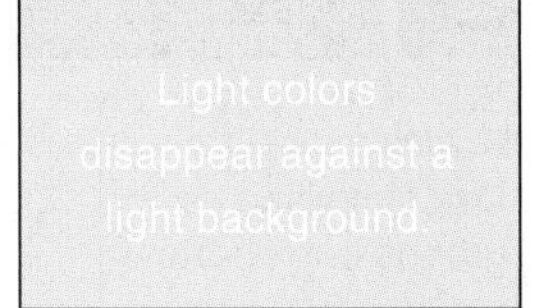

Using Figures and Tables

Visuals for presentations need to be simpler than visuals the audience reads on paper. For example, to adapt a printed data table for a presentation, you might cut out one or more columns or rows of data, round off the data to simplify them, or replace the chart with a graph or other visual. If you have many data tables or charts in your presentation, consider including them on a handout for your audience.

Your presentation visuals should include titles, but don't need figure numbers. As you prepare your presentation, be sure to know where each visual is so that you can return to it easily if someone asks about it during the question period. Rather than reading from your slides, or describing visuals to your audience in detail, summarize the story contained on each slide and elaborate on what it means for your audience.

Using PowerPoint Technology to Involve Your Audience

Projected visuals work only if the technology they depend on works. When you give presentations in your own workplace, check the equipment in advance. When you make a presentation in another location or for another organization, arrive early so that you'll have time to not only check the equipment but also track down a service worker if the equipment isn't working. Be prepared with a backup plan to use if you're unable to show your visuals.

Keep in mind how you will use your presentation slides. Most likely, they will provide visual support for an oral presentation in a face-to-face meeting or videoconference. The slides should visually identify the key points of your presentation in a way that allows you to interact with your audience. Your oral presentation should always include more material than the text on your slides.

Consider ways to stimulate your audience's curiosity, invite questions, and build enthusiasm. For instance, instead of saying, "Sales grew 85% with this program," you could show a graph that shows sales declining up to the introduction of the program; invite the audience to consider what this program might do; and finally, after explaining the program, reveal the full sales graph with an animation that highlights the spike using a dramatic magenta line.

Remember that your audience can look at you or your visual, but not both at the same time. Direct attention to more complex visuals, such as figures, and explain them or give your audience a few seconds to absorb them.

WARNING: Be sure you have a backup plan in case of a technology failure that prevents your use of PowerPoint.

DELIVERING AN EFFECTIVE PRESENTATION LO 19-3

Audiences want the sense that you're talking directly to them and that you care that they understand and are interested. They'll forgive you if you get tangled up in a sentence and end it ungrammatically. They won't forgive you if you seem to have a "canned" talk that you're going to deliver no matter who the audience is or how they respond. You can convey a sense of caring to your audience by making direct eye contact with them and by using a conversational style.

Dealing with Fear

Feeling nervous about public speaking is normal; most people feel some fear about public speaking. But you can harness that nervous energy to help you do your best work. As various trainers have noted, you don't need to get rid of your butterflies. All you need to do is make them fly in formation.

To calm your nerves before you give an oral presentation,

- Be prepared. Analyze your audience, organize your thoughts, prepare visual aids, practice your opener and close, check out the arrangements.
- Have backup plans for various contingencies, including technical problems and likely questions.
- Use only the amount of caffeine you normally use. More or less may make you jumpy.
- Avoid alcoholic beverages.
- Relabel your nerves. Instead of saying, "I'm scared," try saying, "My adrenaline is up." Adrenaline sharpens our reflexes and helps us do our best.

Just before your presentation,

- Consciously contract and then relax your muscles, starting with your feet and calves and going up to your shoulders, arms, and hands.
- Take several deep breaths from your diaphragm; picture stress leaving your body as you exhale.

During your presentation,

- Pause and look at the audience before you begin speaking.
- Concentrate on communicating with your audience, not your feelings.
- Use body energy in strong gestures and movement.

Using Eye Contact

Look directly at the people you're talking to. Make eye contact with individuals in different locations throughout the audience, because you want everyone to feel you are connecting with them. Do not stare at your computer screen or your notes. Researchers have found that observers were more than twice

Avoiding Disastrous PowerPoints

Conference keynote presentations are notoriously boring, with long PowerPoint shows and droning presenters. Participants, bored, fiddle with smartphones and participate in electronic discussions. During one keynote presentation, bored audience members even designed a T-shirt and put it up for sale online. The shirt's message? "I survived the keynote disaster of 09."

How can you keep your presentations from ending up with their own T-shirts? Here are a few tips:

- *Use visuals and words together.* Your PowerPoint slides should augment and enhance your presentation, not distract from or displace it.
- *Keep your slides simple.* An audience should be able to completely understand each slide in two or three seconds.
- *Break complex ideas into multiple slides.* Don't try to get all the information on a single slide. Use several slides that add up to something more complex.
- *Use your slides as a mnemonic device.* Your slides should make your presentation emotionally appealing and memorable to your audience.

Adapted from Nancy Duarte, "Avoiding the Road to PowerPoint Hell," *Wall Street Journal*, January 27, 2011, C12.

http://www.baruch.cuny.edu/tutorials/powerpoint

Want to sharpen your PowerPoint skills? Try out this tutorial that will help improve your preparation design and delivery the next time you have to deliver a presentation. The site also features pros and cons for using PowerPoint and suggests additional resources.

Pressure Presentations

Technology entrepreneurs routinely pitch their ideas to financial investors at the large Tech-Crunch 50 and DEMO conferences. This presentation situation is stressful for many people. These are five tips for presenting under pressure at such conferences.

- *Keep it brief:* Technology conferences charge enormous fees to present, so you are paying thousands of dollars for every minute of your talk. Besides, most audiences get bored within 10 minutes anyway.
- *Don't overload:* The human brain can absorb only so much at one sitting. What is the most important information to guide investors to a favorable decision about your idea?
- *Set the stage:* Define the problem before explaining what your product can do. If there is no problem, your idea lacks impact.
- *Rehearse:* Most people don't spend enough time rehearsing. Practice, practice, practice! Oh, and ditch the notecards, too.
- *Be prepared:* If technology fails, don't stop talking. Acknowledge the issue and move on. Your audience cares about what you have to say, not your slides.

Adapted from Carmine Gallo, "How to Deliver a Presentation under Pressure," *BusinessWeek,* September 19, 2008, http://www.businessweek.com/smallbiz/content/sep2008/sb20080919_919248.htm.

Part of an effective presentation is its setting. Do you think this outdoor setting helps or hinders the presentation?

as likely to notice and comment on poor presentation features, like poor eye contact, than good features, and tended to describe speakers with poor eye contact as disinterested, unprofessional, and poorly prepared.[7]

The point in making eye contact is to establish one-on-one contact with the individual members of your audience. People want to feel that you're talking to them. Looking directly at individuals also enables you to be more conscious of feedback from the audience, so that you can modify your approach if necessary.

Developing a Good Speaking Voice

People will enjoy your presentation more if your voice is easy to listen to. To find out what your voice sounds like, tape-record it. Listen to your voice qualities and delivery.

Voice Qualities

Tone of voice refers to the rising or falling inflection that tells you whether a group of words is a question or a statement, whether the speaker is uncertain or confident, whether a statement is sincere or sarcastic.

When tone of voice and the meaning of words conflict, people "believe" the tone of voice. If you respond to your friends' "How are you?" with the words "I'm dying, and you?" most of your friends will reply "Fine." If the tone of your voice is cheerful, they may not hear the content of the words.

Pitch measures whether a voice uses sounds that are low or high. Low-pitched voices are usually perceived as being more authoritative, sexier, and more pleasant to listen to than are high-pitched voices. Most voices go up in pitch when the speaker is angry or excited; some people raise pitch when they increase volume. Women whose normal speaking voices are high may need to practice projecting their voices to avoid becoming shrill when they speak to large groups.

Stress is the emphasis given to one or more words in a sentence. As the following example shows, emphasizing different words can change the meaning.

I'll give you a raise.

[Implication, depending on pitch and speed: "Another supervisor wouldn't" or "I have the power to determine your salary."]

I'll **give** you a raise.

[Implication, depending on pitch and speed: "You haven't **earned** it" or "OK, all right, you win. I'm saying 'yes' to get rid of you, but I don't really agree," or "I've just this instant decided that you deserve a raise."]

I'll give **you** a raise.

[Implication: "But nobody else in this department is getting one."]

I'll give you **a** raise.

[Implication: "But just one."]

I'll give you a **raise.**

[Implication: "But you won't get the promotion or anything else you want."]

I'll give **you** a **raise.**

[Implication: "You deserve it."]

I'll give you a **raise!**

[Implication: "I've just this minute decided to act, and I'm excited about this idea. The raise will please both of us."]

Speakers who use many changes in tone, pitch, and stress as they speak usually seem more enthusiastic; often they also seem more energetic and more intelligent. Someone who speaks in a monotone may seem apathetic or unintelligent. When you are interested in your topic, your audience is more likely to be also.

Delivery When you speak to a group, talk loudly enough so that people can hear you easily. If you're using a microphone, adjust your volume so you aren't shouting. When you speak in an unfamiliar location, try to get to the room early so you can check the size of the room and the power of the **amplification** equipment. If you can't do that, ask early in your talk, "Can you hear me in the back of the room?"

The bigger the group is, the more carefully you need to **enunciate,** that is, voice all the sounds of each word. Words starting or ending with *f, t, k, v,* and *d* are especially hard to hear. "Our informed and competent image" can sound like "Our informed, incompetent image."

Use your voice as you would use your facial expressions: to create a cheerful, energetic, and enthusiastic impression for your audience. Doing so can help you build rapport with your audience, and can demonstrate the importance of your material. If your ideas don't excite you, why should your audience find them exciting?

Practice your speech over and over, out loud, in front of a mirror or to your family and friends. There are various reasons for doing so. Practice allows you

- To stop thinking about the words and to concentrate instead on emotions you wish to communicate to your audience.
- To work on your transitions that move your speech from one point to the next. Transitions are one of the places where speakers frequently stumble.
- To avoid unintentional negatives. British Petroleum continued to make negative news during the Gulf oil spill with negative public statements from its officials. Its chairman, Carl-Henric Svanberg, told the press "We care about the small people." Its CEO, Tony Hayward, said he "wants his life back."[8]
- To reduce the number of *uhs* you use. **Filler sounds,** which occur when speakers pause searching for the next word, aren't necessarily signs of nervousness. Searching takes longer when people have big vocabularies or talk about topics where a variety of word choices are possible. Practicing your talk makes your word choices automatic, and you'll use fewer *uhs.*[9]

Your Call Is Important to Us

Companies spend thousands of dollars developing detailed automated systems to answer customer calls. Yet many callers bypass the systems to talk to a live agent, which can cost the company $3 to $9 per phone call. How can companies persuade customers to use the automated systems? Some believe the recorded voice can make all the difference.

Aflac, for example, replaced the many different voices on its customer service line with a consistent voice provided by a middle-aged female actress.

The insurance company Asurion conducted a similar change in their system. They coached their new voice actress to sound warmer, more competent, and more like a live customer service agent.

The new voices seem to be working. More customers are using the automated systems than before, and customer satisfaction with the systems in both companies has risen between 5% and 10%.

Adapted from Joe Light, "Automated Lines' Softer Tone," *Wall Street Journal,* November 1, 2010, B10.

Deep Voice Politics

"[Political candidates'] vocal chords—as much as the substance of their words—can influence who becomes the next president, claim the people who study, measure, and coach the human voice.

"'Voice matters—it's what sells,' says John Daly, a University of Texas communications professor who has written a book about persuasion. University of California at Los Angeles psychology professor Albert Mehrabian even claims to have quantified how important a voice is. When we are deciding whether we like the person delivering a message, tone of voice accounts for 38% of our opinion, body language for 55%, and the actual words for just 7%, his studies suggest."

Do you believe that your impressions of public speakers are shaped by vocal tones?

Many presenters spend too much time thinking about what they will say and too little time rehearsing how they will say it. Presentation is important; if it weren't, you would just e-mail your text or PowerPoint to your audience.

Standing and Gesturing

Stand with your feet far enough apart for good balance, with your knees flexed. Unless the presentation is very formal or you're on camera, you can walk if you want to. Some speakers like to come in front of the lectern to remove that barrier between themselves and the audience, or move about the room to connect with more people.

If you use PowerPoint, stand beside the screen so that you don't block it.

Build on your natural style for gestures. Gestures usually work best when they're big and confident. Avoid nervous gestures such as swaying on your feet, jingling coins in your pocket, or twisting a button. These mannerisms distract the audience.

Using Notes and Visuals

If using PowerPoint, use the notes feature. If not using PowerPoint, put your notes on cards or on sturdy pieces of paper and number them. Most speakers like to use 4-by-6-inch or 5-by-7-inch cards because they hold more information than 3-by-5-inch cards.

Your notes need to be complete enough to help you if you go blank, so use long phrases or complete sentences. Under each main point, list the evidence or illustration you'll use.

Look at your notes infrequently. Most of your gaze time should be directed to members of the audience. If using paper note cards, hold them high enough so that your head doesn't bob up and down as you look from the audience to your notes and back again.

If you have lots of visuals and know your topic well, you won't need notes. Face the audience, not the screen. Show the entire visual at once: don't cover up part of it. If you don't want the audience to read ahead, use PowerPoint animation or prepare several slides that build up.

Keep the room lights on if possible; turning them off makes it easier for people to fall asleep and harder for them to concentrate on you.

HANDLING QUESTIONS LO 19-4

Prepare for questions by listing every fact or opinion you can think of that challenges your position. Treat each objection seriously and try to think of a way to deal with it. If you're talking about a controversial issue, you may want to save one point for the question period, rather than making it during the presentation. Speakers who have visuals to answer questions seem especially well prepared.

During your presentation, tell the audience how you'll handle questions. If you have a choice, save questions for the end. In your talk, answer the questions or objections that you expect your audience to have. Don't exaggerate your claims so that you won't have to back down in response to questions later.

During the question period, don't nod your head to indicate that you understand a question as it is asked. Audiences will interpret nods as signs that you agree with the questioner. Instead, look directly at the questioner. As you answer the question, expand your focus to take in the entire group. Don't say, "That's a good question." That response implies that the other questions have been poor ones.

If the audience may not have heard the question or if you want more time to think, repeat the question before you answer it. Link your answers to the points you made in your presentation. Keep the purpose of your presentation in mind, and select information that advances your goals.

If a question is hostile or biased, rephrase it before you answer it. Suppose that during a sales presentation, the prospective client exclaims, "How can you justify those prices?" A response that steers the presentation back to the service's benefits might be: "You're asking about our pricing. The price includes 24-hour, on-site customer support and . . . " Then explain how those features will benefit the prospect. The late Senator Paul Simon was admired for the way he handled hostile questions. Simon would reply, "There are two ways to consider that matter. The way you just mentioned—and a way that starts from a slightly different base." Then Senator Simon would politely explain his point of view. This kind of response respects the questioner by leaving room for more than one viewpoint.[10]

Occasionally someone will ask a question that is really designed to state the speaker's own position. Respond to the question if you want to. Another option is to say, "That's a clear statement of your position. Let's move to the next question now." If someone asks about something that you already explained in your presentation, simply answer the question without embarrassing the questioner. No audience will understand and remember 100% of what you say.

If you don't know the answer to a question, say so. If your purpose is to inform, write down the question so that you can look up the answer before the next session. If it's a question to which you think there is no answer, ask if anyone in the room knows. When no one does, your "ignorance" is vindicated. If an expert is in the room, you may want to refer questions of fact to him or her. Answer questions of interpretation yourself.

At the end of the question period, take two minutes to summarize your main point once more. (This can be a restatement of your close.) Questions may or may not focus on the key point of your talk. Take advantage of having the floor to repeat your message briefly and forcefully.

Attack Responses

In their book, *Buy*In*, John Kotter and Lorne Whitehead suggest 24 common attacks (A) on presentations. They recommend that speakers answer the attacks with brief commonsense responses (R). Here are some examples.

- A: We've never done this in the past, and things have always worked out okay.
  R: True. But surely we have all seen that those who fail to adapt eventually become extinct.
- A: Your proposal doesn't go nearly far enough.
  R: Maybe, but our idea will get us started moving in the right direction and will do so without further delay.
- A: You can't do A without first doing B, yet you can't do B without first doing A. So the plan won't work. R: Well, actually, you can do a little bit of A, which allows a little bit of B, which allows more A, which allows more of B, and so on.

Attacks and responses quoted from John. P. Kotter and Lorne A. Whitehead, "Twenty-Four Attacks and Twenty-Four Responses," chap. 7 in *Buy*In: Saving Your Good Idea from Getting Shot Down* (Boston: Harvard Business Review Press, 2010). Reprinted with permission.

Checklist for Oral Presentations

- ☐ Is the presentation effective for the situation?
- ☐ Is the purpose clear, even if not explicitly stated? Is the purpose achieved?
- ☐ Does the presentation adapt to the audience's beliefs, experiences, and interests?
- ☐ Does the presentation engage the audience?
- ☐ Is the material vivid and specific?
- ☐ Does the material counter common objections without giving them undue weight?
- ☐ Is there an overview of the main points?
- ☐ Does the body contain signposts of the main points?
- ☐ Are there adequate transitions between points? Are the transitions smooth?
- ☐ Are the opening and closing strong and effective?
- ☐ Are there engaging visuals? Do they use an appropriate design or template?
- ☐ Are the visuals readable from a distance?
- ☐ Are visuals free of spelling, punctuation, and grammar mistakes?
- ☐ If the visuals contain data, are the data quickly assimilated?
- ☐ Did the speaker make good eye contact with the audience?
- ☐ Was the speaker positioned effectively? Did the speaker's body block the screen?
- ☐ Did the speaker use engaging vocal delivery?
- ☐ Could you hear and understand what the speaker was saying?

Giving Feedback

Getting feedback from peers is one important part of preparing a presentation, and speakers can't get good feedback without peers who can give good feedback.

Too often peers comment just on simple things, like word choice or body posture, but the most important feedback is frequently about content. Help speakers adapt their material to the audience by asking questions about the people they expect to address. Also, summarize the presenters' message as you understand it, and repeat it back. Doing so can help presenters see where they need to clarify.

No one likes to be criticized, so phrase your critiques in positive terms. Point out changes or suggestions that will make their presentation better, and if you can, back up your advice with tips from professionals.

Think about the way you prepare your own presentations. Do you practice them in front of an audience? What kind of feedback do you get? How could you encourage a practice audience to give you more helpful advice?

Adapted from Kinley Levack, "Talking Head to Rock Star: How You Can Turn Your Top Executives into Polished Presenters," *Successful Meetings* 55, no.13 (December 2006): 28–33.

- ☐ Did the speaker use confident gestures?
- ☐ Did the speaker avoid nervous mannerisms?
- ☐ Did the speaker handle questions effectively?
- ☐ Did the presentation hold your attention? If it was a persuasive presentation, did it convince you?

Additional Points for Group Presentations

- ☐ Were team members introduced to the audience?
- ☐ Were all team members adequately involved in the presentation?
- ☐ Did the presentation move smoothly among the team members?
- ☐ Did the individual presentations coordinate well?
- ☐ Did team members stay tuned in to the person speaking at the time?

MAKING GROUP PRESENTATIONS

Plan carefully to involve as many members of the group as possible in speaking roles.

The easiest way to make a group presentation is to outline the presentation and then divide the topics, giving one to each group member. Another member can be responsible for the opener and the close. During the question period, each member answers questions that relate to his or her topic.

In this kind of divided presentation, be sure to

- Plan transitions.
- Coordinate individual talks to eliminate repetition and contradiction.
- Enforce time limits strictly.
- Coordinate your visuals so that the presentation seems a coherent whole.
- Practice the presentation as a group at least once; more is better.

Some group presentations are even more fully integrated: the group writes a very detailed outline, chooses points and examples, and creates visuals together. Then, within each point, voices trade off. This presentation is effective because each voice speaks only a minute or two before a new voice comes in. However, it works only when all group members know the subject well and when the group plans carefully and practices extensively.

Whatever form of group presentation you use, be sure to introduce each member of the team to the audience and to pay close attention to each other. If other members of the team seem uninterested in the speaker, the audience gets the sense that that speaker isn't worth listening to.

SUMMARY OF KEY POINTS

- **Informative presentations** inform or teach the audience. **Persuasive presentations** motivate the audience to act or to believe. **Goodwill presentations** entertain and validate the audience. Most oral presentations have more than one purpose.
- A written message makes it easier to present extensive or complex information and to minimize undesirable emotions. Oral messages make it easier to use emotion, to focus the audience's attention, to answer questions and resolve conflicts quickly, to modify a proposal that may not be acceptable in its original form, and to get immediate action or response.

- In both oral and written messages, you should
  - Adapt the message to the specific audience.
  - Show the audience how they benefit from the idea, policy, service, or product.
  - Overcome any objections the audience may have.
  - Use you-attitude and positive emphasis.
  - Use visuals to clarify or emphasize material.
  - Specify exactly what the audience should do.
- An oral presentation needs to be simpler than a written message to the same audience.
- In a **monologue presentation,** the speaker plans the presentation in advance and delivers it without deviation. In a **guided discussion,** the speaker presents the questions or issues that both speaker and audience have agreed on in advance. Rather than functioning as an expert with all the answers, the speaker serves as a facilitator to help the audience tap its own knowledge. An **interactive presentation** is a conversation using questions to determine needs, probe objections, and gain provisional and then final commitment to the objective.
- Adapt your message to your audience's beliefs, experiences, and interests.
- Use the beginning and end of the presentation to interest the audience and emphasize your key point.
- Use visuals to seem more prepared, more interesting, and more persuasive.
- Limit your talk to three main points. Early in your talk—perhaps immediately after your opener—provide an overview of the main points you will make. Offer a clear signpost as you come to each new point. A **signpost** is an explicit statement of the point you have reached.
- To calm your nerves as you prepare to give an oral presentation,
  - Be prepared. Analyze your audience, organize your thoughts, prepare visual aids, practice your opener and close, check out the arrangements.
  - Use only the amount of caffeine you normally use. Avoid alcoholic beverages.
  - Relabel your nerves. Instead of saying, "I'm scared," try saying, "My adrenaline is up." Adrenaline sharpens our reflexes and helps us do our best.
- During your presentation,
  - Pause and look at the audience before you begin speaking.
  - Concentrate on communicating, not your feelings.
  - Use body energy in strong gestures and movement.
- Convey a sense of caring to your audience by making direct eye contact with them and by using a conversational style.
- Treat questions as opportunities to give more detailed information than you had time to give in your presentation. Link your answers to the points you made in your presentation.
- Repeat the question before you answer it if the audience may not have heard it or if you want more time to think. Rephrase hostile or biased questions before you answer them.

Under the Big Top

At the Ringling Bros. and Barnum & Bailey's circus, the ringmaster has always played an important role. From the early days of the circus, when consummate showman P. T. Barnum deftly directed the audience's attention to the action in the big top's three rings, the ringmaster has been front and center. Today, after 138 years of the circus, the role has changed in some ways, but the ringmaster is still responsible for managing the experience of the audience. Chuck Wagner, one of the current ringmasters, spoke about his experiences as the primary presenter in The Greatest Show on Earth. Here are some things he's learned:

- To engage an audience, you need to invest energy and enthusiasm.
- If something goes wrong, "stay poised, stay polished, stay calm, and keep that smile on [your] face."
- If something goes really wrong, acknowledge it, but move on with the show.
- In every performance, play to the back row. This means finding a way to draw the people from the top seats of a 20,000-seat arena into the action. Use your voice and motions to address each person individually.
- Be confident and professional.

Most business presentations are not like running a circus. But the lessons learned by a ringmaster have value for every presenter.

Adapted from "Playing to the Back Row: A Conversation with Ringmaster Chuck Wagner," *Harvard Business Review*, January 2009, 41–44.

CHAPTER 19 Exercises and Problems

Go to www.mhhe.com/locker10e for additional Exercises and Problems.

19.1 Reviewing the Chapter

1. What are four major components of planning effective presentations? (LO 19-1)
2. What are four different kinds of presentation openers you can use? (LO 19-1)
3. Name 10 guidelines for creating effective visuals. (LO 19-1)
4. What are some major criteria for choosing the information for your presentation? (LO 19-2)
5. Provide a suitable topic for each of the five common patterns of organization for presentations. (LO 19-2)
6. What are some ways to deal with the common fear of public speaking? Which ways would work for you? (LO 19-3)
7. List some pointers for effectively handling questions during presentations. (LO 19-4)

19.2 Analyzing Openers and Closes

The following openers and closes came from class presentations on information interviews.

- Does each opener make you interested in hearing the rest of the presentation?
- Does each opener provide a transition to the overview?
- Does the close end the presentation in a satisfying way?

a. Opener: I interviewed Mark Perry at AT&T.
   Close: Well, that's my report.

b. Opener: How many of you know what you want to do when you graduate?
   Close: So, if you like numbers and want to travel, think about being a CPA. Ernst & Young can take you all over the world.

c. Opener: You don't have to know anything about computer programming to get a job as a technical writer at CompuServe.
   Close: After talking to Raj, I decided technical writing isn't for me. But it is a good career if you work well under pressure and like learning new things all the time.

d. Opener: My report is about what it's like to work in an advertising agency.
   Middle: They keep really tight security; I had to wear a badge and be escorted to Susan's desk.
   Close: Susan gave me samples of the agency's ads and even a sample of a new soft drink she's developing a campaign for. But she didn't let me keep the badge.

19.3 Developing Points of Interest

One of the keys to preparing an engaging presentation is finding interesting points to share with your audience, either in the form of personal anecdotes to create rapport and build goodwill, or in the form of interesting facts and figures to establish your ethos as a presenter. For each of the following topics, prepare one personal anecdote based on your own experience, and research one interesting fact to share with your audience.

1. Why people need to plan.
2. Dealing with change.
3. The importance of lifelong learning.
4. The importance of effective communication.
5. The value of good customer service.
6. The value of listening.

As your instructor directs,

a. Share your points of interest with a small group of students, and critique each other's work.
b. Turn in your stories in a memo to your instructor.
c. Make a short (1–2 minute) oral presentation featuring your story and fact(s) for one of the assignment topics.

19.4 Evaluating PowerPoint Slides

Evaluate the following drafts of PowerPoint slides.

- Are the slides' background appropriate for the topic?
- Do the slides use words or phrases rather than complete sentences?
- Is the font big enough to read from a distance?
- Is the art relevant and appropriate?
- Is each slide free from errors?

New Construction and Renovations
New buildings
Renovated buildings
Financial Details

a(1)

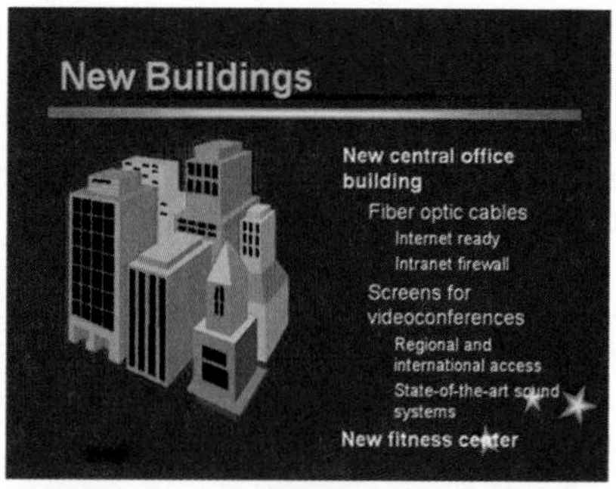
New Buildings
New central office building
Fiber optic cables
Internet ready
Intranet firewall
Screens for videoconferences
Regional and international access
State-of-the-art sound systems
New fitness center

a(2)

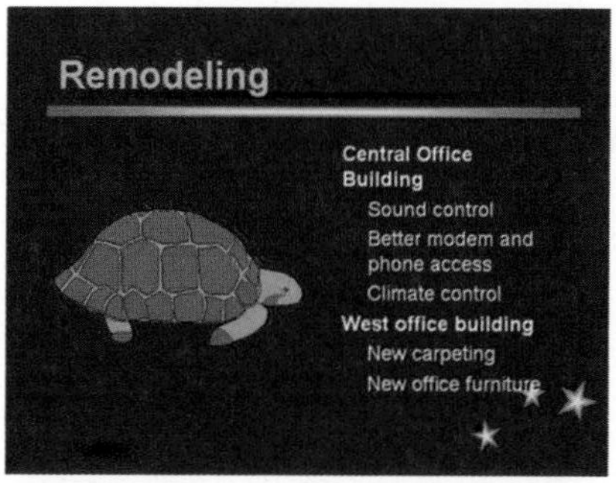
Remodeling
Central Office Building
Sound control
Better modem and phone access
Climate control
West office building
New carpeting
New office furniture

a(3)

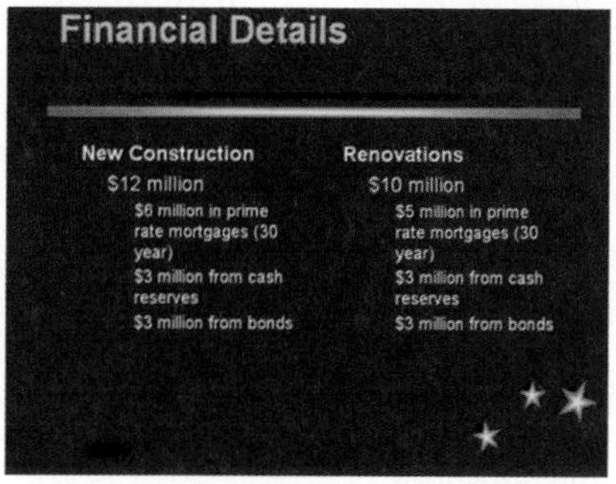
Financial Details
New Construction
$12 million
$6 million in prime rate mortgages (30 year)
$3 million from cash reserves
$3 million from bonds
Renovations
$10 million
$5 million in prime rate mortgages (30 year)
$3 million from cash reserves
$3 million from bonds

a(4)

Niche Marketing
Understanding the Older Buyer

b(1)

Number of Older Buyers Grows
Baby boomers swell over-50 ranks
Older Americans live longer due to better health care
Adults over 50 control most of discretionary wealth
45
40
35
30
25
20
15
10
5
0
1990 1995 2000 2005
45-64
65-79
80+

b(2)

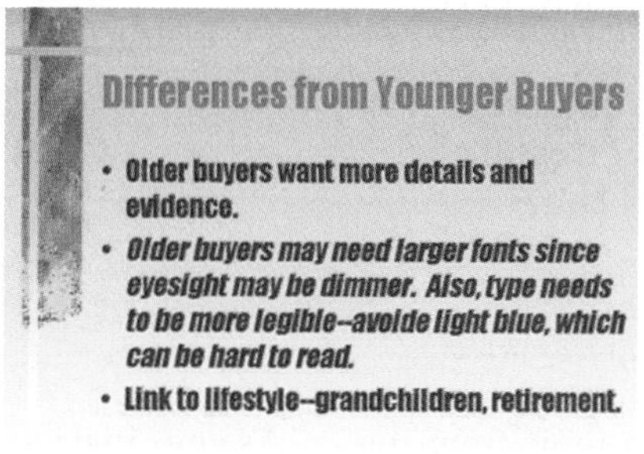
Differences from Younger Buyers
Older buyers want more details and evidence.
Older buyers may need larger fonts since eyesight may be dimmer. Also, type needs to be more legible--avoide light blue, which can be hard to read.
Link to lifestyle--grandchildren, retirement.

b(3)

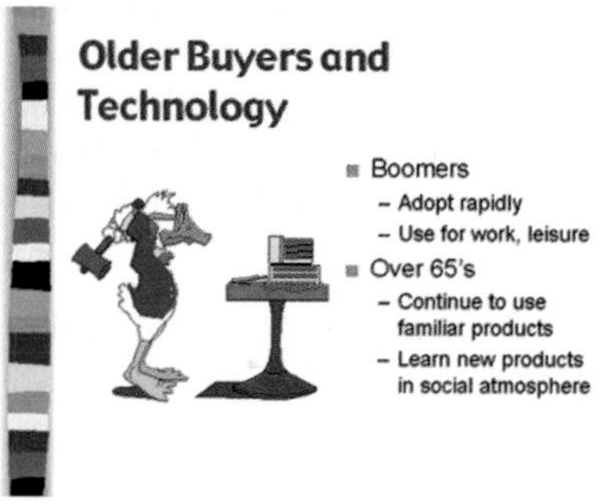
Older Buyers and Technology
Boomers
– Adopt rapidly
– Use for work, leisure
Over 65's
– Continue to use familiar products
– Learn new products in social atmosphere

b(4)

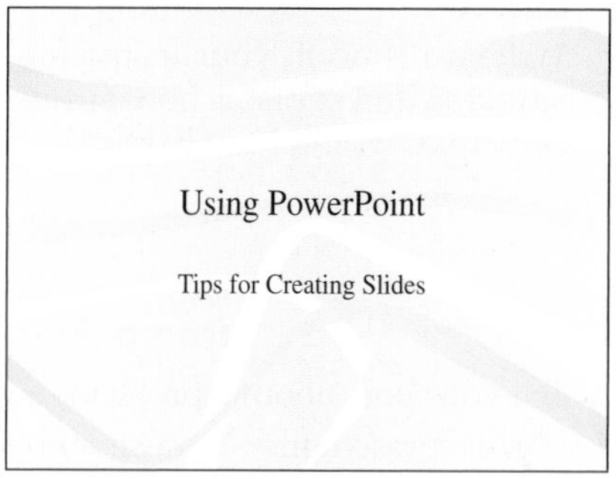
Using PowerPoint
Tips for Creating Slides

c(1)

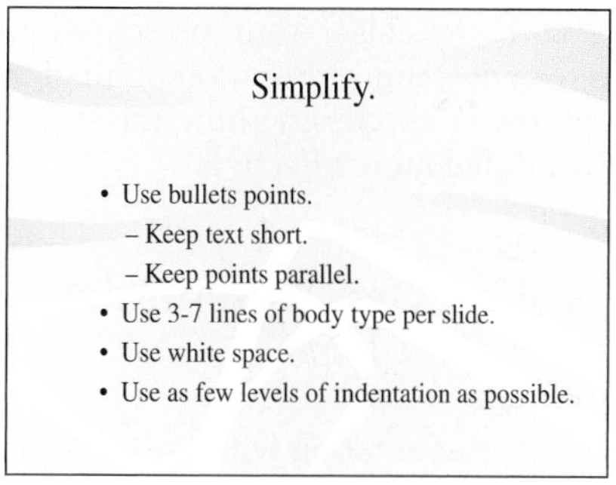
Simplify.
Use bullets points.
– Keep text short.
– Keep points parallel.
Use 3-7 lines of body type per slide.
Use white space.
Use as few levels of indentation as possible.

c(2)

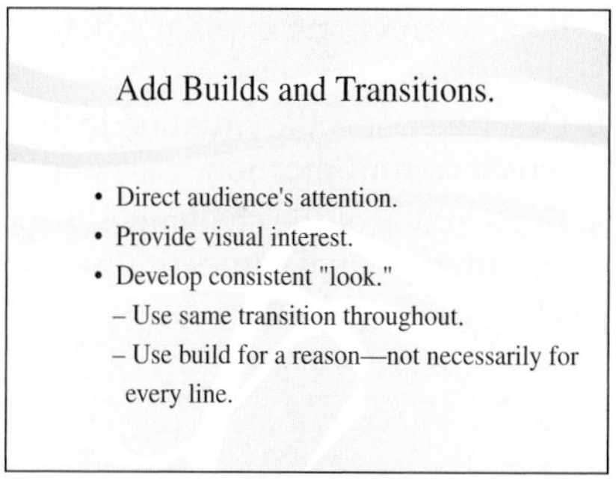
Add Builds and Transitions.
Direct audience's attention.
Provide visual interest.
Develop consistent "look."
– Use same transition throughout.
– Use build for a reason—not necessarily for every line.

c(3)

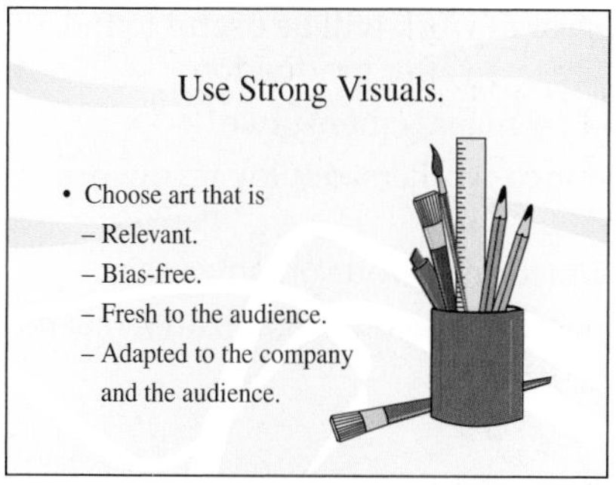
Use Strong Visuals.
Choose art that is
– Relevant.
– Bias-free.
– Fresh to the audience.
– Adapted to the company and the audience.

c(4)

19.5 Evaluating Speakers

Attend a lecture or public presentation on your campus. While the speaker is presenting, don't focus on the content of the message. Instead, focus only on his/her speaking ability and take notes. Pay attention to the speaker's abilities to deal with fear, use eye contact with the audience, and project a clear speaking voice. In addition, notice how the speaker stands and gestures, uses notes and visuals, and handles questions.

As your instructor directs,

a. Deliver your findings to the rest of the class in a short 2–4 minute presentation.

b. Write a memo to your instructor that discusses the presenter's speaking abilities, and how, if at all, they can be improved.

19.6 Evaluating the Way a Speaker Handles Questions

Listen to a speaker talking about a controversial subject. (Go to a talk on campus or in town, or watch a speaker on a TV show like *Face the Nation* or *60 Minutes*.) Observe the way he or she handles questions.

- About how many questions does the speaker answer?
- What is the format for asking and answering questions?
- Are the answers clear? responsive to the question? something that could be quoted without embarrassing the speaker and the organization he or she represents?
- How does the speaker handle hostile questions? Does the speaker avoid getting angry? Does the speaker retain control of the meeting? How?
- If some questions were not answered well, what (if anything) could the speaker have done to leave a better impression?
- Did the answers leave the audience with a more or less positive impression of the speaker? Why?

As your instructor directs,

a. Share your evaluation with a small group of students.

b. Present your evaluation formally to the class.

c. Summarize your evaluation in a memo to your instructor.

19.7 Presenting the News

Research a hot business communication topic from the news (ethics, the economy, job layoffs, communication technology, etc.). Find at least 3–5 sources for your topic. Then, make a short (2–3 minute) presentation where you share your findings with the class. Your presentation should invoke some effective communication strategies you learned in this course by discussing how the situation could have been handled more effectively.

As your instructor directs,

a. Deliver your presentation to the class.

b. Turn in a listing of your sources in APA or MLA format.

c. Write a memo to your instructor that discusses the situation and explains how business communication principles would have helped improve the situation.

19.8 Making a Short Oral Presentation

As your instructor directs,

Make a short (3–5 minute) presentation with PowerPoint slides on one of the following topics:

1. Explain how what you've learned in classes, in campus activities, or at work will be useful to the employer who hires you after graduation.
2. Describe your boss's management style.
3. Describe how your co-workers employ teamwork on the job.
4. Explain a "best-practice" in your organization.
5. Explain what a new hire in your organization needs to know to be successful.
6. Tell your boss about a problem in your unit.
7. Make a presentation to raise funds for a nonprofit organization.
8. Profile someone who is successful in the field you hope to enter and explain what makes him or her successful.
9. Describe a specific situation in an organization in which communication was handled well or badly.
10. Explain one of the challenges (e.g., technology, ethics, international competition) that the field you plan to enter is facing.

11. Profile a company that you would like to work for and explain why you think it would make a good employer.
12. Share the results of an information interview.
13. Share some advice for students currently on the job market.
14. Explain your job interview strategy.

19.9 Making a Longer Oral Presentation

As your instructor directs,

Make a 5- to 12-minute presentation on one of the following. Use visuals to make your talk effective.

1. Persuade your supervisor to make a change that will benefit the organization.
2. Persuade your organization to make a change that will improve the organization's image in the community.
3. Describe the communication process of a person you've interviewed who is working in the field you plan to enter.
4. Evaluate a business document.
5. Evaluate the design of a corporate web page.
6. Present a web page you have designed.
7. Analyze rejection letters that students on your campus have received.
8. Persuade an organization on your campus to make a change.
9. Analyze international messages that your workplace has created or received.
10. Present the results of a survey you conduct.
11. Research an organization you would like to work for.
12. Persuade classmates to donate time or money to a charitable organization.

19.10 Watching Yourself

One of the best ways to improve your presentation skills is to watch yourself present. After you have prepared a presentation on one of the topics listed in exercise 19.8 or 19.9, use a video camera to record your presentation. You should then review your presentation, noting what you did well and what you could improve.

As your instructor directs,

a. Write a two-page memo that discusses your strengths and weaknesses as a presenter. Address how you could improve your weaknesses.
b. Prepare a brief (two-minute) oral summation for your peers about your strengths and weaknesses.
c. Record the presentation a second time to see if you have improved some of your weaknesses.

19.11 Making a Group Oral Presentation

As your instructor directs,

Make an 8- to 12-minute presentation on one of the following. Use visuals to make your talk effective.

1. Explain the role of communication in one or more organizations.
2. Create and present a fund-raising strategy for a nonprofit organization.
3. Report on the nonverbal customs of another country.
4. Report on the written communication styles of another country.
5. Report on the business outlook of another country.
6. Analyze print business materials of an organization and present your findings to the class.
7. Interview the employees of an organization about their teamwork strategies and present the information to the class.
8. Interview an office about their routine communication practices and present your findings to the class.

19.12 Evaluating Oral Presentations

Evaluate an oral presentation given by a classmate or a speaker on your campus. Use the following categories:

Strategy

1. Choosing an effective kind of presentation for the situation.
2. Adapting ideas to audience's beliefs, experiences, and interests.
3. Using a strong opening and close.
4. Using visual aids or other devices to involve audience.

Content

5. Providing a clear, unifying purpose.
6. Using specific, vivid supporting material and language.
7. Providing rebuttals to counterclaims or objections.

Organization

8. Providing an overview of main points.
9. Signposting main points in body of talk.
10. Providing adequate transitions between points and speakers.

Visuals

11. Using an appropriate design or template.
12. Using standard edited English.
13. Being creative.

Delivery

14. Making direct eye contact with audience.
15. Using voice effectively.
16. Using gestures effectively.
17. Handling questions effectively.
18. Positioning (not blocking screen)

As your instructor directs,

a. Fill out a form indicating your evaluation in each of the areas.
b. Share your evaluation orally with the speaker.
c. Write a memo to the speaker evaluating the presentation. Send a copy of your memo to your instructor.

19.13 Evaluating Team Presentations

Evaluate team presentations using the chapter checklist.

As your instructor directs,

a. Fill out a form indicating your evaluation in each of the areas.
b. Share your evaluation orally with the team.
c. Write a memo to the team evaluating the presentation. Send a copy of your memo to your instructor.

APPENDIX

Formatting Letters, Memos, and E-Mail Messages

Appendix Outline

Formats for Letters
Formats for Envelopes
Formats for Memos
Formats for E-Mail Messages
State and Province Abbreviations

Learning objective

After studying this appendix, you will know

LO A-1 Formats for letters.

LO A-2 Formats for envelopes.

LO A-3 Formats for memos.

LO A-4 Formats for e-mail messages.

Letters normally go to people outside your organization; **memos** go to other people in your organization. E-mails go to both audiences. Letters, memos, and e-mails do not necessarily differ in length, formality, writing style, or pattern of organization. However, letters, memos, and e-mails do differ in format. **Format** means the parts of a document and the way they are arranged on the page.

FORMATS FOR LETTERS LO A-1

If your organization has a standard format for letters, use it.

Many organizations and writers choose one of three letter formats: **block format** (see Figure A.2), **modified block format** (see Figure A.3), or the **simplified format** (see Figure A.4). Your organization may make minor changes from the diagrams in margins or spacing.

Figure A.1 shows how the three formats differ.

Use the same level of formality in the **salutation**, or greeting, as you would in talking to someone on the phone: *Dear Glenn* if you're on a first-name basis, *Dear Mr. Helms* if you don't know the reader well enough to use the first name.

Some writers feel that the simplified format is better since the reader is not *Dear.* Omitting the salutation is particularly good when you do not know the reader's name or do not know which courtesy title to use. (For a full discussion on nonsexist salutations and salutations when you don't know the reader's name, see Chapter 3.) However, readers like to see their names. Since the simplified format omits the reader's name in the salutation, writers who use this format but who also want to be friendly often try to use the reader's name early in the body of the letter.

The simplified letter format is good in business-to-business mail, or in letters where you are writing to anyone who holds a job (admissions officer, customer service representative) rather than to a specific person. It is too cold and distancing for cultures that place a premium on relationships.

Sincerely and *Yours truly* are standard **complimentary closes**. When you are writing to people in special groups or to someone who is a friend as well as a business acquaintance, you may want to use a less formal close. Depending on the circumstances, the following informal closes might be acceptable: *Cordially, Thank you,* or even *Ciao.*

In **mixed punctuation**, a colon follows the salutation and a comma follows the close.

A **subject line** tells what the message is about. Subject lines are required in memos and e-mails; they are optional in letters. Good subject lines are specific, concise, and appropriate for your purposes and the response you expect from your reader:

Figure A.1 Comparing and Contrasting Letter Formats

	Block	Modified block	Simplified
Date and signature block	Lined up at left margin	Lined up 1/2 or 2/3 of the way over to the right	Lined up at left margin
Paragraph indentation	None	Optional	None
Salutation and complimentary close	Yes	Yes	None
Subject line	Optional	Rare	Yes
Lists, if any	Indented	Indented	At left margin
Writer's typed name	Upper- and lowercase	Upper- and lowercase	Full capital letters
Paragraph spacing	Single-spaced, double-space between	Single-spaced, double-space between	Single-spaced, double-space between

- When you have good news, put it in the subject line.
- When your information is neutral, summarize it concisely in the subject line.
- When your information is negative, use a negative subject line if the reader may not read the message or needs the information to act. Otherwise, use a neutral subject line.
- When you have a request that will be easy for the reader to grant, put either the subject of the request or a direct question in the subject line.
- When you must persuade a reluctant reader, use a common ground, a benefit, or a neutral subject line.

For examples of subject lines in each of these situations, see Chapters 9, 10, and 11.

A **reference line** refers the reader to the number used on the previous correspondence this letter replies to, or the order or invoice number this letter is about. Very large organizations use numbers on every piece of correspondence they send out so that it is possible to find quickly the earlier document to which an incoming letter refers.

All three formats can use headings, lists, and indented sections for emphasis.

Each of the three formats has advantages. Both block and simplified can be typed quickly since everything is lined up at the left margin. Block format is the format most frequently used for business letters; readers expect it. Modified block format creates a visually attractive page by moving the date and signature block over into what would otherwise be empty white space. Modified block is also a traditional format; readers are comfortable with it.

The examples of the three formats in Figures A.2–A.4 show one-page letters on company letterhead. **Letterhead** is preprinted stationery with the organization's name, logo, address, phone number, and frequently e-mail. Figure A.5 shows how to set up modified block format when you do not have letterhead. (It is also acceptable to use block format without letterhead.)

When your letter runs two or more pages, use a heading on the second page to identify it. Using the reader's name helps the writer, who may be printing out many letters at a time, to make sure the right second page gets in the envelope. The two most common formats are shown in Figures A.6, A.7, A.8, and

Figure A.2 Block Format on Letterhead

Northwest Hardware Warehouse
100 Freeway Exchange Provo, UT 84610 (801) 555-4683 www.northwesthardware.com

3–6 spaces depending on length of letter

Line up everything at left margin

June 20, 2012

2–4 spaces

Mr. James E. Murphy, Accounts Payable Title could be on a separate line
Salt Lake Equipment Rentals
5600 Wasatch Boulevard
Salt Lake City, Utah 84121 ← zip code on same line

1"–1½"

Dear Jim: Colon in mixed punctuation

Use first name in salutation if you'd use it on the phone

The following items totaling $393.09 are still open on your account. ¶ 1 never has a heading

Invoice #01R-784391 Bold heading

After the bill for this invoice arrived on May 14, you wrote saying that the material had not been delivered to you. On May 29, our Claims Department sent you a copy of the delivery receipt signed by an employee of Salt Lake Equipment. You have had proof of delivery for over three weeks, but your payment has not yet arrived.

1", because right margin is justified

Single-space paragraphs
Double-space between paragraphs (one blank space)

Please send a check for $78.42.

Triple-space before a heading (2 blank spaces); double-space after the heading

Voucher #59351

The reference line on your voucher #59351, dated June 16, indicates that it is the gross payment for invoice #01G-002345. However, the voucher was only for $1171.25, while the invoice amount was $1246.37. Please send a check for $75.12 to clear this item.

Do not indent paragraphs

Voucher #55032

Voucher #55032, dated June 16, subtracts a credit for $239.55 from the amount due. Our records do not show that any credit is due on this voucher. Please send either an explanation or a check to cover the $239.55 immediately.

Total Amount Due Headings are optional in letters

Please send a check for $393.09 to cover these three items and to bring your account up to date.

1–2 spaces

Sincerely,

2–4 spaces

Neil Hutchinson

Neil Hutchinson
Credit Representative

cc: Joan Stottlemyer, Credit Manager

Leave bottom margin of 6 spaces—more if letter is short

Figure A.3 Modified Block Format on Letterhead

Bay City Information Systems
151 Bayview Road • San Francisco, CA 81153 • (650) 405-7849 • www.baycity.com

3–6 spaces

September 15, 2012

Line up date with signature block $\frac{1}{2}$ or $\frac{2}{3}$ of the way over to the right

2–4 spaces

Ms. Mary E. Arcas
Personnel Director
Cyclops Communication Technologies
1050 South Sierra Bonita Avenue
Los Angeles, CA 90019 *Zip code on same line*

$1''$–$1\frac{1}{2}''$

Dear Ms. Arcas: *Colon in mixed punctuation*

Indenting ¶ is optional in modified block

1", because right margin is justified

Let me respond to your request for an evaluation of Colleen Kangas. Colleen was hired as a clerk-typist by Bay City Information Systems on April 4, 2010, and was promoted to Administrative Assistant on August 1, 2011. At her review in June, I recommended that she be promoted again. She is an intelligent young woman with good work habits and a good knowledge of computer software.

Single-space paragraphs

As an Adminstrative Assistant, Colleen not only handles routine duties such as processing time cards, ordering supplies, and entering data, but also screens calls for two marketing specialists, answers basic questions about Bay City Information Systems, compiles the statistics I need for my monthly reports, and investigates special assignments for me. In the past eight months, she has investigated freight charges, inventoried department hardware, and transferred files to archives. I need only to give her general directions: she has a knack for tracking down information quickly and summarizing it accurately.

Double-space between paragraphs (one blank line)

Although the department's workload has increased during the year, Colleen manages her time so that everything gets done on schedule. She is consistently poised and friendly under pressure. Her willingness to work overtime on occasion is particularly remarkable considering that she has been going to college part-time ever since she joined our firm.

At Bay City Information Systems, Colleen uses Microsoft Word, Excel, and Access software. She tells me that she also uses PowerPoint in her college classes.

If Colleen were staying in San Francisco, we would want to keep her. She has the potential either to become an Executive Secretary or to move into line or staff work, especially once she completes her degree. I recommend her highly.

1–2 spaces

Sincerely, *Comma in mixed punctuation*

Headings are optional in letters

2–4 spaces

Jeanne Cederlind

Jeanne Cederlind
Vice President, Marketing
jeanne_c@baycity.com

Line up signature block with date

1–4 spaces

Encl.: Evaluation Form for Colleen Kangas

Leave at least 6 spaces at bottom of page—more if letter is short

Figure A.4 Simplified Format on Letterhead

1500 Main Street Iowa City, IA 52232 (319) 555-3113

3–6 spaces

Line up everything at left margin

August 24, 2012

2–4 spaces

Melinda Hamilton
Medical Services Division
Health Management Services, Inc.
4333 Edgewood Road, NE
Cedar Rapids, IA 52401

1"–1 1/2"

Triple-space (two blank spaces) *Subject line in full capital letters*

REQUEST FOR INFORMATION ABOUT COMPUTER SYSTEMS

No salutation

We're interested in upgrading our computer system and would like to talk to one of your marketing representatives to see what would best meet our needs. We will use the following criteria to choose a system:

1. Ability to use our current software and data files.

2. Price, prorated on a three-year expected life.

3. Ability to provide auxiliary services, e.g., controlling inventory of drugs and supplies, monitoring patients' vital signs, and processing insurance forms more quickly.

4. Freedom from downtime.

Double-space (one blank space) between items in list if any items are more than one line long

Triple-space (two blank spaces) between list, next paragraph

Do not indent paragraphs

McFarlane Memorial Hospital has 50 beds for acute care and 75 beds for long-term care. In the next five years, we expect the number of beds to remain the same while outpatient care and emergency room care increase.

3/4"–1" when right margin is not justified

Could we meet the first or the third week in September? We are eager to have the new system installed by Christmas if possible.

Please call me to schedule an appointment.

Headings are optional in letters

No close.

HUGH PORTERFIELD *Writer's name in full capital letters*
Controller

1–4 spaces

Encl.: Specifications of Current System
Databases Currently in Use

cc: Rene Seaburg

Leave 6 spaces at bottom of page—more if letter is short

Figure A.5 Modified Block Format without Letterhead

6–12 spaces

Single-space

11408 Brussels Avenue NE
Albuquerque, NM 87111
November 5, 2012

$1''$–$1\frac{1}{2}''$

2–6 spaces

Mr. Tom Miller, President
Miller Construction
P.O. Box 2900
Lincolnshire, IL 60197-2900

Subject: Invoice No. 664907, 10/29/12

Subject line is optional in block & modified block

Indenting paragraphs is optional in modified block

1",because right margin is justifed

Dear Mr. Miller:

As part of our kitchen remodeling, your crew installed beautiful Sanchez cabinets. The next day they varnished them, but the varnish was not even. It had bubbles and drip marks, and in some places looked and felt rough. My wife complained to the foreman, and he had the crew revarnish the cabinets. If anything, they looked even worse. At that point, the foreman said he could not do any better and if we wanted a better job, we would have to see to it ourselves. So we did. We called Mr. Sancehz, who sent some of his men over, and now the cabinets are lovely.

Because a professional-looking finish on the cabinets is part of what we expected in the remodeling, we ask you to cover Mr. Sanchez's $1050 fee as part of your contract, and to remove it from our bill. The entire kitchen now looks lovely; we love your granite-top counters.

Please send us a new invoice showing Mr. Sanchez's fee removed and our balance paid in full.

Sincerely,

2–4 spaces

William T. Mozing

William T. Mozing

1–4 spaces

Encl.: Check #7587

Line up signature block with date

below. Note even when the signature block is on the second page, it is still lined up with the date.

Reader's Name
Date
Page Number

or

Reader's Name	Page Number	Date

When a letter runs two or more pages, use letterhead only for page 1. (See Figures A.6, A.7, and A.8.) For the remaining pages, use plain paper that matches the letterhead in weight, texture, and color.

Set side margins of 1 inch to 1½ inches on the left and ¾ inch to 1 inch on the right. If you are right justifying, use the 1 inch margin. If your letterhead extends all the way across the top of the page, set your margins even with the ends of the letterhead for the most visually pleasing page. The top margin should be three to six lines under the letterhead, or 1 to 2 inches down from the top of the page if you aren't using letterhead. If your letter is very short, you may want to use bigger side and top margins so that the letter is centered on the page.

The **inside address** gives the reader's name, title (if appropriate), and address: always double check to see the name is spelled correctly. To eliminate typing the reader's name and address on an envelope, some organizations use envelopes with cutouts or windows so that the inside address on the letter shows through and can be used for delivery. If your organization does this, adjust your margins, if necessary, so that the whole inside address is visible.

Many letters are accompanied by other documents. Whatever these documents may be—a multipage report or a two-line note—they are called **enclosures,** since they are enclosed in the envelope. The writer should refer to the enclosures in the body of the letter: "As you can see from my résumé, . . . " The enclosure notation (Encl.:) at the bottom of the letter lists the enclosures. (See Figures A.3, A.4, and A.5.)

Sometimes you write to one person but send copies of your letter to other people. If you want the reader to know that other people are getting copies, list their names on the last page. The abbreviation *cc* originally meant *carbon copy* but now means *computer copy.* Other acceptable abbreviations include *pc* for *photocopy* or simply *c* for *copy.* You can also send copies to other people without telling the reader. Such copies are called **blind copies**. Blind copies are not mentioned on the original; they are listed on the copy saved for the file with the abbreviation *bcc* preceding the names of people getting these copies.

FORMATS FOR ENVELOPES LO A-2

Business envelopes need to put the reader's name and address in the area that is picked up by the Post Office's Optical Character Readers (OCRs). Use side margins of at least 1 inch. Your bottom margin must be at least 5/8 inch but no bigger than 2¼ inches.

Most businesses use envelopes that already have the return address printed in the upper left-hand corner. When you don't have printed envelopes, type

Figure A.6 Second Page of a Two-Page Letter, Block Format

August 11, 2012

2–4 spaces

Ms. Stephanie Voght
Stephen F. Austin High School
1200 Southwest Blvd.
San Antonio, TX 78214

1"–1½"

Dear Ms. Voght: *Colon in mixed punctuation.*

Enclosed are 100 brochures about State University to distribute to your students. The brochures describe the academic programs and financial aid available. When you need additional brochures, just let me know.

1"

Further information about State University

You may also want your students to learn more about life at State University. You

Plain paper for page 2.

½"–1"

Center

Stephanie Voght ← *Reader's name* 2 August 11, 2012

Also OK to line up page number and date at left under reader's name.

campus life, including football and basketball games, fraternities and sororities, clubs and organizations, and opportunities for volunteer work. It stresses the diversity of the student body and the very different lifestyles that are available at State.

Triple-space before each new heading (two blank spaces).

Scheduling a State Squad Speaker *Bold or underline headings.*

To schedule one of the these dynamic speakers for your students, just fill out the enclosed card with your first, second, and third choices for dates, and return it in the stamped, self-addressed envelope. Dates are reserved in the order that requests arrive. Send in your request early to increase the chances of getting the date you want.

Same margins as p 1.

Any one of our State Squad speakers will give your high school students a colorful preview of the college experience. They are also great at answering questions.

1–2 spaces

Sincerely, *Comma in mixed punctuation.*

2–4 spaces

Michael L. Mahler
Director of Admissions

Headings are optional in letters.

1–4 spaces

Encl.: Brochures, Reservation Form

cc: R. J. Holland, School Superintendent
Jose Lavilla, President, PTS Association

Figure A.7 Second Page of a Two-Page Letter, Modified Block Format

November 5, 2012

2–4 spaces

Line up date with signature block.

Mr. Roger B. Castino
Castino Floors and Carpets
418 E. North Street
Brockton, MA 02410

Indenting paragraphs is optional in modified block.

Dear Mr. Castino:

Welcome to the team of Glenarvon Carpet dealers!

Your first shipment of Glenarvon samples should reach you within ten days. The samples include

---

½"–1"

Plain paper for page 2

Mr. Roger B. Castino *← Reader's name* 2 *(Center)* November 5, 2012

territory . In addition, as a dealer you receive

- Sales kit highlighting product features
- Samples to distribute to customers
- Advertising copy to run in local newspapers
- Display units to place in your store.

Indent or center list to emphasize it.

The Annual Sales Meeting each January keeps you up-to-date on new products while you get to know other dealers and Glenarvon executives and relax at a resort hotel.

Use same margins as p 1.

Make your reservations now for Monterey January 10–13 for your first Glenarvon Sales Meeting!

Cordially,

2–4 spaces

Barbara S. Charbonneau

Barbara S. Charbonneau
Vice President, Marketing

Line up signature block with date in heading and on p1.

1–4 spaces

Encl.: Organization Chart
Product List
National Advertising Campaigns in 2011

1–4 spaces

cc: Nancy Magill, Northeast Sales Manager
Edward Spaulding, Sales Representative

6 spaces—more if second page isn't a full page.

Figure A.8 Second Page of a Two-Page Letter, Simplified Format

115 State Street
Ames, IA 50014
515-292-8756
www.optionsforliving.org

2–4 spaces

January 20, 2012

2–4 spaces

Gary Sammons, Editor
Southeastern Home Magazine
253 North Lake Street
Newport News, VA 23612

Triple-space (two blank spaces)

Subject line in full caps

MATERIAL FOR YOUR STORY ON HOMES FOR PEOPLE WITH DISABILITIES

No salutation

Apartments and houses can easily be designed to accommodate people with disabilities. From the outside, the building is indistinguishable from conventional housing. But the modifications inside permit people who use wheelchairs or whose sight or hearing is impaired to do everyday

$\frac{1}{2}$″–1″

Plain paper for page 2

Gary Sammons ← *Reader's name*
January 20, 2012
Page 2

Everything lined up at left margin

in hallways and showers and adjustable cabinets that can be raised or lowered. Cardinal says that the adaptations can run from a few dollars to $5000, depending on what the customer selects.

Same margins as page 1

The Builders Association of Virginia will install many features at no extra cost: 36-inch doorways—8 inches wider than standard—to accommodate wheelchairs and extra wiring for electronic items for people whose sight or hearing is impaired.

If you'd like pictures to accompany your story, just let me know.

No close

MARILYN TILLOTSON *Writer's name in full caps*
Executive Director

Encl.: Blueprints for Housing for People with Disabilities

cc: Douglas Stringfellow, President, BASF
Thomas R. Galliher, President, Cardinal Industries

at least 6 spaces—more if page 2 is not a full page

your name (optional), your street address, and your city, state, and zip code in the upper left-hand corner. Since the OCR doesn't need this information to route your letter, exact margins don't matter. Use whatever is convenient and looks good to you.

FORMATS FOR MEMOS LO A-3

Memos omit both the salutation and the close entirely. Memos rarely use indented paragraphs. Subject lines are required; headings are optional but useful in memos a full page or longer. Each heading must cover all the information until the next heading. Never use a separate heading for the first paragraph.

Figure A.9 illustrates the standard memo format typed on a plain sheet of paper. Note that the first letters of the date, reader's name, writer's name, and subject phrase are lined up vertically. Note also that memos are usually initialed by the To/From block. Initialing tells the reader that you have proofread the memo and prevents someone sending out your name on a memo you did not in fact write.

Some organizations have special letterhead for memos. (See Figure A.10.)

Some organizations alter the order of items in the Date/To/From/Subject block. Some organizations ask employees to sign memos rather than simply initialing them. The signature goes below the last line of the memo and prevents anyone from adding unauthorized information.

If the memo runs two pages or more, set up the second and subsequent pages in one of the following ways (see Figure A.11):

Brief Subject Line
Date
Page Number

or

Brief Subject Line Page Number Date

FORMATS FOR E-MAIL MESSAGES LO A-4

E-mail programs prompt you to supply the various parts of the memo format. See Chapters 9, 10, and 11 for information about designing e-mail subject lines. "Cc:" denotes computer copies; the recipient will see that these people are getting the message. "Bcc:" denotes blind computer copies; the recipient does not see the names of these people. Most e-mail programs also allow you to attach documents from other programs, thus e-mails have attachments rather than enclosures. The computer program supplies the date and time automatically.

Some aspects of e-mail format are still evolving. In particular, some writers treat e-mail messages as if they were informal letters; some treat them as memos. Even though the e-mail screen has a "To" line (as do memos), some writers still use an informal salutation, as in Figure A.12. The writer in Figure A.12 ends the message with a signature block. Signature blocks are particularly useful for e-mail recipients outside the organization who may not know your title or contact information. You can store a signature block in the e-mail program and set the program to insert the signature block automatically.

Figure A.9 Memo Format (on plain paper)

Date: October 7, 2012

To: Annette T. Califero

From: Kyle B. Abrams *KBA*

Subject: A Low-Cost Way to Reduce Energy Use

As you requested, I've investigated low-cost ways to reduce our energy use. Reducing the building temperature on weekends is a change that we could make immediately, that would cost nothing, and that would cut our energy use by about 6%.

The Energy Savings from a Lower Weekend Temperature

Lowering the temperature from 68° to 60° from 8 P.M. Friday evening to 4 A.M. Monday morning could cut our total consumption by 6%. It is not feasible to lower the temperature on weeknights because a great many staff members work late; the cleaning crew also is on duty from 6 P.M. to midnight. Turning the temperature down for only four hours would not result in a significant heat saving.

Turning the heat back up at 4 A.M. will allow the building temperature to be back to 68° by 9 A.M. Our furnace already has computerized controls which can be set to automatically lower and raise the temperature.

How a Lower Temperature Would Affect Employees

A survey of employees shows that only 7 people use the building every weekend or almost every weekend. Eighteen percent of our staff have worked at least one weekend day in the last two months; 52% say they "occasionally" come in on weekends.

People who come in for an hour or less on weekends could cope with the lower temperature just by wearing warm clothes. However, most people would find 60° too cool for extended work. Employees who work regularly on weekends might want to install space heaters.

Action Needed to Implement the Change

Would you also like me to check into the cost of buying a dozen portable space heaters? Providing them would allow us to choose units that our wiring can handle and would be a nice gesture towards employees who give up their weekends to work. I could have a report to you in two weeks.

We can begin saving energy immediately. Just authorize the lower temperature, and I'll see that the controls are reset for this weekend.

Figure A.10 Memo Format (on memo letterhead)

Kimball,
Walls, and
Morganstern

aligned vertically

Date: March 15, 2012 Line up horizontally with printed Date/To/From/Subject

To: Annette T. Califero

From: Kyle B. Abrams KBA Writer's initials added in ink

Capitalize first letter of each major word in subject line

Subject: The Effectiveness of Reducing Building Temperatures on Weekends

Triple-space (two blank spaces)

Reducing the building temperature to 60° on weekends has cut energy use by 4% compared to last year's use from December to February and has saved our firm $22,000.

This savings is particularly remarkable when you consider that this winter has been colder than last year's, so that more heat would be needed to maintain the same temperature.

3/4"–1"

Fewer people have worked weekends during the past three months than during the preceding three months, but snow and bad driving conditions may have had more to do with keeping people home than the fear of being cold. Five of the 12 space heaters we bought have been checked out on an average weekend. On one weekend, all 12 were in use and some people shared their offices so that everyone could be in a room with a space heater.

Fully 92% of our employees support the lower temperature. I recommend that we continue turning down the heat on weekends through the remainder of the heating season and that we resume the practice when the heat is turned on next fall.

Headings are optional in memos

In contrast, the writer in Figure A.13 omits both the salutation and his name. When you send a message to an individual or a group you have set up, the "From:" line will have your name and e-mail address.

If you post a message to a listserv, be sure to give at least your name and e-mail address at the end of your message, as some list-servs strip out identifying information when they process messages.

When you hit "reply," the e-mail program automatically uses "Re:" (Latin for *about*) and the previous subject line. The original message is set off, usually with one or more vertical lines in the left margin or with carats (see Figure A.14). You may want to change the subject line to make it more appropriate for your message.

Use short line lengths in your e-mail message. If the line lengths are too long, they'll produce awkward line breaks, as in Figure A.14.

Figure A.11 Second Page of Two-Page Memo

$1"–1\frac{1}{2}"$

February 18, 2012

To: Dorothy N. Blasingham

Double-space (one blank space)

From: Roger L. Trout **R.L.T.** *Writer's initials added in ink*

Subject: Request for Third-Quarter Computer Training Sessions *Capitalize first letter of all major words in subject line*

Triple-space (two blank spaces)

¶ 1 never has a heading

$\frac{3}{4}"–1"$

Could you please run advanced training sessions on using Excel in April and May and basic training sessions for new hires in June?

Triple-space before a heading (two blank spaces)

Advanced Sessions on Excel

Bold headings

Once the tax season is over, Jose Cisneros wants to have his first- and second-year people take your advanced course on Excel. Plan on about 45–50 people in three sessions. The people in the course already use Excel for basic spreadsheets but need to learn the fine points of macros and charting.

Double-space between paragraphs (one blank space)

If possible, it would be most convenient to have the sessions run for four afternoons rather

Plain paper for page 2

$\frac{1}{2}"–1"$

Dorothy N. Blasingham ← *Brief subject line or reader's name* 2 *Page number* February 18, 2012

Also OK to line up page number, date at left under reader's name

Same margins as p 1.

before the summer vacation season begins.

Orientation for New Hires *Capitalize first letter of all major words in heading*

With a total of 16 full-time and 34 part-time people being hired either for summer or permanent work, we'll need at least two and perhaps three orientation sessions. We'd like to hold these the first, second, and third weeks in June. By May 1, we should know how many people will be in each training session.

Would you be free to conduct training sessions on how to use our computers on June 9, June 16, and June 23? If we need only two dates, we'll use June 9 and June 16, but please block off the 23rd too in case we need a third session.

Triple-space before a heading (two blank spaces)

Request for Confirmation

Let me know whether you're free on these dates in June, and which dates you'd prefer. If you'll let me know by February 25, we can get information out to participants in plenty of time for the sessions.

Thanks!

Headings are optional in memos

Memos are initialed by To/From/Subject block

Figure A.12 A Basic E-Mail Message (direct request)

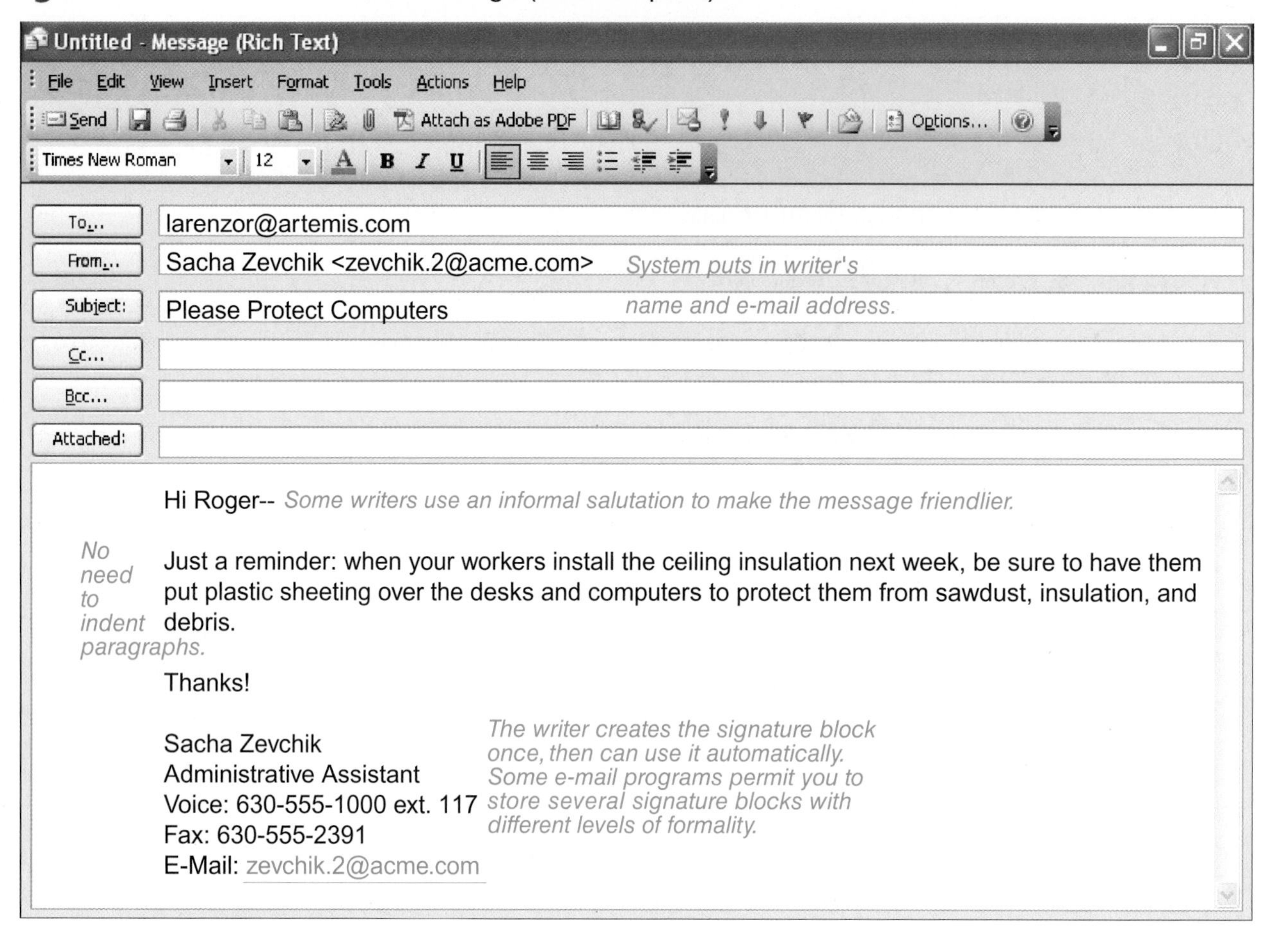

Figure A.13 An E-Mail Message with an Attachment (direct request)

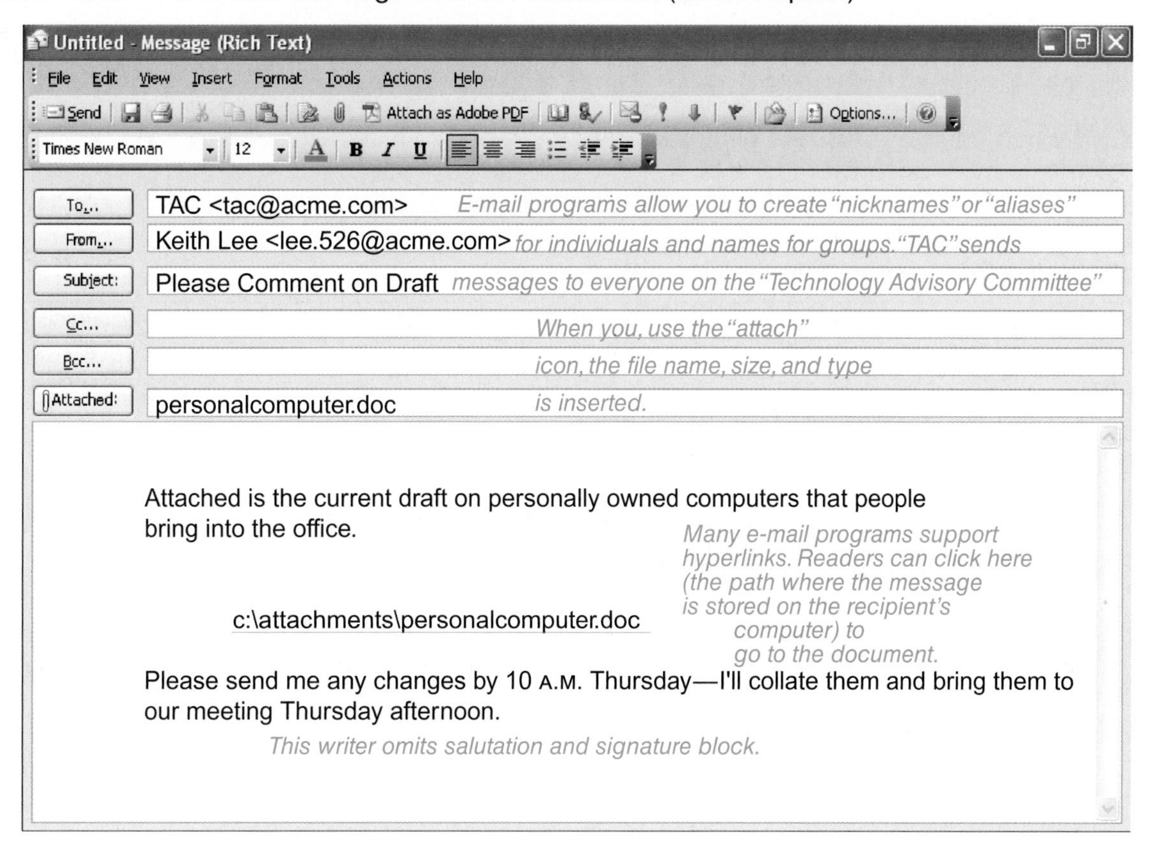

Figure A.14 An E-Mail Reply with Copies (response to a complaint)

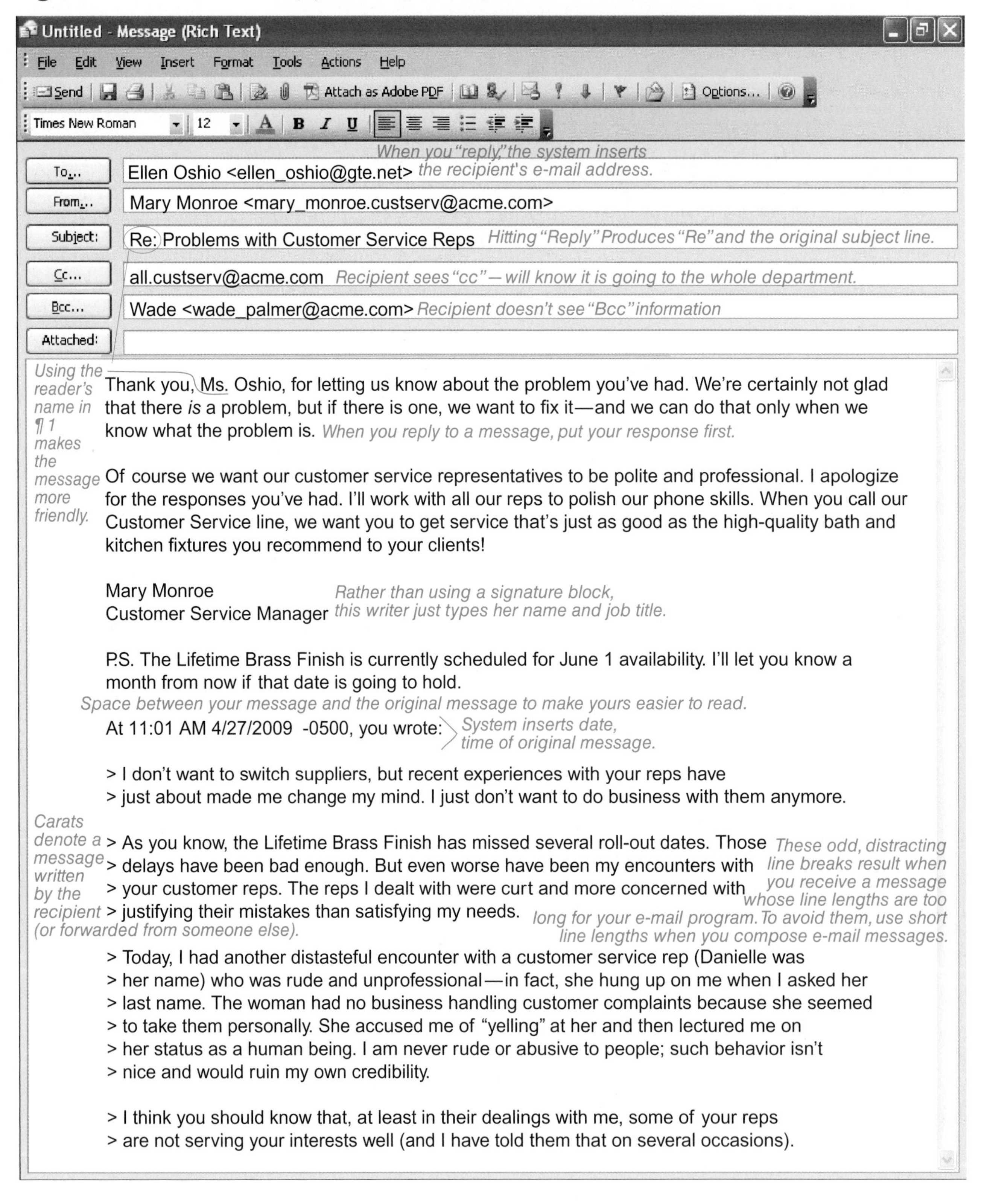

Untitled - Message (Rich Text)

File Edit View Insert Format Tools Actions Help

Send | Attach as Adobe PDF | Options...

Times New Roman | 12

When you "reply," the system inserts the recipient's e-mail address.

To... Ellen Oshio <ellen_oshio@gte.net>

From... Mary Monroe <mary_monroe.custserv@acme.com>

Subject: Re: Problems with Customer Service Reps *Hitting "Reply" Produces "Re" and the original subject line.*

Cc... all.custserv@acme.com *Recipient sees "cc"—will know it is going to the whole department.*

Bcc... Wade <wade_palmer@acme.com> *Recipient doesn't see "Bcc" information*

Attached:

Using the reader's name in ¶ 1 makes the message more friendly.

Thank you, Ms. Oshio, for letting us know about the problem you've had. We're certainly not glad that there *is* a problem, but if there is one, we want to fix it—and we can do that only when we know what the problem is. *When you reply to a message, put your response first.*

Of course we want our customer service representatives to be polite and professional. I apologize for the responses you've had. I'll work with all our reps to polish our phone skills. When you call our Customer Service line, we want you to get service that's just as good as the high-quality bath and kitchen fixtures you recommend to your clients!

Mary Monroe
Customer Service Manager

Rather than using a signature block, this writer just types her name and job title.

P.S. The Lifetime Brass Finish is currently scheduled for June 1 availability. I'll let you know a month from now if that date is going to hold.

Space between your message and the original message to make yours easier to read.

At 11:01 AM 4/27/2009 -0500, you wrote: *System inserts date, time of original message.*

> I don't want to switch suppliers, but recent experiences with your reps have
> just about made me change my mind. I just don't want to do business with them anymore.

Carats denote a message written by the recipient (or forwarded from someone else).

> As you know, the Lifetime Brass Finish has missed several roll-out dates. Those
> delays have been bad enough. But even worse have been my encounters with
> your customer reps. The reps I dealt with were curt and more concerned with
> justifying their mistakes than satisfying my needs.

These odd, distracting line breaks result when you receive a message whose line lengths are too long for your e-mail program. To avoid them, use short line lengths when you compose e-mail messages.

> Today, I had another distasteful encounter with a customer service rep (Danielle was
> her name) who was rude and unprofessional—in fact, she hung up on me when I asked her
> last name. The woman had no business handling customer complaints because she seemed
> to take them personally. She accused me of "yelling" at her and then lectured me on
> her status as a human being. I am never rude or abusive to people; such behavior isn't
> nice and would ruin my own credibility.

> I think you should know that, at least in their dealings with me, some of your reps
> are not serving your interests well (and I have told them that on several occasions).

STATE AND PROVINCE ABBREVIATIONS

States with names of more than five letters are frequently abbreviated in letters and memos. The post office abbreviations use two capital letters with no punctuation. See Figure A.15.

Figure A.15 Post Office Abbreviations for States, Territories, and Provinces

State name	Post office abbreviation	State name	Post office abbreviation
Alabama	AL	Missouri	MO
Alaska	AK	Montana	MT
Arizona	AZ	Nebraska	NE
Arkansas	AR	Nevada	NV
California	CA	New Hampshire	NH
Colorado	CO	New Jersey	NJ
Connecticut	CT	New Mexico	NM
Delaware	DE	New York	NY
District of Columbia	DC	North Carolina	NC
Florida	FL	North Dakota	ND
Georgia	GA	Ohio	OH
Hawaii	HI	Oklahoma	OK
Idaho	ID	Oregon	OR
Illinois	IL	Pennsylvania	PA
Indiana	IN	Rhode Island	RI
Iowa	IA	South Carolina	SC
Kansas	KS	South Dakota	SD
Kentucky	KY	Tennessee	TN
Louisiana	LA	Texas	TX
Maine	ME	Utah	UT
Maryland	MD	Vermont	VT
Massachusetts	MA	Virginia	VA
Michigan	MI	Washington	WA
Minnesota	MN	West Virginia	WV
Mississippi	MS	Wisconsin	WI
		Wyoming	WY

Territory name	Post office abbreviation	Province name	Post office abbreviation
Guam	GU	Alberta	AB
Puerto Rico	PR	British Columbia	BC
Virgin Islands	VI	Manitoba	MB
		New Brunswick	NB
		Newfoundland and Labrador	NL
		Northwest Territories	NT
		Nova Scotia	NS
		Nunavut	NU
		Ontario	ON
		Prince Edward Island	PE
		Quebec	QC
		Saskatchewan	SK
		Yukon Territory	YT

APPENDIX

B

Writing Correctly

Appendix Outline

Using Grammar

- Agreement
- Case
- Dangling Modifier
- Misplaced Modifier
- Parallel Structure
- Predication Errors

Understanding Punctuation

Punctuating Sentences

- Comma Splices
- Run-on Sentences
- Fused Sentences
- Sentence Fragments

Punctuation within Sentences

- Apostrophe
- Colon
- Comma
- Dash
- Hyphen
- Parentheses
- Period
- Semicolon

Special Punctuation Marks

- Quotation Marks
- Square Brackets
- Ellipses
- Underlining and Italics

Writing Numbers and Dates

Words That Are Often Confused

Proofreading Symbols

Learning Objectives

After studying this appendix, you will know

LO B-1 Common grammar usage.

LO B-2 Correct ways to use punctuation.

LO B-3 The right way to use words that are often confused.

Too much concern for correctness at the wrong stage of the writing process can backfire: writers who worry about grammar and punctuation when they're writing a first or second draft are more likely to get writer's block. Wait till you have your ideas on paper to check your draft for correct grammar, punctuation, typing of numbers and dates, and word use. Use the proofreading symbols at the end of this appendix to indicate changes needed in a printed copy.

Most writers make a small number of grammatical errors repeatedly. Most readers care deeply about only a few grammatical points. Keep track of the feedback you get (from your instructors now, from your supervisor later) and put your energy into correcting the errors that bother the people who read what you write. A command of standard grammar will help you build the credible, professional image you want to create with everything you write.

USING GRAMMAR LO B-1

With the possible exception of spelling, grammar is the aspect of writing that writers seem to find most troublesome. Faulty grammar is often what executives are objecting to when they complain that college graduates or MBAs "can't write."

Agreement

Subjects and verbs agree when they are both singular or both plural.

Incorrect: The accountants who conducted the audit was recommended highly.

Correct: The accountants who conducted the audit were recommended highly.

Subject–verb agreement errors often occur when other words come between the subject and the verb. Edit your draft by finding the subject and the verb of each sentence.

American usage treats company names and the words *company* and *government* as singular nouns. British usage treats them as plural:

Correct (US): State Farm Insurance trains its agents well.

Correct (Great Britain): Lloyds of London train their agents well.

Use a plural verb when two or more singular subjects are joined by *and.*

Correct: Larry McGreevy and I are planning to visit the client.

Use a singular verb when two or more singular subjects are joined by *or, nor,* or *but.*

Correct: Either the shipping clerk or the superintendent has to sign the order.

When the sentence begins with *Here* or *There,* make the verb agree with the subject that follows the verb.

Correct: Here is the booklet you asked for.

Correct: There are the blueprints I wanted.

Note that some words that end in *s* are considered to be singular and require singular verbs.

Correct: A series of meetings is planned.

When a situation doesn't seem to fit the rules, or when following a rule produces an awkward sentence, revise the sentence to avoid the problem.

Problematic: The Plant Manager in addition to the sales representative (was, were?) pleased with the new system.

Better: The Plant Manager and the sales representative were pleased with the new system.

Problematic: None of us (is, are?) perfect.

Better: All of us have faults.

Errors in **noun–pronoun agreement** occur if a pronoun is of a different number or person than the word it refers to.

Incorrect: All drivers of leased automobiles are billed $300 if damages to his automobile are caused by a collision.

Correct: All drivers of leased automobiles are billed $300 if damages to their automobiles are caused by collisions.

Incorrect: A manager has only yourself to blame if things go wrong.

Correct: As a manager, you have only yourself to blame if things go wrong.

The following words require a singular verb and pronoun:

everybody	neither
each	nobody
either	a person
everyone	

Correct: Everyone should bring his or her copy of the manual to the next session on changes in the law.

If the pronoun pairs necessary to avoid sexism seem cumbersome, avoid the terms in this list. Instead, use words that take plural pronouns or use second-person *you*.

Each pronoun must refer to a specific word. If a pronoun does not refer to a specific term, add a word to correct the error.

Incorrect: We will open three new stores in the suburbs. This will bring us closer to our customers.

Correct: We will open three new stores in the suburbs. This strategy will bring us closer to our customers.

Hint: Make sure *this* and *it* refer to a specific noun in the previous sentence. If either refers to an idea, add a noun ("this strategy") to make the sentence grammatically correct.

Use *who* and *whom* to refer to people and *which* to refer to objects. *That* can refer to anything: people, animals, organizations, and objects.

Correct: The new Executive Director, who moved here from Boston, is already making friends.

Banished Words

Correct grammar and spelling are basic ways to signal careful, intelligent writing. Another fundamental is to choose words and phrases that say what you mean. Out of habit or carelessness, however, writers may sprinkle their work with meaningless words.

To highlight the problem, Lake Superior State University each January announces its "List of Words Banished from the Queen's English for Mis-Use, Over-Use and General Uselessness." A sample from their lists:

- *Captured alive*—If someone is dead, it's too late to capture him or her.
- *Place stamp here* (on a return envelope)—This phrase states the obvious. Mail requires postage; we know where to put the stamp, don't we?
- *On the ground* (in news broadcasts)—With the exception of the occasional report from a helicopter or battleship, where else would the reporter be?
- *It is what it is*—This phrase says nothing.
- *An accident that didn't need to happen*—Some accidents need to happen?
- *Drug deal gone bad*—Are drug deals ever good?

Adapted from "List of Banished Words," Lake Superior State University, accessed June 28, 2011, http://www.lssu.edu/banished.

Figure B.1 The Case of the Personal Pronoun

	Nominative (subject of clause)	Possessive	Objective	Reflexive/ intensive
Singular				
1st person	I	my, mine	me	myself
2nd person	you	your, yours	you	yourself
3rd person	he/she/it	his/her(s)/its	him/her/it	himself/herself/itself
	one/who	one's/whose	one/whom	oneself/(no form)
Plural				
1st person	we	our, ours	us	ourselves
2nd person	you	your, yours	you	yourselves
3rd person	they	their, theirs	them	themselves

Correct: The information, which she wants now, will be available tomorrow.

Correct: This confirms the price that I quoted you this morning.

Case

Case refers to the grammatical role a noun or pronoun plays in a sentence. Figure B.1 identifies the case of each personal pronoun.

Use **nominative case** pronouns for the subject of a clause.

Correct: Shannon Weaver and I talked to the customer, who was interested in learning more about integrated software.

Use **possessive case** pronouns to show who or what something belongs to.

Correct: Microsoft Office will exactly meet her needs.

Use **objective case** pronouns as objects of verbs or prepositions.

Correct: When you send in the quote, thank her for the courtesy she showed Shannon and me.

Hint: Use *whom* when *him* would fit grammatically in the same place in your sentence.

To (who/whom) do you intend to give this report?

You intend to give this report to him.

Whom is correct.

Have we decided (who, whom?) will take notes?

Have we decided he will take notes?

Who is correct.

Use **reflexive** pronouns to refer to or emphasize a noun or pronoun that has already appeared in the sentence.

Correct: I myself think the call was a very productive one.

Do not use reflexive pronouns as subjects of clauses or as objects of verbs or propositions.

The Errors That Bother People in Organizations

Professor Maxine Hairston constructed a questionnaire with 65 sentences, each with one grammatical error. The administrators, executives, and business people who responded were most bothered by the following:

- Wrong verb forms ("he brung his secretary with him")
- Double negatives
- Objective pronoun used for subject of sentence ("Him and Richards were the last ones hired.")
- Sentence fragments
- Run-on sentences
- Failure to capitalize proper names
- "Would of" for "would have"
- Lack of subject–verb agreement
- Comma between verb and complement ("Cox cannot predict, that street crime will diminish.")
- Lack of parallelism
- Adverb errors ("He treats his men bad.")
- "Set" for "sit"

They also disliked

- Errors in word meaning
- Dangling modifiers
- "I" as objective pronoun ("The army moved my husband and I")
- Not setting off interrupters (e.g., "However") with commas
- Tense switching
- Plural modifiers with singular nouns.

Based on Maxine Hairston, "Not All Errors Are Created Equal: Nonacademic Readers in the Professions Respond to Lapses in Usage," *College English* 43, no. 8 (December 1981), 794–806.

The Fumblerules of Grammar

1. Avoid run-on sentences they are hard to read.
2. A writer must not shift your point of view.
3. Verbs has to agree with their subjects.
4. No sentence fragments.
5. Reserve the apostrophe for it's proper use and omit it when its not needed.
6. Proofread carefully to see if you any words out.
7. Avoid commas, that are unnecessary.
8. Steer clear of incorrect forms of verbs that have snuck in the language.
9. In statements involving two word phrases make an all out effort to use hyphens.
10. Last but not least, avoid clichés like the plague; seek viable alternatives.

Quoted from William Safire, "On Language: The Fumblerules of Grammar," *New York Times Magazine,* November 11, 1979, 16; and "On Language: Fumblerule Follow-up," *New York Times Magazine,* November 25, 1979, 14.

Incorrect: Elaine and myself will follow up on this order.

Correct: Elaine and I will follow up on this order.

Incorrect: He gave the order to Dan and myself.

Correct: He gave the order to Dan and me.

Note that the first-person pronoun comes after names or pronouns that refer to other people.

Dangling Modifier

A **modifier** is a word or phrase that gives more information about the subject, verb, or object in a clause. A **dangling modifier** refers to a wrong word or word that is not actually in the sentence. The solution is to reword the modifier so that it is grammatically correct.

Incorrect: Confirming our conversation, the truck will leave Monday. [The speaker is doing the confirming. But the speaker isn't in the sentence.]

Incorrect: At the age of eight, I began teaching my children about American business. [This sentence says that the author was eight when he or she had children who could understand business.]

Correct a dangling modifier in one of these ways:

- Recast the modifier as a subordinate clause.

Correct: As I told you, the truck will leave Monday.

Correct: When they were eight, I began teaching my children about American business.

- Revise the main clause so its subject or object can be modified by the nowdangling phrase.

Correct: Confirming our conversation, I have scheduled the truck to leave Monday.

Correct: At the age of eight, my children began learning about American business.

Hint: Whenever you use a verb or adjective that ends in *-ing,* make sure it modifies the grammatical subject of your sentence. If it doesn't, reword the sentence.

Misplaced Modifier

A **misplaced modifier** appears to modify another element of the sentence than the writer intended.

Incorrect: Customers who complain often alert us to changes we need to make. [Does the sentence mean that customers must complain frequently to teach us something? Or is the meaning that frequently we learn from complaints?]

Correct a misplaced modifier by moving it closer to the word it modifies or by adding punctuation to clarify your meaning. If a modifier modifies the whole sentence, use it as an introductory phrase or clause; follow it with a comma.

Correct: Often, customers who complain alert us to changes we need to make.

Parallel Structure

Items in a series or list must have the same grammatical structure.

Anguished English

Richard Lederer recorded the following howlers in headlines:

- CEMETERY ALLOWS PEOPLE TO BE BURIED BY THEIR PETS.
- KICKING BABY CONSIDERED TO BE HEALTHY.
- DIRECTOR OF TRUMAN LIBRARY KNOWS NEWSMAN'S PROBLEMS—HE WAS ONE.
- MAN FOUND BEATEN, ROBBED BY POLICE.

Quoted from Richard Lederer, *More Anguished English* (New York: Delacorte Press, 1993), 166–67.

Not parallel: In the second month of your internship, you will

1. Learn how to resolve customers' complaints.
2. Supervision of desk staff.
3. Interns will help plan store displays.

Parallel: In the second month of your internship, you will

1. Learn how to resolve customers' complaints.
2. Supervise desk staff.
3. Plan store displays.

Also parallel: Duties in the second month of your internship include resolving customers' complaints, supervising desk staff, and planning store displays.

Hint: When you have two or three items in a list (whether the list is horizontal or vertical) make sure the items are in the same grammatical form. Put lists vertically to make them easier to see.

Predication Errors

The predicate of a sentence must fit grammatically and logically with the subject. Make sure that the verb describes the action done by or done to the subject.

Incorrect: Our goals should begin immediately.

Correct: Implementing our goals should begin immediately.

In sentences using *is* and other linking verbs, the complement must be a noun, an adjective, or a noun clause.

Incorrect: The reason for this change is because the SEC now requires fuller disclosure.

Correct: The reason for this change is that the SEC now requires fuller disclosure.

UNDERSTANDING PUNCTUATION LO B-2

Punctuation marks are road signs to help readers predict what comes next. (See Figure B.2.)

When you move from the subject to the verb, you're going in a straight line; no comma is needed. When you end an introductory phrase or clause, the comma tells readers the introduction is over and you're turning to the main clause. When words interrupt the main clause, like this, commas tell the reader when to turn off the main clause for a short side route and when to return.

Figure B.2 What Punctuation Tells the Reader

Mark	Tells the reader
Period	We're stopping.
Semicolon	What comes next is closely related to what I just said.
Colon	What comes next is an example of what I just said.
Dash	What comes next is a dramatic example of or a shift from what I just said.
Comma	What comes next is a slight turn, but we're going in the same basic direction.

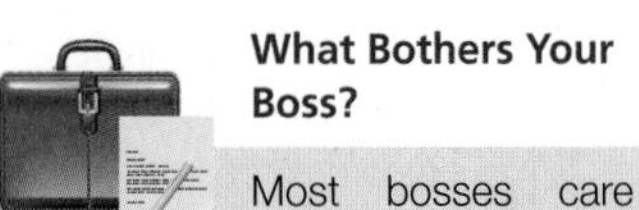

What Bothers Your Boss?

Most bosses care deeply about only a few points of grammar. Find out which errors are your supervisor's pet peeves, and avoid them.

Any living language changes. New usages appear first in speaking. Here are four issues on which experts currently disagree:

1. Plural pronouns to refer to *everybody, everyone,* and *each.* Standard grammar says these words require singular pronouns.
2. Split infinitives. An infinitive is the form of a verb that contains *to: to understand.* An infinitive is split when another word separates the *to* from the rest of an infinitive: *to easily understand.*
3. *Hopefully* to mean *I hope that. Hopefully* means "in a hopeful manner." However, a speaker who says "Hopefully, the rain will stop" is talking about the speaker's hope, not the rain's.
4. *Abbreviations without periods,* Abbreviations such as US or MBA now frequently appear without periods.

Ask your instructor and your boss whether they are willing to accept the less formal usage. When you write to someone you don't know, use standard grammar and usage.

Some people have been told to put commas where they'd take breaths. That's bad advice. How often you'd take a breath depends on how big your lung capacity is, how fast and loud you're speaking, and how much emphasis you want. Commas aren't breaths. Instead, like other punctuation, they're road signs.

PUNCTUATING SENTENCES

A sentence contains at least one main clause. A **main** or **independent clause** is a complete statement. A **subordinate** or **dependent clause** contains both a subject and a verb but is not a complete statement and cannot stand by itself. A phrase is a group of words that does not contain both a subject and a verb.

Main clauses

Your order will arrive Thursday.
He dreaded talking to his supplier.
I plan to enroll for summer school classes.

Subordinate clauses

if you place your order by Monday
because he was afraid the product would be out of stock
since I want to graduate next spring

Phrases

With our current schedule
As a result
After talking to my advisor

A clause with one of the following words will be subordinate:

after	if
although, though	when, whenever
because, since	while, as
before, until	

Using the correct punctuation will enable you to avoid four major sentence errors: comma splices, run-on sentences, fused sentences, and sentence fragments.

Comma Splices

A **comma splice** or **comma fault** occurs when two main clauses are joined only by a comma (instead of by a comma and a coordinating conjunction).

Incorrect: The contest will start in June, the date has not been set.

Correct a comma splice in one of the following ways:

- If the ideas are closely related, use a semicolon rather than a comma. If they aren't closely related, start a new sentence.

Correct: The contest will start in June; the exact date has not been set.

- Add a coordinating conjunction.

Correct: The contest will start in June, but the exact date has not been set.

- Subordinate one of the clauses.

Correct: Although the contest will start in June, the exact date has not been set.

Remember that you cannot use just a comma with the following transitions:

however	nevertheless
therefore	moreover

Instead, either use a semicolon to separate the clauses or start a new sentence.

Incorrect: Computerized grammar checkers do not catch every error, however, they may be useful as a first check before an editor reads the material.

Correct: Computerized grammar checkers do not catch every error; however, they may be useful as a first check before an editor reads the material.

Run-on Sentences

A **run-on sentence** strings together several main clauses using *and, but, or, so,* and *for.* Run-on sentences and comma splices are "mirror faults." A comma splice *uses only* the comma and omits the coordinating conjunction, while a run-on sentence uses *only* the conjunction and omits the comma. Correct a short run-on sentence by adding a comma. Separate a long run-on sentence into two or more sentences. Consider subordinating one or more of the clauses.

Incorrect: We will end up with a much smaller markup but they use a lot of this material so the volume would be high so try to sell them on fast delivery and tell them our quality is very high.

Correct: Although we will end up with a much smaller markup, volume would be high since they use a lot of this material. Try to sell them on fast delivery and high quality.

Fused Sentences

A **fused sentence** results when two sentences or more are *fused,* or joined with neither punctuation nor conjunctions. To fix the error, add the punctuation, add punctuation and a conjunction, or subordinate one of the clauses.

Incorrect: The advantages of Intranets are clear the challenge is persuading employees to share information.

Correct: The advantages of Intranets are clear; the challenge is persuading employees to share information.

Also correct: Although the advantages of Intranets are clear, the challenge is persuading employees to share information.

Sentence Fragments

In a **sentence fragment,** a group of words that is not a complete sentence is punctuated as if it were a complete sentence.

Incorrect: Observing these people, I have learned two things about the program. The time it takes. The rewards it brings.

To fix a sentence fragment, either add whatever parts of the sentence are missing or incorporate the fragment into the sentence before it or after it.

Correct: Observing these people, I have learned that the program is time-consuming but rewarding.

Remember that clauses with the following words are not complete sentences. Join them to a main clause.

Pity the Apostrophe

The apostrophe is so often misused that in England John Richards founded the Apostrophe Protection Society. The society's website, www.apostrophe.org.uk/. summarizes the basic rules for using apostrophes in English. The entertaining part of the website is its examples, photos of signs that have abused apostrophes in many ways, including overuse and omission. Here are some examples:

- In a banquet hall's brochure: "The Ultimate Attraction for all sorts of Function's ranging from, Fair's, Carnival's, Bon Fire Display's, Music Concert's, Party's, Ball's, Corporate Function's and even Wedding's" (and that's just what the ideas range *from; imagine what they range to!*).
- By a parking lot: "Resident's and Visitor's Only" (meaning something belonging to one resident and one visitor).
- By a school parking lot: "Reserved for Principals Office" (a sign that will not enhance the school's reputation).
- In a set of contest rules: "The judges decision is final." (Writer couldn't decide where to put the apostrophe, so he or she didn't try.)
- At a government office building: "Disabled Access (All Depts's) via Dep. of Social Security" (trying all punctuation possibilities at once).

Adapted from The Apostrophe Protection Society Homepage, Floating Lily Designs, last updated February 21, 2011, http://www.apostrophe.org.uk/.

after	if
although, though	when, whenever
because, since	while, as
before, until	

Incorrect: We need to buy a new computer system. Because our current system is obsolete.

Correct: We need to buy a new computer system because our current system is obsolete.

PUNCTUATION WITHIN SENTENCES

The good business and administrative writer knows how to use the following punctuation marks: apostrophes, colons, commas, dashes, hyphens, parentheses, periods, and semicolons.

Apostrophe

1. Use an apostrophe in a contraction to indicate that a letter or symbol has been omitted.

   We're trying to renegotiate the contract.

   The '90s were years of restructuring for our company.

2. To indicate possession, add an apostrophe and an *s* to the word.

   The corporation's home office is in Houston, Texas.

   Apostrophes to indicate possession are especially essential when one noun in a comparison is omitted.

   This year's sales will be higher than last year's.

   When a word already ends in an *s*, add an apostrophe or an apostrophe and *s* to make it possessive.

   The meeting will be held at New Orleans' convention center.

   With many terms, the placement of the apostrophe indicates whether the noun is singular or plural.

   Incorrect: The program should increase the participant's knowledge. [Implies that only one participant is in the program.]

   Correct: The program should increase the participants' knowledge. [Many participants are in the program.]

   Hint: Use "of" in the sentence to see where the apostrophe goes.

   The figures of last year = last year's figures

   The needs of our customers = our customers' needs

   Note that possessive pronouns (e.g., *his, ours*) usually do not have apostrophes. The only exception is *one's*.

   The company needs the goodwill of its stockholders.

   His promotion was announced yesterday.

   One's greatest asset is the willingness to work hard.

3. Do not use an apostrophe to make plurals.

Incorrect:	Use the folder's above the cabinet to file these documents.
Correct:	Use the folders above the cabinet to file these documents.

Colon

1. Use a colon to separate a main clause and a list that explains the last element in the clause. The items in the list are specific examples of the word that appears immediately before the colon.

Please order the following supplies:
Printer cartridges
Computer paper (20-lb. white bond)
Bond paper (25-lb., white, 25% cotton)
Company letterhead
Company envelopes

When the list is presented vertically, capitalize the first letter of each item in the list. When the list is run in with the sentence, you don't need to capitalize the first letter after the colon.

Please order the following supplies: printer cartridges, computer paper (20-lb. white bond), bond paper (25-lb., white, 25% cotton), company letterhead, and company envelopes.

Do not use a colon when the list is grammatically part of the main clause.

Incorrect:	The rooms will have coordinated decors in natural colors such as: eggplant, moss, and mushroom.
Correct:	The rooms will have coordinated decors in natural colors such as eggplant, moss, and mushroom.
Also correct:	The rooms will have coordinated decors in a variety of natural colors: eggplant, moss, and mushroom.

If the list is presented vertically, some authorities suggest introducing the list with a colon even though the words preceding the colon are not a complete sentence.

2. Use a colon to join two independent clauses when the second clause explains or restates the first clause.

Selling is simple: give people the service they need, and they'll come back with more orders.

Comma

1. Use commas to separate the main clause from an introductory clause, the reader's name, or words that interrupt the main clause. Note that commas both precede and follow the interrupting information.

R. J. Garcia, the new Sales Manager, comes to us from the Des Moines office.

A **nonrestrictive** (nonessential) **clause** gives extra information that is not needed to identify the noun it modifies. Because nonrestrictive clauses give extra information, they need extra commas.

The History of Punctuation

WHENWRITING BEGANTHERE WERENOBREAKS BETWEENWORDS

In inscriptions on monuments in ancient Greece, breaks were chosen to create balance and proportion.

WHENWRITI NGBEGANTH EREWERENO BREAKSBET WEENWORDS

In the third century bce, Aristophanes added a dot high in the line (like this •), after a complete thought, or *periodos.* For part of a complete thought, or *colon,* he used a dot on the line (like this .). For a comma, or subdivision of a colon, he used a dot halfway up (like this •).

The monks in the Middle Ages substituted a strong slash for the midway dot. As time went on, the strong slash was shortened and acquired a curl—becoming our comma today.

Based on Lionel Casson, "howandwhy punctuationevercametobeinvented," *Smithsonian* 19, no. 7 (October 1988), 216.

Sue Decker, who wants to advance in the organization, has signed up for the company training program in sales techniques.

Do not use commas to set off information that restricts the meaning of a noun or pronoun. **Restrictive clauses** give essential, not extra, information.

Anyone who wants to advance in the organization should take advantage of on-the-job training.

The clause "who wants to advance in the organization" restricts the meaning of the pronoun *anyone.*

Do not use commas to separate the subject from the verb, even if you would take a breath after a long subject.

Incorrect: Laws requiring registration of anyone collecting $5,000 or more on behalf of another person, apply to schools and private individuals as well to charitable groups and professional fund-raisers.

Correct: Laws requiring registration of anyone collecting $5,000 or more on behalf of another person □ apply to schools and private individuals as well to charitable groups and professional fund-raisers.

2. Use a comma, with a conjunction, after the first clause in a compound sentence.

   This policy eliminates all sick-leave credit of the employee at the time of retirement, and payment will be made only once to any individual.

   Do not use commas to join independent clauses without a conjunction. Doing so produces comma splices.

3. Use commas to separate items in a series. Using a comma before the *and* or *or* is not required by some authorities, but using a comma always adds clarity. The comma is essential if any of the items in the series themselves contain the word *and.*

   The company pays the full cost of hospitalization insurance for eligible employees, spouses, and unmarried dependent children under age 23.

Dash

Use dashes to emphasize a break in thought.

Ryertex comes in 30 grades—each with a special use.

To type a dash, use two hyphens with no space before or after.

Hyphen

1. Use a hyphen to indicate that a word has been divided between two lines.

   Attach the original receipts for lodging, meals, tips, transportation, and registration fees.

   Divide words at syllable breaks. If you aren't sure where the syllables divide, look up the word in a dictionary. When a word has several syllables, divide it after a vowel or between two consonants. Don't divide words of one syllable (e.g., *used*); don't divide a two-syllable word if one of the syllables is only one letter long (e.g., *acre*).

2. Use hyphens to join two or more words used as a single adjective.

   Order five 10- or 12-foot lengths.

   The computer-prepared income and expense statements will be ready next Friday.

The hyphen prevents misreading. In the first example, five lengths are needed, not lengths of 5, 10, or 12 feet. In the second example, without the hyphen, the reader might think that *computer* was the subject and *prepared* was the verb.

Parentheses

1. Use parentheses to set off words, phrases, or sentences used to explain or comment on the main idea.

   For the thinnest Ryertex (.015″) only a single layer of the base material may be used, while the thickest (10″) may contain over 600 greatly compressed layers of fabric or paper. By varying the fabric used (cotton, asbestos, glass, or nylon) or the type of paper, and by changing the kind of resin (phenolic, melamine, silicone, or epoxy), we can produce 30 different grades.

   Any additional punctuation goes outside the second parenthesis when the punctuation applies to the whole sentence. It goes inside when it applies only to the words in the parentheses.

   Please check the invoice to see if credit should be issued. (A copy of the invoice is attached.)

2. Use parentheses for the citations in a text. See Chapter 18 for examples.

Period

1. Use a period at the end of a sentence. Space once before the next sentence.
2. Use a period after some abbreviations. When a period is used with a person's initials, leave one space after the period before the next letter or word. In other abbreviations, no space is necessary.

   R. J. Tebeaux has been named Vice President for Marketing.

   The U.S. division plans to hire 300 new M.B.A.s in the next year.

   The trend is to reduce the use of punctuation. It would also be correct to write

   The US division plans to hire 300 new MBAs in the next year.

Semicolon

1. Use semicolons to join two independent clauses when they are closely related.

   We'll do our best to fill your order promptly; however, we cannot guarantee a delivery date.

   Using a semicolon suggests that the two ideas are very closely connected. Using a period and a new sentence is also correct but implies nothing about how closely related the two sentences are.

2. Use semicolons to separate items in a series when the items themselves contain commas.

   The final choices for the new plant are El Paso, Texas; Albuquerque, New Mexico; Salt Lake City, Utah; Eureka, California; and Eugene, Oregon.

   Hospital benefits are also provided for certain specialized care services such as diagnostic admissions directed toward a definite disease or injury; normal maternity delivery, Caesarean section delivery, or complications of pregnancy; and in-patient admissions for dental procedures necessary to safeguard the patient's life or health.

Hint: A semicolon could be replaced by a period and a capital letter. It has a sentence on both sides.

SPECIAL PUNCTUATION MARKS

Quotation marks, square brackets, ellipses, and underlining are necessary when you use quoted material.

Quotation Marks

1. Use quotation marks around the names of brochures, pamphlets, and magazine articles.

   Enclosed are 30 copies of our pamphlet "Saving Energy."

   You'll find articles like "How to Improve Your Golf Game" and "Can You Keep Your Eye on the Ball?" in every issue.

   In US punctuation, periods and commas go inside quotation marks. Colons and semicolons go outside. Question marks go inside if they are part of the material being quoted.

2. Use quotation marks around words to indicate that you think the term is misleading.

   These "pro-business" policies actually increase corporate taxes.

3. Use quotation marks around words that you are discussing as words.

   Forty percent of the respondents answered "yes" to the first question.

   Use "Ms." as a courtesy title for a woman unless you know she prefers another title.

   It is also acceptable to italicize words instead of using quotation marks.

4. Use quotation marks around words or sentences that you quote from someone else.

   "The Fog Index," says its inventor, Robert Gunning, is "an effective warning system against drifting into needless complexity."

Square Brackets

Use square brackets to add your own additions to or changes in quoted material.

Senator Smith's statement:	"These measures will create a deficit."
Your use of Smith's statement:	According to Senator Smith, "These measures [in the new tax bill] will create a deficit."

The square brackets show that Smith did not say these words; you add them to make the quote make sense in your document.

Ellipses

Ellipses are spaced dots. In typing, use three spaced periods for an ellipsis. When an ellipsis comes at the end of a sentence, use a dot immediately after the last letter of the sentence for a period. Then add three spaced dots, with another space after the last dot.

1. Use ellipses to indicate that one or more words have been omitted in the middle of quoted material. You do not need ellipses at the beginning or end of a quote.

   The Wall Street Journal notes that Japanese magazines and newspapers include advertisements for a "$2.1 million home in New York's posh Riverdale section . . . 185 acres of farmland [and] . . . luxury condos on Manhattan's Upper East Side."

2. In advertising and direct mail, use ellipses to imply the pace of spoken comments.

   If you've ever wanted to live on a tropical island . . . cruise to the Bahamas . . . or live in a castle in Spain . . .

   . . . you can make your dreams come true with Vacations Extraordinaire.

More Anguished English

- Family Physician. Hours: 10:30–12:20; 3:30–4:45 Monday-Friday. 10:30–11:45 Saturday. Limited Amount of Patience.
- Aunt and Roach Killer.
- He is recovering from a near-fatal accident that sent him into a comma.
- The board voted by telephone pole.
- I found a liter of pups.

Quoted from Richard Lederer, *More Anguished English* (New York: Delacorte Press, 1993), 166–67.

Underlining and Italics

1. Underline or italicize the names of newspapers, magazines, and books.

   The Wall Street Journal — *The Wall Street Journal*
   Fortune — *Fortune*
   The Wealth of Nations — *The Wealth of Nations*

   Titles of brochures and pamphlets are put in quotation marks.

2. Underline or italicize words to emphasize them.

   Here's a bulletin that gives you, in handy chart form, workable data on over 50 different types of tubing and pipe.

   You may also use bold to emphasize words. Bold type is better than either underlining or italics because it is easier to read.

WRITING NUMBERS AND DATES

Spell out **numbers** from one to nine. Use figures for numbers 10 and over in most cases. Always use figures for amounts of money (The new office costs $1.7 million). Large numbers frequently use a combination of numbers and words (More than 20 million people are affected by this new federal regulation).

Spell out any number that appears at the beginning of a sentence. If spelling it out is impractical, revise the sentence so that it does not begin with a number.

Fifty students filled out the survey.

In 2002, euro notes and coins entered circulation.

When two numbers follow each other, spell out the smaller number and use figures for the larger number.

In **dates,** use figures for the day and year. The month is normally spelled out. Be sure to spell out the month in international business communication. American usage puts the month first, so that 1/10/12 means *January 10, 2012.* European usage puts the day first, so that 1/10/12 means *October 1, 2012.* Modern punctuation uses a comma before the year only when you give both the month and the day of the month:

May 1, 2012

but

Summers 2009–12

August 2012

Fall 2012

No punctuation is needed in military or European usage, which puts the day of the month first: 13 July 2012. Do not space before or after the slash used to separate parts of the date: 10/05–5/12.

Use a hyphen to join inclusive dates.

March–August 2012 (or write out: March to August 2012)

'08–'09

1999–2001

Note that you do not need to repeat the century in the date that follows the hyphen: 2011–12.

WORDS THAT ARE OFTEN CONFUSED LO B-3

Here's a list of words that are frequently confused. Master them, and you'll be well on the way to using words correctly.

1. accede/exceed
   accede: to yield
   exceed: to go beyond, surpass
      I accede to your demand that we not exceed the budget.
2. accept/except
   accept: to receive; to agree to
   except: to leave out or exclude; but
      I accept your proposal except for point 3.
3. access/excess
   access: the right to use; admission to
   excess: surplus
      As supply clerk, he had access to any excess materials.
4. adapt/adopt
   adapt: adjust
   adopt: to take as one's own
      She would adapt her ideas so people would adopt them.
5. advice/advise
   advice: (noun) counsel
   advise: (verb) to give counsel or advice to someone
      I asked him to advise me, but I didn't like the advice I got.
6. affect/effect
   affect: (verb) to influence or modify
   effect: (verb) to produce or cause; (noun) result
      He hoped that his argument would affect his boss's decision, but so far as he could see, it had no effect.
      The tax relief effected some improvement for the citizens whose incomes had been affected by inflation.
7. affluent/effluent
   affluent: (adjective) rich, possessing in abundance
   effluent: (noun) something that flows out

Affluent companies can afford the cost of removing pollutants from the effluents their factories produce.

8. a lot/allot

   a lot: many (informal)

   allot: divide or give to

   A lot of players signed up for this year's draft. We allotted one first-round draft choice to each team.

9. among/between

   among: (use with more than two choices)

   between: (use with only two choices)

   This year the differences between the two candidates for president are unusually clear.

   I don't see any major differences among the candidates for city council.

10. amount/number

    amount: (use with concepts or items that can be measured but that cannot be counted individually)

    number: (use when items can be counted individually)

    It's a mistake to try to gauge the amount of interest he has by the number of questions he asks.

11. attributed/contributed

    attributed: was said to be caused by

    contributed: gave something to

    The rain probably contributed to the accident, but the police officer attributed the accident to driver error.

12. cite/sight/site

    cite: (verb) to quote

    sight: (noun) vision, something to be seen

    site: (noun) location, place where a building is or will be built

    She cited the old story of the building inspector who was depressed by the very sight of the site for the new factory.

13. complement/compliment

    complement: (verb) to complete, finish; (noun) something that completes

    compliment: (verb) to praise; (noun) praise

    The compliment she gave me complemented my happiness.

14. compose/comprise

    compose: make up, create

    comprise: consist of, be made up of, be composed of

    The city council is composed of 12 members. Each district comprises an area 50 blocks square.

15. confuse/complicate/exacerbate

    confuse: to bewilder

    complicate: to make more complex or detailed

    exacerbate: to make worse

    Because I missed the first 20 minutes of the movie, I didn't understand what was going on. The complicated plot exacerbated my confusion.

16. dependant/dependent

    dependant: (noun) someone for whom one is financially responsible

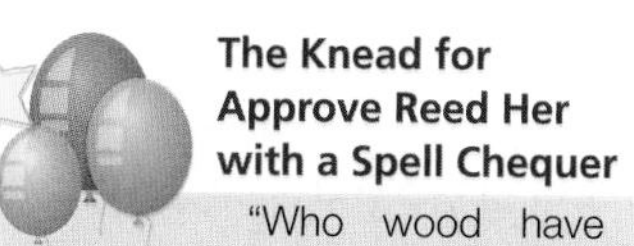

The Knead for Approve Reed Her with a Spell Chequer

"Who wood have guest The Spell Chequer would super seed The assent of the editor Who was once a mane figure? . . . Once, awl sought his council; Now nun prophet from him. How suite the job was; It was all sew fine. . . . Never once was he board As he edited each claws, Going strait to his deer work Where he'd in cyst on clarity. Now he's holy unacceptable, Useless and knot kneaded. . . . This is know miner issue, Fore he cannot urn a wage. Two this he takes a fence, Butt nose naught watt too due. He's wade each option Of jobs he mite dew, But nothing peaks his interest Like making pros clear. Sum will see him silly For being sew upset, But doesn't good righting Go beyond the write spelling?"

Quoted from Jeff Lovill, "On the Uselessness of an Editor in the Presents of a Spell Chequer," *Technical Communication* 35, no. 4 (1988), 267; and Edward M. Chilton, "Various Comments on 4Q88," *Technical Communication* 36, no. 2 (1989), 173.

dependent: (adjective) relying on someone else

IRS regulations don't let us count our 27-year-old son as a dependant, but he is still financially dependent on us.

17. describe/prescribe

describe: list the features of something, tell what something looks like

prescribe: specify the features something must contain

The law prescribes the priorities for making repairs. This report describes our plans to comply with the law.

18. different from/different than

Almost always *different from* (try changing the adjective *different* to the verb *differs*)

Bob's job description is different from mine.

The most common exception is the indirect comparison.

Susan has a different attitude than you and I [*do* is implied].

19. discreet/discrete

discreet: tactful, careful not to reveal secrets

discrete: separate, distinct

I have known him to be discreet on two discrete occasions.

20. disinterested/uninterested

Disinterested: impartial

Uninterested: unconcerned

Because our boss is uninterested in office spats, she makes a disinterested referee.

21. elicit/illicit

elicit: (verb) to draw out

illicit: (adjective) not permitted, unlawful

The reporter could elicit no information from the senator about his illicit love affair.

22. eminent/immanent/imminent

eminent: distinguished

immanent: existing in the mind or consciousness

imminent: about to happen

The eminent doctor believed that death was imminent. The eminent minister believed that God was immanent.

23. farther/further

Farther: use for physical difference

Further: use for metaphoric difference; also use for *additional* or *additionally*

As I traveled farther from the destruction at the plant, I pondered the further evidence of sabotage presented to me today.

24. fewer/less

fewer: (use for objects that can be counted individually)

less: (use for objects that can be measured but not counted individually)

There is less sand in this bucket; there are probably fewer grains of sand, too.

25. forward/foreword

forward: ahead

foreword: preface, introduction

The author looked forward to writing the foreword to the book.

26. good/well

good: (adjective, used to modify nouns; as a noun, means something that is good)

well: (adverb, used to modify verbs, adjectives, and other adverbs)

Her words "Good work!" told him that he was doing well.

He spent a great deal of time doing volunteer work because he believed that doing good was just as important as doing well.

27. i.e./e.g.

i.e.: (*id est*—that is) introduces a restatement or explanation of the preceding word or phrase

e.g.: (*exempli gratia*—for the sake of an example; for example) introduces one or more examples

Although he had never studied Latin, he rarely made a mistake in using Latin abbreviations, e.g., i.e., and etc., because he associated each with a mnemonic device (i.e., a word or image used to help one remember something). He remembered *i.e.* as *in effect,* pretended that *e.g.* meant *example given,* and used *etc.* only when *examples to continue* would fit.

28. imply/infer

imply: suggest, put an idea into someone's head

infer: deduce, get an idea out from something

She implied that an announcement would be made soon. I inferred from her smile that it would be an announcement of her promotion.

29. it's/its

it's: it is, it has

its: belonging to it

It's clear that a company must satisfy its customers to stay in business.

30. lectern/podium

lectern: raised stand with a slanted top that holds a manuscript for a reader or notes for a speaker

podium: platform for a speaker or conductor to stand on

I left my notes on the lectern when I left the podium at the end of my talk.

31. lie/lay

lie: to recline; to tell a falsehood (never takes an object)

lay: to put an object on something (always takes an object)

He was laying the papers on the desk when I came in, but they aren't lying there now.

32. loose/lose

loose: not tight

lose: to have something disappear

If I lose weight, this suit will be loose.

33. moral/morale

moral: (adjective) virtuous, good; (noun: morals) ethics, sense of right and wrong

morale: (noun) spirit, attitude, mental outlook

Studies have shown that coed dormitories improve student morale without harming student morals.

34. objective/rationale

objective: goal

Spelling Demons

The words listed below (in order of increasing difficulty) are among the most frequently misspelled words in English. How many of them do you spell correctly?

1. Grammar
2. Argument
3. Surprise
4. Achieve
5. Definitely
6. Separate
7. Desirable
8. Development
9. Existence
10. Occasion
11. Assistant
12. Repetition
13. Privilege
14. Dependent
15. Consensus
16. Accommodate
17. Occurrence
18. Commitment
19. Allotted
20. Liaison
21. Proceed
22. Harass
23. Dissention
24. Prerogative
25. Inadvertent

Based on Bruce O. Boston, ed., *Stet!* (Alexandria, VA: Editorial Experts, 1986), 267–68

rationale: reason, justification

The objective of the meeting was to explain the rationale behind the decision.

35. personal/personnel

personal: individual, to be used by one person

personnel: staff, employees

All personnel will get personal computers by the end of the year.

36. possible/possibly

possible: (adjective) something that can be done

possibly: (adverb) perhaps

It is possible that we will be able to hire this spring. We can choose from possibly the best graduating class in the past five years.

37. precede/proceed

precede: (verb) to go before

proceed: (verb) to continue; (noun: proceeds) money

Raising the money must precede spending it. Only after we obtain the funds can we proceed to spend the proceeds.

38. principal/principle

principal: (adjective) main; (noun) person in charge; money lent out at interest

principle: (noun) basic truth or rule, code of conduct

The Prince, Machiavelli's principal work, describes his principles for ruling a state.

39. quiet/quite

quiet: not noisy

quite: very

It was quite difficult to find a quiet spot anywhere near the floor of the stock exchange.

40. regulate/relegate

regulate: control

relegate: put (usually in an inferior position)

If the federal government regulates the size of lettering on country road signs, we may as well relegate the current signs to the garbage bin.

41. respectfully/respectively

respectfully: with respect

respectively: to each in the order listed

When I was introduced to the queen, the prime minister, and the court jester, I bowed respectfully, shook hands politely, and winked, respectively.

42. role/roll

role: part in a play or script, function (in a group)

roll: (noun) list of students, voters, or other members; round piece of bread; (verb) move by turning over and over

While the teacher called the roll, George—in his role as class clown—threw a roll he had saved from lunch.

43. simple/simplistic

simple: not complicated

simplistic: watered down, oversimplified

She was able to explain the proposal in simple terms without making the explanation sound simplistic.

44. stationary/stationery

stationary: not moving, fixed

stationery: paper

During the earthquake, even the stationery was not stationary.

45. their/there/they're

their: belonging to them

there: in that place

they're: they are

There are plans, designed to their specifications, for the house they're building.

46. to/too/two

to: (preposition) function word indicating proximity, purpose, time, etc.

too: (adverb) also, very, excessively

two: (adjective) the number 2

The formula is too secret to entrust to two people.

47. unique/unusual

unique: sole, only, alone

unusual: not common

I believed that I was unique in my ability to memorize long strings of numbers until I consulted *Guinness World Records* and found that I was merely unusual: someone else had equaled my feat in 1993.

48. verbal/oral

verbal: using words

oral: spoken, not written

His verbal skills were uneven: his oral communication was excellent, but he didn't write well. His sensitivity to nonverbal cues was acute: he could tell what kind of day I had just by looking at my face.

Hint: Oral comes from the Latin word for mouth, *os.* Think of Oral-B Toothbrushes: for the mouth. Verbal comes from the Latin word for word, *verba.* Nonverbal language is language that does not use words (e.g., body language, gestures).

49. whether/weather

whether: (conjunction) used to introduce possible alternatives

weather: (noun) state of the atmosphere: wet or dry, hot or cold, calm or storm

We will have to see what the weather is before we decide whether to hold the picnic indoors or out.

50. your/you're

your: belonging to you

you're: you are

You're the top candidate for promotion in your division.

PROOFREADING SYMBOLS

Use the proofreading symbols in Figure B.3 to make corrections on paper copies. Figure B.4 shows how the symbols can be used to correct a typed text.

Figure B.3 Proofreading Symbols

Symbol	Meaning	Symbol	Meaning
℘	delete	[	move to left
^	insert a letter	]	move to right
¶	start a new paragraph here	⊓	move up
(stet)	stet (leave as it was before the marked change)	⊔	move down
(tr) ∽	transpose (reverse)	#	leave a space
(lc)	lower case (don't capitalize)	⁀	close up
≡	capitalize	‖	align vertically

Figure B.4 Marked Text

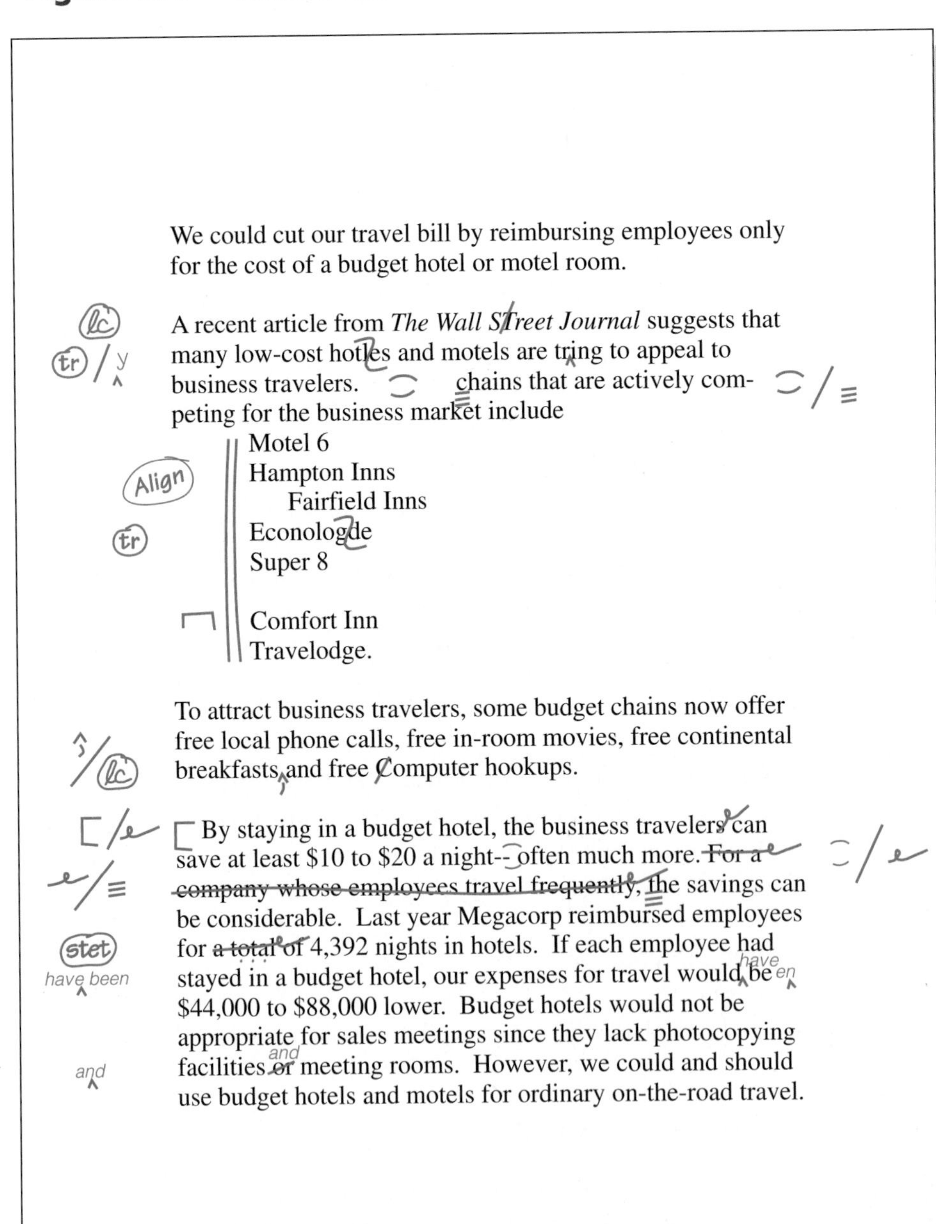

We could cut our travel bill by reimbursing employees only for the cost of a budget hotel or motel room.

A recent article from *The Wall STreet Journal* suggests that many low-cost hotles and motels are tring to appeal to business travelers. chains that are actively com-peting for the business market include

Motel 6
Hampton Inns
Fairfield Inns
Econologde
Super 8

Comfort Inn
Travelodge.

To attract business travelers, some budget chains now offer free local phone calls, free in-room movies, free continental breakfasts and free Computer hookups.

By staying in a budget hotel, the business travelers can save at least $10 to $20 a night--often much more. For a company whose employees travel frequently, the savings can be considerable. Last year Megacorp reimbursed employees for a total of 4,392 nights in hotels. If each employee had stayed in a budget hotel, our expenses for travel would be $44,000 to $88,000 lower. Budget hotels would not be appropriate for sales meetings since they lack photocopying facilities or meeting rooms. However, we could and should use budget hotels and motels for ordinary on-the-road travel.

APPENDIX B

Exercises and Problems

Go to www.mhhe.com/locker10e for additional Exercises and Problems.

B.1 Diagnostic Test on Punctuation and Grammar

Identify and correct the errors in the following passages.

a. Company's are finding it to their advantage to cultivate their suppliers. Partnerships between a company and it's suppliers can yield hefty payoffs for both company and supplier. One example is Bailey Controls an Ohio headquartered company. Bailey make control systems for big factories. They treat suppliers almost like departments of their own company. When a Bailey employee passes a laser scanner over a bins bar code the supplier is instantly alerted to send more parts.

b. Entrepreneur Trip Hawkins appears in Japanese ads for the video game system his company designed. "It plugs into the future! he says in one ad, in a cameo spliced into shots of U.S kids playing the games. Hawkins is one of several US celebrieties and business people whom plug products on Japanese TV. Jodie Foster, harrison ford, and Charlie Sheen adverstises canned coffee beer and cigarettes respectively.

c. Mid size firms employing between 100 and 1000 peopole represent only 4% of companies in the U.S.; but create 33% of all new jobs. One observe attributes their success to their being small enough to take advantage of economic opportunity's agilely, but big enough to have access to credit and to operate on a national or even international scale. The biggest hiring area for midsize company's is wholesale and retail sales (38% of jobs), construction (20% of jobs, manufacturing (19% of jobs), and services (18 of jobs).

B.2 Providing Punctuation

Provide the necessary punctuation in the following sentences. Note that not every box requires punctuation.

1. The system □ s □ user □ friendly design □ provides screen displays of work codes □ rates □ and client information.
2. Many other factors also shape the organization □ s □ image □ advertising □ brochures □ proposals □ stationery □ calling cards □ etc.
3. Charlotte Ford □ author of □ Charlotte Ford □ s □ Book of Modern Manners □ □ says □ □ Try to mention specifics of the conversation to fix the interview permanently in the interviewer □ s □ mind and be sure to mail the letter the same day □ before the hiring decision is made □ □
4. What are your room rates □ and charges for food service □
5. We will need accommodations for 150 people □ five meeting rooms □ one large room and four small ones □ □ coffee served during morning and afternoon breaks □ and lunches and dinners.
6. The Operational Readiness Inspection □ which occurs once every three years □ is a realistic exercise □ which evaluates the National Guard □ s □ ability to mobilize □ deploy □ and fight.
7. Most computer packages will calculate three different sets of percentages □ row percentages □ column percentages □ and table percentages □
8. In today □ s □ economy □ it □ s almost impossible for a firm to extend credit beyond it □ s regular terms.
9. The Department of Transportation does not have statutory authority to grant easements □ however □ we do have authority to lease unused areas of highway right □ of □ way.
10. The program has two goals □ to identify employees with promise □ and to see that they get the training they need to advance.

B.3 Providing Punctuation

Provide the necessary punctuation in the following sentences. Note that not every box requires punctuation.

1. Office work □ □ especially at your desk □ □ can create back □ shoulder □ neck □ or wrist strain.
2. I searched for □ vacation □ and □ vacation planning □ on Google and Bing.
3. I suggest putting a bulletin board in the rear hallway □ and posting all the interviewer □ s □ photos on it.
4. Analyzing audiences is the same for marketing and writing □ you have to identify who the audiences are □ understand how to motivate them □ and choose the best channel to reach them.
5. The more you know about your audience □ □ who they are □ what they buy □ where they shop □ □ the more relevant and effective you can make your ad.
6. The city already has five □ two □ hundred □ bed hospitals.
7. Students run the whole organization □ and are advised by a board of directors from the community.
8. The company is working on three team □ related issues □ interaction □ leadership □ and team size.
9. I would be interested in working on the committee □ however □ I have decided to do less community work so that I have more time to spend with my family.
10. □ You can create you own future □ □ says Frank Montaño □ □ You have to think about it □ crystallize it in writing □ and be willing to work at it □ We teach a lot of goal □ setting and planning in our training sessions □ □

B.4 Creating Agreement

Revise the following sentences to correct errors in noun–pronoun and subject–verb agreement.

1. If there's any tickets left, they'll be $17 at the door.
2. A team of people from marketing, finance, and production are preparing the proposal.
3. Image type and resolution varies among clip art packages.
4. Your health and the health of your family is very important to us.
5. If a group member doesn't complete their assigned work, it slows the whole project down.
6. Baker & Baker was offended by the ad agency's sloppy proposal, and they withdrew their account from the firm.
7. To get out of debt you need to cut up your credit cards, which is hard to do.
8. Contests are fun for employees and creates sales incentives.
9. The higher the position a person has, the more professional their image should be.
10. A new employee should try to read verbal and nonverbal signals to see which aspects of your job are most important.

B.5 Correcting Case Errors

Revise the following sentences to correct errors in pronoun case.

1. I didn't appreciate him assuming that he would be the group's leader.
2. Myself and Jim made the presentation.
3. Employees which lack experience in dealing with people from other cultures could benefit from seminars in intercultural communication.
4. Chandra drew the graphs after her and I discussed the ideas for them.
5. Please give your revisions to Cindy, Tyrone, or myself by noon Friday.
6. Let's keep this disagreement between you and I.

B.6 Improving Modifiers

Revise the following sentences to correct dangling and misplaced modifiers.

1. Originally a group of four, one member dropped out after the first meeting due to a death in the family.
2. Examining the data, it is apparent that most of our sales are to people on the northwest side of the city.
3. As a busy professional, we know that you will want to take advantage of this special offer.
4. Often documents end up in files that aren't especially good.
5. By making an early reservation, it will give us more time to coordinate our trucks to better serve you.

B.7 Creating Parallel Structure

Revise the following sentences to create parallel structure.

1. To narrow a web search,
   - Put quotation marks around a phrase when you want an exact term.
   - Many search engines have wild cards (usually an asterisk) to find plurals and other forms of a word.
   - Reading the instructions on the search engine itself can teach you advanced search techniques.
2. Men drink more alcoholic beverages than women.
3. Each issue of *Hospice Care* has articles from four different perspectives: legislative, health care, hospice administrators, and inspirational authors.
4. The university is one of the largest employers in the community, brings in substantial business, and the cultural impact is also big.
5. These three tools can help competitive people be better negotiators:
   1. Think win–win.
   2. It's important to ask enough questions to find out the other person's priorities, rather than jumping on the first advantage you find.
   3. Protect the other person's self-esteem.
6. These three questions can help cooperative people be better negotiators:
   1. Can you developing a specific alternative to use if negotiation fails?
   2. Don't focus on the bottom line. Spend time thinking about what you want and why you need it.
   3. Saying "You'll have to do better than that because . . . " can help you resist the temptation to say "yes" too quickly.

B.8 Correcting Sentence Errors

Revise the following sentences to correct comma splices, run-on sentences, fused sentences, and sentence fragments.

1. Members of the group are all experienced presenters, most have had little or no experience using PowerPoint.
2. Proofread the letter carefully and check for proper business format because errors undercut your ability to sell yourself so take advantage of your opportunity to make a good first impression.
3. Some documents need just one pass others need multiple revisions.
4. Videoconferencing can be frustrating. Simply because little time is available for casual conversation.
5. Entrepreneurs face two main obstacles. Limited cash. Lack of business experience.
6. The margin on pet supplies is very thin and the company can't make money selling just dog food and the real profit is in extras like neon-colored leashes, so you put the dog food in the back so people have to walk by everything else to get to it.
7. The company's profits jumped 15%. Although its revenues fell 3%.
8. The new budget will hurt small businesses it imposes extra fees it raises the interest rates small businesses must pay.
9. Our phones are constantly being used. Not just for business calls but also for personal calls.
10. Businesses are trying to cut travel costs, executives are taking fewer trips and flying out of alternate airports to save money.

B.9 Editing for Grammar and Usage

Revise the following sentences to eliminate errors in grammar and usage.

1. The number of students surveyed that worked more than 20 hours a week were 60%.
2. Not everyone is promoted after six months some people might remain in the training program a year before being moved to a permanent assignment.
3. The present solutions that has been suggested are not adequate.
4. At times while typing and editing, the text on your screen may not look correct.
5. All employees are asked to cut back on energy waste by the manager.
6. The benefits of an online catalog are
   1. We will be able to keep records up-to-date;
   2. Broad access to the catalog system from any networked terminal on campus;
   3. The consolidation of the main catalog and the catalogs in the departmental and branch libraries;
   4. Cost savings.
7. You can take advantage of several banking services. Such as automatic withdrawal of a house or car payment and direct deposit of your pay check.
8. As a freshman, business administration was intriguing to me.
9. Thank you for the help you gave Joanne Jackson and myself.
10. I know from my business experience that good communication among people and departments are essential in running a successful corporation.

B.10 Writing Numbers

Revise the following sentences to correct errors in writing numbers.

1. 60% percent of the respondents hope to hold internships before they graduate.
2. 1992 marked the formal beginning of the European Economic Community.
3. In the year two thousand, twenty percent of the H-1B visas for immigrants with high-tech skills went to Indians.
4. More than 70,000,000 working Americans lack an employer-sponsored retirement plan.
5. The company's sales have risen to $16 million but it lost five million dollars.

B.11 Using Plurals and Possessives

Choose the right word for each sentence.

1. Many Canadian (companies, company's) are competing effectively in the global market.
2. We can move your (families, family's) furniture safely and efficiently.
3. The (managers', manager's) ability to listen is just as important as his or her technical knowledge.
4. A (memos, memo's) style can build goodwill.
5. (Social workers, social worker's) should tell clients about services available in the community.
6. The (companies, company's) benefits plan should be checked periodically to make sure it continues to serve the needs of employees.
7. Information about the new community makes the (families, family's) move easier.
8. The (managers, manager's) all have open-door policies.
9. (Memos, memo's) are sent to other workers in the same organization.
10. Burnout affects a (social workers', social worker's) productivity as well as his or her morale.

B.12 Choosing the Right Word

Choose the right word for each sentence.

1. Exercise is (good, well) for patients who have had open-heart surgery.
2. This response is atypical, but it is not (unique, unusual).
3. The personnel department continues its (roll, role) of compiling reports for the federal government.
4. The Accounting Club expects (its, it's) members to come to meetings and participate in activities.
5. Part of the fun of any vacation is (cite, sight, site)-seeing.
6. The (lectern, podium) was too high for the short speaker.
7. The (residence, residents) of the complex have asked for more parking spaces.
8. Please order more letterhead (stationary, stationery).
9. The closing of the plant will (affect, effect) house prices in the area.
10. Better communication (among, between) design and production could enable us to produce products more efficiently.

B.13 Choosing the Right Word

Choose the right word for each sentence.

1. The audit revealed a small (amount, number) of errors.
2. Diet beverages have (fewer, less) calories than regular drinks.
3. In her speech, she (implied, inferred) that the vote would be close.
4. We need to redesign the stand so that the catalog is eye-level instead of (laying, lying) on the desk.
5. (Their, There, They're) is some evidence that (their, there, they're) thinking of changing (their, there, they're) policy.
6. The settlement isn't yet in writing; if one side wanted to back out of the (oral, verbal) agreement, it could.
7. In (affect, effect), we're creating a new department.
8. The firm will be hiring new (personal, personnel) in three departments this year.
9. Several customers have asked that we carry more campus merchandise, (i.e., e.g.,) pillows and mugs with the college seal.
10. We have investigated all of the possible solutions (accept, except) adding a turning lane.

B.14 Choosing the Right Word

Choose the right word for each sentence.

1. The author (cites, sights, sites) four reasons for computer phobia.
2. The error was (do, due) to inexperience.
3. (Your, You're) doing a good job motivating (your, you're) subordinates.
4. One of the basic (principals, principles) of business communication is "Consider the reader."
5. I (implied, inferred) from the article that interest rates would go up.
6. Working papers generally are (composed, comprised) of working trial balance, assembly sheets, adjusting entries, audit schedules, and audit memos.
7. Eliminating time clocks will improve employee (moral, morale).
8. The (principal, principle) variable is the trigger price mechanism.
9. (Its, It's) (to, too, two) soon (to, too, two) tell whether the conversion (to, too, two) computerized billing will save as much time as we hope.
10. Formal training programs (complement, compliment) on-the-job opportunities for professional growth.

B.15 Tracking Your Own Mechanical Errors

Analyze the mechanical errors (grammar, punctuation, word use, and typos) in each of your papers.

- How many different errors are marked on each paper?
- Which three errors do you make most often?
- Is the number of errors constant in each paper, or does the number increase or decrease during the term?

As your instructor directs,

a. Correct each of the mechanical errors in one or more papers.

b. Deliberately write two new sentences in which you make each of your three most common errors. Then write the correct version of each sentence.

c. Write a memo to your instructor discussing your increasing mastery of mechanical correctness during the semester or quarter.

d. Briefly explain to the class how to avoid one kind of error in grammar, punctuation, or word use.

APPENDIX C

Citing and Documenting Sources

Appendix Outline

American Psychological Association (APA) Format

Modern Language Association (MLA) Format

Learning Objectives

After studying this appendix, you will know how to

LO C-1 Use APA format for citing and documenting sources.

LO C-2 Use MLA format for citing and documenting sources.

Citing and documenting sources is an important part of any research process. In effective business proposals and reports, sources are cited and documented smoothly and unobtrusively. **Citation** means attributing an idea or fact to its source in the body of the text: "Bill Gates argues that . . ." "According to the John Deere annual report. . . ." **Documentation** means providing the bibliographic information readers would need to go back to the original source. The usual means of documentation are notes (endnotes or footnotes) and lists of references.

Failure to cite and document sources is **plagiarism,** the passing off of the words or ideas of others as one's own. Plagiarism can lead to serious consequences. The news regularly showcases examples of people who have been fired or sued for plagiarism. Now that curious people can type sentences into Google and other search engines and find the sources, plagiarism is easier than ever to catch.

Note that citation and documentation are used in addition to quotation marks. If you use the source's exact words, you'll use the name of the person you're citing and quotation marks in the body of the proposal or report; you'll indicate the source in parentheses and a list of references or in a footnote or endnote. If you put the source's idea into your own words (paraphrasing), or if you condense or synthesize information, you don't need quotation marks, but you still need to tell whose idea it is and where you found it.

Long quotations (four typed lines or more) are used sparingly in business proposals and reports. Since many readers skip quotes, always summarize the main point of the quotation in a single sentence before the quotation itself. End the sentence with a colon, not a period, because it introduces the quote. Indent long quotations on the left to set them off from your text. Indented quotations do not need quotation marks; the indentation shows the reader that the passage is a quote.

To make a quotation fit the grammar of your report, you may need to change one or two words. Sometimes you may want to add a few words to explain something in the longer original. In both cases, use square brackets to indicate words that are your replacements or additions. Omit any words in the original source that are not essential for your purposes. Use ellipses (spaced dots) to indicate your omissions.

Document every fact and idea that you take from a source except facts that are common knowledge. Historical dates and facts are considered common knowledge (e.g., Barack Obama is the 44th president of the United States or the Twin Towers came down on September 11, 2001). Generalizations are considered common knowledge ("More and more women are entering the workforce") even though specific statements about the same topic (such as the percentage of women in the workforce in 1975 and in 2010) would require documentation.

Two widely used formats for citing and documenting sources in proposals and reports are those of the American Psychological Association (APA) and the Modern Language Association (MLA). Each will be discussed in this appendix.

AMERICAN PSYCHOLOGICAL ASSOCIATION (APA) FORMAT LO C-1

The APA format is a widely used documentation style, most notably in the natural and human sciences. *Publication Manual of the American Psychological Association,* 6th edition, second printing, 2009, is the official source for this type of documentation.

For APA in-text citations, the source is indicated by the author's last name and the date of the work in parentheses, unless those items are already in the text. A comma separates the author's name from the date: (Salt, 2009). Page numbers are only given for direct quotations or in cases where the reader may need help to find the location: (Salt, 2009, p. 20). If you have a source with two authors, use an ampersand in the citation: (Locker & Kienzler, 2012). If the author's name is used in the sentence, only the date is given in parentheses. Sec Figure C.1 for a portion of a report that uses APA format.

At the end of your document, include a **References** list that provides the full bibliographic citation for each source used. Arrange the entries alphabetically by the first author's last name. Use only initials for first and middle names. Figure C.2 shows APA format examples of the most often used sources in proposals and reports.

MODERN LANGUAGE ASSOCIATION (MLA) FORMAT LO C-2

The MLA format is another widely used documentation style, most notably in the arts and humanities. *MLA Style Manual and Guide to Scholarly Publishing,* 3rd edition, 2008, is the official source for this type of documentation.

For MLA in-text citations, the source is indicated by the author's last name and page number in parentheses in the text for paraphrases and direct quotations. Unlike APA, the year is not given, unless you're using two or more works by the same author or if the dates are important. No comma separates the name and page number, and the abbreviation "p." is not used: (Salt 20). If you have a source with two authors, use "and" in the citation: (Locker and Kienzler 222). If the author's name is used in the sentence, only the page number is given in parentheses. See Figure C.3 for a portion of a report that uses MLA format and includes a Works Cited section.

At the end of your document, include a **Works Cited** list that provides the full bibliographic citation for each source you have cited. Arrange the entries alphabetically by the first author's last name. Use authors' names as they appear on the source. Note that the Works Cited list gives the medium (e.g., Web, Print, DVD). URLs for web sources are given only when the item may be otherwise hard to find. Figure C.4 shows MLA format examples of the most often used sources in proposals and reports.

Figure C.1 Report Paragraphs with APA Documentation

Headings and paragraph numbers help readers find material in a website without page numbers. If the source does not number the paragraphs, number the paragraphs yourself under each heading.

Numbers at the beginning of sentences must be written out.

This citation for a direct quote uses only year and page number ("p." before number) since author is identified in sentence.

Social media can be defined as "technology facilitated dialogue among individuals or groups, such as blogs, microblogs, forums, wikis," and other unofficial forms of electronic communication (Cone, 2008, What is social media? ¶. 1). In a 2008 study on social media, Cone found that 39% of Americans reported using social media websites at least once a week; 30% reported using them two or more times a week. Additionally, the study found that 34% believed that companies should have a presence on social media websites and use their presence to interact with their customers. Fifty-one percent of users believed that companies should be present on these websites but interact only if customers ask them to do so (Cone). "While the ultimate measure [of most companies' marketing efforts] is sales, social media expands that because of its focus on influencers," says Simon Salt (2009, p. 20), the CEO of Inc-Slingers, a marketing communication firm. For example, he says "cable provider Comcast utilizes social media to monitor existing customer issues. . . . Known on Twitter as @comcastcares, it quickly developed a reputation for engaging its customer base" (p. 20).

Square brackets indicate a change from the original to make the quote fit into the structure of your sentence.

An ellipsis (three spaced dots) indicates some material has been omitted. An extra dot serves as the period of the sentence.

Use page number for direct quote. Author's name already in text, so not repeated here.

The Cone study also found that 25% of users of social media websites reported interacting with companies at least once a week. When asked what kind of role companies should play on these Web sites, 43% said giving virtual customer service, 41% said soliciting customer feedback. Among some of the most popular social media websites are Facebook, My Space, Twitter, Blogger, and Digg.

Because source is adequately identified in text, no parenthetical source citation is needed.

No need to provide a citation for facts that are general or common knowledge.

Twitter, a microblogging website, asks its users a simple question: "What are you doing?" Users can post their own updates and follow others' updates. Twitter has grown at a breathtaking pace in the last few months. It registered a whopping 600% increase in traffic in the 12 months leading up to November 2008. It is estimated that the microblogging website has approximately 3 million registered account holders from across the globe (Salt, 2009). A message or post on Twitter, known as a "tweet," cannot be more than 140 characters long. Companies and organizations are increasingly taking to Twitter.

Basic APA citation: Place author and date in parentheses; separate with a comma. Use page numbers only for a direct quote.

Visible Technologies, a Seattle-based market research firm, helps companies search for valuable market information from a virtual pool of millions of tweets. Some of the firm's clients include Hormel Foods and Panasonic. The computer manufacturer Dell, another customer, asks its customer representatives to interact with customers on Twitter. Recently, the company announced that it increased its sales by $500,000 through the use of Twitter (Baker, 2008, Promotional Tweets, para. 1). Zappos.com, an online shoe seller, encourages its employees to use Twitter to communicate about subjects as wide-ranging as politics to marketing plans (Vascellaro, 2008).

List all works (but only those works) cited in the text. List sources alphabetically.

Article titles use sentence capitalization and no quotation marks.

Date of publication (year, month day) for a weekly source.

Use URL of a specific web page; do not put period after URL. Break long URLs after a /.

Retrieval date is month day, year.

Source by a corporate author.

Italicize volume number.

Only initials for all names except last.

Don't abbreviate month.

References

Baker, S. (2008, May 15). Why Twitter matters. *BusinessWeek.* Retrieved April 15, 2009, from http://www.businessweek.com/technology/content/may2008/tc20080514_269697.htm

Cone. (2008). 2008 business in social media study [Fact sheet]. Retrieved April 15, 2009 from http://www.coneinc.com /stuff /contentmgr/files/0/26ff8eb1d1a9371210502558013fe2a6/files /2008_business_in_social_media_fact_sheet.pdf

Salt, S. (2009, February 15). Track your success. *Marketing News, 43*, 20.

Vascellaro, J. (2008, October 27). Twitter goes mainstream. *Wall Street Journal*, p. R3.

Figure C.2 APA Format for Sources Used Most Often in Proposals and Reports *(Continued)*

In the examples below, headings in green identify the kind of work being referenced. The green headings are not part of the actual citation.

Put authors' last names first. Use only initials for first and middle names.

Note comma after initial, use of ampersand, period after parenthesis.

In titles of articles and books capitalize only (1) first word, (2) first word of subtitle, (3) proper nouns.

No quotation marks around title of article.

Article in a Periodical

Stowers, R. H., & Hummel, J. Y. (2011, June). The use of technology to combat plagiarism in business communication classes. *Business Communication Quarterly, 74,* 164–169. doi:10.1177//1080569911404406

Ampersands join names of coauthors, coeditors.

Use a DOI (Digital Object Identifier) when available because it is more stable than a URL.

Give complete page numbers. No "pp." when journal has a volume number

Volume number is italicized. Provide issue number in parentheses only if each issue begins with page 1.

Date is year, month day

Article in a Newspaper

Trottman, M. (2011, February 8). Facebook firing case is settled. *The Wall Street Journal*, p. B3.

Use "p." for single page, "pp." for multiple pages.

Capitalize all major words in title of journal, magazine, or newspaper.

Author and editor names use initials for first and middle names.

Chapter in an Edited book

Blakeslee, A. M. (2010). Addressing audiences in a digital age. In R. Spilka (Ed.), *Digital literacy for technical communication: 21st century theory and practice* (pp. 199–229). New York, NY: Routledge.

Put editor before book title. Editor names have last names last.

Give state abbreviation

Use full page numbers for article.

Publication date: year, month day.

Article from a Publication on the Web

Lowery, A. (2011, May 20). LinkedIn is worth $9 billion? How the year's hottest IPO is fueling speculation about a new tech bubble. *Slate*. Retrieved from http://www.slate.com/id/2295189/

Only list retrieval date if the source is likely to change (i.e., wikis, blogs); the date would be inserted between "Retrieved" and "from".

No punctuation after URL

Book

Baker, A. C. (2010). *Catalytic conversations: Organizational communication and innovation.* New York, NY: M. E. Sharpe.

Figure C.2 APA Format for Sources Used Most Often in Proposals and Reports *(Concluded)*

Book or Pamphlet with a Corporate Author

American Cancer Society. (2011). *Cancer facts & figures 2010.* [Atlanta, GA:] Author.

Put in brackets information known to you but not printed in document.

Indicates organization authoring document also published it.

E-mail Message

[Identify e-mail messages in the text as personal communication. Give name of author and specific date. Do not list in References.]

Government Document Available on the Web from the GPO Access Database

U.S. Government Accountability Office. (2011, May 19). *Banking regulation: Enhanced guidance on commerical real estate risks needed.* (Publication No. GAO-11-489). Retrieved from Government Accountability Office Reports Online via GPO Access: http://www.gao.gov/htext/d11477r.html

Abbreviate and use periods.

Abbreviate Government Printing Office

Interview Conducted by the Researcher

[Identify interview in the text as personal communication. Give name of interviewee and specific date. Do not list in References.]

Italicize titles of stand-alone works. An article that is part of a larger work is put in Roman type and quotation marks.

n.d. if no date is given

Website

Berry, T. (n.d.). *Getting started on your business plan.* Retrieved May 25, 2011, from http://articles.bplans.com/writing-a-business-plan/getting-started-on-your-business-plan/26

Retrieval dates: Month day, year

Break long URLs after a slash. No period after URL.

Figure C.3 Report Paragraphs with MLA Documentation

Social media can be defined as "technology facilitated dialogue among individuals or groups, such as blogs, microblogs, forums, wikis" and other unofficial forms of electronic communication (Cone). In a 2008 study on social media, Cone found that 39% of Americans reported using social media websites at least once a week; 30% reported using them two or more times a week. Additionally, the study found that 34% believed that companies should have a presence on social media websites and use their presence to interact with their customers. Fifty-one percent of users believed that companies should be present on these websites but interact only if customers ask them to do so (Cone). "While the ultimate measure [of most companies' marketing efforts] is sales, social media expands that because of its focus on influencers," says Simon Salt, the CEO of Inc-Slingers, a marketing communication firm (20). For example, he says "cable provider Comcast utilizes social media to monitor existing customer issues. . . . Known on Twitter as @comcastcares, it quickly developed a reputation for engaging its customer base" (20).

The Cone study also found that 25% of users of social media websites reported interacting with companies at least once a week. When asked what kind of role companies should play on these websites, 43% said giving virtual customer service, 41% said soliciting customer feedback. Among some of the most popular social media websites are Facebook, MySpace, Twitter, Blogger, and Digg.

Twitter, a microblogging website, asks its users a simple question: "What are you doing?" Users can post their own updates and follow others' updates. Twitter has grown at a breathtaking pace in the last few months. It registered a whopping 600% increase in traffic in the 12 months leading up to November 2008. It is estimated that the micro-blogging website has approximately 3 million registered account holders from across the globe (Salt 20). A message or post on Twitter, known as a "tweet," cannot be more than 140 characters long. Companies and organizations are increasingly taking to Twitter.

Visible Technologies, a Seattle-based market research firm, helps companies search for valuable market information from a virtual pool of millions of tweets. Some of the firm's clients include Hormel Foods and Panasonic. The computer manufacturer Dell, another customer, asks its customer representatives to interact with customers on Twitter. Recently, the company announced that it increased its sales by $500,000 through the use of Twitter (Baker). Zappos.com, an online shoe seller, encourages its employees to use Twitter to communicate, about subjects as wide-ranging as politics to marketing plans (Vascellaro R3).

Works Cited

Baker, Stephen. "Why Twitter Matters." *BusinessWeek*. 15 May 2008. Web. 2 Apr. 2009.

Cone. "2008 Business in Social Media Study." 2008. Web. 2 Apr. 2009 <http://www.coneinc.com/stuff/contentmgr/files/0/26ff8eb1d1a9371210502558013fe2a6/files/2008_business_in_social_media_fact_sheet.pdf>.

Salt, Simon. "Track Your Success." *Marketing News*. 2 Apr. 2009: 20. Print.

Vascellaro, Jessica. "Twitter Goes Mainstream." *Wall Street Journal*. 27 Oct. 2008: R3. Print.

Do not list page or paragraph numbers if the source is unnumbered.

Square brackets indicate a change from the original to make the quote fit into the structure of your sentence.

An ellipsis (three spaced dots) indicates some material has been omitted. An extra dot serves as the period of the sentence.

Because source is identified in text and has no page numbers, no citation is needed.

Basic MLA citation: author and page number. Give page number for facts as well as quotes. No comma or "p." between author and number.

Numbers at the beginnings of sentences must be written out.

No "p." before page number; use only page number since author identified in sentence.

Use page number (no "p.") for direct quote. Author's name is already in text, so is not repeated here.

No need to provide a citation for facts that are general or common knowledege.

Do not list headings or paragraph numbers if the source is unnumbered.

List all works (but only those works) cited in the text. List sources alphabetically.

Article titles use title capitalization and quotation marks.

Date of publication: day month (abbreviated) year.

Source by a corporate author.

All names typed as they appear in the source.

Abbrevitate months with five of more letters.

Date you visited site: day month year. Abbreviate months.

Type of source (Print or Web).

URL in angle brackets; period after angle brackets. Break long URLs after a slash. URLs are only given for sites that may be difficult to find otherwise.

Volume and issue number not listed for weekly magazines.

Figure C.4 MLA Format for Sources Used Most Often in Proposals and Reports *(Continued)*

In the examples below, headings in green identify the kind of work being referenced. The green headings are not part of the actual citation.

Use authors' full names as printed in source. First name first for second author

Join authors' names with "and"

Put quotation marks around title of article

Capitalize all major words in titles of articles, books, journals, magazines, and newspapers

Article in a Periodical

Stowers, Robert H., and Julie Y. Hummel. "The Use of Technology to Combat Plagiarism in Busniness Communication Classes." *Business Communication Quarterly 74.2* (2011): 164–69. Print.

Use both volume and issue number; do not italicize

Omit "1" in "169"

Entries designated as Print or Web

Omit introductory articles (e.g. "The") for newspapers and journals.

Article in a Newspaper

Trottman, Melanie. "Facebook Firing Case Is Settled." *Wall Street Journal* 8 Feb. 2011: B3. Print.

Date given as day month (abbreviated) year

Give author's or editor's full name as printed in the source.

Chapter in an Edited Book

Blakeslee, Ann M. "Addressing Audiences in a Digital Age." *Digital Literacy for Technical Communication: 21st Century Theory and Practice*. Ed. Rachel Spilka. New York: Routlege, 2010. 199–229. Print.

Put book title before editor's name.

Editor's first name goes first

City of publication but not state

Article from a Publication on the Web

Lowery, Annie. "LinkedIn Is Worth $9 Billion? How the Year's Hottest IPO Is Fueling Speculation about a New Tech Bubble." *Slate*. Washington Post Co. 20 May 2011. Web. 25 May 2011.

Publication date

Publisher or sponsor of site.

Access date

URLS are given only for sites that may be difficult to find.

Book

Baker, Ann C. *Catalytic Conversations: Organizational Communication and Innovation*. New York: M. E. Sharpe, 2010. Print.

Date after city and publisher

(Continued)

Figure C.4 MLA Format for Sources Used Most Often in Proposals and Reports *(Concluded)*

Book or Pamphlet with a Corporate Author

American Cancer Society. *Cancer Facts & Figures 2010.* [Atlanta, GA:] ACS Publishing, 2011. Print.

Put in brackets information known to you but not printed in source.

E-mail Message

Kienzler, Donna S. "Re: Project Guidelines and New Criteria." Message to Abhijit Rao. 15 July 2011. E-mail.

Government Document Available on the Web from the GPO Access Database

Name of government, not abbreviated, then name of agency

United States. U.S. Government Accountability Office. *Banking Regulation: Enhanced Guidance on Commerical Real Estate Risks Needed.* Rep GAO-11-489. Wahington: GPO, 19 May 2011. Web. 25 May 2011. <http://www.gao.gov/htext/d11477r.html>.

Abbreviate Government Printing Office

URL in angle brackets; period after angle brackets. Separate long URLs after a slash. URLs are given only for site that may be difficult to find.

Interview Conducted by the Researcher

Drysdale, Marissa. Telephone interview. 12 July 2011.

Italicize titles of stand-alone works. An article that is part of a larger work is put in Roman type and quotation marks.

Website

Berry, Tim. "Getting Started on Your Business Plan." *Bplans* Palo Alto Software, Inc., n.d. Web. 25 May 2011. <http://articles.bplans.com/writing-a-business-plan/getting-started-on-your-busines-plan/26>.

Publisher or sponsor of site

n.d. if no date is given

Give URL if source is difficult to find.

APPENDIX D

Formatting a Scannable Résumé

Some people confuse electronic and scannable résumés. The former are résumés you send in or attach to an e-mail. The latter are paper résumés specially formatted for older software. If you need to create a scannable résumé, use these guidelines to increase the chances that your résumé is scanned correctly.

- Use one standard typeface such as Helvetica, Arial, Times New Roman, and Palatino in 11- or 12-point type.
- Eliminate decorative elements such as boxes or vertical or horizontal lines.
- Use a ragged-right margin rather than full justification. Scanners can't always handle the extra spaces between words and letters that full justification creates.
- Start all lines at the left margin.
- Don't use two-column formats.
- Don't italicize or underline words—even titles of books or newspapers that grammatically require such treatment.
- Use full caps for major headings if you wish, but don't overdo them. Make sure the letters do not touch each other.
- Use short, common headings, such as Education, Experience, and Honors.
- Don't use bullets or tabs. You can replace them with keyboard characters such as asterisks, hyphens, or spaces if you wish.
- Eliminate as much punctuation as possible. A computer searching for a particular term may not recognize it if it has a comma or a period behind it.
- List each phone number on its own line. List multiple addresses vertically rather than side by side.
- Print your résumé on high-quality 8-1/2 × 11 white or very light-colored paper. Use a high-quality printer.
- Mail paper copies flat in a page-sized envelope. Don't fold or staple the pages.

Note that these changes may add pages to your résumé. Be sure to put your name at the top of each page.

GLOSSARY

A

abstract A summary of a report, specifying the recommendations and the reasons for them. Also called an executive summary.

acknowledgment responses Nods, smiles, frowns, and words that let a speaker know you are listening.

active listening Feeding back the literal meaning or the emotional content or both so that the speaker knows that the listener has heard and understood.

active voice A verb that describes the action done by the grammatical subject of the sentence.

adjustment A positive response to a claim letter. If the company agrees to grant a refund, the amount due will be adjusted.

agenda A list of items to be considered or acted upon at a meeting.

alliteration A sound pattern occurring when several words begin with the same sound.

alternating pattern (of organization) Discussing the alternatives first as they relate to the first criterion, then as they relate to the second criterion, and so on: ABC, ABC, ABC. Compare *divided pattern.*

analytical report A report that interprets information.

argument The reasons or logic offered to persuade the audience.

assumptions Statements that are not proved in a report, but on which the recommendations are based.

audience benefits Benefits or advantages that the audience gets by using the communicator's services, buying the communicator's products, following the communicator's policies, or adopting the communicator's ideas. Audience benefits can exist for policies and ideas as well as for goods and services.

auxiliary audience People who may encounter your message but will not have to interact with it. This audience includes "read only" people.

average See *mean.*

B

bar chart A visual consisting of parallel bars or rectangles that represent specific sets of data.

behavioral economics A branch of economics that uses social and psychological factors in understanding decision making. It is particularly concerned with the limits of rationality in those decisions.

behavioral interviews Job interviews that ask candidates to describe actual behaviors they have used in the past in specific situations.

bias-free language Language that does not discriminate against people on the basis of sex, physical condition, race, age, or any other category.

blind ads Job listings that do not list the company's name.

blind copies Copies sent to other recipients that are not listed on the original letter, memo or e-mail.

block format In letters, a format in which inside address, date, and signature block are lined up at the left margin; paragraphs are not indented. In résumés, a format in which dates are listed in one column and job titles and descriptions in another.

blocking Disagreeing with every idea that is proposed.

body language Nonverbal communication conveyed by posture and movement, eye contact, facial expressions, and gestures.

boilerplate Language from a previous document that a writer includes in a new document. Writers use boilerplate both to save time and energy and to use language that has already been approved by the organization's legal staff.

boxhead Used in tables, the boxhead is the variable whose label is at the top.

brainstorming A method of generating ideas by recording everything people in a group think of, without judging or evaluating the ideas.

branching question Question that sends respondents who answer differently to different parts of the questionnaire. Allows respondents to answer only those questions that are relevant to their experience.

bridge (in prospecting job letters) A sentence that connects the attention-getter to the body of a letter.

brochure Leaflet (often part of a direct mailing) that gives more information about a product or organization.

buffer A neutral or positive statement designed to allow the writer to delay, or buffer, the negative message.

build goodwill To create a good image of yourself and of your organization–the kind of image that makes people want to do business with you.

bullets Small circles (filled or open) or squares that set off items in a list. When you are giving examples, but the number is not exact and the order does not matter, use bullets to set off items.

business plan A document written to raise capital for a new business venture or to outline future actions for an established business.

businessese A kind of jargon including unnecessary words. Some words were common 200–300 years ago but are no longer part of spoken English. Some have never been used outside of business writing. All of these terms should be omitted.

buying time with limited agreement Agreeing with the small part of a criticism that one does accept as true.

bypassing Miscommunication that occurs when two people use the same language to mean different things.

C

case The grammatical role a noun or pronoun plays in a sentence. The nominative case is used for the subject of a clause, the possessive to show who or what something belongs to, the objective case for the object of a verb or a preposition.

central selling point A strong audience benefit, big enough to motivate people by itself, but also serving as an umbrella to cover other benefits and to unify the message.

channel The physical means by which a message is sent. Written channels include e-mails memos, letters, and billboards.

Oral channels include phone calls, speeches, and face-to-face conversations.

channel overload The inability of a channel to carry effectively all the messages that are being sent.

chartjunk Decoration that is irrelevant to a visual and that may be misleading.

checking for feelings Identifying the emotions that the previous speaker seemed to be expressing verbally or nonverbally.

checking for inferences Trying to identify the unspoken content or feelings implied by what the previous speaker has actually said.

chronological résumé A résumé that lists what you did in a dated order, starting with the most recent events and going backward in reverse chronology.

citation Attributing a quotation or other idea to a source in the body of the report.

claim The part of an argument that the speaker or writer wants the audience to agree with.

claim letter A letter seeking a replacement or refund.

clip art Predrawn images that you can import into your documents.

close The ending of a communication.

closed body position Includes keeping the arms and legs crossed and close to the body. Suggests physical and psychological discomfort, defending oneself, and shutting the other person out. Also called a defensive body position.

closed question Question with a limited number of possible responses.

closure report A report summarizing completed work that does not result in new action or a recommendation.

clowning Making unproductive jokes and diverting the group from its task.

cluster sample A sample of subjects at each of a random sample of locations. This method is usually faster and cheaper than random sampling when face-to-face interviews are required.

clustering A method of thinking up ideas by writing the central topic in the middle of the page, circling it, writing down the ideas that topic suggests, and circling them.

cognitive dissonance A theory which posits that it is psychologically uncomfortable to hold two ideas that are dissonant or conflicting. The theory of cognitive dissonance explains that people will resolve dissonance by deciding that one of the ideas is less important, by rejecting one of the ideas, or by constructing a third idea that has room for both of the conflicting ideas.

cold list A list used in marketing of people with no prior connection to your group.

collaborative writing Working with other writers to produce a single document.

collection letter A letter asking a customer to pay for goods and services received.

collection series A series of letters asking customers to pay for goods and services they have already received. Early letters in the series assume that the reader intends to pay but final letters threaten legal action if the bill is not paid.

comma splice or **comma fault** Using a comma to join two independent clauses. To correct, use a semicolon, use a comma with a conjunction, subordinate one of the clauses, or use a period and start a new sentence.

common ground Values and goals that the communicator and audience share.

communication channel The means by which you convey your message.

communication theory A theory explaining what happens when we communicate and where miscommunication can occur.

competitive proposal A proposal that has to compete for limited resources.

complaint letter A letter that challenges a policy or tries to get a decision changed.

complex sentence Sentence with one main clause and one or more subordinate clauses.

complimentary close The words after the body of the letter and before the signature. *Sincerely* and *Yours truly* are the most commonly used complimentary closes in business letters.

compound sentence Sentence with two main clauses joined by a comma and conjunction.

conclusions Section of a report or other communication that restates the main points.

conflict resolution Strategies for getting at the real issue, keeping discussion open, and minimizing hurt feelings so that people can find a solution that seems good to everyone involved.

connotations The emotional colorings or associations that accompany a word.

consensus Group solidarity supporting a decision.

contact letter Letter written to keep in touch with a customer or donor.

convenience sample A group of subjects to whom the researcher has easy access; not a random sample.

conventions Widely accepted practices.

conversational style Conversational patterns such as speed and volume of speaking, pauses between speakers, whether questions are direct or indirect. When different speakers assign different meanings to a specific pattern, miscommunication results.

coordination The second stage in the life of a task group, when the group finds, organizes, and interprets information and examines alternatives and assumptions. This is the longest of the stages.

corporate culture The values, beliefs, norms, history, and assumptions of an organization that shape behaviors and decisions of individual employees.

counterclaim A statement whose truth would negate the truth of the main claim.

credibility Ability to come across to the audience as believable.

criteria The standards used to evaluate or weigh the factors in a decision.

critical activities (in a schedule) Activities that must be done on time if a project is to be completed by its due date.

critical incident An important event that illustrates behavior or a history.

crop To trim a photograph to fit a specific space, typically to delete visual information that is unnecessary or unwanted.

culture The patterns of behavior and beliefs that are common to a people, nation, or organization.

cutaway drawings Line drawings that depict the hidden or interior portions of an object.

cycling The process of sending a document from writer to superior to writer to yet another superior for several rounds of revisions before the document is approved.

D

dangling modifier A phrase that modifies the wrong word or a word that is not actually in a sentence. To correct a dangling modifier, recast the modifier as a subordinate clause or revise the sentence so its subject or object can be modified by the dangling phrase.

decode To extract meaning from symbols.

decorative visual A visual that makes the speaker's points more memorable but that does not convey numerical data.

defensive body position See *closed body position.*

demographic characteristics Measurable features of an audience that can be counted objectively: age, education level, income, etc.

denotation A word's literal or "dictionary" meaning. Most common words in English have more than one denotation. Context usually makes it clear which of several meanings is appropriate.

dependent clause See *subordinate clause.*

descriptive abstract A listing of the topics an article or report covers that does not summarize what is said about each topic.

deviation bar charts Bar charts that identify positive and negative values, or winners and losers.

devil's advocate Person who defends a less popular viewpoint so that it receives fuller consideration.

dingbats Small symbols such as arrows, pointing fingers, and so forth that are part of a typeface.

direct mail A form of direct marketing that asks for an order, inquiry, or contribution directly from the reader.

direct mail package The outer envelope of a direct mail letter and everything that goes in it: the letter, brochures, samples, secondary letters, reply card, and reply envelope.

direct marketing All advertisements that ask for an order, inquiry, or contribution directly from the audience. Includes direct mail, catalogs, telemarketing (telephone sales), and newspaper and TV ads with 800 numbers to place an order.

direct request pattern A pattern of organization that makes the request directly in the first paragraph.

discourse community A group of people who share assumptions about what channels, formats, and styles to use for communication, what topics to discuss and how to discuss them, and what constitutes evidence.

divided pattern (of organization) Discussing each alternative completely, through all criteria, before going on to the next alternative: AAA, BBB, CCC. Compare *alternating pattern.*

document design The process of writing, organizing, and laying out a document so that it can be easily used by the intended audience.

documentation Full bibliographic information so that interested readers can go to the original source of material used in a report.

dominating (in groups) Trying to run a group by ordering, shutting out others, and insisting on one's own way.

dot chart A chart that shows correlations or other large data sets. Dot charts have labeled horizontal and vertical axes.

dot planning A way for large groups to set priorities; involves assigning colored dots to ideas.

E

editing Checking the draft to see that it satisfies the requirements of good English and the principles of business writing. Unlike revision, which can produce major changes in meaning, editing focuses on the surface of writing.

ego-involvement The emotional commitment that people have to their positions.

elimination of alternatives A pattern of organization for reports that discusses the problem and its causes, the impractical solutions and their weaknesses, and finally the solution the writer favors.

ellipsis Spaced dots used in reports to indicate that words have been omitted from quoted material and in direct mail to give the effect of pauses in speech.

emotional appeal A persuasive technique that uses the audience's emotions to make them want to do what the writer or speaker asks.

empathy The ability to put oneself in someone else's shoes, to feel with that person.

enclosure A document that accompanies a letter.

enunciate To voice all the sounds of each word while speaking.

evaluating Measuring something, such as a document draft or a group decision, against your goals and the requirements of the situation and audience.

evidence Data the audience already accepts.

exaggeration Making something sound bigger or more important than it really is.

executive summary See *abstract.*

expectancy theory A theory that argues that motivation is based on the expectation of being rewarded for performance and the importance of the reward.

external audiences Audiences who are not part of the writer's organization.

external documents Documents that go to people in another organization.

external report Report written by a consultant for an organization of which he or she is not a permanent employee.

extranets Web pages for customers and suppliers.

extrinsic motivators Benefits that are "added on"; they are not a necessary part of the product or action.

eye contact Looking another person directly in the eye.

F

fallacies Common errors in logic that weaken arguments.

feasibility report A report that evaluates a proposed action and shows whether or not it will work.

feedback The receiver's response to a message.

figure Any visual that is not a table.

filler sounds Syllables, such as *um* and *uh,* which some speakers use to fill silence as they mentally search for their next words.

five Ws and H Questions that must be answered early in a press release: who, what, when, where, why, and how.

fixed font A typeface in which each letter has the same width on the page. Sometimes called *typewriter typeface.*

flaming Sending out an angry e-mail message before thinking about the implications of venting one's anger.

focus groups Small groups who come in to talk with a skilled leader about a potential product or process.

font A unified style of type. Fonts come in various sizes.

forecast An overview statement that tells the audience what you will discuss in a section or an entire report.

form letter A prewritten, fill-in-the-blank letter designed to fit standard situations.

formal meetings Meetings run under strict rules, like the rules of parliamentary procedure summarized in *Robert's Rules of Order.*

formal report A report containing formal elements such as a title page, a transmittal, a table of contents, and an abstract.

formalization The third and last stage in the life of a task group, when the group makes its decision and seeks consensus.

format The parts of a document and the way they are arranged on a page.

formation The first stage in the life of a task group, when members choose a leader and define the problem they must solve.

freewriting A kind of writing uninhibited by any constraints. Freewriting may be useful in overcoming writer's block, among other things.

frozen evaluation An assessment that does not take into account the possibility of change.

full justification Making both right and left margins of a text even, as opposed to having a ragged right margin.

fused sentence The result when two or more sentences are joined without punctuation or conjunctions.

G

Gantt charts Bar charts used to show schedules. Gantt charts are most commonly used in proposals.

gatekeeper The audience with the power to decide whether your message is sent on to other audiences.

gathering data Physically getting the background data you need. It can include informal and formal research or simply getting the letter to which you're responding.

general semantics The study of the ways behavior is influenced by the words and other symbols used to communicate.

gerund The *-ing* form of a verb; grammatically, it is a verb used as a noun.

getting feedback Asking someone else to evaluate your work. Feedback is useful at every stage of the writing process, not just during composition of the final draft.

glossary A list of terms used in a document with their definitions.

good appeal An appeal in direct marketing that offers believable descriptions of benefits, links the benefits of the product or service to a need or desire that motivates the audience and makes the audience act.

goodwill The value of a business beyond its tangible assets, including its reputation and patronage. Also, a favorable condition and overall atmosphere of trust that can be fostered between parties conducting business.

goodwill ending Shift of emphasis away from the message to the reader. A goodwill ending is positive, personal, and forward-looking and suggests that serving the reader is the real concern.

goodwill presentation A presentation that entertains and validates the audience.

grammar checker Software program that flags errors or doubtful usage.

grapevine An organization's informal informational network that carries gossip and rumors as well as accurate information.

grid system A means of designing layout by imposing columns on a page and lining up graphic elements within the columns.

ground rules Procedural rules adopted by groups to make meetings and processes run smoothly.

grouped bar chart A bar chart that allows the viewer to compare several aspects of each item or several items over time.

groupthink The tendency for a group to reward agreement and directly or indirectly punish dissent.

guided discussion A presentation in which the speaker presents the questions or issues that both speaker and audience have agreed on in advance. Instead of functioning as an expert with all the answers, the speaker serves as a facilitator to help the audience tap its own knowledge.

H

headings Words or short phrases that group points and divide your letter, memo, e-mail or report into sections.

hearing Perceiving sounds. (Not the same thing as listening.)

hidden job market Jobs that are never advertised but that may be available or may be created for the right candidate.

hidden negatives Words that are not negative in themselves, but become negative in context.

high-context culture A culture in which most information is inferred from the context, rather than being spelled out explicitly in words.

histogram A bar chart using pictures, asterisks, or points to represent a unit of the data.

hypothetical interview question A questions that asks what a person would do in an imaginary situation

I

impersonal expression A sentence that attributes actions to inanimate objects, designed to avoid placing blame on a reader.

indented format A format for résumés in which items that are logically equivalent begin at the same horizontal space, with carryover lines indented.

independent clause See *main clause.*

infinitive The form of the verb that is preceded by *to.*

informal meetings Loosely run meetings in which votes are not taken on every point.

informal report A report using letter or memo format.

information interview An interview in which you talk to someone who works in the area you hope to enter to find out what the day-to-day work involves and how you can best prepare to enter that field.

information overload A condition in which a person cannot process all the messages he or she receives.

information report A report that collects data for the reader but does not recommend action.

informational dimensions Dimensions of group work focusing on the problem, data, and possible solutions.

informative message Message giving information to which the reader's basic reaction will be neutral.

informative presentation A presentation that informs or teaches the audience.

informative report A report that provides information.

inside address The reader's name and address; put below the date and above the salutation in most letter formats.

interactive presentation A presentation that is a conversation between the speaker and the audience.

intercultural competence The ability to communicate sensitively with people from other cultures and countries, based on an understanding of cultural differences.

internal audiences Audiences in the communicator's organization.

internal document Document written for other employees in the same organization.

internal documentation Providing information about a source in the text itself rather than in footnotes or endnotes.

internal report Reports written by employees for use only in their organization.

interpersonal communication Communication between people.

interpersonal dimensions In a group, efforts promoting friendliness, cooperation, and group loyalty.

interview Structured conversation with someone who is able to give you useful information.

intranet A web page just for employees.

intrapreneurs Innovators who work within organizations.

intrinsic motivators Benefits that come automatically from using a product or doing something.

introduction The part of a report that states the purpose and scope of the report. The introduction may also include limitations, assumptions, methods, criteria, and definitions.

J

jargon There are two kinds of jargon. The first kind is the specialized terminology of a technical field. The second is businessese, outdated words that do not have technical meanings and are not used in other forms of English.

judgment See *opinion.*

judgment sample A group of subjects whose views seem useful.

justification report Report that justifies the need for a purchase, an investment, a new personnel line, or a change in procedure.

justified margins Margins that end evenly on both sides of the page.

K

key words Words used in (1) a résumé to summarize areas of expertise, qualifications, and (2) an article or report to describe the content. Key words facilitate computer searches.

L

letter Short document using block, modified, or simplified letter format that goes to readers outside your organization.

letterhead Stationery with the organization's name, logo, address, and telephone number printed on the page.

limitations Problems or factors that constrain the validity of the recommendations of a report.

line graph A visual consisting of lines that show trends or allow the viewer to interpolate values between the observed values.

logical fallacies See *fallacies.*

low-context culture A culture in which most information is conveyed explicitly in words rather than being inferred from context.

M

main clause A group of words that can stand by itself as a complete sentence. Also called an independent clause.

Maslow's hierarchy of needs Five levels of human need posited by Abraham H. Maslow. They include physical needs, the need for safety and security, for love and belonging, for esteem and recognition, and for self-actualization.

mean The average of a group of numbers. Found by dividing the sum of a set of figures by the number of figures.

median The middle number in a ranked set of numbers.

memo Document using memo format sent to readers in your organization.

methods section The section of a report or survey describing how the data were gathered.

minutes Records of a meeting, listing the items discussed, the results of votes, and the persons responsible for carrying out follow-up steps.

mirror question Question that paraphrases the content of the answer an interviewee gave to the last question.

misplaced modifier A word or phrase that appears to modify another element of the sentence than the writer intended.

mixed punctuation Using a colon after the salutation and a comma after the complimentary close in a letter.

mode The most frequent number in a set of numbers.

modified block format A letter format in which the inside address, date, and signature block are lined up with each other one-half or two-thirds of the way over on the page.

modifier A word or phrase giving more information about another word in a sentence.

monochronic culture Culture in which people do only one important activity at a time.

monologue presentation A presentation in which the speaker talks without interruption. The presentation is planned and is delivered without deviation.

multiple graphs Three or more simple stories told by graphs juxtaposed to create a more powerful story.

Myers-Briggs Type Indicator A scale that categorizes people on four dimensions: introvert-extravert; sensing-intuitive; thinking-feeling; and perceiving-judging.

N

negative message A message in which basic information conveyed is negative; the reader is expected to be disappointed or angry.

networking Using your connections with other people to help you achieve a goal.

neutral subject line A subject line that does not give away the writer's stance on an issue.

noise Any physical or psychological interference in a message.

nominative case The grammatical form used for the subject of a clause. *I, we, he, she,* and *they* are nominative pronouns.

nonageist Refers to words, images, or behaviors that do not discriminate against people on the basis of age.

noncompetitive proposal A proposal with no real competition and hence a high probability of acceptance.

nonracist Refers to words, images, or behaviors that do not discriminate against people on the basis of race.

nonrestrictive clause A clause giving extra but unessential information about a noun or pronoun. Because the information is extra, commas separate the clause from the word it modifies.

nonsexist language Language that treats both sexes neutrally, that does not make assumptions about the proper gender for a job, and that does not imply that one sex is superior to or takes precedence over the other.

nonverbal communication Communication that does not use words.

normal interview A job interview with mostly expected questions.

noun–pronoun agreement Having a pronoun be the same number (singular or plural) and the same person (first, second, or third) as the noun it refers to.

O

objective case The grammatical form used for the object of a verb or preposition. *Me, us, him, her,* and *them* are objective pronouns.

omnibus motion A motion that allows a group to vote on several related items in a single vote. Saves time in formal meetings with long agendas.

open body position Includes keeping the arms and legs uncrossed and away from the body. Suggests physical and psychological comfort and openness.

open punctuation Using no punctuation after the salutation and the complimentary close.

open question Question with an unlimited number of possible responses.

opinion A statement that can never be verified, since it includes terms that cannot be measured objectively. Also called a judgment.

organization (in messages) The order in which ideas are arranged.

organizational culture The values, attitudes, and philosophies shared by people in an organization that shape its behaviors and reward structure.

outsourcing Going outside the company for products and services that once were made by the company's employees.

P

package The outer envelope and everything that goes in it in a direct mailing.

paired bar chart A bar chart that shows the correlation between two items.

parallel structure Using the same grammatical and logical form for words, phrases, clauses, and ideas in a series.

paraphrase To repeat in your own words the verbal content of another communication.

passive verb A verb that describes action done to the grammatical subject of the sentence.

people-first language Language that names the person first, then the condition: "people with mental retardation." Used to avoid implying that the condition defines the person's potential.

performance appraisals Supervisors' written evaluations of their subordinates' work.

persona The "author" or character who allegedly writes a document; the voice that a communicator assumes in creating a message.

personal brandings A pop term for marketing yourself, including job searching. It includes an expectation that you will use various options, including social media such as LinkedIn, to market yourself.

personal space The distance someone wants between him- or herself and other people in ordinary, nonintimate interchanges.

personalized A message that is adapted to the individual reader by including the reader's name and address and perhaps other information.

persuade To motivate and convince the audience to act or change a belief.

persuasive presentation A presentation that motivates the audience to act or to believe.

phishing e-mails E-mails that look like messages from official business but actually connect to private sites seeking to acquire data for fraud or identity theft.

pictogram A bar chart using pictures or symbols to represent a unit of data.

pie chart A circular chart whose sections represent percentages of a given quantity.

pitch The highness or lowness of a sound.

plagiarism Passing off the words or ideas of others as one's own.

planning All the thinking done about a subject and the means of achieving your purposes. Planning takes place not only when devising strategies for the document as a whole, but also when generating "miniplans" that govern sentences or paragraphs.

polarization A logical fallacy that argues there are only two possible positions, one of which is clearly unacceptable.

polychronic culture Culture in which people do several things at once.

population The group a researcher wants to make statements about.

positive emphasis Focusing on the positive rather than the negative aspects of a situation.

positive or good news message Message to which the reader's reaction will be positive.

possessive case The grammatical form used to indicate possession or ownership. *My, our, his, hers, its,* and *their* are possessive pronouns.

post office abbreviations Two-letter abbreviations for states and provinces.

prepositions Words that indicate relationships, for example, *with, in, under, at.*

presenting problem The problem that surfaces as the subject of discord. The presenting problem is often not the real problem.

primary audience The audience who will make a decision or act on the basis of a message.

primary research Research that gathers new information.

pro-and-con pattern A pattern of organization that presents all the arguments for an alternative and then all the arguments against it.

probe question A follow-up question designed to get more information about an answer or to get at specific aspects of a topic.

problem-solving pattern A pattern of organization that describes a problem before offering a solution to the problem.

procedural dimensions Dimensions of group work focusing on methods: how the group makes decisions, who does what, when assignments are due.

process of writing What people actually do when they write: planning, gathering, writing, evaluating, getting feedback, revising, editing, and proofreading.

progress report A statement of the work done during a period of time and the work proposed for the next period.

proofreading Checking the final copy to see that it's free from typographical errors.

proportional font A font in which some letters are wider than other letters (for example, *w* is wider than *i*).

proposal Document that suggests a method and personnel for finding information or solving a problem.

prospecting letter A job application letter written to a company that has not announced openings but where you'd like to work.

psychographic characteristics Human characteristics that are qualitative rather than quantitative: values, beliefs, goals, and lifestyles.

psychological description Description of a product or service in terms of audience benefits.

psychological reactance Phenomenon occurring when a person reacts to a negative message by asserting freedom in some other arena.

purpose statement The statement in a proposal or a report specifying the organizational problem, the technical questions that must be answered to solve the problem, and the rhetorical purpose of the report (to explain, to recommend, to request, to propose).

Q

questionnaire List of questions for people to answer in a survey.

R

ragged right margins Margins that do not end evenly on the right side of the page.

random sample A sample for which each member of the population has an equal chance of being chosen.

range The difference between the highest and lowest numbers in a set of figures.

recommendation report A report that evaluates two or more possible alternatives and recommends one of them. Doing nothing is always one alternative.

recommendations Section of a report that specifies items for action.

reference line A *subject line* that refers the reader to another document (usually a numbered one, such as an invoice).

referral interview Interviews you schedule to learn about current job opportunities in your field and to get referrals to other people who may have the power to create a job for you. Useful for tapping into unadvertised jobs and the hidden job market.

reflexive pronoun Refers to or emphasizes a noun or pronoun that has already appeared in the sentence. *Myself, herself,* and *themselves* are reflexive pronouns.

release date Date a report will be made available to the public.

reply card A card or form designed to make it easy for the reader to respond to a direct mail letter. A good reply card repeats the central selling point, basic product information, and price.

request for proposal (RFP) A statement of the service or product that an agency wants; an invitation for proposals to provide that service or product.

respondents The people who fill out a questionnaire; also called *subjects.*

response rate The percentage of subjects receiving a questionnaire who answer the questions.

restrictive clause A clause limiting or restricting the meaning of a noun or pronoun. Because its information is essential, no commas separate the clause from the word it restricts.

résumé A persuasive summary of your qualifications for employment.

résumé blasting Posting your résumé widely—usually by the hundreds—on the web.

reverse chronology Starting with the most recent events, such as job or degree, and going backward in time. Pattern of organization used for chronological résumés.

revising Making changes in the draft: adding, deleting, substituting, or rearranging. Revision can be changes in single words, but more often it means major additions, deletions, or substitutions, as the writer measures the draft against purpose and audience and reshapes the document to make it more effective.

RFP See *request for proposal.*

rhetorical purpose The effect the writer or speaker hopes to have on the audience (to inform, to persuade, to build goodwill).

rhythm The repetition of a pattern of accented and unaccented syllables.

rival hypotheses Alternate explanations for observed results.

rule of three The rule noting a preference for three short parallel examples and explaining that the last will receive the most emphasis.

run-on sentence A sentence containing two or more main clauses strung together with *and, but, or, so,* or *for.*

S

sales pattern A pattern of persuasion that consists of an attention getting opener, a body with reasons and details, and an action close.

salutation The greeting in a letter: "Dear Ms. Smith:"

sample (in marketing) A product provided to the audience to whet their appetite for more.

sample (in research) The portion of the population a researcher actually studies.

sampling frame The list of all possible sampling units.

sampling units Those items/people actually sampled.

sans serif Literally, *without serifs.* Typeface whose letters lack bases or flicks. Helvetica and Geneva are examples of sans serif typefaces.

saves the reader's time The result of a message whose style, organization, and visual impact help the reader to read, understand, and act on the information as quickly as possible.

schematic diagrams Line drawings of objects and their parts.

scope statement A statement in a proposal or report specifying the subjects the report covers and how broadly or deeply it covers them.

secondary audience The audience who may be asked by the primary audience to comment on a message or to implement ideas after they've been approved.

secondary research Research retrieving data someone else gathered. Includes library research.

segmented, subdivided, or stacked bars Bars in a bar chart that sum components of an item.

semantics or general semantics The study of the ways behavior is influenced by the words and other symbols used to communicate.

sentence fragment Words that are not a complete sentence but that are punctuated as if they were a complete sentence.

sentence outline An outline using complete sentences. It contains the thesis or recommendation plus all supporting points.

serif The little extensions from the main strokes on letters. Times Roman and Courier are examples of serif typefaces.

signpost An explicit statement of the place that a speaker or writer has reached: "Now we come to the third point."

simple sentence Sentence with one main clause.

simplified format A letter format that omits the salutation and complimentary close and lines everything up at the left margin.

situational interviews Job interviews in which candidates are asked to describe what they would do in specific hypothetical situations.

skills résumé A résumé organized around the skills you've used, rather than the date or the job in which you used them.

social signals Nonverbal communications such as gestures, facial expressions, voice tone, and proximity.

solicited letter A job letter written when you know that the company is hiring.

spot visuals Informal visuals that are inserted directly into text. Spot visuals do not have numbers or titles.

stereotyping Putting similar people or events into a single category, even though significant differences exist.

storyboard A visual representation of the structure of a document, with a rectangle representing each page or unit. An alternative to outlining as a method of organizing material.

strategy A plan for reaching your specific goals with a specific audience.

stratified random sample A sample generated by first dividing the sample into subgroups in the population and then taking a random sample for each subgroup.

stress (in a communication) Emphasis given to one or more words in a sentence, or one or more ideas in a message.

stress interview A job interview that deliberately puts the applicant under stress, physical or psychological. Here it's important to change the conditions that create physical stress and to meet psychological stress by rephrasing questions in less inflammatory terms and treating them as requests for information.

structured interview An interview that follows a detailed list of questions prepared in advance.

stub The variable listed on the side in a table.

subject line The title of the document, used to file and retrieve the document. A subject line tells readers why they need to read the document and provides a framework in which to set what you're about to say.

subordinate clause A group of words containing a subject and a verb but that cannot stand by itself as a complete sentence. Also called a dependent clause.

summarizing Restating and relating major points, pulling ideas together.

summary abstract The logic skeleton of an article or report, containing the thesis or recommendation and its proof.

summary sentence or paragraph A sentence or paragraph listing in order the topics that following sentences or paragraphs will discuss.

survey A method of getting information from a group of people.

SWOT analysis A method of evaluating a proposed action that examines both internal factors (Strengths, Weaknesses) and external factors (Opportunities, Threats).

T

table Numbers or words arrayed in rows and columns.

talking heads Headings that are detailed enough to provide an overview of the material in the sections they introduce.

template A design or format that serves as a pattern.

10-K report A report filed with the Securities and Exchange Commission summarizing the firm's financial performance.

thank-you note A note thanking someone for helping you.

threat A statement, explicit or implied, that someone will be punished if he or she does or doesn't do something.

360-degree feedback A form of assessment in which an employee receives feedback from peers, managers, subordinates, customers, and suppliers.

tone The implied attitude of the author toward the reader and the subject.

tone of voice The rising or falling inflection that indicates whether a group of words is a question or a statement, whether the speaker is uncertain or confident, whether a statement is sincere or sarcastic.

topic heading A heading that focuses on the structure of a report. Topic headings give little information.

topic outline An outline listing the main points and the subpoints under each main point. A topic outline is the basis for the table of contents of a report.

topic sentence A sentence that introduces or summarizes the main idea in a paragraph.

transitions Words, phrases, or sentences that show the connections between ideas.

transmit To send a message.

transmittal A message explaining why something is being sent.

truncated code Symbols such as asterisks that turn up other forms of a keyword in a computer search.

truncated graphs Graphs with part of the scale missing.

two-margin format A format for résumés in which dates are listed in one column and job titles and descriptions in another. This format emphasizes work history.

U

umbrella sentence or paragraph A sentence or paragraph listing in order the topics that following sentences or paragraphs will discuss.

understatement Downplaying or minimizing the size or features of something.

unity Using only one idea or topic in a paragraph or other piece of writing.

unjustified margins Margins that do not end evenly on the right side of the page.

unstructured interview An interview based on three or four main questions prepared in advance and other questions that build on what the interviewee says.

usability testing Testing a document with users to see that it functions as desired.

V

venting Expressing pent-up negative emotions.

verbal communication Communication that uses words; may be either oral or written.

vested interest The emotional stake readers have in something if they benefit from maintaining or influencing conditions or actions.

vicarious participation An emotional strategy in fund-raising letters based on the idea that by donating money, readers participate in work they are not able to do personally.

visual impact The visual "first impression" you get when you look at a page.

volume The loudness or softness of a voice or other sound.

W

watchdog audience An audience that has political, social, or economic power and that may base future actions on its evaluation of your message.

white space The empty space on the page. White space emphasizes material that it separates from the rest of the text.

widget A software program that can be dropped into social networking sites and other places.

wild card Symbols such as asterisks that turn up other forms of a keyword in a computer search. See also *truncated code*.

withdrawing Being silent, not contributing, not helping with the work, not attending meetings.

wordiness Taking more words than necessary to express an idea.

works cited The sources specifically referred to in a report.

works consulted Sources read during the research for a report but not mentioned specifically in the report.

Y

you-attitude A style of communicating that looks at things from the audience's point of view, emphasizes what the audience wants to know, respects the audience's intelligence, and protects the audience's ego. Using *you* generally increases you-attitude in positive situations. In negative situations or conflict, avoid *you* since that word will attack the audience.

Chapter 1

1. United States Postal Service, "Postal Facts 2010," news release, accessed April 18, 2011, http://www.usps.com/communications/newsroom/postalfacts.htm; Jennifer Valentino-DeVries, "With Catalogs, Opt-Out Policies Vary," *Wall Street Journal*, April 13, 2011, B7; Brian Dunn, "Hard Choices," *Bloomberg Businessweek*, December 6, 2010, 104; and "Internet 2010 in Numbers," *Pingdom* (blog), January 12, 2011, http://royal.pingdom.com/2011/01/12/internet-2010-in-numbers.
2. National Association of Colleges and Employers, "Top Skills for Job Candidates," press release, December 2, 2010, http://www.naceweb.org/Press/Releases/Top_Skills_for_Job_Candidates.aspx.
3. Alex Crippen, "Warren Buffett's $100,000 Offer and $500,000 Advice for Columbia Business School Students," CNBC, November 12, 2009, http://www.cnbc.com/id/33891448/Warren_Buffett_s_100_000_Offer_and_500_000_Advice_for_Columbia_Business_School_Students.
4. Peter Coy, "The Future of Work," *BusinessWeek*, March 22, 2004, 50.
5. The National Commission on Writing for America's Families, Schools, and Colleges, "Writing: A Ticket to Work. . .or a Ticket Out: A Survey of Business Leaders," *College Board* (2004), 7–8.
6. Anne Fisher, "The High Cost of Living and Not Writing Well," *Fortune*, December 7, 1998, 244.
7. Jeffrey Gitomer, *Jeffrey Gitomer's Little Black Book of Connections: 6.5 Assets for Networking Your Way to Rich Relationships* (Austin, TX: Bard Press, 2006), 128–31.
8. Peter D. Hart Research Associate, Inc., *How Should Colleges Assess and Improve Student Learning? Employers' Views on the Accountability Challenge: A Survey of Employers Conducted on Behalf of the Association of American Colleges and Universities* (Washington, DC: The Association of American Colleges and Universities, 2008), 3.
9. The Conference Board et al., *Are They Really Ready To Work? Employers' Perspectives on the Basic Knowledge and Applied Skills of New Entrants to the 21st Century U.S. Workforce*, accessed April 18, 2011, http://www.conference-board.org/pdf_free/BED-06-workforce.pdf.
10. Tom DeMint, "So You Want to be Promoted," *Fire Engineering* 159, no. 7 (2006); Karen M. Kroll, "Mapping Your Career," *PM Network* 19, no. 11 (2005): 28; and Jeff Snyder, "Recruiter: What It Takes," *Security* 43, no. 11 (2006): 70.
11. ". . . Lost Mail," *News & Observer* (Raleigh, NC), April 12, 2011, 8A.
12. "Case Studies," Xerox Corporation, accessed April 19, 2011, http://www.consulting.xerox.com/case-studies/enus.html; and Xerox, *The Optimum Office: How to Achieve Immediate and Guaranteed Cost Savings via a Managed Print Service*, April 2009, http://www.xerox.com/downloads/usa/en/xgs/casestudies/xgs_whitepaper_Optimum_Office_US.pdf.
13. Eric Krell, "The Unintended Word," *HRMagazine* 51, no. 8 (2006): 52.
14. Pui-Wing Tam, "Cutting Files Down to Size: New Approaches Tackle Surplus of Data," *Wall Street Journal*, May 8, 2007, B4.
15. Manuel E. Sosa, Steven D. Eppinger, and Craig M. Rowles, "Are Your Engineers Talking to One Another When They Should?" *Harvard Business Review* 85, no. 11 (2007): 133–42.
16. Peter Sanders, "Boeing Has New Delay for Dreamliner," *Wall Street Journal*, August 28, 2010, B6.
17. The National Commission on Writing for America's Families, Schools, and Colleges, "Writing: A Ticket to Work. . .or a Ticket Out: A Survey of Business Leaders," *College Board* (2004), 29.
18. Michael Lewis, "The End of Wall Street's Boom," Portfolio.com, November 11, 2008, http://www.portfolio.com/news-markets/national-news/portfolio/2008/11/11/The-End-of-Wall-Streets-Boom; and Jean Eaglesham, "Banks Near Deal with SEC: Wall Street Is Keen to Settle Fraud Charges Involving Toxic Mortgage Bonds," *Wall Street Journal*, April 15, 2011, A1.
19. U.S. House of Representatives, *A Failure of Initiative: Final Report of the Select Bipartisan Committee to Investigate the Preparation for and Response to Hurricane Katrina*, 109th Cong., 2d sess. (Washington, DC, February 15, 2006), http://www.gpoaccess.gov/katrinareport/mainreport.pdf; Stephen Power and Ben Casselman, "White House Probe Blames BP, Industry in Gulf Blast," *Wall Street Journal*, January 6, 2011, A2.
20. Janet Adamy, "Advertising: Will a Twist on an Old Vow Deliver for Domino's Pizza?" *Wall Street Journal*, December 17, 2007, B1.
21. Stephen Baker, "A Painful Lesson: E-mail Is Forever," *BusinessWeek*, March 21, 2005, 36; Gary McWilliams, "Wal-Mart Details Roehm Firing," *Wall Street Journal*, March 21, 2007, B11; Peter Waldman and Don Clark, "California Charges Dunn, 4 Others in H-P Scandal; Action Sends Strong Message to Business about Privacy; Precedents for the Web Age?" *Wall Street Journal*, October 5, 2006, A1; and "Will 'Love Factor' Help Make S. C.'s Sanford More Forgivable?" *Des Moines Register*, June 29, 2009, 12A.
22. Elizabeth A. McCord, "The Business Writer, the Law, and Routine Business Communication: A Legal and Rhetorical Analysis," *Journal of Business and Technical Communication* 5, no. 3 (1991): 173–99.
23. The Nielsen Company, "Television, Internet and Mobile Usage in the U.S." Three Screen Report 8, 1st Quarter 2010, http://www.nielsen.com/content/dam/corporate/us/en/reports-downloads/3%20Screen/2010/Three%20Screen%20Report%20%28Q1%202010%29.pdf; Bureau of Labor Statistics, "American Time Use Survey Summary," news release, June 22, 2010, http://www.bls.gov/news.release/atus.nr0.htm; Kristen Purcell, Lee Rainie, Amy Mitchell, Tom Rosenstiel, and Kenny Olmstead, "Understanding the Participatory News Customer," Pew Internet & American Life Project, March 1, 2010, http://www.pewinternet.org/Reports/2010/Online-News.aspx?r=1; and The Nielsen Company, "What Americans Do Online: Social Media and Games Dominate Activity," *Nielsenwire* (blog), August 2, 2010, http://blog.nielsen.com/nielsenwire/online_mobile/what-americans-do-online-social-media-and-games-dominate-activity/.

Chapter 2

1. Isabel Briggs Myers, *Introduction to Type* (Palo Alto, CA: Consulting Psychologists Press, 1980). The material in this section follows Myers's paper.
2. Isabel Briggs Myers and Mary H. McCaulley, *Manual: A Guide to the Development and Use of the Myers-Briggs Type Indicato*r (Palo Alto, CA: Consulting Psychologists Press, 1985), 248–51.
3. Eleanor Laise, "Fund Firms Lower Bar for Younger Investors: Wall Street Unveils Slew of Products with 20-Something Slant; 'My Whatever Plan' Cuts Minimums but Limits Choices," *Wall Street Journal*, July 17, 2007, D1.
4. Miguel Bustillo, "Wal-Mart Adds Guns alongside Butter," *Wall Street Journal*, April 28, 2011, B1.

5. Doug Henschen, "Social Media Shapes Up as Next Analytic Frontier," *InformationWeek,* May 2, 2011, http://www.informationweek.com/news/software/bi/229402598; and Emily Steel, "Exploring Ways to Build a Better Consumer Profile: Nielsen, Digital-Marketing Firm eXelate Form Alliance to Merge Online and Offline Data in Bid to Improve Ad Targeting," *Wall Street Journal,* March 15, 2010, B4.
6. Doug Henschen, "Social Media Shapes Up as Next Analytic Frontier."
7. Ellen Byron, "Big Diaper Makers Square Off," *Wall Street Journal,* April 13, 2009, B7; and Suzanne Vranica, "Tweeting to Sell Cars: Auto Makers Turn to Social Media 'Influencers' for Buzz," *Wall Street Journal,* November 15, 2010, B12.
8. Marc Gunther, "Hard News," *Fortune,* August 6, 2007, 82.
9. "The State of the News Media 2011: An Annual Report on American Journalism: Key Findings," Pew Research Center's Project for Excellence in Journalism, March 14, 2011, http://stateofthemedia.org/2011/overview-2/key-findings/.
10. "The State of the News Media 2011: An Annual Report on American Journalism: Key Findings," Pew Research Center's Project for Excellence in Journalism; and "Peggy Sue Got Old," *Economist,* April 7, 2011, http://www.economist.com/node/18527255?story_id=18527255.
11. "Intel Taps 'Minority Report' for Ad Idea," *Wall Street Journal,* December 13, 2010, B6.
12. John Jurgensen, "How to Make It in the Music Business Today," *Wall Street Journal,* December 17, 2010, D2.
13. Elizabeth Olson, "The Ken Doll Turns 50, and Wins a New Face," *New York Times,* March 21, 2011, http://www.nytimes.com/2011/03/22/business/media/22adco.html.
14. Ben Paynter, "Five Steps to Social Currency," *Fast Company,* May 1, 2010, 45.
15. Emily Steel, "Marketers Test Ads in E-Books," *Wall Street Journal,* December 13, 2010, B1.
16. Stephanie Kang, "Magic of Clorox Sells for a Song," *Wall Street Journal,* March 28, 2008, B4; and "Meet the Newest Rap Recording Artist," *Des Moines Register,* April 16, 2008, 2A.
17. "Steamy Hot Line Raises Pulses, Library Funds," *Des Moines Register,* May 9, 2007, 4A.
18. Suzanne Vranica, "Hanger Ads Ensure Message Gets Home," *Wall Street Journal,* March 12, 2007, B4.
19. Jeffery F. Rayport, "Where Is Advertising Going? Into 'Stitials,'" *Harvard Business Review* 86, no. 5 (2008): 18–19.
20. Lev Grossman, "A Game for All Ages," *Time,* May 15, 2006, 39.
21. Miguel Bustillo and Christopher Lawton, "Best Buy Expands Private-Label Brands," *Wall Street Journal,* April 29, 2009, B1.
22. Cecilie Rohwedder, "Store of Knowledge: No. 1 Retailer in Britain Uses 'Clubcard' to Thwart Wal-Mart: Data from Loyalty Program Help Tesco Tailor Products as It Resists U.S. Invader," *Wall Street Journal,* June 6, 2006, A1.
23. Frederick Herzberg, "One More Time: How Do You Motivate Employees?" *Harvard Business Review* 65, no. 5 (1987): 109–20.
24. John Ketzenberger, "Respect, Not Money, Priceless in Cutting Turnover," *Des Moines Register,* November 20, 2006, 3D.
25. Teri Agins, "Over-40 Finds a Muse," *Wall Street Journal,* December 6, 2008, W4.
26. Ellen Byron, "How P&G Led Also-Ran to Sweet Smell of Success: By Focusing on Fragrance, Gain Detergent Developed a Billion-Dollar Following," *Wall Street Journal,* September 4, 2007, B2.
27. Ryan Chittum, "Price Points: Good Customer Service Costs Money. Some Expenses Are Worth It—and Some Aren't," *Wall Street Journal,* October 30, 2006, R7.
28. David Wessel, "Paper Chase: South Africa's Sun Targets New Class: Tabloid Melds Sex, Soccer with Tales from Townships; Report on Flying Tortoise," *Wall Street Journal,* August 17, 2007, A1.
29. Jeff Eckhoff, "Less Huffing, More Fitness in Meredith's Workout Plan," *Des Moines Register,* June 14, 2009, 1D.
30. Stephen W. Brown, Aners Gustafsson, and Lars Witell, "Beyond Products," *Wall Street Journal,* June 22, 2009, R7.
31. Richard M. Smith, "Stay True to Your Brand: Ad Guru Rance Crain Says the Rules Are Eternal," *Newsweek,* May 5, 2008, E18.
32. James Surowiecki, "The Financial Page Freature Presentation," *The New Yorker,* May 28, 2007, 28.
33. Reuters, "Scientist: Complexity Causes 50% of Product Returns," *Computer World,* May 6, 2006, http://www.computerworld.com/s/article/109254/Scientist_Complexity_causes_50_of_product_returns.
34. Rachael Spilka, "Orality and Literacy in the Workplace: Process- and Text-Based Strategies for Multiple Audience Adaptation," *Journal of Business and Technical Communication* 4, no. 1 (1990): 44–67.

Chapter 3

1. "Amazon Investor Relations," Amazon.com, March 25, 2011, http://phx.corporate-ir.net/phoenix.zhtml?p=irol-irhome&c=97664; and "Video from Jeff Bezos about Amazon and Zappos," YouTube video, 8:10, posted by "07272009july," July 22, 2009, http://www.youtube.com/watch?v=-hxX_Q5CnaA.
2. Linda Kaplan Thaler and Robin Koval, *The Power of Nice: How to Conquer the Business World with Kindness* (New York: Currency, 2006), 3.
3. Aaron Pressman, "When Service Means Survival," *BusinessWeek,* March 2, 2009, 62.
4. John A. Byrne, "How to Lead Now: Getting Extraordinary Performance When You Can't Pay for It," *Fast Company,* August 2003, 65.
5. Timothy Aeppel, "Too Good for Lowe's and Home Depot?" *Wall Street Journal,* July 24, 2006, B1, B6.
6. Annette N. Shelby and N. Lamar Reinsch, "Positive Emphasis and You-Attitude: An Empirical Study," *Journal of Business Communication* 32, no. 4 (1995): 303–27.
7. Martin E. P. Seligman, *Learned Optimism: How to Change Your Mind and Your Life,* 2nd ed. (New York: Pocket Books, 1998), 96–107.
8. Mark A. Sherman, "Adjectival Negation and Comprehension of Multiply Negated Sentences," *Journal of Verbal Learning and Verbal Behavior* 15 (1976): 143–57.
9. Jeffrey Zaslow, "In Praise of Less Praise," *Wall Street Journal,* May 3, 2007, D1.
10. Associated Press, "Florida Police Chief Ousted after 'Jelly Bellies' Memo Telling Cops to Get Fit," *Fox News,* November 2, 2006, http://www.foxnews.com/story/0,2933,226808,00.html.
11. Stephen C. Dillard, "Litigation Nation," *Wall Street Journal,* November 25, 2006, A9.
12. Margaret Baker Graham and Carol David, "Power and Politeness: Administrative Writing in an 'Organized Anarchy,'" *Journal of Business and Technical Communication* 10, no. 1 (1996): 5–27.
13. "Women's History Month: March 2011," U.S. Census Bureau Newsroom, January 26, 2011, http://www.census.gov/newsroom/releases/archives/facts_for_features_

special_editions/cb11-ff04.html; "2010 Census Shows America's Diversity," U.S. Census Bureau Newsroom, March 23, 2011, http://www.census.gov/newsroom/releases/archives/2010_census/cb11-cn125.html; and "Older Americans Month: May 2011," U.S. Census Bureau Newsroom, March 23, 2011, http://www.census.gov/newsroom/releases/archives/facts_for_features_special_editions/cb11-ff08.html.

14. Laura Stevens, "German CEO's Remark on Women Draws Fire," *Wall Street Journal,* February 8, 2011, A9.
15. Frank Newport, "Black or African American?" Gallup, September 28, 2007, http://www.gallup.com/poll/28816/black-african-american.aspx.
16. "20th Anniversary of Americans with Disabilities Act: July 26," U.S. Census Bureau Newsroom, May 26, 2010, http://www.census.gov/newsroom/releases/archives/facts_for_features_special_editions/cb10-ff13.html.
17. M. P. McQueen, "Workplace Disabilities Are on the Rise: Employers Devise Strategies to Accommodate Growing Ranks of Employees Impaired by Age, Obesity, and Disease," *Wall Street Journal,* May 1, 2007, D1.
18. Clark Ansberry, "Erasing a Hurtful Label from the Books," *Wall Street Journal,* November 30, 2010, A6.

Chapter 4

1. Peter Loftus and Jon Kamp, "Glaxo to Pay $750 Million in Pact; Whistleblower Due Big Payment," *Wall Street Journal,* November 27, 2010, B3.
2. Michael Rothfeld, Susan Pulliam, and Chad Bray, " Fund Titan Found Guilty," *Wall Street Journal,* May 12, 2011, A1.
3. Ethics Resource Center, *2009 National Business Ethics Survey* 9, no. 33, accessed May 24, 2011, http://www.ethics.org/nbes/files/nbes-final.pdf.
4. Mary C. Gentile, "Keeping Your Colleagues Honest," *Harvard Business Review* 88, no. 2 (2010): 114–15.
5. "United Nations Global Compact Participants," United Nations Global Compact, accessed May 26, 2011, http://www.unglobalcompact.org/ParticipantsAndStakeholders/index.html.
6. "About Us," Clinton Global Initiative, accessed May 26, 2011, http://www.clintonglobalinitiative.org/aboutus/default.asp.
7. "About Us," Google, accessed May 26, 2011, http://www.google.org/about.html.
8. "Robin Hood: Targeting Poverty in New York City," Robin Hood Foundation, accessed May 26, 2011, http://www.robinhood.org; and Andy Serwer, "The Legend of Robin Hood," *Fortune,* September 18, 2006, 103–14.
9. "Grameen Bank at a Glance," Grameen Bank, last updated March 2011, http://www.grameen-info.org/index.php?option=com_content&task=view&id=26&Itemid=175; and Social Finance.org, "Social Finance Launches First Social Impact Bond," news release, March 18, 2010, http://www.socialfinance.org.uk/sites/default/files/SIB_March18_PR.pdf.
10. Quoted from Tony Hsieh, *Delivering Happiness: A Path to Profits, Passion, and Purpose* (New York: Business Plus, 2010), 243.
11. Leigh Buchanan, "Learning from the Best: Smart Strategies from the Top Small Company Workplaces," *Inc.,* June 2010, 92.
12. Ellen Byron, "Merger Challenge: Unite Toothbrush, Toothpaste: P&G and Gillette Find Creating Synergy Can Be Harder than It Looks," *Wall Street Journal,* April 24, 2007, A1.
13. Phred Dvorak, "Hotelier Finds Happiness Keeps Staff Checked In," *Wall Street Journal,* December 17, 2007, B3.
14. Tony Hsieh, *Delivering Happiness: A Path to Profits, Passion, and Purpose* (New York: Business Plus, 2010), 150–65.
15. Tony Hsieh, *Delivering Happiness: A Path to Profits, Passion, and Purpose,* 148.
16. Daniel Goleman, *Emotional Intelligence: The Tenth Anniversary Edition* (New York: Bantam, 2005), xiv–xv.
17. Deborah Tannen, *That's Not What I Meant!* (New York: William Morrow, 1986).
18. Daniel N. Maltz and Ruth A. Borker, "A Cultural Approach to Male–Female Miscommunication," in *Language and Social Identity,* ed. John J. Gumperz (Cambridge: Cambridge University Press, 1982), 202.
19. Marie Helweg-Larson et al., "To Nod or Not to Nod: An Observational Study of Nonverbal Communication and Status in Female and Male College Students," *Psychology of Women Quarterly* 28, no. 4 (2004): 358–61.
20. Carol Kinsey Goman, "10 Common Body Language Traps for Women in the Workplace," *On Leadership* (blog), *Washington Post,* March 3, 2011, http://www.washingtonpost.com/blogs/on-leadership/post/10-common-body-language-traps-for-women-in-the-workplace/2011/03/03/AFl0GFbF_blog.html.
21. Alex Pentland, "We Can Measure the Power of Charisma," *Business Review,* January 2010, 34.
22. Alex "Sandy" Pentland, "The Power of Nonverbal Communication," *Wall Street Journal,* October 20, 2008, R2.
23. Daniel Goleman, *Emotional Intelligence: The Tenth Anniversary Edition* (New York: Bantam, 2005), 161–62.
24. Daniel Goleman, *Emotional Intelligence: The Tenth Anniversary Edition,* 162.
25. "Social Studies," *Businessweek,* June 14, 2010, 72–3.
26. Jessica Hodgins, "'You Can't Make More Time': Randy Pausch's Heart-felt Views on Using Time to the Fullest," *BusinessWeek,* September 1, 2008, 71.
27. Stephen R. Covey, *The 7 Habits of Highly Effective People: Restoring the Character* (New York: Free Press, 2004), 150–54.
28. Jared Sandberg, "Yes, Sell All My Stocks. No, the 3:15 from JFK. and Get Me Mr. Sister," *Wall Street Journal,* September 12, 2006, B1.
29. Toddi Gutner, "Beat the Clock: E-mails, Faxes, Phone Calls, Oh My. Here's How to Get It All Done," *BusinessWeek SmallBiz,* February/March 2008, 58.
30. Adam Gorlick, "Media Multitaskers Pay Mental Price, Stanford Study Shows," *Stanford Report,* August 24, 2009, http://news.stanford.edu/news/2009/august24/multitask-research-study-082409.html.
31. Maggie Jackson, "May We Have Your Attention, Please?" *BusinessWeek,* June 23, 2008, 56.
32. Sharon Begley, "Will the BlackBerry Sink the Presidency?" *Newsweek,* February 16, 2009, 37.
33. Nick Wingfield, Ian Sherr, and Ben Worthen, "Hacker Raids Sony Videogame Network," *Wall Street Journal,* April 27, 2011, A1.
34. Stephanie Armour, "Employers Look Closely at What Workers Do on Job: Companies Get More Vigilant as Technology Increases their Risks," *USA Today,* November 8, 2006, 2B; and M. P. McQueen, "Laptop Lockdown: Companies Start Holding Employees Responsible for Security of Portable Devices They Use for Work," *Wall Street Journal,* June 28, 2006, D1.
35. "Electronic Monitoring and Surveillance 2007 Survey," American Management Association, February 28, 2008, http://www.amanet.org/training/whitepapers/2007-Electronic-Monitoring-and-Surveillance-Survey-41.aspx.\.

36. Andie Coller, "Grassley Launches Porn Inquiry," Capitol News Company, January 28, 2009, http://dyn.politico.com/members/forums/thread.cfm?catid=1&subcatid=1&threadid=1970273.
37. Chris Newmarker, "On the Off-Ramp to Adultery, There's No Fooling EZ-Pass," *Des Moines Register*, August 12, 2007, 8A.
38. Stephanie Armour, "Employers Look Closely at What Workers Do on Job: Companies Get More Vigilant as Technology Increases their Risks," *USA Today*, November 8, 2006, 2B; M. P. McQueen, "Workers' Terminations for Computer Misuse Rise," *Wall Street Journal*, July 15, 2006, B4; and "Burger King Fires Workers over Blogs," *Wall Street Journal*, May 14, 2008, A18.
39. Dalia Fahmy, "Can You Be Fired for Sending Personal E-Mails at Work?" *ABC News*, December 17, 2009, http://abcnews.go.com/Business/GadgetGuide/supreme-court-employee-rights-privacy-workplace-emails/story?id=9345057.
40. John Markoff, "Armies of Expensive Lawyers, Replaced by Cheaper Software," *New York Times*, March 4, 2011, http://www.nytimes.com/2011/03/05/science/05legal.html.
41. "Twitter Tirades Test Free-Speech Limits," *Des Moines Register*, November 25, 2010, 4A.
42. Lauren A.E. Schuker, "Secret Texting . . . Pass It On," *Wall Street Journal*, February 4, 2011, B11.
43. Nick Wingfield and Julia Angwin, "Microsoft Adds Privacy Tool," *Wall Street Journal*, March 15, 2011, B1.
44. Emily Steel and Jessica E. Vascellaro, "FTC Backs Web-Ad Self-Regulation: Agency Lays Out Principles for Protecting the Privacy of 'Targeted' Users," *Wall Street Journal*, February 13, 2009, B7.
45. Julia Angwin and Tom McGinty, "Sites Feed Personal Details to New Tracking Industry," *Wall Street Journal*, July 31, 2010, A1; Scott Thurm and Yukari Iwatani Kane, "Your Apps Are Watching You," *Wall Street Journal*, December 18, 2010, C1.
46. Christopher W. Hart, "Beating the Market with Customer Satisfaction," *Harvard Business Review* 85, no. 3 (2007): 30–32.
47. "Frequently Asked Questions: What Can ACSI Tell Us," American Customer Satisfaction Index, http://www.theacsi.org/index.php?option=com_content&view=article&id=46&Itemid=124#what_can.
48. Dana Mattioli, "Customer Service as a Growth Engine," *Wall Street Journal*, June 7, 2010, B6.
49. "2010 Working Mother 100 Best Companies: Cisco," Working Mother, accessed May 27, 2011, http://www.workingmother.com/best-companies/cisco-2; and "2010 Working Mother 100 Best Companies: Microsoft," Working Mother, accessed May 27, 2011, http://www.workingmother.com/best-companies/microsoft-0.
50. Scott Adams, "Work–Life Integration," *Dilbert*, March 23, 2011.
51. Betsy McKay and Suzanne Vranica, "Firms Use Earth Day to Show Their Green Side," *Wall Street Journal*, April 22, 2008, B7.
52. Gwendolyn Bounds, "Misleading Claims on 'Green' Labeling," *Wall Street Journal*, October 26, 2010, D4.
53. Ann Zimmerman, "Wal-Mart Boosts Local Produce: Retailer to Expand Purchases from Small Farmers, Monitor Fertilizer, Water Use," *Wall Street Journal*, November 15, 2010, B2; and General Electric Company, "GE Surpassed $5 Billion in Research & Development Investment in Ecomagination Technology," news release, June 24, 2010, http://www.genewscenter.com/Press-Releases/GE-Surpassed-5-Billion-in-Research-Development-Investment-in-Ecomagination-Technology-2902.aspx.
54. "McDonald's Canada: FAQs," McDonald's Corporation, accessed May 27, 2011, http://www.mcdonalds.ca/en/aboutus/faq.aspx.
55. "3M Facts: Year-end 2010," 3M, accessed May 27, 2011, http://multimedia.mmm.com/mws/mediawebserver.dyn?6666660Zjcf6lVs6EVs66S592COrrrrQ-.
56. "Worldwide Facts," United Parcel Service of America, Inc., accessed May 27, 2011, http://www.ups.com/content/us/en/about/facts/worldwide.html.
57. "Growth, Leadership, Sustainability," Coca-Cola Company, accessed May 27, 2011, http://www.thecoca-colacompany.com/ourcompany/index.html.
58. "International," Walmart Corporate, accessed May 27, 2011, http://walmartstores.com/aboutus/246.aspx.
59. Thomas L. Friedman, *The World Is Flat: A Brief History of the Twenty-First Century*, updated and expanded ed. (New York: Farrar, Straus, and Giroux, 2006), 14.
60. Thomas L. Friedman, *The World Is Flat: A Brief History of the Twenty-First Century*, 86.
61. Christine Uber Grosse, "Managing Communication within Virtual Intercultural Teams," *Business Communication Quarterly* (2002): 22; and Linda H. Heuring, "Patients First," *HRMagazine*, July 2003, 67–68.
62. Sue Shellenbarger, "Some Companies Rethink the Telecommuting Trend," *Wall Street Journal*, February 28, 2008, D1.
63. Linda H. Heuring, "Patients First," *HRMagazine*, July 2003, 67–68.
64. Jörgen Sandberg, "Understanding Competence at Work," *Harvard Business Review*, 79, no. 3 (2001): 24–28.
65. L. D. DeSimone et al., "How Can Big Companies Keep the Entrepreneurial Spirit Alive?" *Harvard Business Review* 73, no. 6 (1995): 183–92.
66. Anne Fisher, "America's Most Admired Companies," *Fortune*, March 17, 2008, 65–67.
67. "How Google Fuels Its Idea Factory," *BusinessWeek*, May 12, 2008, 54–55.
68. U.S. Census Bureau, "Census Bureau Reports Nation Has Nearly 350,000 Fewer Nonemployer Business Locations," press release, June 24, 2010, http://www.census.gov/newsroom/releases/archives/business_ownership/cb10-93.html.
69. Max Messmer, "Soft Skills Are Key to Advancing Your Career," *Business Credit* 109, no. 4 (2007): 34.

Chapter 5

1. See especially Linda Flower and John R. Hayes, "The Cognition of Discovery: Defining a Rhetorical Problem," *College Composition and Communication* 31, no. 1 (February 1980): 21–32; Mike Rose, *Writer's Block: The Cognitive Dimension*, published for Conference on College Composition and Communication, 1984.; and essays in two collections: Charles R. Cooper and Lee Odell, *Research on Composing: Points of Departure* (Urbana, IL: National Council of Teachers of English, 1978); Mike Rose, ed., *When a Writer Can't Write: Studies in Writer's Block and Other Composing-Process Problems* (New York: Guilford Press, 1985).
2. Peter Elbow, *Writing with Power: Techniques for Mastering the Writing Process* (New York: Oxford University Press, 1981), 15–20.
3. See Gabriela Lusser Rico, *Writing the Natural Way* (Los Angeles: J. P. Tarcher, 1983), 10.
4. Rachel Spilka, "Orality and Literacy in the Workplace: Process- and Text-Based Strategies for Multiple Audience

Adaptation," *Journal of Business and Technical Communication* 4, no. 1 (January 1990): 44–67.

5. Robert L. Brown, Jr., and Carl G. Herndl, "An Ethnographic Study of Corporate Writing: Job Status as Reflected in Written Text," in *Functional Approaches to Writing: A Research Perspective*, ed. Barbara Couture (Norwood, NJ: Ablex, 1986), 16–19, 22–23.
6. U.S. Securities and Exchange Commission Office of Investor Education and Assistance, *A Plain English Handbook: How to Create Clear SEC Disclosure Documents* (Washington, D.C.: 1998).
7. Eleanor Laise, "Some Consumers Say Wall Street Failed Them," *Wall Street Journal*, November 28, 2008, B1.
8. Gerard Braud, "What Does That Mean?" *Communication World* 24, no. 1 (2007): 34.
9. Warren Buffett, "Letters 2010," Berkshire Hathaway Inc., accessed May 24, 2011, http://www.berkshirehathaway.com/letters/2010ltr.pdf.
10. Richard Lederer and Richard Dowis, *Sleeping Dogs Don't Lay: Practical Advice for the Grammatically Challenged*, (New York: St. Martin's Press, 1999), 91–92.
11. James Suchan and Robert Colucci, "An Analysis of Communication Efficiency between High-Impact and Bureaucratic Written Communication," *Management Communication Quarterly* 2, no. 4 (1989): 464–73.
12. Hilvard G. Rogers and F. William Brown, "The Impact of Writing Style on Compliance with Instructions," *Journal of Technical Writing and Communication* 23, no. 1 (1993): 53–71.
13. Richard Lederer, "The Terrible Ten," *Toastmaster*, July 2003, 28–29.
14. Robert Frank, "The Wealth Report: Millionaires Need Not Apply; SEC and Others Rewrite the Definition of 'Rich'; The Haves and Have-Mores," *Wall Street Journal*, March 16, 2007, W2.
15. Geoff Mullins, "With Wetlands, Words Matter," *Ames Tribune*, April 3, 2008, A4.
16. Arlene Weintraub, "Revenge of the Overworked Nerds," *BusinessWeek*, December 8, 2003, 41.
17. Peter Conrad, *The Medicalization of Society: On the Transformation of Human Conditions into Treatable Disorders* (Baltimore: The Johns Hopkins University Press, 2007).
18. Chad Bray and Anjali Cordeiro, "Tobacco Firms Score Victory as Class-Action Suit Is Denied," *Wall Street Journal*, April 4, 2008, B3; "FDA May Rephrase Pacemaker Warnings," *Wall Street Journal*, September 29, 2006, A8.
19. Melinda Beck, "Getting an Earful: Testing a Tiny, Pricey Hearing Aid," *Wall Street Journal*, January 29, 2008, D1.
20. Jaguar ad, *Wall Street Journal*, September 29, 2000, A20.
21. Betsy Taylor, "Experts: Flood Terms Can Deceive," *Des Moines Register*, July 1, 2008, 9A.
22. Evan Perez, "Mukasey Cites Risk in Using Term 'Torture,'" *Wall Street Journal*, January 17, 2009, A2.
23. Richard C. Anderson, "Concretization and Sentence Learning," *Journal of Educational Psychology* 66, no. 2 (1974): 179–83.
24. Ben Worthen, "Oracle's Hot New Offering: Corporate Technobabble," *Wall Street Journal*, February 12, 2008, B4.
25. Pamela Layton and Adrian J. Simpson, "Deep Structure in Sentence Comprehension," *Journal of Verbal Learning and Verbal Behavior* 14 (1975); Harris B. Savin and Ellen Perchonock, "Grammatical Structure and the Immediate Recall of English Sentences," *Journal of Verbal Learning and Verbal Behavior* 4 (1965): 348–53.
26. Federal Aviation Administration, "Document Checklist for Plain Language," PlainLanguage.gov, accessed May 24, 2011, http://www.plainlanguage.gov/howto/quickreference/checklist.cfm.
27. Bill Walsh, *The Elephants of Style: A Trunkload of Tips on the Big Issues and Gray Areas of Contemporary American English* (New York: McGraw-Hill, 2004), 68.
28. Lloyd Bostian and Ann C. Thering, "Scientists: Can They Read What They Write?" *Journal of Technical Writing and Communication* 17 (1987): 417–27; E. B. Coleman, "The Comprehensibility of Several Grammatical Transformations," *Journal of Applied Psychology* 48, no. 3 (1964): 186–90; Keith Rayner, "Visual Attention in Reading: Eye Movements Reflect Cognitive Processes," *Memory and Cognition* 5 (1977): 443–48.
29. Don Bush, "The Most Obvious Fault in Technical Writing," *Intercom*, July/August 2003, 50.
30. Adam Freedman, "And the Winners Are...," The Party of the First Part (blog), last updated September 21, 2007, http://thepartyofthefirstpart.blogspot.com/2007/09/and-winners-are.html.
31. Thomas N. Huckin, "A Cognitive Approach to Readability," in *New Essays in Technical and Scientific Communication: Research, Theory, Practice*, eds. Paul V. Anderson, R. John Brockmann, and Carolyn R. Miller (Farmingdale, NY: Baywood, 1983), 93–98.
32. James Suchan and Ronald Dulek, "A Reassessment of Clarity in Written Managerial Communications," *Management Communication Quarterly* 4, no. 1 (1990): 93–97.
33. Doris Kearns Goodwin, *Team of Rivals: The Political Genius of Abraham Lincoln* (New York: Simon & Schuster, 2005), 583–87.
34. "Law Typo Allows Children to Marry," *Des Moines Register*, August 18, 2007, 8A.
35. Carol Hymowitz, "Diebold's New Chief Shows How to Lead after a Sudden Rise," *Wall Street Journal*, May 8, 2006, B1.
36. Lynne Truss, *Eats, Shoots & Leaves: The Zero Tolerance Approach to Punctuation* (New York: Gotham Books, 2003), 9–10.
37. Bill Walsh, *Lapsing into a Comma: A Curmudgeon's Guide to the Many Things That Can Go Wrong in Print—and How to Avoid Them* (Lincolnwood (Chicago): Contemporary Books, 2000), 1.
38. Dianna Booher, "Cutting Paperwork in the Corporate Culture," *New York: Facts on File Publications* (1986): 23.
39. Susan D. Kleimann, "The Complexity of Workplace Review," *Technical Communication* 38, no. 4 (1991): 520–26.
40. Glenn J. Broadhead and Richard C. Freed, *The Variables of Composition: Process and Product in a Business Setting*, Conference on College Composition and Communication Studies in Writing and Rhetoric (Carbondale, IL: Southern Illinois University Press, 1986), 57.
41. Janice C. Redish and Jack Selzer, "The Place of Readability Formulas in Technical Communication," *Technical Communication* 32, no. 4 (1985): 46–52.

Chapter 6

1. Edward Tufte, *Beautiful Evidence* (Cheshire, CT: Graphics Press, 2006), 153–55.
2. Charles Kostelnick and Michael Hassett, *Shaping Information: The Rhetoric of Visual Conventions* (Carbondale, IL: Southern Illinois University Press, 2003), 92, 94.
3. Kostelnick and Hassett, *Shaping Information*, 206–07.
4. Charles Kostelnick and David Roberts, *Designing Visual Language*, 2nd ed. (Boston: Allyn & Bacon, 2011), 81–83.
5. George A. Miller, "The Magical Number Seven, Plus or Minus Two: Some Limits on Our Capacity for Processing Information," *Psychological Review* 63, no. 2 (1956): 81–97.
6. Marlee M. Spafford, Catherine F. Schryer, Lorelei Lingard, and Marcellina Mian, "Accessibility and Order: Crossing

Borders in Child Abuse Forensic Reports," *Technical Communication Quarterly* 19, no. 2 (2010): 118–43.

7. Jerry E. Bishop, "Word Processing: Research on Stroke Victims Yields Clues to the Brain's Capacity to Create Language," *Wall Street Journal,* October 12, 1993, A6; Anne Meyer and David H. Rose, "Learning to Read in the Computer Age," in *Reading Research to Practice* ed. Jeanne S. Chall, (Cambridge, MA: Brookline Books, 1998), 4–6.
8. Karen A. Schriver, *Dynamics in Document Design* (New York: Wiley, 1997), 274.
9. Jo Mackiewicz, "What Technical Writing Students Should Know about Typeface Personality," *Journal of Technical Writing and Communication* 34, no. 1–2 (2004): 113–31.
10. Miles A. Kimball and Ann R. Hawkins, *Document Design: A Guide for Technical Communicators* (Boston: Bedford/St. Martin's, 2008), 49, 125.
11. Harald Weinreich et al., "Not Quite the Average: An Empirical Study of Web Use," *ACM Transactions on the Web* 2, no. 1 (2008): 18.
12. Jakob Nielsen, "F-Shaped Pattern for Reading Web Content," Jakob Nielsen's Alertbox, April 17, 2006, http://www.useit.com/alertbox/reading_pattern.html.
13. Jakob Nielsen, "Website Response Time," Jakob Nielsen's Alertbox, June 21, 2010, http://www.useit.com/alertbox/response-times.html.
14. Geoffrey A. Fowler and Scott Morrison, "Ebay Attempts to Clean Up the Clutter," *Wall Street Journal,* November 1, 2010, B3; and Lee Gomes, "Good Site, Bad Site: Evolving Web Design," *Wall Street Journal,* June 12, 2007, B3.
15. Jakob Nielsen, "Top Ten Mistakes in Web Design," Jakob Nielsen's Alertbox, accessed May 23, 2011, http://www.useit.com/alertbox/9605.html; and Emily Steel, "Neglected Banner Ads Get a Second Life," *Wall Street Journal,* June 20, 2007, B4.
16. "Corporate News: Target Settles with Blind Group on Web Access," *Wall Street Journal,* August 28, 2008, B4; and Lauren Pollock, "iTunes Eases Access for Blind," *Wall Street Journal,* September 29, 2008, B5.
17. Stephanie Clifford and Claire Cain Miller, "Retailers Retool Sites to Ease Mobile Shopping," *New York Times,* April 17, 2011, http://www.nytimes.com/2011/04/18/technology/18mobile.html.
18. Jakob Nielsen, "Why You Only Need to Test with 5 Users," Jakob Nielsen's Alertbox, March 19, 2000, www.useit.com/alertbox/20000319.html.
19. Jakob Nielsen "Usability 101: Introduction to Usability," Jakob Nielsen's Alertbox, accessed May 23, 2011, http://www.useiticom/alertbox/20030825.html.

Chapter 7

1. Sharon Begley, "Studies Take Measure of How Stereotyping Alters Performance," *Wall Street Journal,* February 23, 2007, B1; and Claude Steele and Joshua Aronson, "Stereotype Threat and Intellectual Test Performance of African Americans," *Journal of Personality and Social Psychology* 69, no. 5 (1995): 797–811.
2. McDonald's Corporation, *McDonald's 2010 Annual Report,* 9, February 25, 2011, http://www.aboutmcdonalds.com/etc/medialib/aboutMcDonalds/investor_relations3.Par.56096.File.dat/2010%20Annual%20Report%20%28print%29.pdf; "3M at a Glance," 3M Corporation, accessed May 30, 2011, http://solutions.3m.com/wps/portal/3M/en_US/careers/home/about/3M/; "Global Structure & Governance," Proctor and Gamble, accessed May 30, 2011, http://www.pg.com/en_US/company/global_structure_operations/index.shtml; "Unilever Facts," Unilever, accessed May 30, 2011, http://www.unilever.com/aboutus/introductiontounilever/unileverataglance/index.aspx; Walmart Corporation, Walmart's *2011 Annual Report,* 2, http://walmartstores.com/sites/annualreport/2011/financials/Walmart_2011_Annual_Report.pdf.
3. Lauren A. E. Schuker, "Plot Change: Foreign Forces Transform Hollywood Films," *Wall Street Journal,* July 31, 2010, A1.
4. Emily Maltby, "Expanding Abroad? Avoid Cultural Gaffes," *Wall Street Journal,* January 19, 2010, B5.
5. William W. Maddux, Adam D. Galinshky, and Carmit T. Tadmor, "Be a Better Manager: Live Abroad," *Harvard Business Review* 88, no. 9 (2010): 24.
6. Joann S. Lublin, "Hunt Is On for Fresh Executive Talent: Recruiters List Hot Prospects, Cultural Flexibility in Demand," *Wall Street Journal,* April 11, 2011, B1.
7. Diana Middleton, "Schools Set Global Track, for Students and Programs," *Wall Street Journal,* April 7, 2011, B7.
8. Jason DeParle, "Global Migration: A World Ever More on the Move," *New York Times,* June 26, 2010, http://www.nytimes.com/2010/06/27/weekinreview/27deparle.html?pagewanted=2.
9. Jason DeParle, "Global Migration: A World Ever More on the Move."
10. Thomas L. Friedman, *The World Is Flat: A Brief History of the Twenty-first Century,* Updated and Expanded ed. (New York: Farrar, Straus and Giroux, 2006), 8.
11. U.S. Census Bureau, "Statistical Abstract of the United States, Table 9: Resident Population by Race, Hispanic Origin, and Age: 2000 and 2009," accessed May 30, 2011, http://www.census.gov/compendia/statab/2011/tables/11s0009.pdf.
12. U.S. Census Bureau, "Statistical Abstract of the United States, Table 50: Persons Obtaining Legal Permanent Resident Status by Country of Birth: 1981 to 2009," accessed May 30, 2011, http://www.census.gov/compendia/statab/2011/tables/11s0050.pdf.
13. Conor Dougherty, "Whites to Lose Majority Status in U.S. by 2042," *Wall Street Journal,* August 14, 2008, A3.
14. U.S. Census Bureau, "2010 Census Shows America's Diversity," news release, March 24, 2011, http://www.census.gov/newsroom/releases/archives/2010_census/cb11-cn125.html.
15. "About Us," CHIN Radio, accessed May 30, 2011, http://chinradio.com/chin-radio/.
16. U.S. Census Bureau, "2010 Census Shows America's Diversity," news release, March 24, 2011, http://www.census.gov/newsroom/releases/archives/2010_census/cb11-cn125.html.
17. U.S. Census Bureau, "Statistical Abstract of the United States, Table 54: Language Spoken at Home by State: 2008," accessed May 30, 2011, http://www.census.gov/compendia/statab/2011/tables/11s0054.pdf.
18. U.S. Census Bureau, "Statistical Abstract of the United States, Table 54.
19. "Employee Resource Groups and Networks at Microsoft," Microsoft Corporation, accessed May 30, 2011, http://www.microsoft.com/about/diversity/en/us/programs/ergen/default.aspx.
20. Cedric Herring, "Does Diversity Pay?: Race, Gender, and the Business Case for Diversity," *American Sociological Review* 74 (April 2009): 208–224.
21. Abhijit Rao, e-mail message to author, February 15, 2009.
22. "Geert Hofstede™ Cultural Dimensions: United States," ITIM International, last updated 2009, accessed May 30, 2011,

http://www.geert-hofstede.com/hofstede_united_states.shtml.

23. John Webb and Michael Keene, "The Impact of Discourse Communities on International Professional Communication," in *Exploring the Rhetoric of International Professional Communication: An Agenda for Teachers and Researchers,* ed. Carl R. Lovitt and Dixie Goswami (Amityville, NY: Baywood, 1999), 81–109.
24. Richard M. Steers, Carlos J. Sanchez-Runde, Luciara Nardon, *Management across Cultures: Challenges and Strategies* (New York: Cambridge University Press, 2010), 205–6.
25. "Business Cards," *BusinessWeek SmallBiz,* June/July 2008, 28.; and Roy A. Cook and Gwen O. Cook, *Guide to Business Etiquette* (New York: Prentice Hall, 2011), 113.
26. Kathryn King-Metters and Ricard Metters, "Misunderstanding the Chinese Worker: Western Impressions Are Dated—And Probably Wrong," *Wall Street Journal,* July 7, 2008, R11; Jason Leow, "Chinese Bigwigs Are Quick to Reach for the Hair Color: Politicians and Executives Look for Youth in a Bottle of Black Dye on the Sly," *Wall Street Journal,* December 11, 2007, A1, A24.
27. Robert T. Moran, Philip R. Harris, and Sarah V. Moran, *Managing Cultural Differences: Global Leadership Strategies for the 21st Century,* 7th ed. (Boston: Elsevier, 2007), 341–42.
28. Robert T. Moran, Philip R. Harris, and Sarah V. Moran, *Managing Cultural Differences,* 64.
29. Richard M. Steers, Carlos J. Sanchez-Runde, Luciara Nardon, *Management across Cultures: Challenges and Strategies* (New York: Cambridge University Press, 2010), 219.
30. Robert T. Moran, Philip R. Harris, and Sarah V. Moran, *Managing Cultural Differences,* 579.
31. Mike Kilen, "Watch Your Language: Rude or Polite? Gestures Vary with Cultures," *Des Moines Register,* May 30, 2006, E1–2.
32. Martin J. Gannon, *Understanding Global Cultures: Metaphorical Journeys through 23 Nations,* 2nd ed. (Thousand Oaks, CA: Sage, 2001), 13.
33. Edward Twitchell Hall, *Hidden Differences: Doing Business with the Japanese* (Garden City, NY: Anchor-Doubleday, 1987), 25.
34. Robert T. Moran, Philip R. Harris, and Sarah V. Moran, *Managing Cultural Differences: Global Leadership Strategies for the 21st Century,* 7th ed. (Boston: Elsevier, 2007), 445, 78.
35. Malcolm Fleschner, "Worldwide Winner," *Selling Power,* November–December 2001, 54–61.
36. Ira Carnahan, "Presidential Timber Tends to Be Tall," *Forbes,* May 19, 2004, http://www.forbes.com/2004/05/19/cz_ic_0519beltway.html.
37. Craig Storti, *Old World, New World: Bridging Cultural Differences: Britain, France, Germany, and the U.S.* (Yarmouth, ME: Intercultural Press, 2001), 209.
38. Nick Easen, "Don't Send the Wrong Message," *Business 2.0,* August 2005, 102.

Chapter 8

1. Kevin S. Groves, "Leader Emotional Expressivity, Visionary Leadership, and Organizational Change," *Leadership & Organizational Development Journal* 27, no. 7 (2006): 566–83; Ajay Mehra et al., "Distributed Leadership in Teams: The Network of Leadership Perceptions and Team Performance," *The Leadership Quarterly* 17, no. 3 (2006): 232–45; Kenneth David Stand, "Examining Effective and Ineffective Transformational Project Leadership," *Team Performance Management* 11, no. 3/4 (2005): 68–103.
2. Jeswald W. Salacuse, *The Global Negotiator: Making, Managing, and Mending Deals around the World in the Twenty-First Century* (New York: Palgrave Macmillan, 2003), 92.
3. Bob Frisch, "When Teams Can't Decide," *Harvard Business Review* 86, no. 11 (2008): 121–26.
4. Sue Shellenbarger, "Work & Family Mailbox," *Wall Street Journal,* February 9, 2011, D3.
5. Caroline Bailey and Michelle Austin, "360 Degree Feedback and Developmental Outcomes: The Role of Feedback Characteristics, Self-Efficacy and Importance of Feedback Dimensions to Focal Managers' Current Role," *International Journal of Selection and Assessment* 14, no. 1 (2006): 51–66.
6. Kimberly Merriman, "Low-Trust Teams Prefer Individualized Pay," *Harvard Business Review* 86, no. 11 (2008): 32.
7. Sari Lindblom-Ylanne, Heikki Pihlajamaki, and Toomas Kotkas, "What Makes a Student Group Successful? Student-Student and Student–Teacher Interaction in a Problem–Based Learning Environment," *Learning Environments Research* 6, no. 1 (2003): 59–76.
8. Rebecca E. Burnett, "Conflict in Collaborative Decision-Making," in *Professional Communication: The Social Perspective,* ed. Nancy Roundy Blyler and Charlotte Thralls (Newbury Park, CA: Sage, 1993), 144–62; Rebecca E. Burnett, "Productive and Unproductive Conflict in Collaboration," in *Making Thinking Visible: Writing, Collaborative Planning, and Classroom Inquiry,* ed. Linda Flower et al. (Urbana, IL: NCTE, 1994), 239–44.
9. Sue Dyer, "The Root Causes of Poor Communication," *Cost Engineering* 48, no. 6 (2006): 8–10.
10. Solomon F. Asch, "Opinions and Social Pressure," *Scientific American* 193, no. 5 (1955): 31–35. For a review of recent literature on groupthink, see Marc D. Street, "Groupthink: An Examination of Theoretical Issues, Implications, and Future Research Suggestions," *Small Group Research* 28, no. 1 (1997): 72–93.
11. Jared Diamond, *Collapse: How Societies Choose to Fail or Succeed* (New York: Penguin Books, 2005), 439.
12. Francesca Bariela-Chiappini et al., "Five Perspectives on Intercultural Business Communication," *Business Communication Quarterly* 66, no. 3 (2003): 73–96.
13. Ursula Hess and Pierre Philippot, *Group Dynamics and Emotional Expression* (New York: Cambridge University Press, 2007).
14. Kristina B. Dahlin, Laurie R. Weingart, and Pamela J. Hinds, "Team Diversity and Information Use," *Academy of Management Journal* 68, no. 6 (2005): 1107–23; Susannah B. F. Paletz et al., "Ethnic Composition and Its Differential Impact on Group Processes in Diverse Teams," *Small Group Research* 35, no. 2 (2004): 128–57; Leisa D. Sargent and Christina Sue-Chan, "Does Diversity Affect Efficacy? The Intervening Role of Cohesion and Task Interdependence," *Small Group Research* 32, no. 4 (2001): 426–50.
15. Jeswald W. Salacuse, *The Global Negotiator: Making, Managing, and Mending Deals around the World in the Twenty-First Century* (New York: Palgrave Macmillan, 2003), 96–97.
16. Jeanne Brett, Kristin Behfar, and Mary C. Kern, "Managing Multicultural Teams," *Harvard Business Review* 84, no. 11 (2006): 84–91.
17. John E. Tropman, *Making Meetings Work,* 2nd ed. (Thousand Oaks, CA: Sage, 2003), 28.
18. Rebecca E. Burnett, "Productive and Unproductive Conflict in Collaboration," in *Making Thinking Visible: Writing, Collaborative Planning, and Classroom Inquiry,* ed. Linda Flower et al. (Urbana, IL: NCTE, 1994), 239–44.

19. Kitty O. Locker, "What Makes a Collaborative Writing Team Successful? A Case Study of Lawyers and Social Service Workers in a State Agency," in *New Visions in Collaborative Writing,* ed. Janis Forman (Portsmouth, NJ: Boynton, 1991), 37–52.
20. Lisa Ede and Andrea Lunsford, *Singular Texts/Plural Authors: Perspectives on Collaborative Writing* (Carbondale, IL: Southern Illinois Press, 1990), 66.

Chapter 9

1. Drake Bennett, "I'll Have My Robots Talk to Your Robots," *Bloomberg Businessweek,* February 21, 2011, 51–61.
2. Jonathan B. Spira, "The Knowledge Worker's Day: Our Findings," *Basex* (blog), November 4, 2010, http://www.basexblog.com/2010/11/04/our-findings/.
3. Xerox Newsroom, "For Government Workers: Easing Information Overload Will Save," news release, February 19, 2009, http://news.xerox.com/pr/xerox/NR_2009Feb19_Xerox_and_Harris_Interactive_Public_Sector_Survey.aspx
4. Symantec.cloud, "Death to PST Files: The Hidden Costs of Email," *White Paper: Email Management,* Symantec Corporation, March 2011, http://www.radicati.com/?page_id=46.
5. "Internet 2010 in Numbers," *Pingdom* (blog), January 12, 2011, http://royal.pingdom.com/2011/01/12/internet-2010-in-numbers.
6. Jonathan B. Spira and Cody Burke, "Intel's War on Information Overload: A Case Study," *Basex,* August 2009, http://bsx.stores.yahoo.net/inwaroninov.html.
7. Gail Fann Thomas and Cynthia L. King, "Reconceptualizing E-Mail Overload," *Journal of Business and Technical Communication* 20, no. 3 (2006): 252–87.
8. Geoffrey A. Fowler, "Are You Talking to Me?" *Wall Street Journal,* April 25, 2011, R5.
9. Soumitra Dutta, "What's Your Personal Social Media Strategy?" *Harvard Business Review* 88, no. 11 (November 2010): 127; and Emily Glazer, "Fund Firms Cautiously Tweet Their Way into a New World," *Wall Street Journal,* February 7, 2011, R1.
10. Jennifer Saba, "Facebook Tops Google as Most Visited Site in U.S.," Reuters, December 30, 2010, http://www.reuters.com/article/2010/12/30/us-facebook-google-idUSTRE6BT40320101230.
11. Geoffrey A. Fowler, "Are You Talking to Me?" *Wall Street Journal,* April 25, 2011, R5.
12. "11 Career Ending Facebook Faux Pas," *Forbes,* April 13, 2010, http://www.forbes.com/2010/04/13/how-facebook-ruined-my-career-entrepreneurs-human-resources-facebook_slide.html.
13. Serena Dai, "Tweeting Diners Get Quick Response," *Des Moines Register,* September 25, 2010, 3E.
14. William M. Bulkeley, "Playing Well with Others: How IBM's Employees Have Taken Social Networking to an Unusual Level," *Wall Street Journal,* June 18, 2007, R10.
15. Catherine Arnst, "Can Patients Cure Health Care?" *BusinessWeek,* December 15, 2008, 58–61.
16. "Social Networking Rules Vary among Businesses," *Des Moines Register,* October 19, 2009, 6E.
17. Kristin Byron, "Carrying Too Heavy a Load? The Communication and Miscommunication of Emotion by E-Mail," *Academy of Management Review* 33, no.2 (2008): 309–27.
18. Jane Larson, "Be Careful with Business E-Mail Content," *Des Moines Register,* January 21, 2008, 2D.
19. Dinesh Ramde, "Anti-War E-Mail to Soldier Stirs Furor," *Des Moines Register,* January 24, 2007, 5A.
20. Dalia Fahmy, "Can You Be Fired for Sending Personal E-Mails at Work?" *ABC News,* December 17, 2009, http://abcnews.go.com/Business/GadgetGuide/supreme-court-employee-rights-privacy-workplace-emails/story?id=9345057.
21. MailerMailer LLC, *Email Marketing Metrics Report,* July 2010, http://www.mailermailer.com/resources/metrics/index.rwp.
22. Gilbert Ross, "Black Box Backfire," *Wall Street Journal,* April 21, 2007, A8.
23. Jeanne Whalen, "Shareholders Sue Glaxo over Avandia Disclosure," *Wall Street Journal,* June 13, 2007, D7.
24. Mike Spector, "New IRS Rules Help Donors Vet Charities: Revised Tax Form Will Make Nonprofits Reveal More about How They Spend," *Wall Street Journal,* May 29, 2008, D1.
25. Bob Mills, e-mail message to author.
26. "Lighting a Fire under Campbell," *BusinessWeek,* December 4, 2006, 96; and Lee Smith, "Linden Lab's Love Machine," *Talking Internal Communication* (blog), June 15, 2008, http://talkingic.typepad.com/foureightys_lee_smith_tal/2008/06/linden-labs-love-machine.html.
27. Kenneth Blanchard and Spencer Johnson, *The One Minute Manager* (New York: William Morrow, 1982), 19.

Chapter 10

1. Ben Levisohn, "Getting More Workers to Whistle," *BusinessWeek,* January 28, 2008, 18.
2. Robert I. Sutton, *The No Asshole Rule: Building a Civilized Workplace and Surviving One That Isn't* (New York: Warner Business Books, 2007), 45–48.
3. William Ury, *The Power of a Positive No: How to Say No and Still Get to Yes* (New York: Bantam Books, 2007), 41–42.
4. L. Gordon Crovitz, "The Business of Restoring Trust," *Wall Street Journal,* January 31, 2011, A13.
5. Peter D. Timmerman and Wayne Harrison, "The Discretionary Use of Electronic Media: Four Considerations for Bad News Bearers," *Journal of Business Communication* 42, no. 4 (2005): 379–89.
6. Jack Ewing, "Nokia: Bring on the Employee Rants," *BusinessWeek,* June 22, 2009, 50.
7. Kitty O. Locker, "Factors in Reader Responses to Negative Letters: Experimental Evidence for Changing What We Teach," *Journal of Business and Technical Communication* 13, no. 1 (January 1999): 21.
8. Locker, "Factors in Reader Responses to Negative Letters: Experimental Evidence for Changing What We Teach," 25–26.
9. Sharon S. Brehm and Jack W. Brehm, *Psychological Reactance: A Theory of Freedom and Control* (New York: Academic Press, 1981), 3.
10. Elizabeth Bernstein, "I'm Very, Very, Very Sorry. . .Really?" *Wall Street Journal,* October 19, 2010, D1, D2.
11. Melanie Trottman and Andy Pasztor, "Southwest Airlines CEO Apologizes for Lapses," *Wall Street Journal,* March 14, 2008, B1.
12. Norihiko Shirouzu and Yoshio Takahashi, "Toyota Apologizes for Massive Recall," *Wall Street Journal,* February 6, 2010, B1, B5; and Alex Taylor III, "Toyota's No-Show Leadership," *CNNMoney,* February 4, 2010, http://money.cnn.com/2010/02/04/autos/toyota.fortune/index.htm.
13. hallmark@update.hallmark.com, e-mail message to author, May 8, 2007.
14. Scott McCartney, "What Airlines Do When You Complain," *Wall Street Journal,* March 20, 2007, D1; Nick Wingfield,

"Steve Jobs Offers Rare Apology Credit for iPhone," *Wall Street Journal,* September 7, 2007, B1.
15. Laura Landro, "The Informed Patient: Hospitals Own Up to Errors," *Wall Street Journal,* August 25, 2009, D1.
16. Ury, *The Power of a Positive No: How to Say No and Still Get to Yes,* 19.
17. Nathan Becker, "Taco Bell Plans Spin as Critic Drops Beef," *Wall Street Journal,* April 20, 2011, B7.
18. "United Airlines to Unplug Number of Complaints," *Wall Street Journal,* February 11, 2009, D6.
19. Scott McCartney, "The Airlines' Squeaky Wheels Turn to Twitter," *Wall Street Journal,* October 28, 2010, D1, D5.
20. Crovitz, "The Business of Restoring Trust," A13.
21. Stephen W. Gilliland et al., "Improving Applicants' Reactions to Rejection Letters: An Application of Fairness Theory," *Personnel Psychology* 54, no. 3 (2001): 669–704; Robert E. Ployhart, Karen Holcombe Ehrhart, and Seth C. Hayes, "Using Attributions to Understand the Effects of Explanations on Applicant Reactions: Are Reactions Consistent with the Covariation Principle?" *Journal of Applied Social Psychology* 35, no. 2 (2005): 259–96.
22. John P. Hausknecht, David V. Day, and Scott C. Thomas, "Applicant Reactions to Selection Procedures: An Updated Model and Meta-Analysis," *Personnel Psychology* 57, no. 3 (2004): 639–84.
23. Kenneth Blanchard and Spencer Johnson, *The One Minute Manager* (New York: William Morrow, 1982), 59.
24. Carol Hymowitz, "Though Now Routine, Bosses Still Stumble During Layoff Process," *Wall Street Journal,* June 25, 2007, B1.
25. Carol Hymowitz, "Personal Boundaries Shrink as Companies Punish Bad Behavior," *Wall Street Journal,* June 18, 2007, B1.

Chapter 11

1. Jay Heinrichs, "Spot Fallacies," in *Thank You for Arguing: What Aristotle, Lincoln, and Homer Simpson Can Teach Us about the Art of Persuasion* (New York: Three Rivers Press, 2007), chap. 14.
2. Jay A. Conger, "The Necessary Art of Persuasion," *Harvard Business Review* 76, no. 3 (May–June 1998): 88.
3. John Kotter and Holger Rathgeber, *Our Iceberg Is Melting: Changing and Succeeding under Any Conditions* (New York: St. Martin's Press, 2005), 140.
4. Jonah Lehrer, *How We Decide* (New York: Houghton Mifflin Harcourt, 2009), 26, 235.
5. EACA Promotional Marketing Council, "Cyriel (84) Needs a Job," accessed June 22, 2011, http://www.adforum.com/creative_archive/award/reel_detail.asp?tb=1&awy=2006&ID=16&AD=6684218&TDA=VD1tK1qetl.
6. Michael Sanserino, "Peer Pressure and Other Pitches," *Wall Street Journal,* September 14, 2009, B6.
7. Vanessa Fuhrmans, "Training the Brain to Choose Wisely," *Wall Street Journal,* April 28, 2009, D1.
8. Daniel H. Pink, *Drive: The Surprising Truth about What Motivates Us* (New York: Riverhead Books, 2009), 145.
9. Chip Heath and Dan Heath, *Made to Stick: Why Some Ideas Survive and Others Die* (New York: Random House, 2007), 195–98; and Mark Schoofs, "Novel Police Tactic Puts Drug Markets out of Business: Confronted by the Evidence, Dealers in High Point, N.C., Succumb to Pressure," *Wall Street Journal,* September 27, 2006, A1, A16.
10. "'Don't Mess with Texas' Anti-Litter Ad Features Strait," *Des Moines Register,* May 11, 2010, 2A.
11. National Science Foundation, "Why 'Scientific Consensus' Fails to Persuade," news release, September 13, 2010, http://www.nsf.gov/news/news_summ.jsp?cntn_id=117697.
12. Min-Sun Kim and Steven R. Wilson, "A Cross-Cultural Comparison of Implicit Theories of Requesting," *Communication Monographs* 61, no. 3 (September 1994): 210–35; and K. Yoon, C. H. Kim, and M. S. Kim, "A Cross-Cultural Comparison of the Effects of Source Creditability on Attitudes and Behavior Intentions," *Mass Communication and Society* 1, nos. 3 and 4 (1998): 153–73.
13. Daniel D. Ding, "An Indirect Style in Business Communication," *Journal of Business and Technical Communication* 20, no. 1 (2006): 87–100.
14. Peggy E. Chaudhry and Stephen A. Stumpf, "Getting Real about Fakes," *Wall Street Journal,* August 17, 2009, R4.
15. E. L. Fink et al., "The Semantics of Social Influence: Threats vs. Persuasion," *Communication Monographs* 70, no. 4 (2003): 295–316.
16. Malcolm Gladwell, *The Tipping Point: How Little Things Can Make a Big Difference* (New York: Little, Brown and Company, 2002), 96–98.
17. David Wessel, "Inside Dr. Bernanke's E.R." *Wall Street Journal,* July 18, 2009, W3.
18. Judge Baker Children's Center and Campaign for a Commercial-Free Childhood, "Tell Toy Companies: Target Parents, Not Kids, with Holiday Ads," accessed June 22, 2011, http://www.commercialfreechildhood.org/pressreleases/holidaymarketer.htm.
19. Ray Considine and Murray Raphael, *The Great Brain Robbery* (Los Angeles: Rosebud Books, 1980), 95–96.
20. Phred Dvorak, "How Understanding the 'Why' of Decisions Matters," *Wall Street Journal,* March 19, 2007, B3.
21. Chip Heath and Dan Heath, *Made to Stick: Why Some Ideas Survive and Others Die* (New York: Random House, 2007), 165–68.
22. Scott Robinette, "Get Emotional," *Harvard Business Review* 79, no. 5 (May 2001): 24–25.
23. Martin Lindstrom, *Buyology: Truth and Lies about Why We Buy* (New York: Doubleday, 2008), 133–34.
24. "Around the World," *Washington Post,* March 27, 2009, A14.
25. Susan Linn and Alvin Poussaint, "Campaign for a Commercial-Free Childhood," accessed June 22, 2011, http://commercialfreechildhood.org/actions/lettertoceo.pdf.
26. "Fort Hood Suspect's Personnel File Filled with Praise, Despite Problems," *Des Moines Register,* January 20, 2010, 5A.
27. Samuel A. Culbert, "Get Rid of the Performance Review! It Destroys Morale, Kills Teamwork, and Hurts the Bottom Line. And That's Just for Starters," *Wall Street Journal,* October 20, 2008, R4; and Jared Sandberg, "Performance Reviews Need Some Work, Don't Meet Potential," *Wall Street Journal,* November 20, 2007, B1.
28. Jeffrey Zaslow, "The Most-Praised Generation Goes to Work," *Wall Street Journal,* April 20, 2007, W1, W7.
29. Joe Light, "Performance Reviews by the Numbers," *Wall Street Journal,* June 29, 2010, D4.
30. Steve Salerno, "As Seen on TV: But Wait. . . There's More!" *Wall Street Journal,* March 25, 2009, A11.
31. "How to Launch a Direct-Mail Campaign," *BusinessWeek SmallBiz,* August/September 2008, 28.
32. Barbara Kiviat, "Why We Buy: Consumers Tend to Go with What (Little) They Know," *Time,* August 27, 2007, 50–51.

33. Jeffrey Gitomer, *Little Red Book of Sales Answers: 99.5 Real World Answers That Make Sense, Make Sales, and Make Money* (Upper Saddle River, NJ: Prentice Hall, 2005), 112.
34. Beth Negus Viveiros, "Gifts for Life," *Direct,* July (2004): 9.
35. Charity: water homepage, accessed June 22, 2011, http://www.charitywater.org.
36. Lee Rood, "Little Raised over Phone Goes to Charity," *Des Moines Register,* December 14, 2008, 1A.
37. Fund-raising letter from Kevin M Ryan. Undated correspondence.
38. Maxwell Sackheim, *My First Sixty-Five Years in Advertising* (Blue Ridge Summit, PA: Tab Books, 1975), 97–100.

Chapter 12

1. U.S. Department of Labor Bureau of Labor Statistics, "Number of Jobs Held, Labor Market Activity, and Earnings Growth among the Youngest Baby Boomers: Results from a Longitudinal Survey," news release, September 10, 2010, USDL-10-1243, http://www.bls.gov/news.release/pdf/nlsoy.pdf.
2. Richard Nelson Bolles, *What Color Is Your Parachute? A Practical Manual for Job-Hunters and Career-Changers* (Berkeley: Ten Speed Press, 2007), 209.
3. Sarah E. Needleman, "It Isn't Always a Job behind an Online Job Posting: Employment Ads on the Web Can Lead You to Marketing Pitches, or Worse: Ways to See Which Ones Are Sincere," *Wall Street Journal,* February 17, 2009, B14.
4. Anne Fisher, "10 Ways to Use Social Media in Your Job Hunt," CNNMoney, May 20, 2011, http://management.fortune.cnn.com/2011/01/13/10-ways-to-use-social-media-in-your-job-hunt/.
5. Cross-Tab, *Online Reputation in a Connected World, 2010,* accessed April 2, 2011, http://go.microsoft.com/?linkid=9709510.
6. Teri Evans, "Penn State, Texas A&M Top the List: Recruiters Like One-Stop Shopping for Grads with Solid Academics, Job Skills, Record of Success," *Wall Street Journal,* September 13, 2010, B1; and Alexandra Cheney, "Firms Assess Young Interns' Potential: Businesses Look to Pools for Full-Time Hires, Tracking Future Employees as Early as Freshman Year," *Wall Street Journal,* September 13, 2010, B10.
7. Accountemps: A Robert Half Company, "Résumés Inching Up: Survey Shows Longer Résumés Now More Acceptable," news release, March 20, 2010, http://accountemps.rhi.mediaroom.com/index.php?s=189&item=210.
8. Elizabeth Blackburn-Brockman and Kelly Belanger, "One Page or Two? A National Study of CPA Recruiters' Preferences for Résumé Length," *The Journal of Business Communication* 38 (2001): 29–45.
9. CareerBuilder.com,"Nearly Half of Employers Have Caught a Lie on a Résumé, CareerBuider.com Survey Shows," press release, July 30, 2008, http://www.careerbuilder.com/share/aboutus/pressreleasesdetail.aspx?id=pr448&sd=7%2f30%2f2008&ed=12%2f31%2f2008.
10. National Association of Colleges and Employers, "Job Outlook: What Do Employers Look for in Candidates? Spotlight Online for Career Services Professionals," news release, January 6, 2010, http://www.naceweb.org/Publications/Spotlight_Online/2010/0106/Job_Outlook_What_do_employers_look_for_in_candidates_.aspx.
11. Roni Noland, "It's Not a Disaster if Your Old Boss Won't Provide a Reference," *Boston Globe,* March 8, 2009, 5.
12. Phil Elder, "The Trade Secrets of Employment Interviews," paper presented at the Association for Business Communication Midwest Convention, Kansas City, MO, May 2, 1987.
13. "For Job Seekers, Company Sites Beat Online Boards, Social Media," *Wall Street Journal,* April 4, 2011, B8.
14. John B. Killoran, "Self-Published Web Résumés: Their Purposes and Their Genre Systems," *Journal of Business and Technical Communication* 20, no. 4 (2006): 425–59.
15. Keith J. Winstein and Daniel Golden, "MIT Admissions Dean Lied on Résumé in 1979, Quits," *Wall Street Journal,* April 27, 2007, B1.
16. Jon Weinbach, "The Admissions Police," *Wall Street Journal,* April 6, 2007, W1, W10.
17. ". . . And I Invented Velcro," *BusinessWeek,* August 4, 2008; "Nearly Half of Employers Have Caught a Lie on a Résumé, CareerBuilder.com Survey Shows"; and Cari Tuna and Keith J Winstein, "Economy Promises to Fuel Résumé Fraud: Practices Vary for Vetting Prospective Employees, but Executives Usually Face Tougher Background Checks," *Wall Street Journal,* November 17, 2008, B4.

Chapter 13

1. Max Messmer, "Cover Letter Still Important in Online Age," *Pittsburgh Post–Gazette,* August 10, 2008, J1.
2. Jason Fried, "Never Read Another Résumé," *Inc.,* June 2010, 37.
3. Katharine Hansen and Randall Hansen, "The Basics of a Dynamic Cover Letter," in *Cover Letter Resources for Job-Seekers,* accessed April 9, 2011, http://www.quintcareers.com/cover_letter_basics.html.

Chapter 14

1. Robert Half Finance and Accounting, "Tell Me about Yourself," news release, November 8, 2005, http://rhfa.mediaroom.com/index.php?s=305&item=560; and Accountemps, "Hiring Manager to Applicant: 'What Is Your Greatest Weakness?': Accountemps Survey Finds Job Seekers Make Most Mistakes During Interview," news release, September 23, 2010, http://accountemps.rhi.mediaroom.com/interview_mistakes.
2. Accountemps, "The Personal Connection: Survey Shows That in Hiring Process, There's No Substitute for Being There," news release, September 11, 2008, http://accountemps.rhi.mediaroom.com/PersonalConnection.
3. Rachel Emma Silverman, "Choosing the Appropriate Clothes Adds to Stress of the Job Interview," *Wall Street Journal,* April 17, 2001, http://online.wsj.com/article/SB987460110121095208.html.
4. Victoria Knight, "Personality Tests as Hiring Tools," *Wall Street Journal,* March 15, 2006, http://online.wsj.com/article/SB114237811535098217.html.
5. Dana Mattioli, "Sober Thought: How to Mix Work, Alcohol: Taking Cues from Bosses and Clients Can Keep Parties or Meals under Control," *Wall Street Journal,* December 5, 2006, B10.
6. Geoff Smart and Randy Street, *Who: The A Method for Hiring* (New York: Ballantine, 2008).
7. U.S. Department of Commerce Economics and Statistics Administration and Executive Office of the President, Office of Management and Budget, White House Council on Women and Girls, *Women in America: Indicators of Social and Economic Well-Being,* March 2011, 32, http://www.whitehouse.gov/sites/default/files/rss_viewer/Women_in_America.pdf.

Chapter 15

1. "Wikipedia," *Wikipedia,* last modified June 11, 2011, http://en.wikipedia.org/wiki/Wikipedia.

2. Katie Hafner, "Seeing Corporate Fingerprints in Wikipedia Edits," *New York Times,* August 19, 2007, http://www.nytimes.com/2007/08/19/technology/19wikipedia.html?_r=1; and Jonathan Zittrain, Robert McHenry, Benjamin Mako Hill, and Mike Schroepfer, "Ten Years of ~~Inaccuracy and~~ Remarkable Detail: Wikipedia," *Bloomberg Businessweek,* January 10, 2011, 57–61.
3. Julia Angwin and Geoffrey A. Fowler, "Volunteers Log Off as Wikipedia Ages," *Wall Street Journal,* November 23, 2009, A1, A17.
4. "United States: The Ladder of Fame; College Education," *The Economist,* August 26, 2006, 35.
5. Sharon L. Lohr, *Sampling: Design and Analysis* (Pacific Grove, CA: Duxbury Press, 1999), 3.
6. "Television Measurement," The Nielsen Company, accessed June 11, 2011, http://www.nielsen.com/us/en/measurement/television-measurement.html.
7. Cynthia Crossen, "Fiasco in 1936 Survey Brought 'Science' to Election Polling," *Wall Street Journal,* October 2, 2006, B1.
8. Carl Bialik, "Which Is Epidemic—Sexting or Worrying about It? Cyberpolls, Relying on Skewed Samples of Techno-Teen, Aren't Always Worth the Paper They're Not Printed On," *Wall Street Journal,* April 8, 2009, A9.
9. Ann Zimmerman, "Revenge of the Nerds: How Barbie Got Her Geek On," *Wall Street Journal,* April 9, 2010, A1.
10. Andrew O'Connell, "Reading the Public Mind," *Harvard Business Review* 88, no. 10 (October 2010): 28.
11. Carl Bialik, "Online Polling, Once Easily Dismissed, Burnishes Its Image," *Wall Street Journal,* August 7, 2010, A2.
12. Lean Christian, Scott Keeter, Kristen Purcell, and Aaron Smith, "Assessing the Cell Phone Challenge," Pew Research Center, May 20, 2010, http://pewresearch.org/pubs/1601/assessing-cell-phone-challenge-in-public-opinion-surveys.
13. Paul J. Lavrakas, "Nonresponse Issues in U.S. Cell Phone and Landline Telephone Surveys," National Research Council, February 17, 2011, http://www7.nationalacademies.org/cnstat/Lavakas%20Pres.pdf.
14. Carl Bialik, "Making It Count: Alternative Ways to Gather Census Data," *Wall Street Journal,* July 31, 2010, A2; and Paul J. Lavrakas, "Nonresponse Issues in U.S. Cell Phone and Landline Telephone Surveys," National Research Council, February 17, 2011, http://www7.nationalacademies.org/cnstat/Lavakas%20Pres.pdf.
15. Palmer Morrel-Samuels, "Getting the Truth into Workplace Surveys," *Harvard Business Review* 80, no. 2 (February 2002): 111–18.
16. See, for example, "Many Who Say Homosexual Relations Should Be Illegal Change Their Minds When Told It Could Mean That Consenting Adults Could Be Prosecuted for Activities in Their Own Homes," Public Agenda, accessed June 12, 2011, http://www.publicagenda.org/charts/many-who-say-homosexual-relations-should-be-illegal-change-their-minds-when-told-it-could-mean-consenting-adults; Public Agenda, "Now Online—Just the Facts on Gay Rights," news release, February 5, 2002, http://www.publicagenda.org/press-releases/now-online-just-facts-gay-rights; Pew Forum on Religion and Public Life, "Religious Beliefs Underpin Opposition to Homosexuality," November 18, 2003, http://pewforum.org/Gay-Marriage-and-Homosexuality/Religious-Beliefs-Underpin-Opposition-to-Homosexuality.aspx.
17. "20 Questions Journalists Should Ask about Poll Results," Public Agenda, accessed June 12, 2011, http://www.publicagenda.org/pages/20-questions-journalists-should-ask-about-poll-results.
18. Palmer Morrel-Samuels, "Getting the Truth into Workplace Surveys," *Harvard Business Review* 80, no. 2 (February 2002): 116.
19. Carl Bialik, "When Wording Skews Results in Polls," *Wall Street Journal,* September 25, 2010, A2.
20. Earl E. McDowell, Bridget Mrolza, and Emmy Reppe, "An Investigation of the Interviewing Practices of Technical Writers in Their World of Work," in *Interviewing Practices for Technical Writers,* ed. Earl E. McDowell (Amityville, NY: Baywood Publishing, 1991), 207.
21. Thomas Hunter, "Pulitzer Winner Discusses Interviewing," *IABC Communication World,* April 1985, 13–14.
22. Julie Jargon, "Kiwi Goes Beyond Shine in Effort to Step Up Sales," *Wall Street Journal,* December 20, 2007, B1.
23. Peter Noel Murray, "Focus Groups Are Valid When Done Right," *Marketing News,* September 1, 2006, 21, 25.
24. Emily Steel, "The New Focus Groups: Online Networks: Proprietary Panels Help Consumer Companies Shape Products, Ads," *Wall Street Journal,* January 14, 2008, B6.
25. Kelly K. Spors, "The Customer Knows Best," *Wall Street Journal,* July 13, 2009, R5.
26. Andrew O'Connell, "Reading the Public Mind," *Harvard Business Review* 88, no. 10 (October 2010): 28.
27. Louise Witt, "Inside Intent," *American Demographics* 26, no. 2 (2004): 34.
28. The Nielsen Company, "DVR Viewing of Programs and Commercials Varies Based on Time Elapsed between Original Airing and Playback, Nielsen Says," news release, February 15, 2007, http://www.nielsen.com/us/en/insights/press-room/2007/DVR_Viewing_of_Programs_and_Commercials_Varies_Based_on_Time_Elapsed_Between_Original_Airing_and_Playback_Nielsen_Says.html.
29. Emily Steel, "TV Networks Launch Big Campus Push; New Nielsen System Makes College Students Coveted Ratings Draw," *Wall Street Journal,* March 5, 2007, B3.
30. Christopher Meyer and Andre Schwager, "Understanding Customer Experience," *Harvard Business Review* 85, no. 2 (February 2007): 116–26.
31. Daniel Kruger, "You Want Data with That?" *Forbes* 173, no. 6 (2004): 58.

Chapter 16

1. Monica M. Clark, "Nielsen's 'People Meters' Go Top 10: Atlanta Debut Is Milestone for Device That's Redefining Local TV Audiences' Image," *Wall Street Journal,* June 30, 2006, B2.
2. Gerald J. Alred, Charles T. Brusaw, and Walter E. Oliu, *The Business Writer's Handbook,* 8th ed. (New York: St. Martin's Press, 2006), 248–50; William Horton, "The Almost Universal Language: Graphics for International Documents," *Technical Communication* 40, no. 4 (1993): 687; Thyra Rauch, "IBM Visual Interface Design," *The STC Usability PIC Newsletter,* January, 1996, 3; L. G. Thorell and W. J. Smith, *Using Computer Color Effectively: An Illustrated Reference* (Englewood Cliffs, NJ: Prentice Hall, 1990), 12–13.
3. Eric Kenly and Mark Beach, *Getting It Printed: How to Work with Printers & Graphic Imaging Services to Assure Quality, Stay on Schedule, and Control Costs,* 4th ed. (Cincinnati, OH: HOW Design Books, 2004), 68.
4. Miles A. Kimball and Ann R. Hawkins, *Document Design: A Guide for Technical Communicators* (Boston: Bedford/St. Martins, 2008), 253.
5. Edward R. Tufte, *The Visual Display of Quantitative Information,* 2nd ed. (Cheshire, CT: Graphics Press, 2001), 107–21.

6. Charles Kostelnick, "The Visual Rhetoric of Data Displays: The Conundrum of Clarity," *IEEE Transactions on Professional Communication* 51, no. 1 (2008): 116–30.
7. Jerry Bowyer, "In Defense of the Unemployment Rate," *National Review Online,* March 5, 2004, http://article.nationalreview.com/?q=YzNiZGJjYTZlZDNlYzQzZjUxNzFlMWJkNjBiODIzMmI; Mark Gongloff, "Payroll Growth Disappoints," *CNN Money,* December 5, 2003, http://money.cnn.com; and Joint Economic Committee, "Charts: Economy," last updated August 27, 2004 http://jec.senate.gov.
8. Tufte, *The Visual Display of Quantitative Information,* 74–75.
9. Brett Michael Dykes, "British Airways Red-Faced over Faux Image of Bin Laden Boarding Pass," in *Yahoo! News,* June 2, 2010, http://news.yahoo.com/s/ynews/ynews_ts2359/print.
10. Richard B. Woodward, "Debatable 'Evidence,'" *Wall Street Journal,* May 4, 2011, D5.
11. Steven Mufson, "Altered BP Photo Comes into Question," *Washington Post,* July 20, 2010, http://www.washingtonpost.com/wp-dyn/content/article/2010/07/19/AR2010071905256.html.
12. Laura T. Coffey, "Gasp! Babies' Fat Rolls Being Airbrushed Away?" in TodayHealth.com, November 24, 2009, http://today.msnbc.msn.com/id/34046700/ns/today-today_health/t/gasp-babies-fat-rolls-being-airbrushed-away/.
13. John Long, "Ethics in the Age of Digital Photography," in *National Press Photographers Association: Educational Workshops,* accessed June 1, 2011, http://www.nppa.org/professional_development/self-training_resources/eadp_report/index.html.
14. Accenture Advertisement, *Fortune,* August 16, 2010, 17.
15. Lon Tweeten, "Seek & Find," *Time,* June 25, 2007, 64.

Chapter 17

1. "NSF at a Glance," in *About,* accessed May 24, 2011, http://www.nsf.gov/about/glance.jsp; and "NIH Budget," in *About NIH,* accessed May 23, 2011, http://www.nih.gov/about/budget.htm.
2. Julianne Pepitone, "Census Bureau Submits $1B Job Creation Proposal: Agency Received Funds through the Stimulus Measure," *CNNMoney.com,* accessed May 24, 2011, http://money.cnn.com/2009/04/10/news/economy/census_stimulus/index.htm.
3. Susan J. Wells, "Merging Compensation Strategies," *HRMagazine* 49, no. 5 (May 2004): 66.
4. Wells, "Merging Compensation Strategies," 66.
5. Todd Dorman, "No Double-Space? No Grant for You: Preschool Grants Tossed for Failing to Double-Space on Application," *Ames Tribune,* September 12, 2007, B1.
6. "Grant Programs and Details," in *National Endowment for the Humanities,* accessed May 28, 2011, http://www.neh.gov/grants/grants.html.
7. Laura K. Grove, "Finding Funding: Writing Winning Proposals for Research Funds," *Technical Communication* 51 (2004): 25–33.
8. Christine Peterson Barabas, *Technical Writing in a Corporate Culture: A Study of the Nature of Information* (Norwood, NJ: Ablex Publishing, 1990), 327.

Chapter 18

1. Carl Bialik, "Sizing Up Crowds Pushes Limits of Technology," *Wall Street Journal,* February 5, 2011, A4; Constance A. Krach and Victoria A. Velkoff, "Centenarians in the United States," *Current Population Reports, Series P23-199RV,* U.S. Bureau of the Census (Washington, DC: Government Printing Office, 1999), 14; "National Longitudinal Surveys Frequently Asked Questions: Does BLS Have Information on the Number of Times People Change Careers in Their Lives?" Bureau of Labor Statistics, last modified September 23, 2010, http://www.bls.gov/nls/nlsfaqs.htm; and Carl Bialik, "Claims of Thanksgiving Excess Fueled by Feast of Fuzzy Data," *Wall Street Journal,* November 25, 2009, A20.
2. John Hechinger, "Some States Drop Testing Bar," *Wall Street Journal,* October 30, 2009, A3.
3. Thomas Wailgum, "Eight of the Worst Spreadsheet Blunders," *CIO,* August 17, 2007, http://www.cio.com/article/131500/Eight_of_the_Worst_Spreadsheet_Blunders.
4. Jeffrey Zaslow, "An Iconic Report 20 Years Later: Many of Those Women Married After All," *Wall Street Journal,* May 25, 2006, D1.
5. Arlene Weintraub, "What the Doctors Aren't Disclosing: A New Study Shows How Authors of Medical Journal Articles Flout Rules on Revealing Conflicts of Interest," *BusinessWeek,* May 26, 2008, 32.
6. Erick H. Turner et al., "Selective Publication of Antidepressant Trials and Its Influence on Apparent Efficacy," *New England Journal of Medicine* 358, no. 3 (2008): 252.
7. Scott Thurm, "Mind the Gap: Employment Figures Tell Different Stories," *Wall Street Journal,* October 2, 2010, A2.
8. Stephen E. Moore, "655,000 War Dead?" *Wall Street Journal,* October 18, 2006, A20.
9. Neil Munro and Carl M. Cannon, "Data Bomb," *National Journal,* January 4, 2008, http://www.freerepublic.com/focus/f-news/1948378/posts.
10. Malcolm Gladwell, *The Tipping Point: How Little Things Can Make a Big Difference* (New York: Little, Brown and Company, 2002), 146; Steven D. Levitt and Stephen J. Dubner, *Freakonomics: A Rogue Economist Explores the Hidden Side of Everything* (New York: William Morrow, 2005), 119–41.
11. Carl Bialik, "Weddings Are Not the Budget Drains Some Surveys Suggest," *Wall Street Journal,* August 24, 2007, B1.
12. Carl Bialik, "Numbers Show China Beats U.S. in Net Use, but Which Numbers?" *Wall Street Journal,* March 28, 2008, B1.
13. Vivien Beattie, Alpa Dhanani, and Michael John Jones, "Longitudinal Perspective Investigating Presentational Change in U.K. Annual Reports," *Journal of Business Communication* 45, no. 2 (April 2008): 186–95.
14. Frederick F. Reichheld, "The One Number You Need to Grow," *Harvard Business Review* 81, no. 12 (December 2003): 46–54.
15. Jakob Nielsen, "Risks of Quantitative Studies," *Alertbox,* March 1, 2004, http://www.useit.com/alertbox/20040301.html; and Dan Seligman, "The Story They All Got Wrong," *Forbes,* November 25, 2002, 124.
16. "Tiger Effect? Not This Year," *Wall Street Journal,* April 15, 2008, B6.
17. "NASA Releases Information on Federal Survey of Pilots," *Des Moines Register,* January 1, 2008, 2A.
18. George A. Miller, "The Magical Number Seven, Plus or Minus Two: Some Limits on Our Capacity for Processing Information," *Psychological Review* 63, no. 2 (1956): 81–97.
19. Richard J. Connors, ed., *Warren Buffett on Business: Principles from the Sage of Omaha* (Hoboken, NJ: Wiley, 2010), 125.

Chapter 19

1. Sara Silver, "With Its Future Now Uncertain, Bell Labs Turns to Commerce: Storied Font of Basic Research Gets More Practical Focus Amid Worry over a Merger," *Wall Street Journal*, August 21, 2006, A1.
2. Julie Hill, "The Attention Deficit," *Presentations* 17, no. 10 (2003): 26.
3. Patricia Fripp, "Want Your Audiences to Remember What You Say? Learn the Importance of Clear Structure," Fripp and Associates, accessed June 25, 2011, http://www.fripp.com/art.clearstructure.html.
4. Jon Birger et al., "The Best Advice I Ever Got," *Fortune*, May 12, 2008, 70.
5. Chip Heath and Dan Heath, *Made to Stick: Why Some Ideas Survive and Others Die* (New York: Random House, 2007), 7.
6. Heath and Heath, *Made to Stick*, 16–18.
7. Ann Burnett and Diane M. Badzinski, "Judge Nonverbal Communication on Trial: Do Mock Trial Jurors Notice?" *Journal of Communication* 55, no. 2 (2005): 209–24.
8. "Executives' Remarks Annoy Coastal Residents," *Des Moines Register*, June 17, 2010, 4A.
9. Michael Waldholz, "Lab Notes," *Wall Street Journal*, March 19, 1991, B1; and Dave Zielinski, "Perfect Practice," *Presentations* 17, no. 5 (2003): 30–36.
10. G. Michael Campbell, *Bulletproof Presentations* (Franklin Lakes, NJ: Career Press, 2003), 66–67.

Chapter 1

Page 3: Bloomberg via Getty Images; p. 6: The McGraw-Hill Companies, Inc./Jill Braaten, photographer; p. 8: U.S. Coast Guard photograph by Petty Officer 2nd Class NyxoLyno Cangemi; p. 9: AP Images/NASA/JPL/Caltech; p. 27: Roll Call/ Getty Images; p. 31: John Kuntz/The Plain Dealer/Landov.

Chapter 2

Page 33: ©LWA-Dann Tardif/CORBIS; p. 34: MY M&M'S, the letter M and the M&M'S Red Character are registered trademarks of Mars, Incorporated and its affiliates. These trademarks are used with permission. Mars, Incorporated is not associated with McGraw-Hill Higher Education. Advertisement printed with permission of Mars, Incorporated; p. 42: No credit needed; p. 44: Anoek De Groot/AFP/Getty Images.

Chapter 3

Page 57: AP images/Ric Feld; p. 61: AP Images/Orlin Wagner; p. 67: Kitty O. Locker, by permission of Joseph-Beth Booksellers; p. 74: Javier Larrea/AGE Fotostock.

Chapter 4

Page 87: Peter Barreras/AP Images for Pepsi Refresh Project; p. 91: Courtesy of Fujitsu Computer Products of America, Inc.; p. 92: Kelvin Murray/Getty Images/Stone; p. 97: © Jeff Sciortino Photography; p. 97: © Jeff Sciortino Photography; p. 98: Keith Brofsky/Getty Images; p. 102: Courtesy of McAfee.com; p. 105: Getty Images; p. 106: © Medioimages/Alamy; p. 106: Brent Winebrenner/Getty Images/Lonely Planet Images; p. 107: Tim Graham/Getty Images.

Chapter 5

Page 117: AP Images/Jose Luis Magana; p. 120: © The McGraw-Hill Companies, Inc./Lars A. Niki; p. 139: Photodisc/Getty Images; p. 143: © CORBIS.

Chapter 6

Page 157: Brent Stirton/Getty Images; p. 161: 2010Census.gov.

Chapter 7

Page 181: Chris McGrath/Getty Images; p. 184: © Matt Stroshane/epa/Corbis; p. 189: Toru Yamanaka/AFP/Getty Images; p. 190: © Matthew Ashton/Alamy; p. 191: Photo by Harry Baumert, Copyright 2006, The Des Moines Register and Tribune Company. Reprinted with permission; p. 193: © PCL/ Alamy; p. 194: AP Images/Eugene Hoshiko.

Chapter 8

Page 205: U.S. Coast Guard/Getty Images; p. 213: Ryan McVay/ Getty Images; p. 220: ©Bettmann/CORBIS, p. 223: Photo by David Hawe © Blue Man Productions, Inc.

Chapter 9

Page 233: Bloomberg via Getty Images; p. 235T: Digital Vision/ Getty Images; p. 235B: Angelo Cavalli/Getty Images/The Image Bank; p. 242: AAGAMIA/Getty Images; p. 252: AP Images/Candice Choi; p. 253: Courtesy of Toyota Motor North America, Inc.; p. 256: No credit needed.

Chapter 10

Page 277: Bloomberg via Getty Images; p. 279: DreamPictures/Getty Images; p. 282: Bill Pugliano/Getty Images; p. 289: Courtesy, Schwinn Bicycle; p. 291: Christopher Robbins/ Getty Images; p. 292: AP Images/Nick Ut; p. 294: Courtesy of Hallmark Licensing, Inc.; p. 298: Reprinted with permission of the Columbus Dispatch.

Chapter 11

Page 313: AP Images/Air New Zealand, HO; p. 315: Courtesy of Charitywater.org; p. 327: Courtesy of the Central Asia Institute; p. 329: www.savedaruf.org Reprinted with permission of ©Olivier Jobard/SIPA Press; p. 330: Image courtesy of the United States Army and the Ad Council; p. 337: Keith Brofsky/ Getty Images; p. 338: Courtesy of the World Health Organization, http://www.who.int/impact/FinalBrochureWHA2008a.pdf; p. 346: The McGraw-Hill Companies, Inc., Mark Dierker, photographer.

Chapter 12

Page 367: AP Images/Minnesota Public Radio, Tim Post; p. 381: Mark Ralston/AFP/Getty Images.

Chapter 13

Page 409: AP Images/The Indianapolis Star, Matt Detrich.

Chapter 14

Page 439: Win McNamee/Getty Images; p. 443: TL Rubberball Productions; p. 443: TM Jack Hollingsworth/Getty Images/ Photodisc; p. 443: TR Imagewerks/Getty Images; p. 443: BL Jurgen Reisch/Getty Images/Digital Vision; p. 443: BM Digital Vision; p. 443: BR C. Borland/PhotoLink/Getty Images; p. 455: Copyrights ©Danny Turner. All rights reserved; p. 457: © Hans Neleman/zefa/Corbis.

Chapter 15

Page 469: MCT via Getty Images; p. 473: McGraw-Hill Companies, Inc, Jill Braaten, photographer; p. 474: © PhotoAlto; p. 480: Junko Kimura/Getty Images; p. 489: AP Images/Nati Harnik, FILE.

Chapter 16

Page 499: no credit needed public domain; p. 506: Evaristo SA/ AFP/ Getty Images; p. 507: Getty Images (3).

Chapter 17

Page 533: © Banana Stock Ltd.

Chapter 18

Page 553: © Nathaniel Welch Photography; p. 557: Yoshikazu Tsuno/AFP/Getty Images; p. 560: David Woolley/Getty Images/ Digital Vision.

Chapter 19

Page 607: Getty Images; p. 609: The McGraw-Hill Companies, Mark Dierker, photographer; p. 611: © Image Source/PunchStock; p. 620: © Thinkstock/PunchStock.

NAME INDEX

A

Abboud, Leila, 327
Abelson, Max, 249–250
Abkowitz, Alyssa, 167
Ackermann, Josef, 70
Adam, Christine, 16
Adams, John, 220
Agner, Chuck, 625
Ahlgren, Ingrid, 445
Albright, Madeleine, 96
Alred, Gerald J., 510
Alsop, Ron, 32
Alter, Alexandra, 41
Amin, Massoud, 320
Anderson, M., 363
Anson, Chris M., 15
Armstrong, David, 89, 112
Arrowsmith, Ross, 291

B

Badre, Albert N., 165
Baer, Justin, 29
Bakalar, Nicholas, 512
Ballard, Larry, 152
Balsillie, Jim, 610
Bandow, Diane, 305
Barabas, Christine, 545
Barnes, Julian E., 500
Barnum, P. T., 625
Baron, Dennis E., 70
Baron, Renee, 30
Barry, Dave, 92
Barwis, Patrick, 34
Batjargal, Bat, 182
Bauerlein, Valerie, 87
Bazerman, Max H., 332
Beatty, Sally, 343
Beaudette, Marie, 79
Beck, Catherine, 538
Bell, Ted, 415
Berland, Russ, 321
Bernanke, Ben, 121, 321
Bernard, Tara Siegel, 545
Bernstein, Elizabeth, 255
Berzon, Alexandra, 205
Best, Joseph, 67
Best, Robert O., 4
Bezos, Jeff, 8, 266–267
Bialik, Carl, 560
Bieber, Justin, 479
Biederman, Joseph, 112
Bilton, Ricardo, 191
Bin Laden, Osama, 508, 517
Blackmon, Douglas A., 205
Blagojevich, Rod, 103
Blair, John G., 66
Blanchard, Kenneth, 257, 295, 333
Blumenthal, Karen, 339
Bodenberg, Thomas M., 596
Boehret, Katherine, 72
Boice, Robert, 120
Bolles, Richard, 369
Boone, Christian, 490
Boothman, Nicholas, 330
Borker, Ruth A., 95–96
Boroditsky, Lera, 194
Boston, Bruce O., 668
Bowen, Matt, 209
Bowyer, Jerry, 507
Brady, Diane, 610
Brandt, John R., 614
Brat, Illan, 481
Braud, Gerard, 122
Breitbart, Andrew, 490
Brokaw, Tom, 320
Brusaw, Charles T., 510
Bryant Quinn, Jane, 489
Buffett, Warren, 4, 35, 89, 93, 122–124, 219, 340, 570
Buijzen, M., 363
Bumiller, Elisabeth, 499
Burke, Lisa A., 618
Burns, Enid, 526
Burris, Ethan R., 257
Burton, Thomas M., 89
Bush, George H. W., 500
Bush, George W., 128, 141
Butler, Paul, 319
Byron, Ellen, 31, 39, 472

C

Camerer, Colin F., 189
Cameron, James, 560
Campoy, Ana, 205
Capell, Perri, 4
Capelli, Paul, 442
Carnegie, Dale, 340
Cashman, Kevin, 69
Casselman, Ben, 205, 291
Casson, Lionel, 660
Catan, Thomas, 129, 347
Caver, Keith, 183
Chabon, Michael, 140
Chambers, Paul, 103
Chan, Jackie, 479
Chao, Loretta, 32, 53
Cheng, Andria, 184
Churchill, Winston, 125, 190
Clark, Dorie, 371, 496
Clements, Jonathan, 338
Coburn, Tom, 439
Coher, Adam, 327
Colchester, Max, 90
Combs, Sean, 289
Conant, Douglas, 256
Connors, Richard J., 93
Covey, Stephen, 99–100
Crossen, Cynthia, 221
Crovitz, L. Gordon, 159
Cullen, Lisa Takeuchi, 92
Cyrus, Miley, 479

D

Dahl, Cheryl, 81
Daly, John, 622
Davis, Bob, 329
DeBruicker, John, 417
Delaney, Kevin J., 502
Del Ray, Jason, 561
Deshpandé, Rohit, 326
Deter, James R., 257
De Vogue, Ariane, 439
Dooley, Sheena, 511
Dowling, Daisy Wademan, 333
Dreyfack, Raymond, 5
Duarte, Nancy, 499, 619
Dubner, Stephen J., 557
Duffy, Rhonda, 325
Dulek, Ronald, 138
Dunn, Patricia, 11
Dvorak, Phred, 218, 384

E

Eaves, Elisabeth, 97
Echikson, William, 327
Ede, Lisa, 221
Edmondson, Dave, 397
Ehrenfeld, Temma, 290
Elashmawi, Farid, 195–196
Elbert, David, 286
Elder, Phil, 394
Elop, Stephen, 277
Epstein, Stephen, 95
Erard, Michael, 609
Evans, Kelly, 270
Everson, Damen, 320

F

Fahrenthold, David A., 68
Farid, Hany, 508
Farrell, Greg, 543
Felberbaum, Michael, 36
Felten, Eric, 258
Felton, Nicholas, 553
Fieg, John P., 66
Fisher, Anne, 221, 440, 456
Flanagan, Denny, 65
Flesher, Jared, 378
Fleytas, Andrea, 205
Fogg, Piper, 32
Foley, Mark, 11, 239
Forsberg, L. Lee, 15
Foust, Dean, 515
Fowler, Geoffrey A., 185, 191
Francis, Theo, 197
Franklin, Benjamin, 220
Freed, Richard C., 496, 534
Freed, Shervin, 496, 534
Freedman, Adam, 117
Freedman, Aviva, 16
Freedman, David H., 234, 501
Freidman, W., 363
Friedman, Thomas, 107, 184
Frisch, Bob, 210

G

Gallo, Carmine, 607, 620
Galloni, Alessandra, 329
Gardner, Erle Stanley, 117
Gardner, Howard, 91
Gardner, Joe, 316
Garner, Marcus K., 490
Gates, Bill, 89
Gates, Melinda, 89
Gauthier-Villars, David, 341

Gawande. Atul, 212, 250
Gitomer, Jeffrey, 5, 341
Gladwell, Malcolm, 96, 321, 557
Goldman, Matt, 223
Goldstein, Daniel G., 349
Goleman, Daniel, 93, 99
Goman, Carol Kinsey, 99
Goodwin, Doris Kearns, 216
Gordon, Gloria, 12
Gordon, Thomas, 94
Goward, Paul, 69
Graham, Ellen, 70
Grassley, Chuck, 103
Greenberg, Elizabeth, 29
Greenspan, Alan, 121–122
Gremler, Dwayne D., 348
Grisham, John, 117
Guttenburg, Karl-Theodor, 489
Gwinner, Kevin P., 348

H

Hackman, J. Richard, 208
Haefner, Rosemary, 461
Hafner, Katie, 160
Hairston, Maxine, 653
Hall, Edward, 186, 192
Hamm, Jon, 320
Harrington, Richard J., 471
Harris, Philip, R., 186, 195–196
Harrison, David A., 257
Harrison, Wayne, 281–282
Harrison, Scott, 315
Hartley, Greg, 488
Hartley, James, 485
Hasan, Nidal, 333
Hayward, Tony, 621
Hazelton, Michael, 57
Heath, Chip, 319, 321, 614–615
Heath, Dan, 319, 321, 614–615
Hechinger, John, 91, 504, 555
Helft, Miguel, 496
Hempel, Jessi, 367
Herzberg, Frederick, 43
Higgins, Mary, 41
Hoak, Amy, 325
Hofstede, Geert, 186
Holderbaum, Kirk, 569
Holstein, William J., 533
Hopkinson, A., 479
Hsieh, Tony, 37, 58, 91, 452
Hunt, Debra, 305
Hyman, Ira, 235
Hymowitz, Carol, 79, 473

I

Iacocca, Lee, 340
Imus, Don, 70
Inada, Miho, 107
Ip, Greg, 121
Italie, Leanne, 240

J

Jacobs, Frank, 507
Jacques, Susan, 219
James, Judi, 448
James, Karen E., 618
Jefferson, Thomas, 220
Jobs, Steve, 181, 290, 607, 610
Johnson, John H., 12
Johnson, Linda A., 505
Johnson, Spencer, 295, 333
Johnson, Patt, 126
Johnson, Spencer, 257
Jones, Benjamin, 217
Joyce, Susan, 396

K

Kadlec, Daniel, 121
Kagan, Elena, 439
Kanter, Rosabeth Moss, 91
Kapp, Jonathan, 95
Katz, Susan M., 531
Kauffman, Clark, 88
Kazoleas, Dean C., 561
Kendrick, Deborah, 75
Kennedy, John F., 212, 320
Kilen, Mike, 191
Kilpatrick, Kwame, 11
King, W. J., 92
Kingsbury, Kathleen, 101
Kinzie, Susan, 355
Klemperer, Otto, 68
K'naan, 46
Knight, Rebecca, 446
Koppel, Nathan, 35
Kostelnick, Charles, 159
Kotter, John, 318
Kotter, John P., 623
Koval, Robin, 58, 67
Kristof, Nicholas D., 315
Kronholz, June, 143
Kronhoz, June, 622
Kullin, Hans, 479
Kushner, David, 43
Kutner, Mark, 29

L

Labianca, Joe, 100
Landon, Alf, 480
Landro, Laura, 108, 242, 316
Lashinsky, Adam, 506
Lederer, Richard, 655, 663
Lee, Louise, 346
Lehrer, Jonah, 217, 318
Leighton, Ronald, 136
Lencioni, Patrick, 207–208
Lentz, Jim, 3, 287
Levack, Kinley, 624
Levinsky, Dave, 547
Levitt, Steven D., 557
Levitz, Jennifer, 112
Li, Xiangling, 98
Lichtenfeld, J. Leonard, 557
Light, Joe, 621
Lin, Sara, 72
Lincoln, Abraham, 138–139, 216, 617
Lindstrom, Martin, 329
Linn, Susan, 363
Livers, Ancella B., 183
Lockyer, Bill, 144
Lonchar, Kenneth, 397
Long, John, 508
Lorenz, Mary, 381
Lovill, Jeff, 665
Lowry, Tom, 45
Lublin, Joann S., 42
Luhby, Tami, 380
Lunsford, Andrea, 221
Lutz, Peter, 562

M

Mackay, Harvey, 38
Madoff, Bernie, 88
Maltz, Daniel, 95–96
Mandell, Judy, 130
Marr, Merissa, 185
Marshall, Jack, 526
Martin, Joanne, 563
Martin, Timothy W., 252
Martinelli, Rose, 616
Mattews, Robert Guy, 195
Mattioli, Dana, 59
McCabe, Donald, 91
McCartney, Scott, 57, 65
McChrystal, Stanley, 499
McCord, Elizabeth, 571
McGregor, Jena, 58, 556
McGroarty, Patrick, 489
McPherson, John, 68
Meehan, Sean, 34
Meek, James Gordon, 439
Mehrabian, Albert, 622
Microsoft, 499
Middleton, Diana, 119
Mieszkowski, Katherine, 615
Miller, Amy, 455
Miller, Lisa, 44
Mishori, Ranti, 284
Moore, Stephen E., 558
Moran, Robert T., 186
Moran, Sarah V., 186
Morrel-Samuels, Palmer, 483
Morsch, Laura, 370
Mullens, John W., 544
Mundy, Alicia, 112, 220
Murphy, Bruce, 53
Murphy, Tom, 131

N

Nardon, Luciara, 196
Neilsen, Jakob, 296
Nicholson, Rob, 218
Nielsen, Jakob, 169–172, 278, 496
Nooyi, Indra K., 87
Norvig, Peter, 617
Nussbaum, Bruce, 482

O

Obama, Barack, 13, 27, 74–75, 128, 216, 439, 469, 479, 500, 595, 677
O'Connell, Vanessa, 205
O'Dell, Walden, 141
O'Leary, George, 397
Oliu, Walter E., 509

P

Papows, Jeffrey, 397
Patrick, Aaron O., 191
Paulson, Henry, 321
Pausch, Randy, 99
Piëch, Anton, 192
Pink, Daniel, 318–319
Pope, Justin, 616
Poussaint, Alvin, 363
Powell, Mike, 613
Power, Stephen, 205
Powers, Melanie E., 563
Pritchard, Justin, 562

Q

Quattrone, Frank, 11
Quinn, Jennifer, 306

R

Raice, Shayndi, 496
Rajaratnam, Raj, 88
Rand, David, 446
Raskin, Andy, 97
Rathgeber, Holger, 318
Reddy, Sudeep, 309
Reilly, William K., 205
Richards, John, 658
Ricks, David A., 292
Rigdon, Joan E., 221
Roehm, Julie, 11
Romano Joseph D., 496, 534
Roosevelt, Franklin, 480
Rosa, Joe Antonio, 190
Rosales, Lani, 293
Rossi, Lisa, 139
Rumsfeld, Donald, 92
Rundle, Rhonda L., 269

S

Safire, William, 654
Sagario, Dawn, 279
Sanchez-Runde, Carlos J., 196
Sandberg, Sheryl, 559
Sands, Judith Gordon, 94
Sanford, Mark, 11
Saranow, Jennifer, 102
Sauer, Beverly A., 570
Sauer, Patrick J., 536
Scarpelli, Maureen, 317
Schechner, Sam, 140
Schlessinger, Laura, 70
Schryer, Catherine, 297
Schwagler, Nathan, 409
Scott, James Calvert, 138
Seligman, Martin, 64
Sellin, Lawrence, 499
Shah, Neil, 522
Shakur, Tupac, 289
Shaw, Mona, 287
Shaw, Paul, 157
Shea, Christopher, 134
Sherrod, Shirley, 490
Silverman, Rachel, Emma, 343
Singletary, Michelle, 295
Sisario, Ben, 496
Sloan, Allan, 290
Sloan, Ann H., 439
Smart, Geoff, 454
Speizer, Irwin, 47
Spencer, Jane, 506
Spilka, Rachel, 47
Spors, Kelly K., 209
St. Clair, Stacy, 100
Staley, Oliver, 508
Stanford, Duane D., 46
Steel, Emily, 336, 342
Steers, Richard M., 196
Stein, Joel, 612
Steinberg, Brian, 191
Stewart, Julia, 333
Stock, Kyle, 385
Stonecipher, Harry, 11, 296
Stott, Phil, 441
Street, Randy, 454
Stross, Randall, 10
Sturgeon, Julie, 386
Suchan, James, 138
Svanberg, Carl-Henric, 621
Swanson, William, 92

T

Tannen, Deborah, 95–96
Tenbrusel, Ann E., 332
Thaler, Linda Kaplan, 58, 67
Timmerman, Peter D., 281–282
Tischler, Linda, 109
Tonnesen, Gretchen, 417
Toyoda, Akio, 287
Tropman, John, 214
Truss, Lynne, 141
Trust, Michael, 395
Tufte, Edward R., 158, 505, 507, 616
Turow, Scott, 117

U

Ulijn, Jan M., 98

V

Valkenburg, Patti M., 363
Vasicek, Brent, 491
Vazire, Simine, 514
Vella, Matt, 214
Viswanathan, Madhubalan, 190
Vogt, Peter, 424

W

Walker, Joe, 373
Walker, Marcus, 489
Walsh, Bill, 132, 142
Washburn, Carolyn, 64, 474
Watson, Lucinda, 415
Waugh, Barbara, 615
Weber, Roberto A., 189
Weiner, Anthony, 241
Welch, Liz, 223
White, Erin, 213, 222, 328
Whitehead, Lorne A., 623
Wiio, Osmo A., 14
Wildstrom, Stephen H., 144
Wingert, Pat, 557
Winslow, Ron, 220
Winter, Caroline, 249–250
Winters, Dan, 340
Wollner, Herr Fritz, 420
Womack, Sean, 11
Woods, Tiger, 559
Worthen, Ben, 169

Y

Ye, Juliet, 53, 506
Yunus, Muhammad, 89

Z

Ziegler, Chris, 277
Zupek, Rachel, 397, 409
Zweig, Jason, 337

COMPANY INDEX

A

About.com, 371
Absolut Vodka, 507
Accion.org, 351
AcronymFinder.com, 129
ADCouncil, 330, 338
Adobe Photoshop, 508
ADT Security Services, 31
Aflac, 241
Agency for Healthcare Research and Quality, 316
Ahiida, 44
AIG, 88
Airbus, 9
Air New Zealand, 313
Alamo Drafthouse, 293
AlertDriving.com, 183
Alexa.com, 176
Alibaba, 32
Allstate, 36
Aloft Group Inc., 209
AltaVista, 475
Amazon.com, 35, 41–42, 52, 58, 104, 266–267, 318, 373, 470
American Academy of Matrimonial Lawyers, 240
American Express, 59, 74, 109
American Psychological Association (APA), 490, 677–681
American's Job Bank, 370
American Society of Clinical Oncology, 279
Amy's Ice Cream, 455
Angieslist.com, 52, 293
Anglo's, 195
Anheuser-Busch, 504
AOL, 10, 238, 479
Apostrophe Protection Society, 658
Apple, 109, 235, 277, 290, 508, 610
Apple Inc., 181, 191, 607
Apple Store, 478, 610
Arbitron, 488
Architectural Digest, 595
Arm & Hammer, 31
Associated Press, 508
Association for Business Communication, 292
Association for Qualitative Research Newsletter, 488
Association of American Colleges and Universities, 375
AT&T, 108, 550
Author Stream, 618
Automatic Data Processing, 556

B

BabyNameWizard.com, 516
Bank of America, 236, 333
Basex, 236
BBB.org, 411 (fig.)
BearingPoint, 321
Bear Sterns, 88
Bell Atlantic, 538
Bell Labs, 99, 610
Berkshire Hathaway Inc., 93, 122–123, 219
Best Buy, 4, 41–42, 126
Better Business Bureau (bbb.org), 411
Blendtec, 240
BlogHub, 282
Bloomberg Businessweek, 411, 477 (fig.)
Bloomingdale's, 130
Blue Man Group, 223
Boeing, 9, 11, 296, 550
Bon Appétit, 346, 595
Borsheims, 219
Boston College, 504
Bridgestone Firestone, 8
British Airways, 508
British Petroleum (BP), 9, 205, 508, 562, 621
Build-a-Bear, 126
Bureau of Economic Analysis, 477 (fig.)
Burger King, 103

C

Cabela's, 58
Campbell Soup, 256, 481
Campus Career Center, 371, 371 (fig.)
Capital Relocation Services, 151–152
CARE, 341
CareerBuilder, 370–371, 380–381, 396, 409, 412, 442, 447, 458, 461
Career Rookie, 371
Catalyst.org, 531
Catfish Bend Casinos, 88
CBS, 70
Census Bureau, 477 (fig.)
Center for Remote Sensing of Ice Sheets (CReSIS), 516
Center for Science in the Public Interest (CSPI), 614
Centers for Disease Control and Prevention, 516, 519 (fig.)
Central Asia Institute, 327
Central Intelligence Agency, 192
Cerberus Capital Management, 189
Change.org, 351
Charity: water, 315
Chicago Tribune, 370
Chinese Student Association, 472
Chipotle, 240
Choice Hotels, 31
ChooseMyPlate.gov, 525 (fig.)
Chrysler, 282
Church of Scientology, 478
Ciee.org, 421
Cisco, 104–105, 236
Citigroup, 550
Claritas, Inc., 35
ClickZ.com, 531
CLIR. *See* Council of Library and Information Resources (CLIR)
Clorox, 36
CNBC, 442
CNN.com, 411 (fig.)
CNN/FNNFN.com, 477 (fig.)
Coca-Cola, 45–46, 106, 126, 199, 504
College Central, 371
College Grad Job Hunter, 371
Color Hunter, 166
ColorMe Company, 94
Color Palette Generator, 166
Colorschemedesigner.com, 168
Comcast.net, 10, 59, 104, 287
Consumer Affairs, 293
Continental Airlines, 42
Copyworks, 169
CorporateInformation.com, 411 (fig.)
Costco, 184
Costco Taiwan, 184
Council of Library and Information Resources (CLIR), 600
Covenant House, 344
Craigslist, 373
Crate & Barrel, 342
Credit Suisse First Boston, 11
CReSIS. *See* Center for Remote Sensing of Ice Sheets (CReSIS)
CSPI. *See* Center for Science in the Public Interest (CSPI)
CVS, 31
Cyborlink, 194

D

Daimler Chrysler, 144, 189
Danbury Mint, 341
DaVita, 42
Dealer.com, 92
Dell Inc., 239–240
Del Monte, 488
Delta Air Lines, 57, 103, 268, 293
De Tijd, 318
Detroit News, 370
Deutsche Bank, 70
Dictionary.com, 104
Diebold, 141, 478
Direct Marketing Association, 339
Disney, 184
Domino's, 10–11
DonorsChoice, 342
Donorschoose.org, 351
Dosomething.org, 351
Dover Air Force Base, 500
Dow Chemical, 550
Dow Jones & Company, Inc., 520 (fig.)
Dr Pepper, 240
Duke Energy, 483
Dunkin' Donuts, 36

E

Earthwatch, 339
EBay, 32, 170, 373
Education Index, 476 (fig.)
EffectiveMeetings.com, 206
Emcore, 291
Emotiv, 234
EmploymentGuide.com, 370
Enron, 11
Ethics Resource Center, 22
ExecuNet, 378
EZ-Pass, 103

F

Faberge Perfumes, 5
Facebook, 13, 34–36, 101, 103, 240–241, 370, 378, 391, 441, 488
Federal Drug Administration (FDA), 249, 556

Federal Highway Administration Drivers, 164
Federal Jobs Career Central, 370
Federal Trade Commission, 104
FedStats, 477 (fig.)
FEDSTATS.gov, 531
Firestone Tire and Rubber Company, 3
Firstgiving.org, 351
FirstWest Insurance, 347, 350
Five O'Clock Club, The, 371
Flat Earth Society, 124
Flickr, 35
Foote, Cone & Belding, 444
Forbes, 595
Forbes.com, 411 (fig.)
Ford Motor Company, 3, 8–9, 72, 81, 501, 550
Forrester Research Inc., 169
Fortune, 367, 411
Foundation Center, The, 544
Four Seasons Hotels, 58
Frank Davis Fish Company, 347
Frank Lewis Alamo Fruit, 341
FreeOnlineSurvey.com, 495
Friends Committee on National Legislation, 522 (fig.)

G

Gallup Organization, 484
Gamestation, 258
Game-Works, 473
Gap Inc., 81
Gaylord Hotels, 31
General Electric, 106, 373
General Motors, 75, 501
Getsatisfaction.com, 52
Giant Food, 252
Gillette, 92
GlaxoSmithKline, 88, 249
Global Edge, 476 (fig.)
Gmail, 479
Goldman Sachs, 9, 88, 249–250, 269–270
Goodyear, 329
Google, 32, 35, 89, 92, 103, 109–110, 206, 220, 238, 240–241, 277, 372, 378, 414, 441–442, 475, 489, 545, 550, 600, 677
Google Earth, 502
Gorat's, 219
GoToMeeting, 236
Grameen Bank, 89
Growthink, 547
GTE, 536

H

Habitat for Humanity, 344
Halliburton, 9, 205
Hallmark, 61, 294
Hallmark Flowers, 290
Hannaford Bros., 252
Harlem YMCA, 340
Hart Research Associates, 374–375
Hasbro, 473
HBO, 296
Hewlett-Packard, 11, 92, 108, 504, 614
Hewlett-Packard Labs, 615
Holiday Inn, 46
Home Depot, 64, 222, 550
Honda, 326
Hong Kong Disneyland, 184–185
Hook & Ladder Brewing Company, 94
Hoover's Online, 477 (fig.)
Human Resource Management Resources on the Internet, 476 (fig.)
HyVee, 252

I

IBM, 186, 218, 242, 504
ICU Medical, 213
Ideo, 109
Iiepassport.org, 421
IKEA, 479
Inc.com, 411 (fig.)
Indeed.com, 370
Indeed.com/salary, 411 (fig.)
Indoor Tanning Association, 557
Infomap, 158
Information Mapping, 166
Ingram Micro, 409
Intel, 36, 108
InterContinental Hotels Group, 7
Internet Marketing Resources, 476 (fig.)
Interstate Fidelity Insurance (IFI), 257, 595–596
Irin.com, 411 (fig.)

J

JetBlue, 287, 290
Jobbankinof.org, 411 (fig.)
JobHunterBible.com, 371
Jobsboard.com, 421
John Deere, 677
Johnson & Johnson, 142, 183, 278
Joie de Vivre Hospitality, 92
Joseph Best, 67
JPMorgan Chase & Co., 417, 550
Julia Belle Swain, 421
Jumo.com, 351

K

Kaiser Aluminum, 296
Kaiser Permanente, 108–109, 482
Kaplan Thaler Group, 58
Kentucky Fried Chicken, 192
KidSmart, 536
Killian Branding, 426
Kimberly-Clark, 31
Kinkos, 169
Kiva.org, 351
KnowThis: Knowledge Source for Marketing, 476 (fig.)
Kohler, 31
Kwintessential.co.uk, 194

L

Lands' End, 333
LaQuinta Inns & Suites, 78
Lehman Brothers, 88
Linden Labs, 257
LinkedIn, 98, 240–241, 367, 370–371, 380–381, 391, 406
Litterbutt.com, 102
Loews, 42
Logitech, 236
Lorillard Tobacco Company, 356–357
Los Angeles Times, 287, 289, 370
Los Angeles Zoo, 292
Lotus Corporation, 397
Louisiana State University, 504

M

MailerMailer, 247
Management and Entrepreneurship, 476 (fig.)
Map of the Market, 500
Market Metrix, 92
Massachusetts Institute of Technology, 397
Mattel, 36, 481
McAfee, 102
McDonald's, 47, 65, 106–107, 183, 340, 386, 489, 511
McGraw-Hill Companies, Inc., 521
McLellan Marketing Group, 126
McNamara/Salvia, 212
Medtronic Inc., 89
Merck, 220, 249
Meredith Corporation, 46
Meridiaars.com, 611
Merrill Lynch, 88
Met Life, 64
Metropolitan Home, 595
MGT Design Inc., 569
Miami Herald, 370
Michelin, 108, 329
Michigan Lawsuit Abuse Watch (M-LAW), 251
Microsoft, 5, 92, 104–105, 159–160, 185, 277, 373, 377, 499, 615–619
Mizuho, 107
M&M, 34
Modern Language Association (MLA), 490, 677–678, 682–684
Money.com, 411
MonsterCollege, 371
Monster.com, 370–371, 380, 396, 421, 424
MonsterTalk, 370
Moot Corp., 536
Motion Picture Association of America, 144
Mozilla, 104
MSN.com, 104
MTV Arabia, 45
MTV Networks International, 45
Mybikelane.com, 102
Myers-Briggs, 29
MyPyramid.gov, 524 (fig.)
My3cents.com, 52
My Virtual Reference Desk, 477 (fig.)

N

NASA, 560
National Federation of the Blind, 171
National Oceanic and Atmospheric Administration, 617
National Public Radio, 477 (fig.)
National Rifle Association, 361
National Science Foundation, 103

National Transportation Safety Board, 519 (fig.)
NBC, 10, 321
NETability, Inc., 394
NetParty, 241
Networkerforgood.org, 351
New England Journal of Medicine, 556
New Oriental Education & Technology Group, 111
NewsLink, 477 (fig.)
New York City Department of Transportation, 164
New York Times, 477 (fig.)
New York Transit Authority, 157
Nielsen, 31
Nielsen Media Research, 480, 488
Nike, 556
Ning, 240
Nintendo, 41
Nissan, 72, 326
Nokia, 277, 282
Northwest Airlines, 268–269, 295
Notre Dame, 396
Nynex Corporation, 536

O

OkCupid, 561
Open Source Web Design, 469
Optiontechnologies.com, 611
Oregon Forestry Association, 421
Otis Engineering Corporation, 192
OWL (Purdue Online Writing Lab), 371

P

Pacific Bell, 420
Pantone Color Institute, 167
Parisian Water Works, 341
Parker Pen Company, 192
PatientsLikeMe, 242
Payscale.com, 411 (fig.)
PC Gamer, 337
Peace Corps, The, 385
Pearson Education, Inc., 160
PepsiCo Beverages America, 87, 236, 478
Perdue Farms, 192
PETA, 222, 330
Pew Internet & American Life Project, 575, 601
Pew Research Center, 35
Pfizer, 88
Philadelphia Inquirer, 370
Philanthropic Research Inc., 544
Phish, 36
Piccolo's, 219
PlainLanguage.gov, 122, 131, 153
Planet Feedback, 293
Platewire.com, 102
PollDaddy.com, 495
Post-it, 253, 351
Practical Parenting and Pregnancy, 508
Prars.com, 411 (fig.)
Prezi Presentations, 613
Price Chopper, 252
PricewaterhouseCoopers, 373, 420
Procter & Gamble, 36, 39, 46, 53, 92, 183, 236, 472, 488–489, 547, 550, 556
Psychology Today, 337
Public Agenda, 484

Q

QuickBooks, 489
Quintessential Careers, 275, 371
Qwizdom.com, 611

R

Radicati Group, 4, 237
RadioShack, 396
Ratepoint.com, 52
Raytheon, 92
Rensselaer Polytechnic Institute, 397
Report Watch, 564
Resources for Economists on the Internet, 476 (fig.)
ResumeDoctor.com, 393
Riley Guide, The, 371
RIM, 610
Ringling Bros. and Barnum & Bailey's circus, 625
Ripoff Report, 293
Robert Half International, 141, 369, 382, 410, 426–427, 459
Robin Hood, 89
Romano's Macaroni Grill, 160
Rudepeople.com, 102
Rutgers Accounting Web, 476 (fig.)
Ryerson, 6

S

SABMiller, 327
Salary calculators, 411 (fig.)
SalaryExpert.com, 411 (fig.)
Samsung Electronics, 556
San Jose Mercury News, 370
Sarasota Memorial Hospital, 108
Schering-Plough, 220
Schwinn, 289
SCO Group, 144
Scooter Store Inc., 333
Sears, 319
Securities and Exchange Commission Filings and Forms (EDGAR), 477 (fig.)
Sermo, 241
Servision Inc., 505
Sharp, 557
Siemens Global, 380
Sierra Club, 341
Sive Associates, 460
Skype, 206, 236, 440, 445
Small Business Administration, 477 (fig.)
Smartmoney.com, 500
SmartPros, 476 (fig.)
Smithsonian, 595
Smoking Gun website, 289
Social Finance, 89
Sony, 101
Southern Living, 595
Southwest Airlines, 287, 291–292, 550
Speedo, 480
Spherion Career Center, 371
Spy City Café, 130
Spy Museum, 130
Standard & Poor, 58
Statistical Resources on the Web (University of Michigan Documents Center), 476 (fig.)
Staybridge Suites, 46
Steak 'n Shake, 43
Sticky Fingers RibHouses, 130
Stihl, 64
StockMarketYellowPages.com, 411 (fig.)
Stop & Shop, 252
Studyabroad.com, 421
Suggestionbox.com, 52
SurveyMonkey.com, 495
Sylvania, 74
Sysco, 42

T

Taco Bell, 292
Target, 160, 171
Tarsian and Binkley, 536
Tealeaf, 171
Ted.com, 616
Tello, 293
Tencent Holdings, 32
Tesco PLC, 42
Texas A&M, 504
The Net, 477 (fig.)
Thermo Electron, 109
Thesqueakywheel.com, 52
3M, 106, 109, 183
Toastmasters International, 612
TOMS Company, 94
Toro, 69
Toy Industry Association, 364–365
Toyota Motor Company, 3, 253, 287, 326
Transitionsabroad.com, 421
Transocean, 9, 205, 233
TripAdvisor, 476
Turningtechnologies.com, 611
Turnitin.com, 143
Twitter, 13, 34–36, 103, 110, 240–241, 293, 367, 370–371, 441, 479, 488
Tylenol, 46

U

UC Berkeley Career Center, 392
U-Haul, 222
UNICEF, 343–345
Unilever, 183
Unimark International, 157
United Airlines, 65, 268, 293
United Nations Environmental Program, 531
U.S. Armed Forces, 499
U.S. Army, 499
U.S. Bureau of Labor Statistics, 410, 477 (fig.), 555–556
U.S. Census Bureau, 42, 161 (fig.), 185, 535, 555, 559
U.S. Congress Joint Economic Committee, 531
U.S. Department of Health and Human Services, 544
U.S. Department of Transportation, 555

U.S. Fish and Wildlife Service, 617
U.S. Government Printing Office, 477 (fig.)
U.S. Postal Service, 4, 638, 642
U.S. Securities and Exchange Commission, 126
U.S. Small Business Administration, 544
University of Chicago Business School, 616
University of Colorado, 504
University of Illinois Medical Center, 290
University of Michigan, 504
Universum WetFeet, 394
UNUMProvident, 4
UPS, 106, 193, 515
UPS Logistics, 514–515
U.S. News & World Report, 478
USAA, 58
Usable Web, 170

V

VAA. *See* Virgin Atlantic Airlines (VAA)
Vault.com, 371, 411 (fig.), 441, 445
Veritas, 397
Verizon, 36, 536
Virgin Atlantic Airlines (VAA), 34, 240
Vizu.com, 495
Volkswagen, 336

W

Wachovia, 88
Walgreens, 59, 104
Wall Street Journal, 411, 477 (fig.), 520 (fig.), 559
Walmart, 11, 31, 39, 106, 183, 194, 222
Wal-Mart Stores, Inc., 151–152
Walt Disney, 42
Washington Mutual, 88
Washington Post, 35, 477 (fig.)
WebOnlineSurveys.com, 495
Wetfeet.com, 391, 411 (fig.)
White House Briefing Room, 477 (fig.)
Wikipedia, 239, 478
WikiScanner, 478
WithumSmith & Brown, 569
Witness.org, 43
World Health Organization, 515 (fig.), 521 (fig.)
Wowio, 36

X

Xerox, 109
Xerox Global Services Europe, 7
Xing, 241

Y

Yahoo!, 238, 476, 479
Yammer, 241
Yellowstone National Park, 474
Yelp.com, 52, 293
YouGov, 481–482
YouTube, 10, 43, 58, 103, 313, 441

Z

Zappos, 37, 58, 91–92, 448, 452

A

Abbreviations
and punctuation, 656
state and province, 649 (fig.)
ABI/Inform Thesaurus, 475
Abstracts, 595–596, 599
accede/exceed, 664
accept/except, 664
access/excess, 664
Accident report, 470
Accuracy of visuals, 505–509
Accurate denotations, accurate, 126–127
Acknowledgment response, 94
Acronyms, 129
Action, proposals for, 538
Active listening, 94
Active voice, 129–131
Activities, on résumé, 390
ADA; *see* Americans with Disabilities Act (ADA)
adapt/adopt, 664
Address, 380
Administrative documents, 121–124
Advanced Placement (AP) test, 182
Advertising; *see also* Channel
creative uses of, 36
with e-mail, 35
money for, 35
online, 35
on television, 34–35
Advice, career; *see* Job and interview tips
advice/advise, 664
affect/effect, 664
affluent/effluent, 664–665
Afghanistan, 499
Africa, 189, 504
African Americans, 183, 185
Age, 73–74, 193
Agenda, 219
Agreement
noun-pronoun agreement, 652
subject-verb, 651–654
Airline complaint tips, 294 (fig.)
a lot/allot, 665
Alternatives
elimination of alternatives pattern, 561, 563
in negative messages, 286–287, 288 (fig.)
American Psychological Association (APA), 490, 677–681
Americans with Disabilities Act (ADA), 271
among/between, 665
amount/number, 665
Amplification, 621
Analytical report, 470, 491
and/but/or, 133
Anecdotes
in oral presentation, 612
in sales and fund-raising messages, 338–339
Annual report, 471 (fig.), 564, 569
Answering machine, 238
Antipiracy law, 90
APA; *see* American Psychological Association (APA)
Apologies, 287–290
Apostrophe, 658–659
Appalachian Voices, 502
Appeal to authority, 316
Appeal to ignorance, 316
Appeal to popularity, 316
Appendix, for report, 575
Application essay, 427–428
Appraisal; *see* Performance appraisal
Appropriateness, and positive emphasis of words, 65
Argument, 316
Assumptions, 596, 599
Athletes, job opportunities for, 417
Attachment, e-mail, 647 (fig.)
Attire, for interview, 442–443
attributed/contribute, 665
Audience, 478
adapting message to, 36–42
analyzing
customers, 38
group members, 30–32
individuals, 29–30
organizational culture and discourse community, 32–33
questions for, 37
success of, 41–42
auxiliary, 28–29, 48
benefits to, 48
characteristics of, 42–45
identify and develop, 45–46
and negative information, 66–67
success of, 46–47
channel for, choosing, 33–36
expectations of, 40
external, 6
extrinsic motivators, 43, 49
face time with, 45
gatekeeper, 28–29, 48
generational difference at workplace, 32 (fig.)
identifying, 28–29
information use by, 38–39, 41
internal, 6
intrinsic motivators, 43, 49
involving, in PowerPoint presentation, 618–619
multiple needs of, 47
obstacles to overcome, 39
for oral presentation, 610–611, 623, 625
positive aspects for emphasis, 39–40
primary, 28–29, 48, 314
product returns cost, 47
for proposals, 537
reaction to, initial, 37–38
secondary, 28–29, 48
watchdog, 28–29, 48
writing for, 121
you-attitude with international, 61
Audit report, 471 (fig.)
Author, 556
Authoritative body language, 99
Authors, 478
Automated customer service, 621
Auxiliary audience, 28–29, 48
Average, 557–558
Awards; *see* Honors and awards

B

Baby boomers, designing for, 160
Background, of PowerPoint slide, 617
Background or history, for report, 575, 597
BAC website, 144
Bad news; *see* Negative messages
Bangladesh, 191
Bar chart, 503, 511–512
Bastille Day, 188 (fig.)
Bay of Pigs invasion, 212
bcc (blind copy), 244, 638
Behavior, during interview, 446–447, 449 (fig.)
Behavioral economics, 318
Behavioral interview, 455–456, 464
Beijing Olympics, 480
Belgium, 209
Beliefs; *see* Values, beliefs, and practices
Bias-free language, 58, 652
defined, 70
disabilities and diseases, people with, 74–75
nonracist and nonageist, 73–74
nonsexist language, 70–73
people-first language, 75
Bias-free photos and illustrations, 75
Black box warning, 249
Blind copies (bcc), 244, 638
Block format, 632–633, 634 (fig.), 639 (fig.)
Blocking, in teams, 208
Blogs, 241, 371–373; *see also* Social media
Blunders, verbal, 609
Body
of interview, 448
of report, 575, 580 (fig.)–589 (fig.), 596–597, 599
Body language, 97–99; *see also* Nonverbal communication
authoritative, 99
closed (defensive) body position, 97
eye contact, 189, 619–620
gestures, 190, 212
job interviews, 446–447, 449 (fig.), 455–456
mistakes, 447
open body position, 97
Boilerplate, 144
Boolean search, 475, 476 (fig.)
Boxhead, 510–511
Boxing Day, 188 (fig.)
Brackets, square, 662
Brainstorming, 120–121, 145, 209
Branching question, 485, 491
Brazil, 188 (fig.)
British Commonwealth, 188 (fig.)
Brochure, designing, 167
drafting text, 168
printing, 169
visuals, 168
Budget section, of business plan, 544–545
Buffer, 284–285, 300
Burqinis, 44
Business attire, 442–443
Business communication
accuracy of, 17
amount of, 4

Business communication—*Cont.*
bias in, reducing, 70–75
feedback on, 17–18
international, 197
knowledge for, 15
organization of, 16
questions for analysis, 15–16
situations, understanding and analyzing, 14
solving problems, 14–18
style of, 17
trends in
customer service, 104
data security, 101
diversity, 107–108
electronic privacy, 101–104
entrepreneurship, 109
environmental concern, 105–106
globalization, 106–107
innovation, 109
job flexibility, 108
outsourcing, 107
rapid rate of change, 109
teamwork, 108
work/family balance, 104–105
visual attractiveness of, 16–17
you-attitude, 17
Business documents; *see* Report(s)
Businessese, 129
Business plan, 549
defined, 543
evidence to support superlatives in, 547
executive summary of, 543
keys to successful, 544
and MBA students, 536
Business style; *see* Style
Business writing; *see* Writing
but, 133
Buyology, 329
Bypassing, 126–127, 483

C

Cambodia, 188 (fig.)
Campaign for a Commercial-Free Childhood, 330–332, 362–364
Campus interview, 444
Canada, 185, 188 (fig.)
Canada Day, 188 (fig.)
Cancer news, delivering, 279
Capital letters, 164
Captions, for hearing impaired, 171
Carbon copy/computer copy *(cc); see cc* (carbon/computer copy)
Career fair, letter following up from, 419 (fig.)
Career(s); *see also* Job and interview tips
international experience, 184
objective for, 381–382
"Carrot" motivator, 319
Case, 653–654
Catalog, 346
Causation, 559
cc (carbon/computer copy), 245, 638, 639 (fig.)–641 (fig.), 642, 648 (fig.)
Cell phone technology, 35, 235
Central selling point, 167
Challenger space shuttle, 158
Channel
choosing, for audience, 33–36
creative uses of, 36
for customer service, 40
defined, 33
Charity, 342–343, 559; *see also* Sales and fund-raising messages
Chartjunk, 505–506, 517
China, 18, 185, 188 (fig.), 189, 193, 504, 506
Chinese Internet companies, 32
Chinese New Year (Spring Festival), 188 (fig.)
Christmas, 188 (fig.)
Chronological order, for oral presentation, 615
Chronological progress report, 546–548
Chronological report, 561, 656
Chronological résumé, 378–379, 389 (fig.), 398
Chun Ben, 188
Ciao, 632
Cinco de Mayo, 188 (fig.)
Citation, 489–490, 492, 677
cite/sight/site, 665
Claims and complaints, 293–294
Class research projects, proposals for, 537–542
Clause, 656
Clients, giving bad news to, 279–280
Clinton Global Initiative, 89
Clip art, 167, 505, 617
Close
of interview, 448
of oral presentation, 613–614
Closed (defensive) body position, 97
Closed question, 483–484, 491
Closure report, 471, 565
Clothing, 192
Clowning, in teams, 208
Clustering, 121, 145
Cluster points, 558
Cohesiveness, developing team, 207
Collaborative writing, 220–223; *see also* Writing
College colors, 504
College essays, 143
Colon, 655 (fig.), 659
Color
college, 504
and document design, 166–169
in nonverbal communication, 193
in PowerPoint slides, 618
for presentation visuals, 504–505
for résumé, 378
Color Institute, 167
Columbia space shuttle, 17
Comma, 655 (fig.), 659–660
Comma fault, 656
Comma splice, 656–657
Common ground, for problem-solving message, 325
Communication; *see also* Business communication
ability vs. promotability, 4–5
benefits of improving, 12
classroom vs. workplace contexts, 16
cost of, 6–12
failures of, 8, 17
forms of, 4
importance of, 3
interpersonal, 93–99
on the job, 4–6
and misperception, 5–6
personalities in, 30 (fig.)
portable media player, 236
using technology of, 12–13
Communication channel, 33–36; *see also entries for specific channels*
Communication hardware
capital investments in, 234–235
instant messaging and text messaging, 238–239
portable media players, 236
smartphones, 235
videoconferences, 45, 236
Communication laws, 14
Comparison/contrast report, 561–563
Competitive proposal, 534
complement/compliment, 665
Completeness, 556
Complex sentence, 134
Complimentary close (letter), 632–633
Compliments, 195, 255
compose/comprise, 665
Composing process, 118–120
Compound sentence, 133–134
Computer copy *(cc)*, 245, 638–642, 648
Computer printout, 595
Conclusion
of oral presentation, 613–614
for report, 575, 590 (fig.), 597–599
Concreteness, 614
Confidence interval, 480
Conflict resolution, in teams
criticism responses, 216–218
feelings, checking for, 217
inferences, checking for, 217
limited agreement, buying time with, 217–218
negative feelings, repairing, 216
paraphrasing, 217
presenting problem, 216
search for alternatives, 216
steps in, 216
troubleshooting problems, 215 (fig.)
two-meeting rule, 214
you-attitude in, 218
confuse/complicate/exacerbate, 665
Connotations, 127–128
Consents, 209
Contrast, in document design, 169
Convenience sample, 479, 491
Conventions
defined, 13
design and, 159
in visuals, 504
for web pages, 170–171
Conversational style, 95–96
Coordinating conjunction, 656
Coordination, 207
Cordially, 632
Corporate annual meeting, 219, 222

Corporate culture, 91–93, 319
Corporate investors, proposals by, 533
Corporate perks, 92
Correlation, 559
Correspondence, 5
Cost section, of business plan, 544–545
Counterattacking, 216–218
Courtesy titles, 69, 71
Cover, for report, 574–575
Cover letter, 372, 420; *see also* Job application letter
Credibility, 316–317, 351, 614
Credit report, 470
Criteria, 597, 599
Critical activities, 512
Critical incident, 485
Cross-cultural collaboration, 189; *see also* Culture(s)
Cuban Missile Crisis, 212
Culture(s)
  corporate, 91–93, 319
  diversity in North America, 184–185
  and document design, 165
  global business, 183–184
  high-context, 186
  intercultural competence, 107
  international business communication, 197
  international holidays, 188 (fig.)
  local adaptations, 183–184
  low-context, 186
  monochronic, 192
  native, 319–320
  nonverbal communication, 188–194
  oral communication, 194–195
  organizational, 32–33
  polychronic, 192
  safety problems in multiple languages, 195
  social, 319
  understanding different, 182
  and using visuals and data displays, 510
  values, beliefs, and practices, 187–188
  ways to look at, 185–187
  writing to international audiences, 195–197
Currency, 478, 556
Customer analysis, 38; *see also* Audience
Customers and customer service; *see also* Goodwill
  automated, 621
  channels for, 40
  disgruntled customer, 287
  extraordinary, 65
  giving bad news to, 279–280
  how waiting affects business, 286
  improving, 104
  for more sales and market share, 59
  observing, 488–489
  poor and costly, 10
Customs, interview, 445–448
Cycle, 7
Cycling, 142–143

D

Daily Sun, The, 46
Dangling modifier, 653–654
Dash, 655 (fig.), 660
Data
  charity, 559
  checking quality of, 500
  evaluating sources of, 556–557
  managing, 501
  for oral presentation, 614–615
Data displays; *see* Visuals and data displays
Data security, 101
Dates, writing, 663–664
Dating site, online, 561
Davos economic forum, 329
Debt collection, 347
Decision-making strategy, 209–210
Declaration of Independence, 220
Deepwater Horizon, 205, 233, 469
Default response, 349
Defensive (open) body position, 97
Definitions, 597, 599
Demographic characteristics, of audience, 30–31
Demonstrations, for oral presentation, 614–615
Denotations, accurate, 126–127
dependant/dependent, 665–666
Dependent clause, 656
describe/prescribe, 666
Descriptive abstract, 595–596, 599
Design; *see* Document design; PowerPoint
Deviation bar chart, 512–513
Devil's advocate, 209
Diabetes, multicultural education for, 197
different from/different than, 666
Dilbert cartoon, 88, 105
Dingbats, 167
Direct mail, ethics and, 351
Direct marketing, 336
Direct request
  checklist for, 349
  pattern for, 320–323, 351 (*see also* Sales and fund-raising messages)
Disabilities, talking about people with, 74–75; *see also* Diversity
Disability training, 78
Disciplinary notice, 295
Discourse-based interview, 489
Discourse community, 32
discreet/discrete, 666
Discussion, section of report, 497
Diseases, talking about people with, 74–75
disinterested/uninterested, 666
Diversity; *see also* Culture(s)
  and intercultural competence, 107
  in North America, 184–185
  within teams, 108, 213–214
Diwali, 188 (fig.)
Doctors, interpersonal skills for, 96
Documentation, 490, 492, 677
Document design
  for baby boomers, 160
  brochures, 167–169
  and conventions, 159
  cost savings of good design, 158
  creating, 168–169
  cultural differences in, 165
  document with improved visual impact, 163 (fig.)
  document with poor visual impact, 162 (fig.)
  fonts used in, 165
  guidelines for, 161–167
  highlighting decorative devices, and color, 167
  importance of effective, 158
  levels of, 159–161
  margins, 165–166
  position of elements, 166–167
  for résumés, 378
  usability testing, 172
  web pages, 169–171
  white space, 161–164
  writing process and, 158–159
Dominating, in teams, 206
Dominican Republic, 485
Dot chart, 503
Dot planning, 210
Double negative, 65, 653
Drawings, 514, 595
Drive: The Surprising truth about What Motivates Us (Pink), 318
Dynamic displays, 515–516

E

Eats, Shoots & Leaves (Truss), 141
E-card, 284
"E-discovery" software, 103
Editing, 119, 138; *see also* Grammar
  checklist for, 145
  in collaborative writing, 222–223
  defined, 139, 145
  job application letter, 426–427
  what to look for, 140–142
Education, on résumé, 382–384
Egypt, 504
Electronic privacy, 101–104
Electronic résumé, 394–396
Electronic security methods, 101
Elevator speech, 442
elicit/illicit, 666
Elimination of alternatives report, 561, 563
Ellipses, 662–663
E-mail, 5, 11, 13, 242–243
  advertising with, 35
  with attachment, 647 (fig.)
  cc line, 642, 648 (fig.)
  direct request, 646 (fig.)
  job applications letter via, 422–423
  pet peeves, 244
  reply with copies, 648 (fig.)
  request for information interview, 413 (fig.)
  salutations, 243
  signature block in, 642
  subject lines for, 248–249
E-mail address, 381
Email storage, 8
eminent/immanent/imminent, 666
Emotional appeal, 318, 328–330, 344
Emotional Intelligence (Goleman), 99
Emotional purchasing, researching, 481
Emotions, 614

Employee incentive, 47
Employers; *see also* Job search; Résumé
  and employee skills, 374
  expectations of, 375
  and résumés, 374
Enclosures, 635 (fig.)–637 (fig.), 639 (fig.)–641 (fig.)
Enclosures, in fund-raising letters, 344
Entrepreneurship, 109
Enunciate, 621
Environmental concern, among businesses, 105–106
Environmental map, 502
Essays, college, 143
Ethical dilemma, 69
Ethics, 87, 91, 321, 338
  in business environment, 88, 90 (fig.)
  and direct mail, 351
  Encyclopedia of Ethical Failures, 95
  issues in interviewing, 487
  reporting misconduct, 89
  web resources, 90 (fig.)
  and word choice, 128
Etiquette, for interview, 445; *see also* Behavior, during interview
Europe, 191
Exaggeration, 194–195
Excluding alternatives order, for oral presentation, 615
Executive summary, 543, 574–575, 579 (fig.), 595–596, 599
Expatriate experience, 184
Expenses, incurred during job interview, 447
Experience, for résumé, 385
Expression, impersonal, 60
External audience, 6
External document, 7
Extra design level, 160–161
Extrinsic motivators, 43, 49
Extroversion-Introversion dichotomy, 29–30
Eye contact, 189, 619–620

F

Facebook Flight Status app, 34
Face time, with audience, 45
Face-to-face contact, 237–238
Face-to-face survey, 481
Facial expression, 189–190
Fallacies, 316
False cause, 316
False dichotomy, 316
Family; *see* Work/family balance
Fanagolo, 195
farther/further, 666
Fast food chains, adapting to international cultures, 190
Fear, in giving oral presentation, 619
Feasibility, 537
"Feature creep," 47
Feedback, 17–18
  college essays, 143
  getting and using, 142–144
  for oral presentation, 611
  positive feedback notes, 255–257
  team strategies, 210–211
  thank-you notes, 256–257
Female employees, in Japan, 107
fewer/less, 666
Figures, 594–595; *see also* Visuals and data displays
Figures, in PowerPoint presentation, 617–618
Filler sounds, 621
Firings, 292, 296
Five Dysfunctions of a Team, The (Lencioni), 207–208
Fixed font, 165
Flesch Reading Ease Scale, 144
Flow chart, 595
Focused interview, 454
Focus group, 487–488
Fonts
  defined, 165
  for document design, 165
  for résumé, 378
Forecast, 571
Formalization, 207
Formal meeting, 218–219
Formal report, 5, 470
  appendixes, 575
  background or history, 575, 597, 599
  body of, 575, 580 (fig.)–589 (fig.), 596–597, 599
  components, 574–592
  conclusion, 575, 590 (fig.), 597–599
  cover, 574–575
  descriptive abstracts, 595–596, 599
  example of, 576 (fig.)–592 (fig.)
  executive summary, 574–575, 579 (fig.), 595–596, 599
  introduction, 575, 580 (fig.), 599
  letter or memo of transmittal, 574–575, 577 (fig.), 594
  list of illustrations, 574–575, 578 (fig.), 594–595
  recommendations, 575, 590 (fig.), 597–599
  references, 591(fig.)–592 (fig.)
  release date, 593
  summary abstracts, 595, 599
  table of contents, 574–575, 578 (fig.), 594
  title page, 574–576, 576 (fig.), 593–594
Formation, team, 206–207
Formatting
  e-mail messages, 642
    with attachment, 647 (fig.)
    direct request, 646 (fig.)
    reply with copies, 648 (fig.)
  letter, 638
    block format, 632–633, 634 (fig.), 639 (fig.)
    modified block format, 632–633, 635 (fig.), 637 (fig.), 640 (fig.)
    simplified format, 632–633, 636 (fig.), 641 (fig.)
  memo
    headings, 642
    on memo letterhead, 644 (fig.)
    on plain paper, 643 (fig.)
    second page, 645 (fig.)
forward/foreward, 666
Four-color printing, 169
France, 188 (fig.), 192, 209, 504
Fraud victims, 339
Freakonomics (Levitt & Dubner), 557
Freewriting, 120–121, 145
Friends of the Earth, 106
F-shaped pattern, of design, 169
Full justification, 165–166
Functional report, 561, 565
Funding proposals, 543–544
Fund-raising messages; *see* Sales and fund-raising messages
Fused sentence, 657

G

Gantt chart, 503–504, 512–513
Gatekeeper, 28–29, 48
General to particular or particular to general, 561, 564
Geographic or spatial, 561, 564–565
Germany, 189, 195, 209
Gerund, 135
Gestures, 190, 212
Ghana, 188 (fig.)
Global business, 183–184; *see also* Culture(s)
Globalization, 106–107
Global positioning system (GPS), 103
Global Reporting Initiative, 601
Glossary, 597
GMAT, 91
Good news; *see* Positive or good news messages
good/well, 667
Goodwill; *see also* Customers and customer service
  poor communication losses, 10
  positive emphasis, 58, 63–68
  restoring, 57
  solving ethical dilemmas using, 69
  tone, power, and politeness, 68–69
  you-attitude, 17, 45, 58–63
Goodwill ending, 251, 261
Goodwill presentation, 608, 624
Gossip networking, 100
Government plan, executive summary for, 595; *see also* Formal report
GPS; *see* Global Positioning System (GPS)
Graduate Record Examination, 182
Grammar, 140; *see also* Editing; Punctuation; Writing
  agreement, 651–653
  banished words, 652
  case, 653–654
  dangling modifier, 654
  misplaced modifier, 654
  parallel structure, 654–655
  prediction errors, 655
Grapevine, 98
Greenpeace, 106
Grid system, 166–167
Group, analyzing members of, 30–32
Grouped bar chart, 512–513
Group interview, 450, 458
Group presentations, 624

Groupthink, 212
Guided discussion presentation, 610, 625
Gulf of Mexico, 9, 205, 233
Gulf War, 500
Gunning Fog Index, 144

H

Handshaking, 190
Hasty generalization, 316
Head, 598
Headings, 598
 in document design, 164
 in memos, 642
 in reports, 572–574
 on résumé, 378
Head nod, 190
Healthy eating, information for, 252
Height, 193
Helvetica and the New York City Subway System (Shaw), 157
Hidden job market, 428
Hidden negative, 65–67
High-context culture, 186
Histogram, 512–513
Holidays, international, 187
Home page, creating Web, 170
Honesty, 397
Honors and awards, on résumé, 384
hopefully, 656
How They Achieved: Stories of Personal Achievement and Business Success (Watson), 415
HTML, 171
Humiliation, for debt collection, 347
Humor
 in informative messages, 252
 in oral presentation, 614
Hurricane Katrina, 8–9
Hyphen, 660–661
Hypothetical question, 485

I

i.e./e.g., 667
Illustrations, list of, 574–575, 578 (fig.), 594–595; *see also* Visuals and data displays
Impersonal expression, 60
imply/infer, 667
Incentive program
 customer, 47
 employee, 42
Indented format, 386
Independence Day, 188 (fig.)
Independent clause, 656
India, 185
Individuals, as audiences, 29–30
Informal meeting, 218–219
Informal report, 470
Information, 478
Informational dimension, 206
Informational leader, of team, 209
Information interview, 412–413, 428
Information Mapping, 158, 166
Information overload, 236–237
Information report, 470–471, 491
Informative memo report, 566–568 (fig.)
Informative messages, 234; *see also* Negative messages; Positive or good news messages
 checklist for, 259–260
 ending, 251
 humor in, 252
 managing information in, 249–250
 organizing, 244–245, 261
 subject lines for, 245–249
 summaries, 254–255
 transmittals, 253–254 (fig.)
 using benefits in, 250–251
 varieties of, 253–257
Informative presentation, 608, 624
Informative report, 565
Innovation and entrepreneurship, 109
Inside address, 638
Instant messaging, 238–239
Interactive presentation, 610, 625
Intercultural competence, 107
Inter design level, 160–161
Interim report, 471; *see also* Progress report
Internal audience, 6
Internal document, 7
Internal documentation, 490
International business communication, 197
International holidays, 187
International teams, 218
Internet, 12–13, 372–373; *see also* Electronic privacy
 advertising on, 35
 for job search, 370–372
 posting résumé on, 396
 privacy on, 102
 and reporting, 474
 social media, 35
 sources for company facts, 411 (fig.), 414
 sources for research, 476 (fig.)–477 (fig.), 478
Internship, 373–374, 419 (fig.)
Interpersonal communication, 207
 conversational style, 95–96
 listening, 93–95
 networking, 98–99
 nonverbal communication, 96–98
 and teamwork, 206
Interpersonal dimension, 206
Interpersonal leader, of team, 209
Interruption, 101
Interruption interview, 489
Interview, 491; *see also* Research interview; Surveys, analyzing and designing; *entries for specific interview types*
 defined, 478
 for job, 440
  accepting offer, 61
  after, 458–462
  attire, 442–443
  behavioral, 455–456
  behavior during, 446–447, 449 (fig.)
  being memorable, 450
  on campus, 444
  channels for, 444–445
  checklist for, 448
  customs for, 445–448
  elevator speech, 442
  e-mail request for, 413 (fig.)
  expenses, 447
  final research, 441–442
  focused, 454
  follow-up with phone call and written message, 459, 460 (fig.)
  group, 458
  information, 412–413, 428
  Just By Yourself (JBY) syndrome, 448
  kinds of, 454–458
  meals and semisocial occasions, 447
  nervous mannerisms, 447
  note-taking, 447–448
  by phone, 444–445
  practice for, 445
  preparation for, 441–444
  problems, 447
  professional materials, 443–444
  questions and answers, 448–454
  referenced, 454
  referral, 412–414, 428
  and rejection, 465
  screening, 454
  segments of, 448
  situational, 456
  STAR Technique, 457
  strategy for, 441
  stress, 456–458
  topgrading, 454
  travel planning, 442
  video, 445
 survey, defined, 478
Intra design level, 159–161
Intrinsic motivators, 43, 49
Introduction, of report, 575, 580 (fig.), 599
Iran, 191
Iraq, 191
Ireland, 188 (fig.)
Italic type, 169, 663
Italy, 191–192
it's/its, 667

J

Japan, 107, 181, 188 (fig.), 189, 191, 193, 199, 209, 504–505
Jargon, 129–130
Java, 171
JBY; *see* Just Be Yourself (JBY) syndrome
Job and interview tips, 440; *see also* Interview; Job search
 behavior, 446–447, 449 (fig.)
 bloopers, 459
 body language mistakes, 447
 for career fairs, 444
 full-time job, first, 462–463
 Just Be Yourself (JBY), 448
 meals and social occasions, 446–447
 STAR Technique, 457
 You're Hired Interview: Tips and Techniques for a Brilliant Interview, 448
Job application letter
 application essays, 427–428
 content and organization of, 414–422
 editing and proofreading, 426–427
 follow-up, 427
 last paragraph, 421–422

letter length, 426
paragraph length and unity, 426
positive emphasis, 424–425
professional image, 423–427
prospecting letter, 414–415, 417, 418 (fig.)
purpose of, 410
showing how you differ from other applicants, 421
showing knowledge of position and company, 420
solicited letter, 414–416 (fig.)
via e-mail, 422–423
vs. résumé, 410
writing style, 424
you-attitude, 425–426
Job flexibility, 108
Job interview; *see* Interview
Job market, 412–414
Job search; *see also* Interview
accepting offer, 461
blogs, social networking sites, Internet tracking, 372–373
career changes, multiple, 410
cover letter, 372
e-mail guidelines, 395
hidden job market, 428
internship, 373–374
interview questions and answers, 448–454
knowledge of position and companies, 370–372, 411, 414, 420
personal branding, 371–372
problems with, 392–394
rejection, dealing with, 462
unconventional tactics, 409, 461
using Internet in, 370–371
Job titles, nonsexist, 70
Judging-Perceiving dichotomy, 29–30
Judgment sample, 479, 491
Just Be Yourself (JBY) syndrome, 448
Justification report, 471 (fig.), 569
Justify margins, 165–166

K

Keystroke patterning, 101
Key word, 377, 475
Korea, 185, 187, 193, 504

L

Language; *see* Bias-free language; Writing
Last Lecture, The (Pausch), 99
Latin America, 192
Laws, communication, 14
Layoffs, 296
Leadership, in teams, 208–209, 216, 219
Lebanon, 191
lectern/podium, 667
Legal liability, and report drafts, 571
Legal problems, as cost of poor communication, 10–12
Letterhead, 633, 637–638
block format on, 634 (fig.)
modified block format on, 635 (fig.)
simplified format on, 636 (fig.)
Letter or memo of transmittal, 574–575, 577 (fig.), 594
Letters, 242; *see also* E-mail; Memo; Paper memos
blind copies, 638
block format, 632–633, 634 (fig.), 639 (fig.)
comparing and contrasting formats for, 632 (fig.)
complimentary close, 633
copies, 638
enclosures, 635 (fig.)–637 (fig.), 638
formats for, 632–642
inside address, 638
on letterhead, 633–638
mixed punctuation, 633
modified block format, 632–633, 635 (fig.), 637 (fig.), 640 (fig.)
recommendation, 336
simplified format, 632–633, 636 (fig.), 641 (fig.)
subject line, 632–633
Liar detection, 97
lie/lay, 667
Light Revision Checklist, 139–140
Limitations, 596–597, 599
Line graph, 503–504, 513
Listening, 93–95, 208
List of illustrations, 574–575, 578 (fig.), 594–595
Literacy, levels, 29
Literary Digest poll, 480
Local culture adaptations, 183–184
Logic, checking, 559–560
Logical fallacies, 316
loose/lose, 667
Low-context culture, 186

M

Mackay 66, 38
Mail survey, 481
Main clause, 656
Make-good or payback report, 471 (fig.)
Male-female conversation, 95–96
Map, 502, 514–515, 595
Map of the Market, 500
Margin, 165–166
Marketing, combining charity with, 342
Mars Climate Orbiter spacecraft, 9
Meals and semisocial occasions, during job interview, 447
Mean, 557–558
Meaningless sentences, 132; *see also* Unnecessary words
Median, 558
Medical picture boards, 505
Medicine
information about, 242
names for, 131
Meetings
advice for effective, 206
agenda for, 219
being taken seriously in, 221; *see also* Team(s)
corporate annual, 219, 221
formal and informal, 218–219
minutes for, 218–220
omnibus motion, 219
Memo, 5
headings, 642
on memo letterhead, 644 (fig.)
on plain paper, 643 (fig.)
second page, 645 (fig.)
Methods, 596, 599
Mexican-American War, 507
Mexico, 185, 188 (fig.), 191
Microsoft Word conventions, 159
Middle East, 185, 187, 189
Million Random Digits, A, 479
Mine disaster, 570
Minor problems, during job interview, 447
Mirror question, 487, 491
Misplaced modifier, 654
Mixed punctuation, 633
Mode, 558
Modern Language Association (MLA), 490, 677–678, 682–684
Modified block format, 632–633, 635 (fig.), 637 (fig.), 640 (fig.)
Modifier, 654
Monochronic culture, 192
Monologue presentation, 610, 625
moral/morale, 667
Movie rankings, 560
Multicultural diabetes education, 197
Multitasking, 100–101
Muslim countries, 187–189
Myers-Briggs Type Indicator, 29–30
Mystery shopper, 489

N

Names, 380
for medicines, 131
nonsexist, 71–72
Narration
in oral presentation, 612
in sales and fund-raising messages, 338–339
National culture, 187 (fig.)
Native culture, 319–320
Navigation, for website, 170
Negative messages
apologies, 287–290
checklist for, 299
effective, 297
example, 281 (fig.)
metaphors in, 277
organizing to deliver
to clients and customers, 279–280
to peers and subordinates, 280–283
to superiors, 280
parts of
alternatives, 286–287, 288 (fig.)
buffers, 284–285
endings, 287
reasons, 285–286
refusals, 286, 288 (fig.), 294–295
subject lines, 283–284
primary purposes for, 278–279
secondary purpose for, 279
solving sample problem
problem, 296–297
problem analysis, 297
sample solutions, 296–299

Negative messages—*Cont.*
tone in, 291
varieties of
claims and complaints, 293–294
disciplinary notices and performance appraisals, 295
layoffs and firings, 296
rejections and refusals, 294–295
Negatives
defining allowable, 64
double, 65
hidden, 65–67
justify with audience benefit, 66–67
words vs. connotations, 64–65
you-attitude focus, 66
Negative situation
alternative strategies for, 291–293
recasting, as persuasive message, 292–293
recasting, as positive message, 292
Negative team roles, 208
Nervous mannerisms, 447
Netherlands, 209
Networking, 98–100
Newspaper, 35
Nigeria, 189, 191
No Child Left Behind (NCLB) law, 555
Nominative case, 653
Nonageist, making language, 73–74
Noncompetitive proposal, 534–535
Nonracist, making language, 73–74
Nonrestrictive (nonessential) clause, 659–660
Nonsexist language, 70–73, 652
Nonverbal communication, 4, 194
age, 193
body language, 97–98, 189–190
clothing, 192–193
colors, 193
defined, 188
height, 193
during interview, 477
social signals, 96
space, 192
spatial cues, 97
touch, 190–191
North America, 184–185, 192
Norway, 191
Notes, during oral presentations, 622
Note-taking, during job interview, 447–448
Noun-pronoun agreement, 652
Nouns, 131
Numbers
analyzing, 557
writing, 663–664

O

Objections, dealing with, 325–328
Objective case, 653
objective/rationale, 667–668
Objectives, career, 381–382
Objectivity, 478, 556
OCRs; *see* Optical Character Readers (OCRs)
Offshore drilling, 469
Oil spill, 9, 205, 233
Omnibus motion, 219
1-2-3 order, for oral presentation, 615
Online advertising, 35
Online dating site, 561
Online networks, 488
Online reviews, evaluating, 478
Online survey, 481
Open body position, 97
Opening
of interview, 448
of oral presentation, 611–614
Open question, 483–484, 491
Optical Character Readers (OCRs), 638, 642
or, 133
Oral communication, 194–195
informative, 608
written vs., 34, 609, 624
Oral presentation; *see also* Presentations
audience for, 610–611, 623, 625
checklist for, 623–624
choosing demonstrations for, 614–615
choosing information to include in, 613–615
choosing kind of, 610–611
closing, 613–614
delivering, 619–622
eye contact, 619–620
fear, 619
goodwill, 608, 624
group, 624
guided discussion, 610, 625
humor in, 614
identifying purposes in, 608
informative, 608, 624
interactive, 610, 625
mastering toasts, 612
monologue, 610, 625
notes and visuals, using, 622
opening, 611–614
organizing information for, 615–616
persuasive, 608, 624
planning strategy for, 610–613
pressure and stress from, 620
questions, handling, 622–623
speaking voice, developing, 620–622
standing and gesturing, 622
technology for, 611
written message vs., 609
Oral presentations, 608, 624
Organization, of business documents, 120–121
Organizational culture, 32–33, 187 (fig.)
Outsourcing, 107
Overspeaking, in teams, 208
Overview, in oral presentation, 615

P

Page design; *see* Document design
Paired bar chart, 512–513
Palm vein scan, 91
Paper memos, 242
Paragraph
of job application letter, 421–422
length and unity in, 426
of prospecting letter, 417–418 (fig.)
of solicited letter, 415–416 (fig.)
write and revise, 137–138
Parallel structure, 135–136, 654–655
Paraphrase, 217
Parentheses, 661
Passive verb, 60, 570
Passive voice, 129–131
Password authentication, 101
Patterns, analyzing, 558–559
Peer pressure, 212
Peers and subordinates, giving bad news to, 280–283
People-first language, 75
Pepsi Refresh Project, 87
Performance appraisal, 295, 333–335, 335 (fig.)
Period, 655 (fig.), 661
Perks, corporate, 92
Personal branding, 371–372
Personal cultural overlap, 187 (fig.)
personal/personnel, 668
Personal pronoun, case of, 653 (fig.)
Personal space, 192
Personal web page, 371
Persuasion, 196 (fig.)
face-to-face, 345
stories and, 563
Persuasive message
analyzing situation for, 315–320
basis for, 314
letters of recommendation, 336
performance appraisal, 333–335
primary purpose for, 314
problem-solving, 323–332, 347–351
recasting negative situation as, 292–293
safety video, 313
sales and fund-raising, 336–347
sample problem, 347–350
secondary purpose for, 314
threats vs., 320–321
tone in, 332
varieties of, 333–336
Persuasive presentations; *see* Oral presentations
Persuasive strategy, choosing, 320
Pew Internet & American Life Project, 575, 601
Philanthropy, 89; *see also* Ethics
Philippines, 185
Phishing, 101, 370
Phone answering machine, 238
Phone calls, 238
Phone interview, 444–445
Phone number, 381
Photocopy (pc), 638
Photograph, 514, 595
Photos and illustrations, bias-free, 75
Photoshop, 508
Phrase, 656
Physical disabilities; *see* Diversity
Pictogram, 512–513
Pie chart, 503, 510–511, 595
Pitch, 620–621
Plagiarism, 92, 489–490, 677
Plain English Handbook: How to Create Clear SEC Disclosure Documents, A, 122, 153

Planning, for writing, 118–120, 145
Plural pronoun, 656
Politeness, 68–69
Polychronic culture, 192
Population, survey, 479–480
Portable media player, 236
Portfolio, 390
Positive emphasis, 58, 63
  appropriateness of, 68
  check, 67–68
  create, 64–67
  defined, 58, 76
  in job application letter, 424–425
Positive letter, example, 246 (fig.)
Positive memo, subject line example, 247 (fig.)
Positive or good news messages
  audience for, 233
  checklist for, 259–260
  common media, 237–244
  communication hardware, 234–236
  compliments, 255
  defined, 234
  ending, 251
  information overload, 236–237
  managing information in, 249–250
  organizing, 244–245, 261
  positive feedback notes, 255–257
  primary purposes, 234
  recasting negative situation as, 292
  secondary purposes, 234
  solving sample problem, 260
    discussion of solutions, 258–259
    good solution, 260 (fig.)
    problem, 257
    problem analysis, 258
    unacceptable solution, 259 (fig.)
  subject lines for, 245–249
  using benefits in, 250–251
  varieties of, 253–257
Positive team roles, 208
Possessive case, 653
possible/possibly, 668
Postscript (P.S.), 340–341
PowerPoint, 5, 499; *see also* Oral communication; Visuals and data displays
  alternatives to, 615–616
  avoiding disastrous, 619
  designing slides, 616–617
  figures and tables, 618
  involving audience, 618–619
  planning slides, 616–619
  student perceptions of, as instructional tool, 618
Practical Parenting and Pregnancy, 508
Practices; *see* Values, beliefs, and practices
precede/proceed, 668
Prediction errors, 655
Preposition, 124
Presentations, 5, 167; *see also* Oral presentation
Presentation Secrets of Steve Jobs: How to Be Insanely Great in Front of Any Audience, The (Gallo), 607
Presenting problem, 216
Pre-writing, 118–120
Primary audience, 28–29, 48, 314
Primary purpose
  for informative or positive message, 234
  for negative message, 278–279
  for sales and fund-raising messages, 336
Primary research, 474
principal/principle, 668
Print channel, 34–35
Privacy, electronic, 101–104
Probe, 487, 491
Problem–cause–solution order, for oral presentation, 615
Problem/Opportunity, 537
Problem-solution report, 561, 563
Problem-solving message
  checklist for persuasive message, 351
  common ground, developing, 325
  emotional appeal, building, 328–330
  objections, dealing with, 325–328
  organizing, 323–324
  putting it together, 330–332
  reason for audience to act promptly, offering, 328
  subject line for, 324–325
Problem-solving pattern, 320, 351
Problem-solving process, for teams, 209–210
Problem-solving report, 471 (fig.)
Procedural dimension, 206
Procedural leader, of team, 209
Procedure, section of report, 496
Pro–con order, for oral presentation, 615
Product returns, cost of, 47
Professional materials, for interview, 443–444
Progress report, 471
  chronological, 546–548
  political uses of, 546
  recommendation, 547
  task, 547
  writing, 545–548
Projected visual; *see* PowerPoint
Pronoun
  case of personal, 653 (fig.)
  nonsexist, 72–73, 652
  noun-pronoun agreement, 652
  plural, 656
  reflexive, 653–654
  second-person, 136
  third-person, 136
Proofreading, 138, 140
  in collaborative writing, 222–223
  defined, 139, 145
  errors in résumé, 141
  job application letter, 426–427
  of résumé, 398
  spelling errors, 427
  symbols for, 669–670
  typos, 142
Proportional font, 165, 169
Proposal
  for action, 538
  budget and cost sections, 544–545
  business plans and funding, 543–544
  for class research projects, 537–542
  competitive, 534
  by corporate investors, 533
  defined, 534, 549
  noncompetitive, 534–535
  questions, 535
  requests for proposals (RFPs), 536
  sales, 538, 542–543
  styles of, 536
  writing, 534–645
Proposal question, 535
Prospecting job letter, 414–415, 417–418 (fig.), 428
Province abbreviations, 649 (fig.)
P.S.; *see* Postscript (P.S.)
Psychographic characteristics, of audience, 31–32
Psychological description, 330, 346–347
Psychological reactance, 287
Punctuation
  apostrophe, 658–659
  comma, 659–660
  comma splice, 656–657
  dash, 655 (fig.), 660
  ellipses, 662–663
  fused sentence, 657
  history of, 660
  hyphen, 660–661
  italics, 663
  marks of, 655 (fig), 662–663
  parentheses, 661
  period, 655 (fig.), 661
  quotation marks, 662
  run-on sentences, 653–654, 657
  semicolon, 655 (fig.), 661–662
  sentence fragments, 144, 653, 657–658
  in sentences, 656–658
  square brackets, 662
  underlining, 169, 663
Purpose statement, 473, 496, 596, 599

Q

Qualifications, summary of, 382
Quarterly report, 471 (fig.)
Questionnaire, 491
  defined, 478 (*see also* Surveys, analyzing and designing)
  for student report using survey research, 486 (fig.)
Question(s)
  handling, during oral presentation, 622–623
  in opening of oral presentation, 612–613
  in sales and fund-raising messages, 337–338 (*see also* Interview)
  survey, 482–485
quiet/quite, 668
Quotation
  in oral presentation, 612
  in sales and fund-raising messages, 339–341
Quotation marks, 662

R

Race, 73–74
Ragged right margins, 165–166
Ramadan, 187, 188 (fig.)
Random sample, 479–480, 491

Range, 558
Readability formulas, 144
Realistic, 68
Reasons; *see* Negative messages
Rebranding, 371
Recommendation
  letters of, 336
  in report, 575, 590 (fig.), 597–599
Recommendation progress report, 547
Recommendation report, 470, 471 (fig.), 491, 568–569
"Red flag" words, 40
Referenced interview, 454
Reference line (letter), 633
References, 678
  for report, 591 (fig.)–592 (fig.)
  on résumé, 390–391
Referral interview, 412–414, 428
Reflexive pronoun, 653–654
regulate/relegate, 668
Rejections and refusals, 286, 288 (fig.), 294–295, 462
Release date, 593
Religion
  and business communication, 187
  and incentive programs, 47
Repetition, in writing, 571
Replenish Africa Initiative, 46
Report(s); *see also* Proposal; *entries for specific report types*
  accident report, 470
  analytical report, 470, 491
  analyzing data and information for, 554–560
  analyzing numbers, 557–558
  analyzing patterns, 558–559
  analyzing words, 558
  annual report, 471 (fig.), 564, 569
  audit report, 471 (fig.)
  checking logic, 559–560
  choosing information for, 560–561
  chronological progress report, 546–548
  chronological report, 561, 656
  closure report, 471, 565
  comparison/contrast report, 561–563
  credit report, 470
  elimination of alternatives report, 561, 563
  evaluating source of data, 556–557
  example of, 576 (fig.)–592 (fig.)
  formal, 5, 575–592
  functional report, 561, 565
  informal report, 470
  information report, 470–471, 491
  informative memo report, 566–568 (fig.)
  informative report, 565
  interim report, 471 (*see also* Progress report)
  Internet research for, 474
  justification report, 471 (fig.), 569
  legal liability, 571
  make-good or payback report, 471 (fig.)
  organizing information in, 561–569
  presenting information in, 569–574
  problem-solution report, 561, 563
  problem-solving report, 471 (fig.)
  problems with, 472–474
  production process for, 471–472
  purpose statement, 473
  quarterly report, 471 (fig.)
  recommendation progress report, 547
  recommendation report, 470, 471 (fig.), 491, 568–569
  research strategies for
    ABI/Inform Thesaurus, 475
    customers and users, observing, 488–489
    finding information, 474–477
    focus groups, using, 487–488
    interviews, conducting, 485–487
    keywords, 475
    online networks, 488
    primary research, 474
    secondary research, 474
    sources for Web research, 476–477 (fig.)
    surveys, analyzing and designing, 478–485
    Web sources, evaluating, 478
  sales report, 471 (fig.)
  source citation and documentation, 489–491
  sources and visuals, 571
  specific varieties of, 565–568
  task progress report, 547
  technical, 5
  time management for writing, 554
  transmittal, 253–254 (fig.)
  trip report, 471
  varieties of, 470–471
Requests for proposals (RFPs), 535, 545
Research interview, 485–488
Respect for the Aged Day, 188 (fig.)
respectfully/respectively, 668
Respondent, 491
Response rate, 482
Restrictive clause, 660
Results, section of report, 496
Résumé; *see also* Job search
  blunders in, 381
  checklist for, 397
  contents of, 380–390
    activities, 390
    career objective, 381–382
    education, 382–384
    experience, 385–387
    honors and awards, 384
    name and contact information, 380–381
    portfolio, 390
    qualifications summary, 382
    references, 390–391
  cover letter, 372
  defined, 368
  details provided on, 375–376
  emphasis within, 375
  guidelines for, 375–378
  honesty, 397
  how employers use, 374
  indented format, 386
  key words, 377
  kinds of, 378–380, 387–389, 392, 394–396, 398
  layout and design, 378
  length of, 375
  posting, on web, 396
  proofreading errors in, 141
  reverse, 378, 398
  scannable, formatting, 686
  soft skills, 384
  strengths and interests, 369–370
  vs. job application letter, 410
  what not to include in, 391–392
  writing style, 376
Résumé blasting, 393, 396
Revising, 119, 138–142
  checklists for, 140, 145
  in collaborative writing, 222
  defined, 139, 145
  meaningless words, 132
  at sentence level, 129–136
  voice, active and passive, 129–131
  wordiness, 131–132
RFPs; *see* Requests for proposals (RFPs)
Roe v. Wade, 557
role/roll, 668
Roles, team, 207–209
Run-on sentence, 653–654, 657
Russia, 182

S

Safety video, 313
Salary and benefits, negotiating, 459
Sales and fund-raising messages
  direct marketing, 336
  example letter, 345 (fig.)
  organizing
    narration, stories, anecdotes, 338–339
    questions, 337–338
    quotations, 339–341
    startling statements, 339
  primary purpose, 336
  psychological description, 346–347
  secondary purpose, 336
  solving sample problem, 347–350
  strategy in, 341–344
  writing style, 344–347
Sales pattern, 320, 351
Sales proposal, 538, 542–543
Sales report, 471 (fig.)
Salutation, 243, 632
Sample, 479–480
Sample size, 480
Sampling frame, 479
Sampling unit, 479
Sans serif font, 165
Scannable résumé, formatting, 686
Scientific team, 217
Scope, 596, 599
Screening interview, 454
Secondary audience, 28–29, 48
Secondary purpose
  for informative or positive message, 234
  for negative message, 279
  for persuasive message, 314
  for sales and fund-raising messages, 336
Secondary research, 474

Second-person pronoun, 136
Segmented, subdivided, or stacked bars, 512–513
Self-assessment, 369–370; *see also* Résumé
Semicolon, 655 (fig.), 661–662
Sensing-Intuition dichotomy, 29–30
Sentence fragment, 144, 653, 657–658
Sentence outline, 595
Sentences
  combine, to eliminate unnecessary words, 132–133
  complex, 134
  compound, 133–134
  fused, 657
  long- and medium-length, 135
  meaningless sentences, 132
  punctuation in, 655–662
  and readability formulas, 144
  reduce repetition, 134–136
  run-on, 653–654, 657
  simple, 133
  topic, 137
  umbrella, 135
  writing and revising, 129–136
September 11, 2001, 677
7 Habits of Highly Effective People, The (Covey), 99–100
Sexist terms; *see* Bias-free language
Sexting, 480
Sexual orientation; *see* Diversity
Shich-go-san, 189
SiB; *see* Social Impact Bonds (SiB)
Signature block, 638, 642
Signpost, 615, 625
Silent Language of Leaders: How Body Language Can Help—or Hurt—How You Lead, The (Goman), 99
Simple sentence, 133
simple/simplistic, 668
Simplicity, 614
Simplified format, 632–633, 636 (fig.), 641 (fig.)
Sincere, 68
Sincerely, 633
Situational interview, 456, 464
Situational question, 485
Skills résumé, 378, 387–388 (fig.), 388, 398
Smartphone, 171, 235
Social culture, 319
Social Impact Bonds (SiB), 89
Social media, 241
  advertising through, 35
  drawbacks, 242
  popularity of, 239–240
  realm of, 242
Social networking, 372–373, 378, 479; *see also* Internet
Social signal, 96–98
Soft skills, 384
Solicited job letter, 414–416 (fig.), 428
Sources, 490
  citing and documenting, 677–684
  references, 678
  Works Cited list, 678
Space, personal, 192
Spain, 193
Spam, 236
Spam filter, 395
Spatial cues, 97
Speaking voice, developing, 620–622
Special Olympics, 139
Spelling, 138, 427; *see also* Proofreading
Sphere, 282
Split infinitive, 656
Spreadsheet, 555
Square brackets, 662
St. Jean-Baptiste Day, 188 (fig.)
St. Patrick's Day, 188 (fig.)
Standing and gesturing, in oral presentation, 622
STAR Technique (for interviewing), 457
Startling statements
  in oral presentations, 612
  in sales and fund-raising messages, 339
State abbreviations, 649 (fig.)
State of the Union address, 27
stationary/stationery, 669
Stereotype, 183
Stickiness, 614–615
"Stick" motivator, 319
Story
  in oral presentation, 613–614
  in sales and fund-raising messages, 338–339
Storyboard, 121
Strengths, Weaknesses, Opportunities, and Threats (SWOT) analysis, 561, 563
Stress
  from oral presentation, 620
  in voice, 620–621
Stress interview, 456–458, 464
Structured interview, 485
Stub, 510
Student teams, 211–212
Style; *see also* Leadership, in teams
  of job application letter, 424
  organizational preferences for, 138
  for résumé, 376
  writing, 344–347
  of writing, 40, 121–124, 196 (fig.)
Subject line
  appropriate for pattern of organization, 248
  defined, 261
  for letter, 632–633
  make concise, 247–248
  make specific, 245
  in negative messages, 283–284
  points for e-mail, 248–249
  in positive letter, 246 (fig.)
  for problem-solving messages, 324–325
  of progress report, 546
Subject-verb agreement, 651–654
Subordinate clause, 656
Subsistence consumers, communication with, 190
Summaries, in information messages, 254–255
Summary abstract, 595, 599; *see also* Executive summary
Summary sentence, 415–416 (fig.)
Super Bowl, 336
Supercorp: How Vanguard Companies Create Innovation, Profits, Growth, and Social Good (Kanter), 91
Superiors, giving bad news to, 280
Supra design level, 160–161
Surveys, analyzing and designing, 478–485, 491; *see also* Interview; Research interview
  confidence interval, 480
  face-to-face surveys, 481
  interview, defined, 478
  mail surveys, 481
  online surveys, 481
  questionnaire, defined, 478
  questions, characteristics of good, 482–485
  response rates, 482
  samples for, 479–480
  survey, defined, 478
  telephone surveys, 481
Sweden, 189
Swim with the Sharks without Being Eaten Alive (Mackay), 38
SWOT analysis, 561, 563–564
Symbols, for proofreading, 669–670

T

Table; *see also* Visuals and data displays
  boxhead, 509–510
  for identifying exact values, 503
  for list of illustrations, 594–595
  in PowerPoint slides, 618
  stub, 509–510
Table of contents, 574–575, 576 (fig.), 594
Taiwan, 185
Talking heads, 572–573
Task progress report, 547
Team interactions, 206–212
Team(s)
  checklists for, 212
  cohesiveness, developing, 207
  collaborative writing, 220–223
  conflict resolution, 214–218
  coordination, 207
  decision-making strategies, 209–210
  diverse, 213–214
  feedback strategies, 210–211
  formalization, 207
  formation of, 206
  Gulf spill, 205
  informational dimensions, 206
  interaction of, 206–212
  international, 218
  interpersonal communication, 206
  interpersonal dimensions, 206
  leadership in, 208–209
  meetings, 206, 218–219
  myths about, 208
  peer pressure and groupthink, 212
  procedural dimensions, 206
  roles in, 207–208
  scientific, 217
  statistics about, 214
  of students, 211–212

Team(s)—*Cont.*
  successful, 208 (fig.), 211–212, 223
  working in diverse, 213–214
  work preferences, 211
Teamwork, 108
Technology; *see also* E-mail; Internet; PowerPoint
  access for people with visual and hearing impairments, 74
  cell phone, 235
  common media, 237–244
  communication hardware, 234–236
  Deepwater Horizon, 233
  information overload, 236–237
  informative, 234
  for oral presentation, 611, 620
  phone calls, 238
  portable media players, 236
  positive or news message, 234
  smartphones, 235
  social media, 239–242
  telepresence, 236
  thought-conversion, 234
  video conversions, 236
  wikis, 239
Telephone survey, 481
Telepresence, 236
Television advertising, 35
Template, 617
Tesco Clubcard, 42
Text, drafting, 168
Text message, 11, 238–239
Thank you, 633
Thank-you note, 256–257, 414, 459
that/which, 652
their/there/they're, 669
Think-aloud protocol, 489
Thinking-Feeling dichotomy, 29–30
Third-person pronoun, 136
Thorough Revision Checklist, 139–140
Thought-conversion technology, 234
Threats, vs. persuasion, 320–321
360-degree feedback, 211
Thumbs up, 190
Tibet, 506
Time and time management, 99–101, 192
  for report writing, 554
  wasted, 9–10
  for writing, 120
Tipping Point, The (Gladwell), 321, 557
Title page, 574–576, 576 (fig.), 593–594
Titles
  courtesy, 69
  job, 126
Toasts, mastering, 612
To/CC/BCC lines, 245
Tone, 68–69
  in negative messages, 291
  of progress report, 545
  of voice, 620–621
Topgrading interview, 454
Topic heading, 572
Topic sentence, 137, 572
to/too/two, 669
Touch, 190–191
Track Changes, 153
Transition words and phrases, 137–138 (fig.), 572
Translations
  among different cultures, 187
  through nonverbal communication, 194
Translations, and document design, 165
Transmittal, 253–254 (fig.)
Travel award, 47
Travel planning, 442
Trends, color, 167
Trip report, 471
Truncated code, 476
Truncated graph, 507, 517
TV ads, 34–35
Two-meeting rule, 214
Typo, 398

U

Umbrella sentence, 135
Unauthorized use, 597
Underlining, 169, 663
Understatement, 194–195
Unethical sales pitches, 338
Unexpectedness, 614
unique/unusual, 669
United Nations Global Compact, 89
United States, 191, 193, 504
U.S. Census poster (2010), 161 (fig.), 185
U.S. Constitution, Fourth Amendment, 103
Unity, 137
Unnecessary words, 131–133
Unstructured interview, 485
Usability testing, for website, 172

V

Values, beliefs, and practices, 187–188, 196 (fig.)
Venture capitalist, 543
Verb, passive, 60
Verbal blunders, 609
Verbal communication, 4
verbal/oral, 669
Verbs, 131, 133, 135
Vested interest, 316
Vicarious participation, 342
Video conferences, 236
Videoconferencing, 45
Video interview, 445
Video résumé, 392
Vietnam, 185
Violence, workplace, 291
Visuals and data displays; *see also* List of illustrations; PowerPoint; *entries for specific visual types*
  accurate and ethical, 505–509
  bar chart, 503–504, 512–513
  benefits of, 500
  chartjunk, 505–507
  choosing, 502–503
  color and decoration, 504–505
  cultural differences, 510
  data quality, 501
  designing, 509–516
  determining story, 501–502
  deviation bar chart, 512–513
  dot chart, 503–504
  drawings, 514
  dynamic displays, 515–516
  following conventions, 503–504
  Gantt chart, 503–504, 513–514
  grouped bar chart, 512
  guidelines for creating, 501–509
  histogram, 512–513
  integrating, in text, 509
  line graph, 503–504, 513
  maps, 514–515
  during oral presentations, 622
  paired bar chart, 512–513
  photographs, 514
  pictograms, 512–513
  pie chart, 502–504, 510–511
  segmented, subdivided or stacked bars, 512–513
  tables, 502–504, 510–511
  truncated graphs, 506, 508
  use of, 16–17
  when to use, 500–501
Voice, tone of, 620–621
Voting, 209
V-sign, 190

W

Watchdog audience, 28–29, 48
Wavin' Flag, 46
Weak analogy, 316
Web Accessibility Initiative, 171
Web pages, designing, 381
  attracting and maintaining attention, 169
  following conventions, 170–171
  home page, 170
  navigation, 170
  personal, for job search, 371
Web research
  evaluating, 478
  sources for, 476 (fig.)–477 (fig.)
What Color is Your Parachute (Bolles), 369
whether/weather, 669
White pages, 36
White space, 161–164
Who: The Method for Hiring (Smart & Street), 454
who/whom, 652
Widgets, 242
Wikis, 239
Wild card, 476
Withdrawing, from team, 208
Women, 187
Word choice, 125; *see also* Bias-free language; Writing
  accuracy of, 126
  analyzing, 558
  banished words, 652
  businessese, 129
  confused words, 664–669
  connotations, 127–128
  denotations, 126–127
  ethical implications, 128
  insensitive, 139, 652
  jargon, 129
  legal implications, 126
  on menus, 130
  sexist language, 652

similar words, 128–129
transitions, 138
unnecessary words, 131–133
Wordy and wordiness, 59, 131–132
Work/family balance, 104–105
Workplace violence, 291
Work preferences, 211
Works Cited, 678
World Factbook, 192
World Is Flat, The (Friedman), 107, 184
Writer's block, overcoming, 120
Writing; *see also* Job application letter; Punctuation; Sentences; *entries for specific message types*
application essays, 427–428
boilerplate, 144
brainstorming, planning, and organizing business documents, 120–121
brochure text, 168
business and administrative documents, 121–124
collaborative, 220–223
composing process, 118–120
conventions, following, 13
criteria for effective messages, 12
cultural contrasts in persuasive, 196 (fig.)
design as part of process, 158–159
feedback, 142–144
forecasts, 571
formal reports, 575–592
grammar, 140, 651–655
half-truths about, for business, 124–125
headings, 572–574
to international audiences, 195–197
numbers and dates, 663–664
organizational preferences for style, 138
paragraphs, 137–138
practice for, 117
proofreading symbols, 669–670
punctuation marks, 655 (fig.), 662–663
for readability
paragraphs, 137–138
sentences, 129–136
word choice, 125–129
readability formulas, 144
repetition in, 571
report, 569–574
revising, editing, and proofreading, 138–142
rules, evaluating, 124
sources and visuals in, 571
styles of, 40, 121–124, 344–347, 376
talking heads, 572–573
time management, 120
topic heading, 572
topic sentence, 137, 572
transitions, 572
word choice, 125, 126–127, 127–128, 128–129, 130, 131–133, 138–139, 558, 652, 664–669
words often confused, 664–669
written vs. oral message, 34
Writing style, 344–347
Written message, vs. oral communication, 34, 609, 624

X

XML, 171

Y

Yiddish Policemen's Union, The (Chabon), 140
You-attitude
beyond sentence level, 61–62
in business plan, 543
in conflict resolution, 218
create, 59–61, 66
defined, 58–59, 76
with international audience, 61
in job application letter, 425–426
letter lacking in, 62 (fig.)
letter with, 63 (fig.)
and listening, 93
phrase benefits in, 45
in progress reports, 545
You're Hired Interview: Tips and Techniques for a Brilliant Interview (James), 448
Yours truly, 632
your/you're, 669

Z

Z pattern, 166–168